CIVIL PROCEDURE IN PRACTICE

FIRST EDITION

NELSON P. MILLER

CIVIL PROCEDURE IN PRACTICE

FIRST EDITION

NELSON P. MILLER

VANDEPLAS PUBLISHING
UNITED STATES OF AMERICA

Civil Procedure in Practice, First Edition

Nelson P. Miller

Published by:

Vandeplas Publishing – April 2011

801 International Parkway, 5th Floor
Lake Mary, FL. 32746
USA

www.vandeplaspublishing.com

ISBN: 978-1-60042-137-2

Thomas M. Cooley Law School
111 Commerce Avenue S.W.
Grand Rapids, MI 49503
(616) 301-6800 ext. 6963

No free man shall be seized or imprisoned, or stripped of his rights or possessions, or outlawed or exiled, or deprived of his standing in any other way, nor will we proceed with force against him, or send others to do so, except by the lawful judgement of his equals or by the law of the land.

Magna Carta (1215)

WE THE PEOPLE of the United States, in Order to form a more perfect Union, establish Justice, insure domestic Tranquility, provide for the common defence, promote the general Welfare, and secure the Blessings of Liberty to ourselves and our Posterity, do ordain and establish this CONSTITUTION for the United States of America.

U.S. Constitution Preamble

No person shall be ... deprived of life, liberty, or property, without due process of law....

U.S. Constitution 5th Amendment (1791)

No State shall make or enforce any law which shall abridge the privileges or immunities of citizens of the United States; nor shall any State deprive any person of life, liberty, or property, without due process of law... .

U.S. Constitution 14th Am. (1868)

PREFACE

The author developed this text at Thomas M. Cooley Law School. This text is different from the ordinary law school casebook. That difference is due at least in part to Thomas McIntyre Cooley. Justice Cooley had a celebrated (although polite and circumspect) debate with Dean Christopher Columbus Langdell at Harvard Law School on the occasion of Harvard University's 250th anniversary, when Justice Cooley received Harvard's honorary degree. Dean Langdell is credited (or shall we say cursed?) with having created the case method of law school study and, with it, the traditional casebook. He denigrated practical skills studies, and his Harvard comrade-in-arms Justice Oliver Wendell Holmes denigrated ethical studies. By contrast, Justice Cooley expressed concern that the law must not depart from the practical and ethical—hence Cooley Law School's trademark mission of an integrated program of knowledge, skills, and ethics.

Casebooks today do include some introductory text and, often, author notes, questions, and discussion problems. They also include statutes, law review articles, and other commentary. This course book has a design based on pedagogical (teaching), androgogical (learner-centered), and heutogogical (inclusive, learner-controlled) research. This book, like other casebooks, includes excerpts of cases, statutes, and commentary. Yet it also includes learner objectives, case studies, Restatements of the law, skills boxes, technology vignettes, ethics boxes, practice vignettes, practice forms, sample court papers, biographies, and career advice. It also includes all of the *Federal Rules of Civil Procedure* placed in context to the applicable cases and text. Its design is to help you place civil procedure in its practice context, help you develop a professional identity as a member of a community of professional practice, and give you greater control over your learning.

In its much-anticipated report *Educating Lawyers*, the Carnegie Foundation on Higher Education urged precisely these reforms—to integrate skills and ethics into a more explicit study of the knowledge or doctrinal dimension of law, so as to foster an apprenticeship of practice. Although Cooley professors already follow these practices (the Carnegie Foundation report was a vindication of Cooley's educational program), this casebook makes those practices clearer. It is another example of the student-centered innovation that lends Cooley Law School its preeminence at practice preparation. The author hopes you appreciate this design and welcomes your comments, evaluation, and encouragement.

ACKNOWLEDGMENTS

The author thanks and acknowledges the work of many professors at the Thomas M. Cooley Law School. Particular thanks go to: Professors Judy Frank and Gina Torielli for their work on instructional objectives; Professors Jeanette Buttrey and David Tarrien for their work on analytical skills; Professors Charles Senger, Maurice Munroe, Kim O'Leary, and David Finnegan for teaching roundtable support; and Civil Procedure Department Chair Lauren Rousseau and Department members John Scott, Mary D'Isa, Curt Benson, and Christopher Hastings. Particular thanks go to Associate Dean of Faculty Charles Cercone for his support and guidance.

The author also thanks Cooley's founder, Justice Thomas Brennan, and its visionary president and dean, Don LeDuc. Justice Brennan conceived Cooley's distinctive mission. President and Dean LeDuc brought it to unparalleled success as the nation's largest law school. There would not have been the opportunity for this work if it were not for their vision and leadership.

The author also thanks and acknowledges the work of Cooley's Associate Dean for Libraries Duane Strojney and Faculty Center Director Vickie Eggers. Cooley Law School brings extraordinary staff expertise to the study and development of its educational program. The author also thanks and acknowledges the work of Cooley librarians Aletha Honsowitz, John Michaud, Julianne Claydon, and Amy Ash. Cooley's law library is one of the preeminent sources of legal materials in the nation, and its instructional support services are the best within the legal academy.

The author also thanks the many students at Cooley who have contributed to the school's rich learning environment. Teaching law is the greatest of privileges, especially among so committed and engaged body of students. The author also thanks his longtime law partner James Fajen and legal assistants Anne Miller, Sarah Rae, and Katrina Mays. There is no greater professional privilege than the practice of law.

SUMMARY OF CONTENTS

PREFACE vii
ACKNOWLEDGMENTS ix
TABLE OF STATUTES AND RULES xix
TABLE OF CASES xxiii
I. OVERVIEW 1

AUTHORITY TO ADJUDICATE

II. PERSONAL JURISDICTION 23
III. NOTICE AND OPPORTUNITY FOR HEARING. 129
IV. SUBJECT MATTER JURISDICTION. 163
V. VENUE. 205
VI. GOVERNING LAW 229

PROCESS OF ADJUDICATION

VII. PLEADING 259
VIII. JOINDER 361
IX. ALTERNATIVE RESOLUTION 465
X. DISCOVERY 501
XI. ADJUDICATION BEFORE TRIAL 619
XII. TRIAL 665

RESULTS OF ADJUDICATION

XIII. JUDGMENT 745
XIV. APPEAL 789
XV. EFFECT OF JUDGMENT 839
APPENDIX I: FED. R. CIV. P. 895
APPENDIX II: FED. R. APP. P. 949
INDEX 975

TABLE OF CONTENTS

PREFACE vii
ACKNOWLEDGMENTS ix
TABLE OF STATUTES AND RULES xix
TABLE OF CASES xxiii

I. OVERVIEW 1
A. Nature 1
B. Significance 2
C. Structure 4
1. Judicial System. 8
2. Financing Litigation. 10
Christianburg Garment Co. v. EEOC. 11
D. Sources 15
E. Comparison 16
F. Representative Case. 17

AUTHORITY TO ADJUDICATE

II. PERSONAL JURISDICTION. 23
A. Development. 28
1. Traditional Bases. 28
Pennoyer v. Neff. 29
Hess v. Pawlowski 37
2. Modern Bases. 40
International Shoe Co. v. State of Washington 40
B. Specific Jurisdiction. 46
1. Minimum Contacts. 47
McGee v. International Life Ins. Co. 47
Hanson v. Denckla 49
World-Wide Volkswagen Corp. v. Woodson 52
Burger King Corp. v. Rudzewicz 58
Asahi Metal Industry Co. v. Superior Court 63
2. Current Challenges 69
Young v. New Haven Advocate 70
Pebble Beach Co. v. Caddy 75
Mwani v. Bin Laden 80
C. General Jurisdiction 83
1. Introduction 83
Perkins v. Benguet Consolidated Mining Co. 85
Helicopteros Nacionales de Colombia, S.A. v. Hall 86
2. Transient Jurisdiction. 90
Burnham v. Superior Court 90
3. Consent 97
4. Property. 101
Shaffer v. Heitner 102
D. Statutory Authority 110
1. State Long-Arm Statutes. 110

Gray v. American Radiator & Standard Sanitary Corp. 112
World-Wide Volkswagen Corp. v. Woodson (Okla.) 117
2. Reach of the Federal Courts 120
E. Challenging Jurisdiction 122
1. Special Appearance 123
2. Collateral Attack 126
III. NOTICE AND OPPORTUNITY FOR HEARING 129
A. Service of Process 130
1. Constitutional Requirements 131
Mullane v. Central Hanover Bank & Trust Co. 132
Dusenbery v. United States 139
Jones v. Flowers 142
2. Mechanics of Service 148
National Equipment Rental, Ltd. v. Szukhent 151
3. Proving Service 155
B. Opportunity for Hearing 156
Connecticut v. Doehr 158
IV. SUBJECT MATTER JURISDICTION 163
A. Constitutional Framework 163
B. Federal Question 166
Louisville & Nashville R. Co. v. Mottley 168
Grable & Sons Metal Prods., Inc. v. Darue Engineering & Mfg. 170
C. Diversity 174
1. Citizenship 176
Mas v. Perry 176
Saadeh v. Farouki 180
2. Amount in Controversy 184
D. Supplemental Jurisdiction 185
United Mine Workers v. Gibbs 186
Exxon Mobil Corp. v. Allapattah Services, Inc. 190
E. Removal 197
Caterpillar, Inc. v. Lewis 200
V. VENUE 205
A. Original Venue 206
1. State Court 206
2. Federal Court 209
B. Transfer of Venue 215
C. Forum Non Conveniens 220
Piper Aircraft Co. v. Reyno 220
VI. GOVERNING LAW 229
A. State Law in Federal Court 230
Swift v. Tyson 231
1. The *Erie* Doctrine 234
Erie Railroad Co. v. Tompkins 235
Guaranty Trust Co. v. York 243
Byrd v. Blue Ridge Rural Electric Cooperative 246
2. The Rules Enabling Act 249
Hanna v. Plumer 250
Gasperini v. Center for Humanities, Inc. 256
B. Conflict of Laws 264

PROCESS OF ADJUDICATION

VII. PLEADING 267

A. Complaint. 271

1. General Rules. 271
   Conley v. Gibson 282
   Haddle v. Garrison 284
2. Sufficiency. 286
   Bell Atlantic Corp. v. Twombly 289
   Ashcroft v. Iqbal 296
3. Special Rules. 301
   Dura Pharmaceuticals, Inc. v. Broudo 305
   Tellabs, Inc. v. Makor Issues and Rights, Ltd. 307

B. Responding. 313

1. Default. 313
2. Pre-Answer Motion. 321
3. Answer. 325
   Zielinski v. Philadelphia Piers, Inc. 329
4. Defenses. 333
   Jones v. Block 334

C. Amending 338

1. General Rules. 338
   Beeck v. Aquaslide 'N' Dive Corp. 340
2. Relation Back. 344
   Bonerb v. Richard J. Caron Foundation 345
   Worthington v. Wilson 347

D. Abuses. 350

Walker v. Norwest Corp. 352
Christian v. Mattell, Inc. 354

VIII. JOINDER. 361

A. Claims 362

1. Multiple claims. 362
2. Counterclaims. 365
   United States v. Heyward-Robinson Co. 366
3. Crossclaims. 371

B. Parties. 372

1. Permissive joinder. 375
   Mosley v. General Motors Corp. 377
2. Compulsory joinder. 381
   Temple v. Synthes Corp. 382
   Wilbur v. Locke 386
   Republic of the Phillipines v. Pimentel 389
3. Third Parties. 393
   Price v. CTB, Inc. 395
   Owen Equipment & Erection Co. v. Kroger 398

C. Interpleader. 400

State Farm Fire & Casualty Co. v. Tashire 403

D. Intervention. 407

Natural Resources Defense Council v. U.S. Nuclear Reg. Commn. 409
Martin v. Wilks 414

E. Class Actions. 418

1. Certification 420

Communities for Equity v. Michigan High Sch. Athletic Assn. 423
Alston v. Virginia High School League, Inc. 427
Hubler Chevrolet, Inc. v. General Motors Corp. 432
2. Reach. 437
Hansberry v. Lee 442
Phillips Petroleum Co. v. Shutts 446
3. Resolution. 451
Amchem Products, Inc. v. Windsor 454

IX. ALTERNATIVE DISPUTE RESOLUTION 465
A. Negotiation. 469
G. Heileman Brewing Co. v. Joseph Oat Corp. 470
Evans v. Jeff D. 477
Buckhannon Bd. & Care Home, Inc. v. West Va. Dept. H.H.R 480
B. Offers of Judgment. 482
C. Mediation. 484
In re Atlantic Pipe Corp. 485
D. Neutral Evaluation. 490
E. Arbitration. 494
D'Iorio v. Majestic Lanes, Inc. 498

X. DISCOVERY 501
Silvestri v. General Motors Corp. 509
In re Napster Inc. Copyright Litigation 512
A. Scope 518
Thompson v. Department of Housing and Urban Development 519
B. Limitations. 525
Seattle Times Co. v. Rhinehart 526
1. Burden and Proportionality. 529
Gonzales v. Google, Inc. 530
2. Electronically Stored Information. 535
Pension Comm Univ. Montreal Pens. Plan v. Banc of Amer. Secs. ... 537
3. Privilege. 544
Upjohn Co. v. United States 545
Hopson v. Mayor of Baltimore 549
Hickman v. Taylor 556
C. Required Disclosures. 561
Chiquita Intern. Ltd. v. M/V Bolero Reefer 563
Krisa v. Equitable Life Assurance Society 565
D. Devices. 567
1. Production. 567
Williams v. Sprint/United Management Co. 572
2. Interrogatories. 576
In re Convergent Technologies Securities Litigation 581
3. Depositions. 584
4. Admissions. 592
5. Examination. 596
Abdulwali v. Washington Metro Area Transit Authority 598
E. Disputes. 600
Roadway Express, Inc. v. Piper 603
Coca-Cola Bottling Co. v. Coca-Cola Co. 606
Poole v. Textron 611

XI. ADJUDICATION BEFORE TRIAL 619
A. Pretrial Conference and Order. 620
Sanders v. Union Pacific R.R. Co. 624
Rogan v. Menino 625
B. Summary Judgment. 633
Adickes v. S.H. Kress & Co. 636
Celotex Corp. v. Catrett 643
Anderson v. Liberty Lobby, Inc. 648
Matsushita Elec. Industries Co. v. Zenith Radio Corp. 652
Bias v. Advantage International, Inc. 656
Scott v. Harris 660
XII. TRIAL 665
A. Jury Trial 667
1. Right to Jury Trial. 667
Beacon Theatres, Inc. v. Westover 670
Amoco Oil Co. v. Torcomian 677
Chauffeurs, Teamsters & Helpers, Local No. 391 v. Terry 680
2. Drawing Juries. 687
Edmonson v. Leesville Concrete Co. 694
Thompson v. Altheimer & Gray 698
3. Law-Fact Distinction 701
Markman v. Westview Instruments, Inc. 702
4. Instructing Juries 705
5. Judicial Control of Juries. 712
Pennsylvania Railroad v. Chamberlain 714
Reeves v. Sanderson Plumbing Products, Inc. 717
Unitherm Food System, Inc. v. Swift-Ekrich, Inc. 723
Caperton v. A.T. Massey Coal Co. 728
B. Order of Trial. 734
Gilbert v. DaimlerChrysler Corp. 736

RESULTS OF ADJUDICATION

XIII. JUDGMENT. 745
A. Obtaining Judgment. 746
Liberty Mutual Insurance Co. v. Wetzel 748
B. Challenging Judgment. 759
Weisgram v. Marley Co. 761
Dadurian v. Underwriters at Lloyd's of London 765
Peterson v. Wilson 768
C. Enforcing Judgment 775
In re Davis 778
XIV. APPEAL 789
A. Finality 792
1. Time to Appeal. 794
Bowles v. Russell 798
2. Exceptions. 801
Atlantic City Electric Co. v. General Electric Co. 803
Sears, Roebuck & Co. v. Mackey 804
Cohen v. Beneficial Industries Loan Corp. 808
Lauro Lines s.r.l. v. Chasser 810
Kerr v. United States District Court 815

3. State Variations. 820
B. Standard for Review. 821
1. Law and Fact. 822
Anderson v. City of Bessemer City 824
2. Harmless Error. 831
Harnden v. Jayco, Inc. 832
XV. EFFECT OF JUDGMENT 839
A. Claim Preclusion. 841
Mathews v. New York Racing Assn. 841
Migra v. Warren City School District Board of Education 845
1. Same Claim 848
Nestor v. Pratt & Whitney 849
2. Same Parties. 852
Richards v. Jefferson County 853
Taylor v. Sturgell 856
3. Final Judgment on the Merits. 860
Federated Department Stores, Inc. v. Moitie 861
Semtek Intl. Inc. v. Lockheed Martin Corp. 864
B. Issue Preclusion. 870
1. Same Issues 871
Southern Pacific Railroad Co. v. United States 872
2. Actually Litigated. 875
Cromwell v. County of Sac 875
3. Necessary to Decision. 879
Rios v. Davis 879
4. Parties and Non-Mutuality. 882
Bernhard v. Bank of America Nat. Trust & Sav. Assn. 883
Parklane Hosiery Co. v. Shore 886
Conclusion 891

APPENDIX I: FED. R. CIV. P. 895
APPENDIX II: FED. R. CIV. P. 949
INDEX 975

TABLE OF STATUTES & RULES

17 C.F.R. §240.17a-4, 512

10 DEL. CODE §3114, 102

12 OK. Stat.1971, §1701.03, 117

5 U.S.C. §571, 465
9 U.S.C. §1, 494
9 U.S.C. §2, 494,**495**,497
9 U.S.C. §3, **495**
9 U.S.C. §4, **495**
9 U.S.C. §5, **496**
9 U.S.C. §7, 494,**496**
9 U.S.C. §9, 494,**496**
9 U.S.C. §10, 494,**496**
9 U.S.C. §11, 494,**496**
11 U.S.C. §522, 778-783
11 U.S.C. §523, 779-780,782
11 U.S.C. §524, 779
15 U.S.C. §1, 289,670,861
15 U.S.C. §2, 670,723
15 U.S.C. §7, 386
15 U.S.C. §15, 670,861
15 U.S.C. §77p , 203,441
15 U.S.C. §78aa, 120
15 U.S.C. §78bb, 441
15 U.S.C. §78j, 305,863
15 U.S.C. §78n, 886
15 U.S.C. §78t, 886
15 U.S.C. §78u, 304-309,441
15 U.S.C. §78aa,115
15 U.S.C. §1053, 678
15 U.S.C. §1125, 110
20 U.S.C. §1681, 428
26 U.S.C. §527, 729
26 U.S.C. §6335, 170
26 U.S.C. §7402, 546
26 U.S.C. §7602, 545
26 U.S.C. §7604, 529
28 U.S.C. §17, 240
28 U.S.C. §144, 722,**723**
28 U.S.C. §351, 722
28 U.S.C. §455, 268,722,**727**
28 U.S.C. §471, 466,620
28 U.S.C. §473, 483
28 U.S.C. §631, 616
28 U.S.C. §636, 616,628,**630**
28 U.S.C. §651, 465,**466**,483,489,497
28 U.S.C. §652, **466**
28 U.S.C. §653, **466**
28 U.S.C. §654, **466**
28 U.S.C. §655, **467**
28 U.S.C. §656, **467**
28 U.S.C. §657, **467**,496-497
28 U.S.C. §658, **467**
28 U.S.C. §1254, 9
28 U.S.C. §1257, 9
28 U.S.C. §1258, 9
28 U.S.C. §1291, 745,**746**,747,750,787, 792-793,804-806,810
28 U.S.C. §1292, 801,**802**,803,808,810
28 U.S.C. §1331, **166**,167,171,185,189, 203,437
28 U.S.C. §1332, 166,174,**175**,176-185, 189-192,196,257,354,398-399,402,437-438,864
28 U.S.C. §1333, 166
28 U.S.C. §1334, 166,189
28 U.S.C. §1335, 178,390,**401-403**,404
28 U.S.C. §1337, 166
28 U.S.C. §1341, 166,174,386
28 U.S.C. §1350, 81
28 U.S.C. §1359, 179
28 U.S.C. §1367, **189**,190-195,202,363, 365,370-371,376,408
28 U.S.C. §1369, 174
28 U.S.C. §1391, 208,**209**,210-213,406
28 U.S.C. §1392, **210**,213
28 U.S.C. §1397, 406
28 U.S.C. §1404, 215,**216**,217,222-223,226
28 U.S.C. §1406, 214,**215**,217
28 U.S.C. §1407, **210**,217
28 U.S.C. §1441, 171,**197**,198-200,202, 213,864,869
28 U.S.C. §1442, 198
28 U.S.C. §1443, 198
28 U.S.C. §1445, 202
28 U.S.C. §1446, 199-200
28 U.S.C. §1447, 199-200,202
28 U.S.C. §1453, 173,183,196,198,437, **440**
28 U.S.C. §1604, 390
28 U.S.C. §1608, 155
28 U.S.C. §1631, 215,**216**,217
28 U.S.C. §1651, **813**,814,815,865
28 U.S.C. §1652, 229
28 U.S.C. §1673, 777,**778**
28 U.S.C. §1711, 437,**461**
28 U.S.C. §1712, **461**
28 U.S.C. §1713, **462**

28 U.S.C. §1714, **451**
28 U.S.C. §1715, **451**
28 U.S.C. §1738, 48,775,**845**,846-848,850
28 U.S.C. §1861, 687,**688**
28 U.S.C. §1862, **688**
28 U.S.C. §1863, 687,**688**
28 U.S.C. §1864, **689**
28 U.S.C. §1865, 688,**689**
28 U.S.C. §1866, **689**
28 U.S.C. §1867, **689**
28 U.S.C. §1870, 692,**693-695**
28 U.S.C. §1927, 359
28 U.S.C. §2072, 6,121,**248**,250,256,294, 546,807,844
28 U.S.C. §2106, **807**
28 U.S.C. §2107, 792,**795**,797-799
28 U.S.C. §2111, **831**
28 U.S.C. §2201, 170,668,**669**
28 U.S.C. §2202, 667,668,**669**
28 U.S.C. §2241, 848
28 U.S.C. §2283, 407
28 U.S.C. §2361, 130,405,**406**,407
28 U.S.C. §2403, 264
28 U.S.C. §2412, 10
29 U.S.C. §621, 718
29 U.S.C. §623, 719
29 U.S.C. §626, **475**
29 U.S.C. §1132, 121
30 U.S.C. §901, 459
35 U.S.C. §102, 722
40 U.S.C. §270a,367
40 U.S.C. §270b, 367
42 U.S.C. §1981, 376
42 U.S.C. §1982, 518
42 U.S.C. §1983, 10,335-336,347,427,515, 618,628,6655,708,845-847
42 U.S.C. §1985, 282-283,846
42 U.S.C. §1988, 10,476,768
42 U.S.C. §1997e, 333-334
42 U.S.C. §2000e, 377,418,683,747,824
42 U.S.C. §2011, 408
42 U.S.C. §3601, 477
42 U.S.C. §3612, 672
42 U.S.C. §4332, 409
42 U.S.C. §12101, 478
42 U.S.C. §12205, 478
45 U.S.C. §51, 624
47 U.S.C. §231, 528
50 U.S.C.S. App. §521, 317

ABA MODEL R. PROF. CONDUCT 1.1, 417
ABA MODEL R. PROF. CONDUCT 1.2, 166
ABA MODEL R. PROF. CONDUCT 1.5, 417
ABA MODEL R. PROF. CONDUCT 1.7, 372
ABA MODEL R. PROF. CONDUCT 5.5, 36
ABA MODEL R. PROF. CONDUCT 7.3, 458

CAL. CIVIL CODE §1670.5, 493
CAL. CODE CIV. P. §410.10, 111
CAL. CODE CIV. P. §415.30, 148
CAL. CODE CIV. P. §425.10, 274
CAL. CODE CIV. P. §425.11, 274
CAL. CODE CIV. P. §425.13, 311
CAL. CODE CIV. P. §473, 311
CAL. CODE CIV. P. §583.210, 130
CAL. CODE CIV. P. §1021.5, 10
CAL. CODE CIV. P. §1141.21, 492
CAL. CODE CIV. P. §1250.020, 209
CAL. BUS. & PROF. CODE §6068, 358
CAL. FIN. CODE §22341, 209

D.C. CODE ANN. § 35-414, 654

FED. R. APP. P. 1, **791**
FED. R. APP. P. 2, **791**
FED. R. APP. P. 3, **791**
FED. R. APP. P. 4, **794**,796-797
FED. R. APP. P. 5, 801,**802**
FED. R. APP. P. 21, **814**
FED. R. APP. P. 38, **836**
FED. R. APP. P. 58, 796
FED. R. APP. P. FORM 1, **791**

FED. R. CIV. P. 1, **4**,646,660,791,794
FED. R. CIV. P. 2, **4**,269,670,681,791
FED. R. CIV. P. 3, **5**,249,270,790-791,793
FED. R. CIV. P. 4, **24**,81,126,130,148,149, 152,154, 155,250-253,313,392,365,405, 788,835
FED. R. CIV. P. 4.1, **28**
FED. R. CIV. P. 5, **319**
FED. R. CIV. P. 5.1, 262
FED. R. CIV. P. 5.2, 272
FED. R. CIV. P. 6, **312**
FED. R. CIV. P. 7, **267**,270,322,324
FED. R. CIV. P. 7.1, 267,269
FED. R. CIV. P. 8, **271**,273,274-275,281, 283,287,290-291,294,297,301-303,307-309,321,325,329,331-335,337,359,750,852
FED. R. CIV. P. 9, 271,300,**301**,302-303,333
FED. R. CIV. P. 10, **272**,324,332,788
FED. R. CIV. P. 11, 10,269,273,323,332, 350-351,**352**,353-354,788,823
FED. R. CIV. P. 12, 71,99,**124**,174,214,271, 282,284-286,288,293,307,311-312,318-320,324,337,350,353,359,365,386,626,789, 790,852,862-863

FED. R. CIV. P. 13, 365,**366,**367,369-371, 378,462
FED. R. CIV. P. 14, 113,363,393,**394**,395-397,391
FED. R. CIV. P. 15, 271,337,**338**,340-346, 370
FED. R. CIV. P. 16, 469-472,484,547-550, 555,569,620-621,**622**,625-628,662
FED. R. CIV. P. 17, 373,**374**
FED. R. CIV. P. 18, 362,**363**,364-365,395, 462,674
FED. R. CIV. P. 19, 189,214,**381**,383-392, 400,413,415-416,462
FED. R. CIV. P. 20, 189,375,**376**,377-380, 421,462
FED. R. CIV. P. 21, **376**,380
FED. R. CIV. P. 22, **401**,402-403
FED. R. CIV. P. 23, 193,256,379,419,**420,** 422-436,**437**,452,454,457-459,461,463, 476,854,865
FED. R. CIV. P. 23.1, 250,358,373,**374**
FED. R. CIV. P. 23.2, 373,**375**,419
FED. R. CIV. P. 24, 189,**407**,408-412,415, 417,462
FED. R. CIV. P. 25, **375**,790
FED. R. CIV. P. 26, 474,**498**,517-520,526, 527-530,532,534,541,542,546,547-551, 543-554,557-563,568,588,600-601,603, 604,607,851
FED. R. CIV. P. 27, **505**,790
FED. R. CIV. P. 28, 500,585,**586**,790
FED. R. CIV. P. 29, 555,**566,**597
FED. R. CIV. P. 30, 500,585,**586,**591-592, 600,790
FED. R. CIV. P. 31, 500,585,**586,**600
FED. R. CIV. P. 32, 500,585,**586**,790
FED. R. CIV. P. 33, 520,547,577,**578**,580-582,597
FED. R. CIV. P. 34, 520,529,547,**565**,572-573,600
FED. R. CIV. P. 35, 249, 500,561,**596**,597-598,813
FED. R. CIV. P. 36, 592,**593,**613
FED. R. CIV. P. 37, 507,525-526,534,547, 554,600,**601,**604-606,601-604,607
FED. R. CIV. P. 38, **669,**670,673
FED. R. CIV. P. 39, 669,**670,**676
FED. R. CIV. P. 40, **667**
FED. R. CIV. P. 41, 130,214,**322**,323-324, 395,475,624,855,865-867
FED. R. CIV. P. 42, 188,377,380,672-673, 676
FED. R. CIV. P. 43, **734**
FED. R. CIV. P. 44, **734**
FED. R. CIV. P. 44.1, 265
FED. R. CIV. P. 45, **521**,529-530,568
FED. R. CIV. P. 46, 724,**735**,835
FED. R. CIV. P. 47, **691**,696
FED. R. CIV. P. 48, **688**
FED. R. CIV. P. 49, **730**
FED. R. CIV. P. 50, **713**,721-723,725-726, 743,751-765,787
FED. R. CIV. P. 51, 706,**707**,712,835
FED. R. CIV. P. 52, **751**,822,826-828
FED. R. CIV. P. 53, 320,**628**
FED. R. CIV. P. 54, 147,275,481-492,**746**, 749-750,787,792,804-806
FED. R. CIV. P. 55, **315-316**,317-319,323
FED. R. CIV. P. 56, 271,287,294,349,626-627,633,**635**,638-640,643-650,652,654-655,659,661,663,749-750,792,832,841,852
FED. R. CIV. P. 57, 671,675,**676**
FED. R. CIV. P. 58, 754,**756**
FED. R. CIV. P. 59, 723,759,**761**,762,765, 774-775,787
FED. R. CIV. P. 60, 317,624,**774**,775-776, 787
FED. R. CIV. P. 61, **772**,832
FED. R. CIV. P. 62, 750,**770**
FED. R. CIV. P. 62.1, 774
FED. R. CIV. P. 63, **667**
FED. R. CIV. P. 64, 787
FED. R. CIV. P. 65, 407,**758**,759
FED. R. CIV. P. 65.1, **402**
FED. R. CIV. P. 66, **402**
FED. R. CIV. P. 67, **402**
FED. R. CIV. P. 68, 10,**481**,482
FED. R. CIV. P. 69, **777**,778-780,783-784
FED. R. CIV. P. 70, **786**
FED. R. CIV. P. 71.1, **309**,786,**787**
FED. R. CIV. P. 72, **616**
FED. R. CIV. P. 73, 628,**629**
FED. R. CIV. P. 77, 755,**757**,797
FED. R. CIV. P. 78, 616,**617**
FED. R. CIV. P. 79, 755,**757**
FED. R. CIV. P. 80, 734,**735**
FED. R. CIV. P. 81, **5**,199
FED. R. CIV. P. 82, **27**,215
FED. R. CIV. P. 83, 4, **5**,470,485,495
FED. R. CIV. P. 84, **273**,276,282,302,324
FED. R. CIV. P. 85, **6**
FED. R. CIV. P. 86, **6**

FED. R. CIV. P. FORM 1, **276**
FED. R. CIV. P. FORM 2, **349**
FED. R. CIV. P. FORM 3, 147,313
FED. R. CIV. P. FORM 6, 148
FED. R. CIV. P. FORM 7, 185

FED. R. CIV. P. FORM 10, 276,**277**
FED. R. CIV. P. FORM 11, **277-278**
FED. R. CIV. P. FORM 13, **278**
FED. R. CIV. P. FORM 21, 302,**303**
FED. R. CIV. P. FORM 30, 324,**325**
FED. R. CIV. P. FORM 41, **394-395**
FED. R. CIV. P. FORM 50, 566,**567**
FED. R. CIV. P. FORM 51, **594**
FED. R. CIV. P. FORM 70, **754**
FED. R. CIV. P. FORM 71, **754**
FED. R. CIV. P. FORM 80, **632**
FED. R. CIV. P. FORM 81, **632**
FED. R. CIV. P. FORM 82, **632**

FED. R. EVID. 501, 542
FED. R. EVID. 502, **551**
FED. R. EVID. 606, 769-772
FED. R. EVID. 702, 764

FL. CONST. ART. 10, §4, **779**
FL. R. CIV. P. 1.110, 363
FL. R. CIV. P. 1.120, 313
FL. STAT. §768.57, 313
FL. STAT. §768.81, 397
FL. STAT. §768.495, 312

ILL. COMP. STAT. 5/2-301, 123

IOWA CODE ANN. §600B.13, 359

MICH. CT. R. 2.102, 130
MICH. CT. R. 2.103, 149
MICH. CT. R. 2.104, 155
MICH. CT. R. 2.105, 149
MICH. CT. R. 2.111, 275
MICH. CT. R. 2.112, 397
MICH. CT. R. 2.114, 10,350
MICH. CT. R. 2.116, 287,633,640-641
MICH. CT. R. 2.118, 337
MICH. CT. R. 2.203, 363
MICH. CT. R. 2.205, 381
MICH. CT. R. 2.206, 375
MICH. CT. R. 2.221, 219
MICH. CT. R. 2.222, 219
MICH. CT. R. 2.223, 219
MICH. CT. R. 2.403, **490**
MICH. CT. R. 2.405, 481
MICH. CT. R. 3.411, 171
MICH. CT. R. 2.516, **711**
MICH. CT. R. 2.613, **821**
MICH. COMP. L. §37.2302, 424
MICH. COMP. L. §600.1605, **207**
MICH. COMP. L. §600.1611, **207**,209
MICH. COMP. L. §600.1615, **207**
MICH. COMP. L. §600.1621, **208**
MICH. COMP. L. §600.1629, **208**,209
MICH. COMP. L. §600.2912b, 312
MICH. COMP. L. §600.2912d, 312

MINN. CT. R. 13.01, 365

MISSOURI R. CIV. P. 70.02, **701**

N.J. GEN. CT. R. 1:21-7(c), 14
N.J. L. CIV. R. 201.1, 497

N.Y. CIVIL PRAC. L. §302, 112
N.Y. CIVIL PRAC. L. §425.10, **270**
N.Y. CIVIL PRAC. L. §503, **207**
N.Y. CIV. PRAC. L. §504, 209
N.Y. CIV. PRAC. L. §507, 209
N.Y. CIV. PRAC. L. §508, 209
N.Y. CIVIL PRAC. L. §601, 364
N.Y. CIVIL PRAC. L. §1001, 381
N.Y. CIVIL PRAC. L. §1002, 385
N.Y. CIVIL PRAC. L. §3011, **270**
N.Y. CIV. PRAC. L. §3013, **271**
N.Y. CIV. PRAC. L. §3014, **271**
N.Y. CIV. PRAC. L. §5205, 779
N.Y. CIV. PRAC. L. §5501, 256-262
N.Y. CIV. PRAC. L. §5701, **820**
N.Y CODE P. §208, 669
N.Y. COMP. CODES R. & REGS. §500.27, 264
N.Y. CT. R. §212.9, 218-219

R.I. GENERAL L. §9-5-33, 112

TENN. CODE ANN. §36-4-105, 209
TENN. CODE ANN. §36-5-303, 209
TENN. CODE ANN. §36-5-304, 209

TEX. R. CIV. P. 120, 123

U.S. CONST. AM. IV, §1, 34-35
U.S. CONST. AM. VII, **669**
U.S. CONST. ART. I, §8, 240,241,387
U.S. CONST. ART. III, §1, 9
U.S. CONST. ART. III, §2, **165**,166,167,180, 187
U.S. CONST. ART. IV, §4, 848
U.S. CONST. ART. IV, §1, 164
U.S. CONST. ART. IV, §2, 37
U.S. CONST. ART. V, §1, 34

WASH. REV. CODE §4.24.611, 474

TABLE OF CASES

Abdulwali v. Washington Metro Area Trans. Auth., 193 F.R.D. (D. D.C. 2000), **599**

Abney v. United States, 431 U.S. 651 (1977), 811

Abney v. Patten, 696 F.Supp. 567 (W.D. Okla. 1987), 472

Acito v. IMCERA Group, Inc., 47 F.3d 47 (2d Cir. 1995), 302

Adam v. Saenger, 303 U.S. 59 (1938), 37

Adams v. Davison-Paxon Co., 230 S.C. 532, 96 S.E.2d 566 (1957), 246

Adams v. Travelers Indem. Co., 465 F.3d 156 (5th Cir. 2006), 823

Adickes v. S.H. Kress & Co., 398 U.S. 144 (1970), **636**,643-645,648,650,656

Adler v. Wal-Mart Stores, Inc., 144 F.3d 664 (10th Cir. 1998), 649

Aguchak v. Montgomery Ward Co., 520 P.2d 1352 (Alaska 1974), 147

Albemarle Paper Co. v. Moody, 422 U.S. 405 (1975), 11,684

Aldinger v. Howard, 427 U.S. 1 (1976), 179 ALS Scan, Inc. v. Digital Service Consultants, Inc., 293 F.3d 707 (4th Cir.2002), 69-71,79

Allard v. Frizzell, 536 F.2d 1332 (10th Cir. 1976), 410,412

Allen v. McCurry, 449 U.S. 90 (1980), 838-839,846

Allied-Bruce Terminix Cos. v. Dobson, 513 U.S. 265 (1995), 493

Alloy Prods. Corp. v. United States, 302 F.2d 528 (Ct. Cl. 1962), 331

Allstate Ins. Co. v. Hague, 449 U.S. 302 (1981), 265,450

Altec, Inc. v. FWD Corp., 399 F.2d 860 (5th Cir. 1968), 397

Alston v. Virginia High School League, Inc., 184 F.R.D. 574 (1999), **427**

Alyeska Pipeline Service v. Wilderness Society, 421 U.S. 240 (1975), 10,11,605

Amchem Products v. Windsor, 521 U.S. 591 (1997), 217,429,**454**

American Annuity Group., Inc. v. Guaranty Reassurance Corp., 140 F. Supp.2d 859 (S.D. Ohio 2001), 371

American Dredging Co. v. Miller, 510 U.S. 443 (1994), 226

American Fire & Cas. Co. v. Finn, 341 U.S. 6 (1951), 198,201,367

American Life Ins. Co. v. Stewart, 300 U.S. 203 (1937), 668,675

Amoco Oil Co. v. Torcomian, 722 F.2d 1099 (3rd Cir. 1983), **678**

Anderson v. City of Bessemer City, 470 U.S. 564 (1985), 822,**823**

Anderson v. Liberty Lobby, Inc., 477 U.S. 242 (1986), 645,**649**,657,661

Angel v. Bullington, 330 U.S. 183 (1947), 842-843,862

Anheuser-Busch, Inc. v. John Labatt Ltd., 89 F.3d 1339 (8th Cir. 1996), 304

Ankenbrandt v. Richards, 504 U.S. 689 (1992), 183

Arizona v. California, 530 U.S. 392 (2000), 852,868,874

Arizonans for Official English v. Arizona, 520 U.S. 43 (1997), 263

Armstrong v. Pomerance, 423 A.2d 174 (Del. 1980), 109

Asahi Metal Indus. Co. v. Superior Ct., 480 U.S. 102 (1987), **63**,146

Arnold v. Pennsylvania Dept. of Transp., 477 F.3d 105 (3d Cir. 2007), 527

Asea, Inc. v. S. Pac. Transp. Co., 669 F.2d 1242 (9th Cir.1981), 593

Ashcroft v. ACLU, 542 U.S. 656 (2004), 529

Ashcroft v. Iqbal, 129 S. Ct. 1937 (2009), **296**

Associated Gen. Contractors of Cal., Inc. v. Carpenters, 459 U.S. 519 (1983), 292

Atlanta Leasing & Finance, Inc. v. IPM Technology, Inc., 885 F.2d 188 (4th Cir. 1989), 100

Atlantic City Elec. Co. v. General Elec. Co., 337 F.2d 844 (1964), **803**

Altlas Roofing Co. v. Occupational Health & Safety Review Commn., 430 U.S. 442 (1977), 687

Ausherman v. Stump, 643 F.2d 715 (10th Cir. 1981), 282

Avitia v. Metropolitan Club of Chicago, Inc., 49 F.3d 1219 (7th Cir. 1995), 304

Bail v. Cunningham Bros., Inc., 452 F.2d 182 (7th Cir. 1971), 275
Baker v. General Motors Corp., 522 U.S. 222 (1998), 474,840
Baldwin v. Iowa State Traveling Men's Assn., 283 U.S. 522 (1931), 125,862
Baltimore & Carolina Line v. Redman, 295 U.S. 654 (1935), 726,763
Baltimore & Ohio R.R. Co. v. Baugh, 149 U.S. 368, 401 (1893), 238,239
Baltimore S.S. Co. v. Phillips, 274 U.S. 316 (1927), 843,862
Banco Nacional de Cuba v. Sabbatino, 376 U.S. 398 (1964), 241
Bancroft & Masters, Inc. v. Augusta National Inc., 223 F.3d 1082 (9th Cir. 2000), 77
Bank of Augusta v. Earle, 38 U.S. 519 (1839), 39
Bank of India v. Trendi Sportswear, Inc., 239 F.3d 428 (2d Cir. 2000), 400
Bankers Trust Co. v. Mallis, 435 U.S. 381 (1978), 796
Bankers Life & Casualty Co. v. Crenshaw, 486 U.S. 71 (1988), 836
Bankers Life & Casualty Co. v. Holland, 346 U.S. 379 (1953), 803,806-808
Barab v. Menford, 98 F.R.D. 455 (E.D. Pa. 1983), 396
Barnell v Taubman Co., 512 NW2d 13 (Mich. Ct. App. 1993), 641
Bass v. Hoagland, 172 F.2d 205 (5th Cir. 1949), 313
Bateman v. U.S. Postal Service, 231 F.3d 1220 (9th Cir. 2000), 775
Bates v. C & S Adjusters, Inc., 980 F.2d 865 (2d Cir. 1992), 212
Batson v. Kentucky, 476 U.S. 79 (1986), 694,695,697
Beacon Theatres, Inc. v. Westover, 359 U.S. 500 (1959), **671**,676-677,679-680,683, 803
Beattie v. United States, 756 F.2d 91 (D.C. Cir. 1984), 209
Bedingfield v. Jefferson County, 527 So.2d 1270 (1988), 853
Beeck v. Aquaslide 'N' Dive Corp., 350 N.W.2d 149 (Iowa 1984), 342
Beeck v. Aquaslide 'N' Dive Corp., 562 F.2d 537 (8th Cir. 1977), **342**
Behrens v. Pelletier, 516 U.S. 299 (1996), 808
Bell Atlantic Corp. v. Twombly, 550 U.S. 544 (2007), **289**,294,296,298,300-301
Bell v. Hood, 327 U.S. 678 (1946), 862
Ben-Hur v. Cauble, 255 U.S. 356 (1921), 437
Benson and Ford, Inc. v. Wanda Petroleum Co., 833 F.2d 1172 (5th Cir, 1987), 855
Berkovitz v. HBO, Inc., 89 F.3d 24 (1st Cir. 1996), 627
Berner v. British Commonwealth Pac. Airlines, 346 F.2d 532 (2d. Cir. 1965), 887
Bernhard v. Bank of America Nat. Trust & Sav. Assn., 122 P.2d 892 (Cal. Sup. Ct. 1942), **882**,887
Bernhardt v. Polygraphic Co., 350 U.S. 198 (1956), 245-247
Berrety v. Asarco Inc., 439 F.3d 636 (10th Cir. 2006), 848
Bertrand v Alan Ford, Inc., 537 NW2d 185 (Mich. 1995), 641
Best Van Lines, Inc. v. Walker, 490 F.3d 239 (2d Cir. 2007), 79
Bias Advantage Intern., Inc., 905 F.2d 1558 (D.C. Cir. 1990), **654**
Bigelow v. Old Dominion Copper Mining & Smelting Co., 225 U.S. 111 (1912), 383
Bird v. Parsons, 289 F.3d 865 (6th Cir. 2002), 44
Black & White Taxicab & Transfer Co. v.
Black Clawson Co. v. Kroenert Corp., 245 F.3d 759 (8th Cir. 2001), 860
Black Horse Lane Assoc., L.P. v. Dow Chemical Corp., 228 F.3d 275 (3d Cir. 2000), 593
Blackmer v. United States, 284 U.S. 421 (1932), 36
Blair Holdings Corp. v. Rubinstein, 133 F.Supp. 496 (S.D. N.Y. 1955), 179-180
Blanchard v. Bergeron, 489 U.S. 87 (1989), 10
Blank v. Sullivan & Cromwell, 418 F.Supp. 1 (S.D. N.Y. 1975), 727
Blonder-Tongue Laboratories, Inc. v. University of Illinois Foundation, 402 U.S. 313 (1971), 886-887
Blue Chip Stamps v. Manor Drug Stores, 421 U.S. 723 (1975), 306
Boeing Co. v. Van Gemert, 444 U.S. 472 (1980), 460
Bogosian v. Gulf Oil Corp., 738 F.2d 587 (3d Cir. 1984), 563
Bolling v. Sharpe, 347 U.S. 497 (1954), 695
Bonerb v. Richard J. Caron Fdn., 159 F.R.D. 16 (1994), **344**

Bowles v. Russell, 551 U.S. 205 (2007), **798**
Bovis v. Crab Meadow Enterps., Ltd., 889 N.Y.S.2d 634 (N.Y. Sup. Ct. App. Div. 2009), 397
Bowne of New York City, Inc.v. AmBase Corp., 150 F.R.D. 465 (S.D. N.Y. 1993), 546
Boyle v. United Technologies Corp., 487 U.S. 500 (1988), 241
BP Chemicals Ltd. v. Formosa Chemical & Fibre Corp., 229 F.3d 254 (3d Cir. 2000), 122
Braxton v. Litchalk, 223 N.W.2d 316 (Mich. Ct. App. 1974), 877
Brill v. Countrywide Home Loans, Inc., 427 F.3d 446 (7th Cir. 2005), 196
Brooke Group Ltd. v. Brown & Williamson Tobacco Corp., 509 U.S. 209 (1993), 764
Browder v. Director, Dept. of Corrections of Ill., 434 U.S. 257 (1978), 798
Brown & Yellow Taxicab & Transfer Co., 276 U.S. 518 (1928), 236,239
Brown Shoe Co. v. United States, 370 U.S. 294 (1962), 793
Brown v. Board of Education, 347 U.S. 443 (1954), 14
Brown v. Demco, Inc., 792 F.2d 478 (5th Cir. 1986), 202
Brown v. Felsen, 442 U.S. 127 (1979), 840
Brunette Machine Works, Ltd. v. Kockum Indus., Inc., 406 U.S. 706 (1972), 213
Bucher v. Richardson Hosp. Authority, 160 F.R.D. 88 (D.C. Tex. 1994), 527
Buckeye Check Cashing, Inc. v. Cardegna, 546 U.S. 440 (2006), 493
Buckhannon Bd. and Care Home, Inc. v. West Virginia Dept. of Health and Human Resources, 532 U.S. 598 (2001), **478**
Bud Brooks Trucking, Inc. v. Bill Hodges Trucking Co., 909 F.2d 1437 (10th Cir. 1990), 469
Bundy Tubing Co. v. Royal Indemnity Co., 298 F2d 151 (6th Cir. 1962), 642
Burger King Corp. v. Rudzewicz, 471 U.S. 462 (1985), **58**,61,63,67,68,80-82,94
Burlington Northern R. Co. v. Woods, 480 U.S. 1 (1987), 255
Burnham v. Superior Ct., 495 U.S. 604 (1990), **90**
Burrell v. Armijo, 456 F.3d 1159 (10th Cir. 2006), 852
Busch v. Buchman, Buchman & O'Brien, 11 F.3d 1255 (5th Cir. 1994), 121
Bush v. Shabahang, 772 N.W.2d 272 (Mich. Sup. Ct. 2009), 312
Business Guides v. Chromatic Communs. Enterps., 498 U.S. 533 (1991), 359
Byrd v. Blue Ridge Rural Elec. Coop., 356 U.S. 525 (1958), **246**,248,251,260
Byrnie v. Town of Cromwell, 243 F.3d 93 (2d Cir. 2001), 516

Calder v. Jones, 465 U.S. 783 (1984), 65,75
Califano v. Yamasaki, 442 U.S. 682 (1979), 422
California Public Employees' Ret. Sys. v. WorldCom, Inc., 368 F.3d 86 (2d Cir. 2004), 199
Canada Malting Co. v. Paterson Steamships, Ltd., 285 U.S. 413 (1932), 216
Caperton v. A.T. Massey Coal Co., __ U.S. __, 129 S.Ct. 2252 (2009), **728**
Capron v. Van Noorden, 6 U.S. 126 (1804), 173
Carden v. Arkoma Assocs., 494 U.S. 185 (1990), 183
Cardenas v. Dorel Juvenile Group, Inc., 230 F.R.D. 635 (D. Kan. 2005), 528
Carlson v. Green, 446 U.S. 14 (1980), 666
Carnival Cruise Lines, Inc. v. Shute, 499 U.S. 585 (1991), 93
Carrion v. Yeshiva University, 535 F.2d 722 (2d Cir. 1976), 12
Carter v. Countrywide Credit Indus., Inc., 362 F.3d 294 (5th Cir. 2004), 496
Carter v. Jury Commission of Greene County, 396 U.S. 320 (1970), 695
Carter v. United States, 333 F.3d 791 (7th Cir. 2003), 333
Cary v. Curtis, 44 U.S. 236 (1845), 165
Cascade Natural Gas Corp. v. El Paso Natural Gas Co., 386 U.S. 129 (1967), 410
Cash v. Hamilton County Department of Adult Probation, 388 F.3d 539 (6th Cir. 2004), 146
Castano v. The American Tobacco Co., 84 F.3d 734 (5th Cir 1996), 451
Caterpillar, Inc. v. Lewis, 519 U.S. 61 (1996), 199
Caterpillar Inc. v Williams, 482 U.S. 386 (1987), 202
Catlin v. United States, 324 U.S. 229 (1945), 745,792,810,812
Celotex Corp. v. Catrett, 477 U.S. 317 (1986), 627,**643**,648-649,656-657

Centerville ALF, Inc. v. Balanced Care Corp., 197 F.Supp.2d 1039 (S.D. Ohio 2002), 214
Century Wrecker Corp. v. Vulcan Equipment Co., 733 F.Supp. 1170 (E.D. Tenn. 1989), 213
Chambers v. NASCO, Inc., 501 U.S. 32 (1991), 10,359,485,508,511
Chaplaincy of Full Gospel Churches v. England, 454 F.3d 290 (D.C. Cir. 2006), 759
Chase National Bank v. Norwalk, 291 U.S. 431 (1934), 415
Chauffeurs, Teamsters & Helpers, Local No. 391 v. Terry, 494 U.S. 558 (1990), **681**,686
Chavis v. Fidelity Warranty Services, Inc., 415 F.Supp.2d 520 (D. S.C. 2006), 196
Cheney v. United States District Court, 542 U.S. 367 (2004), 816
Chicot County Drainage Dist. v. Baxter State Bank, 308 U.S. 371 (1939), 174
Chiquita Intern. Ltd. v. M/V Bolero Reefer, 1994 WL 177785 (S.D. N.Y. 1994), **561**
Christianburg Garment Co. v. EEOC, 434 U.S. 412 (1978), **11**
Christian v. Mattell, Inc., 286 F.3d 1118 (9th Cir. 2003), 353
Christianson v. Colt Indus. Operating Corp., 486 U.S. 800 (1988), 878
Christopher v. Florida, 449 F.3d 1360 (11th Cir. 2006), 823
Chrysler Corp. v. Varey, 186 F.3d 1016 (8th Cir. 1999), 601
Circuit City Stores, Inc. v. Adams, 279 F.3d 889 (9th Cir. 2002), 497
City of Monterey v. Del Monte Dunes, 526 U.S. 687 (1999), 686
Clark v. Paul Gray, Inc., 306 U.S. 583 (1939), 192,194,437
Clay v. American Tobacco Co., 188 F.R.D. 483 (S.D. Ill. 1999), 434
CNA Fin. Corp. v. Brown, 162 F.3d 1334 (11th Cir.1998), 498
Coastal Video Communs. Corp. v. The Staywell Corp., 59 F.Supp. 562 (Ed. Va. 1999), 84
Cobell v. Norton, 224 F.R.D. 1, 3 (D. D.C. 2004), 321
Coca-Cola Bottling Co. v. Coca-Cola Co., 107 F.R.D. 288 (D. Del. 1985), **606**
Coca-Cola Bottling Co. v. Coca-Cola Co., 110 F.R.D. 363 (D. Del. 1986), 611
Cohen v. Beneficial Indus. Loan Corp., 337 U.S. 541 (1949), 245,249,255,807-808,810-811
Cohen v. The Republic of the Philippines, 146 F.R.D. 90 (S.D. N.Y. 1993), 401
Colby v. Umbrella, Inc., 955 A.2d 1082 (Vt. 2008), 301
Colgrove v. Battin, 413 U.S. 149 (1973), 687,703
Commissioner v. Sunnen, 333 U.S. 591 (1948), 861
Communities for Equity v. Michigan High School Athletic Assn., 192 F.R.D. 568 (W.D. Mich. 1999), **423**
Communities for Equity v. Michigan High School Athletic Assn., 459 F.3d 676 (6th Cir. 2006), 431
Community Dental Services v. Tani, 282 F.3d 1164 (9th Cir. 2002), 775
Cone v. West Virginia Pulp & Paper Co., 330 U.S. 212 (1947), 724-725
Confederated Tribes of Chehalis Indian Reservation v Lujan, 928 F.2d 1496 (9th Cir. 1991), 393
Conley v. Gibson, 355 U.S. 41 (1957), **282**,284,290-292,294,296,306
Connecticut National Bank v. Rytman, 694 A.2d 1246 (Conn. 1997), 851
Connecticut v. Doehr, 501 U.S. 1 (1991), 158,**782**
Consolidated Edison Co. v. Bodman, 445 F.3d 438 (D.C. Cir. 2006), 840
Consolidation Coal Co. v. Bucyrus-Erie Co., 432 N.E.2d 250 (Ill. 1982), 542
Cooke v. United States, 267 U.S. 517 (1925), 604
Cooper Indus., Inc., v. Leatherman Tool Group, Inc., 532 U.S. 424 (2001), 821
Coopers & Lybrand v. Livesay, 437 U.S. 463 (1978), 811
Cooter & Gell v. Harmarx Corp., 496 U.S. 384 (1990), 322,822
County of Suffolk v. Long Island Lighting Co., 122 F.R.D. 120 (E.D. N.Y. 1988), 564
Covey v. Town of Somers, 351 U.S. 141 (1956), 139
Craigie v. General Motors Corp., 740 F.Supp. 353 (E.D. Pa. 1990), 396
Crawford v. Chabot, 202 F.R.D. 223 (W.D. Mich. 1998), 860
Crawford-El v. Britton, 523 U.S. 574 (1998), 664
Cromwell v. County of Sac, 94 U.S. 351 (1877), 861,**874**

Cruz v. Coach Stores, Inc., 202 F.3d 560 (2d Cir. 2000), 343
Cullen v. Auto-Owners Ins. Co., 189 P.3d 344 (2008), 301
Cunningham v. Hamilton County, 527 U.S. 198 (1999), 807
Curtis v. Loether, 415 U.S. 189 (1974), 680,683,686
Curtiss-Wright Corp. v. General Electric Co., 446 U.S. 1 (1980), 751,804
Cybersell, Inc. v. Cybersell, Inc., 130 F.3d 414 (9th Cir.1997), 78

D'Arcy v. Ketchum, 52 U.S. 165 (1850),125
D.H. Overmyer Co. v. Frick Co., 405 U.S. 174 (1972), 100
D'Iorio v. Majestic Lanes, Inc., 370 F.3d 354 (3rd Cir. 2004), 496
Dadurian v. Underwriters at Lloyd's of London, 787 F.2d 756 (1st Cir. 1986), **765**
Dairy Queen, Inc. v. Wood, 369 U.S. 469 (1962), 678-679
Daniel v. American Bd. of Emergency Medicine, 428 F.3d 408 (2d Cir. 2005), 212
Danner v Anskis, 256 F.2d 123 (3d Cir. 1958), 371
Data Disc, Inc. v. Systems Technology Associates, Inc., 557 F.2d 1280 (9th Cir. 1977), 124
Daubert v. Merrell Dow Pharmaceuticals, Inc., 509 U.S. 579 (1993), 762
Davis v. Piper Aircraft Corp., 615 F.2d 606 (4th Cir. 1980), 348
Day & Zimmerman, Inc. v. Challoner, 423 U.S. 3 (1975), 264
Del Vecchio v. Conseco, Inc., 230 F.3d 974 (7th Cir. 2000), 184
Delta Air Lines, Inc. v. August, 450 U.S. 346 (1981), 481
Denny v. Barber, 576 F.2d 465 (2d Cir. 1978), 303
Denny v. Carey, 72 F.R.D. 574 (E.D. Pa. 1976), 303
Deposit Bank v. Frankfort, 191 U.S. 499 (1903), 866
Devlin v. Scardelletti, 536 U.S. 1, 10 (2002), 179,834
Dhamer v. Bristol-Myers Squibb Co., 183 F.R.D. 520 (N.D. Ill. 1998), 434
Diaz v. Paterson, 547 F.3d 88 (2d Cir. 2008), 161
Diaz v. Southern Drilling Corp., 427 F.2d 1118 (5th Cir. 1970), 412
Di Bari v. Incaica Cia Armadora, S.A., 126 F.R.D. 12 (E.D. N.Y. 1989), 599
Dice v. Akron, Canton & Youngstown R. Co., 342 U.S. 359 (1952), 233
Digital Equip. Corp. v. Desktop Direct, Inc., 511 U.S. 863 (1994), 807
DiLeo v. Ernst & Young, 901 F.2d. 624 (7th Cir. 1990), 304
Dimick v. Schiedt, 293 U.S. 474 (1935), 671,768
Dobkin v. Chapman, 236 N.E.2d 451 (N.Y. Ct. App. 1968), 146
Dobson v. Masonite Corp., 359 F.2d 921 (5th Cir. 1966), 702
Doctor's Assocs., Inc. v. Casarotto, 517 U.S. 681 (1996), 494
Doe v. Unocal Corp., 248 F.3d 915 (9th Cir. 2001), 47
Dombrowski v. Eastland, 387 U.S. 82 (1967), 651
Donaldson v. Microsoft Corp., 205 F.R.D. 558 (W.D. Wash. 2001), 422
Donaldson v. United States, 400 U.S. 517 (1971), 410,412
Donatelli v. National Hockey League, 893 F.2d 459 (1st Cir. 1990), 24
Donovan v. Penn Shipping Co., 429 U.S. 648 (1977), 261,766
Douglas v. U.S.A.A., 79 F.3d 1415 (5th Cir. 1996), 835
Dred Scott v. Sandford, 60 U.S. 393 (1856), 174
Duncan v. Upjohn Company, 155 F.R.D. 23 (D. Conn. 1994), 599
Dupasseur v. Rochereau, 88 U.S. 130 (1874), 864
Dura Pharmaceuticals, Inc. v. Broudo, 544 U.S. 336 (2005), 291,**304**,307-308
Durfee v. Duke, 375 U.S. 106 (1963), 173
Dusenbery v. United States, 534 U.S. 161 (2002), **139**,143
Dutkiewicz v. Bartkowiak, 126 N.W.2d 705 (Mich. Sup. Ct. 1964), 304

Edmonson v. Leeville Concrete Co., 500 U.S. 614 (1991), **694**,698,702
EEOC v. Peabody W. Coal Co., 400 F.3d 774 (9th Cir. 2005), 388
Eisen v. Carlisle & Jacquelin, 417 U.S. 156 (1974), 437
Empire Healthchoice Assurance, Inc. v. McVeigh, 547 U.S. 677 (2006), 173
Erickson v. Pardus, 551 U.S. 89 (2007), 296

Erie R. Co. v. Tompkins, 304 U.S. 64 (1938), 201,**235**,241-244,252-253,255-256, 257,261,865
ESAB Group, Inc. v. Centricut, Inc., 126 F.3d 617 (4th Cir.1997), 72
Evans v. Jeff D., 475 U.S. 717 (1986), **475**, 480
Everett v. Verizon Wireless, Inc., 460 F.3d 818 (6th Cir. 2006), 184
Everyday Learning Corp. v. Larson, 242 F.3d 815 (8th Cir. 2001), 601
Executive Software North America, Inc. v United States District Court, 24 F.3d 1545 (9th Cir. 1994), 196
Extra Equipamentos E Exportacao Ltda. v. Case Corp., 361 F.3d 359 (7th Cir. 2004), 393
Exxon Mobil Corp. v. Allapattah Services, Inc., 545 U.S. 546 (2005), 178,184,**190**,195-196,437
Ex parte Fahey, 332 U.S. 258 (1947), 815,817
Ex parte Peru, 318 U.S. 578 (1943), 818
Ex parte Peterson, 253 U.S. 300 (1920), 488

Fahim v. Marriott Hotel Services, Inc., 551 F.3d 344 (5th Cir. 2008), 621
Fauntleroy v. Lum, 210 U.S. 230 (1908), 848
Feder v. Turkish Airlines, 441 F. Supp. 1273 (S.D. N.Y. 1977), 110
Federal Open Market Comm. v. Merrill, 443 U.S. 340 (1979), 609
Federated Dept. Stores, Inc. v. Moitie, 452 U.S. 394 (1981), **860**,863
Ferens v. John Deere Co, 494 U.S. 516 (1990), 217
Ferguson v. Countrywide Credit Indus., Inc., 298 F.3d 778 (9th Cir. 2002), 496
Ferguson v. Writers Guild of America, West, 277 Cal. Rptr. 450 (Cal. Ct. App. 1991), 496
FG Hemisphere Assocs., LLC v. Democratic Republic of Congo, 447 F.3d 835 (D.C. Cir. 2006), 774
Fielding v. Hubert Burda Media, Inc., 415 F.3d 419 (5th Cir. 2005), 68-69
Fields v. Volkswagen of America, Inc., 555 P.2d 48 (Okla. 1976), 111
Finberg v. Sullivan, 634 F.2d 50 (3d Cir. 1980), 147
Finley v. United States, 490 U.S. 545 (1989), 186,191,194
Firestone Tire & Rubber Co. v. Risjord, 449 U.S. 368 (1981), 860
First of Michigan Corp. v. Bramlet, 141 F.3d 260 (6th Cir. 1998), 212
First National Bank of Arizona v. Cities Service Co., 391 U.S. 253 (1968), 650,654
First Options of Chicago, Inc. v. Kaplan, 514 U.S. 938 (1995), 494
FirsTier Mortgage Co. v. Investors Mortgage Ins. Co., 498 U.S. 269 (1991), 797
Fisher v. United States, 425 U.S. 391 (1976), 544
Fisher v. Virginia Electric and Power Co., 243 F.Supp.2d 538 (E.D. Va. 2003), 214
Flexner v. Farson, 248 U. S. 289 (1919), 38,92
Foman v. Davis, 371 U.S. 178 (1962), 340,342,344
Forney v. Apfel, 524 U.S. 266 (1998), 835
Fox v. Capital Co., 299 U.S. 105 (1936), 819
Franchise Tax Bd. v. Construction Laborers Vacation Trust, 463 U.S. 1 (1983), 198
Freedom Natl. Bank v. Northern Illinois Corp., 202 F.2d 601 (7th Cir. 1953), 332
Freeman v. Lester Coggins Trucking, Inc., 771 F.2d 860 (5th Cir. 1985), 855
Friends of the Earth, Inc. v. Laidlaw Environmental Services (TOC), Inc., 528 U.S. 167 (2000), 373
FTC v. Cement Institute, 333 U.S. 683 (1948), 730
Fuentes v. Shevin, 407 U.S. 67 (1972), 157, 783,786

G. Heileman Brewing Co. v. Joseph Oat Corp., 871 F.2d 648 (1989), **469**
Galloway v. Superior Court, 816 F.Supp. 12 (D. D.C. 1993), 688
Galloway v. United States, 319 U.S. 372 (1943), 889
Gargallo v. Merrill, Lynch, Pierce, Fenner & Smith, 918 F.2d 658 (6th Cir. 1990), 869,874
Gasperini v. Center for Humanities, 518 U.S. 415 (1996), **256**
General Dynamics Corp. v. Selb Mfg. Co., 481 F.2d 1204 (8th Cir. 1973), 524
General Elec. Co. v. Wabash Appliance Corp., 304 U.S. 364 (1938), 705
General Elec. v. Joiner, 522 U.S. 136 (1997), 822

General Tel. Co. v. Falcon, 457 U.S. 147 (1982), 423,428
Georgia v. McCollum, 505 U.S. 42 (1992), 693
Gertein v. Pugh, 420 U.S. 103 (1975), 419
Gibson v. National Rail Passenger Corp., 170 F.R.D. 408 (E.D. Pa. 1997), 558
Gilbert v. DaimlerChrysler Corp., 685 N.W.2d 391 (Mich. 2004), **736**
Gillispie v. Goodyear Service Stores, 128 S.E.2d 762 (N.C. 1963), 270
Gilmer v. Interstate/Johnson Lane Corp., 500 U.S. 20 (1991), 493
Glater v. Eli Lilly & Co., 712 F.2d 735 (1st Cir. 1983), 331
Glens Falls Indem. Co. v. Atlantic Bldg. Corp., 199 F.2d 60 (4th Cir. 1952), 396
Glenwood Light & Water Co. v. Mutual Light, Heat & Power Co., 239 U.S. 121 (1915), 184
Globe Liquor Co. v. San Roman, 332 U.S. 571 (1948), 724-725
GMAC Commercial Credit LLC v. Dillard Dept. Stores, Inc., 357 F.3d 827 (8th Cir. 2004), 183
Go-Video, Inc. v. Akai Electric Co., 885 F.2d 1406 (9th Cir. 1989), 213
Goldberg v. Cameron, 482 F.Supp.2d 1136 (N.D. Cal. 2007), 213
Goldberg v. Kelly, 397 U.S. 254 (1970), 157
Golden Eagle Distributing Corp. v. Burroughs Corp, 801 F.2d 584 (9th Cir. 1986), 351
Goldlawr, Inc. v. Heiman, 369 U.S. 463 (1962), 217,225
Gompers v. Bucks Stove & Range Co., 221 U.S. 418 (1911), 604
Gonzales v. Cassidy, 474 F.2d 67 (5th Cir. 1973), 431
Gonzales v. Google, Inc., 234 F.R.D. 674 (N.D. Cal. 2006), **528**,541
Goodwin v. Libbey Glass, Inc., 176 F.Appx. 588 (5th Cir. 2006), 317
Grable & Sons Metal Prods., Inc. v. Darue Engg. & Mfg., 545 U.S. 308 (2005), **169**
Grace v. MacArthur, 170 F.Supp. 442 (E.D. Ark. 1959), 89
Granfinanciera, S.A. v. Nordberg, 492 U.S. 33 (1989), 682,686
Grannis v. Ordean, 234 U.S. 385 (1914), 135
Grasselli Chemical Corp. v. National Aniline & Chemical Co., 282 Fed. 379 (S.D. N.Y. 1920), 609
Grassi v. Ciba-Geigy, Ltd., 894 F.2d 181 (5th Cir. 1990), 179
Gratz v. Bollinger, 539 U.S. 244 (2003), 419
Gray v. American Radiator & Standard Sanitary Corp., 176 N.E.2d 761 (Ill. 1961), 111,**113**,118
Gray v. Mississippi, 481 U.S. 648 (1987), 699
Great Lakes Rubber Corp. v. Herbert Cooper Co., 286 F.2d 631 (3d Cir. 1961), 370
Green Tree Financial Corp. v. Randolph, 531 U.S. 79 (2000), 493
Green v. Advance Ross Electronics Corp., 427 N.E.2d 1203 (Ill. 1981), 117
Green v. Foley, 856 F.2d 660 (4th Cir 1988), 776
Greene v. Lindsey, 456 U.S. 444 (1982), 138
Griffin v. Illinois, 351 U.S. 12 (1956), 789, 836
Griggs v. Provident Consumer Discount Co., 459 U.S. 56 (1982), 799
Grimes v. Mazda North American Operations, 355 F.3d 566 (6th Cir. 2004), 397
Grossmeyer v. McDonald, 128 F.3d 481 (7th Cir. 1997), 198
Grubbs v. General Elec. Credit Corp., 405 U.S. 699 (1972), 201
Grupo Dataflux v. Atlas Global Group, L.P., 541 U.S. 567 (2004), 176,183
Grupo Mexicano de Desarrollo S.A. v. Aliance Bond Fund, Inc., 527 U.S. 308 (1999), 331,758
Guaranty Trust Co. v. York, 326 U.S. 99 (1945), **242**,247-248,250,257
Gulf Ins. Co. v. Glasbrenner, 417 F.3d 353 (2d Cir. 2005), 212
Gulf Oil Co. v. Gilbert, 330 U.S. 501 (1947), 215,222
Gulfstream Aerospace Corp. v. Mayacamas Corp., 485 U.S. 271, 275[] (1988), 810
Gunter v. Atlantic Coast Line R. Co., 200 U.S. 273 (1906), 866
Gutshall v. New Prime, Inc., 196 F.R.D. 43 (W.D. Va. 2000), 558
Guy v. Citizens Fidelity Bank & Trust Co, 429 F.2d 828 (6th Cir. 1970), 401

H.F. Livermore Corp. v. Aktiengeseelschaft Gegruder Loepfe, 432 F.2d 689 (D.C. Cir. 1970), 318

Haddle v. Garrison, 525 U.S. 121 (1998), **284**

Hadges v. Yonkers Racing Corp., 48 F.2d 1320 (2d Cir. 1995), 358

Halaco Eng'g Co. v. Costle, 843 F.2d 376 (9th Cir. 1988), 512

Hall v. Cole, 412 U.S. 1 (1973), 605

Hall Street Assocs., L.L.C. v. Mattel, Inc., 552 U.S. 576 (2008), 493

Hall v. Werthan Bag Corp., 251 F.Supp. 184 (M.D. Tenn. 1966), 379

Hallaba v. Worldcom Network Services, Inc., 196 F.R.D. 630 (N.D. Okla. 2000), 214

Hanlon v. Chrysler Corp., 150 F.3d 1011 (9th Cir. 1997), 459

Hanna v. Plumer, 380 U.S. 460 (1965), **250**,255,259,865

Hansberry v. Lee, 311 U.S. 32 (1940), 415,**439**,852-854,856,858,886

Hanson v. Denckla, 357 U.S. 235 (1958), **49**,56, 60,64,83,114,115

Hanson v. Hunt Oil Co., 398 F.2d 578 (8th Cir. 1968), 340

Harad v. Aetna Cas. & Surety Co., 839 F.2d 979 (3d Cir. 1988), 317

Harnden v. Jayco, Inc., 496 F.3d 579 (2007), **831**

Harris v. Balk, 198 U.S. 215 (1905), 27,101,103

Harrison v. Celotex Corp., 583 F.Supp. 1497 (E.D. Tenn. 1984), 885

Harrison v. Westinghouse Savannah River Co., 176 F.3d 776 (4th Cir. 1999), 302

Harrods Ltd. v. Sixty Internet Domain Names, 302 F.3d 214 (4th Cir. 2002), 110

Hart Steel Co. v. Railroad Supply Co., 244 U.S. 294 (1917), 863

Haywood v. Drown, __ U.S. __, 129 S.Ct. 2108 (2009), 164

Harris v. Secretary, U.S. Dept. of Veterans Affairs, 126 F.3d 339 (D.C. Cir. 1997), 332

Harrison v. Grass, 304 F.Supp.2d 710 (D. Md. 2004), 371

Hartford Accident & Indemnity Co. v. Merrill Lynch, Pierce, Fenner & Smith, Inc., 74 F.R.D. 357 (W.D. Okl. 1976), 287

Havenfield Corp. v. H & R Block, Inc., 67 F.R.D. 93 (W.D. Mo. 1973), 593

Heileman Brewing Co. v. Joseph Oat Corp., 871 F.2d 648 (7th Cir.1989), 485

Heiser v. Woodruff, 327 U.S. 726 (1946), 862

Helicopteros Nacionales de Colombia, S.A. v. Hall, 466 U.S. 408 (1984), 82,**86**,92

Helstoski v. Meanor, 442 U.S. 500 (1979), 811

Helzberg's Diamond Shops, Inc. v. Valley West Des Moines Shopping Ctr., 564 F.2d 816 (8th Cir. 1977), 385

Henderson v. AT&T Corp., 918 F.Supp. 1059 (S.D. Tex. 1996), 380

Henry v. Glaize Md. Orchards, Inc., 103 F.R.D. 589 (D. Md. 1984), 148

Herron v. Southern Pacific Co., 283 U.S. 91 (1931), 248

Hertz v. Friend, __ U.S. __, 130 S.Ct. 1181 (2010), 183

Hess v. Pawlowski, 274 U.S. 352 (1927), **37**,43,49,104

Hetzel v. Prince William County, 523 U.S. 208 (1998), 768

Hiatt v. Yergin, 284 N.E.2d 834 (Ind. Ct. App. 1972), 669

Hickman v. Taylor, 329 U.S. 495 (1947), 517,**553**,563

High River Ltd. Partnership v. Mylan Lab. Inc., 353 F.Supp.2d 487 (M.D. Pa. 2005), 214

Hinderlider v. La Plata River & Cherry Creek Ditch Co., 304 U.S. 92 (1938), 234

Hishon v. King & Spalding, 467 U.S. 69 (1984), 284

Hodgson v. Bowerbank, 9 U.S. 303 (1809), 181

Hoffman v. Blaski, 363 U.S. 335 (1960), 217

Hogan v. Wal-Mart Stores, Inc., 167 F.3d 781, 783 (2d Cir. 1999), 304

Holcomb v. Aetna Life Ins. Co., 228 F.2d 75 (10th Cir. 1955), 407

Holmberg v. State, Division of Risk Management, 796 P.2d 823 (1990), 880

Holmes Group, Inc. v. Vornado Circulation Systems, Inc., 535 U.S. 826 (2002), 167

Honda Power Equip. Mfg., Inc. v. Woodhouse, 219 F.R.D. 2 (D. D.C. 2003), 317

Hopson v. Mayor of Baltimore, 232 F.R.D. 228 (D. Md. 2005), **547**

House v. Hanson, 72 N.W.2d 874 (1955), 365

Howard Motor Co. v. Swint, 448 S.E.2d 713 (Ga. Ct. App. 1994), 379

Howlett v. Rose, 496 U.S. 356 (1990), 164

Hubler Chevrolet, Inc. v. General Motors Corp., 193 F.R.D. 574 (2000), **432**
Hughes Tool Co. v. Trans World Airlines, 409 U.S. 363 (1973), 320
Hughes v. Fetter, 341 U.S. 609 (1951), 164
Hurd v. Monsanto Co., 164 F.R.D. 234 (S.D. Ind. 1995), 433
Hurn v. Oursler, 289 U.S. 238 (1933), 187
Hy Cite Corp. v. Badbusinessbureau.com, L.L.C., 297 F.Supp.2d 1154 (W.D. Wis. 2004), 79

Iglesias v. Mutual Life Ins. Co., 156 F.3d 237 (1st Cir. 1998), 196
Illinois Central Gulf Railroad v. Parks, 390 N.E.2d 1078 (Ind. Ct. App. 1979), 878
In re Asbestos Litigation, 90 F.3d 963 (5th Cir. 1996), 473
In re Atlantic Pipe Corp., 304 F.3d 135 (1st Cir. 2002), **483**
In re Beverly Hills Fire Litigation, 695 F.2d 207 (6th Cir. 1982), 706
In re Chevron U.S.A., 109 F.3d 1016 (5th Cir. 1997), 451
In re Commercial Fin. Services, Inc., 261 B.R. 49 (N.D. Okla. 2000), 350
In re Convergent Techns. Secs. Litig., 108 F.R.D. 328 (N.D. Cal. 1985), **581**
In re Cooper Antitrust Litigation, 196 F.R.D. 348 (W.D. Wis. 2000), 419
In re Davis, 170 F.3d 475 (5th Cir. 1999), **779**
In re Domestic Air Transportation Antitrust Litigation, 148 F.R.D. 297 (N.D. Ga. 1993), 451
In re Dow Co. "Sarabond" Products Liability Litigation, 666 F.Supp. 1466 (D. Colo. 1987), 218
In re Estate of Cochrane, 391 N.E.2d 35 (Ill. Ct. App. 1979), 863
In re Korean Air Lines Disaster of Sept. 1, 1983, 829 F.2d 1171 (D.C. Cir. 1987), 218
In re Napster Inc. Copyright Litigation, 462 F. Supp.2d 1060 (N.D. Cal. 2006), **511**
In re National Presto Indus., Inc., 347 F.3d 662 (7th Cir. 2003), 215
In re Natural Gas Commodities Litigation, 232 F.R.D. 208 (S.D. N.Y. 2005), 559
In re Petition of Sheila Roberts Ford, 170 F.R.D. 504 (1997), 505
In re Primus, 436 U.S. 412 (1978), 460
In re Rhone-Poulenc, Inc., 51 F.3d 1293 (7th Cir. 1995), 451
In re Sammy Daily, 47 F.3d 365 (9th Cir. 1995), 877
In re Sealed Case, 877 F.2d 976 (D.C. Cir. 1989), 546
In re Union Carbide Gas Plant Disaster, 809 F.2d 195 (2d Cir.1987), 227
In re United States Financial Secs. Litigation, 609 F.2d 411 (9th Cir. 1979), 676
In re von Bulow, 828 F.2d 94 (2d Cir 1987), 546
Ingraham v. Carroll, 687 N.E.2d 1293 (N.Y. 1997), 111
Ingraham v. United States, 808 F.2d 1075 (5th Cir. 1987), 332
Inset Systems, Inc. v. Instruction Set, Inc., 937 F. Supp. 161 (D. Conn. 1996), 79
Insurance Corp. of Ireland v. Compagnie des Bauxites de Guinee, 456 U.S. 694 (1982), 99,124, 125
International Harvester Co. v. Kentucky, 234 U.S. 579 (1914), 39
International Shoe Co. v. State of Washington, 326 U.S. 310 (1945), **40**,50,51,53,57,63,64,71,94,96,104,114, 115,447
Interoceania Corp. v. Sound Pilots, Inc., 107 F.3d 86 (2d Cir. 1997), 849
Isbell v. County of Sonoma, 577 P.2d 188 (Cal.), 100
ISI Intl., Inc. v. Borden Ladner Gervais LLP, 256 F.3d 548 (7th Cir. 2001), 122

J.E.B. v. Alabama ex rel. T.B., 511 U.S. 127 (1991), 694,698
James v. Price Stern Sloan, Inc., 283 F.3d 1064 (9th Cir. 2002), 804
Janmark, Inc. v. Reidy, 132 F.3d 1200 (7th Cir. 1997), 68
Janney Montgomery Scott, Inc. v. Shepard Niles, Inc., 11 F.3d 399 (3d Cir. 1993), 384
Jefferson v. Ingersoll Intl. Inc., 195 F.3d 894 (7th Cir. 1999), 433
Jehl v. Southern Pacific Co., 427 P.2d 988 (Cal. 1967), 768
Jin v. Ministry of State Security, 254 F.Supp.2d 61 (D. D.C. 2003), 288
Jinks-Ulmstead v. England, 232 F.R.D. 142 (D. D.C. 2005), 559
Jochims v. Isuzu Motors, Ltd., 148 F.R.D. 624 (S.D. Iowa 1993), 413
John Does 1-100 v. Boyd, 613 F. Supp. 1514 (D. Minn. 1985), 435

Johnson v. California, 545 U.S. 162 (2005), 698
Johnson v. Gmeinder, 191 F.R.D. 638 (D. Kan. 2000), 560
Johnson v. Jones, 515 U.S. 304 (1995), 808
Johnson v. New York, N.H. & H.R. Co., 344 U.S. 48 (1952), 724-725
Jones v. Block, 549 U.S. 199 (2007), **333**
Jones v. Flowers, 547 U.S. 220 (2006), 142
Jones v. Ford Motor Credit Co., 358 F.3d 205 (2d Cir. 2004), 196,370

Kaiser Aluminum & Chem. Sales, Inc. v. Avondale Shipyards, Inc., 677 F.2d 1045 (5th Cir. 1982), 321
Kalb v. Feuerstein, 308 U.S. 433 (1940), 176
Kalinauskas v. Wong, 151 F.R.D. 363 (D. Nev. 1993), 474
Kane v. New Jersey, 242 U.S. 160 (1916), 36-38,41
Karlsson v. Rabinowitz, 318 F.2d 666 (4th Cir. 1963), 150
Karn v. Ingersoll-Rand Co., 168 F.R.D. 633 (N.D. Ind. 1996), 565
Kassner v. 2nd Avenue Delicatessen Inc., 496 F.3d 229 (2d Cir. 2007), 621
Katchen v. Landy, 382 U.S. 323 (1966), 678,686
Keeton v. Hustler Magazine, Inc., 465 U.S. 770 (1984), 82
Keidatz v. Albany, 249 P.2d 264 (1952), 863
Kerr v. United States District Court, 426 U.S. 394 (1976), **815**,818
King Vision Pay Per View, Ltd. v. J.C. Dimitri's Restaurant, Inc., 180 F.R.D. 332 (N.D. Ill. 1998), 331
Kircher v. Putnam Funds Trust, 547 U.S. 633 (2006), 202
Kirk Capital Corp. v. Bailey, 16 F.3d 1485 (8th Cir. 1994), 358
Klaxon Co. v. Stentor Electric Mfg. Co., 313 U.S. 487 (1941), 217,262
Klugh v. United States, 818 F.2d 294 (C.A.4 1987), 857
Knowlton v. Allied Van Lines, Inc., 900 F.2d 1196 (8th Cir. 1990), 100
Knuckles El v. Toombs, 215 F.3d 640 (2000), 334
Kokkonen v. Guardian Life Ins. Co., 511 U.S. 375 (1994), 167,475
Kohl v. Association of Trial Lawyers, 183 F.R.D. 475 (D. Md. 1998), 431
Kossick v. United Fruit Co., 365 U.S. 731 (1961), 241
Koster v. Lumbermens Mut. Cas. Co., 330 U.S. 518 (1947), 223
Kosters v. Seven-Up Co., 595 F.2d 347 (6th Cir. 1979), 400
Kotteakos v. United States, 328 U.S. 750 (1946), 835
Kovach v. District of Columbia, 805 A.2d 957 (D.C. Ct. App. 2002), 880
Kraemer v. Grant County, 892 F.2d 686 (7th Cir. 1990), 351
Kramer v. Caribbean Mills, Inc., 394 U.S. 823 (1969), 179
Kremer v. Chemical Construction Corp., 456 U.S. 461 (1982), 846,850
Krisa v. Equitable Life Assurance Society, 196 F.R.D. 254 (M.D. Pa. 2000), **562**,564
Kulko v. Superior Court, 436 U.S. 84 (1978), 52,83
Kumho Tire Co. v. Carmichael, 526 U.S. 137 (1999), 764

LaBuy v. Howes Leather Co., 352 U.S. 249 (1957), 812
Lafreniere Park Foundation v. Broussard, 221 F.3d 804 (5th Cir. 2000), 852
Lamothe v. Auto Club Ins. Assn., 543 N.W.2d 42 (Mich. Ct. App. 1995), 303
Langfeldt-Haaland v. Saupe Enter., Inc., 768 P.2d 1144 (Alaska 1989), 599
Langley v. Jackson State University, 14 F.3d 1070 (5th Cir. 1994), 475
Larez v. Holcomb, 16 F.2d 1513 (9th Cir. 1994), 349
Latshaw v. Trainer Wortham & Co., 452 F.3d 1097 (9th Cir. 2006), 774
Lattimore v. Citibank Fed. Sav. Bank, 151 F.3d 712 (7th Cir. 1998), 516
Lauro Lines, S.R.L. v. Chaser, 490 U.S. 495 (1989), 807,**809**
Lawlor v. National Screen Service Corp., 349 U.S. 322 (1955), 383,842
Layman v. Southwestern Bell Tel. Co., 554 S.W.2d 477 (Mo. App. 1977), 333
Leatherman v. Tarrant County Narcotics Intelligence & Coordination Unit, 507 U.S. 163 (1993), 284,335
Legault v. Zambarano, 105 F.3d 24 (1st Cir. 1997), 601
Lehman v. Makshian, 453 U.S. 156 (1981), 687

Leroy v. Great Western United Corp., 443 U.S. 173 (1979), 212
Lesnik v. Public Industrials Corp., 144 F.2d 968 (2d Cir. 1944), 368
Lexecon v. Milberg Weiss, 523 U.S. 26 (1998), 217
Liberty Mutual Ins. Co. v. Wetzel, 424 U.S. 737 (1976), **747**
Lightfoot v. Union Carbide Corp., 110 F.3d 898 (2d Cir. 1997), 823
Lincoln Property Co. v. Roche, 546 U.S. 81 (2005), 373
Lindsey v. Normet, 405 U.S. 56 (1972), 836
Link v. Wabash R. Co., 370 U.S. 626 (1962), 324,470,605
Lockett v. Ohio, 438 U.S. 586 (1978), 701
Lockhart v. Patel, 115 F.R.D. 44 (E.D. Ky. 1987), 469
Lorillard v. Pons, 434 U.S. 575 (1978), 684
Louisville & Nashville R. Co. v. Mottley, 211 U.S. 149 (1908), 168,188,198
Lujan v. National Wildlife Federation, 497 U.S. 871 (1990), 764
Lundahl v. Public Storage Mgmt., Inc., 62 Fed. Appx. 217 (10th Cir. 2003), 213
Lyng v. N.W. Indian Cemetery Protective Assn., 485 U.S. 439 (1988), 850

M.L.B. v. S.L.J., 519 U.S. 102 (1996), 836
M.H. Segan Ltd. Partnership v. Hasbro, Inc., 924 F.Supp. 512 (S.D. N.Y. 1996), 303
MacArthur v. San Juan County, 416 F.Supp.2d 1098 (D. Utah 2005), 628
Maher v. Gagne, 448 U.S. 122 (1980), 475
Maher v. GSI Lumonics, Inc., 433 F.3d 123 (1st Cir 2005), 868
Makah Indian Tribe v. Verity, 910 F.2d 555 (9th Cir. 1990), 388
Mansfield, Coldwater & Lake Michigan Ry. Co. v. Swan, 111 U.S. 379 (1884), 357, 748
Mathews v. New York Racing Assn., Inc., 193 F.Supp. 293 (S.D. N.Y. 1961), 840
Marek v. Chesney, 473 U.S. 1 (1985), 482
Marisol v. Giuliani, 126 F.3d 372 (2d Cir. 1997), 422
Markman v. Westview Instruments, Inc., 517 U.S. 370 (1996), **702**
Marrese v. American Acad. of Orthopaedic Surgeons, 470 U.S. 373 (1985), 850,869
Marshall v. Marshall, 547 U.S. 293 (2006), 183
Martin v. Franklin Capital Corp., 546 U.S. 132 (2005), 202
Martin v. Wilks, 490 U.S. 755 (1989), **414,**853,881
Mas v. Perry, 489 F.2d 1396 (5th Cir. 1974), 176
Mathews v. Eldridge, 424 U.S. 319 (1976), 157,159,782
Mathews v. New York Racing Assn., Inc., 193 F. Supp. 293 (S.D. N.Y. 1961), **841**
Matsushita Elec. Indus. Co. v. Zenith Radio Corp., 475 U.S. 574 (1986), **652,** 656-657,659,661
Mattell, Inc. v. Luce, Forward, Hamilton & Scripps, 121 Cal.Rptr.2d 794 (2002), 358
Mayle v. Felix, 545 U.S. 644 (2005), 344
McCarthy v. Amoco Pipeline Co., 595 F.2d 389 (7th Cir. 1979), 184
McCaskey v. Continental Airlines, Inc., 133 F.Supp.2d 514 (S.D. Tex. 2001), 214
McDonald v. Mabee, 243 U. S. 90 (1917), 37, 42, 132
McDonnell Douglas Corp. v. Green, 411 U.S. 792 (1973), 717
McDonough Power Equipment v. Greenwood, 464 U.S 548 (1984), 691
McGee v. International Life Ins. Co., 355 U.S. 220 (1957), **48,**54,60,62,83,95,115
McHenry v. Renne, 84 F.3d 1172 (9th Cir. 1996), 321
Melder v. Morris, 27 F.3d 1097 (5th Cir. 1994), 304
Mennonite Board of Missions v. Adams, 462 U.S. 791 (1983), 138,141,142,145
Merrell Dow Pharms., Inc. v. Thompson, 478 U.S. 804 (1986), 169,170,172
Merrill Lynch, Inc. v. ENC Corp., 464 F.3d 885 (9th Cir. 2006), 385
Merrill v. Yeomans, 94 U.S. 568 (1877), 705
Metro Ford Truck Sales, Inc. v. Ford Motor Co., 145 F.3d 320 (5th Cir, 1998), 198
Metropolitan Life Insurance Co. v. Neaves, 912 F.2d 1062 (9th Cir. 1990), 77
Midland Asphalt Corp. v. United States, 489 U.S. 794 (1989), 810-811
Miedreich v. Lauenstein, 232 U.S. 236 (1914), 155
Migra v. Warren City School Dist. Bd. of Educ., 452 U.S. 394 (1981), 840,844,**845,** 850
Miller v. Fenton, 474 U.S. 104 (1985), 704

Miller-El v. Dretke, 545 U.S. 231 (2005), 698
Milliken v. Meyer, 311 U.S. 457 (1940), 36,42,63,71,90,135
Mills v. Electric Auto-Lite Co., 396 U.S. 375 (1970), 886
Mims v. Central Mfrs. Mut. Ins. Co., 178 F.2d 56 (5th Cir. 1949), 835
Mitchell v. Forsyth, 472 U.S. 511 (1985), 807,811
Mitchell v. W.T. Grant Co., 416 U.S. 600 (1974), 157,159,160,161,783,785-786
Montana v. United States, 440 U.S. 147 (1979), 854-855
Moore v. Chesapeake & Ohio Ry. Co., 291 U.S. 205 (1934), 169
Moore v. New York Cotton Exchange, 270 U.S. 593 (1926), 368,369,378
Moores v. Greenberg, 834 F.2d 1105 (1st Cir. 1987), 263
Moose Lodge No. 107 v. Irvis, 407 U.S. 163 (1972), 696
Morast v. Auble, 519 P.2d 157 (1974), 593
Morris v. Jones, 329 U.S. 545 (1947), 860
Moses H. Cone Memorial Hosp. v. Mercury Constr. Corp., 460 U.S. 1 (1983), 496
Mosley v. General Motors Corp., 497 F.2d 1330 (8th Cir. 1974), **376**
M/S Bremen v. Zapata Off-Shore Co., 407 U.S. 1 (1972), 98-99,812
Mullane v. Central Hanover Bank & Trust Co., 339 U.S. 306 (1950), 81,131,**132**,140, 143-145,156,447,854
Mutual of Omaha Ins. Co. v. Garrigan, 285 N.E.2d 395 (Ohio 1971), 527
Mwani v. Bin Laden, 417 F.3d 1 (2005), **79**

Nasem v. Brown, 595 F.2d 801 (D.C. Cir. 1979), 870
Nash v. Humana Sun Bay Commun. Hosp., 526 So.2d 1036 (Fla. Ct. App. 1988), 312
National Collegiate Athletic Assn. v. Tarkanian, 488 U.S. 179 (1988), 695
National Development Co. v. Triad Holding Corp., 930 F.2d 253, 258 (2d Cir. 1991), 150
National Equipment Rental v. Szukhent, 375 U.S. 311 (1964), 98,**150**,252
National Hockey League v. Metropolitan Hockey Club, 427 U.S. 639 (1976), 604,613
National State Bank v. Federal Reserve bank, 979 F.2d 1579 (3d Cir. 1992), 649
National Ventures, Inc. v. Water Glades 300 Condominium Assn., 847 So.2d 1070 (Fla. Ct. App. 2003), 303
Natural Resources Council, Inc. v. New York State Dept. of Envtl. Conservation, 834 F.2d 60, 61-62 (2d Cir. 1987), 413
Natural Resources Defense Council v. United States Nuclear Regulatory Commn., 578 F.2d 1341 (1978), **408**
Nault's Auto. Sales, Inc. v. American Honda Motor Co., 148 F.R.D. 25 (D. N.H. 1993), 321
Neary v. University of California, 834 P.2d 119 (Ca. 1992), 834,868
Neely v. Martin K. Eby Constr. Co., 386 U.S. 317 (1967), 762-763
Nelson v. Miller, 11 Ill.2d 378, 143 N.E.2d 673 (1957), 113-114
Nemariam v. Federal Democratic Republic of Ethiopia, 315 F.3d 390 (D.C. Cir. 2003), 227
Nesbit v. Independent District of Riverside, 144 U.S. 610 (1892), 849
Nestor v. Pratt & Whitney, 466 F.3d 65 (2nd Cir. 2006), 849
New Hampshire v. Maine, 532 U.S. 742 (2001), 870
New York Gaslight Club, Inc. v. Carey, 447 U.S. 54 (1980), 850
New York Life Ins. Co. v. Dunlevy, 241 U.S. 518 (1916), 401
New York Times Co. v. Sullivan, 376 U.S. 254 (1964), 649
Newman-Green, Inc. v. Alfonzo-Larrain, 490 U.S. 826 (1989), 178
Newman v. Piggie Park Enterprises, 390 U.S. 400 (1968), 11
Newton v. A.C. & S., 918 F.2d 1121, 1126 (3d Cir. 1990), 473
Nguyen v. Excel Corp., 197 F.3d 200 (5th Cir. 1999), 546
Nick v. Morgan's Foods, Inc., 270 F.3d 590 (2001), 469
Nixon v. Fitzgerald, 457 U.S. 731 (1982), 807,811
Nixon v. Sirica, 487 F.2d 700 (D.C. Cir. 1973), 819
Nolan v. Transocean Air Lines, 276 F.2d 280 (2d Cir. 1960), 263
North Georgia Finishing, Inc. v Di-Chem, Inc., 419 U.S. 601 (1975), 157,783-784

Norwood v. Kirkpatrick, 349 U.S. 29 (1955), 217,223

O.J. Distributing, Inc. v. Hornell Brewing Co., 340 F.3d 345 (6th Cir. 2003), 317
O.S.C. Corp. v. Toshiba America, Inc., 491 F.2d 1064 (9th Cir. 1974), 213
Official Airline Guides, Inc. v. Goss, 6 F.3d 1385 (9th Cir. 1993), 469
Ohralik v. Ohio State Bar Assn., 436 U.S. 447 (1978), 460
Oliver v. Swiss Club Tell, 35 Cal.Rptr. 324 (1963), 331
Omni Capital Intl. V. Rudolf Wolff & Co., 484 U.S. 97 (1987), 113
Onvoy, Inc. v. Allete, Inc., 736 N.W.2d 611 (Minn. 2007), 678
Oppenheimer Fund, Inc. v. sanders, 437 U.S. 340 (1978), 528
Oregon v. Corvallis Sand & Gravel Co., 429 U.S. 363 (1977), 234
Ortiz v. Eichler, 794 F.2d 889, 892 (3d Cir. 1986), 147
Ortiz v. Fibreboard Corp., 527 U.S. 815 (1999), 253,432-433,454,865
Osborn v. Bank of the United States, 22 U.S. 738 (1824), 166
Oubre v. Entergy Operations, Inc., 522 U.S. 422 (1998), 474
Oxford First Corp. v. PNC Liquidating Corp., 372 F.Supp. 191 (E.D. Pa. 1974), 121
Owen Equipment and Erection Co. v. Kroger, 437 U.S. 365 (1978), 186,**398**

Paine-Erie Hosp. Supply, Inc. v. Lincoln First Bank, 370 N.Y.S.2d 370 (N.Y. Sup. Ct. 1975), 304
Painter v. Harvey, 863 F.2d 329 (4th Cir. 1988), 369
Panavision Intl. v. Toeppen, 141 F.3d 1316 (9th Cir. 1998), 69,73,76
Papasan v. Allain, 478 U.S. 265 (1986), 290
Parker v. Hulme, 18 F. Cas. 1138 (E.D. Pa. 1849), 704
Parklane Hosiery v. Shore, 439 U.S. 322 (1979), 678,865,**885**
Parr v. United States, 351 U.S. 513 (1956), 816
Parsons Steel, Inc. v. First Alabama Bank, 474 U.S. 518 (1986), 868
Parsons v. Bedford, 28 U.S. 433 (1830), 671,682
Pebble Beach Co. v. Caddy, 453 F.3d 1151 (2006), **75**,122
Pelfrey v. Bank of Greer, 244 S.E.2d. 315 (S.C. 1978), 668
Penland v. Warren County Jail, 797 F.2d 332 (6th Cir.1986), 426
Pennington v. Fourth Natl. Bank, 243 U.S. 269 (1917), 101
Pennoyer v. Neff, 95 U.S. 714 (1877), **28**,38,43, 48,54,90,95,104,114,128,133,443
Peralta v. Heights Medical Center, 485 U.S. 80 (1988), 317,784
Pennsylvania R. v. Chamberlain, 288 U.S. 333 (1933), **714**
Pennzoil Co. v. Texaco, Inc., 481 U.S. 1 (1987), 836
Pension Comm. of Univ. of Montreal Pension Plan v. Banc of America Secs., 685 F. Supp.2d 456 (S.D. N.Y. 2010), **535**
Perkins v. Benguet Consolid. Mining Co., 343 U.S. 437 (1952), 83,**84**,87,114
Peters & Russell v. Dorfman, 188 F.2d 711 (7th Cir. 1951), 331
Peters v. Public Service Corporation, 29 A.2d 189 (N.J. Eq. 1942), 331
Peterson v. Wilson, 141 F.3d 573 (5th Cir. 1998), **769**
Petro-Hunt, L.L.C. v. United States, 365 F.3d 385 (5th Cir. 2004), 848
Philadelphia & Reading Ry. Co. v. McKibbin, 243 U.S. 264 (1917), 39
Phillips Petroleum Co. v. Shutts, 472 U.S. 797 (1985), **446**
Pierre v. Inroads, Inc., 858 F.Supp. 769 (N.D. Ill. 1994), 358
Pingatore v. Montgomery Ward & Co., 419 F.2d 1138 (6th Cir. 1969), 768
Pinker v. Roche Holdings, Ltd., 292 F.3d 361, 369 (3d Cir. 2002), 121
Pioneer Investment Services Co. v. Brunswick Assocs. Ltd. Partnership, 507 U.S. 380 (1993), 775
Piper Aircraft Co., v. Reyno, 454 U.S. 235 (1981), **222**,227
Planned Parenthood of Minnesota, Inc. v. Citizens for Community Action, 558 F.2d 861 (8th Cir. 1977), 412
Plant v. Blazer Financial Services, 598 F.2d 1357 (5th Cir. 1979), 369
Plasse v. Tyco Electronics Corp., 448 F.Supp.2d 302 (D. Mass. 2006), 573
Policci v. Cowles Magazines, Inc., 345 U.S. 663 (1953), 213

Pollux Holding Ltd. v. Chase Manhattan Bank, 329 F.3d 64 (2d Cir. 2003), 230
Poole v. Textron, 192 F.R.D. 494 (D. Md. 2000), **611**
Porn v. National Grange Mut. Ins. Co., 93 F.3d 31 (1st Cir. 1996), 849
Porter v City of Royal Oak, 542 NW2d 905 (Mich. Ct. App. 1995), 641
Porter v. Roosa, 259 F.Supp.2d 638 (S.D. Ohio 2003), 199
Postal Telegraph Cable Co. v. Newport, 247 U.S. 464 (1918), 853
Powers v. Ohio, 499 U.S. 400 (1991), 695,697
Price v. CTB, Inc., 168 F. Supp.2d 1299 (2001), **395**
Provident Tradesmens Bank & Trust Co. v. Patterson, 390 U.S. 102 (1968), 382,385
Publicker Indus., Inc. v. Cohen, 733 F.2d 1059 (3d Cir. 1984), 524
Puerto Rico Aqueduct & Sewer Auth. v. Metcalf & Eddy, 506 U.S. 139 (1993), 807
Pullman-Standard v. Swint, 456 U.S. 273 (1982), 823
Pure Oil v. Suarez, 384 U.S. 202 (1966), 213
Purkett v Elem, 514 U.S 765 (1995), 698
Purnell v. City of Akron, 925 F.2d 941 (6th Cir. 1991), 413

Quackenbush v. Allstate Ins. Co., 517 U.S. 706 (1996), 807
Quercia v. United States, 289 U.S. 466 (1933), 706

Radenbaugh v. Farm Bureau Ins. Co., 610 NW2d 272 (Mich. Ct. App. 2000), 642
Ragan v. Merchants Transfer & Warehouse Co., 337 U.S. 530 (1949), 245,249,251,255
Railroad Co. v. Stout, 84 U.S. 657 (1873), 701
Rakus v. Erie-Lackawanna Railroad, 76 F.R.D. 145 (W.D. N.Y. 1977), 558
Rasmussen v. South Florida Blood Service, Inc., 500 So.2d 533 (Fla. 1987), 527
Ratliff v. Cooper Laboratories, Inc., 444 F.2d 745 (4th Cir. 1971), 100
Reddington v. Staten Island Univ. Hosp., 893 N.E.2d 120 (N.Y. Ct. App. 2008), 263
Redfield v. Parks, 132 U.S. 239 (1889), 679
Reed v. Allen, 286 U.S. 191 (1932), 862
Reeves v. Sanderson, 530 U.S. 133 (2000), **717**
Republic of Mexico v. Hoffman, 324 U.S. 30 (1945), 391
Republic of Panama v. BCCI Holdings (Luxembourg) S.A., 119 F.3d 935 (11th Cir. 1997), 121
Republic of the Philippines v. Pimentel, 553 U.S. 851 (2008), **389**
Reynolds v. Guiliani, 35 F.Supp.2d 331 (S.D. N.Y. 1999), 147
Rhone-Poulenc Rorer Inc. v. Home Indem. Co., 32 F.3d 851 (3d Cir. 1994), 542
Richards v. Jefferson County, 517 U.S. 793 (1996), 431,**852**,857-858
Richardson-Merrell, Inc. v. Koller, 472 U.S. 424 (1985), 806,811
Rio Properties, Inc. v. Rio Int'l Interlink, 284 F.3d 1007 (9th Cir.2000), 77,154
Rios v. Davis, 373 S.W.2d 386 (1963), **879**
Rivet v Regions Bank, 522 U.S. 470 (1998), 167,868
Roadway Express, Inc. v. Piper, 447 U.S. 752 (1980), **603**
Robles v. Exxon Corp., 862 F.2d 1201 (5th Cir. 1989), 771
Rocha v. Great American Ins. Co., 850 F.2d 1095 (6th Cir. 1988), 472
Roche v. Evaporated Milk Assn., 319 U.S. 21 (1943), 816-818
Rodriguez de Quijas v. Shearson/American Express, Inc., 490 U.S. 477 (1989), 468
Rogan v. Menino, 175 F.3d 75 (1st Cir. 1999), **625**
Rogers v. Wal-Mart Stores Inc., 230 F.3d 868 (6th Cir. 2000), 198
Rose v. Giamatti, 721 F.Supp. 906 (S.D. Ohio 1989), 179
Rose v. Mitchell, 443 U.S. 545 (1979), 697
Ross v. A.H. Robins Co., 607 F.2d 545 (2d Cir. 1979), 303
Ross v. Bernhard, 396 U.S. 531 (1970), 678,680,683,686
Ross v. Mather, 51 N.Y. 108 (1872), 270
Rousseau v. Teledyne Movible Offshore, Inc., 812 F.2d 971 (5th Cir. 1987), 770
Roussel v. Tidelands Capital Corp., 438 F.Supp. 684 (N.D. Ala. 1977), 358-359
Rowe Entertainment, Inc. v. William Morris Agency, 205 F.R.D. 421 (S.D. N.Y. 2002), 546
Rozsa v. May Davis Group, Inc., 187 F.Supp.2d 123 (S.D. N.Y. 2002), 287
Ruhrgas AG v. Marathon Oil Co., 526 U.S. 574 (1999), 173

Rush v. City of Maple Heights, 147 N.E.2d 599 (Ohio Sup. Ct. 1958), 841
Russell v. Place, 94 U.S. (4 Otto) 606 (1876), 878
Rynsburger v. Dairymen's Fertilizer Coop., 72 Cal. Rptr. 102 (Cal. Ct. App. 1968), 856

Saadeh v. Farouki, 107 F.3d 52 (D.C. Cir. 1997), 180
St. Mary's Honor Center v. Hicks, 509 U.S. 502 (1993), 719-720
St. Paul Mercury Indemnity Co. v. Red Cab Co., 303 U.S. 283 (1938), 184,198
Salve Regina College v. Russell, 499 U.S. 225 (1991), 263,822
Sanders v. Union Pacific R.R. Co., 193 F.3d 1080 (9th Cir. 1999), **622**
Sanford Construction Co. v. Kaiser Aluminum & Chemical Sales, Inc., 45 F.R.D. 465 (E.D. Ky. 1968), 566
Sarafin v. Sears, Roebuck and Co., 446 F.Supp. 611 (N.D. Ill. 1978), 436
Saucier v. Katz, 533 U.S. 194 (2001), 661
Save Our Sonoran, Inc. v. Flowers, 408 F.3d 1113 (9th Cir. 2005), 759
Scarborough v. Pargoud, 108 U.S. 567 (1883), 799
Scherer v. Equitable Life Assurance Socy., 347 F.3d 394 (2d Cir. 2003), 852
Scheuer v. Rhodes, 416 U.S. 232 (1974), 287,291
Schiavone v. Fortune, 477 U.S. 21 (1986), 347
Schlagenhauf v. Holder, 379 U.S. 104, 121 (1964), 484,597,813,817
Schroeder v. City of New York, 371 U.S. 208 (1962), 138
Schwarzenegger v. Fred Martin Motor Co., 374 F.3d 797 (9th Cir. 2004), 69,77
Scott v. Harris, 550 U.S. 372 (2007), **659**
Scully Signal Co. v. Electrics Corp., 570 F.2d 355 (1st Cir. 1977), 343
Scott v. American Tobacco Co., 949 So.2d 1266 (La. Ct. App. 2007), 451
Scutieri v. Paige, 808 F.2d 785 (11th Cir. 1987), 774
Seamon v. Upham, 563 F.Supp. 396 (E.D. Tex. 1983), 214
Sears, Roebuck & Co. v. Mackey, 351 U.S. 427 (1956), 751-752,**804**
Seattle Times Co. v. Rhinehart, 467 U.S. 20 (1984), **526**
Semtek Intl. Inc. v. Lockheed Martin Corp., 531 U.S. 497 (2001), 256,844,856, **863**,867
Senter v. General Motors Corp., 532 F.2d 511 (6th Cir.1976), 425
Shaffer v. Heitner, 433 U.S. 186 (1977), 81,83,86, 93,95,**101**,103,447
Shamrock Oil & Gas Corp. v. Sheets, 313 U.S. 100 (1941), 198
Shaumyan v. O'Neill, 987 F.2d 122 (2d Cir. 1993), 161
Shearson/American Express, Inc. v. McMahon, 482 U.S. 220 (1987), 468
Shelar v. Shelar, 910 F.Supp. 1307 (N.D. Ohio 1995), 842
Shelley v. Kraemer, 334 U.S. 1 (1948), 430
Sherleigh Assoc. LLC v Sherleigh AssocitES, Inc. Profit-Sharing Plan, 186 F.R.D. 669 (S.D. Fla. 1999), 460
Shields v. Barrow, 58 U.S. 130 (1854), 374
Shoshone Mining Co. v. Rutter, 177 U.S. 505 (1900), 167
Shows v. Jamison Bedding, Inc., 671 F.2d 927 (5th Cir. 1982), 770
Shuffle Master Inc. v. Progressive Games, Inc., 170 F.R.D. 166 (D. Nev. 1996), 600
Sibbach v. Wilson & Co., 312 U.S. 1 (1941), 248,255
Sifers v. Horen, 188 N.W.2d 623 (Mich. 1971), 111
Silvestri v. General Motors Corp., 271 F.3d 583 (4th Cir. 2001), **507**
Simler v. Conner, 372 U.S. 221 (1963), 679
Sinochem Intl. Co. v. Malaysia Intl. Shipping Corp., 549 U.S. 422 (2007), 226
Sisney v. Best Inc., 754 N.W.2d 804 (S.D. 2008), 301
Skelly Oil Co. v. Phillips Petroleum Co., 339 U.S. 667 (1950), 169
Sloan v. State Farm Mut. Auto. Ins. Co., 360 F.3d 1220 (10th Cir. 2004), 473
Smith v. First National Bank in Westfield, 99 Mass. 605 (1868), 716
Smith v. Kansas City Title & Trust Co., 255 U.S. 180 (1921), 167,170
Smith v. United States, 507 U.S. 197 (1993), 213
Smith Kline & French Labs. Ltd. v. Bloch, [1983] 2 All E.R. 72 (Eng. C.A. 1982), 227
Smith v. North American Rockwell Corp., 50 F.R.D. 515 (N.D. Okla. 1970), 377
Sniadach v. Family Finance Corp., 395 U.S. 337 (1969), 156,159,161,783,786

Snyder v. Harris, 394 U.S. 332 (1969), 184, 437
Stafford v. Briggs, 444 U.S. 527 (1980), 121
Sola Electric Co. v. Jefferson Electri Co., 317 U.S. 173 (1942), 233
Sosna v. Iowa, 419 U.S. 393 (1975), 419, 833
Sossamon v. Nationwide Mut. Ins. Co., 135 S.E.2d 87 (1964), 304
Southern Construction Co. v. Pickard, 371 U.S. 57 (1962), 367,368
Southern Pacific R. Co. v. United States, 168 U.S. 1 (1897), **871**
Southland Corp. v. Keating, 465 U.S. 1 (1984), 468
Southwest Airlines Co. v. Texas Intl. Airlines, 546 F.2d 84 (5th Cir. 1977), 856
Spallone v. United States, 493 U.S. 265 (1990), 786
Sparrow v. United Air Lines, Inc., 216 F.3d 1111, 1115 (D.C. Cir. 2000), 284
Spaulding v. Denton, 68 F.R.D. 342 (D. Del. 1975), 558
Stallworth v. Monsanto, 558 F.2d 257 (5th Cir. 1977), 417
State Farm Fire & Cas. Co. v. Century Home Components, 550 P.2d 1185 (Or. Sup. Ct. 1976), 885
State Farm v. Tashire, 386 U.S. 523 (1967), 178,180,**403**
Stearn v. Malloy, 89 F.R.D. 421 (E.D. Wis. 1981), 109
Stewart Organization, Inc. v Ricoh Corp., 487 U.S. 22 (1988), 255
Stoll v. Gottlieb, 305 U.S. 165 (1938), 173
Strawbridge v. Curtiss, 7 U.S. 267 (1806), 177,180,404
Stewart Org., Inc. v. Ricoh Corp., 487 U.S. 22 (1988), 218
Stone v. Dept. of Aviation, 453 F.3d 1271 (10th Cir. 2006), 366
Stoll v. Gottlieb, 305 U.S. 165 (1938), 866
Storms v. Lowe's Home Centers, Inc., 211 F.R.D. 296 (W.D. Va. 2002), 596
Strauss v. Summerhays, 204 Cal.Rptr. 227 (Cal. Ct. App. 1984), 668
Stringfellow v. Concerned Neighbors in Action, 480 U.S. 370 (1987), 413
Styskal v. Weld County Bd. of Commrs., 365 F.3d 855 (10th Cir. 2004), 867
Sullivan v. Stroop, 496 U.S. 478 (1990), 782
Sun Oil Co. v. Wortman, 486 U.S. 717 (1988), 164
Sunfuel Technologies, Inc. v. DHL Express (USA), 463 F.3d 646 (7th Cir. 2006), 451
Surowitz v. Hilton Hotels Corp., 383 U.S. 363 (1966), 359
Swierkiewicz v. Sorema N. A., 534 U.S. 506 (2002), 291,293,308,335
Swift v. Tyson, 41 U.S. 1 (1842), 231,234, 236,240-243,252

Tafflin v. Levitt, 493 U.S. 455 (1990), 166
Tanner v. United States, 483 U.S. 107 (1987), 771
Taylor v. Sturgell, 553 U.S. 880 (2008), **856**
Tellabs, Inc. v. Makor Issues and Rights, Ltd., 551 U.S. 308 (2007), **307**
Temple v. Synthes Corp., 498 U.S. 5 (1990), **382**
Texas Dept. of Community Affairs v. Burdine, 450 U.S. 248 (1981), 719
Textile Workers Union v. Lincoln Mills, 353 U.S. 448 (1957), 241
Thalheim v. Eberheim, 124 F.R.D. 34 (D. Conn. 1988), 593,613
The Evergreens v. Nunan, 141 F.2d 927 (2d. Cir. 1944), 887
Thiel v. Southern Pacific Co., 328 U.S. 217 (1946), 688
Thillens, Inc. v. Community Currency Exchange Assn., 97 F.R.D. 668 (N.D. Ill. 1983), 420
Thompson v. Altheimer & Gray, 248 F.3d 621 (7th Cir. 2003), **699**
Thompson v. Department of Housing and Urban Dev., 199 F.R.D. 168 (D. Md. 2001), **517**
Tirado v. Erosa, 158 F.R.D. 294 (S.D. N.Y.1994), 599
Tomlin v. Holecek, 150 F.R.D. 628 (D. Minn. 1993), 599
Toole v. Baxter Healthcare Corp., 235 F.3d 1307 (11th Cir 2000), 776
Torres v. Commonwealth of Puerto Rico, 485 F.3d 5 (1st Cir 2007), 622
Tracinda Corp. v. DaimlerChrysler AG, 502 F.3d 212 (3d Cir. 2007), 622
Trammel v. United States, 445 U.S. 40 (1980), 544
Travelers Health Assn. v. Commonwealth of Virginia ex rel. State Corporation Comm., 339 U.S. 643 (1950), 49,116

Travis v. Anthes Imperial Ltd., 473 F.2d 515 (8th Cir. 1973), 214
Trbovich v. UMW, 404 U.S. 528 (1972), 411
Troupe v. Chicago, Duluth & Georgian Bay Transit Co., 234 F.2d 253 (2d Cir. 1956), 835
Trowbridge v. Prudential Ins. Co., 322 F.Supp. 190 (S.D. N.Y. 1971), 400
Troy Bank of Troy, Ind. v. G.A. Whitehead & Co., 222 U.S. 39, 40-41 (1911), 184
Trustees v. Greenough, 105 U.S. 527 (1881), 460
Tuchman v. DSC Communications Corp., 14 F.3d 1061 (5th Cir. 1994), 302
Tull v. United States, 481 U.S. 412 (1987), 682,703
Tulsa Professional Collection Services, Inc. v. Pope, 485 U.S. 478 (1988), 138,145,696
Tumey v. Ohio, 273 U.S. 510 (1927), 730,732
Tunick v. Safir, 731 N.E.2d 597 (N.Y. Ct. App. 2000), 263
Twin Disc, Inc. v. Lowell, 69 F.R.D. 64 (E.D. Wis. 1975), 366

U.S. Bancorp Mortgage Co. v. Bonner Mall, 513 U.S. 18 (1994), 834,868
U.S. Steel v. M. DeMatteo Const. Co., 315 F.3d 43 (1st Cir. 2002), 776
Union Paving Co. v. Downer Corp., 276 F.2d 468 (9th Cir. 1960), 365
United Carbon Co. v. Binney & Smith Co., 317 U.S. 228 (1942), 705
Unique Concepts, Inc. v. Manuel, 930 F.2d 573 (7th Cir. 1991), 370
United Artists Corp. v. Masterpiece Productions, 221 F.2d 213 (2d Cir. 1955), 368
United Mine Workers v. Gibbs, 383 U.S. 715 (1966), 185,**186**,191,196,378
United States ex rel. Bernardin v. Duell, 172 U.S. 576 (1899),807
United States F. & G. Co. v. Des Moines National Bank, 145 F.273 (8th Cir. 1906), 716
U.S. Postal Service Bd. of Governors v. Aikens, 460 U.S. 711 (1983), 719
United States Steel Corp. v. United States, 519 F.2d 359 (3d Cir. 1975), 12
United States v. Adlman, 134 F.3d 1194 (2d Cir. 1998), 558
United States v. American Railway Express Co., 265 U.S. 425 (1923), 835
United States v. Bigford, 365 F.3d 859 (10th Cir. 2004), 778
United States v. C.M. Lane Lifeboat Co., 25 F.Supp. 410 (E.D. N.Y. 1938), 413
United States v. Curry, 6 How. 111, 113 (1848), 799
United States v. Deveaux, 9 U.S. 61 (1809), 174,244
United States v. Diebold, Inc., 369 U.S. 654 (1962), 638,654,661
United States v. El Paso Co., 682 F.2d 530 (5th Cir. 1982), 558
United States v. El Paso Natural Gas Co., 376 U.S. 651 (1964), 826
United States v. Employing Plasterers Assn., 347 U.S. 186 (1954), 321
United States v. First National City Bank, 379 U.S. 378 (1965), 63
United States v. Garcia, 936 F.2d 648 (2d Cir.1991), 701
United States v. Gonzalez, 214 F.3d 1109 (9th Cir. 2000), 701
United States v. Heyward Robinson Co., 430 F.2d 1077 (2nd Cir. 1970), **366**
United States v. Hudson, 7 Cranch 32 (1812), 604
United States v. Indrelunas, 411 U.S. 216 (1973), 796
United States v. James Daniel Good Real Property, 510 U.S. 43 (1993), 161
United States v. King, 44 U.S. 773 (1845), 679
United States v. Louisville & Nashville R. Co., 236 U.S. 318 (1915), 544
United States v. MacDonald, 435 U.S. 850 (1978), 811
United States v. Marcus, __ U.S. __ (2010 WL 2025203), 835
United States v. Markwood, 48 F.3d 969 (6th Cir. 1995), 832
United States v. Marine Bancorporation, 418 U.S. 602 (1974), 826
United States v. Mendoza, 464 U.S. 154 (1984), 890
United States v. Mississippi, 380 U.S. 128 (1965), 378
United States v. Nixon, 418 U.S. 683 (1974), 817
United States v. Ryan, 402 U.S. 530 (1971), 819
United States v. Shaffer Equip. Co., 11 F.3d 450 (4th Cir. 1993), 508
United States v. Straits Steel & Wire Co., 810 F.Supp. 208 (W.D. Mich. 1992), 778

United States v. Swiss American Bank, Ltd., 191 F.3d 30 (1st Cir. 1999), 122
United States v. Taylor, 464 F.2d 240 (2d Cir. 1972), 651
United States v. United Shoe Machinery Corp., 89 F. Supp. 357 (D. Mass. 1950), 542
United States v. U.S. Gypsum Co., 333 U.S. 364 (1948), 822,827
United States v. Utah Construction & Mining Co., 384 US. 394 (1966), 880
Unitherm Food Sys., Inc. v. Swift-Ekrich, Inc., 546 U.S. 394 (2006), **723**
Universal Licensing Corp. v. Paoa del Lungo S.p.A., 293 F.3d 579, 581 (2d Cir. 2002), 179
Universal Underwriters Ins. Co. v. Kneeland, 628 NW2d 491, 494 (Mich. 2001), 642
Univ. of Tennessee v. Elliott, 478 U.S. 788 (1986), 851
Upjohn Co. v. United States, 449 U.S. 383 (1981), **543**
Upper Valley Assoc. For Handicapped Citizens v. Mills, 168 F.R.D. 167 (D.Vt.1996), 425

Valente v. Pepsico, Inc., 68 F.R.D. 361 (D. Del. 1975), 542
Van Beek v. Ninkov, 265 F.Supp.2d 1037 (N.D. Iowa 2003), 214
Van Cauwenberghe v. Biard, 486 U.S. 517 (1988), 792,807,810-811
Van Dusen v. Barrack, 376 U.S. 612 (1964), 218,227,265
Virginia v. Westinghouse Elec. Corp., 542 F.2d 214, 216 (4th Cir. 1976), 413
Vodusek v. Bayliner Marine Corp., 71 F.3d 148 (4th Cir. 1995), 509
Voice Systems Marketing Co. v. Appropriate Technology Corp., 153 F.R.D. 117 (E.D. Mich. 1994), 97
Volkswagenwerk Aktiengesellschaft v. Schlunk, 486 U.S. 694 (1988), 153
Volvo North American Corp. v. Men's Intl. Professional Tennis Council, 839 F.2d 69 (2d Cir. 1988), 366
Vreeland v. Ethan Allen, 151 F.R.D. 551 (S.D. N.Y. 1993), 599

Wachovia Bank, N.A. v. Schmidt, 546 U.S. 303 (2006), 183
Waddell v. Hendry County Sheriff's Office, 329 F.3d 1300 (11th Cir 2003), 776
Wagh v. Metris Direct, Inc., 363 F.3d 821, 832 (9th Cir. 2003), 863
Wainwright v. Sykes, 433 U.S. 72 (1977), 827-828
Wainwright v. Witt, 469 U.S. 412 (1985), 828
Walker Process Equipment, Inc. v. Food Machinery & Chemical Corp., 382 U.S. 172 (1965), 724
Walker v. Armco Steel Corp., 446 U.S. 740 (1980), 255
Walker v. City of Hutchinson, 352 U.S. 112 (1956), 138
Walker v. Liggett Group, Inc., 175 F.R.D. 226 (S.D. W.Va. 1997), 451
Walker v. Norwest Corp., 108 F.3d 158 (1996), **351**
Ward v. Board of County Commissioners, 253 U.S. 17 (1920), 233
Ward v. Monroeville, 409 U.S. 57 (1972), 731
Waste Management Holdings, Inc. v. Mowbray, 208 F.3d 288 (1st Cir. 2000), 419
Watergate Landmark Condominium Unit Owners' Assoc. v. Wiss, Janey, Elstner Assoc., 117 F.R.D. 576 (E.D. Va. 1987), 396
Weiss v. St. Paul Fire and Marine Ins. Co., 283 F.3d 790 (6th Cir. 2002), 317
Wenche Siemer v. Learjet Acquisition Corp., 966 F.2d 179, 183 (5th Cir. 1992), 100
Westinghouse Elec. Corp. v. Republic of the Philippines, 951 F.2d 1414 (3d Cir. 1991), 546
Whigham v Beneficial Finance Co., 599 F.2d 1322 (4th Cir. 1979), 370
Williams v. Board of County Commnrs., 192 F.R.D. 698 (D. Kan. 2000), 581
Wilbur v. Locke, 423 F.3d 1101 (2005), **385**
Wilko v. Swan, 346 U.S. (1953), 468
Will v. Hallock, 546 U.S. 345 (2006), 807
Will v. United States, 389 U.S. 90 (1967), 816-818
Williams v. Capital Transit Co., 215 F.2d 487 (D.C. Cir. 1954), 150
Williams v. Sprint/United Mgt. Co., 230 F.R.D. 640 (D. Kan. 2005), **573**
Williamson v. Columbia Gas & Electric Corp., 186 F.2d 464 (3d Cir. 1950), 843
Wilson's Executor v. Deen, 121 U.S. 525 (1887), 862

Winters v. Travia, 495 F.2d 839 (2d Cir. 1974), 594
Wisconsin Dept. of Corrections v. Schacht, 524 U.S. 381 (1998), 198
Withrow v. Larkin, 421 U.S. 35 (1975), 729,730-733
Woodring v. Hall, 438 P.2d 135, 141 (Kan. 1968), 111
Woods v. Interstate Realty Co., 337 U.S. 535 (1949), 245
World-Wide Volkswagen Corp. v. Woodson, 444 U.S. 286 (1980), **52**,60-62, 64,82,95,213,447
World-Wide Volkswagen Corp. v. Woodson, 585 P.2d 351 (1980), **117**
World Wrestling Federation Entertainment, Inc. v. William Morris Agency, Inc., 204 F.R.D. 263 (S.D. N.Y. 2001), 517
Worthington v. Wilson, 8 F.3d 1253 (1993), 345
Wright v. West, 505 U.S. 277 (1992), 721
Wuchter v. Pizzutti, 276 U.S. 13 (1928), 132
Wyman v. Newhouse, 93 F.2d 313 (2d Cir. 1937), 97
Yapp v. Excel Corp., 186 F.3d 1222 (10th Cir. 1999), 776
Young v. New Haven Advocate, 315 F.3d 256 (2002), **69**

Zahn v. International Paper Co., 414 U.S. 291 (1973), 192,194,437
Zenith Radio Corp. v. Hazeltine Research, 401 U.S. 321 (1971), 340-341,827
Zenith Radio Corp. v. Matsushita Elec. Ind. Co., 402 F.Supp. 262 (E.D. Pa. 1975), 214
Zielinski v. Philadelphia Piers, Inc., 139 F. Supp. 408 (1956), **328**
Zippo Manufacturing Co. v. Zippo Dot Com, Inc., 952 F.Supp. 1119 (W.D. Pa. 1997), 79
Zubulake v. UBS Warburg LLC, 216 F.R.D. 280 (S.D. N.Y. 2003), 541
Zubulake v. UBS Warburg LLC, 229 F.R.D. 422 (S.D. N.Y. 2004), 506,512
Zubulake v. UBS Warburg LLC, 217 F.R.D. 309 (S.D. N.Y. 2003), 535,540-541
Zuelke Tool & Eng. Co. v. Anderson Die Castings, Inc., 925 F.2d 226 (7th Cir. 1991), 318

CHAPTER I

OVERVIEW

OBJECTIVE: That you be able to articulate for a client the significance and stages of civil litigation, consistent with your study of this chapter.

Case Study: You are meeting with the president and CEO of a corporate client whom a sheriff's officer just served with a summons and complaint in a civil case filed in the local state circuit court. The complaint alleges a competitor's federal trademark and common law commercial-exploitation claims against your corporate client. The president/CEO explains that the corporate client has traded allegations in a long-running and acrimonious nationwide battle with the competitor. The president/CEO wants to know what to expect in the course of the litigation.

Federal Rules of Civil Procedure this chapter reproduces and addresses

FED. R. CIV. P. 1:	Scope and Purpose.
FED. R. CIV. P. 21:	Misjoinder and Nonjoinder of Parties.
FED. R. CIV. P. 22:	Interpleader.
FED. R. CIV. P. 23:	Class Actions.
FED. R. CIV. P. 24:	Intervention.
FED. R. CIV. P. 81:	Applicability of the Rules in General; Removed Actions.
FED. R. CIV. P. 83:	Rules by District Courts; Judge's Directives.
FED. R. CIV. P. 85:	Title.
FED. R. CIV. P. 86:	Effective Date.

A. Nature

Do not underestimate civil procedure. At its root, civil procedure is not solely or perhaps even primarily about procedure—about processes. It is fundamentally about authority, not the content of authority but its source, nature, exercise, and limits. Civil procedure is about the will of law, not the content of law. Civil procedure is a study in how lawyers properly invoke authority. Novitiates sometimes think that civil procedure is like criminal procedure. Yet criminal procedure has primarily to do with restraints on authority. Civil procedure has much more to do with how to draw on and from authority. The uninformed assume that what makes a great lawyer is great knowledge, performance, or thought. Masterful lawyers are instead those who have a great appreciation for the source and nature of authority. Whatever comes only from the lawyer is valueless because a lawyer has no authority. The lawyer's true authority is what the lawyer derives from the law by knowledge and use of its procedures. The lawyer gains authority only by delegation from the client and judge, each of whom are also under the law's authority and can grant only that which it permits. Judges and law firms beg Civil Procedure professors to teach their students well, as clients should also, because they know that litigators accomplish little or nothing without a well-grounded and thorough knowledge of how to invoke the law's authority through its procedures.

Civil procedure challenges law students because of its unfamiliar nature. Non-lawyers would have a ready sense of law school's other first-year subjects. The public knows about crime. There is even widespread knowledge of criminal procedure given the popularity of entertainment and reality crime shows and the prominence in American society of issues over the treatment of criminal and terrorism suspects. Non-lawyers know about personal suffering and property loss, even if tort is an unfamiliar word for it. Non-lawyers also have a sense of what it means to buy, sell, and own property through promises that both lawyers and non-lawyers call contracts. Constitutional law is familiar because public education includes substantial history and at least some instruction on the formation and powers of government, and there is frequent public debate and widespread public knowledge about individual rights. Legal doctrine taught in Torts, Contracts, Property, and other courses may lie latent in the minds of non-lawyers, but non-lawyers generally have not even a latent perception of civil procedure.

There is little in public education or experience about the way in which lawyers go about enforcing private rights through the civil justice system. Although everyone uses procedure all of the time—just getting out of bed and to school or work in the morning, for example—non-lawyers seldom study, receive training or education in, or even think explicitly about procedure. Indeed, one could make a good argument that what makes a lawyer is explicit knowledge of the nature, source, and value of authority, as invoked by procedure. What, after all, is the central criticism of an unprepared law graduate but that they cannot even find the courthouse? A course in civil procedure tells you how private rights actually work when parties dispute them. It tells you what courts can hear what matters, what law the courts will apply, how parties can discover the facts, and how decisionmakers apply law to facts to reach decisions. As do other chapters, this chapter focuses on the *Federal Rules of Civil Procedure* recognizing that state-court rules supply similar regimes for civil procedure in state-court cases.

B. Significance

Do not underestimate the power of private justice to promote public welfare and private liberty. Civil litigation is enormously powerful as a state-sanctioned means of bringing private disputes to peaceful conclusion. The common law promotes unprecedentedly productive economic rules within quite different societies and cultures, under different political conditions, and with different technologies. The common law is rich stock for economic prosperity and individual liberty. Immigrants come to the United States from all over the world for its social and economic stability, prosperity, and liberty. Yet the common law and its system of private property and individual rights and liberties depend on private enforcement. The American continent is vast, the nation's culture richly diverse, and its social interests healthily disparate. Under these conditions, public enforcement of private rights and centralized protection of private interests would be practically impossible, prohibitively expensive, crudely insensitive, and politically unacceptable. As Karl Llewellyn put it in THE BRAMBLE BUSH 9 (3d ed. 1960), you must read doctrinal courses like Torts, Contracts, and Property "through the spectacles of ... procedure. For what substantive law says should be means nothing except in terms of what procedure says that you can make real." Individual litigants must have ready resort to private, orderly, fair, and efficient means of resolving disputes.

It does not take a modern Alexis de Tocqueville to recognize that American-style civil justice fits American-style industriousness, ingenuity, and independence. Some regard Americans as unduly litigious. It is true that there is more litigation in the United States than any other country. In actuality, though, *per-capita* litigation rates are higher in Austria, Germany, Israel, and Sweden than in the United States. *See* Christian Wollschlager, *Exploring Global Landscapes of Litigation Rates* in JURGEN BRAND & DIETER STREMPEL, EDS., SOZIOLOGIE DES RECHTS: FESTSCHRIFT FUR ERHARD BLANKENBURG 582 (1998). It is just that the United States has a significantly larger population than those other highly developed countries. The prominence of civil litigation in the United States is anything but a defect in the national character. There are at least two other good reasons for it in addition to population. One has to do with the fact that the United States has the world's largest economy. We are a populous nation, though not nearly the most populous. China and India are vastly more populous. Yet we are the most productive, and studies correlate economic activity to litigation rates. *Id.* It makes sense that the more we interact productively around financial and property interests, the more often we would need civil resolution of disagreements over those interests. Increases in litigation over the past 25 years are greater than population growth but much less than economic growth, falling neatly between and correlating to both.

There is a third good reason for American litigiousness. One can readily attribute the prominence of civil litigation in the United States to the desire and willingness of Americans to resolve important issues by private interaction rather than through government administration. Civil litigation is necessarily adversarial, adjusting one individual interest against another. American courts do not reach out and create cases. In a system of private litigation, government does not decide when to take action. Individual parties or (in rare cases classes of parties) bring disputes to courts, at least one of them voluntarily. It is not that Americans like conflict. Studies suggest that the majority of individuals having legal claims (as many as eight out of every nine) decide not to take any action. When disputants do litigate, more than 9 out of 10 cases resolve before trial. When a court enters judgment, parties generally accept that the court has adjudicated the matter, preventing relitigation of the same issues between the same parties.

We trust our ability to adjust private interests with the help of a civil justice system more than we trust bureaucracies to adjust those interests for us. We more often resolve through civil procedures important rights to real and personal property, compensation for personal injury, liberty and regulation of businesses, land and environmental uses, and individual liberties. Procedure, or how the law accomplishes its ends, is as important to us as substance, meaning the ends it preserves and accomplishes. One can hardly separate substance from procedure, for success in one depends on success in the other. Flipping a coin might get the right result half the time but even in those right cases without having achieved public or private confidence because of the arbitrariness of the procedure. Moreover, justice systems should certainly hope to have a higher percentage of correct verdicts. Substantive rights depend on fair procedures. Yet fairness of procedures depends on keeping an eye on the substance. As Grant Gilmore warned in AGES OF AMERICAN LAW 111 (1977), "In Hell there will be nothing but law, and due process will be meticulously observed." Cicero had it right millennia ago in ON DUTIES when he wrote to his son that there is no difference between the virtuous and the expedient, and Sir Henry Maine equally right that substantive law is "secreted in the interstices of Procedure," EARLY LAW AND CUSTOM 389 (1886). The effective litigator practices civil procedure not for its own ends but solely in pursuit of substantive justice. For the American lawyer, civil procedure remains an indispensable tool. As significant as it is, the challenge is to ensure not to mistake it for an end.

C. Structure

To address the law and practice of civil procedure, the author organized this casebook into three parts involving the Authority to Adjudicate, the Process of Adjudication, and the Results of Adjudication. Although the *Federal Rules of Civil Procedure* or equivalent state-court rules become the civil litigator's bible, civil procedure involves much more than process rules. It first raises the question of whether the court that the parties have chosen has the authority to decide the dispute. The court must have authority over the parties, which is an issue that lawyers recognize as personal jurisdiction. A court in one state would ordinarily have no authority to decide the rights of a person who had never been to the state, taken any action toward anyone within the state, or had any property within the state. The court must also have authority over the nature of the dispute, which is an issue that lawyers know as subject-matter jurisdiction. A probate court that a state legislature constituted to decide how to distribute a decedent's property would ordinarily have no authority to decide a business or consumer dispute. As a matter of fundamental fairness, a party must also have notice and an opportunity to be heard. A court should not ordinarily decide a dispute until all parties know about it and have a chance to participate. In addition, if more than one court has personal and subject-matter jurisdiction, then the parties should litigate in the reasonably convenient court. In a federal-court case, the Constitution, Supreme Court case law interpreting the Constitution, federal statutes, and the *Federal Rules of Civil Procedure* may all govern or affect the resolution of these issues, treated in the first part on Authority to Adjudicate. Note here the authority of the *Federal Rules* set forth in FED. R. CIV. P. 1 and the actions to which they apply set forth in FED. R. CIV. P. 81. Note also the authority in FED. R. CIV. P. 83 for a federal judicial district to enact additional local rules.

FED. R. CIV. P. 1. Scope and Purpose. These rules govern the procedure in all civil actions and proceedings in the United States district courts, except as stated in Rule 81. They should be construed and administered to secure the just, speedy, and inexpensive determination of every action and proceeding.

FED. R. CIV. P. 2. One Form of Action. There is one form of action—the civil action.

FED. R. CIV. P. 3. Commencing an Action. A civil action is commenced by filing a complaint with the court.

. . .

FED. R. CIV. P. 81. Applicability of the Rules in General; Removed Actions

(a) APPLICABILITY TO PARTICULAR PROCEEDINGS.

(1) *Prize Proceedings.* These rules do not apply to prize proceedings in admiralty governed by 10 U.S.C. §§7651–7681.

(2) *Bankruptcy.* These rules apply to bankruptcy proceedings to the extent provided by the Federal Rules of Bankruptcy Procedure.

(3) *Citizenship.* These rules apply to proceedings for admission to citizenship to the extent that the practice in those proceedings is not specified in federal statutes and has previously conformed to the practice in civil actions. The provisions of 8 U.S.C. §1451 for service by publication and for answer apply in proceedings to cancel citizenship certificates.

(4) *Special Writs.* These rules apply to proceedings for habeas corpus and for quo warranto to the extent that the practice in those proceedings:

(A) is not specified in a federal statute, the Rules Governing Section 2254 Cases, or the Rules Governing Section 2255 Cases; and

(B) has previously conformed to the practice in civil actions.

(5) *Proceedings Involving a Subpoena.* These rules apply to proceedings to compel testimony or the production of documents through a subpoena issued by a United States officer or agency under a federal statute, except as otherwise provided by statute, by local rule, or by court order in the proceedings.

(6) *Other Proceedings.* These rules, to the extent applicable, govern proceedings under the following laws, except as these laws provide other procedures:

(A) 7 U.S.C. §§292, 499g(c), for reviewing an order of the Secretary of Agriculture;

(B) 9 U.S.C., relating to arbitration;

(C) 15 U.S.C. §522, for reviewing an order of the Secretary of the Interior;

(D) 15 U.S.C. §715d(c), for reviewing an order denying a certificate of clearance;

(E) 29 U.S.C. §§159, 160, for enforcing an order of the National Labor Relations Board;

(F) 33 U.S.C. §§918, 921, for enforcing or reviewing a compensation order under the Longshore and Harbor Workers' Compensation Act; and

(G) 45 U.S.C. §159, for reviewing an arbitration award in a railway-labor dispute.

(b) SCIRE FACIAS AND MANDAMUS. The writs of scire facias and mandamus are abolished. Relief previously available through them may be obtained by appropriate action or motion under these rules.

(c) REMOVED ACTIONS.

(1) *Applicability.* These rules apply to a civil action after it is removed from a state court.

(2) *Further Pleading.* After removal, repleading is unnecessary unless the court orders it. A defendant who did not answer before removal must answer or present other defenses or objections under these rules within the longest of these periods:

(A) 21 days after receiving—through service or otherwise— a copy of the initial pleading stating the claim for relief;

(B) 21 days after being served with the summons for an initial pleading on file at the time of service; or

(C) 7 days after the notice of removal is filed.

(3) *Demand for a Jury Trial.*

(A) *As Affected by State Law.* A party who, before removal, expressly demanded a jury trial in accordance with state law need not renew the demand after removal. If the state law did not require an express demand for a jury trial, a party need not make one after removal unless the court orders the parties to do so within a specified time. The court must so order at a party's request and may so order on its own. A party who fails to make a demand when so ordered waives a jury trial.

(B) *Under Rule 38.* If all necessary pleadings have been served at the time of removal, a party entitled to a jury trial under Rule 38 must be given one if the party serves a demand within 14 days after:

(i) it files a notice of removal; or

(ii) it is served with a notice of removal filed by another party.

(d) LAW APPLICABLE.

(1) *''State Law'' Defined.* When these rules refer to state law, the term ''law'' includes the state's statutes and the state's judicial decisions.

(2) *"State" Defined.* The term "state" includes, where appropriate, the District of Columbia and any United States commonwealth or territory.
(3) *"Federal Statute" Defined in the District of Columbia.* In the United States District Court for the District of Columbia, the term "federal statute" includes any Act of Congress that applies locally to the District.
...

Fed. R. Civ. P. 83. Rules by District Courts; Judge's Directives
(a) LOCAL RULES.
(1) *In General.* After giving public notice and an opportunity for comment, a district court, acting by a majority of its district judges, may adopt and amend rules governing its practice. A local rule must be consistent with—but not duplicate— federal statutes and rules adopted under 28 U.S.C. §§2072 and 2075, and must conform to any uniform numbering system prescribed by the Judicial Conference of the United States. A local rule takes effect on the date specified by the district court and remains in effect unless amended by the court or abrogated by the judicial council of the circuit. Copies of rules and amendments must, on their adoption, be furnished to the judicial council and the Administrative Office of the United States Courts and be made available to the public.
(2) *Requirement of Form.* A local rule imposing a requirement of form must not be enforced in a way that causes a party to lose any right because of a nonwillful failure to comply.
(b) PROCEDURE WHEN THERE IS NO CONTROLLING LAW. A judge may regulate practice in any manner consistent with federal law, rules adopted under 28 U.S.C. §§2072 and 2075, and the district's local rules. No sanction or other disadvantage may be imposed for noncompliance with any requirement not in federal law, federal rules, or the local rules unless the alleged violator has been furnished in the particular case with actual notice of the requirement.
...

Fed. R. Civ. P. 85. Title
These rules may be cited as the Federal Rules of Civil Procedure.

Fed. R. Civ. P. 86. Effective Dates
(a) IN GENERAL. These rules and any amendments take effect at the time specified by the Supreme Court, subject to 28 U.S.C. §2074. They govern:
(1) proceedings in an action commenced after their effective date; and
(2) proceedings after that date in an action then pending unless:
(A) the Supreme Court specifies otherwise; or
(B) the court determines that applying them in a particular action would be infeasible or work an injustice.
(b) DECEMBER 1, 2007 AMENDMENTS. If any provision in Rules 1–5.1, 6–73, or 77–86 conflicts with another law, priority in time for the purpose of 28 U.S.C. §2072(b) is not affected by the amendments taking effect on December 1, 2007.

The second part of this book, on the Process of Adjudication, involves the details of civil litigation. A lawyer's practice of civil procedure depends on familiarity with the *Federal Rules of Civil Procedure* or their state equivalents. The *Federal Rules* and their state equivalents are like statutes. They have specific authoritative promulgators who specify them down to the letter. The rules are rules, with no doubt where to find them. They state broad principles to govern all specific cases. Their promulgators assemble them into sensibly organized codes. They apply to specific proceedings, the *Federal Rules* to federal court civil proceedings and their state equivalents to state court civil proceedings. Yet they are usually not legislative products. The Supreme Court adopts and amends the *Federal Rules of Civil Procedure* through an elaborate two-to-three-year process that requires the consent of Congress. The Supreme Court acts under authority Congress granted it in the Rules Enabling Act, 28 USC §2072. The Rules Enabling Act's process for adopting or amending a rule begins with the Supreme Court establishing a rules committee that produces a draft for public comment and review by other committees ending with Supreme Court approval and review by Congress. State supreme courts have similar legislative authority to enact state court rules often patterned after the *Federal Rules*.

Unlike statutes, the *Federal Rules* are solely procedural. They grant no substantive rights and must not interfere with substantive rights. Congress' Rules Enabling Act, 28 USC §2072(b), states in pertinent part, "Such rules shall not abridge, enlarge, or modify any substantive right." For example, the *Federal Rules* may tell a lawyer how to obtain relief (procedures) but will not tell the lawyer whether relief is available (substantively). One might think that courts have from time to time interpreted the *Federal Rules* in ways that interfere with substantive rights in violation of the Rules Enabling Act. The Supreme Court has not so found in any case. The *Federal Rules of Civil Procedure* or their state equivalent largely controls the process of adjudication, not the Constitution or statutes.

Figure

The Supreme Court originally adopted the *Federal Rules of Civil Procedure* in 1938 after a special committee of judges, lawyers, and law professors drafted them. When the Supreme Court wanted to rewrite the *Federal Rules* recently, it turned to Cooley Law School Professor Joe Kimble, who after several years of leading that work won an award from the Association of American Law Schools for it. Professor Kimble is the dean of the plain English movement in legal writing. For Professor Kimble and others, plain English is more than an issue of style. It is an issue of public access to, understanding of, and appreciation for the law. Rewriting rules of procedure that hundreds of court opinions have interpreted and hundreds of thousands of lawyers have used was no simple task, but after years of commentary, criticism, review, and arduous editing work, the Supreme Court adopted the *Federal Rules* rewrite led by Professor Kimble.

The subject of civil procedure is not complete, though, until the final part on the Results of Adjudication. There is (or should be) a point to civil litigation. The final part addresses the subject of how lawyers obtain orders and judgments, and how they enforce those orders and judgments. Judgments are not self-executing. Just because a judge signs an order requiring a party to pay or act does not mean that the party will do so. Some lawyers and law firms devote their entire practice to the collection or other enforcement of judgments. The final part also addresses how lawyers challenge judgments through post-trial motions and appeals. It also addresses the significant question of whom a judgment governs. Should a judgment against one person affect another person's ability to make or defend the same claim or raise the same issue? The final part addresses when a judgment precludes another claim or issue. The Constitution, case law, statutes, and the *Federal Rules of Civil Procedure* or their state equivalent may all govern or affect the results of adjudication. Appreciate civil procedure's complex and subtle structure. The measure of a lawyer is often in the lawyer's skill at procedure precisely because skill has sufficient nuance to respect varied and important interests.

Knowledge

What you have just read reflects the content structure of civil procedure: (1) procedural rules (2) that parties employ for specific ends (3) constrained by the Constitution's requirement of due process. Each law subject has its own content structure. Tort law involves claims with elements and defenses, organized conceptually in a tree diagram reflecting the choices parties can make to redress their losses and protect their interests. Criminal law has a similar structure of charges and elements. Constitutional law involves a central question of who gets to decide, answered (like peeling an onion) through layers of analysis involving themes like individual rights, separation of powers, and federalism. Lawyers employ their law knowledge, and develop and exercise their legal skills, by drawing on a law field's deep content structure. To ease and organize your civil procedure studies, constantly keep in mind its structure of procedural rules, strategic ends, and constitutional due process.

1. The Judicial System

By far the greater part of civil litigation is in the state rather than federal courts. The Court Statistics Project's report *Examining the Work of State Courts* estimated that there were 18 million new cases in state courts in 2007. About 12 million of those cases were traffic offenses, while 4.2 million were civil cases, and 3.4 million were criminal cases. Federal government statistics show just 257,507 total civil filings in federal district courts in the same year, meaning that federal civil cases represented about 6% or 1/16th of civil cases. Depending on your practice area within civil litigation, you are far more likely to find yourself in state than federal court. According to the Court Statistics Project, of the 4.2 million state-court civil cases (other than traffic offenses), about 1 million were domestic-relations cases, 1 million were contracts cases, and 200,000 were torts cases. Other data from the same source indicate that by far the greater number of civil cases involve contract disputes, then (in descending order) probate and estate matters, small claims, tort cases, cases involving mental health, and finally real property cases. The vast majority of contract cases involve debt collection, then (in descending order) landlord/tenant disputes, mortgage foreclosures, fraud, and employment disputes. Among tort cases, the great majority involve motor-vehicle accidents, then (in descending order) much smaller percentages of malpractice, premises liability, intentional torts, products liability, and defamation. Federal government statistics show that of the 257,507 federal civil cases, 189,311 were original filings, 30,282 were cases removed from state courts, and the remainder involved cases remanded, reopened, or transferred.

Despite that state courts handle much more civil litigation than federal courts, civil-procedure courses focus on the federal judicial system. There are several good reasons for focusing on federal civil procedure, even though many more lawyers practice in state than in federal courts. The federal system is uniform, while state courts vary from state to state in their subject-matter jurisdiction, monetary jurisdictional limits, and appellate structure. The federal system's uniformity makes the *Federal Rules of Civil Procedure* a common point for nationwide study, while students must study state-court rules state-by-state. The Multi-State Bar Examination can test federal civil procedure, while graduates must prepare for and take individual state bar exams on state-court rules. The Federal Rules Decision volumes and other federal reporters collect abundant case law on federal civil procedure, while some states have little or no case authority on significant points of procedure. The Constitution's Supremacy Clause makes federal constitutional and statutory law supreme over state law. For these and other reasons, this book, like other civil procedure casebooks, emphasizes the federal judicial system while including representative state-court procedural rules and cases. Given the prominence of state court over federal court practice, consider closely the select state-court cases and procedural rules.

The Constitution's Article III authorizes the Supreme Court and a federal judiciary. Congress enacted federal statutes establishing that federal judiciary, while the Supreme Court promulgated federal appellate and trial court rules. Most federal cases begin in the United States District Courts. Legislation organizes the federal district courts into 94 federal judicial districts. Each state has at least one federal judicial district such as the District of Mississippi or District of Arkansas. No federal judicial district crosses a state line other than the District of Wyoming, which includes portions of Yellowstone National Park located in Montana and Idaho. (Those who are familiar with the region would understand why.) Many states have more than one federal judicial district, designated by a compass direction such as the Southern District of New York. Each federal district has several judges whom the president appoints and the Senate confirms for life. The federal district courts assign cases to a single judge at a time. The United States District Court judges employ United States District Court magistrate judges for terms of ten years to assist them with specific matters in individual cases.

U.S. Const. Art. III, §1.

The judicial Power of the United States, shall be vested in one supreme Court, and in such inferior Courts as the Congress may from time to time ordain and establish. The Judges, both of the supreme and inferior Courts, shall hold their Offices during good Behaviour, and shall, at stated Times, receive for their Services, a Compensation, which shall not be diminished during their Continuance in Office.

United States Courts of Appeals hear appeals from the United States District Courts. Legislation organizes the federal Courts of Appeals into 12 circuits numbered 1 through 11, as in the United States Court of Appeals for the Sixth Circuit, plus the United States Court of Appeals for the District of Columbia Circuit. Each circuit covers appeals from specific districts within several specific states and, in a few instances, United States territories. For example, the First Circuit hears appeals from the Upper New England states and Puerto Rico. Each circuit has a panel of judges each of whom the president appoints and the Senate confirms for life. The circuit courts initially hear appeals in three-judge panels but may then reconsider cases in en banc panels comprised of all of the circuit's judges. Legislation also establishes the United States Court of Appeals for the Federal Circuit to hear primarily patent appeals. The Supreme Court hears appeals from the United States Courts of Appeals. Most of the Supreme Court's appellate jurisdiction is discretionary. 28 USC §1254(1). Parties file petitions for writs of certiorari, which the Supreme Court grants only when it determines that it should hear and decide the appeal, typically to resolve splits of authority among the circuit courts or for other value as precedent. The Supreme Court may also hear appeals from supreme courts (courts of last resort) in each state and territory, and the District of Columbia, provided that the appeal involves a federal question. 28 USC §§1257(a), 1258.

2. Financing Litigation

One cannot understand and navigate the civil justice system without knowing how the public and parties finance it. The public bears a significant portion of the civil justice system's cost by providing courthouses, court administrators and clerks, judges, judicial staff, and related expenses. Significant public debate occurs at the federal, state, county, and local level over justice-system funding. At the federal and state levels, the debate typically includes judicial compensation, the number of judges, and the most efficient structure of the courts. At the county and local level, the debate may also include whether and when to fill an available new judicial seat, staffing and staff compensation for courthouse personnel, and construction and cost of facilities. Every practitioner knows that courtroom time is precious, counting the hidden costs, as much as $1,000 per judge per hour.

Costs not hidden in the public coffers are those borne by the litigants. Everyone has heard that lawyers are expensive, thinking of the hourly fees charged by top litigators. Yet there are several systems for the delivery of legal services, not all of them based on the hourly fee, and not all of them expensive. These systems are critical to the justice system's credibility and function. The system does not function well in many cases, especially the complex and high-stakes cases, without legal representation. Meaningful access to justice often requires legal representation. Lawyers provide legal services through direct employment by government or government-funded agencies (about 12% of all lawyers), in corporate-counsel offices of businesses (about 8%), and in large and small law firms or sole practice (about 75%). As significant as are the contributions of government, corporate, and big-firm lawyers to the civil justice system's operation, the greater contribution of legal services may be by the majority of lawyers who work alone (about 48% of all lawyers) or in small firms of ten or fewer lawyers (about 22%) providing direct legal services to individuals, families, and small businesses. The private delivery model for most legal services is consistent with American private property, individual rights, and self-responsibility.

A basic challenge that litigants face in obtaining representation is that under the so-called American Rule, parties pay their own lawyers. Under the English Rule (followed in England, Germany, and other countries), the loser would pay the lawyers on both sides. In the vast majority of civil cases in the United States, parties must prepare to pay their own lawyers. The Supreme Court has held that the federal courts have no inherent authority to shift fees based on public interest in the litigation. *See* Alyeska Pipeline Service v. Wilderness Society, 421 U.S. 240, 257 (1975). In some cases, rules or statutes alter the American rule. *See, e.g.,* FED. R. CIV. P. 68 (shift fees for unreasonable rejection of offer of judgment). Fee-shifting statutes promote various public policies. A prime example is 42 U.S.C. §1988(b) authorizing a discretionary award of fees to the prevailing plaintiff in federal civil-rights actions, particularly those under 42 U.S.C. §1983. *See* Blanchard v. Bergeron, 489 U.S. 87 (1989) (award statutory fees to prevailing party promoting public policy unless special circumstances make doing so unjust); *see also* 28 U.S.C. §2412 (fee awards in litigation against the United States); CAL. CODE CIV. PROC. §1021.5 (fee shifting authorized for "the enforcement of an important right affecting the public interest). Other court rules and statutes authorize courts to shift fees as sanctions for party or attorney misconduct. *See, e.g.,* FED. R. CIV. P. 11; MICH. CT. R. 2.114. Federal courts have some inherent authority to shift fees to a party acting in bad faith. *See* Chambers v. NASCO, Inc., 501 U.S. 32 (1991) (nearly $1 million fee award). Courts tend to have relatively broader authority to interpret and apply fee-shifting provisions. For example, the Supreme Court in the following case fashioned the now-settled rule that courts should generally shift fees in federal employment-rights actions only in favor of prevailing plaintiffs, not defendants, even though the statute stated expressly that courts might allow fees to "the prevailing party."

Christianburg Garment Co. v. EEOC,

United States Supreme Court
434 U.S. 412 (1978)

Mr. Justice STEWART delivered the opinion of the Court.

Section 706(k) of Title VII of the Civil Rights Act of 1964 provides: "In any action or proceeding under this title the court, in its discretion, may allow the prevailing party . . . a reasonable attorney's fee... ."[fn]

The question in this case is under what circumstances an attorney's fee should be allowed when the defendant is the prevailing party in a Title VII action—a question about which the federal courts have expressed divergent views. ...

... Rosa Helm ... filed a Title VII charge of racial discrimination against the petitioner Christiansburg Garment Co. ... [T]he Equal Employment Opportunity Commission ... sued the company, alleging that it had engaged in unlawful employment practices... . The District Court ... granted summary judgment in favor of the company. [C][fn]

The company then petitioned for the allowance of attorney's fees against the Commission pursuant to §706(k) of Title VII. Finding that "the Commission's action in bringing the suit cannot be characterized as unreasonable or meritless," the District Court concluded that "an award of attorney's fees to petitioner is not justified in this case."[fn] A divided Court of Appeals affirmed...

.

It is the general rule in the United States that in the absence of legislation providing otherwise, litigants must pay their own attorney's fees. Alyeska Pipeline Co. v. Wilderness Society, 421 U.S. 240[(1975)]. Congress has provided only limited exceptions to this rule "under selected statutes granting or protecting various federal rights." *Id.* at 260[]. Some of these statutes make fee awards mandatory for prevailing plaintiffs;[fn] others make awards permissive but limit them to certain parties, usually prevailing plaintiffs.[fn] But many of the statutes are more flexible, authorizing the award of attorney's fees to either plaintiffs or defendants, and entrusting the effectuation of the statutory policy to the discretion of the district courts.[fn] Section 706(k) of Title VII of the Civil Rights Act of 1964 falls into this last category, providing as it does that a district court may in its discretion allow an attorney's fee to the prevailing party.

In Newman v. Piggie Park Enterprises, 390 U.S. 400[(1968)], the Court considered a substantially identical statute authorizing the award of attorney's fees under Title II of the Civil Rights Act of 1964.[fn] In that case the plaintiffs had prevailed, and the Court of Appeals had held that they should be awarded their attorney's fees "only to the extent that the respondents' defenses had been advanced 'for purposes of delay and not in good faith.'" *Id.* at 401[]. We ruled that this "subjective standard" did not properly effectuate the purposes of the counsel-fee provision of Title II. Relying primarily on the intent of Congress to cast a Title II plaintiff in the role of "a 'private attorney general,' vindicating a policy that Congress considered of the highest priority," we held that a prevailing plaintiff under Title II "should ordinarily recover an attorney's fee unless special circumstances would render such an award unjust." *Id.* at 402[]. We noted in passing that if the objective of Congress had been to permit the award of attorney's fees only against defendants who had acted in bad faith, "no new statutory provision would have been necessary," since even the American common-law rule allows the award of attorney's fees in those exceptional circumstances. *Id.* at 402[].[fn]

In Albemarle Paper Co. v. Moody, 422 U.S. 405[, 415 (1975)], the Court made clear that the *Piggie Park* standard of awarding attorney's fees to a successful plaintiff is equally applicable in an action under Title VII of the Civil Rights Act. [Cc] It can thus be taken as established ... that under § 706(k) of Title VII a prevailing *plaintiff* ordinarily is to be awarded attorney's fees in all but special circumstances.[fn] ...

The question in the case before us is what standard should inform a district court's discretion in deciding whether to award attorney's fees to a successful *defendant* in a Title VII action. ...

Relying on what it terms "the plain meaning of the statute," the company argues that the language of §706(k) admits of only one interpretation: "A prevailing defendant is entitled to an award of attorney's fees on the same basis as a prevailing plaintiff." But the permissive and discretionary language of the statute does not even invite, let alone require, such a mechanical construction. The terms of §706(k) provide no indication whatever of the circumstances under which either a plaintiff *or* a defendant should be entitled to attorney's fees. And a moment's reflection reveals that there are at least two strong equitable considerations counseling an attorney's fee award to a prevailing Title VII plaintiff that are wholly absent in the case of a prevailing Title VII defendant.

First, as emphasized so forcefully in *Piggie Park*, the plaintiff is the chosen instrument of Congress to vindicate "a policy that Congress considered of the highest priority." 390 U.S. at 402[]. Second, when a district court awards counsel fees to a prevailing plaintiff, it is awarding them against a violator of federal law. ... A successful defendant seeking counsel fees under § 706(k) must rely on quite different equitable considerations.

But if the company's position is untenable, the Commission's argument also misses the mark. It seems clear, in short, that in enacting §706(k) Congress did not intend to permit the award of attorney's fees to a prevailing defendant only in a situation where the plaintiff was motivated by bad faith in bringing the action. As pointed out in *Piggie Park*, if that had been the intent of Congress, no statutory provision would have been necessary, for it has long been established that even under the American common-law rule attorney's fees may be awarded against a party who has proceeded in bad faith.[fn] ...

... A fair adversary process presupposes both a vigorous prosecution and a vigorous defense. It cannot be lightly assumed that in enacting § 706(k),

Congress intended to distort that process by giving the private plaintiff substantial incentives to sue, while foreclosing to the defendant the possibility of recovering his expenses in resisting even a groundless action unless he can show that it was brought in bad faith. ...

The first federal appellate court to consider what criteria should govern the award of attorney's fees to a prevailing Title VII defendant was the Court of Appeals for the Third Circuit in United States Steel Corp. v. United States, 519 F.2d 359[(3d Cir. 1975)]. There a District Court had denied a fee award to a defendant that had successfully resisted a Commission demand for documents, the court finding that the Commission's action had not been "'unfounded, meritless, frivolous or vexatiously brought.'" [C] The Court of Appeals concluded that the District Court had not abused its discretion in denying the award. [C] A similar standard was adopted by the Court of Appeals for the Second Circuit in Carrion v. Yeshiva University, 535 F.2d 722[(2d Cir. 1976)]. In upholding an attorney's fee award to a successful defendant, that court stated that such awards should be permitted "not routinely, not simply because he succeeds, but only where the action brought is found to be unreasonable, frivolous, meritless or vexatious." [C][fn]

To the extent that abstract words can deal with concrete cases, we think that the concept embodied in the language adopted by these two Courts of Appeals is correct. We would qualify their words only by pointing out that the term "meritless" is to be understood as meaning groundless or without foundation, rather than simply that the plaintiff has ultimately lost his case, and that the term "vexatious" in no way implies that the plaintiff's subjective bad faith is a necessary prerequisite to a fee award against him. In sum, a district court may in its discretion award attorney's fees to a prevailing defendant in a Title VII case upon a finding that the plaintiff's action was frivolous, unreasonable, or without foundation, even though not brought in subjective bad faith. ...

In denying attorney's fees to the company in this case, the District Court focused on the standards we have discussed. The court found that "the Commission's action in bringing the suit could not be characterized as unreasonable or meritless" because "the basis upon which petitioner prevailed was an issue of first impression requiring judicial resolution" and because the "Commission's statutory interpretation of §14 of the 1972 amendments was not frivolous." The court thus exercised its discretion squarely within the permissible bounds of §706(k). Accordingly, the judgment of the Court of Appeals upholding the decision of the District Court is affirmed.

It is so ordered.

Mr. Justice BLACKMUN took no part in the consideration or decision of this case.

INQUIRY

Indigency. Unlike in criminal cases involving potential incarceration, indigent parties have no constitutional right to legal representation in civil cases. Thus, lawyers must structure their practices to be able to generate sufficient income from their client's matters to continue their work. Lawyers are constantly making judgments about how and to whom to deliver legal services, not out of greed (although lawyers are not immune from that motivation) but out of an appropriately practical stewardship of their legal training and calling. The economic model on which lawyers provide these direct legal services to individuals, families, and small businesses influence the services' quality and availability. Insurance plans (whether private or employer-provided) for pre-paid legal services are rare. Federal, state, and local government supplement the private market for legal services with publicly funded legal-aid organizations and legal assistance centers. Yet legal-aid offices, funded by the federal Legal Services Corporation and by local grants and public support, provide only a fraction of the needed civil legal services and usually only in specific areas such as for domestic violence and termination of parental rights.

Fee Agreements. Instead, lawyers in sole proprietorships or small firms provide the great majority of legal services, through individual retainer agreements offered to individual paying clients. Lawyers base a large percentage of those services on hourly fees charged to the client in monthly bills rendered on specific cases or matters. The flat rates that many lawyers charge for standardized services such as wills, trusts, powers of attorney, and forming a new business, are less suited to litigation with the exception of bankruptcy matters and uncontested divorces. The hourly and flat rates depend on the lawyer's skill, experience, and reputation, the client's ability to pay, the market for legal services in the geographic area and specialty field, and other factors. In certain matters such as personal-injury, wrongful-death, worker's compensation, and Social Security disability cases, lawyers work on contingency fees in which they negotiate at the outset of the representation for a percentage of the client's recovery but receive no fee if there is no recovery. Contingency fees, increasingly regulated by statute, *see, e.g.*, N.J. GEN. CT. R. 1:21-7(c) (fees capped at one-third, 30%, 25%, and 20% based on recovery amoung between zero and $2,000,000), make legal service available to those who cannot afford but critically need it.

Insurance. The way in which lawyer and client structure their fee arrangement often affects the duration, complexity, and resolution of civil litigation. Lawyers must be cognizant of their own ability to continue a representation, meaning that they should also be cognizant, as a strategic matter, of their opposing counsel's ability. For example, insurance companies fund a substantial portion of civil litigation. Automotive, residential, commercial, and other liability policies provide not only for indemnification of the insured up to the policy's stated limits but also for legal representation. The insurers are not being generous. It is their money, and so they choose and pay defense counsel to ensure that it is well spent. Insurance defense counsel typically earn hourly fees, often at somewhat below the rates charged private individuals because of volume discounts. Increasingly, insurers scrutinize bills, institute cost controls, and request fixed fees. When one puts contingency-fee agreements together with insurer-funded defense, one sees that in insured-liability cases, neither plaintiff nor defendant pays their own lawyer. The insurer retains and pays defense counsel, while plaintiff's counsel waits to receive a portion of the recovery. Certainly, the merits of insured-liability claims are important in evaluating and resolving those claims, but given how the parties finance representation in those cases, so, too, can be the defendant's policy limits and deductible (particularly in commercial insurance coverage where deductibles may be substantial), and the plaintiff's percentage fee and costs incurred.

Public-Interest Organizations. Cause litigation attracts other financing. Organizations like Public Citizen Litigation Group, the Alliance Defense Fund, the American Civil Liberties Union, and the Legal Defense Fund of the National Association for the Advancement of Colored People attract contributions from the public. The Legal Defense Fund had primary responsibility for financing Brown v. Board of Education, 347 U.S. 443 (1954), ending de jure public-school segregation. These organizations on occasion also receive fee awards as representatives of the prevailing party in civil-rights litigation. While these public-interest organizations employ skilled civil litigators to represent individual clients in specific cases, they may also benefit from contributions of pro-bono services from lawyers in private practice. Much of these organizations' work may involve recruiting and training cadres of volunteer public-interest lawyers and coordinating demands for their services in cases throughout the country.

Ethics

Despite the variety of public and private delivery mechanisms and the comparatively large number of lawyers in the United States, studies suggest that they do not satisfy all need for legal services. Litigants without a lawyer can increasingly find assistance with legal forms and information through court-based centers supported by a mix of public and private funding and staffed by lawyers, legal assistants, law students, and other volunteers. Lawyers, law firms, and bar associations provide, support, and promote free legal representation through pro-bono programs.

ABA Model Rule of Professional Conduct 6.1 states in part, "Every lawyer has a professional responsibility to provide legal services to those unable to pay." The accompanying Comment adds that the obligation exists "regardless of professional prominence or professional work load... ." Civil litigators fulfill this responsibility by taking pro-bono cases, often by assignment from the local court. Judges respect and appreciate trial lawyers who respond to their calls to represent indigent parties in civil litigation. Lawyers who provide pro-bono service not only increase access to and the credibility of the justice system, provide critical private help and needed public service, and improve the image of the profession. They also improve their skills, expand their knowledge of new practice areas, broaden and deepen their network of client and professional relationsihps, and increase their standing and reputation within the bar and community. Where would you willingly serve?

D. Sources

Civil procedure in the United States fits its citizenry's national and historical commitment to the rule of law. The overleaf quotes Magna Carta invoking "the law of the land" as the great antecedent to the Constitution's 5th and 14th Amendments on "due process of law." These constitutional markers that so foreshadow and underpin American jurisprudence mandate procedure as fundamental to law. Yet American civil procedure has a distinctly more influential history than simply these great constitutional markers of its constraint. There were undoubtedly elaborate ancient procedures. Modern procedure traces its roots to the time of England's King Edward I (1272-1307) when royal judges developed a system of pleading. In what was then primarily an oral rather than written practice of asserting and deciding legal claims, judges began to recognize claims only if they took a certain form of pleading. The practice was for claimants to obtain a writ from the king or king's chancellor requiring the sheriff to bring the respondent before the royal judge. Although technically a writ was simply the paper that began the action, the king and chancellors came to issue only standardized forms of writ, for instance, over possession of land or payment of debt. Writ pleading helped judges to recognize claims, recall arguments, and decide cases that the parties litigated solely or primarily on oral records—not an easy judicial task. In effect, writ pleading clarified the issues for decision. Writs became shorthand for complex law principles and arguments, just as it is still the case today that naming counts of a complaint works as shorthand for pleading elaborate legal theories.

By this practice, writs gradually became the forms or causes of action that the royal judges would recognize. Claimants could separately seek the help of communal (feudal) courts, although in time, three royal courts King's Bench, Common Pleas, and Exchequer (merged into the High Court of Justice in 1873) heard many of the more ordinary matters previously reserved for the feudal courts and not merely those (as was originally the case) offenses against the king. The writ system also helped judges address who would decide after what procedures. Then as now, judges decided matters of law because judges had the requisite legal training and independence. The court would put the parties through some form of investigation or trial to decide fact issues. Writ pleading helped establish whether the judge would decide a case and with what investigation or trial. One of the procedures by which judges made litigants determine disputed fact issues was swearing an oath. (If you are wondering, ordeal and combat were other methods. Be thankful that you are not an 11th-century lawyer or litigant.) Trial by oath required the party to swear an oath following a precise verbal formula, mistake in which could cost the party the verdict. Typically, the party then had to have 12 oath helpers successfully swear the oath. At first, oath helpers swore based on their own knowledge, meaning that the party had to find witness oath helpers. Later, the courts came to accept helpers who swore on belief rather than as witnesses. Hence came the 12-person jury. The fact that claimants and courts had already recognized certain forms of action before jury trial arose meant that courts continued to decide those forms of action without juries.

The historical difference between jury-trial right and no jury right remains today an important distinction among different forms of action. History determines it more so than principle or reason. State and federal judges continue to decide matters of law and grant or deny jury-trial rights based on distinctions between law and equity that arose out of this history. For instance, although diversity jurisdiction would appear to give them the authority to do so in certain cases, federal courts do not hear and decide divorce cases. State-court judges decide divorce and other family-law cases, and they do so without juries. Chapter VI has more discussion of the development of pleading practice. Chapter XII has more discussion of and detail on jury trial.

E. Comparison

Comparative procedure is a fascinating topic. Parties have long resolved disputes by ordinary, if arbitrary, means like drawing straws or flipping a coin. They have also resorted to extraordinary, even if equally arbitrary, means. Officials resolved some ancient Babylonian disputes by tossing one of the parties in the Tigris or Euphrates River to see if they would sink or swim. The Old Testament invokes drawing lots or drinking poisoned water. Feudal England recognized trial by ordeal, combat, or oath. Not just the primitive or ancient but moderns, too, resort to arbitrary and extraordinary dispute resolution. Consider Alexander Hamilton's fatal duel with Aaron Burr. As arbitrary as they sound, these means may have effectively forced the parties to evaluate the significance and alternative resolution of their claims. Some scholars hold that the Old Testament's retributive justice ("eye for an eye, tooth for a tooth"), rather than constituting public punishment, simply gave the victim the means to negotiate fair compensation. Considering the absence of formal justice systems in much of the world today, there certainly remain alternative forms of private justice.

Among developed countries, the major alternative to American-style common-law civil litigation is administrative enforcement of civil codes under a civil-law system. In civil-law countries like France, Germany, and Italy, legislative bodies enact comprehensive codes that administrative bureaucracies then enforce broadly when there are disputes among individuals or private corporate interests. Under the civil law, there are fewer if any opportunities for private litigants to raise and resolve disputes on a case-by-case basis. The civil law proceeds by application and amendment of comprehensive codes, meaning administratively and legislatively, by those who purport to know better. By contrast, the common law proceeds case by case as a battle between private litigants, with its contours drawn from a multitude of cases and constantly adapted as the pattern of cases changes on their individual merits. American-style civil litigation is the ontological (concerned with origins), teleological (purposive), and eschatological (concerned with ends) striving of a people who vest authority within themselves. In that respect, although it has its critics, it is still an unprecedented marvel well worth its study and practice.

F. Representative Case

A caution about your civil-procedure studies: civil procedure is difficult to study piecemeal because it tends to operate as a whole. You might think that you could study procedure (if anything) one piece at a time, from start to finish, because of its orderly nature. Yet you will quickly discern from reading the first cases on the authority of courts to adjudicate cases that decisions about deciding are within themselves strategic and wholistic. Even when, and perhaps especially when, it comes to the seemingly simple first issue of determining what courts can hear what cases, you will see that those decisions are themselves determined by civil procedure. Those who get others to make decisions (what, in essence, civil litigation involves) know that you must first establish a process in order to decide even on the process. Every stage of civil procedure (and every chapter of this book) depends at least in part on how other stages of civil procedure (and thus other chapters of this book) address the particular issue under consideration. The author has done his best to organize and write the text, and edit the cases, to address only the issue under study. The author appreciates the challenge that you face in attempting to learn in discrete chunks that which is ultimately a highly integrated civil justice system.

To remedy in part your sense of disjunction, consider the following representative example as a civil-procedure framework. The claim representative for a nationwide insurance company mailed a copy of a claim file to a small law firm's managing partner. The claim representative and partner had worked together on cases many times before because the small firm was on the insurance company's approved-counsel list. The claim representative's cover letter told the partner that the insurance company was retaining the firm at its usual hourly rate to defend a corporate insured in a products-liability case just filed in the local state circuit court.

The claim representative's cover letter also told the partner the date on which a process server had handed the insured corporate defendant's office manager a summons and complaint. The claim file included the summons issued by the local state circuit court and a copy of the complaint filed there on the plaintiff's behalf by a trial lawyer from another city. (Chapter II addresses the authority of courts to decide a specific person's or entity's matter and the constitutional requirements of notice and opportunity to be heard, including how courts issue summonses and how lawyers arrange for their service.) The partner immediately reviewed the summons and complaint, noting (to ensure no conflicts of interest) that the firm had not previously represented any party to the litigation other than the insured defendant whom the claim representative had instructed the partner to represent. The partner also immediately calendared the dates on which a notice of removal or answer was due, to ensure a timely filed answer. The partner decided that the plaintiff's lawyer, whom the partner knew and respected from prior litigation, had pled and filed a sound complaint under the applicable law. (Chapter III addresses the authority of state and federal courts to hear disputes based on their subject matter. Chapter V addresses which law the courts will apply.)

Skill

Lawyers use different criteria to select or accept civil cases. Although lawyers have an ethical duty to provide representation to the poor, they do not have to take every case. Lawyers are ordinarily quite selective in their cases. Some use economics as the principal criterion. If the case will make the lawyer and law firm money, then the lawyer will take the case. The compensation method can be important. Some law firms take primarily hourly fee cases, while others take primarily contingency-fee cases. The legal field can be important. Most lawyers and firms concentrate in practice areas. Taking a case outside of one's practice area requires developing new skills and efficiencies. The client type can be important. Many law firms serve primarily insurance companies, creating conflicts of interest when the firms take consumers with insurance claims. Consider carefully how your choice of clients and cases reflects your professional identity and commitment.

After completing her review of the claim file, the partner dictated a reply to the claim representative, correspondence to the corporate client's contact person, and memoranda to an associate and office staff. The partner's reply to the claim representative acknowledged the assignment, explained the partner's intent to remove the case from state to federal court, and planned other litigation tasks, estimating their costs. The partner's correspondence to the corporate contact did likewise, also requesting a meeting and information about other potentially responsible parties. (Chapter VII addresses the joinder of other claims and parties.) The partner's memorandum to the associate instructed the associate to review the claim file, summons, and complaint, and another file in which the firm had previously represented the same defendant in a similar case. The memorandum also instructed the associate to draft a notice of removal from state to federal court and the state-court answer and affirmative defenses all for filing within the calendared due dates. Defense counsel removed the case from state to federal court and then filed the corporate client's answer and affirmative defenses. (Chapter VI addresses how lawyers plead complaints and answers, and the default that may enter when a party does not file a timely answer.)

Counsel for both sides then exchanged preliminary lists of witnesses and exhibits. The trial lawyer who filed the case and defense counsel met in a scheduling conference with the trial judge, who ordered that the parties would have six months within which to complete discovery of the other side's evidence. The parties had already begun discovery. Defense counsel's original memorandum to her associate had instructed the associate to draft interrogatories and production requests to the plaintiff and prepare the plaintiff's deposition notice. Over the next six months, the lawyers took 12 depositions of various lay and expert witnesses, and exchanged three rounds of written discovery and responses. In part because the lawyers had a long professional acquaintance, they had only one discovery dispute, resolved by a magistrate judge who ordered the plaintiff's experts to disclose their notes. (Chapter VIII addresses discovery methods and resolution of discovery disputes.) At the close of discovery, defense counsel filed a motion for summary judgment, arguing that the plaintiff's evidence did not establish a prima-facie case that the defendant's product was unreasonably dangerous. Plaintiff's counsel filed a response supported by three experts' affidavits and related exhibits. The trial judge heard arguments of counsel and ordered the motion denied. The pretrial discovery and motions just described often constitutes the bulk of lawyer and party time devoted to civil litigation. (Chapter IX addresses how the courts decide some cases before trial.)

The trial judge then met in pretrial conference with the lawyers for each side. When it appeared to the trial judge that there was some prospect that the parties could reach a settlement, the trial judge ordered them to facilitative mediation before an experienced lawyer mediator on whom the lawyers for both sides had agreed. The plaintiff, plaintiff's counsel, insurance-company claim representative, corporate representative, and defense counsel then spent a day at the mediator's law office attempting to negotiate a settlement. (Chapter X addresses mediation and other forms of dispute resolution.) The lawyers notified the trial judge in writing that the effort had failed, following which the judge set the case for trial. One week before the trial date, the lawyers appeared before the trial judge to argue motions regarding the admissibility of evidence and the content of jury instructions. (Chapter XI addresses how trial judges manage litigation up to trial.)

Practice

The new associate at the large firm knew that she was in for her first big professional challenge when the senior partner told her that a federal judge had asked the partner to find a lawyer in the firm to represent the plaintiff in a civil-rights case over prison conditions.

The partner assigned the associate the case thinking that experienced lawyers in the firm would guide and mentor the associate. He did not realize that the case was on a fast track for trial. The associate knew only that she had a case to try in one month. She poured herself into the case, traveling to the prison to meet the client, reading every detail of his voluminous papers, and developing a lean trial strategy with a strong theme.

When another senior partner learned two days before trial that the associate had prepared the case without more than nominal help, without retaining experts, and with only nominal discovery, the partner sent a scathing message around the firm for its lack of support of a new associate. The associate felt otherwise, that she was well prepared, had made good judgments, and had found the little support that she needed.

The associate was right. She won a rare jury verdict and substantial damages for her client. She also won a bar association award for what would become, in her first year in law practice, her greatest professional triumph.

The trial then took place over two weeks. The plaintiff had demanded a jury trial, so the trial began with counsel questioning, challenging, and striking jurors, and the trial judge ruling on the challenges and seating and preliminarily instructing the jurors. Each side then made an opening statement. Plaintiff's counsel called and examined 9 lay and 5 expert witnesses and offered 40 exhibits in the plaintiff's case in chief, with defense counsel cross-examining each witness. When plaintiff rested, defense counsel moved for a directed verdict, but the trial judge declined to rule and instead took the motion under advisement. Defense counsel then called 2 lay witnesses and 2 expert witnesses in the defendant's case in chief before resting. Plaintiff made no rebuttal case. Defense counsel renewed the motion for directed verdict, but the trial judge this time denied the motion. The trial judge then ruled outside of the jury's presence on several disagreements the lawyers had over the final jury instructions. The trial judge then instructed the jury, following which the lawyers made closing arguments, first plaintiff's counsel for 45 minutes, then defense counsel for an hour, and then plaintiff's counsel in a 15-minute rebuttal. The jury deliberated two hours before returning to the courtroom for the foreperson to read the jury's answers on the written verdict form. (Chapter XII addresses these and other issues having to do with the conduct of trial.)

Defense counsel then worked with a partner and associates to draft and file post-trial motions for judgment notwithstanding the verdict and for new trial. After plaintiff's counsel responded, the trial judge heard arguments and denied the motions. (Chapter XV addresses post-trial motions.) Because the plaintiff had prevailed, the plaintiff's counsel prepared a proposed judgment for defense counsel's review. When the lawyers could not agree on the amount of costs and interest, the plaintiff's counsel filed a motion for entry of judgment and scheduled the motion for hearing. At the hearing, the trial judge made rulings from which the lawyers modified the judgment, signed it approved as to form only, and presented it for the trial judge's signature and for filing with the court. (Chapter XIII addresses how lawyers obtain judgments.) Defense counsel calendared the appeal deadline and then met with representatives of the corporate client and insurer, who agreed that defense counsel should appeal the trial judge's denial of the summary judgment and new trial motions. Defense counsel and an associate prepared and filed the claim and notice of appeal and related papers, and obtained and filed an appeal bond to forestall plaintiff's execution on the judgment. Defense counsel also calculated and calendared the date on which the appeal brief was due. The defense team spent the next few months preparing and filing the appeal brief, reviewing the plaintiff's response brief, preparing and filing a rebuttal brief, and preparing for oral arguments. The oral argument itself was uneventful. (Chapter XVI addresses appeal procedures.)

Two months later, defense counsel received an opinion affirming the judgment. The partner wrote an analysis for representatives of the corporate client and insurer, who agreed that a Supreme Court petition for a writ of certiorari was unwise. The partner calculated the interest on the judgment and contacted plaintiff's counsel requesting a dismissal and confidential settlement agreement in exchange for the settlement draft. Plaintiff's counsel declined the offer but confirmed the interest amount and taxed costs. The partner requested the settlement draft from the insurer while the associate prepared a satisfaction of judgment to exchange for the settlement draft. Three months after the case concluded with the exchange of draft for signed satisfaction, the partner received notice from a health insurance company that it claimed a lien on any amounts that the plaintiff in the case recovered. With the corporate client's authorization, the partner replied indicating that the case had concluded. The partner received a subsequent letter from a law firm representing the health insurer and making a demand for payment of the lien. The partner recommended to the corporate client and its insurer that there be no reply. The partner heard nothing further and subsequently closed the case file. (Chapter XVII addresses the effect of judgment.)

INQUIRY

Representation. Consider relative to the above example how parties commonly retain lawyers for civil litigation. Although there are many unrepresented parties in small matters in local district courts, lawyers conduct complex civil litigation for individual and corporate clients. Insurance companies and other corporate clients typically retain defense counsel at hourly rates, although they increasingly use other case-based billing arrangements such as flat fees and task- or merit-billing to control hourly fee costs. Insurance companies and corporate clients also scrutinize hourly billings. Other lawyers, particularly plaintiff's lawyers in tort litigation, work on contingency fees in which the law firm receives a percentage of the recovery in the case. Under which fee arrangement would you prefer to work, hourly or contingency? Statutes, court rules, ethics rules, and the common law of contracts govern contingency and other fees, which must be reasonable. Assigned counsel is not generally available for the indigent in civil cases.

Career

Where would you prefer to spend your time, in the courtroom or an office? Civil litigators work in offices just like lawyers who specialize in transactional practice. Yet civil litigators also spend at least some time in court. Some lawyers have no interest in going to court. Other lawyers thrive in the courthouse environment, which is often a hive of highly important activity where lawyers readily renew acquaintances. The amount of time a civil litigator will spend in the courthouse may depend on the specific type of civil litigation. Some civil litigators are in the courthouse almost daily over collection and small consumer matters, family law, and landlord-tenant work. Others having larger and more complex civil cases may go to court far less often (once a week or less) but then spend several weeks at court in trial. As you study civil proceudre, consider whether you would appreciate being in court addressing these matters.

AUTHORITY TO ADJUDICATE

CHAPTER II

PERSONAL JURISDICTION

OBJECTIVE: That you be able to determine whether a certain court has the authority to bind a certain party by its decision through the exercise of personal jurisdiction, consistent with the constitutional provisions, statutes, case law and principles in this chapter.

Case Study: The representative of a corporate client meets with you to deliver and discuss a court summons and complaint that the corporate headquarters just received by certified mail, return receipt requested. The complaint alleges a competitor's statutory and common-law unfair-competition claims against the corporate client and one of its managers. The competitor filed the complaint in a state court on the other side of the country from the state in which your office and the corporate client's headquarters and facilities are located. The corporate representative wants to know whether the competitor can make the corporation and its manager litigate in the distant state in which the competitor filed the complaint.

Federal Rules of Civil Procedure this chapter reproduces and addresses
FED. R. CIV. P. 4: Summons.
FED. R. CIV. P. 4.1: Servicing Other Process.
FED. R. CIV. P. 12: Defenses and Objections...; Motion for Judgment on the Pleadings... .
FED. R. CIV. P. 82: Jurisdiction and Venue Unaffected.

This chapter is fundamentally about limits on judicial power—about the reach of courts and their ability to determine matters involving parties who might question why they should be subject to a particular courts' authority. Courts do not simply decide and thereby bind parties. Courts must first have authority over those parties. The law identifies the question of a court's authority to bind parties as a question of *jurisdiction*. No court binds a party without first having jurisdiction. To put the same question in the litigant's perspective, every litigant must first choose a court having the authority to bind the litigant's opponents. If the plaintiff files a complaint in a court that has no jurisdiction over the defendant, then the decision of that court will not bind the defendant. Jurisdiction is the concept through which the law limits the authority of courts, and the opportunity of litigants to invoke that authority, to within appropriate limits. A first skill that civil litigators must have is to choose the right court to bind their clients' opponents with sought-after relief and decisions. To win judgment without jurisdiction is an act of futility. At the most general level, there are two forms of jurisdiction: (1) personal jurisdiction (occasionally also called territorial jurisdiction), meaning that question of the authority of a court to bind a party to its decision; and (2) subject-matter jurisdiction, meaning the separate question of whether the court can hear the type of matter the parties are disputing. A defendant who had no relationship with the court's forum state would challenge the court's personal jurisdiction over the defendant. A defendant might challenge a family or probate court's subject-matter jurisdiction to decide the defendant's business litigation. This chapter addresses personal jurisdiction, while the next chapter addresses subject-matter jurisdiction. As do other chapters, this chapter focuses on the *Federal Rules of Civil Procedure*.

Knowledge

One of the challenges that law students and lawyers face is that courts may use the same legal term to describe different concepts. *Jurisdiction* is one of those terms. You have just seen that jurisdiction may refer to either a court's authority over a person or its authority to decide a subject matter. When a judge or lawyer states that there is no jurisdiction, they may intend either one of those two meanings. The hearer would have to infer the intended meaning from the statement's context, or ask. Jurisdiction may also refer to the state or territory, such as when the reference is to the "law of the jurisdiction," meaning the law of that state. Jurisdiction can also mean the physical boundaries of a state, such as when a lawyer or judge state that an event did not occur "within the jurisdiction." Appreciate the sensitivity of the lawyer's ear for these nuances, and the subtlety and power of legal language.

Personal-jurisdiction doctrine is as complex as any civil-procedure subject gets. Lawyers do make sense of it, even though one federal appellate court labeled it a "riddle wrapped in a mystery inside an enigma." Donatelli v. National Hockey League, 893 F.2d 459, 462 (1st Cir. 1990). For example, notice in one of the examples just given, the reference to the court's forum state. You might question why, if the *Federal Rules of Civil Procedure* govern a national court system, there should be any question whether those national courts have authority over citizens of specific states. There are both substantive and formal reasons why federal courts must, when evaluating personal jurisdiction, consider the relationship of parties to their forum state. The substantive reason is that it might be fundamentally unfair to hale a citizen of a distant state into the federal court's home forum. If you lived and conducted all of your affairs in Maine, would you want someone to be able to force you to litigate in Arizona? This example is the kind of constitutional question personal jurisdiction addresses. The formal reason why federal courts must consider the relationship of parties to their forum state is that the *Federal Rules of Civil Procedure* require federal courts to exercise personal jurisdiction consistent with the jurisdiction of the state courts in the federal court's forum state. Personal jurisdiction in the federal courts ordinarily follows the same analysis as personal jurisdiction in the state courts. Statutes and case law determines, personal jurisdiction, not the *Federal Rules of Civil Procedure*. See if you can find the provisions in the following rules that refer to personal jurisdiction. We will return later to the formal requirements of service of process with which most of the rule deals.

Fed. R. Civ. P. 4. Summons.

(a) CONTENTS; AMENDMENTS.

(1) *Contents.* A summons must:

(A) name the court and the parties;

(B) be directed to the defendant;

(C) state the name and address of the plaintiff's attorney or—if unrepresented—of the plaintiff;

(D) state the time within which the defendant must appear and defend;

(E) notify the defendant that a failure to appear and defend will result in a default judgment against the defendant for the relief demanded in the complaint;

(F) be signed by the clerk; and

(G) bear the court's seal.

(2) *Amendments.* The court may permit a summons to be amended.

(b) ISSUANCE. On or after filing the complaint, the plaintiff may present a summons to the clerk for signature and seal. If the summons is properly completed, the clerk must sign, seal, and issue it to the plaintiff for service on the defendant. A summons—or a copy of a summons that is addressed to multiple defendants—must be issued for each defendant to be served.

(c) SERVICE.

(1) *In General.* A summons must be served with a copy of the complaint. The plaintiff is responsible for having the summons and complaint served within the time allowed by Rule 4(m) and must furnish the necessary copies to the person who makes service.

(2) *By Whom.* Any person who is at least 18 years old and not a party may serve a summons and complaint.

(3) *By a Marshal or Someone Specially Appointed.* At the plaintiff's request, the court may order that service be made by a United States marshal or deputy marshal or by a person specially appointed by the court. The court must so order if the plaintiff is authorized to proceed in forma pauperis under 28 U.S.C. § 1915 or as a seaman under 28 U.S.C. § 1916.

(d) WAIVING SERVICE.

(1) *Requesting a Waiver.* An individual, corporation, or association that is subject to service under Rule 4(e), (f), or (h) has a duty to avoid unnecessary expenses of serving the summons. The plaintiff may notify such a defendant that an action has been commenced and request that the defendant waive service of a summons. The notice and request must:

(A) be in writing and be addressed:

(i) to the individual defendant; or

(ii) for a defendant subject to service under Rule 4(h), to an officer, a managing or general agent, or any other agent authorized by appointment or by law to receive service of process;

(B) name the court where the complaint was filed;

(C) be accompanied by a copy of the complaint, 2 copies of a waiver form, and a prepaid means for returning the form;

(D) inform the defendant, using text prescribed in Form 5, of the consequences of waiving and not waiving service;

(E) state the date when the request is sent;

(F) give the defendant a reasonable time of at least 30 days after the request was sent—or at least 60 days if sent to the defendant outside any judicial district of the United States—to return the waiver; and

(G) be sent by first-class mail or other reliable means.

(2) *Failure to Waive.* If a defendant located within the United States fails, without good cause, to sign and return a waiver requested by a plaintiff located within the United States, the court must impose on the defendant:

(A) the expenses later incurred in making service; and

(B) the reasonable expenses, including attorney's fees, of any motion required to collect those service expenses.

(3) *Time to Answer After a Waiver.* A defendant who, before being served with process, timely returns a waiver need not serve an answer to the complaint until 60 days after the request was sent—or until 90 days after it was sent to the defendant outside any judicial district of the United States.

(4) *Results of Filing a Waiver.* When the plaintiff files a waiver, proof of service is not required and these rules apply as if a summons and complaint had been served at the time of filing the waiver.

(5) *Jurisdiction and Venue Not Waived.* Waiving service of a summons does not waive any objection to personal jurisdiction or to venue.

(e) SERVING AN INDIVIDUAL WITHIN A JUDICIAL DISTRICT OF THE UNITED STATES. Unless federal law provides otherwise, an individual—other than a minor, an incompetent person, or a person whose waiver has been filed—may be served in a judicial district of the United States by:

(1) following state law for serving a summons in an action brought in courts of general

jurisdiction in the state where the district court is located or where service is made; or

(2) doing any of the following:

(A) delivering a copy of the summons and of the complaint to the individual personally;

(B) leaving a copy of each at the individual's dwelling or usual place of abode with someone of suitable age and discretion who resides there; or

(C) delivering a copy of each to an agent authorized by appointment or by law to receive service of process.

(f) SERVING AN INDIVIDUAL IN A FOREIGN COUNTRY. Unless federal law provides otherwise, an individual—other than a minor, an incompetent person, or a person whose waiver has been filed—may be served at a place not within any judicial district of the United States:

w(1) by any internationally agreed means of service that is reasonably calculated to give notice, such as those authorized by the Hague Convention on the Service Abroad of Judicial and Extrajudicial Documents;

(2) if there is no internationally agreed means, or if an international agreement allows but does not specify other means, by a method that is reasonably calculated to give notice:

(A) as prescribed by the foreign country's law for service in that country in an action in its courts of general jurisdiction;

(B) as the foreign authority directs in response to a letter rogatory or letter of request; or

(C) unless prohibited by the foreign country's law, by:

(i) delivering a copy of the summons and of the complaint to the individual personally; or

(ii) using any form of mail that the clerk addresses and sends to the individual and that requires a signed
receipt; or

(3) by other means not prohibited by international agreement, as the court orders.

(g) SERVING A MINOR OR AN INCOMPETENT PERSON. A minor or an incompetent person in a judicial district of the United States must be served by following state law for serving a summons or like process on such a defendant in an action brought in the courts of general jurisdiction of the state where service is made. A minor or an incompetent person who is not within any judicial district of the United States must be served in the manner prescribed by Rule 4(f)(2)(A), (f)(2)(B), or (f)(3).

(h) SERVING A CORPORATION, PARTNERSHIP, OR ASSOCIATION. Unless federal law provides otherwise or the defendant's waiver has been filed, a domestic or foreign corporation, or a partnership or other unincorporated association that is subject to suit under a common name, must be served:

(1) in a judicial district of the United States:

(A) in the manner prescribed by Rule 4(e)(1) for serving an individual; or

(B) by delivering a copy of the summons and of the complaint to an officer, a managing or general agent, or any other agent authorized by appointment or by law to receive service of process and—if the agent is one authorized by statute and the statute so requires—by also mailing a copy of each to the defendant; or

(2) at a place not within any judicial district of the United States, in any manner prescribed by Rule 4(f) for serving an individual, except personal delivery under (f)(2)(C)(i).

(i) SERVING THE UNITED STATES AND ITS AGENCIES, CORPORATIONS, OFFICERS, OR EMPLOYEES.

(1) *United States.* To serve the United States, a party must:

(A)(i) deliver a copy of the summons and of the complaint to the United States attorney for the district where the action is brought—or to an assistant United States attorney or clerical employee whom the United States attorney designates in a writing filed with the court clerk—or

(ii) send a copy of each by registered or certified mail to the civil-process clerk at the United States attorney's office;

(B) send a copy of each by registered or certified mail to the Attorney General of the United States at Washington, D.C.; and

(C) if the action challenges an order of a nonparty agency or officer of the United States, send a copy of each by registered or certified mail to the agency or officer.

(2) *Agency; Corporation; Officer or Employee Sued in an Official Capacity.* To serve a United States agency or corporation, or a United States officer or employee sued only in an official capacity, a party must serve the United States and also send a copy of the summons and of the complaint by registered or certified mail to the agency, corporation, officer, or employee.

(3) *Officer or Employee Sued Individually.* To serve a United States officer or employee sued in an individual capacity for an act or omission occurring in connection with duties performed on the United States' behalf (whether or not the officer or employee is also sued in an official capacity), a party must serve the United States and also serve the officer or employee under Rule 4(e), (f), or (g).

(4) *Extending Time.* The court must allow a party a reasonable time to cure its failure to:

(A) serve a person required to be served under Rule 4(i)(2), if the party has served either the

United States attorney or the Attorney General of the United States; or
(B) serve the United States under Rule 4(i)(3), if the party has served the United States officer or employee.
(j) SERVING A FOREIGN, STATE, OR LOCAL GOVERNMENT.
(1) *Foreign State.* A foreign state or its political subdivision, agency, or instrumentality must be served in accordance with 28 U.S.C. § 1608.
(2) *State or Local Government.* A state, a municipal corporation, or any other state-created governmental organization that is subject to suit must be served by:
(A) delivering a copy of the summons and of the complaint to its chief executive officer; or
(B) serving a copy of each in the manner prescribed by that state's law for serving a summons or like process on such a defendant.
(k) TERRITORIAL LIMITS OF EFFECTIVE SERVICE.
(1) *In General.* Serving a summons or filing a waiver of service establishes personal jurisdiction over a defendant:
(A) who is subject to the jurisdiction of a court of general jurisdiction in the state where the district court is located;
(B) who is a party joined under Rule 14 or 19 and is served within a judicial district of the United States and not more than 100 miles from where the summons was issued; or
(C) when authorized by a federal statute.
(2) *Federal Claim Outside State-Court Jurisdiction.* For a claim that arises under federal law, serving a summons or filing a waiver of service establishes personal jurisdiction over a defendant if:
(A) the defendant is not subject to jurisdiction in any state's courts of general jurisdiction; and
(B) exercising jurisdiction is consistent with the United States Constitution and laws.
(*l*) PROVING SERVICE.
(1) *Affidavit Required.* Unless service is waived, proof of service must be made to the court. Except for service by a United States marshal or deputy marshal, proof must be by the server's affidavit.
(2) *Service Outside the United States.* Service not within any judicial district of the United States must be proved as follows:
(A) if made under Rule 4(f)(1), as provided in the applicable treaty or convention; or
(B) if made under Rule 4(f)(2) or (f)(3), by a receipt signed by the addressee, or by other evidence satisfying the court that the summons and complaint were delivered to the addressee.
(3) *Validity of Service; Amending Proof.* Failure to prove service does not affect the validity of service. The court may permit proof of service to be amended.
(m) TIME LIMIT FOR SERVICE. If a defendant is not served within 120 days after the complaint is filed, the court—on motion or on its own after notice to the plaintiff—must dismiss the action without prejudice against that defendant or order that service be made within a specified time. But if the plaintiff shows good cause for the failure, the court must extend the time for service for an appropriate period. This subdivision (m) does not apply to service in a foreign country under Rule 4(f) or 4(j)(1).
(n) ASSERTING JURISDICTION OVER PROPERTY OR ASSETS.
(1) *Federal Law.* The court may assert jurisdiction over property if authorized by a federal statute. Notice to claimants of the property must be given as provided in the statute or by serving a summons under this rule.
(2) *State Law.* On a showing that personal jurisdiction over a defendant cannot be obtained in the district where the action is brought by reasonable efforts to serve a summons under this rule, the court may assert jurisdiction over the defendant's assets found in the district. Jurisdiction is acquired by seizing the assets under the circumstances and in the manner provided by state law in that district.

FED. R. CIV. P. 4.1. Serving Other Process
(a) IN GENERAL. Process—other than a summons under Rule 4 or a subpoena under Rule 45—must be served by a United States marshal or deputy marshal or by a person specially appointed for that purpose. It may be served anywhere within the territorial limits of the state where the district court is located and, if authorized by a federal statute, beyond those limits. Proof of service must be made under Rule 4(*l*).
(b) ENFORCING ORDERS: COMMITTING FOR CIVIL CONTEMPT. An order committing a person for civil contempt of a decree or injunction issued to enforce federal law may be served and enforced in any district. Any other order in a civil-contempt proceeding may be served only in the state where the issuing court is located or elsewhere in the United States within 100 miles from where the order was issued.

. . .

FED. R. CIV. P. 82. Jurisdiction and Venue Unaffected.
These rules do not extend or limit the jurisdiction of the district courts or the venue of actions in those courts. An admiralty or maritime claim under Rule 9(h) is not a civil action for purposes of 28 U.S.C. §§ 1391–1392.

Skill

FED. R. CIV. P. 4 typifies other *Federal Rules of Civil Procedure* and legal rules in general in that it simultaneously serves several purposes. As you can see from the jurisdiction provision hidden in FED. R. CIV. P. 4(k)(1), one purpose is to carry into effect constitutional requirements and like principles. Rules have a deep purpose. Another purpose of rules is to describe in reasonable detail conventions or protocols that practitioners can follow to structure litigation and other activities in recognizable and efficient means. Some parts of rules have no deep purpose. What is important in those instances is simply that everyone does likewise to forestall chaos. It is like agreeing that everyone should drive on the right-hand side of the road. We could all do just as well driving on the left-hand side of the road (as they do in some countries). The important thing is simply that we all drive on the same side of the road. The skill of a practitioner is to recognize due-process and other principles that a rule's authors hide within the technical requirements of the rule. Lawyers discern what parts of a rule respect deep purposes and what parts are simply conventions. Both can be important, but so can the difference.

A. Development

1. Traditional Bases

American law of personal jurisdiction began in the 1800s when the comparatively rudimentary means of transportation limited interstate travel and commerce. Personal jurisdiction then depended on the person's presence in the state or the presence of the person's property within the state. Presence of person or property within the state provided a categorical, bright-line rule for determining personal jurisdiction. The law divided personal jurisdiction into three types: (1) *in personam* jurisdiction in which the court had full authority over the person; (2) *in rem* jurisdiction in which the court had authority only over the person's property located within the state but not over the person; or (3) *quasi-in-rem* jurisdiction in which the court had authority over the person but could enforce its judgment only by taking the person's property within the state. The important distinction between *in rem* and *quasi in rem* jurisdiction is that for a court to have *in rem* jurisdiction, the dispute had to involve the property located within the court's state, while for *quasi in rem* jurisdiction, the dispute need not relate to the property within the state. *See* Harris v. Balk, 198 U.S. 215 (1905) (*quasi in rem* jurisdiction allows party to execute on unrelated asset within court's jurisdiction). For both *in rem* and *quasi in rem* jurisdiction, the prevailing party could only execute on the property within the state, while for *in personam* jurisdiction, the prevailing party could pursue any of the losing party's assets or income as allowed by the general laws of collection. Claimants obviously preferred *in personam* jurisdiction but might accept *in rem* or *quasi in rem* jurisdiction if that was all that they could obtain. The Supreme Court confirmed this traditional foundation in the following celebrated case. The Supreme Court also articulated its constitutional basis in the full-faith-and-credit clause of Article IV of the

Constitution and the 14th Amendment's due-process clause. As you read the case, consider whether it still makes sense today to base jurisdiction on presence within the state when persons so much more easily move about the country, and persons and entities conduct business across state lines using the Internet and other technology. Consider also whether an action *in rem* against the property is a fiction for an action that is instead against the person who owns the property.

Pennoyer v. Neff,

United States Supreme Court
95 U.S. (5 Otto) 714 (1877)

MR. JUSTICE FIELD delivered the opinion of the court.

This is an action to recover the possession of a tract of land, of the alleged value of $15,000, situated in the State of Oregon. The plaintiff asserts title to the premises by a patent of the United States issued to him in 1866, under the act of Congress of Sept. 27, 1850, usually known as the Donation Law of Oregon. The defendant claims to have acquired the premises under a sheriff's deed, made upon a sale of the property on execution issued upon a judgment recovered against the plaintiff in one of the circuit courts of the State. The case turns upon the validity of this judgment.

It appears from the record that the judgment was rendered in February, 1866, in favor of J. H. Mitchell, for less than $300, including costs, in an action brought by him upon a demand for services as an attorney; that, at the time the action was commenced and the judgment rendered, the defendant therein, the plaintiff here, was a non-resident of the State that he was not personally served with process, and did not appear therein; and that the judgment was entered upon his default in not answering the complaint, upon a constructive service of summons by publication.

The Code of Oregon provides for such service when an action is brought against a non-resident and absent defendant, who has property within the State. It also provides, where the action is for the recovery of money or damages, for the attachment of the property of the non-resident. And it also declares that no natural person is subject to the jurisdiction of a court of the State, "unless he appear in the court, or be found within the State, or be a resident thereof, or have property therein; and, in the last case, only to the extent of such property at the time the jurisdiction attached." Construing this latter provision to mean, that, in an action for money or damages where a defendant does not appear in the court, and is not found within the State, and is not a resident thereof, but has property therein, the jurisdiction of the court extends only over such property, the declaration expresses a principle of general, if not universal, law. The authority of every tribunal is necessarily restricted by the territorial limits of the State in which it is established. Any attempt to exercise authority beyond those limits would be deemed in every other forum, as has been said by this court, an illegitimate assumption of power, and be resisted as mere abuse. [C] In the case against the plaintiff, the property here in controversy sold under the judgment rendered was not attached, nor in any way brought under the jurisdiction of the court. Its first connection with the case was caused by a levy of the execution. It was not, therefore, disposed of pursuant to any adjudication, but only in enforcement of a personal judgment, having no relation to the property, rendered against a non-resident without service of process upon him in the action, or his appearance therein. The court below did not consider that an attachment of the property was essential to its jurisdiction or to the validity of the sale, but held that the judgment was invalid from defects in the affidavit upon which the order of publication was obtained, and in the affidavit by which the publication was proved.

There is some difference of opinion among the members of this court as to the rulings upon these alleged defects. [The Court's difference of opinion, not relevant to the case's outcome, had to do with how to construe a statute requiring an affidavit of the printer that the newspaper had published the order.]

... [I]t was also contended in that court, and is insisted upon here, that the judgment in the State court against the plaintiff was void for want of personal service of process on him, or of his appearance in the action in which it was rendered and that the premises in controversy could not be subjected to the payment of the demand of a resident creditor except by a proceeding *in rem;* that is, by a direct proceeding against the property for that purpose. If these positions are sound, the ruling of the Circuit Court as to the invalidity of that judgment must be sustained, notwithstanding our dissent from the reasons upon which it was made. And that they are sound would seem to follow from two well-established principles of public law respecting the jurisdiction of an independent State over persons and property. The several States of the Union are not, it is true, in every respect independent, many of the right and powers which originally belonged to them being now vested in the government created by the Constitution. But, except as restrained and limited by that instrument, they possess and exercise the authority of independent States, and the principles of public law to which we have referred are applicable to them. One of these principles is, that every State possesses exclusive jurisdiction and sovereignty over persons and property within its territory. As a consequence, every State has the power to determine for itself the civil *status* and capacities of its inhabitants; to prescribe the subjects upon which they may contract, the forms and solemnities with which their contracts shall be executed, the rights and obligations arising from them, and the mode in which their validity shall be determined and their obligations enforced; and also the regulate the manner and conditions upon which property situated within such territory, both personal and real, may be acquired, enjoyed, and transferred. The other principle of public law referred to follows from the one mentioned; that is, that no State can exercise direct jurisdiction and authority over persons or property without its territory. [C] The several States are of equal dignity and authority, and the independence of one implies the exclusion of power from all others. And so it is laid down by jurists, as an elementary principle, that the laws of one State have no operation outside of its territory, except so far as is allowed by comity; and that no tribunal established by it can extend its process beyond that territory so as to subject either persons or property to its decisions. "Any exertion of authority of this sort beyond this limit," says Story, "is a mere nullity, and incapable of binding such persons or property in any other tribunals." Story, Confl. Laws, sect. 539.

But as contracts made in one State may be enforceable only in another State, and property may be held by non-residents, the exercise of the jurisdiction which every State is admitted to possess over persons and property within its own territory will often affect persons and property without it. To any influence exerted in this way by a State affecting persons resident or property situated elsewhere, no objection can be justly taken; whilst any direct exertion of authority upon them, in an attempt to give ex-territorial operation to its laws, or to enforce an ex-territorial jurisdiction by its tribunals, would be deemed an encroachment upon the independence of the State in which the persons are domiciled or the property is situated, and be resisted as usurpation.

Thus the State, through its tribunals, may compel persons domiciled within its limits to execute, in pursuance of their contracts respecting property elsewhere situated, instruments in such form and with such solemnities as to transfer the title, so far as such formalities can be complied with; and the exercise of this jurisdiction in no manner interferes with the supreme control over the property by the State within which it is situated. [Cc]

So the State, through its tribunals, may subject property situated within its limits owned by non-residents to the payment of the demand of its own citizens against them; and the exercise of this jurisdiction in no respect infringes upon the sovereignty of the State where the owners are domiciled. Every State owes protection to its own citizens; and, when non-residents deal with them, it is a legitimate and just exercise of authority to hold and appropriate any property owned by such non-residents to satisfy the claims of its citizens. It is in virtue of the State's jurisdiction over the property of the non-resident situated within its limits that its tribunals can inquire into that non-resident's obligations to its own citizens, and the inquiry can then be carried only to the extent necessary to control the disposition of the property. If the non-resident have no property in the State, there is nothing upon which the tribunals can adjudicate.

These views are not new. They have been frequently expressed, with more or less distinctness, in opinions of eminent judges, and have been carried into adjudications in numerous cases. ... If, without personal service, judgments *in personam*, obtained *ex parte* against non-residents and absent parties, upon mere publication of process, which, in the great majority of cases, would never be seen by the parties interested, could be upheld and enforced, they would be the constant instruments of fraud and oppression. Judgments for all sorts of claims upon contracts and for torts, real or pretended, would be thus obtained, under which property would be seized, when the evidence of the transactions upon which they were founded, if they ever had any existence, had perished.

Substituted service by publication, or in any other authorized form, may be sufficient to inform parties of the object of proceedings taken where property is once brought under the control of the court by seizure or some equivalent act. The law assumes that property is always in the possession of its owner, in person or by agent; and it proceeds upon the theory that its seizure will inform him, not only that it is taken into the custody of the court, but that he must look to any proceedings authorized by law upon such seizure for its condemnation and sale. Such service may also be sufficient in cases where the object of the action is to reach and dispose of property in the State, or of some interest therein, by enforcing a contract or a lien respecting the same, or to partition it among different owners, or, when the public is a party, to condemn and appropriate it for a public purpose. In other words, such service may answer in all actions which are substantially proceedings *in rem*. But where the entire object of the action is to determine the personal rights and obligations of the defendants, that is, where the suit is merely *in personam*, constructive service in this form upon a non-resident is ineffectual for any purpose. Process from the tribunals of one State cannot run into another State, and summon parties there domiciled to leave its territory and respond to proceedings against them. Publication of process or notice within the State where the tribunal sits cannot create any greater obligation upon the non-resident to appear. Process sent to him out of the State, and process published within it, are equally unavailing in proceedings to establish his personal liability.

The want of authority of the tribunals of a State to adjudicate upon the obligations of non-residents, where they have no property within its limits, is not denied by the court below: but the position is assumed, that, where they have property within the State, it is immaterial whether the property is in the first instance brought under the control of the court by attachment or some other equivalent act, and afterwards applied by its judgment to the satisfaction of demands against its owner; or such demands be first established in a personal action, and the property of the non-resident be afterwards seized and sold on execution. But the answer to this position has already been given in the statement, that the jurisdiction of the court to inquire into and determine his obligations at all is only incidental to its jurisdiction over the property. Its jurisdiction in that respect cannot be made to depend upon facts to be ascertained after it has tried the cause and rendered the judgment. If the judgment be previously void, it will not become valid by the subsequent discovery of property of the defendant, or by his subsequent acquisition of it. The judgment, if void when rendered, will always remain void: it cannot occupy the doubtful position of being valid if property be found, and void if there be none. ... [T]he validity of every judgment depends upon the jurisdiction of the court before it is rendered, not upon what may occur subsequently. In *Webster* v. *Reid*, reported in 11th of Howard, the plaintiff claimed title to land sold under judgments recovered in suits brought in a territorial court of Iowa, upon publication of notice under a law of the territory, without service of process; and the court said: "These suits were not a proceeding *in rem* against the land, but were *in personam* against the owners of it. Whether they all resided within the territory or not does not appear, nor is it s matter of any importance. No person is required to answer in a suit on whom process has not been served, or whose property has not been attached. In this case, there was no personal notice, nor an attachment or other proceeding against the land, until after the judgments. The judgments, therefore, are nullities, and did not authorize the executions on which the land was sold."

The force and effect of judgments rendered against non-residents without personal service of process upon them, or their voluntary appearance, have been the subject of frequent consideration in the courts of the United States and of the several States, as attempts have been made to enforce suc judgments in States other than those in which they were rendered, under the provision of the Constitution requiring that "full faith and credit shall be given in each State to the public acts, records, and judicial proceedings of every other State;" and the act of Congress providing for the mode of authenticating such acts, records, and proceedings, and declaring that, when thus authenticated, "they shall have such faith and credit given to them in every court within the United States as they have by law or usage in the courts of the State from which they are or shall or taken." In the earlier cases, it was supposed that the act gave to all judgments the same effect in other States which they had by law in the State where rendered. But this view was afterwards qualified so as to make the act applicable only when the court rendering the judgment had jurisdiction of the parties and of the subject-matter, and not to preclude an inquiry into the jurisdiction of the court in which the judgment was rendered, or the right of the State itself to exercise authority over the person or the subject-matter. [C] ... [T]he courts of the United States ... are tribunals of a different sovereignty, exercising a distinct and independent jurisdiction, and are bound to give to the judgments of the State courts only the same faith and credit which the courts of another State are bound to give to them.

Since the adoption of the Fourteenth Amendment to the Federal Constitution, the validity of such judgments may be directly questioned, and their enforcement in the State resisted, on the ground that proceedings in a court of justice to deter mine the personal rights and obligations of parties over whom that court has no jurisdiction do not constitute due process of law. Whatever difficulty may be experienced in giving to those terms a definition which will embrace every permissible exertion of power affecting private rights, and exclude such as is forbidden, there can be no doubt of their meaning when applied to judicial proceedings. They then mean a course of legal proceedings according to those rules and principles which have been established in our systems of jurisprudence for the protection and enforcement of private rights. To give such proceedings any validity, there must be a tribunal competent by its constitution—that is, by the law of its creation—to pass upon the subject-matter of the suit; and, if that involves merely a determination of the personal liability of the defendant, he must be brought within its jurisdiction by service of process within the State, or his voluntary appearance.

Except in cases affecting the personal *status* of the plaintiff, and cases in which that mode of service may be considered to have been assented to in advance, as hereinafter mentioned, the substituted service of process by publication, allowed by the law of Oregon and by similar laws in other States, where actions are brought against non-residents, is effectual only where, in connection with process against the person for commencing the action, property in the State is brought under the control of the court, and subjected to its disposition by process adapted to that purpose, or where the judgment is sought as a means of reaching such property or affecting some interest therein; in other words, where the action is in the nature of a proceeding *in rem*. As stated by Cooley in his Treatise on Constitutional Limitations, 405, for any other purpose than to subject the property of a non-resident to valid claims against him in the State, "due process of law would require appearance or personal service before the defendant could be personally bound by any judgment rendered."

It is true that, in a strict sense, a proceeding *in rem* is one taken directly against property, and has for its object the disposition of the property, without reference to the title of individual claimants; but, in a larger and more general sense, the terms are applied to actions between parties, where the direct object is to reach and dispose of property owned by them, or of some interest therein. Such are cases commenced by attachment against the property of debtors, or instituted to partition real estate, foreclose a mortgage, or enforce a lien. So far as they affect property in the State, they are substantially proceedings *in rem* in the broader sense which we have mentioned. ...

It follows from the views expressed that the personal judgment recovered in the State court of Oregon against the plaintiff herein, then a non-resident of the State, was without any validity, and did not authorize a sale of the property in controversy.

To prevent any misapplication of the views expressed in this opinion, it is proper to observe that we do not mean to assert, by any thing we have said, that a State may not authorize proceedings to determine the *status* of one of its citizens towards a non-resident, which would be binding within the State, though made without service of process or personal notice to the non-resident. The jurisdiction which every State possesses to determine the civil *status* and capacities of all its inhabitants involves authority to prescribe the conditions on which proceedings affecting them may be commenced and carried on within its territory. The State, for example, has absolute right to prescribe the conditions upon which the marriage relation between its own citizens shall be created, and the causes for which it may be dissolved. One of the parties guilty of acts for which, by the law of the State, a dissolution may be granted, may have removed to a State where no dissolution is permitted. The complaining party would, therefore, fail if a divorce were sought in the State of the defendant; and if application could not be made to the tribunals of the complainant's domicile in such case, and proceedings be there instituted without personal service of process or personal notice to the offending party, the injured citizen would be without redress. [C]

Neither do we mean to assert that a State may not require a non-resident entering into a partnership or association within its limits, or making contracts enforceable there, to appoint an agent or representative in the State to receive service of process and notice in legal proceedings instituted with respect to such partnership, association, or contracts, or to designate a place where such service may be made and notice given, and provide, upon their failure, to make such appointment or to designate such place that service may be made upon a public officer designated for that purpose, or in some other prescribed way, and that judgments rendered upon such service may not be binding upon the non-residents both within and without the State. ... Nor do we doubt that a State, on creating corporations or other institutions for pecuniary or charitable purposes, may provide a mode in which their conduct may be investigated, their obligations enforced, or their charters revoked, which shall require other than personal service upon their officers or members. Parties becoming members of such corporations or institutions would hold their interest subject to the conditions prescribed by law. [C]

In the present case, there is no feature of this kind, and, consequently, no consideration of what would be the effect of such legislation in enforcing the contract of a non-resident can arise. The question here respects only the validity of a money judgment rendered in one State, in an action upon a simple contract against the resident of another, without service of process upon him, or his appearance therein.

Judgment affirmed.

INQUIRY

History. Scholars account for the colorful history of the *Pennoyer v. Neff* parties. *See* Wendy Perdue, *Sin, Scandal and Substantive Due Process: Personal Jurisdiction and Pennoyer Reconsidered,* 62 WASH. L.REV. 479 (1987); Linda Silberman, *Shaffer v. Heitner: The End of an Era*, 53 N.Y.U. L. REV. 33 (1978). Neff sought fortune moving by covered wagon in 1848 from Iowa to claim Oregon lands. For the legal work, Neff eventually needed a lawyer, unfortunately choosing the scoundrel Mitchell. As a young man, Mitchell taught school and practiced law in the East until he had to marry and move West with a 15-year-old student whom he impregnated. Mitchell took with him $4,000 dollars of client money. He abandoned his wife in California to practice law in Oregon, where he took a second wife without divorcing his first and conducted a five-year dalliance with his second wife's sister. When Neff failed to pay Mitchell for legal services relating to Neff's land, Mitchell sued Neff, taking a default judgment and forcing the sale of Neff's land to Mitchell. Mitchell then promptly assigned the land to Pennoyer who, despite the burden of *Pennoyer v. Neff*, rose to become Oregon's governor. For his part, Mitchell won one of Oregon's U.S. Senate seats and, despite the public disclosure of Mitchell's love letters documenting his affair with his second wife's sister, later won re-election. Curiously, the trial judge in *Pennoyer v. Neff* was the person who publicly disclosed Mitchell's love letters. The law finally caught up with Mitchell in 1905 with his conviction for land fraud, removal from the Senate, fine, and incarceration.

Constitution. Notice how *Pennoyer* grounded its jurisdiction rules in the Constitution, effectively federalizing the question of jurisdiction. Article IV's full-faith-and-credit clause requires a state to recognize another state's judgments. Its Section 1 mandates that "Full Faith and Credit ... be given in each State to judicial proceedings of every other State." In direct effect, a Kansas judgment should be good in New York. There is nonetheless a tension in the plain words of full faith and credit. What happens if the Kansas judge is not good in Kansas because of a defect in jurisdiction? Full faith and credit might imply that the Kansas judgment would still be good in New York. The *Pennoyer* opinion shows how the 14th Amendment resolves that tension. The 14th Amendment's due-process clause requires that state law treat individuals with fundamental fairness. Its Section 1 mandates that no "state [shall] deprive any person of life, liberty or property without due process of law." In direct effect, neither Kansas nor New York should enforce a judgment taken without jurisdiction, in a way that would deprive the judgment debtor of a fair opportunity to contest the judgment. If a Kansas judgment is not good in Kansas because of defective jurisdiction, then it should not be good in New York. Taking the full-faith-and-credit clause and due-process clauses together, a state must only recognize a judgment of another state where the judgment is also valid in the issuing state.

Absence. Even under the traditional law of jurisdiction, *in personam* jurisdiction did not require that the party be physically present in the state when the plaintiff filed and attempted to serve the lawsuit. A court could have *in personam* jurisdiction over an absent resident. In Blackmer v. United States, 284 U.S. 421 (1932), the Supreme Court held that a federal court had jurisdiction to convict an American citizen of contempt for failing to comply with a subpoena served on the citizen to force his return from France to testify in a case arising out of the Teapot Dome Scandal. The Court found *in personam* jurisdiction in the binding effect the nation's laws for foreign service of process had on its absent citizen. The Court then applied its *Blackmer* principle for jurisdiction over absent citizens to state-court jurisdiction in Milliken v. Meyer, 311 U.S. 457 (1940). The *Milliken* plaintiff served the Wyoming state court's summons and complaint on the Wyoming-resident defendant in Colorado. Wyoming state law permitted that foreign service of process. The Supreme Court held valid the Wyoming court's default judgment on the basis that "[d]omicile in the state is alone sufficient to bring an absent defendant within the reach of the state's jurisdiction of a personal judgment by means of appropriate substituted service. ... [T]he authority of a state over one of its citizens is not terminated by the mere fact of his absence from the state." *Id.* at 462-63. Domicile means the state where a person lives intending to remain indefinitely—whether or not the person is presently in that state. The *Milliken* case thus took a big step away from the traditional presence test for *in personam* jurisdiction toward what would become the modern approach addressed below.

Ethics

When a party wishes to challenge the jurisdiction of a foreign court (about which there is more detail later), does its own lawyer get to do so? The usual answer is "no." Individual state bars license lawyers. While some lawyers hold licenses in more than one state, most lawyers hold a license in only a single state. Rule 5.5 of the *ABA Model Rules of Professional Conduct* and state statutes generally prohibit lawyers from practicing in a jurisdiction without a license or special permission. The special permission may take the form of pro hac vice (this turn only) admission on motion of local counsel. To comply with these rules and statutes, when a claimant sues a party in a distant state, the party usually hires local counsel in that distant state either to make the challenge or to work with the party's own lawyer in doing so.

Consent. The concept of consent is a core for questions of jurisdiction. It is certainly fair to hold a party responsible to a court in whose state the party has deliberately and voluntarily engaged in litigation-inducing behaviors. Kane v. New Jersey, 242 U.S. 160 (1916), is an example of consent, in which the Supreme Court accepted that a state could, as a condition of using its new motor-vehicle highways, require out-of-state motorists to file certificates consenting to the state's jurisdiction. Adam v. Saenger, 303 U.S. 59 (1938), is another example of consent, in which the Supreme Court held that by instituting a lawsuit within a state, the plaintiff consents to *in personam* jurisdiction as to counterclaims the defendant might bring against the plaintiff, even if the plaintiff had no other contact or relationship with the jurisdiction other than the lawsuit. The defendant's service of the counterclaim by state procedures giving the plaintiff fair notice satisfies the 14th Amendment's due-process requirements for *in personam* jurisdiction. The Court explained that "[t]he plaintiff having, by his voluntary act in demanding justice from the defendant, submitted himself to the jurisdiction of the court, there is nothing arbitrary or unreasonable in treating him as being there for all purposes for which justice to the defendant requires his presence. It is the price which the state may exact as the condition of opening its courts to the plaintiff." *Id.* at 67-68.

Implied Consent. Consent remains a sound and logical basis for jurisdiction, as long as the law defines consent to mean the individual's voluntary and intentional action toward the forum state. The concept of consent grows problematic when the law extends it beyond its core of thoughtful and deliberate action. It was already apparent early in the 20th century, with the advent of new communication and transportation networks, and the advance of modern corporate and financial forms, that presence within the state was no longer a sensible bright-line rule. There were too many disputed transactions and interests that crossed state lines, jurisdiction over which raised questions that the test of presence could not readily answer. In the following case, the Supreme Court adopted the concept of implied consent as an alternative test for *in personam* jurisdiction. Implied consent is one of many concepts that the law uses to analyze and attempt to resolve a tension in competing policies. Here, those competing policies involve the need to make a forum readily available to claimants to promptly and efficiently resolve disputes but while treating respondents fairly in forum selection. As you read the following case, consider whether implied consent captures that tension usefully. Also, keep in mind that personal-jurisdiction doctrine will continue to change as law adjusts to Internet and wireless communications and commerce. The value in studying these cases is not solely to learn about personal jurisdiction. It is also to see how law responds, here and elsewhere, to changes in technology.

Hess v. Pawlowski,

United States Supreme Court
274 U.S. 352 (1927)

MR. JUSTICE BUTLER delivered the opinion of the Court.

This action was brought by defendant in error to recover damages for personal injuries. The declaration alleged that plaintiff in error negligently and wantonly drove a motor vehicle on a public highway in Massachusetts, and that by reason thereof the vehicle struck and injured defendant in error. Plaintiff in error is a resident of Pennsylvania. No personal service was made on him, and no property belonging to him was attached. The service of process was made in compliance with chapter 90, General Laws of Massachusetts, as amended by Stat. 1923, c. 431, §2, the material parts of which follow:

> … [T]he operation by a nonresident of a motor vehicle on a public way in the commonwealth … shall be deemed equivalent to an appointment by such nonresident of the registrar or his successor in office, to be his true and lawful attorney upon whom may be served all lawful processes in any action or proceeding against him, growing out of any accident or collision in which said nonresident may be involved while operating a motor vehicle on such a way, and said acceptance or operation shall be a signification of his agreement that any such process against him which is so served shall be of the same legal force and validity as if served on him personally. Service of such process shall be made by leaving a copy of the process with a fee of two dollars in the hands of the registrar, or in his office, and such

service shall be sufficient service upon the said nonresident: Provided, that notice of such service and a copy of the process are forthwith sent by registered mail by the plaintiff to the defendant, and the defendant's return receipt and the plaintiff's affidavit of compliance herewith are appended to the writ and entered with the declaration. The court in which the action is pending may order such continuances as may be necessary to afford the defendant reasonable opportunity to defend the action.'

Plaintiff in error appeared specially for the purpose of contesting jurisdiction, and filed an answer in abatement and moved to dismiss on the ground that the service of process, if sustained, would deprive him of his property without due process of law, in violation of the Fourteenth Amendment. The court overruled the answer in abatement and denied the motion. The Supreme Judicial Court held the statute to be a valid exercise of the police power, and affirmed the order. [C] At the trial the contention was renewed and again denied. Plaintiff in error excepted. The jury returned a verdict for defendant in error. The exceptions were overruled by the Supreme Judicial Court. [C] Thereupon the superior court entered judgment. The writ of error was allowed by the Chief Justice of that court.

The question is whether the Massachusetts enactment contravenes the due process clause of the Fourteenth Amendment.

The process of a court of one state cannot run into another and summon a party there domiciled to respond to proceedings against him. Notice sent outside the state to a nonresident is unavailing to give jurisdiction in an action against him personally for money recovery. Pennoyer v. Neff, 95 U.S. 714[(1877)]. There must be actual service within the state of notice upon him or upon some one authorized to accept service for him. [C] A personal judgment rendered against a nonresident, who has neither been served with process nor appeared in the suit, is without validity. McDonald v. Mabee, 243 U. S. 90[(1917)]. The mere transaction of business in a state by nonresident natural persons does not imply consent to be bound by the process of its courts. Flexner v. Farson, 248 U. S. 289[(1919)]. The power of a state to exclude foreign corporations, although not absolute, but qualified, is the ground on which such an implication is supported as to them. [C] But a state may not withhold from nonresident individuals the right of doing business therein. The privileges and immunities clause of the Constitution (section 2, art. 4), safeguards to the citizens of one state the right "to pass through, or to reside in any other state for purposes of trade, agriculture, professional pursuits, or otherwise." And it prohibits state legislation discriminating against citizens of other states. [Cc]

Motor vehicles are dangerous machines, and, even when skillfully and carefully operated, their use is attended by serious dangers to persons and property. In the public interest the state may make and enforce regulations reasonable calculated to promote care on the part of all, residents and nonresidents alike, who use its highways. The measure in question operates to require a nonresident to answer for his conduct in the state where arise causes of action alleged against him, as well as to provide for a claimant a convenient method by which he may sue to enforce his rights. Under the statute the implied consent is limited to proceedings growing out of accidents or collisions on a highway in which the nonresident may be involved. It is required that he shall actually receive and receipt for notice of the service and a copy of the process. And it contemplates such continuances as may be found necessary to give reasonable time and opportunity for defense. It makes no hostile discrimination against nonresidents, but tends to put them on the same footing as residents. Literal and precise equality in respect of this matter is not attainable; it is not required. [C] The state's power to regulate the use of its highways extends to their use by nonresidents as well as by residents. [C] And, in advance of the operation of a motor vehicle on its highway by a nonresident, the state may require him to appoint one of its officials as his agent on whom process may be served in proceedings growing out of such use. Kane v. New Jersey, 242 U. S. 160[(1916)]. That case recognized power of the state to exclude a nonresident until the formal appointment is made. And, having the power so to exclude, the state may declare that the use of the highway by the nonresident is the equivalent of the appointment of the registrar as agent on whom process may be served. [Cc] The difference between the formal and implied appointment is not substantial, so far as concerns the application of the due process clause of the Fourteenth Amendment.

Judgment affirmed.

INQUIRY

Doing Business. How should the law treat corporations on the issue of personal jurisdiction? Corporations presented special challenges for courts deciding *in personam* jurisdiction on tests of either presence or consent. A corporation is a legal entity having the rights, obligations, and status defined by the law of the state that authorized the corporation. Odd as it may seem, the law generally gives corporations the status of persons, even though they are fictions that operate through their officers, employees, and agents. The Supreme Court initially held consistent with accepted law that a corporation could exist only within the state that created it. Bank of Augusta v. Earle, 38 U.S. (13 Pet.) 519, 588 (1839). Yet by the mid 19th century corporations were clearly acting interstate. So to ascertain *in personam* jurisdiction, the Supreme Court and lower courts began construing a corporation's doing business within a state as equivalent to its presence in the state and its consent to that state's jurisdiction. International Harvester Co. v. Kentucky, 234 U.S. 579, 589 (1914) ("the presence of a corporation within a state necessary to the service of process is shown when it appears that the corporation is there carrying on business in such sense as to manifest its presence within the state"); *see also* Philadelphia & Reading Ry. Co. v. McKibbin, 243 U.S. 264, 265 (1917) ("A foreign corporation is amenable to process ... in the absence of consent, only if it is doing business within the state in such manner and to such extent as to warrant the inference that it is present there."). A doing-business test gradually substituted for the traditional presence and consent tests that the courts could not easily apply to inanimate corporations. Notice, though, that the question of how much business a corporation does in a state does not necessarily reflect the fairness to the corporation of extending jurisdiction over it or the unfairness to the claimant of denying that jurisdiction.

The courts' difficulty in applying the doing-business test soon led the Supreme Court to articulate the modern basis for personal jurisdiction.

2. Modern Bases

Presence within the state is no longer the basis for personal jurisdiction. The modern basis for personal jurisdiction depends on the relationship of the disputed transaction or event and the parties to the forum state. The Constitution's full-faith-and-credit and due-process clauses require that jurisdiction depend on providing substantial justice for the parties but within fair play as to the respondent. The respondent must have a substantial enough relationship toward the court's state to make it fair to require the respondent to answer and defend there. The court entertaining jurisdiction must determine that the respondent had sufficient minimum contacts with the state to make the proceeding just and fair as to the respondent. The Supreme Court articulated this minimum-contacts test in the following case. It also distinguished two forms of *in personam* jurisdiction. The first form known as specific jurisdiction is one in which the respondent's contacts in the forum state were what gave rise to the litigation, making jurisdiction particularly fair and appropriate. If one does harm within a foreign state, then one should expect to be subject to its jurisdiction to remedy the harm. The second form known as general jurisdiction is one in which the respondent's contacts in the forum state were not what gave rise to the litigation but yet were substantial enough to make jurisdiction fair and appropriate. If one does harm within another state but has such substantial contacts with the forum state as to make it fair to litigate there, then one should expect to be subject to the forum state's jurisdiction. Consider the Supreme Court's rationale for adopting the minimum-contacts test and articulating these two forms of *in personam* jurisdiction.

International Shoe Co. v. State of Washington,

United States Supreme Court
326 U.S. 310 (1945)

MR. CHIEF JUSTICE STONE delivered the opinion of the Court.

The questions for decision are (1) whether, within the limitations of the due process clause of the Fourteenth Amendment, appellant, a Delaware corporation, has by its activities in the State of Washington rendered itself amenable to proceedings in the courts of that state to recover unpaid contributions to the state unemployment compensation fund exacted by state statutes, [c], and (2) whether the state can exact those contributions consistently with the due process clause of the Fourteenth Amendment.

The statutes in question set up a comprehensive scheme of unemployment compensation, the costs of which are defrayed by contributions required to be made by employers to a state unemployment compensation fund. The contributions are a specified percentage of the wages payable annually by each employer for his employees' services in the state. The assessment and collection of the contributions and the fund are administered by respondents. Section 14(c) of the Act, [c], authorizes respondent Commissioner to issue an order and notice of assessment of delinquent contributions upon prescribed personal service of the notice upon the employer if found within the state, or, if not so found, by mailing the notice to the employer by registered mail at his last known address. ... [T]he order of assessment may be administratively reviewed by an appeal tribunal within the office of unemployment upon petition of the employer, and this determination is ... made subject to judicial review on questions of law by the state Superior Court, with further right of appeal in the state Supreme Court as in other civil cases.

In this case notice of assessment for the years in question was personally served upon a sales solicitor employed by appellant in the State of Washington, and a copy of the notice was mailed by registered mail to appellant at its address in St. Louis, Missouri. Appellant appeared specially before the office of unemployment and moved to set aside the order and notice of assessment on the ground that the service upon appellant's salesman was not proper service upon appellant; that appellant was not a corporation of the State of Washington and was not doing business within the state; that it had no agent within the state upon whom service could be made; and that appellant is not an employer and does not furnish employment within the meaning of the statute.

The motion was heard on evidence and a stipulation of facts by the appeal tribunal which denied the motion and ruled that respondent Commissioner was entitled to recover the unpaid contributions. That action was affirmed by the Commissioner; both the Superior Court and the Supreme Court affirmed. [C] Appellant in each of these courts assailed the statute as applied, as a violation of the due process clause of the Fourteenth Amendment, and as imposing a constitutionally prohibited burden on interstate commerce. The cause comes here on appeal... , appellant assigning as error that the challenged statutes as applied infringe the due process clause of the Fourteenth Amendment and the commerce clause.

The facts as found by the appeal tribunal and accepted by the state Superior Court and Supreme Court, are not in dispute. Appellant is a Delaware corporation, having its principal place of business in St. Louis, Missouri, and is engaged in the manufacture and sale of shoes and other footwear. It maintains places of business in several states, other than Washington, at which its manufacturing is carried on and from which its merchandise is distributed interstate through several sales units or branches located outside the State of Washington.

Appellant has no office in Washington and makes no contracts either for sale or purchase of merchandise there. It maintains no stock of merchandise in that state and makes there no deliveries of goods in intrastate commerce. During the years from 1937 to 1940, now in question, appellant employed eleven to thirteen salesmen under direct supervision and control of sales managers located in St. Louis. These salesmen resided in Washington; their principal activities were confined to that state; and they were compensated by commissions based upon the amount of their sales. The commissions for each year totaled more than $31,000. Appellant supplies its salesmen with a line of samples, each consisting of one shoe of a pair, which they display to prospective purchasers. On occasion they rent permanent sample rooms, for exhibiting samples, in business buildings, or rent rooms in hotels or business buildings temporarily for that purpose. The cost of such rentals is reimbursed by appellant.

The authority of the salesmen is limited to exhibiting their samples and soliciting orders from prospective buyers, at prices and on terms fixed by appellant. The salesmen transmit the orders to appellant's office in St. Louis for acceptance or rejection, and when accepted the merchandise for filling the orders is shipped f.o.b. from points outside Washington to the purchasers within the state. All the merchandise shipped into Washington is invoiced at the place of shipment from which collections are made. No salesman has authority to enter into contracts or to make collections.

The Supreme Court of Washington was of opinion that the regular and systematic solicitation of orders in the state by appellant's salesmen, resulting in a continuous flow of appellant's product into the state, was sufficient to constitute doing business in the state so as to make appellant amenable to suit in its courts. But it was also of opinion that there were sufficient additional activities shown to bring the case within the rule frequently stated, that solicitation within a state by the agents of a foreign corporation plus some additional activities there are sufficient to render the corporation amenable to suit brought in the courts of the state to enforce an obligation arising out of its activities there. [Cc] The court found such additional activities in the salesmen's display of samples sometimes in permanent display rooms, and the salesmen's residence within the state, continued over a period of years, all resulting in a substantial volume of merchandise regularly shipped by appellant to purchasers within the state. ...

Appellant ... insists that its activities within the state were not sufficient to manifest its "presence" there and that in its absence the state courts were without jurisdiction, that consequently it was a denial of due process for the state to subject appellant to suit. It refers to those cases in which it was said that the mere solicitation of orders for the purchase of goods within a state, to be accepted without the state and filled by shipment of the purchased goods interstate, does not render the corporation seller amenable to suit within the state. [Cc] And appellant further argues that since it was not present within the state, it is a denial of due process to subject it to taxation or other money exaction. It thus denies the power of the state to lay the tax or to subject appellant to a suit for its collection.

Historically the jurisdiction of courts to render judgment in personam is grounded on their de facto power over the defendant's person. Hence his presence within the territorial jurisdiction of court was prerequisite to its rendition of a judgment personally binding him. Pennoyer v. Neff, 95 U.S. 714, 733[(1878]]. But now that the capias ad respondendum has given way to personal service of summons or other form of notice, due process requires only that in order to subject a defendant to a judgment in personam, if he be not present within the territory of the forum, he have certain minimum contacts with it such that the maintenance of the suit does not offend "traditional notions of fair play and substantial justice." Milliken v. Meyer, 311, U.S. 457, 463[(1940)]. See Holmes, J., in McDonald v. Mabee, 243 U.S. 90, 91[(1917)]. [Cc]

Since the corporate personality is a fiction, although a fiction intended to be acted upon as though it were a fact, [c], it is clear that unlike an individual its "presence" without, as well as within, the state of its origin can be manifested only by activities carried on in its behalf by those who are authorized to act for it.

To say that the corporation is so far "present" there as to satisfy due process requirements, for purposes of taxation or the maintenance of suits against it in the courts of the state, is to beg the question to be decided. For the terms "present" or "presence" are used merely to symbolize those activities of the corporation's agent within the state which courts will deem to be sufficient to satisfy the demands of due process. [C] Those demands may be met by such contacts of the corporation with the state of the forum as make it reasonable, in the context of our federal system of government, to require the corporation to defend the particular suit which is brought there. An"estimate of the inconveniences" which would result to the corporation from a trial away from its "home" or principal place of business is relevant in this connection. [C]

"Presence" in the state in this sense has never been doubted when the activities of the corporation there have not only been continuous and systematic, but also give rise to the liabilities sued on, even though no consent to be sued or authorization to an agent to accept service of process has been given. [Cc] Conversely it has been generally recognized that the casual presence of the corporate agent or even his conduct of single or isolated items of activities in a state in the corporation's behalf are not enough to subject it to suit on causes of action unconnected with the activities there. [Cc] To require the corporation in such circumstances to defend the suit away from its home or other jurisdiction where it carries on more substantial activities has been thought to lay too great and unreasonable a burden on the corporation to comport with due process.

While it has been held in cases on which appellant relies that continuous activity of some sorts within a state is not enough to support the demand that the corporation be amenable to suits unrelated to that activity, [cc], there have been instances in which the continuous corporate operations within a state were thought so substantial and of such a nature as to justify suit against it on causes of action arising from dealings entirely distinct from those activities. [Cc]

Finally, although the commission of some single or occasional acts of the corporate agent in a state sufficient to impose an obligation or liability on the corporation has not been thought to confer upon the state authority to enforce it, [c], other such acts, because of their nature and quality and the circumstances of their commission, may be deemed sufficient to render the corporation liable to suit. Cf. Kane v. New Jersey, 242 U.S. 160[(1916)]; Hess v. Pawloski, [274 US. 352 (1927)]; [c]. True, some of the decisions holding the corporation amenable to suit have been supported by resort to the legal fiction that it has given its consent to service and suit, consent being implied from its presence in the state through the acts of its authorized agents. [Cc] But more realistically it may be said that those authorized acts were of such a nature as to justify the fiction. [Cc]

It is evident that the criteria by which we mark the boundary line between those activities which justify the subjection of a corporation to suit, and those which do not, cannot be simply mechanical or quantitative. The test is not merely, as has sometimes been suggested, whether the activity, which the corporation has seen fit to procure through its agents in another state, is a little more or a little less. [Cc] Whether due process is satisfied must depend rather upon the quality and nature of the activity in relation to the fair and orderly administration of the laws which it was the purpose of the due process clause to insure. That clause does not contemplate that a state may make binding a judgment in personam against an individual or corporate defendant with which the state has no contacts, ties, or relations. Cf. Pennoyer v. Neff, supra; [c].

But to the extent that a corporation exercises the privilege of conducting activities within a state, it enjoys the benefits and protection of the laws of that state. The exercise of that privilege may give rise to obligations; and, so far as those obligations arise out of or are connected with the activities within the state, a procedure which requires the corporation to respond to a suit brought to enforce them can, in most instances, hardly be said to be undue. [Cc]

Applying these standards, the activities carried on in behalf of appellant in the State of Washington were neither irregular nor casual. They were systematic and continuous throughout the years in question. They resulted in a large volume of interstate business, in the course of which appellant received the benefits and protection of the laws of the state, including the right to resort to the courts for the enforcement of its rights. The obligation which is here sued upon arose out of those very activities. It is evident that these operations establish sufficient contacts or ties with the state of the forum to make it reasonable and just according to our traditional conception of fair play and substantial justice to permit the state to enforce the obligations which appellant has incurred there. Hence we cannot say that the maintenance of the present suit in the State of Washington involves an unreasonable or undue procedure.

We are likewise unable to conclude that the service of the process within the state upon an agent whose activities establish appellant's 'presence' there was not sufficient notice of the suit, or that the suit was so unrelated to those activities as to make the agent an inappropriate vehicle for communicating the notice. It is enough that appellant has established such contacts with the state that the particular form of substituted service adopted there gives reasonable assurance that the notice will be actual. [Cc] Nor can we say that the mailing of the notice of suit to appellant by registered mail at its home office was not reasonably calculated to apprise appellant of the suit. [Cc] ...

Appellant having rendered itself amenable to suit upon obligations arising out of the activities of its salesmen in Washington, the state may maintain the present suit in personam to collect the tax laid upon the exercise of the privilege of employing appellant's salesmen within the state. For Washington has made one of those activities, which taken together establish appellant's "presence" there for purposes of suit, the taxable event by which the state brings appellant within the reach of its taxing power. The state thus has constitutional power to lay the tax and to subject appellant to a suit to recover it. The activities which establish its "presence" subject it alike to taxation by the state and to suit to recover the tax. [Cc]

Affirmed.

Mr. Justice JACKSON took no part in the consideration or decision of this case.

Mr. Justice BLACK delivered the following opinion. ...

... Certainly a State, at the very least, has power to tax and sue those dealing with its citizens within its boundaries, as we have held before. [C] Were the Court to follow this principle, it would provide a workable standard for cases where, as here, no other questions are involved. The Court has not chosen to do so, but instead has engaged in an unnecessary discussion in the course of which it has announced vague Constitutional criteria applied for the first time to the issue before us. It has thus introduced uncertain elements confusing the simple pattern and tending to curtail the exercise of State powers to an extent not justified by the Constitution. …

There is a strong emotional appeal in the words "fair play," "justice," and "reasonableness." But they were not chosen by those who wrote the original Constitution or the Fourteenth Amendment as a measuring rod for this Court to use in invalidating State or Federal laws passed by elected legislative representatives. No one, not even those who most feared a democratic government, ever formally proposed that courts should be given power to invalidate legislation under any such elastic standards. … For application of this natural law concept, whether under the terms "reasonableness," "justice," or "fair play," makes judges the supreme arbiters of the country's laws and practices. [Cc] This result, I believe, alters the form of government our Constitution provides. I cannot agree.

True, the State's power is here upheld. But the rule announced means that tomorrow's judgment may strike down a State or Federal enactment on the ground that it does not conform to this Court's idea of natural justice. …

INQUIRY

Judging. What can we learn about judging, from the Supreme Court's articulating but then changing personal-jurisdiction rules? The *International Shoe* opinion and dissent reflect a persistent balance for courts to strike in the nature of judging. On one hand, formal bright-line rules fashioned around understandable categories (like presence and consent) help make law reasonably clear, keep persons well informed about the law, and make judging reasonably efficient. On the other hand, formal categorical approaches can miss the substantive goal and inevitably create arbitrary lines at their boundaries. By contrast, functional tests (like minimum contacts) keep the law focused on its policy goals but give little advance guidance and tend to require inefficient case-by-case determinations. As the *International Shoe* dissent suggests, one's preference for categorical or functional approaches can depend on one's philosophy of judging (whether managerial or adjudicative) and law (whether formal or realist). When it replaced presence and consent tests with the minimum-contacts standard, did the *International Shoe* opinion succeed in creating a more appropriately functional test, or did it simply substitute new for old categories? One scholar has insightfully labeled as "arbitrary particularization" the process by which the lower courts have developed the contours of *International Shoe's* minimum-contacts standard. Geoffrey C. Hazard, Jr., *A General Theory of State-Court Jurisdiction*, 1965 SUP. CT. REV. 241, 283. Consider next how the law developed around the Supreme Court's new categories of general and specific jurisdiction.

Skill

Lawyers frequently advise clients about probable outcomes by applying tests like the minimum-contacts standard of *International Shoe*. Predict whether your defendant client would be subject to jurisdiction in each of the following cases. As you attempt to do so, identify other facts you would like to know to determine the extent of your client's contacts with the forum jurisdiction:

A. The user of your client manufacturer's product sues your client in one of four states into which your client sells the product through a sales representative covering those four states, even though it is not the state in which the user purchased your client's product.

B. A person injured by a careless driver employed by your client distributor sues your client in the state in which the accident occurred, even though not a state into which your client distributes products.

C. A sales representative through whom your client manufacturer deals sues your client in a state in which the sales representative resides but into which your client manufacturer sells no product.

D. A retailer who sells your client manufacturer's products sues your client in a state in which the retailer has its corporate headquarters, even though the retailer does not sell your client's products in that state.

E. A patient allegedly injured by your hospital client's malpractice sues your client in the state in which the patient resides and your client has several medical suppliers but not the state in which the malpractice occurred.

B. Specific Jurisdiction

As stated above and shown in *International Shoe*, the Supreme Court has articulated two forms of *in personam* jurisdiction. Specific jurisdiction is the form in which the respondent's contacts with the forum state gave rise to the litigation, making jurisdiction fair and appropriate. General jurisdiction is the form in which the respondent's contacts in the forum state were *not* what gave rise to the litigation but were still substantial enough to make jurisdiction fair and appropriate. The following sections on Minimum Contacts, Current Challenges, and Statutory Authority address specific jurisdiction. The chapter returns later to general jurisdiction. As you read these cases, watch how the Supreme Court and lower courts use alternative phrases like "gave rise to," "arose out of," and are "related to," to describe the connection between the defendant's actions and the forum state for specific-jurisdiction purposes. Because the Supreme Court has used alternative phrases, the lower courts have split on which relationship is sufficient to make the jurisdictional form specific rather than general jurisdiction. For instance, in the Sixth Circuit, the defendant's contacts with the forum state need only "relate to the operative facts of the controversy" for the court to find specific (rather than general) jurisdiction to be the appropriate form. Bird v. Parsons, 289 F.3d 865, 875 (6th Cir. 2002). By contrast, the Ninth Circuit applies a but-for test requiring the plaintiff to show for specific jurisdiction that the defendant's contacts with the forum state were necessary to the cause of action. Doe v. Unocal Corp., 248 F.3d 915, 924 (9th Cir. 2001). In other words, the line between specific and general jurisdiction may not always be clear.

1. Minimum Contacts

The Supreme Court has developed its *International Shoe* minimum-contacts jurisprudence through a series of cases that continue up to today. The following two early cases, still cited today for contrasting purposes, address (like points at opposite ends of a spectrum) the scope of the minimum-contacts standard. In the first case excerpted below, *McGee v. International Life Insurance Co.*, the Supreme Court adopted an approach examining the defendant's contacts with the jurisdiction in light of the interests of the parties and state to exercise jurisdiction. The case may suggest that if the balance tips in favor of jurisdiction, then fewer contacts may be constitutionally necessary. In the second case, *Hanson v. Denckla*, the Supreme Court considered the defendant's contacts with the jurisdiction in light of the interest of the forum state in applying its own laws to the dispute. Choice of law is a different question from choice of jurisdiction. Just because a court exercises jurisdiction over a dispute will not necessarily mean that the court will apply its forum state's law. The law of a foreign state may apply under different choice-of-law principles. The case may suggest that if the forum state's law applies, then the court of that forum has greater constitutional liberty to exercise jurisdiction. Together, the two cases may indicate that it is not merely the parties' convenience in question but also the sovereignty of the states whose courts must resolve the litigation.

McGee v. International Life Ins. Co.,

United States Supreme Court
355 U.S. 220 (1957)

Opinion of the Court by MR. JUSTICE BLACK announced by MR. JUSTICE DOUGLAS.

Petitioner, Lulu B. McGee, recovered a judgment in a California state court against respondent, International Life Insurance Company, on a contract of insurance[insuring the life husband of her husband who died while so insured. The respondent insurer had refused to pay, maintaining that the husband had committed suicide voiding the policy]. Respondent[, having no office or agent in California,] was not served with process in California but by registered mail at its principal place of business in Texas. The California court based its jurisdiction on a state statute which subjects foreign corporations to suit in California on insurance contracts with residents of that State even though such corporations cannot be served with process within its borders.[fn]

Unable to collect the judgment in California petitioner went to Texas where she filed suit on the judgment in a Texas court. But the Texas courts refused to enforce her judgment holding it was void under the Fourteenth Amendment because service of process outside California could not give the courts of that State jurisdiction over respondent. [C] Since the case raised important questions, not only to California but to other States which have similar laws, we granted certiorari. [C] It is not controverted that if the California court properly exercised jurisdiction over respondent the Texas courts erred in refusing to give its judgment full faith and credit. 28 U.S.C. §1738[].

... [S]o far as the record before us shows, respondent has never solicited or done any insurance business in California apart from the policy involved here.

Since Pennoyer v. Neff, 95 U.S. 714[(1877)], this Court has held that the Due Process Clause of the Fourteenth Amendment places some limit on the power of state courts to enter binding judgments against persons not served with process within their boundaries. But just where this line of limitation falls has been the subject of prolific controversy, particularly with respect to foreign corporations. In a continuing process of evolution this Court accepted and then abandoned "consent," "doing business," and "presence" as the standard for measuring the extent of state judicial power over such corporations. [C] More recently in International Shoe Co. v. State of Washington, 326 U.S. 310[(1945)], the Court decided that "due process requires only that in order to subject a defendant to a judgment in personam, if he be not present within the territory of the forum, he have certain minimum contacts with it such that the maintenance of the suit does not offend 'traditional notions of fair play and substantial justice." Id.[at] 316[].

Looking back over this long history of litigation a trend is clearly discernible toward expanding the permissible scope of state jurisdiction over foreign corporations and other nonresidents. In part this is attributable to the fundamental transformation of our national economy over the years. Today many commercial transactions touch two or more States and may involve parties separated by the full continent. With this increasing nationalization of commerce has come a great increase in the amount of business conducted by mail across state lines. At the same time modern transportation and communication have made it much less burdensome for a party sued to defend himself in a State where he engages in economic activity.

Turning to this case we think it apparent that the Due Process Clause did not preclude the California court from entering a judgment binding on respondent. It is sufficient for purposes of due process that the suit was based on a contract which had substantial connection with that State. Cf. Hess v. Pawloski, 274 U.S. 352[(1927)]; [cc][fn]. The contract was delivered in California, the premiums were mailed from there and the insured was a resident of that State when he died. It cannot be denied that California has a manifest interest in providing effective means of redress for its residents when their insurers refuse to pay claims. These residents would be at a severe disadvantage if they were forced to follow the insurance company to a distant State in order to hold it legally accountable. When claims were small or moderate individual claimants freguently could not afford the cost of bringing an action in a foreign forum-thus in effect making the company judgment proof. Often the crucial witnesses-as here on the company's defense of suicide-will be found in the insured's locality. Of course there may be inconvenience to the insurer if it is held amenable to suit in California where it had this contract but certainly nothing which amounts to a denial of due process. Cf. Travelers Health Ass'n v. Commonwealth of Virginia ex rel. State Corporation Comm., 339 U.S. 643[(1950)]. There is no contention that respondent did not have adequate notice of the suit or sufficient time to prepare its defenses and appear. ...

The judgment is reversed and the cause is remanded to the Court of Civil Appeals of the State of Texas, First Supreme Judicial District, for further proceedings not inconsistent with this opinion.

It is so ordered.
Judgment reversed and cause remanded with directions.

Hanson v. Denckla,

United States Supreme Court
357 U.S. 235 (1958)

MR. CHIEF JUSTICE WARREN delivered the opinion of the Court.

This controversy concerns the right to $400,000, part of the corpus of a trust established in Delaware by a settlor who later became domiciled in Florida. One group of claimants, "legatees," urge that this property passed under the residuary clause of the settlor's will, which was admitted to probate in Florida. The Florida courts have sustained this position. [C] Other claimants, "appointees" and "beneficiaries," contend that the property passed pursuant to the settlor's exercise of the inter vivos power of appointment created in the deed of trust. The Delaware courts adopted this position and refused to accord full faith and credit to the Florida determination because the Florida court had not acquired jurisdiction over an indispensable party, the Delaware trustee. [C] ...

The trust whose validity is contested here was created in 1935. Dora Browning Donner, then a domiciliary of Pennsylvania, executed a trust instrument in Delaware naming the Wilmington Trust Co., of Wilmington, Delaware, as trustee. ... Thereafter she left Pennsylvania, and in 1944 became domiciled in Florida, where she remained until her death in 1952. ... Her will, which was admitted to probate in Florida, ... directed that the balance of her property (the $1,000,000 appointed from the Delaware trust) be paid in equal parts to two trusts for the benefit of her daughters Katherine N. R. Denckla and Dorothy B. R. Stewart[, omitting a third daughter Elizabeth Donner Hanson].

This controversy grows out of the residuary clause that created the lastmentioned trusts. ... Residuary legatees Denckla and Stewart, already the recipients of over $500,000 each, urge that the power of appointment over the $400,000 appointed to sister Elizabeth's children was not "effectively exercised" and that the property should accordingly pass to them. Fourteen months after Mrs. Donner's death these parties petitioned a Florida chancery court for a declaratory judgment "concerning what property passes under the residuary clause" of the will. ... The appearing defendants (Elizabeth Donner Hanson and her children) moved to dismiss the suit because the exercise of jurisdiction over indispensable parties, the Delaware trustees, would offend Section 1 of the Fourteenth Amendment. The Chancellor ruled that he lacked jurisdiction over these nonresident defendants because no personal service was had and because the trust corpus was outside the territorial jurisdiction of the court. The cause was dismissed as to them. As far as parties before the court were concerned, however, he ruled that the power of appointment was testamentary and void under the applicable Florida law[, and] that the $400,000 passed under the residuary clause of the will[to Denckla and Stewart].

After the Florida litigation began, but before entry of the decree, the executrix [Elizabeth Donner Hanson] instituted a declaratory judgment action in Delaware to determine who was entitled to participate in the trust assets held in that State. … [T]he parties were substantially the same as in the Florida litigation. … [T]he Delaware Chancellor ruled that the trust and power of appointment were valid under the applicable Delaware law, and that the trust corpus had properly been paid to the Delaware Trust Co. and the other appointees. [C] [The Florida Supreme Court refused to recognize the Delaware decision, and the Delaware Supreme Court refused to recognize the Florida decision.] …

… Appellees[argue] for in personam jurisdiction over the Delaware trustee. They urge that the circumstances of this case amount to sufficient affiliation with the State of Florida to empower its courts to exercise personal jurisdiction over this nonresident defendant. Principal reliance is placed upon McGee v. International Life Ins. Co., 355 U.S. 220[(1957)]. In McGee the Court noted the trend of expanding personal jurisdiction over nonresidents. As technological progress has increased the flow of commerce between States, the need for jurisdiction over nonresidents has undergone a similar increase. At the same time, progress in communications and transportation has made the defense of a suit in a foreign tribunal less burdensome. In response to these changes, the requirements for personal jurisdiction over nonresidents have evolved from the rigid rule of Pennoyer v. Neff, 95 U.S. 714[(1877)], to the flexible standard of International Shoe Co. v. State of Washington, 326 U.S. 310[(1945)]. But it is a mistake to assume that this trend heralds the eventual demise of all restrictions on the personal jurisdiction of state courts. [C] Those restrictions are more than a guarantee of immunity from inconvenient or distant litigation. They are a consequence of territorial limitations on the power of the respective States. However minimal the burden of defending in a foreign tribunal, a defendant may not be called upon to do so unless he has had the "minimal contacts" with that State that are a prerequisite to its exercise of power over him. See International Shoe Co. v. State of Washington, 326 U.S. [at] 319[].

We fail to find such contacts in the circumstances of this case. The defendant trust company has no office in Florida, and transacts no business there. None of the trust assets has ever been held or administered in Florida, and the record discloses no solicitation of business in that State either in person or by mail. [Cc]

The cause of action in this case is not one that arises out of an act done or transaction consummated in the forum State. In that respect, it differs from McGee v. International Life Ins. Co., [supra], and the cases there cited. … In contrast, this action involves the validity of an agreement that was entered without any connection with the forum State. The agreement was executed in Delaware by a trust company incorporated in that State and a settlor domiciled in Pennsylvania. The first relationship Florida had to the agreement was years later when the settlor became domiciled there, and the trustee remitted the trust income to her in that State. From Florida Mrs. Donner carried on several bits of trust administration that may be compared to the mailing of premiums in McGee. But the record discloses no instance in which the trustee performed any acts in Florida that bear the same relationship to the agreement as the solicitation in McGee. Consequently, this suit cannot be said to be one to enforce an obligation that arose from a privilege the defendant exercised in Florida. [C] …

… The unilateral activity of those who claim some relationship with a nonresident defendant cannot satisfy the requirement of contact with the forum

State. The application of that rule will vary with the quality and nature of the defendant's activity, but it is essential in each case that there be some act by which the defendant purposefully avails itself of the privilege of conducting activities within the forum State, thus invoking the benefits and protections of its laws. International Shoe v. State of Washington, [supra]. ...

... The same reasons that compel reversal of the Florida judgment require affirmance of the Delaware one. Delaware is under no obligation to give full faith and credit to a Florida judgment invalid in Florida because offensive to the Due Process Clause of the Fourteenth Amendment. ...

The judgment of the Delaware Supreme Court is affirmed, and the judgment of the Florida Supreme Court is reversed and the cause is remanded for proceedings not inconsistent with this opinion. ...

[Justices BLACK, BURTON, BRENNAN, and DOUGLAS dissented, the latter separately.]

INQUIRY

Interests. What does it mean for a court to balance the parties' and state's interests? There is a purpose to litigation. Parties litigate for specific relief under laws that preserve and promote certain state interests. The relief that a party seeks defines the party's interest just as the law under which the party seeks the relief defines the state's interest. For instance, the creditor who sues a debtor on a consumer debt has a financial interest in enforcing its customers' obligations. When the creditor chooses a forum convenient to it, it seeks to minimize its transactions costs in enforcing its customers' obligations. The debtor who defends based on the interest being usurious has a financial interest in a fair interest rate. When the debtor challenges jurisdiction, the debtor seeks to reduce the burden of ensuring a fair interest rate. The state's laws regulating the creditor-debtor transaction promote the state's interest in fair and secure consumer commerce. The state's long-arm statute under which the court decides jurisdiction promotes the state's sovereignty in enforcing its laws and regulating access to its courts. Lawyers readily identify interests from which to fashion arguments balancing those interests.

Sovereignty. What does it mean for a court to recognize a state's sovereignty? To be sovereign is to decide for one's self on one's own. State sovereignty involves the authority of a state to define and enforce its own laws. When a court considers state sovereignty in determining whether there is jurisdiction over a case, the court attempts to discern whether by deciding the case the court will be promoting an interest the state has defined through its laws. What interests might a state define? Motor-vehicle laws define the state's interest in safe and efficient travel on its highways. Consumer-protection laws promote the state's interest in fair treatment of its individual buyers of goods and services. A state's ability to enforce these laws and promote the interests they represent together establish and promote the state's sovereignty. A state is not sovereign if it cannot establish and enforce its own laws in ways that promote the interests those laws represent.

Purposeful Acts. What control does a person or entity have over where they must respond to litigation? It is clear in this line of cases articulating the minimum-contacts standard that the Supreme Court looks closely at the purposeful acts of the defendant toward the jurisdiction into which the plaintiff is attempting to hale the defendant. A good (and often-cited) example is Kulko v. Superior Court, 436 U.S. 84 (1978), in which the divorced mother of two children sued the children's father for custody and increased support after having moved from the marital home in New York to California. The Supreme Court held that the California state court had no personal jurisdiction over the father whose only contact with California was the fact that the mother had moved his children there. Justice Marshall's majority opinion in *Kulko* pointed out that the father's only "purposeful act" was his acquiescence in the children's move there. The father had sought no benefit from California, even though California had a strong interest in the then-resident children's support. The absence of defendant's purposeful acts toward the jurisdiction can counter-balance the plaintiff's and state's common interests in resolving the litigation there. Consider the balance of interests, sovereignty of the states, and purposeful acts of the defendant, as you read the following case further developing the Supreme Court's minimum-contacts standard for *in personam* jurisdiction. Consider also whether the Supreme Court is modifying in any substantial respect the minimum-contacts standard of *International Shoe.*

World-Wide Volkswagen Corp. v. Woodson,

United States Supreme Court
444 U.S. 286 (1980)

MR. JUSTICE WHITE delivered the opinion of the Court.

The issue before us is whether, consistently with the Due Process Clause of the Fourteenth Amendment, an Oklahoma court may exercise *in personam* jurisdiction over a nonresident automobile retailer and its wholesale distributor in a products-liability action, when the defendants' only connection with Oklahoma is the fact that an automobile sold in New York to New York residents became involved in an accident in Oklahoma.

I

Respondents Harry and Kay Robinson purchased a new Audi automobile from petitioner Seaway Volkswagen, Inc. (Seaway), in Massena, N. Y., in 1976. The following year the Robinson family, who resided in New York, left that State for a new home in Arizona. As they passed through the State of Oklahoma, another car struck their Audi in the rear, causing a fire which severely burned Kay Robinson and her two children.[fn]

The Robinsons[fn] subsequently brought a products-liability action in the District Court for Creek County, Okla., claiming that their injuries resulted from defective design and placement of the Audi's gas tank and fuel system. They joined as defendants the automobile's manufacturer, Audi NSU Auto Union Aktiengesellschaft (Audi); its importer Volkswagen of America, Inc. (Volkswagen); its regional distributor, petitioner World-Wide Volkswagen Corp. (World-Wide); and its retail dealer, petitioner Seaway. Seaway and World-Wide entered special appearances,[fn] claiming that Oklahoma's exercise of jurisdiction over them would offend the limitations on the State's jurisdiction imposed by the Due Process Clause of the Fourteenth Amendment.[fn]

The facts presented to the District Court showed that World-Wide is incorporated and has its business office in New York. It distributes vehicles, parts, and accessories, under contract with Volkswagen, to retail dealers in New York, New Jersey, and Connecticut. Seaway, one of these retail dealers, is incorporated and has its place of business in New York. Insofar as the record reveals, Seaway and World-Wide are fully independent corporations whose relations with each other and with Volkswagen and Audi are contractual only. Respondents adduced no evidence that either World-Wide or Seaway does any business in Oklahoma, ships or sells any products to or in that State, has an agent to receive process there, or purchases advertisements in any media calculated to reach Oklahoma. In fact, as respondents' counsel conceded at oral argument, [c], there was no showing that any automobile sold by World-Wide or Seaway has ever entered Oklahoma with the single exception of the vehicle involved in the present case.

Despite the apparent paucity of contacts between petitioners and Oklahoma, the District Court rejected their constitutional claim... . Petitioners then sought a writ of prohibition in the Supreme Court of Oklahoma to restrain the District Judge, respondent Charles S. Woodson, from exercising *in personam* jurisdiction over them. They renewed their contention that, because they had no "minimal contacts," [c], with the State of Oklahoma, the actions of the District Judge were in violation of their rights under the Due Process Clause.

The Supreme Court of Oklahoma denied the writ, [c],[fn] holding that personal jurisdiction over petitioners was authorized by Oklahoma's "long-arm" statute, [c].[fn] ... The court's rationale was contained in the following paragraph, [c]:

> "In the case before us, the product being sold and distributed by the petitioners is by its very design and purpose so mobile that petitioners can foresee its possible use in Oklahoma. This is especially true of the distributor, who has the exclusive right to distribute such automobile in New York, New Jersey and Connecticut. The evidence presented below demonstrated that goods sold and distributed by the petitioners were used in the State of Oklahoma, and under the facts we believe it reasonable to infer, given the retail value of the automobile, that the petitioners derive substantial income from automobiles which from time to time are used in the State of Oklahoma. This being the case, we hold that under the facts presented, the trial court was justified in concluding that the petitioners derive substantial revenue from goods used or consumed in this State."

We granted certiorari, [c], to consider an important constitutional question with respect to state-court jurisdiction and to resolve a conflict between the Supreme Court of Oklahoma and the highest courts of at least four other States. We reverse.

II

The Due Process Clause of the Fourteenth Amendment limits the power of a state court to render a valid personal judgment against a nonresident defendant. [C] A judgment rendered in violation of due process is void in the rendering State and is not entitled to full faith and credit elsewhere. Pennoyer v.

Neff, 95 U.S. 714, 732-733[] (1878). Due process requires that the defendant be given adequate notice of the suit, [c], and be subject to the personal jurisdiction of the court, International Shoe Co. v. Washington, 326 U.S. 310[] (1945). In the present case, it is not contended that notice was inadequate; the only question is whether these particular petitioners were subject to the jurisdiction of the Oklahoma courts.

As has long been settled, and as we reaffirm today, a state court may exercise personal jurisdiction over a nonresident defendant only so long as there exist "minimum contacts" between the defendant and the forum State. International Shoe Co. v. Washington, supra, at 316[]. The concept of minimum contacts, in turn, can be seen to perform two related, but distinguishable, functions. It protects the defendant against the burdens of litigating in a distant or inconvenient forum. And it acts to ensure that the States through their courts, do not reach out beyond the limits imposed on them by their status as coequal sovereigns in a federal system.

The protection against inconvenient litigation is typically described in terms of "reasonableness" or "fairness." We have said that the defendant's contacts with the forum State must be such that maintenance of the suit "does not offend 'traditional notions of fair play and substantial justice.'" International Shoe Co. v. Washington, supra, at 316[], quoting Milliken v. Meyer, 311 U.S. 457, 463[] (1940). The relationship between the defendant and the forum must be such that it is "reasonable ... to require the corporation to defend the particular suit which is brought there." [International Shoe Co., supra] at 326 U.S.[]. Implicit in this emphasis on reasonableness is the understanding that the burden on the defendant, while always a primary concern, will in an appropriate case be considered in light of other relevant factors, including the forum State's interest in adjudicating the dispute, see McGee v. International Life Ins. Co., 355 U.S. 220, 223[] (1957); the plaintiff's interest in obtaining convenient and effective relief, [c], at least when that interest is not adequately protected by the plaintiff's power to choose the forum, [c]; the interstate judicial system's interest in obtaining the most efficient resolution of controversies; and the shared interest of the several States in furthering fundamental substantive social policies, [c].

The limits imposed on state jurisdiction by the Due Process Clause, in its role as a guarantor against inconvenient litigation, have been substantially relaxed over the years. As we noted in McGee v. International Life Ins. Co., supra, [c], this trend is largely attributable to a fundamental transformation in the American economy… .

Nevertheless, we have never accepted the proposition that state lines are irrelevant for jurisdictional purposes, nor could we, and remain faithful to the principles of interstate federalism embodied in the Constitution. The economic interdependence of the States was foreseen and desired by the Framers. In the Commerce Clause, they provided that the Nation was to be a common market, a "free trade unit" in which the States are debarred from acting as separable economic entities. [C] But the Framers also intended that the States retain many essential attributes of sovereignty, including, in particular, the sovereign power to try causes in their courts. The sovereignty of each State, in turn, implied a limitation on the sovereignty of all of its sister States-a limitation express or implicit in both the original scheme of the Constitution and the Fourteenth Amendment. ...

Thus, the Due Process Clause "does not contemplate that a state may make binding a judgment *in personam* against an individual or corporate defendant with which the state has no contacts, ties, or relations." International Shoe Co. v. Washington, [supra] at 319[]. Even if the defendant would suffer minimal or no inconvenience from being forced to litigate before the tribunals of another State; even if the forum State has a strong interest in applying its law to the controversy; even if the forum State is the most convenient location for litigation, the Due Process Clause, acting as an instrument of interstate federalism, may sometimes act to divest the State of its power to render a valid judgment. Hanson v. Denckla, supra, []at 251.

III

Applying these principles to the case at hand,[fn] we find in the record before us a total absence of those affiliating circumstances that are a necessary predicate to any exercise of state-court jurisdiction. Petitioners carry on no activity whatsoever in Oklahoma. They close no sales and perform no services there. They avail themselves of none of the privileges and benefits of Oklahoma law. They solicit no business there either through salespersons or through advertising reasonably calculated to reach the State. Nor does the record show that they regularly sell cars at wholesale or retail to Oklahoma customers or residents or that they indirectly, through others, serve or seek to serve the Oklahoma market. In short, respondents seek to base jurisdiction on one, isolated occurrence and whatever inferences can be drawn therefrom: the fortuitous circumstance that a single Audi automobile, sold in New York to New York residents, happened to suffer an accident while passing through Oklahoma.

It is argued, however, that because an automobile is mobile by its very design and purpose it was "foreseeable" that the Robinsons' Audi would cause injury in Oklahoma. Yet "foreseeability" alone has never been a sufficient benchmark for personal jurisdiction under the Due Process Clause. In Hanson v. Denckla, supra, it was no doubt foreseeable that the settlor of a Delaware trust would subsequently move to Florida and seek to exercise a power of appointment there; yet we held that Florida courts could not constitutionally exercise jurisdiction over a Delaware trustee that had no other contacts with the forum State. ...

If foreseeability were the criterion, a local California tire retailer could be forced to defend in Pennsylvania when a blowout occurs there, [c]; a Wisconsin seller of a defective automobile jack could be haled before a distant court for damage caused in New Jersey, [c]; or a Florida soft-drink concessionaire could be summoned to Alaska to account for injuries happening there, [c]. Every seller of chattels would in effect appoint the chattel his agent for service of process. His amenability to suit would travel with the chattel. ...

This is not to say, of course, that foreseeability is wholly irrelevant. But the foreseeability that is critical to due process analysis is not the mere likelihood that a product will find its way into the forum State. Rather, it is that the defendant's conduct and connection with the forum State are such that he should reasonably anticipate being haled into court there. [Cc] The Due Process Clause, by ensuring the "orderly administration of the laws," International Shoe Co. v.

Washington, [supra] at 319[], gives a degree of predictability to the legal system that allows potential defendants to structure their primary conduct with some minimum assurance as to where that conduct will and will not render them liable to suit.

When a corporation "purposefully avails itself of the privilege of conducting activities within the forum State," Hanson v. Denckla, [supra] at 253[], it has clear notice that it is subject to suit there, and can act to alleviate the risk of burdensome litigation by procuring insurance, passing the expected costs on to customers, or, if the risks are too great, severing its connection with the State. Hence if the sale of a product of a manufacturer or distributor such as Audi or Volkswagen is not simply an isolated occurrence, but arises from the efforts of the manufacturer or distributor to serve directly or indirectly, the market for its product in other States, it is not unreasonable to subject it to suit in one of those States if its allegedly defective merchandise has there been the source of injury to its owner or to others. The forum State does not exceed its powers under the Due Process Clause if it asserts personal jurisdiction over a corporation that delivers its products into the stream of commerce with the expectation that they will be purchased by consumers in the forum State. [C]

But there is no such or similar basis for Oklahoma jurisdiction over World-Wide or Seaway in this case. Seaway's sales are made in Massena, N. Y. World-Wide's market, although substantially larger, is limited to dealers in New York, New Jersey, and Connecticut. There is no evidence of record that any automobiles distributed by World-Wide are sold to retail customers outside this tristate area. It is foreseeable that the purchasers of automobiles sold by World-Wide and Seaway may take them to Oklahoma. But the mere "unilateral activity of those who claim some relationship with a nonresident defendant cannot satisfy the requirement of contact with the forum State." Hanson v. Denckla, supra, at 253[]. ...

Because we find that petitioners have no "contacts, ties, or relations" with the State of Oklahoma, International Shoe Co. v. Washington, supra[], at 319[], the judgment of the Supreme Court of Oklahoma is

Reversed.

[Opinions of Justices MARSHALL (with whom Justice BLACKMUN joined) and BLACKMUN are omitted.]

Justice BRENNAN, dissenting.

... Because I believe that the Court reads *International Shoe* and its progeny too narrowly, and because I believe that the standards enunciated by those cases may already be obsolete as constitutional boundaries, I dissent. ...

The Court's opinions ... accord too little weight to the strength of the forum State's interest in the case and fail to explore whether there would be any actual inconvenience to the defendant. ...

... I would find that the forum State has an interest in permitting the litigation to go forward, the litigation is connected to the forum, the defendant is linked to the forum, and the burden of defending is not unreasonable. Accordingly, I would hold that it is neither unfair nor unreasonable to require these defendants to defend in the forum State. ...

… [T]he interest of the forum State and its connection to the litigation is strong. The automobile accident underlying the litigation occurred in Oklahoma. The plaintiffs were hospitalized in Oklahoma when they brought suit. Essential witnesses and evidence were in Oklahoma. [C] The State has a legitimate interest in enforcing its laws designed to keep its highway system safe, and the trial can proceed at least as efficiently in Oklahoma as anywhere else.

The petitioners are not unconnected with the forum. Although both sell automobiles within limited sales territories, each sold the automobile which in fact was driven to Oklahoma where it was involved in an accident.[fn] It may be true, as the Court suggests, that each sincerely intended to limit its commercial impact to the limited territory, and that each intended to accept the benefits and protection of the laws only of those States within the territory. But obviously these were unrealistic hopes that cannot be treated as an automatic constitutional shield.[fn]

An automobile simply is not a stationary item or one designed to be used in one place. An automobile is *intended* to be moved around. Someone in the business of selling large numbers of automobiles can hardly plead ignorance of their mobility or pretend that the automobiles stay put after they are sold. It is not merely that a dealer in automobiles foresees that they will move. [C] The dealer actually intends that the purchasers will use the automobiles to travel to distant States where the dealer does not directly "do business." The sale of an automobile does *purposefully* inject the vehicle into the stream of interstate commerce so that it can travel to distant States. See [c]; Hanson v. Denckla, 357 U.S. 235, 253[] (1958). …

The Court accepts that a State may exercise jurisdiction over a distributor which "serves" that State "indirectly" by "deliver[ing] its products into the stream of commerce with the expectation that they will be purchased by consumers in the forum State." [C] It is difficult to see why the Constitution should distinguish between a case involving goods which reach a distant State through a chain of distribution and a case involving goods which reach the same State because a consumer, using them as the dealer knew the customer would, took them there.[fn] In each case the seller purposefully injects the goods into the stream of commerce and those goods predictably are used in the forum State.[fn] …

It may be that affirmance of the judgments in these cases would approach the outer limits of *International Shoe's* jurisdictional principle. But that principle, with its almost exclusive focus on the rights of defendants, may be outdated. …

The conclusion I draw is that constitutional concepts of fairness no longer require the extreme concern for defendants that was once necessary. …

… Accordingly, I would hold that the Constitution should not shield the defendants from appearing and defending in the plaintiffs' chosen fora.

INQUIRY

Forum Shopping. Why does personal jurisdiction matter in a case like *World-Wide Volkswagen,* knowing that the plaintiff will have some court in which to try the case if not the court that the plaintiff chooses? The *World-Wide Volkswagen* plaintiffs, one of whom the allegedly defective vehicle had trapped long enough to burn 48% of her body, produce severe scarring, and require amputation of most of her fingers, chose an Oklahoma state court in the county where the accident took place. After the Supreme Court ruled that the state court had no jurisdiction over the New York defendants, the remaining defendants removed the case from Oklahoma state court to an Oklahoma federal district court—where the plaintiffs lost, recovering nothing for their severe, permanent, and disfiguring injuries. *See* Charles W. Adams, World-Wide Volkswagen v. Woodson—*The Rest of the Story*, 72 NEB. L.REV. 1122 (1993). (Chapter IV addresses removal.) Practitioners tend to study and be aware of how differing demographics of state and federal jury pools in different regions may potentially influence case outcomes. Is choosing a jurisdiction based on a potentially more favorable outcome (a practice known as forum shopping) a legitimate plaintiffs' strategy? Courts addressing questions of jurisdiction caution plaintiffs and their lawyers against forum shopping. Yet by challenging jurisdiction, the defendant may also be making a strategic judgment that there is a more favorable forum. Is a *defendant's* seeking a more favorable forum a legitimate strategic judgment—as legitimate, for instance, as the convenience or burden on the parties and state sovereignty? There are other reasons why parties and their lawyers might want a case tried here or there, including whether the lawyers have the license to practice in the state or would have to refer away the case. Next, consider two Supreme Court cases, decided just four years after *World-Wide Volkswagen*, each of which reached different conclusions whether there was personal jurisdiction even while applying *World-Wide Volkswagen*.

Burger King Corp. v. Rudzewicz,

United States Supreme Court
471 U.S. 462 (1985)

JUSTICE BRENNAN delivered the opinion of the Court. ...

I

A

Burgr King Corporation is a Florida corporation whose principal offices are in Miami. It is one of the world's largest restaurant organizations, with over 3,000 outlets in the 50 States, the Commonwealth of Puerto Rico, and 8 foreign nations. Burger King conducts approximately 80% of its business through a franchise operation... .

The instant litigation grows out of Burger King's termination of one of its franchisees... . The appellee John Rudzewicz, a Michigan citizen and resident, is the senior partner in a Detroit accounting firm. In 1978, he was approached by Brian MacShara, the son of a business acquaintance, who suggested that they jointly apply to Burger King for a franchise in the Detroit area. ...

Rudzewicz and MacShara jointly applied for a franchise to Burger King's Birmingham, Michigan, district office in the autumn of 1978. Their application was forwarded to Burger King's Miami headquarters, which entered into a preliminary agreement with them in February 1979. During the ensuing four months it was agreed that Rudzewicz and MacShara would assume operation of an existing facility in Drayton Plains, Michigan. ... Even before the final agreements were signed, however, the parties began to disagree over site-development fees, building design, computation of monthly rent, and whether the franchisees would be able to assign their liabilities to a corporation they had formed.[fn] During these disputes Rudzewicz and MacShara negotiated both with the Birmingham district office and with the Miami headquarters.[fn] With some misgivings, Rudzewicz and MacShara finally obtained limited concessions from the Miami headquarters,[fn] signed the final agreements, and commenced operations in June 1979. By signing the final agreements, Rudzewicz obligated himself personally to payments exceeding $1 million over the 20-year franchise relationship.

... Rudzewicz and MacShara soon fell far behind in their monthly payments to Miami. Headquarters sent notices of default, and an extended period of negotiations began among the franchisees, the Birmingham district office, and the Miami headquarters. After several Burger King officials in Miami had engaged in prolonged but ultimately unsuccessful negotiations with the franchisees by mail and by telephone,[fn] headquarters terminated the franchise and ordered Rudzewicz and MacShara to vacate the premises. They refused and continued to occupy and operate the facility as a Burger King restaurant.

B

Burger King commenced the instant action in the United States District Court for the Southern District of Florida in May 1981... . Burger King sought damages, injunctive relief, and costs and attorney's fees. Rudzewicz and MacShara entered special appearances and argued, *inter alia,* that because they were Michigan residents and because Burger King's claim did not "arise" within the Southern District of Florida, the District Court lacked personal jurisdiction over them. The District Court denied their motions[, tried the case, entered judgment against Rudzewicz and MacShara for $228,875 in contract damages, and ordered them to relinquish the premises]. ...

Rudzewicz appealed to the Court of Appeals for the Eleventh Circuit. A divided panel of that Circuit reversed the judgment, concluding that the District Court could not properly exercise personal jurisdiction over Rudzewicz... . [Burger King appealed to the Supreme Court which treated its appeal] as a petition for a writ of certiorari, [c,] [concluding to] grant the petition and now reverse.

II

A

... We have noted several reasons why a forum legitimately may exercise personal jurisdiction over a nonresident who "purposefully directs" his activities toward forum residents. A State generally has a "manifest interest" in providing its residents with a convenient forum for redressing injuries inflicted by out-of-state actors. [Cc] Moreover, where individuals "purposefully derive benefit" from their interstate activities, [c], it may well be unfair to allow them to escape having to account in other States for consequences that arise proximately from such activities; the Due Process Clause may not readily be wielded as a territorial shield to avoid interstate obligations that have been voluntarily assumed. And because "modern transportation and communications have made it much less burdensome for a party sued to defend himself in a State where he engages in economic activity," it usually will not be unfair to subject him to the burdens of litigating in another forum for disputes relating to such activity. McGee v. International Life Insurance Co., 355 U.S.[220], 223[(1957)].

Notwithstanding these considerations, the constitutional touchstone remains whether the defendant purposefully established "minimum contacts" in the forum State. International Shoe Co. v. Washington, 326 U.S.[310], 316[(1945)]. Although it has been argued that foreseeability of causing *injury* in another State should be sufficient to establish such contacts there when policy considerations so require,[fn] the Court has consistently held that this kind of foreseeability is not a "sufficient benchmark" for exercising personal jurisdiction. World-Wide Volkswagen Corp. v. Woodson, 444 U.S.[286], 295[(1980)]. Instead, "the foreseeability that is critical to due process analysis ... is that the defendant's conduct and connection with the forum State are such that he should reasonably anticipate being haled into court there." Id., at 297[]. In defining when it is that a potential defendant should "reasonably anticipate" out-of-state litigation, the Court frequently has drawn from the reasoning of Hanson v. Denckla, 357 U.S. 235, 253[] (1958). …

This "purposeful availment" requirement ensures that a defendant will not be haled into a jurisdiction solely as a result of "random," "fortuitous," or "attenuated" contacts, [cc], or of the "unilateral activity of another party or a third person," [c]. Jurisdiction is proper, however, where the contacts proximately result from actions by the defendant *himself* that create a "substantial connection" with the forum State. [Cc] Thus where the defendant "deliberately" has engaged in significant activities within a State, [c], or has created "continuing obligations" between himself and residents of the forum, [c], he manifestly has availed himself of the privilege of conducting business there, and because his activities are shielded by "the benefits and protections" of the forum's laws it is presumptively not unreasonable to require him to submit to the burdens of litigation in that forum as well. …

Once it has been decided that a defendant purposefully established minimum contacts within the forum State, these contacts may be considered in light of other factors to determine whether the assertion of personal jurisdiction would comport with "fair play and substantial justice." International Shoe Co. v. Washington, [supra], at 320[]. Thus courts in "appropriate case[s]" may evaluate "the burden on the defendant," "the forum State's interest in adjudicating the dispute," "the plaintiff's interest in obtaining convenient and effective relief," "the interstate judicial system's interest in obtaining the most efficient resolution of controversies," and the "shared interest of the several States in furthering fundamental substantive social policies." World-Wide Volkswagen Corp. v. Woodson, supra,[] at 292[]. These considerations sometimes serve to establish the reasonableness of jurisdiction upon a lesser showing of minimum contacts than would otherwise be required. [Cc] On the other hand, where a defendant who purposefully has directed his activities at forum residents seeks to defeat jurisdiction, he must present a compelling case that the presence of some other considerations would render jurisdiction unreasonable. ...

B …

Applying these principles to the case at hand, we believe there is substantial record evidence supporting the District Court's conclusion that the assertion of personal jurisdiction over Rudzewicz in Florida for the alleged breach of his franchise agreement did not offend due process. …

In this case, no physical ties to Florida can be attributed to Rudzewicz other than MacShara's brief training course in Miami. Rudzewicz did not maintain offices in Florida and, for all that appears from the record, has never even visited there. Yet this franchise dispute grew directly out of "a contract which had a *substantial* connection with that State." McGee v. International Life Insurance Co., [supra], at 223[] (emphasis added). Eschewing the option of operating an independent local enterprise, Rudzewicz deliberately "reach[ed] out beyond" Michigan and negotiated with a Florida corporation for the purchase of a long-term franchise and the manifold benefits that would derive from affiliation with a nationwide organization. [C] Upon approval, he entered into a carefully structured 20-year relationship that envisioned continuing and wide-reaching contacts with Burger King in Florida. In light of Rudzewicz' voluntary acceptance of the long-term and exacting regulation of his business from Burger King's Miami headquarters, the "quality and nature" of his relationship to the company in Florida can in no sense be viewed as "random," "fortuitous," or "attenuated." Hanson v. Denckla, [supra], at 253[]; [c]; World-Wide Volkswagen Corp. v. Woodson, [supra], at 299[]. Rudzewicz' refusal to make the contractually required payments in Miami, and his continued use of Burger King's trademarks and confidential business information after his termination, caused foreseeable injuries to the corporation in Florida. For these reasons it was, at the very least, presumptively reasonable for Rudzewicz to be called to account there for such injuries. ...

... [W]e believe the Court of Appeals gave insufficient weight to provisions in the various franchise documents providing that all disputes would be governed by Florida law. ... The Court of Appeals reasoned that choice-of-law provisions are irrelevant to the question of personal jurisdiction, relying on *Hanson v. Denckla* for the proposition that "the center of gravity for choice-of-law purposes does not necessarily confer the sovereign prerogative to assert jurisdiction." [Cc] This reasoning misperceives the import of the quoted proposition. The Court in *Hanson* and subsequent cases has emphasized that choice-of-law *analysis*—which focuses on all elements of a transaction, and not simply on the defendant's conduct—is distinct from minimum-contacts jurisdictional analysis-which focuses at the threshold solely on the defendant's purposeful connection to the forum. Nothing in our cases, however, suggests that a choice-of-law *provision* should be ignored in considering whether a defendant has "purposefully invoked the benefits and protections of a State's laws" for jurisdictional purposes. Although such a provision standing alone would be insufficient to confer jurisdiction, we believe that, when combined with the 20-year interdependent relationship Rudzewicz established with Burger King's Miami headquarters, it reinforced his deliberate affiliation with the forum State and the reasonable foreseeability of possible litigation there. ...

III

Notwithstanding these considerations, the Court of Appeals apparently believed that it was necessary to reject jurisdiction in this case as a prophylactic measure, reasoning that an affirmance of the District Court's judgment would result in the exercise of jurisdiction over "out-of-state consumers to collect payments due on modest personal purchases" and would "sow the seeds of default judgments against franchisees owing smaller debts." [C] We share the Court of

Appeals' broader concerns and therefore reject any talismanic jurisdictional formulas; "the facts of each case must [always] be weighed" in determining whether personal jurisdiction would comport with "fair play and substantial justice." [C] ... We also have emphasized that jurisdiction may not be grounded on a contract whose terms have been obtained through "fraud, undue influence, or overweening bargaining power" and whose application would render litigation "so gravely difficult and inconvenient that [a party] will for all practical purposes be deprived of his day in court." [Cc] ...

... [T]hese dangers are not present in the instant case. Because Rudzewicz established a substantial and continuing relationship with Burger King's Miami headquarters, received fair notice from the contract documents and the course of dealing that he might be subject to suit in Florida, and has failed to demonstrate how jurisdiction in that forum would otherwise be fundamentally unfair, we conclude that the District Court's exercise of jurisdiction ... did not offend due process. The judgment of the Court of Appeals is accordingly reversed, and the case is remanded for further proceedings consistent with this opinion.

It is so ordered.

Justice POWELL took no part in the consideration or decision of this case.

Justice STEVENS, with whom Justice WHITE joins, dissenting.

In my opinion there is a significant element of unfairness in requiring a franchisee to defend a case of this kind in the forum chosen by the franchisor. It is undisputed that appellee maintained no place of business in Florida, that he had no employees in that State, and that he was not licensed to do business there. Appellee did not prepare his French fries, shakes, and hamburgers in Michigan, and then deliver them into the stream of commerce "with the expectation that they [would] be purchased by consumers in" Florida. [C] To the contrary, appellee did business only in Michigan, his business, property, and payroll taxes were payable in that State, and he sold all of his products there.

Throughout the business relationship, appellee's principal contacts with appellant were with its Michigan office. Notwithstanding its disclaimer, [c], the Court seems ultimately to rely on nothing more than standard boilerplate language contained in various documents, [c], to establish that appellee "'purposefully availed himself of the benefits and protections of Florida's laws.'" [C]. Such superficial analysis creates a potential for unfairness not only in negotiations between franchisors and their franchisees but, more significantly, in the resolution of the disputes that inevitably arise from time to time in such relationships.

Judge Vance's opinion for the Court of Appeals for the Eleventh Circuit adequately explains why I would affirm the judgment of that court. I particularly find the following more persuasive than what this Court has written today:

> "Nothing in the course of negotiations gave Rudzewicz reason to anticipate a Burger King suit outside of Michigan. The only face-to-face or even oral contact Rudzewicz had with Burger King throughout months of protracted negotiations was with representatives of the Michigan office. ...
>
> "We discern a characteristic disparity of bargaining power in the facts of this case. There is no indication that Rudzewicz had any latitude to negotiate a reduced rent or franchise fee in exchange for the added risk of suit in

Florida. He signed a standard form contract whose terms were non-negotiable and which appeared in some respects to vary from the more favorable terms agreed to in earlier discussions. In fact, the final contract required a minimum monthly rent computed on a base far in excess of that discussed in oral negotiations. Burger King resisted price concessions, only to sue Rudzewicz far from home. In doing so, it severely impaired his ability to call Michigan witnesses who might be essential to his defense and counterclaim.

"... Jurisdiction under these circumstances would offend the fundamental fairness which is the touchstone of due process." [C]

Accordingly, I respectfully dissent.

Asahi Metal Industry Co. v. Superior Court,

United States Supreme Court
480 U.S. 102 (1987)

Justice O'CONNOR announced the judgment of the Court and delivered the opinion for a unanimous Court with respect to Part I, the opinion of the Court with respect to Part II-B, in which Chief Justice REHNQUIST and JUSTICES BRENNAN, WHITE, MARSHALL, BLACKMUN, POWELL, and STEVENS, joined, and an opinion with respect to Parts II-A and III, in which Chief Justice REHNQUIST and Justices POWELL and SCALIA joined. Justice BRENNAN filed an opinion concurring in part and concurring in the judgment, in which Justices WHITE, MARSHALL, and BLACKMUN joined[]. Justice STEVENS filed an opinion concurring in part and concurring in the judgment, in which Justices WHITE and BLACMUN joined[].

This case presents the question whether the mere awareness on the part of a foreign defendant that the components it manufactured, sold, and delivered outside the United States would reach the forum State in the stream of commerce constitutes "minimum contacts" between the defendant and the forum State such that the exercise of jurisdiction "does not offend 'traditional notions of fair play and substantial justice.'" International Shoe Co. v. Washington, 326 U.S. 310, 316[] (1945), quoting Milliken v. Meyer, 311 U.S. 457, 463[] (1940).

I

On September 23, 1978, on Interstate Highway 80 in Solano County, California, Gary Zurcher lost control of his Honda motorcycle and collided with a tractor. Zurcher was severely injured, and his passenger and wife, Ruth Ann Moreno, was killed. In September 1979, Zurcher filed a product liability action in the Superior Court of the State of California... . Zurcher alleged that the 1978 accident was caused by a sudden loss of air and an explosion in the rear tire of the motorcycle, and alleged that the motorcycle tire, tube, and sealant were defective. Zurcher's complaint named, *inter alia,* Cheng Shin Rubber Industrial Co., Ltd. (Cheng Shin), the Taiwanese manufacturer of the tube. Cheng Shin in turn filed a cross-complaint seeking indemnification from its codefendants and from petitioner, Asahi Metal Industry Co., Ltd. (Asahi), the manufacturer of the tube's valve assembly. Zurcher's claims against Cheng Shin and the other defendants were eventually settled and dismissed, leaving only Cheng Shin's indemnity action against Asahi.

... Asahi moved to quash Cheng Shin's service of summons, arguing the State could not exert jurisdiction over it consistent with the Due Process Clause of the Fourteenth Amendment.

... Asahi is a Japanese corporation. It manufactures tire valve assemblies in Japan and sells the assemblies to Cheng Shin, and to several other tire manufacturers, for use as components in finished tire tubes. Asahi's sales to Cheng Shin took place in Taiwan. The shipments from Asahi to Cheng Shin were sent from Japan to Taiwan. Cheng Shin bought and incorporated into its tire tubes 150,000 Asahi valve assemblies in 1978; 500,000 in 1979; 500,000 in 1980; 100,000 in 1981; and 100,000 in 1982. Sales to Cheng Shin accounted for 1.24 percent of Asahi's income in 1981 and 0.44 percent in 1982. Cheng Shin alleged that approximately 20 percent of its sales in the United States are in California. Cheng Shin purchases valve assemblies from other suppliers as well, and sells finished tubes throughout the world. ...

... An affidavit of a manager of Cheng Shin whose duties included the purchasing of component parts stated: "'In discussions with Asahi regarding the purchase of valve stem assemblies the fact that my Company sells tubes throughout the world and specifically the United States has been discussed. I am informed and believe that Asahi was fully aware that valve stem assemblies sold to my Company and to others would end up throughout the United States and in California.'" [C] An affidavit of the president of Asahi, on the other hand, declared that Asahi "'has never contemplated that its limited sales of tire valves to Cheng Shin in Taiwan would subject it to lawsuits in California.'" [C] The record does not include any contract between Cheng Shin and Asahi. [C]

Primarily on the basis of the above information, the Superior Court denied the motion to quash summons, stating: "Asahi obviously does business on an international scale. It is not unreasonable that they defend claims of defect in their product on an international scale." [C] ...

The Court of Appeal of the State of California issued a peremptory writ of mandate commanding the Superior Court to quash service of summons. ...

The Supreme Court of the State of California reversed and discharged the writ issued by the Court of Appeal. ...

We granted certiorari, [c], and now reverse.

II

A

The Due Process Clause of the Fourteenth Amendment limits the power of a state court to exert personal jurisdiction over a nonresident defendant. "[T]he constitutional touchstone" of the determination whether an exercise of personal jurisdiction comports with due process "remains whether the defendant purposefully established 'minimum contacts' in the forum State." Burger King Corp. v. Rudzewicz, 471 U.S. 462, 474[] (1985), quoting International Shoe Co. v. Washington, 326 U.S.[310,] 316[(1945)]. Most recently we have reaffirmed the oft-quoted reasoning of Hanson v. Denckla, 357 U.S. 235, 253[] (1958), that minimum contacts must have a basis in "some act by which the defendant purposefully avails itself of the privilege of conducting activities within the forum State, thus invoking the benefits and protections of its laws." Burger King, [supra] at 475[]. "Jurisdiction is proper ... where the contacts proximately result from actions by the defendant *himself* that create a 'substantial connection' with the forum State." Ibid., quoting McGee v. International Life Insurance Co., 355 U.S. 220, 223[] (1957) (emphasis in original).

Applying the principle that minimum contacts must be based on an act of the defendant, the Court in World-Wide Volkswagen Corp. v. Woodson, 444 U.S. 286[] (1980), rejected the assertion that a *consumer's* unilateral act of bringing the defendant's product into the forum State was a sufficient constitutional basis for personal jurisdiction over the defendant. ...

... Since *World-Wide Volkswagen,* lower courts have been confronted with cases in which the defendant acted by placing a product in the stream of commerce, and the stream eventually swept defendant's product into the forum State, but the defendant did nothing else to purposefully avail itself of the market in the forum State. Some courts have understood the Due Process Clause, as interpreted in *World-Wide Volkswagen,* to allow an exercise of personal jurisdiction to be based on no more than the defendant's act of placing the product in the stream of commerce. Other courts have understood the Due Process Clause and the above-quoted language in *World-Wide Volkswagen* to require the action of the defendant to be more purposefully directed at the forum State than the mere act of placing a product in the stream of commerce.

The reasoning of the Supreme Court of California in the present case illustrates the former interpretation of *World-Wide Volkswagen.* The Supreme Court of California held that, because the stream of commerce eventually brought some valves Asahi sold Cheng Shin into California, Asahi's awareness that its valves would be sold in California was sufficient to permit California to exercise jurisdiction over Asahi consistent with the requirements of the Due Process Clause. The Supreme Court of California's position was consistent with those courts that have held that mere foreseeability or awareness was a constitutionally sufficient basis for personal jurisdiction if the defendant's product made its way into the forum State while still in the stream of commerce. [Cc]

Other courts, however, have understood the Due Process Clause to require something more than that the defendant was aware of its product's entry into the forum State through the stream of commerce in order for the State to exert jurisdiction over the defendant. ...

We now find this latter position to be consonant with the requirements of due process. The "substantial connection," Burger King, [supra], at 475[]; McGee, [supra], at 223[], between the defendant and the forum State necessary for a finding of minimum contacts must come about by *an action of the defendant purposefully directed toward the forum State.* Burger King, supra, [] at 476[]; [c]. The placement of a product into the stream of commerce, without more, is not an act of the defendant purposefully directed toward the forum State. Additional conduct of the defendant may indicate an intent or purpose to serve the market in the forum State, for example, designing the product for the market in the forum State, advertising in the forum State, establishing channels for providing regular advice to customers in the forum State, or marketing the product through a distributor who has agreed to serve as the sales agent in the forum State. But a defendant's awareness that the stream of commerce may or will sweep the product into the forum State does not convert the mere act of placing the product into the stream into an act purposefully directed toward the forum State.

... [R]espondents have not demonstrated any action by Asahi to purposefully avail itself of the California market. Asahi does not do business in California. It has no office, agents, employees, or property in California. It does not advertise or otherwise solicit business in California. It did not create, control, or employ the distribution system that brought its valves to California. [C] There is no evidence that Asahi designed its product in anticipation of sales in California. [C] On the basis of these facts, the exertion of personal jurisdiction over Asahi by the Superior Court of California[fn] exceeds the limits of due process.

B

... We have previously explained that the determination of the reasonableness of the exercise of jurisdiction in each case will depend on an evaluation of several factors. A court must consider the burden on the defendant, the interests of the forum State, and the plaintiff's interest in obtaining relief. It must also weigh in its determination "the interstate judicial system's interest in obtaining the most efficient resolution of controversies; and the shared interest of the several States in furthering fundamental substantive social policies." World-Wide Volkswagen, [supra], at 292[].

A consideration of these factors in the present case clearly reveals the unreasonableness of the assertion of jurisdiction over Asahi, even apart from the question of the placement of goods in the stream of commerce.

Certainly the burden on the defendant in this case is severe. Asahi has been commanded by the Supreme Court of California not only to traverse the distance between Asahi's headquarters in Japan and the Superior Court of California in and for the County of Solano, but also to submit its dispute with Cheng Shin to a foreign nation's judicial system. The unique burdens placed upon one who must defend oneself in a foreign legal system should have significant weight in assessing the reasonableness of stretching the long arm of personal jurisdiction over national borders.

When minimum contacts have been established, often the interests of the plaintiff and the forum in the exercise of jurisdiction will justify even the serious burdens placed on the alien defendant. In the present case, however, the interests of the plaintiff and the forum in California's assertion of jurisdiction over Asahi are slight. All that remains is a claim for indemnification asserted by Cheng Shin, a Taiwanese corporation, against Asahi. The transaction on which the indemnification claim is based took place in Taiwan; Asahi's components were shipped from Japan to Taiwan. Cheng Shin has not demonstrated that it is more convenient for it to litigate its indemnification claim against Asahi in California rather than in Taiwan or Japan.

Because the plaintiff is not a California resident, California's legitimate interests in the dispute have considerably diminished. ... The dispute between Cheng Shin and Asahi is primarily about indemnification rather than safety standards. ... The possibility of being haled into a California court as a result of an accident involving Asahi's components undoubtedly creates an additional deterrent to the manufacture of unsafe components; however, similar pressures will be placed on Asahi by the purchasers of its components as long as those who use Asahi components in their final products, and sell those products in California, are subject to the application of California tort law.

World-Wide Volkswagen also admonished courts to take into consideration the interests of the "several States," in addition to the forum State, in the efficient judicial resolution of the dispute and the advancement of substantive policies. In the present case, this advice calls for a court to consider the procedural and substantive policies of other *nations* whose interests are affected by the assertion of jurisdiction by the California court. ... "Great care and reserve should be exercised when extending our notions of personal jurisdiction into the international field." United States v. First National City Bank, 379 U.S. 378, 404[] (1965) (Harlan, J., dissenting). [C]

Considering the international context, the heavy burden on the alien defendant, and the slight interests of the plaintiff and the forum State, the exercise of personal jurisdiction by a California court over Asahi in this instance would be unreasonable and unfair.

III

Because the facts of this case do not establish minimum contacts such that the exercise of personal jurisdiction is consistent with fair play and substantial justice, the judgment of the Supreme Court of California is reversed, and the case is remanded for further proceedings not inconsistent with this opinion.

It is so ordered.

Justice BRENNAN, with whom Justice WHITE, Justice MARSHALL, and Justice BLACKMUN join, concurring in part and concurring in the judgment.

I do not agree with the interpretation in Part II-A of the stream-of-commerce theory, nor with the conclusion that Asahi did not "purposely avail itself of the California market." *Ante,* at 1034. I do agree, however, with the Court's conclusion in Part II-B that the exercise of personal jurisdiction over Asahi in this case would not comport with "fair play and substantial justice," International Shoe Co. v. Washington, 326 U.S. 310, 320[] (1945). This is one of those rare cases in which "minimum requirements inherent in the concept of 'fair play and substantial justice' ... defeat the reasonableness of jurisdiction even [though] the defendant has purposefully engaged in forum activities." Burger King Corp. v. Rudzewicz, 471 U.S. 462, 477-478[] (1985). I therefore join Parts I and II-B of the Court's opinion, and write separately to explain my disagreement with Part II-A. ...

The endorsement in Part II-A of what appears to be the minority view among Federal Courts of Appeals[fn] represents a marked retreat from the analysis in World-Wide Volkswagen v. Woodson, 444 U.S. 286[] (1980). ...

The Court in *World-Wide Volkswagen* ... took great care to distinguish "between a case involving goods which reach a distant State through a chain of distribution and a case involving goods which reach the same State because a consumer ... took them there." *Id.,* at 306-307[] (BRENNAN, J., dissenting).[fn] ...

In this case, the facts found by the California Supreme Court support its finding of minimum contacts. The court found that "[a]lthough Asahi did not design or control the system of distribution that carried its valve assemblies into California, Asahi was aware of the distribution system's operation, and it knew that it would benefit economically from the sale in California of products incorporating its components." [C] Accordingly, I cannot join the determination in Part II-A that Asahi's regular and extensive sales of component parts to a manufacturer it knew was making regular sales of the final product in California is insufficient to establish minimum contacts with California.

Justice STEVENS, with whom Justice WHITE and Justice BLACKMUN join, concurring in part and concurring in the judgment.

The judgment of the Supreme Court of California should be reversed for the reasons stated in Part II-B of the Court's opinion. While I join Parts I and II-B, I do not join Part II-A for two reasons. First, it is not necessary to the Court's decision. An examination of minimum contacts is not always necessary to determine whether a state court's assertion of personal jurisdiction is constitutional. See Burger King Corp. v. Rudzewicz, 471 U.S. 462, 476-478[] (1985). Part II-B establishes, after considering the factors set forth in World-Wide Volkswagen Corp. v. Woodson, 444 U.S. 286, 292[] (1980), that California's exercise of jurisdiction over Asahi in this case would be "unreasonable and unfair." [C] This finding alone requires reversal; this case fits within the rule that "minimum requirements inherent in the concept of 'fair play and substantial justice' may defeat the reasonableness of jurisdiction even if the defendant has purposefully engaged in forum activities." Burger King,[supra] at 477-478[] (quoting International Shoe Co. v. Washington, 326 U.S. 310, 320[] (1945)). Accordingly, I see no reason in this case for the plurality to articulate "purposeful direction" or any other test as the nexus between an act of a defendant and the forum State that is necessary to establish minimum contacts.

Second, even assuming that the test ought to be formulated here, Part II-A misapplies it to the facts of this case. The plurality seems to assume that an unwavering line can be drawn between "mere awareness" that a component will find its way into the forum State and "purposeful availment" of the forum's market. [C] Over the course of its dealings with Cheng Shin, Asahi has arguably engaged in a higher quantum of conduct than "[t]he placement of a product into the stream of commerce, without more...." [C] Whether or not this conduct rises to the level of purposeful availment requires a constitutional determination that is affected by the volume, the value, and the hazardous character of the components. In most circumstances I would be inclined to conclude that a regular course of dealing that results in deliveries of over 100,000 units annually over a period of several years would constitute "purposeful availment" even though the item delivered to the forum State was a standard product marketed throughout the world.

INQUIRY

Factors. What controlling law should a lawyer deduce from the above opinions? The only part of the above *Asahi Metal Industry Co. v. Superior Ct.* opinion that garnered a majority of the Supreme Court justices, other than Justice O'Connor's Part I stating the case and announcing the reversal, is Part II.B. of Justice O'Connor's opinion. Part II.B. set forth five factors that courts must consider to determine the reasonableness of the exercise of personal jurisdiction: (1) the plaintiff's interest in relief; (2) the defendant's burden; (3) the forum state's interests; (4) efficient resolution among the states; and (5) shared state interests. Can you give examples of each?

Effects. *World-Wide Volkswagen* emphasized that the defendant must purposefully avail itself of the benefits of contacts, ties, and relations with the forum state. *Burger King Corp. v Rudzewicz* indicates that substantial continuing contacts are enough. *Asahi Metal Industry v. Superior Court* indicates that substantial justice and fair play remain important considerations. What if a defendant does little or nothing in the state but nonetheless causes a harmful effect there? The Supreme Court in Calder v. Jones, 465 U.S. 783 (1984), upheld a California state court's personal jurisdiction over the defendant Florida editor and publisher of the tabloid National Enquirer based on the allegedly defamatory *effects* of the Enquirer's publication in California. The Court noted that although the editor and publisher had no direct contact with California regarding the publication, the article's focal point and effects were in California where the Enquirer aimed much of its readership and circulation. Lower courts have differed over *Calder's* effects test. Some find effects alone to be sufficient, such as when a tort victim suffers injury in the forum state. *See* Janmark, Inc. v. Reidy, 132 F.3d 1200, 1202 (7th Cir. 1997). Other lower courts, probably more consistent with *Calder's* facts, require that the defendant have aimed the harmful conduct into the forum state. *See* Fielding v. Hubert Burda Media, Inc., 415 F.3d 419, 425 (5th Cir. 2005); Schwarzenegger v. Fred Martin Motor Co., 374 F.3d 797, 803 (9th Cir. 2004). It may be best to regard the *Calder* effects test as a subsidiary test most appropriate for defamation and other torts cases. In the following section on contemporary jurisdiction issues, see how *Calder's* effects test may have broader application.

Knowledge

It is a fundamental skill of lawyers to be able to read a series of cases to synthesize from them a comprehensive understanding of the law on the issue at hand. Lawyers identify each case with its core principle, assemble those principles into a concept map, and then use the concept map to recall not only the principles but also each case and its facts. For example, the series of cases you just read beginning with *International Shoe* outline the law of personal jurisdiction. Its concept map might look like the following. Personal jurisdiction over a defendant requires *minimum contacts* (*International Shoe*) determined by *balancing interests* (*McGee*), considering *state sovereignty* (*Hanson*), limiting jurisdiction where the defendant *sought no benefit* (*Kulko*) and engaged in no *purposeful acts* (*World-Wide Volkswagen*) toward the jurisdiction, or for *substantial justice and fair play* (*Asahi Metal Industry*), but finding jurisdiction where the defendant had *substantial continuing contact* (*Burger King*) with or *aimed effects into* (*Calder*) the forum state.

2. Current Challenges

Just as easier means of transportation expanded the jurisdictional reach of courts while creating jurisdiction issues, so, too, have expanded communications. Some of the above cases (*Burger King Corp. v. Rudzewicz*, for instance) determined jurisdiction from the defendant's mail, telephone, and fax transmissions into the forum state. Those direct communications can readily demonstrate purposeful availment, substantial continuing relations, and minimum contacts. Internet websites present a different challenge for determining personal jurisdiction. Websites the creators intend to be primarily or solely local or regional are instead available worldwide. A website or post intended for one audience may reach and affect another audience in a location and manner that the author did not anticipate. In other words, it now pretty clearly appears that formulations based on *Calder's* expressly aimed effects and *World-Wide Volkswagen's* purposeful availment remain the reliable tests. See if you agree, based on the following two cases.

Young v. New Haven Advocate,

United States Court of Appeals for the Fourth Circuit
315 F.3d 256 (2002)

MICHAEL, Circuit Judge.

The question in this appeal is whether two Connecticut newspapers and certain of their staff (sometimes, the "newspaper defendants") subjected themselves to personal jurisdiction in Virginia by posting on the Internet news articles that, in the context of discussing the State of Connecticut's policy of housing its prisoners in Virginia institutions, allegedly defamed the warden of a Virginia prison. Our recent decision in ALS Scan, Inc. v. Digital Service Consultants, Inc., 293 F.3d 707 (4th Cir.2002), supplies the standard for determining a court's authority to exercise personal jurisdiction over an out-of-state person who places information on the Internet. Applying that standard, we hold that a court in Virginia cannot constitutionally exercise jurisdiction over the Connecticut-based newspaper defendants because they did not manifest an intent to aim their websites or the posted articles at a Virginia audience. Accordingly, we reverse the district court's order denying the defendants' motion to dismiss for lack of personal jurisdiction.

I.

Sometime in the late 1990s the State of Connecticut was faced with substantial overcrowding in its maximum security prisons. To alleviate the problem, Connecticut contracted with the Commonwealth of Virginia to house Connecticut prisoners in Virginia's correctional facilities. Beginning in late 1999 Connecticut transferred about 500 prisoners, mostly African-American and Hispanic, to the Wallens Ridge State Prison, a "supermax" facility in Big Stone Gap, Virginia. The plaintiff, Stanley Young, is the warden at Wallens Ridge. Connecticut's arrangement to incarcerate a sizeable number of its offenders in Virginia prisons provoked considerable public debate in Connecticut. Several Connecticut legislators openly criticized the policy, and there were demonstrations against it at the state capitol in Hartford.

Connecticut newspapers, including defendants the New Haven Advocate (the Advocate) and the Hartford Courant (the Courant), began reporting on the controversy. On March 30, 2000, the Advocate published a news article, written by one of its reporters, defendant Camille Jackson, about the transfer of Connecticut inmates to Wallens Ridge. The article discussed the allegedly harsh conditions at the Virginia prison and pointed out that the long trip to southwestern

Virginia made visits by prisoners' families difficult or impossible. In the middle of her lengthy article, Jackson mentioned a class action that inmates transferred from Connecticut had filed against Warden Young and the Connecticut Commissioner of Corrections. The inmates alleged a lack of proper hygiene and medical care and the denial of religious privileges at Wallens Ridge. Finally, a paragraph at the end of the article reported that a Connecticut state senator had expressed concern about the presence of Confederate Civil War memorabilia in Warden Young's office. At about the same time the Courant published three columns, written by defendant-reporter Amy Pagnozzi, questioning the practice of relocating Connecticut inmates to Virginia prisons. The columns reported on letters written home by inmates who alleged cruelty by prison guards. In one column Pagnozzi called Wallens Ridge a "cut-rate gulag." Warden Young was not mentioned in any of the Pagnozzi columns.

On May 12, 2000, Warden Young sued the two newspapers, their editors (Gail Thompson and Brian Toolan), and the two reporters for libel in a diversity action filed in the Western District of Virginia. He claimed that the newspapers' articles imply that he "is a racist who advocates racism" and that he "encourages abuse of inmates by the guards" at Wallens Ridge. Young alleged that the newspapers circulated the allegedly defamatory articles throughout the world by posting them on their Internet websites.

The newspaper defendants filed motions to dismiss the complaint under Federal Rule of Civil Procedure 12(b)(2) on the ground that the district court lacked personal jurisdiction over them. In support of the motions the editor and reporter from each newspaper provided declarations establishing the following undisputed facts. The Advocate is a free newspaper published once a week in New Haven, Connecticut. It is distributed in New Haven and the surrounding area, and some of its content is published on the Internet. The Advocate has a small number of subscribers, and none of them are in Virginia. The Courant is published daily in Hartford, Connecticut. The newspaper is distributed in and around Hartford, and some of its content is published on the Internet. When the articles in question were published, the Courant had eight mail subscribers in Virginia. Neither newspaper solicits subscriptions from Virginia residents. No one from either newspaper, not even the reporters, traveled to Virginia to work on the articles about Connecticut's prisoner transfer policy. The two reporters, Jackson of the Advocate and Pagnozzi of the Courant, made a few telephone calls into Virginia to gather some information for the articles. Both interviewed by telephone a spokesman for the Virginia Department of Corrections. All other interviews were done with people located in Connecticut. The two reporters wrote their articles in Connecticut. The individual defendants (the reporters and editors) do not have any traditional contacts with the Commonwealth of Virginia. They do not live in Virginia, solicit any business there, or have any assets or business relationships there. The newspapers do not have offices or employees in Virginia, and they do not regularly solicit or do business in Virginia. Finally, the newspapers do not derive any substantial revenue from goods used or services rendered in Virginia.

In responding to the declarations of the editors and reporters, Warden Young pointed out that the newspapers posted the allegedly defamatory articles on Internet websites that were accessible to Virginia residents. In addition, Young provided copies of assorted print-outs from the newspapers' websites. ...

The district court denied the newspaper defendants' motions to dismiss, concluding that it could exercise personal jurisdiction over them under Virginia's long-arm statute, [c], because "the defendants' Connecticut-based Internet activities constituted an act leading to an injury to the plaintiff in Virginia." The district court also held that the defendants' Internet activities were sufficient to satisfy the requirements of constitutional due process. With our permission the newspaper defendants are taking this interlocutory appeal. ...

II.

A.

... The question ... is whether the defendant has sufficient "minimum contacts with [the forum] such that the maintenance of the suit does not offend 'traditional notions of fair play and substantial justice.'" Int'l Shoe Co. v. Washington, 326 U.S. 310, 316[] (1945) (quoting Milliken v. Meyer, 311 U.S. 457, 463[] (1940)). A court may assume power over an out-of-state defendant either by a proper "finding [of] specific jurisdiction based on conduct connected to the suit or by [a proper] finding [of] general jurisdiction." ALS Scan, Inc. v. Digital Serv. Consultants, Inc., 293 F.3d 707, 711 (4th Cir. 2002). Warden Young argues only for specific jurisdiction, so we limit our discussion accordingly. When a defendant's contacts with the forum state "are also the basis for the suit, those contacts may establish specific jurisdiction." Id. at 712. In determining whether specific jurisdiction exists, we traditionally ask (1) whether the defendant purposefully availed itself of the privileges of conducting activities in the forum state, (2) whether the plaintiff's claim arises out of the defendant's forum-related activities, and (3) "whether the exercise of personal jurisdiction over the defendant would be constitutionally reasonable." Id. at 712. ...

B.

We turn to whether the district court can exercise specific jurisdiction over the newspaper defendants, namely, the two newspapers, the two editors, and the two reporters. To begin with, we can put aside the few Virginia contacts that are not Internet based because Warden Young does not rely on them. Thus, Young does not claim that the reporters' few telephone calls into Virginia or the Courant's eight Virginia subscribers are sufficient to establish personal jurisdiction over those defendants. Nor did the district court rely on these traditional contacts.

Warden Young argues that the district court has specific personal jurisdiction over the newspaper defendants (hereafter, the "newspapers") because of the following contacts between them and Virginia: (1) the newspapers, knowing that Young was a Virginia resident, intentionally discussed and defamed him in their articles, (2) the newspapers posted the articles on their websites, which were accessible in Virginia, and (3) the primary effects of the defamatory statements on Young's reputation were felt in Virginia. Young emphasizes that he is not arguing that jurisdiction is proper in any location where defamatory Internet content can be accessed, which would be anywhere in the world. Rather, Young argues that personal jurisdiction is proper in Virginia because the newspapers understood that their defamatory articles, which were available to Virginia residents on the Internet, would expose Young to public hatred, contempt, and ridicule in Virginia, where he lived and worked. As the district court put it, "[t]he defendants were all well aware of the fact that the plaintiff was employed as a warden within the Virginia correctional system and resided in Virginia," and they "also should have been aware that any harm suffered by Young from the circulation of these articles on the Internet would primarily occur in Virginia."

Young frames his argument in a way that makes one thing clear: if the newspapers' contacts with Virginia were sufficient to establish personal jurisdiction, those contacts arose solely from the newspapers' Internet-based activities. Recently, in *ALS Scan* we discussed the challenges presented in applying traditional jurisdictional principles to decide when "an out-of-state citizen, through electronic contacts, has conceptually 'entered' the State via the Internet for jurisdictional purposes." [C] There, we held that "specific jurisdiction in the Internet context may be based only on an out-of-state person's Internet activity directed at [the forum state] and causing injury that gives rise to a potential claim cognizable in [that state]." [C] We noted that this standard for determining specific jurisdiction based on Internet contacts is consistent with the one used by the Supreme Court in Calder v. Jones, 465 U.S. 783[] (1984). [C] *Calder,* though not an Internet case, has particular relevance here because it deals with personal jurisdiction in the context of a libel suit. ...

Warden Young argues that *Calder* requires a finding of jurisdiction in this case simply because the newspapers posted articles on their Internet websites that discussed the warden and his Virginia prison, and he would feel the effects of any libel in Virginia, where he lives and works. *Calder* does not sweep that broadly, as we have recognized. For example, in ESAB Group, Inc. v. Centricut, Inc., 126 F.3d 617, 625-26 (4th Cir.1997), we emphasized how important it is in light of *Calder* to look at whether the defendant has expressly aimed or directed its conduct toward the forum state. We said that "[a]lthough the place that the plaintiff feels the alleged injury is plainly relevant to the [jurisdictional] inquiry, it must ultimately be accompanied by the defendant's own [sufficient minimum] contacts with the state if jurisdiction ... is to be upheld." [C] We thus had no trouble in concluding in *ALS Scan* that application of *Calder* in the Internet context requires proof that the out-of-state defendant's Internet activity is expressly targeted at or directed to the forum state. [C] In *ALS Scan* we went on to adapt the traditional standard ... for establishing specific jurisdiction so that it makes sense in the Internet context. We "conclude[d] that a State may, consistent with due process, exercise judicial power over a person outside of the State when that person (1) directs electronic activity into the State, (2) with the manifested intent of engaging in business or other interactions within the State, and (3) that activity creates, in a person within the State, a potential cause of action cognizable in the State's courts." [C]

... We thus ask whether the newspapers manifested an intent to direct their website content-which included certain articles discussing conditions in a Virginia prison-to a Virginia audience. As we recognized in *ALS Scan,* "a person's act of placing information on the Internet" is not sufficient by itself to "subject[ ] that person to personal jurisdiction in each State in which the information is accessed." [C] Otherwise, a "person placing information on the Internet would be subject to personal jurisdiction in every State," and the traditional due process principles governing a State's jurisdiction over persons outside of its borders would be subverted. [Cc] Thus, the fact that the newspapers' websites could be accessed anywhere, including Virginia, does not by itself demonstrate that the newspapers were intentionally directing their website content to a Virginia audience. Something more than posting and accessibility is needed to "indicate that the [newspapers] purposefully (albeit electronically) directed [their] activity in a substantial way to the forum state," Virginia. Panavision Int'l, L.P. v. Toeppen, 141 F.3d 1316, 1321 (9th Cir.1998) (quotation omitted). The newspapers must, through the Internet postings, manifest an intent to target and focus on Virginia readers.

We therefore turn to the pages from the newspapers' websites that Warden Young placed in the record, and we examine their general thrust and content. The overall content of both websites is decidedly local, and neither newspaper's website contains advertisements aimed at a Virginia audience. For example, the website that distributes the Courant, ctnow.com, provides access to local (Connecticut) weather and traffic information and links to websites for the University of Connecticut and Connecticut state government. The Advocate's website features stories focusing on New Haven, such as one entitled "The Best of New Haven." In sum, it appears that these newspapers maintain their websites to serve local readers in Connecticut, to expand the reach of their papers within their local markets, and to provide their local markets with a place for classified ads. The websites are not designed to attract or serve a Virginia audience.

We also examine the specific articles Young complains about to determine whether they were posted on the Internet with the intent to target a Virginia audience. The articles included discussions about the allegedly harsh conditions at the Wallens Ridge prison, where Young was warden. One article mentioned Young by name and quoted a Connecticut state senator who reported that Young had Confederate Civil War memorabilia in his office. The focus of the articles, however, was the Connecticut prisoner transfer policy and its impact on the transferred prisoners and their families back home in Connecticut. The articles reported on and encouraged a public debate in Connecticut about whether the transfer policy was sound or practical for that state and its citizens. Connecticut, not Virginia, was the focal point of the articles. [C] …

The facts in this case establish that the newspapers' websites, as well as the articles in question, were aimed at a Connecticut audience. The newspapers did not post materials on the Internet with the manifest intent of targeting Virginia readers. Accordingly, the newspapers could not have "reasonably anticipate[d] being haled into court [in Virginia] to answer for the truth of the statements made in their article[s]." Calder, 465 U.S. at 790[] (quotation omitted). In sum, the newspapers do not have sufficient Internet contacts with Virginia to permit the district court to exercise specific jurisdiction over them.[fn]

We reverse the order of the district court denying the motions to dismiss for lack of personal jurisdiction made by the New Haven Advocate, Gail Thompson (its editor), and Camille Jackson (its reporter) and by the Hartford Courant, Brian Toolan (its editor), and Amy Pagnozzi (its reporter).

REVERSED.

Pebble Beach Co. v. Caddy,

United States Court of Appeals for the Ninth Circuit
453 F.3d 1151 (2006)

TROTT, Circuit Judge.

Pebble Beach Company ("Pebble Beach"), a golf course resort in California, appeals the dismissal for lack of jurisdiction of its complaint against Michael Caddy ("Caddy"), a small-business owner located in southern England. ... Because Caddy did not expressly aim his conduct at California or the United States, we hold that the district court determined correctly that it lacked personal jurisdiction. ... Thus, we affirm.

I

Pebble Beach is a well-known golf course and resort located in Monterey County, California. The golf resort has used "Pebble Beach" as its trade name for 50 years. Pebble Beach contends that the trade name has acquired secondary meaning in the United States and the United Kingdom. Pebble Beach operates a website located at *www.pebblebeach.com.*

Caddy, a dual citizen of the United States and the United Kingdom occupies and runs a three-room bed and breakfast, restaurant, and bar located in southern England. Caddy's business operation is located on a cliff overlooking the pebbly beaches of England's south shore, in a town called Barton-on-Sea. The name of Caddy's operation is "Pebble Beach," which, given its location, is no surprise. Caddy advertises his services, which do not include a golf course, at his website, *www.pebblebeach-uk.com.* Caddy's website includes general information about the accommodations he provides, including lodging rates in pounds sterling, a menu, and a wine list. The website is not interactive. Visitors to the website who have questions about Caddy's services may fill out an on-line inquiry form. However, the website does not have a reservation system, nor does it allow potential guests to book rooms or pay for services on-line.

Except for a brief time when Caddy worked at a restaurant in Carmel, California, his domicile has been in the United Kingdom.

On October 8, 2003, Pebble Beach sued Caddy under the Lanham Act and the California Business and Professions Code for intentional infringement and dilution of its "Pebble Beach" mark. Caddy moved to dismiss the complaint for lack of personal jurisdiction and insufficiency of service of process. On March 1, 2004, the district court granted Caddy's motion on personal jurisdiction grounds, without addressing the insufficiency of service of process issue. The district court denied also Pebble Beach's request for additional discovery. Pebble Beach timely appealed to the Ninth Circuit.

II ...

The arguments are straight forward. Caddy contends that the district court may not assert personal jurisdiction over him, and, consequently, that the complaint against him was properly dismissed. Pebble Beach argues in return that Caddy is subject to specific personal jurisdiction in California, or, alternatively, in any forum in the United States, because he has expressly aimed tortious conduct at California and the United States.[fn] ...

In this circuit, we employ the following three-part test to analyze whether a party's "minimum contacts" meet the Supreme Court's directive. This "minimum contacts" test is satisfied when,

> (1) the defendant has performed some act or consummated some transaction within the forum or otherwise purposefully availed himself of the privileges of conducting activities in the forum, (2) the claim arises out of or results from the defendant's forum-related activities, and (3) the exercise of jurisdiction is reasonable. [C]

... "If any of the three requirements is not satisfied, jurisdiction in the forum would deprive the defendant of due process of law." [C] ... Here, Pebble Beach's arguments fail under the first prong. ...

[I]n order to satisfy the first prong of the "minimum contacts" test, Pebble Beach must establish either that Caddy (1) purposefully availed himself of the privilege of conducting activities in California, or the United States as a whole, or (2) that he purposefully directed its activities toward one of those two forums. [C]

...

Pebble Beach fails to identify any conduct by Caddy that took place in California or in the United States that adequately supports the availment concept. Evidence of availment is typically action taking place in the forum that invokes the benefits and protections of the laws in the forum. [C] Evidence of direction generally consists of action taking place outside the forum that is directed at the forum. [C] ...

...

In Calder v. Jones, [465 U.S. 783 (1984),] the Supreme Court held that a foreign act that is both aimed at and has effect in the forum satisfies the first prong of the specific jurisdiction analysis. [C] We have commonly referred to this holding as the " *Calder* effects test." [C] To satisfy this test the defendant "must have (1) committed an intentional act, which was (2) expressly aimed at the forum state, and (3) caused harm, the brunt of which is suffered and which the defendant knows is likely to be suffered in the forum state." [C] However, referring to the *Calder* test as an "effects" test can be misleading. For this reason, we have warned courts not to focus too narrowly on the test's third prong—the effects prong—holding that "something more" is needed in addition to a mere foreseeable effect. [C] ...

We conclude that Caddy's actions were not expressly aimed at California. The only acts identified by Pebble Beach as being directed at California are the website and the use of the name "Pebble Beach" in the domain name. These acts were not aimed at California and, regardless of foreseeable effect, are insufficient to establish jurisdiction.

In support of its contention that Caddy has expressly aimed conduct at California, Pebble Beach identifies a list of cases where we have found that a defendant's actions have been expressly aimed at the forum state sufficient to establish jurisdiction over the defendant. Pebble Beach asserts that these cases show that Caddy's website and domain name, coupled by his knowledge of the golf resort as a result of his working in California, are sufficient to satisfy the express aiming standard that it is required to meet. We disagree. If anything, these cases establish that "something more"—the express aiming requirement—has not been met by Pebble Beach.

In Panavision[Intl. v. Toeppen, 141 F.3d 1316, 1318-1319 (9th Cir. 1998)], the defendant, a cybersquatter, registered the plaintiff's trademark as part of a domain name. [C] The use of the domain name by the defendant prevented the plaintiff from registering its own domain name and was part of a plan to obtain money from the plaintiff in exchange for the rights to the domain name. [C] The court found personal jurisdiction, not merely because of the domain name use, but because the plan was expressly aimed at the plaintiff... .

Here, Caddy has hatched no such plan directed at Pebble Beach. He is not a cybersquatter trying to obtain money from Pebble Beach. His operation is legitimate and his website relates directly to that end.

In Metropolitan Life Insurance Co. v. Neaves, [912 F.2d 1062 (9th Cir. 1990),] similar to *Panavision,* the defendant's alleged plan to defraud the insurance company involved direct interaction with the forum state. [C] We held that the action at issue satisfied *Calder's* "effects test" because the defendant sent a letter to the forum state addressed to the plaintiff, thereby defrauding a forum state entity. [C]

In Bancroft & Masters, Inc. v. Augusta National Inc., [223 F.3d 1082 (9th Cir. 2000),] a dispute over the domain name www.masters.org was triggered by a letter sent by Augusta that required Bancroft & Masters, a computer corporation in California, to sue or lose the domain name. [C] We stated that the "expressly aiming" standard was satisfied when "individualized targeting was present." [C] We reasoned that specific jurisdiction was proper and that the expressly aiming requirement was satisfied because the letter sent by Augusta constituted "individualized targeting." [C]

The defendant in both *Bancroft* and *Metropolitan Life* did "something more" than commit a "foreign act with foreseeable effects in the forum state." [C] In both cases this "individualized targeting" was correspondence that was a clear attempt to force the plaintiff to act. Here, Caddy engaged in no "individualized targeting." There is no letter written by Caddy forcing Pebble Beach to act. The only substantial action is a domain name and non-interactive informative web site along with the extraneous fact that Caddy had worked, at some point in his past, in California. This does not constitute "individualized targeting." Indeed, to hold otherwise would be contrary to what we have suggested in earlier case law.

In Rio Properties, Inc. v. Rio Int'l Interlink, 284 F.3d 1007, 1020 (9th Cir.2000), we cited Cybersell, Inc. v. Cybersell, Inc., 130 F.3d 414, 418-20 (9th Cir.1997), for the proposition that when a "website advertiser [does] nothing other than register a domain name and post an essentially passive website" and nothing else is done "to encourage residents of the forum state," there is no personal jurisdiction. Similarly, in *Panavision* we stated, "We agree that simply registering someone else's trademark as a domain name and posting a web site on the Internet is not sufficient to subject a party domiciled in one state to jurisdiction in another." 141 F.3d at 1322. Why? Because "the objectionable webpage simply was not aimed intentionally at the [forum state] knowing that harm was likely to be caused there," and "[u]nder the effects doctrine, 'something more' was required to indicate that the defendant purposefully directed its activity in a substantial way to the forum state." *Rio Properties,* 284 F.3d at 1020 (citing *Cybersell, Inc.,* 130 F.3d at 418, 420) (internal quotation marks omitted).[fn]

These cases establish two salient points. First, there can be no doubt that we still require "something more" than just a foreseeable effect to conclude that personal jurisdiction is proper. [C] Second, an internet domain name and passive website alone are not "something more," and, therefore, alone are not enough to subject a party to jurisdiction. [C]

In contrast to those cases where jurisdiction was proper because "something more" existed, the circumstances here are more analogous to Schwarzenegger v. Fred Martin Motor Co. 374 F.3d 797 (9th Cir.2004). In *Schwarzenegger,* we determined that personal jurisdiction based solely on a non-interactive print advertisement would be improper. [C] In *Schwarzenegger,* the former movie star and current California governor, brought an action in California alleging that an Ohio car dealership used impermissibly his "Terminator" image in a newspaper advertisement in Akron, Ohio. [C] The federal district court in California dismissed the complaint for lack of personal jurisdiction. [C] Applying the *Calder* "effects test," we affirmed, concluding that even though the advertisement might lead to eventual harm in California this "foreseeable effect" was not enough because the advertisement was expressly aimed at Ohio rather than California. [C] We concluded that, without "something more" than possible effect, there was simply no individualized targeting of California, or the type of wrongful conduct, that could be construed as being directed at the forum state. [C] We held that Schwarzenegger had not established jurisdiction over the car dealership.

Pebble Beach, like Schwarzenegger, relies almost exclusively on the possible foreseeable effects. Like Schwarzenegger, Pebble Beach's arguments depend on the possible effects of a non-interactive advertisement-here, Caddy's passive website. Notably absent in both circumstances is action that can be construed as being expressly aimed at California. The fact that Caddy once lived in California and therefore has knowledge of the Pebble Beach golf resort goes to the foreseeable effect prong of the "effects test" and is not an independent act that can be interpreted as being expressly aimed at California. Consistent with the dicta of *Cybersell, Panavision,* and *Rio Properties,* we reject also any contention that a passive website constitutes expressed aiming. Thus, today, we extend the holding of *Schwarzenegger* to the situations described in *Panavision* and *Rio Properties,* where the sole basis for asserting jurisdiction is a non-interactive passive website. As with the print advertisement in Schwarzenegger, the fact that Caddy's website is not directed at California is controlling. …

… The fact that the name "Pebble Beach" is a famous mark known world-wide is of little practical consequence when deciding whether action is directed at a particular forum via the world wide web. …

… Caddy did not expressly aim his conduct at California or the United States and therefore is not subject to the personal jurisdiction of the district court. A passive website and domain name alone do not satisfy the *Calder* effects test and there is no other action expressly aimed at California or the United States that would justify personal jurisdiction. …

AFFIRMED.

Figure

Attorney Mikal J. Condon represented the prevailing defendant in the Ninth Circuit Court of Appeals argument of the above *Pebble Beach v. Caddy's* case. Ms. Condon, now with the San Francisco office of the worldwide law firm K&L Gates, LLP, specializes in complex commercial litigation and white-collar criminal defense. She previously worked as staff counsel for a Washington, D.C.-based nonprofit organization, focusing her work on the First Amendment and Internet law.

INQUIRY

Development. How did the courts reach approaches like that shown by the above two United States Circuit Courts of Appeals cases, on this question of jurisdiction based on websites? The lower courts quickly rejected an early approach, *see* Inset Systems, Inc. v. Instruction Set, Inc., 937 F. Supp. 161 (D. Conn. 1996), that would have recognized jurisdiction based simply on the website's availability within the forum, in favor of tests that required something more, *see* Cybersell, Inc., v. Cybersell, Inc., 130 F.3d 414, 418 (9th Cir. 1997). It was not yet clear what constituted something more. A leading opinion in Zippo Manufacturing Co. v. Zippo Dot Com, Inc., 952 F.Supp. 1119, 1124 (W.D. Pa. 1997), made a valiant effort to provide a conceptual framework. *Zippo* placed websites along a scale from active through interactive to passive. A defendant who used its active website to consummate transactions in the forum state would be subject to that state's jurisdiction. A defendant who had no forum contacts other than a passive website that Internet users could view in the forum state would not be subject to that state's jurisdiction. Interactive websites that facilitated individual communications with potential customers in the forum state could give rise to that state's jurisdiction depending on factors like the total extent of forum-directed commercial activity. The Supreme Court has yet to address directly jurisdiction questions raised by the Internet. Lower courts initially viewed the *Zippo* framework favorably. *See* ALS Scan, Inc., v. Digital Service Consultants, Inc., 293 F.3d 707 (4th Cir. 2002) (rejecting jurisdiction based on passive website and requiring more). Courts have since then relied on *Zippo's* framework only in part, called it into serious question, or rejected it outright. *See* Hy Cite Corp. v. Badbusinessbureau.com, L.L.C., 297 F.Supp.2d 1154, 1160 (W.D. Wis. 2004) (rejecting *Zippo* as not authorized by Supreme Court precedent). Until the Supreme Court rules, it may be best to regard *Zippo's* framework examining the interactivity of the website as a logical approach to the peculiar technology but not as a separately approved legal standard. The above two cases seem to so indicate. *See also* Best Van Lines, Inc. v. Walker, 490 F.3d 239, 252 (2d Cir. 2007). Consider one final case involving a worldwide network of a different type, as a capstone to your specific-jurisdiction studies.

Mwani v. Bin Laden,

United States Court of Appeals for the District of Columbia Circuit
417 F.3d 1 (2005)

GARLAND, Circuit Judge.

On August 7, 1998, a devastating truck bomb exploded outside the American embassy in Nairobi, Kenya. The blast killed more than 200 people, including 12 Americans, and wounded more than 4000 others. Most of the casualties were Kenyan. The plaintiffs in this case are all Kenyan: victims, relatives of victims, and businesses harmed in the attack. They sued defendants Osama bin Laden and al Qaeda for orchestrating the bombing... . The district court dismissed the claims against ... bin Laden and al Qaeda for lack of personal jurisdiction.

... [W]e reverse the dismissal of their actions against bin Laden and al Qaeda. Those defendants "engaged in unabashedly malignant actions directed at [and] felt" in this country. [C] Bin Laden and al Qaeda should therefore "reasonably anticipate being haled into court" here by those injured as a result of those actions, *Burger King Corp. v. Rudzewicz,* 471 U.S. 462, 473-74[] (1985), regardless of the plaintiffs' nationality.

I

In early 1999, Odilla Mutaka Mwani and his fellow plaintiffs filed this action in the United States District Court for the District of Columbia. They sought compensatory damages and other relief from Osama bin Laden[and] the terrorist organization known as al Qaeda... for the injuries they sustained in the embassy bombing.[fn] The plaintiffs predicated subject matter jurisdiction for their claims ... against bin Laden and al Qaeda on the Alien Tort Claims Act (ATCA), 28 U.S.C. §1350[, which] provides that "[t]he district courts shall have original jurisdiction of any civil action by an alien for a tort only, committed in violation of the law of nations or a treaty of the United States." Id.

On February 12, 1999, the plaintiffs moved to serve defendants bin Laden and al Qaeda by publication. On August 2, 1999, the district court granted the plaintiffs leave to serve those defendants by "publishing... notice for six weeks in the Daily Washington Law Reporter, the International Herald Tribune, and Al-Quds Al-Arabi (in Arabic)." [C] The plaintiffs later advised the court that the notice had run in all three newspapers, as well as in two additional East African publications.

To no one's surprise, neither bin Laden nor al Qaeda responded. On August 11, 2000, the plaintiffs moved for entry of default against them. Because the district court was not satisfied that it had personal jurisdiction over bin Laden and al Qaeda, it denied the motion... .

... [The district] court concluded that the plaintiffs had "failed to sustain their burden of proving that this Court can exercise personal jurisdiction over" bin Laden and al Qaeda. [C] That was so, the court said, both because of the quality of the plaintiffs' evidence, and because of its failure to establish sufficient contacts between the defendants and the forum to permit the exercise of jurisdiction under the District of Columbia's long-arm statute and the U.S. Constitution. [C] ...

II

... [W]e now consider whether the plaintiffs have satisfactorily shown that the district court may exercise personal jurisdiction over bin Laden and al Qaeda. In the first section below, we address the sources of authority for such an exercise. In the second section, we consider whether the exercise of that jurisdiction would contravene constitutional due process. ...

... The district court did not dispute that the plaintiffs had accomplished service by an acceptable method. ...

Here, the district court authorized the plaintiffs to serve bin Laden and al Qaeda by publication. The court observed that their "address is not known, nor is it easily ascertainable," [c], and that bin Laden had published at least one *fatwa* in *Al-Quds Al-Arabi,* [c]. It concluded that publication was "reasonably calculated to apprise [bin Laden and al Qaeda] of the lawsuit and afford them an opportunity to present their objections." [C] In *Mullane v. Central Hanover Bank & Trust Co.,* the Supreme Court sanctioned service by publication "where it is not reasonably possible or practicable to give more adequate warning," holding that, "in the case of persons missing or unknown, employment of an indirect and even a probably futile means of notification is all that the situation permits and creates no constitutional bar to a final decree foreclosing their rights." 339 U.S. 306, 317[] (1950). ...

... There also must be "authorization for service of summons on the defendant," and a "constitutionally sufficient relationship between the defendant and the forum." [Cc] ... To determine whether these requirements were satisfied here, the district court undertook a traditional inquiry. It asked first whether there was an applicable long-arm statute that would authorize service on the defendants, and then whether the application of such a statute would comply with the demands of due process. [Cc]

With respect to the availability of a long-arm statute, ... [w]hile it is true that some provisions of the District's long-arm statute reach as far as due process permits,[fn] the only provision applicable here does not. ...

Prior to 1993, the absence of a state long-arm statute reaching the defendants' activity would have denied the district court personal jurisdiction, since the federal cause of action at issue here—the ATCA—contains no long-arm provision of its own. ...

... [T]he Rules now contain their *own* long-arm provision which, in some circumstances, eliminates the need to employ the forum state's long-arm statute. Rule 4(k)(2) now provides: "If the exercise of jurisdiction is consistent with the Constitution and laws of the United States, serving a summons ... is also effective, with respect to claims arising under federal law, to establish personal jurisdiction over the person of any defendant who is not subject to the jurisdiction of the courts of general jurisdiction of any state." [C][fn] Rule 4(k)(2) thus permits a federal court to exercise personal jurisdiction over a defendant (1) for a claim arising under federal law, (2) where a summons has been served, (3) if the defendant is not subject to the jurisdiction of any single state court, (4) provided that the exercise of federal jurisdiction is consistent with the Constitution (and laws) of the United States. ...

Whether the exercise of jurisdiction is "consistent with the Constitution" for purposes of Rule 4(k)(2) depends on whether a defendant has sufficient contacts with the United States as a whole to justify the exercise of personal jurisdiction under the Due Process Clause of the Fifth Amendment. [Cc] The Clause "protects an individual's liberty interest in not being subject to the binding judgments of a forum with which he has established no meaningful 'contacts, ties, or relations,'" *Burger King,* 471 U.S. at 472 (quoting International Shoe Co. v. Washington, 326 U.S. 310, 319[] (1945)), and "requir[es] that individuals have 'fair warning that a particular activity may subject [them] to the jurisdiction of a foreign sovereign,'" *id.* (quoting *Shaffer v. Heitner,* 433 U.S. 186, 218[] (1977)) (second alteration in original). "Where a forum seeks to assert specific jurisdiction over an out-of-state defendant who has not consented to suit there, this 'fair warning' requirement is satisfied if the defendant has 'purposefully directed' his activities at residents of the forum," *id.* (quoting Keeton v. Hustler Magazine, Inc., 465 U.S. 770, 774[] (1984)), "and the litigation results from alleged injuries that 'arise out of or relate to' those activities," *id.* (quoting Helicopteros Nacionales de Colombia, S.A. v. Hall, 466 U.S. 408, 414 [](1984)).

In reaching the conclusion that it lacked personal jurisdiction over bin Laden and al Qaeda, the district court focused on a list of specific, physical contacts that the plaintiffs alleged the defendants had made with the District of Columbia and its environs. Those contacts included: the publication of *fatwas* in a newspaper distributed in the United States; the shipment to Virginia of the power supply for a cell phone that bin Laden used in Afghanistan; the scheduling of a bin Laden interview in Afghanistan through an agent in Washington, D.C.; and the transmission of bin Laden's views to the District via interviews on CNN and ABC. [C] ... [T]he court thought the evidence did not demonstrate "that [bin Laden] and al Qaeda 'purposefully directed' [their] activities at the United States" and "that this litigation *results* from alleged injuries that arise out of or relate to those activities." *Id.* (quoting *Burger King,* 471 U.S. at 472).[fn]

... [T]he fundamental problem with the court's analysis was its focus on specific, *physical* contacts between the defendants and the forum. ... [T]he "foreseeability" of causing injury in the forum can establish such contacts where "the defendant's conduct and connection with the forum ... are such that he should reasonably anticipate being haled into court there." *Id.* (quoting World-Wide Volkswagen Corp. v. Woodson, 444 U.S. 286, 295, 100 S.Ct. 559, 62 L.Ed.2d 490 (1980)). ...

In this case, there is no doubt that the defendants "engaged in unabashedly malignant actions directed at [and] felt in this forum." *Id.* The plaintiffs' allegations and evidence were that bin Laden and al Qaeda orchestrated the bombing of the American embassy in Nairobi, not only to kill both American and Kenyan employees inside the building, but to cause pain and sow terror in the embassy's home country, the United States. Nor were the plaintiffs' allegations and evidence of contacts with the United States limited to the Nairobi bombing. The plaintiffs described an ongoing conspiracy to attack the United States, with overt acts occurring within this country's borders. Putting to one side the acts that took place after the embassy bombing (including the attacks on the World Trade Center and the Pentagon on September 11, 2001), the plaintiffs pointed to the 1993 World Trade Center bombing, as well as to the plot to bomb the United Nations, Federal Plaza, and the Lincoln and Holland Tunnels in New York.[fn]

The plaintiffs thus amply made a prima facie showing that bin Laden and al Qaeda "'purposefully directed' [their] activities at residents" of the United States, *Burger King,* 471 U.S. at 472 (quoting *Keeton,* 465 U.S. at 774), and that this litigation results from injuries to the plaintiffs "that 'arise out of or relate to' those activities," *id.* (quoting *Helicopteros Nacionales,* 466 U.S. at 414). Bin Laden and al Qaeda therefore had "fair warning" that their activities would "subject [them] to the jurisdiction" of the United States. *Id.* (quoting *Shaffer,* 433 U.S. at 218).

The fact that injured Kenyans, not injured Americans, are the plaintiffs in this case does not deny the court personal jurisdiction over the defendants. ... The defendants' decision to purposefully direct their terror at the United States, and the fact that the plaintiffs' injuries arose out of one of those terrorist activities, should suffice to cause the defendants to "reasonably anticipate being haled into" an American court. [Cc] ... Here, ... the plaintiffs have sued under the Alien Tort Claims Act, which the Supreme Court has held to supply both subject matter jurisdiction and a cause of action for a narrow set of claims brought by aliens and involving violation of the law of nations. *See* Sosa v. Alvarez-Machain, 542 U.S. 692[] (2004). ...

... Here, the defendants purposefully directed their activities at forum residents, and the fact that the plaintiffs are Kenyans who were injured in the process is not a consideration that would render the assertion of American jurisdiction incompatible with substantial justice.

In sum, we conclude that there is "authorization for service of summons on the defendant[s]" and a "constitutionally sufficient relationship between the defendant[s] and the forum." [C] As a consequence, the district court "may exercise personal jurisdiction over" them. [C] ...

... We reverse the dismissal of [plaintiffs'] claims against bin Laden and al Qaeda... because the plaintiffs have satisfied their burden of showing that the district court can properly exercise personal jurisdiction over those defendants.

So ordered.

C. General Jurisdiction

1. Introduction

Recall that in *International Shoe*, the Supreme Court articulated two forms of *in personam* jurisdiction. Specific jurisdiction is the form in which the respondent's contacts in the forum state gave rise to the litigation, making jurisdiction fair and appropriate. General jurisdiction is the form in which the respondent's contacts in the forum state were *not* what gave rise to the litigation but are still substantial enough to make jurisdiction fair and appropriate. The above sections addressed specific jurisdiction. *International Shoe* and its progeny excerpted, cited, and discussed above, involved cases in which the litigation arose out of the defendant's contacts with the forum state. That is, they involved specific jurisdiction, as in McGee v. International Life Ins. Co., 355 U.S. 220 (1957), in which the defendant Texas insurer sold the disputed life-insurance policy into the forum state California. By contrast, this section addresses general jurisdiction, as if (for instance), Ms. McGee had sued the Texas life-insurance company in California for a slip-and-fall injury she had suffered at the company's Texas headquarters (an incident having no connection to California). It tracks the application of *International Shoe's* minimum-contacts standard to cases in which the litigation did not arise out of the defendant's contacts with the forum state. Perhaps thankfully, the Supreme Court's fundamental test for determining general jurisdiction is substantially the same as its test for determining specific jurisdiction—the minimum-contacts standard of *International Shoe.*

Yet because the factual circumstances supporting general jurisdiction are different from those supporting specific jurisdiction (the difference being that the litigation did not arise out of forum contacts), one benefits from analyzing general jurisdiction cases somewhat differently. While sufficient contact with the forum state remains the touchstone in determining general jurisdiction, it helps to think of general jurisdiction as grouped into four classes of cases. The simplest class of general jurisdiction cases is the one in which the defendant resides in the forum state (if a person) or is incorporated or has its principal place of business in the forum state (if an entity). There is no question of the fundamental fairness of haling a defendant into the defendant's own state's courts, even if the cause of action arose out of state. It does not really even require applying *International Shoe's* minimum-contacts test because the defendant's contacts with the forum state are whole and continual. The only anomaly is that the defendant happened to have acted outside of the forum state to give rise to the litigation. To put it another way, there will always be the home state (or in the case of corporations, sometimes two home states, if they are incorporated and have their principal place of business in different states), the courts of which will have jurisdiction over the defendant, no matter where the cause of action arose. One might think of this class of cases as *resident* general jurisdiction.

The next class of general jurisdiction cases is one in which the defendant has sufficient contact with the forum state under the usual tests articulated by *International Shoe* and its progeny, even though the defendant does not at the time of the lawsuit continue to reside in the forum state and is not present in the state when served, and is therefore not directly governed by *International Shoe* and its progeny because those cases involved specific, not general, jurisdiction. The Supreme Court has, in *Perkins v. Benguet Consolidated Mining Co., infra,* held that general jurisdiction is appropriate in those cases, so long as the defendant has the minimum contacts required under *International Shoe.* One might think of this class of cases as *non-resident* general jurisdiction. The other case featured in this section, *Helicopteros Nacionales de Colombia, S.A. v Hall,* shows the limits of non-resident general jurisdiction, where the non-resident defendant does not have the requisite minimum contacts. As you read these two cases, keep in mind that the litigation did not in either case arise out of the forum contacts. Sections below address three other classes of general-jurisdiction cases.

Perkins v. Benguet Consolidated Mining Co.,

United States Supreme Court
342 U.S. 437 (1952)

JUSTICE BURTON delivered the opinion of the Court.

This case calls for an answer to the question whether the Due Process Clause of the Fourteenth Amendment to the Constitution of the United States precludes Ohio from subjecting a foreign corporation to the jurisdiction of its courts in this action in personam. ... The cause of action sued upon did not arise in Ohio and does not relate to the corporation's activities there. For the reasons hereafter stated, we hold that the Fourteenth Amendment leaves Ohio free to take or decline jurisdiction over the corporation.

... [P]etitioner, Idonah Slade Perkins, a nonresident of Ohio, filed two actions in personam in the Court of Common Pleas of Clermont County, Ohio, against the several respondents. Among those sued is the Benguet Consolidated Mining Company, here called the mining company. It is [incorporated] under the laws of the Philippine Islands, where it owns and has operated profitable gold and silver mines. In one action petitioner seeks approximately $68,400 in dividends claimed to be due her as a stockholder. In the other she claims $2,500,000 damages largely because of the company's failure to issue to her certificates for 120,000 shares of its stock. ...

The essence of the issue here, at the constitutional level, is ... one of general fairness to the corporation. Appropriate tests for that are discussed in International Shoe Co. v. Washington, [326 U.S. 310, 317-320 (1945)]. The amount and kind of activities which must be carried on by the foreign corporation in the state of the forum so as to make it reasonable and just to subject the corporation to the jurisdiction of that state are to be determined in each case. ... [I]f the ... corporation carries on, in that state, ... continuous and systematic corporate activities as it did here—consisting of directors' meetings, business correspondence, banking, stock transfers, payment of salaries, purchasing of machinery, etc.—those activities are enough to make it fair and reasonable to subject that corporation to proceedings in personam in that state, at least insofar as the proceedings in personam seek to enforce causes of action relating to those very activities or to other activities of the corporation within the state.

The instant case takes us one step further to a proceeding in personam to enforce a cause of action not arising out of the corporation's activities in the state of the forum. Using the tests mentioned above we find no requirement of federal due process that either prohibits Ohio from opening its courts to the cause of action here presented or compels Ohio to do so. This conforms to the realistic reasoning in International Shoe Co. v. Washington, supra, [] at [] 318-319[]... .

It remains only to consider, in more detail, the issue of whether, as a matter of federal due process, the business done in Ohio by the respondent mining company was sufficiently substantial and of such a nature as to permit Ohio to entertain a cause of action against a foreign corporation, where the cause of action arose from activities entirely distinct from its activities in Ohio. ...

... [T]he following facts are substantially beyond controversy: The company's mining properties were in the Philippine Islands. Its operations there were completely halted during the occupation of the Islands by the Japanese.

During that interim the president, who was also the general manager and principal stockholder of the company, returned to his home in Clermont County, Ohio. There he maintained an office in which he conducted his personal affairs and did many things on behalf of the company. He kept there office files of the company. He carried on there correspondence relating to the business of the company and to its employees. He drew and distributed there salary checks on behalf of the company, both in his own favor as president and in favor of two company secretaries who worked there with him. He used and maintained in Clermont County, Ohio, two active bank accounts carrying substantial balances of company funds. A bank in Hamilton County, Ohio, acted as transfer agent for the stock of the company. Several directors' meetings were held at his office or home in Clermont County. From that office he supervised policies dealing with the rehabilitation of the corporation's properties in the Philippines and he dispatched funds to cover purchases of machinery for such rehabilitation. Thus he carried on in Ohio a continuous and systematic supervision of the necessarily limited wartime activities of the company. He there discharged his duties as president and general manager, both during the occupation of the company's properties by the Japanese and immediately thereafter. While no mining properties in Ohio were owned or operated by the company, many of its wartime activities were directed from Ohio and were being given the personal attention of its president in that State at the time he was served with summons. Consideration of the circumstances which, under the law of Ohio, ultimately will determine whether the courts of that State will choose to take jurisdiction over the corporation is reserved for the courts of that State. Without reaching that issue of state policy, we conclude that, under the circumstances above recited, it would not violate federal due process for Ohio either to take or decline jurisdiction of the corporation in this proceeding. ...

Accordingly, the judgment of the Supreme Court of Ohio is vacated and the cause is remanded to that court for further proceedings in the light of this opinion.[fn]

It is so ordered.

Judgment vacated and cause remanded for further proceedings.

Mr. Justice BLACK concurs in the result.

[Omitting Justice MINTON'S dissent in which the Chief Justice joined, arguing that the Ohio Supreme Court should decide, taking the above opinion as advisory.]

Helicopteros Nacionales de Colombia, S.A. v. Hall,

United States Supreme Court
466 U.S. 408 (1983)

JUSTICE BLACKMUN delivered the opinion of the Court.

We granted certiorari in this case, [c], to decide whether the Supreme Court of Texas correctly ruled that the contacts of a foreign corporation with the State of Texas were sufficient to allow a Texas state court to assert jurisdiction over the corporation in a cause of action not arising out of or related to the corporation's activities within the State.

I

Petitioner Helicopteros Nacionales de Colombia, S.A. (Helicol), is a Colombian corporation with its principal place of business in the city of Bogota in that country. It is engaged in the business of providing helicopter transportation for oil and construction companies in South America. On January 26, 1976, a helicopter owned by Helicol crashed in Peru. Four United States citizens were among those who lost their lives in the accident. Respondents are the survivors and representatives of the four decedents.

At the time of the crash, respondents' decedents were employed by Consorcio, a Peruvian consortium, and were working on a pipeline in Peru. ... The venture had its headquarters in Houston, Tex. ... Consorcio was to construct a pipeline for Petro Peru running from the interior of Peru westward to the Pacific Ocean. Peruvian law forbade construction of the pipeline by any non-Peruvian entity.

Consorcio/WSH[fn] needed helicopters to move personnel, materials, and equipment into and out of the construction area. In 1974, upon request of Consorcio/WSH, the chief executive officer of Helicol, Francisco Restrepo, flew to the United States and conferred in Houston with representatives of the three joint venturers. At that meeting, there was a discussion of prices, availability, working conditions, fuel, supplies, and housing. ... The Consorcio/WSH representatives decided to accept the contract proposed by Restrepo. Helicol began performing. ... The contract was written in Spanish on official government stationery and provided that the residence of all the parties would be Lima, Peru. It further stated that controversies arising out of the contract would be submitted to the jurisdiction of Peruvian courts. In addition, it provided that Consorcio/WSH would make payments to Helicol's account with the Bank of America in New York City. [C]

Aside from the negotiation session in Houston between Restrepo and the representatives of Consorcio/WSH, Helicol had other contacts with Texas. During the years 1970-1977, it purchased helicopters (approximately 80% of its fleet), spare parts, and accessories for more than $4 million from Bell Helicopter Company in Fort Worth. In that period, Helicol sent prospective pilots to Fort Worth for training and to ferry the aircraft to South America. It also sent management and maintenance personnel to visit Bell Helicopter in Fort Worth during the same period in order to receive "plant familiarization" and for technical consultation. Helicol received into its New York City and Panama City, Fla., bank accounts over $5 million in payments from Consorcio/WSH drawn upon First City National Bank of Houston.

Beyond the foregoing, there have been no other business contacts between Helicol and the State of Texas. Helicol never has been authorized to do business in Texas and never has had an agent for the service of process within the State. It never has performed helicopter operations in Texas or sold any product that reached Texas, never solicited business in Texas, never signed any contract in Texas, never had any employee based there, and never recruited an employee in Texas. In addition, Helicol never has owned real or personal property in Texas and never has maintained an office or establishment there. Helicol has maintained no records in Texas and has no shareholders in that State.[fn] None of the respondents or their decedents were domiciled in Texas, [c],[fn] but all of the decedents were hired in Houston by Consorcio/WSH to work on the Petro Peru pipeline project.

Respondents instituted wrongful-death actions in the District Court of Harris County, Tex., against Consorcio/WSH, Bell Helicopter Company, and Helicol. Helicol filed special appearances and moved to dismiss the actions for lack of in personam jurisdiction over it. The motion was denied. After a consolidated jury trial, judgment was entered against Helicol on a jury verdict of $1,141,200 in favor of respondents.[fn] [C]

The Texas Court of Civil Appeals, Houston, First District, reversed the judgment of the District Court, holding that in personam jurisdiction over Helicol was lacking. [C] The Supreme Court of Texas, ... with three justices dissenting, reversed the judgment of the intermediate court... ruling that the Texas courts had in personam jurisdiction... .

II

The Due Process Clause of the Fourteenth Amendment operates to limit the power of a State to assert in personam jurisdiction over a nonresident defendant. Pennoyer v. Neff, 95 U.S. 714[] (1878). Due process requirements are satisfied when in personam jurisdiction is asserted over a nonresident corporate defendant that has "certain minimum contacts with [the forum] such that the maintenance of the suit does not offend 'traditional notions of fair play and substantial justice.'" International Shoe Co. v. Washington, 326 U.S. 310, 316[] (1945), quoting Milliken v. Meyer, 311 U.S. 457, 463[] (1940). When a controversy is related to or "arises out of" a defendant's contacts with the forum, the Court has said that a "relationship among the defendant, the forum, and the litigation" is the essential foundation of in personam jurisdiction. Shaffer v. Heitner, 433 U.S. 186, 204[] (1977).[fn]

Even when the cause of action does not arise out of or relate to the foreign corporation's activities in the forum State,[fn] due process is not offended by a State's subjecting the corporation to its in personam jurisdiction when there are sufficient contacts between the State and the foreign corporation. Perkins v. Benguet Consolidated Mining Co., 342 U.S. 437[] (1952); [c]. ...

All parties to the present case concede that respondents' claims against Helicol did not "arise out of," and are not related to, Helicol's activities within Texas.[fn] We thus must explore the nature of Helicol's contacts with the State of Texas to determine whether they constitute the kind of continuous and systematic general business contacts the Court found to exist in Perkins. We hold that they do not.

It is undisputed that Helicol does not have a place of business in Texas and never has been licensed to do business in the State. Basically, Helicol's contacts with Texas consisted of sending its chief executive officer to Houston for a contract-negotiation session; accepting into its New York bank account checks drawn on a Houston bank; purchasing helicopters, equipment, and training services from Bell Helicopter for substantial sums; and sending personnel to Bell's facilities in Fort Worth for training.

The one trip to Houston by Helicol's chief executive officer for the purpose of negotiating the transportation-services contract with Consorcio/WSH cannot be described or regarded as a contact of a "continuous and systematic" nature... , and thus cannot support an assertion of in personam jurisdiction over

Helicol by a Texas court. Similarly, Helicol's acceptance from Consorcio/WSH of checks drawn on a Texas bank is of negligible significance for purposes of determining whether Helicol had sufficient contacts in Texas. There is no indication that Helicol ever requested that the checks be drawn on a Texas bank or that there was any negotiation between Helicol and Consorcio/WSH with respect to the location or identity of the bank on which checks would be drawn. Common sense and everyday experience suggest that, absent unusual circumstances,[fn] the bank on which a check is drawn is generally of little consequence to the payee and is a matter left to the discretion of the drawer. Such unilateral activity of another party or a third person is not an appropriate consideration when determining whether a defendant has sufficient contacts with a forum State to justify an assertion of jurisdiction. See Kulko v. California Superior Court, 436 U.S. 84, 93[] (1978) ...; Hanson v. Denckla, 357 U.S. 235, 253[] (1958) ...; [c].

The Texas Supreme Court focused on the purchases and the related training trips in finding contacts sufficient to support an assertion of jurisdiction. We do not agree with that assessment, for ... purchases and related trips, standing alone, are not a sufficient basis for a State's assertion of jurisdiction.

... [W]e hold that mere purchases, even if occurring at regular intervals, are not enough to warrant a State's assertion of in personam jurisdiction over a nonresident corporation in a cause of action not related to those purchase transactions.[fn] Nor can we conclude that the fact that Helicol sent personnel into Texas for training in connection with the purchase of helicopters and equipment in that State in any way enhanced the nature of Helicol's contacts with Texas. The training was a part of the package of goods and services purchased by Helicol from Bell Helicopter. The brief presence of Helicol employees in Texas for the purpose of attending the training sessions is no[t] a significant contact... .

III

We hold that Helicol's contacts with the State of Texas were insufficient to satisfy the requirements of the Due Process Clause of the Fourteenth Amendment.[fn] Accordingly, we reverse the judgment of the Supreme Court of Texas.

It is so ordered.

Justice BRENNAN, dissenting.

... [A] court's specific jurisdiction should be applicable whenever the cause of action arises out of or relates to the contacts between the defendant and the forum. It is eminently fair and reasonable, in my view, to subject a defendant to suit in a forum with which it has significant contacts directly related to the underlying cause of action. Because Helicol's contacts with the State of Texas meet this standard, I would affirm the judgment of the Supreme Court of Texas.

INQUIRY

Application. The above two cases give one example (*Perkins*) where there was general jurisdiction and one example (*Helicopteros*) where there was not general jurisdiction. Did the Supreme Court get the two cases right or backwards? Were there more (and more significant) contacts with the forum state in *Helicopteros*, and fewer (and less significant) contacts in *Perkins*? Reading all of Justice Brennan's *Helicopteros* dissent might help convince you. Is there something else that might explain why *Perkins* found general jurisdiction? *Perkins* may be an example of jurisdiction by necessity, given that Ms. Perkins had no effective Phillipine court in which to sue the Benguet Consolidated Mining Company. Should courts consider the unavailability of another forum as a factor under *International Shoe's* minimum-contacts standard? Although the appellate courts routinely refer to general jurisdiction as an alternative to specific jurisdiction, finding cases in which there is no specific and only general jurisdiction of the type described (and found) in *Perkins* is just next to impossible, although a few cases permit the plaintiff to attempt to discover evidence to support it. *See, e.g.,* Coastal Video Communs. Corp. v. The Staywell Corp., 59 F.Supp. 562 (Ed. Va. 1999). There may, on the other hand, be other ways to establish general jurisdiction, as the following sections explore.

2. Transient Jurisdiction

The next class of general-jurisdiction cases is one in which a non-resident defendant (or a corporate defendant not incorporated or headquartered in the forum state) does *not* have sufficient contacts with the forum state under *International Shoe* and its progeny, except that the defendant happened to be physically present in the state when served with the summons and complaint commencing the litigation. The traditional view has been that presence in the state at the time of personal service, alone without other forum contacts, establishes jurisdiction. The traditional view, while certainly providing a clear test for jurisdiction, led to a few strange-seeming results. *See* Grace v. MacArthur, 170 F.Supp. 442 (E.D. Ark. 1959) (service of complaint on defendant while passenger on commercial flight from Tennessee to Texas but over Arkansas vests Arkansas federal court with personal jurisdiction). The Supreme Court has, in *Burnham v. Superior Court, infra,* approved that presence in the state at the time of personal service alone satisfies constitutional due process. That is, presence alone meets *International Shoe's* minimum-contacts test. In so holding, the Supreme Court (or more aptly, Justice Brennan's concurrence in the result) gave this form of general jurisdiction the new name *transient* jurisdiction. As you read the *Burnham* opinions, none of which garnered a majority even though all justices concurred in the result, consider whether the Supreme Court would approve jurisdiction in a truly transient instance like that just cited in *Grace v. MacArthur.*

Burnham v. Superior Court,

United States Supreme Court
495 U.S. 604 (1990)

JUSTICE SCALIA announced the judgment of the Court and delivered an opinion in which THE CHIEF JUSTICE and Justice KENNEDY join, and in which Justice WHITE joins with respect to Parts I, II-A, II-B, and II-C.

The question presented is whether the Due Process Clause of the Fourteenth Amendment denies California courts jurisdiction over a nonresident, who was personally served with process while temporarily in that State, in a suit unrelated to his activities in the State.

I

Petitioner Dennis Burnham married Francie Burnham in 1976 in West Virginia. In 1977 the couple moved to New Jersey, where their two children were born. In July 1987 the Burnhams decided to separate. They agreed that Mrs. Burnham, who intended to move to California, would take custody of the children. Shortly before Mrs. Burnham departed for California that same month, she and petitioner agreed that she would file for divorce on grounds of "irreconcilable differences."

... Mrs. Burnham ... brought suit for divorce in California state court in early January 1988.

In late January, petitioner visited southern California on business, after which he went north to visit his children ... [where] petitioner was served with a California court summons and a copy of Mrs. Burnham's divorce petition. He then returned to New Jersey.

Later that year, petitioner made a special appearance in the California Superior Court, moving to quash the service of process on the ground that the court lacked personal jurisdiction over him because his only contacts with California were a few short visits to the State for the purposes of conducting business and visiting his children. The Superior Court denied the motion, and the California Court of Appeal denied mandamus relief... . We granted certiorari. [C]

II

A

... To determine whether the assertion of personal jurisdiction is consistent with due process, we have long relied on the principles traditionally followed by American courts in marking out the territorial limits of each State's authority. That criterion was first announced in Pennoyer v. Neff, [95 U.S. 714, 722 (1878)], in which we stated that due process "mean[s] a course of legal proceedings according to those rules and principles which have been established in our systems of jurisprudence for the protection and enforcement of private rights," [c], including the "well-established principles of public law respecting the jurisdiction of an independent State over persons and property," [c]. In what has become the classic expression of the criterion, we said in International Shoe Co. v. Washington, 326 U.S. 310[, 316] (1945)[(quoting Milliken v. Meyer, 311 U.S. 457, 463 (1940)], that a state court's assertion of personal jurisdiction satisfies the Due Process Clause if it does not violate "'traditional notions of fair play and substantial justice.'" [Cc] Since *International Shoe,* we have only been called upon to decide whether these "traditional notions" permit States to exercise jurisdiction over absent defendants in a manner that deviates from the rules of jurisdiction applied in the 19th century. We have held such deviations permissible, but only with respect to suits arising out of the absent defendant's contacts with the State.[fn] See, *e.g., Helicopteros Nacionales de Colombia v. Hall,* 466 U.S. 408, 414[] (1984). The question we must decide today is whether due process requires a similar connection between the litigation and the defendant's contacts with the State in cases where the defendant is physically present in the State at the time process is served upon him.

B

Among the most firmly established principles of personal jurisdiction in American tradition is that the courts of a State have jurisdiction over nonresidents who are physically present in the State. The view developed early that each State had the power to hale before its courts any individual who could be found within its borders, and that once having acquired jurisdiction over such a person by properly serving him with process, the State could retain jurisdiction to enter judgment against him, no matter how fleeting his visit. [C] That view had antecedents in English common-law practice, which sometimes allowed "transitory" actions, arising out of events outside the country, to be maintained against seemingly nonresident defendants who were present in England. ...

Decisions in the courts of many States in the 19th and early 20th centuries held that personal service upon a physically present defendant sufficed to confer jurisdiction, without regard to whether the defendant was only briefly in the State or whether the cause of action was related to his activities there. [Cc] ... Particularly striking is the fact that, as far as we have been able to determine, *not one* American case from the period (or, for that matter, not one American case until 1978) held, or even suggested, that in-state personal service on an individual was insufficient to confer personal jurisdiction.[fn] ...

C

Despite this formidable body of precedent, petitioner contends, in reliance on our decisions applying the *International Shoe* standard, that in the absence of "continuous and systematic" contacts with the forum, [c], a nonresident defendant can be subjected to judgment only as to matters that arise out of or relate to his contacts with the forum. This argument rests on a thorough misunderstanding of our cases. ...

Nothing in *International Shoe* or the cases that have followed it ... offers support for the ... proposition petitioner seeks to establish today: that a defendant's presence in the forum is ... no longer sufficient to establish jurisdiction. That proposition is unfaithful to both elementary logic and the foundations of our due process jurisprudence. ... The short of the matter is that jurisdiction based on physical presence alone constitutes due process because it is one of the continuing traditions of our legal system that define the due process standard of "traditional notions of fair play and substantial justice." That standard was developed by *analogy* to "physical presence," and it would be perverse to say it could now be turned against that touchstone of jurisdiction.

D

Petitioner's strongest argument, though we ultimately reject it, relies upon our decision in Shaffer v. Heitner, 433 U.S. 186[] (1977). ...

It goes too far to say, as petitioner contends, that *Shaffer* compels the conclusion that a State lacks jurisdiction over an individual unless the litigation arises out of his activities in the State. *Shaffer,* like *International Shoe,* involved jurisdiction over an *absent defendant,* and it stands for nothing more than the proposition that when the "minimum contact" that is a substitute for physical presence consists of property ownership it must, like other minimum contacts, be related to the litigation. Petitioner wrenches out of its context our statement in *Shaffer* that "all assertions of state-court jurisdiction must be evaluated according to the standards set forth in *International Shoe* and its progeny," [c]. ... *Shaffer* was saying ... not that all bases for the assertion of *in personam* jurisdiction (including, presumably, in-state service) must be treated alike and subjected to the "minimum contacts" analysis of *International Shoe;* but rather that *quasi in rem* jurisdiction, that fictional "ancient form," and *in personam* jurisdiction, are really one and the same and must be treated alike—leading to the conclusion that *quasi in rem* jurisdiction, *i.e.,* that form of *in personam* jurisdiction based upon a "property ownership" contact and by definition unaccompanied by personal, in-state service, must satisfy the litigation-relatedness requirement of *International Shoe.* ... *International Shoe* confined its "minimum contacts" requirement to situations in which the defendant "be not present within the territory of the forum," [c], and nothing in *Shaffer* expands that requirement beyond that.

It is fair to say, however, that while our holding today does not contradict *Shaffer,* our basic approach to the due process question is different. We have conducted no independent inquiry into the desirability or fairness of the prevailing in-state service rule, leaving that judgment to the legislatures that are free to amend it; for our purposes, its validation is its pedigree... . While in no way receding from or casting doubt upon the holding of *Shaffer* or any other case, we reaffirm today our time-honored approach, [cc]. ... [A] doctrine of personal jurisdiction that dates back to the adoption of the Fourteenth Amendment and is still generally observed unquestionably meets [the *International Shoe*] standard.

III

A few words in response to Justice BRENNAN'S opinion concurring in the judgment... .

... Justice BRENNAN lists the "benefits" Mr. Burnham derived from the State of California—the fact that, during the few days he was there, "[h]is health and safety [were] guaranteed by the State's police, fire, and emergency medical services; he [was] free to travel on the State's roads and waterways; he likely enjoy[ed] the fruits of the State's economy." [C] Three days' worth of these benefits strike us as powerfully inadequate to establish, as an abstract matter, that it is "fair" for California to decree the ownership of all Mr. Burnham's worldly goods acquired during the 10 years of his marriage, and the custody over his children. We daresay a contractual exchange swapping those benefits for that power would not survive the "unconscionability" provision of the Uniform Commercial Code. Even less persuasive are the other "fairness" factors alluded to by Justice BRENNAN. ...

... Justice BRENNAN'S concurrence is unwilling to confess that the Justices of this Court can possibly be bound by a continuing American tradition that a particular procedure is fair ... .

The difference between us and Justice BRENNAN has nothing to do with whether "further progress [is] to be made" in the "evolution of our legal system." [C] It has to do with whether changes are to be adopted as progressive by the American people or decreed as progressive by the Justices of this Court. Nothing we say today prevents individual States from limiting or entirely abandoning the in-state-service basis of jurisdiction. And nothing prevents an overwhelming majority of them from doing so, with the consequence that the "traditional notions of fairness" that this Court applies may change. But the States have overwhelmingly declined to adopt such limitation or abandonment, evidently not considering it to be progress.[fn] The question is whether, armed with no authority other than individual Justices' perceptions of fairness that conflict with both past and current practice, this Court can compel the States to make such a change on the ground that "due process" requires it. We hold that it cannot.

Because the Due Process Clause does not prohibit the California courts from exercising jurisdiction over petitioner based on the fact of in-state service of process, the judgment is

Affirmed.

Justice WHITE, concurring in part and concurring in the judgment.

I join Parts I, II-A, II-B, and II-C of Justice SCALIA'S opinion and concur in the judgment of affirmance. …

Justice BRENNAN, with whom Justice MARSHALL, Justice BLACKMUN, and Justice O'CONNOR join, concurring in the judgment.

I agree with Justice SCALIA that the Due Process Clause of the Fourteenth Amendment generally permits a state court to exercise jurisdiction over a defendant if he is served with process while voluntarily present in the forum State.[fn] I do not perceive the need, however, to decide that a jurisdictional rule that "'has been immemorially the actual law of the land,'" [cc], automatically comports with due process simply by virtue of its "pedigree." Although I agree that history is an important factor in establishing whether a jurisdictional rule satisfies due process requirements, I cannot agree that it is the *only* factor such that all traditional rules of jurisdiction are, *ipso facto,* forever constitutional. Unlike Justice SCALIA, I would undertake an "independent inquiry into the ... fairness of the prevailing in-state service rule." [C] I therefore concur only in the judgment.

I

I believe that the approach adopted by Justice SCALIA'S opinion today—reliance solely on historical pedigree—is foreclosed by our decisions in International Shoe Co. v. Washington, 326 U.S. 310[] (1945), and Shaffer v. Heitner, 433 U.S. 186[] (1977). … The critical insight of *Shaffer* is that all rules of jurisdiction, even ancient ones, must satisfy contemporary notions of due process. …

While our *holding* in *Shaffer* may have been limited to *quasi in rem* jurisdiction, our mode of analysis was not. …

II

Tradition, though alone not dispositive, is of course *relevant* to the question whether the rule of transient jurisdiction is consistent with due process.[fn]

… [T]he historical background [is] relevant because, however murky the jurisprudential origins of transient jurisdiction, the fact that American courts have announced the rule for perhaps a century (first in dicta, more recently in holdings) provides a defendant voluntarily present in a particular State *today* "clear notice that [he] is subject to suit" in the forum. World-Wide Volkswagen Corp. v. Woodson, 444 U.S.[286, 297 (1980)]. … The transient rule is consistent with reasonable expectations and is entitled to a strong presumption that it comports with due process. "If I visit another State, ... I knowingly assume some risk that the State will exercise its power over my property or my person while there. My contact with the State, though minimal, gives rise to predictable risks." Shaffer, [supra], at 218,[] (STEVENS, J., concurring in judgment); see also Burger King Corp. v. Rudzewicz, 471 U.S. 462, 476[] (1985) ("Territorial presence frequently will enhance a potential defendant's affiliation with a State and reinforce the reasonable foreseeability of suit there"); [c]. ...

By visiting the forum State, a transient defendant actually "avail[s]" himself, Burger King, supra, at 476, [] of significant benefits provided by the State. His health and safety are guaranteed by the State's police, fire, and emergency medical services; he is free to travel on the State's roads and waterways; he likely enjoys the fruits of the State's economy as well. Moreover, the Privileges and Immunities Clause of Article IV prevents a state government from discriminating against a transient defendant by denying him the protections of its law or the right of access to its courts. [C] Subject only to the doctrine of *forum non conveniens,* an out-of-state plaintiff may use state courts in all circumstances in which those courts would be available to state citizens. Without transient jurisdiction, an asymmetry would arise: A transient would have the full benefit of the power of the forum State's courts as a plaintiff while retaining immunity from their authority as a defendant. [C]

The potential burdens on a transient defendant are slight. "'[M]odern transportation and communications have made it much less burdensome for a party sued to defend himself' " in a State outside his place of residence. Burger King, supra[], at 474[], quoting McGee v. International Life Ins. Co., 355 U.S. 220, 223[] (1957). That the defendant has already journeyed at least once before to the forum—as evidenced by the fact that he was served with process there—is an indication that suit in the forum likely would not be prohibitively inconvenient. Finally, any burdens that do arise can be ameliorated by a variety of procedural devices. For these reasons, as a rule the exercise of personal jurisdiction over a defendant based on his voluntary presence in the forum will satisfy the requirements of due process.[fn] [C] ...

In this case, it is undisputed that petitioner was served with process while voluntarily and knowingly in the State of California. I therefore concur in the judgment.

Justice STEVENS, concurring in the judgment.

As I explained in my separate writing, I did not join the Court's opinion in Shaffer v. Heitner, 433 U.S. 186[] (1977), because I was concerned by its unnecessarily broad reach. [C] The same concern prevents me from joining either Justice SCALIA'S or Justice BRENNAN'S opinion in this case. For me, it is sufficient to note that the historical evidence and consensus identified by Justice SCALIA, the considerations of fairness identified by Justice BRENNAN, and the common sense displayed by Justice WHITE, all combine to demonstrate that this is, indeed, a very easy case.[FN] [Footnote: Perhaps the adage about hard cases making bad law should be revised to cover easy cases.] Accordingly, I agree that the judgment should be affirmed.

Figure

Attorney James O. Devereaux, a partner in the California law firm Berding & Weil, LLP, argued for the prevailing respondent Ms. Burnham in the Supreme Court in the above *Burnham v. Superior Court* case. Formerly an adjunct professor at Thomas M. Cooley Law School teaching Conflicts of Law, Mr. Devereaux maintains a Northern California real-estate, business-association, and appellate practice. His ability and willingness to mix transactional with civil-litigation work typifies skilled lawyers. Many civil litigators are members of the Supreme Court bar and, like Mr. Devereaux, draft and file amicus curiae (friend of the court) and other briefs, petitions, and responses in the Supreme Court. Few have the privilege of arguing there, and fewer still have a Supreme Court win to their credit, like Mr. Devereaux.

INQUIRY

Playing Tag. Despite that no *Burnham* opinion garnered a majority, the Supreme Court's unanimity as to the *Burnham* result seems to place beyond present dispute that if the plaintiff can catch the defendant in the forum state to serve the defendant with process, then there will be general (transient) jurisdiction. Do you favor this catch-as-catch-can form of jurisdiction? *Burnham* was a good case in which to approve it because of the sadly binary, win-lose nature of divorce litigation. The case had to be tried either in New Jersey or California—the right coast or left coast, with neither forum being particularly convenient for the non-resident party. The Supreme Court's decision in *Burnham* probably favored the more sympathetic party. Can you imagine a case in which transient jurisdiction looks a lot less reasonable than it did in *Burnham*? Some defendants will dodge service of process whether or not jurisdiction is an issue, to delay, complicate, and frustrate the litigation. In what way does transient jurisdiction up the ante?

Resident Agents. *Burnham* involved an individual rather than corporate defendant. The *Burnham* opinions did not directly address whether a plaintiff may obtain transient jurisdiction over a corporate defendant. Although it may sound strange because corporations are not individuals and cannot travel in a transient fashion from state to state, transient jurisdiction (catching the non-resident defendant in the forum state) over a corporate defendant is not a complete non-sequitur but is instead an important legal issue. State laws require corporations to appoint resident agents for service of process in states in which they do business. When a defendant corporation has appointed in the forum state a resident agent on whom the plaintiff serves process, then the court can apply *International Shoe's* minimum-contacts standard to determine jurisdiction. But what if the resident agent happens to travel into another state in which the corporation does no business and has no resident agent, and the plaintiff serves the resident agent there as the forum state. Does transient jurisdiction apply to the corporation whose careless corporate resident agent blunders into service of process in a distant and highly inconvenient forum state? The answer is anyone's guess, as the courts have split. *See* Note, *Registration Statutes, Personal*

Jurisdiction, and the Problem of Predictability, 103 COLUMBIA L.REV. 1163 (2003).

Back to the Future. Note that *Burnham's* recognition of transient jurisdiction can look a lot like a return to the presence test in *Pennoyer v. Neff* that the Supreme Court abandoned in *International Shoe* in favor of constitutional due-process minimum contacts. Can you see any problems with which the courts may have to deal because of transient jurisdiction? For instance, would you grant or deny transient jurisdiction over a defendant whom the plaintiff tricked into the forum state on false pretenses? *Burnham* itself may nearly have been such a case. Mrs. Burnham had Mr. Burnham served with the divorce complaint when Mr. Burnham returned their oldest child to Mrs. Burnham's California home after Mr. Burnham spent a weekend with the child in San Francisco. Mr. Burnham was in California voluntarily, but it is not hard to imagine a scenario in which a plaintiff could entice a defendant into the forum state with false offers, demands, or emergent circumstances. Courts have denied transient jurisdiction in such cases. *See* Wyman v. Newhouse, 93 F.2d 313 (2d Cir.), cert. denied, 303 U.S. 664 (1937) (no jurisdiction over defendant tricked into the jurisdiction by false story account of family illness); Voice Systems Marketing Co. v. Appropriate Technology Corp., 153 F.R.D. 117 (E.D. Mich. 1994) (quashing service on defendant whom plaintiff induced to stay in the forum state for a putative meeting). What if a subpoena has compelled a defendant into the state to testify as a witness in another case? Should there be transient jurisdiction? Most courts have held witnesses immune from service of process unless they were also parties in the action served.

3. Consent

Another class of general-jurisdiction cases is one in which a non-resident defendant (or a corporate defendant not incorporated or headquartered in the forum state) expressly consents to jurisdiction. Consent can be another way to establish jurisdiction. Defendants can consent to jurisdiction in several different ways including by contract or by appearing in the action. Yet as the history of the doctrine shows and Justice Holmes observed in Flexner v. Farson, 248 U.S. 289 (1919), there is some point along the spectrum of consent cases at which consent becomes merely a problematic fiction. At the point at which the defendant can credibly argue that it did not expressly consent and that the court is instead engaging in an implied-consent fiction, *International Shoe's* minimum-contacts standard must come back into play. The following text explores some of the forms and conventions out of which consent arises and some of the issues consent raises.

Ethics

Just because a defendant has a defense does not mean that the defendant should assert it. Rule __ of the ABA MODEL RULES OF PROFESSIONAL CONDUCT permits a lawyer to give not just legal but also social, moral, economic, and political counsel. There may be several reasons why a defendant should not challenge jurisdiction. For instance, think of Mr. Burnham. Parties to a divorce action might be doing the right thing by sacrificing some measure of personal interest and eschewing technical means by which they could gain a tactical advantage, to ensure instead that their children see them as cooperating parents. Mr. Burnham lost the jurisdiction issue. His lawyers would have been acting ethically by helping him consider carefully his strategic approach's broader effects on his children and relationship with them. Even defendant corporations can choose for moral, social, and political reasons to address directly the claims of those whom corporate actions affect, in inconvenient forums where there would be no personal jurisdiction if challenged.

INQUIRY

Appearance. The most direct example of consent is when the defendant accepts service of process, authorizes defense counsel's general appearance in the action, and answers or otherwise defends without raising lack of jurisdiction as a defense. *See* FED. R. CIV. P. 12(h)(1) (defendant loses lack of jurisdiction as a defense unless asserting it in the first answer or motion). You will read more about how a defendant raises and preserves defenses in the chapter on pleading. Note, though, that the form of the defendant's appearance is important if the defendant intends to preserve a jurisdictional challenge. The defendant may have to make a special (rather than general) appearance, solely to contest jurisdiction. A court may construe a general appearance to be consent to general jurisdiction. A section below addresses specific means of challenging jurisdiction.

Agreement. When the parties have a relationship that predates their dispute, then they have the opportunity to agree contractually to jurisdiction in a state with which the parties do not necessarily have the minimum contacts required by *International Shoe*. The Supreme Court approved jurisdiction by contractual consent in National Equipment Rental v. Szukhent, 375 U.S. 311 (1964). The plaintiff New York corporation had leased equipment to the defendant Michigan farmer under a form agreement that, on its back, appointed for the Michigan lessee farmer a New York resident to accept service of process. The plaintiff corporation then sued the defendant farmer in New York when the farmer defaulted. The Supreme Court construed the appointment clause as the farmer's consent to jurisdiction in a state (New York) with which the farmer may not have the requisite minimum contacts but for the appointment clause. Do you think that the farmer knew when he signed the agreement that he may have to travel to New York to defend a lawsuit arising out of the transaction, even assuming that he read the appointment clause? Would it be due process if the farmer had not read and understood the clause, or would it be contract-law principles (like caveat emptor and a presumption that the signer has read and understands the contract) parading as due process?

Forum Selection. What is not immediately clear from *National Equipment Rental v. Szukhent* is whether, when there is a relationship between the parties that predates their dispute, they may also negotiate and agree on a single jurisdiction—that is, exclude other constitutional jurisdictions—before the dispute arises. In M/S Bremen v. Zapata Off-Shore Co., 407 U.S. 1 (1972), the Supreme Court upheld such a forum-selection clause in an agreement between a Louisiana drilling-rig owner and a German ocean-tow company. When a storm damaged the rig off Florida on its way to Italy, the Louisiana owner sued the German tow company in a Florida federal district court, even though the contract stated that the London Court of Justice would decide disputes. The Supreme Court held that the Florida federal district court had no jurisdiction. The case demonstrates that forum-selection clauses may do more than expand the available jurisdictions. They may also limit them. In so holding, the Supreme Court stated that it was simply honoring the parties' agreement, avoiding "a parochial concept" that American entities should get to resolve all disputes under American law in American courts, and encouraging international respect for American commerce. 407 U.S. at 8-9. Is it sound law that private parties should get to deprive United States courts of jurisdiction when the parties do not yet even know what events may spawn the need for litigation? Do forum-selection clauses really promote commerce, or do they disrupt it by replacing the rule of law with bargained injustice?

Choice of Law. Note that a forum-selection clause chooses the forum, not the law that the forum is to apply. Which forum's law applies depends on choice-of-law principles. Choice of law is a complex subject addressed again (summarily) later in this text and (more comprehensively) in a Conflicts of Law course. Many agreements having forum-selection clauses also have choice-of-law clauses.

Fairness. The Supreme Court's *M/S Bremen v. Zapata Offshore Co.* opinion held forum-selection clauses to be valid unless "'unreasonable' under the circumstances." 407 U.S. at 9. The *M/S Bremen* parties disputing jurisdiction were both large corporations having international businesses, each presumably capable of understanding and negotiating over a forum-selection clause. What, though, if the parties are unequal in bargaining power and sophistication? In Carnival Cruise Lines, Inc. v. Shute, 499 U.S. 585 (1991), the State of Washington plaintiff bought a California-to-Mexico cruise from a State of Washington travel agent. After the cruise, the plaintiff sued the cruise line in Washington alleging the cruise line's carelessness in causing her slip-and-fall injury. The trial court ruled that the cruise line had insufficient contacts with Washington, but the Ninth Circuit Court of Appeals disagreed and reversed, finding minimum contacts. The Supreme Court reversed again, holding (without addressing minimum contacts) that a forum-selection clause on the cruise ticket permitted the plaintiff to sue the cruise line only in Florida. Id. at 593. The Supreme Court that courts should scrutinize forum-selection clauses for "fundamental fairness" but held that cruise passengers benefit in the form of reduced fares, from forum-selection clauses advantageous to the cruise line. Id. at 595. Did the Supreme Court get it right in *Carnival Cruise Lines*? Do you think that the plaintiff cruise passenger had any choice in the forum-selection clause or even knew of it? Why defer to contract-law principles when there is a constitutional due-process issue at stake? Do *M/S Bremen* and *Carnival Cruise Lines* mean that consumers who make online purchases consent to otherwise-unconstitutional jurisdiction simply by navigating through click-wrap and browse-wrap agreements containing hidden forum-selection clauses?

Estoppel. The defendant's act of challenging jurisdiction is itself consent to the extent of the court's power to decide the jurisdictional issue. The Supreme Court held in Insurance Corp. of Ireland v. Compagnie des Bauxites de Guinee, 456 U.S. 694 (1982), that the trial court has the power to sanction a foreign defendant for refusing to respond to the plaintiff's discovery on the jurisdiction issue when the defendant challenged jurisdiction. Recall the mention above that courts occasionally allow preliminary jurisdictional discovery, through interrogatories, document requests, and depositions, of the defendant's contacts with the forum state. The case just cited indicates that the defendant consents to that discovery when appearing to challenge jurisdiction. What do you think the sanction should have been in *Insurance Corp. of Ireland*? The trial court presumed from the insurer's failure to respond to discovery that the plaintiff's assertion of minimum contacts was correct—presumed in other words that if the insurer had responded to discovery that the responses would have established jurisdiction. The Supreme Court affirmed the sanction. Do you have any due-process concerns over courts presuming jurisdiction from a defendant's incomplete challenge to it?

Cognovit. Some agreements, particularly promissory notes, go so far as to grant consent not merely to jurisdiction but also to judgment. The drafters of these so-called cognovit clauses typically authorize the lawyer for the creditor to, on attestation of a default, file the complaint, accept its service on the defendant debtor's behalf, and enter judgment against the debtor. Sound unfair? What cognovit does is to shift the procedural burden of determining the validity of an obligation from the creditor to the debtor. A debtor will typically have a limited opportunity to file the debtor's own subsequent action to challenge and have the court set aside an unjust judgment taken by cognovit. The Supreme Court upheld in D.H. Overmyer Co. v. Frick Co., 405 U.S. 174 (1972), the constitutionality of a cognovit clause contained in a promissory note, while at the same time suggesting that the creditor must in the agreement supply independent consideration for the debtor's knowingly accepting the cognovit. *See also* Atlanta Leasing & Finance, Inc. v. IPM Technology, Inc., 885 F.2d 188 (4th Cir. 1989) (guarantor may confess judgment in advance so long as voluntary and knowing). Do you feel that these restrictions satisfy the due-process concerns surrounding cognovit, especially when the creditor might with an appropriate forum-selection clause take the judgment in a state as to which the debtor did not have constitutional minimum contacts? Despite the Supreme Court's decision in *D.H. Overmyer Co. v. Frick,* state courts have held invalid these confession of judgment clauses. *E.g.,* Isbell v. County of Sonoma, 577 P.2d 188 (Cal.), cert. denied, 439 U.S. 996 (1978).

Registration. As mentioned above in the section on transient jurisdiction, state laws require corporations to register and appoint a resident agent for service of process within the state, whenever they do business there. Is a corporation acknowledging that it has minimum contacts for jurisdiction in a state when it complies with a registration law? To put it another way, can a corporation do so little business in a state that it does not constitute jurisdictional minimum contacts, and yet by registering as required by law have consented to jurisdiction? In Ratliff v. Cooper Laboratories, Inc., 444 F.2d 745 (4th Cir.), cert. denied, 404 U.S. 948 (1971), the Fourth Circuit construed the corporation's registration as merely applying and qualifying to do business in the state, not as actually doing business. Registration was not consent to jurisdiction. Then in Knowlton v. Allied Van Lines, Inc., 900 F.2d 1196, 1200 (8th Cir. 1990), the Eighth Circuit held that registration and appointment of an agent for service of process was consent to jurisdiction, including consent to general jurisdiction over an action unrelated to the forum state. But then in Wenche Siemer v. Learjet Acquisition Corp., 966 F.2d 179, 183 (5th Cir. 1992), the Fifth Circuit held that registration and appointment of an agent was not consent to jurisdiction. The Supreme Court has not ruled on the issue, despite that the lower courts disagree. Should consent by registration depend on the language of the state's registration act, giving the states and the registering corporations the choice over jurisdiction?

4. Property

A final class of potential general-jurisdiction cases is one in which a non-resident defendant (or a corporate defendant not incorporated or headquartered in the forum state) yet has property located in the forum state. This class of cases would be the one to which the courts would traditionally have applied *quasi in rem* jurisdiction. Return for a moment to *Pennoyer v. Neff* decided in 1877. Recall that *Pennoyer* recognized three forms of jurisdiction: *in personam* in which the court had full authority over the person; *in rem* in which the court had authority only over the person's property located within the state but not over the person; and *quasi in rem* in which the court had authority over the person but could enforce its judgment only by taking the person's property within the state. When in 1945 *International Shoe* established a new minimum-contacts framework for *in personam* jurisdiction, it left untouched *in rem* and *quasi in rem* jurisdiction. The availability of *in rem* and *quasi in rem* jurisdiction even after *International Shoe* made for some contradictions. For example, in Harris v. Balk, 198 U.S. 215 (1905), cited above in the introduction to *Pennoyer*, the Supreme Court approved that a plaintiff who had no *in personam* jurisdiction over the out-of-state defendant could nonetheless use *quasi in rem* jurisdiction to attach a debt any person owed the defendant, when that person happened to enter the forum state. The defendant may have had no contacts whatsoever with the forum state, yet if the defendant's debtor (someone who owed the defendant some money) entered the forum state, then the plaintiff could sue the defendant there using *quasi in rem* jurisdiction. *See also* Pennington v. Fourth Natl. Bank, 243 U.S. 269, 271-272 (1917) (upholding *quasi in rem* jurisdiction to garnish defendant's bank account to pay alimony, in a state in which defendant had no other contacts). Both *in rem* and *quasi in rem* jurisdiction skirted *International Shoe's* new minimum-contacts standard. You may have noticed that the more recent cases above did not address *in rem* and *quasi in rem* jurisdiction. That is because in the following case decided in 1977, the Supreme Court eliminated *in rem* and *quasi in rem* jurisdiction. After the following case, claims of general jurisdiction must satisfy *International Shoe's* minimum-contacts test just like claims of specific jurisdiction. As you read the following case, keep in mind that the Supreme Court is addressing jurisdiction over individuals (officers and directors), not merely corporate entities. The substantive law of minority-shareholder derivative actions is complex. Focus on the procedural issues involving minimum contacts with the jurisdiction.

Shaffer v. Heitner,

United States Supreme Court
433 U.S. 186 (1977)

MR. JUSTICE MARSHALL delivered the opinion of the Court.

The controversy in this case concerns the constitutionality of a Delaware statute that allows a court of that State to take jurisdiction of a lawsuit by sequestering any property of the defendant that happens to be located in Delaware. Appellants contend that the sequestration statute as applied in this case violates the Due Process Clause of the Fourteenth Amendment both because it permits the state courts to exercise jurisdiction despite the absence of sufficient contacts among the defendants, the litigation, and the State of Delaware and because it authorizes the deprivation of defendants' property without providing adequate procedural safeguards. We find it necessary to consider only the first of these contentions.

I

Appellee Heitner, a nonresident of Delaware, is the owner of one share of stock in the Greyhound Corp., a business incorporated under the laws of Delaware with its principal place of business in Phoenix, Ariz. On May 22, 1974, he filed a shareholder's derivative suit in the Court of Chancery for New Castle County, Del., in which he named as defendants ... 28 present or former officers or directors of one or both of the corporations. In essence, Heitner alleged that the individual defendants had violated their duties to Greyhound by causing it and its subsidiary to engage in actions that resulted in the corporations being held liable for substantial damages in a private antitrust suit[fn] and a large fine in a criminal contempt action.[fn] The activities which led to these penalties took place in Oregon.

Simultaneously with his complaint, Heitner filed a motion for an order of sequestration of the Delaware property of the individual defendants... . This motion was accompanied by a supporting affidavit of counsel which stated that the individual defendants were nonresidents of Delaware. ...

... The requested sequestration order was signed the day the motion was filed.[fn] Pursuant to that order, the sequestrator[fn] "seized" approximately 82,000 shares of Greyhound common stock belonging to 19 of the defendants,[fn] and options belonging to another 2 defendants.[fn] These seizures were accomplished by placing "stop transfer" orders or their equivalents on the books of the Greyhound Corp. So far as the record shows, none of the certificates representing the seized property was physically present in Delaware. The stock was considered to be in Delaware, and so subject to seizure, [c], which makes Delaware the situs of ownership of all stock in Delaware corporations.[fn]

All 28 defendants were notified of the initiation of the suit by certified mail directed to their last known addresses and by publication in a New Castle County newspaper. The 21 defendants whose property was seized (hereafter referred to as appellants) responded by entering a special appearance for the purpose of moving to quash service of process and to vacate the sequestration order. They contended that the ex parte sequestration procedure did not accord them due process of law and that the property seized was not capable of attachment in Delaware. In addition, appellants asserted that under the rule of

International Shoe Co. v. Washington, 326 U.S. 310[] (1945), they did not have sufficient contacts with Delaware to sustain the jurisdiction of that State's courts.

The Court of Chancery rejected these arguments [by holding that sequestration was not to secure the property but to compel defendants' appearance.] ... The court also found no state-law or federal constitutional barrier... . Finally, the court held that the statutory Delaware situs of the stock provided a sufficient basis for the exercise of quasi in rem jurisdiction by a Delaware court. [C]

On appeal, the Delaware Supreme Court affirmed the judgment of the Court of Chancery. ...

II

The Delaware courts rejected appellants' jurisdictional challenge by noting that this suit was brought as a quasi in rem proceeding. Since quasi in rem jurisdiction is traditionally based on attachment or seizure of property present in the jurisdiction, not on contacts between the defendant and the State, the courts considered appellants' claimed lack of contacts with Delaware to be unimportant. This categorical analysis assumes the continued soundness of the conceptual structure founded on the century-old case of Pennoyer v. Neff, 95 U.S. 714[] (1878). ...

From our perspective, the importance of Pennoyer is not its result, but the fact that its principles and corollaries derived from them became the basic elements of the constitutional doctrine governing state-court jurisdiction. [C] As we have noted, under Pennoyer state authority to adjudicate was based on the jurisdiction's power over either persons or property. This fundamental concept is embodied in the very vocabulary which we use to describe judgments. If a court's jurisdiction is based on its authority over the defendant's person, the action and judgment are denominated "in personam" and can impose a personal obligation on the defendant in favor of the plaintiff. If jurisdiction is based on the court's power over property within its territory, the action is called "in rem" or "quasi in rem." The effect of a judgment in such a case is limited to the property that supports jurisdiction and does not impose a personal liability on the property owner, since he is not before the court.[fn] In Pennoyer's terms, the owner is affected only "indirectly" by an in rem judgment adverse to his interest in the property subject to the court's disposition. ...

The Pennoyer rules generally favored nonresident defendants by making them harder to sue. This advantage was reduced, however, by the ability of a resident plaintiff to satisfy a claim against a nonresident defendant by bringing into court any property of the defendant located in the plaintiff's State. [C] [Here, the Supreme Court cited and discussed Harris v. Balk, 198 U.S. 215 (1905), on *quasi in rem* jurisdiction, Hess v. Pawloski, 274 U.S. 352 (1927), on the theory of implied consent, other cases on the fiction of corporate presence, and then its promulgation of International Shoe Co. v. Washington, 326 U.S. 310 (1945).] ...

Thus [after International Shoe], the relationship among the defendant, the forum, and the litigation, rather than the mutually exclusive sovereignty of the States on which the rules of Pennoyer rest, became the central concern of the inquiry into personal jurisdiction.[fn] The immediate effect of this departure from Pennoyer's conceptual apparatus was to increase the ability of the state courts to obtain personal jurisdiction over nonresident defendants. [Cc]

No equally dramatic change has occurred in the law governing jurisdiction in rem. There have, however, been intimations that the collapse of the in personam wing of Pennoyer has not left that decision unweakened as a foundation for in rem jurisdiction. Well-reasoned lower court opinions have questioned the proposition that the presence of property in a State gives that State jurisdiction to adjudicate rights to the property regardless of the relationship of the underlying dispute and the property owner to the forum. [Cc] The overwhelming majority of commentators have also rejected Pennoyer's premise that a proceeding "against" property is not a proceeding against the owners of that property. Accordingly, they urge that the "traditional notions of fair play and substantial justice" that govern a State's power to adjudicate in personam should also govern its power to adjudicate personal rights to property located in the State. [Cc] ...

It is clear, therefore, that the law of state-court jurisdiction no longer stands securely on the foundation established in Pennoyer.[fn] We think that the time is ripe to consider whether the standard of fairness and substantial justice set forth in International Shoe should be held to govern actions in rem as well as in personam.

III

The case for applying to jurisdiction in rem the same test of "fair play and substantial justice" as governs assertions of jurisdiction in personam is simple and straightforward. It is premised on recognition that "(t)he phrase, 'judicial jurisdiction over a thing', is a customary elliptical way of referring to jurisdiction over the interests of persons in a thing." Restatement (Second) of Conflict of Laws §56, Introductory Note (1971)[].[fn] This recognition leads to the conclusion that in order to justify an exercise of jurisdiction in rem, the basis for jurisdiction must be sufficient to justify exercising "jurisdiction over the interests of persons in a thing."[fn] The standard for determining whether an exercise of jurisdiction over the interests of persons is consistent with the Due Process Clause is the minimum-contacts standard elucidated in International Shoe.

This argument, of course, does not ignore the fact that the presence of property in a State may bear on the existence of jurisdiction by providing contacts among the forum State, the defendant, and the litigation. For example, when claims to the property itself are the source of the underlying controversy between the plaintiff and the defendant,[fn] it would be unusual for the State where the property is located not to have jurisdiction. In such cases, the defendant's claim to property located in the State would normally[fn] indicate that he expected to benefit from the State's protection of his interest.[fn] The State's strong interests in assuring the marketability of property within its borders[fn] and in providing a procedure for peaceful resolution of disputes about the possession of that property would also support jurisdiction, as would the likelihood that important records and witnesses will be found in the State.[fn] The presence of property may also favor jurisdiction in cases such as suits for injury suffered on the land of an absentee owner, where the defendant's ownership of the property is conceded but the cause of action is otherwise related to rights and duties growing out of that ownership.[fn]

It appears, therefore, that jurisdiction over many types of actions which now are or might be brought in rem would not be affected by a holding that any assertion of state-court jurisdiction must satisfy the International Shoe standard.[fn] For the type of quasi in rem action typified by Harris v. Balk and the present case, however, accepting the proposed analysis would result in significant change. These are cases where the property which now serves as the basis for state-court jurisdiction is completely unrelated to the plaintiff's cause of action. Thus, although the presence of the defendant's property in a State might suggest the existence of other ties among the defendant, the State, and the litigation, the presence of the property alone would not support the State's jurisdiction. If those other ties did not exist, cases over which the State is now thought to have jurisdiction could not be brought in that forum.

Since acceptance of the International Shoe test would most affect this class of cases, we examine the arguments against adopting that standard as they relate to this category of litigation.[fn] Before doing so, however, we note that this type of case also presents the clearest illustration of the argument in favor of assessing assertions of jurisdiction by a single standard. For in cases such as Harris and this one, the only role played by the property is to provide the basis for bringing the defendant into court.[fn] Indeed, the express purpose of the Delaware sequestration procedure is to compel the defendant to enter a personal appearance.[fn] In such cases, if a direct assertion of personal jurisdiction over the defendant would violate the Constitution, it would seem that an indirect assertion of that jurisdiction should be equally impermissible.

The primary rationale for treating the presence of property as a sufficient basis for jurisdiction to adjudicate claims over which the State would not have jurisdiction if International Shoe applied is that a wrongdoer "should not be able to avoid payment of his obligations by the expedient of removing his assets to a place where he is not subject to an in personam suit." Restatement §66, Comment a. [C] This justification, however, does not explain why jurisdiction should be recognized without regard to whether the property is present in the State because of an effort to avoid the owner's obligations. Nor does it support jurisdiction to adjudicate the underlying claim. At most, it suggests that a State in which property is located should have jurisdiction to attach that property, by use of proper procedures,[fn] as security for a judgment being sought in a forum where the litigation can be maintained consistently with International Shoe. [C] Moreover, we know of nothing to justify the assumption that a debtor can avoid paying his obligations by removing his property to a State in which his creditor cannot obtain personal jurisdiction over him.[fn] The Full Faith and Credit Clause, after all, makes the valid in personam judgment of one State enforceable in all other States.[fn]

It might also be suggested that allowing in rem jurisdiction avoids the uncertainty inherent in the International Shoe standard and assures a plaintiff of a forum.[fn] [C] We believe, however, that the fairness standard of International Shoe can be easily applied in the vast majority of cases. ...

We are left, then, to consider the significance of the long history of jurisdiction based solely on the presence of property in a State. ... The fiction that an assertion of jurisdiction over property is anything but an assertion of jurisdiction over the owner of the property supports an ancient form without substantial modern justification. Its continued acceptance would serve only to allow state-court jurisdiction that is fundamentally unfair to the defendant.

We therefore conclude that all assertions of state-court jurisdiction must be evaluated according to the standards set forth in International Shoe and its progeny.[fn]

IV

The Delaware courts based their assertion of jurisdiction in this case solely on the statutory presence of appellants' property in Delaware. Yet that property is not the subject matter of this litigation, nor is the underlying cause of action related to the property. Appellants' holdings in Greyhound do not, therefore, provide contacts with Delaware sufficient to support the jurisdiction of that State's courts over appellants. If it exists, that jurisdiction must have some other foundation.[fn]

Appellee Heitner did not allege and does not now claim that appellants have ever set foot in Delaware. Nor does he identify any act related to his cause of action as having taken place in Delaware. Nevertheless, he contends that appellants' positions as directors and officers of a corporation chartered in Delaware[fn] provide sufficient "contacts, ties, or relations," [c], with that State to give its courts jurisdiction over appellants in this stockholder's derivative action. This argument is based primarily on what Heitner asserts to be the strong interest of Delaware in supervising the management of a Delaware corporation. ...

This argument is undercut by the failure of the Delaware Legislature to assert the state interest appellee finds so compelling. Delaware law bases jurisdiction, not on appellants' status as corporate fiduciaries, but rather on the presence of their property in the State. Although the sequestration procedure used here may be most frequently used in derivative suits against officers and directors, [c], the authorizing statute evinces no specific concern with such actions. Sequestration can be used in any suit against a nonresident,[fn] [cc], and reaches corporate fiduciaries only if they happen to own interests in a Delaware corporation, or other property in the State. But as Heitner's failure to secure jurisdiction over seven of the defendants named in his complaint demonstrates, there is no necessary relationship between holding a position as a corporate fiduciary and owning stock or other interests in the corporation.[fn] If Delaware perceived its interest in securing jurisdiction over corporate fiduciaries to be as great as Heitner suggests, we would expect it to have enacted a statute more clearly designed to protect that interest.

Moreover, even if Heitner's assessment of the importance of Delaware's interest is accepted, his argument fails to demonstrate that Delaware is a fair forum for this litigation. The interest appellee has identified may support the application of Delaware law to resolve any controversy over appellants' actions in their capacities as officers and directors.[fn] But we have rejected the argument that if a State's law can properly be applied to a dispute, its courts necessarily have jurisdiction over the parties to that dispute.

Appellee suggests that by accepting positions as officers or directors of a Delaware corporation, appellants performed the acts required by Hanson v. Denckla. He notes that Delaware law provides substantial benefits to corporate officers and directors,[fn] and that these benefits were at least in part the incentive for appellants to assume their positions. It is, he says, "only fair and just" to require appellants, in return for these benefits, to respond in the State of Delaware when they are accused of misusing their power. [C]

But like Heitner's first argument, this line of reasoning establishes only that it is appropriate for Delaware law to govern the obligations of appellants to Greyhound and its stockholders. It does not demonstrate that appellants have "purposefully avail(ed themselves) of the privilege of conducting activities within the forum State," Hanson v. Denckla, supra, at 253[], in a way that would justify bringing them before a Delaware tribunal. Appellants have simply had nothing to do with the State of Delaware. Moreover, appellants had no reason to expect to be haled before a Delaware court. Delaware, unlike some States,[fn] has not enacted a statute that treats acceptance of a directorship as consent to jurisdiction in the State. And "(i)t strains reason ... to suggest that anyone buying securities in a corporation formed in Delaware 'impliedly consents' to subject himself to Delaware's ... jurisdiction on any cause of action." [C] Appellants, who were not required to acquire interests in Greyhound in order to hold their positions, did not by acquiring those interests surrender their right to be brought to judgment only in States with which they had had "minimum contacts."

The Due Process Clause "does not contemplate that a state may make binding a judgment . . . against an individual or corporate defendant with which the state has no contacts, ties, or relations." International Shoe Co. v. Washington, [supra], at 319[].

Delaware's assertion of jurisdiction over appellants in this case is inconsistent with that constitutional limitation on state power. The judgment of the Delaware Supreme Court must, therefore, be reversed.

It is so ordered.

Mr. Justice REHNQUIST took no part in the consideration or decision of this case.

Mr. Justice POWELL, concurring.

I agree that the principles of International Shoe Co. v. Washington, 326 U.S. 310 [] (1945), should be extended to govern assertions of in rem as well as in personam jurisdiction in a state court. I also agree that neither the statutory presence of appellants' stock in Delaware nor their positions as directors and officers of a Delaware corporation can provide sufficient contacts to support the Delaware courts' assertion of jurisdiction in this case.

I would explicitly reserve judgment, however, on whether the ownership of some forms of property whose situs is indisputably and permanently located within a State may, without more, provide the contacts necessary to subject a defendant to jurisdiction within the State to the extent of the value of the property. In the case of real property, in particular, preservation of the common-law concept of quasi in rem jurisdiction arguably would avoid the uncertainty of the general International Shoe standard without significant cost to "'traditional notions of fair play and substantial justice.'" [Cc].

Subject to the foregoing reservation, I join the opinion of the Court.

Mr. Justice STEVENS, concurring in the judgment.

The Due Process Clause affords protection against "judgments without notice." International Shoe Co. v. Washington, 326 U.S. 310, 324 [(1945)] (opinion of Black, J.). ...

One who purchases shares of stock on the open market can hardly be expected to know that he has thereby become subject to suit in a forum remote from his residence and unrelated to the transaction. As a practical matter, the Delaware sequestration statute creates an unacceptable risk of judgment without notice. Unlike the 49 other States, Delaware treats the place of incorporation as the situs of the stock, even though both the owner and the custodian of the shares are elsewhere. Moreover, Delaware denies the defendant the opportunity to defend the merits of the suit unless he subjects himself to the unlimited jurisdiction of the court. Thus, it coerces a defendant either to submit to personal jurisdiction in a forum which could not otherwise obtain such jurisdiction or to lose the securities which have been attached. ... I therefore agree with the Court that on the record before us no adequate basis for jurisdiction exists and that the Delaware statute is unconstitutional on its face.

How the Court's opinion may be applied in other contexts is not entirely clear to me. I agree with Mr. Justice POWELL that it should not be read to invalidate quasi in rem jurisdiction where real estate is involved. I would also not read it as invalidating other long-accepted methods of acquiring jurisdiction over persons with adequate notice of both the particular controversy and the fact that their local activities might subject them to suit. My uncertainty as to the reach of the opinion, and my fear that it purports to decide a great deal more than is necessary to dispose of this case, persuade me merely to concur in the judgment.

Mr. Justice BRENNAN, concurring in part and dissenting in part.

I join Parts I-III of the Court's opinion. I fully agree that the minimum-contacts analysis developed in International Shoe Co. v. Washington, 326 U.S. 310 [] (1945), represents a far more sensible construct for the exercise of state-court jurisdiction than the patchwork of legal and factual fictions that has been generated from the decision in Pennoyer v. Neff, 95 U.S. 714 [] (1878). It is precisely because the inquiry into minimum contacts is now of such overriding importance, however, that I must respectfully dissent from Part IV of the Court's opinion. ...

In this instance, Delaware can point to at least three interrelated public policies that are furthered by its assertion of jurisdiction. First, the State has a substantial interest in providing restitution for its local corporations that allegedly have been victimized by fiduciary misconduct, even if the managerial decisions occurred outside the State. ... Second, state courts have legitimately read their jurisdiction expansively when a cause of action centers in an area in which the forum State possesses a manifest regulatory interest. ... Finally, a State like Delaware has a recognized interest in affording a convenient forum for supervising and overseeing the affairs of an entity that is purely the creation of that State's law. ... I, of course, am not suggesting that Delaware's varied interests would justify its acceptance of jurisdiction over any transaction touching upon the affairs of its domestic corporations. But a derivative action which raises allegations of abuses of the basic management of an institution whose existence is created by the State and whose powers and duties are defined by state law fundamentally implicates the public policies of that forum.

I, therefore, would approach the minimum-contacts analysis differently than does the Court. Crucial to me is the fact that appellants[fn] voluntarily associated themselves with the State of Delaware... by entering into a long-term and fragile relationship with one of its domestic corporations. They thereby elected to assume powers and to undertake responsibilities wholly derived from that State's rules and regulations, and to become eligible for those benefits that Delaware law makes available to its corporations' officials. [Cc] While it is possible that countervailing issues of judicial efficiency and the like might clearly favor a different forum, they do not appear on the meager record before us;[fn] and, of course, we are concerned solely with "minimum" contacts, not the "best" contacts. I thus do not believe that it is unfair to insist that appellants make themselves available to suit in a competent forum that Delaware might create for vindication of its important public policies directly pertaining to appellants' fiduciary associations with the State.

INQUIRY

Subsequent History. Immediately after the Supreme Court's decision in *Shaffer v. Heitner,* Delaware's legislature amended its corporation act to deem corporate directors to have appointed their corporation's resident agent for service of process in any suit alleging the directors' violation of their corporate duties. 10 Del. Code §3114. Delaware's Supreme Court then upheld the constitutionality of jurisdiction over directors having no other forum contacts, in cases covered by the amended statute. Armstrong v. Pomerance, 423 A.2d 174 (Del. 1980). Some states followed Delaware's lead. *See* Stearn v. Malloy, 89 F.R.D. 421 (E.D. Wis. 1981) (upholding jurisdiction in similar case under similar Wisconsin statute). Other states did not. In fact, stung by Delaware's legislative action after *Shaffer v. Heitner,* Greyhound Corporation fled Delaware, reincorporating in Arizona, its corporate headquarters where courts would already have had jurisdiction over its directors based on continuous contacts there. Undeterred, Delaware's legislature in 2004 extended its statutory implied consent provision to cover not only corporate directors but also corporate officers. From this history, do you recognize again the role that state statutes continue to play in determining the jurisdiction of state and federal courts, notwithstanding *International Shoe's* constitutional minimum-contacts standard? In the midst of this subsequent history, just three years after *Shaffer v. Heitner*, the Supreme Court held that a plaintiff cannot constitutionally use *quasi in rem* jurisdiction to attach an insurance obligation in the forum state in which the defendant had no other contacts. Do you think that the Supreme Court would find Delaware's action constitutional or unconstitutional? *In rem* and *quasi in rem* jurisdiction are truly dead. Or are they? *See* Feder v. Turkish Airlines, 441 F. Supp. 1273 (S.D. N.Y. 1977) (upholding, after *Shaffer v. Heitner*, *quasi in rem* jurisdiction over a bank account of a defendant who had no other forum contacts).

Cybersquatting. The commercial value of Internet domain names led some Internet users into the practice of anticipating an organization's need or desire for a certain name and registering the name. The registrant could then charge the organization a (potentially extortionate) fee to relinquish it to the organization, sell the name to a competitor to prevent its use by the organization, or use or sell the name to mislead consumers into associating the website with the organization. Congress regulated these practices under the Anti-Cybersquatting and Consumer Protection Act, 15 U.S.C. §1125(d)(2) (2000). Despite that *Shaffer v. Heitner* effectively abolished *in rem* and *quasi in rem* jurisdiction as grounds for the constitutional exercise of jurisdiction, Congress' Anti-Cybersquatting Act contains an *in rem* jurisdiction provision. Because domain-name registrants might be anywhere in the world and might be difficult for a trademark holder to find and sue under the Act in any reasonably convenient or meaningful forum, the Act permits trademark holders to sue *in rem* in the state in which the registrant registered the domain name. Courts have recognized as constitutional the exercise of *in rem* jurisdiction over a domain name under the Act, even where the registrant had no (other) contact with the forum state. *See* Harrods Ltd. v. Sixty Internet Domain Names, 302 F.3d 214, 225 (4th Cir. 2002). It may be, as the *Harrods* opinion implied, that jurisdiction in such cases is constitutional because the disputed issue involves the right under the Act to create the property itself (that is, to register the domain name that would otherwise have no value) rather than or in addition to the issue of who owns and controls it. Do you think that the Supreme Court would agree if it decided the issue?

D. Statutory Authority

It is not enough that the state and federal trial courts' exercise of personal jurisdiction be constitutional under the various principles you have now studied. Because the state and federal trial courts owe their existence to state and federal statutes, respectively, their exercise of personal jurisdiction also depends on the reach of those statutes. The federal Constitution gives Congress, and the state constitutions give their state legislatures, the authority to establish trial courts. To address personal jurisdiction solely from a constitutional perspective is to miss important statutory aspects. The following sections address state and federal statutory authority for the personal jurisdiction of the state and federal courts, respectively.

1. State Long-Arm Statutes

The Supreme Court in *International Shoe* permitted states to extend their courts' jurisdiction to the constitutional limit allowed under its minimum-contacts standard for due process. Nothing requires that states do so. States may choose whether to extend or limit the reach of their courts, as long as they do not extend their courts' reach beyond the minimum-contacts standard. States have made those choices through long-arm statutes and the interpretation state courts give to those statutes. A long-arm statute is a legislative enactment that defines the jurisdictional reach of the state's courts over non-resident defendants. Although many of the states' long-arm statutes are similar, some statutes have longer arms than others, and each state's courts may give those statutes different interpretations. Thus to determine under *International Shoe* and its progeny whether there is constitutionally permissible jurisdiction, the practitioner must first consider whether the state's long-arm statute authorizes jurisdiction and then ensure that the jurisdiction the statute authorizes is constitutionally permissible under the minimum-contacts standard. Gray v. American Radiator & Standard Sanitary Corp., 176 N.E.2d 761 (Ill. 1961), excerpted below, is an example of a state supreme-court case construing as constitutional the first comprehensive long-arm statute enacted under *International Shoe* and used by other states as a model long-arm statute.

There are two general types of long-arm statutes. The first type of long-arm statute like that Illinois enacted enumerates specific acts that will subject the defendant to the state's jurisdiction. If the defendant's acts fit any of the enumerated categories, then the defendant is subject to the state's jurisdiction. If the defendant's acts do not fall into an enumerated category, then the defendant is not subject to the state's jurisdiction even if *International Shoe* would authorize the state's assertion of jurisdiction. For example, Illinois' long-arm statute cited in the above *Gray* case (but since amended) authorized jurisdiction over any defendant who transacted business, committed a tort, owned real property, or insured a risk within the state. Notice how states having the enumerated-acts type of long-arm statute chose to substitute a categorical approach for *International Shoe's* functional minimum-contacts standard. In doing so, these enumerated-acts statutes may limit the reach of state courts to well short of their constitutionally permissible limit. *See* Ingraham v. Carroll, 687 N.E.2d 1293 (N.Y. 1997) (New York's long-arm statute was deliberately designed to keep jurisdiction "well within constitutional bounds") (internal quotation and citation omitted).

The second type of long-arm statute ties jurisdiction to its constitutional limit, authorizing jurisdiction to the same extent as *International Shoe*. California's long-arm statute is a good example, stating simply, "A Court of this state may exercise jurisdiction on any basis not inconsistent with the Constitution of this state or of the United States." CAL. CODE CIV. P. §410.10. Interestingly, the appellate courts of some states having the enumerated-acts type of long-arm statute have interpreted those statutes to extend jurisdiction to its fullest *International Shoe* reach. *See* Fields v. Volkswagen of America, Inc., 555 P.2d 48, 52 (Okla. 1976); Sifers v. Horen, 188 N.W.2d 623 (Mich. 1971); Woodring v. Hall, 438 P.2d 135, 141 (Kan. 1968). Consider the following examples of an enumerated-acts long-arm statute and a fullest-extent long-arm statute, followed by the representative *Gray* case.

N.Y. Civil Practice Law (McKinney's) §302. Personal jurisdiction by acts of non-domiciliaries.

(a) Acts which are the basis of jurisdiction. As to a cause of action arising from any of the acts enumerated in this section, a court may exercise personal jurisdiction over any non-domiciliary, or his executor or administrator, who in person or through an agent: 1. transacts any business within the state or contracts anywhere to supply goods or services in the state; or 2. commits a tortious act within the state, except as to a cause of action for defamation of character arising from the act; or 3. commits a tortious act without the state causing injury to person or property within the state, except as to a cause of action for defamation of character arising from the act, if he (i) regularly does or solicits business, or engages in any other persistent course of conduct, or derives substantial revenue from goods used or consumed or services rendered, in the state, or (ii) expects or should reasonably expect the act to have consequences in the state and derives

substantial revenue from interstate or international commerce; or 4. owns, uses or possesses any real property situated within the state.
(b) Personal jurisdiction over non-resident defendant in matrimonial actions or family court proceedings. A court in any matrimonial action or family court proceeding involving a demand for support, alimony, maintenance, distributive awards or special relief in matrimonial actions may exercise personal jurisdiction over the respondent or defendant notwithstanding the fact that he or she no longer is a resident or domiciliary of this state ... if the party seeking support is a resident of or domiciled in this state at the time such demand is made, provided that this state was the matrimonial domicile of the parties before their separation, or the defendant abandoned the plaintiff in this state, or the claim for support, alimony, maintenance, distributive awards or special relief in matrimonial actions accrued under the laws of this state or under an agreement executed in this state. ...
(c) Effect of appearance. Where personal jurisdiction is based solely upon this section, an appearance does not confer such jurisdiction with respect to causes of action not arising from an act enumerated in this section. ...

R.I. General Laws §9-5-33. Jurisdiction over foreign corporations and over nonresident individuals, partnerships, or associations.
(a) Every foreign corporation, every individual not a resident of this state or his or her executor or administrator, and every partnership or association, composed of any person or persons not such residents, that shall have the necessary minimum contacts with the state of Rhode Island, shall be subject to the jurisdiction of the state of Rhode Island, and the courts of this state shall hold such foreign corporations and such nonresident individuals or their executors or administrators, and such partnerships or associations amenable to suit in Rhode Island in every case not contrary to the provisions of the constitution or laws of the United States.
(b) Service of process may be made on any such foreign corporation, nonresident individual or his or her executor or administrator, and such partnership or association within or without the state in the manner provided by any applicable procedural rule or in the manner prescribed by order of the court in which the action is brought.
(c) Nothing herein shall limit or affect the right to serve process upon the nonresident individual or his or her executor or administrator, or the partnership or association, or a foreign corporation within this state or without this state in any manner now or hereafter permitted by law.

Gray v. American Radiator & Standard Sanitary Corp.,

Illinois Supreme Court
176 N.E.2d 761 (1961)

KLINGBIEL, JUSTICE. Phyllis Gray appeals from a judgment of the circuit court of Cook County dismissing her action for damages. The issues are concerned with the construction and validity of our statute providing for substituted service of process on nonresidents. Since a constitutional question is involved, the appeal is direct to this court.

The suit was brought against the Titan Valve Manufacturing Company and others, on the ground that a certain water heater had exploded and injured the plaintiff. The complaint charges, inter alia, that the Titan company, a foreign corporation, had negligently constructed the safety valve; and that the injuries were suffered as a proximate result thereof. Summons issued and was duly served on Titan's registered agent in Cleveland, Ohio. The corporation appeared specially, filing a motion to quash on the ground that it had not committed a tortious act in Illinois. Its affidavit stated that it does no business here; that it has no agent physically present in Illinois; and that it sells the completed valves to defendant, American Radiator & Standard Sanitary Corporation, outside Illinois. ... The court granted Titan's motion, dismissing both the complaint and the cross claim.

Section 16 of the Civil Practice Act provides that summons may be personally served upon any party outside the State; and that as to nonresidents who have submitted to the jurisdiction of our courts, such service has the force and effect of personal service within Illinois. [C] Under section 17(1)(b) a nonresident who, either in person or through an agent, commits a tortious act within this State submits to jurisdiction. [C] The questions in this case are (1) whether a tortious act was committed here, within the meaning of the statute, despite the fact that the Titan corporation had no agent in Illinois; and (2) whether the statute, if so construed, violates due process of law.

The first aspect to which we must direct our attention is one of statutory construction. Under section 17(1)(b) jurisdiction is predicated on the committing of a tortious act in this State. It is not disputed, for the purpose of this appeal, that a tortious act was committed. The issue depends on whether it was committed in Illinois, so as to warrant the assertion of personal jurisdiction by service of summons in Ohio.

The wrong in the case at bar did not originate in the conduct of a servant physically present here, but arose instead from acts performed at the place of manufacture. Only the consequences occurred in Illinois. It is well established, however, that in law the place of a wrong is where the last event takes place which is necessary to render the actor liable. Restatement, Conflict of Laws, sec. 377. ... We think it is clear that the alleged negligence in manufacturing the valve cannot be separated from the resulting injury; and that for present purposes, like those of liability and limitations, the tort was committed in Illinois.

Titan seeks to avoid this result by arguing that instead of using the word "tort," the legislature employed the term "tortious act"; and that the latter refers only to the act or conduct, separate and apart from any consequences thereof. We cannot accept the argument. To be tortious an act must cause injury. The concept of injury is an inseparable part of the phrase. ... As we observed in Nelson v. Miller, 11 Ill.2d 378, 143 N.E.2d 673 [(1957)], the statute contemplates the exertion of jurisdiction over nonresident defendants to the extent permitted by the due-process clause.

The Titan company contends that if the statute is applied so as to confer jurisdiction in this case it violates the requirement of due process of law. The precise constitutional question thus presented has not heretofore been considered by this court. In the Nelson case the validity of the statute was upheld in an action against a nonresident whose employee, while physically present in Illinois, allegedly caused the injury. The ratio decidendi was that Illinois has an interest in providing relief for injuries caused by persons having "substantial contacts within the State." A standard of fairness or reasonableness was announced, within the limitation that defendant be given a realistic opportunity to appear and be heard. The case at bar concerns the extent to which due process permits substituted service where defendant had no agent or employee in the State of the forum.

Under modern doctrine the power of a State court to enter a binding judgment against one not served with process within the State depends upon two questions: first, whether he has certain minimum contacts with the State (see International Shoe Co. v. State of Washington, 326 U.S. 310, 316 [(1945)], and second, whether there has been a reasonable method of notification. See [id. at 320.] In the case at bar there is no contention that section 16 provides for inadequate notice or that its provisions were not followed. Defendant's argument on constitutionality is confined to the proposition that applying section 17(1)(b), where the injury is defendant's only contact with the State, would exceed the limits of due process.

A proper determination of the question presented requires analysis of those cases which have dealt with the quantum of contact sufficient to warrant jurisdiction. Since the decision in Pennoyer v. Neff, 95 U.S. 714 [(1877)], the power of a State to exert jurisdiction over nonresidents has been greatly expanded, particularly with respect to foreign corporations. [C] International Shoe Co. v. State of Washington, [supra], was a proceeding to collect unpaid contributions to the unemployment compensation fund of the State of Washington. ... In holding that maintenance of the suit did not violate due process the court pointed out that the activities of the corporation in Washington were not only continuous and systematic but also gave rise to the liability sued on. It was observed that such operations, which resulted in a large volume of business, established "sufficient contacts or ties with the state of the forum to make it reasonable and just according to our traditional conception of fair play and substantial justice to permit the state to enforce the obligations which appellant has incurred there." [C]

Where the business done by a foreign corporation in the State of the forum is of a sufficiently substantial nature, it has been held permissible for the State to entertain a suit against it even though the cause of action arose from activities entirely distinct from its conduct within the State. Perkins v. Benguet Consolidated Mining Co., 342 U.S. 437[(1952)]. But where such business or other activity is not substantial, the particular act or transaction having no connection with the State of the forum, the requirement of "contact" is not satisfied. Hanson v. Denckla, 357 U.S. 235, 253[(1958)].

In the case at bar the defendant's only contact with this State is found in the fact that a product manufactured in Ohio was incorporated in Pennsylvania, into a hot water heater which in the course of commerce was sold to an Illinois consumer. The record fails to disclose whether defendant has done any other business in Illinois, either directly or indirectly; and it is argued, in reliance on the International Shoe test, that since a course of business here has not been shown there are no "minimum contacts" sufficient to support jurisdiction. We do not think, however, that doing a given volume of business is the only way in which a nonresident can form the required connection with this State. Since the International Shoe case was decided the requirements for jurisdiction have been further relaxed, so that at the present time it is sufficient if the act or transaction itself has a substantial connection with the State of the forum.

In McGee v. International Life Insurance Co., 355 U.S. 220 [(1957)], suit was brought in California against a foreign insurance company on a policy issued to a resident of California. The defendant was not served with process in that State but was notified by registered mail at its place of business in Texas, pursuant to a statute permitting such service in suits on insurance contracts. The contract in question was delivered in California, the premiums were mailed from there and the insured was a resident of that State when he died, but defendant had no office or agent in California nor did it solicit any business there apart from the policy sued on. After referring briefly to the International Shoe case the court held that "it is sufficient for purposes of due process that the suit was based on a contract which had substantial connection" with California. ...

In Nelson v. Miller, [supra], the commission of a single tort within this State was held sufficient to sustain jurisdiction under the present statute. The defendant in that case, a resident of Wisconsin, was engaged in the business of selling appliances. It was alleged that in the process of delivering a stove in Illinois, an employee of the defendant negligently caused injury to the plaintiff. [This court held] that the defendant was not denied due process by being required to defend in Illinois[.] ...

Whether the type of activity conducted within the State is adequate to satisfy the requirement depends upon the facts in the particular case. [C] The question cannot be answered by applying a mechanical formula or rule of thumb but by ascertaining what is fair and reasonable in the circumstances. In the application of this flexible test the relevant inquiry is whether defendant engaged in some act or conduct by which he may be said to have invoked the benefits and protections of the law of the forum. See Hanson v. Denckla, [supra at] 253[]; International Shoe Co.[, supra at] 319[]. The relevant decisions since Pennoyer v. Neff show a development of the concept of personal jurisdiction from one which requires service of process within the State to one which is satisfied either if the act or transaction sued on occurs there or if defendant has engaged in a sufficiently substantial course of activity in the State, provided always that reasonable notice and opportunity to be heard are afforded. ...

It is true that courts cannot "assume that this trend heralds the eventual demise of all restrictions on the personal jurisdiction of state courts." Hanson v. Denckla, [supra at] 251[]. An orderly and fair administration of the law throughout the nation requires protection against being compelled to answer claims brought in distant States with which the defendant has little or no association and in which he would be faced with an undue burden or disadvantage in making his defense. It must be remembered that lawsuits can be brought on frivolous demands or groundless claims as well as on legitimate ones, and that procedural rules must be designed and appraised in the light of what is fair and just to both sides in the dispute. Interpretations of basic rights which consider only those of a claimant are not consonant with the fundamental requisites of due process.

In the case at bar defendant does not claim that the present use of its product in Illinois is an isolated instance. While the record does not disclose the volume of Titan's business or the territory in which appliances incorporating its valves are marketed, it is a reasonable inference that its commercial transactions, like those of other manufacturers, result in substantial use and consumption in this

State. To the extent that its business may be directly affected by transactions occurring here it enjoys benefits from the laws of this State, and it has undoubtedly benefited, to a degree, from the protection which our law has given to the marketing of hot water heaters containing its valves. Where the alleged liability arises, as in this case, from the manufacture of products presumably sold in contemplation of use here, it should not matter that the purchase was made from an independent middleman or that someone other than the defendant shipped the product into this State.

With the increasing specialization of commercial activity and the growing interdependence of business enterprises it is seldom that a manufacturer deals directly with consumers in other States. The fact that the benefit he derives from its laws is an indirect one, however, does not make it any the less essential to the conduct of his business; and it is not unreasonable, where a cause of action arises from alleged defects in his product, to say that the use of such products in the ordinary course of commerce is sufficient contact with this State to justify a requirement that he defend here.

As a general proposition, if a corporation elects to sell its products for ultimate use in another State, it is not unjust to hold it answerable there for any damage caused by defects in those products. Advanced means of distribution and other commercial activity have made possible these modern methods of doing business, and have largely effaced the economic significance of State lines. By the same token, today's facilities for transportation and communication have removed much of the difficulty and inconvenience formerly encountered in defending lawsuits brought in other States. ...

The principles of due process relevant to the issue in this case support jurisdiction in the court where both parties can most conveniently settle their dispute. The facts show that the plaintiff, an Illinois resident, was injured in Illinois. The law of Illinois will govern the substantive questions, and witnesses on the issues of injury, damages and other elements relating to the occurrence are most likely to be found here. Under such circumstances the courts of the place of injury usually provide the most convenient forum for trial. [C] In Travelers Health Association v. Commonwealth of Virginia, 339 U.S. 643[(1950)], a Nebraska insurance corporation was held subject to the jurisdiction of a Virginia regulatory commission although it had no paid agents within the State and its only contact there was a mail-order business operated from its Omaha office. The court observed, by way of dictum, that "suits on alleged losses can be more conveniently tried in Virginia where witnesses would most likely live and where claims for losses would presumably be investigated. ... And prior decisions of this Court have referred to the unwisdom, unfairness and injustice of permitting policyholders to seek redress only in some distant state where the insurer is incorporated. The Due Process Clause does not forbid a state to protect its citizens from such injustice." [Id.] at 649[]. We think a similar conclusion must follow in the case at bar.

... We conclude accordingly that defendant's association with this State is sufficient to support the exercise of jurisdiction.

We construe section 17(1)(b) as providing for jurisdiction under the circumstances shown in this case, and we hold that as so construed the statute does not violate due process of law.

The trial court erred in quashing service of summons and in dismissing the complaint and cross claim. The judgment is reversed and the cause is remanded to the circuit court of Cook County, with directions to deny the motion to quash.

Reversed and remanded, with directions.

INQUIRY

Statutory Construction. The above *Gray v. American Radiator & Standard Sanitary Corp.* case suggests the challenges that courts can face in construing long-arm statutes whose language is necessarily general, even when the statute is of the type that enumerates specific acts. Green v. Advance Ross Electronics Corp., 427 N.E.2d 1203 (Ill. 1981), is a subsequent case in which the Illinois Supreme Court again construed the statute's broad language regarding tortious acts committed "within the state" based on what it perceived to be the policy behind that part of the long-arm statute. In *Green,* though, the Illinois Supreme Court found that the defendant's allegedly tortious conduct as an Illinois corporate officer acting in another state, the effects of which the corporation felt within Illinois, was not conduct within the terms of the long-arm statute. The Illinois legislature eventually amended the state's long-arm statute to cover "[t]he performance of duties as a director or officer of a corporation organized under the laws of this State... ," 735 ILCS 5/2-209 (1989), presumably addressing that gap in personal jurisdiction. Expect challenges applying long-arm statutes of either type to the infinity variety of human conduct and misconduct. Also recall that confirming the reach of the state's long-arm statute is just one step in the analysis of personal jurisdiction, as the subsequent history of the following familiar case citing *Gray v. American Radiator & Standard Sanitary Corp.* demonstrates.

World-Wide Volkswagen Corp. v. Woodson,

Oklahoma Supreme Court
585 P.2d 351 (1978),
reversed, 444 U.S. 286 (1980)

BARNES, Justice:

This case concerns an original action brought on behalf of World-Wide Volkswagen Corporation and Seaway Volkswagen, Inc., in which the petitioners ask this Court to assume original jurisdiction and issue a writ of prohibition, prohibiting the respondent trial judge, the Honorable Charles S. Woodson, from exercising personal jurisdiction over the petitioners, through service under the Uniform Interstate and International Procedure Act, as adopted in Oklahoma, [c], commonly referred to as the Oklahoma Long-Arm Statute.

The test for applying Long-Arm jurisdiction in Oklahoma is to determine whether the exercise of jurisdiction is authorized by statute, and, if so, whether such exercise of jurisdiction is consistent with the constitutional requirements of due process.[fn]

After examining Oklahoma'a Long-Arm Statute and the facts present in this case, we conclude that jurisdiction over the non-resident petitioners is authorized by statute.

The facts before us in this case are as follows: In September of 1977, an Audi automobile, driven by Kay Eloise Robinson, was struck in the rear by an automobile being driven by a party not involved in the case before us. Mrs. Robinson and her two children, Eva May and George Samuel, were seriously injured in that collision when the gasoline tank of their Audi automobile ruptured, causing a fire in the passenger compartment of that car. As a result of that collision, manufacturers products liability actions were brought on behalf of Mrs. Robinson, her husband and her children against (1) the manufacturer of the automobile, Volkswagenwerk Aktiengesellschaft; (2) against the U.S. importer of the automobile, Volkswagen of America, Inc.; (3) against the distributor of the automobile, World-Wide Volkswagen Corporation; and (4) against the retail dealer who sold the Robinsons the car, Seaway Volkswagen, Inc.

It is World-Wide Volkswagen, distributor of Audis in Connecticut, New York and New Jersey, and Seaway Volkswagen, Inc., the dealer who sold the car, that petition this Court seeking a writ of prohibition. ...

In the case before us, the respondents contend that the courts of Oklahoma have jurisdiction over the petitioners because they caused a tortious injury in this State, giving rise to jurisdiction under the provisions of 12 O.S.1971, §1701.03(a)(3) or (4)[, which] provides in part:

"(a) A court may exercise personal jurisdiction over a person, who acts directly or by an agent, as to a cause of action or claim for relief arising from the person's: ...

"(3) causing tortious injury in this state by an act or omission in this state;

"(4) causing tortious injury in this state by an act or omission outside this state if he regularly does or solicits business or engages in any other persistent course of conduct, or derives substantial revenue from goods used or consumed or services rendered, in this state ; ... ."

While it is true that the alleged acts or omissions of the petitioners allegedly caused tortious injury in this State, none of the acts or omissions alleged took place in this State. The defects in the product allegedly existed at the time the product left the hands of the petitioners, and at that time the automobile was not, and had not been, in the State of Oklahoma. We therefore conclude that no acts or omissions on the part of the petitioners took place within the State. In attempting to convince us that acts or omissions of the petitioners did take place within the State, the respondents rely upon Gray v. American Radiator & Standard Sanitary Corp., [] 176 N.E.2d 761 (1961).

We do not find the analysis used in Gray v. American Radiator, supra, persuasive. In that case, the Illinois Supreme Court was interpreting a provision of the Illinois Revised Statutes which provided that a nonresident, who either in person or through an agent Commits a tortious act within Illinois, submits to the jurisdiction of Illinois, and may be served by means of the State Long-Arm Statute. In determining whether the manufacturer of a defective safety valve, which was allegedly defective at the time of manufacture in Ohio, committed a "tortious act" in the State of Illinois, the Court held that a tort had been committed within the jurisdiction because the injury which resulted from the defect occurred in Illinois. In so ruling, the Court held that the place of a wrong is where the last event necessary to render the actor liable takes place, and that the last act to render the manufacturer liable was the sustaining of an injury in Illinois by the plaintiff.

Our statute is unlike the Illinois statute. The Illinois statute merely requires that a tortious act be committed within Illinois. The Illinois court ruling makes a party subject to Illinois jurisdiction if his acts ultimately result in tortious injury within Illinois. Our statute requires more than the occurrence of tortious injury within the State before a party is subject to personal jurisdiction. Under the provisions of subsection (a)(3) ... , a person is subject to personal jurisdiction in Oklahoma if he causes tortious injury in the State "by an act or omission in this state." It is not possible to interpret the provisions of subsection (a)(3) ... in the same way in which Illinois interpreted its statute, as such an interpretation would be inconsistent with subsection (a)(4) of the same section, which specifically sets forth the prerequisites for in personam jurisdiction in situations in which tortious injury in this State is caused by acts or omissions outside the State. ...

Because our statute required more contact with the State than the Illinois statute, we are not persuaded by the Illinois court's rationale in Gray v. American Radiator, supra. Accordingly, we hold that the acts or omissions of the petitioners, which are alleged in the petition, were not acts or omissions in this State, and therefore no power to exercise personal jurisdiction over the petitioners existed by virtue of the provisions of 12 O.S.1971, §1701.03(a)(3).

We next consider whether the power to exercise personal jurisdiction over the petitioners existed by virtue of 12 O.S.1971, §1701.03(a)(4). Under the provisions of subsection (a)(4) ... more is required than the mere occurrence of tortious injury in this State. Under the provisions of that subsection, a party causing tortious injury in this State by acts or omissions outside the State is subject to the exercise of personal jurisdiction of this State, if "He regularly does or solicits business or engages in any other persistent course of conduct, or derives substantial revenue from goods used or consumed or services rendered, in this state."

In the case before us, the product being sold and distributed by the petitioners is by its very design and purpose so mobile that petitioners can foresee its possible use in Oklahoma. This is especially true of the distributor, who has the exclusive right to distribute such automobile in New York, New Jersey and Connecticut. The evidence presented below demonstrated that goods sold and distributed by the petitioners were used in the State of Oklahoma, and under the facts we believe it reasonable to infer, given the retail value of the automobile, that the petitioners derive substantial income from automobiles which from time to time are used in the State of Oklahoma. This being the case, we hold that under the facts presented, the trial court was justified in concluding that the petitioners derive substantial revenue from goods used or consumed in this State.

Because the trial court was justified in concluding that the petitioners derived substantial revenue from goods used within the State, and because alleged acts or omissions on the part of petitioners outside the State allegedly caused tortious injury in this State, we hold that the trial court had the power, pursuant to 12 O.S.1971, §1701.03(a)(4), to exercise personal jurisdiction over the petitioners. As the trial court had such power, we refuse to issue a writ of prohibition.

ORIGINAL JURISDICTION ASSUMED AND ORIGINAL PROHIBITION DENIED.

INQUIRY

Other Steps. In the opinion that you read earlier in this chapter in the same *World-Wide Volkswagen v. Woodson, supra,* the United States Supreme Court reversed the Oklahoma Supreme Court, holding that the plaintiff had not established the defendant's constitutional minimum contacts. 444 U.S. 286 (1980). The above opinion of the Oklahoma Supreme Court began by acknowledging that the test for personal jurisdiction "is to determine whether the exercise of jurisdiction is authorized by statute, and, if so, whether such exercise of jurisdiction is consistent with the constitutional requirements of due process." The Oklahoma Supreme Court decided the first question as to the reach of the long-arm statute. Did it decide the second question as to the constitutionality of personal jurisdiction? Are those two questions the only questions to answer to determine jurisdiction, or is there a third question? The next chapter addresses the constitutional requirements of notice and opportunity for hearing.

2. Reach of the Federal Courts

Like state trial courts, legislation establishes the personal-jurisdiction reach of the federal district courts, within constitutional limits. Some federal statutes like the Securities and Exchange Act of 1934, 15 U.S.C. §78aa, and Employee Retirement Income Security Act (ERISA), 29 U.S.C. §1132(e)(2), grant nationwide or even worldwide personal jurisdiction, while others like the Anti-Terrorism Act, 18 U.S.C. §§2300, 2334, grant the district courts personal jurisdiction only over defendants who reside, are in, or have an agent in the district. FED. R. CIV. P. 4(k)(1)(C) recognizes the personal jurisdiction extended by these federal statutes by providing, "Serving a summons or filing a waiver of service establishes personal jurisdiction over a defendant ... when authorized by federal statute." Where no federal statute grants a district court personal jurisdiction over a defendant in an action, FED. R. CIV. P. 4(k)(1)(A) authorizes the district court to extend personal jurisdiction to the same extent as the long-arm statute of the district's state. It provides, "Serving a summons or filing a waiver of service establishes personal jurisdiction over a defendant ... who is subject to the jurisdiction of a court of general jurisdiction in the state where the district court is located... ." The two jurisdiction provisions in Rule 4(k)(1)(A) and (C), and particularly subsection (A)'s grant of jurisdiction co-extensive with the state long-arm statute, establish personal jurisdiction for the vast majority of federal district court cases.

Rule 4 recognizes two other, significantly more rare circumstances in which the federal district courts will have personal jurisdiction. Rule 4(k)(1)(B) recognizes personal jurisdiction in a federal district court over a defendant "who is a party joined under Rule 14 or 19 and is served within a judicial district of the United States and not more than 100 miles from where the summons was issued...

." Rule 14 permits a defendant to plead (third-party) claims against non-parties for the liability that the plaintiff has alleged against the defendant. Rule 19 permits the court to add non-parties to the action when their presence in the action is necessary to the just resolution of the pending claims. In essence, Rule 4(k)(1)(B), known as the 100-mile bulge rule, allows a district court to exercise personal jurisdiction over additional parties to a very modestly greater extent than the other personal-jurisdiction subrules, when they are relatively near the courthouse. Rule 4(k)(2) addresses the even more curious situation of when a foreign defendant has minimum contacts with the United States as a whole but not with any one state. Rule 4(k)(2), added as the result of the Supreme Court's decision in Omni Capital Intl. V. Rudolf Wolff & Co., 484 U.S. 97 (1987), provides for personal jurisdiction over a defendant "if (A) the defendant is not subject to jurisdiction in any state's courts of general jurisdiction; and (b) exercising jurisdiction is consistent with the United States Constitution and laws."

Given Rule 4's prominence in determining personal jurisdiction in the federal district courts, one might think that much of federal district court personal jurisdiction is rule-based rather than statutory. Recall from Chapter I, though, that Congress' Rules Enabling Act, 28 USC §2072, authorizes the Supreme Court to adopt and amend the FEDERAL RULES, meaning that all personal jurisdiction of the federal district courts is ultimately created by federal statute. Rule 4 reads more like a rule for service of process than a grant of personal jurisdiction. Rule 4 has a service-of-process tenor because federal statute, not the FEDERAL RULES, authorize personal jurisdiction. The Supreme Court was not being oblique in drafting Rule 4. It was instead being appropriately deferential to the legislative source of trial court power. Consider the following issues that these federal statutes and Rule 4's provisions raise.

INQUIRY

Nationwide Contacts. When a federal statute grants a federal district court personal jurisdiction over any defendant within the United States (nationwide personal jurisdiction), and the plaintiff serves a defendant consistent with Rule 4(k)(1)(C) invoking that federal statute, what minimum contacts does *International Shoe* and its progeny require before the court can constitutionally exercise personal jurisdiction? Strange as it may seem from the many cases following *International Shoe* in which state contacts were the measure, in the majority of federal circuits nationwide personal jurisdiction requires the federal district court to determine whether the defendant had minimum contacts with the *nation as a whole* rather than with any individual state. *See* Pinker v. Roche Holdings, Ltd., 292 F.3d 361, 369 (3d Cir. 2002); Busch v. Buchman, Buchman & O'Brien, 11 F.3d 1255, 1258 (5th Cir. 1994). The Eleventh Circuit takes the contrary view that nationwide minimum contacts may not satisfy the Fifth Amendment's due-process clause, while acknowledging that its view is a departure. Republic of Panama v. BCCI Holdings (Luxembourg) S.A., 119 F.3d 935, 947 (11th Cir. 1997); *see also* Oxford First Corp. v. PNC Liquidating Corp., 372 F.Supp. 191 (E.D. Pa. 1974) (Fifth Amendment due process requires fairness determined by defendant's contacts and inconvenience, the impact of defendant's conduct, judicial economy, and location of discovery). Why might nationwide contacts not be enough? Why, as to federal district court personal jurisdiction, is it the Fifth Amendment's due-process clause rather than the Fourteenth Amendment's due-process clause that controls? When a United States district court is applying a United States statute to a United States resident, why are nationwide contacts and personal jurisdiction even an issue? *See* Stafford v. Briggs, 444 U.S. 527, 553-554 (1980) (Stewart, J., dissenting) (there is no Fifth Amendment due-process issue for a federal district court exercising personal jurisdiction over a United States resident in a case applying federal law). The unresolved fundamental issue is whether the fairness concerns of *International Shoe* in effect limit national sovereignty within its own borders.

The Internet. Recall the case of Pebble Beach Co. v. Caddy, 453 F.3d 1151 (9th Cir. 2006), applying *International Shoe's* minimum-contacts test to the personal jurisdiction based on Internet contacts. Given the Ninth Circuit's holding in *Pebble Beach Co. v. Caddy* that the foreign defendant did not have minimum contacts with California, what prospects might the plaintiff have had for Rule 4(k)(2) nationwide contacts? The opinion held that not even the fact that the offending website domain name www.pebblebeach-uk.com may have attracted American vacationers to the defendant's resort in England was sufficient to establish nationwide contacts.

Worldwide Contacts. When a federal statute grants a federal district court personal jurisdiction over any defendant worldwide (nationwide personal jurisdiction), and the plaintiff serves a non-U.S.-resident defendant consistent with Rule 4(k)(2) invoking that federal statute, who has to prove or disprove what contacts? Some courts place the burden on the plaintiff to prove that no state court would have personal jurisdiction over the defendant and that the only there is only nationwide minimum contacts. *See* BP Chemicals Ltd. v. Formosa Chemical & Fibre Corp., 229 F.3d 254, 259 (3d Cir. 2000). Other courts place the burden on the defendant to claim a state (presumably other than the state in which the federal district court the plaintiff chose is located) that has personal jurisdiction because of the defendant's minimum contacts there. *See* ISI Intl., Inc. v. Borden Ladner Gervais LLP, 256 F.3d 548, 552 (7th Cir. 2001); *see also* United States v. Swiss American Bank, Ltd., 191 F.3d 30, 41 (1st Cir. 1999) (defendant has burden of proving state personal jurisdiction only after plaintiff makes case for nationwide-only personal jurisdiction).

E. Challenging Jurisdiction

You may already have anticipated from the above cases and discussion some of the issues surrounding just how a defendant can properly go about the curious task of challenging the personal jurisdiction of a court that the defendant claims has no power over the defendant. There are two ways in which a defendant can challenge personal jurisdiction, either (1) directly, by special appearance in the court in which the plaintiff has filed the case, where the defendant maintains that there is no personal jurisdiction, or (2) collaterally, after the plaintiff has taken a default judgment in the court in which the defendant maintains there is no jurisdiction, and when the plaintiff attempts to enforce that judgment in another state (the defendant's state) where there is jurisdiction. As you read the following two sections addressing each of the two approaches, consider in what types of cases and under what circumstances you might advise a client to take one approach over the other approach.

1. Special Appearance

A defendant who makes a direct challenge to jurisdiction asks a court to rule that it has no power to rule—on anything other than its inability to exercise jurisdiction. The defendant who makes that direct challenge must take care not to commit an act that the court will construe as consent to its general jurisdiction. The common-law means by which defendants appeared to contest jurisdiction without submitting unintentionally to the challenged court's general jurisdiction was by special appearance. Depending on the state's particular statutes and court rules, a special appearance might simply be a court paper bearing that title, stating the grounds for the jurisdictional challenge, also stating that the defendant is not making a general appearance, and then not answering, defending, or raising any other issue. *See, e.g.*, ILL. COMP. STAT. 5/2-301(b) (2004); TEX. R. CIV. P. 120a (2003). Although state-court rules vary, the *Federal Rules of Civil Procedure* provide a representative procedure for challenging personal jurisdiction. Read the following FED. R. CIV. P. 12 for the relevant provisions in Subrules 12(b), (g), and (h). Notice that Rule 12(b) requires a defendant to challenge personal jurisdiction by motion before the first responsive pleading and then also to allege lack of personal jurisdiction in any subsequent responsive pleading. Notice also how Rule 12(g) and (h) work together to require a defendant to raise lack of personal jurisdiction in the first motion or consider the defense waived.

FED. R. CIV. P. 12. Defenses and Objections: When and How Presented; Motion for Judgment on the Pleadings; Consolidating Motions; Waiving Defenses; Pretrial Hearing

(a) TIME TO SERVE A RESPONSIVE PLEADING.

(1) *In General.* Unless another time is specified by this rule or a federal statute, the time for serving a responsive pleading is as follows:

(A) A defendant must serve an answer:

(i) within 21 days after being served with the summons and complaint; or

(ii) if it has timely waived service under Rule 4(d), within 60 days after the request for a waiver was sent,

or within 90 days after it was sent to the defendant outside any judicial district of the United States.

(B) A party must serve an answer to a counterclaim or crossclaim within 21 days after being served with the pleading that states the counterclaim or crossclaim.

(C) A party must serve a reply to an answer within 21 days after being served with an order to reply, unless the order specifies a different time.

(2) *United States and Its Agencies, Officers, or Employees Sued in an Official Capacity.* The United States, a United States agency, or a United States officer or employee sued only in an official capacity must serve an answer to a complaint, counterclaim, or crossclaim within 60 days after service on the United States attorney.

(3) *United States Officers or Employees Sued in an Individual Capacity.* A United States officer or employee sued in an individual capacity for an act or omission occurring in connection with duties performed on the United States' behalf must serve an answer to a complaint, counterclaim, or crossclaim within 60 days after service on the officer or employee or service on the United States attorney, whichever is later.

(4) *Effect of a Motion.* Unless the court sets a different time, serving a motion under this rule alters these periods as follows:

(A) if the court denies the motion or postpones its disposition until trial, the responsive pleading must be served within 14 days after notice of the court's action; or

(B) if the court grants a motion for a more definite statement, the responsive pleading must be served within 14 days after the more definite statement is served.

(b) HOW TO PRESENT DEFENSES. Every defense to a claim for relief in any pleading must be asserted in the responsive pleading if one is required. But a party may assert the following defenses by motion:

(1) lack of subject-matter jurisdiction;

(2) lack of personal jurisdiction;

(3) improper venue;

(4) insufficient process;

(5) insufficient service of process;

(6) failure to state a claim upon which relief can be granted; and

(7) failure to join a party under Rule 19.

A motion asserting any of these defenses must be made before pleading if a responsive pleading is allowed. If a pleading sets out a claim for relief that does not require a responsive pleading, an opposing party may assert at trial any defense to that claim. No defense or objection is waived by joining it with one or more other defenses or objections in a responsive pleading or in a motion.

(c) MOTION FOR JUDGMENT ON THE PLEADINGS. After the pleadings are closed—but early enough not to delay trial—a party may move for judgment on the pleadings.

(d) RESULT OF PRESENTING MATTERS OUTSIDE THE PLEADINGS. If, on a motion under Rule 12(b)(6) or 12(c), matters outside the pleadings are presented to and not excluded by the court, the motion must be treated as one for summary judgment under Rule 56. All parties must be given a reasonable opportunity to present all the material that is pertinent to the motion.

(e) MOTION FOR A MORE DEFINITE STATEMENT. A party may move for a more definite statement of a pleading to which a responsive pleading is allowed but which is so vague or ambiguous that the
party cannot reasonably prepare a response. The motion must be made before filing a responsive pleading and must point out the defects complained of and the details desired. If the court orders a more definite statement and the order is not obeyed within 14 days after notice of the order or within the time the court sets, the court may strike the pleading or issue any other appropriate order.

(f) MOTION TO STRIKE. The court may strike from a pleading an insufficient defense or any redundant, immaterial, impertinent, or scandalous matter. The court may act:

(1) on its own; or

(2) on motion made by a party either before responding to the pleading or, if a response is not allowed, within 21 days after being served with the pleading.

(g) JOINING MOTIONS.

(1) *Right to Join.* A motion under this rule may be joined with any other motion allowed by this rule.

(2) *Limitation on Further Motions.* Except as provided in Rule 12(h)(2) or (3), a party that makes a motion under this rule must not make another motion under this rule raising a defense or objection that was available to the party but omitted from its earlier motion.

(h) WAIVING AND PRESERVING CERTAIN DEFENSES.

(1) *When Some Are Waived.* A party waives any defense listed in Rule 12(b)(2)–(5) by:

(A) omitting it from a motion in the circumstances described in Rule 12(g)(2); or

(B) failing to either:

(i) make it by motion under this rule; or

(ii) include it in a responsive pleading or in an amendment allowed by Rule 15(a)(1) as a matter of course.

(2) *When to Raise Others.* Failure to state a claim upon which relief can be granted, to join a person required by Rule 19(b), or to state a legal defense to a claim may be raised:

(A) in any pleading allowed or ordered under Rule 7(a);

(B) by a motion under Rule 12(c); or

(C) at trial.

(3) *Lack of Subject-Matter Jurisdiction.* If the court determines at any time that it lacks subject-matter jurisdiction, the court must dismiss the action.

(i) HEARING BEFORE TRIAL. If a party so moves, any defense listed in Rule 12(b)(1)–(7)—whether made in a pleading or by motion— and a motion under Rule 12(c) must be heard and decided before trial unless the court orders a deferral until trial.

INQUIRY

Procedure. The trial court has substantial discretion to shape the procedures by which it will decide a defendant's challenge to personal jurisdiction by special appearance. *See* Data Disc, Inc. v. Systems Technology Associates, Inc., 557 F.2d 1280, 1285-1286 (9th Cir. 1977). As the case Insurance Corp. of Ireland v. Compagnie des Bauxites de Guinee, 456 U.S. 694 (1982), discussed in a prior section on jurisdiction by estoppel, showed, those procedures may include the plaintiff's right to discover from the defendant the extent of its forum-state contacts. Recall that the Supreme Court in *Insurance Corp. of Ireland* affirmed the trial court's exercise of personal jurisdiction over the insurer defendant challenging it because of the defendant's failure to comply with discovery on the issue. The trial court may permit the plaintiff to serve interrogatories and require the defendant to answer them. The trial court may permit the plaintiff to serve document requests and require the defendant to respond with the documents. The court may permit the plaintiff to take depositions. Then, after appropriate briefing and argument, the court may rule or, if the facts seem too much in dispute, may either hold a summary trial on the disputed jurisdictional issues or may simply set the case over for trial on the merits, reserving the jurisdictional issue for decision after that trial. Indeed, *Data Disc, Inc., supra,* suggested that the trial court may prefer the latter procedure—fullblown trial on the merits—in order that "a plaintiff may present his case in a coherent, orderly fashion and without the risk of prejudicing his case on the merits." Does the trial court's flexibility to design and implement an appropriate procedure beg the question of its power over the defendant who must, as *Insurance Corp. of Ireland* showed, comply with the trial court's reasonable procedures?

Practice

"Go on, take a piece of candy," the old trial judge urged with a grin and gesture when he noticed defense counsel's eyes examining the bowl on the judge's desk as counsel entered the judge's chambers. The local plaintiff's lawyer, who was a longtime acquaintance of the trial judge, grabbed the bowl of candy and rooted through it for a favorite before offering it to the out-of-town defense counsel, who ignored the offer. "Now tell me again about this matter of your making a special appearance to challenge jurisdiction. We don't get that kind of thing around here much even though I've heard of it," the trial judge said with a subtle smile.

Defense counsel took the trial judge's bait, launching into an explanation that sounded like she was lecturing an unprepared student. "Very interesting, counsel," the trial judge nodded as the lecture ended, "Have you heard of this before?" the trial judge asked the plaintiff's lawyer who shrugged without committing. "Well, here's what we'll do. We will set your motion for hearing in two weeks. Is that okay with you, counsel? You don't mind coming all the way back out here again, do you?" the trial judge added with another faint smile.

2. Collateral Attack

The defendant's alternative to a special appearance is a collateral attack on the judgment. When a plaintiff serves a defendant in an action filed in a court that does not have jurisdiction, or the defendant otherwise learns of the pending action, the defendant has the option of not responding, instead allowing the plaintiff to take a default judgment, and then challenging the judgment in any subsequent enforcement action including (especially) one in the defendant's home state where it has assets on which the plaintiff may attempt to execute. *See* D'Arcy v. Ketchum, 52 U.S. 165 (1850) (approving collateral attack on judgment taken without personal jurisdiction). Note that the defendant cannot have it both ways. The Supreme Court in Baldwin v. Iowa State Traveling Men's Assn., 283 U.S. 522 (1931), held that a defendant who makes a special appearance to challenge jurisdiction in the original action but loses that challenge may not later collaterally attack on the same jurisdictional grounds the judgment the defendant suffered in that original action, even if the defendant withdrew after the lost special appearance and suffered only a default judgment. An appearance solely to challenge personal jurisdiction is special but not that special. The defendant gets only one chance at the challenge and must choose at its own peril. The choice indeed seems perilous. For instance, in retrospect, would it have been better for the defendant insurer in Insurance Corp. of Ireland v. Compagnie des Bauxites de Guinee, 456 U.S. 694 (1982), to have just ignored the action rather than make a half-hearted challenge to it? The insurer may have felt that challenging jurisdiction in a state where it claimed not to have even minimum contacts was a "damned if you do or don't" Hobson's choice, especially given the outcome in which its failure to fully participate cost it the jurisdictional challenge. On the other hand, the plaintiff has a somewhat similar problem in deciding whether to proceed with obtaining and attempting to enforce a judgment made worthless because of the absence of personal jurisdiction over the defendant in the issuing state. Why, after all, do parties retain skilled lawyers?

Summary. Personal jurisdiction may seem a complex subject because of its gradual development related to a long history of improvements in transportation and technology. Yet its basic concepts are (at least by now) relatively straightforward. To obtain an enforceable judgment, a plaintiff must choose a court that has personal jurisdiction over the defendant. For personal jurisdiction to meet the Constitution's due-process standard, the defendant must have had minimum contacts with the jurisdiction, meaning that the defendant acted purposefully toward the jurisdiction and that jurisdiction would be reasonable. Determining minimum contacts requires examining the burden on the defendant along with the interests of the plaintiff, state, and community of states, and efficient resolution. Where the defendant's contacts with the state did not give rise to the litigation for purposes of specific jurisdiction, the court may still exercise general jurisdiction over the litigated dispute if the defendant's contacts with the state were sufficiently continuous, systematic, and substantial. In-state service of process continues to satisfy the constitutional requirements through transient jurisdiction. Personal jurisdiction also depends on the court's statutory authority, meaning state long-arm statutes for state trial courts and the statutes of the forum state or another FED. R. CIV. P. 4 basis for the federal district courts. These concepts are fundamental to understanding the limits on a court's authority.

Career

Which do you prefer, criminal or civil law? A good way to explore a career as a trial lawyer is to determine whether you are interested in criminal law and procedure, or civil litigation. Certainly, the skills for each are similar. Yet each field has its own peculiar character. The subject matters are fundamentally different, either crime and the government's responsibility to deter and punish it on the one hand or private civil disputes involving family law, contracts, torts, real property, business interests, and the like on the other hand. Lawyers (and law students) develop an affinity for subject fields. Crime and government conduct fascinate some of us. Other lawyers find private civil disputes to portray more of the richness and meaning of life. Many lawyers practice in both civil- and criminal-law fields. Many more lawyers concentrate solely or primarily in either criminal-justice or civil-litigation work. There are many ways to explore whether you have an affinity for civil litigation including volunteering, interning, and networking.

CHAPTER III

NOTICE AND OPPORTUNITY FOR HEARING

OBJECTIVE: That you be able to determine the methods by which process must be served in order to satisfy constitutional, statutory, and court-rule requirements for an enforceable judgment.

Case Study: You are meeting with a couple whose builder absconded with substantial funds that the couple had paid for an addition to their home. The couple has authorized that you file a civil action against the builder. The couple does not know where the builder is but has heard that he moved to a friend's cabin in a Western state. You must determine how to serve the builder with the summons and complaint in the action so that the judgment you obtain, likely by the builder's default, will be valid in an enforcement action in any state in which investigation discloses the builder has income or assets.

Federal Rules of Civil Procedure this chapter reproduces and addresses:
FED. R. CIV. P. 64: Seizing Person or Property.

The previous chapter addressed the constitutional limits of the power of the state and federal courts authorized by the grant of state long-arm statutes or federal rules and statutes. The statutory authority of courts to decide and the constitutional limits on their reach are just two of three preliminary issues the parties, their lawyers, and the trial courts must address over the power of courts to decide. A third issue has to do with the sufficiency of the notice the plaintiff gives to the defendant in order to enable the defendant to respond to the case, obtaining a hearing. The power of a court to decide, and whether the plaintiff or court have given the defendant adequate notice and opportunity for hearing, are actually distinct constitutional questions, even though for a long time courts treated together the two questions of constitutional power and constitutional notice. Recall Pennoyer v. Neff, 95 U.S. 714 (1878), in which the lower court issue was whether the plaintiff's small-print notice in the legal news met the state statute for service of process. In *Pennoyer v. Neff,* the Supreme Court turned that statutory question into a constitutional question of the trial court's power to exercise jurisdiction. *Pennoyer v. Neff* did not answer the separate question of whether printing a small notice in a local legal news was constitutionally adequate notice giving the defendant fair opportunity for hearing. It was not until much later as personal jurisdiction expanded through *Pennoyer's* concepts that the

Supreme Court began to articulate a separate constitutional standard for notice. There is no question today that notice and opportunity for hearing are separate constitutional issues. Notice and the opportunity for hearing are the fundamentals of due process. The Fifth and Fourteenth Amendment due-process clauses, applicable to the federal and state courts respectively, require fair notice and reasonable opportunity for hearing. The following section on service of process treats notice issues. A later section of this chapter addresses issues around opportunity for hearing.

A. Service of Process

Service of process is the phrase the law uses to describe the way that the plaintiff or court gives the defendant notice that the plaintiff has filed a complaint against the defendant. A lawyer initiates a lawsuit on a plaintiff's behalf by filing a complaint with the trial court clerk. The lawyer will simultaneously prepare a summons for the court clerk to sign and issue. The summons is the court clerk's signed notice demanding that the defendant appear and defend. To *serve process* is to bring the summons and complaint to the defendant's attention in an authorized manner that one can later prove if necessary. A plaintiff who obtains a summons from the court clerk to serve on the defendant along with the complaint will ordinarily want to do so promptly, both to get the litigation moving forward and because summonses may expire, *see* MICH. CT. RULE 2.102(D) (summons expires 91 days after filing of complaint), statute may require service within a certain period, *see* CAL. CODE CIV. P. §583.210(a) (three years within which to serve summons and complaint), or the trial court may dismiss for failure to prosecute, *see* FED. R. CIV. P. 41(b).

A plaintiff might serve a defendant with a summons and complaint in a variety of ways. Those ways fall into a rough hierarchy from surest to least sure to put the defendant on notice. Responsible practitioners naturally tend to prefer the surest and most efficient means of service, which tends to be in-person service using a process server. Another means is to serve by some form of mail (regular, certified, registered, restricted delivery, return receipt, etc.). Another means is to serve by publication in a newspaper and finally by posting (such as by tacking the complaint on the door of the defendant's residence). The manner in which the plaintiff serves process under the case's particular circumstances determines whether notice was constitutionally adequate.

Unfortunately, some cases and statutes use the same or similar phrases, such as nationwide *process* (see the Federal Interpleader Act, 28 U.S.C. §2361), when they mean to refer not to the adequacy or means of notice but to the court's power to decide (its personal jurisdiction). Still other cases refer to lack of jurisdiction when they mean to refer not to the absence of constitutional power to decide but to the failure of the defendant to give constitutionally adequate notice of the case by proper service of process. As you read this chapter, keep separate the concepts of power and notice. Also, keep in mind the difference that the question of notice makes. A subsequent court considering enforcement action outside the forum state whose court issued a judgment need not give that judgment the Constitution's requisite full faith and credit if the plaintiff took the judgment without personal jurisdiction over the defendant including constitutionally appropriate service of process. The federal statutory authority reflected by FED. R. CIV. P. 4 carries that constitutional mandate into full effect. There are few if any constitutional issues when a plaintiff serves a defendant by complying with Rule 4 because the Supreme Court obviously designed the rule to meet its own understanding of the Constitution. The issues around notice and opportunity for hearing instead typically arise around the various state statutes and rules for service of process. In other words, a lawyer must know what (1) the Constitution requires and (2) state law permits, in order to determine how to serve or challenge the service of process. The following two sections address those two subjects.

Practice

"Looks like a home-run case, doesn't it?" the associate asked the partner, employing just the right mix of confident assertion and authentic query.

"Yeah, right," the partner replied with an appreciative but lightly sarcastic tone, adding, "You know what they say about all new cases."

The associate knew what the partner meant because the associate had heard the partner say it several times before. The associate now had just enough experience to begin to understand and believe the partner's aphorism. Whether it involves a new plaintiff's case or new case to defend, lawyers tend to hear from their own clients only the better part of the story. Parties naturally tend to shape their experience to their own viewpoint. Lawyers hear only one side from their own clients. Parties also tend to know less about their case than the lawyers are about to learn through discovery.

And so, the associate replied quickly to the partner before the partner could continue. "I sure do know what they say," the associate chuckled with a broad smile, "No case is better than the day you get it." The associate knew that hard work and disappointments were ahead but still suspected, as the associate knew that the partner also suspected, that the case was a good one for the client.

1. Constitutional Requirement

The Supreme Court held in Mullane v. Central Hanover Bank & Trust Co., 339 U.S. 306 (1950) (excerpted and discussed below), that the Constitution requires a plaintiff to serve process on the defendant in a manner that the plaintiff *reasonably calculates* to effect notice. Notice that the Supreme Court eschewed a bright-line rule, such as that the Constitution requires personal service, in favor of a functional test that requires the courts to look each time to the circumstances. One reason why there is a functional test rather than bright-line rule for determining the constitutionality of service of process is that parties can more easily manipulate bright-line rules. Keep in mind the disincentives both sides have to service of process. Plaintiffs can take default judgments when defendants do not appear and defend. A default judgment ordinarily takes little time and expense, and provides complete and certain relief. Plaintiffs may prefer that defendants not appear and defend, even if it means, by manipulating a service-of-process rule, that the defendant not have notice. Defendants have their own disincentive to service of process. As long as the plaintiff is unable to serve the defendant, the defendant has no legal obligation to appear and defend, and the plaintiff cannot obtain an enforceable judgment. Some defendants dodge service of process to avoid the time, trouble, expense, and sanction of judgment, and to delay and frustrate the plaintiff, burden the plaintiff with additional expense, and deny the plaintiff sought-after relief. The Supreme Court cases on service of process navigate between requiring enough of the plaintiff to assure notice while not requiring too much of the plaintiff when the defendant's actions, intentional or not, frustrate and increase the burden and expense of notice.

Like the personal-jurisdiction doctrine in the previous chapter, there is some history to the Supreme Court's service-of-process jurisprudence. The Supreme Court reached its *Mullane* decision on constitutionally adequate notice not long after deciding *International Shoe* on the minimum-contacts standard for personal jurisdiction. The Supreme Court continues to decide new cases on constitutionally adequate notice, just as it continues to decide new cases on minimum contacts. *International Shoe* and *Mullane* remain the stepping-off points for contemporary decisions on personal jurisdiction and adequate notice. *Mullane's* "reasonably calculated" standard remains the source of the Supreme Court's notice jurisprudence. Even so, some helpful history predates *Mullane.* In McDonald v. Mabee, 243 U.S. 90, 92 (1917), the Supreme Court held constitutionally inadequate a default judgment taken on a promissory note after service of process by publication in the local newspaper once each week for four weeks, after the defendant had already moved out of state, because the service was not the "most likely to reach the defendant... ." Notice the difference between *Mullane's* "reasonably calculated" standard and *McDonald's* "most likely" standard, and recognize that *Mullane's* latter standard is the one that prevails. Also, in Wuchter v. Pizzutti, 276 U.S. 13 (1928), the Supreme Court held constitutionally inadequate a statute that appointed the secretary of state to receive service of process for non-resident motorists but that did not require the secretary of state to then give any notice to those non-resident motorists. *Wuchter* remains an anomaly because the secretary of state actually did give notice to the defendant motorist, notwithstanding the statute's silence. While not the source of today's notice jurisprudence, *McDonald* and *Wuchter* do help to clarify and confirm the currency of *Mullane's* "reasonably calculated" standard.

Mullane v. Central Hanover Bank & Trust Co.,

United States Supreme Court
339 U.S. 306 (1950)

Mr. Justice JACKSON delivered the opinion of the Court.

This controversy questions the constitutional sufficiency of notice to beneficiaries on judicial settlement of accounts by the trustee of a common trust fund established under the New York Banking Law... ., Consol.Laws, c. 2. The New York Court of Appeals considered and overruled objections that the statutory notice contravenes requirements of the Fourteenth Amendment and that by allowance of the account beneficiaries were deprived of property without due process of law. ...

Common trust fund legislation is addressed to a problem appropriate for state action. Mounting overheads have made administration of small trusts undesirable to corporate trustees. In order that donors and testators of moderately sized trusts may not be denied the service of corporate fiduciaries, the District of

Columbia and some thirty states other than New York have permitted pooling small trust estates into one fund for investment administration.[fn] The income, capital gains, losses and expenses of the collective trust are shared by the constituent trusts in proportion to their contribution. By this plan, diversification of risk and economy of management can be extended to those whose capital standing alone would not obtain such advantage.

Statutory authorization for the establishment of such common trust funds is provided in the New York Banking Law… [requiring that] [t]he trust company must keep fund assets separate from its own, and in its fiduciary capacity may not deal with itself or any affiliate. Provisions are made for accountings twelve to fifteen months after the establishment of a fund and triennially thereafter. The decree in each such judicial settlement of accounts is made binding and conclusive as to any matter set forth in the account upon everyone having any interest in the common fund or in any participating estate, trust or fund.

In January, 1946, Central Hanover Bank and Trust Company established a common trust fund in accordance with these provisions, and in March, 1947, it petitioned the Surrogate's Court for settlement of its first account as common trustee. During the accounting period a total of 113 trusts, approximately half inter vivos and half testamentary, participated in the common trust fund, the gross capital of which was nearly three million dollars. The record does not show the number or residence of the beneficiaries, but they were many and it is clear that some of them were not residents of the State of New York.

The only notice given beneficiaries of this specific application was by publication in a local newspaper in strict compliance with the minimum requirements of N.Y. Banking Law §100-c(12): "After filing such petition (for judicial settlement of its account) the petitioner shall cause to be issued by the court in which the petition is filed and shall publish not less than once in each week for four successive weeks in a newspaper to be designated by the court a notice or citation addressed generally without naming them to all parties interested in such common trust fund and in such estates, trusts or funds mentioned in the petition, all of which may be described in the notice or citation only in the manner set forth in said petition and without setting forth the residence of any such decedent or donor of any such estate, trust or fund." Thus the only notice required, and the only one given, was by newspaper publication setting forth merely the name and address of the trust company, the name and the date of establishment of the common trust fund, and a list of all participating estates, trusts or funds.

At the time the first investment in the common fund was made on behalf of each participating estate, however, the trust company, pursuant to the requirements of §100-c(9), had notified by mail each person of full age and sound mind whose name and address was then known to it and who was "entitled to share in the income therefrom … [or] … who would be entitled to share in the principal if the event upon which such estate, trust or fund will become distributable should have occurred at the time of sending such notice." Included in the notice was a copy of those provisions of the Act relating to the sending of the notice itself and to the judicial settlement of common trust fund accounts.

Upon the filing of the petition for the settlement of accounts, appellant was … appointed special guardian and attorney for all persons known or unknown not otherwise appearing who had or might thereafter have any interest in the income of the common trust fund; and appellee Vaughan was appointed to represent those similarly interested in the principal. There were no other appearances on behalf of any one interested in either interest or principal.

Appellant appeared specially, objecting that notice and the statutory provisions for notice to beneficiaries were inadequate to afford due process under the Fourteenth Amendment, and therefore that the court was without jurisdiction to render a final and binding decree. Appellant's objections were entertained and overruled, the Surrogate holding that the notice required and given was sufficient. [C] A final decree accepting the accounts has been entered, affirmed by the Appellate Division of the Supreme Court, [c], and by the Court of Appeals of the State of New York, [c].

The effect of this decree, as held below, is to settle "all questions respecting the management of the common fund." We understand that every right which beneficiaries would otherwise have against the trust company, either as trustee of the common fund or as trustee of any individual trust, for improper management of the common trust fund during the period covered by the accounting is sealed and wholly terminated by the decree. [Cc]

We are met at the outset with a challenge to the power of the State—the right of its courts to adjudicate at all as against those beneficiaries who reside without the State of New York. It is contended that the proceeding is one in personam in that the decree affects neither title to nor possession of any res, but adjudges only personal rights of the beneficiaries to surcharge their trustee for negligence or breach of trust. Accordingly, it is said, under the strict doctrine of Pennoyer v. Neff, 95 U.S. 714[(1878)], the Surrogate is without jurisdiction as to nonresidents upon whom personal service of process was not made.

Distinctions between actions in rem and those in personam are ancient and originally expressed in procedural terms what seems really to have been a distinction in the substantive law of property under a system quite unlike our own. [Cc] The legal recognition and rise in economic importance of incorporeal or intangible forms of property have upset the ancient simplicity of property law and the clarity of its distinctions, while new forms of proceedings have confused the old procedural classification. American courts have sometimes classed certain actions as in rem because personal service of process was not required, and at other times have held personal service of process not required because the action was in rem. [C]

Judicial proceedings to settle fiduciary accounts have been sometimes termed in rem, or more indefinitely quasi in rem, or more vaguely still, "in the nature of a proceeding in rem." It is not readily apparent how the courts of New York did or would classify the present proceeding, which has some characteristics and is wanting in some features of proceedings both in rem and in personam. But in any event we think that the requirements of the Fourteenth Amendment to the Federal Constitution do not depend upon a classification for which the standards are so elusive and confused generally and which, being primarily for state courts to define, may and do vary from state to state. Without disparaging the usefulness of distinctions between actions in rem and those in personam in many branches of law, or on other issues, or the reasoning which underlies them, we do not rest the power of the State to resort to constructive service in this proceeding upon how its courts or this Court may regard this historic antithesis. It is sufficient to observe that, whatever the technical definition of its chosen procedure, the interest of each state in providing means to close trusts that exist by the grace of its laws and are administered under the supervision of its courts is so insistent and rooted in custom as to establish beyond doubt the right of its courts to determine the interests of all claimants, resident or nonresident, provided its procedure accords full opportunity to appear and be heard.

Quite different from the question of a state's power to discharge trustees is that of the opportunity it must give beneficiaries to contest. Many controversies have raged about the cryptic and abstract words of the Due Process Clause but there can be no doubt that at a minimum they require that deprivation of life, liberty or property by adjudication be preceded by notice and opportunity for hearing appropriate to the nature of the case.

In two ways this proceeding does or may deprive beneficiaries of property. It may cut off their rights to have the trustee answer for negligent or illegal impairments of their interests. Also, their interests are presumably subject to diminution in the proceeding by allowance of fees and expenses to one who, in their names but without their knowledge, may conduct a fruitless or uncompensatory contest. Certainly the proceeding is one in which they may be deprived of property rights and hence notice and hearing must measure up to the standards of due process.

Personal service of written notice within the jurisdiction is the classic form of notice always adequate in any type of proceeding. But the vital interest of the State in bringing any issues as to its fiduciaries to a final settlement can be served only if interests or claims of individuals who are outside of the State can somehow be determined. A construction of the Due Process Clause which would place impossible or impractical obstacles in the way could not be justified.

Against this interest of the State we must balance the individual interest sought to be protected by the Fourteenth Amendment. This is defined by our holding that "The fundamental requisite of due process of law is the opportunity to be heard." Grannis v. Ordean, 234 U.S. 385, 394 [(1914)]. This right to be heard has little reality or worth unless one is informed that the matter is pending and can choose for himself whether to appear or default, acquiesce or contest.

The Court has not committed itself to any formula achieving a balance between these interests in a particular proceeding or determining when constructive notice may be utilized or what test it must meet. Personal service has not in all circumstances been regarded as indispensable to the process due to residents, and it has more often been held unnecessary as to nonresidents. We disturb none of the established rules on these subjects. No decision constitutes a controlling or even a very illuminating precedent for the case before us. But a few general principles stand out in the books.

An elementary and fundamental requirement of due process in any proceeding which is to be accorded finality is notice reasonably calculated, under all the circumstances, to apprise interested parties of the pendency of the action and afford them an opportunity to present their objections. Milliken v. Meyer, 311 U.S. 457 [(1941)]; Grannis v. Ordean, [supra]; [cc]. The notice must be of such nature as reasonably to convey the required information, Grannis v. Ordean, supra, and it must afford a reasonable time for those interested to make their appearance, [cc] But if with due regard for the practicalities and peculiarities of the case these conditions are reasonably met the constitutional requirements are satisfied. …

But when notice is a person's due, process which is a mere gesture is not due process. The means employed must be such as one desirous of actually informing the absentee might reasonably adopt to accomplish it. The reasonableness and hence the constitutional validity of any chosen method may be defended on the ground that it is in itself reasonably certain to inform those affected, [cc], or, where conditions do not reasonably permit such notice, that the form chosen is not substantially less likely to bring home notice than other of the feasible and customary substitutes.

It would be idle to pretend that publication alone as prescribed here, is a reliable means of acquainting interested parties of the fact that their rights are before the courts. It is not an accident that the greater number of cases reaching this Court on the question of adequacy of notice have been concerned with actions founded on process constructively served through local newspapers. Chance alone brings to the attention of even a local resident an advertisement in small type inserted in the back pages of a newspaper, and if he makes his home outside the area of the newspaper's normal circulation the odds that the information will never reach him are large indeed. The chance of actual notice is further reduced when as here the notice required does not even name those whose attention it is supposed to attract, and does not inform acquaintances who might call it to attention. In weighing its sufficiency on the basis of equivalence with actual notice we are unable to regard this as more than a feint.

Nor is publication here reinforced by steps likely to attract the parties' attention to the proceeding. It is true that publication traditionally has been acceptable as notification supplemental to other action which in itself may reasonably be expected to convey a warning. The ways or an owner with tangible property are such that he usually arranges means to learn of any direct attack upon his possessory or proprietary rights. Hence, libel of a ship, attachment of a chattel or entry upon real estate in the name of law may reasonably be expected to come promptly to the owner's attention. When the state within which the owner has located such property seizes it for some reason, publication or posting affords an additional measure of notification. A state may indulge the assumption that one who has left tangible property in the state either has abandoned it, in which case proceedings against it deprive him of nothing, [cc], or that he has left some caretaker under a duty to let him know that it is being jeopardized. ...

In the case before us there is, of course, no abandonment. On the other hand these beneficiaries do have a resident fiduciary as caretaker of their interest in this property. But it is their caretaker who in the accounting becomes their adversary. Their trustee is released from giving notice of jeopardy, and no one else is expected to do so. Not even the special guardian is required or apparently expected to communicate with his ward and client, and, of course, if such a duty were merely transferred from the trustee to the guardian, economy would not be served and more likely the cost would be increased.

This Court has not hesitated to approve of resort to publication as a customary substitute in another class of cases where it is not reasonably possible or practicable to give more adequate warning. Thus it has been recognized that, in the case of persons missing or unknown, employment of an indirect and even a probably futile means of notification is all that the situation permits and creates no constitutional bar to a final decree foreclosing their rights. [Cc]

Those beneficiaries represented by appellant whose interests or whereabouts could not with due diligence be ascertained come clearly within this category. As to them the statutory notice is sufficient. However great the odds that publication will never reach the eyes of such unknown parties, it is not in the typical case much more likely to fail than any of the choices open to legislators endeavoring to prescribe the best notice practicable.

Nor do we consider it unreasonable for the State to dispense with more certain notice to those beneficiaries whose interests are either conjectural or future or, although they could be discovered upon investigation, do not in due course of business come to knowledge of the common trustee. Whatever searches might be required in another situation under ordinary standards of diligence, in view of the character of the proceedings and the nature of the interests here involved we think them unnecessary. We recognize the practical difficulties and costs that would be attendant on frequent investigations into the status of great numbers of beneficiaries, many of whose interests in the common fund are so remote as to be ephemeral; and we have no doubt that such impracticable and extended searches are not required in the name of due process. The expense of keeping informed from day to day of substitutions among even current income beneficiaries and presumptive remaindermen, to say nothing of the far greater number of contingent beneficiaries, would impose a severe burden on the plan, and would likely dissipate its advantages. These are practical matters in which we should be reluctant to disturb the judgment of the state authorities.

Accordingly we overrule appellant's constitutional objections to published notice insofar as they are urged on behalf of any beneficiaries whose interests or addresses are unknown to the trustee.

As to known present beneficiaries of known place of residence, however, notice by publication stands on a different footing. Exceptions in the name of necessity do not sweep away the rule that within the limits of practicability notice must be such as is reasonably calculated to reach interested parties. Where the names and post office addresses of those affected by a proceeding are at hand, the reasons disappear for resort to means less likely than the mails to apprise them of its pendency.

The trustee has on its books the names and addresses of the income beneficiaries represented by appellant, and we find no tenable ground for dispensing with a serious effort to inform them personally of the accounting, at least by ordinary mail to the record addresses. [C] Certainly sending them a copy of the statute months and perhaps years in advance does not answer this purpose. The trustee periodically remits their income to them, and we think that they might reasonably expect that with or apart from their remittances word might come to them personally that steps were being taken affecting their interests.

We need not weigh contentions that a requirement of personal service of citation on even the large number of known resident or nonresident beneficiaries would, by reasons of delay if not of expense, seriously interfere with the proper administration of the fund. Of course personal service even without the jurisdiction of the issuing authority serves the end of actual and personal notice, whatever power of compulsion it might lack. However, no such service is required under the circumstances. This type of trust presupposes a large number of small interests. The individual interest does not stand alone but is identical with that of a class. The rights of each in the integrity of the fund and the fidelity of the trustee are shared by many other beneficiaries. Therefore notice reasonably certain to reach most of those interested in objecting is likely to safeguard the interests of all, since any objections sustained would inure to the benefit of all. We think that under such circumstances reasonable risks that notice might not actually reach every beneficiary are justifiable. ...

The statutory notice to known beneficiaries is inadequate, not because in fact it fails to reach everyone, but because under the circumstances it is not reasonably calculated to reach those who could easily be informed by other means at hand. However it may have been in former times, the mails today are recognized as an efficient and inexpensive means of communication. Moreover, the fact that the trust company has been able to give mailed notice to known beneficiaries at the time the common trust fund was established is persuasive that postal notification at the time of accounting would not seriously burden the plan. ...

We hold the notice of judicial settlement of accounts required by the New York Banking Law §100-c(12) is incompatible with the requirements of the Fourteenth Amendment as a basis for adjudication depriving known persons whose whereabouts are also known of substantial property rights. Accordingly the judgment is reversed and the cause remanded for further proceedings not inconsistent with this opinion.

Reversed.

Mr. Justice DOUGLAS took no part in the consideration or decision of this case.

[Mr. Justice BURTON'S dissenting opinion is omitted.]

INQUIRY

Publication. In the context of service of process, publication generally means to pay a newspaper to print a legal notice weekly for a few weeks or on another reasonable timetable. Is there anything in *Mullane* suggesting that the Supreme Court will accept publication as constitutionally adequate constructive notice, when the plaintiff had reasonable alternative means to locate and personally serve the defendant? In several decisions after *Mullane*, the Supreme Court rejected the theory of constructive notice by publication where, although publication may have been meaningful, the plaintiff could and should have used public records to attempt to locate and serve the defendant. *See, e.g.,* Tulsa Professional Collection Services, Inc. v. Pope, 485 U.S. 478 (1988) (publication not sufficient to put estate creditors' on notice when the executrix could ascertain their names and addresses and serve by mail); Mennonite Board of Missions v. Adams, 462 U.S. 791 (1983) (publication of notice of tax sale not sufficient to defeat mortgagee's interest); Schroeder v. City of New York, 371 U.S. 208 (1962) (publication not sufficient for condemnation proceedings where title records showed landowner addresses); Walker v. City of Hutchinson, 352 U.S. 112 (1956) (same). Publication alone, without other efforts, is ordinarily constitutionally inadequate notice.

Posting. In the context of service, posting generally means to tack the legal notice of the proceeding to the door of the defendant's residence. If there is no residence on premises involved in the litigation, then the plaintiff would tack the notice to a sign, tree, or post on those premises. Is there anything in *Mullane* suggesting that the Supreme Court will accept posting as constitutionally adequate constructive notice, when the plaintiff had reasonable alternative means to locate and personally serve the defendant? As was the case with publication, in decisions after *Mullane*, the Supreme Court rejected the theory of constructive notice by posting where the plaintiff could and should have located the defendant for personal service or other actual notice. *See* Greene v. Lindsey, 456 U.S. 444 (1982) (property owner's posting eviction notice on tenant's door not sufficient notice). In two of those decisions, *Mennonite Board of Missions v. Adams, supra*, and *Schroeder v. City of New York, supra*, the Supreme Court held posting constitutionally insufficient even when combined with publication. Posting and publication, even when used in the same case, are ordinarily constitutionally insufficient when not accompanied by other efforts.

Mail. Unlike publication and posting, which tend to be stopgap measures for service of process when all other reasonable means fail, mail is a common means for service of process. Service of process by mail still raises its own constitutional issues. *Mullane's* "reasonably calculated" test remains the constitutional standard for mail service just as it is for publication and posting. When is mail service constitutionally sufficient, and when is it not sufficient? The answer depends in part on the type of mail service that the plaintiff chooses which in any one case can be critical to the outcome. The plaintiff can establish the defendant's actual notice when the defendant signs a certified-mail receipt, and the Postal Service returns that receipt to the plaintiff for filing with the court as proof of service. Certified mail without return of signed receipt is less reliable because it depends on the deliverer's reliability. Regular mail is even less reliable because there is no witness (only a presumption) that the defendant received the mail. Note also that in any service-of-process case, including one involving mailing, an issue arises when the plaintiff knows or has reason to know that the defendant may not be mentally competent to accept service. *See* Covey v. Town of Somers, 351 U.S. 141, 146-147 (1956) (notice of tax forfeiture mailed to property owner known to be insane violates due process). The following two recent Supreme Court cases, one finding mail service constitutional and the other find mail service not constitutional, highlight the tension between the burden of notice on the plaintiff and the due-process rights of the defendant. Unfortunately, the two cases may not clarify the boundaries of constitutional service by mail or illustrate a spectrum along which to judge mail service. Majority and dissenting opinions in the two cases show that the Supreme Court's majority shifted on the issue with a change in its makeup between the two cases.

Dusenbery v. United States,

United States Supreme Court
534 U.S. 161 (2002)

Chief Justice REHNQUIST delivered the opinion of the Court.

This case concerns the adequacy of the means employed by the Federal Bureau of Investigation (FBI) to provide notice to a federal prisoner of his right to contest the administrative forfeiture of property seized during the execution of a search warrant for the residence where he was arrested.

In April 1986, officers of the FBI arrested petitioner Larry Dean Dusenbery at a house trailer in Atwater, Ohio. Later that day, they obtained and executed a search warrant, seizing drugs, drug paraphernalia, several firearms, a ballistic knife, an automobile registered in the name of petitioner's stepmother, and ... $21,939 in cash... .

Two months later, petitioner pleaded guilty in the United States District Court for the Northern District of Ohio to a charge of possession with intent to distribute 813 grams of cocaine... . He was sentenced to 12 years of imprisonment... . The FBI ... began the process of administratively forfeiting the cash and the automobile.

To effect such a forfeiture, the statute required the agency to send written notice of the seizure together with information on the applicable forfeiture procedures to each party who appeared to have an interest in the property. [C] It also required the publication for at least three successive weeks of a similar notice in a newspaper of general circulation in the judicial district in which the forfeiture proceeding was brought. [Cc] The FBI sent letters of its intention to forfeit the cash by certified mail addressed to petitioner care of the Federal Correctional Institution (FCI) in Milan, Michigan, where he was then incarcerated; to the address of the residence where petitioner was arrested; and to an address in Randolph, Ohio, the town where petitioner's mother lived. [C] It placed the requisite legal notice in three consecutive Sunday editions of the Cleveland Plain Dealer. [C] ... The FBI received no response to these notices within the time allotted, and so declared the items administratively forfeited. [Cc] An FBI agent turned over the cash to the United States Marshals Service... .

Nearly five years later, petitioner moved in the District Court ... seeking return of all the property and funds seized in his criminal case. ... The District Court denied the motion... .

The Court of Appeals for the Sixth Circuit vacated the District Court's judgment and remanded for further proceedings. ...

Following remand, the District Court entered an order allowing discovery and subsequently presided over a telephone deposition of James Lawson, an Inmate Systems Officer who began to work in the mailroom at FCI Milan early in 1988 and who had submitted an affidavit in the case. Lawson testified that he signed the certified mail receipt for the FBI's notice to petitioner regarding the cash. [C] He also testified about the procedures within FCI Milan for accepting, logging, and delivering certified mail addressed to inmates. [C] Lawson explained that the procedure would have been for him to log the mail in, for petitioner's "Unit Team" to sign for it, and for it then to be given to petitioner. [C] But he said that a paper trail no longer existed because the Bureau of Prisons (BOP) had a policy of holding prison logbooks for only one year after they were closed.[fn] [C]

Both parties moved for summary judgment. The District Court ruled that the Government's sending of notice by certified mail to petitioner's place of incarceration satisfied his due process rights as to the cash. [C] The Court of Appeals affirmed. [C] Citing *Mullane v. Central Hanover Bank & Trust Co.*, 339 U.S. 306, 314[] (1950), it held that the Government's notice of the cash forfeiture comported with due process even in the absence of proof that the mail actually reached petitioner. [C]

The Due Process Clause of the Fifth Amendment prohibits the United States, as the Due Process Clause of the Fourteenth Amendment prohibits the States, from depriving any person of property without "due process of law." From these "cryptic and abstract words," *Mullane, supra,* at 313[], we have determined that individuals whose property interests are at stake are entitled to "notice and an opportunity to be heard." [C]

We think *Mullane* supplies the appropriate analytical framework. ... Since *Mullane* was decided, we have regularly turned to it when confronted with questions regarding the adequacy of the method used to give notice. [Cc] We see no reason to depart from this well-settled practice. ...

Was the notice in this case "reasonably calculated under all the circumstances" to apprise petitioner of the pendency of the cash forfeiture? The Government here carried its burden of showing the following procedures had been used to give notice. The FBI sent certified mail addressed to petitioner at the correctional facility where he was incarcerated. At that facility, prison mailroom staff traveled to the city post office every day to obtain all the mail for the institution, including inmate mail. [C] The staff signed for all certified mail before leaving the post office. Once the mail was transported back to the facility, certified mail was entered in a logbook maintained in the mailroom. [C] A member of the inmate's Unit Team then signed for the certified mail to acknowledge its receipt before removing it from the mailroom, and either a Unit Team member or another staff member distributed the mail to the inmate during the institution's "mail call." [C]

Petitioner does not seriously contest the FBI's use of the postal service to send its certified letter to him, a method our cases have recognized as adequate for known addressees when we have found notice by publication insufficient.[fn] [C] Instead, he argues that the notice was insufficient because due process generally requires "actual notice" to interested parties prior to forfeiture, which he takes to mean actual receipt of notice.[fn] [Cc] For this proposition he cites Mennonite Bd. of Missions[v. Adams, 462 U.S. 791, 796-797 (1983)]. But ... *Mennonite* ... does not say that the State *must provide* actual notice, but that it *must attempt to provide* actual notice. ...

We note that none of our cases cited by either party has required actual notice in proceedings such as this. Instead, we have allowed the Government to defend the "reasonableness and hence the constitutional validity of any chosen method ... on the ground that it is in itself reasonably certain to inform those affected." *Mullane,* [*supra*], at 315[].

Petitioner argues that because he was housed in a federal prison at the time of the forfeiture, the FBI could have made arrangements with the BOP to assure the delivery of the notice in question to him. ... But the Due Process Clause does not require such heroic efforts [as shown in the movie "Saving Private Ryan"] by the Government; it requires only that the Government's effort be "reasonably calculated" to apprise a party of the pendency of the action; "'[t]he criterion is not the possibility of conceivable injury but the just and reasonable character of the requirements ... .'" *Mullane, supra,* at 315. ...

Justice GINSBURG'S dissent does not contend, as petitioner does, that due process could be satisfied in this case only with actual notice. It makes an alternative argument that the FBI's notice was constitutionally flawed because it was "'substantially less likely to bring home notice' than a feasible substitute,"

[cc]—namely, the methods used currently by the BOP, which generally require an inmate to sign a logbook acknowledging delivery[c] Just how requiring the *end recipient* to sign for a piece of mail substantially improves the reliability of the delivery procedures *leading up to* that person's receipt, Justice GINSBURG'S dissent does not persuasively explain. ...

Here, the use of the mail addressed to petitioner at the penitentiary was clearly acceptable for much the same reason we have approved mailed notice in the past. Short of allowing the prisoner to go to the post office himself, the remaining portion of the delivery would necessarily depend on a system in effect within the prison itself relying on prison staff. We think the FBI's use of the system described in detail above was "reasonably calculated, under all the circumstances, to apprise [petitioner] of the pendency of the action." *Mullane,* [*supra*], at 314[]. Due process requires no more.

The judgment of the Court of Appeals is

Affirmed.

Justice GINSBURG, with whom Justice STEVENS, Justice SOUTER, and Justice BREYER join, dissenting.

... Today's decision diminishes the safeguard of notice, affording an opportunity to be heard, before one is deprived of property. As adequate to notify prisoners that the Government seeks forfeiture of their property, the Court condones a procedure too lax to reliably ensure that a prisoner will receive a legal notice sent to him. The Court does so despite the Government's total control of a prison inmate's location, and the evident feasibility of tightening the notice procedure "as [would] one desirous of actually informing [the prisoner]." [C] Because the Court, without warrant in fact or law, approves a procedure "less likely to bring home notice" than a feasible alternative, [c], I dissent. ...

... Given the circumstances and conditions of imprisonment, the Government must have cause to be confident that legal notices to prisoners will be delivered inside the prison with the care "one desirous of actually informing the [addressee] might reasonably adopt to accomplish it." *Mullane,* [*supra*], at 315[]. The uncertain mailroom to cell delivery system formerly in place at FCI Milan fell short of that mark. Greater reliability could be achieved with modest effort. Because the Court finds that small but significant effort undue, I dissent.

Jones v. Flowers,

United States Supreme Court
547 U.S. 220 (2006)

Chief Justice ROBERTS delivered the opinion of the Court.

Before a State may take property and sell it for unpaid taxes, the Due Process Clause of the Fourteenth Amendment requires the government to provide the owner "notice and opportunity for hearing appropriate to the nature of the case." Mullane v. Central Hanover Bank & Trust Co., 339 U.S. 306, 313[] (1950). We granted certiorari to determine whether, when notice of a tax sale is mailed to the owner and returned undelivered, the government must take additional reasonable steps to provide notice before taking the owner's property.

I

In 1967, petitioner Gary Jones purchased a house at 717 North Bryan Street in Little Rock, Arkansas. ... Jones paid his mortgage each month for 30 years, and the mortgage company paid Jones' property taxes. After Jones paid off his mortgage in 1997, the property taxes went unpaid, and the property was certified as delinquent.

In April 2000, respondent Mark Wilcox, the Commissioner of State Lands (Commissioner), attempted to notify Jones of his tax delinquency, and his right to redeem the property, by mailing a certified letter to Jones at the North Bryan Street address. [C] The packet of information stated that unless Jones redeemed the property, it would be subject to public sale two years later... . Nobody was home to sign for the letter, and nobody appeared at the post office to retrieve the letter within the next 15 days. The post office returned the unopened packet to the Commissioner marked "'unclaimed.'" [C]

Two years later, and just a few weeks before the public sale, the Commissioner published a notice of public sale in the Arkansas Democrat Gazette. No bids were submitted, which permitted the State to negotiate a private sale of the property. [C] Several months later, respondent Linda Flowers submitted a purchase offer. The Commissioner mailed another certified letter to Jones at the North Bryan Street address, attempting to notify him that his house would be sold to Flowers if he did not pay his taxes. Like the first letter, the second was also returned to the Commissioner marked "unclaimed." [C] Flowers purchased the house, which the parties stipulated in the trial court had a fair market value of $80,000, for $21,042.15. [C] Immediately after the 30-day period for postsale redemption passed, [c], Flowers had an unlawful detainer notice delivered to the property. The notice was served on Jones' daughter, who contacted Jones and notified him of the tax sale. [C]

Jones filed a lawsuit in Arkansas state court against the Commissioner and Flowers, alleging that the Commissioner's failure to provide notice of the tax sale and of Jones' right to redeem resulted in the taking of his property without due process. The Commissioner and Flowers moved for summary judgment on the ground that the two unclaimed letters sent by the Commissioner were a constitutionally adequate attempt at notice, and Jones filed a cross-motion for summary judgment. The trial court granted summary judgment in favor of the Commissioner and Flowers. [C] It concluded that the Arkansas tax sale statute, which set forth the notice procedure followed by the Commissioner, complied with constitutional due process requirements.

Jones appealed, and the Arkansas Supreme Court affirmed the trial court's judgment. [C] The court noted our precedent stating that due process does not require actual notice, see Dusenbery v. United States, 534 U.S. 161, 170[] (2002), and it held that attempting to provide notice by certified mail satisfied due process in the circumstances presented... .

II

A

Due process does not require that a property owner receive actual notice before the government may take his property. *Dusenbery, supra,* at 170[]. Rather, we have stated that due process requires the government to provide "notice reasonably calculated, under all the circumstances, to apprise interested parties of the pendency of the action and afford them an opportunity to present their objections." *Mullane,* 339 U.S., at 314[]. ... The Commissioner notes this Court's ample precedent condoning notice by mail, see, *e.g., Dusenbery, supra*[]; Tulsa Professional Collection Services, Inc. v. Pope, 485 U.S. 478, 490[] (1988); Mennonite Bd. of Missions v. Adams, 462 U.S. 791, 798[] (1983); *Mullane, supra*[], and adds that the Arkansas scheme exceeds constitutional requirements by requiring the Commissioner to use certified mail. [C]

... In each of these cases, the government attempted to provide notice and heard nothing back indicating that anything had gone awry, and we stated that "[t]he reasonableness and hence the constitutional validity of [the] chosen method may be defended on the ground that it is in itself reasonably certain to inform those affected." *Id.,* at 315[]; see also *Dusenbery, supra,* at 170[]. But we have never addressed whether due process entails further responsibility when the government becomes aware prior to the taking that its attempt at notice has failed. That is a new wrinkle... . The question presented is whether such knowledge on the government's part is a "circumstance and condition" that varies the "notice required." ...

We do not think that a person who actually desired to inform a real property owner of an impending tax sale of a house he owns would do nothing when a certified letter sent to the owner is returned unclaimed. If the Commissioner prepared a stack of letters to mail to delinquent taxpayers, handed them to the postman, and then watched as the departing postman accidentally dropped the letters down a storm drain, one would certainly expect the Commissioner's office to prepare a new stack of letters and send them again. No one "desirous of actually informing" the owners would simply shrug his shoulders as the letters disappeared and say "I tried." Failure to follow up would be unreasonable, despite the fact that the letters were reasonably calculated to reach their intended recipients when delivered to the postman.

By the same token, when a letter is returned by the post office, the sender will ordinarily attempt to resend it, if it is practicable to do so. [C] This is especially true when, as here, the subject matter of the letter concerns such an important and irreversible prospect as the loss of a house. ... Deciding to take no further action is not what someone "desirous of actually informing" Jones would do; such a person would take further reasonable steps if any were available. ...

It is certainly true, as the Commissioner and Solicitor General contend, that the failure of notice in a specific case does not establish the inadequacy of the attempted notice... . But if a feature of the State's chosen procedure is that it promptly provides additional information to the government about the effectiveness of notice, it [is acceptable] to consider what the government does with that information in assessing the adequacy of the chosen procedure. After all, the State knew *ex ante* that it would promptly learn whether its effort to effect notice through certified mail had succeeded. It would not be inconsistent with the approach the Court has taken in notice cases to ask, with respect to a procedure under which telephone calls were placed to owners, what the State did when no one answered. Asking what the State does when a notice letter is returned unclaimed is not substantively different. ...

Jones should have been more diligent with respect to his property, no question. People must pay their taxes, and the government may hold citizens accountable for tax delinquency by taking their property. But before forcing a citizen to satisfy his debt by forfeiting his property, due process requires the government to provide adequate notice of the impending taking. [Cc]

B

In response to the returned form suggesting that Jones had not received notice that he was about to lose his property, the State did-nothing. For the reasons stated, we conclude the State should have taken additional reasonable steps to notify Jones, if practicable to do so.

We think there were several reasonable steps the State could have taken. What steps are reasonable in response to new information depends upon what the new information reveals. The return of the certified letter marked "unclaimed" meant either that Jones still lived at 717 North Bryan Street, but was not home when the postman called and did not retrieve the letter at the post office, or that Jones no longer resided at that address. One reasonable step primarily addressed to the former possibility would be for the State to resend the notice by regular mail, so that a signature was not required. ... Following up with regular mail might also increase the chances of actual notice to Jones if—as it turned out—he had moved. Even occupants who ignored certified mail notice slips addressed to the owner (if any had been left) might scrawl the owner's new address on the notice packet and leave it for the postman to retrieve, or notify Jones directly. ...

Other reasonable followup measures ... would have been to post notice on the front door, or to address otherwise undeliverable mail to "occupant." ...

Jones believes that the Commissioner should have searched for his new address in the Little Rock phonebook and other government records such as income tax rolls. We do not believe the government was required to go this far. ...

... [W]e disclaim any "new rule" that is "contrary to *Dusenbery* and a significant departure from *Mullane*." [Citing the dissent.]

The Commissioner's effort to provide notice to Jones of an impending tax sale of his house was insufficient to satisfy due process given the circumstances of this case. The judgment of the Arkansas Supreme Court is reversed, and the case is remanded for proceedings not inconsistent with this opinion.

It is so ordered.

Justice ALITO took no part in the consideration or decision of this case.

Justice THOMAS, with whom Justice SCALIA and Justice KENNEDY join, dissenting.

... Adopting petitioner's arguments, the Court holds today that "when mailed notice of a tax sale is returned unclaimed, the State must take additional reasonable steps to attempt to provide notice to the property owner before selling his property, if it is practicable to do so." [C] The Court concludes that it was practicable for Arkansas to take additional steps here—namely, notice by regular mail, posting notice on petitioner's door, and addressing mail to "'occupant.'" [C] Because, under this Court's precedents, the State's notice methods clearly satisfy the requirements of the Due Process Clause, I respectfully dissent. ...

The methods of notice employed by Arkansas were reasonably calculated to inform petitioner of proceedings affecting his property interest and thus satisfy the requirements of the Due Process Clause. The State mailed a notice by certified letter to the address provided by petitioner. The certified letter was returned to the State marked "unclaimed" after three attempts to deliver it. The State then published a notice of public sale containing redemption information in the Arkansas Democrat Gazette newspaper. After Flowers submitted a purchase offer, the State sent yet another certified letter to petitioner at his record address. That letter, too, was returned to the State marked "unclaimed" after three delivery attempts.[fn]

Arkansas' attempts to contact petitioner by certified mail at his "record address," without more, satisfy due process. *Dusenbery, supra*[]. See also *Mullane, supra*[]; Tulsa Professional Collection Services, Inc. v. Pope, 485 U.S. 478, 490[] (1988)...; Mennonite Bd. of Missions v. Adams, 462 U.S. 791, 792[] (1983)... . Because the notices were sent to the address provided by petitioner himself, the State had an especially sound basis for determining that notice would reach him. ...

In Arkansas, approximately 18,000 parcels of delinquent real estate are certified annually. [C] Under the Court's rule, the State will bear the burden of locating thousands of delinquent property owners. These administrative burdens are not compelled by the Due Process Clause. ...

Moreover, the Court's proposed methods are no more reasonably calculated to achieve notice than the methods employed by the State here. Regular mail is hardly foolproof; indeed, it is arguably less effective than certified mail. Certified mail is tracked, delivery attempts are recorded, actual delivery is logged, and notices are posted to alert someone at the residence that certified mail is being held at a local post office. By creating a record, these features give parties grounds for defending or challenging notice. By contrast, regular mail is untraceable; there is no record of either delivery or receipt. Had the State used regular mail, petitioner would presumably argue that it should have sent notice by certified mail because it creates a paper trail.[fn]

... The State's attempts to notify petitioner by certified mail at the address that he provided and, additionally, by publishing notice in a local newspaper satisfy due process. Accordingly, I would affirm the judgment of the Arkansas Supreme Court.

Figure

Attorney Michael Kirkpatrick represented the prevailing petitioner Gary Jones in the above *Jones v. Flowers* Supreme Court case. Public Citizen Litigation Group in Washington, D.C., employs Mr. Kirkpatrick to litigate public-interest cases involving constitutional and administrative law, civil rights and employment law, and access to government. Before joining Public Citizen in 2004, Mr. Kirkpatrick worked as a senior trial attorney for Civil Rights Division of the United States Department of Justice. He began his career in civil litigation as a staff attorney with the Farm Worker Division of Texas Rural Legal Aid—a long way from his two wins in the United States Supreme Court.

INQUIRY

Impracticality. Service can be impractical or impossible. How should the court treat the constitutionality of service of process by the best means possible or reasonably practical, but yet that is also reasonably sure not to reach the defendant because actual notice is so highly impractical or impossible? Courts may find service of process constitutionally adequate in those cases. *See* Dobkin

v. Chapman, 236 N.E.2d 451 (N.Y. Ct. App. 1968) (service by publication and regular mail on motor-vehicle drivers whose current addresses were unknown for leaving the scene held constitutional). Requiring a plaintiff to do the impossible, such as locate and give actual notice to a defendant who wants to remain concealed and is doing an excellent job of it, might itself be a denial of due process. At least, recall that the Supreme Court's five factors in Asahi Metal Industry Co. v. Rudzemicz, 480 U.S. 102 (1980), for constitutional exercise of personal jurisdiction include the plaintiff's interest in obtaining relief. The plaintiff's access to justice is a constitutional issue. On the other hand, that interest will not always be so substantial. For example, in Cash v. Hamilton County Department of Adult Probation, 388 F.3d 539 (6th Cir. 2004), the Sixth Circuit held that there is at least a fact issue as to whether publication in the local newspaper was sufficient to give constitutional notice to the homeless whose personal property the city destroyed as part of a community clean-up program. How would you propose serving the homeless?

Contents. There are also constitutional dimensions to the contents of the notice that the plaintiff provides. It is not simply a matter of getting any notice into the defendant's hands. Constitutionally adequate service of process begins with notifying the defendant of the pending action's title, case number, and court, plus notifying the defendant of how and when to appear and defend. The Constitution may also require a detailed explanation of the grounds for the action. Ortiz v. Eichler, 794 F.2d 889, 892 (3d Cir. 1986); Reynolds v. Guiliani, 35 F.Supp.2d 331 (S.D. N.Y. 1999). It may also require notifying the defendant of what alternatives may exist for requesting transfer of the action to a more convenient venue, Aguchak v. Montgomery Ward Co., 520 P.2d 1352 (Alaska 1974), or what other statutory rights and exemptions the defendant may have to challenge the action, Finberg v. Sullivan, 634 F.2d 50 (3d Cir. 1980). FED. R. CIV. P. 12(b)(4) authorizes a defendant to move to dismiss an action based on "insufficient process," meaning a technical defect on the face of the summons that resulted in inadequate notice. *See* Cranford v. United States, 359 F. Supp.2d 981, 984 (E.D. Cal. 2005). FED. R. CIV. P. FORM 3 offers practitioners a form that, under FED. R. CIV. P. 54, suffices as to the form and contents of a summons. Examine Form 3, keeping mind its purpose in satisfying constitutional due process.

Form 3. Summons

(Caption--See Form 1.)

To <u>*name the defendant*</u>:

A lawsuit has been filed against you.

Within 21 days after service of this summons on you (not counting the day you received it), you must serve on the plaintiff an answer to the attached complaint or a motion under Rule 12 of the Federal Rules of Civil Procedure. The answer or motion must be served on the plaintiff's attorney, __________, whose address is __________. If you fail to do so, judgment by default will be entered against you for the relief demanded in the complaint. You also must file your answer or motion with the court.

Date __________

____
Clerk of Court

(Court Seal)

(Use 60 days if the defendant is the United States or a United States agency, or is an officer or employee of the United States allowed 60 days by Rule 12(a)(3).)

Knowledge

Lawyers commonly build a conceptual spectrum along which to place cases and hypotheticals, to test and illustrate how the courts apply a legal rule to specific cases. For instance, cases on the constitutionality of service of process tend to fall along the spectrum from obviously constitutional at one end (personal service) to obviously not constitutional at the other end (no attempt at service whatsoever). The variety of alternative service methods, and their various failures and successes, place other cases along the spectrum from probably constitutional to probably not constitutional. Changes in the Supreme Court's makeup can alter or obscure the spectrum but at the same time usefully illustrate policies behind the spectrum.

2. Mechanics of Service

The above section treating the constitutional requirements for notice introduces the various means by which plaintiffs serve or attempt to serve process today. The above section has not yet addressed what statutes and court rules authorize as to service of process. FED. R. CIV. P. 4 (already reproduced in the previous chapter for its terms relating to personal jurisdiction) authorizes service of process for the federal district courts. While it is a pattern of sorts for various state-court rules, Rule 4 also incorporates in its subsection (e)(1) procedures used by the state in which the district court is located. In other words, federal litigants may serve process in the manner permitted either by the FEDERAL RULES OF CIVIL PROCEDURE or by the rules of the forum state. FED. R. CIV. P. 4(g) is another such borrowing provision, directing the practitioner to the statutes and court rules of the forum state for service of process on minors and incompetents.

The first means that Rule 4 authorizes for service of process is recognizing the defendant's waiver of formal service. Waiver (or at least a formal rule for waiver) is a relatively new invention. The Supreme Court proposed in 1982 that the FEDERAL RULES OF CIVIL PROCEDURE permit service by registered or certified mail, return receipt requested. Congress instead adopted in 1983 a system for service by acknowledgment like the system still used in California, CAL. CODE CIV. P. §415.30, in which the plaintiff simply mails the summons and complaint to the defendant by regular mail but with an acknowledgment form hoping that the defendant will sign and return the acknowledgment. If the defendant did not return the signed form, then the plaintiff used other methods of service with the defendant having to pay the cost of those other methods. After only modest success, Congress revised Rule 4 to provide in its subsection (d) for the current method of waiver. The plaintiff mails or otherwise delivers by reliable means a notice of the lawsuit's filing together with a request that the defendant waive service. The defendant must respond within 30 days or pay the costs of alternative service, unless the defendant has good cause for not responding, such as that the defendant never received the mailing. *See, e.g.,* Henry v. Glaize Md. Orchards, Inc., 103 F.R.D. 589, 590 (D. Md. 1984). If the defendant does respond, the defendant gets 60 days (longer than the usual 20 days) to answer. A plaintiff does not have to use Rule 4(d)'s waiver method and indeed should not attempt to when a limitations period contingent on service is due to expire. Examine FED. R. CIV. P. Form 6 as the form of notice that will suffice to invoke the Rule 4(d)'s waiver provisions.

Form 6. Waiver of the Service of Summons

(Caption--See Form 1.)

To *name the plaintiff's attorney or the unrepresented plaintiff*:

I have received your request to waive service of a summons in this action along with a copy of the complaint, two copies of this waiver form, and a prepaid means of returning one signed copy of the form to you.

I, or the entity I represent, agree to save the expense of serving a summons and complaint in this case.

I understand that I, or the entity I represent, will keep all defenses or objections to the lawsuit, the court's jurisdiction, and the venue of the action, but that I waive any objections to the absence of a summons or of service.

I also understand that I, or the entity I represent, must file and serve an answer or a motion under Rule 12 within 60 days from _______, the date when this request was sent (or 90 days if it was sent outside the United States). If I fail to do so, a default judgment will be entered against me or the entity I represent.

(Date and sign--See Form 2.)

(Attach the following to Form 6.)

Duty to Avoid Unnecessary Expenses of Serving a Summons

Rule 4 of the Federal Rules of Civil Procedure requires certain defendants to cooperate in saving unnecessary expenses of serving a summons and complaint. A defendant who is located in the United States and who fails to return a signed waiver of service requested by a plaintiff located in the United States will be required to pay the expenses of service, unless the defendant shows good cause for the failure.

"Good cause" does *not* include a belief that the lawsuit is groundless, or that it has been brought in an improper venue, or that the court has no jurisdiction over this matter or over the defendant or the defendant's property.

If the waiver is signed and returned, you can still make these and all other defenses and objections, but you cannot object to the absence of a summons or of service.

If you waive service, then you must, within the time specified on the waiver form, serve an answer or a motion under Rule 12 on the plaintiff and file a copy with the court. By signing and returning the waiver form, you are allowed more time to respond than if a summons had been served.

The favored means for service of process is by personal service, meaning handing to the defendant the court's original summons and a copy of the complaint. The summons demands that the defendant appear and defend. The copy of the complaint then tells the defendant what the defendant must answer. Because court rules may require the plaintiff to serve on the defendant an original summons, a lawyer who represents the plaintiff and files the complaint will obtain several original summonses in a single case all at once, given that the lawyer may need to attempt service several different times in different forms and may have to serve an original (rather than copy) summons. *See, e.g.*, MICH. CT. R. 2.105(A)(1). FED. R. CIV. P. 4(e)(2)(A) authorizes personal service on natural persons. A common limitation among state court rules on personal service is that the plaintiff must have someone else do it. *See, e.g.*, MICH. CT. R. 2.103(A) ("Process in civil actions may be served by any legally competent adult who is not a party or an officer of a corporate party."). This limitation ensures that the plaintiff does not misrepresent the manner, date, and general accomplishment of service. Lawyers may serve process but usually hire others to do so. Private investigators and retired or part-time police officers commonly offer personal service for modest fees, as may other entrepreneurs willing to take the risk that comes with personally serving unhappy defendants. Local law enforcement may also have a service-of-process division. Lawyers will mail or otherwise deliver (perhaps through a box at the court clerk's office) the summons and complaint to the local process server for personal service. Lawyers develop process-server favorites based on price, timeliness, resourcefulness, and other criteria, though ultimately on reliability for establishing personal service.

In addition to authorizing personal service on natural persons by delivering (handing) a copy of the summons and complaint to the defendant, Rule 4(e)(2) provides for alternative forms of personal service. Rule 4(e)(2)(B) authorizes leaving a copy of the summons and complaint at the defendant's "dwelling or usual place of abode with someone of suitable age and discretion who resides there… ." Federal circuit courts have recognized a spouse, Karlsson v. Rabinowitz, 318 F.2d 666, 668 (4th Cir. 1963), and a wealthy world-traveler's housekeeper, National Development Co. v. Triad Holding Corp., 930 F.2d 253, 258 (2d Cir.), cert. denied, 502 U.S. 968 (1991), as suitable persons for service of process but not an estranged wife, Williams v. Capital Transit Co., 215 F.2d 487 (D.C. Cir. 1954). These cases suggest both the convenience and mischief possible under Rule 4(e)(2)(B). Similarly, Rule 4(e)(2)(C) authorizes delivering the summons and complaint to "an agent authorized by appointment or law to receive service of process." Here, too, there is opportunity both for fairness and convenience on the one hand and some mischief on the other. Consider the following case in which the Supreme Court held that signing a form lease agreement appointing a stranger as an agent for service of process is authorized by Rule 4, so long as the agent then mails the summons and complaint to the defendant and the defendant has actual notice.

National Equipment Rental, Ltd. v. Szukhent,

United States Supreme Court
375 U.S. 311 (1964)

Mr. Justice STEWART delivered the opinion of the Court.

The Federal Rules of Civil Procedure provide that service of process upon an individual may be made "by delivering a copy of the summons and of the complaint to an agent authorized by appointment ... to receive service of process."[fn] The petitioner is a corporation with its principal place of business in New York. It sued the respondents, residents of Michigan, in a New York federal court, claiming that the respondents had defaulted under a farm equipment lease. The only question now before us is whether the person upon whom the summons and complaint were served was "an agent authorized by appointment" to receive the same, so as to subject the respondents to the jurisdiction of the federal court in New York.[fn]

The respondents obtained certain farm equipment from the petitioner under a lease... . The lease was on a printed form less than a page and a half in length, and consisted of 18 numbered paragraphs. The last numbered paragraph, appearing just above the respondents' signatures and printed in the same type used in the remainder of the instrument, provided that "the Lessee hereby designates Florence Weinberg... as agent for the purpose of accepting service of any process within the State of New York." The respondents were not acquainted with Florence Weinberg.

In 1962 the petitioner commenced the present action by filing in the federal court in New York a complaint which alleged that the respondents had failed to make any of the periodic payments specified by the lease. The Marshal delivered two copies of the summons and complaint to Florence Weinberg. That same day she mailed the summons and complaint to the respondents, together with a letter stating that the documents had been served upon her as the respondents' agent for the purpose of accepting service of process in New York, in accordance with the agreement contained in the lease.[fn] The petitioner itself also notified the respondents by certified mail of the service of process upon Florence Weinberg.

Upon motion of the respondents, the District Court quashed service of the summons and complaint, holding that, although Florence Weinberg had promptly notified the respondents of the service of process and mailed copies of the summons and complaint to them, the lease agreement itself had not explicitly required her to do so, and there was therefore a "failure of the agency arrangement to achieve intrinsic and continuing reality." [C] The Court of Appeals affirmed, [c] and we granted certiorari, [c]. For the reasons stated in this opinion, we have concluded that Florence Weinberg was "an agent authorized by appointment ... to receive service of process," and accordingly we reverse the judgment before us.

We need not and do not in this case reach the situation where no personal notice has been given to the defendant. Since the respondents did in fact receive complete and timely notice of the lawsuit pending against them, no due process claim has been made. ... [T]his Court's decision in Wuchter v. Pizzutti, 276 U.S. 13[(1928)], is inapposite here. In that case a state nonresident motorist statute which failed to provide explicitly for communication of notice was held unconstitutional, despite the fact that notice had been given to the defendant in that particular case. ... The question presented here, on the other hand, is whether a party to a private contract may appoint an agent to receive service of process... , where the agent is not personally known to the party, and where the agent has not expressly undertaken to transmit notice to the party.

The purpose underlying the contractual provision here at issue seems clear. The clause was inserted by the petitioner and agreed to by the respondents in order to assure that any litigation under the lease should be conducted in the State of New York. ... [I]t is settled, as the courts below recognized, that parties to a contract may agree in advance to submit to the jurisdiction of a given court, to permit notice to be served by the opposing party, or even to waive notice altogether. [Cc]

Under well-settled general principles of the law of agency Florence Weinberg's prompt acceptance and transmittal to the respondents of the summons and complaint pursuant to the authorization was itself sufficient to validate the agency, even though there was no explicit previous promise on her part to do so. ...

We deal here with a Federal Rule, applicable to federal courts in all 50 States. But even if we were to assume that this uniform federal standard should give way to contrary local policies, there is no relevant concept of state law which would invalidate the agency here at issue. In Michigan, where the respondents reside, the statute which validates service of process under the circumstances present in this case contains no provision requiring that the appointed agent expressly undertake to notify the principal of the service of process.[fn] Similarly, New York law, which it was agreed should be applicable to the lease provisions, does not require any such express promise by the agent in order to create a valid agency for receipt of process. ...

It is argued, finally, that the agency sought to be created in this case was invalid because Florence Weinberg may have had a conflict of interest. This argument is based upon the fact that she was not personally known to the respondents at the time of her appointment and upon a suggestion in the record that she may be related to an officer of the petitioner corporation. But such a contention ignores the narrowly limited nature of the agency here involved. Florence Weinberg was appointed the respondents' agent for the single purpose of receiving service of process. An agent with authority so limited can in no meaningful sense be deemed to have had an interest antagonistic to the respondents, since both the petitioner and the respondents had an equal interest in assuring that, in the event of litigation, the latter be given that adequate and timely notice which is a prerequisite to a valid judgment.[fn]

A different case would be presented if Florence Weinberg had not given prompt notice to the respondents, for then the claim might well be made that her failure to do so had operated to invalidate the agency. ...

The judgment of the Court of Appeals is reversed and the case is remanded for further proceedings consistent with this opinion. It is so ordered.

Judgment of Court of Appeals reversed and case remanded.

Mr. Justice BLACK, dissenting.

... [U]pholding service of process in this case raises serious questions as to whether these Michigan farmers have been denied due process of law in violation of the Fifth and Fourteenth Amendments.

... It is hardly likely that these Michigan farmers, hiring farm equipment, were in any position to dicker over what terms went into the contract they signed. Yet holding this service effective inevitably will mean that the Szukhents must go nearly a thousand miles to a strange city, hire New York counsel, pay witnesses to travel there, pay their own and their witnesses' hotel bills, try to explain a dispute over a farm equipment lease to a New York judge or jury, and in other ways bear the burdens of litigation in a distant, and likely a strange, city. The company, of course, must have had this in mind when it put the clause in the contract. It doubtless hoped, by easing into its contract this innocent looking provision for service of process in New York, to succeed in making it as burdensome, disadvantageous, and expensive as possible for lessees to contest actions brought against them. ...

The end result of today's holding is not difficult to foresee. Clauses like the one used against the Szukhents—clauses which companies have not inserted, I suspect, because they never dreamed a court would uphold them—will soon find their way into the "boilerplate" of everything from an equipment lease to a conditional sales contract. Today's holding gives a green light to every large company in this country to contrive contracts which declare with force of law that when such a company wants to sue someone with whom it does business, that individual must go and try to defend himself in some place, no matter how distant, where big business enterprises are concentrated... . The very threat of such a suit can be used to force payment of alleged claims, even though they be wholly without merit. This fact will not be news to companies exerting their economic power to wangle such contracts. ...

I would affirm the judgment.

Mr. Justice BRENNAN, with whom THE CHIEF JUSTICE and Mr. Justice GOLDBERG join, dissenting.

I would affirm. ... I would, first, ... deny validity to the appointment of a purported agent whose interests conflict with those of his supposed principal, [c]. Second, I would require that the appointment include an explicit condition that the agent after service transmit the process forthwith to the principal. ... Third, since the corporate plaintiff prepared the printed form contract, I would not hold the individual purchaser bound by the appointment without proof, in addition to his mere signature on the form, that the individual understandingly consented to be sued in a State not that of his residence. ... It offends common sense to treat a printed form which closes an installment sale as embodying terms to all of which the individual knowingly assented. The sales pitch aims solely at getting the signature on the form and wastes no time explaining or even mentioning the print. Before I would find that an individual purchaser has knowingly and intelligently consented to be sued in another State, I would require more proof of that fact than is provided by his mere signature on the form.

Since these standards were not satisfied in this case, the service of the summons and complaint was properly quashed.

INQUIRY

Corporations. Whom must a plaintiff serve when the defendant is not a natural person but a corporation? As in the case of service on natural persons, the FEDERAL RULES OF CIVIL PROCEDURE authorize, in Rule 4(h)(1)(A), service on a corporation as the statutes and court rules of the forum state would permit such service, so long as that service is within a federal district. Once again, the FEDERAL RULES borrow the forum state's service-of-process rules. Rule 4(h)(1)(B) also authorizes that a plaintiff serve a corporation by personally serving "an officer, a managing or general agent, or any other agent authorized by appointment or by law to receive service of process" within a federal district, so long as the plaintiff also mails the summons and complaint to the corporation. Why do you think the rule also requires mailing? Is it "every little bit helps"? *See* Insurance Co. of North America v. S/S Hellenic Challenger, 88 F.R.D. 545 (S.D. N.Y. 1980) (refusing to set aside default judgment entered after service of process on assistant claims manager who lost it). Keep in mind *Mullane's* "reasonably calculated" standard. If the plaintiff cannot locate an agent for service within a federal district and the forum state's rules do not help, then Rule 4(h)(2) permits a plaintiff to serve a corporate defendant after the manner of foreign service, as the next section addresses.

Foreign Service. FED. R. CIV. P. 4(f) addresses service "not within any judicial district of the United States," meaning service in foreign countries. *See* Volkswagenwerk Aktiengesellschaft v. Schlunk, 486 U.S. 694 (1988) (service within the United States is not effective under rules for foreign service). Rule 4(f)(1) permits service in foreign countries by the terms of "any internationally agreed means of service that is reasonably calculated to give notice, such as those authorized by the Hague Convention... ." The Hague Convention, to which about 65 countries are signatories, permits service through a central authority designated by and within the foreign state, consistent with the laws on service of process of that foreign state. For the rest of the world's nations who are not Hague Convention signatories, the plaintiff must determine what the foreign state's laws permit and then follow those methods without the advantage of a responsible central authority. There are at least two reasons why service should be by means approved by the foreign state: (1) respect for the sovereignty of the foreign country keeping in mind that service of process extends the reach of United States law into that country, which the country might consider an unauthorized and even hostile act; and (2) so that the foreign country where the defendant may have collectible assets recognizes the United States judgment. Improper service in a foreign country is an especially useless act. Rule 4(f)(2) allows other methods of foreign service reasonably calculated to give notice and not contrary to the foreign state's laws, including personal service, mail with signed receipt, as the foreign state may specifically direct on request, or as the federal district court orders. The last option may be the most attractive, given that federal district courts have ordered foreign service by such reasonable means as delivery to the defendant's attorney, ordinary mail to the last known address, and even email. *See* Rio Properties, Inc. v. Rio Intl. Interlink, 284 F.3d 1007, 1016 (9th Cir. 2002) (affirming default judgment on actual notice after regular mail and email service under Rule 4(f)).

Government. The FEDERAL RULES OF CIVIL PROCEDURE include provisions for service of process on the United States, a United States agency, and a foreign government. Rule 4(i) permits the plaintiff to serve the United States by personally serving a United States attorney, assistant United States attorney, or designated clerical employee in the United States attorney's office within the issuing district, or by registered or certified mail to that office's civil-process clerk or to the Attorney General in Washington, D.C. If the suit is against a United States agency, officer, or employee rather than the United States, then Rule 4(i)(2) requires that the plaintiff serve the United States as immediately above and also use registered or certified mail to serve the agency, officer, or employee. Under Rule 4(j), service on state or local government requires delivery to the chief executive officer or service as the forum state's law permits. Service on foreign governments must be as provided under 28 U.S.C. §1608.

Practice

The new associate opened the strangely marked envelope while grinning ear to ear. And yes, inside was an ornate certificate indicating that the associate had successfully served a foreign manufacturer overseas. All that it took was about six months of patient effort researching the Hague Convention, then researching what service the foreign state permitted, having the documents translated into the correct language, obtaining and completing the appropriate forms, locating the foreign state's central authority to whom to send the documentation, and making not-so-patient inquiries as to the reasons for the delay. After savoring the victor for the rest of the day, the associate filed the original of the ornate certificate with the court clerk and had a copy framed to hang on the office wall.

3. Proving Service

To those unfamiliar with civil procedure, the next requirement may seem strange but is actually sensible. Service is not reliable until the plaintiff files a return of service with the court. Filing a service return with the court establishes service to the court's satisfaction and to the satisfaction of anyone (especially the defendant) later examining the court file to investigate the validity of the judgment. When a served defendant fails to answer and the plaintiff requests a default judgment, the court clerk may examine the court file for a return of service confirm that the plaintiff properly served the defendant. The trial judge may do likewise at any hearing in which the defendant later challenges the default judgment. FED. R. CIV. P. 4(*l*)(1) requires that the plaintiff prove service by the server's affidavit unless the defendant waived it. A return of service is a form that includes the server's attestation as to the time, date, place, and means of service. The trial court has issued the summons that the plaintiff has served, and now the plaintiff has returned the service to the trial court from which the summons issued.

What if the attestation on the return of service is false? In Miedreich v. Lauenstein, 232 U.S. 236 (1914), the Supreme Court rejected a collateral attack on a sheriff's return of service, effectively upholding a judgment of foreclosure despite that the judgment debtor showed that the sheriff's return of service was false. That result does not mean that the defendant is helpless against a false return. The Supreme Court noted that the debtor's recourse would be against the process server's bond. The result in *Miedreich v. Lauenstein* might also have been different if the debtor had made a direct challenge to the foreclosure judgment rather than a collateral attack on the service return. What happens if the plaintiff neglects to file a return of service? Interestingly, Rule 4(*l*)(3) states that failing to prove service by filing the requisite return of service in the form of the server's affidavit does make the service invalid. It is, at that point, only incomplete, not invalid. Rule 4(*l*)(3) permits the trial court to allow amended proof of service. *See also* MICH. CT. R. 2.104(B) (failure to file return does not affect service validity).

There remains a situation in which service is invalid even when the attestation on the return of service is true, the service complied with the issuing court's rules, and the notice supplied by the chosen method of service would be constitutional. That situation is where the law grants the defendant immunity from service of process. It would be wrong to think of immunity from process as intended to benefit the defendant. It is not. It is to benefit the justice system or system of governance, meaning to recognize a greater benefit than the plaintiff would presumably realize by obtaining valid service over the immune defendant. Federal diplomatic immunity for representatives of foreign government is an example in which the civil justice system respects the need of foreign officials to travel freely on official government business important to the security and welfare of nations, within reasonable limits. *See* Kadic v. Karadzic, 70 F.3d 232 (2d Cir. 1995) (refusing to extend diplomatic immunity to foreign head of state who was not a designated United Nations representative and whom officer served outside United Nations headquarters district).

Practice

"What do you mean, 'substituted service'?" the client asked the volunteer lawyer at the courthouse's legal-help center. The client had a look of confused hopelessness, probably in part from sensing the lawyer's own concern. The client was trying to serve a complaint against an ex-boyfriend with whom she had borrowed money to buy a car. The client needed the ex-boyfriend's help paying for the car or his signature on the title to sell it but could not locate him for personal service and lately had heard that he had disappeared out of state. The lawyer patiently explained why the court rules required substituted service, as the lawyer helped the client fill out the motion forms. At each opportunity, the lawyer tried to encourage the client to trust the court, knowing that due process must seem a strange thing when owed to a deadbeat ex-boyfriend while also knowing that the client needed the court's help.

B. Opportunity for Hearing

In Mullane v. Central Hanover Bank & Trust Co., 339 U.S. 306 (1950), the Supreme Court recognized that due process requires both notice and opportunity for hearing. This dual requirement means that the plaintiff must give the defendant notice of the action *and* the court must reasonably offer the defendant an adequate hearing, usually before deciding the matter. In practice, opportunity for hearing can mean not only that the court must offer some form of trial or summary proceeding but also that the court give the defendant enough time to gather evidence and prepare to make the hearing meaningful. Due process does not mean that courts are unable to take any action until after hearing. There are certainly instances in civil litigation in which the delay occasioned by notice and hearing could so jeopardize the plaintiff's rights and public's interest that due process will authorize a trial court to make what the law calls a *provisional remedy*. Depending on the applicable state or federal law and the particular circumstances of the case, those remedies may permit the plaintiff to have the court attach, replevin, or sequester the defendant's property, garnish obligations others owe to the defendant, appoint receivers, and issue injunctions and notices of the pending litigation, in ways that interfere substantially with the defendant's ability to benefit from those interests. FED. R. CIV. P. 64 authorizes the federal district courts to adopt the provisional remedies of their forum state.

FED. R. CIV. P. 64. Seizing a Person or Property
(a) REMEDIES UNDER STATE LAW—IN GENERAL. At the commencement of and throughout an action, every remedy is available that, under the law of the state where the court is located, provides for seizing a person or property to secure satisfaction of the potential judgment. But a federal statute governs to the extent it applies.
(b) SPECIFIC KINDS OF REMEDIES. The remedies available under this rule include the following—however designated and regardless of whether state procedure requires an independent action: arrest; attachment; garnishment; replevin; sequestration; and other corresponding or equivalent remedies.

The availability and application of provisional remedies has given rise to a series of significant cases in which the Supreme Court has held the due-process clause applicable to those remedies and has articulated the boundaries of due process. In Sniadach v. Family Finance Corp., 395 U.S. 337 (1969), the Supreme Court held unconstitutional a Wisconsin statute that authorized the trial court to garnish the defendant's wages after the plaintiff's complaint but before trial, at the plaintiff's request. As explained more fully in a subsequent chapter on post-judgment remedies, when the plaintiff serves a garnishment writ on the defendant's employer, the employer must withhold statutory amounts from the defendant's wages. Although federal and state laws prohibit an employer from firing an employee based on wage garnishment, garnishment at any time, and especially before trial, can still wreak havoc on a defendant's finances. The Supreme Court recognized the particular unfairness of that burden when the plaintiff had not yet fully established the right to recover.

Three years later in Fuentes v. Shevin, 407 U.S. 67 (1972), the Supreme Court extended *Sniadach* to hold unconstitutional pre-hearing replevin of defendant's personal property. As explained more fully later, replevin authorizes the trial court to issue a writ commanding a law-enforcement officer to seize the personal property including, if necessary, by breaking into a dwelling. Replevin statutes typically require the plaintiff to post a bond. The defendant may usually get the property back promptly by posting the defendant's own bond. Yet the Supreme Court nonetheless recognized an inherent unfairness to the process at least when applied in consumer settings. The Court concluded that replevin might be available only in extraordinary settings such as where an important public or governmental interest was at stake, there was "special need for very prompt action," and the state maintains "strict control over its monopoly of legitimate force" by, for instance, ensuring that judges or other trained officials rather than clerks issue the writs of replevin. 407 U.S. at 90-91.

Two years later, the Supreme Court appeared to relax *Sniadach's* due-process requirements in Mitchell v. W.T. Grant Co., 416 U.S. 600 (1974), when it approved a sequestration process in which a retailer creditor obtained the trial court's writ and had the defendant consumer's goods seized as security for the consumer debt. The Supreme Court accepted the process because it involved secured property and a judge-authorized writ, and provided prompt post-sequestration hearing. Yet just one year later in North Georgia Finishing, Inc. v Di-Chem, Inc., 419 U.S. 601 (1975), the Supreme Court invalidated another garnishment statute because it provided no prompt post-garnishment hearing and did not require the issuing court to examine closely the plaintiff's request for the writ.

It looked for a time like the Supreme Court might extend *Sniadach* to routinely preclude government from terminating an individual's public benefits without first offering a hearing. In Goldberg v. Kelly, 397 U.S. 254 (1970), the Supreme Court held that the due-process clause entitles the recipient of public benefits to a pre-termination hearing. Yet just six years later in Mathews v. Eldridge, 424 U.S. 319 (1976), the Supreme Court held that the due-process clause does not entitle the recipient of Social Security benefits to a pre-termination hearing. The *Mathews* Court balanced the recipient's private interest against the risk of error in the pre-termination decision and the governmental burden of pre-termination hearing, those three considerations soon recognized as the *Mathews* factors. These cases laid the groundwork for the Supreme Court to apply the *Mathews* factors to disputes between private parties, in the following case representing the current law on the due-process contours of opportunity for hearing.

Connecticut v. Doehr,

United States Supreme Court
501 U.S. 1 (1991)

Justice WHITE delivered an opinion, Parts I, II, and III of which are the opinion of the Court.[fn: The CHIEF JUSTICE, Justice BLACKMUN, Justice KENNEDY, and Justice SOUTER join Parts I, II, and II of this opinion, and Justice SCALIA joins Parts I and III.]

This case requires us to determine whether a state statute that authorizes prejudgment attachment of real estate without prior notice or hearing, without a showing of extraordinary circumstances, and without a requirement that the person seeking the attachment post a bond, satisfies the Due Process Clause of the Fourteenth Amendment. We hold that, as applied to this case, it does not.

I

On March 15, 1988, petitioner John F. DiGiovanni submitted an application to the Connecticut Superior Court for an attachment in the amount of $75,000 on respondent Brian K. Doehr's home… . DiGiovanni took this step in conjunction with a civil action for assault and battery that he was seeking to institute against Doehr in the same court. The suit did not involve Doehr's real estate, nor did DiGiovanni have any pre-existing interest either in Doehr's home or any of his other property.

Connecticut law authorizes prejudgment attachment of real estate without affording prior notice or the opportunity for a prior hearing to the individual whose property is subject to the attachment. The State's prejudgment remedy statute provides, in relevant part: "The court or a judge of the court may allow the prejudgment remedy to be issued by an attorney without hearing ... upon verification by oath of the plaintiff or of some competent affiant, that there is probable cause to sustain the validity of the plaintiff's claims... ." [C][fn]

The statute does not require the plaintiff to post a bond to insure the payment of damages that the defendant may suffer should the attachment prove wrongfully issued or the claim prove unsuccessful.

As required, DiGiovanni submitted an affidavit in support of his application [stating ...] that "I was willfully, wantonly and maliciously assaulted by the defendant, Brian K. Doehr"; that "[s]aid assault and battery broke my left wrist and further caused an ecchymosis to my right eye, as well as other injuries"; and that "I have further expended sums of money for medical care and treatment." [C] The affidavit concluded with the statement, "In my opinion, the foregoing facts are sufficient to show that there is probable cause that judgment will be rendered for the plaintiff." [C]

On the strength of these submissions the Superior Court Judge ... found "probable cause to sustain the validity of the plaintiff's claim" and ordered the attachment on Doehr's home "to the value of $75,000." The sheriff attached the property four days later... . Only after this did Doehr receive notice of the attachment. He also had yet to be served with the complaint... . As the statute further required, the attachment notice informed Doehr that he had the right to a hearing: (1) to claim that no probable cause existed to sustain the claim; (2) to request that the attachment be vacated, modified, or dismissed or that a bond be substituted; or (3) to claim that some portion of the property was exempt from execution. [C]

Rather than pursue these options, Doehr filed suit against DiGiovanni in Federal District Court, claiming that [the statute] was unconstitutional under the Due Process Clause of the Fourteenth Amendment.[fn] The District Court upheld the statute and granted summary judgment in favor of DiGiovanni. [C] On appeal, a divided panel of the United States Court of Appeals for the Second Circuit reversed [citing Sniadach v. Family Finance Corp., 395 U.S. 337 (1969), and relying on Mitchell v. W.T. Grant Co., 416 U.S. 600 (1974), and distinguishing Mathews v. Eldridge, 424 U.S. 319 (1976).]. ...

II

With this case we return to the question of what process must be afforded by a state statute enabling an individual to enlist the aid of the State to deprive another of his or her property by means of the prejudgment attachment or similar procedure. ...

... In *Mathews, [supra,]* we drew upon our prejudgment remedy decisions to determine what process is due when the government itself seeks to effect a deprivation on its own initiative. [C] That analysis resulted in the now familiar threefold inquiry requiring consideration of "the private interest that will be affected by the official action"; "the risk of an erroneous deprivation of such interest through the procedures used, and the probable value, if any, of additional or substitute safeguards"; and lastly "the Government's interest, including the function involved and the fiscal and administrative burdens that the additional or substitute procedural requirement would entail." [C]

Here the inquiry is similar, but the focus is different. Prejudgment remedy statutes ordinarily apply to disputes between private parties rather than between an individual and the government. … For this type of case, therefore, the relevant inquiry requires, as in *Mathews,* first, consideration of the private interest that will be affected by the prejudgment measure; second, an examination of the risk of erroneous deprivation through the procedures under attack and the probable value of additional or alternative safeguards; and third, in contrast to *Mathews,* principal attention to the interest of the party seeking the prejudgment remedy, with, nonetheless, due regard for any ancillary interest the government may have in providing the procedure or forgoing the added burden of providing greater protections.

We now consider the *Mathews* factors in determining the adequacy of the procedures before us, first with regard to the safeguards of notice and a prior hearing, and then in relation to the protection of a bond.

III

We agree with the Court of Appeals that the property interests that attachment affects are significant. For a property owner like Doehr, attachment ordinarily clouds title; impairs the ability to sell or otherwise alienate the property; taints any credit rating; reduces the chance of obtaining a home equity loan or additional mortgage; and can even place an existing mortgage in technical default where there is an insecurity clause. …

… [T]hese effects do not amount to a complete, physical, or permanent deprivation of real property; their impact is less than the perhaps temporary total deprivation of household goods or wages. See *Sniadach, supra,* [c]; *Mitchell, supra*[, c]. But the Court has never held that only such extreme deprivations trigger due process concern. [C] To the contrary, our cases show that even the temporary or partial impairments to property rights that attachments, liens, and similar encumbrances entail are sufficient to merit due process protection. …

… [T]he risk of erroneous deprivation that the State permits here is substantial. By definition, attachment statutes premise a deprivation of property on one ultimate factual contingency—the award of damages to the plaintiff which the defendant may not be able to satisfy. [Cc] For attachments before judgment, Connecticut mandates that this determination be made by means of a procedural inquiry that asks whether "there is probable cause to sustain the validity of the plaintiff's claim." [C] The statute elsewhere defines the validity of the claim in terms of the likelihood "that judgment will be rendered in the matter in favor of the plaintiff." [Cc] What probable cause means in this context, however, remains obscure. … Doehr, citing ambiguous state cases, reads the provision as requiring no more than that a plaintiff demonstrate a subjective good-faith belief that the suit will succeed. [Cc] At oral argument, the State shifted its position to argue that the statute requires something akin to the plaintiff stating a claim with sufficient facts to survive a motion to dismiss.

We need not resolve this confusion since the statute presents too great a risk of erroneous deprivation under any of these interpretations. If the statute demands inquiry into the sufficiency of the complaint, or, still less, the plaintiff's good-faith belief that the complaint is sufficient, requirement of a complaint and a factual affidavit would permit a court to make these minimal determinations. But neither inquiry adequately reduces the risk of erroneous deprivation. Permitting a court to authorize attachment merely because the plaintiff believes the defendant is liable, or because the plaintiff can make out a facially valid complaint, would permit the deprivation of the defendant's property when the claim would fail to convince a jury, when it rested on factual allegations that were sufficient to state a cause of action but which the defendant would dispute, or in the case of a mere good-faith standard, even when the complaint failed to state a claim upon which relief could be granted. The potential for unwarranted attachment in these situations is self-evident and too great to satisfy the requirements of due process absent any countervailing consideration.

Even if the provision requires the plaintiff to demonstrate, and the judge to find, probable cause to believe that judgment will be rendered in favor of the plaintiff, the risk of error was substantial in this case. As the record shows, and as the State concedes, only a skeletal affidavit need be, and was, filed. ... [I]n a case like this involving an alleged assault, even a detailed affidavit would give only the plaintiff's version of the confrontation. Unlike determining the existence of a debt or delinquent payments, the issue does not concern "ordinarily uncomplicated matters that lend themselves to documentary proof." *Mitchell, [supra,]* at 609[]. ...

What safeguards the State does afford do not adequately reduce this risk. Connecticut points out that the statute also provides an "expeditiou[s]" postattachment adversary hearing, [c]; notice for such a hearing, [c]; judicial review of an adverse decision, [c]; and a double damages action if the original suit is commenced without probable cause, [c]. Similar considerations were present in *Mitchell,* where we upheld Louisiana's sequestration statute despite the lack of predeprivation notice and hearing. But in *Mitchell,* the plaintiff had a vendor's lien to protect, the risk of error was minimal because the likelihood of recovery involved uncomplicated matters that lent themselves to documentary proof, [c], and the plaintiff was required to put up a bond. None of these factors diminishing the need for a predeprivation hearing is present in this case. ...

Finally, we conclude that the interests in favor of an *ex parte* attachment, particularly the interests of the plaintiff, are too minimal to supply such a consideration here. The plaintiff had no existing interest in Doehr's real estate when he sought the attachment. His only interest in attaching the property was to ensure the availability of assets to satisfy his judgment if he prevailed on the merits of his action. Yet there was no allegation that Doehr was about to transfer or encumber his real estate or take any other action during the pendency of the action that would render his real estate unavailable to satisfy a judgment. Our cases have recognized such a properly supported claim would be an exigent circumstance permitting postponing any notice or hearing until after the attachment is effected. See *Mitchell, supra*; *Fuentes, supra*; *Sniadach, [supra]*. Absent such allegations, however, the plaintiff's interest in attaching the property does not justify the burdening of Doehr's ownership rights without a hearing to determine the likelihood of recovery.

No interest the government may have affects the analysis. The State's substantive interest in protecting any rights of the plaintiff cannot be any more weighty than those rights themselves. ...

V

Because Connecticut's prejudgment remedy provision, [c], violates the requirements of due process by authorizing prejudgment attachment without prior notice or a hearing, the judgment of the Court of Appeals is affirmed, and the case is remanded to that court for further proceedings consistent with this opinion.

It is so ordered.

INQUIRY

Application. The lower courts appear confident of applying the three *Mathews* factors after the fashion of *Connecticut v. Doehr. See, e.g.,* Shaumyan v. O'Neill, 987 F.2d 122 (2d Cir. 1993) (upholding attachment under same statute as in *Doehr* on balance of *Mathews* factors). *Connecticut v. Doehr* was not the Supreme Court's last word on the due-process requirements of opportunity for hearing, even though it and *Mathews* continue to supply the standard. In United States v. James Daniel Good Real Property, 510 U.S. 43 (1993), the Supreme Court held that the federal government must give notice and opportunity for hearing before seizing the home of a defendant already convicted of the underlying drug crime on which the statute relied for civil forfeiture. The case did not alter the constitutional standard. Lower courts evaluating the constitutionality of pre-judgment provisional remedies continue to use *Connecticut v. Doehr* to help them apply the *Mathews* factors in civil litigation between private parties. *See* Diaz v. Paterson, 547 F.3d 88 (2d Cir. 2008) (upholding state lis pendens statute under balance of *Mathews* factors as in *Doehr*).

Career

Which side do you prefer? Civil litigation's adversarial nature, together with ethical duties that require lawyers to represent parties free from conflicts of interest, means that lawyers take one side or the other side (not both sides) in a dispute. Although lawyers who represent plaintiffs and lawyers who represent defendants certainly share skills and have somewhat similar roles even though on different sides, there also tend to be differences between plaintiffs' and defense work. Some of those differences have to do with the different civil procedures for plaintiffs and defendants involving issues like pleading, service of process, discovery, and the order of trial. Other differences have to do with how the different sides structure and maintain client relationships over issues of authority, direction or control, and reporting. The economics may also be different, whether (for instance) hourly, flat, or contingency fee, making compensation more or less certain and more or less tied to hours, productivity, or success. With careful conflict checking, some lawyers manage to practice simultaneously both plaintiffs' and defense work. Others change sides one or more times during the course of a career. Many others start and finish a career on just one side. Knowing your traits and preferences for one side or the other side is a good strategy to explore civil-litigation careers.

CHAPTER IV

SUBJECT MATTER JURISDICTION

OBJECTIVE: That you be able to determine the state and federal courts that have jurisdiction over the subject matter of a civil case and what opportunity the parties have to choose in which court to litigate.

Case Study: You are teleconferencing with corporate counsel for a national corporation whose resident agent a sheriff just served with a summons and complaint in a products-liability case filed in state court in the county in which you practice. Corporate counsel indicates that the company tries rather than settles these cases and wants to know what options the company has as to the court in which it will try the case.

A. Constitutional Framework

Recall that Part I addresses the authority of courts to adjudicate. So far, in examining the subjects of personal jurisdiction, notice to the defendant, and the defendant's opportunity for hearing, we have focused on the limits of a court's reach and the fairness to the defendant when a court adjudicates. In this chapter, the focus shifts from fair treatment of the defendant to the competence of the court within its delegated authority. By competence, we mean whether the legislature has constituted the particular court to hear the type of action that the plaintiff has filed. It is not whether the trial judge and judicial staff have the knowledge and skill to decide the matter. Once a legislature constitutes a court for a certain type of case, the judge and judicial staff will likely develop and exercise particular expertise in that area. Yet the concept explored in this chapter is that legislatures constitute courts to hear certain types of cases and within certain monetary limits. A delegated authority like a trial court must never assume more authority than that authority it received by delegation. It must exercise only the delegated authority. For a court to decide wrongly is one thing. It happens frequently. Yet for a court to decide where it has no power to decide is a much greater offense, undermining the institutions of law and the court, not simply demonstrating the fallibility of the particular judge who made the error. It happens much more rarely. These questions of a court's statutory authority to hear certain matters are questions of subject-matter jurisdiction, as distinguished from personal jurisdiction.

For instance, a state legislature may constitute small-claims courts to hear matters up to a modest dollar limit such $3,750 without the involvement of lawyers, district courts to hear matters up to a higher limit such as $25,000, and circuit courts to hear matters over $25,000. The legislature may at the same time prohibit the small-claims and district courts from granting any relief other than money damages, reserving declaratory and equitable relief for the circuit courts.

The circuit courts would thus hear any family-law and most real-property matters, effectively making them courts of general subject-matter jurisdiction. A state legislature may separately establish probate or other specialty courts. Despite the fact that state legislatures often divide their subject-matter jurisdiction, state courts are fundamentally courts of general subject-matter jurisdiction. They will hear all matters arising under state law. Indeed, the Supreme Court held in Hughes v. Fetter, 341 U.S. 609 (1951), that the Constitution's full-faith-and-credit clause, Art. IV, §1, requires the courts of one state to hear matters involving the laws of a different state, even though the forum state's courts may apply their own state's procedural laws including their own limitations periods, Sun Oil Co. v. Wortman, 486 U.S. 717 (1988). As is shown further below, state courts will also hear many matters arising under federal law. The Supreme Court held in Howlett v. Rose, 496 U.S. 356 (1990), a federal civil-rights case, that when parties decide to litigate their federal civil claim in state rather than federal court where Congress so permits it, the state court must hear the matter. *See also* Haywood v. Drown, __ U.S. __, 129 S.Ct. 2108 (2009) (state court must not eliminate jurisdiction to avoid hearing federal claim).

This chapter addresses the subject-matter jurisdiction of primarily the federal rather than state courts. Even though the vast majority of civil litigation occurs in the state rather than federal courts, there are good reasons for all practitioners to know the subject-matter jurisdiction of the federal courts. First, the basic concept of subject-matter jurisdiction as determined by legislative authority is the same for the state or federal courts, even if the source or specific nature of the legislation is different. Some of what you learn about the subject-matter jurisdiction of the federal courts also applies to the subject-matter jurisdiction of the state courts. There are, on the other hand, important differences between the subject-matter jurisdiction of the federal and state courts. It is important to keep in mind again that state courts are courts of general subject-matter jurisdiction, whereas federal courts are courts of limited subject-matter jurisdiction. Yet the federal system's uniformity does make it easier to study comprehensively, given the substantial variety in the ways that different states divide up the subject-matter jurisdiction of their courts and even substantial variety within individual states as one moves from metropolitan to rural areas. A large metropolitan area may have several state courts of different subject-matter jurisdiction, while a rural county in the same state may have a unified trial court handling all such matters.

There are also important strategic reasons for civil litigators to know the extent of federal-court subject-matter jurisdiction. Civil litigants in state court must be aware of the opportunity to litigate in federal court, when that opportunity exists. In some cases, plaintiffs may choose either a state or federal forum. When the plaintiff chooses a state over the federal forum, the defendant may have the right to remove the case to federal court. You need to know when a party is able to remove a state case to federal court, how to remove it or challenge removal, and when a party has a right to a remand to state court because the federal court no longer has subject-matter jurisdiction. These considerations are important because there are differences between individual state and federal courts. Many of the differences that practitioners consider more important depend on local circumstances such as whether the state or federal docket has the longer delays, which judge is more likely to allow certain cases to go to the jury, how effective the judge is in helping parties to negotiate and settle, which counsel is more familiar with which court system, and how the state and federal jury pools compare. In a perfect world, justice would not depend on choice of forum. Yet inevitably, the generally more local character of state courts seated in particular counties tends to create a more local character for justice in those courts, whatever those local conditions may mean for the parties and their counsel.

Skills

Civil litigators rely heavily on strategic advice and judgments. As just suggested, many practitioners feel that the judgment as to which court in which to litigate can be critical to a particular case's outcome. How do lawyers develop that sense of judgment? Certainly, one's own professional experience of courts and their judges, judicial staff, and juries can be important, especially as that experience accumulates. Experience is a wise teacher. Yet lawyers also draw constantly on the experience of other lawyers. It is common for a lawyer who has no experience in a certain court to ask a trusted lawyer acquaintance who does. In larger firms, lawyers rely primarily on other lawyers within their own firm. Sole and small-firm practitioners maintain an informal network serving the same purpose. Preparation is everything. What lawyers try to avoid is that sinking feeling, "If I had only known... ."

There are more than just practical and strategic reasons to study federal subject-matter jurisdiction. The line between state and federal authority represents an enormously significant legal and political issue. The states rejected the Articles of Confederation in favor of the new Constitution in order to better divide those powers. The states later fought the Civil War to redivide state and federal power by post-War amendments to the Constitution, having failed to make a lasting division. The limited subject-matter jurisdiction of the federal courts represents a political compromise and judgment as to the most appropriate division of power between the states and federal government. The Supreme Court recognized in Cary v. Curtis, 44 U.S. 236, 245 (1845), that the fact that Congress determines the subject-matter jurisdiction of the federal courts is an important check on federal judicial powers. While the Constitution's Article III creates a United States Supreme Court, it does not expressly create federal district courts, instead enumerating in the following provision a limited scope of their potential powers in the event that Congress chose to do so.

> **U.S. Const., Art. III, §2.** The judicial Power shall extend to all Cases, in Law and Equity, arising under this Constitution, the Laws of the United States, and Treaties made, or which shall be made, under their Authority;—to all Cases affecting Ambassadors, other public Ministers and Consuls;—to all Cases of admiralty and maritime Jurisdiction;—to Controversies to which the United States shall be a Party;—to Controversies between two or more States;—between a State and Citizens of another State;—between Citizens of different States;—between Citizens of the same State claiming Lands under Grants of different States, and between a State, or the Citizens thereof, and foreign States, Citizens or Subjects.

Congress did exercise its constitutional authority under the above provision to create federal district courts but limited their overall subject-matter jurisdiction to less than that permitted by the Constitution. The primary forms of subject-matter jurisdiction that the federal courts exercise are over federal questions, 28 U.S.C. §1331, in cases involving diversity of citizenship, 28 U.S.C. §1332, and for supplemental jurisdiction. As you read the following sections addressing those forms, keep in mind that the federal courts have concurrent jurisdiction (that is, share jurisdiction) with the state courts over these types of cases. The Supreme Court held in Tafflin v. Levitt, 493 U.S. 455, 458-459 (1990), that where Congress is silent on subject-matter jurisdiction arising out of a federal-law dispute, the presumption is for concurrent jurisdiction. Also, keep in mind that Congress has legislated other subject-matter jurisdiction such that only the federal district courts and not the state courts have jurisdiction, *see, e.g.*, 28 U.S.C. §1333 (admiralty); 28 U.S.C. §1334 (bankruptcy); 28 U.S.C. §1337 (antitrust), and also prohibited the federal district courts from exercising jurisdiction in other types of cases, *see, e.g.*, 28 U.S.C. §1341 (state tax collection).

Ethics

Lawyers and their clients share decision-making responsibility. Under Rule 1.2 of the ABA MODEL RULES OF PROFESSIONAL CONDUCT, the client decides on the objectives of the representation, while the lawyer consults with the client about the means of achieving those objectives. For example, clients decide whether to sue and when to settle. A lawyer would ordinarily consult a client over which witnesses to call. Lawyers make their own decisions (without client involvement) about routine matters not likely to directly affect the outcome, such as when to schedule a deposition. The decision whether to litigate in state or federal court is a significant decision that a lawyer would ordinarily discuss with the client.

B. Federal Question

Federal-question jurisdiction is the first form of jurisdiction authorized by the Constitution's Article III, Section 2, above. Interestingly, after a brief period of less than a year under the Midnight Judges Act of 1801 repealed under President Thomas Jefferson, it took most of a century for Congress in 1875 to grant the federal district courts broad subject-matter jurisdiction over claims arising out of federal law. In the meantime, the Supreme Court had decided Osborn v. Bank of the United States, 22 U.S. (9 Wheat.) 738 (1824), in which Justice Marshall wrote for the Court that a statute chartering the plaintiff national bank and authorizing it "to sue and be sued … in any Circuit Court of the United States" had also granted the federal courts Article II, Section 2 subject-matter jurisdiction. *Osborn* effectively established the principle of congressional authorization of Article III, Section 2's potential judicial powers. When in 1875 Congress made its broad grant of federal-question jurisdiction, it presumably did so to develop a coherent body of federal law under an expert federal judiciary, and to ensure access to courts in cases involving federal claims. The statute granting federal-question jurisdiction currently states as follows. Notice that the statute's language is substantially equivalent to the constitutional language.

28 U.S.C. §1331. The district courts shall have jurisdiction of all civil actions arising under the Constitution, laws, or treaties of the United States.

Practitioners readily recognize federal-question jurisdiction at its core, when the plaintiff sues under a federal statute that creates a federal cause of action. Even there, though, there can be close issues as to whether the federal courts will have jurisdiction. For example, in Shoshone Mining Co. v. Rutter, 177 U.S. 505 (1900), the Supreme Court held that the federal courts do not have jurisdiction over land-patent claims filed by miners under a federal statute that relied for the miners' substantive rights on "local customs or rules of miners in the several mining districts... ." There can, in other words, be federal laws that merely provide a means for enforcing what are state substantive rights. Under *Shoshone Mining Co.,* those laws do not confer federal jurisdiction. On the other hand, the Supreme Court in Smith v. Kansas City Title & Trust Co., 255 U.S. 180 (1921), held that the plaintiff could file in federal court a claim arising under a state law permitting a shareholder to sue to prevent a private corporation from investing in unauthorized securities, where the authority of the securities would depend on the application of federal law. There can, in other words, be state laws that merely provide a means for enforcing what are federal substantive rights over which the federal courts have subject-matter jurisdiction. Just what constitutes a federal question can be difficult to determine, given the variety of ways in which federal and state laws interact to create and sustain rights.

Beyond the substantive question of what "arising under" means, the Supreme Court has also decided federal-question cases on the basis of the pleadings through which admittedly federal questions arose. Parties initiate federal civil litigation asserting federal rights through complaints, affirmative defenses, counter- and cross-claims, and third-party claims. Here, the Supreme Court has developed a constellation of rules including that the federal question must arise out of the plaintiff's "well-pleaded complaint," not from the defendant's affirmative defense or counterclaim, and not from a complaint artfully drafted to anticipate a federal defense that the defendant may raise. *See* Holmes Group, Inc. v. Vornado Circulation Systems, Inc., 535 U.S. 826 (2002) (no federal-question jurisdiction based on federal counterclaim); Rivet v Regions Bank, 522 U.S. 470 (1998) (no federal-question jurisdiction based on prior federal judgment as a claim-preclusion defense). For another example of an issue of federal-question jurisdiction arising out of a case's procedural posture, the Supreme Court held in Kokkonen v. Guardian Life Ins. Co., 511 U.S. 375 (1994), that where a plaintiff sues in federal court under a federal statute but settles and dismisses the federal case, the plaintiff only has recourse to state (not federal) court to enforce the settlement agreement because enforcement is merely a question of state contract law. Federal courts have federal-question jurisdiction to enforce federal-court judgments, not private settlement agreements enforceable under state contract law.

The well-pleaded complaint rule and artful-drafting doctrine are useful conceptual tools to determine federal-question jurisdiction. While preserving these interpretive rules, the Supreme Court continues to address what the Constitution's and federal statute's "arising under" language means, most recently looking beyond any bright-line rule to consider the federal elements of the claim, the strength of the federal interests those elements reflect, and the impact of federal judicial resolution of the dispute, as shown in cases below. As you read the cases establishing these rules, remain conscious of which provision the

Supreme Court is interpreting, the Constitution's Article III, Section 2, or the federal-question statute, 28 U.S.C. §1331.

Louisville & Nashville R. Co. v. Mottley,

United States Supreme Court
211 U.S. 149 (1908)

Statement [of the case] by Mr. Justice MOODY:

The appellees (husband and wife), being residents and citizens of Kentucky, brought this suit in equity in the circuit court of the United States for the western district of Kentucky against the appellant, a railroad company and a citizen of the same state. The object of the suit was to compel the specific performance of [a] contract... .

The bill alleged that ... plaintiffs, while passengers upon the defendant railroad, were injured by the defendant's negligence, and released their respective claims for damages in consideration of the agreement for transportation during their lives, expressed in the contract. It is alleged that the contract was performed by the defendant up to January 1, 1907, when the defendant declined to renew the passes. The bill then alleges that the refusal to comply with the contract was based solely upon [an] act of Congress[, ...] which forbids the giving of free passes or free transportation. The bill further alleges: First, that the act of Congress referred to does not prohibit the giving of passes under the circumstances of this case; and, second, that, if the law is to be construed as prohibiting such passes, it is in conflict with the 5th Amendment of the Constitution, because it deprives the plaintiffs of their property without due process of law. The defendant demurred to the bill. The judge of the circuit court overruled the demurrer, entered a decree for the relief prayed for, and the defendant appealed directly to this court.

Mr. Justice MOODY, after making the foregoing statement, delivered the opinion of the court:

... [I]n our opinion, the court below was without jurisdiction of the cause. Neither party has questioned that jurisdiction, but it is the duty of this court to see to it that the jurisdiction of the circuit court, which is defined and limited by statute, is not exceeded. ...

There was no diversity of citizenship, and it is not and cannot be suggested that there was any ground of jurisdiction, except that the case was a "suit . . . arising under the Constitution or laws of the United States." 25 Stat. at L. 434, chap. 866, U. S. Comp. Stat. 1901, p. 509. It is the settled interpretation of these words, as used in this statute, conferring jurisdiction, that a suit arises under the Constitution and laws of the United States only when the plaintiff's statement of his own cause of action shows that it is based upon those laws or that Constitution. It is not enough that the plaintiff alleges some anticipated defense to his cause of action, and asserts that the defense is invalidated by some provision of the Constitution of the United States. Although such allegations show that very likely, in the course of the litigation, a question under the Constitution would arise, they do not show that the suit, that is, the plaintiff's original cause of action, arises under the Constitution. ...

The application of this rule to the case at bar is decisive against the jurisdiction of the circuit court.

It is ordered that the judgment be reversed and the case remitted to the circuit court with instructions to dismiss the suit for want of jurisdiction.

INQUIRY

Artful Pleading. *Mottley* held in what would become the "well-pleaded" complaint rule that the federal question on which the federal district court bases its subject-matter jurisdiction must arise in the complaint, not in the defendant's answer and affirmative defenses. One looks to the complaint for the federal question, not to the pleadings responding to the complaint. One might think, then, that there could be federal-question jurisdiction over a complaint pled under Congress' Declaratory Judgment Act, 28 U.S.C. §§2201 et seq., giving a federal district court statutory authority to declare parties' rights in "a case or controversy within its jurisdiction." Notice, though, that the Act's language implies, correctly, that the federal district court must have some other basis for subject-matter jurisdiction than the Act itself, which is only a procedural provision offering a federal-court forum for resolving by declaratory judgment cases having those other bases for federal jurisdiction. For example, what about when the plaintiff files a declaratory-judgment action asking the federal district court to declare the parties' rights regarding, say, the termination of contracts, implicating only state law? In Skelly Oil Co. v. Phillips Petroleum Co., 339 U.S. 667 (1950), the Supreme Court held that the federal district court would not in that case have federal-question jurisdiction, even though the case pled the federal Declaratory Judgment Act for its jurisdictional basis. Practitioners associate the *Skelly Oil* opinion with the doctrine rejecting federal-question jurisdiction based on artful pleading.

Federal Standards. What if the case is a state-law claim that relies for its cause of action on federal standards? State tort law may permit a plaintiff to rely on the violation of statute for negligence per se or presumption or inference of negligence. If the statute on which the plaintiff relies is a federal statute, then the question becomes whether the case arises under federal law for federal-court subject-matter jurisdiction. In Merrell Dow Pharms., Inc. v. Thompson, 478 U.S. 804 (1986), the Supreme Court rejected federal jurisdiction in such cases. The federal statute in question did not itself create a private right of action, making the state interest in construing and applying its tort laws the greater interest. *Merrell Dow Pharmaceuticals* extended a much earlier case, Moore v. Chesapeake & Ohio Ry. Co., 291 U.S. 205 (1934), in which the Supreme Court held that a state employer-liability system that rejected federal law as a basis for an employee's duty of care remains a state claim over which the federal courts would not have jurisdiction. It looked for a time like the Supreme Court might in *Merrell Dow Pharmaceuticals* have implied a bright-line rule that there would be no federal-court jurisdiction unless the federal statute on which the plaintiff relied actually created a federal cause of action for the plaintiff. After nearly 20 years of circuit splits and scholarly debate, the Supreme Court held otherwise in the following case, that federal elements and interests may still be sufficiently substantial for the plaintiff's state claim to arise under federal law for purposes of federal-question jurisdiction.

Grable & Sons Metal Prods., Inc. v. Darue Engineering & Mfg.,

United States Supreme Court
545 U.S. 308 (2005)

Justice SOUTER delivered the opinion of the Court.

The question is whether want of a federal cause of action to try claims of title to land obtained at a federal tax sale precludes removal to federal court of a state action with nondiverse parties raising a disputed issue of federal title law. We answer no, and hold that the national interest in providing a federal forum for federal tax litigation is sufficiently substantial to support the exercise of federal-question jurisdiction over the disputed issue on removal... .

I

In 1994, the Internal Revenue Service seized Michigan real property belonging to petitioner Grable & Sons Metal Products, Inc., to satisfy Grable's federal tax delinquency. Title 26 U.S.C. § 6335 required the IRS to give notice of the seizure, and there is no dispute that Grable received actual notice by certified mail before the IRS sold the property to respondent Darue Engineering & Manufacturing. ... [Grable] did not exercise its statutory right to redeem the property within 180 days of the sale, [c], and after that period had passed, the Government gave Darue a quitclaim deed, [c].

Five years later, Grable brought a quiet title action in state court, claiming that Darue's record title was invalid because the IRS had failed to notify Grable of its seizure of the property in the exact manner required by §6335(a), which provides that written notice must be "given by the Secretary to the owner of the property [or] left at his usual place of abode or business." Grable said that the statute required personal service, not service by certified mail.

Darue removed the case to Federal District Court as presenting a federal question, because the claim of title depended on the interpretation of the notice statute in the federal tax law. The District Court declined to remand the case at Grable's behest after finding that the "claim does pose a 'significant question of federal law,'" [c], and ruling that Grable's lack of a federal right of action to enforce its claim against Darue did not bar the exercise of federal jurisdiction. On the merits, the court granted summary judgment to Darue, holding that although § 6335 by its terms required personal service, substantial compliance with the statute was enough. [C]

The Court of Appeals for the Sixth Circuit affirmed. [C] On the jurisdictional question, the panel thought it sufficed that the title claim raised an issue of federal law that had to be resolved, and implicated a substantial federal interest (in construing federal tax law). The court went on to affirm the District Court's judgment on the merits. We granted certiorari on the jurisdictional question alone,[fn] [c], to resolve a split within the Courts of Appeals on whether *Merrell Dow Pharmaceuticals Inc. v. Thompson,* 478 U.S. 804[] (1986), always requires a federal cause of action as a condition for exercising federal-question jurisdiction.[fn] We now affirm.

II

Darue was entitled to remove the quiet title action if Grable could have brought it in federal district court originally, 28 U.S.C. § 1441(a), as a civil action "arising under the Constitution, laws, or treaties of the United States," §1331.

This provision for federal-question jurisdiction is invoked by and large by plaintiffs pleading a cause of action created by federal law... . There is, however, another longstanding, if less frequently encountered, variety of federal "arising under" jurisdiction, this Court having recognized for nearly 100 years that in certain cases federal-question jurisdiction will lie over state-law claims that implicate significant federal issues. [C] The doctrine captures the commonsense notion that a federal court ought to be able to hear claims recognized under state law that nonetheless turn on substantial questions of federal law, and thus justify resort to the experience, solicitude, and hope of uniformity that a federal forum offers on federal issues, [c].

The classic example is Smith v. Kansas City Title & Trust Co., 255 U.S. 180[] (1921)... . Although Missouri law provided the cause of action, the Court recognized federal-question jurisdiction because the principal issue in the case was the federal constitutionality of the bond issue. *Smith* thus held, in a somewhat generous statement of the scope of the doctrine, that a state-law claim could give rise to federal-question jurisdiction so long as it "appears from the [complaint] that the right to relief depends upon the construction or application of [federal law]." *Id.* at 199.

The *Smith* statement has been subject to some trimming to fit earlier and later cases recognizing the vitality of the basic doctrine, but shying away from the expansive view that mere need to apply federal law in a state-law claim will suffice to open the "arising under" door. ... It has in fact become a constant refrain in such cases that federal jurisdiction demands not only a contested federal issue, but a substantial one, indicating a serious federal interest in claiming the advantages thought to be inherent in a federal forum. [Cc]

But even when the state action discloses a contested and substantial federal question, the exercise of federal jurisdiction is subject to a possible veto. For the federal issue will ultimately qualify for a federal forum only if federal jurisdiction is consistent with congressional judgment about the sound division of labor between state and federal courts governing the application of §1331. ... Because arising-under jurisdiction to hear a state-law claim always raises the possibility of upsetting the state-federal line drawn (or at least assumed) by Congress, the presence of a disputed federal issue and the ostensible importance of a federal forum are never necessarily dispositive; there must always be an assessment of any disruptive portent in exercising federal jurisdiction. [C]

These considerations have kept us from stating a "single, precise, all-embracing" test for jurisdiction over federal issues embedded in state-law claims between nondiverse parties. [C] ... [T]he question is, does a state-law claim necessarily raise a stated federal issue, actually disputed and substantial, which a federal forum may entertain without disturbing any congressionally approved balance of federal and state judicial responsibilities.

III

A

This case warrants federal jurisdiction. Grable's state complaint must specify "the facts establishing the superiority of [its] claim," Mich. Ct. Rule 3.411(B)(2)(c)[], and Grable has premised its superior title claim on a failure by the IRS to give it adequate notice, as defined by federal law. Whether Grable was given notice within the meaning of the federal statute is thus an essential element of its quiet title claim, and the meaning of the federal statute is actually in dispute;

it appears to be the only legal or factual issue contested in the case. The meaning of the federal tax provision is an important issue of federal law that sensibly belongs in a federal court. The Government has a strong interest in the "prompt and certain collection of delinquent taxes," [c], and the ability of the IRS to satisfy its claims from the property of delinquents requires clear terms of notice to allow buyers like Darue to satisfy themselves that the Service has touched the bases necessary for good title. The Government thus has a direct interest in the availability of a federal forum to vindicate its own administrative action, and buyers (as well as tax delinquents) may find it valuable to come before judges used to federal tax matters. Finally, because it will be the rare state title case that raises a contested matter of federal law, federal jurisdiction to resolve genuine disagreement over federal tax title provisions will portend only a microscopic effect on the federal-state division of labor. [C] ...

B

Merrell Dow Pharmaceuticals Inc. v. Thompson, 478 U.S. 804[] (1986), on which Grable rests its position, is not to the contrary. *Merrell Dow* considered a state tort claim resting in part on the allegation that the defendant drug company had violated a federal misbranding prohibition, and was thus presumptively negligent under Ohio law. [C] The Court assumed that federal law would have to be applied to resolve the claim, but after closely examining the strength of the federal interest at stake and the implications of opening the federal forum, held federal jurisdiction unavailable. Congress had not provided a private federal cause of action for violation of the federal branding requirement... .

Accordingly, *Merrell Dow* should be read in its entirety as treating the absence of a federal private right of action as evidence relevant to, but not dispositive of, the "sensitive judgments about congressional intent" that § 1331 requires. ...

One only needed to consider the treatment of federal violations generally in garden variety state tort law. "The violation of federal statutes and regulations is commonly given negligence per se effect in state tort proceedings."[fn] Restatement (Third) of Torts §14, Reporters' Note, Comment *a*[] (Tentative Draft No. 1, Mar. 28, 2001). [C] A general rule of exercising federal jurisdiction over state claims resting on federal mislabeling and other statutory violations would thus have heralded a potentially enormous shift of traditionally state cases into federal courts. ...

As already indicated, however, a comparable analysis yields a different jurisdictional conclusion in this case. Although Congress also indicated ambivalence in this case by providing no private right of action to Grable, it is the rare state quiet title action that involves contested issues of federal law, [c]. Consequently, jurisdiction over actions like Grable's would not materially affect, or threaten to affect, the normal currents of litigation. Given the absence of threatening structural consequences and the clear interest the Government, its buyers, and its delinquents have in the availability of a federal forum, there is no good reason to shirk from federal jurisdiction over the dispositive and contested federal issue at the heart of the state-law title claim.[fn]

IV

The judgment of the Court of Appeals, upholding federal jurisdiction over Grable's quiet title action, is affirmed.

It is so ordered.

[Concurring opinion by Justice THOMAS omitted.]

INQUIRY

Federal Interests. *Grable* indicates the significance of federal elements and federal interests to determining whether the federal courts have federal-question jurisdiction over the plaintiff's state claim. In short, *Grable* made the exercise of that jurisdiction possible. Yet how probable did *Grable* make the existence of that jurisdiction? The Supreme Court took only one year to answer that question in Empire Healthchoice Assurance, Inc. v. McVeigh, 547 U.S. 677 (2006), where it found no federal-question jurisdiction despite recognizing that the interests in that case were "distinctly federal" and that federal law was also a necessary element. *Empire Healthchoice* involved a private insurer seeking reimbursement in federal court of medical expenses it paid on behalf of a federal worker under a federal health-insurance contract. The insurer sought reimbursement from the worker's estate out of a wrongful-death settlement the estate received after the worker died from the injuries for which the insurer had paid for treatment. The federal contract required the insurer to seek reimbursement. The Supreme Court rejected federal-question jurisdiction despite all of those distinctly federal interests. In doing so, the *Empire Healthchoice* opinion characterized the *Grable*-style state-law claims cognizable in federal court as a "special and small category" of cases restricted to contesting federal-agency action based on federal statute, decisions in which would control "numerous other cases." 547 U.S. at 700-701. Perhaps the lesson is not to expect much of *Grable.*

> ***Knowledge***
>
> As in *Empire Healthchoice* just noted, courts often consider the effects of their decisions to reach and justify those decisions. The law considers prediction and knowledge of effects as an important tool in shaping the law. This instrumentalism balances the common law's stability, making it capable of development, growth, and change. As *Empire Healthchoice* shows, it is also a way in which an appellate court can quickly arrest an undesired trend that one of its own decisions may have unintentionally initiated. Law's knowledge lies in a combination of principle, past, people, and pragmatics.

Challenges. As a later chapter on dispositive motions addresses in more detail, a defendant may challenge subject-matter jurisdiction under either a FED. R. CIV. P. 12(b)(1) motion for failure to state a claim or under Rule 12(b)(6) for lack of jurisdiction, although if the court must look beyond the pleading, then the defendant should choose Rule 12(b)(6). When a defendant challenges both personal and subject-matter jurisdiction, the federal district court may decide on which grounds to grant the motion. Ruhrgas AG v. Marathon Oil Co., 526 U.S. 574 (1999). When must a party challenge subject-matter jurisdiction? The Supreme Court held in Capron v. Van Noorden, 6 U.S. 126 (1804), that a party may challenge subject-matter jurisdiction at any time, even after it has lost. As shown above in *Mottley*, the Supreme Court has extended that rule to allow the federal court to raise the jurisdictional issue sua sponte (on its own motion). In other words, subject-matter jurisdiction is so fundamental that the parties cannot waive it. Does that mean that, as in personal jurisdiction, a defendant can ignore a proceeding over which the federal district court has no subject-matter jurisdiction, and then mount a collateral attack on the judgment when the plaintiff seeks to enforce it? Unfortunately, the answer is not entirely clear. Parties are bound to subject-matter jurisdiction (as they are to personal jurisdiction) when they appear, challenge jurisdiction, and lose. Durfee v. Duke, 375 U.S. 106 (1963); Stoll v. Gottlieb, 305 U.S. 165 (1938). They are also bound when they appear in federal court, fail to challenge jurisdiction, lose, and then attempt a collateral attack in another court. Chicot County Drainage Dist. v. Baxter State Bank, 308 U.S. 371 (1939). Where they are not bound is when they appear in *state* court, challenge or fail to challenge jurisdiction, lose, and then attempt a collateral attack in *federal* court, at least where Congress has implied that it intends to allow such collateral attack. Kalb v. Feuerstein, 308 U.S. 433 (1940). The Supreme Court has not decided whether a defendant may collaterally attack a default judgment where Congress has expressed or implied that intent.

C. Diversity

After federal-question jurisdiction, which accounts for the majority of federal civil cases, a second form of federal-court subject-matter jurisdiction is diversity jurisdiction. Although the number and percentage of diversity cases has increased over the past few years, diversity cases currently account for a little more than one quarter of federal civil cases. Congress created the federal courts' diversity jurisdiction so soon after the Constitution's ratification that time shrouds its reason for having done so. Indeed, the Supreme Court's infamous decision in Dred Scott v. Sandford, 60 U.S. 393 (1856), denying African-American slaves citizenship, arose out of a question of the slaves' ability to invoke federal-court jurisdiction by diversity of citizenship. The earliest asserted and most widely accepted reason, stated by Chief Justice Marshall in United States v. Deveaux, 9 U.S. (5 Cranch) 61 (1809), was to insulate non-resident parties from local bias in state courts. That justification may still be true today. A local county jury in state court might favor a local party over a non-resident, particularly a national corporation. Federal courts draw their juries from all parts of their district, an area much larger than the local county. Equally important is that federal judges are lifetime appointees insulated from political influence, whereas in many states, counties elect their local trial-court judges, keeping them sensitive to local concerns. There is no state-court equivalent for federal-court diversity jurisdiction.

A federal forum for non-residents to enforce state-law obligations may also have encouraged national investment in developing states. Today, diversity jurisdiction may promote a federal forum in which to address state-law issues that nonetheless have a national impact and character, for example, in corporate accountability or as to consumer protection. Congress' recent enactment of the Class Action Fairness Act of 2005, 28 U.S.C. §§1332(d), 1453, and Multiparty, Multiforum Trial Jurisdiction Act of 2002, 28 U.S.C. §§1369, 1441(e)(5), reflect those national interests. The Class Action Fairness Act permits plaintiffs to aggregate the value of their individual class-action claims and have a federal forum if the claims total more than $5 million and at least one plaintiff is a citizen of a different state than at least one defendant. The Multiparty, Multiforum Trial Jurisdiction Act creates a federal forum for mass torts cases in which at least 75 people died in one location, so long as the case has certain aspects of diversity. These acts promote a federal forum for class-action or other multiparty claims brought under state law having potential impact on the national economy. They are extensions of diversity jurisdiction, not its core.

The core of diversity jurisdiction, authorized by 28 U.S.C. §1332(a)(1), is in suits between citizens of different states, whose matter in controversy has a value exceeding $75,000. Keep in mind that §1332's grant of diversity jurisdiction is significantly more limited than what Article III, §2's language would authorize, that "[t]he judicial Power shall extend ... to Controversies ... between Citizens of different States ... and between a State, or the Citizens thereof, and foreign States, Citizens or Subjects." This fact has two consequences for the practitioner. One is that it is §1332's language and the Supreme Court's interpretation of it that will control in most cases, with Article III, §2, acting only as a backstop beyond which §1332 must not reach. The other is that Congress changes diversity jurisdiction every so often and will very likely continue to do so, for instance by extending it to class and multiparty actions as just shown above. It has also periodically increased the amount-in-controversy figure, most recently in 1996 from $50,000 to its current $75,000. Those changes, the variety of new diversity cases, and changes in the Supreme Court's interpretation of §1332, make the diversity issue more dynamic than one might expect, as the following discussion shows. So long as §1332 keeps its current basic structure, though, the central conditions for invoking federal-court diversity jurisdiction should remain diversity of citizenship and satisfying the amount in controversy.

§ 1332. Diversity of citizenship; amount in controversy; ... .

(a) The district courts shall have original jurisdiction of all civil actions where the matter in controversy exceeds the sum or value of $75,000, exclusive of interest and costs, and is between—

(1) citizens of different States;

(2) citizens of a State and citizens or subjects of a foreign state;

(3) citizens of different States and in which citizens or subjects of a foreign state are additional parties; and

(4) a foreign state, defined in section 1603(a) of this title, as plaintiff and citizens of a State or of different States.

For the purposes of this section, section 1335, and section 1441, an alien admitted to the United States for permanent residence shall be deemed a citizen of the State in which such alien is domiciled.

... [Costs provision omitted.]

(c) For the purposes of this section and section 1441 of this title—

(1) a corporation shall be deemed to be a citizen of any State by which it has been incorporated and of the State where it has its principal place of business, except that in any direct action against the insurer of a policy or contract of liability insurance, whether incorporated or unincorporated, to which action the insured is not joined as a party-defendant, such insurer shall be deemed a citizen of the State of which the insured is a citizen, as well as of any State by which the insurer has been incorporated and of the State where it has its principal place of business; and

(2) the legal representative of the estate of a decedent shall be deemed to be a citizen only of the same State as the decedent, and the legal representative of an infant or incompetent shall be deemed to be a citizen only of the same State as the infant or incompetent.

... [Class-action provisions omitted.]

(e) The word "States", as used in this section, includes the Territories, the District of Columbia, and the Commonwealth of Puerto Rico.

1. Citizenship

The diversity of the parties' citizenship must meet literally at least one of §1332(a)'s diversity requirements. It is not enough that prevailing norms might define certain parties as diverse. One must instead determine the citizenship of every party to confirm that every plaintiff has different citizenship from every defendant. Indeed, it is important to note that the Supreme Court has supplied additional requirements not evident from §1332's plain language. The Supreme Court's willingness to and necessity of entering the fray over the contours of diversity jurisdiction means that a diversity case must satisfy both the statute's literal requirements and the Supreme Court's articulation of those requirements based on the statute's purpose. For example, although §1332(a)(1) requires that the case be between "citizens of different States," it does not define citizenship. The Supreme Court has defined citizenship as the party's domicile, meaning the one state where the party resides principally with the intent to remain there indefinitely. The definition means that a party may only have one citizenship state, not multiple states in which the party is a citizen. The definition also means that citizenship does not include a location where a party resides temporarily such as while away at college. The Supreme Court has also held that the federal district courts must determine domicile as of the date that the plaintiff filed the complaint (the time-of-filing rule), not at a later date after a party's domicile changes during the course of litigation. Grupo Dataflux v. Atlas Global Group, L.P., 541 U.S. 567, 569-570 (2004). The case below presents an example of how, and how often, the question of citizenship may arise.

Mas v. Perry,

United States Court of Appeals for the Fifth Circuit
489 F.2d 1396, cert. denied, 419 U.S. 842 (1974)

AINSWORTH, Circuit Judge.

This case presents questions pertaining to federal diversity jurisdiction under 28 U.S.C. § 1332, which, pursuant to article III, section II of the Constitution, provides for original jurisdiction in federal district courts of all civil actions that are between, inter alia, citizens of different States or citizens of a State and citizens of foreign states and in which the amount in controversy is more than $10,000 [today $75,000].

Appellees Jean Paul Mas, a citizen of France, and Judy Mas were married at her home in Jackson, Mississippi. Prior to their marriage, Mr. and Mrs. Mas were graduate assistants, pursuing coursework as well as performing teaching duties, for approximately nine months and one year, respectively, at Louisiana State University in Baton Rouge, Louisiana. Shortly after their marriage, they returned to Baton Rouge to resume their duties as graduate assistants at LSU. They remained in Baton Rouge for approximately two more years, after which they moved to Park Ridge, Illinois. At the time of the trial in this case, it was their intention to return to Baton Rouge While Mr. Mas finished his studies for the degree of Doctor of Philosophy. Mr. and Mrs. Mas were undecided as to where they would reside after that.

Upon their return to Baton Rouge after their marriage, appellees rented an apartment from appellant Oliver H. Perry, a citizen of Louisiana. This appeal arises from a final judgment entered on a jury verdict awarding $5,000 to Mr. Mas and $15,000 to Mrs. Mas for damages incurred by them as a result of the discovery that their bedroom and bathroom contained "two-way" mirrors and that they had been watched through them by the appellant during three of the first four months of their marriage.

At the close of the appellees' case at trial, appellant made an oral motion to dismiss for lack of jurisdiction.[fn] The motion was denied by the district court. Before this Court, appellant challenges the final judgment below solely on jurisdictional grounds, contending that appellees failed to prove diversity of citizenship among the parties and that the requisite jurisdictional amount is lacking with respect to Mr. Mas. Finding no merit to these contentions, we affirm. Under section 1332(a)(2), the federal judicial power extends to the claim of Mr. Mas, a citizen of France, against the appellant, a citizen of Louisiana. Since we conclude that Mrs. Mas is a citizen of Mississippi for diversity purposes, the district court also properly had jurisdiction under section 1332(a)(1) of her claim.

It has long been the general rule that complete diversity of parties is required in order that diversity jurisdiction obtain; that is, no party on one side may be a citizen of the same State as any party on the other side. Strawbridge v. Curtiss, 7 U.S. (3 Cranch) 267[] (1806); [c]. This determination of one's State Citizenship for diversity purposes is controlled by federal law, not by the law of any State. [C] As is the case in other areas of federal jurisdiction, the diverse citizenship among adverse parties must be present at the time the complaint is filed. [Cc] Jurisdiction is unaffected by subsequent changes in the citizenship of the parties. [Cc] The burden of pleading the diverse citizenship is upon the party invoking federal jurisdiction, [c]; and if the diversity jurisdiction is properly challenged, that party also bears the burden of proof, [cc].

To be a citizen of a State within the meaning of section 1332, a natural person must be both a citizen of the United States, [cc], and a domiciliary of that State. [Cc] For diversity purposes, citizenship means domicile; mere residence in the State is not sufficient. [Cc]

A person's domicile is the place of "his true, fixed, and permanent home and principal establishment, and to which he has the intention of returning whenever he is absent therefrom... ." [C] A change of domicile may be effected only by a combination of two elements: (a) taking up residence in a different domicile with (b) the intention to remain there. [Cc]

It is clear that at the time of her marriage, Mrs. Mas was a domiciliary of the State of Mississippi. ...

An American woman is not deemed to have lost her United States citizenship solely by reason of her marriage to an alien. Similarly, we conclude that for diversity purposes a woman does not have her domicile or State Citizenship changed solely by reason of her marriage to an alien.

Mrs. Mas's Mississippi domicile was disturbed neither by her year in Louisiana prior to her marriage nor as a result of the time she and her husband spent at LSU after their marriage, since for both periods she was a graduate assistant at LSU. [C] Though she testified that after her marriage she had no intention of returning to her parents' home in Mississippi, Mrs. Mas did not effect a change of domicile since she and Mr. Mas were in Louisiana only as students and lacked the requisite intention to remain there. [C] Until she acquires a new domicile, she remains a domiciliary, and thus a citizen, of Mississippi. [Cc] ...

Thus the power of the federal district court to entertain the claims of appellees in this case stands on two separate legs of diversity jurisdiction: a claim by an alien against a State citizen; and an action between citizens of different States. We also note, however, the propriety of having the federal district court entertain a spouse's action against a defendant, where the district court already has jurisdiction over a claim, arising from the same transaction, by the other spouse against the same defendant. [C] In the case before us, such a result is particularly desirable. The claims of Mr. and Mrs. Mas arise from the same operative facts, and there was almost complete interdependence between their claims with respect to the proof required and the issues raised at trial. Thus, since the district court had jurisdiction of Mr. Mas's action, sound judicial administration militates strongly in favor of federal jurisdiction of Mrs. Mas's claim.

Affirmed.

INQUIRY

Complete Diversity. Notice that the Supreme Court in *Mas v. Perry, supra,* considered the citizenship of both Mr. and Mrs. Mas to ascertain whether both were diverse from the Louisiana citizenship of Mr. Perry. What if only one of the two plaintiffs in the above case had citizenship diverse (different) from the defendant's state? As the *Mas v. Perry* opinion noted, from time immemorial beginning with Chief Justice Marshall's opinion in Strawbridge v. Curtiss, 7 U.S. 267 (1806), the Supreme Court has required complete diversity between the sides. What supplies the complete diversity requirement, given that it is not in Article III, §2, or the plain language of §1332(a)? The Supreme Court recently acknowledged that complete diversity's source lies (in deference to Chief Justice Marshall) in the Court's interpretation of diversity's purpose. Exxon Mobil Corp. v. Allapattah Services, Inc., 545 U.S. 546, 553 (2005). The Court's reasoning has been that if there are citizens of the same state on both sides (at least one plaintiff and one defendant from the same state), then there is no longer a need to insulate non-resident parties from local bias. Whatever biases exist would work against both sides—or so it goes. A practitioner might disagree in any one case that bias disappears, depending on the number, alignment, and prominence of the parties. Can you imagine such a case in which significant bias may still exist despite the same citizenship of nominal adversaries?

Minimal Diversity. In State Farm v. Tashire, 386 U.S. 523 (1967), the Supreme Court confirmed that its complete-diversity requirement is a product of its interpretation of §1332(a), not Article III, §2. *State Farm v. Tashire* established that the Constitution permits federal courts to exercise jurisdiction where there is only minimal diversity, meaning at least one plaintiff and one defendant who are citizens of different states. Congress soon took advantage of the opportunity to authorize minimal-diversity jurisdiction in the Federal Interpleader Act, 28 U.S.C. §1335. The Act permits a plaintiff who holds a disputed fund to interplead defendants into a federal court case to determine interests in the fund, so long as at least one defendant has citizenship different from the plaintiff. The Class Action Fairness Act and Multiparty, Multiforum Trial Jurisdiction Act, *supra*, are other examples where Congress has authorized minimal-diversity jurisdiction. Those authorizations do not change that the parties must have complete diversity for jurisdiction under §1332(a). When there is only minimal diversity in a case filed under §1332(a) requiring complete diversity, must the federal district court dismiss the case? The Supreme Court held in Newman-Green, Inc. v. Alfonzo-Larrain, 490 U.S. 826 (1989), that the federal district court may instead dismiss the non-diverse party in order to retain jurisdiction, so long as the non-diverse party is dispensable.

Nominal Joinder. When the plaintiff's principal dispute is with a defendant with whom the plaintiff has diversity of citizenship, and yet the plaintiff joins other parties with whom the plaintiff does not have diversity citizenship, does the federal district court lose diversity jurisdiction? Although the plaintiff drafting the complaint largely controls diversity jurisdiction (the master-of-the-complaint rule), the answer may still be "not always." In Rose v. Giamatti, 721 F.Supp. 906 (S.D. Ohio 1989), baseball's alltime hits leader, Ohio resident Pete Rose, filed a state-court suit for an injunction to stop Major League Baseball's commissioner Bartlett Giamatti from investigating and disciplining Rose. Rose joined Major League Baseball and Rose's team the Cincinnati Reds, seeming to defeat diversity jurisdiction. Commissioner Giamatti nonetheless successfully removed the state case to federal court, the federal court holding that parties other than Commissioner Giamatti were "at best" only "nominal parties in this controversy" who "may be disregarded for diversity of citizenship purposes." *Id.* at 923-924. How should the federal district courts determine citizenship for class actions having a few named class representatives but a multitude of unnamed class members? *See* Devlin v. Scardelletti, 536 U.S. 1, 10 (2002) (citizenship based solely on named, not unnamed, class representatives).

Collusive Joinder. Realize from the foregoing discussion that diversity-of-citizenship jurisdiction creates an incentive for mischief in joining nominal parties to create or destroy diversity jurisdiction. With 28 U.S.C. §1359, Congress prohibited collusive joinder to invoke diversity jurisdiction, leaving the federal courts to struggle with when a party has, in the statute's terms, been "improperly or collusively ... joined" for diversity jurisdiction. *See* Kramer v. Caribbean Mills, Inc., 394 U.S. 823 (1969) (foreign corporation's assignment, for one dollar, of interest to Texas attorney on whom diversity jurisdiction relied deemed collusive, where attorney assigned back 95% of interest). Section 1359 by its terms prohibits collusive joinder only to create, not to defeat, diversity jurisdiction. Should the courts prohibit collusive joinder that defeats diversity jurisdiction? *See* Grassi v. Ciba-Geigy, Ltd., 894 F.2d 181 (5th Cir. 1990) (applying same collusion standard to effort to defeat diversity). Section 1359 removed another opportunity for manipulating citizenship when it defined the citizenship of a representative of an estate, minor, or incompetent as the citizenship of the person or estate represented.

Alienage Jurisdiction. Section 1332 bears other evidence of Congress attempting to limit diversity jurisdiction to its intended purpose while reducing its manipulation. For example, in 1988 Congress added to the conclusion of §1332(a) that "an alien admitted to the United States for permanent residence shall be deemed a citizen of the State in which such alien is domiciled." The additional language addresses the alienage jurisdiction authorized under §1332(a)(2) for "citizens of a State and citizens or subjects of a foreign state" and (a)(3) for "citizens of different States and in which citizens or subjects of a foreign state are additional parties." The following case construed §1332(a)'s additional language deeming aliens to also be citizens of the state of their domicile to restrict, not expand, diversity jurisdiction, by eliminating cases in which the alien party has the same state domicile as an opposing party. Lower courts have also held that one alien may not sue another alien under diversity jurisdiction. Diversity jurisdiction in cases brought by aliens requires a plaintiff state citizen who is diverse from all plaintiff aliens and at least one defendant alien. Universal Licensing Corp. v. Paoa del Lungo S.p.A., 293 F.3d 579, 581 (2d Cir. 2002). Aliens without a state (the stateless) probably do not qualify for federal-court diversity jurisdiction. Blair Holdings Corp. v. Rubinstein, 133 F.Supp. 496, 501-502 (S.D. N.Y. 1955). Notice from the following case that each effort to define and restrict diversity jurisdiction creates new opportunity to reinterpret and expand it.

Saadeh v. Farouki,

United States Court of Appeals for the District of Columbia
107 F.3d 52 (D.C. Cir. 1997)

ROGERS, Circuit Judge.

Appellant Fawaz Farouki appeals from a judgment awarding appellee Rafic Saadeh $758,470 for breach of contract for failure to repay a commercial loan. ... We now hold that the district court lacked subject matter jurisdiction, and therefore vacate the judgment of the district court and remand the case with instructions to dismiss the complaint.

I.

Throughout the 1980s, Fawaz Farouki, the owner of several construction companies doing business in the Middle East and Europe, invested millions of dollars in various enterprises through his investment company, Dinavest, Ltd., a United Kingdom corporation with its principal place of business in Monte Carlo, Principality of Monaco. In 1984, hoping to invest in a California company, Four Point Entertainment, Farouki and Dinavest borrowed $550,000 from Rafic Saadeh, a businessman residing in Athens, Greece. Saadeh received a promissory note in exchange for his loan in September 1984. This was the first of three repayment agreements entered into by the parties, all of which resulted in a default by Farouki. ...

In 1992, Saadeh filed suit in the United States District Court for the District of Columbia against Farouki, his wife, Dinavest, and L.R. Holdings, a District of Columbia corporation owned and operated by Mrs. Farouki. He sought damages for breach of contract and an accounting. At that time, Farouki was a citizen of Jordan, and Mrs. Farouki was apparently a citizen of Egypt. Beginning in 1989, however, the Faroukis had become permanent residents of Maryland.[fn] The sole basis of jurisdiction alleged in Saadeh's complaint was diversity of citizenship, 28 U.S.C. § 1332.

II.

Under Article III of the Constitution, the judicial power of the United States extends to "Controversies... between citizens of different States... and between a State, or the Citizens thereof, and foreign States, Citizens or Subjects." U.S. CONST. art. III, §2. Article III requires only minimal diversity, that is, diversity of citizenship between any two parties on opposite sides of an action, regardless of whether other parties may be co-citizens. State Farm Fire & Casualty Co. v. Tashire, 386 U.S. 523, 530-31[] (1967). Congress has never granted the district courts the full measure of diversity jurisdiction permitted by the Constitution, however. In Strawbridge v. Curtiss, 7 U.S. (3 Cranch) 267, 267[] (1806), the Supreme Court construed the diversity provision of the Judiciary Act of 1789 to require that no two parties on opposite sides of an action could be citizens of the same State. The current diversity statute, 28 U.S.C. § 1332,[fn] retains this requirement of "complete diversity." ... The Supreme Court has never addressed the scope of the complete diversity rule in cases involving alien parties. Prior to 1988, however, this court held, as have others, that the diversity statute did not confer jurisdiction over a lawsuit involving an alien on one side, and an alien and a citizen on the other side. [Cc]

As noted, however, Congress amended the diversity statute in 1988 to add what now appears as the last sentence of 28 U.S.C. § 1332(a). This sentence provides in pertinent part that for the purposes of § 1332(a) "an alien admitted to the United States for permanent residence shall be deemed a citizen of the State in which such alien is domiciled." Under this amendment, diversity of citizenship no longer exists in an action between a citizen of State A and an alien admitted to the United States for permanent residence who resides in State A. Read literally, however, the amended statute would create diversity between Saadeh and both Faroukis. As permanent residents of Maryland at the time Saadeh filed his complaint, Mr. and Mrs. Farouki would be "deemed" citizens of Maryland. Thus the amended statute would also appear to abrogate partially the rule of complete diversity by permitting a non-resident alien and a resident alien to be present on opposite sides of this lawsuit. ...

[T]he remaining question is whether, at the time Saadeh filed his complaint, Farouki qualified as a "citizen of a State" under the 1988 amendment to § 1332. In resolving a question of statutory interpretation, a court's starting point is always the language of the statute. [C] If the language is plain on its face, courts do not ordinarily resort to legislative history. [Cc] Nevertheless, there are exceptions. For example, the Supreme Court has observed that "in rare cases, the literal application of a statute will produce a result demonstrably at odds with the intentions of its drafters, and those intentions must be controlling." [C] "Looking beyond the naked text for guidance is perfectly proper when the result it apparently decrees is difficult to fathom or where it seems inconsistent with Congress' intention, since the plain-meaning rule is 'rather an axiom of experience than a rule of law, and does not preclude consideration of persuasive evidence if it exists.'" [Cc] Consequently, "[w]here the literal reading of a statutory term would 'compel an odd result,' ... we must search for other evidence of congressional intent to lend the term its proper scope." [Cc] In addition, the Supreme Court has instructed that "where an otherwise acceptable construction of a statute would raise serious constitutional problems," a court should "construe the statute to avoid such problems unless such construction is plainly contrary to the intent of Congress." [C] While a court "cannot press statutory construction 'to the point of disingenuous evasion,' even to avoid a constitutional question," [cc] where the evidence of congressional intent supports an interpretation that avoids such problems, the court will adopt it. [C]

A literal reading of the 1988 amendment to § 1332(a) would produce an odd and potentially unconstitutional result. It would both partially abrogate the longstanding rule of complete diversity, and create federal diversity jurisdiction over a lawsuit brought by one alien against another alien, without a citizen of a state on either side of the litigation. The judicial power of the United States does not extend to such an action under the Diversity Clause of Article III. Hodgson v. Bowerbank, 9 U.S. (5 Cranch) 303[] (1809); [cc]. Under the circumstances, it behooves the court to examine the legislative history of the 1988 amendment in order to determine congressional intent.

... So far as appears, the idea for the addition of an alienage provision originated in a recommendation of the Judicial Conference of the United States.[fn] [C] The Judicial Conference supported the addition of the alienage provision in order to restrict diversity jurisdiction: "There is no reason why actions involving persons who are permanent residents of the United States should be heard by federal courts merely because one of them remains a citizen or subject of a foreign state or has not yet become a citizen of the United States. ..." ... A section-by-section analysis introduced into the Congressional Record similarly reveals the intent to reduce diversity jurisdiction through the alienage provision. Describing Title II as "mak[ing] modest adjustments to the scope of diversity jurisdiction to relieve the caseload pressures on the Federal Courts," the analysis paralleled the language of the Judicial Conference report... .

Given the reasoning underlying the recommendation for the alienage provision and the general expressions of legislative intent for the Judicial Improvements Act, in the absence of contrary evidence, we conclude that Congress intended to contract diversity jurisdiction through the 1988 amendment to §1332(a), not to expand it by abrogating the longstanding rule that complete diversity is destroyed in lawsuits between aliens. ... It would be illogical to conclude that Congress intended to eliminate diversity jurisdiction in cases between a citizen and an alien permanently residing in the same state, but simultaneously intended to expand diversity jurisdiction in cases between an alien permanently residing in one state and an alien permanently residing in another state. Despite the plain language of §1332(a), the alienage amendment "clearly appears to have been intended only to eliminate subject matter jurisdiction of cases between a citizen and an alien living in the same state." [C] ... [T]his appears to be one of those rare cases where the most literal interpretation of a statute is at odds with the evidence of Congressional intent and a contrary construction is necessary to avoid "formidable constitutional difficulties." [C] ...

... We ... conclude that the 1988 amendment to §1332 did not confer diversity jurisdiction over a lawsuit between an alien on one side, and an alien and a citizen on the other side, regardless of the residence status of the aliens.

Accordingly, we hold that the district court lacked subject matter jurisdiction because Farouki's acquisition of United States citizenship after Saadeh filed his complaint could not cure the defect, and we vacate the judgment and remand the case to the district court with instructions to dismiss the complaint for lack of subject matter jurisdiction... .

Knowledge

It is a curious aspect of legal drafting that ever greater efforts to clarify by adding more words and clauses tend only to produce ever greater ambiguities in the text one is drafting. German-American law professor Francis Lieber wrote of that curiosity in his seminal 1839 work LEGAL AND POLITICAL HERMENEUTICS on which American jurisprudence has based much of its doctrine for construing statutes and other legal writing. Lieber explained that legal language is necessarily imprecise because the human circumstances that it addresses are also fraught with uncertainty and ambiguity. It is not simply that words may convey more than one meaning. It is also that relationships and events have many credible interpretations depending on the observers' perspectives. Events and conditions are objectively real, but we construct our knowledge of them from uncertain personal perspectives using equally uncertain language. Notice how *Saadeh v. Farouki* resolved the uncertainty by looking beyond the language to its purpose. Doing so does not resolve the uncertainty. Instead, it shifts the uncertainty from meaning to purposes.

INQUIRY

Corporations. Section 1332(c)(1) defines a corporation's citizenship as the state of its incorporation *and* the state where it has its principal place of business. Section 1332(c)(1)'s definition means that corporations may have either one or two states of citizenship, depending on whether they are incorporated in a state other than the one in which they have their principal place of business, but no more than two states of citizenship. *See* Wachovia Bank, N.A. v. Schmidt, 546 U.S. 303 (2006) (national bank chartered by the federal government has only one citizenship in the state where it locates its main office). Given the national and even global scope of many corporations' business, you can imagine the difficulty in any particular case of determining where a corporation has its principal place of business. Until the Supreme Court's decision in Hertz v. Friend, __ U.S. __, 130 S.Ct. 1181 (2010), case law articulated three alternative tests known as the nerve-center test where corporate control resides, the corporate-activities test where the corporation's greatest productive capacity exists, or the total-activity test considering control, production, and all other circumstances. In the *Hertz* decision, the Supreme Court adopted the nerve-center test. Interestingly, the Supreme Court has held that for diversity purposes, the citizenship of a partnership depends on the citizenship of each of its individual members. Grupo Dataflux v. Atlas Global Group, L.P., 541 U.S. 567 (2004); *see also* Carden v. Arkoma Assocs., 494 U.S. 185 (1990). The same would be true of an unincorporated association that citizenship would depend on the domicile of each of its individual members. What is the citizenship of a limited liability company? *See* GMAC Commercial Credit LLC v. Dillard Dept. Stores, Inc., 357 F.3d 827, 828-829 (8th Cir. 2004) (citizenship of its members).

Family-Law Cases. The Supreme Court has interpreted diversity jurisdiction not to authorize divorce, child-custody, child-support, and other family-law cases, even when the parties have diverse citizenship, because non-resident bias would not be present. Ankenbrandt v. Richards, 504 U.S. 689 (1992). The underlying concern is that federal-court jurisdiction over divorce and other family-law cases would inundate the federal courts as it does the state courts, significantly altering the character of the federal courts. The Supreme Court maintains a similar exception for probate cases. State probate courts administer decedent's estates including civil litigation over the validity of a will and claims to property administered through probate, even when the parties have diversity of citizenship. There are limits, though, to both exceptions, meaning that there are cases where the federal courts may exercise diversity jurisdiction in matters relating to divorce or probate, even if not over the divorce and probate cases themselves. The Supreme Court recognized jurisdiction in the recent case brought by the young exotic dancer Anna Nicole Smith (now deceased) involving her brief marriage to a 90-year-old tycoon, where the claims were for fraud and tortious interference rather than to annul a will or otherwise control property under probate. Marshall v. Marshall, 547 U.S. 293 (2006).

2. Amount in Controversy

The second requirement for §1332(a) diversity jurisdiction after diversity of citizenship is to establish that "the matter in controversy exceeds the sum or value of $75,000, exclusive of interest and costs... ." This requirement, as in the case of diversity of citizenship, gives the plaintiff substantial control over the litigation (the master-of-the-complaint rule). The plaintiff has relative leeway to allege the amount in controversy. The Supreme Court's standard, established in St. Paul Mercury Indemnity Co. v. Red Cab Co., 303 U.S. 283, 288-289 (1938), requires only that the plaintiff's allegation be "apparently made in good faith. It must appear to a legal certainty that the claim is really for less than the jurisdictional amount to justify dismissal." This standard relieves the lower courts of litigating over the amount in controversy. Cases dismissing on that basis are few and far between. The Supreme Court also stated in *St. Paul Mercury Indemnity Co.* that diversity jurisdiction remains even when "events occurring subsequent to the institution of suit ... reduce the amount recoverable below the statutory limit" or the plaintiff is otherwise unable "to recover an amount adequate to" meet the statutory amount in controversy. *Id.* at 289-290. Section 1332(b) does now include a cost-shifting provision creating a level of accountability for the plaintiff in alleging the amount in controversy. Yet it is the initial complaint that matters, not subsequent events or the ultimate recovery.

Another common question that may arise as to the amount in controversy is how to treat multiple smaller claims that in their aggregate exceed the $75,000 jurisdictional limit. The rule is to permit a single plaintiff to aggregate claims against a single defendant into an amount that exceeds the jurisdictional limit. *See* Everett v. Verizon Wireless, Inc., 460 F.3d 818, 822 (6th Cir. 2006). The plaintiff who has a single claim against the defendant worth in excess of the jurisdictional limit may in the same case maintain a claim against the same defendant worth less than the jurisdictional limit. Exxon Mobil Corp. v. Allapattah Services, Inc., 545 U.S. 546 (2005). On the other hand, the rule is to prohibit a single plaintiff from aggregating claims against multiple defendants to attempt to satisfy the jurisdictional limit and to prohibit multiple plaintiffs from aggregating claims. Only plaintiffs who "have a common and undivided interest" "to enforce [as to] a single title or right" may consider the aggregate value of that interest. Troy Bank of Troy, Ind. v. G.A. Whitehead & Co., 222 U.S. 39, 40-41 (1911). Class-action members whose claims in the aggregate would meet the $75,000 jurisdictional limit but none of whose individual claims would meet that limit have not satisfied the jurisdictional limit. Snyder v. Harris, 394 U.S. 332 (1969); *see also* Del Vecchio v. Conseco, Inc., 230 F.3d 974 (7th Cir. 2000) (no aggregating $5,000 class-member claims to exceed $75,000 jurisdictional limit); *cf.* Class Action Fairness Act of 2005, 28 U.S.C. §§1332(d), 1453 (diversity jurisdiction for class-action aggregate in excess of $5 million).

Not all federal diversity cases have damages as their principal remedy. Some federal diversity cases seek primarily injunctive relief. How does a practitioner determine whether there is federal diversity jurisdiction over a case that has a damages claim that does not exceed the $75,000 jurisdictional limit but yet involves a substantial claim for injunctive relief? The Supreme Court's opinion in Glenwood Light & Water Co. v. Mutual Light, Heat & Power Co., 239 U.S. 121 (1915), indicates that the jurisdictional amount then depends on the monetary value to the plaintiff of the equitable relief. Although *Glenwood Light & Water Co.* did not directly address the question, there is also some federal authority that the district courts may consider the cost to the defendant of the equitable relief as an appropriate alternative measure of the amount in controversy. *See* McCarthy v. Amoco Pipeline Co., 595 F.2d 389, 391-392 (7th Cir. 1979). These questions of subject-matter jurisdiction are obviously complex. Note, though, the simplicity with which the following FED. R. CIV. P. Form 7 indicates that the plaintiff may plead subject-matter jurisdiction.

Federal Rules of Civil Procedure Form 7. Statement of Jurisdiction

a. (*For diversity-of-citizenship jurisdiction.*) The plaintiff is [a citizen of *Michigan*] [a corporation incorporated under the laws of *Michigan* with its principal place of business in *Michigan*]. The defendant is [a citizen of *New York*] [a corporation incorporated under the laws of *New York* with its principal place of business in *New York*]. The amount in controversy, without interest and costs, exceeds the sum or value specified by 28 U.S.C. § 1332.

b. (*For federal-question jurisdiction.*) This action arises under [the United States Constitution, *specify the article or amendment and the section*] [a United States treaty *specify*] [a federal statute, ___ U.S.C. § ___].

c. (*For a claim in the admiralty or maritime jurisdiction.*) This is a case of admiralty or maritime jurisdiction. (*To invoke admiralty status under Rule 9(h) use the following:* This is an admiralty or maritime claim within the meaning of Rule 9(h).)

D. Supplemental Jurisdiction

The above discussion addresses the original jurisdiction of the federal district courts in which the plaintiff's claim, if brought alone, would qualify for federal-court jurisdiction. Federal-question jurisdiction under §1331 and diversity-of-citizenship jurisdiction under §1332 are examples of the federal district courts' original jurisdiction. Beyond their original jurisdiction, the federal courts have supplemental jurisdiction under §1367 over certain claims which, if brought alone, would *not* qualify for federal-court jurisdiction. Until Congress enacted §1367 in 1990, the federal courts entertained supplemental jurisdiction under the doctrines of pendent and ancillary jurisdiction. Section 1367 subsumed the Supreme Court doctrines of pendent and ancillary jurisdiction, turning them into statutory supplemental jurisdiction. One cannot appreciate how Section 1367's supplemental jurisdiction works without at least an outline of pendent and ancillary jurisdiction.

Pendent jurisdiction addressed otherwise non-qualifying claims joined to one or more other claims qualifying for federal jurisdiction. For example, in United Mine Workers v. Gibbs, 383 U.S. 715 (1966), excerpted below, the Supreme Court recognized pendent jurisdiction over a non-qualifying state-law tortious-interference claim the plaintiff pled together with a federal-law Labor Management Relations Act claim that qualified for federal-question jurisdiction. The critical consideration in *United Mine Workers* was that the state and federal claims arose out of a "common nucleus of operative fact," that phrase becoming the standard for when federal courts could exercise pendent jurisdiction over other claims. Then in Aldinger v. Howard, 427 U.S. 1 (1976), the Supreme Court rejected that the plaintiff could file suit against one defendant on a claim implicating a federal question and obtain pendent jurisdiction over another defendant on a non-qualifying state claim. The Court, in other words, rejected pendent *party* jurisdiction, preserving pendent jurisdiction only for pendent *claims*. Two subsequent decisions, Owen Equipment and Erection Co. v. Kroger, 437 U.S. 365 (1978), and Finley v. United States, 490 U.S. 545 (1989), confirmed under other circumstances that pendent jurisdiction was not available for non-qualifying claims against other parties. Ancillary jurisdiction addressed otherwise nonqualifying counterclaims, cross-claims, and third-party claims that a party brought in a case involving one or more other claims qualifying for federal jurisdiction. Consider the following seminal Supreme Court case on pendent jurisdiction as a foundation for §1367's supplemental jurisdiction.

United Mine Workers v. Gibbs,

United States Supreme Court
383 U.S. 715 (1966)

Mr. Justice BRENNAN delivered the opinion of the Court.

Respondent Paul Gibbs was awarded compensatory and punitive damages in this action against petitioner United Mine Workers of America (NMW) for alleged violations of §303 of the Labor Management Relations Act, [c], and of the common law Tennessee. The case grew out of the rivalry between the United Mine Workers and the Southern Labor Union over representation of workers in the southern Appalachian coal fields. Tennessee Consolidated Coal Company, not a party here, laid off 100 miners ... when it closed one of its mines in southern Tennessee during the spring of 1960. Late that summer, Grundy Company, a wholly owned subsidiary of Consolidated, hired respondent as mine superintendent to attempt to open a new mine on Consolidated's property at nearby Gray's Creek through use of members of the Southern Labor Union. As part of the arrangement, Grundy also gave respondent a contract to haul the mine's coal to the nearest railroad loading point.

On August 15 and 16, 1960, armed members of Local 5881 forcibly prevented the opening of the mine, threatening respondent and beating an organizer for the rival union.[fn] The members of the local believed Consolidated had promised them the jobs at the new mine; they insisted that if anyone would do the work, they would. At this time, no representative of the UMW, their international union, was present. ... There was uncontradicted testimony that [UMW's field representative] first learned of the violence [later], and returned with explicit instructions from his international union superiors to establish a limited picket line, to prevent any further violence, and to see to it that the strike did not spread to neighboring mines. There was no further violence at the mine site; a picket line was maintained there for nine months; and no further attempts were made to open the mine during that period.[fn]

Respondent lost his job as superintendent, and never entered into performance of his haulage contract. He testified that he soon began to lose other trucking contracts and mine leases he held in nearby areas. Claiming these effects to be the result of a concerted union plan against him, he sought recovery not against Local 5881 or its members, but only against petitioner, the international union. The suit was brought in the United States District Court for the Eastern District of Tennessee, see, and jurisdiction was premised on allegations of secondary boycotts under §303. The state law claim, for which jurisdiction was based upon the doctrine of pendent jurisdiction, asserted "an unlawful conspiracy and an unlawful boycott aimed at him and (Grundy) to maliciously, wantonly and willfully interfere with his contract of employment and with his contract of haulage."[fn]

... The jury's verdict was that the UMW had violated both §303 and state law. Gibbs was awarded $60,000 as damages under the employment contract and $14,500 under the haulage contract; he was also awarded $100,000 punitive damages. On motion, the trial court set aside the award of damages with respect to the haulage contract on the ground that damage was unproved. It also held that union pressure on Grundy to discharge respondent as supervisor would constitute only a primary dispute with Grundy, as respondent's employer, and hence was not cognizable as a claim under §303. Interference with the employment relationship was cognizable as a state claim, however, and a remitted award was sustained on the state law claim.[fn] [C] The Court of Appeals for the Sixth Circuit affirmed. [C] We granted certiorari. [C] We reverse.

...

A threshold question is whether the District Court properly entertained jurisdiction of the claim based on Tennessee law. ...

... [We must] answer the question whether the state claim was properly adjudicated in the District Court absent diversity jurisdiction. The Court held in Hurn v. Oursler, 289 U.S. 238[(1933)], that state law claims are appropriate for federal court determination if they form a separate but parallel ground for relief also sought in a substantial claim based on federal law. The Court distinguished permissible from non-permissible exercises of federal judicial power over state law claims by contrasting "a case where two distinct grounds in support of a single cause of action are alleged, one only of which presents a federal question, and a case where two separate and distinct causes of action are alleged, one only of which is federal in character. In the former, where the federal question averred is not plainly wanting in substance, the federal court, even though the federal ground be not established, may nevertheless retain and dispose of the case upon the nonfederal ground; in the latter it may not do so upon the nonfederal cause of action." 289 U.S. at 246[]. The question is into which category the present action fell.

Hurn was decided in 1933, before the unification of law and equity by the Federal Rules of Civil Procedure. At the time, the meaning of 'cause of action' was a subject of serious dispute... .

With the adoption of the Federal Rules of Civil Procedure and the unified form of action, Fed. Rule Civ. Proc. 2, much of the controversy over "cause of action" abated. ... Under the Rules, the impulse is toward entertaining the broadest possible scope of action consistent with fairness to the parties; joinder of claims, parties and remedies is strongly encouraged.[fn] Yet because the Hurn question involves issues of jurisdiction as well as convenience, there has been some tendency to limit its application to cases in which the state and federal claims are, as in Hurn, "little more than the equivalent of different epithets to characterize the same group of circumstances." 289 U.S. at 246[].[fn]

This limited approach is unnecessarily grudging. Pendent jurisdiction, in the sense of judicial power, exists whenever there is a claim "arising under (the) Constitution, the Laws of the United States, and Treaties made, or which shall be made, under their Authority... ," U.S. Const., Art. III, §2, and the relationship between that claim and the state claim permits the conclusion that the entire action before the court comprises but one constitutional "case."[fn] The federal claim must have substance sufficient to confer subject matter jurisdiction on the court. [C] The state and federal claims must derive from a common nucleus of operative fact. But if, considered without regard to their federal or state character, a plaintiff's claims are such that he would ordinarily be expected to try them all in one judicial proceeding, then, assuming substantiality of the federal issues, there is power in federal courts to hear the whole.[fn]

That power need not be exercised in every case in which it is found to exist. It has consistently been recognized that pendent jurisdiction is a doctrine of discretion, not of plaintiff's right.[fn] Its justification lies in considerations of judicial economy, convenience and fairness to litigants; if these are not present a federal court should hesitate to exercise jurisdiction over state claims, even though bound to apply state law to them, Erie R. Co. v. Tompkins, 304 U.S. 64[(1938)]. Needless decisions of state law should be avoided both as a matter of comity and to promote justice between the parties, by procuring for them a surer-footed reading of applicable law.[fn] Certainly, if the federal claims are dismissed before trial, even though not insubstantial in a jurisdictional sense, the state claims should be dismissed as well.[fn] Similarly, if it appears that the state issues substantially predominate, whether in terms of proof, of the scope of the issues raised, or of the comprehensiveness of the remedy sought, the state claims may be dismissed without prejudice and left for resolution to state tribunals. There may, on the other hand, be situations in which the state claim is so closely tied to questions of federal policy that the argument for exercise of pendent jurisdiction is particularly strong. In the present case, for example, the allowable scope of the state claim implicates the federal doctrine of pre-emption; while this interrelationship does not create statutory federal question jurisdiction, Louisville & N.R. Co. v. Mottley, 211 U.S. 149[(1908)], its existence is relevant to the exercise of discretion. Finally, there may be reasons independent of jurisdictional considerations, such as the likelihood of jury confusion in treating divergent legal theories of relief, that would justify separating state and federal claims for trial, Fed. Rule Civ. Proc. 42(b). If so, jurisdiction should ordinarily be refused.

The question of power will ordinarily be resolved on the pleadings. But the issue whether pendent jurisdiction has been properly assumed is one which remains open throughout the litigation. Pretrial procedures or even the trial itself may reveal a substantial hegemony of state law claims, or likelihood of jury confusion, which could not have been anticipated at the pleading stage. Although it will of course be appropriate to take account in this circumstance of the already completed course of the litigation, dismissal of the state claim might even then be merited. For example, it may appear that the plaintiff was well aware of the nature of his proofs and the relative importance of his claims; recognition of a federal court's wide latitude to decide ancillary questions of state law does not imply that it must tolerate a litigant's effort to impose upon it what is in effect only a state law case. Once it appears that a state claim constitutes the real body of a case, to which the federal claim is only an appendage, the state claim may fairly be dismissed.

We are not prepared to say that in the present case the District Court exceeded its discretion in proceeding to judgment on the state claim. ... [T]he state and federal claims arose from the same nucleus of operative fact and reflected alternative remedies. Indeed, the verdict sheet sent in to the jury authorized only one award of damages, so that recovery could not be given separately on the federal and state claims. ...

... We thus conclude that although it may be that the District Court might, in its sound discretion, have dismissed the state claim, the circumstances show no error in refusing to do so.

Reversed.

[Justice HARLAN'S concurring opinion, in which Justice CLARK joined, omitted.]

INQUIRY

Statutory Treatment. The Supreme Court's last word on pendent jurisdiction in the 1989 case of *Finley v. United States, supra*, noted that Congress could change Supreme Court doctrine recognizing pendent claims but rejecting pendent parties. Congress did so the following year with §1367. Subsection (a) of §1367 authorized federal district-court supplemental jurisdiction "over all other claims that are so related to" qualifying claims "that they form part of the same case or controversy under Article III of the United States Constitution." In §1367(a), Congress clearly authorized pendent *claim* jurisdiction in substantially the form that the Supreme Court had recognized. Indeed, notice how similar §1367(a) is to the Supreme Court's "common nucleus of operative facts" concept. Section 1367(a) then added that supplemental jurisdiction "shall include claims that involve the joinder or intervention of additional parties," thus appearing to adopt the pendent *party* jurisdiction that the Supreme Court had rejected in *Aldinger, Kroger Equipment and Erection Co.*, and *Finley, supra.*

Exceptions. Yet §1367(a) tells only half of the story. Subsection (b) of §1367 then sets forth certain exceptions to §1367(a)'s seemingly broad grant of supplemental (pendent-party) jurisdiction. By its own terms, §1367(b)'s exceptions to supplemental jurisdiction apply only to §1332 diversity-of-citizenship cases. Supplemental jurisdiction remains for cases filed under the federal district courts' §1331 federal-question jurisdiction, §1334 bankruptcy jurisdiction, or other grant of jurisdiction not based on diversity. When it comes to diversity cases, though, §1367(b) prohibits supplemental jurisdiction over parties whom the plaintiff sues after a defendant impleads them as third parties under FED. R. CIV. P. 19, whom the plaintiff attempts to join as necessary under Rule 19 or joins permissively under Rule 20, or claims against after they intervene under Rule 24. The text returns to these issues Chapter 8 on joinder. For now, examine §1367 below. Then consider an issue in the following case that you may not have recognized from reading the statute.

28 U.S.C. §1367. Supplemental jurisdiction.
(a) Except as provided in subsections (b) and (c) or as expressly provided otherwise by Federal statute, in any civil action of which the district courts have original jurisdiction, the district courts shall have supplemental jurisdiction over all other claims that are so related to claims in the action within such original jurisdiction that they form part of the same case or controversy under Article III of the United States Constitution. Such supplemental jurisdiction shall include claims that involve the joinder or intervention of additional parties.
(b) In any civil action of which the district courts have original jurisdiction founded solely on section 1332 of this title, the district courts shall not have supplemental jurisdiction under subsection (a) over claims by plaintiffs against persons made parties under Rule 14, 19, 20, or 24 of the Federal Rules of Civil Procedure, or over claims by persons proposed to be joined as plaintiffs under Rule 19 of such rules, or seeking to intervene as plaintiffs under Rule 24 of such rules, when exercising supplemental jurisdiction over such claims would be inconsistent with the jurisdictional requirements of section 1332.
(c) The district courts may decline to exercise supplemental jurisdiction over a claim under subsection (a) if—
(1) the claim raises a novel or complex issue of State law,
(2) the claim substantially predominates over the claim or claims over which the district court has original jurisdiction,
(3) the district court has dismissed all claims over which it has original jurisdiction, or
(4) in exceptional circumstances, there are other compelling reasons for declining jurisdiction.

Exxon Mobil Corp. v. Allapattah Services, Inc.,

United States Supreme Court
545 U.S. 546 (2005)

Justice KENNEDY delivered the opinion of the Court.

These consolidated cases present the question whether a federal court in a diversity action may exercise supplemental jurisdiction over additional plaintiffs whose claims do not satisfy the minimum amount-in-controversy requirement, provided the claims are part of the same case or controversy as the claims of plaintiffs who do allege a sufficient amount in controversy. Our decision turns on the correct interpretation of 28 U.S.C. § 1367. ...

We hold that, where the other elements of jurisdiction are present and at least one named plaintiff in the action satisfies the amount-in-controversy requirement, §1367 does authorize supplemental jurisdiction over the claims of other plaintiffs in the same Article III case or controversy, even if those claims are for less than the jurisdictional amount specified in the statute setting forth the requirements for diversity jurisdiction. ...

I

In 1991, about 10,000 Exxon dealers filed a class-action suit against the Exxon Corporation in the United States District Court for the Northern District of Florida. The dealers alleged an intentional and systematic scheme by Exxon under which they were overcharged for fuel purchased from Exxon. The plaintiffs invoked the District Court's §1332(a) diversity jurisdiction. After a unanimous jury verdict in favor of the plaintiffs, the District Court certified the case for interlocutory review, asking whether it had properly exercised §1367 supplemental jurisdiction over the claims of class members who did not meet the jurisdictional minimum amount in controversy.

The Court of Appeals for the Eleventh Circuit upheld the District Court's extension of supplemental jurisdiction to these class members. [C] ... This decision accords with the views of the Courts of Appeals for the Fourth, Sixth, and Seventh Circuits. [Cc] The Courts of Appeals for the Fifth and Ninth Circuits, adopting a similar analysis of the statute, have held that in a diversity class action the unnamed class members need not meet the amount-in-controversy requirement, provided the named class members do. These decisions, however, are unclear on whether all the named plaintiffs must satisfy this requirement. [Cc]

In the other case now before us the Court of Appeals for the First Circuit took a different position on the meaning of §1367(a). [C] In that case, a 9-year-old girl sued Star-Kist in a diversity action in the United States District Court for the District of Puerto Rico, seeking damages for unusually severe injuries she received when she sliced her finger on a tuna can. Her family joined in the suit, seeking damages for emotional distress and certain medical expenses. The District Court granted summary judgment to Star-Kist, finding that none of the plaintiffs met the minimum amount-in-controversy requirement. The Court of Appeals for the First Circuit, however, ruled that the injured girl, but not her family members, had made allegations of damages in the requisite amount.

The Court of Appeals... [also] held that §1367 authorizes supplemental jurisdiction only when the district court has original jurisdiction over the action, and that in a diversity case original jurisdiction is lacking if one plaintiff fails to satisfy the amount-in-controversy requirement. ... The Court of Appeals for the First Circuit's view of §1367 is... shared by the Courts of Appeals for the Third, Eighth, and Tenth Circuits, and the latter two Courts of Appeals have expressly applied this rule to class actions. [Cc]

II

A

The district courts of the United States, as we have said many times, are "courts of limited jurisdiction. They possess only that power authorized by Constitution and statute," [c]. In order to provide a federal forum for plaintiffs who seek to vindicate federal rights, Congress has conferred on the district courts original jurisdiction in federal-question cases-civil actions that arise under the Constitution, laws, or treaties of the United States. 28 U.S.C. § 1331. In order to provide a neutral forum for what have come to be known as diversity cases, Congress also has granted district courts original jurisdiction in civil actions between citizens of different States, between U.S. citizens and foreign citizens, or by foreign states against U.S. citizens. §1332. To ensure that diversity jurisdiction does not flood the federal courts with minor disputes, §1332(a) requires that the matter in controversy in a diversity case exceed a specified amount, currently $75,000.

Although the district courts may not exercise jurisdiction absent a statutory basis, it is well established—in certain classes of cases—that, once a court has original jurisdiction over some claims in the action, it may exercise supplemental jurisdiction over additional claims that are part of the same case or controversy. The leading modern case for this principle is Mine Workers v. Gibbs, 383 U.S. 715[] (1966). ...

As we later noted, the decision allowing jurisdiction over pendent state claims in *Gibbs* did not mention, let alone come to grips with, the text of the jurisdictional statutes and the bedrock principle that federal courts have no jurisdiction without statutory authorization. Finley v. United States, 490 U.S. 545, 548[] (1989). In *Finley,* we nonetheless reaffirmed and rationalized *Gibbs* and its progeny by inferring from it the interpretive principle that, in cases involving supplemental jurisdiction over additional claims between parties properly in federal court, the jurisdictional statutes should be read broadly, on the assumption that in this context Congress intended to authorize courts to exercise their full Article III power to dispose of an "'entire action before the court [which] comprises but one constitutional "case."'" [C]

We have not, however, applied *Gibbs'* expansive interpretive approach to other aspects of the jurisdictional statutes. For instance, we have consistently interpreted §1332 as requiring complete diversity... . The complete diversity requirement is not mandated by the Constitution, [c], or by the plain text of § 1332(a). The Court, nonetheless, has adhered to the complete diversity rule in light of the purpose of the diversity requirement, which is to provide a federal forum for important disputes where state courts might favor, or be perceived as favoring, home-state litigants. ...

In contrast to the diversity requirement, most of the other statutory prerequisites for federal jurisdiction, including the federal-question and amount-in-controversy requirements, can be analyzed claim by claim. ...

Thus, with respect to plaintiff-specific jurisdictional requirements, the Court held in Clark v. Paul Gray, Inc., 306 U.S. 583[] (1939), that every plaintiff must separately satisfy the amount-in-controversy requirement. Though *Clark* was a federal-question case, at that time federal-question jurisdiction had an amount-in-controversy requirement analogous to the amount-in-controversy requirement for diversity cases. ... The Court reaffirmed this rule, in the context of a class action brought invoking § 1332(a) diversity jurisdiction, in Zahn v. International Paper Co., 414 U.S. 291[] (1973). It follows "inescapably" from *Clark,* the Court held in *Zahn,* that "any plaintiff without the jurisdictional amount must be dismissed from the case, even though others allege jurisdictionally sufficient claims." [C] ...

As the jurisdictional statutes existed in 1989, then, here is how matters stood: First, the diversity requirement in §1332(a) required complete diversity; absent complete diversity, the district court lacked original jurisdiction over all of the claims in the action. ... Second, if the district court had original jurisdiction over at least one claim, the jurisdictional statutes implicitly authorized supplemental jurisdiction over all other claims between the same parties arising out of the same Article III case or controversy. [C] Third, even when the district court had original jurisdiction over one or more claims between particular parties, the jurisdictional statutes did not authorize supplemental jurisdiction over additional claims involving other parties. [Cc]

B

In *Finley* we emphasized that "[w]hatever we say regarding the scope of jurisdiction conferred by a particular statute can of course be changed by Congress." [C] In 1990, Congress accepted the invitation[, enacting] §1367, the provision which controls these cases. ...

All parties to this litigation and all courts to consider the question agree that §1367 overturned the result in *Finley.* There is no warrant, however, for assuming that §1367 did no more than to overrule *Finley* and otherwise to codify the existing state of the law of supplemental jurisdiction. ...

Section 1367(a) is a broad grant of supplemental jurisdiction over other claims within the same case or controversy, as long as the action is one in which the district courts would have original jurisdiction. The last sentence of § 1367(a) makes it clear that the grant of supplemental jurisdiction extends to claims involving joinder or intervention of additional parties. The single question before us, therefore, is whether a diversity case in which the claims of some plaintiffs satisfy the amount-in-controversy requirement, but the claims of other plaintiffs do not, presents a "civil action of which the district courts have original jurisdiction." If the answer is yes, §1367(a) confers supplemental jurisdiction over all claims, including those that do not independently satisfy the amount-in-controversy requirement, if the claims are part of the same Article III case or controversy. If the answer is no, § 1367(a) is inapplicable and, in light of our holdings in *Clark* and *Zahn,* the district court has no statutory basis for exercising supplemental jurisdiction over the additional claims.

We now conclude the answer must be yes. When the well-pleaded complaint contains at least one claim that satisfies the amount-in-controversy requirement, and there are no other relevant jurisdictional defects, the district court, beyond all question, has original jurisdiction over that claim. The presence of other claims in the complaint, over which the district court may lack original jurisdiction, is of no moment. If the court has original jurisdiction over a single claim in the complaint, it has original jurisdiction over a "civil action" within the meaning of §1367(a), even if the civil action over which it has jurisdiction comprises fewer claims than were included in the complaint. Once the court determines it has original jurisdiction over the civil action, it can turn to the question whether it has a constitutional and statutory basis for exercising supplemental jurisdiction over the other claims in the action.

Section 1367(a) commences with the direction that §§1367(b) and (c), or other relevant statutes, may provide specific exceptions, but otherwise §1367(a) is a broad jurisdictional grant, with no distinction drawn between pendent-claim and pendent-party cases. In fact, the last sentence of §1367(a) makes clear that the provision grants supplemental jurisdiction over claims involving joinder or intervention of additional parties. The terms of §1367 do not acknowledge any distinction between pendent jurisdiction and the doctrine of so-called ancillary jurisdiction. Though the doctrines of pendent and ancillary jurisdiction developed separately as a historical matter, the Court has recognized that the doctrines are "two species of the same generic problem," [c]. Nothing in § 1367 indicates a congressional intent to recognize, preserve, or create some meaningful, substantive distinction between the jurisdictional categories we have historically labeled pendent and ancillary.

... While §1367(b) qualifies the broad rule of § 1367(a), it does not withdraw supplemental jurisdiction over the claims of the additional parties at issue here. ... Nothing in the text of §1367(b)... withholds supplemental jurisdiction over the claims of plaintiffs permissively joined under Rule 20... or certified as class-action members pursuant to Rule 23... . The natural, indeed the necessary, inference is that §1367 confers supplemental jurisdiction over claims by Rule 20 and Rule 23 plaintiffs. This inference, at least with respect to Rule 20 plaintiffs, is strengthened by the fact that §1367(b) explicitly excludes supplemental jurisdiction over claims against defendants joined under Rule 20. ...

And so we circle back to the original question. When the well-pleaded complaint in district court includes multiple claims, all part of the same case or controversy, and some, but not all, of the claims are within the court's original jurisdiction, does the court have before it "any civil action of which the district courts have original jurisdiction"? It does. Under §1367, the court has original jurisdiction over the civil action comprising the claims for which there is no jurisdictional defect. No other reading of § 1367 is plausible in light of the text and structure of the jurisdictional statute. Though the special nature and purpose of the diversity requirement mean that a single nondiverse party can contaminate every other claim in the lawsuit, the contamination does not occur with respect to jurisdictional defects that go only to the substantive importance of individual claims.

It follows from this conclusion that the threshold requirement of §1367(a) is satisfied in cases, like those now before us, where some, but not all, of the plaintiffs in a diversity action allege a sufficient amount in controversy. We hold that §1367 by its plain text overruled *Clark* and *Zahn* and authorized supplemental jurisdiction over all claims by diverse parties arising out of the same Article III case or controversy, subject only to enumerated exceptions not applicable in the cases now before us. ...

The judgment of the Court of Appeals for the Eleventh Circuit is affirmed. The judgment of the Court of Appeals for the First Circuit is reversed, and the case is remanded for proceedings consistent with this opinion.

It is so ordered.

[The dissent of Justice STEVENS, with whom Justice BREYER joined, omitted.]

Justice GINSBURG, with whom Justice STEVENS, Justice O'CONNOR, and Justice BREYER join, dissenting.

These cases present the question whether Congress, by enacting 28 U.S.C. §1367, overruled this Court's decisions in Clark v. Paul Gray, Inc., 306 U.S. 583[] (1939)... , and Zahn v. International Paper Co., 414 U.S. 291[] (1973). *Clark* held that, when federal-court jurisdiction is predicated on a specified amount in controversy, each plaintiff joined in the litigation must independently meet the jurisdictional amount requirement. *Zahn* confirmed that in class actions governed by Federal Rule of Civil Procedure 23(b)(3), "[e]ach [class member] ... must satisfy the jurisdictional amount, and any [class member] who does not must be dismissed from the case." [C]

Section 1367, all agree, was designed to overturn this Court's decision in Finley v. United States, 490 U.S. 545[] (1989). ...

What more §1367 wrought is an issue on which courts of appeals have sharply divided. ... The Court today holds that §1367, although prompted by *Finley,* a case in which original access to federal court was predicated on a federal question, notably enlarges federal diversity jurisdiction. The Court reads § 1367 to overrule *Clark* and *Zahn,* thereby allowing access to federal court by coplaintiffs or class members who do not meet the now in excess of $75,000 amount-in-controversy requirement, so long as at least one coplaintiff, or the named class representative, has a jurisdictionally sufficient claim. [C]

The Court adopts a plausibly broad reading of § 1367, a measure that is hardly a model of the careful drafter's art. There is another plausible reading, however, one less disruptive of our jurisprudence regarding supplemental jurisdiction. If one reads §1367(a) to instruct, as the statute's text suggests, that the district court must first have "original jurisdiction" over a "civil action" before supplemental jurisdiction can attach, then *Clark* and *Zahn* are preserved, and supplemental jurisdiction does not open the way for joinder of plaintiffs, or inclusion of class members, who do not independently meet the amount-in-controversy requirement. ... I conclude that this narrower construction is the better reading of § 1367. ...

The Court's reading is surely plausible, especially if one detaches §1367(a) from its context and attempts no reconciliation with prior interpretations of § 1332's amount-in-controversy requirement. But §1367(a)'s text ... can be read another way, one that would involve no rejection of *Clark* and *Zahn.*

... [A] complaint must first meet that "original jurisdiction" measurement. If it does not, no supplemental jurisdiction is authorized. If it does, §1367(a) authorizes "supplemental jurisdiction" over related claims. In other words, §1367(a) would preserve undiminished, as part and parcel of §1332 "original jurisdiction" determinations, both the "complete diversity" rule and the decisions restricting aggregation to arrive at the amount in controversy.[fn] Section 1367(b)'s office, then, would be "to prevent the erosion of the complete diversity [and amount-in-controversy] requirement[s] that might otherwise result from an expansive application of what was once termed the doctrine of ancillary jurisdiction." [Cc] In contrast to the Court's construction of §1367, which draws a sharp line between the diversity and amount-in-controversy components of §1332, [cc], the interpretation presented here does not sever the two jurisdictional requirements.

While §1367's enigmatic text[fn] defies flawless interpretation, [c],[fn] the precedent-preservative reading, I am persuaded, better accords with the historical and legal context of Congress' enactment of the supplemental jurisdiction statute, [c], and the established limits on pendent and ancillary jurisdiction, [c]. ... It ... follows the sound counsel that "close questions of [statutory] construction should be resolved in favor of continuity and against change," [c].[fn]

For the reasons stated, I would hold that §1367 does not overrule *Clark* and *Zahn.* I would therefore affirm the judgment of the Court of Appeals for the First Circuit and reverse the judgment of the Court of Appeals for the Eleventh Circuit.

Figure

David Indiano, a partner in the five-lawyer San Juan, Puerto Rico law firm Indiano & Williams, was lead counsel in the district-court case and circuit-court appeal involving the 9-year-old girl who cut herself on the Star-Kist tuna can, that formed one of the two underlying cases in the above *Exxon Mobil Corp.* decision. Mr. Indiano is a civil litigator whose law practice in Puerto Rico serves a wide range of corporate and individual clients on both the plaintiff's and defense sides. Although Mr. Indiano was born and attended law school in Ohio, undergraduate studies in Spain and teaching in Puerto Rico led Mr. Indiano to establish his law practice there. Much of his practice involves diversity-jurisdiction cases in the federal courts in Puerto Rico because of an anomaly in Puerto Rican law that grants broad statutory tort rights but does not offer jury trial, available then only in the federal district court. Mr. Indiano, both a practitioner and published scholar, has been president of the Puerto Rican chapter of the Federal Bar Association. In an arrangement typical for Supreme Court cases, his clients retained a major Washington, D.C. law firm whom Mr. Indiano then assisted with the Supreme Court briefing.

INQUIRY

Class Actions. In the above *Exxon Mobil* case decided in 2005, the Supreme Court held that §1367 supplemental jurisdiction permits class-action members whose individual claims are for less than diversity's $75,000 jurisdictional limit to maintain claims so long as at least one class member's claim exceeds $75,000. In effect, *Exxon Mobil* recognized §1367's supplemental *party* (not merely supplemental *claim*) jurisdiction. *Exxon Mobil* thus recognized that §1367 had overturned the rule of *Finley v. United States* that had refused to recognize pendent party jurisdiction in a federal-question case. Pendent party jurisdiction, today known as supplemental jurisdiction, is alive and well, within the other limitations of §1367(c). Yet between enacting §1367 in 1990 and the Supreme Court's expansive interpretation of it in 2005 in *Exxon Mobil* to reach class-action claims, Congress had already enacted the Class Action Fairness Act, 28 U.S.C. §§1332(d), 1453, mentioned above, to provide for federal jurisdiction over class-action claims aggregating over $5 million even if *none* of the claims had a value in excess of $75,000. Was Congress' enactment of the Class Action Fairness Act an indication that Congress had *not* intended the expansive interpretation that the Supreme Court gave §1367 in *Exxon Mobil*? After *Exxon Mobil*, the Class Action Fairness Act is necessary only for cases not including any individual claims greater than $75,000, whereas before *Exxon Mobil* it provided jurisdiction for class-action members whose individual claims were less than that jurisdictional limit. *See* Brill v. Countrywide Home Loans, Inc., 427 F.3d 446 (7th Cir. 2005) (Class Action Fairness Act jurisdiction available based on aggregate of $1,500 claims exceeding $5 million); Chavis v. Fidelity Warranty Services, Inc., 415 F.Supp.2d 520 (D. S.C. 2006) (Class Action Fairness Act jurisdiction available based on aggregate of $50,000 claims exceeding $50 million). You return to the study of class actions in Chapter 8 on joinder.

Discretionary Denial. Recall that in *United Mine Workers v. Gibbs, supra*, predating §1367, the Supreme Court observed that the federal district courts had discretion whether to recognize pendent jurisdiction. Subsection

(c) of §1367 codified that discretion into four categories in which the federal district courts may decline to exercise supplemental jurisdiction including "if (1) the claim raises a novel or complex issue of State law, (2) the claim substantially predominates over the claim or claims over which the district court has original jurisdiction, (3) the district court has dismissed all claims over which it has original jurisdiction, or (4) in exceptional circumstances, there are other compelling reasons for declining jurisdiction." Courts have noted the relatively broad discretion the "other compelling reasons" category gives to the district courts to decline supplemental jurisdiction. *See* Executive Software North America, Inc. v United States District Court, 24 F.3d 1545, 1556-1559 (9th Cir. 1994).

Counterclaims. There is no question that under §1367's supplemental jurisdiction (and, for that matter, the Supreme Court's prior pendent jurisdiction), the federal district courts have jurisdiction over a defendant's counterclaim that arises out of the same case or controversy (the same common nucleus of operative fact) as the plaintiff's federal-jurisdiction-qualifying claim, whether or not there is an independent basis for federal jurisdiction over the counterclaim. What about counterclaims for which there is no independent basis for federal jurisdiction and that do *not* arise out of the same controversy (meaning, in effect, permissive counterclaims)? In the absence of a Supreme Court decision, the lower federal courts have disagreed over whether the federal district courts have jurisdiction over non-qualifying, independent (permissive) counterclaims. *Contrast* Jones v. Ford Motor Credit Co., 358 F.3d 205 (2d Cir. 2004) (federal jurisdiction but discretionary denial permissible), *with* Iglesias v. Mutual Life Ins. Co., 156 F.3d 237, 241 (1st Cir. 1998) (no federal jurisdiction).

E. Removal

Although the plaintiff has the first opportunity to choose the court (state or federal) in which to litigate, by drafting the complaint to invoke or not invoke federal jurisdiction (the master-of-the-complaint rule), the plaintiff does not always have the final say. Recall that the state and federal courts have concurrent jurisdiction over most claims. The plaintiff could, for instance, file in state rather than federal court diversity of citizenship cases arising out of state law. State courts also have concurrent jurisdiction over many federal-question cases, lacking jurisdiction only in those cases, like bankruptcy, in which a federal statute grants the federal courts exclusive jurisdiction. Much of the time, when the state and federal courts have concurrent jurisdiction over a case, the plaintiff will file the case in federal rather than state court, perhaps to draw on the federal court's greater expertise over certain kinds of federal cases or (in diversity cases) to avoid potential local bias in county state court. When the plaintiff pleads a complaint over which a federal district court could have exercised jurisdiction but files that complaint in state rather than federal court, Congress has provided some defendants with a route to federal court. The defendant may have the right to remove the case from state to federal court. Congress granted defendants that right in the First Judiciary Act of 1789. Read the current version of the removal statute, based on a removal statute first enacted in 1875, before considering some issues it raises.

28 U.S.C. §1441. Actions removable generally
(a) Except as otherwise expressly provided by Act of Congress, any civil action brought in a State court of which the district courts of the United States have original jurisdiction, may be removed by the defendant or the defendants, to the district court of the United States for the district and division embracing the place where such action is pending. For purposes of removal under this chapter, the citizenship of defendants sued under fictitious names shall be disregarded.
(b) Any civil action of which the district courts have original jurisdiction founded on a claim or right arising under the Constitution, treaties or laws of the United States shall be removable without regard to the citizenship or residence of the parties. Any other such action shall be removable only if none of the parties in interest properly joined and served as defendants is a citizen of the State in which such action is brought.
(c) Whenever a separate and independent claim or cause of action within the jurisdiction conferred by section 1331 of this title is joined with one or more otherwise non-removable claims or causes of action, the entire case may be removed and the district court may determine all issues therein, or, in its discretion, may remand all matters in which State law predominates.
[Subsection (d) on removal by foreign state omitted.]
[Subsection (e) on removal under §1369 omitted.]
(f) The court to which a civil action is removed under this section is not precluded from hearing and determining any claim in such civil action because the State court from which such civil action is removed did not have jurisdiction over that claim.

INQUIRY

Strategy. The question of removal begins with the defendant's choice. Just because the defendant has the right to remove a case from state to federal court does not mean that the defendant should or must do so. The right to remove compels no duty to remove. The same considerations that made the plaintiff choose state over federal court may weigh in defendant's favor for leaving the case in state court. Often enough, though, those considerations or other considerations weigh in the opposite direction in favor of defendant removing the case to federal court. Just as the plaintiff had a choice of courts, the defendant may also. In cases that the defendant may remove, defendant has the last choice and can eliminate (trump or frustrate) the plaintiff's choice. Indeed, some plaintiffs who may actually prefer state court will simply file in federal court knowing that the defendant will remove the case.

Basis. The question of removal, though, requires the practitioner to consider carefully whether a defendant may in fact remove under the removal statute, 28 U.S.C. §1441. There are other removal statutes for specific situations. *See* 28 U.S.C. §1442 (federal-officer defendants); 28 U.S.C. §1443 (civil-rights claims); 28 U.S.C. §1453 (interstate class actions). Yet §1441 is the general removal statute. Removal consideration begins with the same well-pleaded-complaint rule articulated in Louisville & Nashville R. Co. v. Mottley, 211 U.S. 149 (1908), for the federal court's original jurisdiction. One looks first to the face of the well-pled complaint. The fact that the defendant may have a federal defense to the action does not establish removal jurisdiction, just as in *Mottley* it did not establish original jurisdiction. Nor will a federal counterclaim help. *See* Metro Ford Truck Sales, Inc. v. Ford Motor Co., 145 F.3d 320, 327 (5th Cir, 1998); *see also* Shamrock Oil & Gas Corp. v. Sheets, 313 U.S. 100 (1941) (plaintiff may not remove based on defendant's federal counterclaim). On the other hand, when the plaintiff omits the federal basis for a complaint from an artfully drafted pleading, that omission will not defeat removal jurisdiction. The defendant may still remove, provided that there is otherwise removal jurisdiction. Franchise Tax Bd. v. Construction Laborers Vacation Trust, 463 U.S. 1, 22-23 (1983). The presence of non-removable supplemental claims does not affect removal jurisdiction. If the plaintiff amends after removal to eliminate the basis for federal jurisdiction, the federal district court retains removal jurisdiction. *See* St. Paul Mercury Indem. Co. v. Red Cab Co., 303 U.S. 283 (1938); Rogers v. Wal-Mart Stores Inc., 230 F.3d 868 (6th Cir. 2000).

Scope. As evident from the statute reproduced above, §1441(a) contains the basic grant of removal jurisdiction, stating in pertinent part that "any civil action brought in a State court of which the district courts of the United States have original jurisdiction, may be removed ... to the district court... ." The next section, §1441(b), contains an important limitation that if any defendant is a citizen of the state in which the plaintiff filed the action, then removal is possible only if federal-question jurisdiction would have been the original basis for jurisdiction. Why the limitation? The answer may lie in part in that the defendant would not have the concern over local bias that was the rationale for diversity jurisdiction. Once the defendant removes a case, the federal district court will have supplemental jurisdiction over those claims just as it would if the plaintiff had filed the case in federal court in the first instance. *See* Grossmeyer v. McDonald, 128 F.3d 481, 488 (7th Cir. 1997). Subsection 1441(c), though, may extend removal jurisdiction beyond supplemental jurisdiction when it states that the federal district court may also determine "a separate and independent claim or cause of action" joined to the removable claim. Subsection 1441(c) does not contain the same-case-or-controversy language of §1367. *See* American Fire & Cas. Co. v. Finn, 341 U.S. 6 (1951) ("separate and independent claim" means an unrelated claim); *see also* Wisconsin Dept. of Corrections v. Schacht, 524 U.S. 381 (1998) (§1441(c) jurisdiction over independent claim for which there is no other federal jurisdiction). Would exercising removal jurisdiction over a completely unrelated claim be beyond what Article III, §2 authorizes (be unconstitutional)? *See* Porter v. Roosa, 259 F.Supp.2d 638, 653-654 (S.D. Ohio 2003) (unconstitutional); *but cf.* California Public Employees' Ret. Sys. v. WorldCom, Inc., 368 F.3d 86, 105-106 (2d Cir. 2004) (permitting §1441(c) removal).

Procedure. Removal procedures appear in §1441, §1446, and §1447. A defendant who wishes to remove a case need simply file a notice of removal under §1446(a) "in the district court of the United States for the district and division within which such action is pending." Notice that the defendant has no opportunity for forum shopping in the removal process. The plaintiff who chooses the state court effectively chooses the federal removal forum. Subsection 1446(b) gives the defendant 30 days from the complaint's service within which to remove or, if the case only later becomes removable (for instance, when the plaintiff amends the complaint), then 30 days from that notice. The same §1446(b) gives the defendant just one year within which to remove a diversity case in the event of the dismissal (for instance) of non-diverse parties. As soon as the defendant files the removal notice, the federal district court has jurisdiction over the case to decide whether removal was proper, a determination the district court must make as of the filing of the notice of removal. FED. R. CIV. P. 81(c) provides that the *Federal Rules* apply to actions removed from state court. Consider the following Supreme Court case exhibiting some of the problems and perils of removal.

Caterpillar, Inc. v. Lewis,

United States Supreme Court
519 U.S. 61 (1996)

Justice GINSBURG delivered the opinion of the Court.

This case, commenced in a state court, involves personal injury claims arising under state law. The case was removed to a federal court at a time when, the Court of Appeals concluded, complete diversity of citizenship did not exist among the parties. Promptly after the removal, the plaintiff moved to remand the case to the state court, but the District Court denied that motion. Before trial of the case, however, all claims involving the nondiverse defendant were settled, and that defendant was dismissed as a party to the action. Complete diversity thereafter existed. The case proceeded to trial, jury verdict, and judgment for the removing defendant. The Court of Appeals vacated the judgment, concluding that, absent complete diversity at the time of removal, the District Court lacked subject-matter jurisdiction.

The question presented is whether the absence of complete diversity at the time of removal is fatal to federal-court adjudication. We hold that a district court's error in failing to remand a case improperly removed is not fatal to the ensuing adjudication if federal jurisdictional requirements are met at the time judgment is entered.

...

Respondent James David Lewis, a resident of Kentucky, filed this lawsuit in Kentucky state court... , after sustaining injuries while operating a bulldozer. Asserting state-law claims based on defective manufacture, negligent maintenance, failure to warn, and breach of warranty, Lewis named as defendants both the manufacturer of the bulldozer-petitioner Caterpillar Inc., a Delaware corporation with its principal place of business in Illinois-and the company that serviced the bulldozer-Whayne Supply Company, a Kentucky corporation with its principal place of business in Kentucky.

Several months later, Liberty Mutual Insurance Group, the insurance carrier for Lewis' employer, intervened in the lawsuit as a plaintiff. A Massachusetts corporation with its principal place of business in that State, Liberty Mutual asserted subrogation claims against both Caterpillar and Whayne Supply for workers' compensation benefits Liberty Mutual had paid to Lewis on behalf of his employer.

Lewis entered into a settlement agreement with defendant Whayne Supply less than a year after filing his complaint. Shortly after learning of this agreement, Caterpillar filed a notice of removal ... in the United States District Court for the Eastern District of Kentucky. Grounding federal jurisdiction on diversity of citizenship, [c], Caterpillar satisfied with only a day to spare the statutory requirement that a diversity-based removal take place within one year of a lawsuit's commencement, see 28 U.S.C. §1446(b). Caterpillar's notice of removal explained that the case was nonremovable at the lawsuit's start: Complete diversity was absent then because plaintiff Lewis and defendant

Whayne Supply shared Kentucky citizenship. [C] Proceeding on the understanding that the settlement agreement between these two Kentucky parties would result in the dismissal of Whayne Supply from the lawsuit, Caterpillar stated that the settlement rendered the case removable. [C]

Lewis objected to the removal and moved to remand the case to state court. Lewis acknowledged that he had settled his own claims against Whayne Supply. But Liberty Mutual had not yet settled its subrogation claim against Whayne Supply, Lewis asserted. Whayne Supply's presence as a defendant in the lawsuit, Lewis urged, defeated diversity of citizenship. [C] Without addressing this argument, the District Court denied Lewis' motion to remand... , treating as dispositive Lewis' admission that he had settled his own claims against Whayne Supply. [C]

... In June 1993, plaintiff Liberty Mutual and defendant Whayne Supply entered into a settlement of Liberty Mutual's subrogation claim, and the District Court dismissed Whayne Supply from the lawsuit. With Caterpillar as the sole defendant adverse to Lewis,[fn] the case proceeded to a six-day jury trial... , ending in a unanimous verdict for Caterpillar. ...

When a plaintiff files in state court a civil action over which the federal district courts would have original jurisdiction based on diversity of citizenship, the defendant or defendants may remove the action to federal court, 28 U.S.C. §1441(a), provided that no defendant "is a citizen of the State in which such action is brought," §1441(b).[fn] In a case not originally removable, a defendant who receives a pleading or other paper indicating the postcommencement satisfaction of federal jurisdictional requirements—for example, by reason of the dismissal of a nondiverse party—may remove the case to federal court within 30 days of receiving such information. §1446(b). No case, however, may be removed from state to federal court based on diversity of citizenship "more than 1 year after commencement of the action." [C][fn]

Once a defendant has filed a notice of removal in the federal district court, a plaintiff objecting to removal "on the basis of any defect in removal procedure" may, within 30 days, file a motion asking the district court to remand the case to state court. §1447(c). ...

... [T]he Sixth Circuit correctly determined that the complete diversity requirement was not satisfied at the time of removal. [C] We accordingly home in on this question: Does the District Court's initial misjudgment still burden and run with the case, or is it overcome by the eventual dismissal of the nondiverse defendant?

Petitioner Caterpillar relies heavily on our decisions in American Fire & Casualty Co. v. Finn, 341 U.S. 6[] (1951), and Grubbs v. General Elec. Credit Corp., 405 U.S. 699[] (1972), urging that these decisions "long ago settled the proposition that remand to the state court is unnecessary even if jurisdiction did not exist at the time of removal, so long as the district court had subject matter jurisdiction at the time of judgment." [C] ... But neither decision resolves dispositively a controversy of the kind we face, for neither involved a plaintiff who moved promptly, but unsuccessfully, to remand a case improperly removed from state court to federal court, and then challenged on appeal a judgment entered by the federal court. ...

... Caterpillar moves too quickly over the terrain we must cover. The *jurisdictional* defect was cured, *i.e.*, complete diversity was established before the trial commenced. ... But a statutory flaw—Caterpillar's failure to meet the §1441(a) requirement that the case be fit for federal adjudication at the time the removal petition is filed—remained in the unerasable history of the case. ...

Having preserved his objection to an improper removal, Lewis urges that an "all's well that ends well" approach is inappropriate here. He maintains that ultimate satisfaction of the subject-matter jurisdiction requirement ought not swallow up antecedent statutory violations. The course Caterpillar advocates, Lewis observes, would disfavor diligent plaintiffs who timely, but unsuccessfully, move to check improper removals in district court. Further, that course would allow improperly removing defendants to profit from their disregard of Congress' instructions, and their ability to lead district judges into error.

Concretely, in this very case, Lewis emphasizes, adherence to the rules Congress prescribed for removal would have kept the case in state court. Only by removing prematurely was Caterpillar able to get to federal court inside the one-year limitation set in § 1446(b).[fn] Had Caterpillar waited until the case was ripe for removal, *i.e.*, until Whayne Supply was dismissed as a defendant, the one-year limitation would have barred the way,[fn] and plaintiff's choice of forum would have been preserved.[fn]

These arguments are hardly meritless, but they run up against an overriding consideration. Once a diversity case has been tried in federal court, with rules of decision supplied by state law under the regime of *Erie R. Co. v. Tompkins,* 304 U.S. 64[] (1938), considerations of finality, efficiency, and economy become overwhelming. ...

Our view is in harmony with a main theme of the removal scheme Congress devised. Congress ordered a procedure calling for expeditious superintendence by district courts. ... To wipe out the adjudication postjudgment, and return to state court a case now satisfying all federal jurisdictional requirements, would impose an exorbitant cost on our dual court system, a cost incompatible with the fair and unprotracted administration of justice. ...

The procedural requirements for removal remain enforceable by the federal trial court judges to whom those requirements are directly addressed. Lewis' prediction that rejection of his petition will "encourag[e] state court defendants to remove cases improperly," [c], rests on an assumption we do not indulge—that district courts generally will not comprehend, or will balk at applying, the rules on removal Congress has prescribed. ... The odds against any gain from a wrongful removal, in sum, render improbable Lewis' projection of increased resort to the maneuver.

For the reasons stated, the judgment of the Court of Appeals is reversed, and the case is remanded for proceedings consistent with this opinion.

It is so ordered.

INQUIRY

Remand. The defendant who has an initial right to remove had best not answer or otherwise defend in state court before attempting removal because the federal district court may construe that action as consent to state-court jurisdiction and waiver of removal. Brown v. Demco, Inc., 792 F.2d 478, 481 (5th Cir. 1986). Under §1447(c), plaintiffs who wish to challenge removal and obtain a remand to state court must do so within 30 days. A defendant may not challenge on appeal a decision to remand, 28 U.S.C. §1447(d); Kircher v. Putnam Funds Trust, 547 U.S. 633 (2006), but a plaintiff may appeal after final judgment a refusal to remand, *see* Caterpillar Inc. v Williams, 482 U.S. 386, 390-391 (1987). The plaintiff may also have the costs and attorney's fees incurred in obtaining remand, when the defendant has removed without reasonable basis. 28 U.S.C. 1447(c); Martin v. Franklin Capital Corp., 546 U.S. 132, 136 (2005). Also, note §1441(c)'s option for the federal district court to remand all matters in which state claims predominate. Keep in mind that Congress controls removal. For example, §1445 forbids removal of claims under the Federal Employers' Liability Act against railroads. Indeed, the Securities Litigation Uniform Standards Act, 15 U.S.C. §77p(b), (c), permits removal but then requires dismissal of removed actions, in effect confirming that federal law preempts state cases.

Summary. Subject-matter jurisdiction, then, involves the question of whether the applicable legislature (state legislature or national Congress) has authorized a particular court to hear the particular type of matter, within constitutional authority for the judicial system of which the particular court is a part. State court systems vary in their constitutional and legislative authority, often by amount in controversy but also by type of claim (probate, family law, etc.) and type of relief (money damages only or also declaratory and injunctive relief). Federal courts have diversity-of-citizenship jurisdiction under §1332 with a $75,000 amount in controversy. Citizenship depends on domicile for individuals and state of incorporation and principal place of business for corporations. Federal courts also have federal-question jurisdiction under §1331, although narrower than the potential Article III, §2 authorization. Federal courts also have supplemental jurisdiction under §1367 over non-qualifying state claims that arise out of a common nucleus of operative fact as claims that qualify for federal jurisdiction. Defendants may remove qualifying federal claims from state to federal court under §1441 following specific procedures. Judges and lawyers respect these limits because not to do so is to undermine the institutions of law and the courts.

Career

Which side do you prefer? Civil litigation's adversarial nature, together with ethical duties that require lawyers to represent parties free from conflicts of interest, means that lawyers take one side or the other side (not both sides) in a dispute. Although lawyers who represent plaintiffs and lawyers who represent defendants certainly share skills and have somewhat similar roles even though on different sides, there also tend to be differences between plaintiffs' and defense work. Some of those differences have to do with the different civil procedures for plaintiffs and defendants involving issues like pleading, service of process, discovery, and the order of trial. Other differences have to do with how the different sides structure and maintain client relationships over issues of authority, direction or control, and reporting. The economics may also be different, whether (for instance) hourly, flat, or contingency fee, making compensation more or less certain and more or less tied to hours, productivity, or success. With careful conflict checking, some lawyers manage to practice simultaneously both plaintiffs' and defense work. Others change sides one or more times during the course of a career. Many others start and finish a career on just one side.

Knowing your traits and preferences for one side or the other side is a good strategy to explore civil-litigation careers.

CHAPTER V

VENUE

OBJECTIVE: That you be able to identify and apply applicable venue statutes, rules, and doctrines, to determine a proper and reasonably convenient court in which to file a civil lawsuit.

Case Study: Your client, a computer consultant, hands you a federal summons and complaint filed against her in a federal district court on the other side of the state, outside of the federal district in which your office, your client's office, and the local office of the plaintiff customer where your client performed consulting work are located. Your client wants to know whether she must travel to the other side of the state to litigate this lawsuit.

The question of venue involves choosing a proper and reasonably convenient forum. It presumes that the court has personal jurisdiction over the defendant and subject-matter jurisdiction over the claims, and that the defendant had notice and opportunity for hearing. Venue is the fourth step of choosing the right court to initiate civil litigation, after (1) personal jurisdiction, (2) subject-matter jurisdiction, and (3) notice/opportunity for hearing. Statutes, rules, and doctrines on venue answer questions about where to litigate a civil case, when there are two or more available locations within the same state or federal district, or different states or federal districts. There are significant differences between personal and subject-matter jurisdiction, on one hand, and venue on the other hand. Venue is not a yes-or-no, constitutional question of a court's permissible reach. Venue is instead a here-or-there, statutory and common-law question of which is the better forum. The venue question is not over the structure of government but instead involves common-sense issues having to do with efficiency of the courts and convenience to parties and witnesses. Venue is the plaintiff's choice initially, within the scope of the applicable venue statutes determining original venue. Defendants may then have the opportunity to seek transfer of venue on statutory grounds or dismissal of a case for inconvenient venue. The following sections address those three subjects of (1) whether a court has original venue (whether venue is proper in the plaintiff's chosen court), (2) whether the defendant may obtain transfer of venue under an applicable statute, and (3) whether the case should be dismissed for inconvenient venue under the common-law doctrine of forum non conveniens.

A. Original Venue

Once a practitioner has confirmed that a certain court has personal and subject-matter jurisdiction over a case, you might think that there would be no question whether the plaintiff could file the case in that court under whatever venue provisions exist. Perhaps then, the only question should be whether there is a more convenient court to which to transfer venue. You would be only half-right in thinking so. There are certainly statutes and rules for the transfer of venue, addressed in the following section. Those venue-transfer provisions are probably more often the fighting issues in venue disputes. Yet sensibly, the statutes and rules for venue first address whether venue is proper (whether there is original venue). Only then do they address whether the trial court should transfer venue to a more convenient forum. Why not make the question of venue simply one of convenience? If plaintiffs could choose any forum having personal jurisdiction, and the only dispute then was whether that forum was reasonably convenient, there would be many such disputes over the convenience of the chosen forum. Venue statutes force the plaintiff to make the more convenient forum choice first (that is, if they restrict original venue to a reasonable scope), making many fewer disputes over venue transfer. Because venue is an issue in both state and federal court, the following two subsections address state and federal original-venue statutes separately. Keep in mind as you study venue provisions that forums make differences in outcomes. One study showed that a defendant is twice as likely to prevail if successful in transferring venue (although note the control issues of any such study that transferred cases may have been better for the defendants for reasons other than the change in the forum). *See* Kevin M. Clermont and Theodore Eisenberg, *Exorcising the Evil of Forum-Shopping*, 80 CORNELL L.REV. 1507 (1995).

Ethics

Rule 3.3 of the ABA MODEL RULES OF PROFESSIONAL CONDUCT requires that counsel disclose adverse authority to the court when opposing counsel has not done so and the trial court appears unaware of that authority. It also requires that counsel speak truthfully to the court and correct any false statements to the conclusion of the proceeding. These and other rules requiring counsel to respect and submit to the court's authority make a motion challenging the court's jurisdiction or venue a delicate proposition. Submission, though, does not mean obedience when there has not yet been a ruling to obey. Lawyers can challenge a court's power without disrespecting the court. Attitude is everything, especially in arguing that the court lacks jurisdiction or that venue is improper.

1. State Court

State venue statutes identify the locations (often counties) in which there is original venue for an action. States tend to administer their court systems at the county level, although some will combine counties, and others will subdivide counties into two or more districts. Beyond that basic similarity, state venue statutes and court rules vary widely within some general patterns. Many venue statutes locate venue in the county where the cause of action arose. Note the difficulty in defining that location. In a tort action, for instance, it could be where the wrongful act occurred or where the injury or damage occurred, those being two different places in many tort cases (often, for instance, for products liability). Some statutes simplify that inquiry by designating the county where a certain event took place relating to the litigation, such as where a motor-vehicle accident occurred. Venue statutes also often place venue in the county where all or part of the subject of the litigation is located. Aside from the general patterns in venue statutes, there may also be general venue statutes to fill gaps in the specific venue provisions so that there is an original venue statute covering every civil case filed. General venue statutes often specify the county where the defendant resides or does business, and then (often as a fallback provision) where the plaintiff resides or does business. Contrast the different manner in which two states address venue, one simple and general, and the other categorical and complex, reflected in the following rules and statutes.

NEW YORK CIV. PRAC. LAW & RULES §503. Venue based on residence.
(a) Generally. Except where otherwise prescribed by law, the place of trial shall be in the county in which one of the parties resided when it was commenced; or, if none of the parties then resided in the state, in any county designated by the plaintiff. A party resident in more than one county shall be deemed a resident of each such county.
(b) Executor, administrator, trustee, committee, conservator, general or testamentary guardian, or receiver. An executor, administrator, trustee, committee, conservator, general or testamentary guardian, or receiver shall be deemed a resident of the county of his appointment as well as the county in which he actually resides.
(c) Corporation. A domestic corporation, or a foreign corporation authorized to transact business in the state, shall be deemed a resident of the county in which its principal office is located; except that such a corporation, if a railroad or other common carrier, shall also be deemed a resident of the county where the cause of action arose.
...

MICH. COMP. LAWS §600.1605. Venue; real actions, replevin.
The county in which the subject of action, or any part thereof, is situated, is a proper county in which to commence and try the following actions:
(a) the recovery of real property, or of an estate or interests therein, or for the determination in any form of such right or interest;
(b) the partition of real property;
(c) the foreclosure of all liens or mortgages on real property; and
(d) the recovery of tangible personal property.

MICH. COMP. LAWS §600.1611. Venue; action on probate bond.
The county in which a probate bond is filed is a proper county in which to commence and try actions upon the bond.

MICH. COMP. LAWS §600.1615. Venue; action against governmental units
Any county in which any governmental unit, including but not limited to a public, municipal, quasi-municipal, or governmental corporation, unincorporated board, public body, or political subdivision, exercises or may

exercise its governmental authority is the proper county in which to commence and try actions against such governmental units, except that if the cause of action arose in the county of the principal office of such governmental unit, that county is the proper county in which to commence and try actions against such governmental units.

MICH. COMP. L. §600.1621. Venue; other actions, county in which defendant resides or conducts business; actions against fiduciary.

Except for actions provided for in sections 1605, 1611, 1615, and 1629, venue is determined as follows:

(a) The county in which a defendant resides, has a place of business, or conducts business, or in which the registered office of a defendant corporation is located, is a proper county in which to commence and try an action.

(b) If none of the defendants meet 1 or more of the criteria in subdivision (a), the county in which a plaintiff resides or has a place of business, or in which the registered office of a plaintiff corporation is located, is a proper county in which to commence and try an action.

(c) An action against a fiduciary appointed by court order shall be commenced in the county in which the fiduciary was appointed.

MICH. COMP. L. §600.1629. Venue; tort and product liability actions; change of venue.

(1) Subject to subsection (2), in an action based on tort or another legal theory seeking damages for personal injury, property damage, or wrongful death, all of the following apply:

(a) The county in which the original injury occurred and in which either of the following applies is a county in which to file and try the action:

(*i*) The defendant resides, has a place of business, or conducts business in that county.

(*ii*) The corporate registered office of a defendant is located in that county.

(b) If a county does not satisfy the criteria under subdivision (a), the county in which the original injury occurred and in which either of the following applies is a county in which to file and try the action:

(*i*) The plaintiff resides, has a place of business, or conducts business in that county.

(*ii*) The corporate registered office of a plaintiff is located in that county.

(c) If a county does not satisfy the criteria under subdivision (a) or (b), a county in which both of the following apply is a county in which to file and try the action:

(*i*) The plaintiff resides, has a place of business, or conducts business in that county, or has its corporate registered office located in that county.

(*ii*) The defendant resides, has a place of business, or conducts business in that county, or has its corporate registered office located in that county.

(d) If a county does not satisfy the criteria under subdivision (a), (b), or (c), a county that satisfies the criteria under section 1621 or 1627 is a county in which to file and try an action.

(2) Any party may file a motion to change venue based on hardship or inconvenience.

(3) For the purpose of this section only, in a product liability action, a defendant is considered to conduct business in a county in which the defendant's product is sold at retail.

Skill

Notice in the venue statutes above the relationship of substance to procedure. Several of the provisions dictate the procedure (the court in which venue lies) based on the nature of the substantive right the plaintiff seeks to enforce (tort recovery for bodily injury, claims to real property, etc.). In the law, substantive rights guard the integrity of a person and the property rights and interests of a person or corporation, while procedures are the means by which persons and entities address impaired substantive rights. Another way to think of it is that procedure represents latent substance, as parties use procedures to attempt to retain, restore, or gain substantive rights (money judgments, specific performance, etc.). Substance represents latent procedure, as parties expend their time and resources (their substance, in a sense) in the use of procedure. Think of Einstein's famous equation, $e = mc^2$, for the conversion of energy (procedure) to mass (substance) and vice versa, with its speed-of-light-squared constant (justice). Clients recognize intuitively the convertible nature of substance and procedure, as they decide when and to what extent to engage in litigation. Lawyers have the responsibility of helping them do so.

INQUIRY

Specific Provisions. Most states will have many specific venue provisions—perhaps dozens. What forms of action do you think would most require specific venue statutes? In any one state, there may be separate statutes dictating original venue for divorce, *see, e.g.,* TENN. CODE ANN. §36-4-105; child custody and support, *see, e.g.,* TENN. CODE ANN. §§36-5-303, 36-5-304(1)(A); probate, *see, e.g.,* MICH.. COMP. L. §600.1611; claim and delivery of personal property, *see, e.g.,* N.Y. CIV. PRAC. L.&R. §508; actions against corporate resident agents; actions against local government units or officials, *see, e.g.,* N.Y. CIV. PRAC. L.&R. §504; tort actions and various forms of tort actions, *see, e.g.,* MICH.. COMP. L. §600.1629; retail loan contracts, *see, e.g.,* CAL. FIN. CODE §22341; and actions involving real property, *see, e.g.,* CAL. CODE CIV. P. §1250.020, N.Y. CIV. PRAC. L.&R. §507. Why might you expect to find a specific venue provision for these specific types of action? For example, what is it about a dispute over real property that makes it sensible to try the case in the county in which the real property is located? What do you think the state legislatures enacting these specific venue provisions were trying to accomplish? Reducing forum shopping and ensuring party convenience are certainly two primary considerations. So, probably, is providing a reasonable degree of certainty over proper venue. Sometimes, the larger consideration is avoiding smaller disputes over matters of procedure that, at least in theory, should not greatly affect the outcome.

2. Federal Court

Venue in federal court begins with a general statute, 28 U.S.C. §1391. Like state venue provisions and rules for personal jurisdiction, §1391 generally requires a connection between the venue and either the parties or the events or property that they dispute. Section 1391's present form is the result of a century-long statutory history resulting in extensive amendments in 1990 and further refinements in 1992 and 1995. The amendments attempted to ensure that the statute provided for venue in every case rather than leaving gaps. Venue is in part a matter of choosing among multiple possible forums and in part ensuring that venue principles and rules provide for at least one proper forum. Section 1391 accomplishes the first end (choosing among possible forums) by dividing its provisions into subsection (a) applying to diversity cases only and subsection (b) applying to all other cases. Notice that subsections (a) and (b) are identical except as to the category of cases (diversity or not) to which they apply and as to one phrase in subsection (3) the significance of which the text below addresses. Under both §1391(a) and (b), the court first has original venue in one of two ways. Either all defendants must reside in the state and at least one in the district or (2) a substantial part of the events giving rise to the claim occurred, or property that is the subject of the dispute is located, in the district. Section 1391 accomplishes the second end (ensuring at least one proper forum) by providing a fallback provision in subsection (3) to each of subsections (a) and (b). As you read the federal general venue statute §1391 (followed by another general venue provision §1392), think of the value of this structure and how it relates to the structure of the state provisions above.

28 U.S.C. §1391. Venue generally

(a) A civil action wherein jurisdiction is founded only on diversity of citizenship may, except as otherwise provided by law, be brought only in (1) a judicial district where any defendant resides, if all defendants reside in the same State, (2) a judicial district in which a substantial part of the events or omissions giving rise to the claim occurred, or a substantial part of property that is the subject of the action is situated, or (3) a judicial district in which any defendant is subject to personal jurisdiction at the time the action is commenced, if there is no district in which the action may otherwise be brought.

(b) A civil action wherein jurisdiction is not founded solely on diversity of citizenship may, except as otherwise provided by law, be brought only in (1) a judicial district where any defendant resides, if all defendants reside in the same State, (2) a judicial district in which a substantial part of the events or omissions giving rise to the claim occurred, or a substantial part of property that is the subject of the action is situated, or (3) a judicial district in which any defendant may be found, if there is no district in which the action may otherwise be brought.

(c) For purposes of venue under this chapter, a defendant that is a corporation shall be deemed to reside in any judicial district in which it is subject to personal jurisdiction at the time the action is commenced. In a State which has more than one judicial district and in which a defendant that is a corporation is subject to personal jurisdiction at the time an action is commenced, such corporation shall be deemed to reside in any district in that State within which its contacts would be sufficient to subject it to personal jurisdiction if that district were a separate State, and, if there is no such district, the corporation shall be deemed to reside in the district within which it has the most significant contacts.

(d) An alien may be sued in any district.

...

28 U.S.C. §1392. Defendants or property in different districts in same State.

Any civil action, of a local nature, involving property located in different districts in the same State, may be brought in any of such districts.

INQUIRY

Residence. Subsections (a)(1) and (b)(1) of §1391 provide for venue in a district where any defendant resides, so long as all defendants reside in that state in which the district is located. Although it gives pause, this restriction makes sense. If subsection (1) allowed for venue in any district in which any defendant resided, then it would be easy to inconvenience seriously several out-of-state defendants, by choosing a district in the state in which only one defendant, and perhaps even a nominal defendant, had residence. Why not provide simply for original venue in the district in which all defendants reside? Many states have two or more federal districts. It might well be no serious inconvenience to require defendants who all reside in one such state to travel across the state to the other district in which at least one defendant resides. Lower federal courts have defined the term "residence" in §1391(a)(1) and (b)(1) to mean domicile, that is, the one permanent home to which the defendant intends to return when absent. *See* Manley v. Engram, 755 F.2d 1463, 1466n.3 (11th Cir. 1985), *citing* Mas v. Perry, 489 F.2d 1396, cert. denied, 419 U.S. 842 (1974) (addressing definition of "citizenship" under diversity subject-matter statute §1332). Thankfully, when it comes to federal statutes on choosing the right court in which to file suit, the federal courts define citizenship and residence as domicile—a consistency that only lawyers could truly appreciate.

Location of Events. Subsections (a)(2) and (b)(2) of §1391 provide for venue in a district where a "substantial part" of the events giving rise to the claim occurred or disputed property is located. May more than one district have venue under §1391(a)(2) or (b)(2)? In other words, can a *substantial part* of events or property be located in more than one district? Subsection (2)'s substantial-part test arose from the following helpful history. The prior statute based venue only on citizenship, not on where a substantial part of the events occurred or property was located. However, the prior statute's fallback provision was for the district "in which the claim arose." The "claim arose" language was similar to but not the same as the "substantial part" language of the current §1391(a)(2) and (b)(2). In Leroy v. Great Western United Corp., 443 U.S. 173 (1979), the Supreme Court interpreted restrictively the "claim arose" language of the prior statute to mean (ordinarily) the *one* district in which the weight or bulk of contacts had occurred. Congress clearly rejected the Supreme Court's restrictive reading in amending the prior statute to provide for the "substantial part" language of §1391(a)(2) and (b)(2). Substantial can certainly mean less than a majority. There may two or more districts in which a substantial part of the claim occurred or disputed property is located. More than one district may have original venue under §1391(a)(2) and (b)(2). *See* Bates v. C & S Adjusters, Inc., 980 F.2d 865 (2d Cir. 1992). Circuit courts have interpreted "substantial part" to mean any district where significant material events occurred, *see* Gulf Ins. Co. v. Glasbrenner, 417 F.3d 353, 357 (2d Cir. 2005), not necessarily where the *most* substantial event occurred, *see* First of Michigan Corp. v. Bramlet, 141 F.3d 260, 263 (6th Cir. 1998).

Fallback Provisions. Notice again the subsection (3) fallback provisions in both subsection (a) and (b) of §1391. When should the plaintiff be able to resort to the fallback provisions to justify choice of venue? The federal courts have construed the language of subsection (3) to mean what it says that the fallback provisions apply only when subsections (1) and (2), and any other venue provisions, do not provide for venue. *See* Daniel v. American Bd. of Emergency Medicine, 428 F.3d 408, 434 (2d Cir. 2005). An enterprising practitioner has no mischief to make with either §1391(a)(3) or (b)(3). Notice also that in subsection (a)(3) the fallback venue is any district in which the defendant "is subject to personal jurisdiction," whereas in subsection (b)(3) the fallback venue is any district in which the defendant "may be found... ." Is there any significance to this difference? Perhaps not, because there is personal (transient) jurisdiction whereever the plaintiff finds (serves) the defendant. At least one notable commentator attributes the difference between subsections (a)(3) and (b)(3) to drafting error. *See* 14D C. WRIGHT, A. MILLER & E. COOPER, FEDERAL PRACTICE AND PROCEDURE JURISPRUDENCE 3d §3802.1.

Corporations. Subsections (a) and (b) of §1391 appear to address venue only as to individuals and not as to corporations. How does §1391 treat corporations compared to individuals? By defining a corporation's residence as any forum in which the court would have personal jurisdiction over the corporation, subsection 1391(c) expands venue for corporations to the limits of personal jurisdiction. Why did Congress include the last clause of subsection (c) addressing the possibility of finding no district that has personal jurisdiction within a state that does have personal jurisdiction? Is it possible to have a state in which the corporation does sufficient business for minimum contacts establishing personal jurisdiction over the corporation, but the corporation so divides its contacts between districts in the state that no individual district would have personal jurisdiction for lack of sufficient contacts? You should now see the challenge that Congress and the state legislatures face in ensuring that venue provisions grant venue in at least some forum. Section 1391(d) grants venue in any United States district court for a case against an alien. Alien corporations face the same unlimited federal venue under §1391 as alien individuals. *See* Go-Video, Inc. v. Akai Electric Co., 885 F.2d 1406, 1410-1411 (9th Cir. 1989); O.S.C. Corp. v. Toshiba America, Inc., 491 F.2d 1064, 1068 (9th Cir. 1974). Is there any limitation, then, to where a plaintiff may sue an alien? Keep in mind that venue is just one consideration. A plaintiff can have proper venue for a case against a defendant without also having personal jurisdiction against the defendant in that district. *See* World-Wide Volkswagen v. Woodson, 444 U.S. 286 (1980). The plaintiff must choose a court having personal jurisdiction over the alien defendant.

Special Venue Statutes. Subsections (a) and (b) of §1391 each begin with the caution that they determine venue only "except as otherwise provided by law... ." This limitation means that the many special federal venue statutes take precedence over §1391(a) and (b) in determining venue if the special statutes so indicate. The removal statute 28 U.S.C. §1441(a) is an example in which the Supreme Court has held that its specific provisions as to which federal district court will have removal jurisdiction also controls venue. *See* Policci v. Cowles Magazines, Inc., 345 U.S. 663, 665-666 (1953); *see also* Lundahl v. Public Storage Mgmt., Inc., 62 Fed. Appx. 217, 218-219 (10th Cir. 2003). The special statute for intellectual-property (copyright and patent) cases, 28 U.S.C. §1400, is another example. *See* Goldberg v. Cameron, 482 F.Supp.2d 1136 (N.D. Cal.

2007) (only the specific provision, not the general, applies). Yet the general provision §1391(c)'s definition of where a corporation resides can provide the definition for a specific provision like the same intellectual-property provision. *See* Century Wrecker Corp. v. Vulcan Equipment Co., 733 F.Supp. 1170 (E.D. Tenn. 1989), affirmed, 923 F.2d 870 (Fed. Cir. 1990), cert. denied, 499 U.S. 962 (1991). If the special venue statute does not indicate its precedence over the general provisions §1391(a) and (b), then the Supreme Court has held (at least as to a prior version of the general venue statute) that the plaintiff may take resort to either the special or the general venue provision. Pure Oil v. Suarez, 384 U.S. 202 (1966). By contrast to the deferential §1391(a) and (b), the alien-venue provision in §1391(d) takes precedence over other special venue statutes. Brunette Machine Works, Ltd. v. Kockum Indus., Inc., 406 U.S. 706, 714 (1972).

Local-Action Doctrine. Traditionally, venue for actions involving real property was proper only in the state where the property was located. The courts came to know this venue rule as the "local-action doctrine." The federal courts will recognize the local-action doctrine in appropriate cases and entertain or not entertain the case depending on whether the real property is located within the district's state. *See* Van Beek v. Ninkov, 265 F.Supp.2d 1037, 1046 (N.D. Iowa 2003); Hallaba v. Worldcom Network Services, Inc., 196 F.R.D. 630, 650 (N.D. Okla. 2000). Congress acknowledged the local-action doctrine in 28 U.S.C. §1392 (reproduced above), although in doing so it referred to actions "of a local nature… ." If one reads §1392 in conjunction with §1391(a)(2) and (b)(2) providing for venue where a substantial part of disputed property is located, the import of §1392 (its acknowledgment of the local-action doctrine) becomes clearer. Was §1392 really necessary, when it is so seldom cited and §1391(a)(2) and (b)(2) already seem to cover venue in real-property cases? For a thorough discussion of the interesting history of the local-action doctrine, see Fisher v. Virginia Electric and Power Co., 243 F.Supp.2d 538 (E.D. Va. 2003).

Multiple Claims. So far, the discussion has assumed that if there is venue over the case, then there is venue over all claims within it. After all, §1391(a) and (b) authorize venue based on the location of defendants' residence or the substantial part of the events or disputed property—not on the nature of individual claims. Yet there is some authority that the plaintiff who pleads two or more claims in a single complaint must establish venue as to each of those claims. *See* Centerville ALF, Inc. v. Balanced Care Corp., 197 F.Supp.2d 1039, 1046 (S.D. Ohio 2002). Predictably, then, there is other authority recognizing a doctrine of pendent venue granting a court venue for claims over which it has supplemental (pendent) jurisdiction. *See* Travis v. Anthes Imperial Ltd., 473 F.2d 515, 528-529 (8th Cir. 1973); High River Ltd. Partnership v. Mylan Lab. Inc., 353 F.Supp.2d 487, 493 (M.D. Pa. 2005); *see also* Beattie v. United States, 756 F.2d 91, 101 (D.C. Cir. 1984), abrogated on other grounds, Smith v. United States, 507 U.S. 197 (1993). Some courts extend pendent venue to any claims supported by related facts, *see* Zenith Radio Corp. v. Matsushita Elec. Ind. Co., 402 F.Supp. 262 (E.D. Pa. 1975), or where judicial economy warrants it, *see* Seamon v. Upham, 563 F.Supp. 396, 399 (E.D. Tex. 1983). Other courts reject the doctrine of pendent venue entirely. McCaskey v. Continental Airlines, Inc., 133 F.Supp.2d 514, 525 (S.D. Tex. 2001). Again, given that §1391 identifies the location of defendants' residence or the substantial part of the events or disputed property as the basis for venue, is there any need for a pendent-venue doctrine?

Challenging Venue. Where venue is improper (not inconvenient but improper), then the means for challenging it is for the defendant to file a motion under FED. R. CIV. P. 12(b)(3) to dismiss for improper venue. Given the significance of the choice of courts to any procedures that follow, it should be no surprise that the timing of that motion, like motions challenging personal jurisdiction, is critical. Rule 12(g) and (h) require that the defendant make the motion as an initial response and not later, on penalty of waiving a venue challenge. A subsequent chapter provides a more detailed discussion of Rule 12 motions. Note, also, that if a party joins a party whose joinder makes venue improper, the district court must dismiss the joined party if the joined party makes that motion. *See* FED. R. CIV. P. 19(a)(3) ("If a joined party objects to venue and the joinder would make venue improper, the court must dismiss that party."). Dismissal of a party or case for improper venue is not a decision on the merits, meaning that it does not bar refiling of the action in a court that has proper venue. *See* FED. R. CIV. P. 41(b) ("a dismissal under this subdivision (b) [for involuntary dismissals] and any dismissal not under this rule—except one for lack of jurisdiction, improper venue, or failure to join a party under Rule 19—operates as an adjudication on the merits"). As is also true in the case of personal jurisdiction, the *Federal Rules of Civil Procedure* on venue simply give the parties means of carrying venue statutes into effect. According to FED. R. CIV. P. 82, the *Federal Rules* "do not extend or limit the jurisdiction of the district courts or the venue of actions in those courts." Consider the next section on how federal district courts may transfer jurisdiction as an alternative to dismissal and refiling, or even to simply hearing the case.

Practice

The lawyer checked in with the judge's secretary well before the crowded cattle-call motion docket began, hoping that opposing counsel would also so that the lawyer could start the long drive back to his office at a reasonable hour. Trouble was, the lawyer had not yet met opposing counsel in this distant county where opposing counsel had his office. Opposing counsel had pretty obviously filed the case here solely because it was her home turf, if the lawyer was right that venue was improper and inconvenient.

"All rise," the bailiff intoned as the judge entered precisely at 8:30 a.m. A good sign, the lawyer thought. A timely judge suggests an efficient motion docket. But then the minutes and hours wore on, without the secretary calling the lawyer's motion. Finally, just before noon, the secretary called the lawyer's motion.

The lawyer had hardly started the argument about how the case had no contacts with the county before the judge interrupted curtly, "Let me hear from opposing counsel," wearily sweeping the back of a hand once across the bench as if to literally brush the lawyer aside. Opposing counsel got maybe two sentences in before the judge looked at the lawyer who had made the motion for the first time and grunted a tired, "Motion granted." The judge then told the secretary to set the rest of the motions over to next week, to audible groans from the many waiting lawyers.

B. Transfer of Venue

Again, one might think that when venue is proper in a certain court, the plaintiff gets to choose it. Yet several federal statutes (representative in some respects of state statutes) grant the district courts authority to transfer a case to a different federal district court or different division within a federal district. The statutes offer various grounds for transfer. The first of those statutes, 28 U.S.C. §1404, authorizes transfer based on convenience to parties and witnesses. The criteria for determining convenience typically include not only the burden of travel to distant forums but also whether the court can compel attendance and related "interests of justice," as §1404(a). Appropriately, ties on convenience (where the transferor and putative transferee courts are equally convenient) go to the plaintiff who, after all, chose the court having original venue. *See* In re National Presto Indus., Inc., 347 F.3d 662, 664 (7th Cir. 2003), citing Gulf Oil Co. v. Gilbert, 330 U.S. 501 (1947). The next section on the doctrine of forum non conveniens further articulates the private and public interest involved in determining convenience. A second statute, 28 U.S.C. §1406, authorizes transfer when the plaintiff simply chose an improper venue (one not authorized by statute). A third statute, 28 U.S.C. §1631, authorizes transfer when the court has no personal jurisdiction. As you read each of these statutes, consider carefully what discretion the federal district courts retain to transfer or not transfer, and what other options they may have when, on any of the above grounds, the court determines that it should not hear the case that the plaintiff filed in that forum.

28 U.S.C. §1404. Change of venue.
(a) For the convenience of parties and witnesses, in the interest of justice, a district court may transfer any civil action to any other district or division where it might have been brought.
(b) Upon motion, consent or stipulation of all parties, any action, suit or proceeding of a civil nature or any motion or hearing thereof, may be transferred, in the discretion of the court, from the division in which pending to any other division in the same district. Transfer of proceedings in rem brought by or on behalf of the United States may be transferred under this section without the consent of the United States where all other parties request transfer.
(c) A district court may order any civil action to be tried at any place within the division in which it is pending.
...

28 U.S.C. §1406. Cure or waiver of defects.
(a) The district court of a district in which is filed a case laying venue in the wrong division or district shall dismiss, or if it be in the interest of justice, transfer such case to any district or division in which it could have been brought.
(b) Nothing in this chapter shall impair the jurisdiction of a district court of any matter involving a party who does not interpose timely and sufficient objection to the venue.
(c) As used in this section, the term "district court" includes the District Court of Guam, the District Court for the Northern Mariana Islands, and the District Court of the Virgin Islands, and the term "district" includes the territorial jurisdiction of each such court.

28 U.S.C. §1407. Multidistrict litigation.

(a) When civil actions involving one or more common questions of fact are pending in different districts, such actions may be transferred to any district for coordinated or consolidated pretrial proceedings. Such transfers shall be made by the judicial panel on multidistrict litigation authorized by this section upon its determination that transfers for such proceedings will be for the convenience of parties and witnesses and will promote the just and efficient conduct of such actions. Each action so transferred shall be remanded by the panel at or before the conclusion of such pretrial proceedings to the district from which it was transferred unless it shall have been previously terminated: *Provided, however*, That the panel may separate any claim, cross-claim, counter-claim, or third-party claim and remand any of such claims before the remainder of the action is remanded.

(b) Such coordinated or consolidated pretrial proceedings shall be conducted by a judge or judges to whom such actions are assigned by the judicial panel on multidistrict litigation. ...

...

28 U.S.C. §1631. Transfer to cure want of jurisdiction.

Whenever a civil action is filed in a court as defined in section 610 of this title or an appeal, including a petition for review of administrative action, is noticed for or filed with such a court and that court finds that there is a want of jurisdiction, the court shall, if it is in the interest of justice, transfer such action or appeal to any other such court in which the action or appeal could have been brought at the time it was filed or noticed, and the action or appeal shall proceed as if it had been filed in or noticed for the court to which it is transferred on the date upon which it was actually filed in or noticed for the court from which it is transferred.

INQUIRY

Discretion. Defendants often move to dismiss or for transfer in the alternative. What discretion do the above venue statutes permit? None of the above federal venue statutes mandate transfer. They each only permit transfer. So what are the court's options? The district court considering a motion for transfer under §§1404, 1406, or 1631 may dismiss the case rather than transfer it. The federal district court has greater discretion whether to transfer under §1404 than it has in a decision whether to dismiss. *See* Norwood v. Kirkpatrick, 349 U.S. 29 (1955). Indeed, a district court may transfer a case even when it does not have personal jurisdiction over the defendant. *See* Goldlawr, Inc. v. Heiman, 369 U.S. 463, 466 (1962). The moving defendant and the ruling district court both recognize that dismissal may result in the plaintiff refiling in the district to which the defendant sought transfer. Interestingly, plaintiffs may also move for transfer under §1404. *See* Ferens v. John Deere Co, 494 U.S. 516 (1990). Given that the plaintiff chooses the original forum, when would a plaintiff seek transfer?

Multi-District Litigation. The final statute, 28 U.S.C. §1407, authorizes transfer by a judicial panel on multi-district litigation, where the panel concludes that convenience and efficiency compel consolidation of cases in different districts for pretrial procedures. Congress designed §1407 for cases arising out of mass torts such as air crash, defective drug, and asbestos litigation. By its own terms, §1407 applies only to pretrial procedures, meaning that a case transferred under §1407 returns to its original forum for trial. *See* Amchem Products v. Windsor, 521 U.S. 591 (1997); Lexecon v. Milberg Weiss, 523 U.S. 26 (1998). Do you see any way in which a federal district court to which a multi-district panel transferred many related multi-district cases could hold onto those cases for trial? In *Lexecon v. Milberg Weiss* (just cited), the Supreme Court prohibited what was until that case a common practice, for a court that had received a case under §1407 multi-district transfer to then transfer that case *to itself* under §1404 in order to try the case along with the rest of its multi-district cases. Was that process (as the *Lexecon v. Milberg Weiss* case held) an unauthorized manipulation of §1407 in a way that Congress had not intended? Congress has not amended §1407 to re-authorize the self-transfer practice that the Supreme Court prohibited in *Lexecon v. Milberg Weiss*.

Limits on Discretion. Does a federal district court have discretion to transfer a case under §1404(a) to a court where the parties want to go but cannot get there without the help of the court? The Supreme Court addressed that situation in Hoffman v. Blaski, 363 U.S. 335 (1960), where a defendant moved for transfer of venue to a court that did not have personal jurisdiction over the defendant. The plaintiff, as it turned out, would have consented to transfer to that court, but the Supreme Court ruled that transfer was not permissible. Can you tell why? The Supreme Court construed §1404(a)'s "where it might have been brought" language to mean that the transferee court must have personal jurisdiction over the case as if the plaintiff had filed it there originally. Given that a defendant may waive a challenge to personal jurisdiction, did the Supreme Court reach the right result in *Hoffman v. Blaski*? Keep in mind that transfer of venue involves more than party convenience. Courts have their own interests. In enacting §1404, Congress may not have intended to expand the number of possible forums in which parties could litigate. What, then, should a district court do when the case involves a contract in which the parties have agreed to a forum-selection clause? Must the court follow the clause? In Stewart Org., Inc. v. Ricoh Corp., 487 U.S. 22 (1988), the Supreme Court held that forum-selection clauses are only a significant but not controlling factor in the district court's decision whether to grant transfer.

Forum Law. When a federal district court orders transfer of venue under §1404, what law should the other court apply, the law of the transferor or transferee forum? The next chapter addresses what law federal district courts apply in diversity cases that the parties could have litigated in state court. As you will see in the next chapter, generally, federal district courts will apply state substantive law in diversity cases. There are often questions, though, as to which state's law to apply. The choice of that law (another topic covered elsewhere) can depend in part on where the parties litigate the case. *See, e.g.,* Klaxon Co. v. Stentor Electric Mfg. Co., 313 U.S. 487 (1941) (federal district courts apply the choice-of-law rules of their forum state). Because the forum can affect the choice of law, transfer of venue can also affect choice of law. A defendant could get better law by obtaining transfer of venue, increasing the prospects for forum shopping. In Van Dusen v. Barrack, 376 U.S. 612 (1964), the Supreme Court held that a federal district court receiving a case on transfer under §1404 must apply the law that the federal district court granting transfer would have applied. Federal circuits and districts can also differ in their interpretation of federal law. Unlike in diversity-jurisdiction cases, when a federal district court transfers a federal-question case from its own to another circuit or district that interprets federal law differently, the transferor court's forum law does not follow the case. The district courts apply their own circuit's and district's interpretation of federal law, not the interpretation in the transferor district. *See* In re Korean Air Lines Disaster of Sept. 1, 1983, 829 F.2d 1171 (D.C. Cir. 1987); *cf.* In re Dow Co. "Sarabond" Products Liability Litigation, 666 F.Supp. 1466, 1468 (D. Colo. 1987) (applying transferor district's law in multi-district litigation in which case will return to transferor district for trial).

State-Court Transfers. State courts have similar state statutory or court-rule authority to transfer venue to courts of other counties within the same state (as well as to dismiss in favor of the plaintiff refiling in another state). Compare the court rules on transfer for the two states whose venue statutes the section above reproduces. New York's single court rule for change of venue is exceedingly simple. By contrast, Michigan has significantly more detailed court rules on transfer of venue addressing (1) the form and timing of venue motions generally, (2) the grounds, form, and handling of motions to transfer venue when venue is proper, and (3) the grounds, form, and handling of motions to transfer venue when venue is improper. As you read and compare the rules, consider whether the additional detail in the Michigan rules is necessary and helpful. Under which set of rules would you prefer to litigate the venue question? How would your answer change depending on which party (moving or responding) you represented?

N.Y. Court Rules §212.9. Venue.
(a) Motions for a Change of Venue. Motions for a change of venue shall be heard in the division of the court in which the action was instituted. An order of transfer shall direct the disposition of the papers then on file.

Mich. Court Rule 2.221 MOTION FOR CHANGE OF VENUE.
(A) Time to File. A motion for change of venue must be filed before or at the time the defendant files an answer.
(B) Late Motion. Untimeliness is not a ground for denial of a motion filed after the answer if the court is satisfied that the facts on which the motion is based were not and could not with reasonable diligence have been known to the moving party more than 14 days before the motion was filed.
(C) Waiver. An objection to venue is waived if it is not raised within the time limits imposed by this rule.

Mich. Court Rule 2.222 CHANGE OF VENUE; VENUE PROPER.
(A) Grounds. The court may order a change of venue of a civil action, or of an appeal from an order or decision of a state board, commission, or agency authorized to promulgate rules or regulations, for the convenience of parties and witnesses or when an impartial trial cannot be had where the action is pending. In the case of appellate review of administrative proceedings, venue may also be changed for the convenience of the attorneys.
(B) Motion Required. If the venue of the action is proper, the court may not change the venue on its own initiative, but may do so only on motion of a party.
(C) Multiple Claims. If multiple claims are joined in an action, and the venue of one or more of them would have been improper if the claims had been brought in separate actions, the defendant may move to separate the claims and

to transfer those as to which venue would have been improper. The court has discretion to
(1) order the transfer of all claims,
(2) order the separation and transfer moved for, or
(3) retain the entire action for trial.
(D) Filing and Jury Fees After Change of Venue.
(1) At or before the time the order changing venue is entered, the party that moved for change of venue shall tender a negotiable instrument in the amount of the applicable filing fee, payable to the court to which the case is to be transferred. The transferring court shall send the negotiable instrument with the case documents to the transferee court.
(2) If the jury fee has been paid, the clerk of the transferring court shall forward it to the clerk of the court to which the action is transferred.
(E) In tort actions filed between October 1, 1986, and March 28, 1996, if venue is changed because of hardship or inconvenience, the action may be transferred only to the county in which the moving party resides.

MICH. COURT RULE 2.223 CHANGE OF VENUE; VENUE IMPROPER.
(A) Motion; Court's Own Initiative. If the venue of a civil action is improper, the court
(1) shall order a change of venue on timely motion of a defendant, or
(2) may order a change of venue on its own initiative with notice to the parties and opportunity for them to be heard on the venue question.
If venue is changed because the action was brought where venue was not proper, the action may be transferred only to a county in which venue would have been proper.
(B) Costs; Fees.
(1) The court shall order the change at the plaintiff's cost, which shall include the statutory filing fee applicable to the court to which the action is transferred, and which may include reasonable compensation for the defendant's expense, including reasonable attorney fees, in attending in the wrong court.
(2) After transfer, no further proceedings may be had in the action until the costs and expenses allowed under this rule have been paid. If they are not paid within 56 days from the date of the order changing venue, the action must be dismissed by the court to which it was transferred.
(3) If the jury fee has been paid, the clerk of the transferring court shall forward it to the clerk of the court to which the action is transferred.
(4) MCL 600.1653 applies to tort actions filed on or after October 1, 1986.

Skills

A motion for change of venue is ordinarily a relatively simple court paper for a lawyer to draft. As with any court paper, the motion will begin with a caption that includes the court, case number, judge's name, and parties' names and alignment. The caption usually includes the names, addresses, and other contact information for all attorneys who have appeared in the case. The motion will then have its title. The text begins with a statement that the party is moving under a certain rule or statute, followed by numbered paragraphs stating the motion's grounds. The motion ends with a paragraph requesting the specific relief, followed by the lawyer's signature block, a date, and likely a certificate of service. Briefs routinely accompany motions. As is true with most motions, the harder part of drafting a motion for change of venue is developing and documenting the supporting facts. The challenge is not locating and articulating the law but justifying a certain outcome on its application. Examine a sample motion for change of venue to see if you can identify the above components and to judge how well the lawyer made the argument.

C. Forum Non Conveniens

The above sections address (1) the state and federal statutes that authorize original venue and then (2) the statutes and court rules that authorize a case's transfer from one venue to another. What, though, when the court has a case in which original venue is technically proper according to the authorizing statutes but there seem overriding reasons for the court not to entertain it? Is the court (and are the defendants) stuck with it? The common-law doctrine of forum non conveniens addresses cases the court should not hear, because of party or witness inconvenience or judicial efficiency, even though there is statutory authority for original venue. The doctrine of forum non conveniens gives the court the legal grounds to dismiss otherwise properly filed actions. It is indeed a doctrine of convenience, and not just for parties and witnesses but also for the courts in maintaining their dockets. Yet here, convenience means more than mere ease. Litigation is never easy. More fundamentally, the doctrine of forum non conveniens enables courts the liberty of refusing to extend their power where to do so would offend the innately local interests of justice. The doctrine of forum non conveniens confirms what might seem surprising to the lay person but experienced lawyers know well, that courts have legitimate ways to avoid asserting their power where doing so might ultimately reduce it. Judgments and orders are primarily self-executing. There are boundaries beyond which a court should not go in ruling, in the event that its rulings carry so little connection with the locale of the dispute that there is inadequate respect for the power of its judgment. Identify in the following seminal case these private and public interests that form the rationale for the doctrine of forum non conveniens.

Piper Aircraft Co. v. Reyno,

United States Supreme Court
454 U.S. 235 (1981)

Justice MARSHALL delivered the opinion of the Court.

These cases arise out of an air crash that took place in Scotland. Respondent, acting as representative of the estates of several Scottish citizens killed in the accident, brought wrongful-death actions against petitioners that were ultimately transferred to the United States District Court for the Middle District of Pennsylvania. Petitioners moved to dismiss on the ground of *forum non conveniens.* After noting that an alternative forum existed in Scotland, the District Court granted their motions. [C] The United States Court of Appeals for the Third Circuit reversed. [C] The Court of Appeals based its decision, at least in part, on the ground that dismissal is automatically barred where the law of the alternative forum is less favorable to the plaintiff than the law of the forum chosen by the plaintiff. Because we conclude that the possibility of an unfavorable change in law should not, by itself, bar dismissal, and because we conclude that the District Court did not otherwise abuse its discretion, we reverse.

I

A

In July 1976, a small commercial aircraft crashed in the Scottish highlands during the course of a charter flight from Blackpool to Perth. The pilot and five passengers were killed instantly. The decedents were all Scottish subjects and residents, as are their heirs and next of kin. There were no eyewitnesses to the accident. At the time of the crash the plane was subject to Scottish air traffic control.

The aircraft, a twin-engine Piper Aztec, was manufactured in Pennsylvania by petitioner Piper Aircraft Co. (Piper). The propellers were manufactured in Ohio by petitioner Hartzell Propeller, Inc. (Hartzell). At the time of the crash the aircraft was registered in Great Britain and was owned and maintained by Air Navigation and Trading Co., Ltd. (Air Navigation). It was operated by McDonald Aviation, Ltd. (McDonald), a Scottish air taxi service. Both Air Navigation and McDonald were organized in the United Kingdom. The wreckage of the plane is now in a hangar in Farnsborough, England.

The British Department of Trade investigated the accident shortly after it occurred[... and] suggested that mechanical failure in the plane or the propeller was responsible. At Hartzell's request, this report was reviewed by a three-member Review Board, which ... found no evidence of defective equipment and indicated that pilot error may have contributed to the accident. The pilot, who had obtained his commercial pilot's license only three months earlier, was flying over high ground at an altitude considerably lower than the minimum height required by his company's operations manual.

In July 1977, a California probate court appointed respondent Gaynell Reyno administratrix of the estates of the five passengers. Reyno is not related to and does not know any of the decedents or their survivors; she was a legal secretary to the attorney who filed this lawsuit. Several days after her appointment, Reyno commenced separate wrongful-death actions against Piper and Hartzell in the Superior Court of California, claiming negligence and strict liability.[fn] Air Navigation, McDonald, and the estate of the pilot are not parties to this litigation. ... Reyno candidly admits that the action against Piper and Hartzell was filed in the United States because its laws regarding liability, capacity to sue, and damages are more favorable to her position than are those of Scotland. Scottish law does not recognize strict liability in tort. Moreover, it permits wrongful-death actions only when brought by a decedent's relatives[who] may sue only for "loss of support and society."[fn]

On petitioners' motion, the suit was removed to the United States District Court for the Central District of California. Piper then moved for transfer to the United States District Court for the Middle District of Pennsylvania, pursuant to 28 U.S.C. §1404(a).[fn] Hartzell moved to dismiss for lack of personal jurisdiction, or in the alternative, to transfer.[fn] ... [T]he District Court quashed service on Hartzell and transferred the case to the Middle District of Pennsylvania. Respondent then properly served process on Hartzell.

B

... [A]fter the suit had been transferred, both Hartzell and Piper moved to dismiss the action on the ground of *forum non conveniens.* The District Court granted these motions... . It relied on the balancing test set forth by this Court in Gulf Oil Corp. v. Gilbert, 330 U.S. 501[] (1947), and its companion case, Koster

v. Lumbermens Mut. Cas. Co., 330 U.S. 518[] (1947). In those decisions, the Court stated that a plaintiff's choice of forum should rarely be disturbed. However, when an alternative forum has jurisdiction to hear the case, and when trial in the chosen forum would "establish ... oppressiveness and vexation to a defendant ... out of all proportion to plaintiff's convenience," or when the "chosen forum [is] inappropriate because of considerations affecting the court's own administrative and legal problems," the court may, in the exercise of its sound discretion, dismiss the case. Koster, supra, at 524[]. To guide trial court discretion, the Court provided a list of "private interest factors" affecting the convenience of the litigants, and a list of "public interest factors" affecting the convenience of the forum. Gilbert, supra, 330 U.S. at 508-509[].[FN6. The factors pertaining to the private interests of the litigants included the "relative ease of access to sources of proof; availability of compulsory process for attendance of unwilling, and the cost of obtaining attendance of willing, witnesses; possibility of view of premises, if view would be appropriate to the action; and all other practical problems that make trial of a case easy, expeditious and inexpensive." Gilbert, 330 U.S., at 508[]. The public factors bearing on the question included the administrative difficulties flowing from court congestion; the "local interest in having localized controversies decided at home"; the interest in having the trial of a diversity case in a forum that is at home with the law that must govern the action; the avoidance of unnecessary problems in conflict of laws, or in the application of foreign law; and the unfairness of burdening citizens in an unrelated forum with jury duty. *Id.*, at 509[].]

C

On appeal, the United States Court of Appeals for the Third Circuit reversed and remanded for trial. The decision to reverse appears to be based on two alternative grounds. First, the Court held that the District Court abused its discretion in conducting the *Gilbert* analysis. Second, the Court held that dismissal is never appropriate where the law of the alternative forum is less favorable to the plaintiff. ...

II

The Court of Appeals erred in holding that plaintiffs may defeat a motion to dismiss on the ground of *forum non conveniens* merely by showing that the substantive law that would be applied in the alternative forum is less favorable to the plaintiffs than that of the present forum. The possibility of a change in substantive law should ordinarily not be given conclusive or even substantial weight in the *forum non conveniens* inquiry.

We expressly rejected the position adopted by the Court of Appeals in our decision in Canada Malting Co. v. Paterson Steamships, Ltd., 285 U.S. 413 (1932). ...

The Court of Appeals' decision is inconsistent with this Court's earlier *forum non conveniens* decisions in another respect. Those decisions have repeatedly emphasized the need to retain flexibility. ...

In fact, if conclusive or substantial weight were given to the possibility of a change in law, the *forum non conveniens* doctrine would become virtually useless. Jurisdiction and venue requirements are often easily satisfied. As a result, many plaintiffs are able to choose from among several forums. Ordinarily, these plaintiffs will select that forum whose choice-of-law rules are most advantageous. Thus, if the possibility of an unfavorable change in substantive law is given substantial weight in the *forum non conveniens* inquiry, dismissal would rarely be proper. ...

Upholding the decision of the Court of Appeals would result in other practical problems. At least where the foreign plaintiff named an American manufacturer as defendant,[fn] a court could not dismiss the case on grounds of *forum non conveniens* where dismissal might lead to an unfavorable change in law. The American courts, which are already extremely attractive to foreign plaintiffs,[fn18., noting that all but 6 of the 50 American States offer strict liability] would become even more attractive. The flow of litigation into the United States would increase and further congest already crowded courts.[fn] ...

The Court of Appeals based its decision, at least in part, on an analogy between dismissals on grounds of *forum non conveniens* and transfers between federal courts pursuant to §1404(a). ... However, §1404(a) transfers are different than dismissals on the ground of *forum non conveniens*.

Congress enacted §1404(a) to permit change of venue between federal courts. Although the statute was drafted in accordance with the doctrine of *forum non conveniens*, [c], it was intended to be a revision rather than a codification of the common law. Norwood v. Kirkpatrick, 349 U.S. 29[] (1955). District courts were given more discretion to transfer under §1404(a) than they had to dismiss on grounds of *forum non conveniens*. *Id.*, at 31-32[]. ...

We do not hold that the possibility of an unfavorable change in law should *never* be a relevant consideration in a *forum non conveniens* inquiry. Of course, if the remedy provided by the alternative forum is so clearly inadequate or unsatisfactory that it is no remedy at all, the unfavorable change in law may be given substantial weight; the district court may conclude that dismissal would not be in the interests of justice.[fn] In these cases, however, the remedies that would be provided by the Scottish courts do not fall within this category. Although the relatives of the decedents may not be able to rely on a strict liability theory, and although their potential damages award may be smaller, there is no danger that they will be deprived of any remedy or treated unfairly.

III

The Court of Appeals also erred in rejecting the District Court's *Gilbert* analysis. ...

A

The District Court acknowledged that there is ordinarily a strong presumption in favor of the plaintiff's choice of forum, which may be overcome only when the private and public interest factors clearly point towards trial in the alternative forum. It held, however, that the presumption applies with less force when the plaintiff or real parties in interest are foreign.

The District Court's distinction between resident or citizen plaintiffs and foreign plaintiffs is fully justified. ... [A] plaintiff's choice of forum is entitled to greater deference when the plaintiff has chosen the home forum. [C][fn] When the home forum has been chosen, it is reasonable to assume that this choice is convenient. When the plaintiff is foreign, however, this assumption is much less reasonable. Because the central purpose of any *forum non conveniens* inquiry is to ensure that the trial is convenient, a foreign plaintiff's choice deserves less deference.[fn] ...

B

The *forum non conveniens* determination is committed to the sound discretion of the trial court. It may be reversed only when there has been a clear abuse of discretion; where the court has considered all relevant public and private interest factors, and where its balancing of these factors is reasonable, its decision deserves substantial deference. [Cc] …

(1)

In analyzing the private interest factors, the District Court stated that the connections with Scotland are "overwhelming." [C] This characterization may be somewhat exaggerated. Particularly with respect to the question of relative ease of access to sources of proof, the private interests point in both directions. As respondent emphasizes, records concerning the design, manufacture, and testing of the propeller and plane are located in the United States. She would have greater access to sources of proof relevant to her strict liability and negligence theories if trial were held here.[fn] However, the District Court did not act unreasonably in concluding that fewer evidentiary problems would be posed if the trial were held in Scotland. A large proportion of the relevant evidence is located in Great Britain. …

The District Court correctly concluded that the problems posed by the inability to implead potential third-party defendants clearly supported holding the trial in Scotland. Joinder of the pilot's estate, Air Navigation, and McDonald is crucial to the presentation of petitioners' defense. If Piper and Hartzell can show that the accident was caused not by a design defect, but rather by the negligence of the pilot, the plane's owners, or the charter company, they will be relieved of all liability. It is true, of course, that if Hartzell and Piper were found liable after a trial in the United States, they could institute an action for indemnity or contribution against these parties in Scotland. It would be far more convenient, however, to resolve all claims in one trial. …

(2)

The District Court's review of the factors relating to the public interest was also reasonable. On the basis of its choice-of-law analysis, it concluded that if the case were tried in the Middle District of Pennsylvania, Pennsylvania law would apply to Piper and Scottish law to Hartzell. It stated that a trial involving two sets of laws would be confusing to the jury. It also noted its own lack of familiarity with Scottish law. Consideration of these problems was clearly appropriate under *Gilbert*; in that case we explicitly held that the need to apply foreign law pointed towards dismissal.[fn] …

Scotland has a very strong interest in this litigation. The accident occurred in its airspace. All of the decedents were Scottish. Apart from Piper and Hartzell, all potential plaintiffs and defendants are either Scottish or English. As we stated in *Gilbert*, there is "a local interest in having localized controversies decided at home." 330 U.S. at 509[]. … The American interest in this accident is simply not sufficient to justify the enormous commitment of judicial time and resources that would inevitably be required if the case were to be tried here.

IV

The Court of Appeals erred in holding that the possibility of an unfavorable change in law bars dismissal on the ground of *forum non conveniens*. It also erred in rejecting the District Court's *Gilbert* analysis. The District Court properly decided that the presumption in favor of the respondent's forum choice applied with less than maximum force because the real parties in interest are foreign. It did not act unreasonably in deciding that the private interests pointed towards trial in Scotland. Nor did it act unreasonably in deciding that the public interests favored trial in Scotland. Thus, the judgment of the Court of Appeals is

Reversed.

Justice POWELL took no part in the decision of these cases.

Justice O'CONNOR took no part in the consideration or decision of these cases.

Justice WHITE[concurred in part and dissented in part. Justice STEVENS also dissented, with Justice BRENNAN joining that dissent.]

INQUIRY

Jurisdiction. There was no dispute in the above *Piper Aircraft v. Reyno* case that the federal district court had personal jurisdiction over all parties. Often, though, disputes over personal jurisdiction coincide with disputes over venue. Can you see why? When a party moves to dismiss based on both lack of personal jurisdiction and forum non conveniens, on which basis should the court rule first? One might think that personal jurisdiction would come first because the court has no power over the party as to whom personal jurisdiction is absent. One might also think that a court having no subject-matter jurisdiction over a case would be especially reticent to entertain a motion regarding venue. Yet in Sinochem Intl. Co. v. Malaysia Intl. Shipping Corp., 549 U.S. 422 (2007), the Supreme Court held that federal district courts may dismiss based on forum non conveniens before deciding whether they have either personal or subject-matter jurisdiction. The Supreme Court relied on American Dredging Co. v. Miller, 510 U.S. 443 (1994), in which the Court had held that forum non conveniens dismissals are not decisions on the merits. Parties remain free to refile in the more convenient jurisdiction. Recall Goldlawr, Inc. v. Heiman, 369 U.S. 463, 466 (1962) (cited above), in which the Supreme Court held that a district court may transfer a case under §1406 even when it does not have personal jurisdiction over the defendant.

Inconvenient Convenience. Consider this anomaly in *Piper Aircraft v. Reyno.* The defendant Piper Aircraft removed the case from California state court to federal district court in California and then obtained transfer from the California federal district court to a Pennsylvania federal district court under 28 U.S.C. §1404. Section 1404 involves transfer for the convenience of the parties. Piper Aircraft's reliance on §1404 to obtain transfer from California to Pennsylvania means that Piper must have convinced the California district court that the Pennsylvania district court was the more convenient. Should Piper Aircraft then have succeeded in convincing the Pennsylvania court and Supreme Court that Pennsylvania was yet so inconvenient as to warrant dismissal? There must be relative levels of convenience, enabling a federal district court to be convenient enough to receive transfer but not sufficiently convenient to overcome a forum non conveniens challenge by the same party who initially claimed that the federal district was the more convenient of two federal district court forums. To put it another way, forum non conveniens may be a more powerful doctrine than the transfer convenience recognized under §1404.

Justice. When they have a choice, why do litigants prefer a forum in the United States? *See* Smith Kline & French Labs. Ltd. v. Bloch, [1983] 2 All E.R. 72 (Eng. C.A. 1982) ("As a moth is drawn to the light, so is a litigant drawn to the United States.") (opinion by Lord Denning). The reasons are both legal and practical. As *Piper Aircraft v. Reyno* reflects, American substantive law (in that case, strict products liability law) may simply be more generous to the party choosing the forum. *Piper Aircraft* held that a federal district court should not consider the favorability of law unless the law in the other forum is "so clearly inadequate or unsatisfactory that it is no remedy at all... ." What criteria determine a law's adequacy? *Compare* Nemariam v. Federal Democratic Republic of Ethiopia, 315 F.3d 390 (D.C. Cir.), cert. denied, 540 U.S. 877 (2003) (damages offset in international claims commission inadequate under *Piper Aircraft* when compared to full relief in federal district court), *with* Gonzales v. Chrysler Corp., 301 F.3d 377 (5th Cir. 2002) (Mexican law capping damages at about $2,500 for loss of a child's life is adequate under *Piper Aircraft* standard) (rejecting economic considerations in determining law's adequacy). American law may also be more highly developed than the law of the more convenient forum, no matter which party it favors. Now reconsider Van Dusen v. Barrack, 376 U.S. 612 (1964), discussed in the previous section on transfer of venue, and holding that the transferee federal district court must apply the law that the transferor federal district court would have applied. What do you think the prospects are that a court hearing a case that the plaintiff re-filed after a forum non conveniens dismissal in another forum would apply the law of that other forum? The point is that defendants who want better law (and have the choice-of-law doctrine for it) will have to obtain a forum non conveniens dismissal, not §1404 transfer.

Access. The practical reasons to seek a United States forum can be just as substantial as the legal reasons. Even with its challenges around funding and crowded dockets, the civil justice system in the United States still has more resources, meaning more courts, courthouses, judges, judicial staff, and lawyers, than many other systems. *See* In re Union Carbide Gas Plant Disaster, 809 F.2d 195 (2d Cir.) (plaintiffs oppose dismissal based on inability of Indian courts to handle mass tort claims), cert. denied, 484 U.S. 871 (1987). Some courts considering forum non conveniens motions have conditioned dismissal on the defendant accept personal service or even waiving defenses in the forum in which the plaintiff would have to refile after dismissal. *See, e.g., id.*; *see also* Pollux Holding Ltd. v. Chase Manhattan Bank, 329 F.3d 64 (2d Cir. 2003), cert. denied, 540 U.S. 1149 (2004). Enforcement of judgments may be another reason for parties to file in United States courts, particularly when the defendant has United States assets. While courts in other nations are likely to enforce a United States judgment because of the integrity of United States law and civil procedure, there may be some question whether a United States court will enforce a judgment taken in another country whose procedures do not look like due process.

Summary. In sum, venue determines the choice of courts based on convenience and efficiency, not on constitutional standards having to do with personal and subject-matter jurisdiction. State and federal statutes control original venue in state and federal courts, respectively. A plaintiff must file the case in a court that has venue under one of those statutes. Statutes and court rules permit defendants to seek transfer of venue to more convenient and efficient forums, so long as defendants challenge venue in the first response. The doctrine of forum non conveniens may permit a defendant to obtain dismissal of an action even where a statute provides for original venue, and even where dismissal may result in less favorable law or other disadvantage to or hardship on the plaintiff, if the interests of justice so require. In making that determination, courts will consider both private interests such as convenience to parties and witnesses and availability of court processes, and public interests such as the efficiency of the court and the interest of the locale in deciding the disputed claims.

Career

Do you prefer to work alone or in teams? The law setting in which you work (whether court or other government agency, corporate counsel or other business setting, or a law firm) can determine whether you will work primarily alone or with others. So can the size of the law firm in which you work, if you choose to work in a firm. The type of civil litigation you do can also affect whether you work alone or with others. Solo and small-firm practices involving less-complex cases tend to be situations in which lawyers work alone. Larger firms handling more-complex cases with greater numbers of parties tend to be places where lawyers work in teams. Working independently and alone energizes some lawyers. Others feel better about their work when they interact frequently with and depend more on others who share in the work. As you study civil procedure, consider what your preference might be. Knowing your preference is a good way to explore a law career.

CHAPTER VI

GOVERNING LAW

OBJECTIVE: That you be able to determine whether state or federal law governs issues arising in a case filed in federal court under its diversity jurisdiction.

Case Study: Corporate counsel has just assigned you the defense of a national corporation in a contract dispute filed in federal court based on diversity-of-citizenship jurisdiction. The contract has both an arbitration clause and a forum-selection clause. The law of the forum state would recognize the arbitration clause but not the forum-selection clause. Federal law would do the opposite, recognizing the forum-selection clause but not the arbitration clause. Corporate counsel wants your opinion on which law governs, state or federal, in order to make strategic judgments about whether to seek a change of venue and arbitrate.

<u>*Federal Rules of Civil Procedure* this chapter reproduces and addresses</u>:
FED. R. CIV. P. 5.1. Constl. Challenge to Statute—Notice, Certific., and Intervention.
FED. R. CIV. P. 44.1. Determining Foreign Law.

This chapter addresses what law the court must apply. The chapter on personal jurisdiction explored limits on the reach of a court's authority, the chapter on notice and opportunity for hearing the fairness of adjudication, and the chapter on subject-matter jurisdiction the circumscribed nature of delegated authority. This chapter addresses how courts share delegated authority. Once you determine a court's reach, fairness, and competence within its delegation, there may still be questions of what law it should apply. The questions arise in two ways, either (1) between the laws of one state and another state or (2) between state and federal law. Traditionally, lawyers identify the question of choosing which state's law applies as *conflicts of law*, in which your law school may have a separate course. Just because the plaintiff files a case in a state does not mean that state's law should apply. Perhaps the case involves parties, events, and interests in a different state such that the other state's law should govern. This chapter concludes with a brief treatment of conflicts of law (the state-versus-state governing-law question).

The other question of the choice between state and federal law arises in federal-court cases involving diversity jurisdiction. If a case involves a claim made under a federal statute, then that federal law will govern whether the parties try the case in state or federal court. When the parties file a state-law case such as a tort or contract claim in federal court based on diversity jurisdiction, one might think that state law should control, as it generally does. The problem involves drawing the line between state law and federal procedure. As courts constituted and governed by federal law, federal courts must apply their own procedures, not state procedures, when they decide diversity cases under state law. Given the impact of procedure on substance and substance on procedure, the Supreme Court has struggled to articulate standards by which the federal courts can respect that line—the subject the first part of this chapter addresses. That struggle reaches all the way back over 200 years to the Judiciary Act of 1789, when Congress created diversity jurisdiction, simultaneously providing in what we know as the Rules of Decision Act that state law would govern:

28 U.S.C. §1652. State laws as rules of decision.

The laws of the several states, except where the Constitution or Acts of Congress otherwise require or provide, shall be regarded as rules of decisions in civil actions in the courts of the United States, in cases where they apply.

Appreciate this chapter's significance. Those who interact in law firms with lawyers and paralegals or other support staff can tell the difference. Support-staff members know the forms and systems of the law, while lawyers know the source and nature of its authority. A lawyer is not different from a paralegal or an unrepresented person because of the lawyer's knowledge of the content of the law. Paralegals and laypersons can readily learn the law's content. Rather, the power of a lawyer lies in the lawyer's knowledge of the source and nature of law's will. Lawyers look for authority, knowing that clients and community depend on authority in the way that it joins and coordinates us. If you join a law firm with experienced staff support, then you may find that your secretary knows more than you do about what papers you must prepare and file where to pursue a civil case. Experienced support-staff members may even know the judges better than the new lawyer. Yet there will be no question that you, and not the secretary, are the lawyer. The substantive difference has to do with your knowledge of the source and nature of the law. A layperson may regard the judge as the authority, while the lawyer knows that judges only execute and enforce authority that lies elsewhere. No subject does more to instill that numinous lawyer's skill and mark out that difference than the *Erie* doctrine and related subjects this chapter covers. The impractical but invaluable and even profound doctrines in this chapter are what make a lawyer. Every law subject has its talisman. In Civil Procedure, that talisman is *Erie*, a fitting name for a doctrine whose mysteries point the student to the source and nature of divided authority.

A. State Law in Federal Court

When Congress constituted the federal trial courts with the Judiciary Act of 1789 and simultaneously provided (in the currently codified §1652) that "the laws of the several states" would govern in federal-court civil actions "in cases where they apply," probably few anticipated the difficulty the Supreme Court would face in articulating how the federal trial courts should discern that line. For you to understand that law as it now exists, you must first appreciate its history.

Initially, the Supreme Court regarded the question of where state law would apply in federal court as solely an issue of statutory construction. To what "laws of the several states" had Congress meant to refer, and in which "civil actions" do "they apply"? These questions looked to the Supreme Court in the following *Swift v. Tyson* case to be questions of statutory construction, not of constitutional dimension. *Swift's* answer, which stood for nearly 100 years until *Erie Railroad Co. v. Tompkins*, was simply that by "laws of the several states," Congress had meant state statutes, not state-court decisions interpreting those statutes. *Swift v. Tyson* did acknowledge the authority of state-judge-made law on peculiarly local matters and encouraged respect for state-court decisions. Yet under *Swift v. Tyson*, while federal courts would decide diversity cases under state statutes, they would interpret those statutes and decide other matters not controlled by state statute under federal common law. As you read *Swift v. Tyson*, query why the Supreme Court might have chosen to abandon its federal common law 100 years later in *Erie*.

Swift v. Tyson,

United States Supreme Court
41 U.S. (16 Pet.) 1 (1842)

STORY, Justice, delivered the opinion of the court.

This cause comes before us from the circuit court of the southern district of New York, upon a certificate of division of the judges of that court. The action was brought by the plaintiff, Swift, as indorsee, against the defendant, Tyson, as acceptor, upon a bill of exchange [that Tyson signed to buy certain lands in Maine from others who, it turned out, had misrepresented that they owned the lands that they sold to Tyson. Tyson refused to honor the bill of exchange when demanded by the assignee Swift]… .

At the trial [of Swift's claim against Tyson on the bill], the aceptance and indorsement of the bill were admitted, and the plaintiff [Swift] there rested his case. … [Swift pled that he] was a *bonâ fide* holder of the bill, not having any notice of anything in the sale or title to the lands, or otherwise impeaching the transaction, and with the full belief that the bill was justly due. … [Tyson argued] that the bill was accepted by [Tyson] as part consideration for the purchase of certain lands in the state of Maine [under fraudulent misrepresentation as to ownership of those lands.] … The judges of the circuit court … divided in opinion upon … [whether Tyson] was entitled to the same defence to the action, as if the suit was between the original parties to the bill… ; and whether the evidence so offered was admissible as against the plaintiff [Swift] in the action. And this is the question certified to us for our decision.

There is no doubt, that a *bonâ fide* holder of a negotiable instrument, for a valuable consideration, without any notice of facts which impeach its validity, as between the antecedent parties, if he takes it under an indorsement made before the same becomes due, holds the title unaffected by these facts, and may recover thereon, although, as between the antecedent parties, the transaction may be without any legal validity. This is a doctrine so long and so well established, and so essential to the security of negotiable paper, that it is laid up among the fundamentals of the law, and requires no authority or reasoning to be now brought in its support. …

In the present case, the plaintiff is a *bonâ fide* holder, without notice, for what the law deems a good and valid consideration, that is, for a preexisting debt; and the only real question in the cause is, whether, under the circumstances of the present case, such a pre-existing debt constitutes a valuable consideration, in the sense of the general rule applicable to negotiable instruments. We say, under the circumstances of the present case, for the acceptance having been made in New York, the argument on behalf of the defendant is, that the contract is to be treated as a New York contract, and therefore, to be governed by the laws of New York...

.

[A]dmitting the doctrine to be fully settled in New York, it remains to be considered, whether it is obligatory upon this court, if it differs from the principles established in the general commercial law. ... It is, however, contended, that the 34th section of the judiciary act of 1789, ch. 20, furnishes a rule obligatory upon this court to follow the decisions of the state tribunals in all cases to which they apply. That section provides "that the laws of the several states, except where the constitution, treaties or statutes of the United States shall otherwise require or provide, shall be regarded as rules of decision, in trials at common law, in the courts of the United States, in cases where they apply." In order to maintain the argument, it is essential, therefore, to hold, that the word 'laws,' in this section, includes within the scope of its meaning, the decisions of the local tribunals. In the ordinary use of language, it will hardly be contended, that the decisions of courts constitute laws. They are, at most, only evidence of what the laws are, and are not, of themselves, laws. They are often re-examined, reversed and qualified by the courts themselves, whenever they are found to be either defective, or ill-founded, or otherwise incorrect. The laws of a state are more usually understood to mean the rules and enactments promulgated by the legislative authority thereof, or long-established local customs having the force of laws. In all the various cases, which have hitherto come before us for decision, this court have uniformly supposed, that the true interpretation of the 34th section limited its application to state laws, strictly local, that is to say, to the positive statutes of the state, and the construction thereof adopted by the local tribunals, and to rights and titles to things having a permanent locality, such as the rights and titles to real estate, and other matters immovable and intra-territorial in their nature and character. It never has been supposed by us, that the section did apply, or was designed to apply, to questions of a more general nature, not at all dependent upon local statutes or local usages of a fixed and permanent operation, as, for example, to the construction of ordinary contracts or other written instruments, and especially to questions of general commercial law, where the state tribunals are called upon to perform the like functions as ourselves, that is, to ascertain, upon general reasoning and legal analogies, what is the true exposition of the contract or instrument, or what is the just rule furnished by the principles of commercial law to govern the case. And we have not now the slightest difficulty in holding, that this section, upon its true intendment and construction, is strictly limited to local statutes and local usages of the character before stated, and does not extend to contracts and other instruments of a commercial nature, the true interpretation and effect whereof are to be sought, not in the decisions of the local tribunals, but in the general principles and doctrines of commercial jurisprudence. Undoubtedly, the decisions of the local tribunals upon such subjects are entitled to, and will receive, the most deliberate attention and respect of this court; but they cannot furnish positive rules, or conclusive authority, by which our own judgments are to be bound up and governed. The law respecting negotiable instruments may be truly declared … to be in a great measure, not the law of a single country only, but of the commercial world. …

It becomes necessary for us, therefore, upon the present occasion, to express our own opinion of the true result of the commercial law upon the question now before us. And we have no hesitation in saying, that a pre-existing debt does constitute a valuable consideration, in the sense of the general rule already stated, as applicable to negotiable instruments. Assuming it to be true … that the holder of a negotiable instrument is unaffected with the equities between the antecedent parties, of which he has no notice, only where he receives it in the usual course of trade and business, for a valuable consideration, before it becomes due; we are prepared to say, that receiving it in payment of, or as security for, a pre-existing debt, is according to the known usual course of trade and business. … It is for the benefit and convenience of the commercial world, to give as wide an extent as practicable to the credit and circulation of negotiable paper, that it may pass not only as security for new purchases and advances, made upon the transfer thereof, but also in payment of, and as security for, pre-existing debts. The creditor is thereby enabled to realize or to secure his debt, and thus may safely give a prolonged credit, or forbear from taking any legal steps to enforce his rights. The debtor also has the advantage of making his negotiable securities of equivalent value to cash. But establish the opposite conclusion, that negotiable paper cannot be applied in payment of, or as security for, pre-existing debts, without letting in all the equities between the original and antecedent parties, and the value and circulation of such securities must be essentially diminished, and the debtor driven to the embarrassment of making a sale thereof, often at a ruinous discount, to some third person, and then, by circuity, to apply the proceeds to the payment of his debts. What, indeed, upon such a doctrine, would become of that large class of cases, where new notes are given by the same or by other parties, by way of renewal or security to banks, in lieu of old securities discounted by them, which have arrived at maturity? Probably, more than one-half of all bank transactions in our country, as well as those of other countries, are of this nature. The doctrine would strike a fatal blow at all discounts of negotiable securities for pre-existing debts.

[Justice CATRON'S concurring opinion omitted.]

INQUIRY

Diversity Jurisdiction. Keep in mind that the question of which law governs arises in federal court in diversity-of-citizenship cases, not in cases brought under the federal courts' federal-question jurisdiction. Why is that so? Federal-question cases involve claims arising under federal law. When a federal court hears those federal-question claims, it has only federal law to apply. There is no conflict with state law for the trial court to resolve. What, though, if the litigants file a case in state court that involves federal questions? Some federal statutes permit enforcement action in either state or federal court. *See, e.g.*, Dice v. Akron, Canton & Youngstown R. Co., 342 U.S. 359 (1952) (federal law held to govern Federal Employer Liability Act action initiated in state court). State courts commonly decide under federal law other matters involving federal rights and interests. *See, e.g.*, Sola Electric Co. v. Jefferson Electri Co., 317 U.S. 173 (1942) (federal Copyright Act defense to contract licensing action); Ward v. Board of County Commissioners, 253 U.S. 17 (1920) (federal real-property-tax exemption litigated in state court). In those instances, the state court would clearly apply federal law because of the Constitution's Article VI supremacy clause. For a good example, the Supreme Court decided Hinderlider v. La Plata River & Cherry Creek Ditch Co., 304 U.S. 92 (1938), the same day as *Erie Railroad Co. v. Tompkins*, ruling that federal law governing interstate waterways applied in a state-court case, even though the federal law was based on cases (federal common law) rather than federal statute. Federal law is supreme in state-court cases. Obviously, state law applies in state-court cases not involving federal questions. What law applies when a state-court case implicates both federal and state interests? In Oregon v. Corvallis Sand & Gravel Co., 429 U.S. 363 (1977), the Supreme Court held that the predominance of state interests in determining title to disputed lands permitted the state court to apply state law despite the presence of potential federal interests. The rest of this section addresses only federal-court diversity-of-citizenship cases.

Constitutional Issues. The rule of *Swift v. Tyson* that federal courts follow only state statutes and not state-court decisions (state common law) on matters of general law seems clear enough from the opinion. However, the rationale that there should be uniform federal law, meaning a federal common law built upon diversity cases, creates a constitutional tension. Some history helps to make more evident the constitutional issues that *Swift v. Tyson* raised. Justice Story's opinion in *Swift v. Tyson* in effect argued the need for national systems of finance and commerce backed by federal law. Yet the late 1800s began a turbulent time in America as corporate and industrial interests expanded, often with the support of federal law and courts, to what many perceived to be the detriment of state, local, and individual interests. The country's 1929 financial meltdown and ensuing Great Depression sharpened that sense. Congress could have clarified the Rules of Decision Act but did not do so. Section 1652 retains the material language today that it did when Congress first enacted it in 1789. Every significant development in this story has depended on the Supreme Court. The Supreme Court could not change the Rules of Decision Act. Yet it had *Marbury v. Madison's* power of judicial review through which it could declare unconstitutional any interpretation of the Act that distorted the constitutional structure of government. After all, the Constitution would not see as a problem the line-drawing made necessary by dividing power between state and federal courts. The correct constitutional view is to see divided and shared judicial power as a necessary check on what some have called the most dangerous branch of government.

1. The *Erie* Doctrine

The Supreme Court addressed and attempted to resolve the constitutional tension created by *Swift v. Tyson* in the *Erie Railroad Co. v. Tompkins* decision below by, in effect, abolishing federal general common law and requiring the federal courts to recognize state-court decisions in diversity cases. In its simplest form (so simple as to distort the ruling), the rule of *Erie* was that federal courts in diversity cases should follow state substantive and federal procedural law. At its most basic level, *Erie* replaced *Swift v. Tyson's* distinction between state statutes (that federal courts must follow) and state-court decisions (that federal courts need not follow) with a distinction between substance (controlled by state law) and procedure (controlled by federal law and rules). Yet subsequent cases would confirm that the distinction is more fundamental than just that. They would also explore the extent to which the Supreme Court was deciding *Erie* on statutory or constitutional grounds. This section treats *Erie* and its progeny, drawing out the deeper nature of that distinction, reflecting the varying interests of the state and federal governments. Keep in mind as you read this section that leading commentators regard it as "impossible to overstate the importance of the *Erie* decision." CHARLES ALAN WRIGHT & MARY KAY KANE, FEDERAL COURTS §55 (6th ed. 2002).

An interesting twist in the story is that it was the national railroad, not the individual plaintiff Tompkins, who in *Erie* argued for applying state rather than federal common law. One of the defendant railroad's trains had severed Tompkins' arm when its open door knocked him under the passing train as he walked along the tracks toward his mother-in-law's Pennsylvania house. As you will see from the *Erie* opinion, the law of Pennsylvania was not so good for the seriously injured Tompkins' negligence claim. So he and his young lawyers (one 27 and the other 21 years old) filed the case in federal court in New York to take advantage of more-favorable federal common law. The forum shopping worked. The generous federal common law helped Tompkins win a verdict that would have been worth over $500,000 in today's dollars. The probability of Supreme Court review of an appellate decision affirming a jury verdict in a simple negligence case must have been miniscule. Even after the Supreme Court took the case and ruled, it took one of the justices writing to the *New York Times* to help the public appreciate the overlooked ruling's broad significance. *See* Irving Younger, *Observation: What Happened in* Erie, 56 TEX. L.REV. 1011 (1978). It might have been a federal court once again protecting a national corporate interest, yet its impact would have the opposite effect. As you read *Erie*, though, focus not on the factual context but on the Supreme Court's rationale. To what extent is *Erie* a constitutional decision and to what extent statutory interpretation of the Rules of Decision Act?

Erie Railroad Co. v. Tompkins,

United States Supreme Court
304 U.S. 64 (1938)

Mr. Justice BRANDEIS delivered the opinion of the court.

The question for decision is whether the oft-challenged doctrine of Swift v. Tyson[fn] shall now be disapproved.

Tompkins, a citizen of Pennsylvania, was injured on a dark night by a passing freight train of the Erie Railroad Company while walking along its right of way at Hughestown in that state. He claimed that the accident occurred through negligence… . To enforce that claim he brought an action in the federal court for Southern New York, which had jurisdiction because the company is a corporation of that state. It denied liability; and the case was tried by a jury.

The Erie ... contended ... that its duty to Tompkins, and hence its liability, should be determined in accordance with the Pennsylvania law; that under the law of Pennsylvania, as declared by its highest court, persons who use pathways along the railroad right of way... are to be deemed trespassers; and that the railroad is not liable for injuries to undiscovered trespassers resulting from its negligence, unless it be wanton or willful. Tompkins ... contended that, since there was no statute of the state on the subject, the railroad's duty and liability is to be determined in federal courts as a matter of general law.

The trial judge refused to rule that the applicable law precluded recovery. The jury brought in a verdict of $30,000; and the judgment entered thereon was affirmed by the Circuit Court of Appeals, which held [c] that it was unnecessary to consider whether the law of Pennsylvania was as contended, because the question was one not of local, but of general, law, and that "upon questions of general law the federal courts are free, in absence of a local statute, to exercise their independent judgment as to what the law is... ."

The Erie had contended that application of the Pennsylvania rule was required, among other things, by section 34 of the Federal Judiciary Act of September 24, 1789, c. 20, [c], which provides: "The laws of the several States, except where the Constitution, treaties, or statutes of the United States otherwise require or provide, shall be regarded as rules of decision in trials at common law, in the courts of the United States, in cases where they apply."

Because of the importance of the question whether the federal court was free to disregard the alleged rule of the Pennsylvania common law, we granted certiorari. [C]

First. Swift v. Tyson, [41 U.S. (16 Pet.) 1 (1842)], held that federal courts exercising jurisdiction on the ground of diversity of citizenship need not, in matters of general jurisprudence, apply the unwritten law of the state as declared by its highest court; that they are free to exercise an independent judgment as to what the common law of the state is... .

... The federal courts assumed, in the broad field of "general law," the power to declare rules of decision which Congress was confessedly without power to enact as statutes. Doubt was repeatedly expressed as to the correctness of the construction given section 34,[fn] and as to the soundness of the rule which it introduced.[fn] But it was the more recent research of a competent scholar, who examined the original document, which established that the construction given to it by the Court was erroneous; and that the purpose of the section was merely to make certain that, in all matters except those in which some federal law is controlling, the federal courts exercising jurisdiction in diversity of citizenship cases would apply as their rules of decision the law of the state, unwritten as well as written.[fn5. Charles Warren, New Light on the History of the Federal Judiciary Act of 1789 (1923) 37 Harv.L.Rev. 49, 51-52, 81-88, 108.]

Criticism of the doctrine became widespread after the decision of Black & White Taxicab & Transfer Co. v. Brown & Yellow Taxicab & Transfer Co., 276 U.S. 518 [(1928)].[fn] There, Brown &Yellow, a Kentucky corporation owned by Kentuckians, and the Louisville & Nashville Railroad, also a Kentucky corporation, wished that the former should have the exclusive privilege of soliciting passenger and baggage transportation at the Bowling Green, Ky., Railroad station; and that the Black & White, a competing Kentucky corporation, should be prevented from interfering with that privilege. Knowing that such a contract would be void under the common law of Kentucky, it was arranged that the Brown & Yellow reincorporate under the law of Tennessee, and that the contract with the railroad should be executed there. The suit was then brought by the Tennessee corporation in the federal court for Western Kentucky to enjoin competition by the Black & White; an injunction issued by the District Court was sustained by the Court of Appeals; and this Court, citing many decisions in which the doctrine of Swift & Tyson had been applied, affirmed the decree.

Second. Experience in applying the doctrine of Swift v. Tyson, had revealed its defects, political and social; and the benefits expected to flow from the rule did not accrue. Persistence of state courts in their own opinions on questions of common law prevented uniformity;[fn] and the impossibility of discovering a satisfactory line of demarcation between the province of general law and that of local law developed a new well of uncertainties.[fn]

On the other hand, the mischievous results of the doctrine had become apparent. Diversity of citizenship jurisdiction was conferred in order to prevent apprehended discrimination in state courts against those not citizens of the state. *Swift v. Tyson* introduced grave discrimination by noncitizens against citizens. It made rights enjoyed under the unwritten "general law" vary according to whether enforcement was sought in the state or in the federal court; and the privilege of selecting the court in which the right should be determined was conferred upon the noncitizen.[fn] Thus, the doctrine rendered impossible equal protection of the law. In attempting to promote uniformity of law throughout the United States, the doctrine had prevented uniformity in the administration of the law of the state.

The discrimination resulting became in practice far-reaching. This resulted in part from the broad province accorded to the so-called "general law" as to which federal courts exercised an independent judgment.[fn] In addition to questions of purely commercial law, 'general law' was held to include the obligations under contracts entered into and to be performed within the state,[fn] the extent to which a carrier operating within a state may stipulate for exemption from liability for his own negligence or that of his employee;[fn] the liability for torts committed within the state upon persons resident or property located there, even where the question of liability depended upon the scope of a property right conferred by the state;[fn] and the right to exemplary or punitive damages.[fn] Furthermore, state decisions construing local deeds,[fn] mineral conveyances,[fn] and even devises of real estate,[fn] were disregarded.[fn]

In part the discrimination resulted from the wide range of persons held entitled to avail themselves of the federal rule by resort to the diversity of citizenship jurisdiction. Through this jurisdiction individual citizens willing to remove from their own state and become citizens of another might avail themselves of the federal rule.[fn] And, without even change of residence, a corporate citizen of the state could avail itself of the federal rule by reincorporating under the laws of another state, as was done in the Taxicab Case.

The injustice and confusion incident to the doctrine of *Swift v. Tyson* have been repeatedly urged as reasons for abolishing or limiting diversity of citizenship jurisdiction.[fn] Other legislative relief has been proposed.[fn] If only a question of statutory construction were involved, we should not be prepared to abandon a doctrine so widely applied throughout nearly a century.[fn] But the unconstitutionality of the course pursued has now been made clear, and compels us to do so.

Third. Except in matters governed by the Federal Constitution or by acts of Congress, the law to be applied in any case is the law of the state. And whether the law of the state shall be declared by its Legislature in a statute or by its highest court in a decision is not a matter of federal concern. There is no federal general common law. Congress has no power to declare substantive rules of common law applicable in a state whether they be local in their nature or "general," be they commercial law or a part of the law of torts. And no clause in the Constitution purports to confer such a power upon the federal courts. As stated by Mr. Justice Field when protesting in Baltimore & Ohio R.R. Co. v. Baugh, 149 U.S. 368, 401[(1893)], against ignoring the Ohio common law of fellow-servant liability: ["]I am aware that what has been termed the general law of the country—which is often little less than what the judge advancing the doctrine thinks at the time should be the general law on a particular subject—has been often advanced in judicial opinions of this court to control a conflicting law of a state. I admit that learned judges have fallen into the habit of repeating this doctrine as a convenient mode of brushing aside the law of a state in conflict with their views. And I confess that, moved and governed by the authority of the great names of those judges, I have, myself, in many instances, unhesitatingly and confidently, but I think now erroneously, repeated the same doctrine. But, notwithstanding the great names which may be cited in favor of the doctrine, and notwithstanding the frequency with which the doctrine has been reiterated, there stands, as a perpetual protest against its repetition, the constitution of the United States, which recognizes and preserves the autonomy and independence of the states,—independence in their legislative and independence in their judicial departments. Supervision over either the legislative or the judicial action of the states is in no case permissible except as to matters by the constitution specifically authorized or delegated to the United States. Any interference with either, except as thus permitted, is an invasion of the authority of the state, and, to that extent, a denial of its independence."

The fallacy underlying the rule declared in *Swift v. Tyson* is made clear by Mr. Justice Holmes.[fn] The doctrine rests upon the assumption that there is "a transcendental body of law outside of any particular State but obligatory within it unless and until changed by statute," that federal courts have the power to use their judgment as to what the rules of common law are; and that in the federal courts "the parties are entitled to an independent judgment on matters of general law":

> "But law in the sense in which courts speak of it today does not exist without some definite authority behind it. The common law so far as it is enforced in a State, whether called common law or not, is not the common law generally but the law of that State existing by the authority of that State without regard to what it may have been in England or anywhere else. …
>
> "The authority and only authority is the State, and if that be so, the voice adopted by the State as its own (whether it be of its Legislature or of its Supreme Court) should utter the last word."

Thus the doctrine of Swift v. Tyson is, as Mr. Justice Holmes said, "an unconstitutional assumption of powers by the Courts of the United States which no lapse of time or respectable array of opinion should make us hesitate to correct." In disapproving that doctrine we do not hold unconstitutional section 34 of the Federal Judiciary Act of 1789 or any other act of Congress. We merely declare that in applying the doctrine this Court and the lower courts have invaded rights which in our opinion are reserved by the Constitution to the several states.

Fourth. The defendant contended that by the common law of Pennsylvania as declared by its highest court… , the only duty owed to the plaintiff was to refrain from willful or wanton injury. The plaintiff denied that such is the Pennsylvania law.[fn] In support of their respective contentions the parties discussed and cited many decisions of the Supreme Court of the state. The Circuit Court of Appeals ruled that the question of liability is one of general law; and on that ground declined to decide the issue of state law. As we hold this was error, the judgment is reversed and the case remanded to it for further proceedings in conformity with our opinion.

Reversed.

Mr. Justice CARDOZO took no part in the consideration or decision of this case.

Mr. Justice BUTLER (dissenting).

… No constitutional question was suggested or argued below or here. And as a general rule, this Court will not consider any question not raised below and presented by the petition. [Cc] Here it does not decide either of the questions presented, but, changing the rule of decision in force since the foundation of the government, remands the case to be adjudged according to a standard never before deemed permissible.

The opinion just announced states that: "The question for decision is whether the oft-challenged doctrine of *Swift v. Tyson*[, *supra,*] shall now be disapproved." …

The doctrine of that case has been followed by this Court in an unbroken line of decisions. So far as appears, it was not questioned until more than 50 years later, and then by a single judge.[fn] Baltimore & O. Railroad Co. v. Baugh, 149 U.S. 368, 390[(1893)]. …

Thereafter, as before, the doctrine was constantly applied.[fn] In Black & White Taxicab Co. v. Brown & Yellow Taxicab Co., 276 U.S. 518[(1928)], three judges dissented. The writer of the dissent, Mr. Justice Holmes said, however [c]: "I should leave Swift v. Tyson undisturbed, as I indicated in Kuhn v. Fairmont Coal Co., but I would not allow it to spread the assumed dominion into new fields." …

This Court has often emphasized its reluctance to consider constitutional questions and that legislation will not be held invalid as repugnant to the fundamental law if the case may be decided upon any other ground. In view of grave consequences liable to result from erroneous exertion of its power to set aside legislation, the Court should move cautiously, seek assistance of counsel, act only after ample deliberation, show that the question is before the Court, that its decision cannot be avoided by construction of the statute assailed or otherwise, indicate precisely the principle or provision of the Constitutional held to have been transgressed, and fully disclose the reasons and authorities found to warrant the conclusion of invalidity. …

So far as appears, no litigant has ever challenged the power of Congress to establish the rule as construed. It has so long endured that its destruction now without appropriate deliberation cannot be justified. …

The course pursued by the Court in this case is repugnant to the Act of Congress of August 24, 1937, 50 Stat. 751, 28 U.S.C.A. §§17[]. It declares that: "Whenever the constitutionality of any Act of Congress affecting the public interest is drawn in question in any court of the United States in any suit or proceeding to which the United States, or any agency thereof, or any officer or employee thereof, as such officer or employee, is not a party, the court having jurisdiction of the suit or proceeding shall certify such fact to the Attorney General. In any such case the court shall permit the United States to intervene and become a party for presentation of evidence (if evidence is otherwise receivable in such suit or proceeding) and argument upon the question of the constitutionality of such Act. In any such suit or proceeding the United States shall, subject to the applicable provisions of law, have all the rights of a party and the liabilities of a party as to court costs to the extent necessary for a proper presentation of the facts and law relating to the constitutionality of such Act." ...

... [T]he Court states that it does not hold section 34 unconstitutional, but merely that, in applying the doctrine of *Swift v. Tyson* construing it, this Court and the lower courts have invaded rights which are reserved by the Constitution to the several states. But, plainly through the form of words employed, the substance of the decision appears; it strikes down as unconstitutional section 34 as construed by our decisions; it divests the Congress of power to prescribe rules to be followed by federal courts when deciding questions of general law. In that broad field it compels this and the lower federal courts to follow decisions of the courts of a particular state.

I am of opinion that the constitutional validity of the rule need not be considered, because under the law, as found by the courts of Pennsylvania and generally throughout the country, it is plain that the evidence required a finding that plaintiff was guilty of negligence that contributed to cause his injuries, and that the judgment below should be reversed upon that ground.

Mr. Justice MCREYNOLDS, concurs in this opinion.

Mr. Justice REED (concurring in part).

I concur in the conclusion reached in this case, in the disapproval of the doctrine of *Swift v. Tyson*, and in the reasoning of the majority opinion, except in so far as it relies upon the unconstitutionality of the "course pursued" by the federal courts.

The "doctrine of *Swift v. Tyson*," as I understand it, is that the words "the laws," as used in section 34, line 1, of the Federal Judiciary Act of September 24, 1789, 28 U.S.C.A. §725, do not included in their meaning "the decisions of the local tribunals." ...

To decide the case now before us and to "disapprove" the doctrine of Swift v. Tyson requires only that we say that the words "the laws" include in their meaning the decisions of the local tribunals. ...

The "unconstitutional" course referred to in the majority opinion is apparently the ruling in *Swift v. Tyson* that the supposed omission of Congress to legislate as to the effect of decisions leaves federal courts free to interpret general law for themselves. I am not at all sure whether, in the absence of federal statutory direction, federal courts would be compelled to follow state decisions. There was sufficient doubt about the matter in 1789 to induce the first Congress to legislate. ... If the opinion commits this Court to the position that the Congress is without power to declare what rules of substantive law shall govern the federal courts, that conclusion also seems questionable. The line between procedural and substantive law is hazy, but no one doubts federal power over procedure. [C] The Judiciary Article, 3, and the "necessary and proper" clause of article 1, §8, may fully authorize legislation, such as this section of the Judiciary Act. ...

INQUIRY

Federal Common Law. Keep in mind that scholars will contest nearly everything one can say about *Erie*, even while one must know and rely on its broad lines and doctrine. The *Erie* opinion states one of those broad lines as, "There is no federal general common law." Notice the Supreme Court's insertion of the adjective *general* between "federal" and "common law." What was the Court pointing out? By holding that federal courts in diversity cases look to state substantive law including state common law, *Erie* abolished much of federal common law that the federal courts had developed under *Swift v. Tyson* to supplant state-court decisions on state-law substantive matters. *Erie* did not abolish all federal common law. Much of federal common law remains, including all of that carrying out powers the Constitution grants directly to federal courts, and that interpreting federal procedural rules and federal substantive statutes. Can you think of examples of each? In one instance having to do with labor law where Congress' statutory grant was so broad as not to give the federal courts any particular guidance, the Supreme Court held in Textile Workers Union v. Lincoln Mills, 353 U.S. 448 (1957), that Congress' intent was to give authority to the federal courts to develop federal common law on the subject. Federal common law also exists independent of federal statute in enclaves comprised of special federal interests. *See* Banco Nacional de Cuba v. Sabbatino, 376 U.S. 398 (1964) (federal-government commercial dispute with foreign parties implicating international relations); Kossick v. United Fruit Co., 365 U.S. 731 (1961) (admiralty and maritime law); Clearfield Trust Co. v. United States, 318 U.S. 363 (1943) (federal contract rights, bonds, and securities). Federal common law can even give rise to a federal defense to a state claim. *See* Boyle v. United Technologies Corp., 487 U.S. 500 (1988) (government-contractor defense to state-law tort action). Federal common law lives after *Erie*, just not on issues governed by state substantive law.

The Constitution. The *Erie* decision asserts that it addressed a constitutional question ("the unconstitutionality of the course pursued has now been made clear"). If so, then on what clause of the Constitution did the Supreme Court rely for its decision in *Erie*? The opinion mentions none. The Supreme Court was instead addressing the structure of government as the Constitution created it. Part of the issue had to do with the federal government's limited power and the Constitution's reservation to the states of general powers over such matters as tort, contract, criminal, and property law. Congress could not then have enacted a general federal tort law governing conduct of individuals within particular states. Yet at least today (given more expansive interpretation of federal commerce powers under U.S. CONST., Art. I, §8), Congress could likely regulate tort law as it applied along an interstate railroad governing Tompkins' circumstance in *Erie*. On its particular facts, perhaps *Erie* might then no longer be good law. Yet the point of *Erie* has nothing in particular to do with tort, contract, or other state substantive law. It instead has everything to do with which law applies, state or federal. Also, while Congress might regulate tort law within railroad rights-of-way, the federal courts could not do so on their own, beyond interpreting federal statutes and regulations.

Statutory Construction. The first step the *Erie* Supreme Court took to reach the constitutional issue was to dispose of *Swift v. Tyson's* statutory construction. To do so, the Supreme Court held based on new scholarly research that *Swift v. Tyson* had misconstrued the language of the Rules of Decision Act that the "laws of the several States" would control to mean only state statutory law. Although the *Erie* opinion did not reflect it, the new research was the discovery of a draft of the Rules of Decision Act under which it would have been "the Statute law of the several States ... and their unwritten or common law" that would control. Charles Warren, *New Light on the History of the Federal Judiciary Act of 1789*, 37 HARV. L.REV. 49 (1923). When Congress adopted the final version of the Rules of Decision Act eliminating *both* the reference to state "statute" law *and* state "unwritten or common law" in favor of simply "state" law, did it really (as the *Erie* opinion concluded) mean that Congress had intended to *include* state common law as controlling in diversity cases? It seems that lawyers could make equally sound arguments that Congress' omission of both statutory and common-law descriptors left the question open for *Swift v. Tyson* to interpret Congress' intent exactly as it had—a stance confirmed by nearly 100 years of congressional inaction to correct that interpretation.

Substance v. Procedure. Notice in the *Erie* decision that it was only Justice Reed's concurrence that referred directly to "[t]he line between procedural and substantive law" as the state-or-federal-law difference maker. Justice Brandeis' majority opinion made no such reference, instead referring more generally to the limited authority of Congress and the federal courts, and related structural interests. The omission of a clear line left it to the lower courts and subsequent Supreme Court decisions to articulate further *Erie's* standard. Just where were the lower courts to draw the line? It also left it to the Supreme Court to begin to develop the limits of *Erie* where state law would no longer prevail. In a series of cases, the Supreme Court balanced deference to state authority with the independence of the federal judicial system. There were also questions to answer over jury-trial rights, statutes of limitation, enforcement of arbitration agreements, and a host of like issues that seem to fall right along the substance/procedure line. Consider the next significant case in which the Supreme Court declined to limit the reach of state law under *Erie*. In the following case, *Guaranty Trust Co. v. York*, the Supreme Court held that state law governs in equity as well as law cases including in providing the limitations period. Keep in mind that the particular rule of the case is not as important as the standard the Supreme Court articulates through it. As you read the following case discussing how courts had misconstrued *Erie* to establish a bright-line substance/ procedure standard, see if you can locate the newly articulated *Erie* standard.

Guaranty Trust Co. v. York,

United States Supreme Court
326 U.S. 99 (1945)

Mr. Justice FRANKFURTER delivered the opinion of the Court. ...

In May, 1930, Van Sweringen Corporation issued notes to the amount of $30,000,000. Under an indenture of the same date, petitioner, Guaranty Trust Co., was named trustee with power and obligations to enforce the rights of the noteholders in the assets of the Corporation and of the Van Sweringen brothers. ... ... Guaranty [later] co-operated in a plan for the purchase of the outstanding notes... .

Respondent York received $6,000 of the notes as a gift... .

The suit, instituted as a class action ... and brought in a federal court solely because of diversity of citizenship, is based on an alleged breach of trust by Guaranty in that it failed to protect the interests of the noteholders... . Petitioner moved for summary judgment, which was granted... . On appeal, the Circuit Court of Appeals ... held that in a suit brought on the equity side of a federal district court that court is not required to apply the State statute of limitations that would govern like suits in the courts of a State where the federal court is sitting even though the exclusive basis of federal jurisdiction is diversity of citizenship. [C] ...

Our starting point must be the policy of federal jurisdiction which Erie R. Co. v. Tompkins, 304 U.S. 64[(1938)], embodies. In overruling Swift v. Tyson, [41 U.S. (16 Pet.) 1 (1841)], *Erie R. Co. v. Tompkins* did not merely overrule a venerable case. It overruled a particular way of looking at law which dominated the judicial process long after its inadequacies had been laid bare. [Cc] Law was conceived as a "brooding omnipresence" of Reason, of which decisions were merely evidence and not themselves the controlling formulations. Accordingly, federal courts deemed themselves free to ascertain what Reason, and therefore Law, required wholly independent of authoritatively declared State law, even in cases where a legal right as the basis for relief was created by State authority and could not be created by federal authority and the case got into a federal court merely because it was "between Citizens of different States" under Art. III, §2 of the Constitution of the United States. ...

... [T]his case reduces itself to the narrow question whether, when no recovery could be had in a State court because the action is barred by the statute of limitations, a federal court in equity can take cognizance of the suit because there is diversity of citizenship between the parties. ...

Matters of "substance" and matters of "procedure" are much talked about in the books as though they defined a great divide cutting across the whole domain of law. ... But ... [n]either "substance" nor "procedure" represents the same invariants. Each implies different variables depending upon the particular problem for which it is used. [C] And the different problems are only distantly related at best... .

Here we are dealing with a right to recover derived not from the United States but from one of the States. When, because the plaintiff happens to be a nonresident, such a right is enforceable in a federal as well as in a State court, the forms and mode of enforcing the right may at times, naturally enough, vary because the two judicial systems are not identic. But since a federal court adjudicating a state-created right solely because of the diversity of citizenship of the parties is for that purpose, in effect, only another court of the State, it cannot afford recovery if the right to recover is made unavailable by the State nor can it substantially affect the enforcement of the right as given by the State.

And so the question is not whether a statute of limitations is deemed a matter of "procedure" in some sense. The question is whether such a statute concerns merely the manner and the means by which a right to recover, as recognized by the State, is enforced, or whether such statutory limitation is a matter of substance in the aspect that alone is relevant to our problem, namely, does it significantly affect the result of a litigation for a federal court to disregard a law of a State that would be controlling in an action upon the same claim by the same parties in a State court? ...

Plainly enough, a statute that would completely bar recovery in a suit if brought in a State court bears on a State-created right vitally and not merely formally or negligibly. As to consequences that so intimately affect recovery or non-recovery a federal court in a diversity case should follow State law. ...

To make an exception to Erie R. Co. v. Tompkins on the equity side of a federal court is to reject the considerations of policy which, after long travail, led to that decision. ...

Diversity jurisdiction is founded on assurance to non-resident litigants of courts free from susceptibility to potential local bias. The Framers of the Constitution, according to Marshall, entertained "apprehensions" lest distant suitors be subjected to local bias in State courts, or, at least, viewed with "indulgence the possible fears and apprehensions" of such suitors. Bank of the United States v. Deveaux, [9 U.S. (5 Cranch 61) 87 (1809)]. And so Congress afforded out-of-State litigants another tribunal, not another body of law. The operation of a double system of conflicting laws in the same State is plainly hostile to the reign of law. ...

Dicta may be cited characterizing equity as an independent body of law. To the extent that we have indicated, it is. But insofar as these general observations go beyond that, they merely reflect notions that have been replaced by a sharper analysis of what federal courts do when they enforce rights that have no federal origin. And so, before the true source of law that is applied by the federal courts under diversity jurisdiction was fully explored, some things were said that would not now be said. ...

The judgment is reversed and the case is remanded for proceedings not inconsistent with this opinion.

So ordered.

Reversed.

Mr. Justice ROBERTS and Mr. Justice DOUGLAS took no part in the consideration or decision of this case.

Mr. Justice RUTLEDGE.

I dissent. ...

... One may give full adherence to the rule of Erie R. Co. v. Tompkins, 304 U.S. 64[(1938)], and its extension to cases in equity in so far as they affect clearly substantive rights, without conceding or assuming that the long tradition, both federal and state, which regards statutes of limitations as falling within the category of remedial rather than substantive law, necessarily must be ruled in the same way; and without conceding further that only a different jurisdprudential climate or a kind of "brooding omnipresence in the sky" has dictated the hitherto unvaried policy of the federal courts in their general attitude toward the strict application of local statutes of limitations in equity causes.

If any characteristic of equity jurisprudence has descended unbrokenly from and within "the traditional scope of equity as historically evolved in the English Court of Chancery," it is that statutes of limitations, often in terms applying only to actions at law, have never been deemed to be rigidly applicable as absolute barriers to suits in equity as they are to actions at law.[fn] That tradition, it would seem, should be regarded as having been incorporated in the various Acts of Congress which have conferred equity jurisdiction upon the federal courts. So incorporated, it has been reaffirmed repeatedly by the decisions of this and other courts.[fn] It is now excised from those Acts. If there is to be excision, Congress, not this Court, should make it. …

The words 'substantive' and 'procedural' or 'remedial' are not talismanic. Merely calling a legal question by one or the other does not resolve it otherwise than as a purely authoritarian performance. But they have come to designate in a broad way large and distinctive legal domains within the greater one of the law and to mark, though often indistinctly or with overlapping limits, many divides between such regions.

One of these historically has been the divide between the substantive law and the procedural or remedial law to be applied by the federal courts in diversity cases, a division sharpened but not wiped out by *Erie R. Co. v. Tompkins* and subsequent decisions extending the scope of its ruling. …

Mr. Justice MURPHY joins in this opinion.

INQUIRY

Realism. Justice Frankfurter's majority opinion in *Guaranty Trust Co. v. York* famously criticized *Swift v. Tyson* specifically and prior legal scholars generally as incorrectly treating law as an artificial "'brooding omnipresence' of Reason." Justice Frankfurter's invitation, associated with a movement identified as Legal Realism, was to look behind words and principles to understand and manipulate better their effects. Before the Supreme Court's decision in *Erie R. Co. v. Tompkins*, were judges and lawyers so naïve? You can see how the dissent already bristled at the Realists' suggestion that there was any such naïvete extant. Scholars today challenge the Realists' assertion, finding a similar degree of pragmatism, instrumentalism, and realism in the statements and opinions of those whom the emerging Realists attacked. *See* BRIAN TAMANAHA, BEYOND THE FORMALIST-REALIST DIVIDE: THE ROLE OF POLITICS IN JUDGING (Princeton Univ. Press 2010). Judges have always fashioned legal rules instrumentally in part, based on predictions of their outcomes and making policy judgments of their best effects, but defining those policies through (and constraining that tendency within) formal rules. What was new about *Guaranty Trust Co. v. York* was that it castigated formal rules while acknowledging its instrumental effects. Yet formal rules are unavoidable. What formal rule did *Guaranty Trust Co. v. York's* Realist judicial philosophy produce? How well or poorly did that rule work?

Outcome-Determinative Test. Of course, Justice Frankfurter's disdain for formalism notwithstanding, *Guaranty Trust Co. v. York* produced its own rule. In *Guaranty Trust Co. v. York*, the Supreme Court articulated that the *Erie* doctrine has to do with whether the law merely dictates the "forms," "mode," "manner," or "means" of enforcing a right or, in contrast, whether it will "significantly affect the result of a litigation." Lower courts over-simplified *Erie* into a substance-versus-procedure standard. Similarly, lower courts over-simplified *Guaranty Trust Co. v. York's* holding into an outcome-determinative test. If the outcome changed depending on which law that the federal court applied, then the federal court would apply state law. The *Guaranty Trust Co. v. York* opinion showed that the substance-versus-procedure standard inadequately reflected the deep meaning and sensitivity of *Erie*. What do you think are the pitfalls of simplifying *Guaranty Trust Co. v. York* into an outcome-determinative test? Can you hypothesize instances where the outcome-determinative test would obviously not make sense? The Supreme Court applied the outcome-determinative test in a series of cases each of which held that the federal courts must apply state law. *See* Cohen v. Beneficial Indus. Loan Corp., 337 U.S. 541 (1949) (requiring bond for expenses in shareholder-derivative suit); Woods v. Interstate Realty Co., 337 U.S. 535 (1949) (barring suit by non-resident corporations not paying in-state taxes); Ragan v. Merchants Transfer & Warehouse Co., 337 U.S. 530 (1949) (determining when cause of action arises for purposes of limitation period); *see also* Bernhardt v. Polygraphic Co., 350 U.S. 198 (1956) (barring employment arbitration). Eventually, though, the Supreme Court tired of *Guaranty Trust Co. v. York's* outcome-determinative test in favor of a more sensitive standard. See if you can discern that standard in the next case.

Byrd v. Blue Ridge Rural Electric Cooperative,

United States Supreme Court
356 U.S. 525 (1958)

Mr. Justice BRENNAN delivered the opinion of the Court. ...

This case was brought in the District Court for the Western District of South Carolina. Jurisdiction was based on diversity of citizenship. [C] The petitioner, a resident of North Carolina, sued respondent, a South Carolina corporation, for damages for injuries allegedly caused by the respondent's negligence. He had judgment on a jury verdict. The Court of Appeals for the Fourth Circuit reversed and directed the entry of judgment for the respondent. [C] We granted certiorari... .

The respondent is in the business of selling electric power to subscribers in rural sections of South Carolina. The petitioner was employed as a lineman in the construction crew of a construction contractor. ... The petitioner was injured while connecting power lines to one of the new substations.

One of respondent's affirmative defenses was that under the South Carolina Workmen's Compensation Act,[fn] the petitioner... was ... barred from suing the respondent at law because obliged to accept statutory compensation benefits as the exclusive remedy for his injuries.[fn] ...

I.

[The Supreme Court remanded for error by the lower federal courts in construing a state statute to bar additional evidence on whether the petitioner-employee was respondent's employee under the statute.]

II.

A question is also presented as to whether on remand the factual issue is to be decided by the judge or by the jury. The respondent argues on the basis of the decision of the Supreme Court of South Carolina in Adams v. Davison-Paxon Co., 230 S.C. 532, 96 S.E.2d 566[(1957)],[fn] that the issue of immunity should be decided by the judge and not by the jury. ...

The respondent argues that this state-court decision governs the present diversity case and "divests the jury of its normal function" to decide the disputed fact question of the respondent's immunity... . This is to contend that the federal court is bound under Erie R. Co. v. Tompkins, 304 U.S. 64[(1938)], to follow the state court's holding to secure uniform enforcement of the immunity created by the State.[fn]

First. It was decided in *Erie R. Co. v. Tompkins* that the federal courts in diversity cases must respect the definition of state-created rights and obligations by the state courts. We must, therefore, first examine the rule in *Adams v. Davison-Paxon Co.* to determine whether it is bound up with these rights and obligations in such a way that its application in the federal court is required. [C]

The Workmen's Compensation Act is administered in South Carolina by its Industrial Commission. The South Carolina courts hold that, on judicial review of actions of the Commission... , the question whether the claim of an injured workman is within the Commission's jurisdiction is a matter of law for decision by the court, which makes its own findings of fact relating to that jurisdiction.[fn] The South Carolina Supreme Court states no reasons in *Adams v. Davison-Paxon Co.* why, although the jury decides all other factual issues raised by the cause of action and defenses, the jury is displaced as to the factual issue raised by the affirmative defense... . [T]he Adams holding is grounded in the practical consideration that the question had theretofore come before the South Carolina courts from the Industrial Commission and the courts had become accustomed to deciding the factual issue of immunity without the aid of juries. We find nothing to suggest that this rule was announced as an integral part of the special relationship created by the statute. Thus the requirement appears to be merely a form and mode of enforcing the immunity, Guaranty Trust Co. of New York v. York, 326 U.S. 99, 108[(1945)], and not a rule intended to be bound up with the definition of the rights and obligations of the parties. ...

Second. But cases following Erie have evinced a broader policy to the effect that the federal courts should conform as near as may be—in the absence of other considerations—to state rules even of form and mode where the state rules may bear substantially on the question whether the litigation would come out one way in the federal court and another way in the state court if the federal court failed to apply a particular local rule.[fn] E.g., Guaranty Trust Co. of New York v. York, supra; Bernhardt v. Polygraphic Co., 350 U.S. 198[(1956)]. Concededly the nature of the tribunal which tries issues may be important in the enforcement of the parcel of rights making up a cause of action or defense, and bear significantly upon achievement of uniform enforcement of the right. It may well be that in the instant personal-injury case the outcome would be substantially affected by whether the issue of immunity is decided by a judge or a jury. Therefore, were "outcome" the only consideration, a strong case might appear for saying that the federal court should follow the state practice.

But there are affirmative countervailing considerations at work here. The federal system is an independent system for administering justice to litigants who properly invoke its jurisdiction. An essential characteristic of that system is the manner in which, in civil common-law actions, it distributes trial functions between judge and jury and, under the influence—if not the command[fn]—of the Seventh Amendment, assigns the decisions of disputed questions of fact to the jury. [C] The policy of uniform enforcement of state-created rights and obligations, see, e.g., *Guaranty Trust Co. of New York v. York, supra*, cannot in every case exact compliance with a state rule[fn]—not bound up with rights and obligations—which disrupts the federal system of allocating functions between judge and jury. [C] Thus the inquiry here is whether the federal policy favoring jury decisions of disputed fact questions should yield to the state rule in the interest of furthering the objective that the litigation should not come out one way in the federal court and another way in the state court.

We think that in the circumstances of this case the federal court should not follow the state rule. It cannot be gainsaid that there is a strong federal policy against allowing state rules to disrupt the judge-jury relationship in the federal courts. ... [I]n light of the influence of the Seventh Amendment, the function assigned to the jury "is an essential factor in the process for which the Federal Constitution provides." [Herron v. Southern Pacific Co., 283 U.S. 91, 95 (1931).]
...

Third. We have discussed the problem upon the assumption that the outcome of the litigation may be substantially affected by whether the issue of immunity is decided by a judge or a jury. But clearly there is not present here the certainty that a different result would follow, cf. *Guaranty Trust Co. of New York v. York, supra*, or even the strong possibility that this would be the case, [c]. There are factors present here which might reduce that possibility. The trial judge in the federal system has powers denied the judges of many States to comment on the weight of evidence and credibility of witnesses, and discretion to grant a new trial if the verdict appears to him to be against the weight of the evidence. We do not think the likelihood of a different result is so strong as to require the federal practice of jury determination of disputed factual issues to yield to the state rule in the interest of uniformity of outcome.[fn] ...

Reversed and remanded.

[Concurring and dissenting opinions of Justices WHITTAKER, FRANKFURTER, and HARLAN omitted.]

INQUIRY

Balancing Interests. Why not decide *Byrd* under *Guaranty Trust Co. v. York's* outcome-determinative test? Justice Brennan's majority opinion makes a good case of it that the outcome could have been the same under either state or federal law, such that the lower court could under, *Guaranty Trust Co. v. York*, have applied federal law to grant a jury-trial right. The *Byrd* Court's willingness to reject the outcome-determinative test when it need not have done so to reach the same result means that something more was afoot in *Byrd.* The *Byrd* Court articulated a new standard. Did you catch it? *Byrd* first considered whether the state rule was "bound up with" state-created rights. It then considered the degree to which the alternative federal rule was an "essential characteristic" of the independent federal judicial system. By considering first the state's interest in the state rule and then the federal interest in the federal rule, Justice Brennan's majority opinion may have articulated an interest-balancing test. Notice now how the three standards that we have so far considered—*Erie's* substance/procedure distinction, *Guaranty Trust Co. v. York's* outcome-determinative test, and *Byrd's* interest-balancing test—could work together to produce a more articulate and comprehensive standard. Or was Justice Brennan's considerating the merely "form and mode" (his own words) nature of the state rule and that it was not "bound up with the definition of" state rights just a fancy way of applying *Erie's* substance/procedure distinction? We are closer to a coherent picture even if not all the way there yet.

Practice

"So, Civil Procedure, is it?" the trial judge asked the lawyer whom she had not seen for some years. Outside of the courtroom, judges and lawyers maintain cordial relationships, keeping up with one another on safe professional subjects having to do with careers, firms, and offices. The judge knew that the lawyer had been teaching at a law school but had not known the subject the lawyer taught.

"Yes, like putting a diaper on a baby with no baby," the lawyer quipped, making both of them laugh.

"Well, teach them well, my friend, teach them well," the trial judge answered. "When I started in practice at the firm, I wished a hundred times over that I had studied my Civil Procedure better. And from the bench, there is not a day that goes by that I do not wish that other lawyers had also studied Civil Procedure better."

2. The Rules Enabling Act

We have not yet directly addressed the question of the *Federal Rules of Civil Procedure* and their effect on the choice of governing law in a federal-court diversity case. The Supreme Court decided *Erie* in 1938, not long after Congress enacted the 1934 Rules Enabling Act presently codified at 28 U.S.C. §2072. The Rules Enabling Act gave the Supreme Court power to prescribe the *Federal Rules of Civil Procedure.* Although the *Federal Rules* were not to interfere with substantive rights, the Rules Enabling Act provided that the *Federal Rules* would be superior to any conflicting provisions. As you review the Rules Enabling Act, think of the place of the *Federal Rules* in light of *Erie's* substance/procedure distinction, *Guaranty Trust Co. v. York's* outcome-determinative test, and *Byrd's* interest-balancing test.

28 U.S.C. §2072. Rules of procedure and evidence; power to prescribe.
(a) The Supreme Court shall have the power to prescribe general rules of practice and procedure and rules of evidence for cases in the United States district courts (including proceedings before magistrate judges thereof) and courts of appeals.

(b) Such rules shall not abridge, enlarge or modify any substantive right. All laws in conflict with such rules shall be of no further force or effect after such rules have taken effect.
(c) Such rules may define when a ruling of a district court is final for the purposes of appeal under section 1291 of this title.

INQUIRY

Constitutionality. Not long after deciding *Erie* in 1938, the Supreme Court upheld the constitutionality of the 1934 Rules Enabling Act in Sibbach v. Wilson & Co., 312 U.S. 1 (1941). In *Sibbach*, the federal District Court for the Northern District of Illinois ordered the personal-injury plaintiff in a diversity case to submit to medical examination under FED. R. CIV. P. 35. Although court-ordered medical examinations are commonly available in personal-injury actions in other states, they were not in Illinois. The Supreme Court recognized the plaintiff's physical integrity and opportunity to make a tort recovery for the violation of that integrity as "substantive rights" with which the Rules Enabling Act would not have allowed a *Federal Rule of Civil Procedure* to interfere. However, the Court rejected that a medical examination under Rule 35 would interfere with those rights. The Court permitted the medical examination to go forward even though doing so put it in conflict with Illinois state law. Oddly (even though, we will see, presciently), the *Sibbach* opinion did not cite *Erie*. Instead, the Court treated *Sibbach* as presenting a question of interpreting the Rules Enabling Act rather than one of constitutional dimensions. Not long after, the Supreme Court decided two cases in which it Cohen v. Beneficial Indus. Loan Corp., 337 U.S. 541 (1949), and Ragan v. Merchants Transfer & Warehouse Co., 337 U.S. 530 (1949) (both mentioned above), in which it held that state law applied rather than two other *Federal Rules of Civil Procedure* (currently Rules 3 and 23.1). *Cohen* and *Ragan* appeared to conflict with *Sibbach*. Do the *Federal Rules* govern over state law in diversity cases or do they not? Moreover, is deciding which law governs a question of statutory interpretation or constitutional import? The Supreme Court answered both questions in the following case, holding that the *Federal Rules* do indeed govern as a question of statutory interpretation. The decision did not overrule *Erie* or fully return us to *Swift v. Tyson*. Yet it clearly de-constitutionalized the governing-law question, at least when applied in a case involving a *Federal Rule of Civil Procedure*. As you read the following case, see if you can discern where *Erie* analysis might still be necessary.

Hanna v. Plumer,

United States Supreme Court
380 U.S. 460 (1965)

Mr. Chief Justice WARREN delivered the opinion of the Court.

The question to be decided is whether, in a civil action where the jurisdiction of the United States district court is based upon diversity of citizenship between the parties, service of process shall be made in the manner prescribed by state law or that set forth in Rule 4(d)(1) of the Federal Rules of Civil Procedure.

... [P]etitioner, a citizen of Ohio, filed her complaint in the District Court for the District of Massachusetts, claiming damages in excess of $10,000 for personal injuries resulting from an automobile accident in South Carolina, allegedly caused by the negligence of one Louise Plumer Osgood, a Massachusetts citizen deceased at the time of the filing of the complaint. Respondent, Mrs. Osgood's executor and also a Massachusetts citizen, was named as defendant. ... [S]ervice was made by leaving copies of the summons and the complaint with respondent's wife at his residence, concededly in compliance with [Fed. R. Civ. P.] 4(d)(1) [(now Rule 4(e)(2)(B)) permitting that form of service.] ...

Respondent filed his answer on February 26, alleging, inter alia, that the action could not be maintained because it had been brought "contrary to and in violation of the provisions of Massachusetts General Laws [c]" [requiring personal service]. ...

... [T]he District Court granted respondent's motion for summary judgment, citing Ragan v. Merchants Transfer & Warehouse Co., 337 U.S. 530[(1949)], and Guaranty Trust Co.[] v. York, 326 U.S. 99[(1945)], in support of its conclusion that the adequacy of the service was to be measured by §9, with which, the court held, petitioner had not complied. ... The Court of Appeals for the First Circuit... concluded that the conflict of state and federal rules was over "a substantive rather than a procedural matter," and unanimously affirmed. ...

We conclude that the adoption of Rule 4(d)(1), designed to control service of process in diversity actions,[fn] neither exceeded the congressional mandate embodied in the Rules Enabling Act nor transgressed constitutional bounds, and that the Rule is therefore the standard against which the District Court should have measured the adequacy of the service. Accordingly, we reverse the decision of the Court of Appeals.

The Rules Enabling Act, 28 U.S.C. §2072 (1958 ed.) [(since amended)], provides, in pertinent part: "The Supreme Court shall have the power to prescribe, by general rules, the forms of process, writs, pleadings, and motions, and the practice and procedure of the district courts of the United States in civil actions. Such rules shall not abridge, enlarge or modify any substantive right and shall preserve the right of trial by jury * * *."

Under the cases construing the scope of the Enabling Act, Rule 4(d)(1) clearly passes muster. Prescribing the manner in which a defendant is to be notified that a suit has been instituted against him, it relates to the "practice and procedure of the district courts." [C] "The test must be whether a rule really regulates procedure,—the judicial process for enforcing rights and duties recognized by substantive law and for justly administering remedy and redress for disregard or infraction of them." Sibbach v. Wilson & Co., 312 U.S. 1, 14[(1941)].[fn] ...

... [W]ere there no conflicting state procedure, Rule 4(d)(1) would clearly control. National Equipment Rental, Ltd. v. Szukhent, 375 U.S. 311, 316[(1964)]. However, respondent, focusing on the contrary Massachusetts rule, calls to the Court's attention another line of cases, a line which—like the Federal Rules—had its birth in 1938. Erie R. Co. v. Tompkins, 304 U.S. 64[(1938)], overruling Swift v. Tyson, [41 U.S. (16 Pet.) 1 (1842)], held that federal courts sitting in diversity cases, when deciding questions of "substantive" law, are bound by state court decisions as well as state statutes. The broad command of Erie was therefore identical to that of the Enabling Act: federal courts are to apply state substantive law and federal procedural law. However, as subsequent cases sharpened the distinction between substance and procedure, the line of cases following Erie diverged markedly from the line construing the Enabling Act. *Guaranty Trust Co.[] v. York*, [*supra*], made it clear that Erie-type problems were not to be solved by reference to any traditional or common-sense substance-procedure distinction… .

Respondent, by placing primary reliance on *York*… , suggests that the Erie doctrine acts as a check on the Federal Rules of Civil Procedure, that despite the clear command of Rule 4(d)(1), *Erie* and its progeny demand the application of the Massachusetts rule. …

In the first place, it is doubtful that, even if there were no Federal Rule making it clear that in-hand service is not required in diversity actions, the *Erie* rule would have obligated the District Court to follow the Massachusetts procedure. "Outcome-determination" analysis was never intended to serve as a talisman. Byrd v. Blue Ridge Rural Elec. Cooperative, 356 U.S. 525, 537[(1958)]. Indeed, the message of *York* itself is that choices between state and federal law are to be made not by application of any automatic, "litmus paper" criterion, but rather by reference to the policies underlying the *Erie* rule. *Guaranty Trust Co. of New York v. York, supra*[].[fn]

The Erie rule is rooted in part in a realization that it would be unfair for the character of result of a litigation materially to differ because the suit had been brought in a federal court. … The decision was also in part a reaction to the practice of "forum-shopping" which had grown up in response to the rule of *Swift v. Tyson*. [C][fn] That the *York* test was an attempt to effectuate these policies is demonstrated by the fact that the opinion framed the inquiry in terms of "substantial" variations between state and federal litigation. [C] Not only are nonsubstantial, or trivial, variations not likely to raise the sort of equal protection problems which troubled the Court in Erie; they are also unlikely to influence the choice of a forum. The "outcome-determination" test therefore cannot be read without reference to the twin aims of the Erie rule: discouragement of forum-shopping and avoidance of inequitable administration of the laws.[fn]

The difference between the conclusion that the Massachusetts rule is applicable, and the conclusion that it is not, is of course at this point "outcome-determinative" in the sense that if we hold the state rule to apply, respondent prevails, whereas if we hold that Rule 4(d)(1) governs, the litigation will continue. But in this sense every procedural variation is "outcome-determinative." [I]t is difficult to argue that permitting service of defendant's wife to take the place of inhand service of defendant himself alters the mode of enforcement of state-created rights in a fashion sufficiently "substantial" to raise the sort of equal protection problems to which the Erie opinion alluded.

There is, however, a more fundamental flaw in respondent's syllogism: the incorrect assumption that the rule of *Erie R. Co. v. Tompkins* constitutes the appropriate test of the validity and therefore the applicability of a Federal Rule of Civil Procedure. The *Erie* rule has never been invoked to void a Federal Rule. It is true that there have been cases where this Court has held applicable a state rule in the face of an argument that the situation was governed by one of the Federal

Rules. But the holding of each such case was not that *Erie* commanded displacement of a Federal Rule by an inconsistent state rule, but rather that the scope of the Federal Rule was not as broad as the losing party urged, and therefore, there being no Federal Rule which covered the point in dispute, *Erie* commanded the enforcement of state law. ... (Here, of course, the clash is unavoidable; Rule 4(d)(1) says—implicitly, but with unmistakable clarity—that inhand service is not required in federal courts.) At the same time, in cases adjudicating the validity of Federal Rules, we have not applied the *York* rule or other refinements of *Erie*, but have to this day continued to decide questions concerning the scope of the Enabling Act and the constitutionality of specific Federal Rules in light of the distinction set forth in *Sibbach*. [C]

Nor has the development of two separate lines of cases been inadvertent. The line between "substance" and "procedure" shifts as the legal context changes. It is true that both the Enabling Act and the *Erie* rule say, roughly, that federal courts are to apply state "substantive" law and federal "procedural" law, but from that it need not follow that the tests are identical. For they were designed to control very different sorts of decisions. When a situation is covered by one of the Federal Rules, the question facing the court is a far cry from the typical, relatively unguided *Erie* choice: the court has been instructed to apply the Federal Rule, and can refuse to do so only if the Advisory Committee, this Court, and Congress erred in their prima facie judgment that the Rule in question transgresses neither the terms of the Enabling Act nor constitutional restrictions.[fn] ...

Erie and its offspring cast no doubt on the long-recognized power of Congress to prescribe housekeeping rules for federal courts even though some of those rules will inevitably differ from comparable state rules. [C] Thus, though a court, in measuring a Federal Rule against the standards contained in the Enabling Act and the Constitution, need not wholly blind itself to the degree to which the Rule makes the character and result of the federal litigation stray from the course it would follow in state courts, [c], it cannot be forgotten that the *Erie* rule, and the guidelines suggested in *York*, were created to serve another purpose altogether. To hold that a Federal Rule of Civil Procedure must cease to function whenever it alters the mode of enforcing state-created rights would be to disembowel either the Constitution's grant of power over federal procedure or Congress' attempt to exercise that power in the Enabling Act.[fn] Rule 4(d)(1) is valid and controls the instant case.

Reversed.

Mr. Justice BLACK concurs in the result.

Mr. Justice HARLAN, concurring. It is unquestionably true that up to now *Erie* and the cases following it have not succeeded in articulating a workable doctrine governing choice of law in diversity actions. I respect the Court's effort to clarify the situation in today's opinion. However, in doing so I think it has misconceived the constitutional premises of *Erie* and has failed to deal adequately with those past decisions upon which the courts below relied.

Erie was something more than an opinion which worried about "forum-shopping and avoidance of inequitable administration of the laws," [c], although to be sure these were important elements of the decision. I have always regarded that decision as one of the modern cornerstones of our federalism, expressing policies that profoundly touch the allocation of judicial power between the state and federal systems. *Erie* recognized that there should not be two conflicting systems of law controlling the primary activity of citizens, for such alternative governing authority must necessarily give rise to a debilitating uncertainty in the planning of everyday affairs.[fn] And it recognized that the scheme of our Constitution envisions an allocation of law-making functions between state and federal legislative processes which is undercut if the federal judiciary can make substantive law affecting state affairs beyond the bounds of congressional legislative powers in this regard. Thus, in diversity cases *Erie* commands that it be the state law governing primary private activity which prevails.

The shorthand formulations which have appeared in some past decisions are prone to carry untoward results that frequently arise from oversimplification. ... To my mind the proper line of approach in determining whether to apply a state or a federal rule... is to stay close to basic principles by inquiring if the choice of rule would substantially affect those primary decisions respecting human conduct which our constitutional system leaves to state regulation. If so, *Erie* and the Constitution require that the state rule prevail, even in the face of a conflicting federal rule.

The Court weakens, if indeed it does not submerge, this basic principle by finding, in effect, a grant of substantive legislative power in the constitutional provision for a federal court system... , and through it, setting up the Federal Rules as a body of law inviolate. ... So long as a reasonable man could characterize any duly adopted federal rule as "procedural," the Court, unless I misapprehend what is said, would have it apply no matter how seriously it frustrated a State's substantive regulation of the primary conduct and affairs of its citizens. Since the members of the Advisory Committee, the Judicial Conference, and this Court who formulated the Federal Rules are presumably reasonable men, it follows that the integrity of the Federal Rules is absolute. Whereas the unadulterated outcome and forum-shopping tests may err too far toward honoring state rules, I submit that the Court's "arguably procedural, ergo constitutional" test moves too fast and far in the other direction. ...

It remains to apply what has been said to the present case. If the Federal District Court in Massachusetts applies Rule 4(d)(1) of the Federal Rules of Civil Procedure instead of the Massachusetts service rule, what effect would that have on the speed and assurance with which estates are distributed? As I see it, the effect would not be substantial. It would mean simply that an executor would have to check at his own house or the federal courthouse as well as the registry of probate before he could distribute the estate with impunity. As this does not seem enough to give rise to any real impingement on the vitality of the state policy which the Massachusetts rule is intended to serve, I concur in the judgment of the Court.

INQUIRY

Reconciliation. How, then, does one reconcile *Hanna v. Plummer* with the long line of decisions following *Erie*? Perhaps the easiest way to reconcile *Hanna* is to allow it to stand for the rule that a *Federal Rule of Civil Procedure* or other rule or statute within the sense of the Rules Enabling Act will govern when it is clearly applicable whether or not in conflict with a state law or rule. In the vast majority of cases, *Hanna* makes civil procedure much simpler for the practitioner: follow the *Federal Rules* where they regulate procedure. *See Sibbach v. Wilson, supra*, at 14 ("[t]he test must be whener a rule really regulates procedure"). Two Supreme Court cases decided after *Hanna* confirm that the holding of *Hanna* applies not just to the *Federal Rules of Civil Procedure* but to other rules and statutes within the sense of the Rules Enabling Act. In Burlington Northern R. Co. v. Woods, 480 U.S. 1 (1987), the Supreme Court held that a *Federal Rule of Appellate Procedure* supplanted a state statute on penalty interest on a judgment. In Stewart Organization, Inc. v Ricoh Corp., 487 U.S. 22 (1988), the Supreme Court held that 28 U.S.C. §1404 supplants state case law on the enforceability of a forum-selection clause. Both federal provisions clearly governed federal-court practice within the sense of the Rules Enabling Act, and so as a matter of statutory interpretation the federal provisions applied.

***Erie's* Relevance.** Has *Erie* disappeared, then? The constitutional concerns, standards, and tests of *Erie*, *Byrd*, and *York* remain relevant in at least two situations. One is where there is no applicable *Federal Rule of Civil Procedure* or other rule or statute within the sense of the Rules Enabling Act. In that instance where state law conflicts with no other federal rule or statute prescribing federal-court practice, then *Erie* analysis (and its great deference to state law) applies. The other situation where *Erie* maintains an influence is in determining the scope of the *Federal Rules of Civil Procedure*. Recall *Cohen* and *Ragan*, in which the Supreme Court held that state law applied rather than two *Federal Rules*. When in *Hanna v. Plummer* the Court stated "there have been cases where this Court has held applicable a state rule in the face of an argument that the situation was governed by one of the Federal Rules," it presumably was referring to *Cohen* and *Ragan*. The *Hanna* opinion clarified that "the holding of each such case [*Cohen* and *Ragan*] was not that *Erie* commanded displacement of a Federal Rule by an inconsistent state rule, but rather that the scope of the Federal Rule was not as broad as the losing party urged... ." *Hanna* may indicate that *Erie* also influences the scope of the *Federal Rules of Civil Procedure*, in addition to applying where there is no *Federal Rule*. *See* Walker v. Armco Steel Corp., 446 U.S. 740 (1980) (reaffirming *Ragan* as involving a state rule comprising "a statement of a substantive decision [that] is an integral part of the several policies served by the statute of limitations" and interpreting Rule 3 narrowly not to apply). Subsequent Supreme Court cases have narrowly construed various *Federal Rules* not to directly apply and control. *See* Semtek Intl. Inc. v. Lockheed Martin Corp., 531 U.S. 497 (2001) (narrow construction of Rule 41(b) not to apply to ultimate issue); Ortiz v. Fibreboard Corp., 527 U.S. 815, 842 (1999) ("limiting construction" of Rule 23(b)(1)(B) to "minimize potential conflict").

***Erie's* Standard.** If, then, *Erie* remains relevant, how did *Hanna v. Plummer* modify *Erie* doctrine? Scholars differ in their interpretations. *Contrast* Westen & Lehman, *Is there Life for* Erie *After the Death of Diversity?*, 78 MICH. L.REV. 311, 314-315 (1980), *with* Ely, *The Irrepressible Myth of* Erie, 87 HARV. L.REV. 693, 697-698 (1974). Yet in outline, a comprehensive *Erie* analysis should begin by determining whether a *Federal Rule of Civil Procedure* or other federal rule or statute clearly prescribes the federal court's procedure (a Rules Enabling Act analysis), in which instance the federal provision controls under *Hanna*. If the implicated federal provision is arguably not so broad and specific that it must apply, then the federal court should examine whether the federal provision is merely procedural rather than substantive, in which event it may still control. If, on the other hand, it has substantive rather than merely procedural aspects, then the court should examine whether the federal-or-state-law decision is outcome determinative in the specific case or a substantial percentage of like cases, in which event *Erie's* structural concerns definitely arise. Given outcome-determinative influence, the court should then balance the degree to which the state provision is an integral part of state-law rights against countervailing federal interests in control over the federal courts. The following case shows one of the Supreme Court's latest attempts to apply this comprehensive framework. As you read the case, see if you can identify each stage of the analysis. Did the Supreme Court miss the first step of ensuring that the applicable *Federal Rule* did not directly govern the question?

Gasperini v. Center for Humanities, Inc.,

United States Supreme Court
518 U.S. 415 (1996)

Justice GINSBURG delivered the opinion of the Court.

Under the law of New York, appellate courts are empowered to review the size of jury verdicts and to order new trials when the jury's award "deviates materially from what would be reasonable compensation." N.Y. Civ. Prac. Law and Rules (CPLR) §5501(c)[]. Under the Seventh Amendment, which governs proceedings in federal court, but not in state court, "the right of trial by jury shall be preserved, and no fact tried by a jury, shall be otherwise re-examined in any Court of the United States, than according to the rules of the common law." [C] The compatibility of these provisions, in an action based on New York law but tried in federal court by reason of the parties' diverse citizenship, is the issue we confront in this case. We hold that New York's law controlling compensation awards for excessiveness or inadequacy can be given effect, without detriment to the Seventh Amendment, if the review standard set out in CPLR §5501(c) is applied by the federal trial court judge, with appellate control of the trial court's ruling limited to review for "abuse of discretion."

I

Petitioner William Gasperini, a journalist for CBS News and the Christian Science Monitor, began reporting on events in Central America in 1984. ... During the course of his seven-year stint in Central America, Gasperini took over 5,000 slide transparencies, depicting active war zones, political leaders, and scenes from daily life. In 1990, Gasperini agreed to supply his original color transparencies to The Center for Humanities, Inc. (Center) for use in an educational videotape, Conflict in Central America. Gasperini selected 300 of his slides for the Center; its videotape included 110 of them. The Center agreed to return the original transparencies, but upon the completion of the project, it could not find them.

Gasperini commenced suit in the United States District Court for the Southern District of New York, invoking the court's diversity jurisdiction pursuant to 28 U.S.C. § 1332.[fn] He alleged several state-law claims for relief, including breach of contract, conversion, and negligence. [C] The Center conceded liability for the lost transparencies and the issue of damages was tried before a jury.

At trial, Gasperini's expert witness testified that the "industry standard" within the photographic publishing community valued a lost transparency at $1,500. ... Gasperini estimated that his earnings from photography totaled just over $10,000 for the period from 1984 through 1993. He also testified that he intended to produce a book containing his best photographs from Central America. [C]

After a three-day trial, the jury awarded Gasperini $450,000 in compensatory damages. This sum, the jury foreperson announced, "is [$]1500 each, for 300 slides." [C] Moving for a new trial under Federal Rule of Civil Procedure 59, the Center attacked the verdict on various grounds, including excessiveness. Without comment, the District Court denied the motion. [C]

The Court of Appeals for the Second Circuit vacated the judgment entered on the jury's verdict. [C] Mindful that New York law governed the controversy, the Court of Appeals endeavored to apply CPLR §5501(c), which instructs that, when a jury returns an itemized verdict, as the jury did in this case, the New York Appellate Division "shall determine that an award is excessive or inadequate if it deviates materially from what would be reasonable compensation." ... Surveying Appellate Division decisions that reviewed damage awards for lost transparencies, the Second Circuit concluded that testimony on industry standard alone was insufficient to justify a verdict; prime among other factors warranting consideration were the uniqueness of the slides' subject matter and the photographer's earning level.[fn]

Guided by Appellate Division rulings, the Second Circuit held that the $450,000 verdict "materially deviates from what is reasonable compensation." [C] ... [T]he Second Circuit set aside the $450,000 verdict and ordered a new trial, unless Gasperini agreed to an award of $100,000.

This case presents an important question regarding the standard a federal court uses to measure the alleged excessiveness of a jury's verdict in an action for damages based on state law. ...

II

Before 1986, state and federal courts in New York generally invoked the same judge-made formulation in responding to excessiveness attacks on jury verdicts: courts would not disturb an award unless the amount was so exorbitant that it "shocked the conscience of the court." ...

In both state and federal courts, trial judges made the excessiveness assessment in the first instance, and appellate judges ordinarily deferred to the trial court's judgment. ...

In 1986, as part of a series of tort reform measures, New York codified a standard for judicial review of the size of jury awards. Placed in CPLR § 5501(c), the prescription reads: "In reviewing a money judgment ... in which it is contended that the award is excessive or inadequate and that a new trial should have been granted unless a stipulation is entered to a different award, the appellate division shall determine that an award is excessive or inadequate if it deviates materially from what would be reasonable compensation."[fn] ...

New York state-court opinions confirm that §5501(c)'s "deviates materially" standard calls for closer surveillance than "shock the conscience" oversight. [Cc]

Although phrased as a direction to New York's intermediate appellate courts, §5501(c)'s "deviates materially" standard, as construed by New York's courts, instructs state trial judges as well. [Cc] Application of § 5501(c) at the trial level is key to this case.

To determine whether an award "deviates materially from what would be reasonable compensation," New York state courts look to awards approved in similar cases. …

III

In cases like Gasperini's, in which New York law governs the claims for relief, does New York law also supply the test for federal-court review of the size of the verdict? …

As the parties' arguments suggest, CPLR §5501(c), appraised under *Erie R. Co. v. Tompkins,* 304 U.S. 64[] (1938), and decisions in *Erie*'s path, is both "substantive" and "procedural": "substantive" in that § 5501(c)'s "deviates materially" standard controls how much a plaintiff can be awarded; "procedural" in that §5501(c) assigns decisionmaking authority to New York's Appellate Division. Parallel application of §5501(c) at the federal appellate level would be out of sync with the federal system's division of trial and appellate court functions, an allocation weighted by the Seventh Amendment. The dispositive question, therefore, is whether federal courts can give effect to the substantive thrust of §5501(c) without untoward alteration of the federal scheme for the trial and decision of civil cases.

A

… Classification of a law as "substantive" or "procedural" for *Erie* purposes is sometimes a challenging endeavor.[fn.7 … [I]t is settled that if [a Federal Rule of Civil Procedure] is consonant with the Rules Enabling Act, 28 U.S.C. §2072, and the Constitution, the Federal Rule applies regardless of contrary state law. … Federal courts have interpreted the Federal Rules … with sensitivity to important state interests and regulatory policies. …] Guaranty Trust Co. v. York, 326 U.S. 99[, 109] (1945), an early interpretation of *Erie,* propounded an "outcome-determination" test: "[D]oes it significantly affect the result of a litigation for a federal court to disregard a law of a State that would be controlling in an action upon the same claim by the same parties in a State court?" … A later pathmarking case, qualifying *Guaranty Trust,* explained that the "outcome-determination" test must not be applied mechanically to sweep in all manner of variations; instead, its application must be guided by "the twin aims of the *Erie* rule: discouragement of forum-shopping and avoidance of inequitable administration of the laws." Hanna v. Plumer, 380 U.S. 460, 468[] (1965).

Informed by these decisions, we address the question whether New York's "deviates materially" standard, codified in CPLR §5501(c), is outcome affective in this sense: Would "application of the [standard] ... have so important an effect upon the fortunes of one or both of the litigants that failure to [apply] it would [unfairly discriminate against citizens of the forum State, or] be likely to cause a plaintiff to choose the federal court"? *Hanna v. Plumer, supra,* at 468n.9[].[fn] …

It … appears that if federal courts ignore the change in the New York standard and persist in applying the "shock the conscience" test to damage awards on claims governed by New York law,[fn] "'substantial' variations between state and federal [money judgments]" may be expected. See *Hanna,* [*supra*,] at 467-468[]. We therefore agree with the Second Circuit that New York's check on excessive damages implicates what we have called *Erie* 's "twin aims." [C] Just as the *Erie* principle precludes a federal court from giving a state-created claim "longer life ... than [the claim] would have had in the state court," [c], so *Erie* precludes a recovery in federal court significantly larger than the recovery that would have been tolerated in state court.

B

CPLR §5501(c) ... is phrased as a direction to the New York Appellate Division. ... Concentrating on the authority §5501(c) gives to the Appellate Division, Gasperini urges that the provision shifts fact-finding responsibility from the jury and the trial judge to the appellate court. Assigning such responsibility to an appellate court, he maintains, is incompatible with the Seventh Amendment's Reexamination Clause, and therefore, Gasperini concludes, §5501(c) cannot be given effect in federal court. [C] Although we reach a different conclusion than Gasperini, we agree that the Second Circuit did not attend to "[a]n essential characteristic of [the federal court] system," Byrd v. Blue Ridge Rural Elec. Cooperative, Inc., 356 U.S. 525, 537[] (1958), when it used §5501(c) as "the standard for [federal] appellate review," [c]. ...

The Seventh Amendment, which governs proceedings in federal court, but not in state court,[fn] bears not only on the allocation of trial functions between judge and jury, the issue in *Byrd;* it also controls the allocation of authority to review verdicts, the issue of concern here. ...

Byrd involved the first Clause of the Amendment, the "trial by jury" Clause. This case involves the second, the "Reexamination" Clause. In keeping with the historic understanding,[fn] the Reexamination Clause does not inhibit the authority of trial judges to grant new trials "for any of the reasons for which new trials have heretofore been granted in actions at law in the courts of the United States." Fed. Rule Civ. Proc. 59(a). That authority is large. [Cc] ... This discretion includes overturning verdicts for excessiveness and ordering a new trial without qualification, or conditioned on the verdict winner's refusal to agree to a reduction (remittitur). [C][fn]

In contrast, appellate review of a federal trial court's denial of a motion to set aside a jury's verdict as excessive is a relatively late, and less secure, development. ...

... We now ... make explicit [that the Seventh Amendment does not preclude appellate review of a trial judge's denial of a motion to set aside a jury verdict as excessive.][fn] ...

C

In *Byrd,* the Court faced a one-or-the-other choice: trial by judge as in state court, or trial by jury according to the federal practice.[fn] In the case before us, a choice of that order is not required, for the principal state and federal interests can be accommodated. The Second Circuit correctly recognized that when New York substantive law governs a claim for relief, New York law and decisions guide the allowable damages. ...

New York's dominant interest can be respected, without disrupting the federal system, once it is recognized that the federal district court is capable of performing the checking function, *i.e.,* that court can apply the State's "deviates materially" standard in line with New York case law evolving under CPLR §5501(c). ...

Within the federal system, practical reasons combine with Seventh Amendment constraints to lodge in the district court, not the court of appeals, primary responsibility for application of §5501(c)'s "deviates materially" check. Trial judges have the "unique opportunity to consider the evidence in the living courtroom context," [c], while appellate judges see only the "cold paper record," [c].

District court applications of the "deviates materially" standard would be subject to appellate review under the standard the Circuits now employ when inadequacy or excessiveness is asserted on appeal: abuse of discretion. [Cc] In light of *Erie*'s doctrine, the federal appeals court must be guided by the damage-control standard state law supplies,[fn] but as the Second Circuit itself has said: "If we reverse, it must be because of an abuse of discretion... . The very nature of the problem counsels restraint... . We must give the benefit of every doubt to the judgment of the trial judge." [C]

IV

It does not appear that the District Court checked the jury's verdict against the relevant New York decisions demanding more than "industry standard" testimony to support an award of the size the jury returned in this case. As the Court of Appeals recognized, [c], the uniqueness of the photographs and the plaintiff's earnings as photographer—past and reasonably projected—are factors relevant to appraisal of the award. [Cc] Accordingly, we vacate the judgment of the Court of Appeals and instruct that court to remand the case to the District Court so that the trial judge, revisiting his ruling on the new trial motion, may test the jury's verdict against CPLR §5501(c)'s "deviates materially" standard.

It is so ordered.

[Justice STEVENS' dissent omitted.]

Justice SCALIA, with whom the CHIEF JUSTICE and Justice THOMAS join, dissenting.

Today the Court overrules a longstanding and well-reasoned line of precedent that has for years prohibited federal appellate courts from reviewing refusals by district courts to set aside civil jury awards as contrary to the weight of the evidence. One reason is given for overruling these cases: that the Courts of Appeals have, for some time now, decided to ignore them. Such unreasoned capitulation to the nullification of what was long regarded as a core component of the Bill of Rights—the Seventh Amendment's prohibition on appellate reexamination of civil jury awards—is wrong. It is not for us, much less for the Courts of Appeals, to decide that the Seventh Amendment's restriction on federal-court review of jury findings has outlived its usefulness.

The Court also holds today that a state practice that relates to the division of duties between state judges and juries must be followed by federal courts in diversity cases. On this issue, too, our prior cases are directly to the contrary.

As I would reverse the judgment of the Court of Appeals, I respectfully dissent.

... The Court's holding that federal courts of appeals may review district-court denials of motions for new trials for error of fact is not the only novel aspect of today's decision. The Court also directs that the case be remanded to the District Court, so that it may "test the jury's verdict against CPLR §5501(c)'s 'deviates materially' standard." [C] This disposition contradicts the principle that "[t]he proper role of the trial and appellate courts in the federal system in reviewing the size of jury verdicts is ... a matter of federal law." Donovan v. Penn Shipping Co., 429 U.S. 648, 649[] (1977) *(per curiam).*

... [C]hanging the standard by which trial judges review jury verdicts ... disrupt[s] the federal system, and is plainly inconsistent with the "strong federal policy against allowing state rules to disrupt the judge-jury relationship in federal court." Byrd v. Blue Ridge Rural Elec. Cooperative, Inc., 356 U.S. 525, 538[] (1958).[fn] ...

... [T]he reason the Court asserts for giving §5501(c) dispositive effect [is that it] ... "is manifestly substantive," [c], since it operates to "contro[l] how much a plaintiff can be awarded" by "tightening the range of tolerable awards," [c]. Although "less readily classified" as substantive than "a statutory cap on damages," [the majority asserts that] it nonetheless "was designed to provide an analogous control," [c], by making a new trial mandatory when the award "deviat[es] materially" from what is reasonable, [c].

I do not see how this can be so. It seems to me quite wrong to regard this provision as a "substantive" rule for *Erie* purposes. The "analog[y]" to "a statutory cap on damages," [c], fails utterly. There is an absolutely fundamental distinction between a *rule of law* such as that, which would ordinarily be imposed upon the jury in the trial court's instructions, and a *rule of review,* which simply determines how closely the jury verdict will be scrutinized for compliance with the instructions. A tighter standard for reviewing jury determinations can no more plausibly be called a "substantive" disposition than can a tighter appellate standard for reviewing trial-court determinations. The one, like the other, provides additional assurance *that the law has been complied with;* but the other, like the one, *leaves the law unchanged.*

The Court commits the classic *Erie* mistake of regarding whatever changes the outcome as substantive, [c]. That is not the only factor to be considered. ... Outcome determination "was never intended to serve as a talisman," Hanna v. Plumer, 380 U.S. 460, 466-467[] (1965), and does not have the power to convert the most classic elements of the *process* of assuring that the law is observed into the substantive law itself. ...

In any event, the Court exaggerates the difference that the state standard will make. It concludes that different outcomes are likely to ensue depending on whether the law being applied is the state "deviates materially" standard of §5501(c) or the "shocks the conscience" standard. [C] Of course it is not the federal *appellate* standard but the federal *district-court* standard for granting new trials that must be compared with the New York standard to determine whether substantially different results will obtain—and it is far from clear that the district-court standard *ought* to be "shocks the conscience."[fn] ... What seems to me far more likely to produce forum shopping is the consistent difference between the state and federal *appellate* standards, which the Court leaves untouched. Under the Court's disposition, the Second Circuit reviews only for abuse of discretion, whereas New York's appellate courts engage in a *de novo* review for material deviation, giving the defendant a double shot at getting the damages award set aside. The only result that would produce the conformity the Court erroneously believes *Erie* requires is the one adopted by the Second Circuit and rejected by the Court: *de novo* federal appellate review under the §5501(c) standard.

To say that application of §5501(c) in place of the federal standard will not consistently produce disparate results is not to suggest that the decision the Court has made today is not a momentous one. The *principle* that the state standard governs is of great importance, since it bears the potential to destroy the uniformity of federal practice and the integrity of the federal court system. Under the Court's view, a state rule that directed courts "to determine that an award is excessive or inadequate if it deviates *in any degree* from *the proper measure of compensation* " would have to be applied in federal courts, effectively requiring federal judges to determine the amount of damages *de novo,* and effectively taking the matter away from the jury entirely. [C] Or consider a state rule that allowed the defendant a second trial on damages, with judgment ultimately in the amount of the lesser of two jury awards. ...

The foregoing describes why I think the Court's *Erie* analysis is flawed. But in my view, one does not even reach the *Erie* question in this case. The standard to be applied by a district court in ruling on a motion for a new trial is set forth in Rule 59 of the Federal Rules of Civil Procedure [(since then amended)], which provides that "[a] new trial may be granted ... for any of the reasons for which new trials have heretofore been granted in actions at law *in the courts of the United States.*" (Emphasis added.) That is undeniably a federal standard.[fn] Federal District Courts in the Second Circuit have interpreted that standard to permit the granting of new trials where "'it is quite clear that the jury has reached a seriously erroneous result'" and letting the verdict stand would result in a "'miscarriage of justice.'" [Cc] Assuming (as we have no reason to question) that this is a correct interpretation of what Rule 59 requires, it is undeniable that the Federal Rule is "'sufficiently broad' to cause a 'direct collision' with the state law or, implicitly, to 'control the issue' before the court, thereby leaving no room for the operation of that law." [C] It is simply not possible to give controlling effect both to the federal standard and the state standard in reviewing the jury's award. That being so, the court has no choice but to apply the Federal Rule, which is an exercise of what we have called Congress's "power to regulate matters which, though falling within the uncertain area between substance and procedure, are rationally capable of classification as either," *Hanna,* [*supra*], at 472[].

There is no small irony in the Court's declaration today that appellate review of refusals to grant new trials for error of fact is "a control necessary and proper to the fair administration of justice," [c]. It is objection to *precisely* that sort of "control" by federal appellate judges that gave birth to the Reexamination Clause of the Seventh Amendment. ...

... I respectfully dissent.

INQUIRY

Guesswork. The above discussion has assumed that when a federal court entertaining a diversity case applies state law, that the state law is clear. What should a federal court do when the state law that it must apply is not clear and, instead, the state-law question is one of first impression? In one such case, the admirable Judge Henry Friendly wryly observed that "this diversity of citizenship case [requires him] to determine what the New York courts would think the

California courts would think on an issue about which neither has thought." Nolan v. Transocean Air Lines, 276 F.2d 280, 281 (2d Cir. 1960). The federal trial judge makes a best effort to do that which the state court would have done. Because appeals of those guesstimates (what one court labeled "informed prophecy," *see* Moores v. Greenberg, 834 F.2d 1105 (1st Cir. 1987)) go to federal rather than state appellate courts, the federal appellate courts then face the same difficulty of making their best judgment. In doing so, the federal appellate courts must not defer to (and must instead make de novo review of) the lower federal court's judgment. Salve Regina College v. Russell, 499 U.S. 225 (1991). The federal courts do not always get it right. One can find instances where later state decisions show the federal courts to have diverged, requiring the federal courts to return in any subsequent cases to the state-law path clarified by the subsequent state-court decisions. Practitioners recognize these anomalies, considering them when advising clients regarding the benefits of alternative jurisdictions.

Certification. Some federal courts have an alternative to guessing (predicting) what a state court would do if faced with a question of first impression. At last count, 45 states permit the Supreme Court and federal Circuit Courts of Appeals to certify a state-law question to the state's highest court for answer, with 36 of those states also permitting certification by federal District Courts. Certification systems permit the federal courts to state questions of law and permit but do not require the state high courts to answer those questions. *See* Tunick v. Safir, 731 N.E.2d 597 (N.Y. Ct. App. 2000) (declining to answer certified question because of delay in resolution of case that certification would cause). Judith S. Kaye and Kenneth L. Weissman, *Interactive Judicial Federalism: Certified Questions in New York*, 69 FORDHAM L.REV. 373, App. A (2000). Certification systems do not transfer the case. They merely certify questions. *See, e.g.*, Reddington v. Staten Island Univ. Hosp., 893 N.E.2d 120 (N.Y. Ct. App. 2008) (entertaining two questions certified from the United States Court of Appeals for the Second Circuit). Like a federal court predicting state-court action, certification is itself an imperfect system, even though the Supreme Court has written favorably of certification. *See* Arizonans for Official English v. Arizona, 520 U.S. 43, 76 (1997). The necessarily abstract nature of the federal court's question of law can lead to confusing or inapplicable state-court answers. Certification can also be an antidote to or an opportunity for forum shopping. *See* Calabresi, *Federal and State Courts: Restoring a Workable Balance*, 78 N.Y.U. L.REV. 1293, 1300 (2003). If you were appellate counsel in a federal appeal of a first-impression state issue, would you try certification? See what you think of the following certification statute. FED. R. CIV. P. 5.1, also reproduced below, provides for a different kind of certification. Can you discern the difference?

22 N.Y. Comp. Codes R. & Regs. §500.27 [Rules of Practice of the N.Y. Court of Appeals]. Discretionary proceedings to review certified questions from Federal courts and other courts of last resort.

(a) Whenever it appears to the Supreme Court of the United States, any United States Court of Appeals, or a court of last resort of any other state that determinative questions of New York law are involved in a case pending before that court for which no controlling precedent of the Court of Appeals exists, the court may certify the dispositive questions of law to the Court of Appeals.

(b) The certifying court shall prepare a certificate which shall contain the caption of the case, a statement of facts setting forth the nature of the case and the circumstances out of which the questions of New York law arise, and the questions of New York law, not controlled by precedent, that may be determinative, together with a statement as to why the issue should be addressed in the Court of Appeals at this time.

...

(g) When a determination is rendered by the court with respect to the questions certified, it shall be sent by the clerk of the court to the certifying court.

FED. R. CIV. P. 5.1. Constitutional Challenge to a Statute—Notice, Certification, and Intervention.

(a) NOTICE BY A PARTY. A party that files a pleading, written motion, or other paper drawing into question the constitutionality of a federal or state statute must promptly:

(1) file a notice of constitutional question stating the question and identifying the paper that raises it, if:

(A) a federal statute is questioned and the parties do not include the United States, one of its agencies, or one of its officers or employees in an official capacity; or

(B) a state statute is questioned and the parties do not include the state, one of its agencies, or one of its officers or employees in an official capacity; and

(2) serve the notice and paper on the Attorney General of the United States if a federal statute is questioned—or on the state attorney general if a state statute is questioned—either by certified or registered mail or by sending it to an electronic address designated by the attorney general for this purpose.

(b) CERTIFICATION BY THE COURT. The court must, under 28 U.S.C. §2403, certify to the appropriate attorney general that a statute has been questioned.

(c) INTERVENTION; FINAL DECISION ON THE MERITS. Unless the court sets a later time, the attorney general may intervene within 60 days after the notice is filed or after the court certifies the challenge, whichever is earlier. Before the time to intervene expires, the court may reject the constitutional challenge, but may not enter a final judgment holding the statute unconstitutional.

(d) NO FORFEITURE. A party's failure to file and serve the notice, or the court's failure to certify, does not forfeit a constitutional claim or defense that is otherwise timely asserted.

Knowledge

Courts face a productive tension when formulating rules and standards. On one hand, they can formulate and apply clear, certain, and predictable rules that nonetheless sometimes produce insensitive and even arbitrary results in borderline cases. On the other hand, courts can formulate sensitive and flexible general standards that nonetheless are expensive around which to litigate, difficult to administer, and hard to predict. Clear rules and general standards each have their advantages and disadvantages. It may depend on how one sees a judge's role and responsibility, whether as judging or managing. You can choose whether to treat purposefully ambiguous standards with frustration or appreciation. You can mock clear rules for their wooden insensitivity or appreciate them for their certainty. We encourage you to appreciate the value of both rules and standards. Your attitude toward law knowledge makes a difference in how effectively you learn.

B. Conflicts of Law

The Supreme Court's first good opportunity to apply *Erie* came in a curiously appropriate place. Recall the mention in the chapter introduction of *conflicts-of-law* doctrine helping courts decide which state's law applies when the case involves residents of different states, matters occurring across state lines, or in another respect two or more states having interests. *Erie* itself presents an example. Just because the railroad's train injured Tompkins in Pennsylvania does not necessarily mean that a New York court should apply Pennsylvania law if (hypothetically) Tompkins resided in and the railroad operated out of New York. Perhaps then, New York rather than Pennsylvania law should apply. *Erie* did not address the conflicts-of-law issue presumably because it was obvious enough that Pennsylvania was the state with the greatest interest whose law should apply. Although there is much consistency state to state, states develop their own conflicts-of-law rules. When a federal court must decide which state's law to apply in a diversity case, whose conflict-of-law rules does the federal court apply? The Supreme Court answered that question in Klaxon Co. v. Stentor Electric Mfg. Co., 313 U.S. 487 (1941), holding that the federal court should apply the conflict-of-law rules of the state in which the federal court is located. *See also* Day & Zimmerman, Inc. v. Challoner, 423 U.S. 3 (1975) (Texas federal court must apply Texas conflict-of-law rules); Van Dusen v. Barrack, 376 U.S. 612 (1964) (transferred case retains the conflict-of-law rules of the transferor court's forum state).

What are the conflict-of-law rules that determine which state's law applies? Lawyers treat this question of governing law under the rubrics *choice of law* and, when there is disagreement over that choice, *conflicts of law*. Choice and conflicts of law raise the questions of (1) when a state should allow its courts to hear matters involving interstate matters and (2) which state's law the court should apply in those cases. The rules governing those questions are the subject of entire law-school Conflict of Laws courses. The rules also vary state to state. Suffice it here to say that the touchstone for deciding conflicts of law is the due-process clause of the Constitution. *See* Allstate Ins. Co. v. Hague, 449 U.S. 302, 312-313 (1981) (requiring significant contacts or aggregation of contacts reflecting state's interests) (plurality opinion). State courts may not apply state law arbitrarily or capriciously in ways that deny litigants due process. A traditional approach favored applying the law of the place where the event occurred as to matters of substance (a doctrine known as lex loci delicti) and the law of the forum for procedural matters (a doctrine known as lex fori). Contemporary approaches tend to examine the strength or closeness of the dispute's connection with each state whose law might possibly apply, to see which state has the strongest policy interest in having its law apply. The traditional categorical rules provide a substantial degree of certainty and predictability, while the contemporary interest-balancing approaches are more sensitive but harder to predict and tend to generate their own rules.

Similar questions over governing law can arise in United States federal and state court cases involving international affairs. Choice and conflicts of law issues can arise when the question is the law of which nation (or the law of which state of which nation) rather than merely the law of which American state. The European lexicon treats the issue as one of *private international law* rather than choice or conflicts of law, even though private-international-law principles can be similar. That law and those principles are also beyond the scope of this civil-procedure course, even if the possibility of these issues is well worth noting. Many practitioners find increasing need to understand international choice-of-law issues in order to serve clients in the United States having global travels and personal, professional, and business interests. FED. R. CIV. P. 44.1 requires that a party notify the trial court in writing whenever the case involves a question of a foreign nation's law. United States courts may not be able to determine a foreign nation's law through the usual research means. Even if writings and translations were within the trial court's reach, foreign nations may not have reduced all of their law to writing. Rule 44.1 recognizes these challenges and permits a federal trial court to consider any material or source including inadmissible testimony.

FED. R. CIV. P. 44.1. Determining Foreign Law
A party who intends to raise an issue about a foreign country's law must give notice by a pleading or other writing. In determining foreign law, the court may consider any relevant material or source, including testimony, whether or not submitted by a party or admissible under the Federal Rules of Evidence. The court's determination must be treated as a ruling on a question of law.

Summary. When a dispute arises in a federal-court diversity case over whether state or federal law governs an issue, then the trial court will determine whether a *Federal Rule of Civil Procedure* or other federal rule or statute clearly prescribes the federal court's procedure. If so (under a straightforward Rules Enabling Act analysis), then the federal provision controls. In determining whether a federal provision applies, the trial court may construe the federal provision narrowly to avoid conflicts with a substantial state interest. The federal court may also examine whether the federal provision is merely procedural rather than substantive, in which event the federal provision may still control. If, on the other hand, it has substantive aspects, then the court should examine whether the federal-or-state-law decision is likely to determine the case's outcome. If so, then the court should determine the degree to which the state provision is an integral part of state-law rights and balance that determination against countervailing federal interests in control over the federal courts. Where there is a question of which state's law to apply, federal courts look to the choice-of-law doctrine of the forum state. State choice-of-law rules tend either to be categorical (the substantive law of the place where the cause of action arose and the procedural law of the forum state) or to involve a balancing of each state's interests in having its own law apply. Lawyers distinguish themselves by knowing the significance of the question of which law governs, in that law is the one source of all delegated authority.

Career

Do you work best in formal or informal environments? Some lawyers prefer a relaxed work environment in which they can perform as best suits their individual style. Other lawyers prefer a structured environment in which the employer communicates clear expectations, and the lawyers know when they have met those expectations. In civil litigation, smaller firms tend to have less structure and encourage their lawyers to work when and how they think best. They value personal initiative. By contrast, larger firms often have management systems, protocols, and lines of supervision that are important to the timing and integrity of their complex litigation work. Freestyling in such an environment can disrupt the work. As you read the civil-procedure cases, think about the type of environment in which the lawyers probably performed the work, and consider your preference.

PROCESS OF ADJUDICATION

CHAPTER VII

PLEADING

OBJECTIVE: That you be able to identify pleading requirements and options for initiating and responding to civil litigation in the state and federal courts.

Case Study: You are meeting with a client who has described the breakup of a business of which the client is a part owner and manager. The client has been unable to agree with the other owner on how to value and divide the business despite (and likely because of) the business' great success. Mediation failed because of disagreement over misrepresentations, misuse of assets, and nonperformance. Both owners are now consulting lawyers. Advise the client about initiating and responding to civil litigation.

Federal Rules of Civil Procedure this chapter reproduces and addresses
FED. R. CIV. P. 5: Serving and Filing Pleadings and Other Papers.
FED. R. CIV. P. 5.2: Privacy Protection for Filings Made with the Court.
FED. R. CIV. P. 6: Computing and Extending Time; Time for Motion Papers.
FED. R. CIV. P. 7: Pleadings Allowed; Form of Motions and Other Papers.
FED. R. CIV. P. 7.1: Disclosure Statement.
FED. R. CIV. P. 8: General Rules of Pleading.
FED. R. CIV. P. 9: Pleading Special Matters.
FED. R. CIV. P. 10: Form of Pleadings.
FED. R. CIV. P. 11: Signing Pleadings... ; Representation... ; Sanctions.
FED. R. CIV. P. 15: Amended and Supplemental Pleadings.
FED. R. CIV. P. 41: Dismissal of Actions.
FED. R. CIV. P. 55: Default; Default Judgment.
FED. R. CIV. P. 71.1: Condemning Real or Personal Property.

This chapter is the first of several on the process of adjudication. You have now completed the first six chapters that together address the authority of the courts to adjudicate. This chapter addresses how lawyers invoke court authority by initiating civil litigation through drafting, filing, and responding to pleadings. Subsequent chapters in this second part of the text address joinder (adding other parties to the litigation not named and other claims not pled in the original pleadings), discovery (determining the evidence before trial), adjudication before trial (by motion), alternative dispute resolution (such as mediation and arbitration), case management (by the court), and trial. The *Federal Rules of Civil Procedure* that you encounter in these chapters on the Process of Adjudication continue to reflect policy and due process concerns, as did the *Federal Rules* that you encountered in the first several chapters on the Authority to Adjudicate. Although in this part you shift from the divine to the mundane (that is, from direct consideration of constitutional issues to the mechanical steps lawyers take to invoke authority), recognizing the underlying policies and due process concerns will aid your learning and practice. Many *Federal Rules* and their state counterparts reflect a tension among policies for the just, efficient, independent, and fair resolution of disputes. The trial courts interpret and apply procedural rules accommodating as best they can those vitalizing policies. As do other chapters, this chapter focuses on the *Federal Rules of Civil Procedure* recognizing that state-court rules supply similar regimes for pleading in state-court cases.

The title of this chapter "Pleading" is appropriate in a couple of respects as a distinct word with which to describe the process of initiating civil litigation. Conventionally, the verb to plead is to ask or implore on specific compelling grounds. Similarly, in legal lexicon, to plead is a party's act of setting out specific claims against other parties and defenses to those claims. Pleadings (the nominal form of the verb to plead) are the court papers that lawyers draft and file asking the trial court for relief on certain legal claims. Court papers include everything that one might file with the court clerk. Pleadings are the subset of court papers that begin the litigation. They frame the legal issue that the trial court must resolve. As you read FED. R. CIV. P. 7 below, notice how it distinguishes pleadings from motions and other court papers. Notice, too, the following FED. R. CIV. P. 7.1. Any idea why corporate parties would have to disclose parent and controlling entities? *See* 28 U.S.C. §455(b) (recusal of judge having financial interest in case).

FED. R. CIV. P. 7. Pleadings Allowed; Form of Motions and Other Papers
(a) PLEADINGS. Only these pleadings are allowed:
(1) a complaint;
(2) an answer to a complaint;
(3) an answer to a counterclaim designated as a counterclaim;
(4) an answer to a crossclaim;
(5) a third-party complaint;
(6) an answer to a third-party complaint; and
(7) if the court orders one, a reply to an answer.
(b) MOTIONS AND OTHER PAPERS.
(1) *In General.* A request for a court order must be made by motion. The motion must:
(A) be in writing unless made during a hearing or trial;
(B) state with particularity the grounds for seeking the order; and
(C) state the relief sought.
(2) *Form.* The rules governing captions and other matters of form in pleadings apply to motions and other papers.

FED. R. CIV. P. 7.1. Disclosure Statement
(a) WHO MUST FILE; CONTENTS. A nongovernmental corporate party must file 2 copies of a disclosure statement that:
(1) identifies any parent corporation and any publicly held corporation owning 10% or more of its stock; or
(2) states that there is no such corporation.
(b) TIME TO FILE; SUPPLEMENTAL FILING. A party must:
(1) file the disclosure statement with its first appearance, pleading, petition, motion, response, or other request addressed to the court; and
(2) promptly file a supplemental statement if any required information changes.

INQUIRY

History. The faintly anachronistic cast to the word pleading also reminds us that the process of initiating civil litigation has a significant history to it. Recall Chapter 1's mention that American civil procedure and, indeed, its common law have their roots in the old English writ system. To begin an action, a claimant obtained a writ from the king, king's chancellor, or feudal court recognizing only limited forms of action that helped judges sort valid from invalid cases. Early reforms of the writ system only worsened its hyper-technical and inflexible forms. Common Law Procedure Acts in the 1850s relaxed some pleading requirements. Parliament finally combined courts and abolished the writ forms of action with the Judicature Acts of 1873 and 1875, establishing. American reforms began in 1848 when New York adopted the first Field Code (advocated by lawyer David Dudley Field). The new American pleading rules eliminated the form of action, instead requiring that the plaintiff plead a statement of facts supporting a claim for relief or cause. Not all was immediately well. Changes in pleading rules did not necessarily mean that the substantive law underlying the old forms of action had also changed. A new pleading identifying the cause or claim could seem a lot like an old pleading identifying the old form of action. *See* Ross v. Mather, 51 N.Y. 108 (1872) (pleading that identified fraud as the cause does not state claim for breach of contract). To remove any lingering doubt that trial judges were not to judge modern pleadings under the old writ system, when the *Federal Rules of Procedure* took effect in 1938, FED. R. CIV. P. 2 explicitly abolished the old forms of action by providing, "There is one form of action—the civil action."

State Rules. State cases decided under modern pleading rules have tended to require that the plaintiff identify who was involved, what happened, and when and where it occurred. *See* Gillispie v. Goodyear Service Stores, 128 S.E.2d 762 (N.C. 1963). Yet, as this chapter shows, courts can construe even that basic pleading requirement for a statement of facts in ways that can look hypertechnical to the lawyer trying to meet the new rules. See if you recognize any opportunity for such mischief in the following representative modern state-court pleading rules:

> **N.Y. CIV. PRAC. LAW & RULES §425.10. Statement of facts; demand for judgment.**
> (a) A complaint or cross-complaint shall contain both of the following:
> (1) A statement of the facts constituting the cause of action, in ordinary and concise language.
> (2) A demand for judgment for the relief to which the pleader claims to be entitled. If the recovery of money or damages is demanded, the amount demanded shall be stated.
> (b) Notwithstanding subdivision (a), where an action is brought to recover actual or punitive damages for personal injury or wrongful death, the amount demanded shall not be stated… .
>
> **N.Y. CIV. PRAC. LAW & RULES §3011. Kinds of pleadings.**
> There shall be a complaint and an answer. An answer may include a counterclaim against a plaintiff and a cross-claim against a defendant. A defendant's pleading against another claimant is an interpleader complaint, or against any other person not already a party is a third-party complaint. There shall be a reply to a

counterclaim denominated as such, an answer to an interpleader complaint or third-party complaint, and an answer to a cross-claim that contains a demand for an answer. If no demand is made, the cross-claim shall be deemed denied or avoided. There shall be no other pleading unless the court orders otherwise.

N.Y. CIV. PRAC. LAW & RULES §3013. Particularity of statements generally.
Statements in a pleading shall be sufficiently particular to give the court and parties notice of the transactions, occurrences, or series of transactions or occurrences, intended to be proved and the material elements of each cause of action or defense.

N.Y. CIV. PRAC. LAW & RULES §3014. Statements.
Every pleading shall consist of plain and concise statements in consecutively numbered paragraphs. Each paragraph shall contain, as far as practicable, a single allegation. Reference to and incorporation of allegations may subsequently be by number. Prior statements in a pleading shall be deemed repeated or adopted subsequently in the same pleading whenever express repetition or adoption is unnecessary for a clear presentation of the subsequent matters. Separate causes of action or defenses shall be separately stated and numbered and may be stated regardless of consistency. Causes of action or defenses may be stated alternatively or hypothetically. A copy of any writing which is attached to a pleading is a part thereof for all purposes.

INQUIRY

Functions. As the above state-court rules suggest, pleading retains its primary function to identify the parties and claims so that all parties have notice and opportunity for fair resolution. Yet a pleading's audience is larger than the opposing parties and their lawyers. Lawyers file pleadings with court clerks as permanent public records. The court clerk, trial judge, and public all have their own use for pleadings. Court clerks use the caption of a pleading to ensure proper administration including opening a case, assigning a case number and judge, filing original pleadings, and routing any copies (to a trial judge, judicial law clerk, Friend of the Court, or process server, for instance). Trial judges also use pleadings to ensure that they have no conflicts (*see* FED. R. CIV. P. 7.1). More significantly, parties can call upon the trial judge to use the pleadings to evaluate whether the case belongs in that court rather than some other court, or in any court. News reporters and other members of the public may also review pleadings for matters of general interest. You may have noticed in the first state-court rule above that a plaintiff pleading a personal-injury or wrongful-death claim must not state a damage amount. Can you articulate why (the concern over publicity)? Opposing parties' interests differ when it comes to the public aspect of pleading. Plaintiffs and defendants may prefer either greater or lesser disclosure, depending on the nature of the claims and interests. Pleading rules have some responsibility in addressing those interests.

Compromise. Pleading once had two additional functions that it no longer has or has only in limited respects. The *Federal Rules of Civil Procedure* and similar state-court rules provide elaborate means of discovering evidence, reducing the need for parties to plead detailed facts. *See* FED. R. CIV. P. 26-37.

The *Federal Rules* and state-court rules also authorize motions to dismiss and for summary judgment, reducing the need for courts to winnow groundless claims on the pleadings. *See* FED. R. CIV. P. 12(b); FED. R. CIV. P. 56. State and federal rules also impose sanctions on parties and lawyers who plead frivolous cases. *See* FED. R. CIV. P. 11. They also permit liberal amendment. *See* FED. R. CIV. P. 15. Yet as pleading rules relaxed, pre-trial procedures and their accompanying cost and burden may have increased beyond an acceptable point. Pleading history helps us appreciate that state and federal pleading rules continue to reflect this tension over the proper role of pleading. Keeping this tension in mind, and the underlying competing goals that it reflects, will help you learn pleading rules and case law. As has been true in the prior chapters, this chapter focuses on the *Federal Rules* because of their uniformity nationwide and similarity to state pleading rules.

A. Complaint

1. General Rules

FED. R. CIV. P. 3 provides, "A civil action is commenced by filing a complaint with the court." FED. R. CIV. P. 7(a)(1), reproduced above in this chapter, identifies a complaint as an allowable pleading but states nothing further as to its form or content. General pleading rules appear in FED. R. CIV. P. 8. Special pleading rules appear in FED. R. CIV. P. 9. The division makes sense. Rule 8 applies to all actions. The special circumstances addressed in Rule 9 apply to only some actions. What the federal-court practitioner must do is to comply in every case with Rule 8 while remaining aware of the possibility that Rule 9's special rules may also apply, maintaining a mental note of Rule 9's special instances. A following section addresses those special circumstances. This section addresses Rule 8's general provisions. The general provisions of Rule 8(a) having to do with a claim for relief are deceptively simple. Rule 8(a)(1) requires a statement of the jurisdictional grounds, (a)(2) a "short and plain statement of the claim," and (a)(3) a demand for relief, also known as a prayer for relief or ad damnum clause. Rule 8(d)(1) requires that allegations be "simple, concise, and direct" and states, "No technical form is required." Nonetheless, the Supreme Court case law interpreting Rule 8(a)'s requirements is surprisingly nuanced. This section first addresses Rule 8(a)'s basic requirements, while the following section addresses cases specifically addressed to the sufficiency of Rule 8(a) pleadings. Read Rule 8 and two associated rules before exploring those issues.

FED. R. CIV. P. 8. General Rules of Pleading
(a) CLAIM FOR RELIEF. A pleading that states a claim for relief must contain:
(1) a short and plain statement of the grounds for the court's jurisdiction, unless the court already has jurisdiction and the claim needs no new jurisdictional support;
(2) a short and plain statement of the claim showing that the pleader is entitled to relief; and
(3) a demand for the relief sought, which may include relief in the alternative or different types of relief.
(b) DEFENSES; ADMISSIONS AND DENIALS.
(1) *In General.* In responding to a pleading, a party must:
(A) state in short and plain terms its defenses to each claim asserted against it; and

(B) admit or deny the allegations asserted against it by an opposing party.
(2) *Denials—Responding to the Substance.* A denial must fairly respond to the substance of the allegation.
(3) *General and Specific Denials.* A party that intends in good faith to deny all the allegations of a pleading—including the jurisdictional grounds—may do so by a general denial. A party that does not intend to deny all the allegations must either specifically deny designated allegations or generally deny all except those specifically admitted.
(4) *Denying Part of an Allegation.* A party that intends in good faith to deny only part of an allegation must admit the part that is true and deny the rest.
(5) *Lacking Knowledge or Information.* A party that lacks knowledge or information sufficient to form a belief about the truth of an allegation must so state, and the statement has the effect of a denial.
(6) *Effect of Failing to Deny.* An allegation—other than one relating to the amount of damages—is admitted if a responsive pleading is required and the allegation is not denied. If a responsive pleading is not required, an allegation is considered denied or avoided.
(c) AFFIRMATIVE DEFENSES.
(1) *In General.* In responding to a pleading, a party must affirmatively state any avoidance or affirmative defense, including: accord and satisfaction; arbitration and award; assumption of risk; contributory negligence; discharge in bankruptcy; duress; estoppel; failure of consideration; fraud; illegality; injury by fellow servant; laches; license; payment; release; res judicata; statute of frauds; statute of limitations; and waiver.
(2) *Mistaken Designation.* If a party mistakenly designates a defense as a counterclaim, or a counterclaim as a defense, the court must, if justice requires, treat the pleading as though it were correctly designated, and may impose terms for doing so.
(d) PLEADING TO BE CONCISE AND DIRECT; ALTERNATIVE STATEMENTS; INCONSISTENCY.
(1) *In General.* Each allegation must be simple, concise, and direct. No technical form is required.
(2) *Alternative Statements of a Claim or Defense.* A party may set out 2 or more statements of a claim or defense alternatively or hypothetically, either in a single count or defense or in separate ones. If a party makes alternative statements, the pleading is sufficient if any one of them is sufficient.
(3) *Inconsistent Claims or Defenses.* A party may state as many separate claims or defenses as it has, regardless of consistency.
(e) CONSTRUING PLEADINGS. Pleadings must be construed so as to do justice.

...

FED. R. CIV. P. 10. Form of Pleadings
(a) CAPTION; NAMES OF PARTIES. Every pleading must have a caption with the court's name, a title, a file number, and a Rule 7(a) designation. The title of the complaint must name all the parties; the title of other pleadings, after naming the first party on each side, may refer generally to other parties.
(b) PARAGRAPHS; SEPARATE STATEMENTS. A party must state its claims or defenses in numbered paragraphs, each limited as far as practicable to a single set of circumstances. A later pleading may refer by number to a paragraph in an earlier pleading. If doing so would promote clarity, each claim founded on a separate transaction or occurrence—and each defense other than a denial—must be stated in a separate count or defense.
(c) ADOPTION BY REFERENCE; EXHIBITS. A statement in a pleading may be adopted by reference elsewhere in the same pleading or in any other pleading or motion. A copy of a written instrument that is an exhibit to a pleading is a part of the pleading for all purposes.

...

FED. R. CIV. P. 84. Forms
The forms in the Appendix suffice under these rules and illustrate the simplicity and brevity that these rules contemplate.

INQUIRY

Form. Rule 8 addresses a pleading's contents. What does the *Federal Rules of Civil Procedure* dictate about a pleading's form? FED. R. CIV. P. 10, reproduced above, is another general pleading rule. It differs from Rule 8 in that

Rule 8 has to do with the content of a pleading while Rule 10 has to do with its form. Rule 10(a) states the required components of the case's caption. Rule 10(b) requires parties to separate their claims and defenses into numbered paragraphs each limited to "a single set of circumstances." Rule 10(c) permits parties to plead by reference to other pleadings and court papers or to attached documents. Rule 10(c) relaxes traditional rules that pleadings must be complete or must recite certain content such as legal descriptions of real property. Rule 11, addressed later in this chapter and requiring that all pleadings be signed, has much more to do with the responsibility for a pleading than merely its signed form. Disclosures made within a pleading can be important for other reasons not directly having to do with the case. Pleadings may require the disclosure of the names of minors, perhaps including when they were involved in circumstances the public disclosure of which could subject them to undue embarrassment or harassment. Pleadings may also require reference to birthdates, Social Security numbers, and financial accounts the public disclosure of which could lead to identify theft. FED. R. CIV. P. 5.2 describes the process a party must follow to redact that information from a pleading. Note the procedure Rule 5.2 provides for listing redactions and identifiers.

FED. R. CIV. P. 5.2. Privacy Protection For Filings Made with the Court

(a) REDACTED FILINGS. Unless the court orders otherwise, in an electronic or paper filing with the court that contains an individual's social-security number, taxpayer-identification number, or birth date, the name of an individual known to be a minor, or a financial-account number, a party or nonparty making the filing may include only:

(1) the last four digits of the social-security number and taxpayer-identification number;

(2) the year of the individual's birth;

(3) the minor's initials; and

(4) the last four digits of the financial-account number.

(b) EXEMPTIONS FROM THE REDACTION REQUIREMENT. The redaction requirement does not apply to the following:

(1) a financial-account number that identifies the property allegedly subject to forfeiture in a forfeiture proceeding;

(2) the record of an administrative or agency proceeding;

(3) the official record of a state-court proceeding;

(4) the record of a court or tribunal, if that record was not subject to the redaction requirement when originally filed;

(5) a filing covered by Rule 5.2(c) or (d); and

(6) a pro se filing in an action brought under 28 U.S.C. §§ 2241, 2254, or 2255.

(c) LIMITATIONS ON REMOTE ACCESS TO ELECTRONIC FILES; SOCIALSECURITY APPEALS AND IMMIGRATION CASES. Unless the court orders otherwise, in an action for benefits under the Social Security Act, and in an action or proceeding relating to an order of removal, to relief from removal, or to immigration benefits or detention, access to an electronic file is authorized as follows:

(1) the parties and their attorneys may have remote electronic access to any part of the case file, including the administrative record;

(2) any other person may have electronic access to the full record at the courthouse, but may have remote electronic access only to:

(A) the docket maintained by the court; and

(B) an opinion, order, judgment, or other disposition of the court, but not any other part of the case file or the administrative record.

(d) FILINGS MADE UNDER SEAL. The court may order that a filing be made under seal without redaction. The court may later unseal the filing or order the person who made the filing to file a redacted version for the public record.

(e) PROTECTIVE ORDERS. For good cause, the court may by order in a case:

(1) require redaction of additional information; or

(2) limit or prohibit a nonparty's remote electronic access to a document filed with the court.

(f) OPTION FOR ADDITIONAL UNREDACTED FILING UNDER SEAL. A person making a redacted filing may also file an unredacted copy under seal. The court must retain the unredacted copy as part of the record.

(g) OPTION FOR FILING A REFERENCE LIST. A filing that contains redacted information may be filed together with a reference list that identifies each item of redacted information and specifies an appropriate identifier that uniquely corresponds to each item listed. The list must be filed under seal and may be amended as of right.

Any reference in the case to a listed identifier will be construed to refer to the corresponding item of information.

(h) WAIVER OF PROTECTION OF IDENTIFIERS. A person waives the protection of Rule 5.2(a) as to the person's own information by filing it without redaction and not under seal.

INQUIRY

Ad Damnum. The prayer for relief or ad damnum clause required by Rule 8(a)(3) has a special function in judgments taken by default (this chapter addresses default in a later section). FED. R. CIV. P. 54(c) expressly prohibits a default judgment from differing in kind or exceeding the amount that the prayer for relief demanded. Note that it is only default judgments that bear that limitation. A party may obtain greater or different relief after hearing or trial than that the prayer for relief demanded. *See* Bail v. Cunningham Bros., Inc., 452 F.2d 182, 187-188 (7th Cir. 1971) ($150,000 jury award on $100,000 ad damnum). Can you articulate why? The question implicates due process. The law should not hold a party who reads and accepts the demand in complaint, and chooses not to appear and defend on that basis, to a judgment different in kind or greater in amount than that demanded. The party would not have had notice. A party who appears and defends will have had full opportunity to evaluate evidence and defend against claims that support relief different in kind or greater in amount than that preliminarily demanded. Interestingly, some states prohibit the plaintiff from pleading a damages figure unless it is for a sum certain, meaning a figure computed from reliable economic losses. *See* CAL. CODE C. P. §§425.10, .11 (personal injury and wrongful death); MICH. CT. RULE 2.111(B)(2) (all matters over $25,000).

Practice

The new small-town civil litigator had initially been ill at ease pursuing the attorney-fee claim on behalf of two very highly experienced and skilled Manhattan criminal-defense lawyers. Quickly sensing the litigator's inexperience, the criminal-defense lawyers had taken to lightly ribbing the litigator to put the litigator at ease over it. The criminal-defense lawyers had earned their substantial fees, obtaining a hung jury in a murder charge against the New York tabloid-famous daughter of a wealthy Midwest financier. The financier felt otherwise. The litigator had pled contract and quantum meruit claims against the financier, with an ad damnum for the total unpaid six-figure amount that the criminal-defense lawyers had billed the financier. To the litigator's pleasant surprise, the jury returned a verdict many tens of thousands of dollars in excess of the ad damnum, finding that although the contract had not anticipated a hung jury, the criminal-defense lawyers had more than earned their billed charges. The criminal-defense lawyers had no end of fun further ribbing the inexperienced litigator that it was the first case they had seen in which the jury returned more than a lawyer had asked for.

Consistency. What happens when a party has several claims or defenses that may or may not apply, depending on how the factfinder interprets the evidence, and some of those claims or defenses are inconsistent? For example, the line between an intentional tort like battery and a tort of negligence such as malpractice can be hard to discern. The difference in claims depends on discerning the defendant's state of mind. May a plaintiff plead both claims in one case, or must the pleading be consistent? Rule 8(d)(2) authorizes alternative or hypothetical claims and defenses, while Rule 8(d)(3) permits a party to state claims or defenses "regardless of consistency." A party may plead legal claims that are inconsistent. Yet do not misunderstand what Rule 8(d)(2) means when it states that a party may plead "hypothetically." Lawyers must not plead frivolous claims. They may plead claims and defenses that are hypothetical only in the sense that they may arise after the factfinder makes a preliminary determination on a disputed issue. For example, a defendant may deny in an answer to a breach-of-contract claim that there was a contract and may then also plead contract defenses. What precautions might you take if you were drafting a pleading that included inconsistent claims or defenses? *See* FED. R. CIV. P. Form 10 (reproduced below).

Forms. Note the frequency with which Rule 8 uses the adjectives "short," "plain," "simple," "concise," and "direct." In case practitioners did not get the central liberalizing theme, Rule 84 (reproduced immediately above) referred to an Appendix to the *Federal Rules of Civil Procedure* that includes forms illustrating the allowable "simplicity and brevity that these rules contemplate." Lawyers and their firms tend to adopt styles and conventions for pleadings and court papers that, while mimicking the federal forms and one another at least in part, often provide additional helpful information. For instance, most pleadings and court papers will include, just beneath the caption but above the title, the names and addresses of all lawyers who have appeared in the litigation. The form of pleadings and court papers reflect other interests. Law firms in particular may deliberately develop, preserve, and regard a distinct pleading style as an important means by which to set apart the lawyers of the firm from other lawyers and firms. Examine the different forms of pleadings and court papers from Internet or other readily available sources. What are the stylistic differences? Which style and convention do you prefer, and why? The Supreme Court amended Rule 84 in 1946 explicitly to state that the forms more than just illustrate. They "suffice." Examine the following official forms to see if you agree that they comply with the above rules while being simple and brief. Look especially closely at the substantive allegations of the contract- and tort-claim forms. Are the allegations too brief? Compare the forms to the sample complaint that follows them, adapted from a case that the author tried to a jury verdict in the plaintiffs' favor.

Federal Rules of Civil Procedure Form 1. Caption

(*Use on every summons, complaint, answer, motion, or other document.)*

United States District Court
for the
_______ District of _______

A B, Plaintiff)
)
v.)

) Civil Action No.

____

C D, Defendant)

)

v.)

)

E F, Third-Party Defendant)

(*Use if needed.*))

)

(*Name of Document*)

____

Federal Rules of Civil Procedure Form 10. Complaint to Recover a Sum Certain

(Caption—See Form 1.)

1. (Statement of Jurisdiction--See Form 7.)

(*Use one or more of the following as appropriate and include a demand for judgment.*)

(a) On a Promissory Note

2. On <u>*date,*</u> the defendant executed and delivered a note promising to pay the plaintiff on <u>*date*</u> the sum of $_______ with interest at the rate of ___ percent. A copy of the note [is attached as Exhibit A] [is summarized as follows: _______.]

3. The defendant has not paid the amount owed.

(b) On an Account

2. The defendant owes the plaintiff $_______ according to the account set out in Exhibit A.

(c) For Goods Sold and Delivered

2. The defendant owes the plaintiff $_______ for goods sold and delivered by the plaintiff to the defendant from <u>*date*</u> to <u>*date*</u>.

(d) For Money Lent

2. The defendant owes the plaintiff $_______ for money lent by the plaintiff to the defendant on <u>*date*</u>.

(e) For Money Paid by Mistake

2. The defendant owes the plaintiff $_______ for money paid by mistake to the defendant on <u>*date*</u> under these circumstances: <u>*describe with particularity in accordance with Rule 9(b).*</u>

(f) For Money Had and Received

2. The defendant owes the plaintiff $_______ for money that was received from <u>*name*</u> on <u>*date*</u> to be paid by the defendant to the plaintiff.

Demand for Judgment

Therefore, the plaintiff demands judgment against the defendant for $_______, plus interest and costs.

(Date and sign—See Form 2.)

Federal Rules of Civil Procedure Form 11. Complaint for Negligence

(Caption—See Form 1.)

1. (Statement of Jurisdiction--See Form 7.)
2. On *date*, at *place*, the defendant negligently drove a motor vehicle against the plaintiff.
3. As a result, the plaintiff was physically injured, lost wages or income, suffered physical and mental pain, and incurred medical expenses of $_______.
Therefore, the plaintiff demands judgment against the defendant for $_______, plus costs.

(Date and sign—See Form 2).

Federal Rules of Civil Procedure Form 13. Complaint for Negligence Under the Federal Employers' Liability Act

(Caption—See Form 1.)

1. (Statement of Jurisdiction--See Form 7.)
2. At the times below, the defendant owned and operated in interstate commerce a railroad line that passed through a tunnel located at _______.
3. On *date*, the plaintiff was working to repair and enlarge the tunnel to make it convenient and safe for use in interstate commerce.
4. During this work, the defendant, as the employer, negligently put the plaintiff to work in a section of the tunnel that the defendant had left unprotected and unsupported.
5. The defendant's negligence caused the plaintiff to be injured by a rock that fell from an unsupported portion of the tunnel.
6. As a result, the plaintiff was physically injured, lost wages or income, suffered mental and physical pain, and incurred medical expenses of $_______.
Therefore, the plaintiff demands judgment against the defendant for $_______, and costs.

(Date and sign—See Form 2.)

UNITED STATES DISTRICT COURT
FOR THE WESTERN DISTRICT OF MICHIGAN

MAYNARD RAY, JOHN W. BAINES, and **PAUL RUTTER,** Plaintiffs,	No. CIV-01-01234 Hon. **************

v

WINDSOR COUNTY and **RON HOOPER** individually and in his official capacity as Sheriff of Windsor County,

Defendants.

PLAINTIFFS' COMPLAINT

[*Names, addresses, and telephone numbers of counsel omitted*]

Plaintiffs Maynard Ray, John Baines, and Paul Rutter complain against defendants Windsor County and Ron Hooper individually and in his official capacity as Sheriff of Windsor County, as follows:

PARTIES, VENUE, AND JURISDICTION

1.Mr. Ray and Mr. Baines reside in Coloma and Mr. Rutter resides in Buckham in Windsor County, Michigan, within the Western District of Michigan.

2.Windsor County is a body of state government located in the Western District.

3. Mr. Hooper resides in Windsor County in the Western District.

4. Mr. Hooper is the newly elected Sheriff of Windsor County and is sued both individually and in his official capacity as Sheriff of Windsor County.

5. This Court has jurisdiction over this case under 28 USC Section 1343(a)(3) and supplemental jurisdiction over other claims under 28 USC Section 1367(a).

6. This Court has venue over this case under 28 USC Section 1391(b) and (c).

FACTUAL ALLEGATIONS

7. Mr. Hooper ran for Windsor County Sheriff in the year 2000.

8. Mr. Hooper was opposed by the incumbent Sheriff Kennard.

9. Mr. Hooper solicited and obtained the endorsement of Sheriff officers.

10. Mr. Ray, Mr. Baines, and Mr. Rutter declined to endorse Mr. Hooper.

11. Mr. Ray, Mr. Baines, and Mr. Rutter endorsed Mr. Hooper's opponent Sheriff Kennard.

12. Mr. Ray', Mr. Baines's, and Mr. Rutter's names were on advertisements for Sheriff Kennard.

13. Mr. Ray', Mr. Baines's, and Mr. Rutter's names were not on an advertisement for Mr. Hooper.

14. Mr. Hooper knew of Mr. Ray', Mr. Baines's, and Mr. Rutter's endorsement of Sheriff Kennard.

15. Mr. Hooper prevailed in the primary and general election.

16. Upon becoming Sheriff, Mr. Hooper transferred Mr. Ray, Mr. Baines, and Mr. Rutter, and demoted Mr. Rutter in rank.

17. Mr. Hooper also transferred others who had not endorsed Mr. Hooper.

18. Mr. Hooper transferred officers who had endorsed his opponent Sheriff Kennard.

19. Mr. Hooper transferred Mr. Ray and Mr. Baines and transferred and demoted Mr. Rutter without evaluation.

20. Mr. Hooper transferred Mr. Ray and Mr. Baines and transferred and demoted Mr. Rutter without finding misconduct.

21. Mr. Hooper transferred Mr. Ray and Mr. Baines and transferred and demoted Mr. Rutter without expressed reason.

22. Mr. Hooper replaced Mr. Ray, Mr. Baines, and Mr. Rutter with Hooper political supporters.

23. Mr. Hooper transferred Mr. Ray, Mr. Baines, and Mr. Rutter out to the road patrol.

24. Because road patrol is typically an entry level position, and for other reasons, transfer out to road patrol is regarded in the law enforcement community and established by past practice as a disciplinary action harmful to one's career.

25. Before their transfer, Mr. Ray, Mr. Baines, and Mr. Rutter had obtained the traditional law enforcement career goals but have now lost their career goals.

26. Transfer out to road patrol changes Mr. Ray', Mr. Baines's, and Mr. Rutter's work hours.

27. Transfer out to road patrol changes Mr. Ray', Mr. Baines's, and Mr. Rutter's work shifts.

28. Transfer out to road patrol changes Mr. Ray', Mr. Baines's, and Mr. Rutter's work days.

29. Transfer out to road patrol means rotating shifts for Mr. Ray, Mr. Baines, and Mr. Rutter.

30. Transfer out to road patrol entirely changes Mr. Ray', Mr. Baines's, and Mr. Rutter's duties.

31. Mr. Ray, Mr. Baines, and Mr. Rutter have suffered humiliation and embarrassment and other similar and related forms of non-economic loss.

32. Mr. Ray, Mr. Baines, and Mr. Rutter have suffered career harm and harm to reputation.

33. These damages are both economic and non-economic.

34. These damages will continue into the future, with costs and attorney's fees.

This reference incorporates the above paragraphs into the following count.

COUNT I: 42 USC SECTION 1983 LIABILITY FOR VIOLATION OF CONSTITUTIONAL RIGHTS

35. Mr. Ray, Mr. Baines, and Mr. Rutter were entitled under the First and Fourteenth Amendments of the United States Constitution not to be discriminated against in the terms, conditions, and privileges of their employment on the basis of their exercise of First Amendment rights to free political association and free speech on political issues.

36. Mr. Ray', Mr. Baines's, and Mr. Rutter's above actions and statements declining to endorse Mr. Hooper and instead endorsing Sheriff Kennard constituted political association and speech.

37. Mr. Hooper through his transition team expressly determined to transfer to less desirable posts officers who did not endorse Mr. Hooper for Sheriff but who endorsed his opponent Sheriff Kennard, acting under color of state law, statute, ordinance, regulation, custom or usage, and in retaliation for the exercise of constitutionally protected rights to freedom of speech and political association.

38. Mr. Hooper did make transfers and demotion motivated in substantial part by the political association and speech of those transferred, in a pattern and practice of discrimination, in retaliation for the exercise of constitutionally protected rights.

39. Mr. Ray, Mr. Baines, and Mr. Rutter were transferred for their political association and speech.

40. Mr. Ray', Mr. Baines's, and Mr. Rutter's political association and speech were substantial and motivating factors in their transfer.

41. Any contrary explanation offered by Mr. Hooper is pretext for discrimination.

42. Mr. Ray', Mr. Baines's, and Mr. Rutter's association and speech were constitutionally protected under these circumstances as a clearly established and well-known right.

43. Mr. Ray', Mr. Baines's, and Mr. Rutter's association and speech were on matters of public and political concern.

44. Mr. Ray', Mr. Baines's, and Mr. Rutter's association and speech were not disruptive.

45. There was no harm to internal discipline or efficiency from the political association and speech.

46. The association and speech was void of any vitriolic or personal attacks.

47. Mr. Ray, Mr. Baines, and Mr. Rutter violated no Department rule.

48. Mr. Ray, Mr. Baines, and Mr. Rutter engaged in no misconduct.

49. Mr. Hooper was acting within the course and scope of his employment as Sheriff of Windsor County, even though in violation of Mr. Ray', Mr. Baines's, and Mr. Rutter's rights.

50. Windsor County endorsed and approved the actions of Mr. Hooper, which were also in his official capacity as Sheriff of Windsor County, and on information and belief, under a policy, trade, or custom of that governmental body.

51. Mr. Hooper is liable under 42 USC Section 1983 for his violations of Mr. Ray', Mr. Baines's, and Mr. Rutter's rights, individually and in his official capacity as Sheriff of Windsor County.

52. The violation of those rights proximately caused Mr. Ray and Mr. Baines the above loss and damage, for which they are entitled to recover under 42 USC Section 1983.

53. Mr. Ray, Mr. Baines, and Mr. Rutter are further entitled to punitive damages to deter Mr. Hooper from engaging in such violation of constitutional rights.

This reference incorporates the above paragraphs into the following count.

COUNT II: VIOLATION OF LABOR AGREEMENT

54. The labor agreement is attached and incorporated by this reference.

55. Article 2 of the labor agreement states in pertinent part that: "[n]either the Employer nor the Union shall discriminate against any employee covered by this agreement in a manner which would violate any applicable laws on the basis of * * * political affiliation."

56. Mr. Hooper and Windsor County violated that provision of the labor agreement in the above manner.

57. Mr. Ray, Mr. Baines, and Mr. Rutter grieved the violation.

58. Mr. Hooper and Windsor County denied the grievance, and the union declined to arbitrate.

59. Mr. Ray, Mr. Baines, and Mr. Rutter have thus exhausted their administrative remedies.

60. The labor agreement permits Mr. Ray, Mr. Baines, and Mr. Rutter to pursue this remedy.

61. Mr. Hooper's and Windsor County's breach of the labor agreement caused Mr. Ray, Mr. Baines, and Mr. Rutter the above consequential loss and damage.

ON THESE GROUNDS, plaintiffs Maynard Ray, John Baines, and Paul Rutter pray that the Court grant judgment in their favor and against defendants Windsor County and Paul Hooper, for all damages, costs, and attorney's fees under 42 USC Section 1988 and other law to which they are found entitled, together with reinstatement to their former positions, with all other appropriate legal and equitable relief.

JURY DEMAND

Plaintiffs demand trial by jury of all issues so triable in this case.
[*Signature block omitted*]
Attorneys for Plaintiffs
Dated: March 6, 2002

Practice

"You know, I hate answering your complaints," the gruff old defense counsel grumbled at the plaintiff's lawyer while they waited in the courthouse hallway for the case-evaluation results.

The plaintiff's lawyer just smiled, knowing exactly what defense counsel meant. The plaintiff's lawyer knew from doing defense work that it was easy to deny the long, compound allegations that most lawyers pled in their complaints. There was always something exaggerated, distorted, or unclear in those complex allegations. So the plaintiff's lawyer had adopted the odd habit of trying to keep the complaint's allegations as short as a *single line*, breaking each allegation down into its simplest undeniable parts. Still, the plaintiff's lawyer could not resist playing along with his grumpy old friend. "Really?" the plaintiff's lawyer answered with just the right degree of bemusement, "What do you mean?"

Defense counsel grunted a profanity. "You know what I mean. The paragraphs are so #8&% short that that I can't deny them." The plaintiff's lawyer laughed easily, his pleading practice fully vindicated. Just then, the clerk handed them the case-evaluation results. Defense counsel grunted another profanity, adding, "What are you doing with it?"

"You know I can't tell you yet," the plaintiff's lawyer smiled back.

"Oh, don't give me that. I know you're so pleased you can't stand yourself. I'll send you the release for your client to sign," defense counsel shot back, adding a final well-placed profanity but this time letting a small smile escape with it.

INQUIRY

Possibility. The Supreme Court referred approvingly to Rule 84's Appendix of forms in the well-known case Conley v. Gibson, 355 U.S. 41 (1957). *Conley v. Gibson* was one of a series of cases involving federal labor-law claims brought by workers to compel bargaining agents to represent them fairly and without racial discrimination. *Conley v. Gibson's* contribution to civil procedure was that it articulated a federal pleading standard that stood for 50 years until *Bell Atlantic Corp. v. Twombly* (excerpted and addressed in the next section). Rule 8(a) requires only a "short and plain statement of the claim showing that the pleader is entitled to relief." The standard that federal courts associate with *Conley v. Gibson* is in its language that a trial court should not dismiss a complaint "unless it appears beyond doubt that the plaintiff can prove no set of facts" supporting the claim. The standard indicates that a complaint that raises the mere possibility of a claim is sufficient. Indeed, there is authority that the federal trial courts may dismiss under Rule 8(a) a complaint that is so long and detailed as to be prolix. *See* Ausherman v. Stump, 643 F.2d 715, 716 (10th Cir. 1981) (63-page complaint with 9 pages of attachments). As you read *Conley v. Gibson,* recognize that, according to its overruling by *Bell Atlantic Corp. v. Twombly,* its "no set of facts" standard overstates the still-liberal nature of Rule 8(a). Also, recognize that the Supreme Court appears prepared to continue to wrestle with replacing *Conley v. Gibson's* standard and that *Conley v. Gibson* may yet retain the generally correct spirit of liberal pleading under the *Federal Rules of Civil Procedure.*

Conley v. Gibson,

United States Supreme Court
355 U.S. 41 (1957)

Mr. Justice BLACK delivered the opinion of the Court.

Once again Negro employees are here under the Railway Labor Act[fn] asking that their collective bargaining agent be compelled to represent them fairly. ...

... In summary, the complaint made the following allegations relevant to our decision: Petitioners were employees of the Texas and New Orleans Railroad at its Houston Freight House ... [when] the Railroad purported to abolish 45 jobs held by petitioners or other Negroes all of whom were either discharged or demoted. In truth the 45 jobs were not abolished at all but instead filled by whites as the Negroes were ousted... . Despite repeated pleas by petitioners, the Union, acting according to plan, did nothing to protect them against these discriminatory discharges and refused to give them protection comparable to that given white employees. The complaint then went on to allege that the Union had failed in general to represent Negro employees equally and in good faith. It charged that such discrimination constituted a violation of petitioners' right under the Railway Labor Act to fair representation from their bargaining agent. And it concluded by asking for relief in the nature of declaratory judgment, injunction and damages.

The respondents appeared and moved to dismiss the complaint on several grounds[including that] the complaint failed to state a claim upon which relief could be given. The District Court granted the motion to dismiss... . The Court of Appeals for the Fifth Circuit... affirmed. [C] ...

... [W]e hold that ... the complaint adequately set forth a claim upon which relief could be granted. In appraising the sufficiency of the complaint we follow, of course, the accepted rule that a complaint should not be dismissed for failure to state a claim unless it appears beyond doubt that the plaintiff can prove no set of facts in support of his claim which would entitle him to relief.[fn] Here, the complaint alleged, in part, that petitioners were discharged wrongfully by the Railroad and that the Union, acting according to plan, refused to protect their jobs as it did those of white employees or to help them with their grievances all because they were Negroes. If these allegations are proven there has been a manifest breach of the Union's statutory duty to represent fairly and without hostile discrimination all of the employees in the bargaining unit. ...

The respondents also argue that the complaint failed to set forth specific facts to support its general allegations of discrimination and that its dismissal is therefore proper. The decisive answer to this is that the Federal Rules of Civil Procedure do not require a claimant to set out in detail the facts upon which he bases his claim. To the contrary, all the Rules require is "a short and plain statement of the claim"[fn] that will give the defendant fair notice of what the plaintiff's claim is and the grounds upon which it rests. The illustrative forms appended to the Rules plainly demonstrate this. Such simplified "notice pleading" is made possible by the liberal opportunity for discovery and the other pretrial procedures established by the Rules to disclose more precisely the basis of both claim and defense and to define more narrowly the disputed facts and issues.[fn] Following the simple guide of Rule 8(f) that "all pleadings shall be so construed as to do substantial justice," we have no doubt that petitioners' complaint adequately set forth a claim and gave the respondents fair notice of its basis. The Federal Rules reject the approach that pleading is a game of skill in which one misstep by counsel may be decisive to the outcome and accept the principle that the purpose of pleading is to facilitate a proper decision on the merits. [C]

The judgment is reversed and the cause is remanded to the District Court for further proceedings not inconsistent with this opinion.

It is so ordered.

Reversed and remanded with direction.

INQUIRY

Heightened Standards. The next 50 years after *Conley v. Gibson* saw periodic attempts by the lower federal courts to deal with meritless claims through pleading challenges. Attempts to heighten pleading standards beyond the very low bar *Conley v. Gibson* established failed. In Hishon v. King & Spalding, 467 U.S. 69 (1984), the Supreme Court cited *Conley v. Gibson* to hold that the plaintiff, a lawyer alleging that a law firm had unlawfully discriminated against her, had adequately alleged an implied contract for partnership. *Hishon* cited *Conley v. Gibson* to recite, "A court may dismiss a complaint only if it is clear that no relief could be granted under any set of facts that could be proved consistent with the allegations." 467 U.S. at 73. For another example, in Leatherman v. Tarrant County Narcotics Intelligence & Coordination Unit, 507 U.S. 163 (1993), the Supreme Court rejected a heightened standard for municipal liability in civil-rights cases that the Fifth Circuit had developed. Citing *Conley v. Gibson, Leatherman* held instead "that [Rule 8(a)(2)] meant what it said: The Federal Rules of Civil Procedure do not require a claimant to set out in detail the facts upon which he bases his claim." 507 U.S. at 168. Then again, in Swierkiewicz v. Sorema, N.A., 534 U.S. 506 (2002), the Supreme Court rejected a heightened standard for race-discrimination cases relying on the *McDonnell Douglas* burden-shifting standard. *Swierkiewicz v. Sorema, N.A.*, asserted that defendants who cannot discern from the complaint allegations sufficient for notice should move under FED. R. CIV. P. 12(e) for more definite statement and then challenge meritless claims through a FED. R. CIV. P. 56 motion for summary judgment. 534 U.S. at 513-514. *Conley v. Gibson* reigned. *See, e.g.*, Sparrow v. United Air Lines, Inc., 216 F.3d 1111, 1115 (D.C. Cir. 2000) (discrimination plaintiff need only allege "I was turned down for my job because of my race"). Consider another brief excerpt of a Supreme Court case reversing unanimously a Rule 12(b)(6) dismissal. As you read the opinion, keep in mind that the district court had dismissed the case in an unpublished opinion and the federal appellate court had affirmed in a brief, three-sentence per curiam opinion, making the Supreme Court's grant of certiorari and unanimous reversal all the more emphatic.

Haddle v. Garrison,

United States Supreme Court
525 U.S. 121 (1998)

Chief Justice REHNQUIST delivered the opinion of the Court.

Petitioner Michael A. Haddle, an at-will employee, alleges that respondents conspired to have him fired from his job in retaliation for obeying a federal grand jury subpoena and to deter him from testifying at a federal criminal trial. We hold that such interference with at-will employment may give rise to a claim for damages under the Civil Rights Act of 1871, Rev. Stat. §1980, 42 U.S.C. §1985(2).

According to petitioner's complaint, a federal grand jury indictment ... charged petitioner's employer, Healthmaster, Inc., and respondents Jeanette Garrison and Dennis Kelly, officers of Healthmaster, with Medicare fraud. Petitioner cooperated with the federal agents in the investigation that preceded the indictment. He also appeared to testify before the grand jury pursuant to a subpoena, but did not testify due to the press of time. Petitioner was also expected to appear as a witness in the criminal trial resulting from the indictment.

Although Garrison and Kelly were barred by the Bankruptcy Court from participating in the affairs of Healthmaster, they conspired ... to bring about petitioner's termination. They did this both to intimidate petitioner and to retaliate against him for his attendance at the federal-court proceedings.

Petitioner sued for damages in the United States District Court for the Southern District of Georgia, asserting a federal claim under 42 U.S.C. §1985(2) and various state-law claims. ... As §1985 demands, he also alleged that he had been "injured in his person or property" by the acts of respondents in violation of § 1985(2) and that he was entitled to recover his damages occasioned by such injury against respondents jointly and severally.

Respondents moved to dismiss for failure to state a claim upon which relief can be granted. ...

... We ... granted certiorari[c] to decide whether petitioner was "injured in his property or person" when respondents induced his employer to terminate petitioner's at-will employment as part of a conspiracy prohibited by §1985(2). ...

Petitioner's action was dismissed pursuant to Federal Rule of Civil Procedure 12(b)(6) because, in the Eleventh Circuit's view, he had not suffered an injury that could give rise to a claim for damages under § 1985(2). We must, of course, assume that the facts as alleged in petitioner's complaint are true and that respondents engaged in a conspiracy prohibited by §1985(2). Our review in this case is accordingly confined to one question: Can petitioner state a claim for damages by alleging that a conspiracy proscribed by §1985(2) induced his employer to terminate his at-will employment?[fn] ...

We hold that the sort of harm alleged by petitioner here-essentially third-party interference with at-will employment relationships-states a claim for relief under §1985(2). Such harm has long been a compensable injury under tort law, and we see no reason to ignore this tradition in this case. As Thomas Cooley recognized:

"One who maliciously and without justifiable cause, induces an employer to discharge an employee, by means of false statements, threats or putting in fear, or perhaps by means of malevolent advice and persuasion, is liable in an action of tort to the employee for the damages thereby sustained. *And it makes no difference whether the employment was for a fixed term not yet expired or is terminable at the will of the employer.*" 2 Law of Torts 589-591 (3d ed.1906) (emphasis added). ...

The kind of interference with at-will employment relations alleged here is merely a species of the traditional torts of intentional interference with contractual relations and intentional interference with prospective contractual relations. [Cc] ... Thus, to the extent that the terms "injured in his person or property" in §1985 refer to principles of tort law, see 3 W. Blackstone, Commentaries on the Laws of England 118 (1768) (describing the universe of common-law torts as "all private wrongs, or civil injuries, which may be offered to the rights of either a man's person or his property"), we find ample support for our holding that the harm occasioned by the conspiracy here may give rise to a claim for damages under §1985(2).

The judgment of the Court of Appeals is reversed, and the case is remanded for further proceedings consistent with this opinion.

It is so ordered.

INQUIRY

Strategy. Did the *Haddle v. Garrison* defendants gain anything by having moved to dismiss on the pleadings? You can discern from the above cases the defenses' available strategies. To appreciate the impact of these Supreme Court rulings and standards, you must know the litigation dynamic. Under *Conley v. Gibson*, there seems little basis on which to challenge a pleading on its face for having failed to plead sufficient facts. Pleading legal conclusions with just enough spare facts to suggest the possibility of a claim might well be enough. Challenging meritless claims would require a motion for summary judgment in which the trial court must examine evidence beyond the face of the pleadings. Examining evidence beyond the face of the pleadings generally means allowing the parties some or even full discovery. Defendants would prefer to avoid discovery in cases that appear meritless on the pleadings because of discovery's burden and expense, and the possibility that the plaintiff may discover evidence that turns an apparently frivolous case into one having merit. Also, motions for summary judgment on the evidence are significantly more challenging for the moving party to prepare and the trial court to decide than are motions to dismiss on the pleadings. Motions to dismiss involve examing the complaint and applying applicable law—relatively simple steps involving relatively limited information. By contrast, motions for summary judgment can involve examining evidence of all kinds including deposition testimony, transactional documents, reports, diagrams, summaries, and even supporting data like photographs and reconstructions, while also construing the pleadings' claims and defenses under the applicable law and regulations. The Supreme Court eventually (and quite recently) came to conclude that *Conley v. Gibson* did not give the lower federal courts the tools that they needed to evaluate claims at the pleading stage so as to avoid unnecessary discovery and motion practice beyond the pleadings. The next section addresses that recent Supreme Court case law. As you read the next section, keep in mind the Supreme Court's challenge not to reinstitute anything like the old writ system in effect requiring a plaintiff to find the magic words of pleading to have meritorious cases heard.

Ethics

Pleading rules are not the only way that the justice system ensures that only meritorious claims and defenses move forward. Rule 3.1 of the ABA MODEL RULES OF PROFESSIONAL CONDUCT prohibits lawyers from bringing or defending a proceeding without "a basis in law and fact for doing so that is not frivolous... ." Rule 3.3 also prohibits lawyers from knowingly making false statements of fact or law to a tribunal. Rule 8.4 also prohibits dishonest, deceitful, and fraudulent conduct. A lawyer can lose the license to practice law over frivolous pleading and, if not that, quickly lose a reputation. The lawyer who invokes court authority by drafting honest pleadings with a strong dose of candor will find success in good reputation.

2. Sufficiency

Before addressing the Supreme Court's emerging pleading standard, consider the means by which parties may challenge pleadings. Chapter 2 already reproduced FED. R. CIV. P. 12 and introduced you to FED. R. CIV. P. 12(b)(2) as the means by which parties challenge personal jurisdiction. You have also seen that parties challenge subject-matter jurisdiction under Rule 12(b)(1). Rule 12 is also the means by which parties challenge pleadings. Rule 12(b) lists seven grounds to dismiss, stating that "a party may assert the following defenses by motion... ." Rule 12(b)(6) provides the specific grounds for a motion to dismiss on the pleadings. Those Rule 12(b)(6) grounds, the "failure to state a claim upon which relief can be granted," are a litany on the tongue of every defense counsel. Federal courts and practitioners call a motion to dismiss on the pleadings a "Rule 12(b)(6) motion," although traditional common-law pleading knew it as a *demurrer*. State courts and practitioners know and follow similar rules, also using their identifying numbers and letters as handy labels. *See, e.g.*, MICH. CT. RULE 2.116(C)(8) ("failed to state a claim on which relief can be granted") (commonly referred to as a "subrule (C)(8)" motion). Keep in mind that Rule 12(b)(6) motions for failure to state a claim test only the facial sufficiency of the complaint. When deciding a Rule 12(b)(6) motion, the trial court must accept as true all allegations made in the challenged complaint (another litany familiar to defense counsel). Summary judgment motions under FED. R. CIV. P. 56 test allegations for supporting evidence, not Rule 12(b)(6) motions to dismiss. One must also read Rule 12(b)(6) "failure to state a claim" together with Rule 8(a)(2) requiring that a pleading contain only a "short and plain statement of the claim showing that the pleader is entitled to relief... ." Practitioners are rightly cautious in bringing Rule 12(b)(6) motions, expecting that in most instances the better challenges are as to whether the pleading has factual support.

There are actually two situations in which a Rule 12(b)(6) may be most appropriate. That is, Rule 12(b)(6)'s "failure to state a claim" language has two connotations. One is that the plaintiff's complaint simply does not say enough about the claim to be intelligible as to what the defendant must defend. When a trial court grants a Rule 12(b)(6) motion to dismiss because the plaintiff has omitted necessary elements of what appears to be a potential claim, a common practice is for the trial court to simultaneously grant leave to amend. *See* Bazroux v. Scott, 136 F.3d 1053, 1054 (5th Cir. 1998). Outright dismissal is more likely when the plaintiff has already failed once or more in amendment. *See* Rozsa v. May Davis Group, Inc., 187 F.Supp.2d 123, 132 (S.D. N.Y. 2002). A subsequent section in this chapter further addresses amendment.

The other connotation to Rule 12(b)(6)'s "failure to state a claim" language is that the law simply does not recognize the claim that the plaintiff has pled, even though the plaintiff has made it adequately clear what the plaintiff asserts. This form of Rule 12(b)(6) motion tests a complaint's legal sufficiency, not its descriptive sufficiency. *See* Scheuer v. Rhodes, 416 U.S. 232, 236 (1974) (Rule 12(b)(6) review standard is "whether the claimant is entitled to offer evidence to support the claim"). Defense lawyers often make the two arguments ("I cannot tell what the plaintiff is alleging" and "what the plaintiff alleging is not a legal claim") together, especially in instances where the complaint raises mixed questions of law and fact. *See, e.g.,* Hartford Accident & Indemnity Co. v. Merrill Lynch, Pierce, Fenner & Smith, Inc., 74 F.R.D. 357 (W.D. Okl. 1976) (granting Rule 12(b)(6) motion where complaint failed to plead facts indicating proximate cause to the trial court's satisfaction).

Rule 12(b) also provides for the timing of the Rule 12(b)(6) motion, that it "must be made before pleading if a responsive pleading is allowed." Rule 12(b)'s time requirement means that defense counsel ordinarily make motions to dismiss on the pleadings immediately in place of the answer. Under Rule 12(a)(4)(A), a Rule 12 motion delays the need to answer until 14 days after notice that the trial court denied the motion or postponed ruling until after trial. What, though, of a situation in which the parties discern, after the defendant answers the complaint, that there is no factual dispute but a dispositive legal issue? Rule 12(c), titled "Motion for Judgment on the Pleadings," provides an alternative to a Rule 12(b)(6) motion to dismiss. Rule 12(c) states, "After the pleadings are closed—but early enough not to delay trial—a party may move for judgment on the pleadings." Rule 12(c) expands the time within which a party may move to dismiss on the pleadings, allowing the parties to contest and the trial court to rule on the statute of limitations, novel legal theories, or other dispositive procedural or substantive legal issues. *See, e.g.,* Jin v. Ministry of State Security, 254 F.Supp.2d 61 (D. D.C. 2003) (defamation claim dismissed under Rule 12(c) as untimely filed applicable limitations period). Following sections of this chapter explore when responsive pleadings are due, when pleading amendment is possible, and thus when "the pleadings are closed" under Rule 12(c). In some cases, it might be shortly after the defendant's answer, early in the case. In other instances, such as where new evidence arises justifying and requiring pleading amendment, it may be much later. The trial court's case-management order (a subject covered in a later chapter) may also have something to do with when the pleadings close in many cases. Strategically, the defense would tend to prefer an earlier date and the plaintiff a later date, given the cost and burden of discovery and the possibility that it will lead the plaintiff to evidence on which to amend the complaint to help defeat a motion on the pleadings.

Skills

Every competent civil litigator knows intimately the dynamic and strategies that these pleading rules create. Indeed, the ability to sort claims that the defense should immediately challenge on the pleadings, from claims the defense should later challenge on the pleadings, on summary judgment, or not at all, are skills that make defense counsel masterful. The skill involves several considerations beyond the strength or weakness of the claims, and the likelihood or unlikelihood that the trial judge will grant the motion. Considerations can include whether to attack all of the claims at once, only to challenge certain of the claims, or to challenge some claims immediately and others later, and if so, in what order. Considerations can also include what disclosure of litigation strategies the defense may have to make in order to challenge the pleadings, what financial cost the client will incur, and how even a losing motion may educate the trial judge to the issues. There are few if any decisions that can carry as great an impact on the overall litigation as how defense counsel determines to challenge the pleadings and claims by motion.

Now that you have a sense of the means and strategy of motions challenging the pleadings, consider the evolving standard under which the Supreme Court requires that lower federal courts evaluate those motions. You will see from the excerpted opinion below that *Bell Atlantic Corp. v. Twombly* established a plausibility standard, even if it did so uneasily. What is the Supreme Court facing here with this emerging issue of a complaint's sufficiency? Trial judges must not substitute their judgment for the judgment of juries on disputed issues of fact. They should also not foreclose a plaintiff from using discovery to obtain evidence in support of fact allegations. Theoretically, if a plaintiff alleges that an event occurred or that certain actors had a certain intent or state of mind satisfying the element of a legal claim, then the trial judge should permit the plaintiff to proceed through discovery. The defendant's motion to dismiss on the pleadings would be premature. The defendant should instead use a Rule 56 motion for summary judgment to challenge a well-pled claim that nonetheless has no evidentiary support. Yet a plaintiff can allege anything. The question is whether a trial judge should have the authority to evaluate allegations that on their face state claims but are so preposterous that it would undermine public confidence in the judicial system if the court were to accept them. The Supreme Court's tentative solution in *Bell Atlantic Corp. v. Twombly* was to permit the trial judge some latitude (how much is not yet clear) to judge a pleading's plausibility. *Bell Atlantic Corp. v. Twombly* had to set aside *Conley v. Gibson's* possibility standard. It clearly did so. The question is how much more it did. Consider what you think as you read the excerpted opinion. Also, recognize the policy concerns over litigation costs that the opinion's evolving standard attempts to address.

Bell Atlantic Corp. v. Twombly,

United States Supreme Court
550 U.S. 544 (2007)

SOUTER, Justice.

Liability under §1 of the Sherman Act, 15 U.S.C. §1, requires a "contract, combination ..., or conspiracy, in restraint of trade or commerce." The question in this putative class action is whether a §1 complaint can survive a motion to dismiss … absent some factual context suggesting agreement… . We hold that such a complaint should be dismissed.

I

The upshot of the 1984 divestiture of the American Telephone & Telegraph Company's (AT & T) local telephone business was a system of regional service monopolies (variously called "Regional Bell Operating Companies," "Baby Bells," or "Incumbent Local Exchange Carriers" (ILECs)), and a separate, competitive market for long-distance service from which the ILECs were excluded. More than a decade later, Congress withdrew approval of the ILECs' monopolies by enacting the Telecommunications Act of 1996 (1996 Act)[], which "fundamentally restructure[d] local telephone markets"… . In recompense, the 1996 Act set conditions for authorizing ILECs to enter the long-distance market. [C]

"Central to the [new] scheme [was each ILEC's] obligation ... to share its network with competitors," [c], which came to be known as "competitive local exchange carriers" (CLECs), [c]. …

Respondents William Twombly and Lawrence Marcus (hereinafter plaintiffs) represent a putative class consisting of all "subscribers of local telephone and/or high speed internet services ... from February 8, 1996 to present." [C] In this action against petitioners, a group of ILECs,[fn] plaintiffs seek treble damages and declaratory and injunctive relief for claimed violations of §1 of the Sherman Act, [c], which prohibits "[e]very contract, combination in the form of trust or otherwise, or conspiracy, in restraint of trade or commerce among the several States, or with foreign nations."

The complaint alleges that the ILECs conspired to restrain trade in two ways, each supposedly inflating charges for local telephone and high-speed Internet services. Plaintiffs say, first, that the ILECs "engaged in parallel conduct" in their respective service areas to inhibit the growth of upstart CLECs. …

Second, the complaint charges agreements by the ILECs to refrain from competing against one another.

The complaint couches its ultimate allegations this way:

"In the absence of any meaningful competition between the [ILECs] in one another's markets, and in light of the parallel course of conduct that each engaged in to prevent competition from CLECs within their respective local telephone and/or high speed internet services markets and the other facts and market circumstances alleged above, Plaintiffs allege upon information and belief that [the ILECs] have entered into a contract, combination or conspiracy to prevent competitive entry in their respective local telephone and/or high speed internet services markets and have agreed not to compete with one another and otherwise allocated customers and markets to one another." [C][fn]

The United States District Court for the Southern District of New York dismissed the complaint for failure to state a claim upon which relief can be granted. …

The Court of Appeals for the Second Circuit reversed, holding that the District Court tested the complaint by the wrong standard. …

We granted certiorari to address the proper standard for pleading an antitrust conspiracy through allegations of parallel conduct, [c], and now reverse.

II

A

Because § 1 of the Sherman Act "does not prohibit [all] unreasonable restraints of trade ... but only restraints effected by a contract, combination, or conspiracy," [c], "[t]he crucial question" is whether the challenged anticompetitive conduct "stem[s] from independent decision or from an agreement, tacit or express," [c]. While a showing of parallel "business behavior is admissible circumstantial evidence from which the fact finder may infer agreement," it falls short of "conclusively establish[ing] agreement or ... itself constitut[ing] a Sherman Act offense." [C] …

The inadequacy of showing parallel conduct or interdependence, without more, mirrors the ambiguity of the behavior: consistent with conspiracy, but just as much in line with a wide swath of rational and competitive business strategy unilaterally prompted by common perceptions of the market. …

B

This case presents the antecedent question of what a plaintiff must plead in order to state a claim under §1 of the Sherman Act. Federal Rule of Civil Procedure 8(a)(2) requires only " a short and plain statement of the claim showing that the pleader is entitled to relief," in order to "give the defendant fair notice of what the ... claim is and the grounds upon which it rests," Conley v. Gibson, 355 U.S. 41, 47[] (1957). While a complaint attacked by a Rule 12(b)(6) motion to dismiss does not need detailed factual allegations, *ibid.;* [c], a plaintiff's obligation to provide the "grounds" of his "entitle[ment] to relief" requires more than labels and conclusions, and a formulaic recitation of the elements of a cause of action will not do, see Papasan v. Allain, 478 U.S. 265, 286[] (1986) (on a motion to dismiss, courts "are not bound to accept as true a legal conclusion couched as a factual allegation"). Factual allegations must be enough to raise a right to relief above the speculative level, [c][fn3], on the assumption that all the allegations in the complaint are true (even if doubtful in fact), see, *e.g.*, Swierkiewicz v. Sorema N. A., 534 U.S. 506, 508n. 1[] (2002); [c]; Scheuer v. Rhodes, 416 U.S. 232, 236[] (1974) (a well-pleaded complaint may proceed even if it appears "that a recovery is very remote and unlikely").

[FN3. The dissent greatly oversimplifies matters by suggesting that the Federal Rules somehow dispensed with the pleading of facts altogether. [C] While, for most types of cases, the Federal Rules eliminated the cumbersome requirement that a claimant "set out *in detail* the facts upon which he bases his claim," Conley v. Gibson, 355 U.S. 41, 47[] (1957) (emphasis added), Rule 8(a)(2) still requires a "showing," rather than a blanket assertion, of entitlement to relief. Without some factual allegation in the complaint, it is hard to see how a claimant could satisfy the requirement of providing not only "fair notice" of the nature of the claim, but also "grounds" on which the claim rests. [C]]

In applying these general standards to a §1 claim, we hold that stating such a claim requires a complaint with enough factual matter (taken as true) to suggest that an agreement was made. Asking for plausible grounds to infer an agreement does not impose a probability requirement at the pleading stage; it simply calls for enough fact to raise a reasonable expectation that discovery will reveal evidence of illegal agreement.[fn] And, of course, a well-pleaded complaint may proceed even if it strikes a savvy judge that actual proof of those facts is improbable, and "that a recovery is very remote and unlikely." [C] ... It makes sense to say, therefore, that an allegation of parallel conduct and a bare assertion of conspiracy will not suffice. Without more, parallel conduct does not suggest conspiracy, and a conclusory allegation of agreement at some unidentified point does not supply facts adequate to show illegality. Hence, when allegations of parallel conduct are set out in order to make a §1 claim, they must be placed in a context that raises a suggestion of a preceding agreement, not merely parallel conduct that could just as well be independent action.

The need at the pleading stage for allegations plausibly suggesting (not merely consistent with) agreement reflects the threshold requirement of Rule 8(a)(2) that the "plain statement" possess enough heft to "sho[w] that the pleader is entitled to relief." A statement of parallel conduct, even conduct consciously undertaken, needs some setting suggesting the agreement necessary to make out a §1 claim; without that further circumstance pointing toward a meeting of the minds, an account of a defendant's commercial efforts stays in neutral territory. An allegation of parallel conduct is thus much like a naked assertion of conspiracy in a §1 complaint: it gets the complaint close to stating a claim, but without some further factual enhancement it stops short of the line between possibility and plausibility of "entitle[ment] to relief." [C][fn]

We alluded to the practical significance of the Rule 8 entitlement requirement in Dura Pharmaceuticals, Inc. v. Broudo, 544 U.S. 336, [347] (2005), when we explained that something beyond the mere possibility of loss causation must be alleged, lest a plaintiff with "'a largely groundless claim'" be allowed to "'take up the time of a number of other people, with the right to do so representing an *in terrorem* increment of the settlement value.'" [Cc] ...

Thus, it is one thing to be cautious before dismissing an antitrust complaint in advance of discovery, [c], but quite another to forget that proceeding to antitrust discovery can be expensive. As we indicated over 20 years ago in Associated Gen. Contractors of Cal., Inc. v. Carpenters, 459 U.S. 519, 528n.17[] (1983), "a district court must retain the power to insist upon some specificity in pleading before allowing a potentially massive factual controversy to proceed." [Cc] ...

It is no answer to say that a claim just shy of a plausible entitlement to relief can, if groundless, be weeded out early in the discovery process through "careful case management," [c], given the common lament that the success of judicial supervision in checking discovery abuse has been on the modest side. ...

Plaintiffs['] ... main argument against the plausibility standard at the pleading stage is its ostensible conflict with an early statement of ours construing Rule 8. Justice Black's opinion for the Court in *Conley v. Gibson* spoke not only of the need for fair notice of the grounds for entitlement to relief but of "the accepted rule that a complaint should not be dismissed for failure to state a claim unless it appears beyond doubt that the plaintiff can prove no set of facts in support of his claim which would entitle him to relief." 355 U.S., at 45-46[]. This "no set of facts" language can be read in isolation as saying that any statement revealing the theory of the claim will suffice unless its factual impossibility may be shown from the face of the pleadings; and the Court of Appeals appears to have read *Conley* in some such way when formulating its understanding of the proper pleading standard, [c].[fn]

On such a focused and literal reading of *Conley's* "no set of facts," a wholly conclusory statement of claim would survive a motion to dismiss whenever the pleadings left open the possibility that a plaintiff might later establish some "set of [undisclosed] facts" to support recovery. So here, the Court of Appeals specifically found the prospect of unearthing direct evidence of conspiracy sufficient to preclude dismissal, even though the complaint does not set forth a single fact in a context that suggests an agreement. [C] It seems fair to say that this approach to pleading would dispense with any showing of a "'reasonably founded hope'" that a plaintiff would be able to make a case, [c]; Mr. Micawber's optimism would be enough.

Seeing this, a good many judges and commentators have balked at taking the literal terms of the *Conley* passage as a pleading standard. [Cc]

We could go on, but there is no need to pile up further citations to show that *Conley'* "no set of facts" language has been questioned, criticized, and explained away long enough. o be fair to the *Conley* Court, the passage should be understood in light of the opinion's preceding summary of the complaint's concrete allegations, which the Court quite reasonably understood as amply stating a claim for relief. But the passage so often quoted fails to mention this understanding on the part of the Court, and after puzzling the profession for 50 years, this famous observation has earned its retirement. The phrase is best forgotten as an incomplete, negative gloss on an accepted pleading standard: once a claim has been stated adequately, it may be supported by showing any set of facts consistent with the allegations in the complaint. [Cc] *Conley,* then, described the breadth of opportunity to prove what an adequate complaint claims, not the minimum standard of adequate pleading to govern a complaint's survival.[fn] ...

III

When we look for plausibility in this complaint, we agree with the District Court that plaintiffs' claim of conspiracy in restraint of trade comes up short. To begin with, the complaint leaves no doubt that plaintiffs rest their §1 claim on descriptions of parallel conduct and not on any independent allegation of actual agreement among the ILECs. [C] Although in form a few stray statements speak directly of agreement,[fn] on fair reading these are merely legal conclusions resting on the prior allegations. ...

We think that nothing contained in the complaint invests either the action or inaction alleged with a plausible suggestion of conspiracy. ...

Plaintiffs say that our analysis runs counter to Swierkiewicz v. Sorema N. A., 534 U.S. 506, 508[] (2002), which held that "a complaint in an employment discrimination lawsuit [need] not contain specific facts establishing a prima facie case of discrimination... ." ... Even though Swierkiewicz's pleadings "detailed the events leading to his termination, provided relevant dates, and included the ages and nationalities of at least some of the relevant persons involved with his termination," the Court of Appeals dismissed his complaint for failing to allege certain additional facts that Swierkiewicz would need at the trial stage to support his claim in the absence of direct evidence of discrimination. [C] We reversed on the ground that the Court of Appeals had impermissibly applied what amounted to a heightened pleading requirement by insisting that Swierkiewicz allege "specific facts" beyond those necessary to state his claim and the grounds showing entitlement to relief. [C]

Here, in contrast, we do not require heightened fact pleading of specifics, but only enough facts to state a claim to relief that is plausible on its face. Because the plaintiffs here have not nudged their claims across the line from conceivable to plausible, their complaint must be dismissed.

The judgment of the Court of Appeals for the Second Circuit is reversed, and the cause is remanded for further proceedings consistent with this opinion.

It is so ordered.

Justice STEVENS, with whom Justice GINSBURG joins except as to Part IV, dissenting.

In the first paragraph of its 24-page opinion the Court states that the question to be decided is whether allegations that "major telecommunications providers engaged in certain parallel conduct unfavorable to competition" suffice to state a violation of § 1 of the Sherman Act. [C] The answer to that question has been settled for more than 50 years. If that were indeed the issue, a summary reversal ... would adequately resolve this case. ... [P]arallel conduct is circumstantial evidence admissible on the issue of conspiracy, but it is not itself illegal. [C]

Thus, this is a case in which there is no dispute about the substantive law. If the defendants acted independently, their conduct was perfectly lawful. If, however, that conduct is the product of a horizontal agreement among potential competitors, it was unlawful. Plaintiffs have alleged such an agreement and, because the complaint was dismissed in advance of answer, the allegation has not even been denied. Why, then, does the case not proceed? Does a judicial opinion that the charge is not "plausible" provide a legally acceptable reason for dismissing the complaint? I think not. ...

Two practical concerns presumably explain the Court's dramatic departure from settled procedural law. Private antitrust litigation can be enormously expensive, and there is a risk that jurors may mistakenly conclude that evidence of parallel conduct has proved that the parties acted pursuant to an agreement when they in fact merely made similar independent decisions. Those concerns merit careful case management, including strict control of discovery, careful scrutiny of evidence at the summary judgment stage, and lucid instructions to juries; they do not, however, justify the dismissal of an adequately pleaded complaint without even requiring the defendants to file answers denying a charge that they in fact engaged in collective decisionmaking. More importantly, they do not justify an interpretation of Federal Rule of Civil Procedure 12(b)(6) that seems to be driven by the majority's appraisal of the plausibility of the ultimate factual allegation rather than its legal sufficiency. ...

I

Rule 8(a)(2) of the Federal Rules requires that a complaint contain "a short and plain statement of the claim showing that the pleader is entitled to relief." The rule did not come about by happenstance and its language is not inadvertent. The English experience with Byzantine special pleading rules ... made obvious the appeal of a pleading standard that was easy for the common litigant to understand and sufficed to put the defendant on notice as to the nature of the claim against him and the relief sought. ...

Under the relaxed pleading standards of the Federal Rules, the idea was not to keep litigants out of court but rather to keep them in. The merits of a claim would be sorted out during a flexible pretrial process and, as appropriate, through the crucible of trial. [C] ...

II

It is in the context of this history that Conley v. Gibson, 355 U.S. 41[] (1957), must be understood. The *Conley* plaintiffs were black railroad workers who alleged that their union local had refused to protect them against discriminatory discharges... . The union sought to dismiss the complaint on the ground that its general allegations of discriminatory treatment by the defendants lacked sufficient specificity. Writing for a unanimous Court, Justice Black rejected the union's claim as foreclosed by the language of Rule 8. [C] In the course of doing so, he articulated the formulation the Court rejects today... .

Consistent with the design of the Federal Rules, *Conley's* "no set of facts" formulation permits outright dismissal only when proceeding to discovery or beyond would be futile. Once it is clear that a plaintiff has stated a claim that, if true, would entitle him to relief, matters of proof are appropriately relegated to other stages of the trial process. Today, however, in its explanation of a decision to dismiss a complaint that it regards as a fishing expedition, the Court scraps *Conley's* "no set of facts" language. ...

If *Conley's* "no set of facts" language is to be interred, let it not be without a eulogy. That exact language, which the majority says has "puzzl[ed] the profession for 50 years," [c], has been cited as authority in a dozen opinions of this Court and four separate writings.[fn] In not one of those 16 opinions was the language "questioned," "criticized," or "explained away." Indeed, today's opinion is the first by any Member of this Court to express *any* doubt as to the adequacy of the *Conley* formulation. ...

Petitioners have not requested that the *Conley* formulation be retired, nor have any of the six *amici* who filed briefs in support of petitioners. I would not rewrite the Nation's civil procedure textbooks and call into doubt the pleading rules of most of its States without far more informed deliberation as to the costs of doing so. Congress has established a process—a rulemaking process—for revisions of that order. See 28 U.S.C. §§2072-2074 (2000 ed. and Supp. IV). ...

Everything today's majority says would therefore make perfect sense if it were ruling on a Rule 56 motion for summary judgment and the evidence included nothing more than the Court has described. But it should go without saying in the wake of *Swierkiewicz* that a heightened production burden at the summary judgment stage does not translate into a heightened pleading burden at the complaint stage. ...

Accordingly, I respectfully dissent.

INQUIRY

Plausibility. Notice how in *Bell Atlantic Corp. v. Twombly* the Supreme Court distinguished its new plausibility standard from possibility or probability standards. Possibility would be the lowest standard, allowing a plaintiff the greatest liberty to plead conceivable but still-meritless claims. The trial court would dismiss a complaint only if the defendant showed that it was impossible for the plaintiff to prevail on the claim as pled. Probability would be the highest standard, requiring that the plaintiff establish that there is a genuine prospect of success on the claim. Plausibility is apparently a standard between possibility and probability, akin to the plaintiff showing a reasonably founded hope for success, in a way that gives the defendant adequate notice of the grounds. What are some of the challenges that practitioners face in meeting the plausibility or any other pleading standard? In some cases, the lawyer's lack of knowledge or skill contributes to inadequate pleading. In other cases, the unavailability of evidence makes for vague pleading allegations. In still other cases, the ambiguity of the substantive claim or sensitive nature of one of its elements can create an insurmountable pleading challenge. Which of these factors or what combination of these factors created the pleading issue in *Bell Atlantic Corp. v. Twombly*?

Knowledge

The Supreme Court's possibility, plausibility, and probability concepts are another example of a conceptual spectrum. Chapter 3 mentioned how lawyers can build a conceptual spectrum out of the various forms of service of process (each increasingly remote from personal service), as well as other facts, circumstances, rules, holdings, and concepts. Notice how helpful a conceptual spectrum is here, too, in understanding and recalling the Supreme Court's emerging pleading standard.

Evolution. How significant is the decision in *Bell Atlantic Corp. v. Twombly*? Literally thousands of federal court cases have now cited it despite its recency. Members of the U.S. House of Representatives introduced a bill for the Open Access to Courts Act of 2009, H.R. 4115, to reject *Bell Atlantic Corp. v. Twombly* and restore *Conley v. Gibson* with the language, "A court shall not dismiss a complaint under subdivision (b)(6), (c), or (e) of Rule 12 of the Federal Rules of Civil Procedure unless it appears beyond doubt that the plaintiff can prove no set of facts in support of the claim which would entitle the plaintiff to relief... [or because] the factual contents of the complaint do not show the plaintiff's claim to be plausible or are insufficient to warrant a reasonable inference that the defendant is liable for the misconduct alleged." Yet two weeks after the Supreme Court decided *Bell Atlantic Corp. v. Twombly*, the Court appeared to back away from the proposition that the case had significantly changed the *Conley v. Gibson* standard. In Erickson v. Pardus, 551 U.S. 89 (2007), a per curiam opinion of the Supreme Court reversed the Rule 12(b)(6)/Rule 8(a)(2) dismissal of a prisoner's civil-rights claim. In doing so, *Erickson v. Pardus* cited and quoted that part of *Conley v. Gibson* that *Bell Atlantic Corp. v. Twombly* had also cited and quoted approvingly, that "Specific facts are not necessary; the statement need only 'give the defendant fair notice of what the ... claim is and the grounds on which it rests.'" 551 U.S. at 93. The federal district and circuit courts had found the prisoner's complaint to have alleged only conclusory allegations as to the deliberate denial of medical care for life-theatening illness. The *Erickson v. Pardus* opinion also repeated the well-established principle that "when ruling on a defendant's motion to dismiss, a judge must accept as true all of the factual allegations in the complaint." *Id.* A Rule 12(b)(6)/Rule 8(a)(2) motion must certainly now cite *Bell Atlantic Corp. v. Twombly*, but it must also be prepared to overcome *Conley v. Gibson's* "fair notice" standard and the traditional "accept as true all allegations" condition. See, then, how the Supreme Court addressed the evolving pleadings standard in the following case.

Ashcroft v. Iqbal,

United States Supreme Court
___ U.S. ___, 129 S.Ct. 1937 (2009)

Justice KENNEDY delivered the opinion of the Court.

Respondent Javaid Iqbal is a citizen of Pakistan and a Muslim. In the wake of the September 11, 2001, terrorist attacks he was arrested in the United States on criminal charges and detained by federal officials. Respondent claims he was deprived of various constitutional protections while in federal custody. To redress the alleged deprivations, respondent filed a complaint against numerous federal officials, including John Ashcroft, the former Attorney General of the United States, and Robert Mueller, the Director of the Federal Bureau of Investigation (FBI). Ashcroft and Mueller are the petitioners in the case now before us. As to these two petitioners, the complaint alleges that they adopted an unconstitutional policy that subjected respondent to harsh conditions of confinement on account of his race, religion, or national origin.

In the District Court petitioners raised the defense of qualified immunity and moved to dismiss the suit, contending the complaint was not sufficient to state a claim against them. The District Court denied the motion to dismiss, concluding the complaint was sufficient to state a claim despite petitioners' official status at the times in question. Petitioners brought an interlocutory appeal in the Court of Appeals for the Second Circuit. The court, without discussion, assumed it had jurisdiction over the order denying the motion to dismiss; and it affirmed the District Court's decision.

Respondent's account of his prison ordeal could, if proved, demonstrate unconstitutional misconduct by some governmental actors. But the allegations and pleadings with respect to these actors are not before us here. This case instead turns on a narrower question: Did respondent, as the plaintiff in the District Court, plead factual matter that, if taken as true, states a claim that petitioners deprived him of his clearly established constitutional rights. We hold respondent's pleadings are insufficient. ...

I

Following the 2001 attacks, the FBI and other entities within the Department of Justice began an investigation of vast reach to identify the assailants and prevent them from attacking anew. The FBI dedicated more than 4,000 special agents and 3,000 support personnel to the endeavor. By September 18 "the FBI had received more than 96,000 tips or potential leads from the public." ...

In the ensuing months the FBI questioned more than 1,000 people with suspected links to the attacks in particular or to terrorism in general. [C] Of those individuals, some 762 were held on immigration charges; and a 184-member subset of that group was deemed to be "of 'high interest'" to the investigation. [C] The high-interest detainees were held under restrictive conditions designed to prevent them from communicating with the general prison population or the outside world. [C]

Respondent was one of the detainees. ...

Respondent pleaded guilty to the criminal charges, served a term of imprisonment, and was removed to his native Pakistan. [C] He then filed a *Bivens* action in the United States District Court for the Eastern District of New York against 34 current and former federal officials... .

The allegations against petitioners are the only ones relevant here. The complaint contends that petitioners designated respondent a person of high interest on account of his race, religion, or national origin, in contravention of the First and Fifth Amendments to the Constitution. ... It further alleges that "[t]he policy of holding post-September-11th detainees in highly restrictive conditions of confinement until they were 'cleared' by the FBI was approved by Defendants ASHCROFT and MUELLER in discussions in the weeks after September 11, 2001." [C] Lastly, the complaint posits that petitioners "each knew of, condoned, and willfully and maliciously agreed to subject" respondent to harsh conditions of confinement "as a matter of policy, solely on account of [his] religion, race, and/or national origin and for no legitimate penological interest." [C] The pleading names Ashcroft as the "principal architect" of the policy, [c], and identifies Mueller as "instrumental in [its] adoption, promulgation, and implementation." [C] ...

... [W]e begin by taking note of the elements a plaintiff must plead to state a claim of unconstitutional discrimination against officials entitled to assert the defense of qualified immunity.

... Because vicarious liability is inapplicable to *Bivens* and §1983 suits, a plaintiff must plead that each Government-official defendant, through the official's own individual actions, has violated the Constitution.

... Where the claim is invidious discrimination in contravention of the First and Fifth Amendments, our decisions make clear that the plaintiff must plead and prove that the defendant acted with discriminatory purpose. [Cc] ... [T]o state a claim based on a violation of a clearly established right, respondent must plead sufficient factual matter to show that petitioners adopted and implemented the detention policies at issue not for a neutral, investigative reason but for the purpose of discriminating on account of race, religion, or national origin. ...

We turn to respondent's complaint. Under Federal Rule of Civil Procedure 8(a)(2), a pleading must contain a "short and plain statement of the claim showing that the pleader is entitled to relief." As the Court held in [Bell Atlantic Corp. v.] Twombly, 550 U.S. 544, [555 (2007)], the pleading standard Rule 8 announces does not require "detailed factual allegations," but it demands more than an unadorned, the-defendant-unlawfully-harmed-me accusation. *Id.*[] A pleading that offers "labels and conclusions" or "a formulaic recitation of the elements of a cause of action will not do." *Id.*[] Nor does a complaint suffice if it tenders "naked assertion[s]" devoid of "further factual enhancement." *Id.*[]

To survive a motion to dismiss, a complaint must contain sufficient factual matter, accepted as true, to "state a claim to relief that is plausible on its face." *Id.* at 557[]. A claim has facial plausibility when the plaintiff pleads factual content that allows the court to draw the reasonable inference that the defendant is liable for the misconduct alleged. *Id.* at 556[]. The plausibility standard is not akin to a "probability requirement," but it asks for more than a sheer possibility that a defendant has acted unlawfully. [*Id.*] Where a complaint pleads facts that are "merely consistent with" a defendant's liability, it "stops short of the line between possibility and plausibility of 'entitlement to relief.'" *Id.* at 557[].

Two working principles underlie our decision in *Twombly.* First, the tenet that a court must accept as true all of the allegations contained in a complaint is inapplicable to legal conclusions. Threadbare recitals of the elements of a cause of action, supported by mere conclusory statements, do not suffice. [C] Rule 8 marks a notable and generous departure from the hyper-technical, code-pleading regime of a prior era, but it does not unlock the doors of discovery for a plaintiff armed with nothing more than conclusions. Second, only a complaint that states a plausible claim for relief survives a motion to dismiss. *Id.* at 556[]. ... [W]here the well-pleaded facts do not permit the court to infer more than the mere possibility of misconduct, the complaint has alleged—but it has not "show[n]"—"that the pleader is entitled to relief." Fed. Rule Civ. Proc. 8(a)(2). ...

Under *Twombly*'s construction of Rule 8, we conclude that respondent's complaint has not "nudged [his] claims" of invidious discrimination "across the line from conceivable to plausible." *Ibid.*

We begin our analysis by identifying the allegations in the complaint that are not entitled to the assumption of truth. Respondent pleads that petitioners "knew of, condoned, and willfully and maliciously agreed to subject [him]" to harsh conditions of confinement "as a matter of policy, solely on account of [his] religion, race, and/or national origin and for no legitimate penological interest." [C] The complaint alleges that Ashcroft was the "principal architect" of this invidious policy, [c], and that Mueller was "instrumental" in adopting and executing it, [c]. These bare assertions, much like the pleading of conspiracy in *Twombly,* amount to nothing more than a "formulaic recitation of the elements" of a constitutional discrimination claim... . As such, the allegations are conclusory and not entitled to be assumed true. [C] ... It is the conclusory nature of respondent's allegations, rather than their extravagantly fanciful nature, that disentitles them to the presumption of truth.

We next consider the factual allegations in respondent's complaint to determine if they plausibly suggest an entitlement to relief. The complaint alleges that "the [FBI], under the direction of Defendant MUELLER, arrested and detained thousands of Arab Muslim men ... as part of its investigation of the events of September 11." [C] It further claims that "[t]he policy of holding post-September-11th detainees in highly restrictive conditions of confinement until they were 'cleared' by the FBI was approved by Defendants ASHCROFT and MUELLER in discussions in the weeks after September 11, 2001." [C] Taken as true, these allegations are consistent with petitioners' purposefully designating detainees "of high interest" because of their race, religion, or national origin. But given more likely explanations, they do not plausibly establish this purpose.

The September 11 attacks were perpetrated by 19 Arab Muslim hijackers who counted themselves members in good standing of al Qaeda, an Islamic fundamentalist group. Al Qaeda was headed by another Arab Muslim—Osama bin Laden—and composed in large part of his Arab Muslim disciples. It should come as no surprise that a legitimate policy directing law enforcement to arrest and detain individuals because of their suspected link to the attacks would produce a disparate, incidental impact on Arab Muslims, even though the purpose of the policy was to target neither Arabs nor Muslims. On the facts respondent alleges the arrests Mueller oversaw were likely lawful and justified by his nondiscriminatory intent to detain aliens who were illegally present in the United States and who had potential connections to those who committed terrorist acts. As between that "obvious alternative explanation" for the arrests, [c], and the purposeful, invidious discrimination respondent asks us to infer, discrimination is not a plausible conclusion.

But even if the complaint's well-pleaded facts give rise to a plausible inference that respondent's arrest was the result of unconstitutional discrimination, that inference alone would not entitle respondent to relief. ... Respondent's constitutional claims against petitioners rest solely on their ostensible "policy of holding post-September-11th detainees" in the ADMAX SHU once they were categorized as "of high interest." [C] To prevail on that theory, the complaint must contain facts plausibly showing that petitioners purposefully adopted a policy of classifying post-September-11 detainees as "of high interest" because of their race, religion, or national origin.

This the complaint fails to do. Though respondent alleges that various other defendants, who are not before us, may have labeled him a person of "of high interest" for impermissible reasons, his only factual allegation against petitioners accuses them of adopting a policy approving "restrictive conditions of confinement" for post-September-11 detainees until they were " 'cleared' by the FBI." [C] Accepting the truth of that allegation, the complaint does not show, or even intimate, that petitioners purposefully housed detainees in the ADMAX SHU due to their race, religion, or national origin. All it plausibly suggests is that the Nation's top law enforcement officers, in the aftermath of a devastating terrorist attack, sought to keep suspected terrorists in the most secure conditions available until the suspects could be cleared of terrorist activity. Respondent does not argue, nor can he, that such a motive would violate petitioners' constitutional obligations. He would need to allege more by way of factual content to "nudg[e]" his claim of purposeful discrimination "across the line from conceivable to plausible." [C] ...

We hold that respondent's complaint fails to plead sufficient facts to state a claim for purposeful and unlawful discrimination against petitioners. The Court of Appeals should decide in the first instance whether to remand to the District Court so that respondent can seek leave to amend his deficient complaint.

The judgment of the Court of Appeals is reversed, and the case is remanded for further proceedings consistent with this opinion.

It is so ordered.

Justice SOUTER, with whom Justice STEVENS, Justice GINSBURG, and Justice BREYER join, dissenting. ...

... [T]he complaint satisfies Rule 8(a)(2). Ashcroft and Mueller admit they are liable for their subordinates' conduct if they "had actual knowledge of the assertedly discriminatory nature of the classification of suspects as being 'of high interest' and they were deliberately indifferent to that discrimination." [C] ... The complaint ... alleges, at a bare minimum, that Ashcroft and Mueller knew of and condoned the discriminatory policy their subordinates carried out. Actually, the complaint goes further in alleging that Ashcroft and Muller affirmatively acted to create the discriminatory detention policy. If these factual allegations are true, Ashcroft and Mueller were, at the very least, aware of the discriminatory policy being implemented and deliberately indifferent to it. ...

... I think the majority is right in saying that these allegations suggest only that Ashcroft and Mueller "sought to keep suspected terrorists in the most secure conditions available until the suspects could be cleared of terrorist activity," [c], and that this produced "a disparate, incidental impact on Arab Muslims," [c]. And I agree that the two allegations selected by the majority, standing alone, do not state a plausible entitlement to relief for unconstitutional discrimination.

But these allegations do not stand alone as the only significant, nonconclusory statements in the complaint, for the complaint contains many allegations linking Ashcroft and Mueller to the discriminatory practices of their subordinates. ...

... By my lights, there is no principled basis for the majority's disregard of the allegations linking Ashcroft and Mueller to their subordinates' discrimination.

I respectfully dissent.

Justice BREYER, dissenting.

I agree with Justice SOUTER and join his dissent. I write separately to point out that, like the Court, I believe it important to prevent unwarranted litigation from interfering with "the proper execution of the work of the Government." [C] But I cannot find in that need adequate justification for the Court's interpretation of *Bell Atlantic Corp. v. Twombly,* 550 U.S. 544[] (2007), and Federal Rule of Civil Procedure 8. The law, after all, provides trial courts with other legal weapons designed to prevent unwarranted interference. ... For this reason, as well as for the independently sufficient reasons set forth in Justice SOUTER's opinion, I would affirm the Second Circuit.

INQUIRY

Case Management. What are the policy considerations that the *Ashcroft v. Iqbal* case presents? To what degree should those considerations influence pleading rules? *Ashcroft v. Iqbal* raises obvious national-security issues, just as the other cases cited and excerpted above raise other important substantive issues. Consider the procedural concerns. As a case's size and complexity increases, so do its costs, yet so may the plaintiff's need to rely on notice pleading and liberal discovery. Defendants wish to avoid incurring significant costs in meritless cases. Plaintiffs need to be able to plead claims without facing the obstacle of arcane or technical requirements, and need reasonable access to evidence. Courts need claims whose boundaries the pleadings clearly enough define to manage the litigation. The dynamic does not resolve itself easily. Where the stakes and challenges are greatest for the plaintiff, the defendant and trial court may have the greatest incentive to look more closely at the plaintiff's pleading. Although no *Federal Rule* directly suggests that the magnitude of the case should change the pleading requirement, FED. R. CIV. P. 8(e) does state, "Pleadings must be construed so as to do justice." As later chapters address, the Supreme Court amended the *Federal Rules of Civil Procedure* in 1983 to expand a federal trial court's authority to manage discovery and other pre-trial procedures. The hope was that increasing trial-court control over a case would decrease unnecessary costs and wasteful litigation, short of imposing technical pleading requirements likely to give rise to arduous pleading challenges. *Bell Atlantic Corp. v. Twombly* and *Ashcroft v. Iqbal* each suggested that case-management measures have not been successful, while the dissent in *Twombly* argued for giving those measures a greater chance. Appreciate this tension when you reach the chapters on discovery and case management.

State Decisions. Some state high courts have adopted *Bell Atlantic Corp. v. Twombly's* pleading standard. *See, e.g.*, Sisney v. Best Inc., 754 N.W.2d 804 (S.D. 2008). Others have explicitly rejected *Bell Atlantic Corp. v. Twombly* and retained *Conley v. Gibson*. See Colby v. Umbrella, Inc., 955 A.2d 1082 (Vt. 2008). Still others follow their own pleading standards different from both *Twombly* and *Conley*. *See* Cullen v. Auto-Owners Ins. Co., 189 P.3d 344 (2008). It is too early to identify a trend.

Technology

Lawyers use forms and patterns when drafting pleadings, just as they do when drafting other documents. An old complaint in a motor-vehicle-accident case may include the traffic statutes and ordinances that a defendant driver violated, providing shortcuts to additional research for drafting a new complaint in a similar case. Another old complaint might remind one to include additional prayers for relief (punitive or exemplary damages, interest, costs, expenses, injunctions, and other orders) beyond the basic compensatory-damages request. Old answers may include long and well-researched lists of available affirmative defenses. Civil litigators may draw from a rich trove of their own pleadings and pleadings drafted by others in their law firms, when drafting a new pleading. They may also use commercial formbooks. Lawyers and law firms once kept folders or notebooks of sample pleadings and purchased formbooks. Today, they keep shared electronic folders organized for convenient review, with each file named to make the folders searchable, and use Internet links and databases. A civil litigator's ability to use technology to locate pattern pleadings is a critical skill.

3. Special Rules

So far, the chapter has addressed general rules of pleading under FED. R. CIV. P. 8. You have seen that much of the debate over those general rules involve whether there are or should be heightened standards for pleading. FED. R. CIV. P. 9 addresses special rules of pleading. Those special rules take two forms. They either (1) relieve a party of pleading when one might think a party needs to plead or (2) require a party to plead when one might think a party needs not plead. Rule 9 is a sensible way of clarifying pleading issues that might arise without it. Rule 9(a) relieving a party of pleading the capacity or authority to sue and Rule 9(g) requiring a party to plead special damages are examples of each function. The rationale for relieving a party of pleading with particularity should be clear from the above discussion. Why, for instance, should there be pleading disputes over whether a guardian has the authority to represent a minor, when discovery and other pre-trial procedures can readily determine that question? Pleading a party's capacity to sue seems redundant when the party is actually suing and the question of capacity will often require examining the circumstances beyond the face of the pleading. Rule 9(a) properly relieves a party of that pleading burden.

Given Rule 8's liberality in pleading and the extensive debate over heightened pleading standards, it may seem curious that Rule 9(b) provides for a heightened pleading standard where the allegations involve fraud or mistake. Rule 9(b) requires that "a party must state with particularity the circumstances constituting fraud or mistake." Can you conjecture why parties and courts might want greater specificity as to fraud allegations? The reasons tend to have to do with how easy fraud is to allege, how hard to rebut, and how damaging the allegation. *See* Christopher M. Fairman, *Heightened Pleading,* 81 TEX. L.REV. 551, 564 (2002), *citing* Harrison v. Westinghouse Savannah River Co., 176 F.3d 776, 784 (4th Cir. 1999); Acito v. IMCERA Group, Inc., 47 F.3d 47, 52 (2d Cir. 1995); Tuchman v. DSC Communications Corp., 14 F.3d 1061, 1067 (5th Cir. 1994). Read Rule 9, and then compare its heightened-pleading standard for fraud in Rule 9(b) to Form 21 of the *Federal Rules of Civil Procedure* alleging a fraudulent-conveyance claim. Does Form 21 plead fraud with sufficient particularity to satisfy Rule 9(b)? Keep in mind that the forms "suffice" under FED. R. CIV. P. 84.

FED. R. CIV. P. 9. Pleading Special Matters
(a) CAPACITY OR AUTHORITY TO SUE; LEGAL EXISTENCE.
(1) *In General.* Except when required to show that the court has jurisdiction, a pleading need not allege:
(A) a party's capacity to sue or be sued;
(B) a party's authority to sue or be sued in a representative capacity; or
(C) the legal existence of an organized association of persons that is made a party.
(2) *Raising Those Issues.* To raise any of those issues, a party must do so by a specific denial, which must state any supporting facts that are peculiarly within the party's knowledge.
(b) FRAUD OR MISTAKE; CONDITIONS OF MIND. In alleging fraud or mistake, a party must state with particularity the circumstances constituting fraud or mistake. Malice, intent, knowledge, and other conditions of a person's mind may be alleged generally.
(c) CONDITIONS PRECEDENT. In pleading conditions precedent, it suffices to allege generally that all conditions precedent have occurred or been performed. But when denying that a condition precedent has occurred or been performed, a party must do so with particularity.
(d) OFFICIAL DOCUMENT OR ACT. In pleading an official document or official act, it suffices to allege that the document was legally issued or the act legally done.
(e) JUDGMENT. In pleading a judgment or decision of a domestic or foreign court, a judicial or quasi-judicial tribunal, or a board or officer, it suffices to plead the judgment or decision without showing jurisdiction to render it.
(f) TIME AND PLACE. An allegation of time or place is material when testing the sufficiency of a pleading.
(g) SPECIAL DAMAGES. If an item of special damage is claimed, it must be specifically stated.
(h) ADMIRALTY OR MARITIME CLAIM.
(1) *How Designated.* If a claim for relief is within the admiralty or maritime jurisdiction and also within the court's subject-matter jurisdiction on some other ground, the pleading may designate the claim as an admiralty or maritime claim for purposes of Rules 14(c), 38(e), and 82 and the Supplemental Rules for Admiralty or Maritime Claims and Asset Forfeiture Actions. A claim cognizable only in the admiralty or

maritime jurisdiction is an admiralty or maritime claim for those purposes, whether or not so designated.
(2) *Designation for Appeal.* A case that includes an admiralty or maritime claim within this subdivision (h) is an admiralty case within 28 U.S.C. § 1292(a)(3).

Federal Rules of Civil Procedure Form 21. Complaint on a Claim for a Debt and to Set Aside a Fraudulent Conveyance Under Rule 18(b).

(Caption—See Form 1.)

1. (Statement of Jurisdiction--See Form 7.)
2. On *date*, defendant *name* signed a note promising to pay to the plaintiff on *date* the sum of $_______ with interest at the rate of ___ percent. [The pleader may, but need not, attach a copy or plead the note verbatim.]
3. Defendant *name* owes the plaintiff the amount of the note and interest.
4. On *date*, defendant *name* conveyed all defendant's real and personal property *if less than all, describe it fully* to defendant *name* for the purpose of defrauding the plaintiff and hindering or delaying the collection of the debt.

Therefore, the plaintiff demands that:
(a) judgment for $_______, plus costs, be entered against defendant(s) *name(s)*; and
(b) the conveyance to defendant *name* be declared void and any judgment granted be made a lien on the property.

(Date and sign—See Form 2.)

INQUIRY

Particularity. What does it mean to plead fraud "with particularity"? One might think that it would include pleading the who, what, when, and where of the allegedly fraudulent statement. Although cases do discuss that possibility, *see* Melder v. Morris, 27 F.3d 1097, 1100n.5 (5th Cir. 1994); DiLeo v. Ernst & Young, 901 F.2d. 624, 627 (7th Cir. 1990), the consensus is instead to temper Rule 9(b) with Rule 8's liberal provisions. Ross v. A.H. Robins Co., 607 F.2d 545, 557 n.20 (2d Cir. 1979); Denny v. Barber, 576 F.2d 465, 467 (2d Cir. 1978). One federal district court opinion suggests that Rule 9(b) requires only "slightly more notice than would be forthcoming under Rule 8" and not "the pleading of detailed evidentiary matter." Denny v. Carey, 72 F.R.D. 574, 578 (E.D. Pa. 1976). Discovery of the alleged nature of the fraud may have the effect of supplementing the pleadings. *See* M.H. Segan Ltd. Partnership v. Hasbro, Inc., 924 F.Supp. 512, 526-527n.20 (S.D. N.Y. 1996). State cases under similar state-court rules may require greater specificity than Rule 9(b) and Form 21. *See* National Ventures, Inc. v. Water Glades 300 Condominium Assn., 847 So.2d 1070, 1074 (Fla. Ct. App. 2003) (insufficient allegations to support claim of fraud); Dutkiewicz v. Bartkowiak, 126 N.W.2d 705, 706 (Mich. Sup. Ct. 1964) ("an action in fraud must definitely and issuably set forth the facts complained of and relied upon for recovery"); Lamothe v. Auto Club Ins. Assn., 543 N.W.2d 42 (Mich. Ct. App. 1995) (dismissing claim for pleading fraud only generally).

Special Damages. Notice again Rule 9(g)'s requirement that a party "specifically state" an item of special damages. Can you articulate the reason? Rule 9(g) properly preserves the traditional pleading rule that while general damages require only a general allegation of loss, *see* Sossamon v. Nationwide Mut. Ins. Co., 135 S.E.2d 87 (1964) (general allegation of personal-injury damages sufficient to include medical expenses), a plaintiff should plead special damages with particularity, *see* Hogan v. Wal-Mart Stores, Inc., 167 F.3d 781, 783 (2d Cir. 1999) (New York law requires alleging aggravation of pre-existing condition). Here, *special damages* probably means either anything out of the ordinary or that specific element required in certain tort cases such as slander or abuse of process. *See* Avitia v. Metropolitan Club of Chicago, Inc., 49 F.3d 1219, 1226 (7th Cir. 1995) (defining special damages to be those unusual to the cause); *see also* Anheuser-Busch, Inc. v. John Labatt Ltd., 89 F.3d 1339, 1349 (8th Cir. 1996) (plaintiff must plead punitive damages or lose them), cert. denied, 519 U.S. 1109 (1997). A plaintiff who claims losses qualifying as special damages should put the defendant on immediate notice, given the unusual additional monetary consequences. Where special damages are an element of the claim (not merely additional damages), the trial court may dismiss for failure to plead them. *See* Paine-Erie Hosp. Supply, Inc. v. Lincoln First Bank, 370 N.Y.S.2d 370 (N.Y. Sup. Ct. 1975).

Statutory Standards. Rule 9(b) is not the only authority to heighten pleading standards for specific claims. Congress is free to establish pleading standards for federal statutory claims. It did so with the Private Securities Litigation Reform Act of 1995, Pub. L. No. 104-67, 109 Stat. 737. The Act applies to private securities-fraud claims. Congress' purpose in adopting the Act had to do with controlling abusive securities-fraud litigation, in which easily alleged strike suits threatened legitimate entities. The Act imposed two heightened pleading requirements. Securities-fraud complaints must first "specify" the defendant's statements that misled the defrauded individual to form a misleading belief and then "state with particularity facts giving rise to a strong inference" of the defendant's fraudulent state of mind. 15 U.S.C. §78u-4(b)(1) and (2). The Supreme Court dealt with these requirements in the two recent cases excerpted below. The first case, *Dura Pharmaceuticals, Inc. v. Broudo*, held that these provisions required the plaintiff to plead specifically the loss that the fraud caused. The second case, *Tellabs, Inc. v. Makor Issues and Rights, Ltd.*, held that pleading to a "strong inference" meant that the complaint should leave the inference that fraud was at least as likely the defendant's intent as any nonfraudulent intent. Consider these two cases in light of the plausibility standard of *Bell Atlantic Corp. v. Twombly* and *Ashcroft v. Iqbal*. How are they alike, and how are they different?

Dura Pharmaceuticals, Inc. v. Broudo,

United States Supreme Court
544 U.S. 336 (2005)

Justice BREYER delivered the opinion of the Court.

A private plaintiff who claims securities fraud must prove that the defendant's fraud caused an economic loss. [C] We consider a Ninth Circuit holding that a plaintiff can satisfy this requirement—a requirement that courts call "loss causation"—simply by alleging in the complaint and subsequently establishing that "the price" of the security " *on the date of purchase* was inflated because of the misrepresentation." [C] In our view, the Ninth Circuit is wrong, both in respect to what a plaintiff must prove and in respect to what the plaintiffs' complaint here must allege.

I

Respondents are individuals who bought stock in Dura Pharmaceuticals, Inc. ... [T]heir detailed amended (181 paragraph) complaint ... says the following (and nothing significantly more than the following) about economic losses attributable to the spray device misstatement: *"In reliance on the integrity of the market, [the plaintiffs] ... paid artificially inflated prices for Dura securities" and the plaintiffs suffered "damage[s]" thereby. [c]* (emphasis added).

The District Court dismissed the complaint. In respect to the plaintiffs' drug-profitability claim, it held that the complaint failed adequately to allege an appropriate state of mind, *i.e.,* that defendants had acted knowingly, or the like. In respect to the plaintiffs' spray device claim, it held that the complaint failed adequately to allege "loss causation."

The Court of Appeals for the Ninth Circuit reversed... [, holding that s]ince the complaint pleaded "that the price at the time of purchase was overstated," and it sufficiently identified the cause, its allegations were legally sufficient. [C]

Because the Ninth Circuit's views about loss causation differ from those of other Circuits that have considered this issue, we granted Dura's petition for certiorari. [Cc] We now reverse.

II

Private federal securities fraud actions are based upon federal securities statutes and their implementing regulations. Section 10(b) of the Securities Exchange Act of 1934 forbids (1) the "use or employ[ment] ... of any ... deceptive device," (2) "in connection with the purchase or sale of any security," and (3) "in contravention of" Securities and Exchange Commission "rules and regulations." 15 U.S.C. §78j(b). Commission Rule 10b-5 forbids, among other things, the making of any "untrue statement of a material fact" or the omission of any material fact "necessary in order to make the statements made ... not misleading." 17 CFR §240.10b-5 (2004).

The courts have implied from these statutes and Rule a private damages action, which resembles, but is not identical to, common-law tort actions for deceit and misrepresentation. [Cc] And Congress has imposed statutory requirements on that private action. *E.g.,* 15 U.S.C. §78u-4(b)(4).

In cases involving publicly traded securities and purchases or sales in public securities markets, the action's basic elements include: (1) *a material misrepresentation (or omission),* [c]; (2) *scienter, i.e.,* a wrongful state of mind, [c]; (3) *a connection with the purchase or sale of a security,* [c]; (4) *reliance,* often referred to in cases involving public securities markets (fraud-on-the-market cases) as "transaction causation," [c]; (5) *economic loss,* [c]; and (6) *"loss causation," i.e.,* a causal connection between the material misrepresentation and the loss, [cc].

Dura argues that the complaint's allegations are inadequate in respect to these last two elements. ...

... The statute insists that securities fraud complaints "specify" each misleading statement; that they set forth the facts "on which [a] belief" that a statement is misleading was "formed"; and that they "state with particularity facts giving rise to a strong inference that the defendant acted with the required state of mind." 15 U.S.C. §§78u-4(b)(1), (2). And the statute expressly imposes on plaintiffs "the burden of proving" that the defendant's misrepresentations "caused the loss for which the plaintiff seeks to recover." §78u-4(b)(4).

The statute thereby makes clear Congress' intent to permit private securities fraud actions for recovery where, but only where, plaintiffs adequately allege and prove the traditional elements of causation and loss. ...

Our holding about plaintiffs' need to *prove* proximate causation and economic loss leads us also to conclude that the plaintiffs' complaint here failed adequately to *allege* these requirements. We concede that the Federal Rules of Civil Procedure require only "a short and plain statement of the claim showing that the pleader is entitled to relief." Fed. Rule Civ. Proc. 8(a)(2). And we assume, at least for argument's sake, that neither the Rules nor the securities statutes impose any special further requirement in respect to the pleading of proximate causation or economic loss. But, even so, the "short and plain statement" must provide the defendant with "fair notice of what the plaintiff's claim is and the grounds upon which it rests." Conley v. Gibson, 355 U.S. 41, 47 (1957). The complaint before us fails this simple test.

As we have pointed out, the plaintiffs' lengthy complaint contains only one statement that we can fairly read as describing the loss caused by the defendants' "spray device" misrepresentations. That statement says that the plaintiffs "paid artificially inflated prices for Dura['s] securities" and suffered "damage[s]." [C] The statement implies that the plaintiffs' loss consisted of the "artificially inflated" purchase "prices." The complaint's failure to claim that Dura's share price fell significantly after the truth became known suggests that the plaintiffs considered the allegation of purchase price inflation alone sufficient. The complaint contains nothing that suggests otherwise.

... [T]he "artificially inflated purchase price" is not itself a relevant economic loss. And the complaint nowhere else provides the defendants with notice of what the relevant economic loss might be or of what the causal connection might be between that loss and the misrepresentation concerning Dura's "spray device."

We concede that ordinary pleading rules are not meant to impose a great burden upon a plaintiff. Swierkiewicz v. Sorema N. A., 534 U.S. 506, 513-515 [] (2002). But it should not prove burdensome for a plaintiff who has suffered an economic loss to provide a defendant with some indication of the loss and the causal connection that the plaintiff has in mind. ... At the same time, allowing a plaintiff to forgo giving any indication of the economic loss and proximate cause that the plaintiff has in mind ... would permit a plaintiff "with a largely groundless claim to simply take up the time of a number of other people, with the right to do so representing an *in terrorem* increment of the settlement value, rather than a reasonably founded hope that the [discovery] process will reveal relevant evidence." Blue Chip Stamps[v. Manor Drug Stores], 421 U.S.[723, 741 (1975)]. Such a rule would tend to transform a private securities action into a partial downside insurance policy. [Cc]

For these reasons, we find the plaintiffs' complaint legally insufficient. We reverse the judgment of the Ninth Circuit, and we remand the case for further proceedings consistent with this opinion.

It is so ordered.

Tellabs, Inc. v. Makor Issues and Rights, Ltd.,

United States Supreme Court
551 U.S. 308 (2007)

Justice GINSBURG delivered the opinion of the Court.

This Court has long recognized that meritorious private actions to enforce federal antifraud securities laws are an essential supplement to criminal prosecutions and civil enforcement actions brought, respectively, by the Department of Justice and the Securities and Exchange Commission (SEC). See, e.g., Dura Pharmaceuticals, Inc. v. Broudo, 544 U.S. 336[] (2005); [c]. Private securities fraud actions, however, if not adequately contained, can be employed abusively to impose substantial costs on companies and individuals whose conduct conforms to the law. [C] As a check against abusive litigation by private parties, Congress enacted the Private Securities Litigation Reform Act of 1995 (PSLRA), 109 Stat. 737.

Exacting pleading requirements are among the control measures Congress included in the PSLRA. The PSLRA Act requires plaintiffs to state with particularity both the facts constituting the alleged violation, and the facts evidencing scienter, i.e., the defendant's intention "to deceive, manipulate, or defraud." [Cc] This case concerns the latter requirement. ... [P]laintiffs must "state with particularity facts giving rise to a strong inference that the defendant acted with the required state of mind." 15 U.S.C. §78u-4(b)(2).

Congress left the key term "strong inference" undefined, and Courts of Appeals have divided on its meaning. In the case before us, the Court of Appeals for the Seventh Circuit held that the "strong inference" standard would be met if the complaint "allege[d] facts from which, if true, a reasonable person could infer that the defendant acted with the required intent." [C]. That formulation, we conclude, does not capture the stricter demand Congress sought to convey... . It does not suffice that a reasonable factfinder plausibly could infer from the complaint's allegations the requisite state of mind. Rather, to determine whether a complaint's scienter allegations can survive threshold inspection for sufficiency, a court governed ... must engage in a comparative evaluation; it must consider, not only inferences urged by the plaintiff, as the Seventh Circuit did, but also competing inferences rationally drawn from the facts alleged. An inference of fraudulent intent may be plausible, yet less cogent than other, nonculpable explanations for the defendant's conduct. To qualify as "strong"... , we hold, an inference of scienter must be more than merely plausible or reasonable—it must be cogent and at least as compelling as any opposing inference of nonfraudulent intent. ...

In an ordinary civil action, the Federal Rules of Civil Procedure require only "a short and plain statement of the claim showing that the pleader is entitled to relief." Fed. Rule Civ. Proc. 8(a)(2). Although the rule encourages brevity, the complaint must say enough to give the defendant "fair notice of what the plaintiff's claim is and the grounds upon which it rests." Dura Pharmaceuticals, 544 U.S.[336, 346 (2005)] (internal quotation marks omitted). Prior to the enactment of the PSLRA, the sufficiency of a complaint for securities fraud was governed not by Rule 8, but by the heightened pleading standard set forth in Rule 9(b). ... Rule 9(b) applies to "all averments of fraud or mistake"; it requires that "the circumstances constituting fraud ... be stated with particularity" but provides that "[m]alice, intent, knowledge, and other condition of mind of a person, may be averred generally." ...

Under the PSLRA's heightened pleading instructions, any private securities complaint alleging that the defendant made a false or misleading statement must: (1) "specify each statement alleged to have been misleading [and] the reason or reasons why the statement is misleading," 15 U.S.C. §78u-4(b)(1); and (2) "state with particularity facts giving rise to a strong inference that the defendant acted with the required state of mind," §78u-4(b)(2). ...

The "strong inference" standard "unequivocally raise[d] the bar for pleading scienter," [c]... .

We establish the following prescriptions: *First,* faced with a Rule 12(b)(6) motion to dismiss a §10(b) action, courts must, as with any motion to dismiss for failure to plead a claim on which relief can be granted, accept all factual allegations in the complaint as true. [C] ...

Second, courts must consider the complaint in its entirety, as well as other sources courts ordinarily examine when ruling on Rule 12(b)(6) motions to dismiss, in particular, documents incorporated into the complaint by reference, and matters of which a court may take judicial notice. [C] The inquiry, as several Courts of Appeals have recognized, is whether *all* of the facts alleged, taken collectively, give rise to a strong inference of scienter, not whether any individual allegation, scrutinized in isolation, meets that standard. [Cc]

Third, in determining whether the pleaded facts give rise to a "strong" inference of scienter, the court must take into account plausible opposing inferences. ... ... Congress did not merely require plaintiffs to "provide a factual basis for [their] scienter allegations," [c], *i.e.,* to allege facts from which an inference of scienter rationally *could* be drawn. Instead, Congress required plaintiffs to plead with particularity facts that give rise to a "strong"—*i.e.,* a powerful or cogent—inference. [Cc]

The strength of an inference cannot be decided in a vacuum. The inquiry is inherently comparative: How likely is it that one conclusion, as compared to others, follows from the underlying facts? ... A complaint will survive, we hold, only if a reasonable person would deem the inference of scienter cogent and at least as compelling as any opposing inference one could draw from the facts alleged.[fn] …

While we reject the Seventh Circuit's approach… , we do not decide whether, under the standard we have described, [c], the Shareholders' allegations warrant "a strong inference that [Notebaert and Tellabs] acted with the required state of mind," [c]. Neither the District Court nor the Court of Appeals had the opportunity to consider the matter in light of the prescriptions we announce today. We therefore vacate the Seventh Circuit's judgment so that the case may be reexamined in accord with our construction… .

The judgment of the Court of Appeals is vacated, and the case is remanded for further proceedings consistent with this opinion.

It is so ordered.

Justice SCALIA, concurring in the judgment.

I fail to see how an inference that is merely "at least as compelling as any opposing inference," [c], can conceivably be called what the statute here at issue requires: a "strong inference," 15 U.S.C. § 78u-4(b)(2). … In my view, the test should be whether the inference of scienter (if any) is *more plausible* than the inference of innocence.[fn] …

Justice ALITO, concurring in the judgment.

… [T]he best interpretation of the statute is that only those facts that are alleged "with particularity" may properly be considered in determining whether the allegations of scienter are sufficient. Second, I agree with Justice SCALIA that a "strong inference" of scienter, in the present context, means an inference that is more likely than not correct. …

I would also hold that a "strong inference that the defendant acted with the required state of mind" is an inference that is stronger than the inference that the defendant lacked the required state of mind. …

[Justice STEVENS' dissenting opinion omitted.]

INQUIRY

Real and Personal Property. Actions involving real property require special pleading rules. A major part of the concern is that the pleadings, orders, judgments, and other court papers affecting interests in real property accommodate state recording systems for title to real property. FED. R. CIV. P. 71.1(c)(1) requires that a party filing a complaint involving real property name both the property and at least one owner in the complaint's caption. The presumed purpose is to increase the probability that unidentified owners or those who claim interests in the property are more likely to receive notice of the action. *See* Rule 71.1(c)(3) (procedure for designating unknown owners). Rule 71.1(c)(2) requires more detail as to the contents of the complaint than general pleading rules, including the authority for taking the real property, the use to which the taker will put the real property, and the real property's description. By *description,* Rule 71.1(c)(2)(C) presumably means the real property's legal description, not merely the street address by which users know the property. The real property's legal description is critical to a trial court's reliable disposition of boundary and other similar ownership disputes. Prevailing parties may wish to record a judgment or order, meaning that the judgment or order will need to include a legal description. Rule 71.1(d) includes special procedures for service of process appropriate to notifying multiple identified or unidentified owners. Other provisions of Rule 71.1 address substitution of parties, amendment of pleadings, and other pre-trial and trial issues. Actions involving personal property also benefit by special pleading rules. Rule 71.1, addressing real-property actions, also addresses actions involving personal property, under the same or parallel provisions.

FED. R. CIV. P. 71.1. Condemning Real or Personal Property

(a) APPLICABILITY OF OTHER RULES. These rules govern proceedings to condemn real and personal property by eminent domain, except as this rule provides otherwise.

(b) JOINDER OF PROPERTIES. The plaintiff may join separate pieces of property in a single action, no matter whether they are owned by the same persons or sought for the same use.

(c) COMPLAINT.

(1) *Caption.* The complaint must contain a caption as provided in Rule 10(a). The plaintiff must, however, name as defendants both the property—designated generally by kind, quantity, and location—and at least one owner of some part of or interest in the property.

(2) *Contents.* The complaint must contain a short and plain statement of the following:

(A) the authority for the taking;

(B) the uses for which the property is to be taken;

(C) a description sufficient to identify the property;

(D) the interests to be acquired; and

(E) for each piece of property, a designation of each defendant who has been joined as an owner or owner of an interest in it.

(3) *Parties.* When the action commences, the plaintiff need join as defendants only those persons who have or claim an interest in the property and whose names are then known. But before any hearing on compensation, the plaintiff must add as defendants all those persons who have or claim an interest and whose names have become known or can be found by a reasonably diligent search of the records, considering both the property's character and value and the interests to be acquired. All others may be made defendants under the designation "Unknown Owners."

(4) *Procedure.* Notice must be served on all defendants as provided in Rule 71.1(d), whether they were named as defendants when the action commenced or were added later. A defendant may answer as provided in Rule 71.1(e). The court, meanwhile, may order any distribution of a deposit that the facts warrant.

(5) *Filing; Additional Copies.* In addition to filing the complaint, the plaintiff must give the clerk at least one copy for the defendants' use and additional copies at the request of the clerk or a defendant

(d) PROCESS.

(1) *Delivering Notice to the Clerk.* On filing a complaint, the plaintiff must promptly deliver to the clerk joint or several notices directed to the named defendants. When adding defendants, the plaintiff must deliver to the clerk additional notices directed to the new defendants.

(2) *Contents of the Notice.*

(A) *Main Contents.* Each notice must name the court, the title of the action, and the defendant to whom it is directed. It must describe the property sufficiently to identify it, but need not describe any property other than that to be taken from the named defendant. The notice must also state:

(i) that the action is to condemn property;

(ii) the interest to be taken;

(iii) the authority for the taking;

(iv) the uses for which the property is to be taken;

(v) that the defendant may serve an answer on the plaintiff's attorney within 21 days after being served with the notice;

(vi) that the failure to so serve an answer constitutes consent to the taking and to the court's authority to proceed with the action and fix the compensation; and

(vii) that a defendant who does not serve an answer may file a notice of appearance.

(B) *Conclusion.* The notice must conclude with the name, telephone number, and e-mail address of the plaintiff's attorney and an address within the district in which the action is brought where the attorney may be served.

(3) *Serving the Notice.*

(A) *Personal Service.* When a defendant whose address is known resides within the United States or a territory subject to the administrative or judicial jurisdiction of the United States, personal service of the notice (without a copy of the complaint) must be made in accordance with Rule 4.

(B) *Service by Publication.*
(i) A defendant may be served by publication only when the plaintiff's attorney files a certificate stating that the attorney believes the defendant cannot be personally served, because after diligent inquiry within the state where the complaint is filed, the defendant's place of residence is still unknown or, if known, that it is beyond the territorial limits of personal service. Service is then made by publishing the notice—once a week for at least 3 successive weeks—in a newspaper published in the county where the property is located or, if there is no such newspaper, in a newspaper with general circulation where the property is located. Before the last publication, a copy of the notice must also be mailed to every defendant who cannot be personally served but whose place of residence is then known. Unknown owners may be served by publication in the same manner by a notice addressed to "Unknown Owners."
(ii) Service by publication is complete on the date of the last publication. The plaintiff's attorney must prove publication and mailing by a certificate, attach a printed copy of the published notice, and mark on the copy the newspaper's name and the dates of publication.
(4) *Effect of Delivery and Service.* Delivering the notice to the clerk and serving it have the same effect as serving a summons under Rule 4.
(5) *Amending the Notice; Proof of Service and Amending the Proof.* Rule 4(a)(2) governs amending the notice. Rule 4(*l*) governs proof of service and amending it.
(e) APPEARANCE OR ANSWER.
(1) *Notice of Appearance.* A defendant that has no objection or defense to the taking of its property may serve a notice of appearance designating the property in which it claims an interest. The defendant must then be given notice of all later proceedings affecting the defendant.
(2) *Answer.* A defendant that has an objection or defense to the taking must serve an answer within 21 days after being served with the notice. The answer must:
(A) identify the property in which the defendant claims an interest;
(B) state the nature and extent of the interest; and
(C) state all the defendant's objections and defenses to the taking.
(3) *Waiver of Other Objections and Defenses; Evidence on Compensation.* A defendant waives all objections and defenses not stated in its answer. No other pleading or motion asserting an additional objection or defense is allowed. But at the trial on compensation, a defendant—whether or not it has previously appeared or answered—may present evidence on the amount of compensation to be paid and may share in the award.
(f) AMENDING PLEADINGS. Without leave of court, the plaintiff may—as often as it wants—amend the complaint at any time before the trial on compensation. But no amendment may be made if it would result in a dismissal inconsistent with Rule 71.1(i)(1) or
(2). The plaintiff need not serve a copy of an amendment, but must serve notice of the filing, as provided in Rule 5(b), on every affected party who has appeared and, as provided in Rule 71.1(d), on every affected party who has not appeared. In addition, the plaintiff must give the clerk at least one copy of each amendment for the defendants' use, and additional copies at the request of the clerk or a defendant. A defendant may appear or answer in the time and manner and with the same effect as provided in Rule 71.1(e).
(g) SUBSTITUTING PARTIES. If a defendant dies, becomes incompetent, or transfers an interest after being joined, the court may, on motion and notice of hearing, order that the proper party be substituted. Service of the motion and notice on a nonparty must be made as provided in Rule 71.1(d)(3).
(h) TRIAL OF THE ISSUES.
(1) *Issues Other Than Compensation; Compensation.* In an action
involving eminent domain under federal law, the court tries all issues, including compensation, except when compensation must be determined:
(A) by any tribunal specially constituted by a federal statute to determine compensation; or
(B) if there is no such tribunal, by a jury when a party demands one within the time to answer or within any additional time the court sets, unless the court appoints a commission.
(2) *Appointing a Commission; Commission's Powers and Report.*
(A) *Reasons for Appointing.* If a party has demanded a jury, the court may instead appoint a three-person commission to determine compensation because of the character, location, or quantity of the property to be condemned or for other just reasons.
(B) *Alternate Commissioners.* The court may appoint up to two additional persons to serve as alternate commissioners to hear the case and replace commissioners who, before a decision is filed, the court finds unable or disqualified to perform their duties. Once the commission renders its final decision, the court must discharge any alternate who has not replaced a commissioner.
(C) *Examining the Prospective Commissioners.* Before making its appointments, the court must advise the parties of the identity and

qualifications of each prospective commissioner and alternate, and may permit the parties to examine them. The parties may not suggest appointees, but for good cause may object to a prospective commissioner or alternate.

(D) *Commission's Powers and Report.* A commission has the powers of a master under Rule 53(c). Its action and report are determined by a majority. Rule 53(d), (e), and (f) apply to its action and report.

(i) DISMISSAL OF THE ACTION OR A DEFENDANT.

(1) *Dismissing the Action.*

(A) *By the Plaintiff.* If no compensation hearing on a piece of property has begun, and if the plaintiff has not acquired title or a lesser interest or taken possession, the plaintiff may, without a court order, dismiss the action as to that property by filing a notice of dismissal briefly describing the property.

(B) *By Stipulation.* Before a judgment is entered vesting the plaintiff with title or a lesser interest in or possession of property, the plaintiff and affected defendants may, without a court order, dismiss the action in whole or in part by filing a stipulation of dismissal. And if the parties so stipulate, the court may vacate a judgment already entered.

(C) *By Court Order.* At any time before compensation has been determined and paid, the court may, after a motion and hearing, dismiss the action as to a piece of property. But if the plaintiff has already taken title, a lesser interest, or possession as to any part of it, the court must award compensation for the title, lesser interest, or possession taken.

(2) *Dismissing a Defendant.* The court may at any time dismiss a defendant who was unnecessarily or improperly joined.

(3) *Effect.* A dismissal is without prejudice unless otherwise stated in the notice, stipulation, or court order.

(j) DEPOSIT AND ITS DISTRIBUTION.

(1) *Deposit.* The plaintiff must deposit with the court any money required by law as a condition to the exercise of eminent domain and may make a deposit when allowed by statute.

(2) *Distribution; Adjusting Distribution.* After a deposit, the court and attorneys must expedite the proceedings so as to distribute the deposit and to determine and pay compensation. If the compensation finally awarded to a defendant exceeds the amount distributed to that defendant, the court must enter judgment against the plaintiff for the deficiency. If the compensation awarded to a defendant is less than the amount distributed to that defendant, the court must enter judgment against that defendant for the overpayment.

(k) CONDEMNATION UNDER A STATE'S POWER OF EMINENT DOMAIN.This rule governs an action involving eminent domain under state law. But if state law provides for trying an issue by jury—or for trying the issue of compensation by jury or commission or both—that law governs.

(*l*) COSTS. Costs are not subject to Rule 54(d).

INQUIRY

State Standards. Like Congress, state legislatures may also alter the pleading requirements for various claims to address policy concerns over the integrity of the civil justice system. Those who seek pleading reform complain of frivolous, harassing, burdensome, embarrassing, and expensive claims that undermine professions, trades, industries, and economies. Those who oppose reform point to the individual and corporate interest the reformers have in closing the courthouse doors to avoid responsibility for just obligations and how reforms unfairly shift the burden and loss to the backs of those least able to bear it. Civil procedures can and do reflect and accommodate important political, moral, social, ideological, and economic interests. For example, some states supplement pleading requirements for medical-malpractice cases, requiring detailed pre-pleading notice to the defendant professional, *see, e.g.,* FL. STAT. ANN. §768.57(2); MICH. COMP. LAWS §600.2912b, detailed affidavits of merit filed with the complaint, MICH. COMP. LAWS §600.2912d, certificates of good faith filed by counsel, FL. STAT. ANN. §768.495, or affidavits showing a substantial probability of prevailing on a claim for punitive damages, CAL. CODE CIV. P. §425.13(a). The plaintiff may have to allege these procedures in the complaint.

See Nash v. Humana Sun Bay Commun. Hosp., 526 So.2d 1036 (Fla. Ct. App. 1988), *citing* FL. R. CIV. P. 1.120(c) ("Pleading Special Matters—Conditions Precedent"). The parties may also engage in substantial pre-trial litigation as to the sufficiency of these pleading and pre-pleading requirements. *See* Bush v. Shabahang, 772 N.W.2d 272 (Mich. Sup. Ct. 2009). Do these measures decrease or increase the cost of litigation? How do they affect access to the courts for those who have suffered loss or injury?

B. Responding

You have now addressed the form and content of the complaint and, in Chapter 3 on Notice and Opportunity for Hearing, service of summons and complaint on the defendant. Turn now to how a defendant may respond to service of summons and complaint. The defendant has several options. The first option, which is to do nothing, may seem unattractive but is actually a common route chosen by defendants. Chapter 1 indicated the huge number of collections actions. Many of those actions involve just debts for which there is no legal defense. There are just defenses in many other of those actions about which the defendants are unaware or as to which they cannot afford or access legal representation. Many defendants simply do not respond to service of a civil action. If the plaintiff's service was proper, then the plaintiff may obtain a judgment against the non-responding defendant through a process the law calls *default*. The next section addresses default and default judgment. The defendant's other options are to file a motion, answer, and raise affirmative defenses, each addressed by subsequent sections of this chapter.

1. Default

Default is a two-step process beginning with the entry of default and ending with obtaining the default judgment. A party may obtain entry of default only after the time period has expired for appearing and defending without the defendant having responded. If the defendant files an answer or motion before the plaintiff requests a default, then the plaintiff no longer has the right to request default, even if the defendant later refuses to continue in the defense. *See* Bass v. Hoagland, 172 F.2d 205 (5th Cir. 1949), cert. denied, 338 U.S. 816 (1949). As you have already seen in Chapter 3 on Notice and Opportunity for Hearing, FED. R. CIV. P. 4 dictates the contents of the summons and means of serving it. Rule 4(a)(1)(D) requires that the summons "state the time within which the defendant must appear and defend[.]" Rule 4(a)(1)(E) requires that the summons "notify that a failure to appear and defend will result in a default judgment against the defendant for the relief demanded in the complaint[.]" The time period within which the defendant must appear and defend depends on FED. R. CIV. P. 12. Rule 12(a)(1)(A)(i) requires in general that the defendant serve an answer within 21 days after receiving service of the summons and complaint. Other subrules of Rule 12 modify the 21-day rule. Rule 12(a)(1)(A)(ii) reminds us that Rule 4(d)(3) extends the 21-day period to 60 days if the defendant waived service (90 days if outside any judicial district). Rule 12(a)(2) and (3) give the federal government and officers 60 days to answer. Other subrules of Rule 12 require the defendant who plans to file one of the Rule 12 motions to do so "before pleading," ordinarily meaning within the 21-day period. When the defendant does file a Rule 12 motion, Rule 12(a)(4) effectively suspends the time within which the defendant has to answer until after the trial court rules or indicates that it does not intend to rule. Examine again FED. R. CIV. P. Form 3 (reproduced in Chapter 3) to ensure that it meets the requirements of Rule 4 for stating the time within which to appear and defend.

Skill

Lawyers who defend clients in civil litigation maintain systems to ensure timely answer of complaints. There must be few things worse in law practice than the embarrassment, fear, and financial consequences of a default occurring because of the carelessness of defense counsel. Defense counsel open mail immediately and review faxes and emails routinely and promptly, to ensure that they are aware of a client's tender of any complaint for defense. They calculate the due date for any complaint and enter the due date on an electronic calendar shared with their legal assistant or secretary. They determine promptly what they must do to respond to or answer a complaint, estimate the time involved, and plan accordingly to have the appropriate pleading or court paper filed timely. They also maintain malpractice insurance and notify their insurer promptly whenever a potential claim arises over a default entered against one of their clients. Courts have some discretion to set aside defaults, and judges appreciate a practitioner's challenges, but favorable exercise of discretion depends on demonstrating sound systems for managing deadlines.

Identifying the correct period is the first step for defense counsel to ensure a timely response. When one considers the anomalies of the calendar, though, it is not always clear from FED. R. CIV. P. 12 alone on precisely what date a time period may end. For instance, what if the 21-day period ends on a weekend or legal holiday? FED. R. CIV. P. 6 serves three functions. It helps the practitioner compute the precise day on which a response is due, provides for calendar anomalies, and gives the practitioner procedures for requesting extension when it looks like a timely response may not be reasonably possible. For example, Rule 6(a)(1)(C) extends the due date to the next day after weekends or legal holidays. Rule 6(b)'s procedures for extending time depend generally on a party showing good cause by motion. Rule 6(b) favors those who file the motion to extend before the period expires. Rule 6(b) is also the means by which the trial court will recognize and accept counsels' agreement for an extension, which is a common courtesy among practitioners. Read the following Rule 6 to appreciate how sensitive practitioners must be to the proper computation of these times, what relief Rule 6 provides when the clerk's office is inaccessible, and how and when a practitioner may extend due dates.

Fed. R. Civ. P. 6. Computing and Extending Time; Time for Motion Papers

(a) COMPUTING TIME. The following rules apply in computing any time period specified in these rules, in any local rule or court order, or in any statute that does not specify a method of computing time.

(1) *Period Stated in Days or a Longer Unit.* When the period is stated in days or a longer unit of time:

(A) exclude the day of the event that triggers the period;

(B) count every day, including intermediate Saturdays, Sundays, and legal holidays; and

(C) include the last day of the period, but if the last day is a Saturday, Sunday, or legal holiday, the period continues to run until the end of the next day that is not a Saturday, Sunday, or legal holiday.

(2) *Period Stated in Hours.* When the period is stated in hours:

(A) begin counting immediately on the occurrence of the event that triggers the period;

(B) count every hour, including hours during intermediate Saturdays, Sundays, and legal holidays; and

(C) if the period would end on a Saturday, Sunday, or legal holiday, the period continues to run until the same time on the next day that is not a Saturday, Sunday, or legal holiday.

(3) *Inaccessibility of the Clerk's Office.* Unless the court orders otherwise, if the clerk's office is inaccessible:

(A) on the last day for filing under Rule 6(a)(1), then the time for filing is extended to the first accessible day that is not a Saturday, Sunday, or legal holiday; or

(B) during the last hour for filing under Rule 6(a)(2), then the time for filing is extended to the same time on the first accessible day that is not a Saturday, Sunday, or legal holiday.

(4) *''Last Day'' Defined.* Unless a different time is set by a statute, local rule, or court order, the last day ends:

(A) for electronic filing, at midnight in the court's time zone; and

(B) for filing by other means, when the clerk's office is scheduled to close.

(5) *''Next Day'' Defined.* The ''next day'' is determined by continuing to count forward when the period is measured after an event and backward when measured before an event.

(6) *''Legal Holiday'' Defined.* ''Legal holiday'' means:

(A) the day set aside by statute for observing New Year's Day, Martin Luther King Jr.'s Birthday, Washington's Birthday, Memorial Day, Independence Day, Labor Day, Columbus Day, Veterans' Day, Thanksgiving Day, or Christmas Day;

(B) any day declared a holiday by the President or Congress; and

(C) for periods that are measured after an event, any other day declared a holiday by the state where the district court is located.

(b) EXTENDING TIME.

(1) *In General.* When an act may or must be done within a specified time, the court may, for good cause, extend the time:

(A) with or without motion or notice if the court acts, or if a request is made, before the original time or its extension expires; or

(B) on motion made after the time has expired if the party failed to act because of excusable neglect.

(2) *Exceptions.* A court must not extend the time to act under Rules 50(b) and (d), 52(b), 59(b), (d), and (e), and 60(b).

(c) MOTIONS, NOTICES OF HEARING, AND AFFIDAVITS.

(1) *In General.* A written motion and notice of the hearing must be served at least 14 days before the time specified for the hearing, with the following exceptions:

(A) when the motion may be heard ex parte;

(B) when these rules set a different time; or

(C) when a court order—which a party may, for good cause, apply for ex parte—sets a different time.

(2) *Supporting Affidavit.* Any affidavit supporting a motion must be served with the motion. Except as Rule 59(c) provides otherwise, any opposing affidavit must be served at least 7 days before the hearing, unless the court permits service at another time.

(d) ADDITIONAL TIME AFTER CERTAIN KINDS OF SERVICE. When a party may or must act within a specified time after service and service is made under Rule 5(b)(2)(C), (D), (E), or (F), 3 days are added after the period would otherwise expire under Rule 6(a).

FED. R. CIV. P. 55 governs the process of entering a default and the means of obtaining default judgment. Although lawyers use the word in different ways, a *default* is technically a court paper signed by the court clerk noting a party's failure to appear and defend as the rules require. The convention is to say that a clerk *enters* a default because a default is technically neither filed by a party nor ordered by the court. It is instead the clerk's notation (entry) in the court file that the defendant has failed to timely appear and defend. One might therefore think that clerks enter defaults through their own automated processes. They ordinarily do not. There are reasons why a party may not have appeared and defended as required. For example, it is common for a plaintiff's lawyer to grant defense counsel an extension of time within which to answer, without notifying the clerk. A court clerk may also not be aware at the moment that the period expires of the means and timing of the plaintiff's service of process on the defendant. Instead, the lawyer who arranged, achieved, and documented service of process will request that the court clerk enter the default, when that lawyer determines under all the circumstances that entry of default is most appropriate. Rule 55(a) makes quite clear that the clerk has no discretion but must enter default when shown that default is proper. As you read Rule 55 and the following vignette, discern the strategies counsel employ and considerations they face when determining whether to obtain entry of default.

FED. R. CIV. P. 55. Default; Default Judgment

(a) ENTERING A DEFAULT. When a party against whom a judgment for affirmative relief is sought has failed to plead or otherwise defend, and that failure is shown by affidavit or otherwise, the clerk must enter the party's default.

(b) ENTERING A DEFAULT JUDGMENT.

(1) *By the Clerk.* If the plaintiff's claim is for a sum certain or a sum that can be made certain by computation, the clerk—on the plaintiff's request, with an affidavit showing the amount due—must enter judgment for that amount and costs against a defendant who has been defaulted for not appearing and who is neither a minor nor an incompetent person.

(2) *By the Court.* In all other cases, the party must apply to the court for a default judgment. A default judgment may be entered against a minor or incompetent person only if represented by a general guardian, conservator, or other like fiduciary who has appeared. If the party against whom a default judgment is sought has appeared personally or by a representative, that party or its representative must be served with written notice of the application at least 7 days before the hearing. The court may conduct hearings or make referrals—preserving any federal statutory right to a jury trial—when, to enter or effectuate judgment, it needs to:

(A) conduct an accounting;

(B) determine the amount of damages;

(C) establish the truth of any allegation by evidence; or

(D) investigate any other matter.

(c) SETTING ASIDE A DEFAULT OR A DEFAULT JUDGMENT. The court may set aside an entry of default for good cause, and it may set aside a default judgment under Rule 60(b).

(d) JUDGMENT AGAINST THE UNITED STATES. A default judgment may be entered against the United States, its officers, or its agencies only if the claimant establishes a claim or right to relief by evidence that satisfies the court.

Practice

When the client left, leaving the complaint behind for the defense lawyer to answer, the defense lawyer dutifully faxed and mailed the plaintiff's lawyer requesting a two-week extension until the second week after New Year's Day. The client had delayed a couple of weeks in meeting with the defense lawyer. The answer was due just a few days later on Christmas Eve, and the defense lawyer had planned to be out of the office between Christmas and New Year's. When the plaintiff's lawyer did not respond to the fax or mail, the defense lawyer telephoned, leaving messages requesting extension, but again received no reply. The defense lawyer thought briefly about just trusting the plaintiff's lawyer, whom the defense lawyer knew of from some other litigation. Yet something the client had said about bad feelings between the client and the opposing-party plaintiff made the defense lawyer even more cautious than usual. So the defense lawyer drafted an answer and affirmative defenses and, when the defense lawyer had still received no extension by December 23rd, had the answer and affirmative defenses hand delivered to the court clerk for filing, retaining a file-stamped copy. Two weeks later when the defense lawyer returned to the office, there was the plaintiff's default entered by the court clerk on December 26th. The defense lawyer blanched before remembering the copy of the answer file stamped December 23rd, securely in the defense lawyer's file. The court clerk should have rejected the default request but had mistakenly overlooked the timely filed answer. The court promptly set aside the default when the defense lawyer brought the clerk's mistake to the trial judge's attention. The plaintiff's lawyer was sheepish about having been responsible for the whole embarrassing and time-consuming affair, regretted having allowed the plaintiff client to manipulate procedural rules and professional relationships, and so soon resolved the litigation.

INQUIRY

Affidavit. FED. R. CIV. P. 55(a) permits entry of default when the plaintiff shows "by affidavit or otherwise" the defendant's failure to appear and defend. Affidavit is the usual means by which the plaintiff's lawyer requests entry of default. The plaintiff's lawyer will attest that the plaintiff has properly served process on defendant and that defendant has not appeared or defended as Rule 12 requires. The attestation will typically include that the defendant is not an unrepresented minor or incompetent, is not on active duty military service, and is not protected from default by other rule or statute, to satisfy Rule 55(b)(1) and other statutory protections. *See* Servicemembers Civil Relief Act, 50 U.S.C.S. App. §521(b). Incidentally, Rule 55(a) is intentionally ambiguous as to who will request default and against whom it may enter. Although it is usually the plaintiff requesting default and the defendant who suffers it, Rule 55 applies equally to counterclaims, crossclaims, and third-party practice, meaning that any party who serves a pleading requiring response may request default, and any party whom Rule 12 requires to respond but who fails to do so may suffer default.

Setting Aside Default. As expedient as defaults may seem, courts disfavor default for policy and practical reasons. The law favors disposition of claims on their merits rather than on technical or procedural grounds. *See* Harad v. Aetna Cas. & Surety Co., 839 F.2d 979, 982 (3d Cir. 1988). Parties should have their claims and defenses heard, not disposed by fiat. A party whose lawyer misses a deadline by mistake in computation or simple oversight may have a good argument that a resulting substantial default judgment is an injustice. *See* Goodwin v. Libbey Glass, Inc., 176 F.Appx. 588, 593n.6 (5th Cir. 2006) (proper to set aside default when defendant's only error was to miss a time requirement); *see also* CAL. CODE CIV. P. §473(b) (set aside default due to attorney's mistake if defaulted party pays opposing side's attorney's fees); *cf.* Honda Power Equip. Mfg., Inc. v. Woodhouse, 219 F.R.D. 2 (D. D.C. 2003) (default judgment appropriate where defaulted party refused to respond to lawyer's requests and had already suffered related judgment). Defaults are also not necessarily so expedient. Defaults breed additional litigation over procedure rather than substance, as parties implore the court to enter them, set them aside, or enforce them on grounds having little or nothing to do with the merits of claims or defenses. FED. R. CIV. P. 55(c) thus provides that the court may set aside a default on the defaulted party's showing good cause. As this discussion suggests, the abundant state and federal authority on what constitutes good cause tends to consider the culpability of the defaulted party's inaction and whether the defaulted party has a good defense to the action. *See* O.J. Distributing, Inc. v. Hornell Brewing Co., 340 F.3d 345, 353 (6th Cir. 2003). The court must set aside the default if it was technically improper such as for lack of proper service, *see id.*, especially if service would not have satisfied due process, *see* Peralta v. Heights Medical Center, 485 U.S. 80 (1988). Rule 55(c) also provides for setting aside a default judgment, referring to the standard in FED. R. CIV. P. 60(b) for setting aside judgments generally. The courts have understandably shown greater willingness to set aside a default judgment under Rule 60(b) than a judgment taken on the merits after the losing party appeared and defended. *See* Weiss v. St. Paul Fire and Marine Ins. Co., 283 F.3d 790 (6th Cir. 2002). In *Peralta v. Heights Medical Center, supra*, the Supreme Court held that if service is constitutionally defective, then the trial court must set aside the default judgment whether or not the defendant is able to demonstrate a meritorious defense.

Appearance. FED. R. CIV. P. 55(b) distinguishes the procedure for obtaining a default judgment depending on whether the defendant appeared in the action. An appearance is a notice to the court clerk that a lawyer representing a certain party or non-party has a sufficient interest in the case as to require all parties to serve on the lawyer copies of court papers filed in the case and the clerk to serve all orders and notices. An appearance ensures that the lawyer knows who is filing what in the court file. Although filing any pleading or other court paper on behalf of a party constitutes an appearance, *see* Zuelke Tool & Eng. Co. v. Anderson Die Castings, Inc., 925 F.2d 226, 230 (7th Cir. 1991), some lawyers nonetheless make a practice of separately filing a court paper titled "Appearance" when they file the defendant's answer, motion, or other initial responsive pleading. There are also occasions when a lawyer will file only an appearance without filing an answer, motion, or other initial response. *See, e.g.,* H.F. Livermore Corp. v. Aktiengeseelschaft Gegruder Loepfe, 432 F.2d 689, 691 (D.C. Cir. 1970). Can you think of such an occasion? If a client who already had a lawyer who had appeared and defended in the action retained you to assist that lawyer, would you file an appearance in the case? Parties often have more than one lawyer and law firm representing them in a single case, in which case the lawyers and firms who do not file the initial responsive pleading will instead file an appearance. If a lawyer has appeared for the defaulted defendant before the plaintiff has requested a default judgment, then Rule 55(b)(2) requires that the plaintiff's application for default judgment give the defendant notice. Defense counsel would then have the opportunity to move to set aside the default before the court enters judgment.

Service. Chapter 3 on Notice and Opportunity for Hearing addressed the constitutional aspects of service of process on the defendant. Service of process is an important subject when it comes to giving the defendant initial notice of the action. How do the *Federal Rules of Civil Procedure* and their state-court equivalents ensure that parties receive notice of subsequent matters? You have just seen that Rule 55(b)(2) requires a party to serve an application for a default judgment on an opposing party who has appeared. FED. R. CIV. P. 5 states the rules for when a party or the court must serve other parties with pleadings, notices, and other court papers after the initial service of process. For example, Rule 5(a)(2) specifically provides that if neither the party nor the party's lawyer has appeared in the action, then the plaintiff's lawyer need not serve the defendant with subsequent papers requesting default judgment. Rule 5 serves the important function of ensuring that parties receive notice and copies of pleadings and court papers when they should and that they do not when they should not. As you read Rule 5, see if you can appreciate the distinction. Why, for instance, would Rule 5(a)(2) not require the plaintiff to serve a non-appearing defendant with an application for default judgment? As a practitioner, would you do so anyway?

FED. R. CIV. P. 5. Serving and Filing Pleadings and Other Papers

(a) SERVICE: WHEN REQUIRED.

(1) *In General.* Unless these rules provide otherwise, each of the following papers must be served on every party:

(A) an order stating that service is required;

(B) a pleading filed after the original complaint, unless the court orders otherwise under Rule 5(c) because there are numerous defendants;

(C) a discovery paper required to be served on a party, unless the court orders otherwise;

(D) a written motion, except one that may be heard ex parte; and

(E) a written notice, appearance, demand, or offer of judgment, or any similar paper.

(2) *If a Party Fails to Appear.* No service is required on a party who is in default for failing to appear. But a pleading that asserts a new claim for relief against such a party must be served on that party under Rule 4.

(3) *Seizing Property.* If an action is begun by seizing property and no person is or need be named as a defendant, any service required before the filing of an appearance, answer, or claim must be made on the person who had custody or possession of the property when it was seized.

(b) SERVICE: HOW MADE.

(1) *Serving an Attorney.* If a party is represented by an attorney, service under this rule must be made on the attorney unless the court orders service on the party.

(2) *Service in General.* A paper is served under this rule by:

(A) handing it to the person;

(B) leaving it:

(i) at the person's office with a clerk or other person in charge or, if no one is in charge, in a conspicuous
place in the office; or

(ii) if the person has no office or the office is closed, at the person's dwelling or usual place of abode with someone of suitable age and discretion who resides there;

(C) mailing it to the person's last known address—in which event service is complete upon mailing;

(D) leaving it with the court clerk if the person has no known address;

(E) sending it by electronic means if the person consented in writing—in which event service is complete upon transmission, but is not effective if the serving party learns that it did not reach the person to be served; or

(F) delivering it by any other means that the person consented to in writing—in which event service is complete when the person making service delivers it to the agency designated to make delivery.

(3) *Using Court Facilities.* If a local rule so authorizes, a party may use the court's transmission facilities to make service under Rule 5(b)(2)(E).

(c) SERVING NUMEROUS DEFENDANTS.

(1) *In General.* If an action involves an unusually large number of defendants, the court may, on motion or on its own, order that:
(A) defendants' pleadings and replies to them need not be served on other defendants;
(B) any crossclaim, counterclaim, avoidance, or affirmative defense in those pleadings and replies to them will be treated as denied or avoided by all other parties; and
(C) filing any such pleading and serving it on the plaintiff constitutes notice of the pleading to all parties.
(2) *Notifying Parties.* A copy of every such order must be served on the parties as the court directs.
(d) FILING.
(1) *Required Filings; Certificate of Service.* Any paper after the complaint that is required to be served—together with a certificate of service—must be filed within a reasonable time after service. But disclosures under Rule 26(a)(1) or (2) and the following discovery requests and responses must not be filed until they are used in the proceeding or the court orders filing: depositions, interrogatories, requests for documents or tangible things or to permit entry onto land, and requests for admission.
(2) *How Filing Is Made—In General.* A paper is filed by delivering it:
(A) to the clerk; or
(B) to a judge who agrees to accept it for filing, and who must then note the filing date on the paper and promptly send it to the clerk.
(3) *Electronic Filing, Signing, or Verification.* A court may, by local rule, allow papers to be filed, signed, or verified by electronic means that are consistent with any technical standards established by the Judicial Conference of the United States. A local rule may require electronic filing only if reasonable exceptions are allowed. A paper filed electronically in compliance with a local rule is a written paper for purposes of these rules.
(4) *Acceptance by the Clerk.* The clerk must not refuse to file a paper solely because it is not in the form prescribed by these rules or by a local rule or practice.

INQUIRY

Judgment. FED. R. CIV. P. 55(b) also distinguishes procedures for entry of default judgment depending on whether the claim was for a sum certain. If the complaint's ad damnum clause named a sum certain (specific figure computed reliably on economic losses), then the clerk must enter the default judgment. Otherwise, in the event of uncertain damages or a damages request different from the complaint's prayer for relief, Rule 55(b)(2) authorizes the court to hold a hearing or refer the matter to a special magistrate or other authority to determine damages. Rule 55(b)(2) gives the trial court broad power to investigate and challenge the truth of allegations, and account for and compute damages. It also requires the trial court to preserve the defaulted party's right to jury trial. That broad authority does not mean that the plaintiff must prove liability anyway, despite the default. The default establishes liability, leaving damages the only contestable issue. Hughes Tool Co. v. Trans World Airlines, 409 U.S. 363 (1973). If the defendant has appeared, then plaintiff's counsel can expect and should prepare for a full trial on damages. If the defendant has not appeared, then the practice tends to be for the court to conduct only a truncated hearing or to refer the matter to a trusted damages expert. *See* FED. R. CIV. P. 53(a)(1)(B)(ii) (special masters to "perform an accounting or resolve a difficult computation of damages"). Chapter XIV addresses other issues having to do with obtaining judgments while Chapter XV addresses enforcing judgments and Chapter XVIII the effect of judgments.

2. Pre-Answer Motion

You should now understand the procedure for filing and serving a complaint, and obtaining a default judgment when the defendant fails or refuses to appear and defend. What are the defendant's options when the defendant does intend to appear and defend? FED. R. CIV. P. 12(b) catalogs several motions that the defendant may file in response to service of the complaint and, indeed, must file if the defendant wishes to preserve the associated defenses. These Rule 12(b) defenses include personal and subject-matter jurisdiction, the propriety of venue, the sufficiency of process and service of process, whether the complaint states a claim, and whether the plaintiff has failed to join an indispensable party. The text has already addressed most of the Rule 12(b) defenses. You have already seen in the discussion above having to do with the sufficiency of a complaint how a defendant may challenge it by motion under FED. R. CIV. P. 12(b)(6) for failure to state a claim on which relief can be granted. Earlier chapters addressed several other of the Rule 12(b) defenses because of their close relationship to the constitutional authority of the trial court to adjudicate. Chapter II addressed how a defendant may challenge personal jurisdiction with a motion under Rule 12(b)(2). Chapter III addressed how a defendant challenges insufficient process (a technical defect in the contents of the summons) or service of process with motions under Rule 12(b)(4) and (5). Chapter IV addressed how a defendant challenges subject-matter jurisdiction with a Rule 12(b)(1) motion. Chapter V addressed how a defendant challenges improper or inconvenient venue with a Rule 12(b)(3) motion. The next chapter, Chapter VIII, addresses challenges to joinder by motion under Rule 12(b)(7). This section addresses the remaining Rule 12 motions.

More Definite Statement. Rule 12(e), titled "Motion for More Definite Statement," authorizes dismissal on motion when a pleading "is so vague or ambiguous that the party cannot reasonably prepare a response." The practitioner must read Rule 12(e) together with Rule 8(a)(2) that a pleading need only include "a short and plain statement of the claim." In other words, a lawyer should not read Rule 12(e) with the false hope of inducing a pleading that includes a comprehensive and detailed statement of the factual support for the claim. Rule 12(e) motions are relatively rare, especially when filed alone, and rarely successful. More commonly, the moving party will combine a Rule 12(b)(6) motion to dismiss with an alternative Rule 12(e) motion for more definite statement, to highlight for the court the difficulty that the moving party has in responding to the complaint. Rule 12(e) requires expressly that the moving party "point out the defects complained of and the details desired." Even more commonly, the practitioner who must defend vague allegations within a complaint will serve interrogatories requesting the facts and evidence supporting each paragraph of the complaint. The availability of discovery may be why practitioners are reluctant to request and trial judges seldom grant Rule 12(e) motions, even though there are instances when they do so. *See* McHenry v. Renne, 84 F.3d 1172, 1175 (9th Cir. 1996); *see also* United States v. Employing Plasterers Assn., 347 U.S. 186, 189 (1954) (Rule 12(e) gives a party "a right to call for" more facts). When a trial court does grant a motion for more definite statement, Rule 12(a)(4)(B) requires the defendant to answer the more-definite complaint within 14 days after the plaintiff files it.

To Strike. Rule 12(f), titled "Motion to Strike," authorizes a motion to strike when a pleading includes "an insufficient defense or any redundant, immaterial, impertinent, or scandalous matter." Rule 12(f) has two different purposes. The first is to authorize the plaintiff to move to dismiss "an insufficient defense," which the federal courts have interpreted to mean one for which there is no support as a matter of law. *See* Kaiser Aluminum & Chem. Sales, Inc. v. Avondale Shipyards, Inc., 677 F.2d 1045, 1047 (5th Cir. 1982). In that sense, Rule 12(f) is the plaintiff's equivalent of a defendant's Rule 12(b)(6) motion for failure to state a claim. Defendants are often at a disadvantage in answering a complaint within a short time period with incomplete information. Defense lawyers plead affirmative defenses as a matter of caution, sometimes when they anticipate the need for them more than the need is apparent from the face of the complaint. Rule 12(f) gives the plaintiff an opportunity to winnow defenses to those for which there is a legal basis within the scope of the complaint. Rule 12(f)'s other function is to clean up pleadings that are legally sufficient but contain distracting and even damaging allegations having nothing to do with the merits of a claim or defense. *See* Cobell v. Norton, 224 F.R.D. 1, 3 (D. D.C. 2004). A Rule 12(f) motion is particularly appropriate when a pleading depicts unnecessarily a party in a cruelly negative light, lowering the dignity of the proceeding and court. *See* Nault's Auto. Sales, Inc. v. American Honda Motor Co., 148 F.R.D. 25 (D. N.H. 1993) (scandalous allegations of "perjury" and "contempt" by "liars"); Hughes v. Kaiser Jeep Corp., 40 F.R.D. 89, 93 (D. S.C. 1966) (defendant's product alleged to be a "death trap"). Practitioners may find Rule 12(f) motions particularly appropriate when an unrepresented party fails to appreciate the decorum with which the courts conduct civil proceedings, including in the tone of pleadings, even when substantial interests are at stake.

Delays. As noted above, when a defendant files a Rule 12 motion, Rule 12(a)(4) suspends the usual 21-day period or other time within which that defendant must answer until the trial court denies the motion or indicates that it is postponing ruling. Because defendants file Rule 12 motions before answering, and the filing of a Rule 12 motion suspends the time within which to answer, Rule 12 motions carry the prospect for delaying the proceeding. A Rule 12 motion can effectively move the proceeding into a state of suspended animation of unknown duration. Defendants are quite aware of that potential advantage, as plaintiffs are aware of their disadvantage. The *Federal Rules* limit the opportunity for delay through Rules 12(g) and (h). Rule 12(g)(1) permits a party to join Rule 12 motions. Rule 12(g)(2) then provides that a party who "makes a motion under this rule must not make another motion under this rule raising a defense or objection that was available to the party but omitted from its earlier motion." Rule 12(g) in effect prohibits seriatim motions. It requires that a party make all of its Rule 12 motions at once. Rule 12(g) works together with Rule 12(h)(1), which provides that a party waives Rule 12(b)(2)-(5) defenses if not included in a (first and only) Rule 12 motion. In short, Rule 12's drafters eliminated opportunities for defendants to delay a proceeding beyond the time within which the trial court either decides the first Rule 12 motion or indicates its intent to postpone decision.

Voluntary Dismissal. Another situation, one that may not have occurred to you, remains, requiring its own procedures. In an appreciable percentage of cases, the plaintiff's act of filing and serving the lawsuit will cause the parties to reevaluate their interests and either settle their dispute without further recourse to litigation, or otherwise induce the plaintiff to decide not to pursue the litigation. FED. R. CIV. P. 41 provides for those situations. Rule 41(a) addresses voluntary dismissals by the plaintiff. One might think that the plaintiff could dismiss a lawsuit at any time. Rule 41(a) provides otherwise, and for good reason. Although under Rule 41(a)(1) a plaintiff may dismiss most actions at any time before the defendant appears and defends, once the defendant makes that effort Rule 41(a)(2) requires the plaintiff to obtain the court's order for dismissal. The difference has to do with the terms and effects of the dismissal. A plaintiff's voluntary dismissal before the defendant has appeared is ordinarily without prejudice, meaning that the plaintiff may refile the case again later, unless it is a second dismissal. *See* Cooter & Gell v. Harmarx Corp., 496 U.S. 384, 394 (1990) (second Rule 41(a)(1) dismissal is with prejudice). Where on the other hand the defendant has appeared, the defendant may have expended considerable time, effort, and expense in defense of the action and so may desire that the dismissal be with prejudice, meaning a final adjudication on the merits. Rule 41(a)(2) requiring court order for dismissal after the defendant appears and defends, permits the trial judge to impose terms including not only whether the dismissal will be with or without prejudice but also whether the plaintiff should pay costs and whether the defendant may preserve counterclaims. Read Rule 41 for these voluntary-dismissal procedures.

FED. R. CIV. P. 41. Dismissal of Actions

(a) VOLUNTARY DISMISSAL.

(1) *By the Plaintiff.*

(A) *Without a Court Order.* Subject to Rules 23(e), 23.1(c), 23.2, and 66 and any applicable federal statute, the plaintiff may dismiss an action without a court order by filing:

(i) a notice of dismissal before the opposing party serves either an answer or a motion for summary judgment; or

(ii) a stipulation of dismissal signed by all parties who have appeared.

(B) *Effect.* Unless the notice or stipulation states otherwise, the dismissal is without prejudice. But if the plaintiff previously dismissed any federal- or state-court action based on or including the same claim, a notice of dismissal operates as an adjudication on the merits.

(2) *By Court Order; Effect.* Except as provided in Rule 41(a)(1), an action may be dismissed at the plaintiff's request only by court order, on terms that the court considers proper. If a defendant has pleaded a counterclaim before being served with the plaintiff's motion to dismiss, the action may be dismissed over the defendant's objection only if the counterclaim can remain pending for independent adjudication. Unless the order states otherwise, a dismissal under this paragraph (2) is without prejudice.

(b) INVOLUNTARY DISMISSAL; EFFECT. If the plaintiff fails to prosecute or to comply with these rules or a court order, a defendant may move to dismiss the action or any claim against it. Unless the dismissal order states otherwise, a dismissal under this subdivision (b) and any dismissal not under this rule—except one for lack of jurisdiction, improper venue, or failure to join a party under Rule 19—operates as an adjudication on the merits.

(c) DISMISSING A COUNTERCLAIM, CROSSCLAIM, OR THIRD-PARTY CLAIM. This rule applies to a dismissal of any counterclaim, crossclaim, or third-party claim. A claimant's voluntary dismissal under Rule 41(a)(1)(A)(i) must be made:

(1) before a responsive pleading is served; or

(2) if there is no responsive pleading, before evidence is introduced at a hearing or trial.

(d) COSTS OF A PREVIOUSLY DISMISSED ACTION. If a plaintiff who previously dismissed an action in any court files an action based on or including the same claim against the same defendant, the court:

(1) may order the plaintiff to pay all or part of the costs of that previous action; and

(2) may stay the proceedings until the plaintiff has complied.

INQUIRY

Discretion. Rule 41(a)(2)'s permissive language makes it clear that the trial court has discretion whether to grant or deny a plaintiff's request for voluntary dismissal. *See* Hamm v. Rhone-Poulenc Rorer Pharm., Inc., 187 F.3d 941, 950 (8th Cir. 1999) (voluntary dismissal within trial court's discretion). Relevant factors in that determination include good cause for the dismissal, burden to the defendant, and judicial economy. Should the plaintiff's ability to obtain a better result elsewhere be a factor? *See* McCants v. Ford Motor Co., 781 F.2d 855, 857-859 (11th Cir. 1986) (affirming voluntary dismissal where plaintiff seeks more favorable limitations period elsewhere); *see also* Texaco Inc. v. Pennzoil, 481 U.S. 1 (1987) (voluntary dismissal after denial of preliminary injunction, with case refiled elsewhere resulting in $10 billion judgment). Or is it better to refuse voluntary dismissal if the plaintiff is merely trying to avoid an impending loss? *See Hamm v. Rhone-Polenc Rorer Pharm., Inc., supra* (barring voluntary dismissals to avoid losing). Rule 41(a)(2) also permits the trial court to impose terms for voluntary dismissal. What terms might a trial court impose? Costs are a common term. *See* Rogers v. Wal-Mart Stores, 230 F.3d 868, 874 (6th Cir. 2000), cert. denied, 532 U.S. 953 (2001). Some cases also allow the trial court to impose attorney's fees, *see* Evans v. Safeway Stores, 623 F.2d 121, 122 (8th Cir. 1980), especially if the underlying claim would have allowed the prevailing defendant to recover attorney's fees, *see* Esposito v. Piatowski, 223 F.3d 497, 500-501 (7th Cir. 2000).

Involuntary Dismissal. Rule 41(b) also addresses involuntary dismissal. It authorizes a defendant to move for dismissal where the plaintiff fails to prosecute a civil action. Although the language of Rule 41(b) is actually broader than the mere failure to prosecute, also including failure to "comply with these rules or a court order," do not confuse Rule 41(b) with Rule 11 motions for sanctions or Rule 12 motions to dismiss. Rule 41(b) involuntary dismissals have to do with the plaintiff's delay or inattention, not misconduct or lack of merit in the claims. Think of Rule 41(b) as a corollary to the duties Rule 55 imposes on a defendant to timely appear and defend or suffer default and default judgment. The plaintiff, too, has a duty to respect the authority of the court and the interest of the opposing party in the case's expeditious resolution. Plaintiff delay happens. Plaintiffs occasionally have other circumstances develop (including financial, health, and management problems, and disagreements with retained counsel) that make pursuing or dismissing the litigation less attractive options than simply delaying or ignoring it. Rule 41(b) gives the defendant the opportunity to request involuntary dismissal and the court express authority to grant the request. The Supreme Court has also interpreted Rule 41(b) to give the trial court implied authority to order involuntary dismissal without motion. *See* Link v. Wabash R. Co., 370 U.S. 626, 629-630 (1962) (affirming dismissal for failure to attend pretrial conference). Unlike the common treatment of voluntary dismissals, Rule 41(b) provides that involuntary dismissals are ordinarily with prejudice, meaning treated as adjudications on the merits barring relitigation, unless the trial court orders otherwise. Can you discern the reason for the differing treatment?

3. Answer

Unless the defendant succeeds in resolving the case by agreement or obtaining the case's Rule 12 dismissal, the complaint will require an answer. The complaint and answer, together with any cross-claims, counterclaims, third-party complaints, and their answers, frame the legal and factual issues in a case. Much like the rules for the complaint, Rules 7, 8, 10, and 11 work together to define the form and contents of an answer. Rule 7(a)(2) identifies an answer as a pleading. Rules 8(b) and 8(c) are most significant in determining the substance of an answer. Rule 8(b) enables a defendant to contest (in outdated common-law vernacular, to *traverse*) the complaint's allegations. Rule 8(b) states general and specific rules under which a party may admit, deny, or otherwise answer the allegations of a pleading. Rule 8(c) enables a defendant to accept or ignore the complaint's allegations (in outdated common-law vernacular, *confession and avoidance*) in favor of pleading separate affirmative defenses. Rule 8(c) authorizes a defendant to assert affirmative defenses in response to a complaint—or lose them. Rule 10 provides the form and content of the answer's caption and the numbered and focused form of its paragraphs. Rule 11 provides for signing the answer and certifying that the law and facts on which the answer relies are well grounded.

The case and inquiries that follow explore the rules for answering. First, though, consider the form of an answer. FED. R. CIV. P. Form 30, reproduced below, offers a form of answer that, under FED. R. CIV. P. 84, will officially suffice. Yet Form 30 is not how practitioners style answers. Instead, defense lawyers title the pleading "Answer and Affirmative Defenses" and, in cases involving multiple defendants, add "of Defendant ..." to distinguish their client's answer from other defendants' answers. Defense lawyers then use like headings and numbered paragraphs mimicking the plaintiff's complaint, *separately answering each paragraph*. The defense lawyer who followed Form 30 by answering multiple paragraphs of the complaint in one collective denial, admission, or mixed denial and admission, would have adopted so highly unconventional a practice as to risk confusion, challenge, and even malpractice. Defense lawyers then list separately their defendant client's affirmative defenses, typically under a subtitle "Affirmative Defenses" and by lettered paragraphs to distinguish them from the answers to the complaint's numbered paragraphs. Compare the unconventional and exceedingly brief style of Form 30 with the conventional form of the sample answer (drawn from a products liability case) that follows it.

Federal Rules of Civil Procedure Form 30. Answer Presenting Defenses Under Rule 12(b)

(Caption—See Form 1.)

Responding to Allegations in the Complaint

1. Defendant admits the allegations in paragraphs _______.
2. Defendant lacks knowledge or information sufficient to form a belief about the truth of the allegations in paragraphs _______.

3. Defendant admits *identify part of the allegation* in paragraph _______ and denies or lacks knowledge or information sufficient to form a belief about the truth of the rest of the paragraph.

Failure to State a Claim

4. The complaint fails to state a claim upon which relief can be granted.

Failure to Join a Required Party

5. If there is a debt, it is owed jointly by the defendant and *name* who is a citizen of _______. This person can be made a party without depriving this court of jurisdiction over the existing parties.

Affirmative Defense-Statute of Limitations

6. The plaintiff's claim is barred by the statute of limitations because it arose more than _______ years before this action was commenced.

Counterclaim

7. (*Set forth any counterclaim in the same way a claim is pleaded in a complaint. Include a further statement of jurisdiction if needed.*)

Crossclaim

8. (*Set forth a crossclaim against a coparty in the same way a claim is pleaded in a complaint. Include a further statement of jurisdiction if needed.*)

(Date and sign—See Form 2.)

UNITED STATES DISTRICT COURT
EASTERN DISTRICT OF MICHIGAN
SOUTHERN DIVISION

CARLOS GUITERREZ and DEBORAH GUITERREZ,
Plaintiffs,

v

MACON DISTRIBUTING COMPANY, an Indiana corporation, and YUHANG STEEL PRODUCTS CO., a Chinese corporation,
Defendants.

No. 08-******-NP
Hon. __________________

ANSWER OF DEFENDANT MACON DISTRIBUTING CO.

AFFIRMATIVE DEFENSES

CROSS-COMPLAINT

[*Names, law firms, addresses, and telephones of counsel omitted*]

Attorneys for Plaintiffs

Attorneys for Defendant Macon

Answer

Defendant Macon Distributing Company ("Macon") answers plaintiffs' complaint by like headings and numbered paragraphs saying:

GENERAL ALLEGATIONS

1. No contest as to plaintiffs' residence.

2. Admitted as to Macon's incorporation and principal place of business.

3.-10. No contest as to the incorporation and place of business of the Chinese corporation defendant.

11. No contest as to Macon's corporate status.

12. Denied as untrue as to the allegation of product failure, on information and belief and for lack of knowledge, pending plaintiffs' proofs.

13. Denied as untrue as to the allegation of damages in excess of $75,000, that allegation being disputed both as to liability and amount of damages.

14. The jurisdictional allegation is denied as untrue as to the allegation of damages in excess of $75,000, that allegation being disputed both as to liability and amount of damages.

COUNT I

This reference incorporates the above paragraphs into this count.

15. Denied as untrue as to the allegation of an injury event, both as to liability and damages, on information and belief and for lack of knowledge, pending plaintiffs' proofs.

16. Denied as untrue as to Macon's alleged design, manufacture, testing, and supplying. The allegation with respect to sale and distribution is denied on information and belief and for lack of knowledge, pending plaintiffs' proofs.

17. Denied as untrue as to the allegation of product failure, on information and belief and for lack of knowledge, pending plaintiffs' proofs.

18. This paragraph and each of its subparagraphs a) through f) are denied as untrue as to Macon's alleged design, manufacture, testing, and supplying. The allegations with respect to sale and distribution are denied on information and belief and for lack of knowledge, pending plaintiffs' proofs.

19. Denied as untrue as to Macon's alleged breach of duties, cause-in-fact, proximate cause, and damages, including subparagraphs a) through j), on information and belief and for lack of knowledge, pending plaintiffs' proofs.

20. Denied as untrue as to the allegations of negligence, gross negligence, and consortium loss, both as to liability and damages as to Macon, on information and belief and for lack of knowledge, pending plaintiffs' proofs.

COUNT II

21. This reference incorporates the above paragraphs into this count.

22. Denied as untrue as to Macon's alleged implied and express warranties, on information and belief and for lack of knowledge, pending plaintiffs' proofs.

23. Denied as untrue as to Macon's alleged breaches of implied and express warranties, on information and belief and for lack of knowledge, pending plaintiffs' proofs.

24. Denied as untrue as to Macon's alleged implied and express warranties, and as to cause-in-fact, proximate cause, and damages, on information and belief and for lack of knowledge, pending plaintiffs' proofs.

ON THESE GROUNDS, defendant Macon Distributing Company prays for judgment in its favor and dismissal of plaintiffs' first amended complaint as to this defendant, with prejudice and with allowable costs and attorney's fees.

Affirmative Defenses

For its separate affirmative defenses, defendant Macon Distributing Company states as follows:

A. Plaintiffs may have failed to state a claim against these defendants.

B. Plaintiffs may fail to establish the requisite amount in controversy, such that this Court would not have jurisdiction.

C. These defendants are entitled to an allocation of fault and an apportionment of damages among the plaintiffs and defendants.

D. If the proofs show that the product was manufactured long enough ago, then plaintiffs' claims may be barred by repose, these defendants are entitled to statutory presumptions with respect to the product's reasonably safe design, manufacture, sale, distribution, and use, and plaintiffs are entitled to no presumptions.

E. If the proofs show that plaintiff Carlos Guiterrez or others were misusing the product at the time of his injury, then plaintiffs' claims are barred.

F. If the proofs show that plaintiff Carlos Guiterrez was comparatively negligent in the selection, position, use, maintenance, or repair of the product, or in the failure to use other secure means of protection as redundancy against product failure, or in other ways, then plaintiffs' claims will be barred in whole or in part.

G. If the proofs show that plaintiff Carlos Guiterrez has failed to mitigate damages, then plaintiffs' damages would be barred in whole or in part.

H. If the proofs show that the plaintiffs' failed to timely file their complaint within the statutory three-year period, then their claims are barred.

I. These defendants reserve defenses pending discovery.

ON THESE DEFENSES, defendant Macon Distributing Company prays for judgment in its favor and dismissal of plaintiffs' first amended complaint as to this defendant, with prejudice and with allowable costs and attorney's fees.

Cross-Complaint

Defendant Macon Distributing Company cross-complains against defendant Yuhang Steel Products Co. saying:

1. The first amended complaint alleges that the Chinese corporation cross-defendant designed, manufactured, imported, and sold a defective product causing plaintiffs' injury, loss, and damage.

2. The first amended complaint further alleges that Macon distributed the allegedly defective product.

COUNT I—INDEMNITY

3. Assuming solely for purposes of this cross-complaint that the plaintiffs' allegations are true, and without admitting those allegations, then if true the plaintiffs' allegations would establish the right of cross-plaintiff Macon to the Chinese corporation cross-defendant's common law and express and implied contractual indemnity as to any damages owed by Macon to the plaintiffs in this litigation, together with costs, expenses, interest, and attorney's fees.

ON THESE GROUNDS, defendant Macon Distributing Company prays for judgment in its favor and against the other defendant Yuhang Steel Products Co. for all amounts to which Macon is found liable to the plaintiffs in this case, together with costs, expenses, interest, and attorney's fees.

[*signature block of counsel omitted*]
Attorneys for Defendant Macon

Dated:

Technology

Lawyers once handwrote or dictated pleadings for secretaries to type. Lawyers today are generally able to draft and type their own pleadings using their own computers and word processing software. Yet lawyers rarely type an entire pleading. Instead, they assemble pleadings from prior pleadings using electronic cut-and-paste functions, macros for signature blocks, styles, and other technology tools. In the case of standardized pleadings, lawyers may use document-assembly software or electronic forms. Lawyers depend on the efficiencies gained by well-designed and smartly employed electronic document-assembly tools. Locate your state bar's practice-management resource center, and explore its technology links and tools.

INQUIRY

Admissions. Admissions are simple enough, as paragraph 2 of the above sample pleading shows. The single word "Admitted" would have been sufficient. Why, though, did the sample answer plead "No contest" to paragraphs 1 and 3-11 of the complaint rather than simply admit them? In the case in which the party makes the allegation, there is no difference between admitting and refusing to contest an allegation. The admission or refusal to contest establishes the allegation for all purposes in that proceeding. It is a *judicial* admission, not merely an *evidentiary* admission. Not only may the opposing party read the admission to the jury to establish matters in the litigation, but the opposing party may also require that the court prevent the party who admitted or refused to contest from later contesting the allegation. In other words, the court may entirely remove those matters from dispute, taking them as established. The difference between admitting and refusing to contest an allegation has to do with the effect on future proceedings. Judicial admissions in one proceeding can bind a party in a subsequent proceeding, whereas refusals to contest do not.

Denials. The rules for denials are more complex than for admissions. Rule 8(b)(1)'s general rules for answers mimick Rule 8(a)'s "short and plain" statement requirement. Yet Rule 8(b)(2) requires that a "denial must fairly respond to the substance of the allegation." What does that term mean? Complaint paragraphs often contain compound allegations. An artful answer could make a general denial of a compound allegation in a way that would not help the pleader to understand which particular of the allegation was incorrect. The case below shows how detrimental a general denial can be to the party who makes it, when it does not respond to the allegation's substance. The trial court may construe the overly general denial to be an admission of the allegation's substance. In short, Rule 8(b)(2) prohibits artful indirection. Rule 8(b)(3) permits the defendant to plead denials either paragraph-by-paragraph or collectively. Rule 8(b)(2) works together with Rule 8(b)(4), requiring that a party who "intends in good faith to deny only part of an allegation must admit the part that is true and deny the rest." Why are such detailed rules for answering necessary? There are few if any litigation tasks requiring greater care and circumspection than answering a complaint, given the foreclosing effect of inadvertent admissions or omissions. Rule 8(b)(5) is in some respects the defense lawyer's relief valve, permitting an answer that the party "lacks knowledge or information sufficient to form a belief as to the truth of an allegation," which Rule 8(b)(5) further construes as a denial. Rule 8(b)(6) provides that the answering party admits an allegation to which the answer does not respond. Consider a case whose outcome depended on Rule 8(b).

Zielinski v. Philadelphia Piers, Inc.,

United States District Court for the Eastern District of Pennsylvania
139 F. Supp. 408 (1956)

VAN DUSEN, District Judge.

Plaintiff requests a ruling that, for the purposes of this case, the motordriven fork lift operated by Sandy Johnson on February 9, 1953, was owned by defendant and that Sandy Johnson was its agent acting in the course of his employment on that date. The following facts are established by the pleadings, interrogatories, depositions and uncontradicted portions of affidavits:

1. Plaintiff filed his complaint on April 28, 1953, for personal injuries received on February 9, 1953, while working on Pier 96, Philadelphia, for J. A. McCarthy, as a result of a collision of two motor-driven fork lifts.

2. Paragraph 5 of this complaint stated that "a motor-driven vehicle known as a fork lift or chisel, owned, operated and controlled by the defendant, its agents, servants and employees, was so negligently and carelessly managed * * * that the same * * * did come into contact with the plaintiff causing him to sustain the injuries more fully hereinafter set forth."

3. The "First Defense" of the Answer stated "Defendant * * * (c) denies the averments of paragraph 5 * * *."

4. The motor-driven vehicle known as a fork lift or chisel, which collided with the McCarthy fork lift on which plaintiff was riding, had on it the initials "P.P.I."

5. On February 10, 1953, Carload Contractors, Inc. made a report of this accident to its insurance company, whose policy No. CL 3964 insured Carload Contractors, Inc. against potential liability for the negligence of its employees contributing to a collision of the type described in paragraph 2 above.

6. By letter of April 29, 1953, the complaint served on defendant was forwarded to the above-mentioned insurance company. This letter read as follows:

> "Gentlemen:
>
> "As per telephone conversation today with your office, we attach hereto 'Complaint in Trespass' as brought against Philadelphia Piers, Inc. by one Frank Zielinski for supposed injuries sustained by him on February 9, 1953.
>
> "We find that a fork lift truck operated by an employee of Carload Contractors, Inc., also insured by yourselves was involved in an accident with another chisel truck, which, was alleged, did cause injury to Frank Zielinski, and same was reported to you by Carload Contractors, Inc. at the time, and you assigned Claim Number OL 0153-94 to this claim.
>
> "Should not this Complaint in Trespass be issued against Carload Contractors, Inc. and not Philadelphia Piers, Inc.?
>
> "We forward for your handling."

7. Interrogatories 1 to 5 and the answers thereto,[fn] which were sworn to by defendant's General Manager on June 12, 1953, and filed on June 22, 1953, read as follows:

> "1. State whether you have received any information of an injury sustained by the plaintiff on February 9, 1953, South Wharves. If so, state when and from whom you first received notice of such injury. A. We were first notified of this accident on or about February 9, 1953 by Thomas Wilson.
>
> "2. State whether you caused an investigation to be made of the circumstances of said injury and if so, state who made such investigation and when it was made. A. We made a very brief investigation on February 9, 1953 and turned the matter over to (our insurance company) for further investigation. ...

8. At a deposition taken August 18, 1953, Sandy Johnson testified that he was the employee of defendant on February 9, 1953, and had been their employee for approximately fifteen years.[fn]

9. At a pre-trial conference held on September 27, 1955,[FN3. The applicable statute of limitations prevented any suit against Carload Contractors, Inc. after February 9, 1955, [c].] plaintiff first learned that over a year before February 9, 1953, the business of moving freight on piers in Philadelphia, formerly conducted by defendant, had been sold by it to Carload Contractors, Inc. and Sandy Johnson had been transferred to the payroll of this corporation without

apparently realizing it, since the nature or location of his work had not changed. ...

11. Defendant now admits that on February 9, 1953, it owned the fork lift in the custody of Sandy Johnson and that this fork lift was leased to Carload Contractors, Inc. It is also admitted that the pier on which the accident occurred was leased by defendant.

12. There is no indication of action by either party in bad faith and there is no proof of inaccurate statements being made with intent to deceive. Because defendant made a prompt investigation of the accident (see answers to Interrogatories 1, 2, 16 and 17), its insurance company has been representing the defendant since suit was brought, and this company insures Carload Contractors, Inc. also, requiring defendant to defend this suit, will not prejudice it.[fn]

Under these circumstances, and for the purposes of this action, it is ordered that the following shall be stated to the jury at the trial: "It is admitted that, on February 9, 1953, the towmotor or fork lift bearing the initials 'P.P.I.' was owned by defendant and that Sandy Johnson was a servant in the employ of defendant and doing its work on that date."

This ruling is based on ... the circumstances of this case, [that] the answer contains an ineffective denial of that part of paragraph 5 of the complaint which alleges that "a motor driven vehicle known as a fork lift or chisel (was) owned, operated and controlled by the defendant, its agents, servants and employees."

F.R.Civ.P. 8(b), 28 U.S.C. provides: "A party shall state in short and plain terms his defenses to each claim asserted and shall admit or deny the averments upon which the adverse party relies. * * * Denials shall fairly meet the substance of the averments denied. When a pleader intends in good faith to deny only a part or a qualification of an averment, he shall specify so much of it as is true and material and shall deny only the remainder."

For example, it is quite clear that defendant does not deny the averment in paragraph 5 that the fork lift came into contact with plaintiff, since it admits, in the answers to interrogatories,[fn] that an investigation of an occurrence of the accident had been made and that a report dated February 10, 1953, was sent to its insurance company stating "While Frank Zielinski was riding on bumper of chisel and holding rope to secure cargo, the chisel truck collided with another chisel truck operated by Sandy Johnson causing injuries to Frank Zielinski's legs and hurt head of Sandy Johnson." Compliance with the above-mentioned rule required that defendant file a more specific answer than a general denial. A specific denial of parts of this paragraph and specific admission of other parts would have warned plaintiff that he had sued the wrong defendant. ...

Under circumstances where an improper and ineffective answer has been filed, the Pennsylvania courts have consistently held that an allegation of agency in the complaint requires a statement to the jury that agency is admitted where an attempt to amend the answer is made after the expiration of the period of limitation. [Cc] Although the undersigned has been able to find no federal court decisions on this point, he believes the principle of these Pennsylvania appellate court decisions may be considered in view of all the facts of this case, where jurisdiction is based on diversity of citizenship, the accident occurred in Pennsylvania, and the federal district court is sitting in Pennsylvania. ...

... Under the circumstances of this case, principles of equity[fn] require that defendant be estopped from denying agency because, otherwise, its inaccurate statements and statements in the record, which it knew (or had the means of knowing within its control) were inaccurate, will have deprived plaintiff of his right of action.

If Interrogatory 2 had been answered accurately[fn] by saying that employees of Carload Contractors, Inc. had turned the matter over to the insurance company,[fn] it seems clear that plaintiff would have realized his mistake. The fact that if Sandy Johnson had testified accurately, the plaintiff could have brought its action against the proper party defendant within the statutory period of limitations is also a factor to be considered, since defendant was represented at the deposition and received knowledge of the inaccurate testimony.

At least one appellate court has stated that the doctrine of equitable estoppel will be applied to prevent a party from taking advantage of the statute of limitations where the plaintiff has been misled by conduct of such party. See, Peters v. Public Service Corporation, [] 29 A.2d 189, 195 ([N.J. Eq.] 1942).[fn] In that case, the court said, 29 A.2d at page 196: "Of course, defendants were under no duty to advise complainants' attorney of his error, other than by appropriate pleadings, but neither did defendants have a right, knowing of the mistake, to foster it by its acts of omission." …

Since this is a pre-trial order, it may be modified at the trial if the trial judge determines from the facts which then appear that justice so requires. [Cc][fn]

INQUIRY

Lack of Information. As indicated briefly above, Rule 8(b)(5) permits a party to answer that the party is "without knowledge or information sufficient to form a belief as to the truth of an averment." The Supreme Court confirmed recently what Rule 8(b)(5) itself states, that this non-answer constitutes a denial. Grupo Mexicano de Desarrollo S.A. v. Aliance Bond Fund, Inc., 527 U.S. 308, 320n.5 (1999). Practitioners must not take Rule 8(b)(5) as an opportunity for mischief, that is, to plead no knowledge or information when there is knowledge or information with which to admit or deny the allegation. *See* Glater v. Eli Lilly & Co., 712 F.2d 735, 737 (1st Cir. 1983) (noting that lack of knowledge or information must be "defendant's good faith answer"). Read the section below on how Rule 11 discourages pleading abuses. There are some allegations that a defendant simply must know, such as a corporate defendant's fact and home state of incorporation. *See* Oliver v. Swiss Club Tell, 35 Cal.Rptr. 324 (1963) (construing corporate defendant's lack-of-information answer as admitting fact and home state of incorporation). Some defense lawyers make a practice to "neither admit nor deny" an allegation and instead "leave plaintiff to its proofs." Rule 8(b) does not contemplate that highly equivocal form of non-answer, which at least one court has condemned. *See* King Vision Pay Per View, Ltd. v. J.C. Dimitri's Restaurant, Inc., 180 F.R.D. 332 (N.D. Ill. 1998). How close do some of the answers in the sample answer above come to conflicting with Rule 8(b) and this holding?

Indirection. There are also ways in which specific admissions and denials, not just general denials or non-answers, can mislead. A defendant might specifically admit *one part* but not all of an allegation. For example, the defendant might admit having been present at the scene while not responding to the associated allegation that the defendant undertook some action there. Rule 8(b)(6) would construe the failure to respond as an admission. A defendant might also deny *all parts* of an allegation in a way that leaves room for a negative pregnant that some parts of the allegation are true. For example, the defendant might deny having been present, taken an action, and produced a result, leaving open the possibility that the defendant was present and took an action but did not produce the result, or was present and produced a result but took a different action. There is authority construing a compound denial as an admission of an otherwise undisputed fact. *See* Freedom Natl. Bank v. Northern Illinois Corp., 202 F.2d 601, 605 (7th Cir. 1953) (denial that value exceeded specific figure construed to admit that value equalled figure otherwise established).

More Pleading. Subrules (3), (4), and (6) of Rule 8(a) provide for answering counterclaims, cross-claims, and third-party complaints, respectively. Rules 8, 9, 10, and 11 on the general and special rules for pleading, and their form, contents, and signing, apply equally to these pleadings as they do to the initial complaint and answer. The plaintiff who fails to answer a counterclaim admits its allegations. *See* Alloy Prods. Corp. v. United States, 302 F.2d 528, 531 (Ct. Cl. 1962); Peters & Russell v. Dorfman, 188 F.2d 711, 712 (7th Cir. 1951). Ordinarily, a plaintiff need make no reply to an answer. The defendant gets the last word. There may be instances, though, when the plaintiff wishes to reply to an answer or even when the defendant desires an answer to the defendant's answer. FED R. CIV. P. 7(a)(7) anticipates those possibilities by permitting the court to order a reply to an answer. Some state-court rules permit the defendant to demand in the answer that the plaintiff reply. *See* MICH. CT. RULES 2.110(B)(5). Thankfully, there is no reply to a reply. *See* FED. R. CIV. P. 7(a). FED. R. CIV. P. 8(b)(6), providing, "If a responsive pleading is not required, an allegation is considered denied or avoided," deems the allegations of a reply denied. *See* Radio Shack Corp. v. Radio Shack, 180 F.2d 200, 206 (7th Cir. 1950).

4. Defenses

As already indicated above, Rule 8(c) more than authorizes a defendant to plead affirmative defenses. Rule 8(c) requires a defendant to "affirmatively state any avoidance or affirmative defense... ." The practice convention, shown in the sample pleading above, is to allege affirmative defenses in the same pleading, separately after the numbered paragraphs constituting the answer. Rule 8(c) specifies no fewer than 19 defenses that the defendant must affirmatively plead in the answer but makes clear by its "any ... defense, including" language that the list is non-exhaustive. Rule 8(c)'s effect is to bar from further consideration any defenses not pled. Use it, or lose it. *See* Harris v. Secretary, U.S. Dept. of Veterans Affairs, 126 F.3d 339, 343 (D.C. Cir. 1997) (statute of limitations is an affirmative defense that defendant must plead); Ingraham v. United States, 808 F.2d 1075 (5th Cir. 1987) (damages cap is affirmative defense that defendant must plead); *see also* Layman v. Southwestern Bell Tel. Co., 554 S.W.2d 477 (Mo.

App. 1977) (easement is an affirmative defense to trespass). Some courts require the plaintiff to show prejudice before barring a defense that the defendant failed to plead in the answer. *See* Carter v. United States, 333 F.3d 791, 796 (7th Cir. 2003) (failure to plead damages cap not a waiver of defense, where plaintiff was not prejudiced by delay); *see also* Harris v. Secretary, U.S. Dept. of Veterans Affairs, supra (trial court may consider motion for leave to amend to add defenses). Prejudice might entail the way in which the plaintiff goes about preparing the case for trial, not accounting for the unpled defense, or the plaintiff devoting more time and effort to an aspect of the case than warranted if the defendant had pled the defense. *Id.* Yet trying to show no prejudice to the plaintiff is an unenviable position no defense counsel wants to be in. The 19 defenses Rule 8(c) lists make a good (although not an exhaustive) checklist. They include "accord and satisfaction; arbitration and award; assumption of risk; contributory negligence; discharge in bankruptcy; duress; estoppel; failure of consideration; fraud; illegality; injury by fellow servant; laches; license; payment; release; res judicata; statute of frauds; statute of limitations; and waiver." Prudent defense lawyers will procure, develop, and maintain an exhaustive list of affirmative defenses, and refer to that list and to prior pleadings to ensure that the answer pleads all potential defenses. Consider the following case highlighting the question of what is and is not an affirmative defense and the peril of not pleading one.

Jones v. Block,

United States Supreme Court
549 U.S. 199 (2007)

Chief Justice ROBERTS delivered the opinion of the Court.

In an effort to address the large number of prisoner complaints filed in federal court, Congress enacted the Prison Litigation Reform Act of 1995 (PLRA)[], 42 U.S.C. §1997e *et seq.* Among other reforms, the PLRA mandates early judicial screening of prisoner complaints and requires prisoners to exhaust prison grievance procedures before filing suit. [C] The Sixth Circuit, along with some other lower courts, adopted several procedural rules designed to implement this exhaustion requirement and facilitate early judicial screening. These rules require a prisoner to allege and demonstrate exhaustion in his complaint... . Other lower courts declined to adopt such rules. We granted certiorari to resolve the conflict and now conclude that these rules are not required by the PLRA, and that crafting and imposing them exceeds the proper limits on the judicial role.

I

Prisoner litigation continues to "account for an outsized share of filings" in federal district courts. [C] In 2005, nearly 10 percent of all civil cases filed in federal courts nationwide were prisoner complaints challenging prison conditions or claiming civil rights violations.[fn] Most of these cases have no merit; many are frivolous. Our legal system, however, remains committed to guaranteeing that prisoner claims of illegal conduct by their custodians are fairly handled according to law. The challenge lies in ensuring that the flood of nonmeritorious claims does not submerge and effectively preclude consideration of the allegations with merit. [C]

Congress addressed that challenge in the PLRA. What this country needs, Congress decided, is fewer and better prisoner suits. [C] To that end, Congress enacted a variety of reforms designed to filter out the bad claims and facilitate consideration of the good. Key among these was the requirement that inmates complaining about prison conditions exhaust prison grievance remedies before initiating a lawsuit.

The exhaustion provision of the PLRA states:

"No action shall be brought with respect to prison conditions under [42 U.S.C. §1983], or any other Federal law, by a prisoner confined in any jail, prison, or other correctional facility until such administrative remedies as are available are exhausted." 42 U.S.C. §1997e(a).

Requiring exhaustion allows prison officials an opportunity to resolve disputes concerning the exercise of their responsibilities before being haled into court. This has the potential to reduce the number of inmate suits, and also to improve the quality of suits that are filed by producing a useful administrative record. [C] In an attempt to implement the exhaustion requirement, some lower courts have imposed procedural rules that have become the subject of varying levels of disagreement among the federal courts of appeals.

The first question presented centers on a conflict over whether exhaustion under the PLRA is a pleading requirement the prisoner must satisfy in his complaint or an affirmative defense the defendant must plead and prove.[fn] The Sixth Circuit, adopting the former view, requires prisoners to attach proof of exhaustion—typically copies of the grievances—to their complaints to avoid dismissal. If no written record of the grievance is available, the inmate must plead with specificity how and when he exhausted the grievance procedures. Knuckles El v. Toombs, 215 F.3d 640, 642 (2000). …

[A vehicle accident injured petitioner Jones while prison officials held him at a Michigan correctional facility. Jones claimed to have aggravated his vehicle injuries when a prison official ordered him to his prison work over his protests that his injuries prevented it. Jones also alleged retaliation over his protests. He sued under 42 U.S.C. §1983 for deliberate indifference to medical needs, retaliation, and harassment, naming prison officials as defendants. The federal district court dismissed and Sixth Circuit affirmed, holding that Jones' complaint had not pled exhaustion of administrative remedies under the PLRA. Other inmates filed similar suits in Michigan federal courts and suffered similar dismissals affirmed by the Sixth Circuit.]

II

There is no question that exhaustion is mandatory under the PLRA and that unexhausted claims cannot be brought in court. [C] What is less clear is whether it falls to the prisoner to plead and demonstrate exhaustion in the complaint, or to the defendant to raise lack of exhaustion as an affirmative defense. The minority rule, adopted by the Sixth Circuit, places the burden of pleading exhaustion in a case covered by the PLRA on the prisoner; most courts view failure to exhaust as an affirmative defense. [C]

We think petitioners, and the majority of courts to consider the question, have the better of the argument. Federal Rule of Civil Procedure 8(a) requires simply a "short and plain statement of the claim" in a complaint, while Rule 8(c) identifies a nonexhaustive list of affirmative defenses that must be pleaded in response. The PLRA itself is not a source of a prisoner's claim; claims covered by the PLRA are typically brought under 42 U.S.C. §1983, which does not require exhaustion at all, [c]. ... The PLRA dealt extensively with the subject of exhaustion, [c], but is silent on the issue whether exhaustion must be pleaded by the plaintiff or is an affirmative defense. This is strong evidence that the usual practice should be followed, and the usual practice under the Federal Rules is to regard exhaustion as an affirmative defense.

In a series of recent cases, we have explained that courts should generally not depart from the usual practice under the Federal Rules on the basis of perceived policy concerns. Thus, in Leatherman v. Tarrant County Narcotics Intelligence and Coordination Unit, 507 U.S. 163[] (1993), we unanimously reversed the Court of Appeals for imposing a heightened pleading standard in §1983 suits against municipalities. We explained that "[p]erhaps if [the] Rules ... were rewritten today, claims against municipalities under §1983 might be subjected to the added specificity requirement.... But that is a result which must be obtained by the process of amending the Federal Rules, and not by judicial interpretation." *Id.* at 168[].

In Swierkiewicz v. Sorema N.A., 534 U.S. 506[] (2002), we unanimously reversed the Court of Appeals for requiring employment discrimination plaintiffs to specifically allege the elements of a prima facie case of discrimination. We explained that "the Federal Rules do not contain a heightened pleading standard for employment discrimination suits," and a "requirement of greater specificity for particular claims" must be obtained by amending the Federal Rules. *Id.* at 515[] (citing *Leatherman*). And just last Term, in Hill v. McDonough, 547 U.S. 573[] (2006), we unanimously rejected a proposal that §1983 suits challenging a method of execution must identify an acceptable alternative: "Specific pleading requirements are mandated by the Federal Rules of Civil Procedure, and not, as a general rule, through case-by-case determinations of the federal courts." *Id.* at 582[] (citing *Swierkiewicz*). ...

The argument that screening would be more effective if exhaustion had to be shown in the complaint proves too much; the same could be said with respect to any affirmative defense. ...

We conclude that failure to exhaust is an affirmative defense under the PLRA, and that inmates are not required to specially plead or demonstrate exhaustion in their complaints. We understand the reasons behind the decisions of some lower courts to impose a pleading requirement on plaintiffs in this context, but that effort cannot fairly be viewed as an interpretation of the PLRA. ... Given that the PLRA does not itself require plaintiffs to plead exhaustion, such a result "must be obtained by the process of amending the Federal Rules, and not by judicial interpretation." *Leatherman,* [*supra*], at 168[]. ...

We are not insensitive to the challenges faced by the lower federal courts in managing their dockets and attempting to separate, when it comes to prisoner suits, not so much wheat from chaff as needles from haystacks. We once again reiterate, however—as we did unanimously in *Leatherman, Swierkiewicz,* and *Hill*—that adopting different and more onerous pleading rules to deal with particular categories of cases should be done through established rulemaking procedures, and not on a case-by-case basis by the courts.

The judgments of the United States Court of Appeals for the Sixth Circuit are reversed, and the cases are remanded for further proceedings consistent with this opinion.

It is so ordered.

Practice

The defense lawyer loved the aspect of practice involved in drafting and filing an answer. Accepting an assignment and answering a new case was like opening a new book, surveying the table of contents, and leafing through its chapters with relish and anticipation. There were also the economic aspects of it. A new assignment meant more work. It also meant renewing old acquaintances with opposing counsel. It also meant meeting new clients, learning about their lives and businesses, encountering witnesses, and challenging opposing parties. The lawyer mused about these things while finishing drafting the answer, opening the desk drawer, and brushing aside the pens and pencils in it to study the list of affirmative defenses taped to the bottom of the desk drawer.

INQUIRY

Burdens. The issue in *Jones v. Block* of whether the plaintiff must plead exhaustion of administrative remedies as an element of a prisoner civil-rights claim, or whether the failure to exhaust is instead an affirmative defense for the defendant to raise, highlights pleading burdens. Lawyers and law students grow accustomed to speaking of the burden of proof. Lawyers and law students know the difference between the typical preponderance-of-the-evidence burden of proof for civil cases and the beyond-a-reasonable-doubt burden required by the Constitution in criminal cases. The burdens of pleading and production are less obvious. The plaintiff who has the burden of proof on each element of a claim will have concomitant burdens to plead those elements of the claim and to produce evidence in support of them. The defendant who has the burden of proof on an affirmative defense will have the concomitant burden of pleading the defense and of producing evidence in support of it. To fail to meet a burden is to lose the claim or defense. As the chapter on trials addresses, to fail to meet a proof burden means an adverse jury verdict. To fail to meet a burden of production can mean summary judgment before trial, directed verdict at trial, or judgment notwithstanding the verdict after trial. To fail to meet a pleading burden can mean a Rule 12(b)(6) dismissal.

Shifting Burdens. The law in some states conflates these burdens on some claims and defenses. For example, contract law might require the defendant on a claim made on a promissory note to plead and prove the note's payment rather than require the plaintiff to prove its nonpayment (perhaps because it is easier to prove a positive, in this instance by receipt, than to prove a negative). For another example, tort law may require the plaintiff to plead and prove falsity for a defamatory statement or, alternatively, require the defendant to plead and prove the statement's truth as a defense. State-court rules of civil procedure or case law alert the practitioner to the need to plead an unexpected element of a claim or defense shifted to recognize some policy or interest. If a defendant mistakenly identifies a defense as a counterclaim or counterclaim as a defense,

FED. R. CIV. P. 8(c)(2) has the trial court overlook the mistake "if justice requires" and authorizes the trial court to impose accompanying conditions.

C. Amending

The lawyer who pleads a complaint or answer does not always get it right the first time. The reasons why tend to fall into three categories. Even with as much care as they take and knowing the significance of getting the pleadings right, lawyers do make mistakes. The mistakes may be ones of law, such as omitting a necessary party, claim, or element, or of fact, such as getting wrong a date, place, action, or identity. The mistakes may be due to inexperience or carelessness, or they may have occurred despite reasonable care, due to incomplete or inaccurate information provided by others and reasonably relied upon by counsel. Pleadings can also be inaccurate because the party and its lawyer are working from their own view of the case, without the benefit of the differing perspectives of other parties expressed in their responsive pleadings. Responsive pleadings can certainly alter the contested issues, making the pleading lawyer want to amend at the peril of being accused of presenting a moving target. Pleadings can also become inaccurate because of events occurring after the lawyer drafted and filed the pleading. Life goes on during and outside of litigation, affecting the litigation's parties and their litigated relationships and interests. The following section shows that the *Federal Rules of Civil Procedure* and state-court rules give lawyers an early unfettered opportunity to amend pleadings but then later limit correction to obtaining the opposing party's consent or trial court's leave. Trial courts grant leave freely when justice requires, which tends to depend on the reasons for the inaccuracy including especially the culpability of the pleading party or lawyer, and prejudice to the opposing party. When the trial court does allow amendment, limitations periods can raise the question of when the amendment takes effect. The next section on *relation back* addresses this peculiar but important question.

1. General Rules

FED. R. CIV. P. 15, reproduced immediately below, provides for amending and supplementing pleadings. Rule 15 divides itself into four subrules having to do with amendments before trial, amendments during and after trial, relation back of amendments, and supplemental pleadings. Rule 15(a)(1)(A) permits a party to amend once as a matter of course before the opposing party responds or, if the *Federal Rules* require no response, then within 20 days after serving the pleading. One might question the need for Rule 15(a)(1)(A) other than as an "oops" provision, which the pleasant phrase "as a matter of course" may suggest. It is not all that uncommon that when a lawyer files a pleading and provides copies of it to a client or insurer, someone involved in the litigation (the lawyer's partner, insurer's claim representative, or client's risk manager, for instance) will see or think of something that warrants the pleading's amendment. Rule 15(a)(1)(A) presumes that no opposing party or other interested person or entity has yet detrimentally relied on the pleading, and so it permits one unrestricted amendment. Some state-court rules allow a party to amend once in response to a responsive pleading. *See* MICH. CT. RULE 2.118(A)(1) ("A party may amend a pleading once as a matter of course within 14 days after being served with a responsive pleading... ."). This measure addresses one of the most common reasons for the need to amend, that the opposing party has brought forth unanticipated information or taken an unexpected position that the original pleading did not address. FED. R. CIV. P. 15 does not offer this accommodation.

Rule 15(a)(2) addresses all other amendments before trial. It does so by requiring the party seeking amendment to obtain the opposing party's consent or trial court's leave. Rule 15(a)(2) further provides, "The court should freely give leave when justice so requires." The trial courts embrace this language. They do tend to grant leave when parties request it, surely to comply with Rule 15(a)(2)'s exhorting language but probably also loathing another pretrial skirmish. Trial courts are more reluctant to grant leave in two instances: (1) where amendment would be futile (would not resolve the pleading's deficiency); and (2) where amendment would prejudice the defendant. Parties can and do closely contest these exceptions, as the following cases show. Why, though, would an opposing party consent to amendment? Lawyers commonly recommend that their clients consent to an opposing party's amendment, certainly when the amendment affects no substantive rights, such as to correct the misspelling of a party's name after the party has already accepted service. The fighting issues arise when amendment would save or add claims or defenses in a way that might prove dispositive of the litigation. Skirmishes over amendment can become decisive battles. Read Rule 15 in its entirety and the introductory case that follows it, before turning to its other provisions.

FED. R. CIV. P. 15. Amended and Supplemental Pleadings

(a) AMENDMENTS BEFORE TRIAL.

(1) *Amending as a Matter of Course.* A party may amend its pleading once as a matter of course within:

(A) 21 days after serving it, or

(B) if the pleading is one to which a responsive pleading is required, 21 days after service of a responsive pleading or 21 days after service of a motion under Rule 12(b), (e), or (f), whichever is earlier.

(2) *Other Amendments.* In all other cases, a party may amend its pleading only with the opposing party's written consent or the court's leave. The court should freely give leave when justice so requires.

(3) *Time to Respond.* Unless the court orders otherwise, any required response to an amended pleading must be made within the time remaining to respond to the original pleading or within 14 days after service of the amended pleading, whichever is later.

(b) AMENDMENTS DURING AND AFTER TRIAL.

(1) *Based on an Objection at Trial.* If, at trial, a party objects that evidence is not within the issues raised in the pleadings, the court may permit the pleadings to be amended. The court should freely permit an amendment when doing so will aid in presenting the merits and the objecting party fails to satisfy the court that the evidence would prejudice that party's action or defense on the merits. The court may grant a continuance to enable the objecting party to meet the evidence.

(2) *For Issues Tried by Consent.* When an issue not raised by the pleadings is tried by the parties' express or implied consent, it must be treated in all respects as if raised in the pleadings. A party may move—at any time, even after judgment—to amend the pleadings to conform them to the evidence and to raise an unpleaded issue. But failure to amend does not affect the result of the trial of that issue.

(c) RELATION BACK OF AMENDMENTS.

(1) *When an Amendment Relates Back.* An amendment to a pleading relates back to the date of the original pleading when:

(A) the law that provides the applicable statute of limitations allows relation back;

(B) the amendment asserts a claim or defense that arose out of the conduct, transaction, or occurrence set out—or attempted to be set out—in the original pleading; or

(C) the amendment changes the party or the naming of the party against whom a claim is asserted, if Rule 15(c)(1)(B) is satisfied and if, within the period provided by Rule 4(m) for serving the summons and complaint, the party to be brought in by amendment:

(i) received such notice of the action that it will not be prejudiced in defending on the merits; and

(ii) knew or should have known that the action would have been brought against it, but for a mistake concerning the proper party's identity.

(2) *Notice to the United States.* When the United States or a United States officer or agency is added as a defendant by amendment, the notice requirements of Rule 15(c)(1)(C)(i) and (ii) are satisfied if, during the stated period, process was delivered or mailed to the United States attorney or the United States attorney's designee, to the Attorney General of the United States, or to the officer or agency.

(d) SUPPLEMENTAL PLEADINGS. On motion and reasonable notice, the court may, on just terms, permit a party to serve a supplemental pleading setting out any transaction, occurrence, or event that happened after the date of the pleading to be supplemented. The court may permit supplementation even though the original pleading is defective in stating a claim or defense. The court may order that the opposing party plead to the supplemental pleading within a specified time.

Beeck v. Aquaslide 'N' Dive Corp.,

United States Court of Appeals for the Eighth Circuit
562 F.2d 537 (8th Cir. 1977)

BENSON, District Judge[, by designation].

This case is an appeal from the trial court's[fn] exercise of discretion on procedural matters in a diversity personal injury action.

Jerry A. Beeck was severely injured on July 15, 1972, while using a water slide. He and his wife, Judy A. Beeck, sued Aquaslide 'N' Dive Corporation (Aquaslide), a Texas corporation, alleging it manufactured the slide involved in the accident, and sought to recover substantial damages on theories of negligence, strict liability and breach of implied warranty.

Aquaslide initially admitted manufacture of the slide, but later moved to amend its answer to deny manufacture… . The district court granted leave to amend.[fn] On motion of the defendant, a separate trial was held on the issue of "whether the defendant designed, manufactured or sold the slide in question." … The … jury… returned a verdict for the defendant, after which the trial court entered summary judgment of dismissal of the case. Plaintiffs took this appeal, and stated the issues presented for review to be:

1. Where the manufacturer of the product, a water slide, admitted in its Answer and later in its Answer to Interrogatories both filed prior to the running of the statute of limitations that it designed, manufactured and sold the water slide in question, was it an abuse of the trial court's discretion to grant leave to amend to the manufacturer in order to deny these admissions after the running of the statute of limitations?

2. After granting the manufacturer's Motion for Leave to Amend in order to deny the prior admissions of design, manufacture and sale of the water slide in question, was it an abuse of the trial court's discretion to further grant the manufacturer's Motion for a Separate Trial on the issue of manufacture?

I. Facts.

In 1971 Kimberly Village Home Association of Davenport, Iowa, ordered an Aquaslide product from one George Boldt, who was a local distributor handling defendant's products. The order was forwarded by Boldt to Sentry Pool and Chemical Supply Co. in Rock Island, Illinois, and Sentry forwarded the order to Purity Swimming Pool Supply in Hammond, Indiana. A slide was delivered from a Purity warehouse to Kimberly Village, and was installed by Kimberly employees. On July 15, 1972, Jerry A. Beeck was injured while using the slide at a social gathering sponsored at Kimberly Village by his employer, Harker Wholesale Meats, Inc. Soon after the accident investigations were undertaken by representatives of the separate insurers of Harker and Kimberly Village. On October 31, 1972, Aquaslide first learned of the accident through a letter sent by a representative of Kimberly's insurer to Aquaslide, advising that "one of your Queen Model #Q-3D slides" was involved in the accident. Aquaslide forwarded this notification to its insurer. Aquaslide's insurance adjuster made an on-site investigation of the slide in May, 1973, and also interviewed persons connected with the ordering and assembly of the slide. An inter-office letter dated September 23, 1973, indicates that Aquaslide's insurer was of the opinion the "Aquaslide in question was definitely manufactured by our insured." The complaint was filed October 15, 1973.[fn] Investigators for three different insurance companies, representing Harker, Kimberly and the defendant, had concluded that the slide had been manufactured by Aquaslide, and the defendant, with no information to the contrary, answered the complaint on December 12, 1973, and admitted that it "designed, manufactured, assembled and sold" the slide in question.[fn]

The statute of limitations on plaintiff's personal injury claim expired on July 15, 1974. About six and one-half months later Carl Meyer, president and owner of Aquaslide, visited the site of the accident prior to the taking of his deposition by the plaintiff.[fn] From his on-site inspection of the slide, he determined it was not a product of the defendant. Thereafter, Aquaslide moved the court for leave to amend its answer to deny manufacture of the slide.

II. Leave to Amend.

Amendment of pleadings in civil actions is governed by Rule 15(a), F.R.Civ.P., which provides in part that once issue is joined in a lawsuit, a party may amend his pleading "only by leave of court or by written consent of the adverse party; and leave shall be freely given when justice so requires."

In Foman v. Davis, 371 U.S. 178[, 182] (1962), the Supreme Court had occasion to construe that portion of Rule 15(a) set out above:

> Rule 15(a) declares that leave to amend "shall be freely given when justice so requires," this mandate is to be heeded. . . . If the underlying facts or circumstances relied upon by a plaintiff may be a proper subject of relief, he ought to be afforded an opportunity to test his claim on the merits. In the absence of any apparent or declared reason such as undue delay, bad faith or dilatory motive on the part of the movant, repeated failure to cure deficiencies by amendments previously allowed, undue prejudice to the opposing party by virtue of allowance of the amendment, futility of amendment, etc. the leave sought should, as the rules require, be "freely given." Of course, the grant or denial of an opportunity to amend is within the discretion of the District Court… .

This Court in Hanson v. Hunt Oil Co., 398 F.2d 578, 582 (8th Cir. 1968), held that "(p)rejudice must be shown." (Emphasis added). The burden is on the party opposing the amendment to show such prejudice. In ruling on a motion for leave to amend, the trial court must inquire into the issue of prejudice to the opposing party, in light of the particular facts of the case. [C]

Certain principles apply to appellate review of a trial court's grant or denial of a motion to amend pleadings. First, as noted in Foman v. Davis, allowance or denial of leave to amend lies within the sound discretion of the trial court, Zenith Radio Corp. v. Hazeltine Research, 401 U.S. 321, 330[], rehearing denied, 401 U.S. 1015[] (1971); [c], and is reviewable only for an abuse of discretion. [C] The appellate court must view the case in the posture in which the trial court acted in ruling on the motion to amend. [C]

It is evident from the order of the district court that in the exercise of its discretion in ruling on defendant's motion for leave to amend, it searched the record for evidence of bad faith, prejudice and undue delay which might be sufficient to overbalance the mandate of Rule 15(a)[], and Foman v. Davis, that leave to amend should be "freely given." Plaintiffs had not at any time conceded that the slide in question had not been manufactured by the defendant, and at the time the motion for leave to amend was at issue, the court had to decide whether the defendant should be permitted to litigate a material factual issue on its merits.

In inquiring into the issue of bad faith, the court noted the fact that the defendant, in initially concluding that it had manufactured the slide, relied upon the conclusions of three different insurance companies,[fn] each of which had conducted an investigation into the circumstances surrounding the accident. This reliance upon investigations of three insurance companies, and the fact that "no contention has been made by anyone that the defendant influenced this possibly erroneous conclusion," persuaded the court that "defendant has not acted in such bad faith as to be precluded from contesting the issue of manufacture at trial." The court further found "(t)o the extent that 'blame' is to be spread regarding the original identification, the record indicates that it should be shared equally."

In considering the issue of prejudice that might result to the plaintiffs from the granting of the motion for leave to amend, the trial court held that the facts presented to it did not support plaintiffs' assertion that, because of the running of the two year Iowa statute of limitations on personal injury claims, the allowance of the amendment would sound the "death knell" of the litigation. In order to accept plaintiffs' argument, the court would have had to assume that the defendant would prevail at trial on the factual issue of manufacture of the slide, and further that plaintiffs would be foreclosed, should the amendment be allowed, from proceeding against other parties if they were unsuccessful in pressing their claim against Aquaslide. On the state of the record before it, the trial court was unwilling to make such assumptions,[fn] and concluded "(u)nder these circumstances, the Court deems that the possible prejudice to the plaintiffs is an insufficient basis on which to deny the proposed amendment." The court reasoned that the amendment would merely allow the defendant to contest a disputed factual issue at trial, and further that it would be prejudicial to the defendant to deny the amendment.

The court also held that defendant and its insurance carrier, in investigating the circumstances surrounding the accident, had not been so lacking in diligence as to dictate a denial of the right to litigate the factual issue of manufacture of the slide.

On this record we hold that the trial court did not abuse its discretion in allowing the defendant to amend its answer. …

[The opinion then held that the district court had not abused its discretion by holding a separate trial on the issue of who manufactured the slide. The jury found that Aquaslide did not manufacture the slide.]

The judgment of the district court is affirmed.

INQUIRY

History. Was the above *Beeck v. Aquaslide* case over? The case has additional relevant context and history. Injured sliders sued Aquaslide 'N' Dive Corp. in several other lawsuits in which, it turned out, Aquaslide had not made the product. Given that knockoff products were apparently common, the Beecks sued Aquaslide again in state court after losing in federal court, this time alleging Aquaslide's reckless misrepresentation. After several more years of litigation, the Iowa Supreme Court gave the Beecks the opportunity to prove that claim so long as they also showed causation that, if Aquaslide had disclosed that it was not the manufacturer, then the Beecks would have discovered and collected from the true manufacturer. Beeck v. Aquaslide 'N' Dive Corp., 350 N.W.2d 149 (Iowa 1984). How happy do you think the Beecks were with that result? In other words, what were their prospects for locating and recovering from the knockoff manufacturer?

Culpability. Note first from *Beeck v. Aquaslide* that it is not only the plaintiff who may need to amend the complaint. Defendants may need to amend their answers. Rule 15 applies generally to any party and pleading. *Beeck v. Aquaslide* also indicates the two standards or criteria the courts tend to consider when deciding motions for leave to amend: (1) the culpability of the pleading party in creating the need for amendment; and (2) the prejudice to the opposing party if the trial court grants leave to amend. The first standard can implicate either the pleading party or its lawyer. Bad faith in pleading certainly makes it easy to deny leave. Carelessness can also make denying leave easier, particularly when it is the party's carelessness but also when it is the lawyer's. *See* Foman v. Davis, 371 U.S. 178, 182 (1962) ("undue delay, bad faith, or dilatory motive [such as] repeated failure to cure deficiencies"). Courts will occasionally observe that a party aggrieved by its lawyer's carelessness may have a malpractice action. The hardest question is when the culpability is mere inadvertence. For instance, when a secretary inadvertently files a superseded draft of a pleading, the party and lawyer are hardly to blame, and the trial court should be more willing to grant leave, justice so requiring. There may also be many instances where these is no culpability, not even inadvertence, where the need to amend arose out of subsequent events or information beyond the reasonable reach of the pleading party and its lawyers. *Beeck v. Aquaslide* also suggests that blame can work both ways, implicating the responding party as much as the pleading party. The party who knows or should know of an opposing party's pleading error and yet fails to disclose it may be more culpable than the inadvertent pleader, making leave to amend even more warranted.

Prejudice. The other consideration is the degree to which the responding party has suffered prejudice due to the inaccurate pleading, relying on the erroneous pleading to the responding party's detriment. *Beeck v. Aquaslide* illustrates how practitioners can struggle with articulating detriment. What, after all, can be more prejudicial than losing not only the case but also the ability to pursue a meritorious claim against the proper party? *Beeck v. Aquaslide* suggested that the plaintiff may actually not have been without remedy against the actual manufacturer, even though the limitations period had appeared to have run. What statute or equitable doctrine might still have given the Beecks an opportunity to sue the actual manufacturer? In addition to losing the ability to pursue other claims, a party might prove prejudice by having incurred litigation expense, wasted effort preparing, lost the opportunity to prepare, lost the opportunity to identify and list witnesses and exhibits, lost the opportunity to add other parties, claims, or defenses, and resolved other claims against other parties on less favorable terms or lost that opportunity to resolve them. Prejudice is less likely to make the difference when the trial court can relieve the prejudice by amending pretrial orders.

During or After Trial. Given the above discussion on the problems late amendment can create, it may seem odd that Rule 15(b) would authorize and a trial court would entertain amendments during or after trial. The question of amendment during trial arises when a party presents evidence that expands the claims or defenses or alters their nature. Trial lawyers plan statements, evidence, and argument around the claims and issues raised by the pleadings. Yet trials do not always go according to plan. Exhibits are predictable. Witnesses are not. Lawyers sometimes have to try cases on claims, defenses, and issues that the pleadings did not anticipate. Rule 15(b)(1) addresses that contingency by providing that "[t]he court should freely permit an amendment when doing so will aid in presenting the merits and the objecting party fails to satisfy the court that the evidence would prejudice that party's action or defense on the merits." *See, e.g.,* Cruz v. Coach Stores, Inc., 202 F.3d 560, 569 (2d Cir. 2000) (permitting Rule 15(b) amendment during trial to add hostile-work-environment claim). Note Rule 15(b)(1)'s reference to "the objecting party." Trial lawyers know the pleadings and wisely object to evidence that raises claims beyond them. If they do not object, then Rule 15(b)(2) permits amendments to "conform … to the evidence" on unpled claims tried by "express or implied consent[.]" Assiduous pretrial preparation can go for naught in the heat of a trial in which unanticipated testimony raises new claims and defenses. When parties dispute amendment at trial, Rule 15(b)(1) establishes an amendment standard much like that employed by Rule 15(a), urging free leave for good reason but permitting the trial court to consider prejudice to the objecting party. The objecting party's needing to present additional unavailable evidence may constitute prejudice. *See* Scully Signal Co. v. Electrics Corp., 570 F.2d 355, 362 (1st Cir. 1977), cert. denied, 436 U.S. 945 (1978).

2. Relation Back

The above *Beeck v. Aquaslide 'N' Dive Corp.* case illustrates a significant hazard that plaintiffs can face when they discover that they have sued the wrong defendant or on the wrong claim. The limitations period may bar the claim that the plaintiff should have maintained from the outset by the time that the plaintiff discovers the need for amendment. The relation-back doctrine removes that hazard in some cases. Rule 15(c)(1) provides three circumstances when an amendment will relate back to the date of the original complaint. The first of those, in Rule 15(c)(1)(A), is when the statute establishing the limitations period so provides. The next, stated in Rule 15(c)(1)(B), is when the amendment "asserts a claim or defense that arose out of the conduct, transaction, or occurrence set out—or attempted to be set out—in the original pleading[.]" The Supreme Court has interpreted this form of the relation-back doctrine to depend on a showing that the added claim arose out of "a common core of operative facts" shared with the original claim. Mayle v. Felix, 545 U.S. 644, 644 (2005). The case immediately below, *Bonerb v. Richard J. Caron Foundation*, illustrates how a trial court will apply the relation-back doctrine based on the added claim arising out of the same occurrence. The third opportunity for relation back, stated in Rule 15(c)(1)(C), is when the original complaint misnamed a party who knew of the action within the time for its service and knew that the complaint should have named it but for the mistake. The second case below, *Worthington v. Wilson*, illustrates the challenges a party faces in meeting all of the particular requirements of Rule 15(c)(1)(C). It is always better to get it right the first time.

Bonerb v. Richard J. Caron Foundation,

United States District Court for the Western District of New York
159 F.R.D. 16 (1994)

HECKMANN, United States Magistrate Judge.

... Plaintiff has moved to amend his complaint pursuant to Rule 15 of the Federal Rules of Civil Procedure. For the following reasons, plaintiff's motion is granted. ...

In this diversity action, plaintiff seeks damages for personal injuries allegedly sustained when he slipped and fell while playing basketball on defendant's recreational basketball court on November 29, 1991. Defendant is a not-for-profit corporation licensed and doing business as a drug and alcohol rehabilitation facility in Westfield, Pennsylvania. Plaintiff is a resident of Western New York.

The original complaint, filed on October 1, 1993, alleges that plaintiff was injured while he was a rehabilitation patient at defendant's Westfield facility, and was participating in a mandatory exercise program. Plaintiff claims that the basketball court was negligently maintained by defendant.

On July 25, 1994, this court granted plaintiff's motion for substitution of new counsel. On September 1, 1994, plaintiff moved to amend his complaint to add a new cause of action for "counseling malpractice" [c]. According to plaintiff's counsel, investigation and discussions undertaken after his substitution as counsel indicated to him that a malpractice claim was warranted under the circumstances. [C] Defendant objects to the amendment on the grounds that the counseling malpractice claim does not relate back to the original pleading and is therefore barred by Pennsylvania's two-year statute of limitations.

DISCUSSION

Rule 15 of the Federal Rules of Civil Procedure provides that once time for amending a pleading as of right has expired, a party may request leave of court to amend, which "shall be freely given when justice so requires." Fed.R.Civ.P. 15(a). This provision has been liberally construed, and leave to amend should be granted absent undue prejudice to the party opposing the amendment, undue delay on the part of the party seeking the amendment, or bad faith. Foman v. Davis, 371 U.S. 178, 182[] (1962); [c]. ...

Rule 15(c)(2) provides that where a party seeks to amend its pleading to assert a claim that would otherwise be time-barred, the claim may be saved by "relation back" to the date of the original pleading when "the claim or defense asserted in the amended pleading arose out of the conduct, transaction, or occurrence set forth or attempted to be set forth in the original pleading...." In determining whether a claim relates back, courts look to the "operational facts" set forth in the original complaint to determine whether the defendant was put on notice of the claim that the plaintiff later seeks to add. [C] ...

An amendment which changes the legal theory of the case is appropriate if the factual situation upon which the action depends remains the same and has been brought to the defendant's attention by the original pleading. [Cc] Thus, an amendment "that changes only the legal theory of the action, or adds another claim arising out of the same transaction or occurrence, will relate back." [Cc]

In this case, the original complaint alleges that plaintiff was injured when he slipped and fell on a wet, muddy basketball court "while participating in a mandatory exercise program ..." at defendant's rehabilitation facility [c]. Plaintiff alleges several instances of defendant's negligent conduct, such as failure to maintain the premises safely, failure to warn, failure to inspect and failure to "properly supervise and/or instruct plaintiff ..." [c]. The proposed amendment seeks to allege that plaintiff "was caused to fall while playing in an outdoor basketball court ... in an exercise program mandated as part of his treatment in the rehabilitation program ..." [c], and that "the rehabilitation and counseling care rendered ... was negligently, carelessly and unskillfully performed" [c].

The allegations in the original and amended complaints derive from the same nucleus of operative facts involving the injury suffered by plaintiff on November 29, 1991. It is true that a claim for professional malpractice invokes an entirely different duty and conduct on the part of the defendant than does a claim for negligent maintenance of the premises. However, the original complaint advised defendant of the same transaction or occurrence giving rise to these different theories of negligence. Indeed, the original complaint alleged that participation in the exercise program was mandatory, and that the injury was caused by defendant's failure to "properly supervise and/or instruct plaintiff...." These allegations not only gave defendant sufficient notice of the general facts surrounding the occurrence, but also alerted defendant to the possibility of a claim based on negligent performance of professional duties. [C] This is all that is required for relation back under Rule 15(c).

Defendant contends that it will be unduly prejudiced by the amendment because it will have to return to the drawing board to prepare an entirely new defense. However, as plaintiff points out, the period for discovery has not yet expired, depositions of defendant's personnel have not yet been taken, and expert witness information has not been exchanged. ...

Finally, there has been no showing of undue delay or bad faith on the part of plaintiff.

CONCLUSION

For the reasons set forth above, plaintiff's motion for leave to amend the complaint (Item 16) is granted. The amended complaint attached as Exhibit A to Item 16 shall be deemed filed and served as of the date of this order, and defendant shall plead in response in accordance with Fed.R.Civ.P. 15(a).

SO ORDERED.

Worthington v. Wilson,

United States Court of Appeals for the Seventh Circuit
8 F.3d 1253 (1993)

MANION, Circuit Judge:

In his 42 U.S.C. § 1983 complaint, Richard Worthington claimed that while being arrested the arresting officers purposely injured him. When he filed suit on the day the statute of limitations expired, he named "three unknown named police officers" as defendants. Worthington later sought to amend the complaint to substitute police officers Dave Wilson and Jeff Wall for the unknown officers. The district court concluded that the relation back doctrine of Fed.R.Civ.P. 15(c) did not apply, and dismissed the amended complaint. [C] We affirm.

I.

On February 25, 1989, Richard Worthington was arrested by a police officer in the Peoria Heights Police Department. At the time of his arrest, Worthington had an injured left hand, and he advised the arresting officer of his injury. According to Worthington's complaint, the arresting officer responded by grabbing Worthington's injured hand and twisting it, prompting Worthington to push the officer away and tell him to "take it easy." A second police officer arrived at the scene, and Worthington was wrestled to the ground and handcuffed. The police officers then hoisted Worthington from the ground by the handcuffs, which caused him to suffer broken bones in his left hand.

Exactly two years later, on February 25, 1991, Worthington filed a five-count complaint in the Circuit Court of Peoria County, Illinois, against the Village of Peoria Heights and "three unknown named police officers," stating the above facts and alleging that he was deprived of his constitutional rights in violation of 42 U.S.C. §1983. Counts one through three of the complaint named the police officers in their personal and official capacities, and alleged a variety of damages. ...

The Village removed the action to federal court... .

On June 17, 1991, Worthington filed an amended complaint in which he substituted as the defendants Dave Wilson and Jeff Wall, two of the twelve or so members of the Peoria Heights Police Department, for the "unknown named police officers" who arrested him on February 25, 1989. Wilson and Wall moved to dismiss the amended complaint primarily on grounds that Illinois' two-year statute of limitations expired, [c], and that the amendment did not relate back to the filing of the original complaint under Rule 15(c). ...

... [T]he district judge granted Wilson's and Wall's motion to dismiss the amended complaint under revised Rule 15(c)... . Worthington appeals this dismissal. ...

II.

Rule 15(c) was amended to provide broader "relation back" of pleadings when a plaintiff seeks to amend his complaint to change defendants. Rule 15(c) as amended December 1, 1991, provides, in pertinent part:

> An amendment of a pleading relates back to the date of the original pleading when (1) relation back is permitted by the law that provides the statute of limitations applicable to the action, or (2) the claim or defense asserted in the amended pleading arose out of the conduct, transaction, or occurrence set forth or attempted to be set forth in the original pleadings, or (3) the amendment changes the party or the naming of the party against whom a claim is asserted if the foregoing provision (2) is satisfied and, within the period provided by Rule 4(j) for service of the summons and complaint, the party to be brought in by amendment (A) has received such notice of the institution of the action that the party will not be prejudiced in maintaining a defense on the merits, and (B) knew or should have known that, but for a mistake concerning the identity of the proper party, the action would have been brought against the party.

Prior to this amendment, the standard for relation back under Rule 15(c) was set out in Schiavone v. Fortune, 477 U.S. 21[] (1986):

> The four prerequisites to a 'relation back' amendment under Rule 15(c) are: (1) the basic claim must have arisen out of the conduct set forth in the original pleading; (2) the party to be brought in must have received such notice that it will not be prejudiced in maintaining its defense; (3) that party must or should have known that, but for a mistake concerning identity, the action would have been brought against it; and (4) the second and third requirements must have been fulfilled within the proscribed limitations period. [*Id.* at 29.]

The Advisory Committee Notes to amended Rule 15(c) indicate that the amendment repudiates the holding in *Schiavone* that notice of a lawsuit's pendency must be given within the applicable statute of limitations period. ...

In this case, Wilson and Wall did not know of Worthington's action before the limitations period expired, as was required by *Schiavone,* but they were aware of its pendency within the extra 120 days provided by new Rule 15(c). ...

Both versions of Rule 15(c) require that the new defendants "knew or should have known that, but for a mistake concerning the identity of the proper party, the action would have been brought against the party." ...

The record shows that there was no mistake concerning the identity of the police officers. At oral argument, counsel for Worthington indicated that he did not decide to file suit until one or two days before the statute of limitations had expired. At that point, neither Worthington nor his counsel knew the names of the two police officers who allegedly committed the offense. Thus, the complaint was filed against "unknown police officers." Because Worthington's failure to name Wilson and Wall was due to a lack of knowledge as to their identity, and not a mistake in their names, Worthington was prevented from availing himself of the relation back doctrine of Rule 15(c). ...

Worthington argues alternatively that equitable tolling should bar Wilson and Wall from asserting a statute of limitations defense because the officers fraudulently concealed their identity from him. ...

Under Illinois law, a plaintiff who alleges fraudulent concealment to toll the statute of limitations must set forth affirmative acts or words by the defendants which prevented him from discovering their identity. [C] "Mere silence of the defendant and the mere failure on the part of the plaintiff to learn of a cause of action do not amount to fraudulent concealment." [C] ... [T]he failure to name Wilson and Wall was due to Worthington's own lack of diligence in learning their identity. ...

III.

We conclude that the amendment adding Wilson and Wall failed to satisfy the "mistake" requirement of Rule 15(c). As a result, relation back was precluded, and Worthington's complaint was time-barred under Illinois law. ...

AFFIRMED.

INQUIRY

Supplemental Pleadings. FED. R. CIV. P. 15(d) addresses instances when a party needs to amend a pleading because of events occurring after the party filed the original pleading. Rule 15(d) requires the party wishing to supplement a pleading to file a motion giving reasonable notice, after which the trial court may permit supplementation "on just terms[.]" Note that Rule 15(d) provides that the trial court "may" grant the motion, suggesting a degree of discretion. Rule 15(d)'s reasonable-notice requirement, its permissive rather than mandatory language as to the trial court's action, and the trial judge's authority to impose just terms, all suggest that supplementation is not a foregone conclusion. The supplementing party should act promptly when the need for supplementation arises, demonstrate the need including the prejudice if the trial court refuses supplementation, and be prepared to meet terms like scheduling extensions and award of costs. There is authority that supplemental pleadings can also relate back to the original filing. *See* Davis v. Piper Aircraft Corp., 615 F.2d 606, 609n.3 (4th Cir. 1980) (appointment of ancillary administrator after appointment period had expired).

Evaluation. Now that you have studied pleading rules and the standards and principles under which the trial courts interpret and apply them, how effective do you think that they are in achieving their goals of framing the issues for fair and efficient discovery and trial, while retaining an appropriate degree of flexibility? Surely, modern pleading rules are an improvement over writ pleading. They are comparatively concise in their form and direct in their application. Do they appear to you to retain any unnecessarily arcane or technical aspects? New practitioners can still find daunting their occasionally complex requirements, particularly when a defendant must move to dismiss on which defense. Are the pleading rules too rigid or, on the other hand, too flexible? Practitioners find that they can be either depending on the occasion. For instance, a party's inability to raise a defense omitted from the first responsive pleading can seem overly strict, while on the other hand a party's right to amend pleadings at trial to conform to the evidence can seem to gut notice requirements. On the whole, modern pleading rules probably find the middle course down a litigation path that can have many twists and turns to it. Consider one final issue having just as much or more to do with the integrity and value of pleadings: to what degree do they depend on the good faith of and fair use by practitioners?

D. Abuses

Pleading abuses are presumably as old as pleadings. All that one has to do to appreciate the nature of those abuses is to examine the rules against them. It is in the nature of rules that they exist for a reason, as a record of their violation. In the federal courts, FED. R. CIV. P. 11 regulates the abuse of "a pleading, written motion, or other paper" presented to the court. Practitioners know what papers are and are not subject to Rule 11. For instance, correspondence between lawyers is not within Rule 11 because correspondence is not a paper "presented to the court." By Rule 11(d)'s express terms, discovery papers filed or served under Rules 26 through 37 are also not subject to Rule 11. Rule 11 instead regulates pleadings, meaning in general the complaint, answer, and any counterclaims, cross-claims, and third-party claims, and their answers. It also regulates dispositive motions, briefs, and responses filed under FED. R. CIV. P. 12 or 56. Pleadings and other court papers are *what* Rule 11 regulates, but *whom* does it regulate? Rule 11(a) requires that at least one attorney of record (or, if a party has no attorney, then the party personally) sign every pleading or other court paper. Rule 11 applies to signers. Subrule (b) then expands Rule 11's application to anyone who signs, files, submits, or later advocates the pleading or other court paper, while subrule (c) authorizes the trial court to impose Rule 11 sanctions on "any attorney, law firm, or party that violated the rule or is responsible for the violation." In short, Rule 11 casts a wide net extending to any lawyer, law firm, or party responsible for the violation. Still, it is the signer who should take extra care that every pleading or other court papers meets all Rule 11 requirements.

Federal Rules of Civil Procedure Form 2. Date, Signature, Address, E-Mail Address, and Telephone Number

(Use at the conclusion of pleadings and other papers that require a signature.)

Date __________

____
(Signature of the attorney or unrepresented party)

____
(Printed name)

____
(Address)

____
(E-mail address)

____
(Telephone number)

Rule 11(b) identifies and prohibits four specific abuses and one general abuse. Rule 11(b)(1) prohibits pleadings and other court papers "presented for any improper purpose, such as to harass, cause unnecessary delay, or needlessly increase the cost of litigation[.]" Rule 11(b)(2) prohibits legal contentions that are not "warranted by existing law or by a nonfrivolous argument for extending, modifying, or reversing existing law or for establishing new law[.]" Note the room that Rule 11(b)(2) gives lawyers to advocate for law changes. *See* Larez v. Holcomb, 16 F.2d 1513, 1522 (9th Cir. 1994) (do not allow Rule 11 to "chill vigorous advocacy"). Rule 11(b)(3) prohibits factual contentions that have no evidentiary support or are not likely to garner evidentiary support "after a reasonable opportunity for further investigation or discovery[.]" *See, e.g.,* In re Commercial Fin. Services, Inc., 261 B.R. 49, 53-54 (N.D. Okla. 2000) (Rule 11(b)(3) violation for no evidentiary support for complaints). Rule 11(b)(4) prohibits equally unfounded denials of factual contentions. Rule 11(b)'s introduction to each of these four subrules includes its own general caution that assertions in these court papers must be "formed afer an inquiry reasonable under the circumstances[.]" Taken together, Rule 11(b) and its four subrules require lawyers to make reasonable inquiry, maintain proper motivation, make only sound arguments, assert only supported facts, and make only supported fact denials. State-court rules include similar provisions. *See, e.g.,* MICH. COURT RULE 2.114. Read FED. R. CIV. P. 11 for this structure.

FED. R. CIV. P. 11. Signing Pleadings, Motions, and Other Papers; Representations to the Court; Sanctions

(a) SIGNATURE. Every pleading, written motion, and other paper must be signed by at least one attorney of record in the attorney's name—or by a party personally if the party is unrepresented. The paper must state the signer's address, e-mail address, and telephone number. Unless a rule or statute specifically states otherwise, a pleading need not be verified or accompanied by an affidavit. The court must strike an unsigned paper unless the omission is promptly corrected after being called to the attorney's or party's attention.

(b) REPRESENTATIONS TO THE COURT. By presenting to the court a pleading, written motion, or other paper—whether by signing, filing, submitting, or later advocating it—an attorney or unrepresented party certifies that to the best of the person's knowledge, information, and belief, formed after an inquiry reasonable under the circumstances:

(1) it is not being presented for any improper purpose, such as to harass, cause unnecessary delay, or needlessly increase the cost of litigation;

(2) the claims, defenses, and other legal contentions are warranted by existing law or by a nonfrivolous argument for extending, modifying, or reversing existing law or for establishing new law;

(3) the factual contentions have evidentiary support or, if specifically so identified, will likely have evidentiary support after a reasonable opportunity for further investigation or discovery; and

(4) the denials of factual contentions are warranted on the evidence or, if specifically so identified, are reasonably based on belief or a lack of information.

(c) SANCTIONS.

(1) *In General.* If, after notice and a reasonable opportunity to respond, the court determines that Rule 11(b) has been violated, the court may impose an appropriate sanction on any attorney, law firm, or party that violated the rule or is responsible for the violation. Absent exceptional circumstances, a law firm must be held jointly responsible for a violation committed by its partner, associate, or employee.

(2) *Motion for Sanctions.* A motion for sanctions must be made separately from any other motion and must describe the specific conduct that allegedly violates Rule 11(b). The motion must be served under Rule 5, but it must not be filed or be presented to the court if the challenged paper, claim, defense, contention, or denial is withdrawn or appropriately corrected within 21 days after service or within another time the court sets. If warranted, the court may award to the prevailing party the reasonable expenses, including attorney's fees, incurred for the motion.

(3) *On the Court's Initiative.* On its own, the court may order an attorney, law firm, or party to show cause why conduct specifically described in the order has not violated Rule 11(b).
(4) *Nature of a Sanction.* A sanction imposed under this rule must be limited to what suffices to deter repetition of the conduct or comparable conduct by others similarly situated. The sanction may include nonmonetary directives; an order to pay a penalty into court; or, if imposed on motion and warranted for effective deterrence, an order directing payment to the movant of part or all of the reasonable attorney's fees and other expenses directly resulting from the violation.
(5) *Limitations on Monetary Sanctions.* The court must not impose a monetary sanction:
(A) against a represented party for violating Rule 11(b)(2); or
(B) on its own, unless it issued the show-cause order under Rule 11(c)(3) before voluntary dismissal or settlement of the claims made by or against the party that is, or whose attorneys are, to be sanctioned.
(6) *Requirements for an Order.* An order imposing a sanction must describe the sanctioned conduct and explain the basis for the sanction.
(d) INAPPLICABILITY TO DISCOVERY. This rule does not apply to disclosures and discovery requests, responses, objections, and motions under Rules 26 through 37.

INQUIRY

Reasonable Inquiry. A substantial percentage of pleadings must in the end be legally untenable or factually inaccurate. Both sides in every dispute cannot always be right. It is thus important to recognize that FED. R. CIV P. 11 does not sanction every legally insufficient or factually incorrect allegation. Rule 11 applies to misconduct, not losers. Rule 11(b)'s general requirement that the signer make "an inquiry reasonable under the circumstances" is a safe harbor within which lawyers can err legally and factually in their pleadings and court papers. What constitutes a reasonable investigation? Trial courts may consider several factors including the lawyer's time available to investigate (not relating to workload but to the urgency of the filing of the court paper), the parties or persons on whom the lawyer relied to investigate, whether the lawyer was relying on pleadings drafted by other lawyers who were bound under the same rules, the factual complexities of the case, and to what extent discovery was available and would have benefited the investigation. *See* Kraemer v. Grant County, 892 F.2d 686, 689 (7th Cir. 1990). Rule 11 is not draconian. It is also not meant to be a tool with which opposing lawyers attempt to intimidate a just advocate, although lawyers have surely attempted to misuse it in that fashion. It is also not meant to chill meritorious litigation. *See* Golden Eagle Distributing Corp. v. Burroughs Corp, 801 F.2d 584 (9th Cir. 1986) (reversing Rule 11 sanctions for failure to disclose legal authority, where sanctions based on judicial hindsight might chill advocacy). Read the following two cases to get a better sense of the general types of misconduct, either egregiously bumbling or sadistically manipulative, to which Rule 11 does very clearly apply.

Walker v. Norwest Corp.,

United States Circuit Court for the Eighth Circuit
108 F.3d 158 (1996)

JOHN R. GIBSON, Circuit Judge.

Jimmy Lee Walker, III, his guardian, Cynthia Walker, and their attorney, James Harrison Massey, appeal from the district court's[fn] award of sanctions against Massey for filing a diversity case in which he failed to plead complete diversity of citizenship, and indeed, pleaded facts which tended to show there was not complete diversity. The Walkers and Massey contend that the district court erred in awarding sanctions at all, in determining the amount of sanctions, and in not allowing the Walkers to amend their complaint. We affirm.

Massey filed a complaint in the district court for the District of South Dakota on behalf of the Walkers, alleging breach of fiduciary duty and other state law causes of action in connection with the administration of a trust fund held for Jimmy Lee Walker at Norwest Bank South Dakota, N.A. The complaint stated that jurisdiction was based on diversity, since "the Plaintiff and *some of the Defendants* are citizens of different states." (Emphasis added). The Walkers are both South Dakotans. The complaint averred that one of the defendants, Norwest Corporation, was a Minnesota corporation. The complaint did not allege the other defendants'[fn] citizenship precisely, but stated that many of them were South Dakota "residents." …

Upon receiving the complaint, the attorney for Norwest Corporation and its subsidiaries and officers wrote Mr. Massey informing him that his complaint showed on its face that there was no diversity jurisdiction. The letter asked Massey to dismiss the complaint, and warned that if he did not, Norwest would seek sanctions, including attorneys' fees. Massey's only answer was a letter that acknowledged Norwest's correspondence, but made no substantive response to the deficiency counsel had pointed out.

After Massey failed to offer any explanation for his defective complaint or to move to amend or dismiss it, Norwest moved to dismiss and for an award of sanctions, as it had promised to do. …

The district court granted the Fed.R.Civ.P. 12(b)(1) motion to dismiss for lack of jurisdiction and sanctioned attorney Massey under Fed.R.Civ.P. 11. [C] The court held that there was no diversity jurisdiction because there was not complete diversity among plaintiffs and defendants, since plaintiffs were South Dakotans and numerous defendants were alleged to be South Dakota "residents." The court ordered the defendants to file an accounting of their fees and expenses incurred in defending against the suit[, ordering Massey to pay the two sets of defendants the full amount each had requested, $2,794.52 and $2,050.75, respectively.] …

The Walkers and Massey appeal.

I.

They first argue that the district court abused its discretion in determining that Massey had filed a complaint that was not warranted by existing law or a nonfrivolous argument for the extension, modification, or reversal of existing law or the establishment of new law. They contend that their allegations that the defendants were South Dakota residents were not determinative of the defendants citizenship, since they could be living in South Dakota without intent to stay there. [C] They contend that Rule 11 does not require the kind of "complicated, in-depth, and possibly impossible inquiry" that would have been necessary to determine the defendants' citizenship before filing a complaint based on diversity of citizenship. …

It was the Walkers' burden to plead the citizenship of the parties in attempting to invoke diversity jurisdiction. [C] They failed to carry that burden, since they did not allege the domicile[fn] of the individual defendants or the place of incorporation and principal place of business of all the corporate defendants. [C] …

… [The Walkers and Massey also] argue that finding out the defendants' citizenship would be more trouble than they should be expected to take. This is a burden that plaintiffs desiring to invoke diversity jurisdiction have assumed since the days of Chief Justice Marshall. *See* Strawbridge v. Curtiss, 7 U.S. at 267. The fact that the Walkers did not allege the citizenship of the defendants convinces us that the district court did not abuse its discretion in determining that Rule 11 sanctions were appropriate.

II.

The Walkers and Massey next contend that the district court abused its discretion in awarding monetary sanctions, since dismissal of the complaint would have been adequate. They argue that the award of monetary sanctions in this case would discourage "novel legal arguments." Their legal argument in the district court was contrary to the established statutory requirements for diversity. *See* 28 U.S.C. §1332(a)(1)[]. They also argue that the district court should have inquired into Massey's financial circumstances, and that if it had done so, it would have found that he "is presently experiencing financial hardships and is unable to pay this sanction." Not only did Massey fail to argue this point to the district court, but there is no record evidence to support the argument before this court. Finally, they argue that the defendants have no need for compensation for their fees and expenses, since they are "multi-billion/million dollar defendants." There is no record evidence of the defendants' financial condition, but there is evidence that they incurred fees and expenses because of the Walkers' lawsuit. We see no abuse of discretion in awarding monetary sanctions. …

V.

The Walkers and Massey argue that the district court erred in awarding the full amount of fees and expenses defendants requested, since the defendants' counsel did more work than was justified. Massey was persistent in filing baseless and uninformed pleadings, motion papers, and briefs, which drove up the defendants' fees. The district court did not abuse its discretion in entering sanctions for the full amount of expenses and fees claimed. …

We affirm the district court's entry of Rule 11 sanctions in the amounts provided.

Christian v. Mattell, Inc.,

United States Circuit Court for the Ninth Circuit
286 F.3d 1118 (2003)

McKEOWN, Circuit Judge.

It is difficult to imagine that the Barbie doll, so perfect in her sculpture and presentation, and so comfortable in every setting, from "California girl" to "Chief Executive Officer Barbie," could spawn such acrimonious litigation and such egregious conduct on the part of her challenger. In her wildest dreams, Barbie could not have imagined herself in the middle of Rule 11 proceedings. But the intersection of copyrights on Barbie sculptures and the scope of Rule 11 is precisely what defines this case.

James Hicks appeals from a district court order requiring him, pursuant to Federal Rule of Civil Procedure 11, to pay Mattel, Inc., $501,565 in attorneys' fees that it incurred in defending against what the district court determined to be a frivolous action. Hicks brought suit on behalf of Harry Christian, claiming that Mattel's Barbie dolls infringed Christian's Claudene doll sculpture copyright. In its sanctions orders, the district court found that Hicks should have discovered prior to commencing the civil action that Mattel's dolls could not have infringed Christian's copyright because, among other things, the Mattel dolls had been created well prior to the Claudene doll and the Mattel dolls had clearly visible copyright notices on their heads. After determining that Hicks had behaved "boorishly" during discovery and had a lengthy rap sheet of prior litigation misconduct, the district court imposed sanctions.

We hold that the district court did not abuse its discretion in determining that the complaint filed by Hicks was frivolous under Rule 11. ...

Mattel is a toy company that is perhaps best recognized as the manufacturer of the world-famous Barbie doll. ... Mattel has sought to protect its intellectual property by registering various Barbie-related copyrights, including copyrights protecting the doll's head sculpture. Mattel has vigorously litigated against putative infringers.

In 1990, Claudene Christian, then an undergraduate student at the University of Southern California ("USC"), decided to create and market a collegiate cheerleader doll. The doll, which the parties refer to throughout their papers as "Claudene," had blonde hair and blue eyes and was outfitted to resemble a USC cheerleader. ...

... In the complaint, which Hicks signed, Christian alleged that Mattel obtained a copy of the copyrighted Claudene doll in 1996, the year of its creation,[fn] and then infringed its overall appearance, including its face paint, by developing a new Barbie line called "Cool Blue" that was substantially similar to Claudene. ...

Two months after the complaint was filed, Mattel moved for summary judgment. In support of its motion, Mattel proffered evidence that the Cool Blue Barbie doll contained a 1991 copyright notice on the back of its head, indicating that it predated Claudene's head sculpture copyright by approximately six years.[fn] Mattel therefore argued that Cool Blue Barbie could not as a matter of law infringe Claudene's head sculpture copyright. ...

At a follow-up counsel meeting required by a local rule, Mattel's counsel attempted to convince Hicks that his complaint was frivolous. During the videotaped meeting, they presented Hicks with copies of various Barbie dolls that not only had been created prior to 1996 (the date of Claudene's creation), but also had copyright designations on their heads that pre-dated Claudene's creation. Additionally, Mattel's counsel noted that the face paint on some of the earlier-created Barbie dolls was virtually identical to that used on Claudene. Hicks declined Mattel's invitation to inspect the dolls and, later during the meeting, hurled them in disgust from a conference table.

Having been unsuccessful in convincing Hicks to dismiss Christian's action voluntarily, Mattel served Hicks with a motion for Rule 11 sanctions. In its motion papers, Mattel argued, among other things, that Hicks had signed and filed a frivolous complaint based on a legally meritless theory that Mattel's prior-created head sculptures infringed Claudene's 1997 copyright. Hicks declined to withdraw the complaint during the 21-day safe harbor period provided by Rule 11, and Mattel filed its motion.

Seemingly unfazed by Mattel's Rule 11 motion, Hicks proceeded with the litigation.... .

Hicks ... began filing ... papers that were characterized by frequency and volume. ...

The district court granted Mattel's motions for summary judgment and Rule 11 sanctions. The court ruled that Mattel did not infringe the 1997 Claudene copyright because it could not possibly have accessed the Claudene doll at the time it created the head sculptures of the Cool Blue (copyrighted in 1991) and Virginia Tech (copyrighted in 1976) Barbies. ...

As for Mattel's Rule 11 motion, the district court found that Hicks had "filed a meritless claim against defendant Mattel. A reasonable investigation by Mr. Hicks would have revealed that there was no factual foundation for [Christian's] copyright claim." Indeed, the district court noted that Hicks needed to do little more than examine "the back of the heads of the Barbie dolls he claims were infringing," because such a perfunctory inquiry would have revealed "the pre-1996 copyright notices on the Cool Blue and [Virginia Tech] Barbie doll heads."

Additionally, the district court made other findings regarding Hicks' misconduct in litigating against Mattel, all of which demonstrated that his conduct fell "below the standards of attorneys practicing in the Central District of California." The district court singled out the following conduct:

- Sanctions imposed by the district court against Hicks in a related action against Mattel for failing, among other things, to file a memorandum of law in support of papers styled as a motion to dismiss and failing to appear at oral argument;
- Hicks' behavior during the Early Meeting of Counsel, in which he "toss[ed] Barbie dolls off a table";
- Hicks' interruption of Christian's deposition after Christian made a "damaging admission ... that a pre-1996 Barbie doll allegedly infringed the later created Claudene doll head...." When asked whether the prior-created Pioneer Barbie doll infringed Claudene, Christian stated, "I think so ... [b]ecause it's got the look...." At that juncture, Hicks requested an immediate recess, during which he lambasted his client in plain view of Mattel's attorneys and the video camera;
- Hicks' misrepresentations during oral argument on Mattel's summary judgment motion about the number of dolls alleged in the complaint to be infringing and whether he had ever reviewed a particular Barbie catalogue (when a videotape presented to the district court by Mattel demonstrated that Hicks had reviewed it during a deposition);
- Hicks' misstatement of law in a summary judgment opposition brief about the circuit's holdings regarding joint authorship of copyrightable works.

After Mattel submitted a general description of the fees that it incurred in defending against Christian's action, the court requested Mattel to submit a more specific itemization and description of work performed by its attorneys. Mattel complied.

The district court awarded Mattel $501,565 in attorneys' fees. ...

Filing a complaint in federal court is no trifling undertaking. An attorney's signature on a complaint is tantamount to a warranty that the complaint is well grounded in fact and "existing law" (or proposes a good faith extension of the existing law) and that it is not filed for an improper purpose. ...

The attorney has a duty prior to filing a complaint not only to conduct a reasonable factual investigation, but also to perform adequate legal research that confirms whether the theoretical underpinnings of the complaint are "warranted by existing law or a good faith argument for an extension, modification or reversal of existing law." [C] One of the fundamental purposes of Rule 11 is to "reduce frivolous claims, defenses or motions and to deter costly meritless maneuvers, ... [thereby] avoid[ing] delay and unnecessary expense in litigation." [C] Nonetheless, a finding of significant delay or expense is not required under Rule 11. Where, as here, the complaint is the primary focus of Rule 11 proceedings, a district court must conduct a two-prong inquiry to determine (1) whether the complaint is legally or factually "baseless" from an objective perspective, and (2) if the attorney has conducted "a reasonable and competent inquiry" before signing and filing it. [C] ...

The district court did not abuse its discretion in concluding that Hicks' failure to investigate fell below the requisite standard established by Rule 11. ...

Hicks argues that even if the district court were justified in sanctioning him under Rule 11 based on Christian's complaint and the follow-on motions, its conclusion was tainted because it impermissibly considered other misconduct that cannot be sanctioned under Rule 11, such as discovery abuses, misstatements made during oral argument, and conduct in other litigation.

Hicks' argument has merit. While Rule 11 permits the district court to sanction an attorney for conduct regarding "pleading[s], written motion[s], and other paper[s]" that have been signed and filed in a given case, Fed.R.Civ.P. 11(a), it does not authorize sanctions for, among other things, discovery abuses or misstatements made to the court during an oral presentation. ...

The orders clearly demonstrate that the district court decided, at least in part, to sanction Hicks because he signed and filed a factually and legally meritless complaint and for misrepresentations in subsequent briefing. But the orders, coupled with the supporting examples, also strongly suggest that the court considered extra-pleadings conduct as a basis for Rule 11 sanctions. Although the court also referenced conduct in related litigation, it is unlikely that the court based its order on such conduct because Hicks had already been sanctioned for violating local rules in the context of the related litigation and the court noted that fact.

The laundry list of Hicks' outlandish conduct is a long one and raises serious questions as to his respect for the judicial process. Nonetheless, Rule 11 sanctions are limited to "paper[s]" signed in violation of the rule. Conduct in depositions, discovery meetings of counsel, oral representations at hearings, and behavior in prior proceedings do not fall within the ambit of Rule 11. Because we do not know for certain whether the district court granted Mattel's Rule 11 motion as a result of an impermissible intertwining of its conclusion about the complaint's frivolity and Hicks' extrinsic misconduct, we must vacate the district court's Rule 11 orders.[fn] ...

Hicks raises various challenges to the quantum of attorneys' fees. Because we are vacating the district court's Rule 11 orders on other legal grounds, we express no opinion at this stage about the particular reasonableness of any of the fees the district court elected to award Mattel. We do, however, encourage the district court on remand to ensure that the time spent by Mattel's attorneys was reasonably and appropriately spent in relation to both the patent frivolousness of Christian's complaint and the services directly caused by the sanctionable conduct.[fn] [C] ...

We vacate the district court's Rule 11 orders and remand for further proceedings consistent with this opinion.

VACATED and REMANDED.

INQUIRY

Safe Harbors. Rule 11 offers a second means of protection or escape from the threat of Rule 11 sanctions, in addition to Rule 11(b)'s "reasonable inquiry" safe harbor. Rule 11(c)(2) requires that a party seeking sanctions move separately from any other motion. This provision is significant. Some state-court practitioners adopt the practice of requesting sanctions as a matter of routine in the prayer for relief accompanying every pleading or other court paper. Doing so is not necessarily an uncivil or unwise practice. Practitioners have had the displeasure of having been stung in one proceeding or another at having failed to make a formal sanction request when the court later indicated that it would otherwise have sanctioned opposing counsel. Recitals requesting sanctions are routine in some state-court settings. Rule 11(c)(2) effectively prohibits such routine recitals. Rule 11(c)(2) then gives the offending lawyer a chance to withdraw or correct the offending pleading or other court paper, by requiring that the lawyer who seeks sanctions first serve the Rule 11 motion on the offending lawyer without also filing the motion. Rule 11(c)(2)'s procedure gives counsel 21 days within which to decide whether and how to proceed in advocating, correcting, or withdrawing the challenged pleading or other court paper. We all make mistakes. Most of us are also capable in various situations of using poor judgment. Rule 11(c)(2)'s fair-warning provision gives a lawyer a chance to seek the review and advice of other lawyers, and to avoid Rule 11 sanctions where warranted. *See* Hadges v. Yonkers Racing Corp., 48 F.2d 1320 (2d Cir. 1995) (reversing sanction for moving party's failure to offer Rule 11(c) safe-harbor period).

Other Sanctions. Each of the two above cases, *Walker v. Norwest Corp.* and *Christian v. Mattell, Inc.*, in their own way indicate the sensitivity and accountability the trial court must show in determining the form and assessing the amount of a Rule 11 sanction. Rule 11(c)(3) admonishes the trial court that any sanctions "must be limited to what suffices to deter repetition of the conduct or comparable conduct by others similarly situated." *See* Kirk Capital Corp. v. Bailey, 16 F.3d 1485, 1490 (8th Cir. 1994) (impose the least severe sanction necessary to deter). Rule 11(c)(3) also makes clear that the sanction need not be monetary. *See* Pierre v. Inroads, Inc., 858 F.Supp. 769, 775 (N.D. Ill. 1994) (publication of opinion identifying lawyer and Rule 11 misconduct is sufficient to deter). A Rule 11 sanction, though, may be just the start of trouble for offending counsel. Some states require lawyers who suffer Rule 11 and similar state-court-rule sanctions to report those events to state-bar grievance authorities for investigation. *See* CAL. BUS. & PROF. CODE §6068(o)(3). There is also potential civil liability. The lawyer Hicks and his law firm in the above *Christian v. Mattell, Inc.* case suffered a malicious-civil-prosecution action arising out of that case. Mattell, Inc. v. Luce, Forward, Hamilton & Scripps, 121 Cal.Rptr.2d 794 (2002).

Other Authority. The Rule 11(c)(2) safe-harbor process just described is not the only authority for sanctions. Rule 11(c)(3) permits the trial court to impose sanctions on its own initiative, provided that it first order the lawyer, law firm, or party to show cause why it should not impose a sanction for conduct it describes in the order. Rule 11(c)(5)(B) reiterates that the trial court may not impose sanctions on its own initiative without that show-cause order. There is other authority for sanctions outside of Rule 11, in areas of perceived abuse. FED. R. CIV. P. 23.1 requires counsel to certify the truth of allegations in a shareholder derivative action. *See* Roussel v. Tidelands Capital Corp., 438 F.Supp. 684, 688 (N.D. Ala. 1977) (dismissal as sanction for violating Rule 23.1 certification requirement). Lawyers who multiply proceedings in bad faith are subject to sanction under 28 U.S.C. §1927. State law may impose certification requirements in other areas of perceived abuse. *See, e.g.,* IOWA CODE ANN. §600B.13 (verification requirement for paternity and child support actions). The Supreme Court held in Chambers v. NASCO, Inc., 501 U.S. 32, 44-45 (1991), that the federal courts have inherent authority to punish party or lawyer misconduct.

Rule 11 Abuses. The threat of Rule 11 sanctions can intimidate advocates, and not just because the power to request sanctions lies in the hands of an opponent. Scholarship questions whether the federal courts should be trusted to apply evenhandedly Rule 11 and their other inherent sanctioning authority. *See* Danielle Kie Hart, *And the Chill Goes on—Federal Civil Rights Plaintiffs Beware: Rule 11 vis-à-vis 28 U.S.C. §1927 and the Court's Inherent Power,* 37 LOY. L.A. L.REV. 645, 646-647 (2004). The Supreme Court held to the contrary in Business Guides v. Chromatic Communs. Enterps., 498 U.S. 533, 552 (1991), that any affect that Rule 11 has on substantive rights is incidental and therefore does not violate the Rules Enabling Act's prohibition in 28 U.S.C. §2072(b) that the *Federal Rules of Civil Procedure* must not modify any substantive right. Yet in one case, Surowitz v. Hilton Hotels Corp., 383 U.S. 363 (1966), the Supreme Court found itself compelled to reverse the district court's imposition of Rule 11 sanctions and Court of Appeals' affirmance of those sanctions. The lower courts had sanctioned the immigrant plaintiff, who spoke very limited English and had little education, for not understanding the allegations filed on her behalf. The shareholders' derivative action in which she was the named representative alleged grave charges of fraud without "one iota of evidence" that her lawyer Mr. Brilliant (yes, literally) had intended the action as a strike suit to injure the defendant corporation. *Id.* at 372. The current version of Rule 11 (discussed above) softens the prior Rule 11's chilling effect by instituting the 21-day safe-harbor period, eliminating a good-faith requirement, allowing greater advocacy for change in the law, and shifting the sanction from compensation to deterrence.

Summary. Lawyers invoke court authority by drafting and filing pleadings. Those pleadings typically begin with a complaint comprised of a caption, numbered paragraphs containing the allegations, a prayer for relief, and a signature block. FED. R. CIV. P. 8 authorizes notice pleading, meaning that the complaint's simple, short, and concise allegations need only put the defendant on notice of the claims against which it must defend. Rule 8 does not require detailed factual allegations. Once the plaintiff serves the complaint, the defendant must timely appear and defend or suffer default and default judgment. The defendant may file a Rule 12 motion to dismiss for defects on the face of the complaint such as lack of jurisdiction, improper venue, or failure to state a claim. The Supreme Court is currently refining the Rule 12(b)(6) standard for failure to state a claim, from where no claim is possible toward where the claim is not plausible. The defendant must answer a facially sufficient complaint, responding to each substantive allegation of each paragraph and alleging separately all available affirmative defenses. An answer may include counterclaims, crossclaims, and third-party claims, to which the identified party must timely respond. Parties may amend pleadings once before the response and later on motion and court order, with leave to amend freely granted except where an amendment would be futile or prejudicial. Rule 11 binds lawyers, law firms, and parties to reasonable investigation and good faith in pleading on penalty of monetary or other sanction.

Career

Would you prefer to work more with clients or with lawyers and judges? Civil litigation tends to involve lots of interaction with other professionals especially including judges, lawyers, and court staff but often also involving law enforcement, medical, engineering, and other expert witnesses. By contrast, transactional practice in estate planning, real property, and business organizations can involve significantly more interaction with clients and less interaction with judges and other lawyers. Working with other lawyers and developing a reputation within a vibrant professional community energizes some lawyers who for that reason may prefer civil litigation. Other lawyers prefer to serve clients directly in transactional practice without depending on judges or drawing from other lawyers. As you read the civil-procedure cases, consider the role of reputation and your preference for professional interaction.

CHAPTER VIII

JOINDER

OBJECTIVE: That you be able to determine which claims and parties a single case may include and the procedure through which a party includes other parties and claims in an ongoing action.

Case Study: You are meeting with a corporate client's litigation committee about an interference-with-contract and unfair-competition lawsuit in which the client is one of two defendants. The committee's members have articulated several potential claims against the plaintiff, other defendant, and various non-parties. Advise the committee what information you would need to determine whether the client could or must bring those claims in the same action, and describe the procedures by which it would do so.

Federal Rules of Civil Procedure this chapter reproduces and addresses:
FED. R. CIV. P. 18: Joinder of Claims.
FED. R. CIV. P. 19: Required Joinder of Parties.
FED. R. CIV. P. 20: Permissive Joinder of Parties.
FED. R. CIV. P. 21: Misjoinder and Nonjoinder of Parties.
FED. R. CIV. P. 22: Interpleader.
FED. R. CIV. P. 23: Class Actions.
FED. R. CIV. P. 24: Intervention.

You now have a sense of how lawyers initiate civil litigation through pleadings that frame the issues. You have not yet seen how courts keep the scope of a civil case to within reasonable limits while still allowing multiple parties to resolve efficiently multiple claims in a single proceeding. Under the old common-law system of writ pleading, the law organized cases around the legal theory or theories recognized by the form of the writ, even if it meant joining in one case two or more different fact scenarios providing the basis for seeking the writ. Writ pleading, based as it was on the allowable legal theories, limited the number of parties that a case could reasonably accommodate. Litigation tended to proceed piecemeal between opposing parties on specific claims involving specific theories. By contrast, modern civil procedure organizes cases around occurrences or transactions involving a common nucleus of operative fact. Modern procedure, organized around occurrences or transactions, expands the number of potential parties while permitting different legal theories and varying party alignments but restricting the facts to a single transaction or occurrence. In short, modern civil procedure allows for relatively broad joinder of claims and parties but fewer discrete events, while courts must still apply rules to keep cases within a manageable scope.

This chapter explores those rules for joinder. It begins with the study of a single plaintiff joining multiple claims against one or more defendants and associated rules allowing defendants to counterclaim or crossclaim. The chapter then moves to issues surrounding multiple parties, including when a plaintiff may join multiple parties (permissive joinder), when a plaintiff must join multiple parties (compulsory joinder), and when defendants may join additional parties (third-party practice). The chapter then addresses when a plaintiff may bring in other parties to contest an issue in which the plaintiff has no stake or only a nominal interest (interpleader) and when a non-party may join the action of its own initiative (intervention). The chapter ends by treating cases in which a limited number of plaintiffs wish to represent the interests of many other identified or unidentified plaintiffs in class actions. Much if not most of civil litigation involves joinder rules at least to some degree. Cases that do not involve the joinder of multiple claims and parties are not the rule but more nearly the exception. All civil litigators need a basic understanding of the subjects addressed in this chapter. As do other chapters, this chapter focuses on the *Federal Rules of Civil Procedure* recognizing that state-court rules supply similar regimes for joinder in state-court cases.

A. Claims

The issue of multiple claims involves, first, what claims a plaintiff can join in an action against a *single* defendant, then, what claims a plaintiff can join in an action against *multiple* defendants, and, finally, what claims *defendants* can bring in an action against either the plaintiff or one another. As odd as it may seem initially, the rules are somewhat different for each situation and depend on a mix of the *Federal Rules of Civil Procedure* (or, for state cases, equivalent state-court rules) and common-law doctrine. The first section below addresses the circumstances under which a plaintiff can join multiple claims in an action. The second and third sections address claims by defendants first against the plaintiff and then against one another.

1. Multiple Claims

FED. R. CIV. P. 18 makes the question of a plaintiff's joinder of multiple claims against a single defendant look easy: join as many or as few claims as you wish. The *Federal Rules* do not require a party to join claims. Nor do the *Federal Rules* prohibit a party from joining claims. Read Rule 18 below, noting the permissive language of Rule 18(a) that a party *may* join as many claims as it has against an opposing party. Rule 18(b) then deals with the special situation in which the second claim that a party joins is contingent on the court's deciding the first claim. Rule 18(b) permits a party to join contingent claims, removing another possible impediment to joinder and making the joinder rules even more liberal. Rule 18(b) includes as an illustrative (rather than limiting) example that a party might plead, all in one action, both the right to money damages and the contingent right to set aside a conveyance that the opposing party allegedly made to avoid paying those money damages. Rule 18 has the purpose and effect of reducing litigation procedures and hence litigation expense by eliminating unnecessary replication of proceedings. The tenor Rule 18 is to encourage a party to resolve in one proceeding all claims it has against an opposing party. It is usually efficient to do so whether or not it is strategically wise. Rule 18 gives a party the option. The issues surrounding joinder of claims come not from the *Federal Rules* but from other directions.

FED. R. CIV. P. 18. Joinder of Claims
(a) IN GENERAL. A party asserting a claim, counterclaim, crossclaim, or third-party claim may join, as independent or alternative claims, as many claims as it has against an opposing party.
(b) JOINDER OF CONTINGENT CLAIMS. A party may join two claims even though one of them is contingent on the disposition of the other; but the court may grant relief only in accordance with the parties' relative substantive rights. In particular, a plaintiff may state a claim for money and a claim to set aside a conveyance that is fraudulent as to that plaintiff, without first obtaining a judgment for the money.

INQUIRY

Jurisdiction. The complexity of claim-joinder rules arises not from Rule 18 but from the jurisdictional issues that joining state claims to federal claims raise in the federal courts. Recall the chapter on subject-matter jurisdiction. Federal courts have limited jurisdiction. If a plaintiff files a claim in federal court for which there is federal-question jurisdiction but then tries to join to that federal claim a second claim for which there is no federal jurisdiction, then the plaintiff may not join the second claim. The question is not merely whether the second claim raises a federal question or would qualify under diversity-of-citizenship jurisdiction. Recall that federal courts also have supplemental jurisdiction under 28 U.S.C. §1367(a) (addressed in Chapter 4. Part D) over claims "that are so related to" the claim over which the federal court has jurisdiction "that they form part of the same case or controversy… ." What subject-matter jurisdiction does is give constitutional and statutory dimensions to the claim-joinder question in federal courts. Rule 18 tells a party to join claims as the party pleases, but the Constitution's Article III limit on the jurisdiction of the federal courts and Congress' statutory circumspection in granting jurisdiction mean that the party must ensure that added state-law claims meet §1367(a)'s same-case-or-controversy requirement for supplemental jurisdiction or some other jurisdictional boost like those in FED. R. CIV. P. 4(k)(1)(B) (the 100-mile rule) or FED. R. CIV. P. 14 (third-party practice). State claims must arise out of the same case or controvery or find some other federal-jurisdiction basis for a party to join them to other federal-jurisdiction-qualifying claims in federal court. The following section on counterclaims shows how courts interpret the same-case-or-controversy requirement in a related joinder setting.

State Courts. The jurisdictional limitation does not apply to claim joinder in state courts because state courts do not have the same constitutional limit on their jurisdiction. State-court rules on claim joinder have the same generous scope as FED. R. CIV. P. 18. *See, e.g.,* FLA. R. CIV. P. 1.110(g) ("A pleader may set up in the same action as many claims or causes of action or defenses in the same right as the pleader has… ."); MICH. CT. RULE 2.203(B) ("A pleader may join … as many claims, legal or equitable, as the pleader has against an opposing party."); N.Y. CIVIL PRAC. LAW & RULES §601 ("The plaintiff … may join as many claims as he may have against an adverse party."). That scope does not limit claims to the same case or controversy. For example, a plaintiff in a single state-court case may sue a defendant for breach of contract relating to one transaction and for fraud relating to an entirely different transaction. State rules on claim joinder may, on the other hand, raise their own subject-matter jurisdiction issues, having to do with the limits of state-court jurisdiction under applicable state-court rules and statutes. States often constitute separate family courts, probate courts, and courts based on the amount in question. Different matters involving the same parties may require participating in different actions in different courts having different subject-matter jurisdiction. For example, civil litigation over a wrongful death caused by medical malpractice would entail the tort action in the state court of general jurisdiction plus a separate probate proceeding in probate court to approve any settlement and disburse any litigation proceeds. A family court would have the authority to divide marital property between divorcing spouses but likely not to resolve at the same time claims and interests of third parties in that property, which a court of general jurisdiction would instead resolve. Moreover, parties may divide claims between state and federal courts. A state family court would divorce spouses, but a federal bankruptcy court would dictate the terms of their contemporaneous bankruptcy filing, plan, and discharge.

Claim Preclusion. There is another reason why claim joinder is complex and parties need to give the decision whether to join or not join claims more careful consideration. Common-law rules on claim preclusion may bar a party from litigating non-joined claims in a subsequent case between the same parties. Again, it is not that FED. R. CIV. P. 18 is at all complex. It is not. Under Rule 18, plaintiffs may join or not join claims as they please. Yet if a party decides not to join a claim that arose out of the same case or controversy (the same common nucleus of operative fact), then the claim-preclusion rules of the applicable law may bar non-joined claims. Technically, claim preclusion does not arise from Rule 18 itself. What, after all, should a *Federal Rule of Civil Procedure* say about a party's right to raise a state claim in a subsequent state proceeding? Claim preclusion is instead a creature of the common law developed to ensure that parties do not bring seriatim claims in multiple actions all arising out of a single transaction or occurrence. Claim-preclusion rules force parties to make appropriate use of judicial resources through consolidated legal proceedings. The connection between claim preclusion and Rule 18's joinder provisions is that they use similar same-transaction-or-occurrence standards. A claim that a party must join under Rule 18 is likely to be a claim that the common law would bar under claim-preclusion rules if not litigated in the first proceeding arising between the same parties out of the same transaction or occurrence. Chapter 18 on Effect of Judgment addresses claim preclusion in detail.

Knowledge

At this point in your law studies and study of civil procedure, you must appreciate the vast law knowledge that law students must learn to graduate, pass the bar exam, and enter practice. It is true of much law knowledge and especially of the knowledge of civil procedure that lawyers tend to form and retain latent cognitive structures for it rather than know it explicitly. It is a bit like driving a motor vehicle. Have you ever driven a familiar route and realized, at reaching your destination, that your mind was completely occupied by matters other than negotiating the route that you were driving? Once you acquire and put into regular use cognitive structures having to do with pleading and joinder of parties, you may nearly forget the explicit rules and instead perform with confidence within the experience of those structures. Lawyers research issues such as pleading and joinder rules when they sense that the issue that they have encountered does not lie within the usual patterns. Build and use these structures now, knowing that in time they can become second nature to you.

2. Counterclaims

Chapter 7 on pleading addressed only some of the options—file a Rule 12 motion, answer, and raise affirmative defenses—that a defendant has when responding to a complaint. The facts and law may also support a defendant's counterclaim against the plaintiff. Joinder rules may either permit or require a counterclaim. FED. R. CIV. P. 13 defines which counterclaims a party must file or lose (called *compulsory* counterclaims), and which counterclaims a party may file or not file, without any effect on the party's ability to bring those same claims in a subsequent proceeding (called *permissive* counterclaims). The basic distinction is the same as it is for joinder of claims addressed immediately above. In general, under Rule 13(a)(1) a party must join counterclaims that arise "out of the transaction or occurrence that is the subject matter of the opposing party's claim" so long as it does not require adding another party over whom the federal court cannot acquire jurisdiction. Rule 13(a)(2) states two exceptions, one obvious (when there is already a pending action including the non-pled counterclaim, *see* Union Paving Co. v. Downer Corp., 276 F.2d 468 (9th Cir. 1960) (omission of counterclaim already pled in another action not preclusive)) and one not so obvious (involving attachment). Rule 13(b) permits a party to plead any non-compulsory counterclaims, in that sense being a broad grant for unrelated counterclaims like the grant of Rule 18 to join any claims. Rule 13(c) makes it explicit that counterclaims need not relate to the claim in the relief that they request but may request more, less, or different relief. Rule 13 is broader than at least some state-court rules for joining counterclaims. *See* House v. Hanson, 72 N.W.2d 874 (1955) (omission of word "occurrence" from MINN. CT. RULE 13.01 intended to ensure that courts read state rule restrictively to prohibit tort counterclaims).

The same two concerns discussed immediately above regarding joinder of claims—(1) whether a federal court will have jurisdiction over the joined counterclaims when there is no independent basis for jurisdiction and (2) the preclusive effect of a judgment when a party does not join compulsory counterclaims—apply to joinder of counterclaims. If a state-law counterclaim is compulsory under Rule 13(a)'s same-transaction-or-occurrence language and meets §1367(a) supplemental jurisdiction's same-case-or-controversy requirement (or finds another jurisdictional boost such as Rule 4(k)(1)'s 100-mile rule), then the federal court will have jurisdiction over that state-law counterclaim. Similarly, if the counterclaim is compulsory, then common-law rules for claim preclusion will likely bar the party who fails to join that counterclaim from bringing it in a subsequent action. *See* Stone v. Dept. of Aviation, 453 F.3d 1271, 1275 (10th Cir. 2006); Twin Disc, Inc. v. Lowell, 69 F.R.D. 64, 68 (E.D. Wis. 1975). Other considerations are easier when it comes to counterclaims. There is no need to analyze personal jurisdiction over the plaintiff or the propriety of the venue when a defendant brings a counterclaim. *See* Volvo North American Corp. v. Men's Intl. Professional Tennis Council, 839 F.2d 69, 72 (2d Cir. 1988) (plaintiff's filing federal case consents to jurisdiction and venue as to counterclaim). Read Rule 13, followed by a case demonstrating how a court will apply the same-case-or-controversy rule for supplemental jurisdiction over a counterclaim joined under Rule 13(a).

FED. R. CIV. P. 13. Counterclaim and Crossclaim

(a) COMPULSORY COUNTERCLAIM.

(1) *In General.* A pleading must state as a counterclaim any claim that—at the time of its service—the pleader has against an opposing party if the claim:

(A) arises out of the transaction or occurrence that is the subject matter of the opposing party's claim; and

(B) does not require adding another party over whom the court cannot acquire jurisdiction.

(2) *Exceptions.* The pleader need not state the claim if:

(A) when the action was commenced, the claim was the subject of another pending action; or

(B) the opposing party sued on its claim by attachment or other process that did not establish personal jurisdiction over the pleader on that claim, and the pleader does not assert any counterclaim under this rule.

(b) PERMISSIVE COUNTERCLAIM. A pleading may state as a counterclaim against an opposing party any claim that is not compulsory.

(c) RELIEF SOUGHT IN A COUNTERCLAIM. A counterclaim need not diminish or defeat the recovery sought by the opposing party. It may request relief that exceeds in amount or differs in kind from the relief sought by the opposing party.

(d) COUNTERCLAIM AGAINST THE UNITED STATES. These rules do not expand the right to assert a counterclaim—or to claim a credit— against the United States or a United States officer or agency.

(e) COUNTERCLAIM MATURING OR ACQUIRED AFTER PLEADING. The court may permit a party to file a supplemental pleading asserting a counterclaim that matured or was acquired by the party after serving an earlier pleading.

(f) [ABROGATED.]

(g) CROSSCLAIM AGAINST A COPARTY. A pleading may state as a crossclaim any claim by one party against a coparty if the claim arises out of the transaction or occurrence that is the subject matter of the original action or of a counterclaim, or if the claim relates to any property that is the subject matter of the original action. The crossclaim may include a claim that the coparty is or may be liable to the crossclaimant for all or part of a claim asserted in the action against the crossclaimant.

(h) JOINING ADDITIONAL PARTIES. Rules 19 and 20 govern the addition of a person as a party to a counterclaim or crossclaim.

(i) SEPARATE TRIALS; SEPARATE JUDGMENTS. If the court orders separate trials under Rule 42(b), it may enter judgment on a counterclaim or crossclaim under Rule 54(b) when it has jurisdiction to do so, even if the opposing party's claims have been dismissed or otherwise resolved.

United States v. Heyward-Robinson Co.,

United States Court of Appeals for the Second Circuit
430 F.2d 1077 (1970)

FREDERICK VAN PELT BRYAN, District Judge[, sitting by designation].

This is an appeal from a judgment for the plaintiff entered in the United States District Court for the District of Connecticut upon a jury verdict after trial… .

The action involves two subcontracts for excavation work between D'Agostino Excavators, Inc. (D'Agostino) and The Heyward-Robinson Company, Inc. (Heyward) as prime contractor on two construction jobs in Connecticut. One of the prime contracts, for the construction of barracks at the Naval Submarine Base in New London, Groton, was with the federal government (the Navy job). The other, a non-federal job, was for the construction of a plant for Stelma, Inc. at Stamford (the Stelma job).

D'Agostino brought this action against Heyward and its surety, Maryland Casualty Company (Maryland) under the Miller Act, 40 U.S.C. §§270a and 270b, to recover payments alleged to be due on the Navy job. Heyward answered, denying liability on the Navy job and counterclaiming for alleged overpayments and extra costs of completing both the Navy job and the Stelma job. In reply, D'Agostino denied liability on the Heyward counterclaims and interposed a reply counterclaim to recover from Heyward monies alleged to be due on the Stelma job.

At the trial, the two subcontracts in suit were treated together. D'Agostino claimed that Heyward had breached both subcontracts by failing to make progress payments as required and that substantial sums were owing to it from Heyward on both jobs. Heyward claimed that D'Agostino had breached both subcontracts by permitting its compensation and employee liability insurance to lapse; that, as a result, Heyward on October 19, 1965 had terminated both; and that D'Agostino was liable for overpayments and costs of completion on both. ...

... Heyward and Maryland appeal from the judgment against them... .

Appellants' initial contention is that the District Court had no jurisdiction over the counterclaims on the Stelma job. ...

Appellants urge that the Stelma counterclaims are not compulsory counterclaims over which the federal court acquired jurisdiction ancillary to the jurisdiction which it had over D'Agostino's Miller Act claim stated in the complaint. They say that these are permissive counterclaims over which the court had no ancillary jurisdiction and which lacked the required independent basis of federal jurisdiction.

This jurisdictional issue is raised for the first time in this Court. In the Court below appellants affirmatively urged that the Stelma counterclaims were compulsory. Nevertheless, it is well settled that lack of federal jurisdiction may be raised for the first time on appeal, even by a party who originally asserted that jurisdiction existed or by the Court sua sponte. E.g., American Fire & Casualty Co. v. Finn, 341 U.S. 6, 17-18[] (1951); Mansfield, Coldwater & Lake Michigan Ry. Co. v. Swan, 111 U.S. 379, 384[] (1884); [cc]. We turn, then, to the jurisdictional issue.

It is apparent from the record that there is no independent basis of federal jurisdiction over the Stelma counterclaims. Both D'Agostino and Heyward are New York corporations with offices in New York. There is thus no diversity jurisdiction. Clearly there is no jurisdiction under the Miller Act over these counterclaims since the Stelma contract did not involve public work for the federal government.

The question is whether the Stelma counterclaims are compulsory or are permissive. Under the rule in this circuit, if they are permissive there is no Federal jurisdiction over them unless they rest on independent jurisdictional grounds. [Cc] ... On the other hand, if they are compulsory counterclaims, they are ancillary to the claim asserted in the complaint and no independent basis of Federal jurisdiction is required. [Cc]

Under Rule 13(a) Fed. R. Civ. P. a counterclaim is compulsory "if it arises out of the transaction or occurrence that is the subject matter of the opposing party's claim." In United Artists Corp. v. Masterpiece Productions, [221 F.2d 213 (2d Cir. 1955)], Chief Judge Clark said:

> In practice this criterion has been broadly interpreted to require not an absolute identity of factual backgrounds for the two claims, but only a logical relationship between them. Lesnik v. Public Industrials Corp., []144 F.2d 968, 975[(2d Cir. 1944)], citing and quoting, inter alia, Moore v. New York Cotton Exchange, 270 U.S. 593, 610[(1926)], thus: "'Transaction' is a word of flexible meaning. It may comprehend a series of many occurrences, depending not so much upon the immediateness of their connection as upon their logical relationship." [Cc]

Thus "* * * courts should give the phrase 'transaction or occurrence that is the subject matter' of the suit a broad realistic interpretation in the interest of avoiding a multiplicity of suits." 3 J. Moore, supra, P13.13 at 33-36 (2d ed. 1969). As the Supreme Court said in [Southern Construction Co. v.] Pickard[, 371 U.S. 57, 60 (1962)]: "The requirement that counterclaims arising out of the same transaction or occurrence as the opposing party's claim 'shall' be stated in the pleadings was designed to prevent multiplicity of actions and to achieve resolution in a single lawsuit of all disputes arising out of common matters." [C]

In the case at bar the counterclaims were compulsory within the meaning of Rule 13(a). There was such a close and logical relationship between the claims on the Navy and Stelma jobs that the Stelma counterclaims arose out of the same "transaction or occurrence" as those terms are now broadly defined. Both subcontracts were entered into by the same parties for the same type of work and carried on during substantially the same period. Heyward had the right to terminate both subcontracts in the event of a breach by D'Agostino of either. Heyward also had the right to withhold monies due on one to apply against any damages suffered on the other. Progress payments made by Heyward were not allocated as between jobs and were made on a lump sum basis for both as though for a single account.

A single insurance policy covered both jobs. The letters of Heyward to D'Agostino of October 8 and 19, 1965 threatening termination and terminating both jobs, allegedly because of the cancellation by D'Agostino of this joint insurance coverage and failure to properly man both projects, treated both jobs together. These letters formed the basis of one of Heyward's major claims at the trial.

The controversy between the parties which gave rise to this litigation was with respect to both jobs and arose from occurrences affecting both. Indeed, it would seem to have been impossible for Heyward to have fully litigated the claims against it on the Navy job without including the Stelma job, because the payments it made to D'Agostino could not be allocated between the two jobs.

As the appellants themselves point out in their brief, the "Stelma and Navy claims were so interwoven at the trial that they are now absolutely incapable of separation." The proof as to payments and alleged defaults in payments was made without any differentiation between the two claims and neither of the parties was able to offer any evidence of apportionment. Finally, the evidence as to the breaches of contract claimed by the respective parties related in the main to both contracts rather than to one or the other.

The jurisdictional question so belatedly raised by the appellants must be viewed in light of the record as a whole. So viewed, it is plain that the Stelma counterclaims bare a logical and immediate relationship to the claims on the Navy job. Thus they arose out of the "transaction or occurrence which is the subject matter" of the suit instituted by D'Agostino on the Navy job and are compulsory counterclaims under Rule 13(a). The Stelma counterclaims were thus ancillary to the claims asserted in the complaint over which the Federal Court had acquired jurisdiction under the Miller Act, and there is jurisdiction over them. [Cc] To require that the closely related Navy and Stelma claims must be litigated separately would result in fragmentation of litigation and multiplicity of suits contrary to one of the major purposes of Rule 13(a). [Cc]. ...

The judgment below is affirmed. ...

FRIENDLY, Circuit Judge (concurring) [Opinion omitted. Judge Friendly's concurrence disagreed that breach of the second subcontract was a compulsory counterclaim but would have held that the federal courts can hear permissive counterclaims without independent jurisdiction over them, for which there has been some federal authority constituting a minority position.].

INQUIRY

Logical Relationship. Did the outcome in *Heyward-Robinson* surprise you? As the above *Heyward-Robinson* case indicates, the federal courts apply a generous logical-relationship test to decide whether a counterclaim arises out of the same transaction or occurrence and is therefore compulsory under Rule 13(a). *Heyward-Robinson* cited Moore v. New York Cotton Exchange, 270 U.S. 593, 610 (1926), for its broad definition that the same transaction has "flexible meaning" including "a series of many occurrences, depending not so much upon the immediateness of their connection as upon their logical relationship." In *Moore v. New York Cotton Exchange*, the Supreme Court held compulsory a defendant's counterclaim accusing the plaintiff of stealing price quotations from defendant's exchange, where the plaintiff had sued to force the defendant exchange to install a price-quotation ticker. Can you appreciate how logical relationship is broader than immediate connection? Can you are articulate a functional test instead? A leading treatise suggests that case law and policy support three functional tests giving purpose to the logical-relationship test, that a claim and counterclaim arise out of the same transaction or occurrence if (1) they raise the same issues of law and fact, (2) they rely on the same evidence, or (3) res judicata would bar the counterclaim if brought separately. 6 WRIGHT & MILLER, FEDERAL PRACTICE AND PROCEDURE §1410 (1971); *see also* Painter v. Harvey, 863 F.2d 329, 331 (4th Cir. 1988) (same).

Policy. The above case *Heyward-Robinson Co.* case and the Supreme Court case Southern Construction Co. v. Pickard, 371 U.S. 57 (1962), that *Heyward-Robinson* cites indicate Rule 13(a)'s policy to promote the efficient resolution of counterclaims in a single proceeding. Is it truly efficient, though, to force parties to bring counterclaims that they might otherwise not bring? Can you think of an example where it would be better for everyone involved to let a sleeping counterclaim lie? Rule 13(a)'s policy to promote efficient resolution of counterclaims in a single proceeding can work against the policies reflected in the substantive federal law under which the plaintiff brings the claim, resulting in conflicting decisions on how the federal courts should apply Rule 13(a). *Contrast* Plant v. Blazer Financial Services, 598 F.2d 1357 (5th Cir. 1979) (lender must counterclaim on loan default when borrower brings Truth-in-Lending Act claim), *with* Whigham v Beneficial Finance Co., 599 F.2d 1322, 1323-1324 (4th Cir. 1979) (lender need not counterclaim on loan default when borrower brings Truth-in-Lending Act claim). Can you see why borrower, lender, and trial court all might prefer that the lender not bring its counterclaim for the loan's default when the borrower's claim raises a disclosure issue? Forcing parties to bring and dispute counterclaims is not always in the best interest of those parties or of the trial courts.

Case or Controversy. Even if parties who hold counterclaims might prefer to decide whether to pursue them in a pending federal case or bring them later in another proceeding in state or federal court (that is, prefer that they be permissive rather than compulsory), there is a benefit to Rule 13(a)'s compulsory joinder. As noted above, counterclaims, like joined claims, must also qualify for federal-court jurisdiction. If they are compulsory under Rule 13(a), meaning that they arise out of the same transaction or occurrence, then one might assume that they qualify for §1367(a) supplemental jurisdiction. Yet §1367(a)'s language offers supplemental jurisdiction for claims arising out of the same "case or controversy," not the same "transaction or occurrence." Is there any difference? Some courts may find the tests to be essentially the same, meaning that §1367(a) supplemental jurisdiction would exist over all Rule 13(a) compulsory counterclaims and no Rule 13(b) permissive counterclaims. *See* Unique Concepts, Inc. v. Manuel, 930 F.2d 573, 574 (7th Cir. 1991). There is some contrary authority that §1367's same-case-or-controversy standard for supplemental jurisdiction is broader than Rule 13(a)'s same-transaction-or-occurrence standard for compulsory counterclaims. *See* Jones v. Ford Motor Credit Co., 358 F.3d 205, 213-214 (2d Cir. 2004) (permissive collection-action claim may arise from the same federal equal-credit-law case or controversy, for permissive supplemental jurisdiction).

Pleading. A practice convention is to plead the counterclaim in the same pleading immediately after the answer and affirmative defenses. Defense counsel will also file a counterclaim as a separate pleading at the same time as the defendant's answer. Yet it is not only defendants who may plead counterclaims. Rule 13(a) and (b) speak of a "party" raising a counterclaim in a "pleading," not limiting counterclaims to defendants answering a plaintiff's complaint. The lesson here may be for all pleaders, not merely plaintiffs, to take care in the claims that they plead lest there result an onerous counterclaim. Great Lakes Rubber Corp. v. Herbert Cooper Co., 286 F.2d 631 (3d Cir. 1961), may be an example. The plaintiff pled claims in that case that the plaintiff alleged satisfied federal-question jurisdiction. The federal court later dismissed plaintiff's claims for lack of federal jurisdiction. But for the defendant's federal counterclaims, the dismissal would have ended the federal action. Yet because the defendant's counterclaims preserved the federal court's jurisdiction, the plaintiff was able to counterclaim against the defendant making the same claims that the court had just dismissed but qualifying them for §1367's same-case-or-controversy standard for supplemental jurisdiction. FED. R. CIV. P. 13(e) authorizes the trial court to permit a party to add a counterclaim with a supplemental pleading if the party later acquires it. FED. R. CIV. P. 15 on amended pleadings in general also applies to the amendment and relation back of counterclaims. Interestingly, a compulsory counterclaim may relate back to the filing date of the complaint, not merely to the filing date of an answer and counterclaim in which it could first have been asserted. *See* Harrison v. Grass, 304 F.Supp.2d 710, 715 (D. Md. 2004); *but cf.* American Annuity Group., Inc. v. Guaranty Reassurance Corp., 140 F. Supp.2d 859, 872 (S.D. Ohio 2001) (amended counterclaim does not relate back).

3. Crossclaims

When a plaintiff sues two or more defendants, then in addition to an answer, affirmative defenses, and counterclaim, the defendant may also file a crossclaim against other defendants. A crossclaim is a claim by a party against another party who is similarly aligned with respect to the pleading that first brought the parties into the action. FED. R. CIV. P. 13(g) states that a crossclaim is against a "coparty," although that term misleads if it is taken to suggest any particular relationship other than the fortuity of similar alignment. For example, when a plaintiff sues two or more defendants, depending on the case the defendants may have no relationship, may have directly opposing interests, may have a substantial relationship, or may have identical interests. Crossclaims allow parties whom a pleading aligned to plead and resolve claims between them. A common example is the action in which the plaintiff sues two or more defendants alleging their tort liability, and a defendant crossclaims against a codefendant for contribution or indemnity to ensure that it does not pay the plaintiff for that codefendant's liability.

Note that in the example just given about the tort action that the crossclaim arose out of the occurrence alleged in the complaint. Rule 13(g) expressly limits crossclaims to those that "arise[] out of the transaction or occurrence that is the subject matter of the original action or of a counterclaim" or "relates to property that is the subject matter of the original action. In that respect, Rule 13 is quite unlike Rule 18(a) permitting joinder of any claims whether related or unrelated and Rule 13(b) permitting permissive joinder of unrelated counterclaims. Can you articulate why claims and counterclaims can be unrelated but not crossclaims? Rule 13(g)'s relatedness requirement effectively eliminates any subject-matter jurisdiction issues, given §1367's same-case-or-controversy standard for supplemental jurisdiction. Note also that Rule 13(g) does not limit crossclaims to defendants. Third-party defendants and other parties may also file crossclaims. Can you think of an instance when two plaintiffs might crossclaim between them? That part of Rule 13(g) just quoted about crossclaims arising out of the occurrence that is the subject "of a counterclaim" provides a clue. When a defendant pleads a counterclaim against one or more of multiple plaintiffs, it may trigger one plaintiff's crossclaim against another plaintiff. For example, if a complaint alleges that the defendant driver negligently injured the plaintiff driver and plaintiff passenger in the same vehicle, and the defendant driver counterclaims against the plaintiff driver for the defendant driver's own injuries or for contribution, then the plaintiff passenger may at that point wish to entertain a crossclaim against the plaintiff driver. *See* Danner v Anskis, 256 F.2d 123 (3d Cir. 1958) (crossclaim of plaintiff passenger against co-plaintiff driver). Can you imagine why the plaintiff driver might not have sued the plaintiff driver in the original action?

Ethics

Rule 1.7 of the ABA MODEL RULES OF PROFESSIONAL CONDUCT prohibits lawyers from representing multiple parties in an action where those parties maintain claims between them or otherwise have non-waiveable conflicts of interest. Lawyers often do represent two or more parties in litigation when they are similiarly aligned (that is, when they are coparties) and have similar interests. For example, a defendant employer will often retain counsel to defend both the employer and a defendant employee whose actions involved the employer in litigation. The example just given above involving the plaintiff driver and passenger in a motor-vehicle negligence case is another example. The plaintiffs in that case might retain the same lawyer to pursue the action, especially if the plaintiffs were family members. However, an opposing party's counterclaim can drive a figurative wedge between parties whose interests may initially appear similar. The right of one coparty to maintain crossclaims against other coparties accentuates their differing interests. The wise lawyer anticipates counterclaims and represents only one coparty if a counterclaim is going to create a conflict between coparties. The lawyer who begins by representing coparties may end up representing *no* parties if their interests suddenly differ because of a counterclaim. For a contingency-fee lawyer, that mistake can be very expensive. Any lawyer deigning to represent both a plaintiff driver and passenger in a motor-vehicle negligence case should carefully consider that possibility.

B. Parties

This chapter on joinder focuses on multiple claims and multiple parties. There may be multiple plaintiffs and multiple defendants in a single action. The rules for when plaintiffs may join together in a single action and when one or more plaintiffs may join multiple defendants in a single action share some of the concepts for multiple claims. Like joinder-of-claims rules, joinder of parties may depend on whether the rights on which they are joined arise out of the same transaction or occurrence. Like joinder-of-claim rules, joinder-of-parties rules also divide into permissive and compulsory joinder. Joinder-of-parties strategies and consequences also depend on a mix of *Federal Rules of Civil Procedure* or equivalent state-court rules and common-law claim-preclusion concepts. Yet multiple-party rules deploy joinder concepts in a somewhat different fashion from multiple-claim rules. Joinder of parties also calls into play other strategic interests and questions of the number and representation of potential parties. This section on multiple parties includes subsections on permissive joinder, compulsory joinder, and third parties. Sections on interpleader, intervention, and class actions follow.

In turning from joinder of claims to joinder of parties, we should first spend a moment on two doctrines, (1) standing and (2) capacity, that affect who may bring an action. Standing doctrine has several purposes. One has to do with ensuring that any action that the court entertains involves a sufficiently personal interest to warrant giving the party who wishes to maintain it the use of the courts. It has, in other words, to do with preserving the integrity of the courts against vain claims and preserving limited judicial resources for meaningful actions. It also enables courts to respect the separation of powers when parties attempt to invoke judicial authority to challenge executive or legislative actions that have not caused the putative litigant a concrete injury. Another purpose for standing doctrine has to do with ensuring that the party who maintains an action has a sufficient interest in the action to do a good job of it. One party should not be able to maintain a claim in which another party has the more substantial interest, lest the representative party do it less than ample justice. Standing doctrine also protects the responding party from a multiplicity of actions, when only the party who has suffered the concrete injury and has the authentic interest in the action may maintain it. In the federal courts, standing takes on a constitutional dimension under Article III. The Supreme Court has held that to establish standing satisfying Article III's requirement, the plaintiff must show a concrete and particularized "injury in fact" that is either actual or imminent, must trace the injury to the defendant's action, and must show that a favorable decision will redress the injury. Friends of the Earth, Inc. v. Laidlaw Environmental Services (TOC), Inc., 528 U.S. 167, 180-181 (2000).

State and federal courts use the common-law concept of the *real party in interest* to state and apply standing rules. *See, e.g.*, FLA. R. CIV. P. 1.210(a); MICH. CT. RULE 2.201(B). FED. R. CIV. P. 17(a) bears that title, although given its somewhat inarticulate and redundant form, *interested party* is a preferred form. Rule 17(a)(1), stating that "[a]n action must be prosecuted in the name of the real party in interest," in effect incorporates common-law standing doctrine. By "prosecuted," Rule 17(a)(1) means that the *plaintiff* must be the interested party, not that the defendant has any duty to identify the interested defendant. *See* Lincoln Property Co. v. Roche, 546 U.S. 81, 90 (2005). The balance of Rule 17(a)(1) then disposes of some easy standing issues, that executors, administrators, guardians, bailees, trustees, and parties whom a contract or statute authorize to represent another's interest may do so without joining the beneficiary. One might think that this provision defeats standing's purpose to ensure that the party with the greatest interest participates, until one recalls that these representatives have duties like loyalty, diligence, and competence that promote if not ensure the quality of their representation. Rule 17(a)(3) ensures that the federal court gives the interested party an opportunity to "ratify, join, or be substituted into the action" before the court dismisses for lack of standing. FED. R. CIV. P. 23.1 states standing rules for shareholder derivative actions and FED. R. CIV. P. 23.2 standing rules for actions on behalf of unincorporates associations, both potentially troublesome issues warranting rule definition.

Capacity is the other issue that, like standing doctrine, ensures the integrity of a party to conduct civil litigation. Capacity rules differ from standing rules and doctrine in that the capacity question is not the sufficiency of the party's injury and interest but instead the party's ability to maintain the action. The capacity of minors and incompetent persons are two good examples. Minors presumably lack the maturity, objectivity, and experience, and incompetents by definition lack the mental acuity, to conduct litigation on their own behalf. The *Federal Rules of Civil Procedure* do not define who is a minor (whether a person under age 18, 21, or some other age) or incompetent. Instead, FED. R. CIV. P. 17(b)-(d) states a few specific rules having to do with capacity and refers to state law for other capacity rules. Specifically, Rule 17(b)(1)-(3) states choice-of-law rules adopting the law of the state of domicile, incorporation, or court location depending on whether the party is an individual or corporation, or has another status. Under Rule 17(b)(1), a practitioner would look to the law of the domicile of the party to determine whether the party was a minor or incompetent. Rule 17(c) states other specific rules for representatives to sue on behalf of minors and incompetents. Rule 17(d) states similar rules for suits by and against public officers. FED. R. CIV. P. 25 addresses other specific capacity issues by providing for substitution of parties upon death, incompetency, transfer of the litigated interest, or separation from office. Before moving on to issues surrounding joinder of multiple parties, read these standing and capacity rules, appreciating the sensitivity practitioners must show to ensure the integrity of parties, representation, litigation, and the civil justice system.

FED. R. CIV. P. 17. Plaintiff and Defendant; Capacity; Public Officers

(a) REAL PARTY IN INTEREST.

(1) *Designation in General.* An action must be prosecuted in the name of the real party in interest. The following may sue in their own names without joining the person for whose benefit the action is brought:

(A) an executor;

(B) an administrator;

(C) a guardian;

(D) a bailee;

(E) a trustee of an express trust;

(F) a party with whom or in whose name a contract has been made for another's benefit; and

(G) a party authorized by statute.

(2) *Action in the Name of the United States for Another's Use or Benefit.* When a federal statute so provides, an action for another's use or benefit must be brought in the name of the United States.

(3) *Joinder of the Real Party in Interest.* The court may not dismiss an action for failure to prosecute in the name of the real party in interest until, after an objection, a reasonable time has been allowed for the real party in interest to ratify, join, or be substituted into the action. After ratification, joinder, or substitution, the action proceeds as if it had been originally commenced by the real party in interest.

(b) CAPACITY TO SUE OR BE SUED. Capacity to sue or be sued is determined as follows:

(1) for an individual who is not acting in a representative capacity, by the law of the individual's domicile;

(2) for a corporation, by the law under which it was organized; and

(3) for all other parties, by the law of the state where the court is located, except that:

(A) a partnership or other unincorporated association with no such capacity under that state's law may sue or be sued in its common name to enforce a substantive right existing under the United States Constitution or laws; and

(B) 28 U.S.C. §§ 754 and 959(a) govern the capacity of a receiver appointed by a United States court to sue or be sued in a United States court.

(c) MINOR OR INCOMPETENT PERSON.

(1) *With a Representative.* The following representatives may sue or defend on behalf of a minor or an incompetent person:

(A) a general guardian;

(B) a committee;

(C) a conservator; or

(D) a like fiduciary.

(2) *Without a Representative.* A minor or an incompetent person who does not have a duly appointed representative may sue by a next friend or by a guardian ad litem. The court must appoint a guardian ad litem—or issue another appropriate order—to protect a minor or incompetent person who is unrepresented in an action.

(d) PUBLIC OFFICER'S TITLE AND NAME. A public officer who sues or is sued in an official capacity may be designated by official title rather than by name, but the court may order that the officer's name be added.

....

FED. R. CIV. P. 23.1. Derivative Actions

(a) PREREQUISITES. This rule applies when one or more shareholders or members of a corporation or an unincorporated association bring a derivative action to enforce a right that the corporation or association may properly assert but has failed to enforce. The derivative action may not be maintained if it appears that the plaintiff does not fairly and adequately represent the interests of shareholders or members who are similarly situated in enforcing the right of the corporation or association.

(b) PLEADING REQUIREMENTS. The complaint must be verified and must:

(1) allege that the plaintiff was a shareholder or member at the time of the transaction complained of, or that the plaintiff's share or membership later devolved on it by operation of law;

(2) allege that the action is not a collusive one to confer jurisdiction that the court would otherwise lack; and

(3) state with particularity:

(A) any effort by the plaintiff to obtain the desired action from the directors or comparable authority and, if necessary, from the shareholders or members; and

(B) the reasons for not obtaining the action or not making the effort.

(c) SETTLEMENT, DISMISSAL, AND COMPROMISE. A derivative action may be settled, voluntarily dismissed, or compromised only with the court's approval. Notice of a proposed settlement, voluntary dismissal, or compromise must be given to shareholders or members in the manner that the court orders.

FED. R. CIV. P. 23.2. Actions Relating to Unincorporated Associations

This rule applies to an action brought by or against the members of an unincorporated association as a class by naming certain members as representative parties. The action may be maintained only if it appears that those parties will fairly and adequately protect the interests of the association and its members. In conducting the action, the court may issue any appropriate orders corresponding with those in Rule 23(d), and the procedure for settlement, voluntary dismissal, or compromise must correspond with the procedure in Rule 23(e).

FED. R. CIV. P. 25. Substitution of Parties

(a) DEATH.

(1) *Substitution if the Claim Is Not Extinguished.* If a party dies and the claim is not extinguished, the court may order substitution of the proper party. A motion for substitution may be made by any party or by the decedent's successor or representative. If the motion is not made within 90 days after service of a statement noting the death, the action by or against the decedent must be dismissed.

(2) *Continuation Among the Remaining Parties.* After a party's death, if the right sought to be enforced survives only to or against the remaining parties, the action does not abate, but proceeds in favor of or against the remaining parties. The death should be noted on the record.

(3) *Service.* A motion to substitute, together with a notice of hearing, must be served on the parties as provided in Rule 5 and on nonparties as provided in Rule 4. A statement noting death must be served in the same manner. Service may be made in any judicial district.

(b) INCOMPETENCY. If a party becomes incompetent, the court may, on motion, permit the action to be continued by or against the party's representative. The motion must be served as provided in Rule 25(a)(3).

(c) TRANSFER OF INTEREST. If an interest is transferred, the action may be continued by or against the original party unless the court, on motion, orders the transferee to be substituted in the action or joined with the original party. The motion must be served as provided in Rule 25(a)(3).

(d) PUBLIC OFFICERS; DEATH OR SEPARATION FROM OFFICE. An action does not abate when a public officer who is a party in an official capacity dies, resigns, or otherwise ceases to hold office while the action is pending. The officer's successor is automatically substituted as a party. Later proceedings should be in the substituted party's name, but any misnomer not affecting the parties' substantial rights must be disregarded. The court may order substitution at any time, but the absence of such an order does not affect the substitution.

---

1. Permissive Joinder

FED. R. CIV. P. 20 states the federal-court rules for permissive joinder of parties, meaning when parties may join together in a single action as plaintiffs and when one or more plaintiffs may join multiple defendants in a single action. States have analogous rules. *See, e.g.,* MICH. CT. RULE 2.206; N.Y. CIVIL PRAC. LAW & RULES §1002. Unlike the generous rules for permissive joinder of claims, there is no unfettered right to join as many parties in a single action as the plaintiff or plaintiffs may desire. When you have a single plaintiff and single defendant, there is efficiency to joining unrelated claims and counterclaims between them, that the parties may resolve all claims in a single proceeding. The parties are already invested in the action, and the claims and counterclaims that they maintain may work as offsets, resulting in net settlements and judgments that provide comprehensive and coordinate rather than piecemeal justice. Yet when it comes to joining parties, a broad rule for permissive joinder of unrelated parties would offer no such efficiencies. If one joins in a single action multiple parties that have no interest in a core transaction or occurrence and instead have discrete claims and counterclaims among them in differing alignments, then there is no prospect for comprehensive and coordinate resolution. The parties also gain no efficiencies around presenting evidence and addressing legal issues. The parties may as well maintain separate actions. Thus in its subrules (a)(1) and (2), Rule 20 permits joinder of multiple plaintiffs or multiple defendants only when their rights and obligations "arise out of the same transaction, occurrence, or series of transactions or occurrences" under a "question of law or fact common to all" plaintiffs or all defendants. Because even this limitation may still allow for a relatively complex action burdening one or more parties, Rule 20(b) permits the court to order separate trials or other protective action. FED. R. CIV. P. 21 further authorizes the court to add or drop parties or sever claims on just terms to control multiple-party actions. Read Rules 20 and 21, followed by a case applying rules for permissive joinder of multiple parties.

FED. R. CIV. P. 20. Permissive Joinder of Parties

(a) PERSONS WHO MAY JOIN OR BE JOINED.

(1) *Plaintiffs.* Persons may join in one action as plaintiffs if:

(A) they assert any right to relief jointly, severally, or in the alternative with respect to or arising out of the same transaction, occurrence, or series of transactions or occurrences; and

(B) any question of law or fact common to all plaintiffs will arise in the action.

(2) *Defendants.* Persons—as well as a vessel, cargo, or other property subject to admiralty process in rem—may be joined in one action as defendants if:

(A) any right to relief is asserted against them jointly, severally, or in the alternative with respect to or arising out of the same transaction, occurrence, or series of transactions or occurrences; and

(B) any question of law or fact common to all defendants will arise in the action.

(3) *Extent of Relief.* Neither a plaintiff nor a defendant need be interested in obtaining or defending against all the relief demanded. The court may grant judgment to one or more plaintiffs according to their rights, and against one or more defendants according to their liabilities.

(b) PROTECTIVE MEASURES. The court may issue orders—including an order for separate trials—to protect a party against embarrassment, delay, expense, or other prejudice that arises from including a person against whom the party asserts no claim and who asserts no claim against the party.

FED. R. CIV. P. 21. Misjoinder and Nonjoinder of Parties

Misjoinder of parties is not a ground for dismissing an action. On motion or on its own, the court may at any time, on just terms, add or drop a party. The court may also sever any claim against a party.

Mosley v. General Motors Corp.,

United States Court of Appeals for the Eighth Circuit
497 F.2d 1330 (1974)

ROSS, Circuit Judge.

Nathaniel Mosley and nine other persons joined in bringing this action individually and as class representatives alleging that their rights guaranteed under 42 U.S.C. §2000e et seq. and 42 U.S.C. §1981 were denied by General Motors and Local 25, United Automobile, Aerospace and Agriculture Implement Workers of America (Union) by reason of their color and race. Each of the ten named plaintiffs had, prior to the filing of the complaint, filed a charge with the Equal Employment Opportunity Commission (EEOC)[, which] made a reasonable cause finding that General Motors, Fisher Body Division and Chevrolet Division, and the Union had engaged in unlawful employment practices in violation of Title VII of the Civil Rights Act of 1964. Accordingly, the charging parties were notified by EEOC of their right to institute a civil action in the appropriate federal district court… .

In each of the first eight counts of the twelve-count complaint, eight of the ten plaintiffs alleged that General Motors, Chevrolet Division, had engaged in unlawful employment practices by: "discriminating against Negroes as regards promotions, terms and conditions of employment"; "retaliating against Negro employees who protested actions made unlawful by Title VII of the Act and by discharging some because they protested said unlawful acts"; "failing to hire Negro employees as a class on the basis of race"; "failing to hire females as a class on the basis of sex"; "discharging Negro employees on the basis of race"; and "discriminating against Negroes and females in the granting of relief time." Each additionally charged that the defendant Union had engaged in unlawful employment practices "with respect to the granting of relief time to Negro and female employees" and "by failing to pursue 6a grievances." The remaining two plaintiffs made similar allegations against General Motors, Fisher Body Division. All of the individual plaintiffs requested injunctive relief, back pay, attorneys fees and costs. …

… The district court ordered that "insofar as the first ten counts are concerned, those ten counts shall be severed into ten separate causes of action," and each plaintiff was directed to bring a separate action based upon his complaint, duly and separately filed. …

In reaching this conclusion on joinder, the district court followed the reasoning of Smith v. North American Rockwell Corp., 50 F.R.D. 515 (N.D. Okla. 1970), which, in a somewhat analogous situation, found there was no right to relief arising out of the same transaction, occurrence or series of transactions or occurrences, and that there was no question of law or fact common to all plaintiffs sufficient to sustain joinder under Federal Rule of Civil Procedure 20(a), Similarly, the district court here felt that the plaintiffs' joint actions against General Motors and the Union presented a veriety of issues having little relationship to one another; that they had only one common problem, i.e., the defendant; and that as pleaded the joint actions were completely unmanageable. … We granted the application to permit this interlocutory appeal and for the following reasons we affirm in part and reverse in part.

Rule 20(a) of the Federal Rules of Civil Procedure provides: "All persons may join in one action as plaintiffs if they assert any right to relief jointly, severally, or in the alternative in respect of or arising out of the same transaction, occurrence, or series of transactions or occurrences and if any question of law or fact common to all these persons will arise in the action. ..."

Additionally, Rule 20(b) and Rule 42(b) vest in the district court the discretion to order separate trials or make such other orders as will prevent delay or prejudice. ... To determine whether the district court's order was proper herein, we must look to the policy and law that have developed around the operation of Rule 20.

The purpose of the rule is to promote trial convenience and expedite the final determination of disputes, thereby preventing multiple lawsuits. [C] Single trials generally tend to lessen the delay, expense and inconvenience to all concerned. Reflecting this policy, the Supreme Court has said: "Under the Rules, the impulse is toward entertaining the broadest possible scope of action consistent with fairness to the parties; joinder of claims, parties and remedies is strongly encouraged." United Mine Workers of America v. Gibbs, 383 U.S. 715, 724[] (1966).

Permissive joinder is not, however, applicable in all cases. The rule imposes two specific requisites to the joinder of parties: (1) a right to relief must be asserted by, or against, each plaintiff or defendant relating to or arising out of the same *transaction or occurrence, or series of transactions or occurrences*; and (2) some *question of law or fact common* to all the parties must arise in the action.

In ascertaining whether a particular factual situation constitutes a single transaction or occurrence for purposes of Rule 20, a case by case approach is generally pursued. [C] No hard and fast rules have been established under the rule. However, construction of the terms "transaction or occurrence" as used in the context of Rule 13(a) counterclaims offers some guide to the application of this test. For the purposes of the latter rule, "'Transaction' is a word of flexible meaning. It may comprehend a series of many occurrences, depending not so much upon the immediateness of their connection as upon their logical relationship." Moore v. New York Cotton Exchange, 270 U.S. 593, 610[] (1926). Accordingly, all "logically related" events entitling a person to institute a legal action against another generally are regarded as comprising a transaction or occurrence. [C] The analogous interpretation of the terms as used in Rule 20 would permit all reasonably related claims for relief by or against different parties to be tried in a single proceeding. Absolute identity of all events is unnecessary.

This construction accords with the result reached in United States v. Mississippi, [380 U.S. 128 (1965),] a suit brought by the United States against the State of Missippi, the election commissioners, and six voting registrars of the State, charging them with engaging in acts and practices hampering and destroying the right of black citizens of Mississippi to vote. The district court concluded that the complaint improperly attempted to hold the six county registrars jointly liable for what amounted to nothing more than individual torts committed by them separately against separate applicants. In reversing, the Supreme Court said:

> But the complaint charged that the registrars had acted and were continuing to act as part of a state-wide system designed to enforce the registration laws in a way that would inevitably deprive colored people of the right to

> vote solely because of their color. On such an allegation the joinder of all the registrars as defendants in a single suit is authorized by Rule 20(a) of the Federal Rules of Civil Procedure. ... These registrars were alleged to be carrying on activities which were part of a series of transactions or occurrences the validity of which depended to a large extent upon "question(s) of law or fact common to all of them." [Id. at 142-143.]

Here too, then, the plaintiffs have asserted a right to relief arising out of the same transactions or occurrences. Each of the ten plaintiffs alleged that he had been injured by the same general policy of discrimination on the part of General Motors and the Union. Since a "state-wide system designed to enforce the registration laws in a way that would inevitably deprive colored people of the right to vote" was determined to arise out of the same series of transactions or occurrences, we conclude that a company-wide policy purportedly designed to discriminate against blacks in employment similarly arises out of the same series of transactions or occurrences. Thus the plaintiffs meet the first requisite for joinder under Rule 20(a).

The second requisite necessary to sustain a permissive joinder under the rule is that a question of law or fact common to all the parties will arise in the action. The rule does not require that all questions of law and fact raised by the dispute be common. Yet, neither does it establish any qualitative or quantitative test of commonality. For this reason, cases construing the parallel requirement under Federal Rule of Civil Procedure 23(a) provide a helpful framework for construction of the commonality required by Rule 20. In general, those cases that have focused on Rule 23(a)(2) have given it a permissive application so that common questions have been found to exist in a wide range of context. [C] Specifically, with respect to employment discrimination cases under Title VII, courts have found that the discriminatory character of a defendant's conduct is basic to the class, and the fact that the individual class members may have suffered different effects from the alleged discrimination is immaterial for the purposes of the prerequisite. [Cc] In this vein, one court has said: "Although the actual effects of a discriminatory policy may thus vary throughout the class, the existence of the discriminatory policy threatens the entire class. And whether the Damoclean threat of a racially discriminatory policy hangs over the racial class is a question of fact common to all the members of the class." Hall v. Werthan Bag Corp., 251 F.Supp. 184, 186 (M.D. Tenn. 1966). [Cc]

The right to relief here depends on the ability to demonstrate that each of the plaintiffs was wronged by racially discriminatory policies on the part of the defendants General Motors and the Union. The discriminatory character of the defendants' conduct is thus basic to each plaintiff's recovery. The fact that each plaintiff may have suffered different effects from the alleged discrimination is immaterial for the purposes of determining the common question of law or fact. Thus, we conclude that the second requisite for joinder under Rule 20(a) is also meet by the complaint.

For the reasons set forth above, we conclude that the district court abused its discretion in severing the joined actions. The difficulties in ultimately adjudicating damages to the various plaintiffs are not so overwhelming as to require such severance. If appropriate, separate trials may be granted as to any particular issue after the determination of common questions.

The judgment of the district court disallowing joinder of the plaintiffs' individual actions is reversed and remanded with directions to permit the plaintiffs to proceed jointly …

INQUIRY

Tactics. General Motors' decision to oppose the plaintiffs' permissive joinder of race-discrimination claims in the above *Mosley* case was almost certainly tactical rather than efficient. Can you articulate why? Why did the plaintiffs join together in the *Mosley* case as multiple plaintiffs? Some courts may be more sensitive to the possible prejudice against a defendant who faces similar claims by multiple plaintiffs, than appreciative of the efficiencies to the court and advantage to the plaintiffs. *See* Howard Motor Co. v. Swint, 448 S.E.2d 713, 714 (Ga. Ct. App. 1994) (prohibiting joinder of five plaintiffs' sexual-harassment claims against the same company president despite similar state-court rule for permissive joinder). Do FED. R. CIV. P. 20 and 21 give the trial court any authority to sever parties and try their claims separately to prevent prejudice? *See* Henderson v. AT&T Corp., 918 F.Supp. 1059, 1061 (S.D. Tex. 1996) (allowing joinder of five plaintiffs' sex-discrimination claims but severing three cases for trial, where they involved different direct supervisors). A court cannot eliminate all tactical considerations, but Rule 20(b) and 21 each grant the trial court broad authority to keep tactical considerations to a reasonable minimum or at least to balance them between opposing parties. Is the kind of prejudice that can accrue from the trial of multiple plaintiffs' claims against the same defendant doing the same illegal acts against those plaintiffs *undue* prejudice?

Consolidation. Just as Rules 20(b) and 21 authorize the trial court to sever parties' claims into separate actions, so, too, may the trial court consolidate separate actions. FED. R. CIV. P. 42(a) authorizes the federal trial courts to either join separate actions for hearing or trial or simply consolidate them into a single proceeding, so long as they have a common question of law or fact. To consolidate actions means to take what the plaintiffs filed as separate cases and bring them together into a single case, literally opening a new court file, assigning a new case number, and requiring all parties in the separate cases to henceforth conduct their previously separate proceedings in the new case as if they had filed it together as multiple parties. Notice that Rule 42(a) does not require that separate actions arise out of the same transaction or occurrence, or series of transactions or occurrences, for the trial court to join them for hearing or trial or consolidate them. Rule 42(a) consolidation may thus occur even where the plaintiffs could not have originally joined their separate actions in a single multiple-plaintiff proceeding. You can see from the three discrimination cases *Mosley v. General Motors Corp., Howard Motor Co. v. Swint,* and *Henderson v. AT&T* immediately above that although the plaintiffs have the first opportunity to choose the most advantageous joinder or non-joinder of parties, defendants can challenge that joinder, and the court has the means to sever or join parties or join or consolidate actions. The parties make their best effort, but the court has the last laugh. Read Rule 42 on consolidation before moving on to compulsory joinder.

FED. R. CIV. P. 42. Consolidation; Separate Trials
(a) CONSOLIDATION. If actions before the court involve a common question of law or fact, the court may:
(1) join for hearing or trial any or all matters at issue in the actions;
(2) consolidate the actions; or
(3) issue any other orders to avoid unnecessary cost or delay.
(b) SEPARATE TRIALS. For convenience, to avoid prejudice, or to expedite and economize, the court may order a separate trial of one or more separate issues, claims, crossclaims, counterclaims, or third-party claims. When ordering a separate trial, the court must preserve any federal right to a jury trial.

---

2. Compulsory Joinder

As with joinder of claims, there are circumstances when parties must be joined. Unlike joinder-of-claims rules, the authority for compulsory joinder of parties in the federal courts is within the *Federal Rules of Civil Procedure*. Recall that joinder of claims is sometimes compulsory only in the sense that the failure to join those claims would bar the party who holds them from asserting them in a subsequent proceeding. Common-law claim-preclusion rules would bar those non-pled claims and counterclaims in subsequent proceedings. The law makes joinder of parties compulsory in some cases not in the sense that the law would bar those claims against them in subsequent proceedings but instead that the court must order them joined, voluntarily or involuntarily. Compulsory joinder of parties means what it says, that the court will permit (if they are willing) or compel (if they are unwilling) *necessary* parties to join the proceeding, or dismiss the action if joinder is not feasible and they are *indispensable* parties. If the court can join them, then the proceeding will not continue without them. If the court cannot join them, then it may dismiss the proceeding if it determines them to be indispensable. Both state and federal courts follow compulsory joinder rules. *See, e.g.,* MICH. CT. RULE 2.205; N.Y. CIVIL PRAC. LAW & RULES §1001. FED. R. CIV. P. 19 addresses compulsory joinder in the federal courts. State-court compulsory-joinder rules are similar in form and content, although as is true with other rules of procedure, the federal courts' limited jurisdiction implicates additional considerations. Rule 19(a)(1) relieves the federal trial court from joining a party when doing so would deprive the court of subject-matter jurisdiction, meaning when it would destroy diversity of citizenship.

The important question remains as to when joinder of a party is compulsory. Rule 19(a) provides three different standards for compulsory joinder of parties in the federal courts. Rule 19(a)(1)(A) provides for compulsory joinder of a party without whom the trial court "cannot accord complete relief among existing parties… ." Incomplete relief is one ground for compulsory joinder. If the relief that the court can order would not resolve the dispute, the court must join the party whose presence would accord complete relief under the court's orders. Rule 19(a)(1)(B) provides two other grounds for compulsory joinder, when relief among existing parties may "as a practical matter impair or impede" the non-party's ability to protect an interest in the action's subject matter or "leave an existing party subject to a substantial risk of" multiple or inconsistent obligations. Impaired rights or inconsistent obligations are other grounds for compulsory joinder. Read Rule 19 with an eye toward the options of the parties and court when the plaintiff has not joined a necessary or indispensable party. Then consider a Supreme Court case on its application.

FED. R. CIV. P. 19. Required Joinder of Parties
(a) PERSONS REQUIRED TO BE JOINED IF FEASIBLE.
(1) *Required Party.* A person who is subject to service of process and whose joinder will not deprive the court of subject-matter jurisdiction must be joined as a party if:
(A) in that person's absence, the court cannot accord complete relief among existing parties; or
(B) that person claims an interest relating to the subject of the action and is so situated that disposing of the action in the person's absence may:
(i) as a practical matter impair or impede the person's ability to protect the interest; or
(ii) leave an existing party subject to a substantial risk of incurring double, multiple, or otherwise inconsistent obligations because of the interest.
(2) *Joinder by Court Order.* If a person has not been joined as required, the court must order that the person be made a party. A person who refuses to join as a plaintiff may be made either a defendant or, in a proper case, an involuntary plaintiff.
(3) *Venue.* If a joined party objects to venue and the joinder would make venue improper, the court must dismiss that party.
(b) WHEN JOINDER IS NOT FEASIBLE. If a person who is required to be joined if feasible cannot be joined, the court must determine whether, in equity and good conscience, the action should proceed among the existing parties or should be dismissed. The factors for the court to consider include:
(1) the extent to which a judgment rendered in the person's absence might prejudice that person or the existing parties;
(2) the extent to which any prejudice could be lessened or avoided by:
(A) protective provisions in the judgment;
(B) shaping the relief; or
(C) other measures;
(3) whether a judgment rendered in the person's absence would be adequate; and
(4) whether the plaintiff would have an adequate remedy if the action were dismissed for nonjoinder.
(c) PLEADING THE REASONS FOR NONJOINDER. When asserting a claim for relief, a party must state:
(1) the name, if known, of any person who is required to be joined if feasible but is not joined; and
(2) the reasons for not joining that person.
(d) EXCEPTION FOR CLASS ACTIONS. This rule is subject to Rule 23.

Temple v. Synthes Corp.,

United States Supreme Court
498 U.S. 5, rehg. denied, 498 U.S. 1092 (1990)

PER CURIAM.

Petitioner Temple, a Mississippi resident, underwent surgery in October 1986 in which a "plate and screw device" was implanted in his lower spine. The device was manufactured by respondent Synthes Corp., Ltd. (U.S.A.) (Synthes), a Pennsylvania corporation. Dr. S. Henry LaRocca performed the surgery at St. Charles General Hospital in New Orleans, Louisiana. Following surgery, the device's screws broke off inside Temple's back.

Temple filed suit against Synthes in the United States District Court for the Eastern District of Louisiana. The suit, which rested on diversity jurisdiction, alleged defective design and manufacture of the device. At the same time, Temple filed a state administrative proceeding against Dr. LaRocca and the hospital for malpractice and negligence. At the conclusion of the administrative proceeding, Temple filed suit against the doctor and the hospital in Louisiana state court.

Synthes did not attempt to bring the doctor and the hospital into the federal action by means of a third-party complaint, as provided in Federal Rule of Civil Procedure 14(a). Instead, Synthes filed a motion to dismiss Temple's federal suit for failure to join necessary parties pursuant to Federal Rule of Civil Procedure 19. Following a hearing, the District Court ordered Temple to join the doctor and the hospital as defendants within 20 days or risk dismissal of the lawsuit. According to the court, the most significant reason for requiring joinder was the interest of judicial economy. [C] The court relied on this Court's decision in Provident Tradesmens Bank & Trust Co. v. Patterson, 390 U.S. 102[, 111] (1968), wherein we recognized that one focus of Rule 19 is "the interest of the courts and the public in complete, consistent, and efficient settlement of controversies." [C] When Temple failed to join the doctor and the hospital, the court dismissed the suit with prejudice.

Temple appealed, and the United States Court of Appeals for the Fifth Circuit affirmed. [C] The court deemed it "obviously prejudicial to the defendants to have the separate litigations being carried on," because Synthes' defense might be that the plate was not defective but that the doctor and the hospital were negligent, while the doctor and the hospital, on the other hand, might claim that they were not negligent but that the plate was defective. [C] The Court of Appeals found that the claims overlapped and that the District Court therefore had not abused its discretion in ordering joinder under Rule 19. A petition for rehearing was denied.

In his petition for certiorari to this Court, Temple contends that it was error to label joint tortfeasors as indispensable parties under Rule 19(b) and to dismiss the lawsuit with prejudice for failure to join those parties. We agree. Synthes does not deny that it, the doctor, and the hospital are potential joint tortfeasors. It has long been the rule that it is not necessary for all joint tortfeasors to be named as defendants in a single lawsuit. See Lawlor v. National Screen Service Corp., 349 U.S. 322, 329-330[] (1955); Bigelow v. Old Dominion Copper Mining & Smelting Co., 225 U.S. 111, 132[] (1912). [C] Nothing in the 1966 revision of Rule 19 changed that principle. See *Provident Bank, supra,* 390 U.S. at 116-117n. 12[]. The Advisory Committee Notes to Rule 19(a) explicitly state that "a tortfeasor with the usual 'joint-and-several' liability is merely a permissive party to an action against another with like liability." [C] There is nothing in Louisiana tort law to the contrary. [Cc].

The opinion in *Provident Bank, supra,* does speak of the public interest in limiting multiple litigation, but that case is not controlling here. There, the estate of a tort victim brought a declaratory judgment action against an insurance company. We assumed that the policyholder was a person "who, under §(a), should be 'joined if feasible.'" 390 U.S. at 108[], and went on to discuss the appropriate analysis under Rule 19(b), because the policyholder could not be joined without destroying diversity. *Id.,* at 109-116[]. After examining the factors set forth in Rule 19(b), we determined that the action could proceed without the policyholder; he therefore was not an indispensable party whose absence required dismissal of the suit. [C]

Here, no inquiry under Rule 19(b) is necessary, because the threshold requirements of Rule 19(a) have not been satisfied. As potential joint tortfeasors with Synthes, Dr. LaRocca and the hospital were merely permissive parties. The Court of Appeals erred by failing to hold that the District Court abused its discretion in ordering them joined as defendants and in dismissing the action when Temple failed to comply with the court's order. For these reasons, we grant the petition for certiorari, reverse the judgment of the Court of Appeals for the Fifth Circuit, and remand for further proceedings consistent with this opinion.

It is so ordered.

Skill

The final skill that law students learn when reading cases is to discern trends or tendencies. Lawyers will read a single case for its holding or a collection of cases to understand the elements of a claim or how courts define a rule's standard. These questions are determinate, having clear answers. Yet lawyers also read cases for their indeterminacies. A single case may yield an unresolved or uneasily resolved issue more so than a definite holding. Lawyers know how to recognize and employ an issue (for instance, to question and soften an opposing party's position, injecting enough uncertainty to promote compromise resolution) just as much as they employ rules and holdings. Lawyers also know how to read cases to recognize a trend that the law may be moving in another direction and for a tendency of courts to rule a certain way in a certain situation. Lawyers use trends and tendencies constantly when deciding whether to file claims, join parties, file motions, and make arguments.

INQUIRY

Necessary Parties. The fact that the Supreme Court published *Temple v. Synthes Corp.* as a per curiam opinion (generally meaning a unanimous opinion so clear in principle that it does not warrant individual authorship) sets the tone for applying the incomplete-relief, impaired-rights, or inconsistent-obligations standards of FED. R. CIV. P. 19(a). The federal courts will interpret Rule 19(a) narrowly to find fewer necessary parties than Rule 19(a) might suggest if read broadly. What policy compelled the Supreme Court to that conclusion in *Temple v. Synthes Corp.*? The unarticulated policy presumably has to do with party autonomy. It is the plaintiff's cause, not the court's. The plaintiff should have the liberty of determining its contours within reasonable bounds. The trial court should not judge a party to be necessary for joinder unless Rule 19(a)'s factors compel the trial court to that conclusion. The circumstance that a defendant might be able to blame another, shifting some part or all of the loss, is clearly not sufficient to make that other a compulsory party. That the case might establish precedent controlling another case is also clearly not enough. *See* Janney Montgomery Scott, Inc. v. Shepard Niles, Inc., 11 F.3d 399, 407 (3d Cir. 1993). The standards require something more in the nature of connected property or contract rights or obligations. Joint ownership of real or personal property is a good example, where the case would affect ownership, and all joint owners would be necessary parties. Other examples include multiple claimants to an insurance policy or other limited fund that the case will deplete and joint parties to a contract that the case will enforce or void. Compulsory joinder can arise as an issue under many different circumstances. The case of *Wilbur v. Locke* excerpted below illustrates one of those other examples.

Feasibility. Before considering another case, though, recognize how the issue of non-joinder often arises. In a substantial percentage of these non-joinder cases, there is a reason why the plaintiff has not joined a party whom others might judge necessary to the action, and that reason is because joinder was not feasible. Often, the obstacle to joinder is that it would destroy diversity of citizenship. The plaintiff cannot join a defendant in a federal-court case resting on diversity jurisdiction if the defendant is domiciled, incorporated, or headquartered in the same state as the plaintiff. In other cases, the obstacle to joinder is the non-party's immunity from suit. Rule 19(a) states the rules for joinder when joinder is feasible. Rule 19(b) states the rules for joinder when joinder is not feasible for one of these reasons or for other reasons. What must the trial court do when a party is necessary to the action but the court cannot join the party? Rule 19(b) treats the question as one of whether the necessary party is indispensable to the action, that is, whether the trial court must dismiss the action in the non-party's absence. (Rule 19 actually used the term *indispensable* up until its 2007 amendment. Much of the applicable case law reflects that term which still makes sensible shorthand.) Feasibility of joinder is important because it may mean the difference between whether the action can go forward at all. Some parties who would be necessary if the court could join them are indispensable when the court cannot, meaning the court must dismiss, while other parties who would be necessary if the court could join them are not indispensable when the court cannot, meaning the action will continue.

Indispensable Parties. Before Rule 19's adoption, the Supreme Court defined who was necessary and who was indispensable based on whether their substantive rights were joint or severable. *See* Shields v. Barrow, 58 U.S. (17 How.) 130 (1854). Rule 19(b) replaced that categorical approach focusing on the non-parties rights with a functional approach focused on the effects of the trial court's proceeding or not proceeding. The four factors of Rule 19(b) define when the trial court may dismiss a case for non-joinder of an indispensable party. The trial court must consider Rule 19(b)'s four factors of whether judgment would be prejudicial, whether protective provisions in the judgment can lessen that prejudice, the adequacy of judgment without the person as a party, and available remedies for the plaintiff if the trial court dismisses instead of proceeding to judgment. The Supreme Court applied an earlier version of Rule 19(b) in Provident Tradesmens Bank & Trust Co. v. Patterson, 390 U.S. 102 (1968), cited in *Temple v. Synthes Corp., supra.* The Supreme Court in *Provident Tradesmens Bank & Trust Co. v. Patterson* made a detailed analysis of the workings of Rule 19(b)'s factors, reversing the Circuit Court of Appeals' holding that a non-party was indispensable but remanding for redetermination by the federal district court. The import of that decision was clearly to require the lower courts to take a flexible and functional approach, eschewing categorical reasoning.

Equity and Conscience. The first Rule 19(b) factor on whether a judgment would prejudice a non-party is certainly the logical starting point. *See* Helzberg's Diamond Shops, Inc. v. Valley West Des Moines Shopping Ctr., 564 F.2d 816 (8th Cir. 1977) (no Rule 19(b) dismissal where no prejudice to non-party because case would prejudice none of its rights). Rule 19(b) exhorts the federal trial courts to use "equity and good conscience" when determining whether to dismiss for non-joinder of an indispensable party. Why the special exhortation, when presumably trial judges always act equitably while exercising good conscience? The exhortation to equity and good conscience suggests more than the usual discretion in fashioning remedies. *See* Merrill Lynch, Inc. v. ENC

Corp., 464 F.3d 885, 891 (9th Cir. 2006) (exhortation is meant to emphasize flexibility of solutions). It also reinforces the functional and case-specific nature of the determination whether to proceed at all. As you read the following case for the orderly way in which it analyzes the compulsory-joinder issue, evaluate whether it avoids inflexible categories and instead follows a functional approach.

Wilbur v. Locke,

United States Court of Appeals for the Ninth Circuit
423 F.3d 1101 (2005)

WALLACE, Senior Circuit Judge:

The plaintiffs sought relief from an anticipated contract between the State of Washington and the Swinomish Indian Tribe (Tribe) regarding taxation of cigarette sales by Indian retailers. The district court held that the Tax Injunction Act (TIA), 28 U.S.C. §1341, barred the action and dismissed it. ... We affirm, but on grounds different from the district court.

I.

Washington law authorizes the Governor "to enter into contracts concerning the sale of cigarettes" with certain Indian tribes. [C] Such contracts must "provide for a tribal cigarette tax in lieu of all state cigarette taxes and state and local sales and use taxes on sales of cigarettes in Indian country by Indian retailers," but the tribe may "allow an exemption for sales to tribal members." [C] The contracts must also "provide that the tribal cigarette tax rate be one hundred percent of the state cigarette and state and local sales and use taxes within three years of enacting the tribal tax." [C] Tax revenue retained by a tribe must be used for certain statutorily defined "essential government services." [C] Thus, cigarette tax contracts must provide that the state will not impose any tax, and must require a tribe to collect taxes effectively equal to the previously imposed state taxes, and use the revenue for essential government services. In addition, cigarette tax contracts must include a number of provisions regulating Indian retailers' activities, such as provisions requiring tax stamps, governing the purchase of cigarettes by retailers, and ensuring compliance. [C]

Marvin Wilbur, Jr., Marvin Wilbur, Sr., and Joan Wilbur are enrolled members of the Tribe and the operators of a retail store located on trust land within the Swinomish Indian Reservation. In April 2003, the Wilburs filed an action against various Washington officials and the Department of Revenue (State) alleging that the State and the Tribe were negotiating a cigarette tax contract. They alleged that the statutes governing cigarette tax contracts and the proposed agreement violated the Indian Commerce Clause, U.S. Const. art. I, §8, cl. 3, the Sherman Antitrust Act, 15 U.S.C. §§7-276, the Treaty of Point Elliot, 12 Stat. 927 (Jan. 22, 1855), and a host of other constitutional and statutory provisions. The Tribe was not named as a defendant.

The complaint requested, among other relief, ... an injunction "preventing the Defendants from enforcing any provision of the statutes or contracting in any way with the Swinomish Tribe or any person or entity regarding a cigarette tax on any cigarettes to be received or sold by Indian-owned retail businesses within the exterior boundaries of the Swinomish Reservation"; and a "declaration that any agreement or contract entered into by the Swinomish Tribe with Defendants is invalid when attempted to be imposed or any way applied to Plaintiffs."

The State filed a motion to dismiss the Wilburs' complaint, arguing that the Wilburs lacked standing, that the TIA and the Eleventh Amendment barred the Wilburs' action, that the Tribe was an indispensable party, and that the complaint failed to state a claim for which relief could be granted. While that motion was pending, the State and the Tribe executed a cigarette tax contract (Compact). ... [The court first resolved jurisdictional issues in the Wilburs' favor.]

VII.

With these jurisdictional issues behind us, we can now address the Rule 19 question. In the district court, the State argued that the action should be dismissed pursuant to Federal Rule of Civil Procedure 12(b)(7) because the Tribe is an indispensable party pursuant to Rule 19. The district court held that the Tribe was not a necessary party. We generally review for an abuse of discretion the district court's decision regarding joinder, but review de novo any legal conclusions underlying that decision. [C]

Application of Rule 19 involves "three successive inquiries"[:]

> First, the court must determine whether a nonparty should be joined under Rule 19(a). We and other courts use the term "necessary" to describe those "[p]ersons to [b]e [j]oined if[f]easible." ...
>
> If an absentee is a necessary party under Rule 19(a), the second stage is for the court to determine whether it is feasible to order that the absentee be joined. ...
>
> Finally, if joinder is not feasible, the court must determine at the third stage whether the case can proceed without the absentee, or whether the absentee is an "indispensable party" such that the action must be dismissed. ... Rule 19 uses "the word 'indispensable' only in a conclusory sense, that is, a person is 'regarded as indispensable' when he cannot be made a party and, upon consideration of the factors [in Rule 19(b)], it is determined that in his absence it would be preferable to dismiss the action, rather than to retain it." [EEOC v. Peabody W. Coal Co., 400 F.3d 774, 779-780 (9th Cir. 2005) (citations omitted.]

We address each of these inquiries in turn.

A.

The State argues that the Tribe is a "necessary" party because the Tribe "claims an interest relating to the subject of the action and is so situated that the disposition of the action in the [Tribe's] absence may ... as a practical matter impair or impede the [Tribe's] ability to protect that interest." Fed. R. Civ. P. 19(a)(2)(i). In deciding whether Rule 19(a)(2)(i) is satisfied, we "must determine whether the absent party has a *legally protected interest* in the suit," and, if so, whether "that interest will be *impaired or impeded* by the suit." Makah Indian Tribe v. Verity, 910 F.2d 555, 558 (9th Cir. 1990). ...

Here, the Wilburs must establish the illegality of the Compact in order to succeed on the merits of any of their claims. Because the Tribe has an interest in retaining the rights granted by the Compact, the requirement of a "legally protected" interest is satisfied. [C]

In addition, disposition of this action in the Tribe's absence may impair or impede the Tribe's ability to protect its interest. If the Compact is invalidated, the State would be released from its contractual obligation to refrain from taxing cigarette sales by Indian retailers to non-Indians and non-Tribe members. If the State resumed imposing such taxes, the Tribe would be forced to choose between double-taxing its own retailers or foregoing tax revenue for essential government services. Thus, "the instant litigation threatens to impair the [Tribe's] contractual interests, and ... its fundamental economic relationship with [the State]." [C] ...

B.

We now address whether joinder is feasible. "Federally recognized Indian tribes enjoy sovereign immunity from suit, and may not be sued absent an express and unequivocal waiver of immunity by the tribe or abrogation of tribal immunity by Congress." [C] The Wilburs offer no persuasive argument that the Tribe's immunity has either been waived or abrogated. Accordingly, joinder is not feasible. [C]

C.

We now address "whether in equity and good conscience the action should proceed among the parties before it, or should be dismissed, the absent person being thus regarded as indispensable." Fed. R. Civ. P. 19(b). In making this determination, we consider four issues:

> first, to what extent a judgment rendered in the person's absence might be prejudicial to the person or those already parties; second, the extent to which, by protective provisions in the judgment, by the shaping of relief, or other measures, the prejudice can be lessened or avoided; third, whether a judgment rendered in the person's absence will be adequate; fourth, whether the plaintiff will have an adequate remedy if the action is dismissed for nonjoinder. *Id.*

The first three tests point toward dismissal. "[T]he first factor of prejudice, insofar as it focuses on the absent party, largely duplicates the consideration that made a party necessary under Rule 19(a): a protectible interest that will be impaired or impeded by the party's absence." [Cc] If the Compact is invalidated in the Tribe's absence, the Tribe will be prejudiced to a great extent.

As to the second test, it is not possible to lessen or avoid any prejudice by the shaping of relief or protective provisions in the judgment. The Wilburs want nothing less than nullification of the Compact. If they succeed, the Tribe will be deprived of the contractual benefits for which it bargained. Moreover, although the Wilburs stress that the Tribe could have intervened if it wished, "we cannot require the [Tribe] to intervene to minimize the potential prejudice, since intervention would require a waiver of sovereign immunity." [C]

The third test, whether a judgment rendered in the Tribe's absence will be adequate, also "does not favor the plaintiffs," because if the Compact is invalidated, the Tribe's "protectible interests [would be] impaired." [Cc]

The fourth test supports proceeding in the Tribe's absence, as it is unclear whether the Wilburs will have an adequate remedy if the action is dismissed. Nonetheless, even assuming the Wilburs have no other forum in which to pursue a remedy, we have "regularly held that the tribal interest in immunity overcomes the lack of an alternative remedy or forum for the plaintiffs." [Cc] Thus, a balance of the four tests in Rule 19(b) supports dismissal of the action. ...

DISMISSAL AFFIRMED.

Republic of the Philippines v. Pimentel,

United States Supreme Court
553 U.S. 851 (2008)

Justice KENNEDY delivered the opinion of the Court.

This case turns on the interpretation and proper application of Rule 19 of the Federal Rules of Civil Procedure and requires us to address the Rule's operation in the context of foreign sovereign immunity.

This interpleader action was commenced to determine the ownership of property allegedly stolen by Ferdinand Marcos when he was the President of the Republic of the Philippines. Two entities named in the suit invoked sovereign immunity. They are the Republic of the Philippines and the Philippine Presidential Commission on Good Governance, referred to in turn as the Republic and the Commission. They were dismissed, but the interpleader action proceeded to judgment over their objection. Together with two parties who remained in the suit, the Republic and the Commission now insist it was [the district and circuit courts'] error to allow the litigation to proceed. Under Rule 19, they contend, the action should have been dismissed once it became clear they could not be joined as parties without their consent. …

In 1972, Ferdinand Marcos, then President of the Republic, incorporated Arelma, S.A. (Arelma), under Panamanian law. Around the same time, Arelma opened a brokerage account with Merrill Lynch, Pierce, Fenner & Smith Inc. (Merrill Lynch) in New York, in which it deposited $2 million. As of the year 2000, the account had grown to approximately $35 million.

Alleged crimes and misfeasance by Marcos during his presidency became the subject of worldwide attention and protest. A class action by and on behalf of some 9,539 of his human rights victims was filed against Marcos and his estate, among others. The class action was tried in the United States District Court for the District of Hawaii and resulted in a nearly $2 billion judgment for the class. [C] We refer to that litigation as the Pimentel case and to its class members as the Pimentel class. …

The Pimentel class claims a right to enforce its judgment by attaching the Arelma assets held by Merrill Lynch. The Republic and the Commission claim a right to the assets under a 1955 Philippine law providing that property derived from the misuse of public office is forfeited to the Republic from the moment of misappropriation. [C]

After Marcos fled the Philippines in 1986, the Commission was created to recover any property he wrongfully took. … In 1991, the Commission asked the Sandiganbayan, a Philippine court of special jurisdiction over corruption cases, to declare forfeited to the Republic any property Marcos had obtained through misuse of his office. That litigation is still pending in the Sandiganbayan. …

The Republic and the Commission requested that Merrill Lynch … transfer the Arelma assets to an escrow account at [the Philippine National Bank] PNB. Merrill Lynch did not do so. Facing claims from various Marcos creditors, including the Pimentel class, Merrill Lynch instead filed an interpleader action under 28 U.S.C. §1335. The named defendants in the interpleader action were, among others, the Republic and the Commission, Arelma, PNB, and the Pimentel class (the respondents here). …

After being named as defendants in the interpleader action, the Republic and the Commission asserted sovereign immunity under the Foreign Sovereign Immunities Act of 1976 (FSIA), 28 U.S.C. §1604. They moved to dismiss pursuant to Rule 19(b), based on the premise that the action could not proceed without them. Arelma and PNB also moved to dismiss pursuant to Rule 19(b). …

Subdivision (a) of Rule 19 states the principles that determine when persons or entities must be joined in a suit. The Rule instructs that nonjoinder even of a required person does not always result in dismissal. Subdivision (a) opens by noting that it addresses joinder "if feasible." Where joinder is not feasible, the question whether the action should proceed turns on the factors outlined in subdivision (b). … [T]he determination whether to proceed will turn upon factors that are case specific, which is consistent with a Rule based on equitable considerations. This is also consistent with the fact that the determination of who may, or must, be parties to a suit has consequences for the persons and entities affected by the judgment; for the judicial system and its interest in the integrity of its processes and the respect accorded to its decrees; and for society and its concern for the fair and prompt resolution of disputes. [C] For these reasons, the issue of joinder can be complex, and determinations are case specific. [C] …

… The Republic and the Commission are required entities because "[w]ithout [them] as parties in this interpleader action, their interests in the subject matter are not protected." [C] …

[The Supreme Court began by addressing the first of Rule 19(b)'s four factors, which is the prejudice to absent and present parties.]

Comity and dignity interests take concrete form in this case. The claims of the Republic and the Commission arise from events of historical and political significance for the Republic and its people. The Republic and the Commission have a unique interest in resolving the ownership of or claims to the Arelma assets and in determining if, and how, the assets should be used to compensate those persons who suffered grievous injury under Marcos. There is a comity interest in allowing a foreign state to use its own courts for a dispute if it has a right to do so. The dignity of a foreign state is not enhanced if other nations bypass its courts without right or good cause. Then, too, there is the more specific affront that could result to the Republic and the Commission if property they claim is seized by the decree of a foreign court. Cf. Republic of Mexico v. Hoffman, 324 U.S. 30, 35-36[] (1945) (pre-FSIA, common-law doctrine dictated that courts defer to executive determination of immunity because "[t]he judicial seizure" of the property of a friendly state may be regarded as "an affront to its dignity and may ... affect our relations with it"). …

As explained above, the decision to proceed in the absence of the Republic and the Commission ignored the substantial prejudice those entities likely would incur. This most directly implicates Rule 19(b)'s first factor, which directs consideration of prejudice both to absent persons and those who are parties. We have discussed the absent entities. As to existing parties, we do not discount the Pimentel class' interest in recovering damages it was awarded pursuant to a judgment. Furthermore, combating public corruption is a significant international policy. The policy is manifested in treaties providing for international cooperation in recovering forfeited assets. [Cc] This policy does support the interest of the Pimentel class in recovering damages awarded to it.

But it also underscores the important comity concerns implicated by the Republic and the Commission in asserting foreign sovereign immunity. ...

As to the second Rule 19(b) factor—the extent to which any prejudice could be lessened or avoided by relief or measures alternative to dismissal, Fed. Rule Civ. Proc. 19(b)(2)—there is no substantial argument to allow the action to proceed. No alternative remedies or forms of relief have been proposed to us or appear to be available. [C] If the Marcos estate did not own the assets, or if the Republic owns them now, the claim of the Pimentel class likely fails; and in all events, if there are equally valid but competing claims, that too would require adjudication in a case where the Republic and the Commission are parties. [Cc] ...

As to the third Rule 19(b) factor—whether a judgment rendered without the absent party would be adequate, Fed. Rule Civ. Proc. 19(b)(3)—the Court of Appeals understood "adequacy" to refer to satisfaction of the Pimentel class' claims. But adequacy refers to the "public stake in settling disputes by wholes, whenever possible." [C] ... Going forward with the action without the Republic and the Commission would not further the public interest in settling the dispute as a whole because the Republic and the Commission would not be bound by the judgment in an action where they were not parties. ...

As to the fourth Rule 19(b) factor—whether the plaintiff would have an adequate remedy if the action were dismissed for nonjoinder, Fed. Rule Civ. Proc. 19(b)(4)—the Court of Appeals made much of what it considered the tort victims' lack of an alternative forum should this action be dismissed. This seems to assume the plaintiff in this interpleader action was the Pimentel class. It is Merrill Lynch, however, that has the statutory status of plaintiff as the stakeholder in the interpleader action. ...

... A dismissal of the action on the ground of nonjoinder ... will protect Merrill Lynch in some respects. That disposition will not provide Merrill Lynch with a judgment determining the party entitled to the assets, but it likely would provide Merrill Lynch with an effective defense against piecemeal litigation and inconsistent, conflicting judgments. As matters presently stand, in any later suit against it Merrill Lynch may seek to join the Republic and the Commission and have the action dismissed under Rule 19(b) should they again assert sovereign immunity. Dismissal for nonjoinder to some extent will serve the purpose of interpleader, which is to prevent a stakeholder from having to pay two or more parties for one claim.

Any prejudice to Merrill Lynch in this regard is outweighed by prejudice to the absent entities invoking sovereign immunity. Dismissal under Rule 19(b) will mean, in some instances, that plaintiffs will be left without a forum for definitive resolution of their claims. But that result is contemplated under the doctrine of foreign sovereign immunity. [C] ...

... This leaves the Pimentel class, which has waited for years now to be compensated for grievous wrongs, with no immediate way to recover on its judgment against Marcos. And it leaves Merrill Lynch, the stakeholder, without a judgment.

The balance of equities may change in due course. One relevant change may occur if it appears that the Sandiganbayan cannot or will not issue its ruling within a reasonable period of time. Other changes could result when and if there is a ruling. If the Sandiganbayan rules that the Republic and the Commission have no right to the assets, their claims in some later interpleader suit would be less substantial than they are now. If the ruling is that the Republic and the Commission own the assets, then they may seek to enforce a judgment in our courts; or consent to become parties in an interpleader suit, where their claims could be considered; or file in some other forum if they can obtain jurisdiction over the relevant persons. We do note that if Merrill Lynch, or other parties, elect to commence further litigation in light of changed circumstances, it would not be necessary to file the new action in the District Court where this action arose, provided venue and jurisdictional requirements are satisfied elsewhere. The present action, however, may not proceed.

The judgment of the Court of Appeals for the Ninth Circuit is reversed, and the case is remanded with instructions to order the District Court to dismiss the interpleader action.

It is so ordered.

Justice STEVENS, concurring in part and dissenting in part. …

I am persuaded that the Court's judgment today represents a more "inflexible approach" than the Rule contemplates. [C] All parties have an interest in the prompt resolution of the disposition of the Arelma assets. A remand would allow a new judge to handle the matter in an expeditious fashion rather than requiring a brand new proceeding. The Court suggests that Merrill Lynch may file in another District Court—presumably in New York—if it seeks to commence further litigation. [C] While this solution would put the matter before another District Judge, it requires the initiation of a new proceeding that may unnecessarily delay the final resolution.

Accordingly, I respectfully dissent.

Justice SOUTER, concurring in part and dissenting in part.

… I differ as to relief because a conclusion of the matter pending before the Sandiganbayan may simplify the issues raised in this case and render one disposition or another more clearly correct. I would therefore vacate the judgment and remand for a stay of proceedings for a reasonable time to await a decree of the Philippine court. …

Biography

Solo practitioner Sherry Broder of the Honolulu, Hawaii Law Offices of Sherry P. Broder was one of the lawyers representing the Pimentel class in the above Supreme Court case. She was a key part of a nationwide team of lawyers who represented victims tortured, and the estates of victims killed, under the Marcos regime. Their work resulted in a $2 billion verdict, what was then the largest civil trial verdict in the United States. Ms. Broder spent more than two decades on that civil litigation, finally helping to win the release in 2006 of $40 million to specific victims and their estates. The American Bar Association recognized Ms. Broder as Solo Practitioner of the Year, and the Hawaii State Bar Association made her its first woman president. Ms. Broder has won many other professional awards for her courageous work in civil litigation.

INQUIRY

Relief. This chapter addresses interpleader in a following section. The above *Republic of the Philippines v. Pimentel* and *Wilbur v. Locke* decisions show the hazard that plaintiffs face under Rule 19(b)—that the trial court's dismissal for nonjoinder may leave them with no remedy. Is that justice, to have a right without a remedy? *See* Extra Equipamentos E Exportacao Ltda. v. Case Corp., 361 F.3d 359, 361 (7th Cir. 2004) (whether the plaintiff has another remedy is one of the most important factors); Confederated Tribes of Chehalis Indian Reservation v Lujan, 928 F.2d 1496, 1505 (9th Cir. 1991) (fact of no alternative forum alone makes dismissal too severe). The last of the four Rule 19(b) factors is whether the plaintiff has an adequate remedy after dismissal for nonjoinder. Did *Republic of the Philippines v. Pimentel* and *Wilbur v. Locke* give that last factor adequate consideration, when, for instance, the Supreme Court recognized in the *Republic of the Philippines* case that human-rights-abuse victims might go uncompensated for "grievous wrongs"? The Supreme Court left the door open to a future action if the victims found no other recourse through the Philippine justice system but dismissed the current action. Do you now discern a trend or tendency as to whether the federal courts will find a non-party indispensable?

3. Third Parties

Sometimes, we are blamed for others' wrongs. Third-party practice enables a defendant to shift some or all of the liability that a plaintiff claims from the defendant to a third-party defendant. Compulsory joinder of parties, joinder-of-claim rules, and the ability of a defendant to counterclaim are not the only constraints on the plaintiff's right to determine the scope of a proceeding. While the plaintiff still has a relative advantage over the defendant in determining the scope of and alignment of parties within a proceeding, defendants have an additional opportunity to broaden that scope and change that alignment by bringing third parties into the case. FED. R. CIV. P. 14 states the rules for third-party practice in the federal district courts. State courts follow similar rules. The law refers to bringing in a third party as *impleader*. Impleader is not a broad but instead a limited right. Rule 14(a)(1) authorizes a defendant to act as a third-party plaintiff to bring into the case only a third-party defendant "who is or may be liable to it for all or part of the claim against it." Rule 14(a)(1) limits the defendant's right to add a third party to alleging the third-party defendant's liability for the liability of the defendant that the plaintiff has alleged. Rule 14(a)(1) also states the procedure and timetable for adding the third-party. A defense counsel will typically file the third-party complaint with the answer, when no leave to do so is required. Rule 14(a)(1) gives defendants an additional 14 days after answering within which to file a third-party complaint. It also permits a third-party complaint later than 14 days on motion and order. The practice in those instances, indicated by FED. R. CIV. P. Form 41, is to include the proposed third-party complaint with the motion justifying its late filing. Real Rule 14, review the simple Form 41, and consider the case that follows to gain a sense of third-party practice and the issues it raises.

Fed. R. Civ. P. 14. Third-Party Practice

(a) WHEN A DEFENDING PARTY MAY BRING IN A THIRD PARTY.

(1) *Timing of the Summons and Complaint.* A defending party may, as third-party plaintiff, serve a summons and complaint on a nonparty who is or may be liable to it for all or part of the claim against it. But the third-party plaintiff must, by motion, obtain the court's leave if it files the third-party complaint more than 14 days after serving its original answer.

(2) *Third-Party Defendant's Claims and Defenses.* The person served with the summons and third-party complaint—the ''third-party defendant'':

(A) must assert any defense against the third-party plaintiff's claim under Rule 12;

(B) must assert any counterclaim against the third-party plaintiff under Rule 13(a), and may assert any counterclaim against the third-party plaintiff under Rule 13(b) or any crossclaim against another third-party defendant under Rule 13(g);

(C) may assert against the plaintiff any defense that the third-party plaintiff has to the plaintiff's claim; and

(D) may also assert against the plaintiff any claim arising out of the transaction or occurrence that is the subject matter of the plaintiff's claim against the third-party plaintiff.

(3) *Plaintiff's Claims Against a Third-Party Defendant.* The plaintiff may assert against the third-party defendant any claim arising out of the transaction or occurrence that is the subject matter of the plaintiff's claim against the third-party plaintiff. The third-party defendant must then assert any defense under Rule 12 and any counterclaim under Rule 13(a), and may assert any counterclaim under Rule 13(b) or any crossclaim under Rule 13(g).

(4) *Motion to Strike, Sever, or Try Separately.* Any party may move to strike the third-party claim, to sever it, or to try it separately.

(5) *Third-Party Defendant's Claim Against a Nonparty.* A thirdparty defendant may proceed under this rule against a nonparty who is or may be liable to the third-party defendant for all or part of any claim against it.

(6) *Third-Party Complaint In Rem.* If it is within the admiralty or maritime jurisdiction, a third-party complaint may be in rem. In that event, a reference in this rule to the ''summons'' includes the warrant of arrest, and a reference to the defendant or third-party plaintiff includes, when appropriate, a person who asserts a right under Supplemental Rule C(6)(a)(i) in the property arrested.

(b) WHEN A PLAINTIFF MAY BRING IN A THIRD PARTY. When a claim is asserted against a plaintiff, the plaintiff may bring in a third party if this rule would allow a defendant to do so.

(c) ADMIRALTY OR MARITIME CLAIM.

(1) *Scope of Impleader.* If a plaintiff asserts an admiralty or maritime claim under Rule 9(h), the defendant or a person who asserts a right under Supplemental Rule C(6)(a)(i) may, as a third-party plaintiff, bring in a third-party defendant who may be wholly or partly liable—either to the plaintiff or to the third-party plaintiff—for remedy over, contribution, or otherwise on account of the same transaction, occurrence, or series of transactions or occurrences.

(2) *Defending Against a Demand for Judgment for the Plaintiff.* The third-party plaintiff may demand judgment in the plaintiff's favor against the third-party defendant. In that event, the third-party defendant must defend under Rule 12 against the plaintiff's claim as well as the third-party plaintiff's claim; and the action proceeds as if the plaintiff had sued both the third-party defendant and the third-party plaintiff.

Fed. R. Civ. P. Form 41. Motion to Bring in a Third-Party Defendant

(Caption--See Form 1.)

The defendant, as third-party plaintiff, moves for leave to serve on <u>*name*</u> a summons and third-party complaint, copies of which are attached.

(Date and sign--See Form 2.)

Price v. CTB, Inc.,

United States District Court for the Middle District of Alabama
168 F.Supp.2d 1299 (2001)

DE MENT, District Judge.

Before the court is Third Party Defendant Illinois Tool Work, Inc.'s ("ITW") Motion to Dismiss... [the claim of] Third Party Plaintiff Latco, Inc. ("Latco")... .

Latco, a building contractor, is an original defendant in the underlying action concerning the quality of its workmanship when it constructed chicken houses for various Alabama farmers. The causes of action against Latco include breach of the construction contract, fraudulent misrepresentation of the caliber of materials to be used, and negligence and wantonness in the construction. ... In the Third Party Complaint, Latco alleges that ITW, a nail manufacturer, defectively designed the nails used in the construction of the chicken houses. The specific causes of action include breach of warranty, violation of the Alabama Extended Manufacturer's Liability Doctrine, and common law indemnity. ITW argues that it was improperly impleaded under Rule 14 of the Federal Rules of Civil Procedure... .

Under Rule 14(a), a defendant may assert a claim against anyone not a party to the original action if that third party's liability is in some way dependent upon the outcome of the original action. [C] There is a limitation on this general statement, however. Even though it may arise out of the same general set of facts as the main claim, a third party claim will not be permitted when it is based upon a separate and independent claim. [C][fn] Rather, the third party liability must in some way be derivative of the original claim; a third party may be impleaded only when the original defendant is trying to pass all or part of the liability onto that third party. [C]

Latco argues that ITW is the prototypical third party defendant under Rule 14. It asserts that ITW can be found liable for the warranty surrounding its products if Latco is first found liable for faulty construction. Furthermore, insists Latco, this derivative liability merely involves a shift in the overall responsibility of the allegedly defective chicken houses. ITW contends, however, that because Rule 14 is merely a procedural rule, the propriety of its application depends upon the existence of a right to indemnity under the substantive law. ITW accurately states the law in this regard, [c], but its conclusion that there is no viable substantive claim under Alabama law is incorrect.

Conceding that Alabama does not recognize a right to contribution among joint tortfeasors, Latco directs the court's attention to the concept of implied contractual indemnity. Under this doctrine, Alabama courts recognize that a manufacturer of a product has impliedly agreed to indemnify the seller when 1) the seller is without fault, 2) the manufacturer is responsible, and 3) the seller has been required to pay a monetary judgment. [C] Under Latco's theory, should it be found liable for its construction of the chicken houses, it can demonstrate that the true fault lies with the nailguns and the nails manufactured by ITW.

... Illinois courts have applied the doctrine in similar cases, and the court finds no reason to believe that Alabama courts would interpret the common law principles in a different manner. ...

... The court finds that Alabama law provides Latco a cause of action under common law indemnity against ITW.

It must be noted, however, that, under Alabama law, the doctrine permits recovery only when the party to be indemnified is "without fault." [C] Whether, in fact, such a factual scenario will be proven at trial is irrelevant for present purposes. The only issue before the court is whether there exists a legal basis to implead ITW, not whether ITW is, in fact, liable to Latco. Since Rule 14 permits Latco to implead any party who "may be liable," Fed. R. Civ. P. 14(a), it follows that the court must permit development of the factual record so the extent of that liability may be determined. [Cc]

Furthermore, since Latco has established a basis upon which it may properly implead ITW, the court need not address the applicability of Rule 14 to the other claims in Latco's Third Party Complaint. It is well established that a properly impleaded claim may serve as an anchor for separate and independent claims under Rule 18(a). [Cc] In short, the court finds that Latco has properly impleaded ITW under Rule 14(a). ...

Accordingly, it is CONSIDERED and ORDERED that ITW's Motion To Dismiss be and the same is hereby DENIED.

INQUIRY

Derivative Liability. May a defendant implead a person who or entity that bears direct liability to the plaintiff but none to the defendant? Rule 14(a) makes it quite clear that a defendant may only add third parties who are liable *to the defendant* for all or part of the claim. The cases tend to say that the defendant's liability must be *derivative* of the liability of the third-party whom the defendant adds, or that the third-party defendant is *secondarily* liable to the defendant. *See* Watergate Landmark Condominium Unit Owners' Assoc. v. Wiss, Janey, Elstner Assoc., 117 F.R.D. 576, 578 (E.D. Va. 1987); Barab v. Menford, 98 F.R.D. 455, 456 (E.D. Pa. 1983). As the above *Price v. CTB, Inc.* case illustrates, a defendant's right to indemnity from a non-party is a common claim on which defendants add third parties. There is also authority for impleading third parties on claims for contribution, *see, e.g.,* Craigie v. General Motors Corp., 740 F.Supp. 353 (E.D. Pa. 1990), breach of warranty, *see, e.g.,* Altec, Inc. v. FWD Corp., 399 F.2d 860 (5th Cir. 1968), and subrogation, *see, e.g.,* Glens Falls Indem. Co. v. Atlantic Bldg. Corp., 199 F.2d 60 (4th Cir. 1952). The rule to keep in mind is that the defendant must seek to transfer all or part of its liability to the third party, not merely that the third party's liability arises out of the same transaction or occurrence.

Indemnity. Indemnity is the right of one who is liable to require another to pay for that liability. Insurance is the classic form of contractual indemnity (that the insurer has promised to pay for the defendant's liability), but indemnity clauses are common in other contracts such as between manufacturers and distributors or retailers. Common-law indemnity of the type alleged in *Price v. CTB, Inc., supra,* implies indemnity from a relationship in which the one owing indemnity introduced the wrong while the one receiving indemnity was held liable for it. What would a defendant do, then, when the defendant believes that the plaintiff has sued the wrong party and that someone else (other than the defendant) is liable *to the plaintiff*? Nothing forecloses the defendant from blaming a non-party. The "empty chair" defense, in which the defendant figuratively points blame toward the chair in which the non-party would have sat if the plaintiff had sued that non-party, is a relatively common argument. Can you see the tactical advantage to the defendant that the chair remains empty? In many instances, the plaintiff could have joined the non-party as a defendant if the plaintiff had so wished. Why do plaintiffs not join potentially liable non-parties as additional defendants? It makes little sense to add as a defendant an uncollectible person or entity.

Contribution. In addition to indemnity, contribution is another common ground on which defendants implead third parties. As your torts studies indicated, contribution is the right of one party to make another party pay its fair share of a joint liability. With the advent of comparative negligence and the allocation of fault among defendants, many jurisdictions have abolished contribution, as the above *Price v. CTB, Inc.* case illustrates. Other states still permit defendants to implead third-party defendants on contribution claims. *See, e.g.*, Bovis v. Crab Meadow Enterps., Ltd., 889 N.Y.S.2d 634 (N.Y. Sup. Ct. App. Div. 2009). Some states go so far as to permit the defendant to file a notice of non-party fault, following which the plaintiff may add the non-party as a defendant, or if the plaintiff does not add the non-party, then the trial court will apportion fault to the non-party. *See, e.g.,* FLA. STAT. §768.81(3); MICH. CT. RULE 2.112(K). Tort reform has introduced variety among the states in the way that state courts handle third-party practice.

Jurisdiction. States have the liberty of fashioning rules for third-party practice without concern for the limited subject-matter jurisdiction that federal courts face. In federal court, may a defendant implead under FED. R. CIV. P. 14 a third party whom the plaintiff could not have joined as a defendant because doing so would destroy diversity-of-citizenship jurisdiction? Recall from Chapter 4 that 28 U.S.C. §1367(a) authorizes supplemental jurisdiction for claims forming part of the same case or controversy. Defendants may implead third parties under Rule 14(a) without concern for federal-question or diversity-of-citizenship jurisdiction because §1367 grants supplemental jurisdiction. *See, e.g.,* Grimes v. Mazda North American Operations, 355 F.3d 566, 572 (6th Cir. 2004). Once a defendant impleads a third-party defendant, may a plaintiff use Rule 14(a)(3) to make a direct claim against that third-party defendant? If so, then you can readily see how easy it would be for parties to skirt the federal courts' limited jurisdiction. The plaintiff could then make the claim against the third-party defendant that the plaintiff could not have made without destroying diversity jurisdiction. In the following case, the Supreme Court rejected what the court then called ancillary jurisdiction and now calls supplemental jurisdiction for plaintiffs' third-party claims for which there is no jurisdictional basis. Congress later incorporated this bar into §1367(b), which states explicitly that the federal district courts do not have supplemental jurisdiction over claims by plaintiffs against persons made third parties under Rule 14. When the defendant brings in through the side door a third party whom the plaintiff could not bring in through the front door, the plaintiff has no recourse against that third party.

Owen Equipment & Erection Co. v. Kroger,

United States Supreme Court
437 U.S. 365 (1978)

Mr. Justice STEWART delivered the opinion of the Court. ...

In an action in which federal jurisdiction is based on diversity of citizenship, may the plaintiff assert a claim against a third-party defendant when there is no independent basis for federal jurisdiction over that claim? The Court of Appeals for the Eighth Circuit held in this case that such a claim is within the ancillary jurisdiction of the federal courts. ...

On January 18, 1972, James Kroger was electrocuted when the boom of a steel crane next to which he was walking came too close to a high-tension electric power line. The respondent (his widow, who is the administratrix of his estate) filed a wrongful-death action in the United States District Court ... against the Omaha Public Power District (OPPD). Her complaint alleged that OPPD's negligent construction, maintenance, and operation of the power line had caused Kroger's death. Federal jurisdiction was based on diversity of citizenship, since the respondent was a citizen of Iowa and OPPD was a Nebraska corporation.

OPPD then filed a third-party complaint pursuant to Fed. Rule Civ. Proc. 14(a)[fn] against the petitioner, Owen Equipment and Erection Co. (Owen), alleging that the crane was owned and operated by Owen, and that Owen's negligence had been the proximate cause of Kroger's death.[Footnote 3 here noted that OPPD relied on the state-law common-law right of contribution.] [OPPD was dismissed, and petitioner Kroger tried the case against Owen.] ...

... On the third day of trial, ... it was disclosed that the petitioner[Owen]'s principal place of business was in Iowa, not Nebraska,[fn] and that the petitioner and the respondent were thus both citizens of Iowa.[fn] The petitioner then moved to dismiss the complaint for lack of jurisdiction. The District Court ... denied the petitioner's motion to dismiss the complaint.

The judgment was affirmed on appeal. [C] The Court of Appeals held that ... the District Court had jurisdictional power, in its discretion, to adjudicate the respondent's claim against the petitioner because that claim arose from the "core of 'operative facts' giving rise to both [respondent's] claim against OPPD and OPPD's claim against Owen." [C] ...

It is undisputed that there was no independent basis of federal jurisdiction over the respondent's state-law tort action against the petitioner, since both are citizens of Iowa. And although Fed. Rule Civ. Proc. 14(a) permits a plaintiff to assert a claim against a third-party defendant, [c], it does not purport to say whether or not such a claim requires an independent basis of federal jurisdiction. ...

The relevant statute in this case, 28 U.S.C. §1332(a)(1), confers upon federal courts jurisdiction over "civil actions where the matter in controversy exceeds the sum or value of $10,000 ... and is between ... citizens of different States." This statute and its predecessors have consistently been held to require complete diversity of citizenship.[fn] That is, diversity jurisdiction does not exist unless *each* defendant is a citizen of a different State from *each* plaintiff. Over the years Congress has repeatedly re-enacted or amended the statute conferring diversity jurisdiction, leaving intact this rule of complete diversity.[fn] Whatever may have been the original purposes of diversity-of-citizenship jurisdiction,[fn] this subsequent history clearly demonstrates a congressional mandate that diversity jurisdiction is not to be available when any plaintiff is a citizen of the same State as any defendant. [C]

Thus it is clear that the respondent could not originally have brought suit in federal court naming Owen and OPPD as codefendants, since citizens of Iowa would have been on both sides of the litigation. Yet the identical lawsuit resulted when she [asserted a claim against Owen]. Complete diversity was destroyed just as surely as if she had sued Owen initially. In either situation, in the plain language of the statute, the "matter in controversy" could not be "between ... citizens of different States."

It is a fundamental precept that federal courts are courts of limited jurisdiction. The limits upon federal jurisdiction, whether imposed by the Constitution or by Congress, must be neither disregarded nor evaded. Yet under the reasoning of the Court of Appeals in this case, a plaintiff could defeat the statutory requirement of complete diversity by the simple expedient of suing only those defendants who were of diverse citizenship and waiting for them to implead nondiverse defendants.[fn] ...

... [T]he claim here arises in a setting quite different from the kinds of nonfederal claims that have been viewed in other cases as falling within the ancillary jurisdiction of the federal courts.

First, the nonfederal claim in this case was simply not ancillary to the federal one in the same sense that, for example, the impleader by a defendant of a third-party defendant always is. A third-party complaint depends at least in part upon the resolution of the primary lawsuit. [C] Its relation to the original complaint is thus not mere factual similarity but logical dependence. [C] The respondent's claim against the petitioner, however, was entirely separate from her original claim against OPPD, since the petitioner's liability to her depended not at all upon whether or not OPPD was also liable. Far from being an ancillary and dependent claim, it was a new and independent one.

Second, the nonfederal claim here was asserted by the plaintiff, who voluntarily chose to bring suit upon a state-law claim in a federal court. By contrast, ancillary jurisdiction typically involves claims by a defending party haled into court against his will, or by another person whose rights might be irretrievably lost unless he could assert them in an ongoing action in a federal court.[fn] A plaintiff cannot complain if ancillary jurisdiction does not encompass all of his possible claims in a case such as this one, since it is he who has chosen the federal rather than the state forum and must thus accept its limitations. ...

... [N]either the convenience of litigants nor considerations of judicial economy can suffice to justify extension of the doctrine of ancillary jurisdiction to a plaintiff's cause of action against a citizen of the same State in a diversity case. ... To allow the requirement of complete diversity to be circumvented as it was in this case would simply flout the congressional command.[fn]

Accordingly, the judgment of the Court of Appeals is reversed.

It is so ordered.

Mr. Justice WHITE, with whom Mr. Justice BRENNAN joins, dissenting.

... [I]t seems to me appropriate to view §1332 as requiring complete diversity only between the plaintiff and those parties he actually brings into the suit. Beyond that, I would hold that in a diversity case the District Court has power, both constitutional and statutory, to entertain all claims among the parties arising from the same nucleus of operative fact as the plaintiff's original, jurisdiction-conferring claim against the defendant. Accordingly, I dissent from the Court's disposition of the present case.

INQUIRY

Further Pleading. After the defendant serves the third-party defendant with the third-party complaint, Rule 14 in effect authorizes and requires the parties to proceed again under the usual pleading rules. The third-party defendant may answer, raise affirmative defenses of its own, counterclaim against the defendant, and make a direct claim against the plaintiff, or add other parties. Rule 14(a)(5) creates the prospect for a fourth party and beyond by allowing the third-party defendant to add non-parties. *See, e.g.,* Bank of India v. Trendi Sportswear, Inc., 239 F.3d 428 (2d Cir. 2000). Rule 14(a)(3) authorizes the plaintiff to claim against the third-party defendant, although it limits those claims to ones related to the plaintiff's claims against the defendant. Rule 14(a) impleader stands to broaden the scope of a proceeding so far as to make its resolution unwieldy. Parties can influence and trial courts control the scope of the proceeding to keep it within manageable limits. Rule 14(a)(4) authorizes a party to move, and thus the court to grant a motion, to strike or sever the third-party claim or to try it separately. *See, e.g.,* Kosters v. Seven-Up Co., 595 F.2d 347 (6th Cir. 1979) (affirming third-party claim's severance for separate trial). Also, parties do not have to pursue Rule 14 third-party claims but may instead pursue them in separate cases.

C. Interpleader

Sometimes, others' disputes catch us in the middle. Interpleader enables a person or entity to initiate civil litigation and then stand aside to let others resolve their disputes. Interpleader is a useful form of action that depends not on substantive law but instead on the intermediate position of the plaintiff who brings the interpleader action. To interplead is for a plaintiff to name as defendants two or more other persons or entities whose competing claims seek an asset held by the plaintiff. Interpleader is available to a person or entity facing claims that compete on contrary grounds for the same asset, not actions on consistent or multiple independent claims. *See* Trowbridge v. Prudential Ins. Co., 322 F.Supp. 190 (S.D. N.Y. 1971) (dismissal of putative interpleader action not based on competing claims). Interpleader is both a procedure and form of action. The interpleader plaintiff need not allege a substantive claim or right but need only invoke interpleader to allow the court to decide among competing claimants who assert their own substantive rights and claims to the asset held by the plaintiff. The *Republic of the Philippines v. Pimentel* case above is an excellent example of the value of interpleader, even though the issue before the Supreme Court in that case involved indispensable parties under FED. R. CIV. P. 19(b), not the rule and statute governing interpleader. In that case, the plaintiff broker held $35 million in an account owned by one entity but to which a class of thousands and a foreign government made competing claims. The interpleading broker could not release the funds to any one of those interested parties without risking liability to the other competing parties. *See also* Cohen v. The Republic of the Philippines, 146 F.R.D. 90 (S.D. N.Y. 1993) (interpleader action involving $5 million in paintings claimed by former Philippine president's wife Imelda Marcos).

State and federal rules and statutes authorize interpleader actions in the state and federal courts. As is the case with other pleading and joinder issues, the limited subject-matter jurisdiction of the federal courts complicates interpleader in the federal courts. The *Federal Rules of Civil Procedure* addresses that complication by having its interpleader rule, FED. R. CIV. P. 22, supplement rather than supersede or limit federal-court interpleader actions. Rule 22 does *not* create federal-court subject-matter jurisdiction. A plaintiff bringing an interpleader action under Rule 22 must establish an independent basis for jurisdiction, such as in diversity of citizenship in the usual interpleader case, claims to a common fund typically arising under state rather than federal law. Interpleader may also arise in the rare case under federal law, in which a federal court may rely on its federal-question jurisdiction. *See, e.g.*, Guy v. Citizens Fidelity Bank & Trust Co, 429 F.2d 828 (6th Cir. 1970). There is also direct statutory authority under 28 U.S.C. §1335, granting the federal courts subject-matter jurisdiction over interpleader actions. Congress enacted the Federal Interpleader Act in response to the Supreme Court's ruling in New York Life Ins. Co. v. Dunlevy, 241 U.S. 518 (1916), in which an insurer suffered double liability because of an anomaly having to do with a state court's lack of personal jurisdiction in an interpleader action. Congress later broadened federal interpleader provisions. There is both rule interpleader under Rule 22 and statutory interpleader under §1335. When the federal courts have subject-matter jurisdiction to entertain an interpleader claim joined pled under §1335, then Rule 22 will govern the conduct of that interpleader action. Compare Rule 22 with the interpleader statute §1335 to appreciate how they work together. Notice also the *Federal Rules* that follow, providing for jurisdiction over claims involving sureties and receivers.

FED. R. CIV. P. 22. Interpleader

(a) GROUNDS.

(1) *By a Plaintiff.* Persons with claims that may expose a plaintiff to double or multiple liability may be joined as defendants and required to interplead. Joinder for interpleader is proper even though:

(A) the claims of the several claimants, or the titles on which their claims depend, lack a common origin or are adverse and independent rather than identical; or

(B) the plaintiff denies liability in whole or in part to any or all of the claimants.

(2) *By a Defendant.* A defendant exposed to similar liability may seek interpleader through a crossclaim or counterclaim.

(b) RELATION TO OTHER RULES AND STATUTES. This rule supplements—and does not limit—the joinder of parties allowed by Rule 20. The remedy this rule provides is in addition to—and does not supersede or limit—the remedy provided by 28 U.S.C. §§1335, 1397, and 2361. An action under those statutes must be conducted under these rules.

28 U.S.C. §1335. Interpleader

(a) The district courts shall have original jurisdiction of any civil action of interpleader or in the nature of interpleader filed by any person, firm, or corporation, association, or society having in his or its custody or possession money or property of the value of $500 or more, or having issued a note, bond, certificate, policy of insurance, or other instrument of value or amount of $500 or more, or providing for the delivery or payment or the loan of money or property of such amount or value, or being under any obligation written or unwritten to the amount of $500 or more, if (1) two or more adverse claimants, of diverse citizenship as defined in subsection (a) or (d) of section 1332 of this title, are claiming or may claim to be entitled to such money or property, or to any one or more of the benefits arising by virtue of any note, bond, certificate, policy or other instrument, or arising by virtue of any such obligation; and if (2) the plaintiff has deposited such money or property or has paid the amount of or the loan or other value of such instrument or the amount due under such obligation into the registry of the court, there to abide the judgment of the court, or has given bond payable to the clerk of the court in such amount and with such surety as the court or judge may deem proper, conditioned upon the compliance by the plaintiff with the future order or judgment of the court with respect to the subject matter of the controversy.

(b) Such an action may be entertained although the titles or claims of the conflicting claimants do not have a common origin, or are not identical, but are adverse to and independent of one another.

FED. R. CIV. P. 65.1. Proceedings Against a Surety

Whenever these rules (including the Supplemental Rules for Admiralty or Maritime Claims and Asset Forfeiture Actions) require or allow a party to give security, and security is given through a bond or other undertaking with one or more sureties, each surety submits to the court's jurisdiction and irrevocably appoints the court clerk as its agent for receiving service of any papers that affect its liability on the bond or undertaking. The surety's liability may be enforced on motion without an independent action. The motion and any notice that the court orders may be served on the court clerk, who must promptly mail copy of each to every surety whose address is known.

FED. R. CIV. P. 66. Receivers

These rules govern an action in which the appointment of a receiver is sought or a receiver sues or is sued. But the practice in administering an estate by a receiver or a similar court-appointed officer must accord with the historical practice in federal courts or with a local rule. An action in which a receiver has been appointed may be dismissed only by court order.

FED. R. CIV. P. 67. Deposit into Court

(a) DEPOSITING PROPERTY. If any part of the relief sought is a money judgment or the disposition of a sum of money or some other deliverable thing, a party—on notice to every other party and by leave of court—may deposit with the court all or part of the money or thing, whether or not that party claims any of it. The depositing party must deliver to the clerk a copy of the order permitting deposit.

(b) INVESTING AND WITHDRAWING FUNDS. Money paid into court under this rule must be deposited and withdrawn in accordance with 28 U.S.C. §§ 2041 and 2042 and any like statute. The money must be deposited in an interest-bearing account or invested in a court-approved, interest-bearing instrument.

INQUIRY

Diversity of Citizenship. How is the above statute 28 U.S.C. §1335, creating subject-matter jurisdiction for federal-court interpleader actions, the same as and different from 28 U.S.C. §1332 authorizing diversity-of-citizenship jurisdiction for other actions not involving interpleader? The interpleader statute §1335(a) requires diversity of citizenship, as does the general statute §1332. Section 1335(a)(2) even refers explicitly to §1332's definitions for diverse citizenship. In that respect, jurisdiction for interpleader is like general diversity-of-citizenship jurisdiction. Yet there are at least two important differences between subject-matter jurisdiction for statutory interpleader under §1335 and subject-matter jurisdiction in general under §1332, and thus for rule interpleader under FED. R. CIV. P. 22. You likely noticed the first difference that while the general diversity-of-citizenship statute §1332 requires an amount in controversy of at least $75,000, the interpleader statute §1335 authorizes actions having a value of as little as $500. Thus, rule interpleader under Rule 22 without the boost of the interpleader statute §1335 requires at least $75,000 in controversy, while statutory interpleader under §1335 requires only $500 or more in controversy. Did you notice the other significant difference? A close reading of §1335(a)(1) indicates that it requires only minimal diversity among "two or more adverse claimants," not complete diversity between the interpleading plaintiff and all defendants. Thus, statutory interpleader requires only minimal diversity, while rule interpleader requires complete diversity. The Supreme Court confirmed this interpretation in the following case, illustrating a more common interpleader issue than the extraordinary *Republic of Philippines v. Pimentel* case, and further illustrating the scope and purpose of an interpleader action.

State Farm Fire & Casualty Co. v. Tashire,

United States Supreme Court
386 U.S. 523 (1967)

Mr. Justice FORTAS delivered the opinion of the Court.

Early one September morning in 1964, a Greyhound bus proceeding northward through Shasta County, California, collided with a southbound pickup truck. Two of the passengers aboard the bus were killed. Thirty-three others were injured, as were the bus driver, the driver of the truck and its lone passenger. One of the dead and 10 of the injured passengers were Canadians; the rest of the individuals involved were citizens of five American States. The ensuing litigation led to the present case, which raises important questions concerning administration of the interpleader remedy in the federal courts.

The litigation began when four of the injured passengers filed suit in California state courts, seeking damages in excess of $1,000,000. Named as defendants were Greyhound Lines, Inc., a California corporation; Theron Nauta, the bus driver; Ellis Clark, who drove the truck; and Kenneth Glasgow, the passenger in the truck who was apparently its owner as well. Each of the individual defendants was a citizen and resident of Oregon. Before these cases could come to trial and before other suits were filed in California or elsewhere, petitioner State Farm Fire & Casualty Company, an Illinois corporation, brought this action in the nature of interpleader in the United States District Court for the District of Oregon.

In its complaint State Farm asserted that at the time of the Shasta County collision it had in force an insurance policy with respect to Ellis Clark, driver of the truck, providing for bodily injury liability up to $10,000 per person and

$20,000 per occurrence and for legal representation of Clark in actions covered by the policy. It asserted that actions already filed in California and others which it anticipated would be filed far exceeded in aggregate damages sought the amount of its maximum liability under the policy. Accordingly, it paid into court the sum of $20,000 and asked the court (1) to require all claimants to establish their claims against Clark and his insurer in this single proceeding and in no other, and (2) to discharge State Farm from all further obligations under its policy-including its duty to defend Clark in lawsuits arising from the accident. ...

Joined as defendants were Clark, Glasgow, Nauta, Greyhound Lines, and each of the prospective claimants. Jurisdiction was predicated upon 28 U.S.C. §1335, the federal interpleader statute,[fn] and upon general diversity of citizenship, there being diversity between two or more of the claimants to the fund and between State Farm and all of the named defendants.

An order issued, requiring the defendants to show cause why they should not be restrained from filing or prosecuting "any proceeding in any state or United States Court affecting the property or obligation involved in this interpleader action, and specifically against the plaintiff and the defendant Ellis D. Clark." ...

... [A] temporary injunction along the lines sought by State Farm was issued by the United States District Court for the District of Oregon... . The injunction... provided that all suits against Clark, State Farm, Greyhound, and Nauta be prosecuted in the interpleader proceeding.

On interlocutory appeal,[fn] the Court of Appeals for the Ninth Circuit reversed. [C] It held that in States like Oregon which do not permit "direct action" suits against insurance companies until judgments are obtained against the insured, the insurance companies may not invoke federal interpleader until the claims against the insured, the alleged tortfeasor, have been reduced to judgment. Until that is done, said the court, claimants with unliquidated tort claims are not "claimants" within the meaning of §1335... .

I.

Before considering the issues presented by the petition for certiorari, we find it necessary to dispose of a question neither raised by the parties nor passed upon by the courts below. Since the matter concerns our jurisdiction, we raise it on our own motion. [C] The interpleader statute, 28 U.S.C. §1335, applies where there are "two or more adverse claimants, of diverse citizenship... ." This provision has been uniformly construed to require only "minimal diversity," that is, diversity of citizenship between two or more claimants, without regard to the circumstance that other rival claimants may be co-citizens.[fn] The language of the statute, the legislative purpose broadly to remedy the problems posed by multiple claimants to a single fund, and the consistent judicial interpretation tacitly accepted by Congress, persuade us that the statute requires no more. There remains, however, the question whether such a statutory construction is consistent with Article III of our Constitution, which extends the federal judicial power to "Controversies ... between citizens of different States ... and between a State, or the Citizens thereof, and foreign States, Citizens or Subjects." In Strawbridge v. Curtiss, [7 U.S. (3 Cranch) 267 (1806)], this Court held that the diversity of citizenship statute required "complete diversity": where co-citizens appeared on both sides of a dispute, jurisdiction was lost. But Chief Justice Marshall there purported to construe only "The words of the act of congress," not the Constitution itself.[fn] And in a variety of contexts this Court and the lower courts have concluded that Article III poses no obstacle to the legislative extension of federal jurisdiction, founded on diversity, so long as any two adverse parties are not co-citizens.[fn] Accordingly, we conclude that the present case is properly in the federal courts.

II.

We do not agree with the Court of Appeals that, in the absence of a state law or contractual provision for "direct action" suits against the insurance company, the company must wait until persons asserting claims against its insured have reduced those claims to judgment before seeking to invoke the benefits of federal interpleader. ...

Considerations of judicial administration demonstrate the soundness of this view which, in any event, seems compelled by the language of the present statute, which is remedial and to be liberally construed. Were an insurance company required to await reduction of claims to judgment, the first claimant to obtain such a judgment or to negotiate a settlement might appropriate all or a disproportionate slice of the fund before his fellow claimants were able to establish their claims. The difficulties such a race to judgment pose for the insurer,[fn] and the unfairness which may result to some claimants, were among the principal evils the interpleader device was intended to remedy.[fn]

III.

The fact that State Farm had properly invoked the interpleader jurisdiction under §1335 did not, however, entitle it to an order both enjoining prosecution of suits against it outside the confines of the interpleader proceeding and also extending such protection to its insured, the alleged tortfeasor. Still less was Greyhound Lines entitled to have that order expanded so as to protect itself and its driver, also alleged to be tortfeasors, from suits brought by its passengers in various state or federal courts. Here, the scope of the litigation, in terms of parties and claims, was vastly more extensive than the confines of the "fund," the deposited proceeds of the insurance policy. In these circumstances, the mere existence of such a fund cannot, by use of interpleader, be employed to accomplish purposes that exceed the needs of orderly contest with respect to the fund.

There are situations, of a type not present here, where the effect of interpleader is to confine the total litigation to a single forum and proceeding. One such case is where a stakeholder, faced with rival claims to the fund itself, acknowledges-or denies-his liability to one or the other of the claimants.[fn] In this situation, the fund itself is the target of the claimants. It marks the outer limits of the controversy. It is, therefore, reasonable and sensible that interpleader, in discharge of its office to protect the fund, should also protect the stakeholder from vexatious and multiple litigation. In this context, the suits sought to be enjoined are squarely within the language of 28 U.S.C. §2361... .

But the present case is another matter. Here, an accident has happened. Thirty-five passengers or their representatives have claims which they wish to press against a variety of defendants: the bus company, its driver, the owner of the truck, and the truck driver. The circumstance that one of the prospective defendants happens to have an insurance policy is a fortuitous event which should not of itself shape the nature of the ensuing litigation. ... [A]n insurance company whose maximum interest in the case cannot exceed $20,000 and who in fact asserts that it has no interest at all, should not be allowed to determine that dozens of tort plaintiffs must be compelled to press their claims—even those claims which are not against the insured and which in no event could be satisfied out of the meager insurance fund—in a single forum of the insurance company's choosing. There is nothing in the statutory scheme, and very little in the judicial and academic commentary upon that scheme, which requires that the tail be allowed to wag the dog in this fashion.

State Farm's interest in this case, which is the fulcrum of the interpleader procedure, is confined to its $20,000 fund. That interest receives full vindication when the court restrains claimants from seeking to enforce against the insurance company any judgment obtained against its insured, except in the interpleader proceeding itself. To the extent that the District Court sought to control claimants' lawsuits against the insured and other alleged tortfeasors, it exceeded the powers granted to it by the statutory scheme. ...

... [W]e hold that the interpleader statute did not authorize the injunction entered in the present case. Upon remand, the injunction is to be modified consistently with this opinion.[fn]

IV.

The judgment of the Court of Appeals is reversed, and the case is remanded to the United States District Court for proceedings consistent with this opinion.

It is so ordered.

Judgment of Court of Appeals reversed and case remanded to the District Court.

Mr. Justice DOUGLAS, dissenting[, omitted. Justice Douglas argued that the defendants were not claimants within §1335 because state law did not authorize a direct action and the policy prohibited direct action until a judgment entered against the insured].

INQUIRY

Other Differences. There are other differences between rule and statutory interpleader having to do with where and against whom the plaintiff may bring the case. Statutory interpleader under §1335 follows its own statutory venue provision, 28 U.S.C. §1397. Section 1397 provides, "Any civil action of interpleader or in the nature of interpleader under section 1335 of this title may be brought in the judicial district in which one or more of the claimants reside." Section 1397, applying only to statutory interpleader, is broader than the general venue statute 28 U.S.C. §1391 (discussed in Chapter 5), applying to rule interpleader. Unless all defendants reside in the same state, the general venue statute §1391 requires the rule-interpleader plaintiff to file in the district in which a substantial part of the events occurred or property is situated, while the interpleader venue statute §1397 allows the statutory-interpleader plaintiff to choose a district where any claimant resides. Personal jurisdiction for statutory interpleader is also broader than for rule interpleader. Under 28 U.S.C. §2361, there is nationwide personal jurisdiction for statutory interpleader, while personal jurisdiction for rule interpleader must follow personal jurisdiction's general rules (discussed in Chapter 2). Under FED. R. CIV. P. 4(k)(1)(A), those general rules often depend on the reach of the state's long-arm statute. Review §2361 below for its nationwide service-of-process provisions for interpleader actions.

28 U.S.C. §2361. Process and procedure
In any civil action of interpleader or in the nature of interpleader under section 1335 of this title, a district court may issue its process for all claimants and enter its order restraining them from instituting or prosecuting any proceeding in any State or United States court affecting the property, instrument or obligation involved in the interpleader action until further order of the court. Such process and order shall be returnable at such time as the court or judge thereof directs, and shall be addressed to and served by the United States marshals for the respective districts where the claimants reside or may be found. Such district court shall hear and determine the case, and may discharge the plaintiff from further liability, make the injunction permanent, and make all appropriate orders to enforce its judgment.

INQUIRY

Injunctions. You can see from the *State Farm Fire & Cas. Co. v. Tashire* case above that whether the court entertaining the interpleader action will grant an injunction against other actions can be critical to the interpleader action's success. An interpleader action may not do much good to the plaintiff who files it if it does not enjoin other litigation. Notice that §2361 immediately above authorizes orders restraining claimants from starting or continuing other actions affecting the interest that is the interpleader action's subject. Although general rules under FED. R. CIV. P. 65 for obtaining injunctions are more complex than §2361 suggests, Rule 65(e)(2) states explicitly that its provisions do not modify the preliminary-injunction provisions of §2361, perhaps meaning that injunctions in interpleader actions do not require Rule 65's notice provisions. *See* Holcomb v. Aetna Life Ins. Co., 228 F.2d 75, 82 (10th Cir. 1955). Notice also that §2361 limits its authority to enjoin other actions, to statutory-interpleader actions. The federal courts may have authority in rule-interpleader actions to enjoin other actions under 28 U.S.C. §2283. Section 2283 provides, "A court of the United States may not grant an injunction to stay proceedings in a State court except as expressly authorized by Act of Congress, or where necessary in aid of its jurisdiction, or to protect or effectuate its judgments." On the other hand, *State Farm Fire & Cas. Co. v. Tashire* probably contributed to the federal courts' reluctance to enjoin state proceedings. Chapter XIV addresses injunctions in detail.

D. Intervention

Litigation does not always involve willing plaintiffs and unwilling defendants. Sometimes, a plaintiff will omit a person or entity, either intentionally or mistakenly, from a proceeding in which the person or entity would like to join. Intervention is the procedure by which non-parties may voluntarily join an action with or without the plaintiff's consent. Intervention involves considering (1) the interest of the non-party in joining the litigation, (2) the interest of the existing parties in opposing intervention, and (3) the interest of the court in the efficient management of the litigation. Non-parties may intervene either to preserve rights that would otherwise be lost or for the convenience of resolving claims in the pending litigation rather than subsequent litigation. On some occasions, plaintiffs are ambivalent about a non-party's intervention. The plaintiff may have pled claims against solvent or insured defendants who are fully capable of providing the plaintiff with full relief, and yet a non-party may have an interest in intervening as a defendant to resolve relative rights and claims among the defendants or with potential third-party defendants. In those cases, the plaintiff may choose to consent to intervention. In other instances, intervention may increase opposition to the plaintiff's claims, increase the resources available to oppose the plaintiff, and increase the plaintiff's administrative work in conducting litigation involving additional parties.

State and federal rules authorize intervention in ways that account for each of these interests and strategic considerations. As is the case for other joinder rules, intervention in federal cases is like intervention under most state rules except for the complicating aspect of the federal courts' limited subject-matter jurisdiction. FED. R. CIV. P. 24 divides intervention into intervention of right and permissive intervention, stating different standards for each and the same procedures for both. Rule 24(a) makes intervention a right whenever authorized by federal statute or when disposition of the action without the intervening party may impair that non-party's interest. Rule 24(b) permits intervention whenever a federal statute grants a conditional right to intervene or when the intervening party's claim or defense has a common question of law or fact with the pending action. When a non-party seeks permissive intervention under Rule 24(b), Rule 24(b)(3) requires the court to consider whether intervention will unduly delay or prejudice resolution of the parties' rights. Rule 24(c) provides in both cases (intervention of right and permissive intervention) that the intervening party must file a motion and state the grounds, presumably including the basis for jurisdiction. The intervening party must show independent grounds for jurisdiction, although supplemental jurisdiction under 28 U.S.C. §1367 may be available. Rule 24(c)'s requirement that the non-party who moves to intervene must attach the proposed pleading demonstrates the adversarial nature of intervention that the intervening party will either be claiming or defending in the action. Read Rule 24 followed by a case illustrating its structures and standards.

FED. R. CIV. P. 24. Intervention

(a) INTERVENTION OF RIGHT. On timely motion, the court must permit anyone to intervene who:

(1) is given an unconditional right to intervene by a federal statute; or

(2) claims an interest relating to the property or transaction that is the subject of the action, and is so situated that disposing of the action may as a practical matter impair or impede the movant's ability to protect its interest, unless existing parties adequately represent that interest.

(b) PERMISSIVE INTERVENTION.

(1) *In General.* On timely motion, the court may permit anyone to intervene who:

(A) is given a conditional right to intervene by a federal statute; or

(B) has a claim or defense that shares with the main action a common question of law or fact.

(2) *By a Government Officer or Agency.* On timely motion, the court may permit a federal or state governmental officer or agency to intervene if a party's claim or defense is based on:

(A) a statute or executive order administered by the officer or agency; or

(B) any regulation, order, requirement, or agreement issued or made under the statute or executive order.

(3) *Delay or Prejudice.* In exercising its discretion, the court must consider whether the

intervention will unduly delay or prejudice the adjudication of the original parties' rights.

(c) NOTICE AND PLEADING REQUIRED. A motion to intervene must be served on the parties as provided in Rule 5. The motion must state the grounds for intervention and be accompanied by a pleading that sets out the claim or defense for which intervention is sought.

Natural Resources Defense Council v. United States Nuclear Regulatory Commission,

United States Circuit Court of Appeals for the Tenth Circuit
578 F.2d 1341 (1978)

DOYLE, Justice.

The American Mining Congress and Kerr-McGee Nuclear Corporation seek review of the order of the United States District Court for the District of New Mexico denying their motions to intervene was a matter of right or on a permissive basis, pursuant to Rule 24(a)(2) and (b), Fed. R. Civil Proc.

The underlying action in which the movants requested intervention was instituted by the Natural Resources Defense Council, Inc., and others. In the action, declaratory and injunctive relief is directed to the United States Nuclear Regulatory Commission (NRC) and the New Mexico Environmental Improvement Agency (NMEIA), prohibiting those agencies from issuing licenses for the operation of uranium mills in New Mexico without first preparing environmental impact statements. Kerr-McGee and United Nuclear are potential recipients of the licenses.

Congress, in the Atomic Energy Act of 1954, 42 U.S.C. §§2011-2296, has authorized the NRC to issue such licenses. NMEIA is involved because under §274(b) of the Act, [c], the NRC is authorized to enter into agreements with the states allowing the states to issue licenses. Such agreements have been made with about 25 states including New Mexico. Thus, the action below in effect seeks to prevent the use of §274(b) of the Act so as to avoid the requirement of an impact statement for which provision is made in the National Environmental Policy Act.

42 U.S.C. §4332(2)(C) (1970) requires that a detailed environmental impact statement must be prepared by all federal agencies "in every recommendation or report on proposals for legislation and other major Federal actions significantly affecting the quality of the human environment." The complaint cites this requirement and alleges that an environmental impact statement would ordinarily be required here as a prerequisite to the issuance of licenses for the operation of uranium mills were it not for the arrangement which gives jurisdiction to the state. It further alleges that such statements are now prepared by the NRC in states that have not entered into agreements with the NRC, but that the NRC does not prepare such statements where there is an agreement with a state such as New Mexico. ...

The relief sought by the plaintiffs' complaint is, First, that NRC's involvement in the licensing procedure in New Mexico is, notwithstanding the delegation to the state, sufficient to constitute major federal action, whereby the impact statement requirement is not eliminated. Second, that if an impact statement is not required in connection with the granting of licenses, the New Mexico program is in conflict with §274(d)(2) of the Atomic Energy Act... .

The motion of United Nuclear Corporation to intervene is not opposed by the parties and was granted. On May 3, 1977, the date that the complaint herein was filed, NMEIA granted a license to United Nuclear to operate a uranium mill at Church Rock, New Mexico. The complaint seeks to enjoin the issuance of the license thus granted.

It was after that that Kerr-McGee Nuclear Corporation, Anaconda Company, Gulf Oil Corporation, Phillips Petroleum Company, and the American Mining Congress filed motions to intervene. These motions, insofar as they sought intervention as of right, were denied on the ground that the interests of the parties or movants would be adequately represented by United Nuclear. Permissive intervention was also denied. Kerr-McGee and the American Mining Congress both appeal denial of both intervention as of right and permissive intervention.

Our issue is a limited one. We merely construe and weigh Rule 24(a) of the Fed. R. Civ. P. (intervention as of right) and decide in light of the facts and considerations presented whether the denial of intervention was correct. ... We do not have a subsection (1) situation involving a statutory conferring of right to intervene. Accordingly, we must consider the standards set forth in subsection (2), which are:

1. Whether the applicant claims an interest relating to the property or transaction which is the subject of the action.

2. Whether the claimants are so situated that the disposition of the action may as a practical matter impair or impede their ability to protect that interest.

3. Whether their interest is not adequately represented by existing parties.

...

Our conclusion is that the interests of movants in the subject matter is sufficient to satisfy the requirements of Rule 24 and that the threat of loss of their interest and inability to participate is of such magnitude as to impair their ability to advance their interest.

I.

... Strictly to require that the movant in intervention have a Direct interest in the outcome of the lawsuit strikes us as being too narrow a construction of Rule 24(a)(2). Kerr-McGee argues that the meaning of interest is one which, if they do not prevail in the intervention, threatens them with a disposition of the action which may, as a practical matter, impair or impede their efforts to protect the interest. Thus, we are asked to interpret interest in relationship to the second criterion in Rule 24(a)(2), impairment or impeding ability to protect the interest.

The Supreme Court has said that the interest must be a significantly protectable interest. See Donaldson v. United States, 400 U.S. 517[] (1971). The Supreme Court held that a taxpayer did not have a right to intervene in a judicial enforcement proceeding seeking issuance of an Internal Revenue summons ordering production of business records of his employer. The narrowness of the Summons proceeding was noted, and it was said that an objection of the taxpayer could be raised at the proper time in a subsequent trial.

Cascade Natural Gas Corp. v. El Paso Natural Gas Co., 386 U.S. 129, 135-36[] (1967), held that the interest claimed by the applicant in intervention did not have to be a direct interest in the property or transaction at issue provided that it was an interest that would be impaired by the outcome. There Cascade's source of supply would have been a new company created by an antitrust divestiture, a significant change. In view of this consequence of the litigation, it was held that Cascade had a sufficient interest. ...

In our case the matter of immediate interest is, of course, the issuance and delivery of the license sought by United Nuclear. However, the consequence of the litigation could well be the imposition of the requirement that an environmental impact statement be prepared before granting any uranium mill license in New Mexico, or, secondly, it could result in an injunction terminating or suspending the agreement between NRC and NMEIA. Either consequence would be felt by United Nuclear and to some degree, of course, by Kerr-McGee, which is said to be one of the largest holders of uranium properties in New Mexico. It operates a uranium mill in Grants, New Mexico, pursuant to an NMEIA license, which application for renewal is pending. A decision in favor of the plaintiffs, which is not unlikely, could have a profound effect upon Kerr-McGee. Hence, it does have an interest within the meaning of Rule 24(a)(2). This interest of Kerr-McGee is in sharp contrast to the minimal interest which was present in Allard[v. Frizzell, 536 F.2d 1332 (10th Cir. 1976)], wherein it was an interest of environmental groups in the protection of living birds. This was considered insufficient to justify intervention in a case involving feathers which are part of Indian artifacts. Their interest was said to be limited to a general interest in the public. [C] The interest asserted on behalf of Kerr-McGee and the American Mining Congress is one which is a genuine threat to Kerr-McGee and the members of the American Mining Congress to a substantial degree. ...

We do not suggest that Kerr-McGee could expect better treatment from state authorities than federal. We do recognize that a change in procedure would produce impairing complications.

II.

The next question is whether, assuming the existence of an interest, the chance of impairment is sufficient to fulfill the requirement of Rule 24(a)(2).

As already noted, the question of impairment is not separate from the question of existence of an interest. The appellants both claim an interest in licenses that are now before NMEIA or will be in the future. If the relief sought by the plaintiffs is granted, there can be little question but that the interests of the American Mining Congress and of Kerr-McGee would be affected. Plaintiffs contend, however, that appellants would not be bound by such a result if they are not participants. Kerr-McGee points out that even though it may not be res judicata, still it would have a stare decisis effect. Moreover, with NRC and NMEIA as parties, the result might be more profound than stare decisis.

It should be pointed out that the Rule refers to impairment "as a practical matter." Thus, the court is not limited to consequences of a strictly legal nature. The court may consider any significant legal effect in the applicant's interest and it is not restricted to a rigid res judicata test. Hence, the stare decisis effect might be sufficient to satisfy the requirement. [C] It is said that where, as here, the case is of first impression, the stare decisis effect would be important. [C]

Finally, the considerations for requiring an environmental impact statement will be relatively the same in respect to the issuance of a uranium mining license in every instance. Hence, to say that it can be repeatedly litigated is not an answer, for the chance of getting a contrary result in a case which is substantially similar on its facts to one previously adjudicated seems remote. [Cc]

We are of the opinion, therefore, that appellants have satisfied the impairment criterion.

III.

The final question is whether the trial court was correct in its conclusion that United Nuclear would adequately represent Kerr-McGee and the American Mining Congress.

The finding and conclusion was that the representation would be adequate because United Nuclear, a fellow member of the industry, has interests which were the same as those of the appellants and possessed the same level of knowledge and experience with the ability and willingness to pursue the matter and could adequately represent Kerr-McGee and the members of the American Mining Congress.

We have held in accordance with Trbovich v. UMW, 404 U.S. 528, 538 n.10[] (1972), that the burden continues to be on the petitioner or movant in intervention to show that the representation by parties may be inadequate. [C] We have also recognized the holding in *Trbovich* that the burden is minimal; that it is enough to show that the representation "may be" inadequate.

United Nuclear is situated somewhat differently in this case than are the other members of the industry since it has been granted its license. From this it is urged by Kerr-McGee that United Nuclear may be ready to compromise the case by obtaining a mere declaration that while environmental impact statements should be issued, this requirement need be prospective only, whereby it would not affect them. While we see this as a remote possibility, we gravely doubt that United Nuclear would opt for such a result. It is true, however, that United Nuclear has a defense of laches that is not available to Kerr-McGee or the others.

7A C. Wright & A. Miller, Federal Practice & Procedure, §1909, at 524 (1972), says: "(I)f (an applicant's) interest is similar to, but not identical with, that of one of the parties, a discriminating judgment is required on the circumstances of the particular case, but he ordinarily should be allowed to intervene unless it is clear that the party will provide adequate representation for the absentee." While the interest of the two applicants may appear similar, there is no way to say that there is no possibility that they will not be different and the possibility of divergence of interest need not be great in order to satisfy the burden of the applicants… .

There are other reasons for allowing intervention. There is some value in having the parties before the court so that they will be bound by the result. American Mining Congress represents a number of companies having a wide variety of interests. This can, therefore, provide a useful supplement to the defense of the case. The same can be said of Kerr-McGee.

The trial court was concerned that the addition of these movants would make the litigation unwieldy. If the intervenors are limited to this group, unwieldiness does not become a problem which the trial court cannot control. … The two appellants here have satisfied their burden of the three requirements of Rule 24(a)(2). Consequently, they should be and they are hereby allowed to intervene. Accordingly, we need not determine whether the district court erred in denying permissive intervention under Rule 24(b).

The order of the district court is reversed and the cause is remanded with instructions to the trial court to grant the appellants, Kerr-McGee's and American Mining Congress', motions to intervene.

INQUIRY

Interest. Notice the Supreme Court's "significantly protectable interest" standard that the above *Natural Resources Defense Council* opinion attributed to Donaldson v. United States, 400 U.S. 517 (1971). As the above *Natural Resources Defense Council* case indicates, real property interests are probably the most obviously protectable interests. *See, e.g.,* Planned Parenthood of Minnesota, Inc. v. Citizens for Community Action, 558 F.2d 861 (8th Cir. 1977) (value of residential real estate warrants neighbors' intervention). Interests in personal property or funds can also warrant intervention. *See, e.g.,* Diaz v. Southern Drilling Corp., 427 F.2d 1118 (5th Cir. 1970) (interest in challenging tax lien on joint funds warrants intervention). As the case of Allard v. Frizzell, 536 F.2d 1332 (10th Cir. 1976), cited in the above case indicates, it is harder to use a policy or advocacy interest to justify intervention.

Alignment. As the above *Natural Resources Council* case also indicates, it may be more important to the outcome whether the intervening party's interests align with the interests of one or more of the current litigants. If no party represents the intervening party's interest, then the court should entertain intervention. *See* Purnell v. City of Akron, 925 F.2d 941 (6th Cir. 1991). Greater alignment means less likely intervention because existing parties will already adequately represent the interest. If the interests of party and non-party align, the non-party will not be able to satisfy the last condition of Rule 24(a)(2), as in the above *Natural Resources Council* case. Yet as the *Natural Resources Council* opinion admits, a party may have similar property rights and financial interests to a non-party but a very different motivation to litigate. *See also* Natural Resources Council, Inc. v. New York State Dept. of Envtl. Conservation, 834 F.2d 60, 61-62 (2d Cir. 1987) (the standard is whether there is sufficient motivation to litigate, not perfect identity of interests); United States v. C.M. Lane Lifeboat Co., 25 F.Supp. 410 (E.D. N.Y. 1938) (party antagonistic toward intervenor does not adequately represent intervenor's interests). The two *Natural Resources Council* cases, the one excerpted above and the one just cited, together suggest that courts may broadly construe the interests of existing parties when they are state and federal agencies and units of government, and accept the adequacy of their representation, even when the private interests of the non-parties seeking intervention are economic rather than governmental. Think of interest less in its property and more in its strategic sense. Overall objectives may also help to define interests. Courts may deny intervention where the objectives of the non-party seeking intervention align with the objectives of a party. *See, e.g.,* Virginia v. Westinghouse Elec. Corp., 542 F.2d 214, 216 (4th Cir. 1976). Courts may also permit limited intervention for specific stages of the litigation, where the intervening party has a special but limited interest. *See, e.g.,* Jochims v. Isuzu Motors, Ltd., 148 F.R.D. 624 (S.D. Iowa 1993) (intervention to oppose protective order).

Joinder. What is the relationship of Rule 24 on intervention to Rule 19 on compulsory joinder? Rules 19 and 24 use the identical operative language that non-parties should participate in an action when it "may as a practical matter impair or impede" their interest. If Rule 19 requires joinder of parties whose interests the litigation may impede, then why have Rule 24 authorizing intervention of right? Or vice versa, if Rule 24 authorizes intervention of right, why have Rule 19 compelling joinder? One reason has to do with who is requesting to add parties to the action. With Rule 19 compulsory joinder, the defendants are generally the parties who want non-parties joined. With Rule 24 intervention of right, the non-party wants to become a party. Rules 19 and 24 differ in other respects. Rule 19(a)(1)(A) provides for compulsory joinder not only when an action may impair a non-party's right but also when the trial court "cannot accord complete relief among existing parties... ." by contrast, Rule 24 on intervention of right assumes that the trial court can accord complete relief without intervention or is unconcerned whether it can, instead expressly requiring (in subrule (a)(2)) that the court consider whether existing parties adequately represent the intervening party's interest. Rule 19(a) compulsory joinder is in that sense more powerful than Rule 24(a) on intervention of right, addressing a narrower but more compelling argument for joining the non-party. Rule 24(a) provides the more compelling ground for intervention than Rule 24(b) on permissive intervention, the latter not even requiring that the action threaten to impair or impede the intervening party's interest. *See* Stringfellow v. Concerned Neighbors in Action, 480 U.S. 370, 381-383 (1987) (distinguishing forms of intervention). The Supreme Court addressed this distinction again in the following case.

Martin v. Wilks,

United States Supreme Court
490 U.S. 755 (1989)

Chief Justice REHNQUIST delivered the opinion of the Court.

A group of white firefighters sued the city of Birmingham, Alabama (City), and the Jefferson County Personnel Board (Board) alleging that they were being denied promotions in favor of less qualified black firefighters. They claimed that the City and the Board were making promotion decisions on the basis of race in reliance on certain consent decrees, and that these decisions constituted impermissible racial discrimination in violation of the Constitution and federal statutes. The District Court held that the white firefighters were precluded from challenging employment decisions taken pursuant to the decrees, even though these firefighters had not been parties to the proceedings in which the decrees were entered. We think this holding contravenes the general rule that a person cannot be deprived of his legal rights in a proceeding to which he is not a party.

The litigation in which the consent decrees were entered began in 1974, when ... seven black individuals filed separate class-action complaints against the City and the Board. They alleged that both had engaged in racially discriminatory hiring and promotion practices in various public service jobs... . After a bench trial on some issues, but before judgment, the parties entered into two consent decrees... . These proposed decrees set forth an extensive remedial scheme, including long-term and interim annual goals for the hiring of blacks as firefighters. The decrees also provided for goals for promotion of blacks within the fire department.

The District Court entered an order provisionally approving the decrees and directing publication of notice of the upcoming fairness hearings. [C] Notice of the hearings, with a reference to the general nature of the decrees, was published in two local newspapers. At that hearing, the Birmingham Firefighters Association (BFA) appeared and filed objections as *amicus curiae*. After the hearing, but before final approval of the decrees, the BFA and two of its members also moved to intervene on the ground that the decrees would adversely affect their rights. The District Court denied the motions as untimely and approved the decrees. [C] ...

A new group of white firefighters, the *Wilks* respondents, then brought suit against the City and the Board in District Court. They too alleged that, because of their race, they were being denied promotions in favor of less qualified blacks in violation of federal law. The Board and the City admitted to making race-conscious employment decisions, but argued that the decisions were unassailable because they were made pursuant to the consent decrees. A group of black individuals, the *Martin* petitioners, were allowed to intervene in their individual capacities to defend the decrees.

The defendants moved to dismiss the reverse discrimination cases as impermissible collateral attacks on the consent decrees. ... After trial the District Court granted the motion to dismiss. [C] The court concluded that ... the defendants had "establish[ed] that the promotions of the black individuals ... were in fact required by the terms of the consent decree." [C]

On appeal, the Eleventh Circuit reversed. It held that, "[b]ecause ... [the *Wilks* respondents] were neither parties nor privies to the consent decrees, ... their independent claims of unlawful discrimination are not precluded." [C] ... Although it recognized a "strong public policy in favor of voluntary affirmative action plans," the panel acknowledged that this interest "must yield to the policy against requiring third parties to submit to bargains in which their interests were either ignored or sacrificed." [C] ...

We granted certiorari [c] and now affirm the Eleventh Circuit's judgment. All agree that "[i]t is a principle of general application in Anglo-American jurisprudence that one is not bound by a judgment *in personam* in a litigation in which he is not designated as a party or to which he has not been made a party by service of process." Hansberry v. Lee, 311 U.S. 32, 40[] (1940). [CC] This rule is part of our "deep-rooted historic tradition that everyone should have his own day in court." 18 C. Wright, A. Miller, & E. Cooper, Federal Practice and Procedure §4449, p. 417 (1981)[]. A judgment or decree among parties to a lawsuit resolves issues as among them, but it does not conclude the rights of strangers to those proceedings.[fn]

Petitioners argue that, because respondents failed to timely intervene in the initial proceedings, their current challenge to actions taken under the consent decree constitutes an impermissible "collateral attack." They argue that respondents were aware that the underlying suit might affect them, and if they chose to pass up an opportunity to intervene, they should not be permitted to later litigate the issues in a new action. The position has sufficient appeal to have commanded the approval of the great majority of the Federal Courts of

Appeals,[fn] but we agree with the contrary view expressed by the Court of Appeals for the Eleventh Circuit in these cases.

We begin with the words of Justice Brandeis in Chase National Bank v. Norwalk, 291 U.S. 431[, 441] (1934): "The law does not impose upon any person absolutely entitled to a hearing the burden of voluntary intervention in a suit to which he is a stranger.... Unless duly summoned to appear in a legal proceeding, a person not a privy may rest assured that a judgment recovered therein will not affect his legal rights." [C] While these words were written before the adoption of the Federal Rules of Civil Procedure, we think the Rules incorporate the same principle; a party seeking a judgment binding on another cannot obligate that person to intervene; he must be joined. [C] Against the background of permissive intervention set forth in *Chase National Bank,* the drafters cast Rule 24, governing intervention, in permissive terms. See Fed. Rule Civ. Proc. 24(a) (intervention as of right) ...; Fed. Rule Civ. Proc. 24(b) (permissive intervention)... . They determined that the concern for finality and completeness of judgments would be "better [served] by mandatory joinder procedures." 18 Wright §4452, p. 453. Accordingly, Rule 19(a) provides for mandatory joinder in circumstances where a judgment rendered in the absence of a person may "leave ... persons already parties subject to a substantial risk of incurring ... inconsistent obligations...."[fn] Rule 19(b) sets forth the factors to be considered by a court in deciding whether to allow an action to proceed in the absence of an interested party.[fn]

Joinder as a party, rather than knowledge of a lawsuit and an opportunity to intervene, is the method by which potential parties are subjected to the jurisdiction of the court and bound by a judgment or decree. The parties to a lawsuit presumably know better than anyone else the nature and scope of relief sought in the action, and at whose expense such relief might be granted. It makes sense, therefore, to place on them a burden of bringing in additional parties where such a step is indicated, rather than placing on potential additional parties a duty to intervene when they acquire knowledge of the lawsuit. The linchpin of the "impermissible collateral attack" doctrine—the attribution of preclusive effect to a failure to intervene—is therefore quite inconsistent with Rule 19 and Rule 24. ...

Petitioners contend that a different result should be reached because the need to join affected parties will be burdensome and ultimately discouraging to civil rights litigation. Potential adverse claimants may be numerous and difficult to identify; if they are not joined, the possibility for inconsistent judgments exists. Judicial resources will be needlessly consumed in relitigation of the same question.

Even if we were wholly persuaded by these arguments as a matter of policy, acceptance of them would require a rewriting rather than an interpretation of the relevant Rules. ...

... Rule 19's provisions for joining interested parties are designed to accommodate the sort of complexities that may arise from a decree affecting numerous people in various ways. We doubt that a mandatory intervention rule would be any less awkward. ...

Nor do we think that the system of joinder called for by the Rules is likely to produce more relitigation of issues than the converse rule. The breadth of a lawsuit and concomitant relief may be at least partially shaped in advance through Rule 19 to avoid needless clashes with future litigation. ...

For the foregoing reasons we affirm the decision of the Court of Appeals for the Eleventh Circuit. That court remanded the case for trial of the reverse discrimination claims. ...

Affirmed.

Justice STEVENS, with whom Justice BRENNAN, Justice MARSHALL, and Justice BLACKMUN join, dissenting.

As a matter of law there is a vast difference between persons who are actual parties to litigation and persons who merely have the kind of interest that may as a practical matter be impaired by the outcome of a case. Persons in the first category have a right to participate in a trial and to appeal from an adverse judgment; depending on whether they win or lose, their legal rights may be enhanced or impaired. Persons in the latter category have a right to intervene in the action in a timely fashion,[fn] or they may be joined as parties against their will.[fn] But if they remain on the sidelines, they may be harmed as a practical matter even though their legal rights are unaffected.[fn] One of the disadvantages of sideline-sitting is that the bystander has no right to appeal from a judgment no matter how harmful it may be.

In these cases the Court quite rightly concludes that the white firefighters who brought the second series of Title VII cases could not be deprived of their legal rights in the first series of cases because they had neither intervened nor been joined as parties. [Cc] The consent decrees obviously could not deprive them of any contractual rights... . There is no reason, however, why the consent decrees might not produce changes in conditions at the white firefighters' place of employment that, as a practical matter, may have a serious effect on their opportunities for employment or promotion even though they are not bound by the decrees in any legal sense. The fact that one of the effects of a decree is to curtail the job opportunities of nonparties does not mean that the nonparties have been deprived of legal rights or that they have standing to appeal from that decree without becoming parties. ...

There is nothing unusual about the fact that litigation between adverse parties may, as a practical matter, seriously impair the interests of third persons who elect to sit on the sidelines. Indeed, in complex litigation this Court has squarely held that a sideline-sitter may be bound as firmly as an actual party if he had adequate notice and a fair opportunity to intervene and if the judicial interest in finality is sufficiently strong. [Cc] ...

... I would vacate the judgment of the Court of Appeals and remand for further proceedings consistent with this opinion.

INQUIRY

Timing. In the above *Martin v. Wilks* case, the Supreme Court kept the burden on the parties to join persons and entities who have an interest in the litigation, if those parties hope to bind the non-parties by judgment in the litigation. Congress effectively limited the rule of *Martin v. Wilks* to other contexts, when in response to the decision it enacted 42 U.S.C. §2000e2(n) prohibiting non-parties from challenging civil-rights consent decrees about which they had actual notice and as to which they had a reasonable opportunity to object, or where a party adequately represented their interests.

There is no sitting on the sidelines in civil-rights actions heading toward consent decrees. In all cases involving intervention, both FED. R. CIV. P. 24(a) on intervention of right and Rule 24(b) on permissive intervention require that the non-party seeking to intervene do so by "timely motion... ." How will a court define "timely," when the person or entity seeking to intervene received no formal notice of the proceeding triggering any particular response period? One court suggested the following sensible factors: (1) how long the non-party knew about the proceeding before moving to intervene; (2) what prejudice the parties suffered from any delay by the non-party from the moment of notice to the moment of moving; (3) the prejudice to the non-party if the court denies the motion for untimeliness; and (4) any other unusual circumstances warranting grant or denial of the motion. Stallworth v. Monsanto, 558 F.2d 257, 264-266 (5th Cir. 1977).

E. Class Actions

The claim- and party-joinder issues and procedures addressed by the above sections are relatively common and routine in civil litigation practice. Any one or more of those joinder issues could arise during the course of relatively routine cases. By contrast, class actions are a subject apart. Class actions involve resources, staffing, and skills that make their conduct a decision thoughtfully addressed well in advance of their initiation. Treatment of the subject here is necessarily topical because of the depth and breadth of the subject. Law schools address entire seminars to class actions, and class action scholarship inundates the law journals because class action procedures, the social and technical matters that they address, and the policies they implicate fascinate. It is appropriate to treat class actions in this chapter on joinder. Class actions still fundamentally involve questions regarding who and how many the litigation will bind to the court's judgment. Given their prevalence and impact, every lawyer should know something about class actions. Yet practitioners do not usually fall incidentally into class action practice. They seek and prepare for it or refer it to experienced class-action counsel.

Ethics

Rule 1.1 of the ABA MODEL RULES OF PROFESSIONAL CONDUCT requires competence of lawyers in any representation that they undertake. One way that lawyers develop competence in new fields like class-action litigation is to associate with experienced counsel. The Comment to Rule 1.1 states, "A lawyer can provide adequate represetnation in a wholly novel field through necessary study. Competent representation can also be provided through the association of a lawyer of established competence in the field in question." It is common for a lawyer in one firm to refer a case to a lawyer in another firm while continuing the representation and appearing in the action as co-counsel. The experienced lawyer will then lead the litigation while the inexperienced lawyer helps with specific tasks, gains experience, and develops the requisite competence to manage similar litigation alone in the future. Rule 1.5(e) on referral fees also applies. Because of their joint responsibility and liability, lawyers who make referrals and appear as co-counsel are cautious to ensure that their co-counsel is indeed competent and acts diligently—and is insured for malpractice.

Collective litigation of one type or another has been around at least since the dawn of the common law, memorialized in England's Courts of Chancery in the form of a bill of peace. Today, mass consumer class actions have a uniquely American cast, although there is increasing recent interest in class-action devices even in civil law countries. Class actions have certainly taken on a greater role recently than in the jurisprudential past. Their rise may in part be from changes in the national economy, in which national and international corporations engage in more transactions impacting more lives in small measure and large ways that litigants cannot effectively address through individual cases. When Congress and the Supreme Court adopted the *Federal Rules of Civil Procedure* in 1938, they probably intended FED. R. CIV. P. 23 to increase the number and scope of class actions. It took a substantial rewrite of Rule 23 in 1966, giving it clearer form and more functional basis, to open class actions to the mass torts and public-interest cases for which we now know them. The American Law Institute has made three major studies of class actions since 1987, indicating how fluid is their current use and form. Today, depending on the cause, grounds, and requested relief, and the particular party's interest and viewpoint, participants in class actions tend to view them as either tools for social justice or harbingers of social demise, even though empirical study has shown large percentages of them to be effective and routine. Willging, Hooper, and Niemic, *Empirical Analysis of Rule 23 to Address the Rulemaking Challenges*, 71 N.Y.U. L.REV. (1996). People have strong opinions, both positive and negative, about the substantive issues that class actions address, and lawmakers have strong opinions, both positive and negative, about the procedural advantages and disadvantages of class actions. Yet in this section you will see the courts consistently treating their maintenance as a matter of law and authority—that Congress has provided for class actions in their present form, and so they remain until Congress provides otherwise.

A class action is a case conducted in the name of one or more class representatives who adequately represent numerous other class members whom the court's judgment will bind even though they are not parties to the action in the usual sense. Class actions begin with a defined class whose members the court and parties must be able to identify objectively without substantial inquiry. *See* In re Cooper Antitrust Litigation, 196 F.R.D. 348 (W.D. Wis. 2000). Class actions also depend on a class representative who is a member of the class and adequately represents its interests. The class representative must meet constitutional requirements for standing. *See* Gratz v. Bollinger, 539 U.S. 244 (2003) (transfer student adequately represents freshmen-student interests because university used same criteria to admit freshmen and transfer students). Class representatives whose claims expire naturally before the class action's conclusion may still satisfy standing and defeat a mootness challenge. *See* Gertein v. Pugh, 420 U.S. 103, 110-111n.11 (1975); Sosna v. Iowa, 419 U.S. 393 (1975). From this introduction, you can sense both the power and improbability of class actions—the tension along which the law defines them—that they decide for many based on the actions and stories of a few. The law uses the concept of *certification* to control that power and reduce the improbability of class actions.

This section begins with grounds and procedures for the certification of class actions. Practitioners have the liberty to plan and plead class actions through putative class representatives, but the trial court decides whether to certify the class. Certification is critical in both its procedural and practical effects, so much so that since 2003, Rule 23(f) has authorized interlocutory appeal of certification decisions with appellate-court permission. Certification is ordinarily the most significant step in a class action. With certification, the case takes on broad scope and powerful effect of discovery, proof, advocacy, and social or financial interest. Without class certification, plaintiffs proceed alone acting only for their own benefit or (as is often the case) choose to dismiss. *See* Waste Management Holdings, Inc. v. Mowbray, 208 F.3d 288, 293 (1st Cir. 2000) (grant interlocutory appeal when certification denial effectively ends case). Yet while the failure to achieve certification breaks a class action, obtaining certification is only an important first step. This section continues with important issues having to do with the class action's reach, including notice requirements, constitutional rules for jurisdiction, choice of law, and venue. Even once the parties and court resolve all legal issues, there remain important considerations surrounding settlement, addressed in the final part of this section. Appreciate the power, significance, uncertainty, and nuance of class actions.

1. Certification

The conduct of class-action litigation generally and the proof of certification specifically are sufficiently complex tasks that state and federal courts follow elaborate rules. FED. R. CIV. P. 23 governing class actions in federal courts (states have similar rules) includes much detail especially as to certification. Rule 23(c)(1)(A) makes clear that certification is a first step, requiring at "an early practicable time," although under Rule 23(c)(1)(C) the trial court may modify its certification order at any time up to judgment. Rule 23(a) then states four prerequisites to certification. Lawyers label these prerequisites numerosity, commonality, typicality, and representation. All class actions must satisfy all four of Rule 23(a)'s prerequisites. Satisfying the four prerequisites of Rule 23(a), though, is just the first step toward certification. Just because one has many potential parties with common issues whom a typical party could adequately represent does not warrant a class action. There must also be something in a sense unjust about requiring parties to resolve the action without including the class. Rule 23(b) complicates the analysis. Rule 23(b) permits certification only if the action would be one of four types. All class actions must fit at least one of Rule 23(b)'s four types. In a sense, Rule 23(a) states the positive conditions for certification while Rule 23(b) states its negative conditions. Rule 23(a) assumes a class, imposing terms that would ensure the class action's proper conduct. By contrast, Rule 23(b) assumes *no* class, requiring the court to determine the injustice that would result by the conduct of individual actions. Read Rule 23 for this structure while appreciating how it enables the courts to balance the tension between class-action power and purpose. Notice that Rule 23(a) permits a single class representative or multiple class representatives. Notice also that Rule 23(a) authorizes a plaintiff or defendant class, although defendant classes are rare. *See* Thillens, Inc. v. Community Currency Exchange Assn., 97 F.R.D. 668, 674 (N.D. Ill. 1983) (defendant classes arise primarily in patent-infringement and securities litigation).

FED. R. CIV. P. 23. Class Actions

(a) PREREQUISITES. One or more members of a class may sue or be sued as representative parties on behalf of all members only if:

(1) the class is so numerous that joinder of all members is impracticable;

(2) there are questions of law or fact common to the class;

(3) the claims or defenses of the representative parties are typical of the claims or defenses of the class; and

(4) the representative parties will fairly and adequately protect the interests of the class.

(b) TYPES OF CLASS ACTIONS. A class action may be maintained if Rule 23(a) is satisfied and if:

(1) prosecuting separate actions by or against individual class members would create a risk of:

(A) inconsistent or varying adjudications with respect to individual class members that would establish incompatible standards of conduct for the party opposing the class; or

(B) adjudications with respect to individual class members that, as a practical matter, would be dispositive of the interests of the other members not parties to the individual adjudications or would substantially impair or impede their ability to protect their interests;

(2) the party opposing the class has acted or refused to act on grounds that apply generally to the class, so that final injunctive relief or corresponding declaratory relief is appropriate respecting the class as a whole; or

(3) the court finds that the questions of law or fact common to class members predominate over any questions affecting only individual members, and that a class action is superior to other available methods for fairly and efficiently adjudicating the controversy. The matters pertinent to these findings include:

(A) the class members' interests in individually controlling the prosecution or defense of separate actions;

(B) the extent and nature of any litigation concerning the controversy already begun by or against class members;

(C) the desirability or undesirability of concentrating the litigation of the claims in the particular forum; and

(D) the likely difficulties in managing a class action.

(c) CERTIFICATION ORDER; NOTICE TO CLASS MEMBERS; JUDGMENT; ISSUES CLASSES; SUBCLASSES.

(1) *Certification Order.*

(A) *Time to Issue.* At an early practicable time after a person sues or is sued as a class representative, the court must determine by order whether to certify the action as a class action.

(B) *Defining the Class; Appointing Class Counsel.* An order that certifies a class action must define the class and the class claims, issues, or defenses, and must appoint class counsel under Rule 23(g).

(C) *Altering or Amending the Order.* An order that grants or denies class certification may be altered or amended before final judgment.

(2) *Notice.*

(A) *For (b)(1) or (b)(2) Classes.* For any class certified under Rule 23(b)(1) or (b)(2), the court may direct appropriate notice to the class.

(B) *For (b)(3) Classes.* For any class certified under Rule 23(b)(3), the court must direct to class members the best notice that is practicable under the circumstances, including individual notice to all members who can be identified through reasonable effort. The notice must clearly and concisely state in plain, easily understood language:

(i) the nature of the action;

(ii) the definition of the class certified;

(iii) the class claims, issues, or defenses;

(iv) that a class member may enter an appearance through an attorney if the member so desires;

(v) that the court will exclude from the class any member who requests exclusion;

(vi) the time and manner for requesting exclusion; and

(vii) the binding effect of a class judgment on members under Rule 23(c)(3).

(3) *Judgment.* Whether or not favorable to the class, the judgment in a class action must:

(A) for any class certified under Rule 23(b)(1) or (b)(2), include and describe those whom the court finds to be class members; and

(B) for any class certified under Rule 23(b)(3), include and specify or describe those to whom the Rule 23(c)(2) notice was directed, who have not requested exclusion, and whom the court finds to be class members.

(4) *Particular Issues.* When appropriate, an action may be brought or maintained as a class action with respect to particular issues.

(5) *Subclasses.* When appropriate, a class may be divided into subclasses that are each treated as a class under this rule.

(d) CONDUCTING THE ACTION.

(1) *In General.* In conducting an action under this rule, the court may issue orders that:

(A) determine the course of proceedings or prescribe measures to prevent undue repetition or complication in presenting evidence or argument;

(B) require—to protect class members and fairly conduct the action—giving appropriate notice to some or all class members of:

(i) any step in the action;

(ii) the proposed extent of the judgment; or

(iii) the members' opportunity to signify whether they consider the representation fair and adequate, to intervene and present claims or defenses, or to otherwise come into the action;
(C) impose conditions on the representative parties or on intervenors;
(D) require that the pleadings be amended to eliminate allegations about representation of absent persons and that the action proceed accordingly; or
(E) deal with similar procedural matters.
(2) *Combining and Amending Orders.* An order under Rule 23(d)(1) may be altered or amended from time to time and may be combined with an order under Rule 16.
(e) SETTLEMENT, VOLUNTARY DISMISSAL, OR COMPROMISE. The claims, issues, or defenses of a certified class may be settled, voluntarily dismissed, or compromised only with the court's approval. The following procedures apply to a proposed settlement, voluntary dismissal, or compromise:
(1) The court must direct notice in a reasonable manner to all class members who would be bound by the proposal.
(2) If the proposal would bind class members, the court may approve it only after a hearing and on finding that it is fair, reasonable, and adequate.
(3) The parties seeking approval must file a statement identifying any agreement made in connection with the proposal.
(4) If the class action was previously certified under Rule 23(b)(3), the court may refuse to approve a settlement unless it affords a new opportunity to request exclusion to individual class members who had an earlier opportunity to request exclusion but did not do so.
(5) Any class member may object to the proposal if it requires court approval under this subdivision (e); the objection may be withdrawn only with the court's approval.
(f) APPEALS. A court of appeals may permit an appeal from an order granting or denying class-action certification under this rule if a petition for permission to appeal is filed with the circuit clerk within 14 days after the order is entered. An appeal does not stay proceedings in the district court unless the district judge or the court of appeals so orders.
(g) CLASS COUNSEL.
(1) *Appointing Class Counsel.* Unless a statute provides otherwise, a court that certifies a class must appoint class counsel. In appointing class counsel, the court:
(A) must consider:
(i) the work counsel has done in identifying or investigating potential claims in the action;
(ii) counsel's experience in handling class actions, other complex litigation, and the types of claims asserted in the action;
(iii) counsel's knowledge of the applicable law; and
(iv) the resources that counsel will commit to representing the class;
(B) may consider any other matter pertinent to counsel's ability to fairly and adequately represent the interests of the class;
(C) may order potential class counsel to provide information on any subject pertinent to the appointment and to propose terms for attorney's fees and nontaxable costs;
(D) may include in the appointing order provisions about the award of attorney's fees or nontaxable costs under Rule 23(h); and
(E) may make further orders in connection with the appointment.
(2) *Standard for Appointing Class Counsel.* When one applicant seeks appointment as class counsel, the court may appoint that applicant only if the applicant is adequate under Rule 23(g)(1) and (4). If more than one adequate applicant seeks appointment, the court must appoint the applicant best able to represent the interests of the class.
(3) *Interim Counsel.* The court may designate interim counsel to act on behalf of a putative class before determining whether to certify the action as a class action.
(4) *Duty of Class Counsel.* Class counsel must fairly and adequately represent the interests of the class.
(h) ATTORNEY'S FEES AND NONTAXABLE COSTS. In a certified class action, the court may award reasonable attorney's fees and nontaxable costs that are authorized by law or by the parties' agreement. The following procedures apply:
(1) A claim for an award must be made by motion under Rule 54(d)(2), subject to the provisions of this subdivision (h), at a time the court sets. Notice of the motion must be served on all parties and, for motions by class counsel, directed to class members in a reasonable manner.
(2) A class member, or a party from whom payment is sought, may object to the motion.
(3) The court may hold a hearing and must find the facts and state its legal conclusions under Rule 52(a).
(4) The court may refer issues related to the amount of the award to a special master or a magistrate judge, as provided in Rule 54(d)(2)(D).

INQUIRY

Prerequisites. Consider in detail Rule 23(a)'s four prerequisites of numerosity, commonality, typicality, and representation. Rule 23(a)(2)'s commonality requirement that "there are questions of law or fact common to the class" should be familiar from Rule 20 on permissive joinder providing (with other conditions) that parties may join on "any question of law or fact common to all" parties. Class members must be alike in ways that matter to the claim. *See* Califano v. Yamasaki, 442 U.S. 682 (1979) (commonality ensures that class-member differences do not affect legal issue controlling case's outcome); *see also* Donaldson v. Microsoft Corp., 205 F.R.D. 558, 565 (W.D. Wash. 2001) (allegation of individualized discrimination destroys commonality requirement). The other three prerequisites are unique to class actions. Rule 23(a)(1)'s numerosity requirement that "the class is so numerous that joinder of all members is impracticable" captures the essence of class actions. Why, after all, not just join all members of the class under Rule 20 for permissive joinder? A case with multiple parties becomes a class-action candidate only when there are so many potential parties—usually at least several dozen—that their joinder is impracticable. Rule 23(a)(3)'s typicality requirement that "the claims or defenses of the representative parties are typical of the claims or defenses of the class" ensures an alignment of interests between those parties in whose name the litigation proceeds and the non-parties whom they represent. Class representatives must be typical, rather than unusual, to the class. *See* Marisol v. Giuliani, 126 F.3d 372, 376 (2d Cir. 1997) (typicality means a claim arising from the same events). Rule 23(a)(4)'s representation requirement that "the representative parties will fairly and adequately protect the interests of the class" ensures proper motivation and sufficient skill and resources to protect the non-party members of the class. Both the class representatives and their lawyers must adequately represent the class. Questions over the class-action lawyers' qualifications, resources, and relationship to the representatives and class are fair game in certification hearings. *See* FED. R. CIV. P. 23(g) (procedure for appointing class counsel). Rule 23(a) states that "[o]ne or more members of a class may sue or be sued as representative parties on behalf of all members only if" satisfying those four prerequisites. Consider two Rule 23(a) certification opinions resulting in opposite decisions on the same issue.

Communities for Equity v. Michigan High School Athletic Assn.,

United States District Court for the Western District of Michigan
192 F.R.D. 568 (1999)

ENSLEN, Chief Judge.

This matter is before the Court on the Plaintiffs' Motion for Class Certification. For the reasons which follow, the motion will be granted.

BACKGROUND

Plaintiffs bring this suit against the Michigan High School Athletic Association and its Representative Council, alleging that they have been excluded from opportunities to participate in interscholastic athletic programs and have received unequal treatment and benefits in these programs. They contend that this putative exclusion and unequal treatment constitute gender discrimination, in violation of (1) Title IX of the Education Amendments of 1972; (2) the Equal Protection Clause of the Fourteenth Amendment; and (3) [Michigan's Elliott Larsen Civil Rights Act]. The alleged discrimination is made manifest, according to Plaintiffs, in MHSAA's: (1) refusing to sanction girls ice hockey and water polo; (2) requiring that the Plaintiff Class play its sports in non-traditional seasons; (3) operating shorter athletic seasons for some girls' sports than for boys' sports; (4) scheduling the competitions of the Plaintiff Class on inferior dates; (5) providing, assigning, and operating inferior athletic facilities to the Plaintiff Class in which to play MHSAA-sanctioned games; (6) requiring that the Plaintiff Class play some sports under rules and/or conditions different from those in the NCAA or other governing organizations, unlike boys; and (7) allocating more resources for the support and promotion of male interscholastic athletic programs than for female programs.

Plaintiffs' Motion for Class Certification asks the Court to define the proposed class as follows: all present and future female students enrolled in MHSAA member schools who participate in interscholastic athletics or who are deterred from participating in interscholastic athletics because of Defendants' discriminatory conduct and who are adversely affected by that conduct.

STANDARD FOR CLASS CERTIFICATION

According to the United States Supreme Court, this Court must conduct a "rigorous analysis" into whether the prerequisites of Federal Rule of Civil Procedure 23 are met before certifying a class action. General Tel. Co. v. Falcon, 457 U.S. 147, 161[] (1982). ... The "rigorous analysis requirement" means that a class is not maintainable merely because the complaint parrots the legal requirements of Rule 23. [C] Although a hearing prior to the class determination is not always required, "it may be necessary for the court to probe behind the pleadings before coming to rest on the certification question." *Falcon,[supra,]* at 160[]; [c]. In this case, the extensive briefing filed by the parties, the Court's past review of motions, and the documentary evidence and affidavits filed make the hearing of evidence unnecessary because the Court is able to probe behind the pleadings without additional evidence or argument.[fn] ...

CLASS CERTIFICATION

Rule 23(a)(1)-Numerosity/Impracticability of Joinder

First, the Court must determine whether the class is sufficiently numerous that joinder is impracticable. Numbers alone are not dispositive when the numbers are small, but will dictate impracticability when the numbers are large. [C] ... In this case, the numbers themselves justify a conclusion of numerosity and impracticability of joinder. Under Plaintiffs' theory of liability, thousands of female high school athletes and would-be athletes are subjected to Defendants' alleged discriminatory practices. In terms of specific numbers, Plaintiffs provide, for instance, evidence of 177 female ice hockey players, and 188 female water polo players, all of whom are allegedly discriminated against by Defendants' refusal to sanction those sports. Similarly, almost 20,000 female basketball players are allegedly injured by a season which is purportedly shorter than that played by boys. ...

Rule 23(a)(2)-Commonality

Next, the Rule requires commonality-that there are questions of law and fact common to class members. Not every common question suffices. [C] What is necessary for certification are common issues the resolution of which will advance the litigation. [C] In cases involving the question of whether a defendant has acted through an illegal policy or procedure, commonality is readily shown because the common question becomes whether the defendant in fact acted through the illegal policy or procedure. [C] Where the nature of the legal claims are such that individuals would have to submit separate proofs to establish liability, class actions are disapproved due to lack of commonality. [C] However, the presence of individual questions need not defeat certification. [C] This should be obvious, since Rule 23 requires common questions, not the absence of individual ones. Once it is determined that there are common questions of law and fact as to a legal claim, differences in damages sustained by class members will usually not defeat certification. [Cc]

Here, the common questions of fact and law are obvious enough. The overarching question is, did MHSAA and its Representative Council act in a manner inconsistent with Title IX, the Equal Protection Clause of the Fourteenth Amendment; and/or Mich. Comp. Laws §§ 37.2302 and 37.2402? The answer turns on the resolution of factual questions regarding Defendants' decisionmaking process and outcomes, and determination of the legal consequences of those facts.

Rule 23(a)(3)-Typicality

... The typicality requirement is the one demanding the closest attention in this matter. The Court must determine whether, on the facts of this case, the Supreme Court's *Falcon* decision precludes a finding of typicality, given the breadth of Plaintiffs' claims. In *Falcon,* a Mexican-American employee who alleged that he had been denied a promotion because of race discrimination brought a class action against his employer. The class included all Mexican-American employees and Mexican-American applicants for employment who had not been hired. The class was certified pursuant to a Fifth Circuit rule which permitted "across-the-board" attacks on all racially discriminatory employment practices. The Fifth Circuit had held that it was permissible for "'an employee complaining of one employment practice to represent another complaining of another practice, if the plaintiff and the members of the class suffer from essentially the same injury. In this case, all of the claims are based on discrimination because of national origin.'" *Falcon, [supra,]* at 153[(internal quotation omitted)]. The Supreme Court reversed, holding that:

> Respondent's complaint provided an insufficient basis for concluding that the adjudication of his claim of discrimination in promotion would require the decision of any common question concerning the failure of petitioner to hire more Mexican-Americans. Without any specific presentation identifying the questions of law or fact that were common to the claims of respondent and of the members of the class he sought to represent, it was error for the District Court to presume that respondent's claim was typical of other claims against petitioner by Mexican-American employees and applicants. If one allegation of specific discriminatory treatment were sufficient to support an across-the-board attack, every Title VII case would be a potential company wide class action. [457 U.S. at 158-59[].]

At first blush, the Supreme Court's criticism of the class certification challenged in *Falcon* appears applicable in a case such as this. After all, a number of different harms are alleged here, which have not been suffered uniformly among the proposed class representatives. There are two reasons, however, that *Falcon* does not bar the certification of this class.

First, the various discrete harms alleged by Plaintiffs are all allegedly suffered by members of Communities for Equity, a proposed class representative. [C] "Numerous decisions have recognized the ability of associations, both incorporated and unincorporated, to act as class representatives under Rule 23. These entities are afforded representative status, provided that the underlying purpose of the organization is to represent the interests of the class." Upper Valley Assoc. For Handicapped Citizens v. Mills, 168 F.R.D. 167, 171 (D.Vt.1996). Since CFE exists for the very purpose of achieving gender equity in high school sports, and since its members allege the manifold harms contained in its complaint, it achieves typicality of injury and claims through its membership.

More importantly, however, the mere fact of some distinction between the particular claims of named Plaintiffs and the diverse manifestations of discrimination alleged here is insufficient to extinguish typicality. The *Falcon* Court provided for the possibility of broad-based attacks on discrimination if there were proof of an underlying policy of discrimination. [C] Here, the variety of alleged manifestations of discrimination, such as inequitable facilities, scheduling, sanctioning, and rules, present a sufficient case of an underlying policy or practice of discrimination.[fn] The Court determines that differences between sanctioning water polo and scheduling basketball are less significant in this matter than the typicality of claims that female high school athletes are discriminated against in violation of the various laws invoked by Plaintiffs. [Cc] The typicality requirement is therefore satisfied.

Rule 23(a)(4)-Adequacy of Representation

Rule 23(a) requires that the class members and their counsel be prepared to provide fair and adequate representation to the class. In *Senter v. General Motors Corp.*, 532 F.2d 511, 525 (6th Cir.1976), the Sixth Circuit Court of Appeals articulated two criteria for determining adequacy of representation: "1) the representative must have common interests with unnamed members of the class, and 2) it must appear that the representatives will vigorously prosecute the interests of the class through qualified counsel." [Cc] The 23(a)(4) requirement includes a requirement that there be no conflicts between the class representatives and the class. [C] Two issues in this matter raise the potentiality for conflict.

First, it is quite possible that members of the class have no desire to pursue this action, and are not unhappy with the status quo. However, the proposed class purports to include only those who are "adversely affected." While this term is problematic, in that it is unclear whether it should be assessed subjectively or objectively, it appears to limit the class in a way to avoid conflict. As well, even without the limiting language, this sort of putative conflict generally fails to bar class certification. [Cc]

Moreover, as suggested by Plaintiffs, the interests of those class members who do not consider themselves adversely affected will be adequately represented by Defendants.[fn] ...

A second type of potential conflict may be that achieving certain types of relief in this case could come at the expense of other types. For instance, MHSAA may experience legally justifiable financial constraints which make it impossible for it to sanction tournaments in both ice hockey and water polo.[fn] Should a conflict arise from the limited availability of resources, however, it may be resolved by the creation of subclasses. [C] In this case, the Court believes that the appropriate course is to defer consideration of any subclasses until the relief stage, if any, of this litigation. [C] To the extent that the underlying issue in this case is one of unequal treatment and discrimination, the matter of whether to sanction a particular sport appears to be one relating to relief, rather than liability.

Adequacy of representation is also measured by the quality of class counsel. There is no argument here that counsel for Plaintiffs are unqualified. They are experienced in both Title IX litigation, and litigation generally. The Court determines that the requirements of Rule 23(a)(4) are satisfied.

Rule 23(b)(2)-Injunctive or Declaratory Relief

... Defendants argue that a class is unnecessary, because relief granted to named Plaintiffs would inure to the benefit of the class. The Sixth Circuit has disclaimed any necessity requirement for Rule 23(b)(2) certification. Penland v. Warren County Jail, 797 F.2d 332, 334 (6th Cir.1986). Even if such a requirement existed, mootness concerns would suggest the necessity of certification.[fn]

To the extent that Defendants discriminate against female high school athletes through unequal treatment, Defendants act or refuse to act on grounds generally applicable to the class. Injunctive relief is, of course, an appropriate remedy for discriminatory treatment. Rule 23(b)(2) certification is therefore appropriate.

CONCLUSION

Therefore, it is the conclusion of this Court that the Motion for Class Certification shall be granted.[fn] An order shall issue consistent with this Opinion.

Biography

Carole Bos of the Grand Rapids, Michigan law firm Bos & Glazier was trial counsel for the Michigan High School Athletic Association in the above case. Ms. Bos is a nationally recognized civil litigator, having co-chaired the ABA Section of Litigation Insurance Coverage Committee and authored books on balancing professional and family life. She represents individual plaintiffs in medical-malpractice and other personal-injury litigation, businesses in intellectual-property and other disputes, and corporate defendants in civil-rights and other complex civil litigation. Ms. Bos and her law partner Brad Glazier, an adjunct professor at Cooley Law School, have won and settled several multi-million dollar cases including a recent $6.1 million jury verdict for a woman paralyzed by medical treatment. Ms. Bos also maintains diverse outside and public interests including a popular Internet site Awesomestories.com applying her courtroom approach to create interest around stories on history and pop culture.

Alston v. Virginia High School League, Inc.,

United States District Court for the Western District of Virginia
184 F.R.D. 574 (1999)

MEMORANDUM OPINION

MICHAEL, Senior District Judge.

Before the court is plaintiffs' motion for class certification... . Because the court finds that plaintiffs have failed to meet their burden of demonstrating that plaintiffs' claims are typical of those of the proposed class and that plaintiffs will adequately protect the interests of the class, the court will deny plaintiffs' motion for class certification.

I.

On August 19, 1997, plaintiffs, as next friends of their minor daughters, brought this action under Title IX of the Education Amendments of 1972 ("Title IX"), 20 U.S.C. §1681 *et seq.*, and 42 U.S.C. §1983, alleging that the defendant has denied certain female athletes in the Commonwealth of Virginia's public high schools equal treatment, opportunities and benefits based on their sex in violation of Title IX and the Equal Protection Clause of Amendment XIV of the United States Constitution. According to the complaint, plaintiffs in this action are the parents of minor girls enrolled in various public high schools in Virginia. The defendant, the Virginia High School League, Inc. ("VHSL"), is an incorporated association of several hundred high schools which administers interscholastic athletic competition in Virginia. The plaintiffs allege that VHSL's system of scheduling athletic seasons constitutes intentional sex discrimination against certain female athletes. …

Preliminary to trial, plaintiffs seek class action certification pursuant to Rule 23(a) and (b)(2) of the Federal Rules of Civil Procedure. Plaintiffs propose the following class definition: "All present and future female students enrolled in Virginia public schools who participate in interscholastic athletics or who are deterred from participating in interscholastic athletics because of Defendants' discriminatory scheduling practices."[fn]

The court heard testimony and oral argument on the issue of class certification at a hearing… .

II.

… Only two of the prerequisites to class certification are contested here: typicality and adequacy. Therefore, the court will presume all other requirements for class certification have been met and discuss only these two contested requirements.

The typicality and adequacy requirements overlap such that discussion of each separately, particularly in this case, makes little sense. Both requirements "look to the potential for conflicts in the class." Amchem Products, Inc. v. Windsor, 521 U.S. 591, 611[] (1997) [(internal quotation omitted)].

In making the appropriate inquiry as to Rule 23(a)(4), adequacy, the district court should seek to "uncover conflicts of interest between named parties and the class they seek to represent," and ask whether class representatives "'possess the same interest and suffer the same injury' as the class members.'" *Id.* at 625-26[] [(internal quotation omitted)]; [c] …

Similarly, the existence of adversity between named representatives and absent class members usually undermines attempts to meet the typicality requirement. [C] …

Even in the context of class actions alleging discrimination on the basis of sex or gender, the typicality and adequacy requirements must still be met with something more than a mere allegation of across-the board discrimination. [C] A putative class representative cannot succeed in meeting the typicality requirement just because discrimination is alleged. [C] The "across-the board" theory for class certification has been rejected by the Supreme Court as well as the Fourth Circuit. [C] (citing Gen. Tel. Co. v. Falcon, 457 U.S. 147[] (1982)). If the mere allegation that discriminatory practices in general cause injury to all members of the class could suffice to show typicality, the typicality requirement would be eviscerated by allowing even the most remote similarity of interests between class representatives and other members of the class to qualify as the basis for class certification. [Cc] ...

In this case, there is unrebutted evidence of a conflict of interests between the named plaintiffs and other members of the class which precludes certification under Rule 23. The results of the survey related to the court by defendant's expert indicate that plaintiffs do not adequately represent the interests of all the members of their class and that plaintiffs' claims are not typical of their class. A majority of the female public school athletes surveyed expressed a desire to preserve the status quo, meaning that most would not favor the injunctive relief sought by plaintiffs. There is a clear division in the class between those girls whose schools have already been subject to reclassification and those girls whose schools could, potentially, at some future time, be subject to reclassification. Those who have never experienced reclassification prefer not to have the entire system changed to suit the student athletes who have had to stop playing one or more of their preferred sports due to reclassification. Logically, if statewide realignment occurred, many more girls would be faced with the necessity of changing which sports they play. ...

This conflict prevents plaintiffs from satisfying the typicality requirement as well as the adequacy of representation requirement. Plaintiffs have presented nothing to dispel the defendant's suggestion that there is a schism between girls who may benefit from reclassification and those who are injured by reclassification. A girl who could not previously play two sports because they occurred in the same season may be able to play those two sports when a school is reclassified and the seasons for some sports change. Such girls would not bring claims like the ones brought here by plaintiffs. Thus it cannot be said that as goes the claim of these plaintiffs, so go the claims of all others in the class. ...

... Plaintiffs go so far as to assert that what other members of the class want is irrelevant. Clearly, Rule 23(a), with its typicality and adequacy requirements, does not allow certification of a class without regard for the interests of all members of that class. Regard for the interests of all members includes not only regard for legal theories viewed in a vacuum or notions that alignment would be more fair in the abstract, but also regard for the specific remedies sought by class representatives as compared to the remedies favored by other members of the class.

Plaintiffs also propose that because other courts have certified classes in cases alleging violations of Title IX, this court must certify the class in this Title IX suit as well. None of the factors described in the Federal Rules, as interpreted by the courts, suggests that this consideration should be weighed by the court to the slightest degree. Certification is a case-by-case analysis and there are no legal claims which automatically bind the court to certify any and every class bringing those claims. ...

For all of these reasons, the class proposed by plaintiffs for certification cannot be accepted by this court as one which fits all the requirements of the Federal Rules. These plaintiffs will not be able to adequately represent the interests of other members of the class who clearly do not favor the remedies sought be plaintiffs. Furthermore, because there is a possibility, unrebutted by plaintiffs, that some girls benefit from and prefer the current scheduling practices of the defendant, the claims of these plaintiffs are not typical of those that would be brought by other members of the proposed class.

III.

Plaintiffs have proposed, in the event that this court declines to certify the class described in their motion for class certification, that a narrower sub-class be certified. This narrower class would consist of "all present and future female athletes enrolled in Virginia public schools who are forced to choose between or among sports because of Defendant's discriminatory scheduling practices." Plaintiffs contend that so defining the class will eliminate any problems in meeting the typicality and adequacy of representation requirements.

Where it is clear that a sub-class is not adequately represented by the named plaintiffs, the court may dismiss the action, or allow it to continue as an action solely for the benefit of the named plaintiffs, or establish sub-classes or narrow the class to those who would be adequately represented by named plaintiffs. [C] However, the narrowed sub-class must still meet all four of the requirements of Rule 23.

Even this narrower class-proposed by plaintiffs ... fails to meet all of the prerequisites to certification. ... [C]onflicts of interests exist even among members of the narrower class. ... [T]he results of the survey suggest that there is a strong chance that some girls who declined to join the lawsuit did so because they, like a majority of female high school athletes in Virginia, do not share the goals and interests of these plaintiffs.

... Therefore, the court will decline to certify the narrower, sub-class proposed by plaintiffs in the alternative. The court will allow the suit to go forward with plaintiffs as representatives only of themselves.

IV.

Plaintiffs have not succeeded in showing that they will adequately represent the interests of all members of any of the classes they have described. They also fail to meet the typicality requirement for class certification. Because adequacy and typicality are both prerequisites to class certification, these failings are dispositive of their motion for class certification.

INQUIRY

Adequacy. Although it took a Supreme Court review and remand, the plaintiffs eventually prevailed in the above *Michigan High School Athletic Assn.* case, establishing constitutional, federal civil-rights act, and state civil-rights act violations. *See* Communities for Equity v. Michigan High School Athletic Assn., 459 F.3d 676 (6th Cir. 2006), cert. denied, 549 U.S. 1322 (2007). Michigan high school girls now play sports during traditional rather than non-traditional seasons because of the case. The above *Virginia High School League* opinion intimates just how divided public opinion and potential class members were on these cases. Although the courts are not to consider the merits of a case, the *Virginia High School League* opinion shows how disagreements within the class over the proper cause and relief can implicate Rule 23(a)'s adequacy-of-representation factor. Changes in the interim relief afforded one or more of the class representatives, or interim actions or omissions by class representatives, can make continued representation inadequate. *See* Gonzales v. Cassidy, 474 F.2d 67 (5th Cir. 1973) (representative's failure to appeal initial judgment grounds to review adequacy). You may also already sense the constitutional dimension (due process' notice and opportunity for hearing) that adequacy of representation can implicate, considering that the class representative's results will bind class members. The text in the next section addresses this issue through the Supreme Court's decision in *Hansberry v. Lee*. *See also* Richards v. Jefferson County, 517 U.S. 793 (1996) (due process prohibits binding class members to judgment where they were inadequately represented). Both of the above high-school-athletic cases cited another Supreme Court case, *General Telephone Co. v. Falcon*, which held that the class representative, allegedly passed over for promotion, was not typical of the class for which the representative sought certification because they had allegedly been discriminated against in hiring, not promotion. In cases where there are typicality and adequacy issues, the trial court may certify a smaller-than-requested class or subclasses. FED. R. CIV. P. 25(c)(5); *see, e.g.,* Kohl v. Association of Trial Lawyers, 183 F.R.D. 475 (D. Md. 1998) (certifying class of current but not future retirees).

Types. You now have a sense of how the courts treat whether the class representative can satisfy Rule 23(a)'s numerosity, commonality, typically, and representation conditions. The next step in the analysis is under which Rule 23(b) type the class actions would qualify. Can you tell yet which Rule 23(b) type of action the above two cases represented? Consider then Rule 23(b)'s four types, one of which the class action must meet for certification. Rule 23(b)(1)(A) defines a first incompatible-standards type where conducting the litigation without the class "would create a risk of ... inconsistent or varying adjudications ... that would establish incompatible standards of conduct for the party opposing the class." If the party opposing the class might suffer two or more contradictory individual judgments, then certify the class (assuming satisfaction of all Rule 23(a) conditions) to obtain a single consistent judgment. Rule 23(b)(1)(B) defines a second insufficient-fund type where "individual adjudications ... would substantially impair or impede" the ability of other non-party claimants "to protect their interests." If individual adjudications would deplete a common but insufficient fund, then certify the class to divide equitably the insufficient fund. *See, e.g.,* Ortiz v. Fibreboard Corp., 527 U.S. 815, 838-839 (1999). Rule 23(b)(2) defines a third injunctive-relief type where "the party opposing the class has acted or refused to act on grounds that apply generally to the class ... as a whole." If the party opposing the class would continue to do to non-parties what it could not do to the party in an individual action after injunctive relief, then certify the class to ensure that the opposing party does not skirt and frustrate the injunction. Rule 23(b)(3) defines a fourth damages type where "questions of law or fact common to class members predominate over any questions affecting only individual members, and ... a class action is superior" to individual actions "for fairly and efficiently adjudicating the controversy." If the claims are so small or uniform that individual actions would be impossible or inefficient, then certify the class to enable their resolution as a whole on sensible economics. Consider next an opinion classifying a case under a Rule 23(b) type to grant certification.

Hubler Chevrolet, Inc. v. General Motors Corp.,

United States District Court for the Southern District of Indiana
193 F.R.D. 574 (2000)

BARKER, Chief Judge.

Plaintiffs, a group of Indiana automobile dealers who sell vehicles manufactured by General Motors (GM), a Delaware corporation, brought this action against GM on behalf of all Indiana dealers alleging that GM's marketing scheme violates the Indiana Deceptive Franchise Practices Act ([c]) and constitutes criminal conversion and unjust enrichment.[fn] Plaintiffs claim that GM unlawfully altered its marketing program, under which it collects from dealers an extra one (1) percent of the Manufacturer's Suggested Retail Price (MSRP) of new cars sold. Formerly, the dealers authorized GM's collection of the one percent charge because GM redistributed the money to regional dealer marketing groups (DMGs) for use in local advertising campaigns. In April of 1999, GM began to retain the monies previously earmarked for local marketing efforts, announcing that it would now spend this money on national advertising. Plaintiffs' Complaint seeks to enjoin GM from assessing the alleged marketing charge against Indiana GM dealers... . Pursuant to Federal Rule of Civil Procedure 23, Plaintiffs moved for certification of a class defined as all GM dealers located in Indiana. Because the parties more than sufficiently communicated their arguments in support of and in opposition to class certification in their briefs, we have determined that a hearing regarding Plaintiffs' motion is unnecessary... .

Discussion

1. Rule 23(a)

... The first step is to satisfy the prerequisites of Rule 23(a)... . The party seeking class certification bears the burden of proving that these prerequisites have been met and that class certification is appropriate. ...

a. Numerosity

... Plaintiffs must show that the putative class is so numerous that "joinder of all [class] members is *impracticable.*" Fed. R.Civ.P. 23(a)(1) (emphasis added). While there is no magic number held to satisfy this requirement, classes of forty or more members have generally been found to be sufficiently numerous. [Cc] In light of the circumstances of this action, including the geographic dispersion of the dealers and the difficulties of administering a case involving over 200 plaintiffs, we believe that joinder is impracticable and that Plaintiffs have satisfied the numerosity requirement.

b. Commonality and Typicality

Rule 23(a)(2) requires that "there are questions of law or fact common to the class," and Rule 23(a)(3) requires that the plaintiff's claim be typical of those of the class. ...

Plaintiffs readily fulfill the element of commonality in this case. All members of the proposed class share an identical legal claim: that the one percent charge collected by GM, formerly distributed to the DMGs, belongs to them. The legality in Indiana of General Motors' marketing practices, namely its retention of the assessment against all new cars sold by its dealers, forms the common basis of the suit.

Similarly, typicality is shown… . As we have previously noted, all of the class members' claims are based on the same legal theory regarding the marketing charge and Rule 23(a)(3) is satisfied.

c. Adequacy of Representation

Rule 23(a)(4) requires that the representative parties fairly and adequately protect the interests of the class. … General Motors provides no evidence that Plaintiffs' counsel is inadequate… .

Similarly unavailing are GM's suggestions that the named plaintiffs are not adequate representatives of the class. …

… We find that Plaintiffs have met the requirement of adequacy of representation. Plaintiffs have established that they meet all of Rule 23(a)'s prerequisites; thus, we turn to consideration of 23(b).

2. Rule 23(b)

It is not enough that the threshold requirements of Rule 23(a) are met; the action must also be maintainable under one of Rule 23(b)'s subparts. [Cc] Plaintiffs seek certification under Rule 23(b)(1), 23(b)(2) and 23(b)(3).

a. Rule 23(b)(1)

Class certification under Rule 23(b)(1) is typically appropriate in cases where there exists either a common fund that may limit recovery to individual plaintiffs or a risk of establishing inconsistent standards of conduct for the defendant. *See* Jefferson v. Ingersoll Intl. Inc., 195 F.3d 894, 897 (7th Cir. 1999) (commenting that "domain of Rule 23(b)(1)" is "limited fund that must be distributed ratably," citing Ortiz v. Fibreboard Corp., 527 U.S. 815[] (1999)). We discern no allegation of a limited fund that would demonstrate why this type of certification should apply in the instant case. Plaintiffs note that "the prosecution of separate actions will create the risk of varying adjudications with respect to individual dealers" that could "be dispositive of the interests of other GM dealers in the State of Indiana who are not parties to this action or will substantially impair or impede their ability to protect their interests." [C] However, "that some plaintiffs may ultimately be successful against a defendant while others may not is simply not a ground for invoking Rule 23(b)(1)(A)." Hurd[v. Monsanto Co., 164 F.R.D. 234, 239 (S.D. Ind. 1995)].

b. Rule 23(b)(2)

Under Rule 23(b)(2), a class may be certified when "the party opposing the class has acted or refused to act on grounds generally applicable to the class," and the representatives are seeking "final injunctive relief or corresponding declaratory relief." [Cc] The primary limitation imposed by this subsection is that injunctive or declaratory relief must predominate as the remedy being sought on behalf of the class. [Cc] The subsection is not fulfilled where the plaintiffs are seeking predominantly money damages. [Cc]

Plaintiffs have alleged conduct by General Motors clearly applicable to all members of the class: illegal conversion of one percent of the price of new vehicles, an amount formerly contributed to local advertising funds, for use in its own national marketing efforts. Thus, any obstacle to Plaintiffs' attempt to certify this class action under Rule 23(b)(2) would come from the type of relief they are seeking, that is, whether it is a form of final injunctive or corresponding declaratory relief. To determine whether the relief sought is primarily equitable or money damages, "the plaintiffs' specific request for relief must be closely scrutinized and consideration must be given to whether the 'crux of the action is for money damages.'" Clay[v. American Tobacco Co., 188 F.R.D. 483, 494 (S.D. Ill. 1999)] (quoting Dhamer v. Bristol-Myers Squibb Co., 183 F.R.D. 520, 528 (N.D. Ill. 1998)).

Deciding whether Plaintiffs' case fits the (b)(2) paradigm presents a close issue because Plaintiffs want to prevent future economic harm and would be entitled to equitable recovery of the amounts paid under an unjust enrichment theory, but they also pursue treble damages on the conversion count and an award of attorney fees as provided for by Indiana statute. In one sense Plaintiffs seek a declaration that the one percent is their money, and relief would seem to flow directly from that proposition. ... Declaratory relief is not to be used simply to "lay the basis for a later damage award." Sarafin v. Sears, Roebuck and Co., 446 F.Supp. 611, 615 (N.D. Ill. 1978); [c]. "The use of a declaratory judgment in a class action where the real goal is a damage award undermines the purpose of Rule 23(b)(2)." *Sarafin, [supra,]* at 615. We do not think that Plaintiffs' prayer for declaratory relief is presented only to lay the basis for an award of treble damages and attorneys fees, but we cannot ignore the large amount of money involved in the potential recovery to class members.

In *Jefferson v. Ingersoll International,* Judge Easterbrook offered guidance to district courts deciding between 23(b)(2) and (b)(3) class certification. 195 F.3d 894, 898 (7th Cir.1999). ... [H]e pointed out that ... "... A court should endeavor to select the most appropriate [Rule 23(b) type] in the list. When substantial damages have been sought, the most appropriate approach is that of Rule 23(b)(3), because it allows notice and an opportunity to opt out." *Jefferson,* 195 F.3d at 898. ... Because of the importance of money damages to Plaintiffs' claims, we believe that class members should have the opportunity to receive notice and opt out. We therefore decline to certify a (b)(2) class, though we recognize that any grant of injunctive relief may affect those who choose not to participate in the suit.

c. Rule 23(b)(3)

A class action is maintainable under Rule 23(b)(3) if we find that "the questions of law or fact common to the members of the class *predominate* over any questions affecting only individual members, and that a class action is *superior* to other available methods for the fair and efficient adjudication of the controversy." Fed. R. Civ. P. 23(b)(3) (emphasis added). The underlying purpose of Rule 23(b)(3)'s requirements is to assure that a class action has "practical utility" in the suit. [C] Rule 23(b)(3) lays out four factors which we consider in analyzing these issues: "(A) the interest of members of the class in individually controlling the prosecution ... of separate actions; (B) the extent and nature of any litigation concerning the controversy already commenced by ... members of the class; (C) the desirability or undesirability of concentrating the litigation of the claims in the particular forum; (D) the difficulties likely to be encountered in the management of a class action." [C]

i. Predominance

Predominance is met when "'one or more of the central issues in the action are common to the class and can be said to predominate... .'" John Does 1-100 v. Boyd, 613 F.Supp. 1514, 1530 (D. Minn. 1985) [(internal quotation omitted)]. Satisfying this criterion "normally turns on the answer to one basic question: is there an essential factual link between all class members and the defendant for which the law provides a remedy?" *Johns,* 145 F.R.D. at 484-85.

We have determined that putative class members share a common basis for their suit: the issue of whether GM's marketing practices violate Indiana law. Each of the plaintiffs involved herein alleges that a one percent charge that he or she formerly agreed to pay for use in local advertising has been diverted to GM's national marketing without his or her consent. The legality of this alleged marketing assessment program under Indiana law is the "dominant, central focus" of the proposed class action. While their objections to General Motors' various marketing initiatives may differ, every member of the proposed class shares the desire to reassert control over what it believes is its marketing money and a common belief that General Motors has in essence stolen its money by exerting exclusive control over the marketing funds. ...

Rule 23(b)(3) class actions commonly involve numerous levels of damages and injury for different class members. [Cc] In *Johns, supra,* [at 485,] the court certified a class action despite dissimilar damage amounts because "the extent of damages is not an issue" when certifying the class, rather it is a question for the merits of the lawsuit. [C] Similarly, the court in *John Does 1-100, supra,* [at 1530,] found that common questions of law and fact predominated despite the fact that varying damage levels were involved in the putative class action. *Id.* Finally, determining damages in this case will not necessitate minitrials because damages can be calculated easily from General Motors computer records tracking the number of vehicles sold by dealers.

The only possibility that Plaintiffs will need to present individualized proof lies in their IDFPA claim, an element of which is "coercion." Assuming that actual coercion must be shown to establish the IDFPA violation, Plaintiffs need not present individualized proof if coercion can be proven on a classwide basis, for example through contracts, agreements and promotional materials uniformly applicable to all members of the proposed class. ...

We conclude that the common legal questions affecting General Motors' liability predominate over any individualized factual and legal questions involved in this case; however, we note that a class could be decertified if it became evident that Plaintiffs must rely upon facts unique to each dealer to show GM forced dealers to participate in the marketing scheme. To the extent the relevant communications differed according to GM division (e.g., different contracts or letters sent to Oldsmobile versus Pontiac dealers) we can create subclasses if material differences prevent their consideration as a single group... .

ii. Superiority

Rule 23(b)(3) also requires Plaintiffs to establish that a class action would be the "superior" manner in which to resolve the controversy. It does not appear that individual class members have any particular interest in pursuing separate actions, and we are unaware of any other litigation surrounding this issue already commenced by class members. Thus, the two most relevant issues regarding the superiority of the class action form highlighted by Rule 23(b)(3) are the desirability of concentrating the actions in this forum and the difficulty that management of such a class action would impose upon us. *See* Fed. R.Civ.P. 23(b)(3)(C), (D).

One reason to favor a class action is to avoid duplicative lawsuits, which would thereby waste the parties' and the courts' time and resources. [Cc] It is without question that allowing this case to proceed as a class action would allow economies of scale to operate and ultimately reduce the overall burden on the courts associated with pursuing the claims versus maintaining individual actions. Assuming for the moment that all of the potential plaintiffs filed suit individually, the federal courts would be open to an avalanche of suits involving duplicitous discovery and a repetition of legal determinations.

A class action allows discovery to proceed on all of the potential claims jointly. A class action also eliminates the potential that the defendants will be subject to contradictory resolutions of the ultimate legal issue; to wit, the validity of the marketing program, because the issue is resolved vis-a-vis all class members at once. A class action simplifies discovery because the defendants and the court will have to deal with only one plaintiffs' counsel, rather than a separate attorney for each individual plaintiff. Discovery disputes can be resolved and legal determinations made with respect to all of the parties at once instead of one plaintiff at a time.

While class actions may present undue pressure upon defendants to settle cases, this factor alone does not outweigh the advantages we have discussed. For these reasons, we hold that Plaintiffs' putative class action is superior to alternative methods of adjudicating the claims and thus this class action may be maintained under Rule 23(b)(3).

Conclusion

Plaintiffs' proposed class satisfies the demands of Rule 23(a) and is maintainable under Rule 23(b)(3). Plaintiffs' motion for class certification is therefore *GRANTED.* The class shall be defined, and the action maintained, on behalf of all General Motors dealers in Indiana affected by the marketing program instituted in April of 1999. Plaintiffs shall provide notice to class members pursuant to Rule 23(c)(2)... . Certification of the class is conditional, subject to our power at any time prior to final judgment to revoke or alter class certification in the interests of justice and to insure compliance with the requirements of Rule 23. [Cc]

INQUIRY

Notice. Certification succeeded under Rule 23(b)(3)'s damages-type class action in the above *Hubler Chevrolet, Inc. v. General Motors Corp.* case, despite Rule 23(b)'s predominance and superiority requirements. Can you articulate why Rule 23(b)(3) discourages damages-type class actions? The prospect for a plaintiff's lawyer to multiply the potential damages several fold, and the risk that prospect creates for solvent or insured defendants (meaning the target they become), makes damages-type class actions powerful for inducing early settlements and capable of abuses. To the predominance and superiority requirements, Rule 23(b)(3) also adds several factors intended to make damages-type class certification more difficult, including the individual interest of class members, whether they are already involved in other litigation, and the manageability of the class action. Rule 23(c)(2)(B) also dictates opt-out-notice requirements that do not apply to the other three types of class action. The Supreme Court has held that the individual class representatives who institute the suit must pay the cost of Rule 23(b)(3) opt-out notice, Eisen v. Carlisle & Jacquelin, 417 U.S. 156, 177 (1974), increasing the plaintiffs' cost and risk in pursuing a damages-type class action. In Oppenheimer Fund, Inc. v. Sanders, 437

U.S. 340 (1978), the Supreme Court disapproved of class-action plaintiffs' increasing practice, in response to *Eisen v. Carlisle & Jacquelin*, of using discovery to force defendant to disclose contact information for class members in a way that substantially reduced the plaintiffs' notice costs (and increased the defendants' costs). The other Rule 23(b) types do not require Rule 23(c)(2)(B) opt-out notice. Indeed, there is no opting out for members of the other Rule 23(b) classes. Can you articulate why the presence of all potential class members is necessary in the incompatible-standards, insufficient-fund, and injunctive-relief types? Rule 23(c)(2)(A) permits but does not require the trial court to order notice for Rule 23(b)(1)(A), (b)(1)(B), and (b)(2) classes. When might notice be most appropriate for incompatible-standards, insufficient-fund, and injunctive-relief classes?

2. Reach

As already intimated, certification is not the only significant issue in class-action litigation. Class actions create unique issues for each of the issues Chapters II through VI address on the authority of courts to adjudicate. Personal jurisdiction, notice and opportunity for hearing, personal jurisdiction, venue, and choice of law each require somewhat different considerations for class actions than for other litigation. For example, consider again subject-matter jurisdiction. Federal courts must generally have independent subject-matter jurisdiction for joined claims including class actions. If a class action arises under federal rather than state law, then federal-question jurisdiction under 28 U.S.C. §1331 makes subject-matter jurisdiction a non-issue. By contrast, diversity jurisdiction under 28 U.S.C. §1332 should be problematic for class actions. The Supreme Court long ago held in Supreme Tribe of Ben-Hur v. Cauble, 255 U.S. 356 (1921), that the trial courts must look only to the citizenship of class representatives to determine diversity. The Supreme Court also long ago held that the claim of each class member had to exceed the requisite $75,000 amount in controversy. *See* Clark v. Paul Gray, Inc., 306 U.S. 583 (1939); *see also* Zahn v. International Paper Co., 414 U.S. 291 (1973); Snyder v. Harris, 394 U.S. 332 (1969) (individually joined plaintiffs may not aggregate claim values).

Then, in Exxon Mobil Corp. v. Allapattah Services, Inc., 545 U.S. 546 (2005), excerpted in Chapter 4 on subject-matter jurisdiction, the Supreme Court ruled that supplemental jurisdiction under 28 U.S.C. §1367 eliminated the amount in controversy requirement for class members, so long as the class representative had a qualifying $75,000 claim. The same year as the Supreme Court decided *Exxon Mobil Corp. v. Allapattah,* Congress enacted the Class Action Fairness Act of 2005, 28 U.S.C. §§1332(d), 1453, 1711-1715, also mentioned in Chapter 4. The Act expanded federal-court subject-matter jurisdiction over class actions, even without supplemental jurisdiction. Under the Act, so long as the claims aggregate to at least $5 million and there is minimal diversity between at least one plaintiff and one defendant, the federal courts will have subject-matter jurisdiction. 28 U.S.C. §1332(d)(2). The Act then gives the federal courts discretion to decline some of these class actions, 28 U.S.C. §1332(d)(3), while requiring them to decline other such class actions, 28 U.S.C. §1332(d)(4), based on factors that tend to reflect the litigation's national character.

Why did Congress make federal subject-matter jurisdiction over class actions so broad and then give the federal courts the opportunity or obligation to decline it? One might think from this seeming invitation to additional damages-type class actions that Congress favored them. Not so fast. State law in general has fewer restrictions than FED. R. CIV. P. 23(b)(3) on damages-type class actions. When Congress broadened subject-matter jurisdiction for class actions in federal courts, it also broadened the statutory provisions that allow defendants to remove class actions from state to federal court. As you studied in Chapter 4, removal ordinarily requires that all defendants agree, none be a citizen of the forum state, and removal occur within one year of filing. Under the Class Action Fairness Act, it takes just one of multiple defendants to remove, whether or not one or more defendants are citizens of the forum state or removal occurs within one year. Congress made it easier for defendants to move state class actions into the federal courts where the federal courts would more often dismiss them for not meeting Rule 23's certification requirements. *See* Myriam Gilles, *Class Dismissed: Contemporary Judicial Hostility to Small-Claims Consumer Class Actions*, 59 DEPAUL L.REV. 305 (2010). With the Class Action Fairness Act, Congress favored national and corporate interests over local and individual interests, much as the broad reach of federal common law had done until *Erie Railroad Co. v. Tompkins* overruled *Swift v. Tyson*. Review the following sections of the Class Action Fairness Act, codified at 28 U.S.C. §§1332(d) and 1453, for these provisions.

28 U.S.C.A. § 1332. Diversity of citizenship; amount in controversy; costs.

...

(d)(1) In this subsection—

(A) the term "class" means all of the class members in a class action;

(B) the term "class action" means any civil action filed under rule 23 of the Federal Rules of Civil Procedure or similar State statute or rule of judicial procedure authorizing an action to be brought by 1 or more representative persons as a class action;

(C) the term "class certification order" means an order issued by a court approving the treatment of some or all aspects of a civil action as a class action; and

(D) the term "class members" means the persons (named or unnamed) who fall within the definition of the proposed or certified class in a class action.

(2) The district courts shall have original jurisdiction of any civil action in which the matter in controversy exceeds the sum or value of $5,000,000, exclusive of interest and costs, and is a class action in which—

(A) any member of a class of plaintiffs is a citizen of a State different from any defendant;

(B) any member of a class of plaintiffs is a foreign state or a citizen or subject of a foreign state and any defendant is a citizen of a State; or

(C) any member of a class of plaintiffs is a citizen of a State and any defendant is a foreign state or a citizen or subject of a foreign state.

(3) A district court may, in the interests of justice and looking at the totality of the circumstances, decline to exercise jurisdiction under paragraph (2) over a class action in which greater than one-third but less than two-thirds of the members of all proposed plaintiff classes in the aggregate and the primary defendants are citizens of the State in which the action was originally filed based on consideration of—

(A) whether the claims asserted involve matters of national or interstate interest;

(B) whether the claims asserted will be governed by laws of the State in which the action was originally filed or by the laws of other States;
(C) whether the class action has been pleaded in a manner that seeks to avoid Federal jurisdiction;
(D) whether the action was brought in a forum with a distinct nexus with the class members, the alleged harm, or the defendants;
(E) whether the number of citizens of the State in which the action was originally filed in all proposed plaintiff classes in the aggregate is substantially larger than the number of citizens from any other State, and the citizenship of the other members of the proposed class is dispersed among a substantial number of States; and
(F) whether, during the 3-year period preceding the filing of that class action, 1 or more other class actions asserting the same or similar claims on behalf of the same or other persons have been filed.
(4) A district court shall decline to exercise jurisdiction under paragraph (2)—
(A)(i) over a class action in which—
(I) greater than two-thirds of the members of all proposed plaintiff classes in the aggregate are citizens of the State in which the action was originally filed;
(II) at least 1 defendant is a defendant—
(aa) from whom significant relief is sought by members of the plaintiff class;
(bb) whose alleged conduct forms a significant basis for the claims asserted by the proposed plaintiff class; and
(cc) who is a citizen of the State in which the action was originally filed; and
(III) principal injuries resulting from the alleged conduct or any related conduct of each defendant were incurred in the State in which the action was originally filed; and
(ii) during the 3-year period preceding the filing of that class action, no other class action has been filed asserting the same or similar factual allegations against any of the defendants on behalf of the same or other persons; or
(B) two-thirds or more of the members of all proposed plaintiff classes in the aggregate, and the primary defendants, are citizens of the State in which the action was originally filed.
(5) Paragraphs (2) through (4) shall not apply to any class action in which—
(A) the primary defendants are States, State officials, or other governmental entities against whom the district court may be foreclosed from ordering relief; or
(B) the number of members of all proposed plaintiff classes in the aggregate is less than 100.
(6) In any class action, the claims of the individual class members shall be aggregated to determine whether the matter in controversy exceeds the sum or value of $5,000,000, exclusive of interest and costs.
(7) Citizenship of the members of the proposed plaintiff classes shall be determined for purposes of paragraphs (2) through (6) as of the date of filing of the complaint or amended complaint, or, if the case stated by the initial pleading is not subject to Federal jurisdiction, as of the date of service by plaintiffs of an amended pleading, motion, or other paper, indicating the existence of Federal jurisdiction.
(8) This subsection shall apply to any class action before or after the entry of a class certification order by the court with respect to that action.
(9) Paragraph (2) shall not apply to any class action that solely involves a claim—
(A) concerning a covered security as defined under 16(f)(3) of the Securities Act of 1933 (15 U.S.C. 78p(f)(3)) and section 28(f)(5)(E) of the Securities Exchange Act of 1934 (15 U.S.C. 78bb(f)(5)(E));
(B) that relates to the internal affairs or governance of a corporation or other form of business enterprise and that arises under or by virtue of the laws of the State in which such corporation or business enterprise is incorporated or organized; or

(C) that relates to the rights, duties (including fiduciary duties), and obligations relating to or created by or pursuant to any security (as defined under section 2(a)(1) of the Securities Act of 1933 (15 U.S.C. 77b(a)(1)) and the regulations issued thereunder).

(10) For purposes of this subsection and section 1453, an unincorporated association shall be deemed to be a citizen of the State where it has its principal place of business and the State under whose laws it is organized.

(11)(A) For purposes of this subsection and section 1453, a mass action shall be deemed to be a class action removable under paragraphs (2) through (10) if it otherwise meets the provisions of those paragraphs.

(B)(i) As used in subparagraph (A), the term "mass action" means any civil action (except a civil action within the scope of section 1711(2)) in which monetary relief claims of 100 or more persons are proposed to be tried jointly on the ground that the plaintiffs' claims involve common questions of law or fact, except that jurisdiction shall exist only over those plaintiffs whose claims in a mass action satisfy the jurisdictional amount requirements under subsection (a).

(ii) As used in subparagraph (A), the term "mass action" shall not include any civil action in which—

(I) all of the claims in the action arise from an event or occurrence in the State in which the action was filed, and that allegedly resulted in injuries in that State or in States contiguous to that State;

(II) the claims are joined upon motion of a defendant;

(III) all of the claims in the action are asserted on behalf of the general public (and not on behalf of individual claimants or members of a purported class) pursuant to a State statute specifically authorizing such action; or

(IV) the claims have been consolidated or coordinated solely for pretrial proceedings.

(C)(i) Any action(s) removed to Federal court pursuant to this subsection shall not thereafter be transferred to any other court pursuant to section 1407, or the rules promulgated thereunder, unless a majority of the plaintiffs in the action request transfer pursuant to section 1407.

(ii) This subparagraph will not apply—

(I) to cases certified pursuant to rule 23 of the Federal Rules of Civil Procedure; or

(II) if plaintiffs propose that the action proceed as a class action pursuant to rule 23 of the Federal Rules of Civil Procedure.

(D) The limitations periods on any claims asserted in a mass action that is removed to Federal court pursuant to this subsection shall be deemed tolled during the period that the action is pending in Federal court.

...

---

28 U.S.C. §1453. Removal of class actions

(a) Definitions.—In this section, the terms "class," "class action," "class certification order," and "class member" shall have the meanings given such terms under section 1332(d)(1).

(b) In general.—A class action may be removed to a district court of the United States in accordance with section 1446 (except that the 1-year limitation under section 1446(b) shall not apply), without regard to whether any defendant is a citizen of the State in which the action is brought, except that such action may be removed by any defendant without the consent of all defendants.

(c) Review of remand orders.—

(1) In general.—Section 1447 shall apply to any removal of a case under this section, except that notwithstanding section 1447(d), a court of appeals may accept an appeal from an order of a district court granting or denying a motion to remand a class action to the State court from which it was removed if application is made to the court of appeals not more than 10 days after entry of the order.

(2) Time period for judgment.—If the court of appeals accepts an appeal under paragraph (1), the court shall complete all action on such appeal, including rendering judgment, not later than 60 days after the date on which such appeal was filed, unless an extension is granted under paragraph (3).

(3) Extension of time period.—The court of appeals may grant an extension of the 60-day period described in paragraph (2) if—

(A) all parties to the proceeding agree to such extension, for any period of time; or

(B) such extension is for good cause shown and in the interests of justice, for a period not to exceed 10 days.

(4) Denial of appeal.—If a final judgment on the appeal under paragraph (1) is not issued before the end of the period described in paragraph (2), including any extension under paragraph (3), the appeal shall be denied.

(d) Exception.—This section shall not apply to any class action that solely involves—

(1) a claim concerning a covered security as defined under section 16(f)(3) of the Securities Act of 1933 (15 U.S.C. 78p(f)(3)) and section 28(f)(5)(E) of the Securities Exchange Act of 1934 (15 U.S.C. 78bb(f)(5)(E));

(2) a claim that relates to the internal affairs or governance of a corporation or other form of business enterprise and arises under or by virtue of the laws of the State in which such corporation or business enterprise is incorporated or organized; or

(3) a claim that relates to the rights, duties (including fiduciary duties), and obligations relating to or created by or pursuant to any security (as defined under section 2(a)(1) of the Securities Act of 1933 (15 U.S.C. 77b(a)(1)) and the regulations issued thereunder).

INQUIRY

Securities Litigation. Class-action securities litigation bears a somewhat similar history of Congress federalizing certain actions to limit the impact of more plaintiff-generous state law. Concerned with an increase in federal securities litigation invoking class-action status, Congress first tightened pleading requirements in those cases making it harder to plead a federal action and required a lead plaintiff with a large financial stake interested in ensuring appropriate process and outcome. *See* Privatre Securities Litigation Reform Act of 1995, 15 U.S.C. §78u4(b)(1)(B). Practitioners responded to the tighter federal pleading requirements by bringing the claims in state court under state securities laws. What recourse did Congress then have to control the state-court litigation? Congress responded by enacting the Uniform Securities Litigation Standards Act of 1998, 15 U.S.C. §77p(c). The Act preempted state securities-law claims in class actions, granted defendants broad rights to remove those state-court class-action securities-law claims to federal court, and mandated their dismissal with certain limited exceptions. Did Congress overdo it? Where Congress intends to preempt state law, it ordinarily simply so provides in substantive-law legislation. State courts must recognize federal preemption. With securities class actions, though, Congress mandated the actions' removal for the federal courts to dismiss, presumably to ensure that state courts do not frustrate its goals of eliminating judicial remedies. In its two recent federal class-action acts, the Class Action Fairness Act and the Uniform Securities Litigation Standards Act, Congress has deployed federal judicial powers to prevent large numbers of individuals from challenging national corporate actions and interests. In the past few years since then, have national corporations acted more or less responsibly regarding individual rights and interests?

Due Process. As the above discussion reflects, subject-matter jurisdiction is largely statutory. The other issues on authority to adjudicate, including personal jurisdiction, notice and opportunity for hearing, venue, and choice of law, have clearer constitutional dimensions. To fully appreciate the impact of the Constitution's due-process clause on class-action litigation, consider the progenitor Supreme Court case excerpted below, *Hansberry v. Lee.* With the help of white real estate agents, the African-American banker and real estate broker Carl Hansberry bought a house in a white Chicago neighborhood in violation of racially restrictive covenants. The Illinois Supreme Court upheld the covenant, forcing Mr. Hansberry and his family to leave. The United States Supreme Court reversed in the following opinion, followed a few years later by its seminal *Shelly v. Kraemer* opinion holding racially restrictive covenants unconstitutional. An interesting note to the history of *Hansberry v. Lee* is that Mr. Hansberry's daughter Lorraine, who was almost hit by a brick thrown through the residence's window when the family lived there briefly, later wrote the first Broadway play by an African American, *A Raisin in the Sun*, drawing on her experience living in Chicago's then-segregated South Side. Read the following case for the way in which it resolves the tension between the need of a class action to bind class members and the constitutional right of a non-party to due process even in class actions. As a matter of due process, class-action judgments bind class members only when they are adequately represented.

Hansberry v. Lee,

United States Supreme Court
311 U.S. 32 (1940)

Mr. Justice STONE delivered the opinion of the Court.

The question is whether the Supreme Court of Illinois, by its adjudication that petitioners in this case are bound by a judgment rendered in an earlier litigation to which they were not parties, has deprived them of the due process of law guaranteed by the Fourteenth Amendment.

Respondents brought this suit in the Circuit Court of Cook County, Illinois, to enjoin the breach by petitioners of an agreement restricting the use of land within a described area of the City of Chicago, which was alleged to have been entered into by some five hundred of the land owners. The agreement stipulated that for a specified period no part of the land should be "sold, leased to or permitted to be occupied by any person of the colored race" [(a provision that the Supreme Court later held unenforceable in Shelley v. Kraemer, 334 U.S. 1 (1948)], and provided that it should not be effective unless signed by the "owners of 95 per centum of the frontage" within the described area. The bill of complaint set up that the owners of 95 per cent of the frontage had signed; that respondents are owners of land within the restricted area who have either signed the agreement or acquired their land from others who did sign and that petitioners Hansberry, who are Negroes, have, with the alleged aid of the other petitioners and with knowledge of the agreement, acquired and are occupying land in the restricted area formerly belonging to an owner who had signed the agreement.

To the defense that the agreement had never become effective because owners of 95 per cent of the frontage had not signed it, respondents pleaded that that issue was res judicata by the decree in an earlier suit. [C] To this petitioners pleaded, by way of rejoinder, that they were not parties to that suit or bound by its decree, and that denial of their right to litigate, in the present suit, the issue of performance of the condition precedent to the validity of the agreement would be a denial of due process of law guaranteed by the Fourteenth Amendment. ...

The circuit court, after a trial on the merits, found that owners of only about 54 per cent of the frontage had signed the agreement, and that the only support of the judgment in the Burke case was a false and fraudulent stipulation of the parties that 95 per cent had signed. But it ruled that the issue of performance of the condition precedent to the validity of the agreement was res judicata as alleged and entered a decree for respondents. The Supreme Court of Illinois affirmed. [C] We granted certiorari to resolve the constitutional question. [C] ...

State courts are free to attach such descriptive labels to litigations before them as they may choose and to attribute to them such consequences as they think appropriate under state constitutions and laws, subject only to the requirements of the Constitution of the United States. But when the judgment of a state court, ascribing to the judgment of another court the binding force and effect of res judicata, is challenged for want of due process it becomes the duty of this Court to examine the course of procedure in both litigations to ascertain whether the litigant whose rights have thus been adjudicated has been afforded such notice and opportunity to be heard as are requisite to the due process which the Constitution prescribes. [C]

It is a principle of general application in Anglo-American jurisprudence that one is not bound by a judgment in personam in a litigation in which he is not designated as a party or to which he has not been made a party by service of process. Pennoyer v. Neff, 95 U.S. 714[(1877)]; [c]. A judgment rendered in such circumstances is not entitled to the full faith and credit which the Constitution and statute of the United States, [c], prescribe, [cc], and judicial action enforcing it against the person or property of the absent party is not that due process which the Fifth and Fourteenth Amendments requires. [Cc]

To these general rules there is a recognized exception that, to an extent not precisely defined by judicial opinion, the judgment in a "class" or "representative" suit, to which some members of the class are parties, may bind members of the class or those represented who were not made parties to it. [Cc]

The class suit was an invention of equity to enable it to proceed to a decree in suits where the number of those interested in the subject of the litigation is so great that their joinder as parties in conformity to the usual rules of procedure is impracticable. Courts are not infrequently called upon to proceed with causes in which the number of those interested in the litigation is so great as to make difficult or impossible the joinder of all because some are not within the jurisdiction or because their whereabouts is unknown or where if all were made parties to the suit its continued abatement by the death of some would prevent or unduly delay a decree. In such cases where the interests of those not joined are of the same class as the interests of those who are, and where it is considered that the latter fairly represent the former in the prosecution of the litigation of the issues in which all have a common interest, the court will proceed to a decree. [Cc]

... [T]here is scope within the framework of the Constitution for holding in appropriate cases that a judgment rendered in a class suit is res judicata as to members of the class who are not formal parties to the suit. Here, as elsewhere, the Fourteenth Amendment does not compel state courts or legislatures to adopt any particular rule for establishing the conclusiveness of judgments in class suits; [cc], nor does it compel the adoption of the particular rules thought by this court to be appropriate for the federal courts. With a proper regard for divergent local institutions and interests, [c], this Court is justified in saying that there has been a failure of due process only in those cases where it cannot be said that the procedure adopted, fairly insures the protection of the interests of absent parties who are to be bound by it. [C]

It is familiar doctrine of the federal courts that members of a class not present as parties to the litigation may be bound by the judgment where they are in fact adequately represented by parties who are present, or where they actually participate in the conduct of the litigation in which members of the class are present as parties, [cc], or where the interest of the members of the class, some of whom are present as parties, is joint, or where for any other reason the relationship between the parties present and those who are absent is such as legally to entitle the former to stand in judgment for the latter. [C]

In all such cases, so far as it can be said that the members of the class who are present are, by generally recognized rules of law, entitled to stand in judgment for those who are not, we may assume for present purposes that such procedure affords a protection to the parties who are represented though absent, which would satisfy the requirements of due process and full faith and credit. [Cc] Nor do we find it necessary for the decision of this case to say that, when the only circumstance defining the class is that the determination of the rights of its members turns upon a single issue of fact or law, a state could not constitutionally adopt a procedure whereby some of the members of the class could stand in judgment for all, provided that the procedure were so devised and applied as to insure that those present are of the same class as those absent and that the litigation is so conducted as to insure the full and fair consideration of the common issue. [Cc] We decide only that the procedure and the course of litigation sustained here by the plea of res judicata do not satisfy these requirements.

The restrictive agreement did not purport to create a joint obligation or liability. If valid and effective its promises were the several obligations of the signers and those claiming under them. The promises ran severally to every other signer. It is plain that in such circumstances all those alleged to be bound by the agreement would not constitute a single class in any litigation brought to enforce it. Those who sought to secure its benefits by enforcing it could not be said to be in the same class with or represent those whose interest was in resisting performance, for the agreement by its terms imposes obligations and confers rights on the owner of each plot of land who signs it. If those who thus seek to secure the benefits of the agreement were rightly regarded by the state Supreme Court as constituting a class, it is evident that those signers or their successors who are interested in challenging the validity of the agreement and resisting its performance are not of the same class in the sense that their interests are identical so that any group who had elected to enforce rights conferred by the agreement could be said to be acting in the interest of any others who were free to deny its obligation.

Because of the dual and potentially conflicting interests of those who are putative parties to the agreement in compelling or resisting its performance, it is impossible to say, solely because they are parties to it, that any two of them are of the same class. Nor without more, and with the due regard for the protection of the rights of absent parties which due process exacts, can some be permitted to stand in judgment for all.

It is one thing to say that some members of a class may represent other members in a litigation where the sole and common interest of the class in the litigation, is either to assert a common right or to challenge an asserted obligation. [C] It is quite another to hold that all those who are free alternatively either to assert rights or to challenge them are of a single class, so that any group merely because it is of the class so constituted, may be deemed adequately to represent any others of the class in litigating their interests in either alternative. Such a selection of representatives for purposes of litigation, whose substantial interests are not necessarily or even probably the same as those whom they are deemed to represent, does not afford that protection to absent parties which due process requires. ... Apart from the opportunities it would afford for the fraudulent and collusive sacrifice of the rights of absent parties, we think that the representation in this case no more satisfies the requirements of due process than a trial by a judicial officer who is in such situation that he may have an interest in the outcome of the litigation in conflict with that of the litigants. [C]

The plaintiffs in the Burke case sought to compel performance of the agreement in behalf of themselves and all others similarly situated. They did not designate the defendants in the suit as a class or seek any injunction or other relief against others than the named defendants, and the decree which was entered did not purport to bind others. In seeking to enforce the agreement the plaintiffs in that suit were not representing the petitioners here whose substantial interest is in resisting performance. The defendants in the first suit were not treated by the pleadings or decree as representing others or as foreclosing by their defense the rights of others, and even though nominal defendants, it does not appear that their interest in defeating the contract outweighed their interest in establishing its validity. For a court in this situation to ascribe to either the plaintiffs or defendants the performance of such functions on behalf of petitioners here, is to attribute to them a power that it cannot be said that they had assumed to exercise, and a responsibility which, in view of their dual interests it does not appear that they could rightly discharge.

Reversed.

Mr. Justice McREYNOLDS, Mr. Justice ROBERTS, and Mr. Justice REED concur in the result.

INQUIRY

Personal Jurisdiction. Chapter XVIII addresses in detail the binding effect of judgments. Subject-matter jurisdiction and notice and opportunity for hearing are not the only additional issue that class actions raise on unique terms.

You should have recognized from your studies in the earlier chapters the constitutional due-process issues lurking behind each of these traditional issues touching on the authority of the courts to adjudicate. Consider also personal jurisdiction. Without personal jurisdiction, the courts would have no constitutional authority to bind individual class members. Does the Constitution require making minimum-contacts analyses for each individual class member? Doing so would be impossible or impractical, destroying the convenience and value of class actions. Class actions require some other categorical standard under which the courts can classify class-action members or some other streamlined procedure by which representatives can satisfy due process. In the following case, the Supreme Court addressed both the constitutionally requisite standard and procedure. Class representatives need not show each class member's minimum contacts with the forum state. They need only show minimal procedures under which the parties and court can distinguish class members and non-class members based on notice and opportunity for hearing. The Supreme Court confirmed as constitutionally adequate a procedure in which regular mail notice binds a class member unless the putative class member opts out. As you read the following case, appreciate the sensibility of this solution while examining its rationale.

Phillips Petroleum Co. v. Shutts,

United States Supreme Court
472 U.S. 797 (1985)

Justice REHNQUIST delivered the opinion of the Court.

Petitioner is a Delaware corporation which has its principal place of business in Oklahoma. During the 1970's it produced or purchased natural gas from leased land located in 11 different States, and sold most of the gas in interstate commerce. Respondents are some 28,000 of the royalty owners possessing rights to the leases from which petitioner produced the gas. They reside in all 50 States, the District of Columbia, and several foreign countries. Respondents brought a class action against petitioner in the Kansas state court, seeking to recover interest on royalty payments which had been delayed by petitioner. They recovered judgment in the trial court, and the Supreme Court of Kansas affirmed the judgment over petitioner's contentions that the Due Process Clause of the Fourteenth Amendment prevented Kansas from adjudicating the claims of all the respondents, and that the Due Process Clause and the Full Faith and Credit Clause of Article IV of the Constitution prohibited the application of Kansas law to all of the transactions between petitioner and respondents. [C] ... We reject petitioner's jurisdictional claim, but sustain its claim regarding the choice of law. ...

Respondents Irl Shutts, Robert Anderson, and Betty Anderson filed suit against petitioner in Kansas state court, seeking interest payments on their suspended royalties which petitioner had possessed pending the Commission's approval of the price increases. ... Over petitioner's objection the Kansas trial court granted respondents' motion to certify the suit as a class action under Kansas law. [C] The class as certified was comprised of 33,000 royalty owners who had royalties suspended by petitioner. The average claim of each royalty owner for interest on the suspended royalties was $100.

After the class was certified respondents provided each class member with notice through first-class mail. The notice described the action and informed each class member that he could appear in person or by counsel; otherwise each member would be represented by Shutts and the Andersons, the named plaintiffs. The notices also stated that class members would be included in the class and bound by the judgment unless they "opted out" of the lawsuit by executing and returning a "request for exclusion" that was included with the notice. The final class as certified contained 28,100 members; 3,400 had "opted out" of the class by returning the request for exclusion, and notice could not be delivered to another 1,500 members, who were also excluded. Less than 1,000 of the class members resided in Kansas. Only a minuscule amount, approximately one quarter of one percent, of the gas leases involved in the lawsuit were on Kansas land. …

… The court found petitioner liable under Kansas law for interest on the suspended royalties to all class members. …

Petitioner raised two principal claims in its appeal to the Supreme Court of Kansas. It first asserted that the Kansas trial court did not possess personal jurisdiction over absent plaintiff class members as required by International Shoe Co. v. Washington, 326 U.S. 310[] (1945), and similar cases. Related to this first claim was petitioner's contention that the "opt-out" notice to absent class members, which forced them to return the request for exclusion in order to avoid the suit, was insufficient to bind class members who were not residents of Kansas or who did not possess "minimum contacts" with Kansas. Second, petitioner claimed that Kansas courts could not apply Kansas law to every claim in the dispute. The trial court should have looked to the laws of each State where the leases were located to determine, on the basis of conflict of laws principles, whether interest on the suspended royalties was recoverable, and at what rate. …

Reduced to its essentials, petitioner's argument is that unless out-of-state plaintiffs affirmatively consent, the Kansas courts may not exert jurisdiction over their claims. Petitioner claims that failure to execute and return the "request for exclusion" provided with the class notice cannot constitute consent of the out-of-state plaintiffs; thus Kansas courts may exercise jurisdiction over these plaintiffs only if the plaintiffs possess the sufficient "minimum contacts" with Kansas as that term is used in cases involving personal jurisdiction over out-of-state defendants. E.g., International Shoe Co. v. Washington, 326 U.S. 310[] (1945); Shaffer v. Heitner, 433 U.S. 186[] (1977); World-Wide Volkswagen Corp. v. Woodson, 444 U.S. 286[] (1980). Since Kansas had no prelitigation contact with many of the plaintiffs and leases involved, petitioner claims that Kansas has exceeded its jurisdictional reach and thereby violated the due process rights of the absent plaintiffs. …

Although the cases like *Shaffer* and *Woodson* which petitioner relies on for a minimum contacts requirement all dealt with out-of-state defendants or parties in the procedural posture of a defendant, [cc], petitioner claims that the same analysis must apply to absent class-action plaintiffs. In this regard petitioner correctly points out that a chose in action is a constitutionally recognized property interest possessed by each of the plaintiffs. Mullane v. Central Hanover Bank & Trust Co., 339 U.S. 306[] (1950). An adverse judgment by Kansas courts in this case may extinguish the chose in action forever through res judicata. Such an adverse judgment, petitioner claims, would be every bit as onerous to an absent plaintiff as an adverse judgment on the merits would be to a defendant. Thus, the same due process protections should apply to absent plaintiffs: Kansas should not be able to exert jurisdiction over the plaintiff's claims unless the plaintiffs have sufficient minimum contacts with Kansas.

We think petitioner's premise is in error. The burdens placed by a State upon an absent class-action plaintiff are not of the same order or magnitude as those it places upon an absent defendant. An out-of-state defendant summoned by a plaintiff is faced with the full powers of the forum State to render judgment *against* it. The defendant must generally hire counsel and travel to the forum to defend itself from the plaintiff's claim, or suffer a default judgment. The defendant may be forced to participate in extended and often costly discovery, and will be forced to respond in damages or to comply with some other form of remedy imposed by the court should it lose the suit. The defendant may also face liability for court costs and attorney's fees. These burdens are substantial, and the minimum contacts requirement of the Due Process Clause prevents the forum State from unfairly imposing them upon the defendant.

A class-action plaintiff, however, is in quite a different posture. ... [T]he class action was an invention of equity to enable it to proceed to a decree in suits where the number of those interested in the litigation was too great to permit joinder. The absent parties would be bound by the decree so long as the named parties adequately represented the absent class and the prosecution of the litigation was within the common interest.[fn] [C]

Modern plaintiff class actions follow the same goals, permitting litigation of a suit involving common questions when there are too many plaintiffs for proper joinder. Class actions also may permit the plaintiffs to pool claims which would be uneconomical to litigate individually. For example, this lawsuit involves claims averaging about $100 per plaintiff; most of the plaintiffs would have no realistic day in court if a class action were not available.

In sharp contrast to the predicament of a defendant haled into an out-of-state forum, the plaintiffs in this suit were not haled anywhere to defend themselves upon pain of a default judgment. ... As commentators have noted, from the plaintiffs' point of view a class action resembles a "quasi-administrative proceeding, conducted by the judge." 3B J. Moore & J. Kennedy, Moore's Federal Practice ¶23.45[4.-5] (1984); [c].

A plaintiff class in Kansas and numerous other jurisdictions cannot first be certified unless the judge, with the aid of the named plaintiffs and defendant, conducts an inquiry into the common nature of the named plaintiffs' and the absent plaintiffs' claims, the adequacy of representation, the jurisdiction possessed over the class, and any other matters that will bear upon proper representation of the absent plaintiffs' interest. [C] Unlike a defendant in a civil suit, a class-action plaintiff is not required to fend for himself. [C] The court and named plaintiffs protect his interests. Indeed, the class-action defendant itself has a great interest in ensuring that the absent plaintiff's claims are properly before the forum. ...

The concern of the typical class-action rules for the absent plaintiffs is manifested in other ways. Most jurisdictions, including Kansas, require that a class action, once certified, may not be dismissed or compromised without the approval of the court. ...

Besides this continuing solicitude for their rights, absent plaintiff class members are not subject to other burdens imposed upon defendants. They need not hire counsel or appear. They are almost never subject to counterclaims or cross-claims, or liability for fees or costs.[fn] Absent plaintiff class members are not subject to coercive or punitive remedies. Nor will an adverse judgment typically bind an absent plaintiff for any damages, although a valid adverse judgment may extinguish any of the plaintiff's claims which were litigated.

Unlike a defendant in a normal civil suit, an absent class-action plaintiff is not required to do anything. He may sit back and allow the litigation to run its course, content in knowing that there are safeguards provided for his protection. In most class actions an absent plaintiff is provided at least with an opportunity to "opt out" of the class, and if he takes advantage of that opportunity he is removed from the litigation entirely. This was true of the Kansas proceedings in this case. ...

Because States place fewer burdens upon absent class plaintiffs than they do upon absent defendants in nonclass suits, the Due Process Clause need not and does not afford the former as much protection from state-court jurisdiction as it does the latter. The Fourteenth Amendment does protect "persons," not "defendants," however, so absent plaintiffs as well as absent defendants are entitled to some protection from the jurisdiction of a forum State which seeks to adjudicate their claims. In this case we hold that a forum State may exercise jurisdiction over the claim of an absent class-action plaintiff, even though that plaintiff may not possess the minimum contacts with the forum which would support personal jurisdiction over a defendant. If the forum State wishes to bind an absent plaintiff concerning a claim for money damages or similar relief at law,[fn3: Our holding today is limited to those class actions which seek to bind known plaintiffs concerning claims wholly or predominately for money judgments. ...] it must provide minimal procedural due process protection. The plaintiff must receive notice plus an opportunity to be heard and participate in the litigation, whether in person or through counsel. The notice must be the best practicable, "reasonably calculated, under all the circumstances, to apprise interested parties of the pendency of the action and afford them an opportunity to present their objections." *Mullane, [supra]*, at 314-315[]; [c]. The notice should describe the action and the plaintiffs' rights in it. Additionally, we hold that due process requires at a minimum that an absent plaintiff be provided with an opportunity to remove himself from the class by executing and returning an "opt out" or "request for exclusion" form to the court. Finally, the Due Process Clause of course requires that the named plaintiff at all times adequately represent the interests of the absent class members. [C] ...

We think that the procedure followed by Kansas, where a fully descriptive notice is sent first-class mail to each class member, with an explanation of the right to "opt out," satisfies due process. Requiring a plaintiff to affirmatively request inclusion would probably impede the prosecution of those class actions involving an aggregation of small individual claims, where a large number of claims are required to make it economical to bring suit. ...

In this case over 3,400 members of the potential class did "opt out," which belies the contention that "opt out" procedures result in guaranteed jurisdiction by inertia. Another 1,500 were excluded because the notice and "opt out" form was undeliverable. We think that such results show that the "opt out" procedure provided by Kansas is by no means *pro forma,* and that the Constitution does not require more to protect what must be the somewhat rare species of class member who is unwilling to execute an "opt out" form, but whose claim is nonetheless so important that he cannot be presumed to consent to being a member of the class by his failure to do so. ...

We therefore hold that the protection afforded the plaintiff class members by the Kansas statute satisfies the Due Process Clause. ... We conclude that the Kansas court properly asserted personal jurisdiction over the absent plaintiffs and their claims against petitioner. ...

The Kansas courts applied Kansas contract and Kansas equity law to every claim in this case, notwithstanding that over 99% of the gas leases and some 97% of the plaintiffs in the case had no apparent connection to the State of Kansas except for this lawsuit.[fn] ...

Petitioner contends that total application of Kansas substantive law violated the constitutional limitations on choice of law mandated by the Due Process Clause of the Fourteenth Amendment and the Full Faith and Credit Clause of Article IV, §1. ...

The conflicts on the applicable interest rates, alone—which we do not think can be labeled "false conflicts" without a more thoroughgoing treatment than was accorded them by the Supreme Court of Kansas—certainly amounted to millions of dollars in liability. We think that the Supreme Court of Kansas erred in deciding on the basis that it did that the application of its laws to all claims would be constitutional. ...

Four Terms ago we addressed a similar situation in Allstate Ins. Co. v. Hague, 449 U.S. 302[] (1981). ...

Kansas must have a "significant contact or significant aggregation of contacts" to the claims asserted by each member of the plaintiff class, contacts "creating state interests," in order to ensure that the choice of Kansas law is not arbitrary or unfair. Allstate[Ins. Co. v. Hague], 449 U.S.[302,] 312-313[(1981)]. Given Kansas' lack of "interest" in claims unrelated to that State, and the substantive conflict with jurisdictions such as Texas, we conclude that application of Kansas law to every claim in this case is sufficiently arbitrary and unfair as to exceed constitutional limits.[fn]

We therefore affirm the judgment of the Supreme Court of Kansas insofar as it upheld the jurisdiction of the Kansas courts over the plaintiff class members in this case, and reverse its judgment insofar as it held that Kansas law was applicable to all of the transactions which it sought to adjudicate. We remand the case to that court for further proceedings not inconsistent with this opinion.

It is so ordered.

Justice POWELL took no part in the decision of this case.

Justice STEVENS, concurring in part and dissenting in part[, omitted].

INQUIRY

Choice of Law. Opt-out rather than opt-in procedures augur more frequent and less expensive class actions with larger classes and broader reach. In that sense, *Phillips Petroleum Co. v. Shutts* was a clear victory for class-action proponents. By contrast, how much of an obstacle to class actions was the

Supreme Court's choice-of-law holding in *Phillips Petroleum Co. v. Shutts*? Choice-of-law issues can easily arise in damages-type class actions due to their typically broad geographic scope. The Supreme Court in *Phillips Petroleum Co. v. Shutts* held that the state must have a sufficiently significant contact or aggregation of contacts creating state interests so as to ensure that application of that state's law is not arbitrary or unfair. The Supreme Court's choice-of-law rule can create class-action obstacles in one of two ways. In some cases, the trial court may have to apply different state law to different subclasses of claims. Doing so may not be difficult in cases (like *Phillips Petroleum Co. v. Shutts*) where the differences in law from state to state involve damages calculations or categories. In other cases, the trial court will not be able to certify the class at all. When, for instance, the differences in law from state to state have to do with establishing liability rather than calculating damages, subclassification of claims may be impossible or impractical, meaning that the trial court must deny certification. *See, e.g.*, Castano v. The American Tobacco Co., 84 F.3d 734, 749 (5th Cir 1996) (rejecting nationwide 50-million-member class for tobacco-addiction claims where "immature" liability theories differed state to state); *see also* In re Chevron U.S.A., 109 F.3d 1016 (5th Cir. 1997) (resist certification for immature torts); In re Rhone-Poulenc, Inc., 51 F.3d 1293 (7th Cir. 1995) (same); Walker v. Liggett Group, Inc., 175 F.R.D. 226 (S.D. W.Va. 1997) (same). After the above tobacco class-action litigation failed, state attorneys general filed individual actions resulting in a $206 billion settlement (paid over 25 years) with 46 states. Class actions are not a panacea. There can be more than one route to similar relief. *But see* Scott v. American Tobacco Co., 949 So.2d 1266 (La. Ct. App. 2007) (affirming $600 million class-action smoking-cessation fund), cert. denied, __ U.S. __, 128 S.Ct. 2908 (2008).

3. Resolution

It should come as no surprise that settlement of class actions raise other unique issues. The risk of large damages awards, widespread injunctive relief, or both, create significant power for class actions to induce settlement. The survival of national corporations or even whole industries may depend on resolving the class action early and on favorable terms. Class representatives and their trial lawyers have their own incentives for early resolution, given the substantial burden and expense, and concomitant risk, of class-action litigation. Not every case can or should be litigated. Courts also favor early resolution. Given this dynamic, class-action practitioners developed a practice of negotiating settlements even before instituting class-action litigation and obtaining certification of the class. The opposing parties and their lawyers would file suit and simultaneously request court approval of the negotiated settlement for what is known as a settlement-only class. Yet this extraordinary alignment of the opposing parties' interests can create risks that class members would suffer an unfavorable settlement—a giveaway of their rights in exchange for a resolution that benefits the plaintiffs' lawyers and defendants more so than the class members. The risk becomes acute in small-claim damages-type class actions in which the defendants receive absolution, the lawyers receive substantial fees, and the class members only coupons for discounts on additional products. *See* In re Domestic Air

Transportation Antitrust Litigation, 148 F.R.D. 297 (N.D. Ga. 1993) (settlement for airline flight coupons); *see also* Sunfuel Technologies, Inc. v. DHL Express (USA), 463 F.3d 646 (7th Cir. 2006) (vacating class-action package-delivery-coupon settlement for trial court's inadequate assessment of its fairness).

In the ordinary non-class-action case, parties settle on terms they alone choose, without court involvement, review, or approval, and without even disclosure of those terms. Not so for class actions. FED. R. CIV. P. 23(e) dictates procedures to settle, voluntary dismiss, or compromise class actions. Each of those procedures responds to a specific concern. Rule 23(e)(1) requires notice to class membes whom the action would bind, thus satisfying due-process issues. Rule 23(e)(2) requires the court to hold a hearing and approve only those actions that are fair, reasonable, and adequate, reducing the prospect for settlements that favor class representatives, their lawyers, and the defendants while not providing adequate relief for the class. Rule 23(e)(3) requires the parties to file a statement of any side agreements inducing the action, to enable the trial court to ensure that defendants have not co-opted class representatives' loyalty. Rule 23(e)(4) authorizes the court to order a second opt-out procedure specifically as to the settlement, to enable class members to decide for themselves when the circumstances warrant it. Rule 23(e)(5) permits a class member to object, giving the trial court a means of hearing concerns that the class representatives and their counsel might not have disclosed to the court. Beyond parties and class members, the public may also have an interest in the settlement. The Class Action Fairness Act requires that parties notify any state or federal agencies whose regulations govern the defendant's actions giving rise to the alleged liability. 28 U.S.C. §1715. The provision is presumably so that the agency can raise at the settlement hearing any issues that the settlement does not address. Review the following sections of the Class Action Fairness Act for these and other provisions.

28 U.S.C. §1714. Protection against discrimination based on geographic location

The court may not approve a proposed settlement that provides for the payment of greater sums to some class members than to others solely on the basis that the class members to whom the greater sums are to be paid are located in closer geographic proximity to the court.

28 U.S.C. §1715. Notifications to appropriate Federal and State officials

(a) Definitions.—

(1) Appropriate Federal official.—In this section, the term "appropriate Federal official" means—

(A) the Attorney General of the United States; or

(B) in any case in which the defendant is a Federal depository institution, a State depository institution, a depository institution holding company, a foreign bank, or a nondepository institution subsidiary of the foregoing (as such terms are defined in section 3 of the Federal Deposit Insurance Act (12 U.S.C. 1813)), the person who has the primary Federal regulatory or supervisory responsibility with respect to the defendant, if some or all of the matters alleged in the class action are subject to regulation or supervision by that person.

(2) Appropriate State official.—In this section, the term "appropriate State official" means the person in the State who has the primary regulatory or supervisory responsibility with respect to the defendant, or who licenses or otherwise authorizes the defendant to conduct business in the State, if some or all of the matters alleged in the class action are subject to regulation by that person. If there is no primary regulator, supervisor, or licensing authority, or the matters alleged in the class action are not subject to regulation or supervision by that person, then the appropriate State official shall be the State attorney general.

(b) In general.—Not later than 10 days after a proposed settlement of a class action is filed in court, each defendant that is participating in the proposed settlement shall serve upon the appropriate State official of each State in which a class member resides and the appropriate Federal official, a notice of the proposed settlement consisting of—

(1) a copy of the complaint and any materials filed with the complaint and any amended complaints (except such materials shall not be required to be served if such materials are made electronically available through the Internet and such service includes notice of how to electronically access such material);

(2) notice of any scheduled judicial hearing in the class action;

(3) any proposed or final notification to class members of—

(A)(i) the members' rights to request exclusion from the class action; or

(ii) if no right to request exclusion exists, a statement that no such right exists; and

(B) a proposed settlement of a class action;

(4) any proposed or final class action settlement;

(5) any settlement or other agreement contemporaneously made between class counsel and counsel for the defendants;

(6) any final judgment or notice of dismissal;

(7)(A) if feasible, the names of class members who reside in each State and the estimated proportionate share of the claims of such members to the entire settlement to that State's appropriate State official; or

(B) if the provision of information under subparagraph (A) is not feasible, a reasonable estimate of the number of class members residing in each State and the estimated proportionate share of the claims of such members to the entire settlement; and

(8) any written judicial opinion relating to the materials described under subparagraphs (3) through (6).

(c) Depository institutions notification.—

(1) Federal and other depository institutions.—In any case in which the defendant is a Federal depository institution, a depository institution holding company, a foreign bank, or a non-depository institution subsidiary of the foregoing, the notice requirements of this section are satisfied by serving the notice required under subsection (b) upon the person who has the primary Federal regulatory or supervisory responsibility with respect to the defendant, if some or all of the matters alleged in the class action are subject to regulation or supervision by that person.

(2) State depository institutions.—In any case in which the defendant is a State depository institution (as that term is defined in section 3 of the Federal Deposit Insurance Act (12 U.S.C. 1813)), the notice requirements of this section are satisfied by serving the notice required under subsection (b) upon the State bank supervisor (as that term is defined in section 3 of the Federal Deposit Insurance Act (12 U.S.C. 1813)) of the State in which the defendant is incorporated or chartered, if some or all of the matters alleged in the class action are subject to regulation or supervision by that person, and upon the appropriate Federal official.

(d) Final approval.—An order giving final approval of a proposed settlement may not be issued earlier than 90 days after the later of the dates on which the appropriate Federal official and the appropriate State official are served with the notice required under subsection (b).

(e) Noncompliance if notice not provided.—

(1) In general.—A class member may refuse to comply with and may choose not to be bound by a settlement agreement or consent decree in a class action if the class member demonstrates that the notice required under subsection (b) has not been provided.
(2) Limitation.—A class member may not refuse to comply with or to be bound by a settlement agreement or consent decree under paragraph (1) if the notice required under subsection (b) was directed to the appropriate Federal official and to either the State attorney general or the person that has primary regulatory, supervisory, or licensing authority over the defendant.
(3) Application of rights.—The rights created by this subsection shall apply only to class members or any person acting on a class member's behalf, and shall not be construed to limit any other rights affecting a class member's participation in the settlement.
(f) Rule of construction.—Nothing in this section shall be construed to expand the authority of, or impose any obligations, duties, or responsibilities upon, Federal or State officials.

INQUIRY

Settlement-Only Classes. Another issue arises when parties attempt to use a settlement-only class to resolve numerous claims that nonetheless do not otherwise qualify under Rule 23 for class-action treatment. Settlement-only classes have an inherently collusive nature to them. Because no lawsuit is filed until the parties reach settlement, the court exercises no supervision, the entire process is essentially secret, and there is nothing transparently adversarial in the parties' roles. The parties to the negotiation may even attempt to settle claims that would not qualify for class treatment. Even where a settlement is fair to a settlement-only class, the trial court may not be able to certify the class lacking one or more Rule 23(a) conditions. The Supreme Court addressed these issues in the following case, rejecting settlement-only classes that cannot meet all Rule 23 requirements for certification. The Supreme Court reached the same result two years later, in Ortiz v. Fibreboard Corp., 527 U.S. 815 (1999), decertifying another asbestos class. As you read the following case, appreciate the limitation that the Supreme Court recognizes on the power of the federal courts.

Amchem Products, Inc. v. Windsor,

United States Supreme Court
521 U.S. 591 (1997)

Justice GINSBURG delivered the opinion of the Court.

This case concerns the legitimacy under Rule 23 of the Federal Rules of Civil Procedure of a class-action certification sought to achieve global settlement of current and future asbestos-related claims. The class proposed for certification potentially encompasses hundreds of thousands, perhaps millions, of individuals tied together by this commonality: Each was, or some day may be, adversely affected by past exposure to asbestos products manufactured by one or more of 20 companies. Those companies, defendants in the lower courts, are petitioners here.

The United States District Court for the Eastern District of Pennsylvania certified the class for settlement only, finding that the proposed settlement was fair and that representation and notice had been adequate. That court enjoined class members from separately pursuing asbestos-related personal-injury suits in any court, federal or state, pending the issuance of a final order. The Court of Appeals for the Third Circuit vacated the District Court's orders, holding that the class certification failed to satisfy Rule 23's requirements in several critical respects. We affirm the Court of Appeals' judgment.

I

A

The settlement-class certification we confront evolved in response to an asbestos-litigation crisis. [C] A United States Judicial Conference Ad Hoc Committee on Asbestos Litigation, appointed by THE CHIEF JUSTICE in September 1990, described facets of the problem in a 1991 report:

> [This] is a tale of danger known in the 1930s, exposure inflicted upon millions of Americans in the 1940s and 1950s, injuries that began to take their toll in the 1960s, and a flood of lawsuits beginning in the 1970s. On the basis of past and current filing data, and because of a latency period that may last as long as 40 years for some asbestos related diseases, a continuing stream of claims can be expected. The final toll of asbestos related injuries is unknown. Predictions have been made of 200,000 asbestos disease deaths before the year 2000 and as many as 265,000 by the year 2015.
>
> The most objectionable aspects of asbestos litigation can be briefly summarized: dockets in both federal and state courts continue to grow; long delays are routine; trials are too long; the same issues are litigated over and over; transaction costs exceed the victims' recovery by nearly two to one; exhaustion of assets threatens and distorts the process; and future claimants may lose altogether. [C]

Real reform, the report concluded, required federal legislation creating a national asbestos dispute-resolution scheme. [C] ... To this date, no congressional response has emerged.

In the face of legislative inaction, the federal courts—lacking authority to replace state tort systems with a national toxic tort compensation regime—endeavored to work with the procedural tools available to improve management of federal asbestos litigation. ... [T]he Judicial Panel on Multidistrict Litigation (MDL Panel)... transferred all asbestos cases then filed but not yet on trial in federal courts to a single district, the United States District Court for the Eastern District of Pennsylvania... . [C][fn] The order aggregated pending cases only; no authority resides in the MDL Panel to license for consolidated proceedings claims not yet filed.

B

After the consolidation, attorneys for plaintiffs and defendants formed separate steering committees and began settlement negotiations. ... [S]ettlement negotiations included efforts to find a "means of resolving ... future cases." [C] ...

[Because defendants would not settle pending claims without protection against future claims, s]ettlement talks thus concentrated on devising an administrative scheme for disposition of asbestos claims not yet in litigation. In these negotiations, counsel for masses of inventory plaintiffs endeavored to represent the interests of the anticipated future claimants, although those lawyers then had no attorney-client relationship with such claimants.

Once negotiations seemed likely to produce an agreement purporting to bind potential plaintiffs, [a consortium of defendants] CCR agreed to settle, through separate agreements, the claims of plaintiffs who had already filed asbestos-related lawsuits. In one such agreement, CCR defendants promised to pay more than $200 million to gain release of the claims of numerous inventory plaintiffs. After settling the inventory claims, CCR, together with the plaintiffs' lawyers CCR had approached, launched this case, exclusively involving persons outside the MDL Panel's province-plaintiffs without already pending lawsuits.[fn]

C

The class action thus instituted was not intended to be litigated. Rather, within the space of a single day, January 15, 1993, the settling parties—CCR defendants and the representatives of the plaintiff class described below—presented to the District Court a complaint, an answer, a proposed settlement agreement, and a joint motion for conditional class certification.[fn]

The complaint identified nine lead plaintiffs, designating them and members of their families as representatives of a class comprising all persons who had not filed an asbestos-related lawsuit against a CCR defendant as of the date the class action commenced, but who (1) had been exposed-occupationally or through the occupational exposure of a spouse or household member-to asbestos or products containing asbestos attributable to a CCR defendant, or (2) whose spouse or family member had been so exposed.[fn] Untold numbers of individuals may fall within this description. All named plaintiffs alleged that they or a member of their family had been exposed to asbestos-containing products of CCR defendants. More than half of the named plaintiffs alleged that they or their family members had already suffered various physical injuries as a result of the exposure. The others alleged that they had not yet manifested any asbestos-related condition. The complaint delineated no subclasses; all named plaintiffs were designated as representatives of the class as a whole. ...

A stipulation of settlement accompanied the pleadings; it proposed to settle, and to preclude nearly all class members from litigating against CCR companies, all claims not filed before January 15, 1993, involving compensation for present and future asbestos-related personal injury or death. An exhaustive document exceeding 100 pages, the stipulation presents in detail an administrative mechanism and a schedule of payments to compensate class members who meet defined asbestos-exposure and medical requirements. The stipulation describes four categories of compensable disease: mesothelioma; lung cancer; certain "other cancers" (colon-rectal, laryngeal, esophageal, and stomach cancer); and "non-malignant conditions" (asbestosis and bilateral pleural thickening). Persons with "exceptional" medical claims-claims that do not fall within the four described diagnostic categories-may in some instances qualify for compensation, but the settlement caps the number of "exceptional" claims CCR must cover.

For each qualifying disease category, the stipulation specifies the range of damages CCR will pay to qualifying claimants. Payments under the settlement are not adjustable for inflation. Mesothelioma claimants—the most highly compensated category—are scheduled to receive between $20,000 and $200,000. The stipulation provides that CCR is to propose the level of compensation within the prescribed ranges; it also establishes procedures to resolve disputes over medical diagnoses and levels of compensation.

Compensation above the fixed ranges may be obtained for "extraordinary" claims. But the settlement places both numerical caps and dollar limits on such claims.[fn] The settlement also imposes "case flow maximums," which cap the number of claims payable for each disease in a given year.

Class members are to receive no compensation for certain kinds of claims, even if otherwise applicable state law recognizes such claims. Claims that garner no compensation under the settlement include claims by family members of asbestos-exposed individuals for loss of consortium, and claims by so-called "exposure-only" plaintiffs for increased risk of cancer, fear of future asbestos-related injury, and medical monitoring. "Pleural" claims, which might be asserted by persons with asbestos-related plaques on their lungs but no accompanying physical impairment, are also excluded. Although not entitled to present compensation, exposure-only claimants and pleural claimants may qualify for benefits when and if they develop a compensable disease and meet the relevant exposure and medical criteria. Defendants forgo defenses to liability, including statute of limitations pleas.

Class members, in the main, are bound by the settlement in perpetuity, while CCR defendants may choose to withdraw from the settlement after ten years. A small number of class members-only a few per year-may reject the settlement and pursue their claims in court. Those permitted to exercise this option, however, may not assert any punitive damages claim or any claim for increased risk of cancer. Aspects of the administration of the settlement are to be monitored by the AFL-CIO and class counsel. Class counsel are to receive attorneys' fees in an amount to be approved by the District Court.

D

On January 29, 1993, as requested by the settling parties, the District Court conditionally certified, under Federal Rule of Civil Procedure 23(b)(3), an encompassing opt-out class. ... In a separate order, Judge Weiner assigned to Judge Reed, also of the Eastern District of Pennsylvania, "the task of conducting fairness proceedings and of determining whether the proposed settlement is fair to the class." [C] ...

E

... The Court of Appeals ... found that "serious intra-class conflicts preclude[d] th[e] class from meeting the adequacy of representation requirement" of Rule 23(a)(4) ... [because the settlement "]makes important judgments on how recovery is to be *allocated* among different kinds of plaintiffs, decisions that necessarily favor some claimants over others." [C] ...

III

To place this controversy in context, we briefly describe the characteristics of class actions for which the Federal Rules provide. Rule 23, governing federal-court class actions, stems from equity practice and gained its current shape in an innovative 1966 revision. [C] ...

In the 1966 class-action amendments, Rule 23(b)(3), the category at issue here, was "the most adventuresome" innovation. [C] Rule 23(b)(3) added to the complex-litigation arsenal class actions for damages designed to secure judgments binding all class members save those who affirmatively elected to be excluded. [Cc] ...

Framed for situations in which "class-action treatment is not as clearly called for" as it is in Rule 23(b)(1) and (b)(2) situations, Rule 23(b)(3) permits certification where class suit "may nevertheless be convenient and desirable." Adv. Comm. Notes, 28 U.S.C.App., p. 697. To qualify for certification under Rule 23(b)(3), a class must meet two requirements beyond the Rule 23(a) prerequisites: Common questions must "predominate over any questions affecting only individual members"; and class resolution must be "superior to other available methods for the fair and efficient adjudication of the controversy." ...

In the decades since the 1966 revision of Rule 23, class-action practice has become ever more "adventuresome" as a means of coping with claims too numerous to secure their "just, speedy, and inexpensive determination" one by one. [C] ...

Among current applications of Rule 23(b)(3), the "settlement only" class has become a stock device. [C] Although all Federal Circuits recognize the utility of Rule 23(b)(3) settlement classes, courts have divided on the extent to which a proffered settlement affects court surveillance under Rule 23's certification criteria. ...

IV

... [C]ourts must be mindful that the Rule as now composed sets the requirements they are bound to enforce. Federal Rules take effect after an extensive deliberative process involving many reviewers... . The text of a rule thus proposed and reviewed limits judicial inventiveness. ...

Rule 23(e), on settlement of class actions, reads in its entirety: "A class action shall not be dismissed or compromised without the approval of the court, and notice of the proposed dismissal or compromise shall be given to all members of the class in such manner as the court directs." This prescription was designed to function as an additional requirement, not a superseding direction, for the "class action" to which Rule 23(e) refers is one qualified for certification under Rule 23(a) and (b). [C] ...

No settlement class called to our attention is as sprawling as this one. [C] Predominance is a test readily met in certain cases alleging consumer or securities fraud or violations of the antitrust laws. [C] Even mass tort cases arising from a common cause or disaster may, depending upon the circumstances, satisfy the predominance requirement. ... The Advisory Committee for the 1966 revision of Rule 23... advised that such cases are "ordinarily not appropriate" for class treatment. [C] But the text of the Rule does not categorically exclude mass tort cases from class certification, and District Courts, since the late 1970's, have been certifying such cases in increasing number. [C] The Committee's warning, however, continues to call for caution when individual stakes are high and disparities among class members great. As the Third Circuit's opinion makes plain, the certification in this case does not follow the counsel of caution. That certification cannot be upheld, for it rests on a conception of Rule 23(b)(3)'s predominance requirement irreconcilable with the Rule's design. ...

Nor can the class approved by the District Court satisfy Rule 23(a)(4)'s requirement that the named parties "will fairly and adequately protect the interests of the class." The adequacy inquiry under Rule 23(a)(4) serves to uncover conflicts of interest between named parties and the class they seek to represent. ...

As the Third Circuit pointed out, named parties with diverse medical conditions sought to act on behalf of a single giant class rather than on behalf of discrete subclasses. In significant respects, the interests of those within the single class are not aligned. Most saliently, for the currently injured, the critical goal is generous immediate payments. That goal tugs against the interest of exposure-only plaintiffs in ensuring an ample, inflation-protected fund for the future. ...

The settling parties, in sum, achieved a global compromise with no structural assurance of fair and adequate representation for the diverse groups and individuals affected. Although the named parties alleged a range of complaints, each served generally as representative for the whole, not for a separate constituency. ...

The Third Circuit found no assurance here—either in the terms of the settlement or in the structure of the negotiations—that the named plaintiffs operated under a proper understanding of their representational responsibilities. [C] That assessment, we conclude, is on the mark. ...

... In accord with the Third Circuit, ... we recognize the gravity of the question whether class action notice sufficient under the Constitution and Rule 23 could ever be given to legions so unselfconscious and amorphous.

V

The argument is sensibly made that a nationwide administrative claims processing regime would provide the most secure, fair, and efficient means of compensating victims of asbestos exposure.[fn] Congress, however, has not adopted such a solution. And Rule 23, which must be interpreted with fidelity to the Rules Enabling Act and applied with the interests of absent class members in close view, cannot carry the large load CCR, class counsel, and the District Court heaped upon it. As this case exemplifies, the rulemakers' prescriptions for class actions may be endangered by "those who embrace [Rule 23] too enthusiastically just as [they are by] those who approach [the Rule] with distaste." C. Wright, Law of Federal Courts 508 (5th ed.1994); [c].

For the reasons stated, the judgment of the Court of Appeals for the Third Circuit is

Affirmed.

Justice O'CONNOR took no part in the consideration or decision of this case.

Justice BREYER, with whom Justice STEVENS joins, concurring in part and dissenting in part.

Although I agree with the Court's basic holding that "[s]ettlement is relevant to a class certification," [c], I find several problems in its approach that lead me to a different conclusion. First, I believe that the need for settlement in this mass tort case, with hundreds of thousands of lawsuits, is greater than the Court's opinion suggests. Second, I would give more weight than would the majority to settlement-related issues for purposes of determining whether common issues predominate. Third, I am uncertain about the Court's determination of adequacy of representation, and do not believe it appropriate for this Court to second-guess the District Court on the matter without first having the Court of Appeals consider it. Fourth, I am uncertain about the tenor of an opinion that seems to suggest the settlement is unfair. And fifth, in the absence of further review by the Court of Appeals, I cannot accept the majority's suggestions that "notice" is inadequate. ...

INQUIRY

Approval. *Amchem Products, Inc. v. Windsor* does not rule out settlement-only classes. Where a trial court can certify the class, it can still approve a settlement-only class. Under *Amchem Products, Inc. v. Windsor*, the trial court must carefully ensure that both that the class qualifies under Rule 23(a) and (b) and that the settlement is fair, reasonable and adequate under Rule 23(e). Approval presents fewer problems for classes that do not present *Amchem Products'* allocation dilemma between present and future class claimants and where class representatives represent all subclasses. *See, e.g.*, Hanlon v. Chrysler Corp., 150 F.3d 1011, 1020-1021 (9th Cir. 1997). Settlement-only classes create unusual tensions between competing policies. On one hand, policy prefers early, negotiated, reduced-cost, and efficient resolution. On the other hand, policy also prefers adversarial, conflict-free, and transparent resolution, and full and fair compensation. The unusual tension in these settlement-only class actions should remind us that the civil justice system's liability model might not always be the best way in which to resolve broad public policy issues. Where administration predominates over adversarial litigation, the law prefers administrative procedures. Congress can act to create alternative administrative systems, *see* Black Lung Benefits Act, 30 U.S.C. §§901 et seq., just as it has acted to attempt to regulate class actions. Can you imagine another even more appropriate forum? The administrative law, structure, and procedures of bankruptcy courts may be peculiarly effective in resolving class actions that threaten the financial viability of the corporate entities whose actions gave rise to the class claims. Rule 23(b)(1) limited-fund type settlement-only classes operate somewhat like the claims of unsecured creditors in bankruptcy cases.

Fees. The above *Amchem Products, Inc. v. Windsor* case intimates an important question that remains: how much should the class pay its lawyers when their work carries small or even incidental benefit to many of its members but greater benefit to the class as a whole? The trial court plays a special role in approving the fees of class counsel. There is no fee-shifting provision for the usual class action. The class representatives and members must ordinarily pay the fees. In the ordinary, non-class-action case, lawyer and client determine fees by a contingency, hourly, or other fee agreement. In class actions, there may be some opportunity to set the guidelines for fees at the case's outset. Rule 23(g)(1)(C) permits counsel to include a fee request when seeking the court's approval as class counsel. *See* Sherleigh Assoc. LLC v Sherleigh Associtès, Inc. Profit-Sharing Plan, 186 F.R.D. 669 (S.D. Fla. 1999) (trial court considers fee bids when selecting class counsel). Yet a fee agreement between the class representatives and their lawyers does not resolve the interests of the class members who were not parties to that agreement but who derived the greater part of the benefit from it and should contribute to the fee.

Ethics

Rule 7.3 of the ABA MODEL RULES OF PROFESSIONAL CONDUCT prohibits in-person or live telephone solicitation of prospective clients "when a significant motive for the lawyer's doing so is the lawyer's pecuniary gain." Interpreting similar anti-solicitation rules adopted by specific states, the Supreme Court has held as constitutional, prohibitions on in-person solicitation of tort victims for private gain.

See Ohralik v. Ohio State Bar Assn., 436 U.S. 447 (1978). When communicating with prospective class representatives, lawyers must respect state conduct rules prohibiting solicitation. Yet, the Supreme Court has also recognized a First Amendment right to offer pro-bono services in pursuit of public-interest actions. See In re Primus, 436 U.S. 412 (1978). Rule 7.3's prohibition on solicitation only applies when the lawyer's motive is the lawyer's own pecuniary gain. Lawyers acting for public interest organizations may have the latitude to initiate communications with prospective class representatives, where lawyers pursuing class actions for pecuniary gain would not.

Common Fund. Where the lawyers' efforts created a settlement fund for distribution to the class, the lawyers will ordinarily draw their fees from that fund. *See* Boeing Co. v. Van Gemert, 444 U.S. 472 (1980) (fee distribution from settlement fund does not violate American rule that parties pay their own fees); Trustees v. Greenough, 105 U.S. 527 (1881) (approving common-fund theory for fees in case benefiting similarly-situated others). For certified class actions, FED. R. CIV. P. 23(h) requires that the lawyers file a motion for fees and serve it on the class members, giving them an opportunity to object and the court the opportunity for hearing. Rule 23(e)'s requirement that the court approve the settlement at a hearing finding it "fair, reasonable, and adequate" would also include its fee provisions. In some cases, the trial court can determine the amount of the fee using a percentage like that used in ordinary contingency fee cases. In other cases where injunctive relief predominates, there is no settlement fund for distribution, or the fund does not represent the full value of the case, the trial court may use the lodestar method used to set fee awards where statutes award fees to the prevailing parties. The lodestar method begins by determining fees from the hours expended and a reasonable hourly rate, and then adjusts the figure for factors including the case's risk, expenses, and complexity, the qualifications, expertise, reputation, and forgone earnings of the lawyers, and the nature, duration, and quality of the lawyer-client relationship. In coupon settlements, the Class Action Fairness Act requires that the court determine fees based not on the value of all distributed or available coupons but on those coupons that class members redeem, as the below provision shows.

28 U.S.C. §1711. Definitions

In this chapter:

(1) Class.—The term "class" means all of the class members in a class action.

(2) Class action.—The term "class action" means any civil action filed in a district court of the United States under rule 23 of the Federal Rules of Civil Procedure or any civil action that is removed to a district court of the United States that was originally filed under a State statute or rule of judicial procedure authorizing an action to be brought by 1 or more representatives as a class action.

(3) Class counsel.—The term "class counsel" means the persons who serve as the attorneys for the class members in a proposed or certified class action.

(4) Class members.—The term "class members" means the persons (named or unnamed) who fall within the definition of the proposed or certified class in a class action.

(5) Plaintiff class action.—T he term "plaintiff class action" means a class action in which class members are plaintiffs.

(6) Proposed settlement.—The term "proposed settlement" means an agreement regarding a class action that is subject to court approval and that, if approved, would be binding on some or all class members.

. . .

28 U.S.C. §1712. Coupon settlements

(a) Contingent fees in coupon settlements.—If a proposed settlement in a class action provides for a recovery of coupons to a class member, the portion of any attorney's fee award to class counsel that is attributable to the award of the coupons shall be based on the value to class members of the coupons that are redeemed.

(b) Other attorney's fee awards in coupon settlements.—

(1) In general.--If a proposed settlement in a class action provides for a recovery of coupons to class members, and a portion of the recovery of the coupons is not used to determine the attorney's fee to be paid to class counsel, any attorney's fee award shall be based upon the amount of time class counsel reasonably expended working on the action.

(2) Court approval.—Any attorney's fee under this subsection shall be subject to approval by the court and shall include an appropriate attorney's fee, if any, for obtaining equitable relief, including an injunction, if applicable. Nothing in this subsection shall be construed to prohibit application of a lodestar with a multiplier method of determining attorney's fees.

(c) Attorney's fee awards calculated on a mixed basis in coupon settlements.—If a proposed settlement in a class action provides for an award of coupons to class members and also provides for equitable relief, including injunctive relief—

(1) that portion of the attorney's fee to be paid to class counsel that is based upon a portion of the recovery of the coupons shall be calculated in accordance with subsection (a); and

(2) that portion of the attorney's fee to be paid to class counsel that is not based upon a portion of the recovery of the coupons shall be calculated in accordance with subsection (b).

(d) Settlement valuation expertise.—In a class action involving the awarding of coupons, the court may, in its discretion upon the motion of a party, receive expert testimony from a witness qualified to provide information on the actual value to the class members of the coupons that are redeemed.

(e) Judicial scrutiny of coupon settlements.—In a proposed settlement under which class members would be awarded coupons, the court may approve the proposed settlement only after a hearing to determine whether, and making a written finding that, the settlement is fair, reasonable, and adequate for class members. The court, in its discretion, may also require that a proposed settlement agreement provide for the distribution of a portion of the value of unclaimed coupons to 1 or more charitable or governmental organizations, as agreed to by the parties. The distribution and redemption of any proceeds under this subsection shall not be used to calculate attorneys' fees under this section.

28 U.S.C. §1713. Protection against loss by class members

The court may approve a proposed settlement under which any class member is obligated to pay sums to class counsel that would result in a net loss to the class member only if the court makes a written finding that nonmonetary benefits to the class member substantially outweigh the monetary loss.

INQUIRY

Summary. This chapter on joinder has shown that Rule 18 permits a party to join related or unrelated claims in a single proceeding, in federal courts keeping in mind that there must be subject-matter jurisdiction (including supplemental jurisdiction) for each claim. Rule 13 requires a responding party to join related counterclaims and permits unrelated counterclaims, provided in federal court that there is subject-matter jurisdiction for unrelated counterclaims. Rule 13 also permits crossclaims so long as they arise out of the same transaction or occurrence as the original claim. Rule 20 permits parties to join as plaintiffs or to sue defendants jointly so long as there is a common question of law or fact among the joint parties. Rule 19 requires parties to join a non-party whose absence will adversely affect a party or the non-party, so long as joinder is feasible as to jurisdiction and venue. Where a non-party is indispensable but the non-party cannot be joined, the trial court must dismiss the action. Rule 14 permits responding parties to sue third parties for liability derivative to the responded-to claim. Rule 24 authorizes non-parties to intervene to preserve rights that the litigation will otherwise impair or impede, unless parties already adequately represent the non-parties' interests. Rule 24 permits the court to allow non-parties to intervene to maintain claims having common questions of law or fact with the main claim. Rule 23 authorizes the trial courts to certify class actions fitting one of four types, on conditions of numerosity, commonality, typicality, and representation.

Career

Do you prefer the big city or a small town? Every community, large or small, has its share of civil litigation. Yet litigation practices can and do differ between small-town, rural areas and the larger metropolitan regions. Because of the larger numbers of lawyers and clients in larger metropolitan areas, civil-litigation practice there can be relatively more anonymous. You may often work with opposing counsel whom you have never met before and will not meet again, making for fresh but less predictable encounters. Each case depends on your performance—on proving yourself over again rather than relying on your professional reputation and relationships. In small-town practice, you tend to know and have significant professional experience with all of the lawyers and judges. Relationship case-to-case may be as or more important than performance in any one case. As you study civil procedure, consider your practice preference, whether big city or small town.

CHAPTER IX

ALTERNATIVE DISPUTE RESOLUTION

OBJECTIVE: That you be able to articulate alternative forms of resolving disputes outside of civil litigation.

Case Study: You are meeting with the sole proprietor of a small business against whom a customer has filed a civil-rights complaint. The business owner's insurer has declined coverage for the liability that the complaint alleges. The business owner has asked what alternatives there are to litigating the case that might avoid some or all of the adverse publicity, risk, and expense. Describe those alternatives and their advantages and disadvantages to litigation.

Federal Rules of Civil Procedure this chapter reproduces and addresses: FED. R. CIV. P. 68. Offer of Judgment.

Civil litigation is not the only way to resolve disputes. Alternative dispute resolution, or "ADR" as lawyers commonly know it, is a legal field unto itself. Depending on who defines it, the field includes at least mediation, arbitration, neutral evaluation, and principles of negotiation. It may also include summary jury trial and trial by special master. Some lawyers devote their full time or a substantial percentage of their practice to serving as mediators or arbitrators. Certifications are available for case evaluators, mediators, and arbitrators. Law schools offer courses in Alternative Dispute Resolution, Negotiation and Confrontation, Advanced Mediation, and Commercial Arbitration. What relationship does alternative dispute resolution have to civil procedure? Rules and practices of civil procedure assume that the parties are engaging in forms of alternative dispute resolution. In some instances, state and federal rules of civil procedure and related statutes authorize or mandate and govern alternative dispute resolution in court-annexed procedures. Appreciate that this chapter introduces alternative dispute resolution as it relates to civil procedure, without purporting to prepare you fully for alternative dispute resolution practice.

The Alternative Dispute Resolution Act, 28 U.S.C. §§651-658, is a prime example of second-generation legislation designed to promote alternative dispute resolution. *See also* The Administrative Dispute Resolution Act, 5 U.S.C. §§571-583 (alternative dispute resolution for administrative proceedings). The Alternative Dispute Resolution Act followed earlier federal legislation, the Civil Justice Reform Act, 28 U.S.C. §§471-482, requiring study of similar measures.

Congress adopted the Alternative Dispute Resolution Act in 1998, requiring that each judicial district adopt some form of alternative dispute resolution procedure by local rule. Under the Act, local federal rules may require parties to participate in mediation or early neutral evaluation conducted by private professionals or may permit the parties to move the litigation to arbitration. Review the Act before exploring popular forms of alternative dispute resolution in the following sections. As you review the act and the forms of alternative dispute resolution that it describes, see if you can discern for each alternative forum (1) who guides each process, (2) what authority they have, (3) what is the source of their authority, (4) who chose them, (5) what presentation the participants make, (6) what rules constrain those presentations, (7) what decisions result, and (8) what is the effect of those decisions. Notice that these questions are the fundamentals of civil procedure. Appreciate that alternative dispute resolution involves mini truncated civil-justice systems bearing the hallmarks, if not the full measure, of due process.

28 U.S.C. §651. Authorization of alternative dispute resolution
(a) Definition.—For purposes of this chapter, an alternative dispute resolution process includes any process or procedure, other than an adjudication by a presiding judge, in which a neutral third party participates to assist in the resolution of issues in controversy, through processes such as early neutral evaluation, mediation, minitrial, and arbitration as provided in sections 654 through 658.
(b) Authority.—Each United States district court shall authorize, by local rule adopted under section 2071(a), the use of alternative dispute resolution processes in all civil actions, including adversary proceedings in bankruptcy, in accordance with this chapter, except that the use of arbitration may be authorized only as provided in section 654. Each United States district court shall devise and implement its own alternative dispute resolution program, by local rule adopted under section 2071(a), to encourage and promote the use of alternative dispute resolution in its district. ...

28 U.S.C. §652. Jurisdiction
(a) Consideration of alternative dispute resolution in appropriate cases.—Notwithstanding any provision of law to the contrary and except as provided in subsections (b) and (c), each district court shall, by local rule adopted under section 2071(a), require that litigants in all civil cases consider the use of an alternative dispute resolution process at an appropriate stage in the litigation. Each district court shall provide litigants in all civil cases with at least one alternative dispute resolution process, including, but not limited to, mediation, early neutral evaluation, minitrial, and arbitration as authorized in sections 654 through 658. Any district court that elects to require the use of alternative dispute resolution in certain cases may do so only with respect to mediation, early neutral evaluation, and, if the parties consent, arbitration.
(b) Actions exempted from consideration of alternative dispute resolution.—Each district court may exempt from the requirements of this section specific cases or categories of cases in which use of alternative dispute resolution would not be appropriate. In defining these exemptions, each district court shall consult with members of the bar, including the United States Attorney for that district. ...

28 U.S.C. §653. Neutrals
(a) Panel of neutrals.—Each district court that authorizes the use of alternative dispute resolution processes shall adopt appropriate processes for making neutrals

available for use by the parties for each category of process offered. Each district court shall promulgate its own procedures and criteria for the selection of neutrals on its panels.
(b) Qualifications and training.—Each person serving as a neutral in an alternative dispute resolution process should be qualified and trained to serve as a neutral in the appropriate alternative dispute resolution process. ...

28 U.S.C. §654. Arbitration
(a) Referral of actions to arbitration.—Notwithstanding any provision of law to the contrary and except as provided in subsections (a), (b), and (c) of section 652 and subsection (d) of this section, a district court may allow the referral to arbitration of any civil action (including any adversary proceeding in bankruptcy) pending before it when the parties consent, except that referral to arbitration may not be made where—
(1) the action is based on an alleged violation of a right secured by the Constitution of the United States;
(2) jurisdiction is based in whole or in part on section 1343 of this title; or
(3) the relief sought consists of money damages in an amount greater than $150,000. ...

28 U.S.C. §655. Arbitrators
(a) Powers of arbitrators.—An arbitrator to whom an action is referred under section 654 shall have the power, within the judicial district of the district court which referred the action to arbitration—
(1) to conduct arbitration hearings;
(2) to administer oaths and affirmations; and
(3) to make awards. ...

28 U.S.C. §656. Subpoenas
Rule 45 of the Federal Rules of Civil Procedure (relating to subpoenas) applies to subpoenas for the attendance of witnesses and the production of documentary evidence at an arbitration hearing under this chapter.

28 U.S.C. §657. Arbitration award and judgment
(a) Filing and effect of arbitration award.—An arbitration award made by an arbitrator under this chapter, along with proof of service of such award on the other party by the prevailing party or by the plaintiff, shall be filed promptly after the arbitration hearing is concluded with the clerk of the district court that referred the case to arbitration. Such award shall be entered as the judgment of the court after the time has expired for requesting a trial de novo. The judgment so entered shall be subject to the same provisions of law and shall have the same force and effect as a judgment of the court in a civil action, except that the judgment shall not be subject to review in any other court by appeal or otherwise.
(b) Sealing of arbitration award.—The district court shall provide, by local rule adopted under section 2071(a), that the contents of any arbitration award made under this chapter shall not be made known to any judge who might be assigned to the case until the district court has entered final judgment in the action or the action has otherwise terminated.
(c) Trial de novo of arbitration awards.—
(1) Time for filing demand.—Within 30 days after the filing of an arbitration award with a district court under subsection (a), any party may file a written demand for a trial de novo in the district court.

(2) Action restored to court docket.—Upon a demand for a trial de novo, the action shall be restored to the docket of the court and treated for all purposes as if it had not been referred to arbitration.
(3) Exclusion of evidence of arbitration.—The court shall not admit at the trial de novo any evidence that there has been an arbitration proceeding, the nature or amount of any award, or any other matter concerning the conduct of the arbitration proceeding, unless—
(A) the evidence would otherwise be admissible in the court under the Federal Rules of Evidence; or
(B) the parties have otherwise stipulated.

28 U.S.C. §658. Compensation of arbitrators and neutrals
(a) Compensation.—The district court shall, subject to regulations approved by the Judicial Conference of the United States, establish the amount of compensation, if any, that each arbitrator or neutral shall receive for services rendered in each case under this chapter. ...

INQUIRY

Voluntariness. Alternative dispute resolution has always existed. To most individuals, civil litigation is no more than the remotest of possibilities, a last-ditch option in desperate situations after all else fails. Yet you can see from the above Alternative Dispute Resolution Act that once parties find themselves engaged in civil litigation, the courts are likely to force them to consider getting out. That was not always the case. *See, e.g.,* Wilko v. Swan, 346 U.S. (1953) (disfavoring compulsory arbitration of certain securities claims). An alternative-dispute-resolution movement arose in the 1970s, spawning significant study of the subject. As alternative dispute resolution became an identified legal subject and field, state and federal legislatures and courts, taking notice, began to make parties participate. *See, e.g.,* Rodriguez de Quijas v. Shearson/American Express, Inc., 490 U.S. 477 (1989) (reversing *Wilko v. Swan* and compelling arbitration of securities claims); Shearson/American Express, Inc. v. McMahon, 482 U.S. 220 (1987) (compelling arbitration of racketeering claims); Southland Corp. v. Keating, 465 U.S. 1 (1984) (reversing California Supreme Court and requiring arbitration of franchise-act claims). Alternative-dispute-resolution scholars and practitioners appreciated the growth in the field but simultaneously regretted the compulsory aspect. Forcing parties to participate in alternative forums when they have chosen to litigate can change their attitudes about those alternative forums. Civil litigators have love/hate relationships with alternative dispute resolution. The following sections on settlement, mediation, offers of judgment, and arbitration reflect that productive tension. How well or poorly does the above Alternative Dispute Resolution Act manage that tension? Does it preserve an adequate degree of voluntariness while adequately promoting ADR participation? Who should choose the form of alternative dispute resolution, the parties, the judge, or a professional administrator trained in ADR? No matter the attitudes, alternative dispute resolution is here to stay, and competent litigators master its several forms.

A. Negotiation

Most cases settle by negotiation. They should. Because parties control the outcome, negotiated resolution tends to be more sensitive to the parties' needs and interests than court-imposed judgments. Judgments tend to produce clear winners and losers. The conventional saying is that with settlement, everyone goes home equally unhappy. In negotiated resolution, parties can often construct compromises that courts would have no legal authority to impose, where the law will provide either a full remedy or none at all. Settlement can also save the parties time and expense, and help parties avoid or control adverse publicity affecting internal and external relationships. Most of all, settlements eliminate risk. For plaintiffs, they eliminate the prospect of obtaining no relief and perhaps owing substantial costs and attorney's fees. For individual defendants, they eliminate the risk of an adverse judgment exceeding any available insurance and perhaps resulting in garnishment of wages and execution on personal assets. For corporate defendants, they eliminate the prospect of a judgment that would exhaust corporate assets or destroy corporate interests. Parties seek control through the resolution of civil litigation, even while litigation and its resolution depend on recognizing the prospect of having no control—that is, of having ceded authority to decide to an independent decisionmaker.

Courts, too, have an interest in settlement. Many courts are busy, some swamped, as Chapter I's introduction indicates. Judges and court administrators plan that a certain percentage of cases will settle. They expect cases to settle. They save justice-system resources when a larger percentage settles than planned, and they incur additional unbudgeted costs when a small percentage settles. Clearance rates comparing cases filed to cases removed from a court's docket determine how many judges and courtrooms a jurisdiction may need, not to mention the speed and quality of justice. Thus, judges and court administrators study, promote, and support settlement.

Civil procedures encourage settlement in a variety of ways. FED. R. CIV. P. 16(a)(5) and similar state-court rules authorize the trial courts to order attorneys and unrepresented parties to appear for a pretrial conference to facilitate settlement. Rule 16(f) gives the trial court the authority to enforce with monetary and other sanctions its order to prepare for, attend, and participate in a settlement conference. *See, e.g.,* Nick v. Morgan's Foods, Inc., 270 F.3d 590 (2001) (affirming monetary sanction for party's failure to attend court-ordered mediation in good faith effort to settle); Official Airline Guides, Inc. v. Goss, 6 F.3d 1385, 1396 (9th Cir. 1993) (sanction of costs and fees); Bud Brooks Trucking, Inc. v. Bill Hodges Trucking Co., 909 F.2d 1437, 1440 (10th Cir. 1990) (sanction of dismissal). It is standard practice for courts to exercise their Rule 16(a)(5) authority to order attorneys and unrepresented parties to attend settlement conferences and, indeed, to do more. For instance, although Rule 16(a)(5) refers explicitly only to ordering the attendance of "the attorneys and any unrepresented parties," trial courts also commonly order the attendance of represented parties. In the case of corporate parties, trial courts may order the attendance of a corporate representative with authority to settle. *See, e.g.,* Lockhart v. Patel, 115 F.R.D. 44 (E.D. Ky. 1987) (striking defendants' pleadings as sanction for failure of corporate representative to attend with settlement authority). Trial judges (and lawyers and mediators) know that settlement negotiations do not succeed when those who are negotiating have no authority to settle. Where applicable procedural rules do not, as in the case of Rule 16(a)(5), give the trial court express authority to order the attendance of party or party representatives with full authority to settle, the trial court may have inherent authority to do so and to sanction parties for violating that order. Consider the following case so holding. There are few greater ways in which to earn the ire of an experienced trial judge than to attend an ordered settlement conference without authority to settle.

G. Heileman Brewing Co. v. Joseph Oat Corp.,

United States Court of Appeals for the Seventh Circuit
871 F.2d 648 (1989)

KANNE, Circuit Judge[, in rehearing en banc].

May a federal district court order litigants-even those represented by counsel-to appear before it in person at a pretrial conference for the purpose of discussing the posture and settlement of the litigants' case? After reviewing the Federal Rules of Civil Procedure and federal district courts' inherent authority to manage and control the litigation before them, we answer this question in the affirmative and conclude that a district court may sanction a litigant for failing to comply with such an order. ...

A federal magistrate ordered Joseph Oat Corporation to send a "corporate representative with authority to settle" to a pretrial conference to discuss disputed factual and legal issues and the possibility of settlement. Although counsel for Oat Corporation appeared, accompanied by another attorney who was authorized to speak on behalf of the principals of the corporation, no principal or corporate representative personally attended the conference. The court determined that the failure of Oat Corporation to send a principal of the corporation to the pretrial conference violated its order. Consequently, the district court imposed a sanction of $5,860.01 upon Oat Corporation pursuant to Federal Rule of Civil Procedure 16(f). This amount represented the costs and attorneys' fees of the opposing parties attending the conference. …

… Oat Corporation contends that, by negative implication, the language of Rule 16(a)(5) prohibits a district court from directing represented litigants to attend pretrial conferences.[fn] That is, because Rule 16 expressly refers to "attorneys for the parties and any unrepresented parties" in introductory paragraph (a), a district court may not go beyond that language to devise procedures which direct the pretrial appearance of parties represented by counsel. …

Rule 16 addresses the use of pretrial conferences to formulate and narrow issues for trial as well as to discuss means for dispensing with the need for costly and unnecessary litigation. …

The pretrial settlement of litigation has been advocated and used as a means to alleviate overcrowded dockets, and courts have practiced numerous and varied types of pretrial settlement techniques for many years. [Cc] Since 1983, Rule 16 has expressly provided that settlement of a case is one of several subjects which should be pursued and discussed vigorously during pretrial conferences.[fn]

The language of Rule 16 does not give any direction to the district court upon the issue of a court's authority to order litigants who are represented by counsel to appear for pretrial proceedings. Instead, Rule 16 merely refers to the participation of trial advocates-attorneys of record and *pro se* litigants. However, the Federal Rules of Civil Procedure do not completely describe and limit the power of the federal courts. [C]

The concept that district courts exercise procedural authority outside the explicit language of the rules of civil procedure is not frequently documented, but valid nevertheless. [C] The Supreme Court has acknowledged that the provisions of the Federal Rules of Civil Procedure are not intended to be the exclusive authority for actions to be taken by district courts. Link v. Wabash R.R., 370 U.S. 626[] (1962).

In *Link*, the Supreme Court noted that a district court's ability to take action in a procedural context may be grounded in "'inherent power,' governed not by rule or statute but by the control necessarily vested in courts to manage their own affairs so as to achieve the orderly and expeditious disposition of cases." 370 U.S. at 630-31[].[fn] This authority likewise forms the basis for continued development of procedural techniques designed to make the operation of the court more efficient, to preserve the integrity of the judicial process, and to control courts' dockets.[fn] Because the rules form and shape certain aspects of a court's inherent powers, yet allow the continued exercise of that power where discretion should be available, the mere absence of language in the federal rules specifically authorizing or describing a particular judicial procedure should not, and does not, give rise to a negative implication of prohibition. *See Link*, 370 U.S. at 629-30[];[fn] *see also* Fed.R.Civ.P. 83 ("In all cases not provided for by rule, the district judges and magistrates may regulate their practice in any manner not inconsistent with these rules or those of the district in which they act.").

In this case, we are required to determine whether a court's power to order the pretrial appearance of litigants who are represented by counsel is inconsistent with, or in derogation of, Rule 16. We must remember that Rule 1 states, with unmistakable clarity, that the Federal Rules of Civil Procedure "shall be construed to secure the just, speedy, and inexpensive determination of every action." This language explicitly indicates that the federal rules are to be liberally construed. [C] There is no place in the federal civil procedural system for the proposition that rules having the force of statute, though in derogation of the common law, are to be strictly construed. [C] ...

... The wording of the rule and the accompanying commentary make plain that the entire thrust of the amendment to Rule 16 was to urge judges to make wider use of their powers and to manage actively their dockets from an early stage. We therefore conclude that our interpretation of Rule 16 to allow district courts to order represented parties to appear at pretrial settlement conferences merely represents another application of a district judge's inherent authority to preserve the efficiency, and more importantly the integrity, of the judicial process.

To summarize, we simply hold that the action taken by the district court in this case constituted the proper use of inherent authority to aid in accomplishing the purpose and intent of Rule 16. We reaffirm the notion that the inherent power of a district judge—derived from the very nature and existence of his judicial office—is the broad field over which the Federal Rules of Civil Procedure are applied.[fn] Inherent authority remains the means by which district judges deal with circumstances not proscribed or specifically addressed by rule or statute, but which must be addressed to promote the just, speedy, and inexpensive determination of every action. ...

Having determined that the district court possessed the power and authority to order the represented litigants to appear at the pretrial settlement conference,[fn] we now must examine whether the court abused its discretion to issue such an order.

At the outset, it is important to note that a district court cannot coerce settlement. [C][fn] In this case, considerable concern has been generated because the court ordered "corporate representatives with authority to settle" to attend the conference. In our view, "authority to settle," when used in the context of this case, means that the "corporate representative" attending the pretrial conference was required to hold a position within the corporate entity allowing him to speak definitively and to commit the corporation to a particular position in the litigation. We do not view "authority to settle" as a requirement that corporate representatives must come to court willing to settle on someone else's terms, but only that they come to court in order to consider the possibility of settlement.

If this case represented a situation where Oat Corporation had sent a corporate representative and was sanctioned because that person refused to make an offer to pay money—that is, refused to submit to settlement coercion—we would be faced with a decidely different issue—a situation we would not countenance.

The Advisory Committee Notes to Rule 16 state that "[a]lthough it is not the purpose of Rule 16(b)(7) to impose settlement negotiations on unwilling litigants, it is believed that providing a neutral forum for discussing [settlement] might foster it." [C] These Notes clearly draw a distinction between being required to attend a settlement conference and being required to participate in settlement negotiations. Thus, under the scheme of pretrial settlement conferences, the corporate representative remains free, on behalf of the corporate entity, to propose terms of settlement independently—but he may be required to state those terms in a pretrial conference before a judge or magistrate. ...

We recognize, as did the district court, that circumstances could arise in which requiring a corporate representative (or any litigant) to appear at a pretrial settlement conference would be so onerous, so clearly unproductive, or so expensive in relation to the size, value, and complexity of the case that it might be an abuse of discretion. ... However, the facts and circumstances of this case clearly support the court's actions to require the corporate representatives of the litigants to attend the pretrial conference personally.

This litigation involved a claim for $4 million—a claim which turned upon the resolution of complex factual and legal issues.[fn] The litigants expected the trial to last from one to three months and all parties stood to incur substantial legal fees and trial expenses. This trial also would have preempted a large segment of judicial time—not an insignificant factor. Thus, because the stakes were high, we do not believe that the burden of requiring a corporate representative to attend a pretrial settlement conference was out of proportion to the benefits to be gained, not only by the litigants but also by the court. ...

Furthermore, no objection to the magistrate's order was made prior to the date the pretrial conference resumed. Oat Corporation contacted the magistrate's office concerning the order's requirements and was advised of the requirements now at issue. However, Oat Corporation never objected to its terms, either when it was issued or when Oat Corporation sought clarification. Consequently, Oat

Corporation was left with only one course of action: it had to comply fully with the letter *and* intent of the order and argue about its reasonableness later.[fn] …

… The judgment of the district court is hereby AFFIRMED.

POSNER, Circuit Judge, dissenting. …

Oat had made clear that it was not prepared to settle the case on any terms that required it to pay money. That was its prerogative, which once exercised made the magistrate's continued insistence on Oat's sending an executive to Madison arbitrary, unreasonable, willful, and indeed petulant. …

Sufficient unto the day is the evil thereof: We should reverse the district court without reaching the question whether there are any circumstances in which a district court may compel a party represented by counsel to attend a pretrial conference.

COFFEY, Circuit Judge, with whom EASTERBROOK, RIPPLE, and MANION, Circuit Judges, join, dissenting[, arguing that Rule 16 leaves a necessary negative inference that only lawyers and unrepresented parties must appear, omitted.]

EASTERBROOK, Circuit Judge, with whom POSNER, COFFEY, and MANION, Circuit Judges, join, dissenting[, omitted.].

RIPPLE, Circuit Judge, with whom COFFEY, Circuit Judge, joins, dissenting[, omitted].

MANION, Circuit Judge, joined by COFFEY, EASTERBROOK, and RIPPLE, Circuit Judges, dissenting[, omitted].

INQUIRY

Judge's Role. *Heileman, supra,* and other cases indicate a trial court's inherent authority to require parties to participate in settlement efforts, even if not to impose settlement terms. *See, e.g.,* Abney v. Patten, 696 F.Supp. 567, 568 (W.D. Okla. 1987) ("The horses may be led to water. Whether they drink is up to them."). What may a trial judge do when the parties attend a pretrial settlement conference? Practitioners know quite well the willingness of some trial judges, endorsed by Rule 16(a)(5) on "facilitating settlement," to help along a settlement negotiation by discussing uncertainties in the outcome. For instance, trial judges will comment from professional experience on the unpredictability of juries. Trial judges have less room to express personal opinions about the case. *Compare* Rocha v. Great American Ins. Co., 850 F.2d 1095, 1100 (6th Cir. 1988) (trial judge's remarks prejudging merits of case invalidate judgment for personal bias and prejudice), *with* Sloan v. State Farm Mut. Auto. Ins. Co., 360 F.3d 1220, 1227 (10th Cir. 2004) (commenting outside of the jury's presence on the case's probable value was not judicial error). There is authority holding that a trial judge may impose a deadline within which the parties must settle or suffer sanctions for settling later after trial begins. *See* Newton v. A.C. & S., 918 F.2d 1121, 1126 (3d Cir. 1990). Trial judges must not, on the other hand, order settlement conferences for other claims and defenses that the parties have not asserted in the case out of which the trial judge issues the order, even if those unasserted claims are holding up the settlement. *See* In re Asbestos Litigation, 90 F.3d 963, 1015 (5th Cir. 1996).

Form. Courts and parties also have an interest in the technical aspects of settlement, not simply in its substantive provisions. There are protocols for settling, just as there are procedures for pleading, discovery, pretrial, and trial. A settlement properly documented and administered should accomplish the parties' intention, clearing the court's docket of the case and giving the parties the requisite degree of finality. A settlement not properly documented may lead to reopening the case and relitigating previously resolved issues. A common means of completing a settlement is for the lawyers to draft and the parties to execute a detailed settlement agreement, one term of which is that the court will dismiss the case. The lawyers then execute a short stipulation which may refer to the settlement agreement, and the court signs a short order dismissing the case, typically with prejudice based on the settlement. The particular form of the settlement agreement will have more to do with the form of requested and negotiated relief (declaratory relief, injunctions, damages) and with contract law as to standard clauses (integration of terms, authority for execution, severability), than with civil procedure. Consider a sample form below.

SETTLEMENT AGREEMENT AND RELEASE

In consideration for the payment to them of the amount of $____________, receipt of which is hereby acknowledged, **CLAIMANTS** release and forever discharge **RESPONDENT**, and its agents, employees, attorneys, insurers, representatives, officers, directors, predecessors, successors, and assigns, from all claims, demands, and causes of action for loss, damages, injuries, claims, and liability, whether known or unknown, and whether past or present, arising out of the fire incident on **INCIDENT DATE**, involving **CLAIMANTS** and their residence at **ADDRESS**, and further release these entities from all other liability which was alleged or which could have been alleged in the case entitled **CLAIMANTS** v **RESPONDENT**, ________ Circuit Court No. **CASE NUMBER**. **CLAIMANTS** further agree to promptly dismiss with prejudice and without costs that pending case and any other case or legal proceeding against the released entities and to forebear from filing or causing to be filed any other legal claim or proceeding to enforce the rights, claims, and interests released by this agreement.

It is expressly understood and agreed that this settlement agreement and release is entered into between the parties as a compromise and resolution of disputed claims. This settlement agreement and release is not to be construed as an admission of liability or of the validity of any of the claims, which are instead expressly denied.

Any persons signing this agreement on behalf of any other individuals or corporate entities represent and warrant that they have obtained all authorizations, resolutions, and approvals, have met the requirements for any insurance or bond, and have otherwise met all other rules and legal requirements necessary to their binding and effective release of the above persons and entities. They further represent and warrant that in signing this agreement they have relied on themselves or on the advice of their own chosen representatives and counsel and not on any representation or omission made by the opposing parties or their representatives and counsel. This paper contains all the terms of the settlement agreement and release between these parties. The parties make no representation beyond the scope of this writing, on which the opposing party is entitled to rely as a basis for entering into this agreement. This agreement is voluntarily made.

CLAIMANT HUSBAND	CLAIMANT WIFE
Signed: ______________________	Signed:

Content. Legal issues can arise around the substantive terms, scope, or content of a settlement agreement and release. For instance, may the parties release in a settlement agreement claims that they could not have maintained in the case that induced the release? The answer in the federal courts appears to be yes. In Matsushita Elec. Indus. Co. v. Epstein, 516 U.S. 367 (1996), the Supreme Court held that the full-faith-and-credit statute 28 U.S.C. §1738 requires the federal courts to recognize state-court judgments that settle claims within the exclusive jurisdiction of the federal courts. The plaintiff class in *Matsushita Elec. Indus. Co. v. Epstein* had pled state-court claims for breach of fiduciary duty and then, when settling those state-law claims, agreed to release federal securities-law claims cognizable only in federal court. So long as state law would recognize the release, the federal courts must give full faith and credit to the state-court judgment incorporating it. Other statutory schemes address settlement terms directly. For example, a provision of the Age Discrimination in Employment Act requires that settlement agreements for claims brought under the Act must be clear, advise the party to consult a lawyer, and permit revocation within one week after signing. *See* 29 U.S.C. §626(f); *see also* Oubre v. Entergy Operations, Inc., 522 U.S. 422 (1998) (claimant may keep settlement funds and pursue claims after signing release without statutory terms).

Confidentiality. Confidentiality is a term that parties on both sides often wish to include in a settlement agreement. Defendants may want to eliminate adverse publicity and avoid publicizing incentives for others to raise claims. Plaintiffs may want to reduce equally adverse publicity and to avoid publicizing to friends, family members, and creditors their sudden monetary gains. Some agreements require parties to return or destroy discovery materials, not to disclose the terms of settlement (particularly amounts paid), and not even to disclose the fact of suit or settlement. Some agreements purport to impose liquidated damages for breach of confidentiality. Confidentiality agreements tend to grant exceptions where court or law requires disclosure, such as to file tax returns disclosing the financial consequences of settlement or to respond to subpoenas. Other agreements require notice of disclosure so that the party entitled to confidentiality can challenge its necessity and limit its scope. Confidentiality agreements tend to bind the parties and hold them responsible for disclosures by their counsel, employees, agents, and representatives. Although confidentiality agreements are in general enforceable, the public and courts may have a contrary interest in disclosure. While confidentiality promotes settlement, a defendant who buys secrecy from one plaintiff may be concealing evidence of wrongs from other claimants. Courts balance these competing interests when deciding whether, under FED. R. CIV. P. 26(c) on protective orders, to require disclosure contrary to express agreement. *See* Kalinauskas v. Wong, 151 F.R.D. 363 (D. Nev. 1993) (permitting deposition of sex-discrimination claimant in other lawsuit but limiting disclosure of terms of her settlement). The public concern is greatest when the settlement purports to prohibit a party's testimony as a witness in subsequent independent litigation. *See* Baker v. General Motors Corp., 522 U.S. 222 (1998) (refusing to enforce settlement agreement prohibiting witness testimony); *see also* WASH. REV. CODE §4.24.611(1)(c)(2) (requiring courts to weigh public interest when deciding on protective orders against disclosing settlement information).

Breach. When a party breaches a term of the settlement agreement, what relief does the opposing party have? Notice from the above example that the trial court does not ordinarily review and approve terms of the settlement, at least when the parties agree to a dismissal with prejudice. The trial court may certainly decide the form of its order for voluntary dismissal under FED. R. CIV. P. 41(a). Chapter VII addresses voluntary dismissal. Yet a dismissal with prejudice pursuant to a settlement agreement leaves a party no clear opportunity to reopen the case when a party breaches the agreement. The trial court has no order to enforce other than its dismissal. A settlement based on a private agreement and dismissal makes enforcement depend on a breach of contract action. State law governs contract actions. Even if the settlement was of a federal case alleging federal-law claims, the federal courts will no longer have jurisdiction to decide a state-law dispute over enforcement of the private agreement resolving the federal litigation. *See* Langley v. Jackson State University, 14 F.3d 1070 (5th Cir. 1994). In cases where parties desire enforcement in the same court in which the case was initially filed and settled, they must incorporate the settlement into the dismissal order. When they do so, the court will maintain jurisdiction to enforce its own judgments and orders. *See* Kokkonen v. Guardian Life Ins. Co., 511 U.S. 375 (1994).

Fees. Recall the brief discussion in Chapter I's overview about how the financing of litigation can influence its resolution. When a fee-shifting statute creates the potential for a prevailing plaintiff to receive an attorney's fee award, that award becomes a part of the settlement calculus. Or does it? Clients decide on the goals of litigation including when and the terms on which to settle litigation. When it comes to receiving a reasonable fee for their efforts, lawyers can have interests that differ from their clients' interests, especially in the settlement of litigation. Depending on the nature of the case, attorney's fees can equal or substantially exceed the anticipated damages, especially in cases where the plaintiffs seek primarily injunctive relief. Defendants and their counsel are quite well aware of the potential for differing interests and may divide plaintiff from plaintiff's counsel to make a more favorable settlement. In the following case, the Supreme Court held that a federal trial court has the statutory authority to decline a fee award where the defendant settles a case by consent decree in which the plaintiff waives fees. The conclusion that a defendant should not pay the plaintiff's attorney fees when the parties so agree may seem obvious. Yet as you read the following case, appreciate the difficult position in which it puts the plaintiff's lawyer and the way in which the ruling might affect the availability of legal representation for plaintiffs.

Evans v. Jeff D.,

United States Supreme Court
475 U.S. 717 (1986)

Justice STEVENS delivered the opinion of the Court.

The Civil Rights Attorney's Fees Awards Act of 1976 (Fees Act) provides that "the court, in its discretion, may allow the prevailing party ... a reasonable attorney's fee" in enumerated civil rights actions. [] 42 U.S.C. §1988. In Maher v. Gagne, 448 U.S. 122[] (1980), we held that fees *may* be assessed against state officials after a case has been settled by the entry of a consent decree. In this case, we consider the question whether attorney's fees *must* be assessed when the case has been settled by a consent decree granting prospective relief to the plaintiff class but providing that the defendants shall not pay any part of the prevailing party's fees or costs. We hold that the District Court has the power, in its sound discretion, to refuse to award fees. ...

The petitioners are the Governor and other public officials of the State of Idaho responsible for the education and treatment of children who suffer from emotional and mental handicaps. Respondents are a class of such children who have been or will be placed in petitioners' care.[fn]

... The factual allegations in the complaint described deficiencies in both the educational programs and the health care services provided respondents. These deficiencies allegedly violated the United States Constitution, the Idaho Constitution, four federal statutes, and certain provisions of the Idaho Code. The complaint prayed for injunctive relief and for an award of costs and attorney's fees, but it did not seek damages.

... The District Court ... appoint[ed] Charles Johnson as [respondents'] next friend for the sole purpose of instituting and prosecuting the action. At that time Johnson was employed by the Idaho Legal Aid Society... . Because the Idaho Legal Aid Society is prohibited from representing clients who are capable of paying their own fees,[fn] it made no agreement requiring any of the respondents to pay for the costs of litigation or the legal services it provided through Johnson. ...

... [O]ne week before trial, petitioners presented respondents with a new settlement proposal[that ...] "offered virtually all of the injunctive relief [they] had sought in their complaint." [C] ... [P]etitioners' offer included a provision for a waiver by respondents of any claim to fees or costs.[fn] ... Johnson ultimately determined that his ethical obligation to his clients mandated acceptance of the proposal. ...

After the stipulation was signed, Johnson filed a written motion requesting the District Court to approve the settlement "except for the provision on costs and attorney's fees," and to allow respondents to present a bill of costs and fees for consideration by the court. [C] At the oral argument on that motion, Johnson contended that petitioners' offer had exploited his ethical duty to his clients—that he was "forced," by an offer giving his clients "the best result [they] could have gotten in this court or any other court," to waive his attorney's fees.[fn] The District Court ... concluded that "it doesn't violate any ethical considerations for an attorney to give up his attorney fees in the interest of getting a better bargain for his client[s]." [C] Accordingly, the District Court approved the settlement and denied the motion to submit a costs bill.

... The Court of Appeals... invalidated the fee waiver and left standing the remainder of the settlement; it then instructed the District Court to "make its own determination of the fees that are reasonable" and remanded for that limited purpose. [C] ...

... Rule 23(e) wisely requires court approval of the terms of any settlement of a class action, but the power to approve or reject a settlement negotiated by the parties before trial does not authorize the court to require the parties to accept a settlement to which they have not agreed. ... The question we must decide, therefore, is whether the District Court had a duty to reject the proposed settlement because it included a waiver of statutorily authorized attorney's fees.

... Although respondents contend that Johnson, as counsel for the class, was faced with an "ethical dilemma" when petitioners offered him relief greater than that which he could reasonably have expected to obtain for his clients at trial (if only he would stipulate to a waiver of the statutory fee award), ... [p]lainly, Johnson had no *ethical* obligation to seek a statutory fee award. His ethical duty was to serve his clients loyally and competently.[fn] Since the proposal to settle the merits was more favorable than the probable outcome of the trial, Johnson's decision to recommend acceptance was consistent with the highest standards of our profession. ...

The defect, if any, in the negotiated fee waiver must be traced not to the rules of ethics but to the Fees Act.[fn] ...

The question this case presents, then, is whether the Fees Act requires a district court to disapprove a stipulation seeking to settle a civil rights class action under Rule 23 when the offered relief equals or exceeds the probable outcome at trial but is expressly conditioned on waiver of statutory eligibility for attorney's fees. For reasons set out below, we are not persuaded that Congress has commanded that all such settlements must be rejected by the District Court. Moreover, on the facts of record in this case, we are satisfied that the District Court did not abuse its discretion by approving the fee waiver. ...

The text of the Fees Act provides no support for the proposition that Congress intended to ban all fee waivers offered in connection with substantial relief on the merits.[fn] On the contrary, the language of the Act, as well as its legislative history, indicates that Congress bestowed on the "prevailing *party* " (generally plaintiffs[fn]) a statutory eligibility for a discretionary award of attorney's fees in specified civil rights actions.[fn] ... Thus, while it is undoubtedly true that Congress expected fee shifting to attract competent counsel to represent citizens deprived of their civil rights,[fn] it neither bestowed fee awards upon attorneys nor rendered them nonwaivable or nonnegotiable; instead, it added them to the arsenal of remedies available to combat violations of civil rights, a goal not invariably inconsistent with conditioning settlement on the merits on a waiver of statutory attorney's fees.[fn]

In fact, we believe that a general proscription against negotiated waiver of attorney's fees in exchange for a settlement on the merits would itself impede vindication of civil rights, at least in some cases, by reducing the attractiveness of settlement. ...

Most defendants are unlikely to settle unless the cost of the predicted judgment, discounted by its probability, plus the transaction costs of further litigation, are greater than the cost of the settlement package. If fee waivers cannot be negotiated, the settlement package must either contain an attorney's fee component of potentially large and typically uncertain magnitude, or else the parties must agree to have the fee fixed by the court. Although either of these alternatives may well be acceptable in many cases, there surely is a significant number in which neither alternative will be as satisfactory as a decision to try the entire case.[fn]

The adverse impact of removing attorney's fees and costs from bargaining might be tolerable if the uncertainty introduced into settlement negotiations were small. But it is not. The defendants' potential liability for fees in this kind of litigation can be as significant as, and sometimes even more significant than, their potential liability on the merits. ...

The question remains whether the District Court abused its discretion in this case by approving a settlement which included a complete fee waiver. As noted earlier, Rule 23(e) wisely requires court approval of the terms of any settlement of a class action. The potential conflict among members of the class-in this case, for example, the possible conflict between children primarily interested in better educational programs and those primarily interested in improved health care-fully justifies the requirement of court approval. ...

In light of the record, respondents must—to sustain the judgment in their favor—confront the District Court's finding that the extensive structural relief they obtained constituted an adequate *quid pro quo* for their waiver of attorney's fees.[fn] ...

What the outcome of this settlement illustrates is that the Fees Act has given the victims of civil rights violations a powerful weapon that improves their ability to employ counsel, to obtain access to the courts, and thereafter to vindicate their rights by means of settlement or trial. For aught that appears, it was the "coercive" effect of respondents' statutory right to seek a fee award that motivated petitioners' exceptionally generous offer. Whether this weapon might be even more powerful if fee waivers were prohibited in cases like this is another question,[fn] but it is in any event a question that Congress is best equipped to answer. Thus far, the Legislature has not commanded that fees be paid whenever a case is settled. Unless it issues such a command, we shall rely primarily on the sound discretion of the district courts to appraise the reasonableness of particular class-action settlements on a case-by-case basis, in the light of all the relevant circumstances.[fn] In this case, the District Court did not abuse its discretion in upholding a fee waiver which secured broad injunctive relief, relief greater than that which plaintiffs could reasonably have expected to achieve at trial.[fn]

The judgment of the Court of Appeals is reversed.

It is so ordered.

Justice BRENNAN, with whom Justice MARSHALL and Justice BLACKMUN join, dissenting[, omitted, arguing that the announced rule would shrink the pool of lawyers willing to take on such litigation].

INQUIRY

Results. The above *Evans v. Jeff D.* case involved a consent decree as to which the defendant avoided paying the other side's attorney fees. Few cases end up in consent decrees. Yet the case highlights that a defendant may, to avoid paying substantial statutory attorney's fees or for other like reasons, decide to correct on its own the illegal practices that the plaintiffs allege as a basis for a statutory fee request. When it is apparent that the litigation induced the defendant's change in position, should the trial court award attorney's fees even though the case did not result in a formal consent decree or other order or judgment reflecting that the plaintiff prevailed? A majority of federal circuits recognized this "catalyst theory" for fee awards until the Supreme Court rejected it in the following case. Once again, as you read the case, consider how it may affect the willingness of lawyers to undertake litigation in which their compensation, if any, would need to depend on shifting fees.

Buckhannon Board and Care Home, Inc. v. West Virginia Dept. of Health and Human Resources,

United States Supreme Court
532 U.S. 598 (2001)

Chief Justice REHNQUIST delivered the opinion of the Court.

Numerous federal statutes allow courts to award attorney's fees and costs to the "prevailing party." The question presented here is whether this term includes a party that has failed to secure a judgment on the merits or a court-ordered consent decree, but has nonetheless achieved the desired result because the lawsuit brought about a voluntary change in the defendant's conduct. We hold that it does not.

Buckhannon Board and Care Home, Inc., which operates care homes that provide assisted living to their residents, failed an inspection by the West Virginia Office of the State Fire Marshal because some of the residents were incapable of "self-preservation" as defined under state law. [Cc] ... [A]fter receiving cease and desist orders requiring the closure of its residential care facilities within 30 days, Buckhannon Board and Care Home, Inc., on behalf of itself and other similarly situated homes and residents (hereinafter petitioners), brought suit ... against the State of West Virginia, two of its agencies, and 18 individuals (hereinafter respondents), seeking declaratory and injunctive relief[fn] that the "self-preservation" requirement violated the Fair Housing Amendments Act of 1988 (FHAA), [] 42 U.S.C. §3601 *et seq.* , and the Americans with Disabilities Act of 1990 (ADA), [] 42 U.S.C. § 12101 *et seq.*

Respondents agreed to stay enforcement of the cease-and-desist orders pending resolution of the case... In 1998, the West Virginia Legislature enacted two bills eliminating the "self-preservation" requirement, [cc], and respondents moved to dismiss the case as moot. The District Court granted the motion, finding that the 1998 legislation had eliminated the allegedly offensive provisions... .

Petitioners requested attorney's fees as the "prevailing party" under the FHAA, 42 U.S.C. §3613(c)(2) ("[T]he court, in its discretion, may allow the prevailing party ... a reasonable attorney's fee and costs"), and ADA, 42 U.S.C. §12205 ("[T]he court ..., in its discretion, may allow the prevailing party ... a reasonable attorney's fee, including litigation expenses, and costs"). Petitioners argued that they were entitled to attorney's fees under the "catalyst theory," which posits that a plaintiff is a "prevailing party" if it achieves the desired result because the lawsuit brought about a voluntary change in the defendant's conduct. ... Although most Courts of Appeals recognize the "catalyst theory,"[fn] the Court of Appeals for the Fourth Circuit rejected it... . The District Court accordingly denied the motion and, for the same reason, the Court of Appeals [for the Fourth Circuit] affirmed... .

In addition to judgments on the merits, we have held that settlement agreements enforced through a consent decree may serve as the basis for an award of attorney's fees. ...

We think, however, the "catalyst theory" falls on the other side of the line from these examples. It allows an award where there is no judicially sanctioned change in the legal relationship of the parties. ... A defendant's voluntary change in conduct, although perhaps accomplishing what the plaintiff sought to achieve by the lawsuit, lacks the necessary judicial *imprimatur* on the change. Our precedents thus counsel against holding that the term "prevailing party" authorizes an award of attorney's fees *without* a corresponding alteration in the legal relationship of the parties. ...

Petitioners nonetheless argue that the legislative history of the Civil Rights Attorney's Fees Awards Act supports a broad reading of "prevailing party" which includes the "catalyst theory." We doubt that legislative history could overcome what we think is the rather clear meaning of "prevailing party"—the term actually used in the statute. ...

... We think the legislative history cited by petitioners is at best ambiguous as to the availability of the "catalyst theory" for awarding attorney's fees. Particularly in view of the "American Rule" that attorney's fees will not be awarded absent "explicit statutory authority," such legislative history is clearly insufficient to alter the accepted meaning of the statutory term. [C]

Petitioners finally assert that the "catalyst theory" is necessary to prevent defendants from unilaterally mooting an action before judgment in an effort to avoid an award of attorney's fees. They also claim that the rejection of the "catalyst theory" will deter plaintiffs with meritorious but expensive cases from bringing suit. We are skeptical of these assertions, which are entirely speculative and unsupported by any empirical evidence... .

Petitioners discount the disincentive that the "catalyst theory" may have upon a defendant's decision to voluntarily change its conduct, conduct that may not be illegal. "The defendants' potential liability for fees in this kind of litigation can be as significant as, and sometimes even more significant than, their potential liability on the merits," Evans v. Jeff D., 475 U.S. 717, 734[] (1986), and the possibility of being assessed attorney's fees may well deter a defendant from altering its conduct.

And petitioners' fear of mischievous defendants only materializes in claims for equitable relief, for so long as the plaintiff has a cause of action for damages, a defendant's change in conduct will not moot the case.[fn] Even then, it is not clear how often courts will find a case mooted: "It is well settled that a defendant's voluntary cessation of a challenged practice does not deprive a federal court of its power to determine the legality of the practice" unless it is "absolutely clear that the allegedly wrongful behavior could not reasonably be expected to recur." Friends of Earth, Inc. v. Laidlaw Environmental Services (TOC), Inc., 528 U.S. 167, 189[] (2000) (internal quotation marks and citations omitted). If a case is not found to be moot, and the plaintiff later procures an enforceable judgment, the court may of course award attorney's fees. Given this possibility, a defendant has a strong incentive to enter a settlement agreement, where it can negotiate attorney's fees and costs. [C]

The judgment of the Court of Appeals is

Affirmed.

Justice SCALIA, with whom Justice THOMAS joins, concurring[, omitted].

Justice GINSBURG, with whom Justice STEVENS, Justice SOUTER, and Justice BREYER join, dissenting.

The Court today holds that a plaintiff whose suit prompts the precise relief she seeks does not "prevail," and hence cannot obtain an award of attorney's fees, unless she also secures a court entry memorializing her victory. The entry need not be a judgment on the merits. Nor need there be any finding of wrongdoing. A court-approved settlement will do. ...

The Court's insistence that there be a document filed in court—a litigated judgment or court-endorsed settlement—upsets long-prevailing Circuit precedent applicable to scores of federal fee-shifting statutes. The decision allows a defendant to escape a statutory obligation to pay a plaintiff's counsel fees, even though the suit's merit led the defendant to abandon the fray, to switch rather than fight on, to accord plaintiff sooner rather than later the principal redress sought in the complaint. Concomitantly, the Court's constricted definition of "prevailing party," and consequent rejection of the "catalyst theory," impede access to court for the less well heeled, and shrink the incentive Congress created for the enforcement of federal law by private attorneys general. ...

Biography

At the time that she represented the successful respondents in the above *Buckhannon* case, Beth Brinkmann was a partner in the Washington, D.C. law firm Morrison & Foerster, later the head of its appellate and Supreme Court practice group. She is a member of the rare group of lawyers who has argued multiple times (in her case, 24 times) before the Supreme Court, in her case often representing corporate and government interests including the United States Chamber of Commerce, U.S. Bank, JPMorgan Chase Bank, the Airports Council International—North America, and the Governor of Guam. In 2010, she left Morrison & Foerster to become Deputy Assistant Attorney General of the United States, leading the appellate staff in the Civil Division. She has been recognized as one of the top 50 women lawyers in Washington.

B. Offers of Judgment

Civil procedure promotes settlement in other ways, in addition to settlement conferences. FED. R. CIV. P. 68 and similar state-court rules, *see, e.g.,* MICH. CT. R. 2.405, allow for offers of judgment. Offer-of-judgment rules are to induce settlement. As Rule 68 below shows, their basic structure is to permit a party to serve an offer of judgment on the opposing party and then to collect costs if the opposing party who rejects the offer subsequently fails to obtain a judgment more favorable than the offer. Parties make settlement offers in many cases through their attorneys. There is ordinarily no formal consequence for a party to reject or fail to respond to a settlement offer. However, if an attorney for a party serves an offer of judgment under Rule 68 or state-rule equivalent, then the opposing party must consider the potential formal consequences of the offer, which could be fee shifting if the opposing party fails to improve its position by rejecting the offer. Offer-of-judgment rules in effect give a party the opportunity to make the other side think more seriously about settling a case, by imposing the risk of fee shifting through an offer-of-judgment rule where there is no other fee-shifting provision.

Practitioners know that the bark of offer-of-judgment rules is greater than their bite. Although parties exchange frequent settlement offers, parties seldom invoke offer-of-judgment rules. It may be that neither side is particularly interested in raising already-high stakes for settlement. If one side invokes an offer-of-judgment rule, then the other side is likely to do the same, whether or not the offers are reasonable. There may also remain a measure of discretion in the trial court's application of an offer-of-judgment rule. In Delta Air Lines, Inc. v. August, 450 U.S. 346 (1981), the Supreme Court held that the federal trial court retains the discretion granted it under Rule 54(d) to award or not to award costs, even in the face of Rule 68 offer of judgment. The defendant in *Delta Air Lines, Inc. v. August* had made a sham $450 offer of judgment in a significant civil-rights case. Although the defendant ultimately prevailed and would, under a strict application of Rule 68's sanction, have been entitled to costs, the Supreme Court held otherwise. Offers need not be reasonable, but the federal district courts retain Rule 54(d)'s discretion. The dearth of formal offers of judgment may also have to do with the fact that so few cases result in judgments to which to compare a formal offer of judgment. Offer-of-judgment rules fall into disuse because offers of judgment are of no consequence when the parties subsequently settle. They require that the case proceed to judgment. Confirm your understanding of offers of judgment by reading Rule 68.

FED. R. CIV. P. 68. Offer of Judgment

(a) MAKING AN OFFER; JUDGMENT ON AN ACCEPTED OFFER. At least 14 days before the date set for trial, a party defending against a claim may serve on an opposing party an offer to allow judgment on specified terms, with the costs then accrued. If, within 14 days after being served, the opposing party serves written notice accepting the offer, either party may then file the offer and notice of acceptance, plus proof of service. The clerk must then enter judgment.

(b) UNACCEPTED OFFER. An unaccepted offer is considered withdrawn, but it does not preclude later offer. Evidence of an unaccepted offer is not admissible except in a proceeding to determine costs.

(c) OFFER AFTER LIABILITY IS DETERMINED. When one party's liability to another has been determined but the extent of liability remains to be determined by further proceedings, the party held liable may make an offer of judgment. It must be served within a reasonable time—but at least 14 days—before the date set for a hearing to determine the extent of liability.

(d) PAYING COSTS AFTER AN UNACCEPTED OFFER. If the judgment that the offeree finally obtains is not more favorable than the unaccepted offer, the offeree must pay the costs incurred after the offer was made.

INQUIRY

Fees. Rule 68(d) provides that the "offeree must pay the costs incurred after the offer was made" as a sanction if the judgment is not more favorable than the offer. What are the costs? As Chapter XIV on judgments addresses, FED. R. CIV. P. 54(d)(1) allows costs to the prevailing party. Rule 54(d)(1) states expressly that costs do not include attorney's fees. The costs allowable under Rule 54 are ordinarily modest expenses like court filing fees, not substantial attorney's fees. However, the Supreme Court recognized in Marek v. Chesney, 473 U.S. 1 (1985), that some statutes such as 42 U.S.C. §1988(b) define costs expressly to include attorney's fees. Thus, when the plaintiff's claim is one for which a statute would shift fees, the costs allowable as a sanction under Rule 68 include attorney's fees. Do you now see a way around the problem presented by the decision in *Buckhannon, supra,* that after a plaintiff files a case for injunctive relief, the defendant might simply adopt its demanded relief, thereby defeating a statutory right of a prevailing plaintiff to shift attorney's fees? Rule 68(a) on offers of judgment states expressly that the offer may include "the costs then accrued." A judgment of dismissal because the defendant changed its conduct to meet the plaintiff's demands could conceivably include an award of reasonable attorney's fees to the plaintiff, if the plaintiff made an offer or judgment before the defendant's change in conduct.

C. Mediation

Mediation is a non-binding alternative-dispute-resolution process in which a trained professional meets with the parties in an effort to gain agreement resolving all or portions of the dispute. Parties retain control of the outcome in mediation, even though courts may order parties in certain cases to participate in and pay for mediation, depending on their statutory, court-rule, or inherent authority. The case below explores that authority and the terms under which trial courts may exercise it. While these legal issues are interesting, mediation is so common in civil litigation that to the practitioner its practical aspects are more significant than the legal issues it occasionally raises. From the practitioners' standpoint, mediation begins with choosing or influencing the choice of the mediator. Mediators ordinarily conduct mediations alone. There are co-mediators only in rare cases, meaning that there is usually no opportunity for the parties to each choose their own. Counsel will often exchange names of proposed mediators and confer until they agree on a mediator whom the parties will respect and trust. Because mediators do not decide issues and bind parties to their decisions, the choice depends more on identifying a mediator with the experience, skill, and standing to work well with the parties and their counsel. The mediator then sets the date for the mediation, which often takes place in the mediator's law office or another neutral, private location.

The lawyers then prepare relatively short written statements of the case for the mediator to review before the mediation. Mediators will sometimes offer confidentiality of submissions to obtain greater candor. The mediation will then ordinarily last a half or full day. Parties or party representatives, their counsel, and insurance representatives will attend with full authority to settle. The mediator will establish the ground rules in a brief gathering at the beginning of the day and then separate the opposing sides for private caucuses. The ground rules will include that the mediator will meet privately with each side, going back and forth between rooms while holding confidential any communication not authorized for disclosure to the other side. In those private caucuses, the mediator alternately listens to and commisserates with the parties while helping the parties evaluate the case's strengths and weaknesses drawing on the mediator's independence and experience. The lawyers for the parties participate in the private caucuses by endorsing, contradicting, and otherwise interpreting the mediator's views to meet the client's needs for loyalty, support, and understanding.

In this manner, the mediator can gain a fuller picture of each side's circumstances and interests, in order to generate settlement discussions and options. Theories of mediation abound, but the interest-based theory just alluded to is a popular model. If the parties reach agreement that day, the mediator will ordinarily write it then for the parties to sign in preliminary form, with more complete documentation to follow. Consider the following case on the authority of a court to order parties to participate in this process.

In re Atlantic Pipe Corp.,

United States Court of Appeals for the First Circuit
304 F.3d 135 (2002)

SELYA, Circuit Judge.

This mandamus proceeding[fn] requires us to resolve an issue of importance to judges and practitioners alike: Does a district court possess the authority to compel an unwilling party to participate in, and share the costs of, non-binding mediation conducted by a private mediator? We hold that a court may order mandatory mediation pursuant to an explicit statutory provision or local rule. We further hold that where, as here, no such authorizing medium exists, a court nonetheless may order mandatory mediation through the use of its inherent powers as long as the case is an appropriate one and the order contains adequate safeguards. Because the mediation order here at issue lacks such safeguards (although it does not fall far short), we vacate it and remand the matter for further proceedings. ...

I. BACKGROUND

In January 1996, Thames-Dick Superaqueduct Partners (Thames-Dick) entered into a master agreement with the Puerto Rico Aqueduct and Sewer Authority (PRASA) to construct, operate, and maintain the North Coast Superaqueduct Project (the Project). Thames-Dick granted subcontracts for various portions of the work, including a subcontract for construction management to Dick Corp. of Puerto Rico (Dick-PR), a subcontract for the operation and maintenance of the Project to Thames Water International, Ltd. (Thames Water), and a subcontract for the fabrication of pipe to Atlantic Pipe Corp. (APC). After the Project had been built, a segment of the pipeline burst. Thames-Dick incurred significant costs in repairing the damage. Not surprisingly, it sought to recover those costs from other parties. In response, one of PRASA's insurers filed a declaratory judgment action in a local court to determine whether Thames-Dick's claims were covered under its policy. The litigation ballooned, soon involving a number of parties and a myriad of issues above and beyond insurance coverage.

On April 25, 2001, the hostilities spilled over into federal court. …

… Thames-Dick asked that the case be referred to mediation and suggested Professor Eric Green as a suitable mediator. The district court granted the motion over APC's objection and ordered non-binding mediation to proceed before Professor Green. The court pronounced mediation likely to conserve judicial resources; directed all parties to undertake mediation in good faith; stayed discovery pending completion of the mediation; and declared that participation in the mediation would not prejudice the parties' positions vis-à-vis the pending motion or the litigation as a whole. The court also stated that if mediation failed to produce a global settlement, the case would proceed to trial. …

III. THE MERITS

There are four potential sources of judicial authority for ordering mandatory non-binding mediation of pending cases, namely, (a) the court's local rules, (b) an applicable statute, (c) the Federal Rules of Civil Procedure, and (d) the court's inherent powers. Because the district court did not identify the basis of its assumed authority, we consider each of these sources.

A. *The Local Rules.*

A district court's local rules may provide an appropriate source of authority for ordering parties to participate in mediation. [C] In Puerto Rico, however, the local rules contain only a single reference to any form of alternative dispute resolution (ADR)… [stating,] "Pursuant to 28 U.S.C. §473(b)(4), this Court shall adopt a method of Alternative Dispute Resolution ("ADR") through mediation by a judicial officer. Such a program would allow litigants to obtain from an impartial third party—the judicial officer as mediator—a flexible non-binding, dispute resolution process to facilitate negotiations among the parties to help them reach settlement." …

The respondents concede that the mediation order in this case falls outside the boundaries of the mediation program envisioned by Rule V. It does so most noticeably because it involves mediation before a private mediator, not a judicial officer. … [W]e conclude that the District of Puerto Rico has no local rule in force that dictates the permissible characteristics of mediation orders. …

B. *The ADR Act.*

There is only one potential source of statutory authority for ordering mandatory non-binding mediation here: the Alternative Dispute Resolution Act of 1998 (ADR Act), 28 U.S.C. §§651-658. Congress passed the ADR Act to promote the utilization of alternative dispute resolution methods in the federal courts and to set appropriate guidelines for their use. The Act lists mediation as an appropriate ADR process. [C] Moreover, it sanctions the participation of "professional neutrals from the private sector" as mediators. [C] Finally, the Act requires district courts to obtain litigants' consent only when they order arbitration, [c], not when they order the use of other ADR mechanisms (such as non-binding mediation).

Despite the broad sweep of these provisions, the Act is quite clear that some form of the ADR procedures it endorses must be adopted in each judicial district by local rule. [C] In the absence of such local rules, the ADR Act itself does not authorize any specific court to use a particular ADR mechanism.

Because the District of Puerto Rico has not yet complied with the Act's mandate, the mediation order here at issue cannot be justified under the ADR Act. ...

C. *The Civil Rules.*

The respondents next argue that the district court possessed the authority to require mediation by virtue of the Federal Rules of Civil Procedure. They concentrate their attention on Fed.R.Civ.P. 16, which states in pertinent part that "the court may take appropriate action[ ] with respect to ... (9) settlement and the use of special procedures to assist in resolving the dispute when authorized by statute or local rule...." Fed. R. Civ. P. 16(c)(9). But the words "when authorized by statute or local rule" are a frank limitation on the district courts' authority to order mediation thereunder,[fn] and we must adhere to that circumscription. *See* Schlagenhauf v. Holder, 379 U.S. 104, 121[] (1964) (explaining that the Civil Rules "should not be expanded by disregarding plainly expressed limitations"). Because there is no statute or local rule authorizing mandatory private mediation in the District of Puerto Rico, [c], Rule 16(c)(9) does not assist the respondents' cause.[fn]

D. *Inherent Powers.*

Even apart from positive law, district courts have substantial inherent power to manage and control their calendars. [Cc] This inherent power takes many forms. *See* Fed. R. Civ. P. 83(b) (providing that judges may regulate practice in any manner consistent with federal law and applicable rules). By way of illustration, a district court may use its inherent power to compel represented clients to attend pretrial settlement conferences, even though such a practice is not specifically authorized in the Civil Rules. *See* Heileman Brewing Co. v. Joseph Oat Corp., 871 F.2d 648, 650 (7th Cir.1989) (en banc).

Of course, a district court's inherent powers are not infinite. There are at least four limiting principles. First, inherent powers must be used in a way reasonably suited to the enhancement of the court's processes, including the orderly and expeditious disposition of pending cases. [C] Second, inherent powers cannot be exercised in a manner that contradicts an applicable statute or rule. Chambers[v. NASCO, Inc., 501 U.S. 32, 47 (1991).] Third, the use of inherent powers must comport with procedural fairness. Id. at 50[]. And, finally, inherent powers "must be exercised with restraint and discretion." Id. at 44[].

At one time, the inherent power of judges to compel unwilling parties to participate in ADR procedures was a hot-button issue for legal scholars. [Cc] Although many federal district courts have forestalled further debate by adopting local rules that authorize specific ADR procedures and outlaw others, [cc], the District of Puerto Rico is not among them. Thus, we have no choice but to address the question head-on.

We begin our inquiry by examining the case law. [The court reviewed federal circuit court authority holding that the federal district courts do not have inherent authority to compel parties to participate in alternative dispute resolution.] ...

... When mediation is forced upon unwilling litigants, it stands to reason that the likelihood of settlement is diminished. Requiring parties to invest substantial amounts of time and money in mediation under such circumstances may well be inefficient. [C]

The fact remains, however, that none of these considerations establishes that mandatory mediation is always inappropriate. There may well be specific cases in which such a protocol is likely to conserve judicial resources without significantly burdening the objectors' rights to a full, fair, and speedy trial. Much depends on the idiosyncracies of the particular case and the details of the mediation order.

In some cases, a court may be warranted in believing that compulsory mediation could yield significant benefits even if one or more parties object. After all, a party may resist mediation simply out of unfamiliarity with the process or out of fear that a willingness to submit would be perceived as a lack of confidence in her legal position. [C] In such an instance, the party's initial reservations are likely to evaporate as the mediation progresses, and negotiations could well produce a beneficial outcome, at reduced cost and greater speed, than would a trial. While the possibility that parties will fail to reach agreement remains ever present, the boon of settlement can be worth the risk.

This is particularly true in complex cases involving multiple claims and parties. The fair and expeditious resolution of such cases often is helped along by creative solutions-solutions that simply are not available in the binary framework of traditional adversarial litigation. Mediation with the assistance of a skilled facilitator gives parties an opportunity to explore a much wider range of options, including those that go beyond conventional zero-sum resolutions. Mindful of these potential advantages, we hold that it is within a district court's inherent power to order non-consensual mediation in those cases in which that step seems reasonably likely to serve the interests of justice. [C]

E. *The Mediation Order.*

Our determination that the district courts have inherent power to refer cases to non-binding mediation is made with a recognition that any such order must be crafted in a manner that preserves procedural fairness and shields objecting parties from undue burdens. We thus turn to the specifics of the mediation order entered in this case. ...

As an initial matter, we agree with the lower court that the complexity of this case militates in favor of ordering mediation. ...

In an effort to parry this thrust, APC raises a series of objections. Its threshold claim is that the district court erred in ordering mediation before resolving a pending motion to dismiss for lack of subject-matter jurisdiction (or, alternatively, to abstain). [C]

Given what has transpired, this argument is fruitless. While this proceeding was pending, the district court denied the motion in question and confirmed the existence of its subject-matter jurisdiction. [C]

Next, APC posits that the appointment of a private mediator proposed by one of the parties is per se improper (and, thus, invalidates the order). We do not agree. The district court has inherent power to "appoint persons unconnected with the court to aid judges in the performance of specific judicial duties." Ex parte Peterson, 253 U.S. 300, 312[] (1920). In the context of non-binding mediation, the mediator does not decide the merits of the case and has no authority to coerce settlement. Thus, in the absence of a contrary statute or rule, it is perfectly acceptable for the district court to appoint a qualified and neutral private party as a mediator. ...

We hasten to add that the litigants are free to challenge the qualifications or neutrality of any suggested mediator (whether or not nominated by a party to the case). ...

APC also grouses that it should not be forced to share the costs of an unwanted mediation. We have held, however, that courts have the power under Fed. R. Civ. P. 26(f) to issue pretrial cost-sharing orders in complex litigation. [C] Given the difficulties facing trial courts in cases involving multiple parties and multiple claims, we are hesitant to limit that power to the traditional discovery context. [C] This is especially true in complicated cases, where the potential value of mediation lies not only in promoting settlement but also in clarifying the issues remaining for trial.

The short of the matter is that, without default cost-sharing rules, the use of valuable ADR techniques (like mediation) becomes hostage to the parties' ability to agree on the concomitant financial arrangements. This means that the district court's inherent power to order private mediation in appropriate cases would be rendered nugatory absent the corollary power to order the sharing of reasonable mediation costs. To avoid this pitfall, we hold that the district court, in an appropriate case, is empowered to order the sharing of reasonable costs and expenses associated with mandatory non-binding mediation.

The remainder of APC's arguments are not so easily dispatched. Even when generically appropriate, a mediation order must contain procedural and substantive safeguards to ensure fairness to all parties involved. The mediation order in this case does not quite meet that test. In particular, the order does not set limits on the duration of the mediation or the expense associated therewith.[fn]

We need not wax longiloquent. As entered, the order simply requires the parties to mediate; it does not set forth either a timetable for the mediation or a cap on the fees that the mediator may charge. The figures that have been bandied about in the briefs—$900 per hour or $9,000 per mediation day—are quite large and should not be left to the mediator's whim. Relatedly, because the mediator is to be paid an hourly rate, the court should have set an outside limit on the number of hours to be devoted to mediation. Equally as important, it is trite but often true that justice delayed is justice denied. An unsuccessful mediation will postpone the ultimate resolution of the case—indeed, the district court has stayed all discovery pending the completion of the mediation—and, thus, prolong the litigation. For these reasons, the district court should have set a definite time frame for the mediation. ...

A court intent on ordering non-consensual mediation should take other precautions as well. For example, the court should make it clear (as did the able district court in this case) that participation in mediation will not be taken as a waiver of any litigation position. The important point is that the protections we have mentioned are not intended to comprise an exhaustive list, but, rather, to illustrate that when a district court orders a party to participate in mediation, it should take care to assuage legitimate concerns about the possible negative consequences of such an order.

To recapitulate, we rule that a mandatory mediation order issued under the district court's inherent power is valid in an appropriate case. We also rule that this is an appropriate case. We hold, however, that the district court's failure to set reasonable limits on the duration of the mediation and on the mediator's fees dooms the decree. ...

Practice

"I congratulate the parties and their counsel on a successful mediation and appreciate the patience you have all shown," the mediator intoned in a brief final gathering after an arduous day of private caucuses. "As I indicated earlier today, I have a dinner engagement and so am leaving it counsel to draft the settlement agreement and obtain their clients' signatures. Please stay in touch, and enjoy your weekend."

Defense counsel had a strong sense of foreboding, knowing that the mediator, though highly skilled and experienced, was breaking mediation's prime rule that you get the signatures when you reach agreement. Defense counsel tried but failed to parry politely the mediator's reluctance to draft a skeleton agreement and get signatures. During the protracted litigation's course, defense counsel had pegged plaintiffs' counsel as naïve of his client entrepreneurs' dishonesty.

Sure enough, the following Monday plaintiffs refused to sign any agreement documenting the fair results of what had been an expensive mediation. When learning of it, the chagrined mediator heavily discounted his invoice. Plaintiffs later induced plaintiffs' counsel, who had still not learned his lesson, to accept a case-evaluation award but then terminated, sued, and grieved plaintiffs' counsel for having done so. Live and learn. Trust the process, but get a signed agreement.

INQUIRY

Results. Practitioners hold differing views of the benefits of mediation. Some practitioners regard mediation as an expensive and distracting waste of time. Experienced lawyers tend to be skilled negotiators. It makes little sense to some practitioners to hire mediators at hundreds of dollars an hour to do that which lawyers do on their own in every case. Parties abuse mediation, using it to gain information about the other side's case theories while increasing the cost and delay of litigation. Other lawyers appreciate that mediation can give the parties a less adversarial forum in which to tell their stories while looking for meaningful and balanced resolution. Mediations often begin with apologies or expressions of concern or regret that would not happen at trial. They often end with novel or creative settlement terms that add value. Although many lawyers take mediation training and obtain certification as a mediator, those who develop full-time or significant mediation practices often have education, training, skills, and experience in mediation that a civil litigator does not share. Successful mediators tend to have masterful skill in reading situations and people. Studies of the cost, efficiency, and effect of mediation support both sides who favor and disfavor mediation.

D. Neutral Evaluation

The Alternative Dispute Resolution Act, 28 U.S.C. §651(a), refers specifically to "early neutral evaluation" without defining it. Early neutral evaluation is like mediation in that it relies on the skill of one or more independent professionals to help the parties along toward settlement. Early neutral evaluation differs from mediation in that the evaluator or evaluators do express a specific opinion about the case's settlement value. Mediators reserve judgments, intimating risks but allowing the parties to form and follow their own opinions. By contrast, evaluators state a specific case value. The parties then have the opportunity to accept or reject the evaluator's figure after reevaluating their own views of settlement based on it. Sometimes parties just need to hear someone else's settlement figure, especially when the evaluator has credibility and relevant experience. Evaluators set case values with the purpose of helping the parties decide whether to settle for that figure or one approaching it. Thus, an evaluator's figure tends to reflect the parties' views at least in part. An evaluator would not ordinarily set a case value higher than the plaintiff's demand or lower than the defendant's last offer. Doing so would not bring the parties any closer. It would drive them apart. Evaluators tend to pick a figure between the lowest demand and highest offer, not necessarily splitting the difference but instead incorporating the evaluator's sense of where the parties may really stand relative to their last figure and the evaluator's own judgment of actual case value.

Beyond these basics, there is a variety of formal and informal neutral evaluation schemes. Some states have adopted elaborate evaluation schemes, by statute requiring all civil litigants having certain kinds of cases (typically torts cases) to participate. Some of those schemes like the one below adopt a carrot-and-stick approach. The carrot is the evaluator's figure. If the parties accept it, then the case resolves. If one or more parties do not accept it, then rejecting parties face the prospect of sanctions if they fail to improve their position by proceeding. Sanctions typically include the costs and reasonable attorney's fees that the other side incurs due to the rejection. As you read the following scheme, consider the steps that you would need to take as a practitioner having a case evaluated by a neutral panel. The following scheme depends on practitioners serving as neutral evaluators. Evaluators will hear from 10 to 20 cases in a single day, serving a few times each year in rotation. The practitioners who serve as evaluators have their own cases evaluated by other panel members. Serving as an evaluator exposes one to a rich store of information on local lawyers, law practices, and judges, legal theories, expert witnesses, and local treating physicians. It also ensures that a practitioner is accountable to the local professional community and that the community is accountable to the practitioner. These subsidiary benefits may be as great as the direct benefits in settlement.

MICHIGAN COURT RULE 2.403. CASE EVALUATION

(A) Scope and Applicability of Rule.

(1) A court may submit to case evaluation any civil action in which the relief sought is primarily money damages or division of property.

(2) Case evaluation of tort cases filed in circuit court is mandatory ...; however, the court may except an action from case evaluation on motion for good cause shown if it finds that case evaluation of that action would be inappropriate.

(3) Cases filed in district court may be submitted to case evaluation under this rule.

...

(B) Selection of Cases.

(1) The judge to whom an action is assigned or the chief judge may select it for case evaluation by written order no earlier than 91 days after the filing of the answer

(a) on written stipulation by the parties,

(b) on written motion by a party, or

(c) on the judge's own initiative.

(2) Selection of an action for case evaluation has no effect on the normal progress of the action toward trial. ...

(D) Case Evaluation Panel.

(1) Case evaluation panels shall be composed of 3 persons.

(2) The procedure for selecting case evaluation panels is as provided in MCR 2.404.

(3) A judge may be selected as a member of a case evaluation panel, but may not preside at the trial of any action in which he or she served as a case evaluator.

(4) A case evaluator may not be called as a witness at trial.

(E) Disqualification of Case Evaluators. The rule for disqualification of a case evaluator is the same as that provided in MCR 2.003 for the disqualification of a judge. ...

(G) Scheduling Case Evaluation Hearing.

(1) The ADR clerk shall set a time and place for the hearing and send notice to the case evaluators and the attorneys at least 42 days before the date set. ...

(H) Fees.

(1) Within 14 days after the mailing of the notice of the case evaluation hearing, unless otherwise ordered by the court, each party must send to the ADR clerk a check for $75 made payable in the manner specified in the notice of the case evaluation hearing. ... The ADR clerk shall arrange payment to the case evaluators. Except by stipulation and court order, the parties may not make any other payment of fees or expenses to the case evaluators than that provided in this subrule. ...

(I) Submission of Documents.

(1) At least 14 days before the hearing, each party shall file with the ADR clerk 3 copies of documents pertaining to the issues to be mediated and 3 copies of a concise summary setting forth that party's factual and legal position on issues presented by the action, and shall serve one copy of the documents and summary on each attorney of record. ...

(J) Conduct of Hearing.

(1) A party has the right, but is not required, to attend a case evaluation hearing. If scars, disfigurement, or other unusual conditions exist, they may be demonstrated to the panel by a personal appearance; however, no testimony will be taken or permitted of any party.

(2) The rules of evidence do not apply before the case evaluation panel. Factual information having a bearing on damages or liability must be supported by documentary evidence, if possible.

(3) Oral presentation shall be limited to 15 minutes per side unless multiple parties or unusual circumstances warrant additional time. Information on applicable insurance policy limits and settlement negotiations shall be disclosed at the request of the case evaluation panel. ...

(K) Decision.

(1) Within 14 days after the hearing, the panel will make an evaluation and notify the attorney for each party of its evaluation in writing. If an award is not unanimous, the evaluation must so indicate. ...

(L) Acceptance or Rejection of Evaluation.

(1) Each party shall file a written acceptance or rejection of the panel's evaluation with the ADR clerk within 28 days after service of the panel's evaluation. Even if there are separate awards on multiple claims, the party must either accept or reject the evaluation in its entirety as to a particular opposing party. The failure to file a written acceptance or rejection within 28 days constitutes rejection.

(2) There may be no disclosure of a party's acceptance or rejection of the panel's evaluation until the expiration of the 28-day period, at which time the ADR clerk

shall send a notice indicating each party's acceptance or rejection of the panel's evaluation. ...

(M) Effect of Acceptance of Evaluation.

(1) If all the parties accept the panel's evaluation, judgment will be entered in accordance with the evaluation, unless the amount of the award is paid within 28 days after notification of the acceptances, in which case the court shall dismiss the action with prejudice. The judgment or dismissal shall be deemed to dispose of all claims in the action and includes all fees, costs, and interest to the date it is entered. ...

(N) Proceedings After Rejection.

(1) If all or part of the evaluation of the case evaluation panel is rejected, the action proceeds to trial in the normal fashion. ...

(O) Rejecting Party's Liability for Costs.

(1) If a party has rejected an evaluation and the action proceeds to verdict, that party must pay the opposing party's actual costs unless the verdict is more favorable to the rejecting party than the case evaluation. However, if the opposing party has also rejected the evaluation, a party is entitled to costs only if the verdict is more favorable to that party than the case evaluation. ...

(6) For the purpose of this rule, actual costs are

(a) those costs taxable in any civil action, and

(b) a reasonable attorney fee based on a reasonable hourly or daily rate as determined by the trial judge for services necessitated by the rejection of the case evaluation. ...

(7) Costs shall not be awarded if the case evaluation award was not unanimous. ...

Practice

"What's wrong with him?" one of the three case evaluators asked the other two, as the plaintiff's lawyer stormed out of the hearing room, uttering an expletive over the award. The evaluators, who were longtime acquaintances drawn from the local bar, had heard the lawyer's exaggerated arguments and exorbitant demand, a style they equated with the distant large metropolitan area from which the lawyer haled. Yet juries in this rural locale were notoriously conservative, and the defense counsel and insurer knew it. The evaluators had to pick a figure that might help the parties to compromise. Approaching the out-of-town lawyer's exorbitant demand would have done no one any good.

"Don't worry about him," one of the evaluators rejoined, "He'll get over it. He knows the market better than we do. I've seen him before. It's all an act, anyway. You watch—his client will accept that award." The three evaluators smiled at one another with a new appreciation for the lawyer's theatrics and their own wisdom in ignoring it.

INQUIRY

Factfinding. The neutral evaluation scheme shown above produces information—a dollar figure—that can help the parties determine whether to settle. If experienced evaluators say that the case is worth only $5,000 or is worth $500,000, then perhaps the parties ought to listen when they had other thoughts about case value. What might be the merits of producing other information to help parties toward settlement? In some cases, particularly those involving a discrete field or industry where there are conventional practices not well understood by the public, parties employ a factfinder or ombudsperson to investigate, hear, and reach conclusions on matters subsidiary to the outcome. Ombudspersons are more common in government, academia, and the media. The institution against which the claimant complains employs the ombudsperson who then uses intimate knowledge of the institution while taking the perspective of the claimant. A factfinder or ombudsperson may decide matters involving who did or said what when to whom, what norms, rules, or regulations those actions violated, and what the parties might do about it. Factfinders and ombudspersons have no authority to decide, but their findings can influence the parties' willingness to settle.

E. Arbitration

Arbitration is a more elaborate form of alternative dispute resolution than mediation or early neutral evaluation. In arbitration, the parties retain a private professional to hear and decide the dispute following modified trial-like procedures. Some arbitrations involve a panel of three arbitrators, each side choosing one and the two choosing a third, although doing so significantly increases the cost. Parties pay arbitrators at substantial hourly or daily rates reflecting the arbitrators' reputation and experience. Why, then, arbitrate? Although each side ordinarily presents testimony under oath and offers exhibits, arbitrations may relax or suspend evidentiary rules, and the parties may even agree to permit testimony by affidavit. Parties may be able to schedule the arbitration sooner than obtain a court trial date and may complete the arbitration more efficiently. They may also be able to agree on an arbitrator who has and will apply special expertise in the field, reaching a more predictable decision. Arbitrators are more able and likely to reach compromise decisions, reducing the risks to both sides. Arbitration is also private, whereas court trials and records are public. Like judicial adjudication, arbitration is typically (though not always) binding on the parties. Indeed, state and federal laws governing enforcement of arbitration decisions limit court review to determining whether the arbitrator showed evident bias or exceeded an arbitrator's powers.

The Federal Arbitration Act, 9 U.S.C. §§1 et seq., is easily the most significant piece of arbitration legislation. The Supreme Court stated in Gilmer v. Interstate/Johnson Lane Corp., 500 U.S. 20, 24 (1991), that the Act "was to reverse the longstanding judicial hostility to arbitration agreements that had existed at English common law and had been adopted by American courts, and to place arbitration agreements upon the same footing as other contracts." *Gilmer* was one of a long line of Supreme Court cases (the first three of which the introduction to this chapter cites) expanding the reach of arbitration and authority of its decisions. *Gilmer* required employees alleging age discrimination to arbitrate those claims based on arbitration clauses in predispute employment agreements. Then, in Allied-Bruce Terminix Cos. v. Dobson, 513 U.S. 265 (1995), the Supreme Court held valid under the Federal Arbitration Act an arbitration clause in a predispute agreement even where state law would have invalidated it. Then, in Green Tree Financial Corp. v. Randolph, 531 U.S. 79, 82 (2000), the Court held valid an arbitration agreement that did not "affirmatively protect a party from potentially steep arbitration costs." In Green Tree Financial Corp. v. Bazzle, 539 U.S. 444 (2003), the Court held that an arbitrator may decide whether a contract forbids class arbitration. In Buckeye Check Cashing, Inc. v. Cardegna, 546 U.S. 440 (2006), the Court held that an arbitrator may decide a contract's legality. The Federal Arbitration Act plainly has broad reach and authority. *Cf.* Hall Street Assocs., L.L.C. v. Mattel, Inc., 552 U.S. 576 (2008) (parties may not alter by contract the Federal Arbitration Act's grounds to vacate or modify decision).

The Federal Arbitration Act first declares valid and enforceable agreements to arbitrate. *See* 9 U.S.C. §2. Parties may agree to arbitrate before a claim first arises, after the claim arises, and even after litigation commences. The Federal Arbitration Act holds that such agreements are enforceable to the same extent as other contracts. In First Options of Chicago, Inc. v. Kaplan, 514 U.S. 938, 944 (1995), the Supreme Court held that under the Act, federal courts should determine the enforceability of arbitration clauses by applying "ordinary state-law principles that govern the formation of contracts." Specifically, "applicable defenses, such as unconscionability, may be applied to invalidate arbitration agreements without contravening the [Federal Arbitration Act]." Doctor's Assocs., Inc. v. Casarotto, 517 U.S. 681, 687 (1996). The Act then authorizes the federal courts to enforce agreements to arbitrate and to stay judicial proceedings. *See* 9 U.S.C. §§3, 4. The Act states some basic procedures for selecting arbitrators and authorizes arbitrators to compel attendance of witnesses. *See* 9 U.S.C. §§5, 7. More significantly, the Act provides for entering arbitration awards as court judgments and for courts to vacate or modify them. *See* 9 U.S.C. §§9, 10, 11. As you review the Act's following selected provisions, appreciate what the Act accomplishes, creating a body of federal substantive law making it a duty comply with arbitration agreements.

9 U.S.C. §2. Validity, irrevocability, and enforcement of agreements to arbitrate

A written provision in any maritime transaction or a contract evidencing a transaction involving commerce to settle by arbitration a controversy thereafter arising out of such contract or transaction, or the refusal to perform the whole or any part thereof, or an agreement in writing to submit to arbitration an existing controversy arising out of such a contract, transaction, or refusal, shall be valid, irrevocable, and enforceable, save upon such grounds as exist at law or in equity for the revocation of any contract.

9 U.S.C. §3. Stay of proceedings where issue therein referable to arbitration

If any suit or proceeding be brought in any of the courts of the United States upon any issue referable to arbitration under an agreement in writing for such arbitration, the court in which such suit is pending, upon being satisfied that the issue involved in such suit or proceeding is referable to arbitration under such an agreement, shall on application of one of the parties stay the trial of the action until such arbitration has been had in accordance with the terms of the agreement, providing the applicant for the stay is not in default in proceeding with such arbitration.

9 U.S.C. §4. Failure to arbitrate under agreement; petition to United States court having jurisdiction for order to compel arbitration; ...

A party aggrieved by the alleged failure, neglect, or refusal of another to arbitrate under a written agreement for arbitration may petition any United States district court which, save for such agreement, would have jurisdiction under Title 28, in a civil action or in admiralty of the subject matter of a suit arising out of the controversy between the parties, for an order directing that such arbitration proceed in the manner provided for in such agreement. ... The court shall hear the parties, and upon being satisfied that the making of the agreement for arbitration or the failure to comply therewith is not in issue, the court shall make an order directing the parties to proceed to arbitration in accordance with the terms of the agreement. …

9 U.S.C. §5. Appointment of arbitrators or umpire
If in the agreement provision be made for a method of naming or appointing an arbitrator or arbitrators or an umpire, such method shall be followed; but if no method be provided therein, or if a method be provided and any party thereto shall fail to avail himself of such method, or if for any other reason there shall be a lapse in the naming of an arbitrator or arbitrators or umpire, or in filling a vacancy, then upon the application of either party to the controversy the court shall designate and appoint an arbitrator or arbitrators or umpire, as the case may require, who shall act under the said agreement with the same force and effect as if he or they had been specifically named therein; and unless otherwise provided in the agreement the arbitration shall be by a single arbitrator.

9 U.S.C. §7. Witnesses before arbitrators; fees; compelling attendance
The arbitrators selected either as prescribed in this title or otherwise, or a majority of them, may summon in writing any person to attend before them or any of them as a witness and in a proper case to bring with him or them any book, record, document, or paper which may be deemed material as evidence in the case. …

9 U.S.C. §9. Award of arbitrators; confirmation; jurisdiction; procedure
If the parties in their agreement have agreed that a judgment of the court shall be entered upon the award made pursuant to the arbitration, and shall specify the court, then at any time within one year after the award is made any party to the arbitration may apply to the court so specified for an order confirming the award, and thereupon the court must grant such an order unless the award is vacated, modified, or corrected as prescribed in sections 10 and 11 of this title. …

9 U.S.C. §10. Same; vacation; grounds; rehearing
(a) In any of the following cases the United States court in and for the district wherein the award was made may make an order vacating the award upon the application of any party to the arbitration—
(1) where the award was procured by corruption, fraud, or undue means;
(2) where there was evident partiality or corruption in the arbitrators, or either of them;
(3) where the arbitrators were guilty of misconduct in refusing to postpone the hearing, upon sufficient cause shown, or in refusing to hear evidence pertinent and material to the controversy; or of any other misbehavior by which the rights of any party have been prejudiced; or
(4) where the arbitrators exceeded their powers, or so imperfectly executed them that a mutual, final, and definite award upon the subject matter submitted was not made. …

9 U.S.C. §11. Same; modification or correction; grounds; order
In either of the following cases the United States court in and for the district wherein the award was made may make an order modifying or correcting the award upon the application of any party to the arbitration—
(a) Where there was an evident material miscalculation of figures or an evident material mistake in the description of any person, thing, or property referred to in the award.

(b) Where the arbitrators have awarded upon a matter not submitted to them, unless it is a matter not affecting the merits of the decision upon the matter submitted.
(c) Where the award is imperfect in matter of form not affecting the merits of the controversy.
The order may modify and correct the award, so as to effect the intent thereof and promote justice between the parties.

INQUIRY

Jurisdiction. While the above Federal Arbitration Act clearly establishes a body of federal substantive law, what courts have jurisdiction to enforce it? The Act does not have a jurisdictional provision. It does not make any agreement having an arbitration clause a subject for federal-question jurisdiction. Instead, its terms only allow the federal courts to order arbitration, enter judgments on arbitration awards, or modify those awards where there is some other basis for federal jurisdiction such as diversity of citizenship or a federal question arising out of the substantive dispute. It only allows a federal court to stay its own judicial proceeding, not state-court proceedings, in favor of arbitration. Because it is federal law, the Act applies in federal and state courts. State courts must follow the Act rather than contrary state law if the agreement containing the arbitration clause affects interstate commerce. Yet the federal courts have no independent jurisdiction to enforce it. The Supreme Court noted these anomalies in Moses H. Cone Memorial Hosp. v. Mercury Constr. Corp., 460 U.S. 1, 24 (1983), concluding, "Nevertheless, although enforcement of the Act is left in large part to the state courts, it nevertheless represents federal policy to be vindicated by the federal courts where appropriate."

Unconscionability. Not all arbitration agreements are enforced. The Federal Arbitration Act requires enforcement only to the extent of governing contract-law principles. *See* 9 U.S.C. §2. One of those principles is not to enforce unconscionable contracts. *See also* CAL. CIVIL CODE §1670.5(a) (the court may refuse to enforce an unconscionable contract clause). What constitutes an unconscionable arbitration clause depends on the fairness of its arbitration terms and procedures, and the extent to which it interferes with enforcement of statutory rights. Arbitration clauses appear in consumer agreements, employment agreements, business contracts, and other transactions. The more sophisticated the parties and extensive the contract negotiations, the more likely will the court enforce its arbitration clause. On the other hand, courts are less likely to enforce an arbitration clause that grants a sophisticated contract drafter important rights or advantages not enjoyed by the unsuspecting signer. For example, in Circuit City Stores, Inc. v. Adams, 279 F.3d 889, 892 (9th Cir.), cert. denied, 535 U.S. 1112 (2002), the federal appellate court held it unconscionable for imbalance of bargaining power, when a large employer required nearly all of its employees to accept a standard arbitration clause governing employment rights. For another example, in Ferguson v. Countrywide Credit Indus., Inc., 298 F.3d 778 (9th Cir. 2002), the appellate court held that the federal district court properly refused to enforce an "insidious" arbitration agreement that required the employee to arbitrate her sex-discrimination claims without discovery while allowing the employer to litigate its own potential claims with discovery. The

Federal Arbitration Act still favors enforcement of arbitration agreements. Where the rights are not so substantial as those respecting employment, one-sided arbitration clauses may still be enforceable. *See* Ferguson v. Writers Guild of America, West, 277 Cal. Rptr. 450 (Cal. Ct. App. 1991) (upholding arbitration before anonymous panel by written submission); *see also* Carter v. Countrywide Credit Indus., Inc., 362 F.3d 294 (5th Cir. 2004) (unfavorable arbitration clauses in consumer mortgage loans held enforceable).

Nonbinding Arbitration. The above provisions of the Federal Arbitration Act make it quite clear that arbitrations within its purview bind the parties. As indicated in the text above, though, arbitration is not always binding. The Alternative Dispute Resolution Act expressly mentions nonbinding arbitration as an alternative to mediation or early neutral evaluation. The Act ensures that the results will not bind a party. Under the Act, either or both sides may require trial rather than accept the arbitration results. *See* 28 U.S.C. §657(c). As is true of early neutral evaluation, some states maintain schemes in which a party who rejects a nonbinding arbitration award may have to pay the other side's costs and reasonable attorney's fees in the event that the rejecting party fails to improve its position after trial. *See, e.g.,* CAL. CIV. CODE P. §1141.21.

D'Iorio v. Majestic Lanes, Inc.,

United States Court of Appeals for the Third Circuit
370 F.3d 354 (2004)

NYGARD, Circuit Judge.

Under Alternative Dispute Resolution Act of 1998 ("the Act"), 28 U.S.C. §651 *et seq.,* District Courts must enact local rules authorizing "the use of alternative dispute resolution processes in all civil actions" in accordance with the Act's provisions. [C] The District of New Jersey complied with this command and enacted N.J. L. Civ. R. 201.1(h)(1), which reads: "Any party may demand a trial *de novo* in the District Court by filing with the Clerk a written demand, containing a short and plain statement of each ground in support thereof, and serving a copy upon all counsel of record or other parties. Such a demand must be filed within 30 days after the arbitration award... . *Withdrawal of a demand for a trial* de novo *shall reinstate the arbitrator's award*" (emphasis added).

Section 657(c) of the Act reads: "... Within 30 days after the filing of an arbitration award with a district court under subsection(a), any party may file a written demand for a trial de novo in the district court. ... *Upon a demand for a trial de novo, the action shall be restored to the docket of the court and treated for all purposes as if it had not been referred to arbitration"* [c] (emphasis added).

Majestic argues that by allowing D'Iorio to resurrect his arbitration award by withdrawing his demand for a trial *de novo,* the emphasized portion of Rule 201.1(h)(1) is inconsistent with § 657(c)'s requirement that once a demand for a trial is made, the action be treated "for all purposes as if it had not been referred to arbitration." We agree, hold that it is inconsistent, and in so holding will reverse the judgment of the District Court.

I.

John D'Iorio alleges that he slipped and fell at a bowling alley owned by Majestic Lanes and sued Majestic in the United States District Court for the

District of New Jersey. The Court referred the lawsuit to compulsory arbitration pursuant to New Jersey Local Rule 201.1.

D'Iorio prevailed in arbitration and was awarded $274,488. ... The very next day, D'Iorio filed a demand for a trial *de novo.* Following the passage of the thirty-day limitation on demands for trial de novo, D'Iorio filed a document styled as a "Notice of Withdrawal of Demand for Trial *De Novo,"* requesting that the District Court withdraw his demand for a trial *de novo* and reinstate the arbitration award. Majestic sent a letter to the District Court objecting to the reinstatement of the arbitration award. However, the District Court had already granted D'Iorio's motions, and had entered judgment in his favor in the amount of the arbitrator's award.

Then, Majestic filed its own demand for a trial *de novo* to which D'Iorio objected. Upon instructions from the District Court, Majestic also filed a formal motion to strike the reinstatement of the arbitration award and the entry of judgment. The District Court denied this motion, but granted D'Iorio's cross-motion to strike Majestic's demand for a trial *de novo,* because Majestic had not filed it "within thirty days after the filing of [the] arbitration award." It is from this order that Majestic appeals.[fn]

II.

We need not labor long on this issue. It is axiomatic that the local rules of a District Court must be consistent with Acts of Congress. Fed.R.Civ.P. 83(a)(1); [c]. The plain language of §657(c) is that once " *a* demand for a trial de novo" is made, "the action shall be restored to the docket of the court and treated for *all purposes* as if it had not been referred to arbitration." 28 U.S.C. § 657(c)(2) (emphasis added). ...

D'Iorio ... [argues] that all Majestic had to do to make this situation equitable was file its own demand for a trial *de novo* within the thirty-day period provided in both the local rules and §657(c)(1). This argument is true, but misses the point. First, Majestic is entitled to the assurances of the Act that once D'Iorio filed his demand for a trial *de novo,* the arbitration award was a nullity, and the cause would be tried. Second and equally as important, ... Rule 201.1(h)(1) is fundamentally inconsistent with the plain language of §657(c)(2). We hold, as did the Court of Appeals for the Eleventh Circuit, that "[the language of Section 657(c)(2)] implies that all parties to the arbitration are treated as if the arbitration never occurred; thus, once [one party] filed a demand for a trial *de novo,* [the remaining party] was relieved of the obligation to file such a demand." CNA Fin. Corp. v. Brown, 162 F.3d 1334, 1337 n. 3 (11th Cir.1998).

In summary, we hold that the District Court erred by denying Majestic's motion to strike D'Iorio's request to withdraw his demand for a trial *de novo,* and by failing to vacate both the reinstatement of the arbitration award and the entry of judgment. We will reverse and remand for a trial *de novo.*

INQUIRY

Summary Trials. Nonbinding arbitration is not the only way to generate helpful information about a case's strengths and weaknesses, and its likely outcome. In complex cases that will take significant time and resources to fully litigate, the parties may elect to employ a neutral advisor, often a retired judge or lawyer with an influential reputation, to hear a portion of the case (a particular liability theory or damages issue, for instance) or to hear the whole case in summary fashion. To shorten trial procedures, the parties may submit opening and closing statements in writing, accept exhibits as admitted, and permit witnesses to testify in the narrative. The advisor can then reach conclusions about the case to guide the parties in further settlement discussions and can make recommendations for how to resolve all or portions of it. Summary jury trial is a similar procedure in which the parties try a portion or all of the case in summary fashion before a privately empaneled jury. The parties then use the jury's nonbinding decision as an indicator of the likely outcome, to help the parties consider resolution. There is, in sum, no end of creativity in the way that practitioners can help parties evaluate case merits in alternative forums outside of civil litigation, to produce surer, sooner, and more sensitive resolution.

Career

Have you met with your faculty advisor? Your faculty advisor may have significant experience in civil litigation. You can ask your faculty advisor questions about the personal and professional rewards and challenges of a civil-litigation practice. Consider meeting with your faculty advisor early to get a better sense of how civil litigation fits into your educational and career goals. Prepare a list of questions in advance. Imagine yourself a reporter who is trying to write a profile of a civil litigator including the highs and lows of trial practice.

CHAPTER X

DISCOVERY

OBJECTIVE: That you be able to identify the methods of discovering and obligation of disclosing evidence including their scope, limits, and devices, and means for resolving discovery disputes.

Case Study: You have the responsibility of formulating a discovery plan to defend a commercial tenant's claim against your client mall owner for allegedly misrepresenting occupancy commitments to induce the tenant to sign a mall lease, and for the client property owner's counterclaim for rent. What discovery devices will you use in what order on what subjects?

Federal Rules of Civil Procedure this chapter reproduces and addresses:
FED. R. CIV. P. 26. Duty to Disclose; General Provisions Governing Discovery.
FED. R. CIV. P. 27. Depositions to Perpetuate Testimony.
FED. R. CIV. P. 28. Persons Before Whom Depositions May Be Taken.
FED. R. CIV. P. 29. Stipulations About Discovery Procedure.
FED. R. CIV. P. 30. Depositions by Oral Examination.
FED. R. CIV. P. 31. Depositions by Written Questions.
FED. R. CIV. P. 32. Using Depositions in Court Proceedings.
FED. R. CIV. P. 33. Interrogatories to Parties.
FED. R. CIV. P. 34. Producing Documents ... and ... Entering ... for Inspection...
FED. R. CIV. P. 35. Physical and Mental Examinations.
FED. R. CIV. P. 36. Requests for Admission.
FED. R. CIV. P. 37. Failure to Make Disclosures or to Cooperate ...; Sanctions.
FED. R. CIV. P. 45. Subpoena.
FED. R. CIV. P. 72. Magistrate Judges: Pretrial Order.
FED. R. CIV. P. 78. Hearing Motions; Submission on Briefs.

Discovery is that stage of civil litigation following the initial pleadings during which the parties learn what relevant and admissible evidence the other side holds or controls. Civil litigators devote a great deal of time to discovery, which plays an inordinate role in contemporary civil litigation. Lawyers develop, estimate the cost and duration of, implement, and assess discovery plans. Fundamentally, the parties use discovery to evaluate their own and their opposition's case. A substantial percentage of cases settle during discovery because of the information discovery produces—positive or negative, with theories confirmed or denied, or evidence simply lacking. Reciprocal discovery gives the parties access to the same evidence, even if it does not always bring parties closer to the same view of the case. Yet discovery also has a lot to do with testing a party's resources and resolve. Parties abuse discovery for a variety of purposes including to burden, embarrass, and harass, or obtain proprietary business information for competitive or other non-litigation purposes. Even without discovery abuse, discovery's duration from three months at minimum in the simplest of cases to (more typically) six to nine months and often longer in complex cases, will alone reveal helpful information regarding a party's willingness and ability to continue the litigation. Discovery's expense does likewise, involving at a minimum hours of attorney time but often also the out-of-pocket cost of document preparation, deposition transcripts, travel, and expert witnesses. It is not unusual for a plaintiff's lawyer to advance and incur tens of thousands of dollars in case expenses during discovery. Discovery can also be a test of will and skill between counsel over the order, timing, priority, appropriateness, and terms of disclosures, and a test of the trial judge's disposition toward the case, parties, and counsel.

This chapter begins by addressing the scope of discovery. FED. R. CIV. P. 26 is the general federal rule that governs discovery. Rule 26(b) and equivalent state-court rules use relevance as a general test for the scope of discovery. Discovery requests must be likely to lead to admissible evidence relevant to the claims and defenses or, in some cases, the broader subject matter of the case. The chapter then addresses limitations on discovery. Rule 26(b) limits discovery first in that it prohibits unduly burdensome discovery. Electronically stored information creates such unique discovery burdens that the chapter addresses that topic separately in this section. Rule 26(b) also limits discovery in that it allows discovery only of "nonprivileged" matters. This chapter addresses discovery issues raised by the attorney-client privilege and attorney work product. Rule 26(c) backs up its limitations by offering parties the right to move for protective orders. The chapter then addresses disclosures required by Rule 26(a) without formal discovery request. The chapter then addresses the individual forms and devices for discovery including requests for production (Rule 34), interrogatories (Rule 33), depositions (Rules 28, 30, 31, and 32), requests to admit (Rule 36), and requests for examination (Rule 35). The chapter ends with a study of how parties resolve discovery disputes under Rule 37. Before you study the scope, limits, devices, and enforcement of discovery, read the general Rule 26 governing discovery, and consider issues relating to presuit investigation.

FED. R. CIV. P. Duty to Disclose; General Provisions Governing Discovery

(a) Required Disclosures.

(1) *Initial Disclosure.*

(A) *In General.* Except as exempted by Rule 26(a)(1)(B) or as otherwise stipulated or ordered by the court, a party must, without awaiting a discovery request, provide to the other parties:

(i) the name and, if known, the address and telephone number of each individual likely to have discoverable information--along with the subjects of that information--that the disclosing party may use to support its claims or defenses, unless the use would be solely for impeachment;

(ii) a copy--or a description by category and location--of all documents, electronically stored information, and tangible things that the disclosing party has in its possession, custody, or control and may use to support its claims or defenses, unless the use would be solely for impeachment;

(iii) a computation of each category of damages claimed by the disclosing party--who must also make available for inspection and copying as under Rule 34 the documents or other evidentiary material, unless privileged or protected from disclosure, on which each computation is based, including materials bearing on the nature and extent of injuries suffered; and

(iv) for inspection and copying as under Rule 34, any insurance agreement under which an insurance business may be liable to satisfy all or part of a possible judgment in the action or to indemnify or reimburse for payments made to satisfy the judgment.

(B) *Proceedings Exempt from Initial Disclosure.* The following proceedings are exempt from initial disclosure:

(i) an action for review on an administrative record;

(ii) a forfeiture action in rem arising from a federal statute;

(iii) a petition for habeas corpus or any other proceeding to challenge a criminal conviction or sentence;

(iv) an action brought without an attorney by a person in the custody of the United States, a state, or a state subdivision;

(v) an action to enforce or quash an administrative summons or subpoena;

(vi) an action by the United States to recover benefit payments;

(vii) an action by the United States to collect on a student loan guaranteed by the United States;

(viii) a proceeding ancillary to a proceeding in another court; and

(ix) an action to enforce an arbitration award.

(C) *Time for Initial Disclosures--In General.* A party must make the initial disclosures at or within 14 days after the parties' Rule 26(f) conference unless a different time is set by stipulation or court order, or unless a party objects during the conference that initial disclosures are not appropriate in this action and states the objection in the proposed discovery plan. In ruling on the objection, the court must determine what disclosures, if any, are to be made and must set the time for disclosure.

(D) *Time for Initial Disclosures--For Parties Served or Joined Later.* A party that is first served or otherwise joined after the Rule 26(f) conference must make the initial disclosures within 30 days after being served or joined, unless a different time is set by stipulation or court order.

(E) *Basis for Initial Disclosure; Unacceptable Excuses.* A party must make its initial disclosures based on the information then reasonably available to it. A party is not excused from making its disclosures because it has not fully investigated the case or because it challenges the sufficiency of another party's disclosures or because another party has not made its disclosures.

(2) ***Disclosure of Expert Testimony.***

(A) *In General.* In addition to the disclosures required by Rule 26(a)(1), a party must disclose to the other parties the identity of any witness it may use at trial to present evidence under Federal Rule of Evidence 702, 703, or 705.

(B) *Witnesses Who Must Provide a Written Report.* Unless otherwise stipulated or ordered by the court, this disclosure must be accompanied by a written report--prepared and signed by the witness--if the witness is one retained or specially employed to provide expert testimony in the case or one whose duties as the party's employee regularly involve giving expert testimony. The report must contain:

(i) a complete statement of all opinions the witness will express and the basis and reasons for them;

(ii) the facts or data considered by the witness in forming them;

(iii) any exhibits that will be used to summarize or support them;

(iv) the witness's qualifications, including a list of all publications authored in the previous 10 years;

(v) a list of all other cases in which, during the previous 4 years, the witness testified as an expert at trial or by deposition; and

(vi) a statement of the compensation to be paid for the study and testimony in the case.

(C) *Witnesses Who Do Not Provide a Written Report.* Unless otherwise stipulated or ordered by the court, if the witness is not required to provide a written report, this disclosure must state:

(i) the subject matter on which the witness is expected to present evidence under Federal Rule of Evidence 702, 703, or 705; and

(ii) a summary of the facts and opinions to which the witness is expected to testify.

(D) *Time to Disclose Expert Testimony.* A party must make these disclosures at the times and in the sequence that the court orders. Absent a stipulation or a court order, the disclosures must be made:

(i) at least 90 days before the date set for trial or for the case to be ready for trial; or

(ii) if the evidence is intended solely to contradict or rebut evidence on the same subject matter identified by another party under Rule 26(a)(2)(B) or (C), within 30 days after the other party's disclosure.

(E) *Supplementing the Disclosure.* The parties must supplement these disclosures when required under Rule 26(e).

(3) ***Pretrial Disclosures.***

(A) *In General.* In addition to the disclosures required by Rule 26(a)(1) and (2), a party must provide to the other parties and promptly file the following information about the evidence that it may present at trial other than solely for impeachment:

(i) the name and, if not previously provided, the address and telephone number of each witness--separately identifying those the party expects to present and those it may call if the need arises;

(ii) the designation of those witnesses whose testimony the party expects to present by deposition and, if not taken stenographically, a transcript of the pertinent parts of the deposition; and

(iii) an identification of each document or other exhibit, including summaries of other evidence--separately identifying those items the party expects to offer and those it may offer if the need arises.

(B) *Time for Pretrial Disclosures; Objections.* Unless the court orders otherwise, these disclosures must be made at least 30 days before trial. Within 14 days after they are made, unless the court sets a different time, a party may serve and promptly file a list of the following objections: any objections to the use under Rule 32(a) of a deposition designated by another party under Rule 26(a)(3)(A)(ii); and any objection, together with the grounds for it, that may be made to the admissibility of materials identified under Rule 26(a)(3)(A)(iii). An objection not so made--except for one under Federal Rule of Evidence 402 or 403--is waived unless excused by the court for good cause.

(4) ***Form of Disclosures.*** Unless the court orders otherwise, all disclosures under Rule 26(a) must be in writing, signed, and served.

(b) Discovery Scope and Limits.

(1) ***Scope in General.*** Unless otherwise limited by court order, the scope of discovery is as follows: Parties may obtain discovery regarding any nonprivileged matter that is relevant to any party's claim or defense--including the existence, description, nature, custody, condition, and location of any documents or other tangible things and the identity and location of persons who know of any discoverable matter. For good cause, the court may order discovery of any matter relevant to the subject matter involved in the action. Relevant information need not be admissible at the trial if the discovery appears reasonably calculated to lead to the discovery of admissible evidence. All discovery is subject to the limitations imposed by Rule 26(b)(2)(C).

(2) ***Limitations on Frequency and Extent.***

(A) *When Permitted.* By order, the court may alter the limits in these rules on the number of depositions and interrogatories or on the length of depositions under Rule 30. By order or local rule, the court may also limit the number of requests under Rule 36.

(B) *Specific Limitations on Electronically Stored Information.* A party need not provide discovery of electronically stored information from sources that the party identifies as not reasonably accessible because of undue burden or cost. On motion to compel discovery or for a protective order, the party from whom discovery is sought must show that the information is not reasonably accessible because of undue burden or cost. If that showing is made, the court may nonetheless order discovery from such sources if the requesting party shows good cause, considering the limitations of Rule 26(b)(2)(C). The court may specify conditions for the discovery.

(C) *When Required.* On motion or on its own, the court must limit the frequency or extent of discovery otherwise allowed by these rules or by local rule if it determines that:

(i) the discovery sought is unreasonably cumulative or duplicative, or can be obtained from some other source that is more convenient, less burdensome, or less expensive;

(ii) the party seeking discovery has had ample opportunity to obtain the information by discovery in the action; or

(iii) the burden or expense of the proposed discovery outweighs its likely benefit, considering the needs of the case, the amount in controversy, the parties' resources, the importance of the issues at stake in the action, and the importance of the discovery in resolving the issues.

(3) ***Trial Preparation: Materials.***

(A) *Documents and Tangible Things.* Ordinarily, a party may not discover documents and tangible things that are prepared in anticipation of litigation or for trial by or for another party or its representative (including the other party's attorney, consultant, surety, indemnitor, insurer, or agent). But, subject to Rule 26(b)(4), those materials may be discovered if:

(i) they are otherwise discoverable under Rule 26(b)(1); and

(ii) the party shows that it has substantial need for the materials to prepare its case and cannot, without undue hardship, obtain their substantial equivalent by other means.

(B) *Protection Against Disclosure.* If the court orders discovery of those materials, it must protect against disclosure of the mental impressions, conclusions, opinions, or legal theories of a party's attorney or other representative concerning the litigation.

(C) *Previous Statement.* Any party or other person may, on request and without the required showing, obtain the person's own previous statement about the action or its subject matter. If the request is refused, the person may move for a court order, and Rule 37(a)(5) applies to the award of expenses. A previous statement is either:

(i) a written statement that the person has signed or otherwise adopted or approved; or

(ii) a contemporaneous stenographic, mechanical, electrical, or other recording--or a transcription of it--that recites substantially verbatim the person's oral statement.

(4) *Trial Preparation: Experts.*

(A) *Deposition of an Expert Who May Testify.* A party may depose any person who has been identified as an expert whose opinions may be presented at trial. If Rule 26(a)(2)(B) requires a report from the expert, the deposition may be conducted only after the report is provided.

(B) *Trial-Preparation Protection for Draft Reports or Disclosures.* Rules 26(b)(3)(A) and (B) protect drafts of any report or disclosure required under Rule 26(a)(2), regardless of the form in which the draft is recorded.

(C) *Trial-Preparation Protection for Communications Between a Party's Attorney and Expert Witnesses.* Rules 26(b)(3)(A) and (B) protect communications between the party's attorney and any witness required to provide a report under Rule 26(a)(2)(B), regardless of the form of the communications, except to the extent that the communications:

(i) relate to compensation for the expert's study or testimony;

(ii) identify facts or data that the party's attorney provided and that the expert considered in forming the opinions to be expressed; or

(iii) identify assumptions that the party's attorney provided and that the expert relied on in forming the opinions to be expressed.

(D) *Expert Employed Only for Trial Preparation.* Ordinarily, a party may not, by interrogatories or deposition, discover facts known or opinions held by an expert who has been retained or specially employed by another party in anticipation of litigation or to prepare for trial and who is not expected to be called as a witness at trial. But a party may do so only:

(i) as provided in Rule 35(b); or

(ii) on showing exceptional circumstances under which it is impracticable for the party to obtain facts or opinions on the same subject by other means.

(E) *Payment.* Unless manifest injustice would result, the court must require that the party seeking discovery:

(i) pay the expert a reasonable fee for time spent in responding to discovery under Rule 26(b)(4)(A) or (D); and

(ii) for discovery under (D), also pay the other party a fair portion of the fees and expenses it reasonably incurred in obtaining the expert's facts and opinions.

(5) *Claiming Privilege or Protecting Trial-Preparation Materials.*

(A) *Information Withheld.* When a party withholds information otherwise discoverable by claiming that the information is privileged or subject to protection as trial-preparation material, the party must:

(i) expressly make the claim; and

(ii) describe the nature of the documents, communications, or tangible things not produced or disclosed--and do so in a manner that, without revealing information itself privileged or protected, will enable other parties to assess the claim.

(B) *Information Produced.* If information produced in discovery is subject to a claim of privilege or of protection as trial-preparation material, the party making the claim may notify any party that received the information of the claim and the basis for it. After being notified, a party must promptly return, sequester, or destroy the specified information and any copies it has; must not use or disclose the information until the claim is resolved; must take reasonable steps to retrieve the information if the party disclosed it before being notified; and may promptly present the information to the court under seal for a determination of the claim. The producing party must preserve the information until the claim is resolved.

(c) Protective Orders.

(1) *In General.* A party or any person from whom discovery is sought may move for a protective order in the court where the action is pending--or as an alternative on matters relating to a deposition, in the court for the district where the deposition will be taken. The motion must include a certification that the movant has in good faith conferred or attempted to confer with other affected parties in an effort to resolve the dispute without court action. The court may, for good cause, issue an order to protect a party or person from annoyance, embarrassment, oppression, or undue burden or expense, including one or more of the following:

(A) forbidding the disclosure or discovery;

(B) specifying terms, including time and place, for the disclosure or discovery;

(C) prescribing a discovery method other than the one selected by the party seeking discovery;

(D) forbidding inquiry into certain matters, or limiting the scope of disclosure or discovery to certain matters;

(E) designating the persons who may be present while the discovery is conducted;

(F) requiring that a deposition be sealed and opened only on court order;

(G) requiring that a trade secret or other confidential research, development, or commercial information not be revealed or be revealed only in a specified way; and

(H) requiring that the parties simultaneously file specified documents or information in sealed envelopes, to be opened as the court directs.

(2) *Ordering Discovery.* If a motion for a protective order is wholly or partly denied, the court may, on just terms, order that any party or person provide or permit discovery.

(3) *Awarding Expenses.* Rule 37(a)(5) applies to the award of expenses.

(d) Timing and Sequence of Discovery.

(1) *Timing.* A party may not seek discovery from any source before the parties have conferred as required by Rule 26(f), except in a proceeding exempted from initial disclosure under Rule 26(a)(1)(B), or when authorized by these rules, by stipulation, or by court order.

(2) *Sequence.* Unless, on motion, the court orders otherwise for the parties' and witnesses' convenience and in the interests of justice:

(A) methods of discovery may be used in any sequence; and

(B) discovery by one party does not require any other party to delay its discovery.

(e) Supplementing Disclosures and Responses.

(1) *In General.* A party who has made a disclosure under Rule 26(a)--or who has responded to an interrogatory, request for production, or request for admission--must supplement or correct its disclosure or response:

(A) in a timely manner if the party learns that in some material respect the disclosure or response is incomplete or incorrect, and if the additional or corrective information has not otherwise been made known to the other parties during the discovery process or in writing; or

(B) as ordered by the court.

(2) *Expert Witness.* For an expert whose report must be disclosed under Rule 26(a)(2)(B), the party's duty to supplement extends both to information included in the report and to information given during the expert's deposition. Any additions or changes to this information must be disclosed by the time the party's pretrial disclosures under Rule 26(a)(3) are due.

(f) Conference of the Parties; Planning for Discovery.

(1) *Conference Timing.* Except in a proceeding exempted from initial disclosure under Rule 26(a)(1)(B) or when the court orders otherwise, the parties must confer as soon as practicable--and in any event at least 21 days before a scheduling conference is to be held or a scheduling order is due under Rule 16(b).

(2) *Conference Content; Parties' Responsibilities.* In conferring, the parties must consider the nature and basis of their claims and defenses and the possibilities for promptly settling or resolving the case; make or arrange for the disclosures required by Rule 26(a)(1); discuss any issues about preserving discoverable information; and develop a proposed discovery plan. The attorneys of record and all unrepresented parties that have appeared in the case are jointly responsible for arranging the conference, for attempting in good faith to agree on the proposed discovery plan, and for submitting to the court within 14 days after the conference a written report outlining the plan. The court may order the parties or attorneys to attend the conference in person.

(3) *Discovery Plan.* A discovery plan must state the parties' views and proposals on:

(A) what changes should be made in the timing, form, or requirement for disclosures under Rule 26(a), including a statement of when initial disclosures were made or will be made;

(B) the subjects on which discovery may be needed, when discovery should be completed, and whether discovery should be conducted in phases or be limited to or focused on particular issues;

(C) any issues about disclosure or discovery of electronically stored information, including the form or forms in which it should be produced;

(D) any issues about claims of privilege or of protection as trial-preparation materials, including--if the parties agree on a procedure to assert these claims after production--whether to ask the court to include their agreement in an order;

(E) what changes should be made in the limitations on discovery imposed under these rules or by local rule, and what other limitations should be imposed; and

(F) any other orders that the court should issue under Rule 26(c) or under Rule 16(b) and (c).

(4) *Expedited Schedule.* If necessary to comply with its expedited schedule for Rule 16(b) conferences, a court may by local rule:

(A) require the parties' conference to occur less than 21 days before the scheduling conference is held or a scheduling order is due under Rule 16(b); and

(B) require the written report outlining the discovery plan to be filed less than 14 days after the parties' conference, or excuse the parties from submitting a written report and permit them to report orally on their discovery plan at the Rule 16(b) conference.

(g) Signing Disclosures and Discovery Requests, Responses, and Objections.

(1) *Signature Required; Effect of Signature.* Every disclosure under Rule 26(a)(1) or (a)(3) and every discovery request, response, or objection must be signed by at least one attorney of record in the attorney's own name--or by the party personally, if unrepresented--and must state the signer's address, e-mail address, and telephone number. By signing, an attorney or party certifies that to the best of the person's knowledge, information, and belief formed after a reasonable inquiry:

(A) with respect to a disclosure, it is complete and correct as of the time it is made; and

(B) with respect to a discovery request, response, or objection, it is:

(i) consistent with these rules and warranted by existing law or by a nonfrivolous argument for extending, modifying, or reversing existing law, or for establishing new law;
(ii) not interposed for any improper purpose, such as to harass, cause unnecessary delay, or needlessly increase the cost of litigation; and
(iii) neither unreasonable nor unduly burdensome or expensive, considering the needs of the case, prior discovery in the case, the amount in controversy, and the importance of the issues at stake in the action.
(2) ***Failure to Sign.*** Other parties have no duty to act on an unsigned disclosure, request, response, or objection until it is signed, and the court must strike it unless a signature is promptly supplied after the omission is called to the attorney's or party's attention.
(3) ***Sanction for Improper Certification.*** If a certification violates this rule without substantial justification, the court, on motion or on its own, must impose an appropriate sanction on the signer, the party on whose behalf the signer was acting, or both. The sanction may include an order to pay the reasonable expenses, including attorney's fees, caused by the violation.

INQUIRY

Presuit Investigation. Before studying discovery in detail, recognize first that a plaintiff must have a factual basis on which to file a lawsuit. A plaintiff may not initiate litigation simply to engage in discovery—to conduct the proverbial "fishing expedition." Plaintiff's lawyers investigate and obtain evidence from a variety of sources presuit to establish a factual basis for filing a lawsuit. In the simplest of cases such as a motor-vehicle accident, the plaintiff may have made the requisite observations from which to initiate a lawsuit, needing no other evidence to trust that the plaintiff has a claim. For medical-malpractice claims, the plaintiff will have a statutory right to the plaintiff's own medical records long before filing a lawsuit, from which the plaintiff's lawyer may glean evidence and retained experts may find support for a claim. In employment disputes, the plaintiff will have a statutory right to obtain from the defendant employer, at any time before or after suit, a copy of the plaintiff's employment file. In each of these cases and other cases, the plaintiff's lawyer may make Freedom of Information Act requests to government agencies for such evidence as motor-vehicle accident reports, Occupational Safety and Health Administration investigations, criminal record checks from law-enforcement agencies, and driver's license and motor-vehicle registration information, and driving histories, from the Secretary of State. The plaintiff's lawyer may also consult with experts, obtain industry standards from trade associations, make Internet searches, and hire an investigator to interview witnesses. What lawyers cannot do is to invoke discovery procedures before filing suit. Lawyers generally have no authority to serve discovery requests and interrogatories, take depositions, demand medical examinations, and serve subpoenas until they first file a lawsuit. Presuit investigation can be critical to the selection and early pursuit of new cases, and affect the discovery to follow.

Perpetuating Testimony. Do the *Federal Rules of Civil Procedure* or equivalent state-court rules give prospective claimants any aid in presuit discovery? Not really. FED. R. CIV. P. 27 is the only rule that addresses the right of a party before suit to take a deposition, which is an action that is ordinarily associated with discovery. Yet Rule 27 makes clear that when a party takes a deposition before the lawsuit is filed, it must be to perpetuate the deponent's testimony, not to discover what that testimony is. *See* In re Petition of Sheila Roberts Ford, 170 F.R.D. 504 (1997) (denying presuit petition to depose sheriff over shooting death where deposition was for discovery). Examples include where a witness has a terminal illness or is entering the military service or otherwise moving away and not expecting to be available until after the conclusion of the litigation. Rule 27 also requires that before taking the deposition, the party must file a petition in the district court, obtain a hearing date, and notify each expected adverse party, thus eliminating potential tactical advantages and substantially increasing the cost. A pre-suit Rule 27 deposition may lead to discovery of some new information, but Rule 27(a)(1)(C) requires the petitioner to show "the facts that the petitioner wants to establish by the proposed testimony," meaning that one must know in advance much of what the witness will say. As you read Rule 27, speculate whether and when you might someday invoke it.

FED. R. CIV. P. 27. Depositions to Perpetuate Testimony

(a) BEFORE AN ACTION IS FILED.

(1) *Petition.* A person who wants to perpetuate testimony about any matter cognizable in a United States court may file a verified petition in the district court for the district where any expected adverse party resides. The petition must ask for an order authorizing the petitioner to depose the named persons in order to perpetuate their testimony. The petition must be titled in the petitioner's name and must show:

(A) that the petitioner expects to be a party to an action cognizable in a United States court but cannot presently bring it or cause it to be brought;

(B) the subject matter of the expected action and the petitioner's interest;

(C) the facts that the petitioner wants to establish by the proposed testimony and the reasons to perpetuate it;

(D) the names or a description of the persons whom the petitioner expects to be adverse parties and their addresses, so far as known; and

(E) the name, address, and expected substance of the testimony of each deponent.

(2) *Notice and Service.* At least 21 days before the hearing date, the petitioner must serve each expected adverse party with a copy of the petition and a notice stating the time and place of the hearing. The notice may be served either inside or outside the district or state in the manner provided in Rule 4. If that service cannot be made with reasonable diligence on an expected adverse party, the court may order service by publication or otherwise. The court must appoint an attorney to represent persons not served in the manner provided in Rule 4 and to cross-examine the deponent if an unserved person is not otherwise represented. If any expected adverse party is a minor or is incompetent, Rule 17(c) applies.

(3) *Order and Examination.* If satisfied that perpetuating the testimony may prevent a failure or delay of justice, the court must issue an order that designates or describes the persons whose depositions may be taken, specifies the subject matter of the examinations, and states whether the depositions will be taken orally or by written interrogatories. The depositions may then be taken under these rules, and the court may issue orders like those authorized by Rules 34 and 35. A reference in these rules to the court where an action is pending means, for purposes of this rule, the court where the petition for the deposition was filed.

(4) *Using the Deposition.* A deposition to perpetuate testimony may be used under Rule 32(a) in any later-filed district court action involving the same subject matter if the deposition either was taken under these rules or, although not so taken, would be admissible in evidence in the courts of the state where it was taken.

(b) PENDING APPEAL.

(1) *In General.* The court where a judgment has been rendered may, if an appeal has been taken or may still be taken, permit a party to depose witnesses to perpetuate their testimony for use in the event of further proceedings in that court.

(2) *Motion.* The party who wants to perpetuate testimony may move for leave to take the depositions, on the same notice and service as if the action were pending in the district court. The motion must show:

(A) the name, address, and expected substance of the testimony of each deponent; and

(B) the reasons for perpetuating the testimony.

(3) *Court Order.* If the court finds that perpetuating the testimony may prevent a failure or delay of justice, the court may permit the depositions to be taken and may issue orders like those authorized by Rules 34 and 35. The depositions may be taken and used as any other deposition taken in a pending district- court action.

(c) PERPETUATION BY AN ACTION. This rule does not limit a court's power to entertain an action to perpetuate testimony.

INQUIRY

Spoliation. There is one other pre-suit subject to address before studying discovery. It has to do with a party's willingness and ability to produce evidence in response to discovery. Not only plaintiffs have an interest in pre-suit investigation. Those who anticipate litigation against them also conduct presuit investigation, especially to preserve evidence. When there are grounds to anticipate that an opponent will file a lawsuit raising claims provable by certain items of evidence, there is a duty to take reasonable steps to preserve that evidence. The evidence may include anything. Often it includes failed products, test results, photographs, incident reports, security videotapes, business records, and email or other electronic files and records. *See, e.g.,* Zubulake v. UBS Warburg LLC, 229 F.R.D. 422 (S.D. N.Y. 2004) (destruction of emails after counsel instructed retention). It may simply be routine practice to dispose of the item or information which because of some unusual occurrence has become evidence. Its destruction may even be automatic as in the case of the overwriting of electronic memory used to store still or video security images. It does not matter. There remains a duty of reasonable care to preserve evidence. A factfinder may also later infer intentional destruction from the incentive the anticipated litigation creates. Courts have the authority to sanction parties for the destruction or "spoliation" of evidence. Consider the following two cases.

Silvestri v. General Motors Corp.,

United States Court of Appeals for the Fourth Circuit
271 F.3d 583 (2001)

NIEMEYER, Circuit Judge:

Mark Silvestri filed this products liability action against General Motors Corporation, alleging that the airbag in a 1995 Chevrolet Monte Carlo he was driving did not deploy as warranted when he crashed into a utility pole and that, as a result, his injuries from the accident were enhanced. Because Silvestri failed, before the vehicle was repaired, to give General Motors notice of his claim and an opportunity to inspect the vehicle—which the district court concluded was "the sole piece of evidence in this case"—the court dismissed Silvestri's action, finding dismissal to be the appropriate sanction for the spoliation of evidence in this case. For the reasons that follow, we affirm.

... While Silvestri was in the hospital, his parents retained attorney William G. Moench to protect Silvestri's legal interests... .

... Moench retained two accident reconstructionists[who] ... inspected and photographed the vehicle and inspected the site, and each prepared a report of his findings. Because [one expert] considered it important that General Motors have an opportunity to see the car, [the expert] "suggested" to Attorney Moench, at the time he conducted his inspection, that "the car has to be kept"; and [the expert] stated, "General Motors needs to see the car." ...

Notwithstanding the anticipation of litigation against General Motors, neither Moench nor Silvestri took any steps to preserve the vehicle or to notify

General Motors of the existence of the vehicle and Silvestri's potential claim. Indeed, General Motors was not notified about the accident until almost three years later when Silvestri commenced this action against the corporation. ... General Motors ultimately found the vehicle in June 1998 in Quebec, Canada. ... When, in 1998, General Motors inspected the airbag sensing and diagnostic module, which monitors and retains in its memory defects in the airbag system, it found that the module had not been damaged in the accident. The module revealed that there had been no defect in the airbag system. Silvestri's expert, however, questioned whether this was the original module that had been in the vehicle at the time of the accident. ...

Following discovery, General Motors ... asked that the case be dismissed based on Silvestri's spoliation of evidence.

... [T]he district court addressed General Motors' spoliation claim and dismissed the case on that basis. The district court concluded that Silvestri had breached his duty either to preserve the vehicle or to notify General Motors about its availability and his claim. The court concluded that Silvestri's failure to discharge this duty caused General Motors to be "highly prejudiced." ... [T]he court noted that General Motors was prejudiced in its examination of the sensing and diagnostic module which monitored the airbag deployment system because Silvestri's expert challenged the results of the examination. ...

On appeal, Silvestri contends that he is not responsible for any spoliation of evidence because (1) he had no duty to preserve the vehicle in question as he was not its owner, and (2) any act of spoliation was that of attorney Moench, hired by his parents, not him, and therefore was not imputable to him. He also argues that the sanction of dismissal was too harsh because General Motors was not so severely prejudiced that it could not adequately defend itself in the action.

In their briefs and at oral argument, the parties have agreed that the law of New York—where the accident occurred—supplies the applicable principles of spoliation, and they have cited that law to the court. We conclude, however, that a federal law of spoliation applies because, as we note below, the power to sanction for spoliation derives from the inherent power of the court, not substantive law. ...

Spoliation refers to the destruction or material alteration of evidence or to the failure to preserve property for another's use as evidence in pending or reasonably foreseeable litigation. [Cc] The right to impose sanctions for spoliation arises from a court's inherent power to control the judicial process and litigation, but the power is limited to that necessary to redress conduct "which abuses the judicial process." Chambers v. NASCO, Inc., 501 U.S. 32, 45-46[]7 (1991)[]; *see also* United States v. Shaffer Equip. Co., 11 F.3d 450, 462 (4th Cir. 1993); *cf.* Fed.R.Civ.P. 37(b)(2) (authorizing sanctions for violations of discovery orders).

The policy underlying this inherent power of the courts is the need to preserve the integrity of the judicial process in order to retain confidence that the process works to uncover the truth. "[B]ecause no one has an exclusive insight into truth, the process depends on the adversarial presentation of evidence, precedent and custom, and argument to reasoned conclusions-all directed with unwavering effort to what, in good faith, is believed to be true on matters material to the disposition." *Shaffer Equipment, [supra]*, at 457. The courts must protect the integrity of the judicial process because, "[a]s soon as the process falters ... the people are then justified in abandoning support for the system." *Id.*

Thus, while the spoliation of evidence may give rise to court imposed sanctions deriving from this inherent power, the acts of spoliation do not themselves give rise in civil cases to substantive claims or defenses.

... In addition, a court must find some degree of fault to impose sanctions. We have recognized that when imposing spoliation sanctions, "the trial court has discretion to pursue a wide range of responses both for the purpose of leveling the evidentiary playing field and for the purpose of sanctioning the improper conduct." Vodusek v. Bayliner Marine Corp., 71 F.3d 148, 156 (4th Cir. 1995). But dismissal should be avoided if a lesser sanction will perform the necessary function. [C] ...

Silvestri contends first that he had no duty to preserve the vehicle because he was not its owner and because neither he nor his agents were in any way engaged in the destruction of the evidence. This argument assumes too narrow an understanding of the duty at issue.

The duty to preserve material evidence arises not only during litigation but also extends to that period before the litigation when a party reasonably should know that the evidence may be relevant to anticipated litigation. [C] If a party cannot fulfill this duty to preserve because he does not own or control the evidence, he still has an obligation to give the opposing party notice of access to the evidence or of the possible destruction of the evidence if the party anticipates litigation involving that evidence. [C]

In this case, it is true that Silvestri did not own the vehicle, nor did he even control it in a legal sense after the accident because the vehicle belonged to his landlady's husband. But it is apparent that Silvestri had access to the vehicle, as his attorney Moench and his retained experts were given apparently unlimited access to the vehicle for inspection purposes. Moreover, the vehicle was preserved in its post-accident condition for perhaps two to three months, or more, a period during which Silvestri, his lawyer, and his experts recognized not only that they would be suing General Motors but also that General Motors should be given an opportunity to inspect the vehicle. Within a couple of weeks of the accident, Silvestri's counsel had a conversation with his experts about the need to preserve the vehicle and have General Motors inspect it. ...

In sum, we agree with the district court that Silvestri failed to preserve material evidence in anticipation of litigation or to notify General Motors of the availability of this evidence, thus breaching his duty not to spoliate evidence.

Silvestri contends that dismissal was an unduly harsh sanction for the spoliation that occurred in this case and that the district court could have, instead, entered an order that designated facts be taken as established for purposes of the action or that presumptions be applied in connection with the burden of proof. ...

We agree with Silvestri that dismissal is severe and constitutes the ultimate sanction for spoliation. It is usually justified only in circumstances of bad faith... . But even when conduct is less culpable, dismissal may be necessary if the prejudice to the defendant is extraordinary, denying it the ability to adequately defend its case. ...

In the case before us, the conduct of the spoliator may have been either deliberate or negligent. We know that Silvestri's attorney knew that the vehicle was the central piece of evidence in his case against General Motors and that he had been reminded that this piece of evidence should be preserved or that General Motors should be notified. As it turned out, the vehicle was not preserved, and neither Silvestri nor his attorneys notified General Motors of Silvestri's claim until almost three years after the accident; by then, the evidence had been destroyed by the repair of the vehicle. Whether Silvestri's counsel believed he was securing advantage to his client's case by deliberately remaining silent for three years or whether he simply ignored his responsibilities through carelessness is not revealed in the record. But what is revealed is a level of culpability that was at least negligent and may have been deliberate. …

When we turn to the prejudice suffered by General Motors, we agree with the district court's finding that the spoliation was "highly prejudicial." It denied General Motors access to the only evidence from which it could develop its defenses adequately. …

In addition, because of the spoliation, General Motors could not resolve the critical question of how Silvestri injured his head. General Motors asserts that Silvestri's injuries were actually caused by pieces of wood that entered the vehicle from the side when the vehicle struck the fence. It points out that if the accident was caused by the fencing, then the airbag would not have prevented Silvestri's injuries. …

In short, we conclude that the district court's finding that General Motors was "highly prejudiced" was not clearly erroneous and that in the peculiar circumstances of this case, the court's order dismissing this case, although severe, was not an abuse of discretion. Accordingly, the judgment of the district court is

AFFIRMED.

TRAXLER, Circuit Judge, concurring in part and dissenting in part[, omitted.]

In re Napster Inc. Copyright Litigation,

United States District Court for the Northern District of California
462 F.Supp.2d 1060 (2006)

MARILYN HALL PATEL, District Judge.

The above-captioned actions arise from the litigation involving alleged copyright infringement by Napster, Inc. and its customers. Now before the court is plaintiffs UMG and EMI's ("plaintiffs") motion … seeking sanctions against defendant Hummer Winblad ("Hummer") for alleged intentional spoliation of evidence. …

… Hummer invested in Napster in May 2000. At that time, several lawsuits were pending against Napster (collectively "the Napster I litigation"). The litigation prompted Hummer to enter into a Common Interest and Defense Agreement with Napster as part of its investment. On June 1, 2000, deposition and document subpoenas were issued for Hummer officers … in the Napster I litigation, calling for all communications regarding Napster. Two days later, Hummer officer Ann Winblad sent an email to nine Hummer employees, copying Hummer's counsel, with the subject line "a/c: E-mails regarding Napster and review of our long standing doc retention policies." The email read … :

> Hank [one of the officers served a subpoena] has asked me to send this out to everyone.
>
> All emails re napster at this point are related to the litigation and should contain the "a/c" (attorney communications) symbol in the subject line... We should not be sending e-mails on this subject anyway. ...
>
> Please also be aware of our e-mail policy. As we have all been required to surrender Napster e-mails, this should reinforce compliance with our longstanding policies.
>
> 1. we do not retain e-mails, it is your responsibility to delete your handled e-mails immediately
>
> 2. we do not us e-mail to chat about matters related to public companies or matters such as the above
>
> 3. we do not retain written copies of e-mails in our files
>
> 4. our document retention policy is that we do not retain documents on any public or acquired company and retain limited information on private companies. all retained information is stored in central files, pls do not retain other docs in your own files unnecessarily
>
> 5. we do not retain files separate from our central files which are periodically checked for compliance to policies... [C]

That same month, ... [the] CEO of Universal Music Corp. ... advised Hummer that the recording companies intended to sue Napster's investment firms if the alleged copyright infringement continued. ...

On July 26, 2000, an additional lawsuit was filed against Napster ("the Katz lawsuit"), naming Hummer Winblad ... as defendant[]. ...

On August 10, 2000, this court entered an order preliminarily enjoining Napster from "engaging in, or facilitating others in copying, downloading, uploading, transmitting, or distributing plaintiffs' copyrighted musical compositions and sound recordings... ." [C] ... Napster ceased operations on July 1, 2001. ...

... In April 2002, ... John Hummer stated in an email that "We [Hummer Winblad] know we are going to be sued." [C] The instant action was filed a year later in April 2003. ...

In February 2004, plaintiffs served Hummer with discovery requests in the instant action requesting all Napster-related communications up through the filing of plaintiffs' complaint in 2003. ...

... [P]laintiffs now allege that Hummer personnel continued to communicate with each other via email regarding Napster, including discussions about issues relevant to the claims and defenses in this action. Plaintiffs further allege that Hummer personnel willfully deleted all of their Napster-related emails in order to avoid turning them over in this litigation.

Hummer does not seem to dispute that they deleted any Napster-related emails on the Hummer Winblad system that were generated after June 3, 2000. Hummer acknowledges that its personnel routinely deleted emails on their system without regard to whether the deleted emails were relevant to the instant litigation. ... Hummer further claims that no Napster-related communications were deleted willfully or intentionally, and that any relevant communications that were deleted were deleted by inadvertence or mistake.

LEGAL STANDARD

District courts may impose sanctions as part of their inherent power "to manage their own affairs so as to achieve the orderly and expeditious disposition of cases." Chambers v. NASCO, Inc., 501 U.S. 32, 43[] (1991); [c]. ...

Courts may sanction parties responsible for spoliation of evidence in three ways. First, a court can instruct the jury that it may draw an inference adverse to the party or witness responsible for destroying the evidence. [Cc] Second, a court can exclude witness testimony proffered by the party responsible for destroying the evidence and based on the destroyed evidence. [Cc] Finally, a court may dismiss the claim of the party responsible for destroying the evidence. [Cc]

A party's destruction of evidence need not be in "bad faith" to warrant a court's imposition of sanctions. [C] District courts may impose sanctions against a party that merely had notice that the destroyed evidence was potentially relevant to litigation. [Cc] However, a party's motive or degree of fault in destroying evidence is relevant to what sanction, if any, is imposed. [Cc]

DISCUSSION ...

I. *Hummer's Obligation to Preserve Documents*

As soon as a potential claim is identified, a litigant is under a duty to preserve evidence which it knows or reasonably should know is relevant to the action. [Cc] ...

A. *Hummer's Obligation Before Fall 2000*

In support of their position that Hummer's obligation to preserve attached in May 2000, plaintiffs point to deposition testimony by Hummer officer Todd Forrest in which Forrest states that, as early as May 2000, individuals were instructed to keep documents surrounding Napster, instructions which continued throughout the relevant period. In addition, plaintiffs point to the fact that Hummer was well aware of Napster's legal troubles based on its pre-investment diligence, and entered into a Common Interest Defense Agreement with Napster at the time of investment. Finally, plaintiffs point to the June 3, 2000 email as evidence that Hummer was taking specific actions with an eye toward litigation during this time period. ...

... [T]here is evidence that John Hummer, at least, knew or should have known that litigation was probable as early as June 3, 2000. Hummer testified to being told by Edgar Bronfman, Jr., CEO of Universal Music Corp., at that time that if Hummer did not "instantaneously comply with the injunction, we will sue the venture firm and you people personally." [C] ... Given the already pending litigation against Napster and the clear indication from Mr. Bronfman that the recording industry would be targeting Napster's investors, Hummer Winblad should reasonably have believed that litigation against it was probable if it continued its involvement with Napster. Therefore, Hummer's duty to preserve evidence attached in June 2000. ...

II. *Sanctions*

Once Hummers duty to preserve took effect in June 2000, Hummer was required to suspend any existing policies related to deleting or destroying files and preserve all relevant documents related to the litigation. *Zubulake,* 220 F.R.D. at 218 ("Once a party reasonably anticipates litigation, it must suspend its routine document retention/destruction policy and put in place a 'litigation hold' to ensure the preservation of relevant documents."); *see also* National Assn. of Radiation Survivors, 115 F.R.D. at 557-58 ("The obligation to retain discoverable materials is an affirmative one; it requires that the agency or corporate officers having notice of discovery obligations communicate those obligations to employees in possession of discoverable materials."). Therefore, even if Hummer's "long standing policies" included deleting emails, Hummer was required to cease deleting emails once the duty to preserve attached in May 2000. Since Hummer acknowledges that it did not cease its document policy, the court may impose sanctions for Hummer's deletion of documents. *Zubulake,* 220 F.R.D. at 220 ("Once the duty to preserve attaches, any destruction of documents is, at a minimum, negligent.").

Plaintiffs have requested a default judgment against Hummer or, in the alternative, an issue preclusion order and an adverse inference instruction. Plaintiffs have also requested monetary sanctions independent of any other sanctions the court may impose. The appropriate sanction, if any, depends largely on the culpability of Hummer and the resulting prejudice to plaintiffs. [Cc]

A. *Default Sanction*

When considering a default sanction in response to spoliation of evidence, the court must determine "(1) the existence of certain extraordinary circumstances, (2) the presence of willfulness, bad faith, or fault by the offending party, (3) the efficacy of lesser sanctions, [and] (4) the relationship or nexus between the misconduct drawing the [default] sanction and the matters in controversy in the case." Halaco Eng'g Co. v. Costle, 843 F.2d 376, 380 (9th Cir. 1988). …

1. *Extraordinary Circumstances*

… Plaintiffs argue that Hummer engaged in deceptive practices by willfully destroying relevant documents and subsequently claiming that all responsive documents had been retained and produced. Specifically, plaintiffs assert that they spent three years attempting to glean an explanation from Hummer regarding the small number of Hummer Winblad emails produced during discovery, and that Hummer deceived them during this period by failing to admit to their document destruction policy and by withholding the June 3, 2000 email until the close of discovery. …

Hummer claims that it failed to produce the June 3, 2000 email due to a mistake as to its relevance and privileged status, claiming that such errors are to be expected in large-scale document production. Hummer claims to have belatedly located the June 3, 2000 email in a box of miscellaneous files during one of a number of repeated searches for responsive documents. Furthermore, because Hummer denies any wrongdoing with respect to its document preservation duties, it denies that it made any bad-faith representations to plaintiffs regarding its production.

It is difficult to say whether Hummer's conduct in this regard resulted from willful deception or simple incompetence. …

2. *Willfulness, Bad Faith, or Fault*

… Plaintiffs argue that Hummer willfully destroyed relevant documents in order to prevent them from being produced in this litigation. Specifically, plaintiffs allege that the June 3, 2000 email clearly amounts to an instruction to delete all Napster-related emails rather than comply with the outstanding subpoena… .

Hummer denies that the June 3, 2000 email indicates any intentional deletion of Napster-related emails. Rather, Hummer asserts that the portion of the email concerning Hummer's document retention policy has "nothing to do with Napster," despite the portion of the email that explicitly addresses the Napster I subpoena. ... In seeking to make this distinction, Hummer glaringly ignores the sentence between the two portions of the email that explicitly ties the retention policy to the Napster production: "*As we have all been required to surrender Napster e-mails, this* should reinforce compliance with our long standing policies." [C] (emphasis added). The very first tenet of the policy, "reinforce[d]" by the requirement to surrender Napster emails, is "we do not retain e-mails, *it is your responsibility to delete your handled e-mails immediately* [.]" *Id.* (emphasis added). This was clearly designed to instruct the recipients to delete all of their Napster-related emails going forward in order to avoid surrendering them. Hummer offers no plausible explanation to the contrary. ...

... Absent a clear explanation for why Hummer employees were instructed to "delete all emails" in conjunction with being apprised of a pending subpoena, the court concludes that the June 3, 2000 email served as an command to delete Napster-related emails going forward.

Separate from the June 3, 2000 email, Hummer apparently acknowledges that it routinely deleted Napster-related emails that resided on Hummer's servers. ...

Hummer's deletion of Napster-related emails may not have been willful, but willfulness is not strictly required for the imposition of default sanctions. Instead, a default sanction requires "willfulness, fault, or bad faith." At worst, Hummer mounted a knowing and concerted effort to destroy Napster-related emails that it had a duty to preserve and produce. At best, however, Hummer was grossly negligent in executing its duties to preserve evidence, by failing to implement a litigation hold and instead relying on Napster to preserve Hummer's emails. Hummer was therefore at fault in failing to preserve Napster-related emails. ...

3. *Efficacy of Lesser Sanctions*

Plaintiffs have requested the alternative relief of preclusion and an adverse inference instruction in the event that the court does not grant a default sanction. If such sanctions would be effective, a default sanction is inappropriate. Given the standard of applying the least onerous effective sanction, plaintiffs must justify the default sanction by either showing that (1) no lesser sanction would adequately punish Hummer and deter other parties from engaging in the same conduct or (2) Hummer has engaged in deceptive conduct and will continue to do so. [Cc]

... [P]laintiffs make no specific showing regarding the inadequacy of lesser sanctions in this case.[fn] For the reasons set forth below, the court concludes that lesser sanctions would be adequate given the level of demonstrable culpability on the part of Hummer, and there is nothing in the current representation or conduct to suggest a recurrence. Therefore, this factor weighs against default sanctions.

4. *Nexus Between Misconduct and Matters in Controversy*

In order for default sanctions to be imposed for Hummer's destruction of documents, there must be a nexus between Hummer's conduct and the merits such that the conduct interferes with the rightful decision of the action. [C] In the context of spoliation of evidence, a nexus exists if the party destroyed documents that were relevant to discovery requests. [Cc] As discussed above, Hummer systematically failed to preserve emails on its company servers, thereby destroying Napster-related communications that resided on the servers during the relevant time period. Accordingly, there is a nexus between Hummer's misconduct and the matters in controversy.

5. *Prejudice*

Prejudice is an "optional" consideration when determining whether default sanctions are appropriate.[fn] [C] …

Plaintiffs contend that Hummer's document destruction policy resulted in the loss of "volumes" of documents over the relevant time period. … Hummer has produced … fewer than 300 … emails. Plaintiffs also point out that, in response to the Napster I subpoena, Hummer produced 271 emails … from the seven-day period from May 20, 2000 to May 26, 2000. This, according to plaintiffs, suggests that there should be many more emails generated after that time period, and that these emails were destroyed by Hummer. In addition, plaintiffs point to several emails collected from other sources which, they claim, demonstrate that Hummer was engaged in communications regarding every aspect of the action. …

Plaintiffs further claim that they have been prejudiced because the Hummer Winblad witnesses have exhibited "litigation amnesia" in claiming an inability to recall facts that would be memorialized in the deleted emails. …

At this stage of the proceedings, when the full evidentiary record has not yet been considered by the court or by a jury, the court cannot determine the extent of prejudice created by Hummer's failure to preserve its emails. … The court will therefore engage in a full analysis of the evidence regarding the quality and quantity of emails improperly deleted by Hummer at the Summary Judgment or trial stage. At this point the court can only conclude that plaintiffs have not produced sufficient evidence of prejudice to justify default sanctions. …

B. *Evidentiary Sanctions*

Plaintiffs have requested two forms of evidentiary sanctions. First, plaintiffs request that Hummer be precluded from contesting all or some of a number of issues related to the parties' claims and defenses. Second, plaintiffs request that the jury be given an adverse inference instruction. …

… [P]laintiffs have shown sufficient prejudice to warrant some degree of preclusion sanctions. The nature and extent of these sanctions will be determined at the Summary Judgment or trial stage. …

… [P]laintiffs are entitled to an adverse inference instruction. The precise wording of the instruction will be determined at trial.

C. *Monetary Sanctions*

Monetary sanctions may be imposed where one party has wrongfully destroyed evidence. [C] Plaintiffs claim that they are entitled to their attorneys' fees associated with bringing this motion, and with the meet and confer process involved in determining the availability of Hummer's Napster-related emails. The court finds that monetary sanctions are warranted here. Hummer could have forestalled a great deal of time and effort by simply acknowledging early on that it was not preserving its internally generated Napster-related communications.

Plaintiffs are entitled to an award of attorney fees that is *reasonable* in light of the degree of Hummer's culpability. Plaintiffs are ordered to submit a request for a specific amount of fees, with evidentiary support, for the court's consideration. …

IT IS SO ORDERED.

INQUIRY

Statutes. The above cases show that a court has inherent power to sanction the spoliation of evidence relating to pending or anticipated litigation, once that litigation is filed in the sanctioning court. A party's duty to preserve evidence is a duty arising out of the party's relationship to the sanctioning court. Ordinarily, if there is no eventual action, then there is no duty because there is no offended court. Is there any other source for the duty to preserve evidence other than the relationship with the sanctioning court? Statutes and regulations occasionally impose duties to preserve certain evidence, particularly business records relating to important transactions. *See, e.g.,* 17 C.F.R. 240.17a-4(b)(4) (securities brokers and dealers must retain all business communications for three years). Violation of a statute or regulation to retain records is not always spoliation. The party seeking a spoliation sanction based on the violation of statute or regulation rather than anticipated litigation may have to establish that the party was a member of the class that the statute or regulation protected. *Compare* Lattimore v. Citibank Fed. Sav. Bank, 151 F.3d 712, 716 (7th Cir. 1998) (general inference of spoliation), *with* Byrnie v. Town of Cromwell, 243 F.3d 93, 109 (2d Cir. 2001) (party seeking inference of spoliation must be member of statute's protected class).

A. Scope

It is natural that parties expect to receive all evidence from the other side while hesitating to disclose all evidence of their own. Litigation is, after all, adversarial and strategic. The grounds on which parties tend not to produce evidence include (a) that the opposing party did not ask for it, (b) that it has nothing to do with the litigation, meaning that it is not relevant, and (c) that the opposing party has no right to it, meaning that it is privileged, inadmissible, and not discoverable even if relevant. FED. R. CIV. P. 26 addresses each of these concerns. Rule 26(b)(1) begins by stating that "[p]arties may obtain discovery regarding any nonprivileged matter that is relevant... ." A party may discover relevant evidence so long as it is not privileged. Relevance determines the scope of discovery. One should ask, though, relevant to what? Rule 26(b)(1) continues that the evidence must be "relevant to any party's claim or defense... ." The party seeking discovery must thus be able to show that the requested discovery seeks evidence that will make proof of a claim or defense more or less likely. *See, e.g.,* World Wrestling Federation Entertainment, Inc. v. William Morris Agency, Inc., 204 F.R.D. 263 (S.D. N.Y. 2001) (contracts with other entertainers not relevant to contract dispute between parties).

Given this restriction, discovery is not a search for new claims or defenses. Until recently, Rule 26(b)(1) allowed discovery of anything relevant to the subject matter of the action, not merely the asserted claims and defenses. Under the old rule, the Supreme Court construed discovery rights so broadly that it once stated, "No longer can the time-honored cry of 'fishing expedition' serve to preclude a party from inquiring into the facts underlying his opponent's case."

Hickman v. Taylor, 329 U.S. 495, 507 (1947). Today, the pleadings determine the scope of discovery in the first instance. A party must be able to connect discovery requests to pled claims or defenses. Yet in its latest version, Rule 26(b)(1) continues that "[f]or good cause, the court may order discovery of any matter relevant to the subject matter involved in the action." There is thus some opportunity for a party to seek evidence that, though not specifically tied to a pled claim or defense, yet relates to the action's subject matter, perhaps including latent, unpled claims or defenses. Read the following case articulating why these two definitions of relevance arose, advocating their significance, and illustrating how difficult they can be in their application.

Thompson v. Department of Housing and Urban Dev.,

United States District Court for the District of Maryland
199 F.R.D. 168, 172 (2001)

GRIMM, United States Magistrate Judge.

Plaintiffs are class representatives of African American residents of Baltimore's public housing developments. They filed suit in January, 1995 against the U.S. Department of Housing and Urban Development and its' secretary (the "federal defendants") and the Housing Authority of Baltimore City ("HABC"), its executive director and the Mayor and City Council of Baltimore (the "local defendants"). The class action lawsuit alleged that the defendants and their predecessors, from 1933 through the present, established and perpetuated *de jure* racial segregation in Baltimore's public housing, in violation of the 5th, 13th, and 14th Amendments to the United States Constitution, as well as Title VI of the Civil Rights Act of 1964, Title VIII of the Civil Rights Act of 1968, 42 U.S.C. Sections 1981, 1982, and 1983, the U.S. Housing Act of 1937 and the Housing and Community Development Act of 1974. Plaintiffs seek declaratory, injunctive, and equitable relief, and attorneys' fees.

In the spring of 1996, the parties entered into a partial consent decree that settled certain claims against the defendants. The decree is ambitious in its scope, and to oversee its implementation a special master was appointed by the court. From the approval of the consent decree until the middle of 2000, most of the attention of the parties has been devoted to its implementation. However, in mid-2000 the plaintiffs initiated discovery against the defendants, and the undersigned was referred the case for resolution of discovery disputes. Pending is the motion by the plaintiffs to compel the local defendants to provide responsive answers to Rule 33 and 34 discovery requests. ... [T]he dispute presents issues of first impression regarding the December 1, 2000 changes to the Rules of Civil Procedure governing the scope of discovery. ...

For the reasons that follow, I am denying the plaintiffs' motion, without prejudice, and returning this dispute to the parties to meet, confer, and take the further action discussed below.

DISCUSSION

The July 1, 1970 changes to the Rules of Civil Procedure transformed Rule 26 from one governing only depositions, to a rule that regulated "the discovery obtainable through any of the discovery devices" listed in the rules. [C] The "new" Rule 26 remained in place until December 1, 2000, and established the scope of discovery broadly as follows: "[p]arties may obtain discovery regarding any matter, *not privileged,* which is *relevant* to the *subject matter involved in the pending action...* . It is not ground for objection that the information sought will be inadmissible at the trial if the information sought appears *reasonably calculated to lead to the discovery of admissible evidence.*" (Emphasis added). The 1993 changes to the rules of procedure added provisions to Rule 26(b)(2)... . Following these changes, Rule 26(b)(2) stated:

> The frequency or extent of use of the discovery methods otherwise permitted under these rules and by any local rule *shall* be limited by the court if it determines that: ... (iii) *the burden or expense of the proposed discovery outweighs its likely benefit, taking into account the needs of the case, the amount in controversy, the parties' resources, the importance of the issues at stake in the litigation, and the importance of the proposed discovery in resolving the issues.* The court may act upon its *own initiative* after reasonable notice or pursuant to a motion under subdivision (c) (Emphasis added).

The combined effect of the changes to Rule 26(b)(1) and (2) was to create a procedural syllogism of sorts, which defined the contours of the scope of discovery. Under it, facts were discoverable if: (1) relevant to the subject matter of the litigation; and (2) not privileged; and (3) if not themselves admissible, then reasonably calculated to lead to admissible evidence, UNLESS the court, *sua sponte,* or at the request of a party, determined that the discovery sought was: (a) unreasonably cumulative, duplicative, or obtainable from another more convenient, less burdensome or less expensive source; or (b) the party seeking the discovery had had sufficient opportunity by discovery in the pending action to obtain it; or, (c) following a costs-benefits analysis that balanced (i) the burden or expense associated with the requested discovery; (ii) the likely benefit to the requesting party of the challenged discovery; (iii) taking into account the following factors: (aa) the needs of the case; (bb) the amount in controversy, (cc) the parties resources, (dd) the importance of the issues at stake in the litigation, and (ee) the importance of the proposed discovery in resolving the issues, the court determined that the requested discovery should not be allowed. ...

Despite the obvious utility of the Rule 26(b)(2) factors in tailoring discovery to accommodate fair disclosure without imposing undue burden or expense, they have tended largely to be ignored by litigants, and, less frequently than desirable, used by the courts, *sua sponte,* to manage discovery.[fn] Instead, particularly with respect to disputes involving Rule 33 and Rule 34 discovery, the focus of the litigants tends to be the party seeking discovery's perceived "right" to all information relating to the broad "subject matter" of the litigation, without any reflection as to the real usefulness of the information sought, or the burden or expense required to produce it, countered by the party resisting the discovery's unparticularized claims of burden, expense, irrelevance, and privilege. ...

The most recent revisions to the discovery rules imposed changes intended to reach lingering concerns about the overbreadth and expense of discovery, and remind the courts and litigants of the fact that in determining what discovery should take place in a particular case, Rule 26(b)(1) is but the first step, necessarily followed by balancing the Rule 26(b)(2) factors. Accordingly, the December 1, 2000 changes to Rule 26(b)(1) restricted the scope of discovery to unprivileged facts relevant to "the claim or defense of any party," unless the court determines that there is "good cause" to permit broader discovery relevant to the subject matter of the action, but not more directly connected to the particular claims and defenses. They additionally required that discovery of inadmissible facts that appear reasonably calculated to lead to the discovery of admissible evidence also must be within the scope of permissible discovery. Furthermore, they emphasize that "all discovery is subject to the limitations imposed by Rule 26(b)(2)(i), (ii), and (iii)", the cost-benefit balancing factors. [C]

The commentary to the rule changes clarifies that the amendment to the scope of discovery provisions of Rule 26(b)(1) "is designed to involve the court more actively in regulating the breadth of sweeping or contentious discovery," so that, if there is "an objection that discovery goes beyond material relevant to the parties' claims or defenses, the court would become involved to determine whether the discovery is relevant to the claims or defenses and, if not, whether good cause exists for authorizing it so long as it is relevant to the subject matter of the action." [C] It also emphasizes the desirability of courts more vigorously applying the Rule 26(b)(2) cost-benefit factors in determining allowable discovery. [C]

Although the rule changes do not specifically explain the difference in scope between discovery relevant to "claims and defenses" in the litigation, and discovery relevant to the "subject matter,"[fn] it is clear that the former is intended to be narrower than the later, and that the broader discovery is only to be allowed for "good cause." Further, it seems clear that the most valuable reference to use in implementing the new change in the scope of discovery is the pleadings that have been filed, as that is where the claims and defenses are stated. ...

... While the pleadings will be important, it would be a mistake to argue that no fact may be discovered unless it directly correlates with a factual allegation in the complaint or answer. ...

Lest litigants and the court become consumed with the philosophical exercise of debating the difference between discovery relevant to the "claims and defenses" as opposed to the "subject matter" of the pending action—the juridical equivalent to debating the number of angels that can dance on the head of a pin—the practical solution to implementing the new rule changes may be to focus more on whether the requested discovery makes sense in light of the Rule 26(b)(2) factors, than to attempt to divine some bright line difference between the old and new rule. ...

The pending discovery dispute illustrates the points raised above. The plaintiffs have filed a sweeping lawsuit alleging discriminatory action by the defendants covering three-quarters of a century, and involving all aspects of the public housing programs in Baltimore. Within a year or so of suit being filed, the parties entered into a comprehensive partial consent decree, itself broad in scope, which settled many, but by no means all, of the claims originally filed. After a hiatus in discovery of several years, plaintiffs initiated renewed discovery requests, under Rules 33 and 34. The local defendants objected to certain of these requests, asserting: overbreadth and burden, without giving particulars to permit either plaintiffs or the court meaningfully to evaluate this claim; and that the challenged requests exceeded the scope of permissible discovery as they were not tailored to the existing "claims and defenses" remaining in the litigation following the consent decree. Plaintiffs, justifying their discovery requests, argue their broad entitlement to discovery relating to the whole of the dispute that is the basis for the litigation, without once attempting to identify which claims that survived the partial consent decree will be furthered by the requested information, or addressing the burden to the local defendants to produce it. Both parties seem content to leave it to the court to sift through the 56 page complaint and the 74 page partial consent decree to determine what discovery should be allowed. ... This will not do.

I am returning this dispute to the parties with guidance as to how they should meet and confer to attempt to resolve or narrow their differences. ... [T]he parties are expected to focus their discussions ... on a particularized analysis of the burden/benefit factors of Rule 26(b)(2). ... If the local defendants claim that they cannot produce requested information because of burden, they must justify this claim with specific details that can be evaluated by the plaintiffs, and, if necessary, the court.

This means that the parties must set aside their differences as adversaries and make a good faith effort to reach common ground on the disputes. ...

If, following their consultations, counsel find that there still are differences that cannot be overcome by negotiation, as likely will be the case, they will contact me, and a discovery conference will be set promptly. While I am mindful of the fact that the commentary to the recent rule changes emphasizes the need for the court actively to be involved in applying the Rule 26(b)(2) factors, this involvement necessarily must follow, not precede, the parties own good faith efforts to do so. Therefore, if there is to be a discovery conference, the court will expect counsel to demonstrate that they have fully considered the cost/benefit factors, and made reasonable modifications of their positions to accommodate them.

Accordingly, it is ... ordered that the plaintiffs' motion to compel discovery from the local defendants is denied, without prejudice, and the parties are to take further action in accordance with this order.

INQUIRY

Reasonably Calculated. Must the evidence that a party seeks by request be admissible evidence? FED. R. CIV. P. 26(b)(1) adds another important dimension to the permissible scope of discovery requests when it states, "Relevant information need not be admissible at the trial if the discovery appears reasonably calculated to lead to the discovery of admissible evidence." How does this sentence broaden the scope of discovery? Practitioners who engage in discovery quickly realize that there is all sorts of information that one would never wish to present to a jury but that can be very useful in locating admissible evidence. Social Security numbers, driver's license numbers, and other identifying information of that type, while having no probative value on any claim or defense, may yet be utterly necessary to locate histories and records. The court, case number, and identity of opposing parties and counsel for other similar litigation may not only be irrelevant but prejudicial and yet can lead to discovery of relevant information within the other case. Rule 26(b)(1) authorizes discovery of information that is not itself admissible evidence but that is reasonably calculated to lead to discovery of admissible evidence. Can you think of other examples?

Non-Parties. Rule 26 stating the general rules of discovery and the following rules governing specifics authorize parties to make discovery of other parties. What discovery can a party make of a non-party? The *Federal Rules of Civil Procedure* limits the methods of discovery as to non-parties, not the scope. Parties may discover relevant evidence from non-parties just as they may from parties, but they may do so only through depositions and inspection of documents, not through interrogatories or medical examinations. Non-parties have no direct interest in the litigation. While their evidence should be available to the parties, discovery requests should not put non-parties to undue burden or expense. The two authorized methods of discovery of non-parties, deposition and document production, are relatively passive compared to the burden of answering detailed interrogatories and the invasiveness of medical examination. One finds this limitation on the discovery of non-parties in an unlikely place, in FED. R. CIV. P. 45 governing subpoenas and, more specifically, in Rule 45(a)(1)(A). Parties make production requests of other parties simply by serving the request. Parties make production requests of non-parties by including the request within a subpoena. Read Rule 45 to get a sense of how powerful subpoenas for discovery materials can be. Also, notice the care with which practitioners must issue discovery subpoenas, the way that a non-party can obtain relief from one, and the way that a party can have one enforced.

FED. R. CIV. P. 45. Subpoena
(a) IN GENERAL.
(1) *Form and Contents.*
(A) *Requirements—In General.* Every subpoena must:
(i) state the court from which it issued;
(ii) state the title of the action, the court in which it is pending, and its civil-action number;
(iii) command each person to whom it is directed to do the following at a specified time and place: attend and testify; produce designated documents, electronically stored information, or tangible things in that person's possession, custody, or control; or permit the inspection of premises; and
(iv) set out the text of Rule 45(c) and (d).
(B) *Command to Attend a Deposition—Notice of the Recording Method.* A subpoena commanding attendance at a deposition must state the method for recording the testimony.
(C) *Combining or Separating a Command to Produce or to Permit Inspection; Specifying the Form for Electronically Stored Information.* A command to produce documents, electronically stored information, or tangible things or to permit the inspection of premises may be included in a subpoena commanding attendance at a deposition, hearing, or trial, or may be set out in a separate subpoena. A subpoena may specify the form or forms in which electronically stored information is to be produced.
(D) *Command to Produce; Included Obligations.* A command in a subpoena to produce documents, electronically stored information, or tangible things requires the responding party to permit inspection, copying, testing, or sampling of the materials.
(2) *Issued from Which Court.* A subpoena must issue as follows:
(A) for attendance at a hearing or trial, from the court for the district where the hearing or trial is to be held;
(B) for attendance at a deposition, from the court for the district where the deposition is to be taken; and
(C) for production or inspection, if separate from a subpoena commanding a person's attendance, from the court for the district where the production or inspection is to be made.
(3) *Issued by Whom.* The clerk must issue a subpoena, signed but otherwise in blank, to a party who requests it. That party must complete it before service. An attorney also may issue and sign a subpoena as an officer of:
(A) a court in which the attorney is authorized to practice; or
(B) a court for a district where a deposition is to be taken or production is to be made, if the attorney is authorized to practice in the court where the action is pending.
(b) SERVICE.
(1) *By Whom; Tendering Fees; Serving a Copy of Certain Subpoenas.* Any person who is at least 18 years old and not a party may serve a subpoena. Serving a subpoena requires delivering a copy to the named person and, if the subpoena requires that person's attendance, tendering the fees for 1 day's attendance and the mileage allowed by law. Fees and mileage need not be tendered when the subpoena issues on behalf of the United States or any of its officers or agencies. If the subpoena commands the production of documents, electronically stored information, or tangible things or the inspection

of premises before trial, then before it is served, a notice must be served on each party.

(2) *Service in the United States.* Subject to Rule 45(c)(3)(A)(ii), a subpoena may be served at any place:

(A) within the district of the issuing court;

(B) outside that district but within 100 miles of the place specified for the deposition, hearing, trial, production, or inspection;

(C) within the state of the issuing court if a state statute or court rule allows service at that place of a subpoena issued by a state court of general jurisdiction sitting in the place specified for the deposition, hearing, trial, production, or inspection; or

(D) that the court authorizes on motion and for good cause, if a federal statute so provides.

(3) *Service in a Foreign Country.* 28 U.S.C. § 1783 governs issuing and serving a subpoena directed to a United States national or resident who is in a foreign country.

(4) *Proof of Service.* Proving service, when necessary, requires filing with the issuing court a statement showing the date and manner of service and the names of the persons served. The statement must be certified by the server.

(c) PROTECTING A PERSON SUBJECT TO A SUBPOENA.

(1) *Avoiding Undue Burden or Expense; Sanctions.* A party or attorney responsible for issuing and serving a subpoena must take reasonable steps to avoid imposing undue burden or expense on a person subject to the subpoena. The issuing court must enforce this duty and impose an appropriate sanction—which may include lost earnings and reasonable attorney's fees—on a party or attorney who fails to comply.

(2) *Command to Produce Materials or Permit Inspection.*

(A) *Appearance Not Required.* A person commanded to produce documents, electronically stored information, or tangible things, or to permit the inspection of premises, need not appear in person at the place of production or inspection unless also commanded to appear for a deposition, hearing, or trial.

(B) *Objections.* A person commanded to produce documents or tangible things or to permit inspection may serve on the party or attorney designated in the subpoena a written objection to inspecting, copying, testing or sampling any or all of the materials or to inspecting the premises— or to producing electronically stored information in the form or forms requested. The objection must be served before the earlier of the time specified for compliance or 14 days after the subpoena is served. If an objection is made, the following rules apply:

(i) At any time, on notice to the commanded person, the serving party may move the issuing court for an order compelling production or inspection.

(ii) These acts may be required only as directed in the order, and the order must protect a person who is neither a party nor a party's officer from significant expense resulting from compliance.

(3) *Quashing or Modifying a Subpoena.*

(A) *When Required.* On timely motion, the issuing court must quash or modify a subpoena that:

(i) fails to allow a reasonable time to comply;

(ii) requires a person who is neither a party nor a party's officer to travel more than 100 miles from where that person resides, is employed, or regularly transacts business in person—except that, subject to Rule 45(c)(3)(B)(iii), the person may be commanded to attend a trial by traveling from any such place within the state where the trial is held;

(iii) requires disclosure of privileged or other protected matter, if no exception or waiver applies; or

(iv) subjects a person to undue burden.

(B) *When Permitted.* To protect a person subject to or affected by a subpoena, the issuing court may, on motion, quash or modify the subpoena if it requires:

(i) disclosing a trade secret or other confidential research, development, or commercial information;

(ii) disclosing an unretained expert's opinion or information that does not describe specific occurrences in dispute and results from the expert's study that was not requested by a party; or

(iii) a person who is neither a party nor a party's officer to incur substantial expense to travel more than 100 miles to attend trial.

(C) *Specifying Conditions as an Alternative.* In the circumstances described in Rule 45(c)(3)(B), the court may, instead of quashing or modifying a subpoena, order appearance or production under specified conditions if the serving party:

(i) shows a substantial need for the testimony or material that cannot be otherwise met without undue hardship; and

(ii) ensures that the subpoenaed person will be reasonably compensated.

(d) DUTIES IN RESPONDING TO A SUBPOENA.

(1) *Producing Documents or Electronically Stored Information.* These procedures apply to producing documents or electronically stored information:

(A) *Documents.* A person responding to a subpoena to produce documents must produce them as they are kept in the ordinary course of business or must organize and label them to correspond to the categories in the demand.

(B) *Form for Producing Electronically Stored Information Not Specified.* If a subpoena does not specify a form for producing electronically stored information, the person responding must produce it in a form or forms in which it is ordinarily maintained or in a reasonably usable form or forms.
(C) *Electronically Stored Information Produced in Only One Form.* The person responding need not produce the same electronically stored information in more than one form.
(D) *Inaccessible Electronically Stored Information.* The person responding need not provide discovery of electronically stored information from sources that the person identifies as not reasonably accessible because of undue burden or cost. On motion to compel discovery or for a protective order, the person responding must show that the information is not reasonably accessible because of undue burden or cost. If that showing is made, the court may nonetheless order discovery from such sources if the requesting party shows good cause, considering the limitations of Rule 26(b)(2)(C). The court may specify conditions for the discovery.
(2) *Claiming Privilege or Protection.*
(A) *Information Withheld.* A person withholding subpoenaed information under a claim that it is privileged or subject to protection as trial-preparation material must:
(i) expressly make the claim; and
(ii) describe the nature of the withheld documents, communications, or tangible things in a manner that, without revealing information itself privileged or protected, will enable the parties to assess the claim.
(B) *Information Produced.* If information produced in response to a subpoena is subject to a claim of privilege or of protection as trial-preparation material, the person making the claim may notify any party that received the information of the claim and the basis for it. After being notified, a party must promptly return, sequester, or destroy the specified information and any copies it has; must not use or disclose the information until the claim is resolved; must take reasonable steps to retrieve the information if the party disclosed it before being notified; and may promptly present the information to the court under seal for a determination of the claim. The person who produced the information must preserve the information until the claim is resolved.
(e) CONTEMPT. The issuing court may hold in contempt a person who, having been served, fails without adequate excuse to obey the subpoena. A nonparty's failure to obey must be excused if the subpoena purports to require the nonparty to attend or produce at a place outside the limits of Rule 45(c)(3)(A)(ii).

B. Limitations

FED. R. CIV. P. 26 places several other limitations on discovery in addition to the basic limitation on scope that the request must seek relevant evidence. You have already seen that the sought-after evidence must also be nonprivileged. Information that would be probative of a claim or defense but privileged because of a policy interest is not discoverable. For example, even though it would likely contain relevant and highly interesting information parties do not make discovery requests for the opposing side's correspondence between attorney and client because of the attorney-client privilege. You have also already seen that the sought-after evidence must be admissible. Information that would be probative of a claim or defense but inadmissible under FRE 403 because of its unduly prejudicial effect is not discoverable.

Rule 26(b) also imposes procedural limitations in addition to the substantive evidentiary limitations of privilege and inadmissibility. Rule 26(b)(1) on the scope of discovery ends by stating, "All discovery is subject to the limitations imposed by Rule 26(b)(2)(C)." Rule 26(b)(2)(C) then lists three limitations that have to do with the procedural fairness of the discovery request rather than what it is that the request seeks. The first procedural limitation is where the request is "unreasonably cumulative or duplicative," or the requesting party can obtain the evidence "from some other source that is more convenient, less burdensome, or less expensive." Discovery is not available when a party has already asked and received or should ask someone else. The second procedural limitation is where "the party seeking discovery has had ample opportunity to obtain the information by discovery in the action." Discovery is not available when a party asks too late. The third procedural limitation is when "the burden or expense of the proposed discovery outweighs its likely benefit" measured against factors relating to the particular case.

Rule 26 includes other similar limitations on discovery in its subrule (c) providing for the means to enforce discovery limitations. Parties and non-parties may prevent unauthorized discovery by moving for protective order under Rule 26(c). Rule 26(c) first requires that a person wishing to prohibit unauthorized discovery meet and confer with the party requesting the discovery. If the conference does not result in a satisfactory explanation, narrowing, or withdrawal of the discovery request, then the person may move under Rule 26(c) showing the court good cause to protect the person "from annoyance, embarrassment, oppression, or undue burden or expense." Just any annoyance is not sufficient for protective order. The party moving for protection under Rule 26(c) must show specific injury. *See* Publicker Indus., Inc. v. Cohen, 733 F.2d 1059, 1071 (3d Cir. 1984); General Dynamics Corp. v. Selb Mfg. Co., 481 F.2d 1204, 1212 (8th Cir. 1973). Consider as an introduction the following Supreme Court case illustrating how annoyance, embarrassment, and oppression may overcome First Amendment interests to protect a party from discovery disclosures. This section then continues with a look at specific issues surrounding burdens, proportionality, and privilege.

Seattle Times Co. v. Rhinehart,

United States Supreme Court
467 U.S. 20 (1984)

Justice POWELL delivered the opinion of the Court.

This case presents the issue whether parties to civil litigation have a First Amendment right to disseminate, in advance of trial, information gained through the pretrial discovery process.

I

Respondent Rhinehart is the spiritual leader of a religious group, the Aquarian Foundation. The Foundation has fewer than 1,000 members, most of whom live in the State of Washington. Aquarian beliefs include life after death and the ability to communicate with the dead through a medium. Rhinehart is the primary Aquarian medium.

In recent years, the Seattle Times and the Walla Walla Union-Bulletin have published stories about Rhinehart and the Foundation. ... They described seances conducted by Rhinehart in which people paid him to put them in touch with deceased relatives and friends. The articles also stated that Rhinehart had sold magical "stones" that had been "expelled" from his body. One article referred to Rhinehart's conviction, later vacated, for sodomy. The four articles that appeared in 1978 concentrated on an "extravaganza" sponsored by Rhinehart at the Walla Walla State Penitentiary. The articles stated that he had treated 1,100 inmates to a 6-hour-long show, during which he gave away between $35,000 and

$50,000 in cash and prizes. One article described a "chorus line of girls [who] shed their gowns and bikinis and sang...." [C] The two articles that appeared in 1979 referred to a purported connection between Rhinehart and Lou Ferrigno, star of the popular television program, "The Incredible Hulk."

II

Rhinehart brought this action in the Washington Superior Court on behalf of himself and the Foundation against the Seattle Times, the Walla Walla Union-Bulletin, the authors of the articles, and the spouses of the authors. Five female members of the Foundation who had participated in the presentation at the penitentiary joined the suit as plaintiffs.[fn] The complaint alleges that the articles contained statements that were "fictional and untrue," and that the defendants—petitioners here—knew, or should have known, they were false. ...

... Petitioners promptly initiated extensive discovery. ... Respondents turned over a number of financial documents, including several of Rhinehart's income tax returns. Respondents refused, however, to disclose certain financial information,[fn] the identity of the Foundation's donors during the preceding 10 years, and a list of its members during that period.

Petitioners filed a motion under the State's Civil Rule 37 requesting an order compelling discovery.[fn] ... Respondents opposed the motion [and] ... moved for a protective order preventing petitioners from disseminating any information gained through discovery. Respondents noted that petitioners had stated their intention to continue publishing articles about respondents and this litigation, and their intent to use information gained through discovery in future articles.

In a lengthy ruling, the trial court initially granted the motion to compel and ordered respondents to identify all donors who made contributions during the five years preceding the date of the complaint, along with the amounts donated. The court also required respondents to divulge enough membership information to substantiate any claims of diminished membership. ...

Respondents filed a motion for reconsideration in which they renewed their motion for a protective order. They submitted affidavits of several Foundation members to support their request. The affidavits detailed a series of letters and telephone calls defaming the Foundation, its members, and Rhinehart—including several that threatened physical harm to those associated with the Foundation. The affiants also described incidents at the Foundation's headquarters involving attacks, threats, and assaults directed at Foundation members by anonymous individuals and groups. In general, the affidavits averred that public release of the donor lists would adversely affect Foundation membership and income and would subject its members to additional harassment and reprisals.

Persuaded by these affidavits, the trial court issued a protective order covering all information obtained through the discovery process that pertained to "the financial affairs of the various plaintiffs, the names and addresses of Aquarian Foundation members, contributors, or clients, and the names and addresses of those who have been contributors, clients, or donors to any of the various plaintiffs." [C] The order prohibited petitioners from publishing, disseminating, or using the information in any way except where necessary to prepare for and try the case. ...

Respondents appealed from the trial court's production order, and petitioners appealed from the protective order. The Supreme Court of Washington affirmed both. ...

III

Most States, including Washington, have adopted discovery provisions modeled on Rules 26 through 37 of the Federal Rules of Civil Procedure. [C] ...

The Rules do not differentiate between information that is private or intimate and that to which no privacy interests attach. Under the Rules, the only express limitations are that the information sought is not privileged, and is relevant to the subject matter of the pending action. Thus, the Rules often allow extensive intrusion into the affairs of both litigants and third parties.[fn] ...

Petitioners argue that the First Amendment imposes strict limits on the availability of any judicial order that has the effect of restricting expression. ... We think the rule urged by petitioners would impose an unwarranted restriction on the duty and discretion of a trial court to oversee the discovery process.

IV

It is, of course, clear that information obtained through civil discovery authorized by modern rules of civil procedure would rarely, if ever, fall within the classes of unprotected speech identified by decisions of this Court. In this case, as petitioners argue, there certainly is a public interest in knowing more about respondents. This interest may well include most—and possibly all—of what has been discovered as a result of the court's order under Rule 26(b)(1). It does not necessarily follow, however, that a litigant has an unrestrained right to disseminate information that has been obtained through pretrial discovery. ...

A

... As in all civil litigation, petitioners gained the information they wish to disseminate only by virtue of the trial court's discovery processes. ...

... [P]retrial depositions and interrogatories are not public components of a civil trial.[fn] ... Much of the information that surfaces during pretrial discovery may be unrelated, or only tangentially related, to the underlying cause of action. Therefore, restraints placed on discovered, but not yet admitted, information are not a restriction on a traditionally public source of information. ...

... Liberal discovery is provided for the sole purpose of assisting in the preparation and trial, or the settlement, of litigated disputes. Because of the liberality of pretrial discovery permitted by Rule 26(b)(1), it is necessary for the trial court to have the authority to issue protective orders conferred by Rule 26(c). It is clear from experience that pretrial discovery by depositions and interrogatories has a significant potential for abuse.[fn] ... The Rules do not distinguish between public and private information. Nor do they apply only to parties to the litigation, as relevant information in the hands of third parties may be subject to discovery. ...

There is an opportunity, therefore, for litigants to obtain—incidentally or purposefully—information that not only is irrelevant but if publicly released could be damaging to reputation and privacy. ... The prevention of the abuse that can attend the coerced production of information under a State's discovery rule is sufficient justification for the authorization of protective orders.[fn]

V

The facts in this case illustrate the concerns that justifiably may prompt a court to issue a protective order. As we have noted, the trial court's order allowing discovery was extremely broad. It compelled respondents—among other things—to identify all persons who had made donations over a 5-year period to Rhinehart and the Aquarian Foundation, together with the amounts donated. ... The Supreme Court of Washington found that dissemination of this information would "result in annoyance, embarrassment and even oppression." [C] It is sufficient for purposes of our decision that the highest court in the State found no abuse of discretion in the trial court's decision to issue a protective order pursuant to a constitutional state law. We therefore hold that where, as in this case, a protective order is entered on a showing of good cause as required by Rule 26(c), is limited to the context of pretrial civil discovery, and does not restrict the dissemination of the information if gained from other sources, it does not offend the First Amendment.[fn]

The judgment accordingly is

Affirmed.

Justice BRENNAN, with whom Justice MARSHALL joins, concurring[, omitted].

INQUIRY

Balancing. Courts balance a range of factors when determining whether to grant a protective order under FED. R. CIV. P. 26(c). Although high-ranking officials would ordinarily be subject to discovery only in rare cases so as not to paralyze the workings of government, *see* Arnold v. Pennsylvania Dept. of Transp., 477 F.3d 105 (3d Cir. 2007), in an appropriate case even a sitting president has responded to discovery in a civil case including giving a deposition and answering interrogatories. *See* Clinton v. Jones, 520 U.S. 681, 691n.14 (1997). Should a blood bank have to disclose donor identities to a person who alleges having received an HIV-tainted infusion? *See* Rasmussen v. South Florida Blood Service, Inc., 500 So..2d 533 (Fla. 1987). Should a life insurance company be able to disinter a body to prove that the death was a suicide? *See* Mutual of Omaha Ins. Co. v. Garrigan, 285 N.E.2d 395, 396-397 (Ohio 1971). Should a defendant hospital be permitted to depose a suicidal minor whose parents allege that she was sexually abused there? *See* Bucher v. Richardson Hosp. Authority, 160 F.R.D. 88 (D.C. Tex. 1994). Stipulated orders limiting the scope, duration, disclosure, and uses of discovery may help parties resolve issues where the interests are shared, compelling, or likely to be protected by the trial court.

1. Burden and Proportionality

In many discovery disputes, parties and non-parties resist disclosure not because the disclosure will affect the litigation but affect the discloser's own interests. Responding to discovery can take substantial time, personnel, resources, and attention away from more productive activities. Responding to discovery can have direct financial costs as personnel search for, gather, copy, organize, and produce documents and things. It can also destroy the proprietary value of confidential business information. *See, e.g.,* Cardenas v. Dorel Juvenile Group, Inc., 230 F.R.D. 635, 638 (D. Kan. 2005) (protecting trade secrets). It can also cause indirect business goodwill or personal loss. How should a trial court decide the limits of discovery when there are obvious burdens on the discloser but also obvious need for the disclosure? Rule 26(b)(2)(C) urges the trial court to consider the benefit and burden of disclosure, its need, the resources of the one responding, the amount in controversy, and the significance of the issues and request. It is a case-specific inquiry. While the technique does not solve all problems, one way in which trial courts relieve some of the burden is to condition compliance with a discovery request on the requester paying the discloser's costs. *See* Oppenheimer Fund, Inc. v. sanders, 437 U.S. 340, 358 (1978). Consider the following case illustrating the discretion that a trial court has in shaping the appropriate limits of discovery and imposing reasonable terms.

Gonzales v. Google, Inc.,

United States District Court for the Northern District of California
234 F.R.D. 674 (2006)

WARE, District Judge.

I. INTRODUCTION

This case raises three vital interests: (1) the national interest in a judicial system to reach informed decisions through the power of a subpoena to compel a third party to produce relevant information; (2) the third-party's interest in not being compelled by a subpoena to reveal confidential business information and devote resources to a distant litigation; and (3) the interest of individuals in freedom from general surveillance by the Government of their use of the Internet or other communications media.

... United States Attorney General Alberto R. Gonzales has subpoenaed Google, Inc., ("Google") to compile and produce a massive amount of information from Google's search index, and to turn over a significant number of search queries entered by Google users. ... [T]he Government filed the present Miscellaneous Action in this District to compel Google to comply with the subpoena. ... At that hearing, the Government made a significantly scaled-down request from the information it originally sought. For the reasons explained in this Order, the motion to compel, as modified, is GRANTED as to the sample of URLs from Google search index and DENIED as to the sample of users' search queries from Google's query log.

II. PROCEDURAL BACKGROUND

In 1998, Congress enacted the Child Online Protection Act ("COPA"), which is now codified as 47 U.S.C. § 231. COPA prohibits the knowing making of a communication by means of the World Wide Web, "for commercial purposes that is available to any minor and that includes material that is harmful to minors," subject to certain affirmative defenses. [C] For this purpose, the statute defines the phrase "material that is harmful to minors" to mean material that is ... obscene... .

Upon enactment of COPA, the American Civil Liberties Union and several other plaintiffs ("Plaintiffs") filed an action in the Eastern District of Pennsylvania, challenging the constitutionality of the Act. The district court granted Plaintiffs' motion for a preliminary injunction on the grounds that COPA is likely to be found unconstitutional on its face for violating the First Amendment rights of adults. ...

The Supreme Court affirmed the preliminary injunction and held that there was an insufficient record before it by which the Government could carry its burden to show that less restrictive alternatives may be more effective than the provisions of COPA. Ashcroft v. ACLU, 542 U.S. 656, 673[] (2004). Of these alternatives directed at preventing minors from viewing "harmful to minors" material on the Internet, the Court focused on blocking and filtering software programs which "impose selective restrictions on speech at the receiving end, not universal restrictions at the source." [C] To "allow the parties to update and supplement the factual record to reflect current technological realities," the Court remanded the case for a trial on the merits. [C]

... [I]n preparing its defense, the Government initiated a study designed to somehow test the effectiveness of blocking and filtering software. To provide it with data for its study, the Government served a subpoena on Google... [requiring it to] produce a designated listing of the URLs which would be available to a user of their services. ...

... Following further negotiations with Google, the Government narrowed this request to all queries that have been entered on the Google search engine during a one-week period. During the course of the present Miscellaneous Action, the Government further restricted the scope of its request, and now represents that it only requires 5,000 entries from Google's query log in order to meet its discovery needs.

Despite these modifications in the scope of the subpoena, Google maintained its objection to the Government's requests. Before the Court is a motion to compel Google to comply with the modified subpoena, namely, for a sample of 50,000 URLs from Google's search index and 5,000 search queries entered by Google's users from Google's query log.

III. STANDARDS

Rule 45 of the Federal Rules of Civil Procedure governs discovery of nonparties by subpoena. [C] The Advisory Committee Notes to the 1970 Amendment to Rule 45 state that the "scope of discovery through a subpoena is the same as that applicable to Rule 34 and other discovery rules." [C] Under Rule 34, the rule governing the production of documents between parties, the proper scope of discovery is as specified in Rule 26(b). [Cc]

Rule 26(b), in turn, permits the discovery of any non-privileged material "relevant to the claim or defense of any party," where "relevant information need not be admissible at trial if the discovery appears reasonably calculated to lead to the discovery of admissible evidence." [C] ...

Rule 26 also specifies that "[a]ll discovery is subject to the limitations imposed by Rule 26(b)(2)[(C)](i), (ii), and (iii)" which requires that discovery methods be limited where: "(i) the discovery sought is unreasonably cumulative or duplicative, or is obtainable from some source that is more convenient, less burdensome, or less expensive; (ii) the party seeking discovery has had ample opportunity by discovery in the action to obtain the information sought; or (iii) the burden or expense of the proposed discovery outweighs its likely benefit, taking into account the needs of the case, the amount in controversy, the parties' resources, the importance of the issues at stake in the litigation, and the importance of the proposed discovery in resolving the issues." The Advisory Committee Notes to the 1983 amendments to Rule 26 state that "[t]he objective is to guard against redundant or disproportionate discovery by giving the court authority to reduce the amount of discovery that may be directed to matters that are otherwise proper subjects of inquiry." …

In addition to the discovery standards under Rule 26 incorporated by Rule 45, Rule 45 itself provides that "on timely motion, the court by which a subpoena was issued shall quash or modify the subpoena if it ... subjects a person to undue burden." Rule 45(3)(A). … Thus, a court determining the propriety of a subpoena balances the relevance of the discovery sought, the requesting party's need, and the potential hardship to the party subject to the subpoena. [C]

IV. DISCUSSION

Google primarily argues that the information sought by the subpoena is not reasonably calculated to lead to evidence admissible in the underlying litigation, and that the production of information is unduly burdensome. …

A. Relevance

Any information sought by means of a subpoena must be relevant to the claims and defenses in the underlying case. …

1. Sample of URLs

As narrowed by negotiations with Google and through the course of this Miscellaneous Action, the Government now seeks a sample of 50,000 URLs from Google's search index. In determining whether the information sought is reasonably calculated to lead to admissible evidence, the party seeking the information must first provide the Court with its plans for the requested information. [C] …

Based on the Government's statement that this information is to act as a "test set for the study" (Reply at 3:20) and a general statement that the purpose of the study is to "evaluate the effectiveness of content filtering software," (Reply at 3:2-5) the Court is able to envision a study whereby a sample of 50,000 URLs from the Google search index may be reasonably calculated to lead to admissible evidence on measuring the effectiveness of filtering software. …

… Given the broad definition of relevance in Rule 26, and the current narrow scope of the subpoena, despite the vagueness with which the Government has disclosed its study, the Court gives the Government the benefit of the doubt. The Court finds that 50,000 URLs randomly selected from Google's data base for use in a scientific study of the effectiveness of filters is relevant to the issues in the [underlying] case… .

2. Search Queries

In its original subpoena the Government sought a listing of the text of all search queries entered by Google users over a two month period. … The Government has narrowed its request so that it now seeks only a sample of 5,000 such queries from Google's query log. … To the extent that the URLs obtained by the researchers as a result of running the search queries provided are then used to create "a sample of a relevant population of websites that can be categorized and used to test filtering software" [c] similar to the sample created from URLs from Google's search index, the Court finds that were the Government to run these URLs through the filtering software and analyze the results, the information sought would be reasonably calculated to lead to admissible evidence.

B. Undue Burden

This Court is particularly concerned anytime enforcement of a subpoena imposes an economic burden on a non-party. Under Rule 45(3)(a), a court may modify or quash a subpoena even for relevant information if it finds that there is an undue burden on the non-party. ...

1. Technological Burden of Production

Google argues that it faces an undue burden because it does not maintain search query or URL information in the ordinary course of business in the format requested by the Government. [C] As a general rule, non-parties are not required to create documents that do not exist, simply for the purposes of discovery. [C] In this case, however, Google has not represented that it is unable to extract the information requested from its existing systems. ... Because the Government has agreed to compensate Google for the reasonable costs of production, and given the extremely scaled-down scope of the subpoena as modified, the Court does not find that the technical burden of production excuses Google from complying with the subpoena. ...

2. Potential for Loss of User Trust

Google also argues that it will be unduly burdened by loss of user trust if forced to produce its users' queries to the Government. ...

Google's own privacy statement indicates that Google users could not reasonably expect Google to guard the query log from disclosure to the Government. ... Google's privacy policy indicates that it has not suggested to its users that non-"personal information" such as that sought by the Government is kept confidential.

However, even if an expectation by Google users that Google would prevent disclosure to the Government of its users' search queries is not entirely reasonable, the statistic cited by Dr. Stark that over a quarter of all Internet searches are for pornography ([c]), indicates that at least some of Google's users expect some sort of privacy in their searches.[fn] The expectation of privacy by some Google users may not be reasonable, but may nonetheless have an appreciable impact on the way in which Google is perceived, and consequently the frequency with which users use Google. ...

3. Trade Secret

Rule 45(c)(3)(B) provides additional protections where a subpoena seeks trade secret or confidential commercial information from a nonparty. Once the nonparty shows that the requested information is a trade secret or confidential commercial information, the burden shifts to the requesting party to show a "substantial need for the testimony or material that cannot be otherwise met without undue hardship and assures that the person to whom the subpoena is addressed will be reasonably compensated." Rule 45(c)(3)(B). ...

a. Search Index and Query Log as Trade Secrets

The disclosure of a statistically significant sample of Google's search index or query log may permit competitors to estimate information about Google's indexing methods or Google's users. [C] By declaration, Google represents that it does not share this information with third parties and it has security procedures to maintain the confidentiality of this information. [C] ...

b. Entanglement in the Underlying Litigation

Google's remaining trade secret argument is that despite the narrowness of the sample provided, it would become entangled in the underlying litigation where further discovery would risk trade secret disclosure. ...

... In litigation where the ultimate question is not whether there is adult material on the Internet, but fundamentally about limiting the access by minors to such adult material, it is quite likely that Plaintiffs will challenge the sample produced by Google as not representative of what minors search for or encounter on the Internet. Such an inquiry would require additional discovery, some of which may implicate Google's confidential commercial information. ... [T]his Court is concerned that a narrow sample of Google's proprietary index and query log, while in itself not likely to lead to the disclosure of confidential information, may act as the thin blade of the wedge in exposing Google to potential disclosure of its confidential commercial information.

c. Substantial Need

The burden thus shifts to the Government to demonstrate that the requested discovery is relevant and essential to a judicial determination of its case. [C] ... [T]he district court's role in this inquiry is to balance the need for the trade secrets against the claim of injury resulting from disclosure. ...

Google contends that it should not be compelled to produce its search index or query log because the information sought by the Government is readily available from open URL databases such as Alexa and transparent search engines such as Dogpile, or that the Government already has sufficient information from AOL, Yahoo, and Microsoft. ...

... In this case, the Government has demonstrated a substantial need for some information from Google in creating a set of URLs to run through filtering software. It is uncontested that Google is the market leader with over 45% of the search engine market. [C] Because Google has the greatest market share, the Government's study may be significantly hampered if it did not have access to some information from the most often used search engine.

4. Cumulative and Duplicative Discovery

What the Government has not demonstrated, however, is a substantial need for *both* the information contained in the sample of URLs and sample of search query text. ... From this Court's interpretation of the Government's general statements of purpose for the information requested, both the sample of URLs and the set of search queries are aimed at providing a list of URLs which will be categorized and run through the filtering software in an effort to determine the effectiveness of filtering software as to certain categories. ...

Faced with duplicative discovery, and with the Government not expressing a preference as to which source of the test set of URLs it prefers, this Court exercises its discretion pursuant to Rule 26(b)(2) and determines that the marginal burden of loss of trust by Google's users based on Google's disclosure of its users' search queries to the Government outweighs the duplicative disclosure's likely benefit to the Government's study. Accordingly, the Court grants the Government's motion to compel only as to the sample of 50,000 URLs from Google's search index.

C. Protective Order

As trade secret or confidential business information, Google's production of a list of URLs to the Government shall be protected by protective order. ...

The Court grants the motion to compel as to a set of 50,000 URLs from Google's search index and orders the parties to show cause... why a designation of the produced information as "Confidential" under the existing protective order is insufficient protection for Google's confidential commercial information.

D. Privacy

The Court raises, sua sponte, its concerns about the privacy of Google's users apart from Google's business goodwill argument. …

The Government contends that there are no privacy issues raised by its request for the text of search queries because the mere text of the queries would not yield identifiable information. …

… In the end, the Court need not express an opinion on this *688 issue because the Government's motion is granted only as to the sample of URLs and not as to the log of search queries. …

V. CONCLUSION

… With these limitations, for the reasons stated in this Order, unless the parties agree otherwise on or before April 3, 2006, Google is ordered to confer with the Government to develop a protocol for the random selection and afterward immediate production of a listing of 50,000 URLs in Google's database on the following conditions:

1. In the development or implementation of the protocol, Google shall not be required to disclose proprietary information with respect to its database;

2. The Government shall pay the reasonable cost incurred by Google in the formulation and implementation of the extraction protocol;

3. Any information disclosed in response to this Order shall be subject to the protective order in the underlying case;

To the extent the motion seeks an order compelling Google to disclose search queries of its users the motion is DENIED. The Court retains jurisdiction to enforce this Order.

Biography

Albert Gidari, Jr., who successfully defended Google, Inc., in the above case, is a partner in the Seattle law firm Perkins Coie. He represents corporate clients on privacy, Internet, security, electronic surveillance, and communications law. His practice includes both civil and criminal litigation, while also editing his law firm's Internet blog DigestibleLaw.com. Most recently, he developed a best-practices guide adopted by the wireless services industry for location-based services for asset tracking, public safety, and law enforcement. He is also a co-founder of the Internet Law and Policy Forum addressing issues raised by the global nature of the Internet.

2. Electronically Stored Information

Much of the case law and many of the rules and conventions on discovery practice assume that the burdens have to do with locating, searching, copying, organizing, and producing large quantities of paper documents. The above case intimates the new environment in which discovery disputes often arise today, having to do with electronically stored information. One might think that discovery would become easier with the advent of electronic storage. It does not. While the physical aspects of storage, search, retrieval, copying, and production may ease with electronically stored information when compared to paper documents, the time and technical aspects do not. Persons and entities generate and store vastly larger quantities of information using electronic production and communication than they once did with paper. The format of electronic information is also vastly more diverse, fluid, and fast-changing, meaning that it is much more capable of intentional destruction or unintentional loss. The highly trained personnel and sophisticated software and hardware necessary to locating, searching, copying, organizing, and producing electronically stored information can be vastly more expensive than the labor and equipment necessary to reproducing paper documents. Whereas complex discovery of voluminous documents was once the preserve of skilled experienced lawyers directing office managers and clerks, technology consultants having special litigation expertise dominate its electronic iteration.

The *Federal Rules of Civil Procedure* responded to this challenge with amendments to FED. R. CIV. P. 26 effective December 1, 2006. Those amendments added Rule 26(b)(2)(B) titled "Specific Limitations on Electronically Stored Information." Rule 26(b)(2)(B) permits a party to refuse discovery when electronically stored information is "not reasonably accessible because of undue burden or cost." Rule 26(b)(2)(B) sounds simple enough in limiting burdensome disclosure. FED. R. CIV. P. 37(e), constituting a provision of the general Rule 37 on enforcement of discovery requests, even offers a safe harbor when "electronically stored information [is] lost as a result of the routine, good-faith operation of an electronic system." In such cases, Rule 37(e) provides that the trial court may not impose sanctions for the failure to produce such evidence "[a]bsent exceptional circumstances" warranting those sanctions. The Advisory Committee Note to Rule 37(e) recognizes that the "routine operation" of electronic information systems "includes the alteration and overwriting of information, often without the operator's specific direction or awareness, a feature with no direct counterpart in hard-copy documents." The *Federal Rules of Civil Procedure* clearly appreciate the difficulty of capturing, preserving, and producing electronically stored information, especially when for corporate entities when it is produced by and within the electronic control of many employees.

In practice, though, the subject of the discovery of electronically stored information is far more complex. Recall the principle of spoliation that intentional or negligent destruction of evidence can lead to sanctions. Although persons and entities, or the electronic information systems that they use, routinely destroy electronically stored information in the ordinary course, when those persons or entities should anticipate that the information may be or become evidence in civil litigation, routine destruction becomes sanctionable spoliation. Thus the emerging practice of competent counsel is to immediately notify a client to institute a litigation hold on electronically stored information whenever it is or may become evidence in litigation. A litigation hold communicates the nature of the evidence, where it is likely to be located, how to preserve it, and who is responsible for collecting it and ensuring compliance with the hold procedure. Credit for Rule 26's amendment and for bringing attention to discovery procedures for electronically stored information goes to United States District Court Judge Shira Scheindlin of the Southern District of New York for her several *Zubulake* opinions. *See, e.g.*, Zubulake v. UBS Warburg LLC, 217 F.R.D. 309 (S.D. N.Y. 2003). Read her most recent opinion reflecting on *Zubulake* and summarizing the field.

Pension Committee of University of Montreal Pension Plan v. Banc of America Securities,

United States District Court for the Southern District of New York
685 F.Supp.2d 456 (2010)

SHIRA A. SCHEINDLIN, District Judge:

Zubulake Revisited: Six Years Later

I. INTRODUCTION

In an era where vast amounts of electronic information is available for review, discovery in certain cases has become increasingly complex and expensive. Courts cannot and do not expect that any party can meet a standard of perfection. Nonetheless, the courts have a right to expect that litigants and counsel will take the necessary steps to ensure that relevant records are preserved when litigation is reasonably anticipated, and that such records are collected, reviewed, and produced to the opposing party. As discussed six years ago in the *Zubulake* opinions, when this does not happen, the integrity of the judicial process is harmed and the courts are required to fashion a remedy. Once again, I have been compelled to closely review the discovery efforts of parties in a litigation, and once again have found that those efforts were flawed. As famously noted, "[t]hose who cannot remember the past are condemned to repeat it."[Fn1. GEORGE SANTAYANA, REASON IN COMMON SENSE.] By now, it should be abundantly clear that the duty to preserve means what it says and that a failure to preserve records—paper or electronic—and to search in the right places for those records, will inevitably result in the spoliation of evidence.

In February, 2004, a group of investors brought this action to recover losses of 550 million dollars stemming from the liquidation of two British Virgin Islands based hedge funds in which they held shares... . Plaintiffs[fn] have asserted claims under the federal securities laws ... against ... the Funds.[fn] ... The Funds retained Citco Fund Services (Curacao) N.V. ("Citco NV") to perform certain administrative duties... .

... [D]uring the discovery process, Citco NV, its parent company, the Citco Group Limited, and former Lancer Offshore directors who were Citco officers (collectively with Citco NV, the "Citco Defendants") claimed that substantial gaps were found in plaintiffs' document productions. ... Following the close of this discovery, the Citco Defendants moved for sanctions, alleging that each plaintiff failed to preserve and produce documents—including those stored electronically—and submitted false and misleading declarations regarding their document collection and preservation efforts. ...

... Based on my review of the evidence, I conclude that all of these plaintiffs were either negligent or grossly negligent in meeting their discovery obligations. As a result, sanctions are required.

II. AN ANALYTICAL FRAMEWORK AND APPLICABLE LAW

From the outset, it is important to recognize what this case involves and what it does not. This case does not present any egregious examples of litigants purposefully destroying evidence. This is a case where plaintiffs failed to timely institute written litigation holds and engaged in careless and indifferent collection efforts after the duty to preserve arose. As a result, there can be little doubt that some documents were lost or destroyed.

The question, then, is whether plaintiffs' conduct requires this Court to impose a sanction for the spoliation of evidence. To answer this question, there are several concepts that must be carefully reviewed and analyzed. The first is plaintiffs' level of culpability—that is, was their conduct of discovery acceptable or was it negligent, grossly negligent, or willful. The second is the interplay between the duty to preserve evidence and the spoliation of evidence. The third is which party should bear the burden of proving that evidence has been lost or destroyed and the consequences resulting from that loss. And the fourth is the appropriate remedy for the harm caused by the spoliation.

A. Defining Negligence, Gross Negligence, and Willfulness in the Discovery Context

… *[N]egligence* involves unreasonable conduct in that it creates a risk of harm to others, but *willfulness* involves intentional or reckless conduct that is so unreasonable that harm is highly likely to occur. …

… In the discovery context, the[se] standards have been set by years of judicial decisions analyzing allegations of misconduct and reaching a determination as to what a party must do to meet its obligation to participate meaningfully and fairly in the discovery phase of a judicial proceeding. …

… [T]he first step in any discovery effort is the preservation of relevant information. A failure to preserve evidence resulting in the loss or destruction of relevant information is surely negligent, and, depending on the circumstances, may be grossly negligent or willful.[fn] … Possibly after October, 2003, when *Zubulake IV* was issued,[fn] and definitely after July, 2004, when the final relevant *Zubulake* opinion was issued,[fn] the failure to issue a *written* litigation hold constitutes gross negligence because that failure is likely to result in the destruction of relevant information.[fn]

The next step in the discovery process is collection and review. Once again, depending on the extent of the failure to collect evidence, or the sloppiness of the review, the resulting loss or destruction of evidence is surely negligent, and, depending on the circumstances may be grossly negligent or willful. For example, the failure to collect records-either paper or electronic-from key players constitutes gross negligence or willfulness as does the destruction of email or certain backup tapes after the duty to preserve has attached. By contrast, the failure to obtain records from all those employees who had any involvement with the issues raised in the litigation or anticipated litigation, as opposed to key players, could constitute negligence. Similarly, the failure to take all appropriate measures to preserve ESI likely falls in the negligence category.[fn] …

B. The Duty to Preserve and Spoliation

Spoliation refers to the destruction or material alteration of evidence or to the failure to preserve property for another's use as evidence in pending or reasonably foreseeable litigation. … The common law duty to preserve evidence relevant to litigation is well recognized.[fn] The case law makes crystal clear that the breach of the duty to preserve, and the resulting spoliation of evidence, may result in the imposition of sanctions by a court because the court has the obligation to ensure that the judicial process is not abused.[fn]

It is well established that the duty to preserve evidence arises when a party reasonably anticipates litigation.[fn] … A plaintiff's duty is more often triggered before litigation commences, in large part because plaintiffs control the timing of litigation.[fn]

C. Burdens of Proof

The third preliminary matter that must be analyzed is what can be done when documents are no longer available. ...

The burden of proof question differs depending on the severity of the sanction. For less severe sanctions—such as fines and cost-shifting—the inquiry focuses more on the conduct of the spoliating party than on whether documents were lost, and, if so, whether those documents were relevant and resulted in prejudice to the innocent party. As explained more thoroughly below, for more severe sanctions—such as dismissal, preclusion, or the imposition of an adverse inference—the court must consider, in addition to the conduct of the spoliating party, whether any missing evidence was relevant and whether the innocent party has suffered prejudice as a result of the loss of evidence. ...

In short, the innocent party must prove the following three elements: that the spoliating party (1) had control over the evidence and an obligation to preserve it at the time of destruction or loss; (2) acted with a culpable state of mind upon destroying or losing the evidence; and that (3) the missing evidence is relevant to the innocent party's claim or defense.[fn]

Relevance and prejudice may be presumed when the spoliating party acted in bad faith or in a grossly negligent manner. ... However, when the spoliating party was merely negligent, the innocent party must prove both relevance and prejudice in order to justify the imposition of a severe sanction.[fn] ...

No matter what level of culpability is found, any presumption is rebuttable and the spoliating party should have the opportunity to demonstrate that the innocent party has not been prejudiced by the absence of the missing information.[fn] ... While requiring the innocent party to demonstrate the relevance of information that it can never review may seem unfair, the party seeking relief has some obligation to make a showing of relevance and eventually prejudice, lest litigation become a "gotcha" game rather than a full and fair opportunity to air the merits of a dispute. If a presumption of relevance and prejudice were awarded to every party who can show that an adversary failed to produce any document, even if such failure is completely inadvertent, the incentive to find such error and capitalize on it would be overwhelming. This would not be a good thing. ...

D. Remedies

The remaining question is what remedy should the court impose. ... Where the breach of a discovery obligation is the non-production of evidence, a court has broad discretion to determine the appropriate sanction.[fn] ...

It is well accepted that a court should always impose the least harsh sanction that can provide an adequate remedy. The choices include—from least harsh to most harsh—further discovery,[fn] cost-shifting,[fn] fines,[fn] special jury instructions,[fn] preclusion,[fn] and the entry of default judgment or dismissal (terminating sanctions).[fn] ...

The Citco Defendants request dismissal—the most extreme sanction. However, a terminating sanction is justified in only the most egregious cases,[fn] such as where a party has engaged in perjury, tampering with evidence, or intentionally destroying evidence by burning, shredding, or wiping out computer hard drives.[fn] As described below, there is no evidence of such misconduct in this case.

Instead, the appropriate sanction here is some form of an adverse inference instruction that is intended to alleviate the harm suffered by the Citco Defendants. Like many other sanctions, an adverse inference instruction can take many forms, again ranging in degrees of harshness. The harshness of the instruction should be determined based on the nature of the spoliating party's conduct-the more egregious the conduct, the more harsh the instruction.

In its most harsh form, when a spoliating party has acted willfully or in bad faith, a jury can be instructed that certain facts are deemed admitted and must be accepted as true.[fn] …

The least harsh instruction *permits* (but does not require) a jury to *presume* that the lost evidence is both relevant and favorable to the innocent party. …

Monetary sanctions are also appropriate in this case. … This sanction is imposed in order to compensate the Citco Defendants for reviewing the declarations, conducting the additional depositions, and bringing this motion.

Three final notes. *First,* I stress that at the end of the day the judgment call of whether to award sanctions is inherently subjective. A court has a "gut reaction" based on years of experience as to whether a litigant has complied with its discovery obligations and how hard it worked to comply. *Second,* while it would be helpful to develop a list of relevant criteria a court should review in evaluating discovery conduct, these inquiries are inherently fact intensive and must be reviewed case by case. Nonetheless, I offer the following guidance.

… [A]fter the final relevant *Zubulake* opinion in July, 2004, the following failures support a finding of gross negligence, when the duty to preserve has attached: to issue a written litigation hold; to identify all of the key players and to ensure that their electronic and paper records are preserved; to cease the deletion of email or to preserve the records of former employees that are in a party's possession, custody, or control; and to preserve backup tapes when they are the sole source of relevant information or when they relate to key players, if the relevant information maintained by those players is not obtainable from readily accessible sources. …

IV. PLAINTIFFS' EFFORTS AT PRESERVATION AND PRODUCTION

Shortly after its retention in October or November, 2003, Counsel contacted plaintiffs to begin document collection and preservation.[fn] Counsel telephoned and emailed plaintiffs and distribute memoranda instructing plaintiffs to be over, rather than under, inclusive, and noting that emails and electronic documents should be included in the production.[fn] Counsel indicated that the documents were necessary to draft the complaint, although they did not expressly direct that the search be limited to those documents.[fn]

This instruction does not meet the standard for a litigation hold. It does not direct employees to *preserve* all relevant records—both paper and electronic—nor does it create a mechanism for *collecting* the preserved records so that they can be searched by someone other than the employee.[fn] Rather, the directive places total reliance on the employee to search and select what that employee believed to be responsive records without any supervision from Counsel.[fn] Throughout the litigation, Counsel sent plaintiffs monthly case status memoranda, which included additional requests for Lancer-related documents, including electronic documents. But these memoranda never specifically instructed plaintiffs not to destroy records so that Counsel could monitor the collection and production of documents.[fn] ...

... In May, 2007, the Citco Defendants made their first document requests.[fn]

... Depositions ... revealed that there were gaps in plaintiffs' document production.[fn] ... In response to a request from the Citco Defendants, the Court ordered plaintiffs to provide declarations regarding their efforts to preserve and produce documents.[fn]

Counsel spent a huge amount of time preparing the declarations, including drafting, questioning plaintiffs' employees, and attempting to locate documents that had not yet been produced.[fn] Counsel emphasized to each declarant the importance of the declarations' accuracy and that each should be carefully reviewed prior to its execution.[fn] ... Each declarant states that he or she believes the company located, preserved, and produced "all" Lancer-related documents in its possession at the time of either the 2003/2004 search, the 2007/2008 search, or both. Each declarant also states that no responsive documents in plaintiff's possession, custody, or control were discarded or destroyed following a specific point in time—either after the "request to preserve them," a specified date, or after the declarant arrived at the company. ... The Citco Defendants then sought to depose certain declarants and other relevant individuals. The Court granted that request.[fn] The Citco Defendants found additional gaps in plaintiffs' productions. ... In addition, the Citco Defendants discovered that almost all of the declarations were false and misleading and/or executed by a declarant without personal knowledge of its contents.

V. DISCUSSION

A. Duty to Preserve and Document Destruction

By April, 2003, ... Plaintiffs had retained counsel... [and] initiated communication with a number of other plaintiffs. ... Accordingly, each plaintiff was under a duty to preserve at that time. While, as discussed below, the duty to issue a written litigation hold might not have been well established at that time, it was beyond cavil that the duty to preserve evidence included a duty to preserve electronic records.[fn]

The burden then falls to the Citco Defendants to demonstrate that documents were destroyed after the duty to preserve arose. ...

All plaintiffs had a fiduciary duty to conduct due diligence before making significant investments in the Funds. Surely records must have existed documenting the due diligence, investments, and subsequent monitoring of these investments. The paucity of records produced by some plaintiffs[fn] and the admitted failure to preserve some records or search at all for others by all plaintiffs leads inexorably to the conclusion that relevant records have been lost or destroyed.[fn]

B. Culpability**[fn]**

... The Citco Defendants contend that plaintiffs acted willfully or with reckless disregard, such that the sanction of dismissal is warranted.[fn] Plaintiffs admit that they failed to institute written litigation holds until 2007 when they returned their attention to discovery after a four year hiatus. Plaintiffs should have done so no later than 2005, when the action was transferred to this District. This requirement was clearly established in this District by mid 2004, after the last relevant *Zubulake* opinion was issued.[fn] Thus, the failure to do so as of that date was, at a minimum, grossly negligent. The severity of this misconduct would have justified severe sanctions had the Citco Defendants demonstrated that any documents were destroyed *after* 2005. They have not done so.[fn] It is likely that most of the evidence was lost before that date due to the failure to institute written litigation holds. ...

From my review of the evidence... , I conclude that no plaintiff engaged in willful misconduct. However, as outlined below, I find that 2M, Hunnicutt, Coronation, the Chagnon Plaintiffs, Bombardier Trusts, and the Bombardier Foundation acted with gross negligence, and the Altar Fund, L'Ecole Polytechnique, Okabena, the Corbett Foundation, Commonfund, KMEFIC, and UM acted in a negligent manner.

C. Relevance and Prejudice

For those plaintiffs that were grossly negligent, I find that the Citco Defendants have "adduced enough evidence" that plaintiffs have failed to produce relevant documents and that the Citco Defendants have been prejudiced as a result. Thus, a jury will be permitted to presume, if it so chooses, both the relevance of the missing documents and resulting prejudice to the Citco Defendants, subject to the plaintiffs' ability to rebut the presumption to the satisfaction of the trier of fact.

For those plaintiffs that were negligent, the Citco Defendants must demonstrate that any destroyed documents were relevant and the loss was prejudicial. ...

... [I]t is impossible to know the extent of the prejudice suffered by the Citco Defendants as a result of those emails and documents that have been permanently lost due to plaintiffs' conduct. The volume of missing emails and documents can never be learned, nor can their substance be known. ... Given the facts and circumstances presented here, I can only conclude that the Citco Defendants have carried their limited burden[fn] of demonstrating that the lost documents would have been relevant. The documents that no longer exist were created during the critical time period. Key players must have engaged in correspondence regarding the relevant transactions. There can be no serious question that the missing material would have been relevant.

Prejudice is another matter. The Citco Defendants have gathered an enormous amount of discovery—both from documents and witnesses.[fn] Unless they can show through extrinsic evidence that the loss of the documents has prejudiced their ability to defend the case, then a lesser sanction than a spoliation charge is sufficient to address any lapse in the discovery efforts of the negligent plaintiffs. ...

VI. CONCLUSION

For the reasons discussed above, the Citco Defendant's motion for sanctions is granted in part. While litigants are not required to execute document productions with absolute precision, at a minimum they must act diligently and search thoroughly at the time they reasonably anticipate litigation. All of the plaintiffs in this motion failed to do so and have been sanctioned accordingly. ...

INQUIRY

Accessibility. Electronically stored information falls into a range of accessibility. Judge Scheindlin's *Zubulake I* opinion cited above listed five categories of electronic data storage from most to least accessible: (1) active online magnetic disk; (2) near-line robotic library; (3) offline storage archives on removable optical disk or magnetic tape; (4) sequential-format backup tapes; and (5) erased, fragmented, or damaged data. Cost shifting is more appropriate the less accessible is the data. *Zubulake I* listed seven factors for determining when retrieval entails undue burden and expense: (1) the extent to which the requester tailored the request; (2) whether the evidence is available elsewhere; (3) total cost of discovery compared to amount in controversy; (4) total cost of discovery compared to party resources; (5) party ability to control costs; (6) significance of the litigated issues; and (7) benefit of obtaining the information. Notice that these seven factors are a lot like the factors in FED. R. CIV. P. 26(b)(2)(C)(iii) regarding production of non-ESI evidence. The "not reasonably accessible" standard of FED. R. CIV. P. 26(b)(2)(B) is essentially like the undue-burden-and-expense standard for discovering non-ESI evidence. When in *Zubulake III* Judge Scheindlin applied her seven factors, Judge Scheindlin shifted to the individual plaintiffs 25% of the production costs of restoring defendants' backup tapes. Zubulake v. UBS Warburg LLC, 216 F.R.D. 280 (S.D. N.Y. 2003).

Sampling. There are differences, though, in the most efficient manner of responding to a request for electronically stored information. The two cases excerpted above, both *Zubulake I* and *Gonzales v. Google Inc.*, approved a sampling process in which the discloser produces only a portion of the requested electronically stored information—say, a few out of dozens of backup tapes—in order for the requester to determine whether it contains relevant evidence. *See also* McPeek v. Ashcroft, 202 F.R.D. 31 (D. D.C. 2001) (sampling of backup tapes). Sampling can help the parties and court determine whether production is worthwhile. Can you see any hazards to sampling? In many cases involving large organizations and enormous quantities of electronically stored information in which sampling is most appropriate, there is nearly bound to be some arguably privileged (confidential or proprietary) information within the sample. When a party mistakenly produces privileged information, the party may have waived the privilege. (See below for a discussion of privilege waiver.)

Claw Back. To promote sampling without extensive privilege review, parties may negotiate a "quick peek" agreement under which inadvertent disclosure is not a waiver of the privilege. The parties acknowledge in their Rule 26(f)(3)(D) discovery plan that the discloser has not engaged in a pre-production privilege review. The requester agrees to return any privileged information within the sample and not to use it in the litigation. The requester must also designate and seal any arguably privileged information in order for the discloser to advocate to the trial court that it order the information returned. The parties may also agree, or the court may impose, a "claw back" term in which, when the discloser discovers that it disclosed privileged information, it may instruct that the requester return and not use it. The court may condition sampling on the requester agreeing to quick-peek and claw-back terms. *See, e.g.*, Zubulake v. UBS Warburg, LLC (*Zubulake III*), 216 F.R.D. 280, 290 (S.D. N.Y. 2003). Together, these terms loosen traditional restraints on disclosure, reducing the cost of production by eliminating or decreasing pre-production privilege review. Rule 26(b)(5)(B) adopts a similar claw-back approach without restricting it to negotiated agreements involving discovery of electronically stored information. Before exploring these issues further in the context of the discovery of electronically stored information, consider the following introduction on discovery practices surrounding the law of privilege.

3. Privilege

FED. R. CIV. P. 26 requires production only of that relevant evidence which is not privileged. With privilege, the evidence that the person or entity holds is relevant, but there are other stronger reasons not to require the person or entity to disclose it. The party seeking the evidence must obtain it from some other source. The law grants privileges around relationships—inter-spousal, attorney-client, physician-patient—having greater value than the discovery and dispute-resolution process would gain by ignoring them. It also grants privileges to protect the integrity of judicial processes, such as the Fifth Amendment privilege against self-incrimination. FED. R. EVID. 501 identifies the common law as the source of privileges. Privilege is the subject of substantive state or federal law. Rule 501 states that "privilege ... shall be governed by the principles of the common law as they may be interpreted by the courts of the United States in the light of reason and experience," unless state laws supply the rule of decision, in which case "privilege ... shall be determined in accordance with State law." Although discovery requests may impinge upon any privilege, this section addresses only the attorney-client and attorney-work-product privileges, both of which are present in most cases. Nearly any time that a party makes a discovery request, the potential exists for it to involve one of those two privileges. Practitioners tend to have these two privileges in mind whenever responding and objecting to discovery requests.

The attorney-client privilege protects confidential communications between attorney and client (including prospective clients) regarding the subject matter of the representation, so long as they maintain the communication as confidential and do not engage in it to commit a crime or tort. *See* Rhone-Poulenc Rorer Inc. v. Home Indem. Co., 32 F.3d 851, 862 (3d Cir. 1994); *see also* United States v. United Shoe Machinery Corp., 89 F. Supp. 357, 358-359 (D. Mass. 1950). The privilege is not so complex when the client is an individual. A party would not produce copies of confidential correspondence or emails between lawyer and client regarding the subject matter of the representation. The privilege grows substantially more complex when the client is a corporation. One might think that the privilege would apply only to communications between the corporation's lawyers and corporate managers, as is true in some state courts applying a "control group" test. *See, e.g.,* Consolidation Coal Co. v. Bucyrus-Erie Co., 432 N.E.2d 250 (Ill. 1982). Yet as the following Supreme Court opinion established for federal proceedings (other than those involving diversity jurisdiction, *see* Valente v. Pepsico, Inc., 68 F.R.D. 361, 366n.10 (D. Del. 1975)), there are good reasons to extend the privilege to communications between the corporation's lawyers and any corporate employee. Indeed, the attorney-client privilege applies not only to communications between the lawyer and any employee of the corporation regarding the representation but also to confidential communications among employees for providing the lawyer with information on which to provide legal counsel. Consider the reasons articulated by the following case.

Upjohn Co. v. United States,

United States Supreme Court
449 U.S. 383 (1981)

Justice REHNQUIST delivered the opinion of the Court.

We granted certiorari in this case to address important questions concerning the scope of the attorney-client privilege in the corporate context... . [C] ... We ... conclude that the attorney-client privilege protects the communications involved in this case from compelled disclosure... .

I

Petitioner Upjohn Co. manufactures and sells pharmaceuticals here and abroad. In January 1976 independent accountants conducting an audit of one of Upjohn's foreign subsidiaries discovered that the subsidiary made payments to or for the benefit of foreign government officials in order to secure government business. The accountants so informed petitioner, Mr. Gerard Thomas, Upjohn's Vice President, Secretary, and General Counsel. Thomas is a member of the Michigan and New York Bars, and has been Upjohn's General Counsel for 20 years. He consulted with outside counsel and R. T. Parfet, Jr., Upjohn's Chairman of the Board. It was decided that the company would conduct an internal investigation of what were termed "questionable payments." As part of this investigation the attorneys prepared a letter containing a questionnaire which was sent to "All Foreign General and Area Managers" over the Chairman's signature. The letter began by noting recent disclosures that several American companies made "possibly illegal" payments to foreign government officials and emphasized that the management needed full information concerning any such payments made by Upjohn. The letter indicated that the Chairman had asked Thomas, identified as "the company's General Counsel," "to conduct an investigation for the purpose of determining the nature and magnitude of any payments made by the Upjohn Company or any of its subsidiaries to any employee or official of a foreign government." The questionnaire sought detailed information concerning such payments. Managers were instructed to treat the investigation as "highly confidential" and not to discuss it with anyone other than Upjohn employees who might be helpful in providing the requested information. Responses were to be sent directly to Thomas. Thomas and outside counsel also interviewed the recipients of the questionnaire and some 33 other Upjohn officers or employees as part of the investigation.

On March 26, 1976, the company voluntarily submitted a preliminary report to the Securities and Exchange Commission on Form 8-K disclosing certain questionable payments.[fn] A copy of the report was simultaneously submitted to the Internal Revenue Service, which immediately began an investigation to determine the tax consequences of the payments. ... [T]he Service issued a summons pursuant to 26 U.S.C. § 7602 demanding production of: "All files relative to the investigation conducted under the supervision of Gerard Thomas to identify payments to employees of foreign governments... . The records should include but not be limited to written questionnaires sent to managers of the Upjohn Company's foreign affiliates, and memorandums or notes of the interviews conducted in the United States and abroad with officers and employees of the Upjohn Company and its subsidiaries." [C] The company declined to produce the documents ... on the grounds that they were protected from disclosure by the attorney-client privilege and constituted the work product of attorneys prepared in anticipation of litigation. ... [T]he United States filed a petition seeking enforcement of the summons under 26 U.S.C. §§7402(b) and 7604(a) in the United States District Court for the Western District of Michigan[, which] ... concluded that the summons should be enforced. ... [T]he Sixth Circuit ... agreed that the privilege did not apply "[t]o the extent that the communications were made by officers and agents not responsible for directing Upjohn's actions in response to legal advice ... for the simple reason that the communications were not the 'client's.'" [C] ...

II

Federal Rule of Evidence 501 provides that "the privilege of a witness ... shall be governed by the principles of the common law as they may be interpreted by the courts of the United States in light of reason and experience." The attorney-client privilege is the oldest of the privileges for confidential communications known to the common law. [C] Its purpose is to encourage full and frank communication between attorneys and their clients and thereby promote broader public interests in the observance of law and administration of justice. The privilege recognizes that sound legal advice or advocacy serves public ends and that such advice or advocacy depends upon the lawyer's being fully informed by the client. As we stated last Term in Trammel v. United States, 445 U.S. 40, 51[] (1980): "The lawyer-client privilege rests on the need for the advocate and counselor to know all that relates to the client's reasons for seeking representation if the professional mission is to be carried out." And in Fisher v. United States, 425 U.S. 391, 403[] (1976), we recognized the purpose of the privilege to be "to encourage clients to make full disclosure to their attorneys." ... Admittedly complications in the application of the privilege arise when the client is a corporation, which in theory is an artificial creature of the law, and not an individual; but this Court has assumed that the privilege applies when the client is a corporation. United States v. Louisville & Nashville R. Co., 236 U.S. 318, 336[] (1915), and the Government does not contest the general proposition.

The Court of Appeals, however, considered the application of the privilege in the corporate context to present a "different problem," since the client was an inanimate entity and "only the senior management, guiding and integrating the several operations, ... can be said to possess an identity analogous to the corporation as a whole" ... [known as] the so-called "control group test" ... . Such a view, we think, overlooks the fact that the privilege exists to protect not only the giving of professional advice to those who can act on it but also the giving of information to the lawyer to enable him to give sound and informed advice. [Cc] The first step in the resolution of any legal problem is ascertaining the factual background and sifting through the facts with an eye to the legally relevant. ...

In the case of the individual client the provider of information and the person who acts on the lawyer's advice are one and the same. In the corporate context, however, it will frequently be employees beyond the control group as defined by the court below—"officers and agents ... responsible for directing [the company's] actions in response to legal advice"—who will possess the information needed by the corporation's lawyers. Middle-level-and indeed lower-level-employees can, by actions within the scope of their employment, embroil the corporation in serious legal difficulties, and it is only natural that these employees would have the relevant information needed by corporate counsel if he is adequately to advise the client with respect to such actual or potential difficulties. ...

The control group test adopted by the court below thus frustrates the very purpose of the privilege by discouraging the communication of relevant information by employees of the client to attorneys seeking to render legal advice to the client corporation. The attorney's advice will also frequently be more significant to noncontrol group members than to those who officially sanction the advice, and the control group test makes it more difficult to convey full and frank legal advice to the employees who will put into effect the client corporation's policy. [Cc]

The narrow scope given the attorney-client privilege by the court below not only makes it difficult for corporate attorneys to formulate sound advice when their client is faced with a specific legal problem but also threatens to limit the valuable efforts of corporate counsel to ensure their client's compliance with the law. In light of the vast and complicated array of regulatory legislation confronting the modern corporation, corporations, unlike most individuals, "constantly go to lawyers to find out how to obey the law," [c] ... .

The communications at issue were made by Upjohn employees[fn] to counsel for Upjohn acting as such, at the direction of corporate superiors in order to secure legal advice from counsel. ... Information, not available from upper-echelon management, was needed to supply a basis for legal advice concerning compliance with securities and tax laws, foreign laws, currency regulations, duties to shareholders, and potential litigation in each of these areas.[fn] The communications concerned matters within the scope of the employees' corporate duties, and the employees themselves were sufficiently aware that they were being questioned in order that the corporation could obtain legal advice. ... Consistent with the underlying purposes of the attorney-client privilege, these communications must be protected against compelled disclosure.

... Here the Government was free to question the employees who communicated with Thomas and outside counsel. Upjohn has provided the IRS with a list of such employees, and the IRS has already interviewed some 25 of them. While it would probably be more convenient for the Government to secure the results of petitioner's internal investigation by simply subpoenaing the questionnaires and notes taken by petitioner's attorneys, such considerations of convenience do not overcome the policies served by the attorney-client privilege. ...

... [W]e conclude that the narrow "control group test" sanctioned by the Court of Appeals, in this case cannot, consistent with "the principles of the common law as ... interpreted ... in the light of reason and experience," Fed. Rule Evid. 501, govern the development of the law in this area. ...

Accordingly, the judgment of the Court of Appeals is reversed, and the case remanded for further proceedings.

It is so ordered.

Chief Justice BURGER, concurring in part and concurring in the judgment[, omitted].

> ***Practice***
>
> The lawyer flipped the interrogatories open to the first numbered demand. Predictably, it asked that the lawyer's client disclose the identity and role of every person who helped to prepare each answer to each of the following interrogatories, and the information those persons provided. Lawyers and their staff prepare interrogatory answers based on a variety of client and file information before the client reviews, corrects, approves, and attests to the answers. So the lawyer began typing the stock objection to this predictable first request, that the client was entitled to the assistance of counsel who also had duties with respect to the preparation of the answers, and that the nature of that assistance and legal advice communicated in the course of it were subject to the attorney-client privilege.

INQUIRY

Waiver. A party waives the attorney-client privilege by intentionally disclosing the information outside of the privilege. *See, e.g.*, Nguyen v. Excel Corp., 197 F.3d 200, 206 (5th Cir. 1999) (intentional disclosure of a portion waives privilege as to remainder). A party may also waive the attorney-client privilege by inadvertent disclosure. The courts disagree over whether purely inadvertent disclosures waive the attorney-client privilege. They also disagree over whether, once a party discloses a particular communication within the attorney-client privilege, the party has waived the privilege as to all other communications on the same subject matter. *See* In re Sealed Case, 877 F.2d 976, 980-981 (D.C. Cir. 1989) (waiver covers all communications on same subject); *but see* In re von Bulow, 828 F.2d 94, 102 (2d Cir 1987) (waiver extends only to disclosed communication, not non-disclosed communications on same subject matter). Can you foresee how the doctrine of waiver can increase the cost of discovery production in certain cases? Attorneys are rightly reluctant to produce by mistake privileged information, given the law of waiver. Yet the cost of pre-production review can be enormous—larger than any other cost associated with discovery of electronically stored information—when the quantity of information a party must produce is large. *See, e.g.,* Rowe Entertainment, Inc. v. William Morris Agency, 205 F.R.D. 421, 425-426 (S.D. N.Y. 2002) ($395,944 estimated cost for pre-production review of sample of email and $9,750,000 estimated cost for full review). What is a party to do?

Non-Waiver Agreements. The quick-peek and claw-back terms described above in the section on electronically stored information ameliorate some of the concern regarding inadvertent waiver of privileges. Yet protective quick-peek and claw-back terms may only bind parties to the agreements containing those terms. *See* Bowne of New York City, Inc.v. AmBase Corp., 150 F.R.D. 465, 478-479 (S.D. N.Y. 1993) (non-party not bound by non-waiver agreement). Rule 26(b)(5)(B) adopting a similar claw-back approach for privilege disputes in general might seem to broaden the protection against waiver. Yet recall that under the Rules Enabling Act, 28 U.S.C.

§2072, the *Federal Rules of Civil Procedure* do not "abridge, enlarge, or modify" substantive rights. The applicable law of privilege waiver, not Rule 26(b)(5)(B), would govern in unrelated proceedings. *See* Westinghouse Elec. Corp. v. Republic of the Philippines, 951 F.2d 1414, 1426-1427 (3d Cir. 1991). Negotiated non-waiver agreements, imposed non-waiver terms, and reliance on Rule 26(b)(5)(B) still makes sense to bind parties. In the end, though, pre-production privilege review may be the only way to ensure non-waiver as to non-parties. Consider the following case.

Hopson v. Mayor of Baltimore,

United States District Court for the District of Maryland
232 F.R.D. 228 (2005)

GRIMM, United States Magistrate Judge.

This case has been referred to me for resolution of all discovery disputes. ... Plaintiffs have asserted putative class claims and individual claims against the City of Baltimore ("The City") and the Baltimore City Police Department ("BCPD") alleging that BCPD engaged in racial discrimination against African American police officers in connection with the administration of the disciplinary system for Baltimore police officers. It is alleged that the disparate impact and disparate treatment claims extend back to 1992, the commencement date for the misconduct that is the focus of the class claims.

When the court issued its scheduling order and discovery commenced, Plaintiffs promptly served interrogatories and document production requests on the Defendants. ... Companion interrogatories included more than 15 specifically designed to discover the nature, extent, and location of electronically stored records, the Defendants' IT capabilities, the nature of archived data, e-mail, and records retention policies—in short, all of the computer generated information that is the subject of so much discussion these days. ...

... [T]his case highlights significant unresolved issues relating to the nature of privilege review that must be performed by a party producing electronically stored information, whether non-waiver agreements entered into by counsel to permit post-production assertion of privilege are permissible, and effective for their intended purpose, as well as the application of principles of substantive evidence law related to the waiver of privilege by inadvertent production. These issues, among the most talked about by lawyers, judges, and the parties who are affected by their resolution, have yet to be fully developed by the courts. ...

This case vividly illustrates one of the most challenging aspects of discovery of electronically stored information—how properly to conduct Rule 34 discovery within a reasonable pretrial schedule, while concomitantly insuring that requesting parties receive appropriate discovery, and that producing parties are not subjected to production timetables that create unreasonable burden, expense, and risk of waiver of attorney-client privilege and work product protection. ...

... [T]he recent report of the Judicial Conference Committee on Rules of Practice and Procedure to the Chief Justice of the United States and the Members of the Judicial Conference of the United States that forwarded proposed revisions to Federal Rules of Civil Procedure 16, 26, 33, 34, and 37, addresses this same issue:

> The problems that can result from efforts to guard against privilege waiver often become more acute when discovery of electronically stored information is sought. The volume of the information and the forms in which it is stored make privilege determinations more difficult and privilege review correspondingly more expensive and time-consuming, yet less likely to detect all privileged information. Inadvertent production is increasingly likely to occur. Because the failure to screen out even one privileged item may result in an argument that there has been a waiver as to all other privileged materials related to the same subject matter, early attention to this problem is more important as electronic discovery becomes more common. Under the proposed amendments to Rules 26(f) and 16, if the parties are able to reach an agreement to adopt protocols for asserting privilege and work-product protection claims that will facilitate discovery that is faster and at lower cost, they may ask the court to include such arrangements in a case-management or other order.[fn]

… [T]he proposed changes to Rule 26(b)(5) would allow a party to raise post-production claims of privilege and work product protection for electronically stored information, and further establish a procedure for resolving disputes regarding such an assertion. The commentary for this proposed rule change again notes the longstanding complaint that the delay and expense associated with privilege review for electronic records is excessive.[fn] The proposed rule changes appear to be ideal, were it not for the following cautionary language in the comment: "The proposed amendment does not address the substantive questions whether privilege or work product protection has been waived or forfeited [by the procedures in the proposed amendment to Rule 26(b)(5)]. Instead, the amendment sets up a procedure to allow the responding party to assert a claim of privilege or of work-product protection after production. ..."

… [T]he procedures proposed to address the burdens of privilege review associated with production of electronically stored information surely would ameliorate them, but at the price of risking waiver or forfeiture of privilege/work product protection,[fn] depending on the substantive law of the jurisdiction in which the litigation was pending. Absent a definitive ruling on the waiver issue, no prudent party would agree to follow the procedures recommended in the proposed rule. And, as already noted, parties, with the apparent encouragement of courts,[fn] have been using these procedures even in advance of the adoption of rule changes authorizing them. …

The changes recommended to Rules 16 and 26 encourage the party receiving the electronic discovery to agree not to assert waiver of privilege/work product protection against an opposing party that agrees to provide expedited production of electronically stored information without first doing a full-fledged privilege review. Similar agreements have been approved by a number of courts in the past. [Cc][fn]

Although the use of "non-waiver" agreements presently may be growing—and if the proposed changes to the discovery rules are adopted they can be expected to increase significantly—they certainly are not risk-free. Some commentators appear to be openly skeptical of their ability to insulate the parties from waiver,[fn] and even if they are enforceable as between the parties that enter into them, it is questionable whether they are effective against third-parties.[fn] [Cc] …

... [T]hree distinct positions have been taken by the courts: the "strict accountability" approach followed by the Federal Circuit and the First Circuit[fn] (which almost always finds waiver, even if production was inadvertent, because "once confidentiality is lost, it can never be restored");[fn] the lenient/"to err is human" approach, followed by the Eighth Circuit and a handful of district courts[fn] (which views waiver as requiring intentional and knowing relinquishment of the privilege, and finds waiver in circumstances of inadvertent disclosure only if caused by gross negligence);[fn] and the third approach, adopting a "'balancing' test that requires the court to make a case-by-case determination of whether the conduct is excusable so that it does not entail a necessary waiver."[fn] ...

... [There is within the waiver question] an unavoidable clash of important policies. On the one hand is the substantive law narrowly confining the attorney-client privilege to its essential purpose, with subject-matter waiver as the price for unprotected disclosure. On the other is the distinct trend towards limiting the nature and amount of discovery to the needs of the particular case, given the issues in the case, the importance of the facts sought to be discovered, and the resources of the parties, such as embodied in Fed.R.Civ.P. 26(b)(2), and the proposed changes to the rules of civil procedure relating to discovery of electronically stored information. In attempting to resolve this clash, it is important to have a clear appreciation of what is at stake. This requires an awareness of the enormous costs that would accompany a requirement that in all civil cases the production of electronically stored information could not be accomplished until after a comprehensive privilege review and particularized assertion of privilege and work product claims.

The commentary to the proposed changes to Rules 16 and 26, quoted above, speak of the costs associated with discovery of electronically stored information in general, and privilege review prior to production specifically: "The volume of the information and the forms in which it is stored make privilege determinations more difficult and privilege review correspondingly more expensive and time-consuming, yet less likely to detect all privileged information."[fn] ...

Those who bear the administrative and financial costs of responding to voluminous discovery requests for electronically stored information are mindful of the potential burden and expense. A publication of the Association for Information Systems (AIS) has observed: "... Since e-mail can provide especially devastating evidence, the use of e-evidence is increasing. In a survey of 1,100 U.S. Companies conducted by the American Management Association and the ePolicy Institute, 14% of respondents said they were ordered by a court or regulator to produce employee e-mail in 2002, which was up from 9% in 2001.[fn]" The same study estimates that "discovery of e-mail occurs in nearly 100% of federal civil ... cases and major employment disputes"[fn] with the following impact on the responding party: "... The cost of responding to a discovery request can be in the millions of dollars if several years' worth of archived e-mail and files must be located, restored, sorted through and cleansed to remove non-relevant confidential material. Those costs are often in the millions of dollars."[fn]

... With regard to the process of assembling electronic information responsive to discovery requests, an entire industry of consultants has developed to provide services to litigants.[fn] ...

... [T]here is a viable method of dealing with the practical challenges to privilege review of electronically stored information without running an unacceptable risk of subject-matter waiver. It lies with the courts issuing scheduling orders under Fed. R. Civ. P. 16, protective orders under Fed. R. Civ. P. 26(c), or discovery management orders under Fed. R. Civ. P. 26(b)(2) that incorporate procedures under which electronic records will be produced without waiving privilege or work product that the courts have determined to be reasonable given the nature of the case, and that have been agreed to by the parties. ... As will be seen, it is essential to the success of this approach in avoiding waiver that the production of inadvertently produced privileged electronic data must be at the compulsion of the court, rather than solely by the voluntary act of the producing party, and that the procedures agreed to by the parties and ordered by the court demonstrate that reasonable measures were taken to protect against waiver of privilege and work product protection. ...

... First, to the extent that parties already are negotiating "non-waiver" electronic records production agreements, a practice encouraged by the proposed changes to Rule 16(f), they would be unwise to assume that such agreements will excuse them from undertaking any pre-production privilege review, or doing less of a pre-production review than is reasonable under the circumstances. In circuits that have adopted the "strict waiver" approach to inadvertent production, such an agreement would be fatal. And, even in those jurisdictions that have adopted the more lenient "balancing test," the producing party still must show that reasonable measures were taken to screen for privileged information.[fn] The better approach is to assume that complete pre-production privilege review is required, unless it can be demonstrated with particularity that it would be unduly burdensome or expensive to do so. ...

Second, ... as the proposed changes to Rule 16(f) make clear, counsel have a duty to take the initiative in meeting and conferring to plan for appropriate discovery of electronically stored information at the commencement of any case in which electronic records will be sought. ... At a minimum, they should discuss: the type of information technology systems in use and the persons most knowledgeable in their operation; preservation of electronically stored information that may be relevant to the litigation; the scope of the electronic records sought (i.e. e-mail, voice mail, archived data, back-up or disaster recovery data, laptops, personal computers, PDA's, deleted data); the format in which production will occur (will records be produced in "native" or searchable format, or image only; is metadata sought); whether the requesting party seeks to conduct any testing or sampling of the producing party's IT system; the burdens and expenses that the producing party will face based on the Rule 26(b)(2) factors, and how they may be reduced ...; the amount of pre-production privilege review that is reasonable for the producing party to undertake, and measures to preserve post-production assertion of privilege within a reasonable time; and any protective orders or confidentiality orders that should be in place regarding who may have access to information that is produced.

It cannot be emphasized enough that the goal of the meeting to discuss discovery is to reach an agreement that then can be proposed to the court. The days when the requesting party can expect to "get it all" and the producing party to produce whatever they feel like producing are long gone. In many cases, such as employment discrimination cases or civil rights cases, electronic discovery is not played on a level field. The plaintiff typically has relatively few electronically stored records, while the defendant often has an immense volume of it. In such cases, it is incumbent upon the plaintiff to have reasonable expectations as to what should be produced by the defendant. ...

... As I ordered during the hearing, the meeting that should have occurred months ago will be held within 30 days. A follow-up hearing with the court will be scheduled at which time a reasonable electronic discovery plan will be ordered. ...

... [I will] independently determine, using the Rule 26(b)(2) factors, the amount of electronic discovery that would be permitted; whether less than full privilege review was reasonable given the extent of electronic discovery allowed and the time to do so and, if full privilege review was not feasible, whether the procedures agreed to by counsel are reasonable. If so, I will issue an order approving them that includes language that compliance with the approved procedures will not result in the waiver of any privilege or work product claim for any inadvertently produced privileged material. ... [T]he issuance of such an order is essential to protecting against subject matter waiver of attorney-client privileged or work product protected information. ... If I eventually am proved wrong, then the Defendants still will be able to argue that their production of privileged information was under the erroneous belief that this order immunized them from waiver... .

It is so ordered.

INQUIRY

Evidence Rule. Congress addressed the waiver issue for federal cases in 2008 by adopting new FED. R. EVID. 502 set out in full below. Unlike the *Federal Rules of Civil Procedure,* a *Federal Rule of Evidence* can modify substantive law. Rule 502 clearly does so, extending not only to federal cases governed under federal law but also to diversity-of-citizenship cases in which state law provides the rule of decision. Rule 502 begins by limiting inadvertent waivers to the communication itself and not to the entire subject matter of the disclosed communication, providing in Rule 502(a) that only intentional waivers reach undisclosed information on the same subject. Rule 502(b) then provides that inadvertent disclosures do not waive a privilege so long as the discloser "took reasonable steps to prevent disclosure" and "to rectify the error... ." Moreover, Rule 502 refers expressly to FED. R. CIV. P. 26(b)(5)(B) containing the claw-back procedure. Thus, Rule 502 appears to protect a party who enters into a quick-peek agreement permitting sampling with limited or no pre-production privilege review (at least where that review would be unduly burdensome) and who invokes Rule 26(b)(5)(B)'s claw-back provision within a reasonable time after discovering the disclosure of privileged information. Rule 502(e) also approves the *Hopson v. Mayor of Baltimore* approach of binding non-parties when the trial court incorporates into a discovery order the quick-peek, claw-back, or other terms of the parties' discovery agreement.

FED. R. EVID. 502. Attorney-Client Privilege and Work Product; Limitations on Waiver

The following provisions apply, in the circumstances set out, to disclosure of a communication or information covered by the attorney-client privilege or work-product protection.

(a) Disclosure made in a Federal proceeding or to a Federal office or agency; scope of a waiver.—When the disclosure is made in a Federal proceeding or to a Federal office or agency and waives the attorney-client privilege or work-product protection, the waiver extends to an undisclosed communication or information in a Federal or State proceeding only if:

(1) the waiver is intentional;

(2) the disclosed and undisclosed communications or information concern the same subject matter; and

(3) they ought in fairness to be considered together.

(b) Inadvertent disclosure.—When made in a Federal proceeding or to a Federal office or agency, the disclosure does not operate as a waiver in a Federal or State proceeding if:

(1) the disclosure is inadvertent;

(2) the holder of the privilege or protection took reasonable steps to prevent disclosure; and

(3) the holder promptly took reasonable steps to rectify the error, including (if applicable) following Federal Rule of Civil Procedure 26(b)(5)(B).

(c) Disclosure made in a State proceeding.—When the disclosure is made in a State proceeding and is not the subject of a State-court order concerning waiver, the disclosure does not operate as a waiver in a Federal proceeding if the disclosure:

(1) would not be a waiver under this rule if it had been made in a Federal proceeding; or

(2) is not a waiver under the law of the State where the disclosure occurred.

(d) Controlling effect of a court order.—A Federal court may order that the privilege or protection is not waived by disclosure connected with the litigation pending before the court—in which event the disclosure is also not a waiver in any other Federal or State proceeding.

(e) Controlling effect of a party agreement.—An agreement on the effect of disclosure in a Federal proceeding is binding only on the parties to the agreement, unless it is incorporated into a court order.

(f) Controlling effect of this rule.—Notwithstanding Rules 101 and 1101, this rule applies to State proceedings and to Federal court-annexed and Federal court-mandated arbitration proceedings, in the circumstances set out in the rule. And notwithstanding Rule 501, this rule applies even if State law provides the rule of decision.

(g) Definitions.—In this rule:

(1) "attorney-client privilege" means the protection that applicable law provides for confidential attorney-client communications; and

(2) "work-product protection" means the protection that applicable law provides for tangible material (or its intangible equivalent) prepared in anticipation of litigation or for trial.

INQUIRY

Attorney Work Product. The other major protection this chapter addresses after the attorney-client privilege is for attorney work product. Attorney work product addresses a somewhat different interest than the attorney-client privilege. Unlike the attorney-client privilege, attorney work product does not involve confidential communications with the client. Rather, it involves information that an attorney develops in the course of a representation anticipating litigation or in furtherance of the litigation itself. Think of the possibility of simply making a discovery request for a copy of the opposing counsel's file sans attorney-client communications. Lawyers take witness statements and photographs, obtain records, summarize deposition testimony, and prepare chronologies, diagrams, databases, and spreadsheets reflecting their theories and impressions of the case. There is something fundamentally unfair about requiring lawyers to disclose that work product. It would interfere with a lawyer's ability to prepare if the lawyer had to anticipate and protect against the opposing side discovering everything that the lawyer created or obtained. It would shift preparation costs from one side to the other. In addition, it could make the lawyer a witness in the case, creating a conflict in roles. Litigators must do their own work in order not to interfere with the work of opponents, at least when that work remains possible. The law must protect attorney work product at least to some degree to preserve the adversarial nature of the civil justice system.

Scope. FED. R. CIV. P. 26(b)(3) defines the protection for attorney work product. Rule 26(b)(3)(A) states that "[o]rdinarily, a party may not discover documents and tangible things that are prepared in anticipation of litigation or for trial by or for another party or its representative... ." Rule 26(b)(3)(A)(ii) then gives the unusual circumstance under which discovery of attorney work product is possible, when "the party shows that it has substantial need for the materials to prepare its case and cannot, without undue hardship, obtain their substantial equivalent by other means." Thus, attorney work product is not a true privilege. Its protection is not absolute. There are circumstances in which an attorney may discover aspects of an opposing attorney's work, such as when a critical witness becomes unavailable after an attorney has taken the witness' statement. On the other hand, when a trial court does order disclosure of attorney work product, Rule 26(b)(3)(B) requires the court to "protect against disclosure of the mental impressions, conclusions, opinions, or legal theories of a party's attorney... ." An attorney might be able to obtain from opposing counsel the statement of an unavailable witness, but the attorney would not be able to obtain opposing counsel's evaluation of that statement. Consider as illustration the progenitor Supreme Court case defining the scope, justification, and workings of the attorney-work-product privilege. Rule 26(b)(3), memorializing the following decision, took effect in 1970.

Hickman v. Taylor,

United States Supreme Court
329 U.S. 495 (1947)

Mr. Justice MURPHY delivered the opinion of the Court.

This case presents an important problem under the Federal Rules of Civil Procedure, [c], as to the extent to which a party may inquire into oral and written statements of witnesses, or other information, secured by an adverse party's counsel in the course of preparation for possible litigation after a claim has arisen. Examination into a person's files and records, including those resulting from the professional activities of an attorney, must be judged with care. It is not without reason that various safeguards have been established to preclude unwarranted excursions into the privacy of a man's work. At the same time, public policy supports reasonable and necessary inquiries. Properly to balance these competing interests is a delicate and difficult task.

On February 7, 1943, the tug "J.M. Taylor" sank while engaged in helping to tow a car float of the Baltimore & Ohio Railroad across the Delaware River at Philadelphia. ... Five of the nine crew members were drowned. Three days later the tug owners and the underwriters employed a law firm, of which respondent Fortenbaugh is a member, to defend them against potential suits by representatives of the deceased crew members and to sue the railroad for damages to the tug.

A public hearing was held on March 4, 1943, before the United States Steamboat Inspectors, at which the four survivors were examined. This testimony was recorded and made available to all interested parties. Shortly thereafter, Fortenbaugh privately interviewed the survivors and took statements from them with an eye toward the anticipated litigation; the survivors signed these statements on March 29. Fortenbaugh also interviewed other persons believed to have some information relating to the accident and in some cases he made memoranda of what they told him. At the time when Fortenbaugh secured the statements of the survivors, representatives of two of the deceased crew members had been in communication with him. Ultimately claims were presented by representatives of all five of the deceased; four of the claims, however, were settled without litigation. The fifth claimant, petitioner herein, brought suit in a federal court under the Jones Act on November 26, 1943, naming as defendants the two tug owners, individually and as partners, and the railroad.

One year later, petitioner filed 39 interrogatories directed to the tug owners. The 38th interrogatory read: "State whether any statements of the members of the crews of the Tugs 'J. M. Taylor' and 'Philadelphia' or of any other vessel were taken in connection with the towing of the car float and the sinking of the Tug 'John M. Taylor.' Attach hereto exact copies of all such statements if in writing, and if oral, set forth in detail the exact provisions of any such oral statements or reports." ...

The tug owners, through Fortenbaugh, answered all of the interrogatories except No. 38 and ... supplemental ones... . While admitting that statements of the survivors had been taken, they declined to summarize or set forth the contents. They did so on the ground that such requests called "for privileged matter obtained in preparation for litigation" and constituted "an attempt to obtain indirectly counsel's private files." It was claimed that answering these requests "would involve practically turning over not only the complete files, but also the telephone records and, almost, the thoughts of counsel." ...

The District Court for the Eastern District of Pennsylvania, sitting en banc, held that the requested matters were not privileged. [C] The court then decreed that the tug owners and Fortenbaugh ... forthwith "Answer Plaintiff's 38th interrogatory and supplemental interrogatories; produce all written statements of witnesses obtained by Mr. Fortenbaugh, as counsel and agent for Defendants; state in substance any fact concerning this case which Defendants learned through oral statements made by witnesses to Mr. Fortenbaugh whether or not included in his private memoranda[;] and produce Mr. Fortenbaugh's memoranda containing statements of fact by witnesses or to submit these memoranda to the Court for determination of those portions which should be revealed to Plaintiff." Upon their refusal, the court adjudged them in contempt and ordered them imprisoned until they complied.

The Third Circuit Court of Appeals, also sitting en banc, reversed the judgment of the District Court. [C] It held that the information here sought was part of the "work product of the lawyer" and hence privileged from discovery under the Federal Rules of Civil Procedure. ...

The pre-trial deposition-discovery mechanism established by Rules 26 to 37 is one of the most significant innovations of the Federal Rules of Civil Procedure. Under the prior federal practice, the pre-trial functions of notice-giving issue-formulation and fact-revelation were performed primarily and inadequately by the pleadings.[fn] Inquiry into the issues and the facts before trial was narrowly confined and was often cumbersome in method.[fn] The new rules, however, restrict the pleadings to the task of general notice-giving and invest the deposition-discovery process with a vital role in the preparation for trial. The various instruments of discovery now serve (1) as a device, along with the pre-trial hearing under Rule 16, to narrow and clarify the basic issues between the parties, and (2) as a device for ascertaining the facts, or information as to the existence or whereabouts of facts, relative to those issues. Thus civil trials in the federal courts no longer need be carried on in the dark. The way is now clear, consistent with recognized privileges, for the parties to obtain the fullest possible knowledge of the issues and facts before trial.[fn] ...

In urging that he has a right to inquire into the materials secured and prepared by Fortenbaugh, petitioner emphasizes that the deposition-discovery portions of the Federal Rules of Civil Procedure are designed to enable the parties to discover the true facts and to compel their disclosure wherever they may be found. It is said that inquiry may be made under these rules, epitomized by Rule 26, as to any relevant matter which is not privileged; and since the discovery provisions are to be applied as broadly and liberally as possible, the privilege limitation must be restricted to its narrowest bounds. On the premise that the attorney-client privilege is the one involved in this case, petitioner argues that it must be strictly confined to confidential communications made by a client to his attorney. And since the materials here in issue were secured by Fortenbaugh from third persons rather than from his clients, the tug owners, the conclusion is reached that these materials are proper subjects for discovery under Rule 26. ...

We agree, of course, that the deposition-discovery rules are to be accorded a broad and liberal treatment. No longer can the time-honored cry of "fishing expedition" serve to preclude a party from inquiring into the facts underlying his opponent's case.[fn] Mutual knowledge of all the relevant facts gathered by both parties is essential to proper litigation. To that end, either party may compel the other to disgorge whatever facts he has in his possession. The deposition-discovery procedure simply advances the stage at which the disclosure can be compelled from the time of trial to the period preceding it, thus reducing the possibility of surprise. But discovery, like all matters of procedure, has ultimate and necessary boundaries. ...

We also agree that the memoranda, statements and mental impressions in issue in this case fall outside the scope of the attorney-client privilege and hence are not protected from discovery on that basis. It is unnecessary here to delineate the content and scope of that privilege as recognized in the federal courts. For present purposes, it suffices to note that the protective cloak of this privilege does not extend to information which an attorney secures from a witness while acting for his client in anticipation of litigation. Nor does this privilege concern the memoranda, briefs, communications and other writings prepared by counsel for his own use in prosecuting his client's case; and it is equally unrelated to writings which reflect an attorney's mental impressions, conclusions, opinions or legal theories.

But the impropriety of invoking that privilege does not provide an answer to the problem before us. Petitioner has made more than an ordinary request for relevant, non-privileged facts in the possession of his adversaries or their counsel. He has sought discovery as of right of oral and written statements of witnesses whose identity is well known and whose availability to petitioner appears unimpaired. ... In addition, petitioner was free to examine the public testimony of the witnesses taken before the United States Steamboat Inspectors. We are thus dealing with an attempt to secure the production of written statements and mental impressions contained in the files and the mind of the attorney Fortenbaugh without any showing of necessity or any indication or claim that denial of such production would unduly prejudice the preparation of petitioner's case or cause him any hardship or injustice. For aught that appears, the essence of what petitioner seeks either has been revealed to him already through the interrogatories or is readily available to him direct from the witnesses for the asking. ...

In our opinion, neither Rule 26 nor any other rule dealing with discovery contemplates production under such circumstances. That is not because the subject matter is privileged or irrelevant, as those concepts are used in these rules.[fn] Here is simply an attempt, without purported necessity or justification, to secure written statements, private memoranda and personal recollections prepared or formed by an adverse party's counsel in the course of his legal duties. As such, it falls outside the arena of discovery and contravenes the public policy underlying the orderly prosecution and defense of legal claims. Not even the most liberal of discovery theories can justify unwarranted inquiries into the files and the mental impressions of an attorney.

Historically, a lawyer is an officer of the court and is bound to work for the advancement of justice while faithfully protecting the rightful interests of his clients. In performing his various duties, however, it is essential that a lawyer work with a certain degree of privacy, free from unnecessary intrusion by opposing parties and their counsel. Proper preparation of a client's case demands that he assemble information, sift what he considers to be the relevant from the irrelevant facts, prepare his legal theories and plan his strategy without undue and needless interference. That is the historical and the necessary way in which lawyers act within the framework of our system of jurisprudence to promote justice and to protect their clients' interests. This work is reflected, of course, in interviews, statements, memoranda, correspondence, briefs, mental impressions, personal beliefs, and countless other tangible and intangible ways—aptly though roughly termed by the Circuit Court of Appeals in this case ([c]) as the "Work product of the lawyer." Were such materials open to opposing counsel on mere demand, much of what is now put down in writing would remain unwritten. An attorney's thoughts, heretofore inviolate, would not be his own. Inefficiency, unfairness and sharp practices would inevitably develop in the giving of legal advice and in the preparation of cases for trial. The effect on the legal profession would be demoralizing. And the interests of the clients and the cause of justice would be poorly served.

We do not mean to say that all written materials obtained or prepared by an adversary's counsel with an eye toward litigation are necessarily free from discovery in all cases. Where relevant and non-privileged facts remain hidden in an attorney's file and where production of those facts is essential to the preparation of one's case, discovery may properly be had. Such written statements and documents might, under certain circumstances, be admissible in evidence or give clues as to the existence or location of relevant facts. Or they might be useful for purposes of impeachment or corroboration. And production might be justified where the witnesses are no longer available or can be reached only with difficulty. ... But the general policy against invading the privacy of an attorney's course of preparation is so well recognized and so essential to an orderly working of our system of legal procedure that a burden rests on the one who would invade that privacy to establish adequate reasons to justify production through a subpoena or court order. That burden, we believe, is necessarily implicit in the rules as now constituted.[fn]

Denial of production of this nature does not mean that any material, non-privileged facts can be hidden from the petitioner in this case. He need not be unduly hindered in the preparation of his case, in the discovery of facts or in his anticipation of his opponents' position. Searching interrogatories directed to Fortenbaugh and the tug owners, production of written documents and statements upon a proper showing and direct interviews with the witnesses themselves all serve to reveal the facts in Fortenbaugh's possession to the fullest possible extent consistent with public policy. ...

We therefore affirm the judgment of the Circuit Court of Appeals.

Affirmed.

Mr. Justice JACKSON, concurring. ...

The primary effect of the practice advocated here would be on the legal profession itself. But it too often is overlooked that the lawyer and the law office are indispensable parts of our administration of justice. Law-abiding people can go nowhere else to learn the ever changing and constantly multiplying rules by which they must behave and to obtain redress for their wrongs. The welfare and tone of the legal profession is therefore of prime consequence to society, which would feel the consequences of such a practice as petitioner urges secondarily but certainly. ...

The real purpose and the probable effect of the practice ordered by the district court would be to put trials on a level even lower than a "battle of wits." I can conceive of no practice more demoralizing to the Bar than to require a lawyer to write out and deliver to his adversary an account of what witnesses have told him. ... The lawyer who delivers such statements often would find himself branded a deceiver afraid to take the stand to support his own version of the witness's conversation with him, or else he will have to go on the stand to defend his own credibility—perhaps against that of his chief witness, or possibly even his client.

Every lawyer dislikes to take the witness stand and will do so only for grave reasons. This is partly because it is not his role; he is almost invariably a poor witness. But he steps out of professional character to do it. He regrets it; the profession discourages it. But the practice advocated here is one which would force him to be a witness, not as to what he has seen or done but as to other witnesses' stories, and not because he wants to do so but in self-defense. ...

Mr. Justice FRANKFURTER joins in this opinion.

INQUIRY

Anticipation. Courts have construed Rule 26(b)(3)'s language that the attorney-work-product privilege protects documents and things prepared "in anticipation of litigation" to mean that the party claiming the privilege must show a "because of" relationship between the created document or thing and the anticipated litigation. *See* United States v. Adlman, 134 F.3d 1194 (2d Cir. 1998). This construction, consistent with Rule 26(b)(3)'s language, suggests a relatively strict but-for condition relating the document or thing to the specific litigation. A minority of courts would also protect documents and things generally created to assist a party to be prepared for some litigation. *See* United States v. El Paso Co., 682 F.2d 530 (5th Cir. 1982) (prepared to ready a party for litigation). Must a party disclose accident reports? Whether an opposing party may discover an accident report probably depends whether the party prepared it in the regular course of business, *see* Spaulding v. Denton, 68 F.R.D. 342 (D. Del. 1975) (regular report to insurers discoverable), or for circulation internally between departments, *see* Rakus v. Erie-Lackawanna Railroad, 76 F.R.D. 145 (W.D. N.Y. 1977) (report to claim department discoverable). Only when corporate employees prepare such reports at the request of counsel in anticipation of litigation are they likely to be attorney work product. Must a defendant disclose surveillance video taken of a plaintiff to evaluate and potentially challenge a claimed disability? *See* Gutshall v. New Prime, Inc., 196 F.R.D. 43 (W.D. Va. 2000) (surveillance video discoverable only if defendant plans to exhibit it at trial); Gibson v. National Rail Passenger Corp., 170 F.R.D. 408 (E.D. Pa. 1997) (same).

Privilege Logs. Technically, by defining the scope of discovery as relevant *nonprivileged* matters, FED. R. CIV. P. 26 excludes attorney-client privilege and attorney work product from discovery's scope. Rule 26(b)(5) nonetheless requires that parties list attorney-client and attorney-work-product information when they withhold it. Parties ordinarily do so in what practitioners know as a *privilege log* in a manner that must, according to Rule 26(b)(5), "enable other parties to assess the claim." A privilege log will typically identify the communication's author, recipient, date, form (letter, email, memorandum, etc.), general description (legal advice, data compilation, etc.), and claimed privileged (attorney-client or attorney-work-product privilege). Privilege logs have a twofold advantage. They give the opposing party an opportunity to evaluate the privilege claim, but they also ensure that there is no dispute later over whether the party claiming the privilege concealed the existence of the document.

> ***Skill***
>
> Probably more than anything, discovery skill involves a lawyer's willingness to attend to detail, both in the making of discovery requests and in responding. Lawyers are properly data driven. They make decisions based on information rather than speculation. They are also detail driven. Accurate data is important to sound decision-making. Accurately representing data is a mark not only of respect for informed decision-making but also a mark of a lawyer's integrity. Carelessness with data implies carelessness with thinking. Deliberate misrepresentation of data is dishonesty. A deliberate failure to disclose information is concealment. Lawyers recognize that skill in making and responding to discovery requests is necessary to reflect both knowledge of the law and rules, and ethical character. Discovery is a test of a lawyer's knowledge, skill, and ethics.

Substantial Need. Rule 26(b)(3) permits a party to discover attorney work product (not including the attorney's mental impressions) where the party can show a substantial need for it. Rule 26(b)(3) ties substantial need to the inability to obtain the information elsewhere without "undue hardship." A party having to depose witnesses at some burden and expense is not a substantial hardship sufficient to obtain interview memoranda protected by the work-product privilege. *See* In re Natural Gas Commodities Litigation, 232 F.R.D. 208, 212-213 (S.D. N.Y. 2005). The information's relevance to a triable issue is also a consideration in determining substantial need, not that the information will simply aid a party in making a strategic decision. *See* Jinks-Ulmstead v. England, 232 F.R.D. 142, 147 (D. D.C. 2005) (determining scope of opposing side's discovery requests is not a substantial need sufficient to overcome work-product privilege).

C. Required Disclosures

Discovery was once the practitioner's province. Practitioners could largely choose whether and when to make discovery requests, and make discovery disclosures only when the other side asked. Courts got involved only when there were discovery disputes. Although that counsel may retain that liberty in state-court proceedings depending on the particular rules of the state, the *Federal Rules of Civil Procedure* no longer permit practitioners to exercise that degree of control over discovery. FED. R. CIV. P. 26(a)(1) now requires parties to make initial disclosures in all federal cases other than a specific list of cases, like actions to review an administrative proceeding, for forfeiture, to quash a subpoena, and to enforce an arbitration award, exempted by Rule 26(a)(1)(B). The initial disclosures required by Rule 26(a)(1)(A) include: the name and contact information for individuals likely to have discoverable information, and the subject of that information; copies or descriptions and locations of documents, electronically stored information, and tangible things that a party may use to support claims or defenses; damages computations and supporting evidence; and insurance policies covering the alleged claims. Rule 26(a)(1)(A)(ii)'s requirement that a party need disclose only *supporting* documents preserves an important adversarial aspect of civil litigation generally and discovery practice in particular. Despite the broad scope of the required initial disclosures, when it comes to document disclosure, civil litigators need not voluntarily make the other side's case.

As to the timing of initial disclosures, Rule 26(a)(1)(C) requires that in the usual case, a party must make the disclosures within 14 days after a discovery conference required by Rule 26(f). Rule 26(a)(1)(E) recognizes that initial disclosures may be incomplete but requires, in essence, that a party do the best that it can. Indeed, Rule 26(g) requires that an attorney of record sign initial and other discovery disclosures certifying that they are complete, correct, and consistent with law and rule, and not interposed for improper purposes such as to burden or harass. Rule 26(g)(3) authorizes the trial court to sanction attorneys and parties for violating that certification. Doing the best one can includes considering the reason for the discovery requests and the burden that they will impose. Rule 26(a)(3) requires other pretrial disclosures, discussed in Chapter XI, including trial witnesses and exhibits not previously disclosed. Rule 26(e) also requires that a party supplement in a timely manner any disclosure or discovery response that the party later learns is incomplete or incorrect. A party must not rest on prior responses that, over time, become incomplete or inaccurate and therefore potentially misleading. Practitioners remain aware of the duty to supplement as they discover new information and may periodically review their prior disclosures and discovery responses to determine whether they require supplementation.

As just indicated, Rule 26(a)(1)'s initial disclosures anticipate that the parties will hold a Rule 26(f) initial conference. Rule 26(f)(1) requires that the conference take place "as soon as practicable" but no less than 21 days before the Rule 16(b) scheduling conference or order. Rule 16(b) requires that the trial judge hold that scheduling conference within 90 days after the defendant appears or 120 days after service. Although Rule 26(f) leaves open the possibility that the parties will confer by video- or teleconference, Rule 26(f)(2) permits the trial court to order parties or attorneys to attend in person. Rule 26(f)(2) requires that the parties use the conference to produce and submit to the trial court a proposed discovery plan, after making or arranging for initial disclosures, discussing preservation of evidence, and discussing settlement. Under Rule 26(f)(3), the parties' proposed discovery plan must address initial disclosures, subjects of and timing for discovery, issues relating to electronically stored information, privilege issues, and limitations on discovery. Discovery plans are important. They are where litigants first realize what can be substantial imbalances in resources. Parties with few resources (in many cases, individual plaintiffs) may be able to hold parties who have substantial resources to the strict limits of the discovery rules or even negotiate helpful accommodations. For example, a party having the resources to engage in substantial discovery may agree to share copies or bear other expenses usually incurred separately by each party or shared by the parties.

Rule 26 also requires disclosures as to retained experts. In complex litigation, lawyers may retain experts of all kinds such as for accident reconstruction, data interpretation, and testimony on standard of care, industry custom, factual and medical causation, medical prognosis, work disability, vocational rehabilitation, life-care costs, appraisals, repair and replacement costs, wage and benefits loss, and similar issues. Rule 26(a)(2) requires parties to disclose the identity of experts whom they retained to call at trial and for those experts to produce a report. Rule 26(a)(2) requires these disclosures only as to specially retained experts, not non-retained experts such as on-the-scene police officers as to accident reconstruction and treating physicians as to medical diagnosis. Parties and their counsel presumably have equal access to non-retained experts who are fact witnesses. The retained expert's Rule 26(a)(2) report must include the expert's qualifications, compensation, opinions, basis for opinions, exhibits in support, and a list of cases in the previous four years in which the expert testified. As is true with other required disclosures, parties may discover additional evidence relating to the expert's anticipated testimony including all case materials that the expert reviewed. *See* Johnson v. Gmeinder, 191 F.R.D. 638, 646 (D. Kan. 2000). Counsel need not disclose information related to experts whom counsel consulted but will not call as an expert at trial. Can you articulate why not? Lawyers may consult several experts before choosing one to retain for testimony at trial. Similarly, Rule 26(b)(4) permits a party to depose an opposing side's retained and testifying experts but prohibits deposition of an opposing side's non-testifying expert unless there are exceptional circumstances. Consider the following case on discovery of a non-testifying expert, followed by a case on discovery of a testifying expert's file.

Chiquita Intern. Ltd. v. M/V Bolero Reefer,

United States District Court for the Southern District of New York
1994 WL 177785 (1994)

FRANCIS, United States Magistrate Judge.

This is a maritime action in which the shipper, Chiquita... , sues the carrier, International Reefer... , for cargo loss and damage. Chiquita alleges that International Reefer was engaged to transport 154,660 boxes of bananas from Puerto Bolivar Ecuador, to Bremerhaven, Germany aboard the M/V Bolero Reefer. However, because of alleged malfunctions of the vessel's loading cranes and side-ports, only 111,660 boxes were loaded. Thus, 43,000 boxes of bananas were left on the wharf and were later disposed of. The cargo that did arrive in Germany was allegedly in poor condition.

International Reefer has submitted a letter in support of an application to compel discovery of Joseph Winer. Mr. Winer is a marine surveyor who examined the vessel and loading gear at Chiquita's request shortly after the vessel arrived in Bremerhaven. International Reefer seeks Mr. Winer's deposition and production of the file he assembled in connection with his inspection. Chiquita has objected to these demands on the ground that Mr. Winer is a non-testifying expert as to whom discovery is closely circumscribed by Rule 26(b)(4)(B) of the Federal Rules of Civil Procedure. International Reefer replies that Mr. Winer is a fact witness rather than an expert. Moreover, even if he is an expert, International

Reefer argues that the fact that he is the only surveyor who observed the vessel shortly after it docked is an exceptional circumstance warranting discovery. ...

Rule 26(b)(4)(B) states: "A party may, through interrogatories or by deposition, discover facts known or opinions held by an expert who has been retained or specially employed by another party in anticipation of litigation or preparation for trial and who is not expected to be called as a witness at trial only as provided in Rule 35(b) or upon a showing of exceptional circumstances under which it is impracticable for the party seeking discovery to obtain facts or opinions on the same subject by other means."

Thus, a non-testifying expert is generally immune from discovery.

Mr. Winer qualifies as such an expert. He is a marine engineer who was specifically engaged by Chiquita to examine the vessel in connection with the cargo loss claim. He is clearly an "expert" in that he brought his technical background to bear in observing the condition of the gear and offering his opinion to Chiquita. He does not forfeit this status merely because he made a personal examination of the vessel and therefore learned "facts," rather than simply offering an opinion based on the observations of others. Rule 26(b)(4)(B) generally precludes discovery of "*facts known* or opinions held" by a non-testifying expert, and so it anticipates that such an expert may make his or her own investigation. Thus, the relevant distinction is not between fact and opinion testimony but between those witnesses whose information was obtained in the normal course of business and those who were hired to make an evaluation in connection with expected litigation. [Cc] Here, Mr. Winer falls into the latter category and Rule 26(b)(4)(B) therefore applies.

International Reefer nevertheless contends that discovery should be permitted under the "exceptional circumstances" clause of the rule, since no other marine surveyor viewed the vessel shortly after docking. This argument would have merit if International Reefer had been precluded from sending its own expert to the scene by forces beyond its control. Thus, for example, in *Sanford Construction Co. v. Kaiser Aluminum & Chemical Sales, Inc.*, 45 F.R.D. 465, 466 (E.D. Ky. 1968), the court found there to be exceptional circumstances where the plaintiff allowed its own expert to examine the item at issue while barring the defendant's experts until the item was no longer accessible.

However, that is not the case here. The vessel and equipment were at least as available to International Reefer as to Chiquita from the time of loading. Indeed, during the three-week voyage to Bremerhaven, International Reefer's employees had the exclusive opportunity to examine the loading cranes. Under these circumstances, the failure of International Reefer to engage its own marine surveyor in a timely manner should not be rewarded by permitting discovery of Chiquita's expert. To do so would permit the exceptional circumstances exception to swallow Rule 26(b)(4)(B).

Finally, International Reefer maintains that even if it is foreclosed from deposing Mr. Winer, it should be given access to his file. However, Rule 26(b)(4)(B) applies to document discovery as well as to depositions. [C] Nevertheless, International Reefer is correct that information does not become exempt from discovery merely because it is conveyed to a non-testifying expert. Thus, while the file may contain Mr. Winer's recorded observations and opinions which need not be disclosed, it may also include discoverable information provided to Mr. Winer by others. Such documents shall be produced.

Conclusion

For the reasons set forth above, International Reefer's application to take the deposition of Joseph Winer is denied. By May 13, 1994, Chiquita shall produce from Mr. Winer's file those documents that do not reflect his observations and opinions or are otherwise privileged. Chiquita shall prepare a log of any documents withheld, identifying them with the specificity required by Local Rule 46(e).

SO ORDERED.

Krisa v. Equitable Life Assurance Society,

United States District Court for the Middle District of Pennsylvania
196 F.R.D. 254 (2000)

VANASKIE, Chief Judge.

Presently at issue in the above-captioned matter is plaintiff John Krisa's demand that defendant Equitable Life Assurance Society ("Equitable") produce drafts of reports prepared by Equitable's expert witnesses and other documents for which Equitable claims protection under the work product doctrine, as well as correspondence between Equitable's counsel and its expert witnesses… .

This case concerns Equitable's decision to deny Krisa's application for disability benefits under insurance policies issued to Krisa by Equitable. Krisa, an attorney, contends that he is entitled to benefits because labile hypertension renders him unable to pursue his chosen avocation of a litigation lawyer. …

Krisa seeks production of preliminary reports and other documents created by Equitable's experts in connection with this litigation. Equitable responds that it need not produce the draft reports and written analyses generated by its experts because such documents are protected by the work product doctrine codified in Rule 26(b)(3)… .

Equitable's argument disregards the fact that the protection afforded by Rule 26(b)(3) is subject to Rule 26(b)(4), which generally authorizes discovery of testifying expert witnesses. …

Consistent with this analysis, a number of courts have held that draft reports of testifying expert witnesses are discoverable. [Cc] As succinctly stated in County of Suffolk v. Long Island Lighting Co., 122 F.R.D. 120, 122 (E.D. N.Y. 1988): "In general, the work-product privilege has been held not to apply to opinions and documents generated or consulted by an expert retained to testify at trial." …

The conclusion that the draft reports and other documents prepared by Equitable's witnesses in this case are not covered by the work product privilege is consistent with the policy considerations underlying the privilege. The work product privilege is based upon "the general policy against invading the privacy of an attorney's course of preparation." Bogosian v. Gulf Oil Corp., 738 F.2d 587, 592 (3d Cir. 1984) (*citing* Hickman v. Taylor, 329 U.S. 495, 512[] (1947)). … Equitable's representations indicate that counsel's mental processes and opinions are not contained in the experts' draft reports. Thus, requesting production of these documents will not invade the privacy to be accorded Equitable's trial counsel in developing litigation theories and strategies.[fn] Moreover, Krisa could be deprived of a information that would be material to effective cross-examination of Equitable's experts if deprived of the expression of the evolution of the experts' opinions. Accordingly, Equitable will be required to produce the draft expert reports and other documents prepared by the experts it intends to present at trial.[fn] ...

... I find that disclosure of core work product to a testifying expert does not abrogate the protection accorded such information. Accordingly, the documents embodying communications between counsel and Equitable's expert witnesses have been reviewed to ascertain whether they contain core attorney work product. ...

Only document numbered 1 on the Davison privilege log, Mr. Davison's handwritten notes of a telephone conversation with Equitable's counsel, reflects a communication between Equitable's lawyer and Mr. Davison that encompasses counsel's mental impressions. Equitable will not be required to produce this document. ...

Krisa seeks production of cover letters sent from Equitable's attorney to its experts. Equitable does not contend that such documents are covered by the work product privilege. Instead, Equitable maintains that, because the transmittal letters were not "considered" by the expert witnesses in forming their opinions, the cover letters are outside the scope of discovery authorized by Rule 26(a)(2)(B). ...

... The transmittal letters in question tend to establish the identification of documents that were made available to Equitable's experts. The fact that an expert witnesses was presented with a certain document but did not consider it may be highly relevant in testing the expert's conclusions. Because Equitable does not claim any privilege with respect to the transmittal letters, and they fall within the permissible limits of discovery, Equitable will be ordered to produce them.[fn] ...

INQUIRY

Attorney Work Product. As the above *Krisa v Equitable Life Assurance Society* case suggests, when lawyers retain and consult with testifying experts, they necessarily share their theories of the case. Ordinarily, the lawyers take care in what they ask the expert to review. There are two concerns. First, the expert should have all relevant evidence. To withhold relevant evidence from an expert when the expert is forming an opinion opens the expert up to damaging cross-examination based on the withheld evidence. On the other hand, anything that a testifying expert reviews may be subject to discovery. Lawyers must take care in sharing privileged information with experts because the opposing side may then be able to obtain that privileged information. The federal courts disagree on whether a party must produce attorney work product that a testifying expert has reviewed. *Compare Krisa v Equitable Life Assurance Society, supra, with* Karn v. Ingersoll-Rand Co., 168 F.R.D. 633 (N.D. Ind. 1996) (parties are required to produce attorney work product reviewed by testifying experts).

D. Devices

Now that you have an understanding of the scope and limits of discovery, and required disclosures, consider the specific forms of discovery devices that parties may use to obtain evidence. This section addresses five forms of discovery: (1) requests to produce; (2) interrogatories; (3) depositions; (4) requests to admit; and (5) examinations. The *Federal Rules of Civil Procedure* and equivalent state-court rules provide for each of these five forms of discovery. The three forms of discovery most often used are requests to produce, interrogatories, and depositions. Even in the simplest of cases involving, say, a motor-vehicle accident in which liability is assured and injuries are clear, the parties will routinely exchange elaborate interrogatories and requests to produce, and usually take one or more depositions. Admission requests are also relatively common though often significantly less critical and effective. Examinations of the mental or physical condition of a party are relatively infrequent except in special classes of cases.

It should be obvious to you by now that discovery skills are critical in civil litigation. Knowledge of the applicable rules gives a lawyer a good start on those skills, although competent practice can also depend on knowledge of the local customs and conventions. Efficient and effective discovery can also depend on the quality of the relationship with opposing counsel. In a contentious counsel relationship, discovery can too easily become a tit-for-tat situation in which one side serving burdensome discovery or refusing to accommodate reasonable requests for time extension becomes the other side's license to do likewise. By contrast, experienced lawyers who have litigated multiple cases with opposing counsel will often conduct discovery with little or no dispute and without much attention given to the formal requirements of the applicable discovery rules, drawing instead on respect for and trust in the integrity of opposing counsel. FED. R. CIV. P. 29 authorizes the parties to accommodate one another with discovery stipulations. Before studying each of the five discovery devices, read Rule 29, appreciating the value of professional relationship.

FED. R. CIV. P. 29. Stipulations About Discovery Procedure
Unless the court orders otherwise, the parties may stipulate that:
(a) a deposition may be taken before any person, at any time or place, on any notice, and in the manner specified—in which event it may be used in the same way as any other deposition; and
(b) other procedures governing or limiting discovery be modified—but a stipulation extending the time for any form of discovery must have court approval if it would interfere with the time set for completing discovery, for hearing a motion, or for trial.

1. Production

FED. R. CIV. P. 34 authorizes a party to request another party to produce for inspection, copying, and testing any documents, electronically stored information, or tangible things, and to permit entry onto property for similar purposes. Rule 34(a) states explicitly that the request must be "within the scope of Rule 26(b)," meaning that Rule 34 requests are subject to Rule 26(b)'s scope and privilege limitations. In practice, lawyers draft both broad and narrow requests to produce in a single court paper typically titled "Plaintiff's First Requests to Produce to Defendant" or "Defendant's First Requests to Produce to Plaintiff." Broad requests ensure that a party obtains all relevant evidence. Narrow requests ensure that a party obtains evidence on specific issues. For instance, a single court paper filed under Rule 34 in a workplace dispute might include both the broad request to produce all trial exhibits and a narrow request to produce the plaintiff's employment application, together with many similarly broad and narrow requests.

A Rule 34 request to produce compels the recipient to respond within 30 days by producing the requested documents and things or objecting to each request. A usual form of response is to state "see attached" and then attach copies of requested documents, indicating which documents respond to which request as Rule 34(b)(2)(E)(i) requires. Another common response is to sign and attach an authorization for release of the requested records from the independent source holding them pursuant to the responder's privilege. For example, when a party requests the opposing party's medical records, the opposing will respond by listing the medical recordskeepers and attaching a signed authorization for release of those records, recognizing that the requesting party would ordinarily prefer to receive the full records from that independent source. The responding party will keep a copy of the response and attached records to be able later to prove compliance with the request. Read Rule 34 for these and other particulars. Then review FED. R. CIV. P. Form 50 and a sample request to produce, drawn from a state-court case over the denial of disability insurance, before considering some issues requests to produce raise.

FED. R. CIV. P. 34. Producing Documents, Electronically Stored Information, and Tangible Things, or Entering onto Land, for Inspection and Other Purposes

(a) IN GENERAL. A party may serve on any other party a request within the scope of Rule 26(b):

(1) to produce and permit the requesting party or its representative to inspect, copy, test, or sample the following items in the responding party's possession, custody, or control:

(A) any designated documents or electronically stored information—including writings, drawings, graphs, charts, photographs, sound recordings, images, and other data or data compilations—stored in any medium from which information can be obtained either directly or, if necessary, after translation by the responding party into a reasonably usable form; or

(B) any designated tangible things; or

(2) to permit entry onto designated land or other property possessed or controlled by the responding party, so that the requesting party may inspect, measure, survey, photograph, test, or sample the property or any designated object or operation on it.

(b) PROCEDURE.

(1) *Contents of the Request.* The request:

(A) must describe with reasonable particularity each item or category of items to be inspected;

(B) must specify a reasonable time, place, and manner for the inspection and for performing the related acts; and

(C) may specify the form or forms in which electronically stored information is to be produced.

(2) *Responses and Objections.*

(A) *Time to Respond.* The party to whom the request is directed must respond in writing within 30 days after being served. A shorter or longer time may be stipulated to under Rule 29 or be ordered by the court.

(B) *Responding to Each Item.* For each item or category, the response must either state that inspection and related activities will be permitted as requested or state an objection to the request, including the reasons.

(C) *Objections.* An objection to part of a request must specify the part and permit inspection of the rest.

(D) *Responding to a Request for Production of Electronically Stored Information.* The response may state an objection to a requested form for producing electronically stored information. If the responding party objects to a requested form—or if no form was specified in the

request—the party must state the form or forms it intends to use.
(E) *Producing the Documents or Electronically Stored Information.* Unless otherwise stipulated or ordered by the court, these procedures apply to producing documents or electronically stored information:
(i) A party must produce documents as they are kept in the usual course of business or must organize and label them to correspond to the categories in the request;
(ii) If a request does not specify a form for producing electronically stored information, a party must produce it in a form or forms in which it is ordinarily maintained or in a reasonably usable form or forms; and
(iii) A party need not produce the same electronically stored information in more than one form.
(c) NONPARTIES. As provided in Rule 45, a nonparty may be compelled to produce documents and tangible things or to permit an inspection.

FED. R. CIV. P. FORM 50. Request to Produce Documents and Tangible Things, or to Enter Onto Land Under Rule 34.

(Caption—See Form 1.)

The plaintiff _name_ requests that the defendant _name_ respond within ____ days to the following requests:

1. To produce and permit the plaintiff to inspect and copy and to test or sample the following documents, including electronically stored information:
(*Describe each document and the electronically stored information, either individually or by category.*) (*State the time, place, and manner of the inspection and any related acts.*)

2. To produce and permit the plaintiff to inspect and copy—and to test or sample—the following tangible things:
(*Describe each thing, either individually or by category.*) (*State the time, place, and manner of the inspection and any related acts.*)

3. To permit the plaintiff to enter onto the following land to inspect, photograph, test, or sample the property or an object or operation on the property.
(*Describe the property and each object or operation.*) (*State the time and manner of the inspection and any related acts.*)

(Date and sign—See Form 2.)

[Case caption]

DEFENDANT'S FIRST REQUESTS TO PLAINTIFF TO PRODUCE

Defendant Ronald Franken serves the following requests to produce under MICH. CT. R. 2.310 on plaintiff Charles Parker, M.D., for response within 28 days. These requests are continuing, and supplemental responses are due within 28 days or such shorter period as necessary to give reasonable notice:

1. All disability insurance policies you obtained through Mr. Franken's agency, together with any cover letters or other correspondence, memoranda, addenda, explanations, other papers, or electronically stored information in its native format relating to those policies.

2. Any other claims, demands, or complaints you have made against any other person or entity for any loss, breach, damage, or injury of any kind in the past seven years.

3. If you claim mental or emotional distress or any other form of non-economic damages in this case, or if you claim or in the past seven years have claimed disability from employment, then your complete medical, psychiatric, psychological, and counseling records for the past seven years.

4. Any damages calculation you intend to show to any decision-maker including but not limited to case evaluator, mediator, judge, or jury, in this case.

5. The curriculum vitae, report or opinions, materials from which the report or opinions were prepared, correspondence, memoranda, and time and billing records of any expert on whose testimony or other evidence you intend to rely in this case.

6. All communications (including email or other electronic communication), letters, contracts, applications, manuals, diaries, memoranda, other records or papers, or electronically stored information in its native format relating in any way to the employment relationship you allege in this case.

7. Each exhibit you will or may offer at trial.

8. All letters, memoranda, reports, affidavits, draft affidavits, emails, and other communications between you or your attorney or agents and any expert witness you will or may call on your behalf in this case.

9. Any evidence you have of your efforts to mitigate your damages in this case.

10. All legal documents prepared for you during the time that you had any insurance in place through Mr. Franken. If you maintain that the requested documentation is privileged, then prepare a privilege log indicating the document date, document type, subject of the document, and basis for the privilege.

11. Any insurance policy, quote, proposal, advice, explanation, or other documentation you received from any other insurance agent, at any time during the time you had any insurance in place through Mr. Franken.

12. Your buy-sell agreement with your partner in your professional practice, together with any correspondence, memoranda, or other papers relating to its effectuation, interpretation, termination, or alteration.

[Signature block]

INQUIRY

Non-Parties. Although the drafters of FED. R. CIV. P. 34 wrote it explicitly in terms of requesting documents and things from parties ("A party may serve on any other party a request…"), Rule 34 ends with a subrule (c) stating that a party may also compel a nonparty to produce documents and things and permit entry for inspection. Rule 34(c) refers to Rule 45 (reproduced above) titled "Subpoenas." Rule 45(a)(1) includes explicit reference to serving requests to produce and permit inspection on nonparties. In fact, practitioners routinely serve subpoenas on nonparties including a list of the requested documents, while also serving a copy on the opposing party to give the opposing party an opportunity to object as required by Rule 45(b)(1). Because the nonparty may be unfamiliar with the case and reason for the request, the requesting lawyer may include a cover letter with a very brief explanation that, for instance, the requested medical records are for use in a motor-vehicle-accident personal-injury action. Otherwise, nonparties who receive subpoenas for records may suspect that the case implicates their own conduct and may resist making a complete and timely response on that mistaken basis.

Things. Rule 34(a)(1)(B) authorizes requests to produce "any designated tangible things" in addition to documents and electronically stored information. The word "things" may seem inarticulate (Rule 34(a)(1) uses the more general term "items") but illustrates the rule's broad scope. Anything can become the subject of litigation. Can you imagine some of the common and uncommon things for which parties serve requests to produce, for example in personal-injury litigation? Defense counsel, suspicious of malingering, may request a plaintiff who alleges disability to produce at a deposition assistive devices, medical equipment, and prescription bottles. In products-liability cases, defense counsel uniformly request production of the allegedly defective product. One should read Rule 34(a)(1)(B) in conjunction with Rule 34(a)(2) authorizing requests to produce or permit inspection of property so that a party may "inspect, measure, survey, photograph, test, or sample the property or any designated object or operation on it." Parties commonly retain experts to make those inspections. Lawyers commonly negotiate the terms for inspection, especially when it entails the possibility of alterating the evidence or destroying all or any part of it as a necessary incident to testing.

Format of ESI. One major dispute that requests to produce electronically stored information can generate is the electronic format of the disclosure. Does the discloser have to produce the electronically stored information in a certain format convenient to the requester or in its native (original) format, or may the discloser produce it in a less easily modifiable format? For example, the original electronic file may have been in WordPerfect format, when the requester would prefer to read it in Word, and when the discloser would prefer to secure it in non-modifiable Portable Document Format (pdf). The format can be important not only to how secure it is (whether, for instance, the requester could modify it to make it appear other than it was in its original) but also whether it is easily searched for words and phrases significant to the litigation. FED. R. CIV. P. 26(f)(3) requires parties to discuss format issues at their initial discovery conference. FED. R. CIV. P. 16(b) permits the trial court to incorporate production format requirements into the case scheduling order. In the absence of an agreement or order, Rule 34(b)(1)(C) permits the requester to designate a preferred format, although Rule 34(b)(2)(D) permits the discloser to object to the requested form, then requiring the discloser to state its preferred form. If the requester designates no form, then Rule 34(b)(2)(E)(ii) requires the discloser to produce electronically stored information in its native form or reasonably useable forms.

Metadata. The format for production of electronically stored information raises an additional concern. Electronic files, particularly word-processing files, contain more information than the screen or printed copy reveals. That information may include data about: the date and time of the file's creation, and identity of creator; the date, time, and nature of revisions, and identity of revisers; the date and time of deletion, and identity of the deleter; and the dates and times that users accessed and printed the file, and their identities. This metadata can be critical evidence, for example, in cases involving contract formation and interpretation, and around spoliation of evidence. *See, e.g.,* Plasse v. Tyco

Electronics Corp., 448 F.Supp.2d 302 (D. Mass. 2006). Yet parties can also scrub metadata from files. How should discovery rules handle metadata? The *Federal Rules of Civil Procedure* make no specific statement regarding metadata. Rule 34(b)(2)(E)(ii)'s presumption that disclosers should ordinarily produce electronically stored information in its native format or other reasonably useable form may leave an inference in favor of the disclosure of metadata. The better interpretation, though, is that the *Federal Rules* leave the question of the disclosure of metadata to the general discovery standards of scope (relevance) and privilege under Rule 26. If the requesting party can demonstrate metadata's relevance, then it should be discoverable. No scrubbing of metadata should occur without a privilege log so indicating and giving the basis for the file alteration. Consider the following case so holding.

Williams v. Sprint/United Management Co.,

United States District Court for the District of Kansas
230 F.R.D. 640 (2005)

WAXSE, United States Magistrate Judge.

Plaintiff Shirley Williams filed this suit on behalf of herself and others similarly situated, asserting that her age was a determining factor in Defendant's decision to terminate her employment during a reduction-in-force (RIF). ... The parties are presently engaged in discovery concerning the merits of Plaintiffs' pattern and practice allegations. This matter is presently before the Court ... which ordered Defendant to show cause why it should not produce electronic Microsoft Excel spreadsheets in the manner in which they were maintained and why it should not be sanctioned for "scrubbing" the metadata and locking certain data on the electronic spreadsheets prior to producing them to Plaintiffs without either the agreement of the parties or the approval of the Court. ...

... Due to the highly contentious nature of this litigation, the Magistrate Judge has conducted discovery conferences twice a month since March 2005 to resolve discovery issues identified by the parties. One of the ongoing discovery disputes has been Defendant's production of spreadsheets that relate to the RIFs at issue in this case. ...

... Plaintiffs requested that the Court enter an order requiring Defendant to produce candidate selection spreadsheets and other basic RIF documents... .

... [L]ater, at the May 19, 2005 discovery conference, Plaintiffs requested that Defendant be required to produce the actual electronic "active file" version of all the Excel RIF spreadsheets. Plaintiffs' stated reason for requesting that the spreadsheets be produced in their electronic form was so Plaintiffs could perform "statistical or manipulative things without taking the spreadsheets and going through the laborious process of keying in all that data again."[fn] When the Court asked Defendant whether it was now producing the active file of the spreadsheets requested by Plaintiffs, Defendant reported that it was continuing to produce the TIFF [(Tagged Image File Format)][fn] images of the spreadsheets as previously agreed by the parties. The Court then stated that: "[G]enerally, when things are maintained in the regular course of business in electronic form, they should be produced in that form, unless there's an agreement otherwise. And it sounds like what you're telling me, there was an agreement otherwise, until May

11, and then it was pointed out you want them in the form they were maintained."[fn]

... [Later,] the Court further clarified its position on electronic document production of the spreadsheets: "What I'm talking about is if you're talking about documents maintained on Excel, you've got that in some form, whether it's on disk or paper, whatever it's on. It's an electronic form of Excel containing the data. The only thing you would have to do is review it for privilege and then give it to them."[fn] ... [Additional conferences followed at which native format was discussed and apparently assumed or required.]

On June 23, 2005, Defendant tendered to Plaintiffs' counsel 3083 Excel spreadsheets in electronic form and indicated that there were 983 additional spreadsheets identified that had not been fully processed for production and would be produced no later than June 27, 2005.[fn]

At the July 7, 2005 discovery conference, Plaintiffs' counsel advised the Court that Defendant, prior to producing the electronic versions of the Excel spreadsheets, had utilized software to scrub the spreadsheet files to remove the metadata. Plaintiffs claim this metadata would have contained information such as file names, dates of the file, authors of the file, recipients of the file, print-out dates, changes and modification dates, and other information. Plaintiffs' counsel stated that Defendant did not provide them with any type of log of what information was scrubbed. Plaintiffs' counsel also advised the Court that Defendant had locked certain cells and data on the Excel spreadsheets prior to producing them so that Plaintiffs could not access those cells.

Defendant admitted that it had scrubbed the metadata from and locked certain data on the spreadsheets prior to producing them. It argued that the spreadsheets' metadata is irrelevant and contains privileged information. Defendant further argued that Plaintiffs never requested the metadata be included in the electronic Excel spreadsheets it produced and that metadata was never discussed at any of the discovery conferences.

After hearing the respective arguments of counsel, the Court ordered Defendant to show cause why it should not be sanctioned for not complying with "what at least I understood my Order to be, which was that electronic data be produced in the manner in which it was maintained, and to me that did not allow for the scrubbing of metadata because when I talk about electronic data, that includes the metadata."[fn] The Court then gave Defendant seven days to show cause why it had scrubbed metadata and locked data, "because my intent from the two previous Orders was to do as I said, produce it in the format it's maintained, not modify it and produce it."[fn] The Court advised Defendant that if it could show justification for scrubbing the metadata and locking the cells, the Court would certainly consider it, but cautioned that "it's going to take some clear showing or otherwise there are going to be appropriate sanctions, which at least will be the production of the information in the format it was maintained."[fn] ...

... Defendant claims that it scrubbed the metadata from the spreadsheets to preclude the possibility that Plaintiffs could "undelete" or recover privileged and protected information properly deleted from the spreadsheets and to limit the information in the spreadsheets to those pools from which it made the RIF decisions currently being litigated. In an attempt to justify its actions, Defendant contends that emerging standards of electronic discovery articulate a presumption against the production of metadata, which is not considered part of a document, unless it is both specifically requested and relevant. Defendant next argues that Plaintiffs never sought the production of metadata. …

Metadata, commonly described as "data about data," is defined as "information describing the history, tracking, or management of an electronic document."[fn] Some examples of metadata for electronic documents include: a file's name, a file's location (e.g., directory structure or pathname), file format or file type, file size, file dates (e.g., creation date, date of last data modification, date of last data access, and date of last metadata modification), and file permissions (e.g., who can read the data, who can write to it, who can run it).[fn] Some metadata, such as file dates and sizes, can easily be seen by users; other metadata can be hidden or embedded and unavailable to computer users who are not technically adept.[fn] …

Certain metadata is critical in information management and for ensuring effective retrieval and accountability in record-keeping. Metadata can assist in proving the authenticity of the content of electronic documents, as well as establish the context of the content. Metadata can also identify and exploit the structural relationships that exist between and within electronic documents, such as versions and drafts. Metadata allows organizations to track the many layers of rights and reproduction information that exist for records and their multiple versions. Metadata may also document other legal or security requirements that have been imposed on records; for example, privacy concerns, privileged communications or work product, or proprietary interests.[fn] …

Due to the hidden, or not readily visible, nature of metadata, commentators note that metadata created by any software application has the potential for inadvertent disclosure of confidential or privileged information in both a litigation and non-litigation setting, which could give rise to an ethical violation.[fn] One method commonly recommended to avoid this inadvertent disclosure is to utilize software that removes metadata from electronic documents.[fn] The process of removing metadata is commonly called "scrubbing" the electronic documents.[fn] In a litigation setting, the issue arises of whether this can be done without either the agreement of the parties or the producing party providing notice through an objection or motion for protective order. …

The narrow issue currently before the Court is whether, under emerging standards of electronic discovery, the Court's Order directing Defendant to produce electronic spreadsheets as they are kept in the ordinary course of business requires Defendant to produce those documents with the metadata intact. As noted above, the Court finds insufficient guidance in either the federal rules or case law, and thus relies primarily on the Sedona Conference Principles and comments for guidance on the emerging standards of electronic document production, specifically with regard to metadata. While recognizing that the Sedona Principles and comments are only persuasive authority and are not binding, the Court finds the Sedona Principles and comments particularly instructive in how the Court should address the electronic discovery issue currently before it. …

… With regard to metadata in general, the Court looks to Principle 12 and Comment 12.a. to the Sedona Principles. Based upon this Principle and Comment, emerging standards of electronic discovery appear to articulate a general presumption against the production of metadata, but provide a clear caveat when the producing party is aware or should be reasonably aware that particular metadata is relevant to the dispute.

Based on these emerging standards, the Court holds that when a party is ordered to produce electronic documents as they are maintained in the ordinary course of business,[fn] the producing party should produce the electronic documents with their metadata intact, unless that party timely objects to production of metadata, the parties agree that the metadata should not be produced, or the producing party requests a protective order.[fn] The initial burden with regard to the disclosure of the metadata would therefore be placed on the party to whom the request or order to produce is directed. The burden to object to the disclosure of metadata is appropriately placed on the party ordered to produce its electronic documents as they are ordinarily maintained because that party already has access to the metadata and is in the best position to determine whether producing it is objectionable. Placing the burden on the producing party is further supported by the fact that metadata is an inherent part of an electronic document, and its removal ordinarily requires an affirmative act by the producing party that alters the electronic document. …

… While the Court cannot fashion an exhaustive list of the spreadsheet metadata that may be relevant, the Court does find that metadata associated with any changes to the spreadsheets, the dates of any changes, the identification of the individuals making any changes, and other metadata from which Plaintiffs could determine the final versus draft version of the spreadsheets appear relevant. … Defendant should reasonably have known that Plaintiffs were expecting the electronic spreadsheets to contain their metadata intact. Furthermore, if Defendant believed the metadata to be irrelevant, it should have asserted a relevancy objection instead of making the unilateral decision to produce the spreadsheets with the metadata removed. …

In this case, Defendant has failed to object and has not provided a privilege log identifying the electronic documents that it claims contain privileged metadata. Defendant has not provided the Court with even a general description of the purportedly privileged metadata that was scrubbed from the spreadsheets. As Defendant has failed to provide any privilege log for the electronic documents it claims contain metadata that will reveal privileged communications or attorney work product, the Court holds that Defendant has waived[fn] any attorney-client privilege or work product protection with regard to the spreadsheets' metadata… .

… While metadata was never mentioned during any of the discovery conferences or in any of the Court's orders, the Court finds that Defendant should reasonably have been aware that the spreadsheets' metadata was encompassed within the Court's directive that it produce the electronic Excel spreadsheets as they are maintained in the regular course of business. …

The Court [also] finds that Defendant has failed to show sufficient cause for its unannounced and unilateral actions in locking certain data and cells on the Excel spreadsheets the Court ordered it to produce to Plaintiffs in the manner in which they were maintained. … While the Court's Order did not expressly state that the spreadsheets should be produced "unlocked," Defendant should have been reasonably aware that locking the spreadsheets' cells and data was not complying with the spirit of the Court's directive that the spreadsheets be produced as they are kept in the ordinary course of business. …

The Court concludes that Defendant has shown cause why it should not be sanctioned for its actions in scrubbing the metadata and locking spreadsheet cells and data. Although the Court intended its ruling requiring Defendant to produce the electronic RIF-related spreadsheets in the manner in which they were ordinarily maintained to include the metadata, the Court recognizes that the production of metadata is a new and largely undeveloped area of the law. This lack of clear law on production of metadata, combined with the arguable ambiguity in the Court's prior rulings, compels the Court to conclude that sanctions are not appropriate here.

The Court, however, wants to clarify the law regarding the production of metadata in this case. When the Court orders a party to produce an electronic document in the form in which it is regularly maintained, i.e., in its native format or as an active file, that production must include all metadata unless that party timely objects to production of the metadata, the parties agree that the metadata should not be produced, or the producing party requests a protective order. ...

---

2. Interrogatories

FED. R. CIV. P. 33 and equivalent state-court rules authorize parties to serve interrogatories on another party for that other party to answer in writing within a specified time. Interrogatories are questions written in a court paper requiring a party to state facts and opinions or contentions on the application of law to fact. An advantage of interrogatories over depositions is that Rule 33(b)(1)(B) requires corporate parties to answer using all information available to the entity after reasonable investigation, not merely that information available to the individual corporate representative who signs the answers. Deponents answer only what they know. Representative signers of interrogatory answers certify that the answers include information available to the corporation after reasonable investigation. Rule 33(b)(2) gives a party 30 days within which to answer or object to the interrogatories. As just indicated, Rule 33(b)(5) requires the party to sign the answers, while Rule 33(b)(3) requires the signature to be under oath, meaning with a notary public also signing. The signature and oath requirements highlight that practitioners use interrogatory answers for more than broad discovery. Rule 33(c) provides, "An answer to an interrogatory may be used to the extent allowed by the Federal Rules of Evidence," meaning that depending on the circumstance, a party may use an opposing party's interrogatory answers for impeachment or evidence at trial. Read Rule 33, and then review sample interrogatories that were served in the same state-court disability claim as the above sample requests to produce.

FED. R. CIV. P. 33. Interrogatories to Parties
(a) IN GENERAL.
(1) *Number.* Unless otherwise stipulated or ordered by the court, a party may serve on any other party no more than 25 written interrogatories, including all discrete subparts. Leave to serve additional interrogatories may be granted to the extent consistent with Rule 26(b)(2).
(2) *Scope.* An interrogatory may relate to any matter that may be inquired into under Rule 26(b). An interrogatory is not objectionable merely because it asks for an opinion or contention that relates to fact or the application of law to fact, but the court may order that the interrogatory need not be answered until designated discovery is complete, or until a pretrial conference or some other time.

(b) ANSWERS AND OBJECTIONS.
(1) *Responding Party.* The interrogatories must be answered:
(A) by the party to whom they are directed; or
(B) if that party is a public or private corporation, a partnership, an association, or a governmental agency, by any officer or agent, who must furnish the information available to the party.
(2) *Time to Respond.* The responding party must serve its answers and any objections within 30 days after being served with the interrogatories. A shorter or longer time may be stipulated to under Rule 29 or be ordered by the court.
(3) *Answering Each Interrogatory.* Each interrogatory must, to the extent it is not objected to, be answered separately and fully in writing under oath.
(4) *Objections.* The grounds for objecting to an interrogatory must be stated with specificity. Any ground not stated in a timely objection is waived unless the court, for good cause, excuses the failure.
(5) *Signature.* The person who makes the answers must sign them, and the attorney who objects must sign any objections.
(c) USE. An answer to an interrogatory may be used to the extent allowed by the Federal Rules of Evidence.
(d) OPTION TO PRODUCE BUSINESS RECORDS. If the answer to an interrogatory may be determined by examining, auditing, compiling, abstracting, or summarizing a party's business records (including electronically stored information), and if the burden of deriving or ascertaining the answer will be substantially the same for either party, the responding party may answer by:
(1) specifying the records that must be reviewed, in sufficient detail to enable the interrogating party to locate and identify them as readily as the responding party could; and
(2) giving the interrogating party a reasonable opportunity to examine and audit the records and to make copies, compilations, abstracts, or summaries.

[Case caption]

DEFENDANT'S FIRST INTERROGATORIES TO PLAINTIFF

Defendant Ronald Franken serves the following interrogatories under MICH. CT. RULE 2.309 on plaintiff Charles Parker, M.D., to answer under oath within 28 days of service using all information available to him or his attorneys or agents after reasonable inspection and investigation. These interrogatories are continuing, and supplemental answers are due within 28 days or such shorter period as necessary to give reasonable notice:

1. State your full name including any former names or aliases used, Social Security number, and driver's license number. ANSWER:
2. State all addresses at which you have resided or you have used for residential addresses for any purpose within the past ten years. ANSWER:
3. State your employment history for the past ten years including name and address of your employer and supervisor, job duties, compensation including wages and benefits, and reason for termination of employment. ANSWER:
4. Describe by number, issue date, coverage type, and coverage limits or amount, all insurance policies you obtained through Mr. Franken's agency. ANSWER:
5. State where (including address, office or room, precise location within the office or room, and custodian name and relationship to you) you maintained each insurance policy described in your previous answer. ANSWER:
6. Describe whether, when, and why you read each insurance policy described in your answer 4. above including by giving the dates, places, and purposes of each reading. ANSWER:
7. Identify who provided you with any explanation or interpretation of each insurance policy described in your answer 4. above, and what, when, where, with whom, and why, meaning that you include in your answer the precise nature of the explanation or interpretation, the date and place it occurred, the persons present, and the reason why it was provided. ANSWER:

8. Describe by whom, when, where, how, and why you were advised as to your legal rights and duties under each insurance policy described in answer 4. above. ANSWER:

9. What is the complete factual basis for your allegation that you had an exclusive or special relationship with Mr. Franken with respect to your insurance needs, including in your answer the terms of any agreement you claim was formed, any consideration exchanged with respect to that agreement, the duration of the agreement, how it was memorialized, the names of the witnesses who will testify to it, how it was documented, and any other detail. ANSWER:

10. Identify by name, company, and address, any other insurance agents from whom you obtained any insurance, quote, proposal, advice, explanation, or information, at any time during the time you had any insurance in place through Mr. Franken, giving the date and substance of each such communication. ANSWER:

11. Identify by name, firm, and address, any lawyer from whom you obtained any advice, interpretation, explanation, or other counsel during the time you had any insurance in place through Mr. Franken, giving the date and substance of each such communication. If you maintain that any of the requested information is privileged, then prepare a privilege log indicating the date, place, persons present, subject of the consultation, and basis for the privilege. ANSWER:

12. Describe by author, date, contents, and present location all legal documents prepared for you during the time that you had any insurance in place through Mr. Franken. If you maintain that any of the requested information is privileged, then prepare a privilege log indicating the document date, document type, subject of the document, and basis for the privilege. ANSWER:

13. Describe your last in-person communication with Mr. Franken before you filed your lawsuit, including your and Mr. Franken's verbatim statements, or the contents of the communication as closely as you can recall, including the time, place, and other persons present. ANSWER:

14. State verbatim or as closely as you can recall any admissions or other statements you claim were made by Mr. Franken relating in any way to the matters your complaint alleges, and identify the time and place of, and the persons present for, those admissions or other statements. ANSWER:

15. State the beginning and ending dates of each of your marriages together with the names and current or last known addresses of your wife or former wives and the reason for the termination of any marriage. ANSWER:

16. What is your factual basis, if any, for alleging that Franken & Moyer is a legal entity? ANSWER:

17. Identify by name, current or last known address, and telephone number each individual with whom you have resided during the time of the events you describe in the complaint, and for each state their family or other relationship to you. ANSWER:

18. Describe your economic and non-economic damages in as much detail as you are able. ANSWER:

19. State the amount of damages you claim in this case, and give your manner of calculating those damages including each category and amount and each entry on the standard civil jury verdict form. If you claim not to know this information as yet, be sure that you timely supplement this answer. Calculations made for the jury will be objected to if not first disclosed in response to this interrogatory. ANSWER:

20. State the name, address, and qualifications of each expert witness whom you will or may call on your behalf, the compensation paid or payable to

that expert including the total amount and rate, and the facts and opinions to which each expert will testify. ANSWER:

21. State the name, address, and relationship to you of each lay witness whom you will or may call on your behalf, and for each state the testimony you anticipate. ANSWER:

22. State the name, address, and relationship to you of each other person having any knowledge or information of the matters you allege in your complaint, and for each describe that knowledge or information. ANSWER:

23. Describe any other claims, demands, or complaints you have made against any other person or entity for any loss, breach, damage, or injury of any kind in the past seven years. Include in your answer the respondent's or defendant's name, address, attorney, and insurer, as well as the nature and substance of the claim and a description of its result including the date and amount of any recovery, settlement, or judgment. ANSWER:

24. Describe in detail the "trustworthy and accurate information regarding the amount of funding available" you allege in paragraph 29 of your first amended complaint should have been provided to you by Mr. Franken and Mr. Moyer. ANSWER:

25. Describe the terms of your buy-sell agreement with your partner in your professional practice. ANSWER:

26. Explain why you did not elect to retire under the buy-sell agreement you had with your partner in your professional practice. ANSWER:

27. Describe the medical and factual basis for the disability you claimed under your policy of disability insurance, including by describing the medical or other condition you claim to have had, describing how it affected your employment, and giving the name, address, and specialty of any medical or other care provider who supported those claims. ANSWER:

28. Disclose by date and amount the benefits you received under that disability insurance policy. ANSWER:

29. Disclose by nature, date, and amount any payment or other consideration you received from, through, or on behalf of your partner in your professional practice relating in any way to the withdrawal from or termination of your professional practice and relationship. ANSWER:

30. With respect to your first amended complaint's allegation in paragraph 27 that Mr. Franken participated in annual meetings, state the date of each annual meeting held relating to your insurance, financial, and legal matters, in the last ten years before you filed your complaint (whether or not Mr. Franken attended), and state the names of each participant (including whether Mr. Franken attended). ANSWER:

31. With respect to your first amended complaint's allegation in paragraph 27 that Mr. Franken participated in other meetings, state the date of each such other meeting held relating to your insurance, financial, and legal matters, in the last ten years before you filed your complaint (whether or not Mr. Franken attended), and state the names of each participant (including whether Mr. Franken attended). ANSWER:

32. With respect to your first amended complaint's allegation in paragraph 30 that Mr. Franken participated in "multiple planning meetings with other professional advisors," state the date of each such planning meeting in the last ten years before you filed your complaint (whether or not Mr. Franken attended), and state the names of each participant (including whether Mr. Franken attended). ANSWER:

33. Describe for each such meeting in answers 30, 31, and 32 in which Mr. Franken participated, the information and opinions Mr. Franken provided. ANSWER:

34. Describe for each such meeting in answers 30, 31, and 32 in which Mr. Franken did not participate, the information and opinions provided by anyone else relating in any way to insurance. ANSWER:

[Signature block]

Technology

Technology can be a great leveler. With technical proficiency, small law firms representing individual clients with few resources can level the playing field against law large firms representing corporate interests with abundant resources. Technology plays a role at all stages of litigation from initial marketing and client communications through presuit investigation, filing and service of pleadings, to pretrial, trial, appeal, and enforcement of judgments. Yet the power of technology is nowhere more evident in litigation than in discovery stages. Lawyers today depend on information technology to draft and assemble discovery requests, gather and assemble information to respond to discovery requests, and analyze and represent the information produced through discovery requests. Understanding what word-processing, document-assembly, case-management, database, spreadsheet, and other functions can perform what discovery-related tasks can go a long way to making a civil litigator more efficient, productive, and effective. It can also make the work more satisfying and meaningful.

INQUIRY

Number. Practitioners know that interrogatories can be easy to draft but hard to answer. Notice the large number of interrogatories (34) in the above sample. Relatively recent amendments to FED. R. CIV. P. 33(a)(1) limited the number of interrogatories in federal cases to 25 including subparts. The drafters did so because of the large number of interrogatories practitioners had typically served—often over 50 and occasionally up to 100 or more, and then in successive waves. Practitioners would also include large numbers of subparts (a., b., c., etc., then i., ii., iii., etc.) to ensure that an opposing party disclosed all requested information without gloss. These practices placed a heavy burden on opposing parties both in the time that answering required and in attorney's fees incurred in drafting and revising answers and objections. Lawyers draft interrogatory answers from information supplied by the client and other sources. Before signing, the client must ensure that each answer is complete and fully accurate, meaning that the client must first make reasonable investigation. The client will work closely with the lawyer to do so in what can be a time-consuming process, especially considering that one wrong, incomplete, or inartful answer can cost a party a case. Limiting to 25 the number of interrogatories available in federal court eliminated most of the burden. *See* Williams v. Board of County Commissioners, 192 F.R.D. 698, 701-02 (D. Kan. 2000) (117 subparts to 7 interrogatories exceeds allowable 25 limit). Many states do not limit the number of interrogatories. Would you prefer a limited or unlimited number of interrogatories? On what factors would your answer depend? Can a party obtain adequate discovery with only 25 interrogatories in its arsenal? Might this limit influence your advice to a defendant whether to remove a case from state to federal court?

Theories. Practitioners use interrogatories not only to discover evidence and information likely to lead to evidence but also to discern another party's legal theories and positions. Rule 33(a)(2) permits an interrogatory to ask not only for facts but also "for an opinion or contention that relates to fact or the application of law to fact… ." The ability of a party to ask for opinions and contentions helps to narrow the triable issues. Can you discern any disadvantages to the practice? Early in the discovery process, a party may not yet have determined its ultimate position on every possible issue. Opinions and contentions can change as discovery brings to light new evidence and, indeed, as it reveals the opinions and contentions of other parties. Rule 33(a)(2) protects against a party using interrogatories to pin down an opponent before the evidence is fully developed, by providing that "the court may order that the interrogatory" requesting opinions and contentions "not be answered until designated discovery is complete, or until a pretrial conference or some other time." Read the following opinion further explaining this dynamic, while recognizing that it came at a time when the federal courts were addressing emerging trends in discovery and its abuse.

In re Convergent Technologies Securities Litigation,

United States District Court for the Northern District of California
108 F.R.D. 328 (1985)

WAYNE D. BRAZIL, United States Magistrate.

The principal[fn] issue in this discovery dispute can be simply framed: *when* (at which juncture in the pretrial period) should plaintiffs answer "contention"[fn] interrogatories served by defendants. The parties do *not* disagree about *whether* the questions should be answered. The sole question is when.

Counsel already have spent upwards of *$40,000* of their clients' money on this *one discovery dispute.*[fn] That fact strikes this court as strong evidence that there has been in this case a major breakdown in what is supposed to be the self-executing system of pretrial discovery. …

The fact that counsel have spent so much money on this one discovery dispute raises troubling questions in this court's mind that reach beyond the confines of this particular litigation. In little more than a year this court has been forced to intervene in discovery disputes in many cases involving big economic stakes. I have emerged from my contacts with these matters with an uneasy sense that the discovery system in large commercial cases more than occasionally may be perverted into an arena for economic power plays, that parties use discovery tools (or cast their responses to discovery requests) not so much to learn what the facts are, but more to muscle one another into attitudes conducive to favorable settlements. While I do not have sufficient evidence to make a fair judgment about whether the discovery process has been so perverted in this case, my fear that discovery has been distorted by economic combat in this type of litigation compels me to make it absolutely clear that it is irresponsible, unethical, and unlawful to use discovery for the purpose of flexing economic muscle. …

At the outset I point out that the phrase "contention interrogatory" is used imprecisely to refer to many different kinds of questions. Some people would classify as a contention interrogatory any question that asks another party to indicate *what* it contends. Some people would define contention interrogatories as embracing only questions that ask another party *whether* it makes some specified contention. Interrogatories of this kind typically would begin with the phrase "Do you contend that... ." ... Some contention interrogatories ask the responding party to take a position, and then to explain or defend that position, with respect to *how the law applies to facts.* A variation on this theme involves interrogatories that ask parties to spell out the *legal basis* for, or theory behind, some specified contention.

It is not uncommon for a set of "contention interrogatories" to include *all* of these kinds of questions. ...

Despite assertions to the contrary by defendants, no party has an absolute right to have answers to contention interrogatories, or to any kind of interrogatory. ... [A] court can determine whether any given interrogatory is "otherwise proper" ... after considering, among other things, whether it is interposed for any improper purpose, and whether it is "unreasonable or unduly burdensome or expensive, given the needs of the case, the discovery already had in the case, the amount in controversy, and the importance of the issues at stake in the litigation."[fn] If it were clear, for example, that by using some other discovery tool a party could acquire information of comparable quality while imposing less of a burden on an opponent, a court would be constrained to rule that a contention interrogatory need not be answered, regardless of when in the pretrial period it was served.[fn]

Rule 33(b) and the Advisory Committee Notes accompanying the 1970 amendments thereto clearly confer on the courts considerable discretion in deciding when (if ever) a party must answer contention interrogatories. After declaring that an otherwise proper interrogatory is not *necessarily* objectionable merely because it calls for an opinion or contention, the Rule immediately adds: "but the court may order that such an interrogatory need not be answered until after designated discovery has been completed or until a pretrial conference or other later time."[fn] Commenting on this passage, the Advisory Committee notes that "Since interrogatories involving mixed questions of law and fact may create disputes between the parties which are best resolved after much or all of the other discovery has been completed, the court is expressly authorized to defer an answer."[fn] ...

... [T]here is considerable recent authority for the view that the wisest general policy is to defer propounding and answering contention interrogatories until near the end of the discovery period. ...

Because the benefits that can flow from clarifying and narrowing the issues in litigation *early* in the pretrial period are potentially significant, and because it is possible that in some circumstances answers to some kinds of contention interrogatories might contribute meaningfully toward these objectives, it would be unwise to create a rigid rule, even if applicable to only certain categories of cases, that would always protect parties from having to answer contention interrogatories until some predetermined juncture in the pretrial period.

On the other hand, there is substantial reason to believe that the *early* knee jerk filing of sets of contention interrogatories that systematically track all the allegations in an opposing party's pleadings is a serious form of discovery abuse. Such comprehensive sets of contention interrogatories can be almost mindlessly generated, can be used to impose great burdens on opponents, and can generate a great deal of counterproductive friction between parties and counsel. Moreover, at least in cases where defendants presumably have access to most of the evidence about their own behavior, it is not at all clear that forcing plaintiffs to answer these kinds of questions, early in the pretrial period, is sufficiently likely to be productive to justify the burden that responding can entail.

This follows in part from the court's skepticism about the *quality* of the information that *early* responses to contention interrogatories are likely to contain. Counsel drafting responses to these kinds of interrogatories early in the pretrial period may fear being boxed into a position that later embarasses them, or that might be used to try to limit the subject areas of their subsequent discovery. Lawyers generally attempt to maximize and preserve their options while providing as little tactical help to their opponents as possible; so motivated, they are likely to search for ways to give opponents as little information as they can get away with when they respond to contention interrogatories early in the pretrial period. The "substance" of their responses to such questions might reduce to phrases like "research and investigation continuing." …

Given all of the above considerations, this court believes that the wisest course is not to preclude entirely the *early* use of contention interrogatories, but to place a burden of justification on a party who seeks answers to these kinds of questions before substantial documentary or testimonial discovery has been completed. … The Court will be especially vigilant in its evaluation of proffered justifications when a complaint is not facially infirm and when defendants appear to have control over or adequate access to much of the evidence relevant to their alleged misconduct. …

The court concludes that the following procedure is appropriate with respect to contention interrogatories filed before most other discovery has been completed. The propounding party must craft specific, limited (in number) questions. The responding party must examine such questions in good faith and, where it appears that answering them would materially contribute to any of the goals discussed in this opinion, must answer the interrogatories. If answering some, but not all, of the questions would materially contribute to any of the goals described above, the responding party must answer those questions. Where the responding party feels, in good faith, that providing early answers would not contribute enough to justify the effort involved, that party should telephone or write opposing counsel to explain the basis for his position. If opposing counsel continues to press for early answers, the responding party should enter objections… . Thereafter, the burden would fall on the propounding party to seek an order compelling answers. In seeking such an order, the propounding party would bear the burden of justification described above. …

Defendant Burroughs Corporation has filed a set of 15 interrogatories which, counting subparts, add up to at least 52 questions, many of which are compound and expansive, in part because the allegations against Burroughs in plaintiffs' Complaint are more than occasionally compound and expansive. …

Burroughs says that its "interrogatories track the specific allegations relating to Burroughs… ."[fn] That sounds like a classic characterization of contention interrogatories. …

… The court fails to see how substantial interests of Burroughs will be harmed it if is forced to wait until no more than 60 days after completion of that document production for answers to its interrogatories. …

Defendants have suggested several other possible justifications for compelling plaintiffs to answer their contention interrogatories prior to substantial completion of the document productions by defendants. ... The court alludes here, in particular, to the defendants' arguments that prompt answers to their contention interrogatories might expose grounds for a statute of limitations defense... . To put the matter simply, defendants have failed to show, by carefully developing the applicable law, and by applying that law to the facts as alleged by plaintiffs or as supported in competent declarations or documentary evidence from defendants, that there is a real likelihood that *early* answers from plaintiffs to questions in these areas will result in a significant re-shaping of the litigation or a significant savings to one or more of the defendants. ... If *early* answers would advance any such interests, it is up to defendants to show the court how. ...

Defendants also argued at the hearing on these motions that early answers to their contention interrogatories would materially help their economic experts develop their analysis of the plaintiffs' fraud on the market theory. ... This court's review of the relevant law[fn] suggests that the kind of information defendants appear to be seeking is most likely to be useful, if at all, in connection with affirmative defenses that might be available in response to the fraud on the market theory. But it is not clear why defendants should be permitted to press plaintiffs, *early* in the discovery period, *through this problematic type of interrogatory,* for help developing affirmative defenses. ...

In sum, the court ... orders plaintiffs to answer the remaining contention interrogatories that are the subjects of these motions within 60 days after substantial completion of the document production initiated by plaintiffs First Consolidated Request for Production of documents, dated March 13, 1985.

INQUIRY

Business Records. Are there any alternatives to either answering or objecting to interrogatories? FED. R. CIV. P. 33(d) permits a party to produce business records from which the requesting and disclosing parties would have substantially the same burden of deriving an answer, so long as the producing party specifies the records sufficiently for the requesting party to derive the answer. In other words, a party may not use interrogatories to make the opposing party analyze records that the requesting party could just as readily analyze itself. Yet practitioners are rightly cautious of invoking Rule 33(d)'s alternative. Lawyers tend to want to know an answer before the other side discovers it, both to place the answer in its proper context and to prepare for any consequences to its disclosure. Would a safe alternative to Rule 33(d)'s incautious alternative be for counsel to analyze the records in order to derive a preliminary answer before deciding whether to answer or produce?

3. Depositions

FED. R. CIV. P. 30 and equivalent state-court rules permit parties to take depositions of party and non-party witnesses. A deposition is an oral examination under oath before a court reporter who can then prepare and certify a transcript of the witness' testimony. Lawyers take depositions at their office or another location convenient to the lawyers and witness. FED. R. CIV. P. 28 specifies the "officers" before whom parties may take depositions, as those whom federal law or the state law of the place of examination authorizes to administer oaths. In practice, that means a notary public specially trained to record testimony. Lawyers retain independent court reporters (sole proprietors or a company or network of reporters) to attend with the appropriate equipment, which may be an old-fashioned stenograph machine or more often today recording equipment, computer, and transcription software. Rule 30(b)(3)(A) also permits audiovisual recording, a relatively common tactic for key witnesses whose testimony a party may want to exhibit. Rule 30 sets forth abundant additional detail regarding the notice and conduct of depositions. Lawyers for all parties receive notice and usually attend, with the lawyer noticing the deposition then examining the witness as if in court, and lawyers for the other parties free also to examine. Rule 30(a)(2)(A)(i) limits depositions to 10 per side and Rule 30(d)(1) to 7 hours in duration in 1 day. State-court rules do not necessarily include those limitations, meaning that there may be many more depositions in any one state-court case, some lasting more than one day.

FED. R. CIV. P. 31 authorizes a seldom-used alternative in which the reporter would read the deponent questions written by the lawyer, who would not attend. Lawyers tend not to use Rule 31 depositions on written questions because of the deponent's ability to evade answering questions, without the lawyer present to ask follow-up questions.

FED. R. CIV. P. 32 governs the use of depositions. Depositions have several practical uses and some advantages over interrogatories and requests to produce. Lawyers first conduct depositions to obtain information. A lawyer may conduct a discovery deposition in an informal, relaxed, and even friendly manner completely unlike a trial cross-examination. Yet lawyers will also use depositions to test witnesses. Depositions help lawyers evaluate party and non-party witnesses. A witness who appears perfectly at ease and credible in an office or other informal setting may be ill at ease and unconvincing under oath on cross-examination. Cross-examination is a powerful tool in the hands of a masterful examiner. Depositions also permit the lawyers to determine and later prove the limits of a witness' knowledge and observations. Lawyers also conduct depositions to acquire and preserve testimony for trial. Parties typically use depositions at trial to impeach testifying witnesses, under Rule 32(a)(2). Parties occasionally have an opposing party's deposition read at trial as if the deponent were testifying, as permitted under Rule 32(a)(3). The lawyers will submit the deposition transcript to the trial judge if it is a bench trial. For a jury trial, the lawyers will read aloud their questions from the deposition transcript, using the witness or a stand-in to read aloud the deposition answers. Reading depositions aloud in court makes for poor attention, concentration, and retention, but Rule 32(c) requires that parties present depositions "in nontranscript form" (meaning read aloud or audiovisual) if a party so requests, which is the usual practice.

FED. R. CIV. P. 28. Persons Before Whom Depositions May Be Taken

(a) WITHIN THE UNITED STATES.

(1) *In General.* Within the United States or a territory or insular possession subject to United States jurisdiction, a deposition must be taken before:

(A) an officer authorized to administer oaths either by federal law or by the law in the place of examination; or

(B) a person appointed by the court where the action is pending to administer oaths and take testimony.

(2) *Definition of "Officer."* The term "officer" in Rules 30, 31, and 32 includes a person appointed by the court under this rule or designated by the parties under Rule 29(a).

(b) IN A FOREIGN COUNTRY.

(1) *In General.* A deposition may be taken in a foreign country:

(A) under an applicable treaty or convention;

(B) under a letter of request, whether or not captioned a "letter rogatory";

(C) on notice, before a person authorized to administer oaths either by federal law or by the law in the place of examination; or

(D) before a person commissioned by the court to administer any necessary oath and take testimony.

(2) *Issuing a Letter of Request or a Commission.* A letter of request, a commission, or both may be issued:

(A) on appropriate terms after an application and notice of it; and

(B) without a showing that taking the deposition in another manner is impracticable or inconvenient.

(3) *Form of a Request, Notice, or Commission.* When a letter of request or any other device is used according to a treaty or convention, it must be captioned in the form prescribed by that treaty or convention. A letter of request may be addressed "To the Appropriate Authority in [name of country]." A deposition notice or a commission must designate by name or descriptive title the person before whom the deposition is to be taken.

(4) *Letter of Request—Admitting Evidence.* Evidence obtained in response to a letter of request need not be excluded merely because it is not a verbatim transcript, because the testimony was not taken under oath, or because of any similar departure from the requirements for depositions taken within the United States.

(c) DISQUALIFICATION. A deposition must not be taken before a person who is any party's relative, employee, or attorney; who is related to or employed by any party's attorney; or who is financially interested in the action.

Fed. R. Civ. P. 30. Depositions by Oral Examination

(a) WHEN A DEPOSITION MAY BE TAKEN.

(1) *Without Leave.* A party may, by oral questions, depose any person, including a party, without leave of court except as provided in Rule 30(a)(2). The deponent's attendance may be compelled by subpoena under Rule 45.

(2) *With Leave.* A party must obtain leave of court, and the court must grant leave to the extent consistent with Rule 26(b)(2):

(A) if the parties have not stipulated to the deposition and:

(i) the deposition would result in more than 10 depositions being taken under this rule or Rule 31 by the plaintiffs, or by the defendants, or by the third-party defendants;

(ii) the deponent has already been deposed in the case; or

(iii) the party seeks to take the deposition before the time specified in Rule 26(d), unless the party certifies in the notice, with supporting facts, that the deponent is expected to leave the United States and be unavailable for examination in this country after that time; or

(B) if the deponent is confined in prison.

(b) NOTICE OF THE DEPOSITION; OTHER FORMAL REQUIREMENTS.

(1) *Notice in General.* A party who wants to depose a person by oral questions must give reasonable written notice to every other party. The notice must state the time and place of the deposition and, if known, the deponent's name and address. If the name is unknown, the notice must provide a general description sufficient to identify the person or the particular class or group to which the person belongs.

(2) *Producing Documents.* If a subpoena duces tecum is to be served on the deponent, the materials designated for production, as set out in the subpoena, must be listed in the notice or in an attachment. The notice to a party deponent may be accompanied by a request under Rule 34 to produce documents and tangible things at the deposition.

(3) *Method of Recording.*

(A) *Method Stated in the Notice.* The party who notices the deposition must state in the notice the method for recording the testimony. Unless the court orders otherwise, testimony may be recorded by audio, audiovisual, or stenographic means. The noticing party bears the recording costs. Any party may arrange to transcribe a deposition.

(B) *Additional Method.* With prior notice to the deponent and other parties, any party may designate another method for recording the testimony in addition to that specified in the original notice. That party bears the expense of the additional record or transcript unless the court orders otherwise.

(4) *By Remote Means.* The parties may stipulate—or the court may on motion order—that a deposition be taken by telephone or other remote means. For the purpose of this rule and Rules

28(a), 37(a)(2), and 37(b)(1), the deposition takes place where the deponent answers the questions.

(5) *Officer's Duties.*

(A) *Before the Deposition.* Unless the parties stipulate otherwise, a deposition must be conducted before an officer appointed or designated under Rule 28. The officer must begin the deposition with an on-the-record statement that includes:

(i) the officer's name and business address;

(ii) the date, time, and place of the deposition;

(iii) the deponent's name;

(iv) the officer's administration of the oath or affirmation to the deponent; and

(v) the identity of all persons present.

(B) *Conducting the Deposition; Avoiding Distortion.* If the deposition is recorded nonstenographically, the officer must repeat the items in Rule 30(b)(5)(A)(i)–(iii) at the beginning of each unit of the recording medium. The deponent's and attorneys' appearance or demeanor must not be distorted through recording techniques.

(C) *After the Deposition.* At the end of a deposition, the officer must state on the record that the deposition is complete and must set out any stipulations made by the attorneys about custody of the transcript or recording and of the exhibits, or about any other pertinent matters.

(6) *Notice or Subpoena Directed to an Organization.* In its notice or subpoena, a party may name as the deponent a public or private corporation, a partnership, an association, a governmental agency, or other entity and must describe with reasonable particularity the matters for examination. The named organization must then designate one or more officers, directors, or managing agents, or designate other persons who consent to testify on its behalf; and it may set out the matters on which each person designated will testify. A subpoena must advise a nonparty organization of its duty to make this designation. The persons designated must testify about information known or reasonably available to the organization. This paragraph (6) does not preclude a deposition by any other procedure allowed by these rules.

(c) EXAMINATION AND CROSS-EXAMINATION; RECORD OF THE EXAMINATION; OBJECTIONS; WRITTEN QUESTIONS.

(1) *Examination and Cross-Examination.* The examination and cross-examination of a deponent proceed as they would at trial under the Federal Rules of Evidence, except Rules 103 and 615. After putting the deponent under oath or affirmation, the officer must record the testimony by the method designated under Rule 30(b)(3)(A). The testimony must be recorded by the officer personally or by a person acting in the presence and under the direction of the officer.

(2) *Objections.* An objection at the time of the examination—whether to evidence, to a party's conduct, to the officer's qualifications, to the manner of taking the deposition, or to any other aspect of the deposition—must be noted on the record, but the examination still proceeds; the testimony is taken subject to any objection. An objection must be stated concisely in a nonargumentative and nonsuggestive manner. A person may instruct a deponent not to answer only when necessary to preserve a privilege, to enforce a limitation ordered by the court, or to present a motion under Rule 30(d)(3).

(3) *Participating Through Written Questions.* Instead of participating in the oral examination, a party may serve written questions in a sealed envelope on the party noticing the deposition, who must deliver them to the officer. The officer must ask the deponent those questions and record the answers verbatim.

(d) DURATION; SANCTION; MOTION TO TERMINATE OR LIMIT.

(1) *Duration.* Unless otherwise stipulated or ordered by the court, a deposition is limited to 1 day of 7 hours. The court must allow additional time consistent with Rule 26(b)(2) if needed to fairly examine the deponent or if the deponent, another person, or any other circumstance impedes or delays the examination.

(2) *Sanction.* The court may impose an appropriate sanction—including the reasonable expenses and attorney's fees incurred by any party—on a person who impedes, delays, or frustrates the fair examination of the deponent.

(3) *Motion to Terminate or Limit.*

(A) *Grounds.* At any time during a deposition, the deponent or a party may move to terminate or limit it on the ground that it is being conducted in bad faith or in a manner that unreasonably annoys, embarrasses, or oppresses the deponent or party. The motion may be filed in the court where the action is pending or the deposition is being taken. If the objecting deponent or party so demands, the deposition must be suspended for the time necessary to obtain an order.

(B) *Order.* The court may order that the deposition be terminated or may limit its scope and manner as provided in Rule 26(c). If terminated, the deposition may be resumed only by order of the court where the action is pending.

(C) *Award of Expenses.* Rule 37(a)(5) applies to the award of expenses.

(e) REVIEW BY THE WITNESS; CHANGES.

(1) *Review; Statement of Changes.* On request by the deponent or a party before the deposition is completed, the deponent must be allowed 30 days after being notified by the officer that the transcript or recording is available in which:

(A) to review the transcript or recording; and

(B) if there are changes in form or substance, to sign a statement listing the changes and the reasons for making them.

(2) *Changes Indicated in the Officer's Certificate.* The officer must note in the certificate prescribed by Rule 30(f)(1) whether a

review was requested and, if so, must attach any changes the deponent makes during the 30-day period.

(f) CERTIFICATION AND DELIVERY; EXHIBITS; COPIES OF THE TRANSCRIPT OR RECORDING; FILING.

(1) *Certification and Delivery.* The officer must certify in writing that the witness was duly sworn and that the deposition accurately records the witness's testimony. The certificate must accompany the record of the deposition. Unless the court orders otherwise, the officer must seal the deposition in an envelope or package bearing the title of the action and marked "Deposition of [witness's name]" and must promptly send it to the attorney who arranged for the transcript or recording. The attorney must store it under conditions that will protect it against loss, destruction, tampering, or deterioration.

(2) *Documents and Tangible Things.*

(A) *Originals and Copies.* Documents and tangible things produced for inspection during a deposition must, on a party's request, be marked for identification and attached to the deposition. Any party may inspect and copy them. But if the person who produced them wants to keep the originals, the person may:

(i) offer copies to be marked, attached to the deposition, and then used as originals—after giving all parties a fair opportunity to verify the copies by comparing them with the originals; or

(ii) give all parties a fair opportunity to inspect and copy the originals after they are marked—in which event the originals may be used as if attached to the deposition.

(B) *Order Regarding the Originals.* Any party may move for an order that the originals be attached to the deposition pending final disposition of the case.

(3) *Copies of the Transcript or Recording.* Unless otherwise stipulated or ordered by the court, the officer must retain the stenographic notes of a deposition taken stenographically or a copy of the recording of a deposition taken by another method. When paid reasonable charges, the officer must furnish a copy of the transcript or recording to any party or the deponent.

(4) *Notice of Filing.* A party who files the deposition must promptly notify all other parties of the filing.

(g) FAILURE TO ATTEND A DEPOSITION OR SERVE A SUBPOENA; EXPENSES. A party who, expecting a deposition to be taken, attends in person or by an attorney may recover reasonable expenses for attending, including attorney's fees, if the noticing party failed to:

(1) attend and proceed with the deposition; or

(2) serve a subpoena on a nonparty deponent, who consequently did not attend.

Fed. R. Civ. P. 31. Depositions by Written Questions

(a) WHEN A DEPOSITION MAY BE TAKEN.

(1) *Without Leave.* A party may, by written questions, depose any person, including a party, without leave of court except as provided in Rule 31(a)(2). The deponent's attendance may be compelled by subpoena under Rule 45.

(2) *With Leave.* A party must obtain leave of court, and the court must grant leave to the extent consistent with Rule 26(b)(2):

(A) if the parties have not stipulated to the deposition and:

(i) the deposition would result in more than 10 depositions being taken under this rule or Rule 30 by the plaintiffs, or by the defendants, or by the third-party defendants;

(ii) the deponent has already been deposed in the case; or

(iii) the party seeks to take a deposition before the time specified in Rule 26(d); or

(B) if the deponent is confined in prison.

(3) *Service; Required Notice.* A party who wants to depose a person by written questions must serve them on every other party, with a notice stating, if known, the deponent's name and address. If the name is unknown, the notice must provide a general description sufficient to identify the person or the particular class or group to which the person belongs. The notice must also state the name or descriptive title and the address of the officer before whom the deposition will be taken.

(4) *Questions Directed to an Organization.* A public or private corporation, a partnership, an association, or a governmental agency may be deposed by written questions in accordance with Rule 30(b)(6).

(5) *Questions from Other Parties.* Any questions to the deponent from other parties must be served on all parties as follows: cross-questions, within 14 days after being served with the notice and direct questions; redirect questions, within 7 days after being served with cross-questions; and recross-questions, within 7 days after being served with redirect questions. The court may, for good cause, extend or shorten these times.

(b) DELIVERY TO THE OFFICER; OFFICER'S DUTIES. The party who noticed the deposition must deliver to the officer a copy of all the questions served and of the notice. The officer must promptly proceed in the manner provided in Rule 30(c), (e), and (f) to:

(1) take the deponent's testimony in response to the questions;

(2) prepare and certify the deposition; and

(3) send it to the party, attaching a copy of the questions and of the notice.

(c) NOTICE OF COMPLETION OR FILING.

(1) *Completion.* The party who noticed the deposition must notify all other parties when it is completed.
(2) *Filing.* A party who files the deposition must promptly notify all other parties of the filing.

Fed. R. Civ. P. 32. Using Depositions in Court Proceedings
(a) USING DEPOSITIONS.
(1) *In General.* At a hearing or trial, all or part of a deposition may be used against a party on these conditions:
(A) the party was present or represented at the taking of the deposition or had reasonable notice of it;
(B) it is used to the extent it would be admissible under the Federal Rules of Evidence if the deponent were present and testifying; and
(C) the use is allowed by Rule 32(a)(2) through (8).
(2) *Impeachment and Other Uses.* Any party may use a deposition to contradict or impeach the testimony given by the deponent as a witness, or for any other purpose allowed by the Federal Rules of Evidence.
(3) *Deposition of Party, Agent, or Designee.* An adverse party may use for any purpose the deposition of a party or anyone who, when deposed, was the party's officer, director, managing agent, or designee under Rule 30(b)(6) or 31(a)(4).
(4) *Unavailable Witness.* A party may use for any purpose the deposition of a witness, whether or not a party, if the court finds:
(A) that the witness is dead;
(B) that the witness is more than 100 miles from the place of hearing or trial or is outside the United States, unless it appears that the witness's absence was procured by the party offering the deposition;
(C) that the witness cannot attend or testify because of age, illness, infirmity, or imprisonment;
(D) that the party offering the deposition could not procure the witness's attendance by subpoena; or
(E) on motion and notice, that exceptional circumstance make it desirable—in the interest of justice and with due regard to the importance of live testimony in open court—to permit the deposition to be used.
(5) *Limitations on Use.*
(A) *Deposition Taken on Short Notice.* A deposition must not be used against a party who, having received less than 14 days' notice of the deposition, promptly moved for a protective order under Rule 26(c)(1)(B) requesting that it not be taken or be taken at a different time or place—and this motion was still pending when the deposition was taken.
(B) *Unavailable Deponent; Party Could Not Obtain an Attorney.* A deposition taken without leave of court under the unavailability provision of Rule 30(a)(2)(A)(iii) must not be used against a party who shows that, when served with the notice, it could not, despite diligent efforts, obtain an attorney to represent it at the deposition.
(6) *Using Part of a Deposition.* If a party offers in evidence only part of a deposition, an adverse party may require the offeror to introduce other parts that in fairness should be considered with the part introduced, and any party may itself introduce any other parts.
(7) *Substituting a Party.* Substituting a party under Rule 25 does not affect the right to use a deposition previously taken.
(8) *Deposition Taken in an Earlier Action.* A deposition lawfully taken and, if required, filed in any federal- or state-court action may be used in a later action involving the same subject matter between the same parties, or their representatives or successors in interest, to the same extent as if taken in the later action. A deposition previously taken may also be used as allowed by the Federal Rules of Evidence.
(b) OBJECTIONS TO ADMISSIBILITY. Subject to Rules 28(b) and 32(d)(3), an objection may be made at a hearing or trial to the admission of any deposition testimony that would be inadmissible if the witness were present and testifying.
(c) FORM OF PRESENTATION. Unless the court orders otherwise, a party must provide a transcript of any deposition testimony the party offers, but may provide the court with the testimony in nontranscript form as well. On any party's request, deposition testimony offered in a jury trial for any purpose other than impeachment must be presented in nontranscript form, if available, unless the court for good cause orders otherwise.
(d) WAIVER OF OBJECTIONS.
(1) *To the Notice.* An objection to an error or irregularity in a deposition notice is waived unless promptly served in writing on the party giving the notice.
(2) *To the Officer's Qualification.* An objection based on disqualification of the officer before whom a deposition is to be taken is waived if not made:
(A) before the deposition begins; or
(B) promptly after the basis for disqualification becomes known or, with reasonable diligence, could have been known.
(3) *To the Taking of the Deposition.*
(A) *Objection to Competence, Relevance, or Materiality.* An objection to a deponent's competence—or to the competence, relevance, or materiality of testimony—is not waived by a

failure to make the objection before or during the deposition, unless the ground for it might have been corrected at that time.

(B) *Objection to an Error or Irregularity.* An objection to an error or irregularity at an oral examination is waived if:

(i) it relates to the manner of taking the deposition, the form of a question or answer, the oath or affirmation, a party's conduct, or other matters that might have been corrected at that time; and

(ii) it is not timely made during the deposition.

(C) *Objection to a Written Question.* An objection to the form of a written question under Rule 31 is waived if not served in writing on the party submitting the question within the time for serving responsive questions or, if the question is a recross-question, within 7 days after being served with it.

(4) *To Completing and Returning the Deposition.* An objection to how the officer transcribed the testimony—or prepared, signed, certified, sealed, endorsed, sent, or otherwise dealt with the deposition—is waived unless a motion to suppress is made promptly after the error or irregularity becomes known or, with reasonable diligence, could have been known.

UNITED STATES DISTRICT COURT
FOR THE WESTERN DISTRICT OF MICHIGAN

JENNIFER MURPHY and **WILL MAYS**,

Plaintiffs,

v

DAKE COUNTY and **RAOUL BAYLOR**, individually and in his official capacity as Sheriff of Dake County,

Defendants.

No. CIV-07-1234

Hon. ****** *******

DEPOSITION NOTICE AND NOTICE TO PRODUCE

[Names and addresses of all attorneys of record]

PLEASE TAKE NOTICE that plaintiffs will take the deposition under FED. R. CIV. P. 30 of defendant Raoul Baylor, under oath, before a certified court reporter, for discovery, for use at trial, and for all uses permitted by the *Federal Rules of Civil Procedure* and *Rules of Evidence*, at 9:00 a.m. on Monday, August 13, 2008, in the office of defense counsel, 1001 State Street, Lake Worth, Michigan. This time, date, and place were arranged between counsel.

PLEASE TAKE FURTHER NOTICE of this request that the witness produce under FED. R. CIV. P. 34 at the deposition all of those documents and things that plaintiffs previously requested.

[Signature block for plaintiffs' counsel]

July 12, 2008

[Certificate of service]

INQUIRY

Objections. FED. R. CIV. P. 30(c)(1) requires that "examination and cross-examination of a deponent proceed as they would at trial." Lawyers and witnesses generally observe record consciousness and decorum at depositions. When instead they speak over one another, or when witnesses make inaudible gestures or incomprehensible grunts for answers, the court reporter necessarily corrects them. Consistent with Rule 30(c)(1), Rule 30(c)(2) provides that lawyers must note their objections on the record at a deposition in nonargumentative manner, but further, that the deposition still proceeds. The problem with deposition objections is that there is no judge at a deposition. Lawyers should make short and infrequent objections when necessary to alert the examining counsel to correctible defects in questions. Objections as to form and foundation are particularly appropriate. Lawyers often agree to waive the necessity of making other objections, reserving those objections in the event that they later use the transcript at hearing or trial. As Rule 30(c)(2) notes, lawyers must object and should instruct the witness not to answer when the objection involves a privilege, unless they plan to waive the privilege.

Ethics

Witness coaching is a controversial subject. On one hand, lawyers properly prepare their clients when those clients face deposition. Clients are entitled to know in advance, what a deposition is like and what its uses are. Yet as ABA MODEL RULE OF PROFESSIONAL CONDUCT 3.4 provides, lawyers must not obstruct another party's access to evidence, counsel or assist another person in so doing, or counsel or assist a witness to testify falsely. Rule 3.5(d) prohibits lawyers from engaging in conduct intended to disrupt a tribunal. There have been infamous instances of lawyers obstructing and attempting to intimidate opposing lawyers who are taking depositions. In the hands of unethical counsel, objections can escalate into poorly hidden hints to the witness and outright obstruction. Rule 30(d)(2) subjects lawyers to sanctions for disrupting depositions. Rule 30(d)(3) permits a party to move to terminate or limit an abusive deposition.

Priority. When should a party take a deposition relative to other forms of discovery? The convention is to obtain responses to requests to produce and answers to interrogatories before deposing witnesses, especially party witnesses. A good deposition often depends on having first obtained the documents and other records and files on which to examine the deponent. Lawyers tend to write rough outlines for areas of deposition inquiry while spending equal or greater time determining which exhibits on which to examine the deponent. Interrogatory answers can also help guide a deposition examination, giving a lawyer a foundational understanding from which to make detailed inquiries. Lawyers tend to want to know everything that they can about a case before they examine a witness, so that they can elicit, control, impeach, and explore the witness' testimony. Yet in some cases, taking a deposition first, before engaging in other forms of discovery, makes more strategic sense. Can you discern which cases? Pre-deposition discovery can educate the deponent as much as the lawyer who takes the deposition. Some cases benefit by capturing witness testimony early before other discovery and litigation procedures (motions, settlement efforts, etc.) inform and shape it. FED. R. CIV. P. 26(d)(2) provides that parties may employ discovery methods in any sequence and that discovery by one party does not delay discovery by another.

Cost. Interrogatories and requests to produce are inexpensive forms of discovery to initiate. Depositions are costly both in terms of the time that they take (including any required travel) and for the services and transcripts provided by the independent court reporter. Lawyers may travel all over the country or to distant lands to secure deposition testimony for discovery or trial, billing clients for time and travel or, in contingency-fee cases, incurring the travel costs as advanced expenses. Court reporters typically charge a modest appearance fee but then charge substantial per-page rates for both the sealed original of the transcript and each copy. Lawyers have the option of ordering or not ordering transcripts at the deposition's conclusion, but a deposition without them does little good. A single deposition can easily cost several hundred dollars in advanced expenses simply to pay the court reporter. It is relatively common for plaintiffs' lawyers to incur and advance many thousands of dollars in deposition expenses on a single case while bearing those expenses all at once in many cases. Successful law practice, case management, and client relationships depend on prudent use of these resources.

Corporations. Rule 30(b)(6) authorizes a party to notice the deposition of an unidentified corporate representative to testify concerning a specific subject matter. The provision has two purposes. Parties, particularly individual plaintiffs, often cannot know who within a large corporation knows of the information they seek. Interrogatories may confirm the identity of those individuals, whose depositions the party seeking discovery can then notice, but Rule 30(b)(6) gives a party the option of requiring the corporate party to produce those corporate representatives for deposition. Indeed, if the representative whom the corporation produces in response to a Rule 30(b)(6) deposition notice lacks knowledge on the designated subject, then the trial court may construe it for sanction purposes as a failure of any witness to appear. *See* Black Horse Lane Assoc., L.P. v. Dow Chemical Corp., 228 F.3d 275 (3d Cir. 2000). The other purpose to requiring the corporate party to produce deponents on specific subject matters is to prevent the corporation from later claiming that the party seeking discovery asked the questions of the wrong deponent. When the corporate party produces the deponent, it makes it hard for the corporate party to later claim that a different witness had more complete or better information on the specified subject.

4. Admissions

FED. R. CIV. P. 36 and equivalent state-court rules authorize parties to serve requests to admit on other parties for those other parties to admit or deny within 30 days or like period. Rule 36(b) provides that admissions under the rule conclusively establish those matters for the case in which they are admitted. Admission requests hold much promise, seldom realized. They are easy to prepare. Yet they are easier to reasonably deny, given the adversarial nature of litigation, the ambiguity of statements, the uncertainty of continuing discovery, differing views of the law, and different assessments of the law's application to disputed evidence. Requests to admit are particularly ineffective in discovering new evidence. Indeed, that is not their role. Their role is in large part to narrow disputed issues. Notice pleading affords only minimum opportunity for the parties to determine the disputed issues. Broad allegations earn broad denials. Requests to admit permit a lawyer to write specific statements of fact and of the application of law to fact, to see how the opposing party will answer. Requests to admit can effectively shape issues more so than rule them in or out. The art of requests to admit is in counsel's ability to make the requests precise and discrete enough to force a helpful denial or admission. Rule 36(a)(1)(B) authorizes another helpful practice of requiring a party to admit the genuineness of a document. Judicious use of this provision often enables a trial lawyer to avoid having to call witnesses solely to authenticate documents, which can be a time-consuming and distracting effort.

Rule 36 appears to add teeth to its winnowing power in another manner. Rule 36(a)(3) deems the matter admitted unless the responding party answers the request within the prescribed time. Lawyers take that prospect seriously. Some case authority takes the deemed-admitted rule literally. *See, e.g.,* Asea, Inc. v. S. Pac. Transp. Co., 669 F.2d 1242, 1245 (9th Cir.1981); Morast v. Auble, 519 P.2d 157 (1974). Failing to answer admission requests could in theory result in legal malpractice, through inadvertent admissions causing a party to lose a winnable and case-dispositive issue. Rule 36(a)(4) permits a party to qualify an answer in good faith, so long as the qualifications are necessary and clear, and not to undermine Rule 36's goal in clarifying issues. *See* Thalheim v. Eberheim, 124 F.R.D. 34, 35 (D. Conn. 1988) (rejecting "hair-splitting distinctions" intended to burden the requesting party); Havenfield Corp. v. H & R Block, Inc., 67 F.R.D. 93, 96 (W.D. Mo. 1973) ("part denial must be clear."). Some courts skirt Rule 36's literal language, either limiting admissions to non-central issues, *see* Pickens v. Equitable Life Assurance Society, 413 F.2d 1390 (5th Cir. 1969), or giving ground where there is good cause for the failure to answer. Rule 36 does not expressly authorize this action, but Rule 36(b) does permit the trial court to permit withdrawal or amendment of an answer to promote decisions on the merits. The tendency of courts to soften the effect of requests deemed admitted leads some practitioners to file motions to determine the effect of a non-answer, although Rule 36(a)(6) actually only authorizes motions to determine the sufficiency of answers or objections. Read Rule 36, and then review the official form and a sample request to admit following it. Do you think that the sample requests were specific enough to generate meaningful admissions?

FED. R. CIV. P. 36. Requests for Admission

(a) SCOPE AND PROCEDURE.

(1) *Scope.* A party may serve on any other party a written request to admit, for purposes of the pending action only, the truth of any matters within the scope of Rule 26(b)(1) relating to:

(A) facts, the application of law to fact, or opinions about either; and

(B) the genuineness of any described documents.

(2) *Form; Copy of a Document.* Each matter must be separately stated. A request to admit the genuineness of a document must be accompanied by a copy of the document unless it is, or has been, otherwise furnished or made available for inspection and copying.

(3) *Time to Respond; Effect of Not Responding.* A matter is admitted unless, within 30 days after being served, the party to whom the request is directed serves on the requesting party a written answer or objection addressed to the matter and signed by the party or its attorney. A shorter or longer time for responding may be stipulated to under Rule 29 or be ordered by the court.

(4) *Answer.* If a matter is not admitted, the answer must specifically deny it or state in detail why the answering party cannot truthfully admit or deny it. A denial must fairly respond to the substance of the matter; and when good faith requires that a party qualify an answer or deny only a part of a matter, the answer must specify the part admitted and qualify or deny the rest.

The answering party may assert lack of knowledge or information as a reason for failing to admit or deny only if the party states that it has made reasonable inquiry and that the information it knows or can readily obtain is insufficient to enable it to admit or deny.

(5) *Objections.* The grounds for objecting to a request must be stated. A party must not object solely on the ground that the request presents a genuine issue for trial.

(6) *Motion Regarding the Sufficiency of an Answer or Objection.* The requesting party may move to determine the sufficiency of an answer or objection. Unless the court finds an objection justified, it must order that an answer be served. On finding that an answer does not comply with this rule, the court may order either that the matter is admitted or that an amended answer be served. The court may defer its final decision until a pretrial conference or a specified time before trial. Rule 37(a)(5) applies to an award of expenses.

(b) EFFECT OF AN ADMISSION; WITHDRAWING OR AMENDING IT. A matter admitted under this rule is conclusively established unless the court, on motion, permits the admission to be withdrawn or amended. Subject to Rule 16(e), the court may permit withdrawal or amendment if it would promote the presentation of the merits of the action and if the court is not persuaded that it would prejudice the requesting party in maintaining or defending the action on the merits. An admission under this rule is not an admission for any other purpose and cannot be used against the party in any other proceeding.

FED. R. CIV. P. Form 51. Request for Admissions Under Rule 36.

(Caption—See Form 1.)

The plaintiff _name_ asks the defendant _name_ to respond within 30 days to these requests by admitting, for purposes of this action only and subject to objections to admissibility at trial:

1. The genuineness of the following documents, copies of which [are attached] [are or have been furnished or made available for inspection and copying].

(*List each document.*)

2. The truth of each of the following statements:

(*List each statement.*)

(Date and sign—See Form 2.)

[Case caption]

PLAINTIFF'S FIRST REQUESTS TO DEFENDANT TO ADMIT

Plaintiff requests pursuant to MICH. CT. RULE 2.312 that defendant Michael LeBeau admit the truth of the following facts and the application of law to facts, and the genuineness and admissibility of the described documents:

1. Mr. LeBeau executed the Loan Agreement attached as Exhibit A to the complaint.
2. At the time Mr. LeBeau executed the Loan Agreement attached as Exhibit A to the complaint, he understood and voluntarily accepted its terms.
3. Mr. LeBeau executed the Secured Promissory Note attached as Exhibit B to the complaint.
4. At the time Mr. LeBeau executed the Secured Promissory Note attached as Exhibit B to the complaint, he understood and voluntarily accepted its terms.

5. Mr. LeBeau executed the personal Guaranty attached as Exhibit C to the complaint.

6. At the time Mr. LeBeau executed the personal Guaranty attached as Exhibit C to the complaint, he understood and voluntarily accepted its terms.

7. Under the Loan Agreement and as consideration for the Secured Promissory Note and personal Guaranty, Mr. Denton as Trustee for the Amended and Restated Denton Revocable Trust conveyed $100,000 to Mr. LeBeau.

8. Mr. LeBeau received and accepted the benefit of the $100,000 that Mr. Denton conveyed on behalf of the Amended and Restated Denton Revocable Trust.

9. Mr. LeBeau intended at the time of his receipt of the $100,000 to repay that $100,000 according to the terms of the Loan Agreement, Secured Promissory Note, and personal Guaranty attached to the complaint.

10. But for the "economic conditions" Mr. LeBeau alleges in his Answer at ¶10, Mr. LeBeau would have complied with the terms of the Loan Agreement, Secured Promissory Note, and personal Guaranty attached to the complaint.

11. But for the "economic conditions" Mr. LeBeau alleges in his Answer at ¶10, Mr. LeBeau would have repaid to the Amended and Restated Denton Revocable Trust the loaned amount of $100,000.

12. The "economic conditions" Mr. LeBeau alleges in his Answer at ¶10 were Mr. LeBeau's risks under the Loan Agreement, Secured Promissory Note, and personal Guaranty attached to the complaint.

13. Mr. LeBeau did not condition on favorable economic conditions his performance of the obligations imposed on Mr. LeBeau by the Loan Agreement, Secured Promissory Note, and personal Guaranty attached to the complaint.

14. The maturity date on which Mr. LeBeau was to repay Mr. Denton the $100,000 loan amount was to be 120 days after the documents' August 6, 2009 execution, that date being December 4, 2009.

15. Mr. LeBeau failed to repay Mr. Denton the full $100,000 loan amount by on or about December 4, 2009.

16. Mr. Denton and the Amended and Restated Denton Revocable Trust have satisfied all conditions to Mr. LeBeau's performance of the Loan Agreement, Secured Promissory Note, and personal Guaranty attached to the complaint.

17. Mr. LeBeau has waived all conditions to his performance of the Loan Agreement, Secured Promissory Note, and personal Guaranty attached to the complaint.

18. Mr. LeBeau acknowledged in a signed writing the business purpose of the Loan Agreement, Secured Promissory Note, and personal Guaranty attached to the complaint.

19. The Loan Agreement and accompanying documents provided for the securing of Mr. LeBeau's loan-repayment obligations by mortgage against Mr. LeBeau's real property, as shown by Exhibit D to the complaint.

20. Mr. LeBeau's mortgaged interest under Exhibit D to the complaint was in a four-house development project.

21. Mr. LeBeau represented to Mr. Denton that Mr. LeBeau would use the Loan Agreement's proceeds to complete the four-house development project mortgaged under Exhibit D to the complaint.

22. Mr. LeBeau used the Loan Agreement proceeds for purposes unrelated to the four-house development project.

[Signature block]

---

5. Examination

The most invasive form of discovery device is the right to obtain a physical or mental examination of a party by a qualified diagnostician. FED. R. CIV. P. 35 and equivalent state-court rules grant that right within protective procedures. As Rule 35(a)(1) provides, the right to an examination exists, of course, only when the claims and defenses in the case make a party's mental or physical condition an issue. *See* Storms v. Lowe's Home Centers, Inc., 211 F.R.D. 296 (W.D. Va. 2002) (no authority for vocational assessment of party independent of physical or mental examination). Examinations are most common in guardianship or other similar cases in which a ward's mental competence is in issue and in personal-injury or other disability cases in which a plaintiff's or claimant's physical condition and capability is in issue. Just because a party conducts litigation in a manner that seems irrational does not give the opposing party a right to a mental examination. The right to an examination arises in response to claims and defenses, not the conduct of the litigation. Discovery by examination has other procedural safeguards. Rule 35(a)(1) permits examination only by "a suitably licensed or certified examiner." If, for instance, the party's condition were neurological, then the examiner would ordinarily be a neurologist. If it were orthopedic, then the examiner would ordinarily be an orthopedist. If it were mental, then the examiner would ordinarily be a psychiatrist or psychologist.

Although the practice in some state courts is to treat orders for examination as routine, under Rule 35 examinations require a showing of good cause. The party may have already submitted to examination by others including especially treating medical care providers. A party who wishes to avoid examination may also abandon claims that depend on proving mental or physical disability. *See, e.g.,* Winters v. Travia, 495 F.2d 839 (2d Cir. 1974) (abandoning that part of damage claim having to do with physical injury). Requesters may establish good cause by showing that there is a genuine dispute as to the party's condition. Ordinarily, the requesting party uses a Rule 35 examination to prepare an opposing medical expert whose opinions will contradict at least in part prior examinations by treating physicians or other physicians selected by the party whose condition is in issue. There is also no sandbagging in the examination process. Rule 35(b) requires the examiner to write a report "set[ting] out in detail the examiner's findings, including diagnoses, conclusions, and the results of any tests," and to disclose the report to the examined party. Rule 35(b)(6) recognizes that in some cases the parties will agree to an examination but requires the examiner to produce a report in those cases. As you read Rule 35, notice the sensitivity with which it treats this invasive form of discovery and the safeguards that it offers against abuse.

FED. R. CIV. P. 35. Physical and Mental Examinations

(a) ORDER FOR AN EXAMINATION.

(1) *In General.* The court where the action is pending may order a party whose mental or physical condition—including blood group—is in controversy to submit to a physical or mental examination by a suitably licensed or certified examiner. The court has the same authority to order a party to produce for examination a person who is in its custody or under its legal control.

(2) *Motion and Notice; Contents of the Order.* The order:

(A) may be made only on motion for good cause and on notice to all parties and the person to be examined; and

(B) must specify the time, place, manner, conditions, and scope of the examination, as well as the person or persons who will perform it.

(b) EXAMINER'S REPORT.

(1) *Request by the Party or Person Examined.* The party who moved for the examination must, on request, deliver to the requester a copy of the examiner's report, together with like reports of all earlier examinations of the same condition. The request may be made by the party against whom the examination order was issued or by the person examined.

(2) *Contents.* The examiner's report must be in writing and must set out in detail the examiner's findings, including diagnoses, conclusions, and the results of any tests.

(3) *Request by the Moving Party.* After delivering the reports, the party who moved for the examination may request—and is entitled to receive—from the party against whom the examination order was issued like reports of all earlier or later examinations of the same condition. But those reports need not be delivered by the party with custody or control of the person examined if the party shows that it could not obtain them.

(4) *Waiver of Privilege.* By requesting and obtaining the examiner's report, or by deposing the examiner, the party examined waives any privilege it may have—in that action or any other action involving the same controversy—concerning testimony about all examinations of the same condition.

(5) *Failure to Deliver a Report.* The court on motion may order—on just terms—that a party deliver the report of an examination. If the report is not provided, the court may exclude the examiner's testimony at trial.

(6) *Scope.* This subdivision (b) applies also to an examination made by the parties' agreement, unless the agreement states otherwise. This subdivision does not preclude obtaining an examiner's report or deposing an examiner under other rules.

INQUIRY

In Controversy. May a party place an opposing party's mental or physical condition in controversy and then demand an examination, or is examination available only when a party places the party's own mental or physical condition in issue? Ordinarily, just because a party alleges as a claim or defense that the opposing party is incompetent or disabled does not give that party a right to have the opposing party examined. In the usual case where a trial court orders examination, the party who is subject to examination must have asserted the claim or defense putting the party's mental or physical condition in issue. Parties thus usually get to make their own judgments about whether to assert claims or defenses that will subject them to examination. There is some authority, though, that the right to an examination is reciprocal and does not depend on who placed a party's mental or physical condition in issue. In Schlagenhauf v. Holder, 379 U.S. 104, 121 (1964), the Supreme Court approved vision examination of a bus driver in a motor-vehicle-accident case but rejected internal-medicine and pyschiatric examinations, stating "The 'good cause' and 'in controversy' requirements of Rule 35 make it very apparent that sweeping examinations of a party who has not affirmatively put into issue his own mental or physical condition are not to be automatically ordered merely because the person has been involved in an accident... . Mental and physical examinations are only to be ordered upon a discriminating application by the district judge of the limitations prescribed by the Rule."

Conditions. Some practitioners are reluctant to agree to examinations of their clients without negotiating a stipulated order including protective terms, particularly when they have reason to suspect the credibility of the examiner. Rule 35(a)(2)(B) authorizes the trial court to establish not only the time, time, place, manner, and scope of the examination but also its conditions. Some aspects of medical examination, such as blood draws, radiographs, and even strength testing, can carry some risks. Examiners must often rely on prior imaging and laboratory reports and restrict their examination to physical observation, range of motion, questioning, and other non-invasive means. One common additional term that practitioners will request is to permit the party's spouse or another independent witness to attend the examination in the event that the examiner exaggerates or otherwise misreports the nature and results of the examination. Consider the following case denying a similar request.

Abdulwali v. Washington Metro Area Transit Authority,

United States District Court for the District of Columbia
193 F.R.D. 10 (2000)

DEBORAH ANN ROBINSON, United States Magistrate Judge.

... The subject of the cross motions for protective order is an independent psychiatric examination of plaintiff... . Defendant seeks an order precluding plaintiff from having her attorney present and recording the examination. [C] By her cross motion, plaintiff seeks an order allowing her counsel to be present at the examination and allowing her to record the examination. [C] Plaintiff also requests the following "additional safeguards": (1) that the examiner be precluded from asking any questions concerning the accident, and restrict his examination to prior and subsequent mental history; (2) that the examiner be required to supply counsel with a copy of any notes the examiner takes during the examination, a typewritten copy of any handwritten notes and the raw data of any tests performed; (3) that the examiner be required to provide copies of tapes if the examiner routinely records examinations for his own use; (4) that the examination be by interview only and that the plaintiff not be required to complete any form, questionnaire or interrogatory; and (5) that the examination be limited to three hours. [C]

Plaintiff is the mother of ... a six year old boy who died from injuries sustained during an accident on a Metro train on February 5, 1999. Tyri was separated from his mother when he boarded a Metro train and his mother remained on the platform. He attempted to cross between cars to get closer to his mother on the platform and sustained fatal injuries. Plaintiff ... seeks damages for ... negligent infliction of mental anguish, on a bystander theory of liability... .

Plaintiff concedes that the defendant has the right to conduct the psychiatric examination of plaintiff pursuant to Rule 35 of the Federal Rules of Civil Procedure. [C] In her written memorandum, plaintiff repeatedly maintains that the examination "could easily be transformed into a *de facto* deposition." [C] As the basis of her motion for a protective order, plaintiff states that she is "currently pregnant and ... [t]he stress of the accident coupled with her late term pregnancy puts her in a debilitated condition. She is no match for an experienced psychiatrist who may deliberately or inadvertently seek to explore areas not relevant or material to arriving at a diagnosis which could lead to difficulties for the plaintiff in the on-going litigation." ...

At the hearing before the undersigned, counsel for the defendant agreed that given plaintiff's condition and the absence of a firm trial date, the examination of the plaintiff could take place after she gives birth. When the undersigned specifically asked counsel for the plaintiff to articulate any need for the accommodations requested other than her pregnancy, counsel stated that defendant "should not have a second opportunity to depose the plaintiff." ...

... [Defendant] asserts that ... "Dr. Berger like any other physician has a right to take a history from Ms. Abdulwali regarding how she believes the incident occurred and any part she may have played which resulted in the tragic event in order to form his opinion as to the sole or multiple causes of Ms. Abdulwali's present emotional state."

For the reasons set forth below, the undersigned finds that plaintiff has failed to demonstrate that the protections she seeks are warranted. Accordingly, her motion for protective order will be denied. ...

While the federal courts which have considered this issue are divided, the "greater weight of authority favors the exclusion of the Plaintiff's attorney from the conduct of a Rule 35 examination." Tomlin v. Holecek, 150 F.R.D. 628, 631 (D. Minn. 1993) (surveying authority and holding that plaintiff was not entitled to have her counsel present during psychological examination); [cc]. *But see* Vreeland v. Ethan Allen, 151 F.R.D. 551 (S.D. N.Y. 1993) (holding that authorizing presence of plaintiff's attorney at psychological exam was not abuse of discretion); Langfeldt-Haaland v. Saupe Enter., Inc., 768 P.2d 1144, 1146 (Alaska 1989) (holding that counsel are allowed to attend and record court-ordered medical examinations as a matter of course).

In the instances in which the presence of a third party has been allowed, "[e]ach of these rulings has been grounded in the particular facts of the case. None has found an absolute right to have an attorney present during a psychiatric examination." Tirado v. Erosa, 158 F.R.D. 294, 295 (S.D. N.Y.1994) (*comparing* Vreeland v. Ethan Allen, 151 F.R.D. 551 (S.D. N.Y. 1993) (permitting plaintiffs' attorney to attend psychological examinations), *and* Di Bari v. Incaica Cia Armadora, S.A., 126 F.R.D. 12 (E.D. N.Y. 1989) (allowing a court reporter, but not an attorney, to be present at a psychiatric examination), *with* Duncan v. Upjohn Company, 155 F.R.D. 23 (D. Conn. 1994) (plaintiff's physician not permitted to attend psychiatric examination)... .

The undersigned finds that in the instant case, plaintiff has failed to show a compelling need for the presence of her attorney during her psychiatric examination. ... Due to the agreement that the examination will not take place until after she has given birth, plaintiff's concerns regarding her "debilitated condition" are no longer relevant. The only other concern articulated by plaintiff is that the examination will turn into a "second deposition" of the plaintiff. This concern is allayed by counsel's ability to confer with plaintiff regarding the exam, review Dr. Berger's report in accordance with Rule 35 of the Federal Rules of Civil Procedure, depose Dr. Berger, and cross-examine Dr. Berger at trial. [Cc] ...

With respect to plaintiff's request for "additional safeguards" limiting the scope of the examination, the undersigned finds that the requirements of Rule 35(b) of the Federal Rules of Civil Procedure adequately safeguard the interests of the plaintiff, and that further safeguards are unwarranted. ...

In the instant case, plaintiff has offered no compelling reason to intrude upon the examining doctor's discretion regarding the scope, means and timing of her psychiatric examination; nor has she shown that any of the components of the psychiatric examination as described by Dr. Berger are unduly intrusive or overbroad. ... Accordingly, plaintiff's requests to limit the scope and duration of the examination will be denied. ...

E. Disputes

As the above case law indicates, discovery disputes do arise. It is not that lawyers are overly contentious. In complex cases, discovery can require substantial coordination between opposing counsel. Conducting the FED. R. CIV. P. 26 discovery conference and drafting its discovery plan require at least some and often substantial cooperation. Counsel may require time extensions to comply with requests to produce voluminous documents, to locate and produce electronically stored information, and to draft detailed and complete answers to interrogatories calling for broad disclosure. Lawyers are routinely understanding of opposing counsel's discovery obligations and burdens, and often employ informally their Rule 26(a)(1)(A) and Rule 29 authority to modify discovery requirements by stipulation. Even something as simple as scheduling the date, time, and place of a deposition can require professional courtesy when schedules conflict or, conversely, an unfortunate level of contention when counsel are unable or unwilling to cooperate. The large quantity of interaction over important yet highly uncertain matters is bound to lead to occasional disputes. The *Federal Rules of Civil Procedure* expects that the lawyers will conduct discovery without direct court supervision (save for the timetables and structure provided for by the Rule 26 discovery order) while also anticipating that they will occasionally need the court's help in resolving disputes. Unsupervised discovery with court involvement only to resolve discovery disputes can lead to greater understanding, clarity, agreement, and trust.

It can also lead to complete breakdowns in the litigation process, to the point of dismissal or default. In its worst form (setting aside the possibility of outright lies and falsification or destruction of evidence), discovery practice can involve stalling (unnecessary delays), sandbagging (producing some but less-than-complete discovery), and stonewalling (refusing to produce anything until forced to do so). In the other direction, it can involve inundating an opponent with discovery demands or even with discovery responses, making it difficult and expensive for the requesting party to find the relevant evidence within the volume of produced information. A significant percentage of cases resolve at least in part because of the way in which discovery disputes reveal not just the factual and legal authority behind claims and defenses but the character, preparedness, professionalism, tactics, and commitment of the parties and their counsel, and of the court's ability and willingness to respond.

FED. R. CIV. P. 37 accounts for this dynamic with a carrot-and-stick approach for resolving discovery disputes before enforcing discovery rights. Rule 37(a)(1) first requires that when moving for an order to compel discovery, a party must certify having attempted to confer with the party or non-party who resists discovery, to resolve the dispute. *See* Shuffle Master Inc. v. Progressive Games, Inc., 170 F.R.D. 166 (D. Nev. 1996) (no sanctions without certifying attempt to confer). Sometimes, getting what you need simply requires that you ask in a different way. Even a perfunctory, rule-required telephone call to opposing counsel can occasionally produce positive results when a formal written request failed to do so. Rule 37(a)(1) requires the lawyers to talk first and to certify to the court that they have done so. Rule 37(a)(3) then authorizes specific motions to enforce the various discovery rules addressed above including to compel witnesses to attend and answer on depositions under Rules 30 and 31, parties to answer interrogatories under Rule 33, and parties to produce documents and things for inspection under Rule 34. Rule 37(a)(5)(A) then raises the stakes for discovery disputes by requiring the party who loses a discovery motion to pay the other side's expenses unless the resister was substantially justified or other circumstances make an award unjust.

Rule 37(b) further raises the stakes by authorizing sanctions up to dismissal or default for disobeying a discovery order. Discovery abuses warranting dismissal or default as a sanction are understandably rare. *See, e.g.,* Chrysler Corp. v. Varey, 186 F.3d 1016, 1020-1022 (8th Cir. 1999) (default judgment as a discovery sanction). Courts are rightly reluctant to impose a sanction that would deny a party its day in court and, moreover, could be inconsistent with a decision on the merits of the case. Ordinarily, dismissal or default is inappropriate if lesser sanctions will prevent further abuses and adequately deter others, but the sanction can depend on a variety of factors and is within the discretion of the trial court. *Cf.* Everyday Learning Corp. v. Larson, 242 F.3d 815 (8th Cir. 2001) (approving of dispositive sanction). The much more common sanction, though, is an award of costs and attorney's fees necessarily incurred by the party prevailing in the discovery dispute. Trial courts have the authority to impose monetary discovery sanctions on both the party and its attorney. *See, e.g.,* Legault v. Zambarano, 105 F.3d 24, 28 (1st Cir. 1997).

As some of the following case law shows, Rule 37's enforcement mechanisms work in coordination with Rule 26(g)'s provision that an attorney's signature or unrepresented party's signature on a discovery paper certifies its integrity. Rule 26(g)(3) provides for sanctions. Importantly, Rule 26(g) sanctions are available even before the trial court first orders a party to comply with discovery requests, whereas Rule 37 tends to reserve its enforcement mechanisms for failures or refusals to comply with discovery orders. Read Rule 37 for these and other provisions, and then consider a Supreme Court case that encouraged the federal district courts to make greater use of its sanctions.

FED. R. CIV. P. 37. Failure to Make Disclosures or to Cooperate in Discovery; Sanctions

(a) MOTION FOR AN ORDER COMPELLING DISCLOSURE OR DISCOVERY.

(1) *In General.* On notice to other parties and all affected persons, a party may move for an order compelling disclosure or discovery. The motion must include a certification that the movant has in good faith conferred or attempted to confer with the person or party failing to make disclosure or discovery in an effort to obtain it without court action.

(2) *Appropriate Court.* A motion for an order to a party must be made in the court where the action is pending. A motion for an order to a nonparty must be made in the court where the discovery is or will be taken.

(3) *Specific Motions.*

(A) *To Compel Disclosure.* If a party fails to make a disclosure required by Rule 26(a), any other party may move to compel disclosure and for appropriate sanctions.

(B) *To Compel a Discovery Response.* A party seeking discovery may move for an order compelling an answer, designation, production, or inspection. This motion may be made if:

(i) a deponent fails to answer a question asked under Rule 30 or 31;

(ii) a corporation or other entity fails to make a designation under Rule 30(b)(6) or 31(a)(4);

(iii) a party fails to answer an interrogatory submitted under Rule 33; or

(iv) a party fails to respond that inspection will be permitted—or fails to permit inspection—as requested under Rule 34.

(C) *Related to a Deposition.* When taking an oral deposition, the party asking a question may complete or adjourn the examination before moving for an order.

(4) *Evasive or Incomplete Disclosure, Answer, or Response.* For purposes of this subdivision

(a), an evasive or incomplete disclosure, answer, or response must be treated as a failure to disclose, answer, or respond.

(5) *Payment of Expenses; Protective Orders.*

(A) *If the Motion Is Granted (or Disclosure or Discovery Is Provided After Filing).* If the motion is granted—or if the disclosure or requested discovery is provided after the motion was filed—the court must, after giving an opportunity to be heard, require the party or deponent whose conduct necessitated the motion, the party or attorney advising that conduct, or both to pay the movant's reasonable expenses incurred in making the motion, including attorney's fees. But the court must not order this payment if:

(i) the movant filed the motion before attempting in good faith to obtain the disclosure or discovery without court action;

(ii) the opposing party's nondisclosure, response, or objection was substantially justified; or

(iii) other circumstances make an award of expenses unjust.

(B) *If the Motion Is Denied.* If the motion is denied, the court may issue any protective order authorized under Rule 26(c) and must, after giving an opportunity to be heard, require the movant, the attorney filing the motion, or both to pay the party or deponent who opposed the motion its reasonable expenses incurred in opposing the motion, including attorney's fees. But the court must not order this payment if the motion was substantially justified or other circumstances make an award of expenses unjust.

(C) *If the Motion Is Granted in Part and Denied in Part.* If the motion is granted in part and denied in part, the court may issue any protective order authorized under Rule 26(c) and may, after giving an opportunity to be heard, apportion the reasonable expenses for the motion.

(b) FAILURE TO COMPLY WITH A COURT ORDER.

(1) *Sanctions in the District Where the Deposition Is Taken.* If the court where the discovery is taken orders a deponent to be sworn or to answer a question and the deponent fails to obey, the failure may be treated as contempt of court.

(2) *Sanctions in the District Where the Action Is Pending.*

(A) *For Not Obeying a Discovery Order.* If a party or a party's officer, director, or managing agent—or a witness designated under Rule 30(b)(6) or 31(a)(4)—fails to obey an order to provide or permit discovery, including an order under Rule 26(f), 35, or 37(a), the court where the action is pending may issue further just orders. They may include the following:

(i) directing that the matters embraced in the order or other designated facts be taken as established for purposes of the action, as the prevailing party claims;

(ii) prohibiting the disobedient party from supporting or opposing designated claims or defenses, or from introducing designated matters in evidence;

(iii) striking pleadings in whole or in part;

(iv) staying further proceedings until the order is obeyed;

(v) dismissing the action or proceeding in whole or in part;

(vi) rendering a default judgment against the disobedient party; or

(vii) treating as contempt of court the failure to obey any order except an order to submit to a physical or mental examination.

(B) *For Not Producing a Person for Examination.* If a party fails to comply with an order under Rule 35(a) requiring it to produce another person for examination, the court may issue any of the orders listed in Rule 37(b)(2)(A)(i)–(vi), unless the disobedient party shows that it cannot produce the other person.

(C) *Payment of Expenses.* Instead of or in addition to the orders above, the court must order the disobedient party, the attorney advising that party, or both to pay the reasonable expenses, including attorney's fees, caused by the failure, unless the failure was substantially justified or other circumstances make an award of expenses unjust.

(c) FAILURE TO DISCLOSE, TO SUPPLEMENT AN EARLIER RESPONSE, OR TO ADMIT.

(1) *Failure to Disclose or Supplement.* If a party fails to provide information or identify a witness as required by Rule 26(a) or (e), the party is not allowed to use that information or witness to supply evidence on a motion, at a hearing, or at a trial, unless the failure was substantially justified or is harmless. In addition to or instead of this sanction, the court, on motion and after giving an opportunity to be heard:

(A) may order payment of the reasonable expenses, including attorney's fees, caused by the failure;

(B) may inform the jury of the party's failure; and

(C) may impose other appropriate sanctions, including any of the orders listed in Rule 37(b)(2)(A)(i)–(vi).

(2) *Failure to Admit.* If a party fails to admit what is requested under Rule 36 and if the requesting party later proves a document to be genuine or the matter true, the requesting party may move that the party who failed to admit pay the reasonable expenses, including attorney's

fees, incurred in making that proof. The court must so order unless:
(A) the request was held objectionable under Rule 36(a);
(B) the admission sought was of no substantial importance;
(C) the party failing to admit had a reasonable ground to believe that it might prevail on the matter; or
(D) there was other good reason for the failure to admit.
(d) PARTY'S FAILURE TO ATTEND ITS OWN DEPOSITION, SERVE ANSWERS TO INTERROGATORIES, OR RESPOND TO A REQUEST FOR INSPECTION.
(1) *In General.*
(A) *Motion; Grounds for Sanctions.* The court where the action is pending may, on motion, order sanctions if:
(i) a party or a party's officer, director, or managing agent—or a person designated under Rule 30(b)(6) or 31(a)(4)—fails, after being served with proper notice, to appear for that person's deposition; or
(ii) a party, after being properly served with interrogatories under Rule 33 or a request for inspection under Rule 34, fails to serve its answers, objections, or written response.
(B) *Certification.* A motion for sanctions for failing to answer or respond must include a certification that the movant has in good faith conferred or attempted to confer with the party failing to act in an effort to obtain the answer or response without court action.
(2) *Unacceptable Excuse for Failing to Act.* A failure described in Rule 37(d)(1)(A) is not excused on the ground that the discovery sought was objectionable, unless the party failing to act has a pending motion for a protective order under Rule 26(c).
(3) *Types of Sanctions.* Sanctions may include any of the orders listed in Rule 37(b)(2)(A)(i)–(vi). Instead of or in addition to these sanctions, the court must require the party failing to act, the attorney advising that party, or both to pay the reasonable expenses, including attorney's fees, caused by the failure, unless the failure was substantially justified or other circumstances make an award of expenses unjust.
(e) FAILURE TO PROVIDE ELECTRONICALLY STORED INFORMATION.
Absent exceptional circumstances, a court may not impose sanctions under these rules on a party for failing to provide electronically stored information lost as a result of the routine, good-faith operation of an electronic information system.
(f) FAILURE TO PARTICIPATE IN FRAMING A DISCOVERY PLAN. If a party or its attorney fails to participate in good faith in developing and submitting a proposed discovery plan as required by Rule 26(f), the court may, after giving an opportunity to be heard, require that party or attorney to pay to any other party the reasonable expenses, including attorney's fees, caused by the failure.

Roadway Express, Inc. v. Piper,

United States Supreme Court
447 U.S. 752 (1980)

Mr. Justice POWELL delivered the opinion of the Court.

This case presents the question whether federal courts have statutory or inherent power to tax attorney's fees directly against counsel who have abused the processes of the courts.

I

In June 1975, two former employees and one unsuccessful job applicant brought a civil rights class action against petitioner Roadway Express, Inc. (Roadway). The complaint filed in the United States District Court for the Western District of Louisiana alleged that Roadway's employment policies discriminated on the basis of race… .

Counsel for the plaintiffs—Robert E. Piper, Jr., Frank E. Brown, Jr., and Bobby Stromile—are the respondents in the present case. In September 1975, respondents served interrogatories on Roadway. Having secured an extension from the District Court, Roadway answered the interrogatories on January 5,

1976, and served its own set of interrogatories at the same time. Thereafter, however, the litigation was stalled by respondents' uncooperative behavior.

On April 13, 1976, Roadway moved for an order compelling answers to its interrogatories. The motion was set for argument on the morning of April 21, but counsel for the plaintiffs did not appear. They did attend a rescheduled hearing that afternoon, and the Magistrate ordered that the interrogatories be answered by May 24. Respondents ignored that deadline and, in fact, never answered the interrogatories. Roadway also served notice in April that it would take depositions from all three plaintiffs in early May. One of the plaintiffs did not appear on the appointed days, however, and he never was deposed.

The respondents showed no greater respect for the orders of the District Court than for the requests of their adversaries. On April 7, the court instructed counsel for both sides to file briefs evaluating the impact of a recent decision in a related case. Although respondents' brief was due within 10 days, nothing arrived for six weeks. On May 19, the District Court gave respondents 10 additional days to file a brief or face dismissal of the action. No brief was ever submitted.

On June 14, Roadway moved to dismiss the suit under Federal Rule of Civil Procedure 37.[fn] Roadway also requested an award of attorney's fees and court costs. On June 30, the District Court heard argument and dismissed the action with prejudice. A second hearing, limited to the question of costs and attorney's fees, was held in October 1976.

The District Court's opinion sharply criticized the respondents for their "deliberate inaction" in handling the case. [C] ... [T]he court concluded that the three lawyers "improvidently enlarged and inadequately prosecuted" the action, [c]. As a sanction, the court ordered them to pay Roadway's costs and attorney's fees for the entire lawsuit. The total assessment exceeded $17,000. [C] ...

Federal Rule of Civil Procedure 37(b) authorizes sanctions for failure to comply with discovery orders. The District Court may bar the disobedient party from introducing certain evidence, or it may direct that certain facts shall be "taken to be established for the purposes of the action. ..." The Rule also permits the trial court to strike claims from the pleadings, and even to "dismiss the action ... or render a judgment by default against the disobedient party." See National Hockey League v. Metropolitan Hockey Club, 427 U.S. 639[] (1976) (*per curiam*); [c]. Both parties and counsel may be held personally liable for expenses, "including attorney's fees," caused by the failure to comply with discovery orders.[fn] Rule 37 sanctions must be applied diligently both "to penalize those whose conduct may be deemed to warrant such a sanction, [and] to deter those who might be tempted to such conduct in the absence of such a deterrent." *National Hockey League v. Metropolitan Hockey Club, supra*, at 643[].

The respondents in this case never have complied with the District Court's order that they answer Roadway's interrogatories. That failure was the immediate ground for dismissing the case, [c], and it also exposed respondents and their clients to liability under Rule 37(b) for the resulting costs and attorney's fees. Indeed, Roadway's motion for dismissal sought recovery of those expenses under Rule 37. On the remand of this action, the District Court will have the authority to act upon that request. ...

Roadway also contends that the District Court's ruling was a proper exercise of the court's inherent powers.[fn] The inherent powers of federal courts are those which "are necessary to the exercise of all others." United States v. Hudson, 7 Cranch 32, 34[] (1812). The most prominent of these is the contempt sanction, "which a judge must have and exercise in protecting the due and orderly administration of justice and in maintaining the authority and dignity of the court . ..." Cooke v. United States, 267 U.S. 517, 539[] (1925); [c]. Because inherent powers are shielded from direct democratic controls, they must be exercised with restraint and discretion. See Gompers v. Bucks Stove & Range Co., 221 U.S. 418, 450-451[] (1911); [c]. There are ample grounds for recognizing, however, that in narrowly defined circumstances federal courts have inherent power to assess attorney's fees against counsel.

In Link v. Wabash R. Co., 370 U.S. 626, 632[] (1962), this Court recognized the "well-acknowledged" inherent power of a court to levy sanctions in response to abusive litigation practices. The trial court had dismissed an action for failure to prosecute. ... Since the assessment of counsel fees is a less severe sanction than outright dismissal, *Link* strongly supports Roadway's contention here.

Of course, the general rule in federal courts is that a litigant cannot recover his counsel fees. See *Alyeska Pipeline Co. v. Wilderness Society, [supra,]* at 257[]. But that rule does not apply when the opposing party has acted in bad faith. ...

The bad-faith exception for the award of attorney's fees is not restricted to cases where the action is filed in bad faith. "'[B]ad faith' may be found, not only in the actions that led to the lawsuit, but also in the conduct of the litigation." Hall v. Cole, 412 U.S. 1, 15[] (1973). [C] This view coincides with the ruling in *Link, supra*, which approved judicial power to dismiss a case not because the substantive claim was without merit, but because the plaintiff failed to pursue the litigation.

The power of a court over members of its bar is at least as great as its authority over litigants.[fn] If a court may tax counsel fees against a party who has litigated in bad faith, it certainly may assess those expenses against counsel who willfully abuse judicial processes. [C] Like other sanctions, attorney's fees certainly should not be assessed lightly or without fair notice and an opportunity for a hearing on the record.[fn] But in a proper case, such sanctions are within a court's powers.

... Since the District Court did not consider the costs and fees that Roadway might recover under Rule 37, that question must be addressed on remand. Similarly, the trial court did not make a specific finding as to whether counsel's conduct in this case constituted or was tantamount to bad faith, a finding that would have to precede any sanction under the court's inherent powers. The case is remanded to the Court of Appeals with directions to return it to the District Court for proceedings consistent with this opinion.

So ordered.

Mr. Justice BLACKMUN, concurring in part and dissenting in part[, omitted].

Mr. Justice STEVENS, concurring in part and dissenting in part[, omitted].

Mr. Chief Justice BURGER, dissenting[, omitted].

INQUIRY

Ignoring Requests. FED. R. CIV. P. 37(a) authorizes motions to enforce discovery requests and provides for sanctions against losers of those motions. Most motions involve objections to discovery, refusals to provide discovery, conditional offers of discovery (only on the offeror's terms), or incomplete discovery responses. What happens when a party simply ignores a discovery request? Rule 37(d) has its own sanctions regime when a party fails to appear for a Rule 30 or 31 deposition, answer Rule 33 interrogatories, or respond to a Rule 34 production request. In those instances of non-response, Rule 37(d)(3) provides that the court may award the sanctions listed in Rule 37(b)(2)(A)(i)-(vi) (everything from taking matters as established and striking pleadings up to dismissal or default) without considering arguments of good faith or substantial justification for the non-response. Only when it comes to monetary awards of expenses does the non-responding party get a chance to explain the non-response. The effect of Rule 37(d) is to compel a party to attend to discovery without forcing the other party to make them do so. Rule 37(d) effectively counteracts the dilatory practice of not doing anything until the other side makes one do so. Next consider a case in which the party resisting discovery was clearly attentive to the request but claimed a most substantial reason for doing so. As you read the case, consider whether there is any greater interest in resisting discovery than the interest claimed in this case. Given its outcome, also consider whether there is any case in which the court would not compel similar discovery.

Coca-Cola Bottling Co. v. Coca-Cola Co.,

United States District Court for the District of Delaware
107 F.R.D. 288 (1985)

MURRAY M. SCHWARTZ, Chief Judge.

The complete formula for Coca-Cola is one of the best-kept trade secrets in the world. Although most of the ingredients are public knowledge, [c], the ingredient that gives Coca-Cola its distinctive taste is a secret combination of flavoring oils and ingredients known as "Merchandise 7X." The formula for Merchandise 7X has been tightly guarded since Coca-Cola was first invented and is known by only two persons within The Coca-Cola Company ("the Company"). The only written record of the secret formula is kept in a security vault at the Trust Company Bank in Atlanta, Georgia, which can only be opened upon a resolution from the Company's Board of Directors.

The impregnable barriers which the Company has erected to protect its valuable trade secret are now threatened by pretrial discovery requests in two connected cases before this Court. Plaintiffs in these lawsuits are bottlers of Coca-Cola products who seek declaratory, injunctive and monetary relief against the Company based upon allegations of breach of contract, violation of two 1921 Consent Decrees, trademark infringement, dilution of trademark value, and violation of federal antitrust laws, all of which allegedly occurred when the Company introduced diet Coke in 1982. Stripped to bare essentials, the plaintiffs' contention is that the Company is obligated to sell them the syrup used in the bottling of diet Coke under the terms of their existing contracts covering the syrup used in the bottling of Coca-Cola. The primary issue arising from this contention is whether the contractual term "Coca-Cola Bottler's Syrup" includes the syrup used to make diet Coke. Plaintiffs contend that in order to prevail on this issue, they need to discover the complete formula, including the secret ingredients, for Coca-Cola, as well as the complete formulae, also secret, for diet Coke and other Coca-Cola soft drinks. Accordingly, plaintiffs have filed a motion to compel production of the complete formulae under Fed.R.Civ.P. 37(a). Defendant, which has resisted disclosure of its secret formulae at every turn, contests the relevance of the complete formulae to the instant litigation and avers that disclosure of the secret formulae would cause great damage to the Company.

The issue squarely presented by plaintiffs' motion to compel is whether plaintiffs' need for the secret formulae outweighs defendant's need for protection of its trade secrets. In considering this dispute, I am well aware of the fact that disclosure of trade secrets in litigation, even with the use of an appropriate protective order, could "become by indirection the means of ruining an honest and profitable enterprise." 8 J. Wigmore, *Evidence* §2212, at 155 (McNaughton rev. 1961). Moreover, I am also aware that an order compelling disclosure of the Company's secret formulae could be a bludgeon in the hands of plaintiffs to force a favorable settlement. On the other hand, unless defendant is required to respond to plaintiffs' discovery, plaintiffs will be unable to learn whether defendant has done them a wrong. [C] Except for a few privileged matters, nothing is sacred in civil litigation; even the legendary barriers erected by The Coca-Cola Company to keep its formulae from the world must fall if the formulae are needed to allow plaintiffs and the Court to determine the truth in these disputes. ...

On July 8, 1982, the Company introduced diet Coke to the market with great fanfare. The name was chosen carefully and focused on the descriptive nature of the word "diet" and the tremendous market recognition of "Coke." The advertising emphasized the taste of the new cola and its relationship to Coke. The public response to diet Coke has been phenomenal—in just three years, it has become the third largest selling soft drink in the United States and the best-selling diet soft drink in the world.

The introduction of diet Coke immediately gave rise to a dispute between Coke bottlers and the Company over what price bottlers must pay for diet Coke syrup. The Company took the position that diet Coke was not within the scope of the existing contracts, and a new contract term with flexible pricing would have to be developed. Many of the bottlers ... believed that the Company was obligated to provide diet Coke under the terms of their existing Bottler's Contracts for Coca-Cola. This dispute led to the filing of these lawsuits in early 1983. ...

After extensive discovery, plaintiffs filed the instant motion that, in essence, seeks to compel the Company to produce the complete formulae, including secret ingredients, for Coca-Cola, diet Coke, caffeine free Coca-Cola, caffeine free diet Coke, TAB, and every experimental cola formula developed and tested by the Company for possible marketing under the Coca-Cola or Coke trademarks.[fn] Defendant... has objected to plaintiffs' discovery wherever it approached matters related to the secret formulae. Thus, plaintiffs have been foreclosed both from learning the formulae themselves and from learning about other matters that relate to the formulae.

In support of their motion to compel, plaintiffs have contended that the secret formulae are relevant and necessary to prove their contentions and respond to defendant's argument that Coca-Cola and diet Coke are two different products.

In response, the Company denies that the formulae are relevant and essential to resolve the central issues in these cases, and also contends that disclosure of these trade secrets is inappropriate at this stage of the litigation. On May 8, 1985, the Court heard extensive oral argument on these issues and received evidence concerning the introduction of new Coke. At the hearing, the Court explored with the parties the possibility of resolving the formula discovery issues by a suitable stipulation, which would obviate the need for the Company to disclose its secrets. A stipulation that the secret ingredients in diet Coke and Coke are identical was used to avoid the disclosure of the secret formulae at the preliminary injunction stage, but plaintiffs indicated at the hearing that the same stipulation was no longer acceptable, in part because it is not true. …

It is well established that trade secrets are not absolutely privileged from discovery in litigation. *See, e.g.,* Federal Open Market Committee v. Merrill, 443 U.S. 340, 362[] (1979); [cc]. In order to resist discovery of a trade secret, a party must first demonstrate by competent evidence that the information sought through discovery is a trade secret and that disclosure of the secret might be harmful. [Cc] If this showing is made, … [t]he level of necessity that must be shown is that the information must be necessary for the movant to prepare its case for trial, which includes proving its theories and rebutting its opponent's theories. [Cc]

Once relevancy and need have been established, the Court must balance the need for the information against the injury that would ensue if disclosure is ordered. *Federal Open Market Committee v. Merrill, [supra,]* at 362[]; [cc]. Because protective orders are available to limit the extent to which disclosure is made, the relevant injury to be weighed in the balance is not the injury that would be caused by public disclosure, but the injury that would result from disclosure under an appropriate protective order. …

The balance between the need for information and the need for protection against the injury caused by disclosure is tilted in favor of disclosure once relevance and necessity have been shown. As the Supreme Court has recognized, "orders forbidding any disclosure of trade secrets or confidential commercial information are rare." *Federal Open Market Committee v. Merrill, [supra,]* at 362n.24[]; [cc]. A survey of the relevant case law reveals that discovery is virtually always ordered once the movant has established that the secret information is relevant and necessary. [Cc] … As Judge Learned Hand stated in one of the earliest trade secret cases: "It is true that the result may be to compel the defendant to disclose [trade secrets], and that that may damage the defendant ... That is, however, an inevitable incident to any inquiry in such a case; unless the defendant may be made to answer, the plaintiff is deprived of its right to learn whether the defendant has done it a wrong." Grasselli Chemical Corp. v. National Aniline & Chemical Co., 282 Fed. 379, 381 (S.D. N.Y. 1920). …

To satisfy its burden of proving that the Coca-Cola formulae qualify for trade secret protection, defendant has submitted the affidavit of Robert A. Keller, Senior Vice President and General Counsel of the Company. [C] According to the Keller affidavit, the Company has taken every precaution to prevent disclosure of the formula for "Merchandise 7X," the secret ingredient in old Coke. The written version of the secret formula is kept in a security vault at the Trust Company Bank in Atlanta, and that vault can only be opened by a resolution from the Company's Board of Directors. It is the Company's policy that only two persons in the Company shall know the formula at any one time, and that only those persons may oversee the actual preparation of Merchandise 7X. The Company refuses to allow the identity of those persons to be disclosed or to allow those persons to fly on the same airplane at the same time. The same precautions are taken regarding the secret formulae of the Company's other cola drinks-diet Coke, caffeine free diet Coke, TAB, caffeine free TAB, and caffeine free Coca-Cola. ...

The Keller affidavit further states that these secret formulae are highly valued assets of the Company and have never been disclosed to persons outside the Company. As an indication of the value the Company places on its secret formulae, Keller avers that the Company elected to forego producing Coca-Cola in India, a potential market of 550 million persons, because the Indian government required the Company to disclose the secret formula for Coca-Cola as a condition of doing business there. ...

Although some of the mystique surrounding the Coca-Cola formulae is the creation of marketing hype, it is beyond dispute that, behind the hype, the Company possesses trade secrets which have been carefully safeguarded and which are extremely valuable. It is also evident that any disclosure of those trade secrets would be harmful to the Company. Accordingly, I find that defendant's secret formulae are trade secrets and subject to the maximum protection that the law ... allows. ...

Plaintiffs contend that discovery of these secret formulae is required because they are relevant and necessary to the presentation of plaintiffs' case. ...

A major issue common to both actions is whether diet Coke and Coca-Cola are the same product. The Company's primary defense has been that Coca-Cola and diet Coke are two separate and distinct products. Plaintiffs contend that the complete formulae for diet Coke and Coca-Cola would be relevant to rebut this defense by showing that the two colas share common attributes and that any differences between the two are insignificant and merely reflect attempts to achieve taste identity. ...

... When this Court previously addressed the merits of this litigation in the context of a motion for preliminary injunction, the first issue addressed was whether Coke and diet Coke are two versions of the same product. ... [A]ll the ingredients are relevant to determine whether the two colas are the same product. In fact, the secret ingredients may be the most relevant ones because the secret ingredients are what gives these drinks their distinctive tastes. ...

Plaintiffs could use the secret formulae to prove one of several product identity theories. ... The complete formulae, once known, will tend to make a disputed fact more (or less) likely: that, for purposes of this litigation, diet Coke syrup is Bottler's Syrup. ...

As in most disputes over the discoverability of trade secrets, [cc], the necessity of the discovery of the complete formulae follows logically from the determination that the formulae are relevant. Plaintiffs need the complete formulae in order to address the product identity issue by comparing the ingredients of the various soft drinks involved. Plaintiffs cannot respond to the assertions of defendant's experts that diet Coke and Coca-Cola are two products unless plaintiffs' experts can analyze the complete formulae and explain why the products are the same.[fn] ... Without the complete formulae, plaintiffs will be foreclosed from presenting all the relevant evidence in support of their position. ...

After the hearing, defendant attempted to remove the necessity for the information by offering to stipulate that the secret ingredients in old Coke, new Coke and diet Coke are identical. Defendant contends that this result is the most favorable set of facts that plaintiffs could hope to find through discovery. It is evident, however, that the actual formulae could be more favorable to plaintiffs than this stipulation. For example, if the secret ingredients in new Coke and diet Coke are very similar but different than the secret ingredients in old Coke, that would favor plaintiffs, as indicated above. ...

The final part of the test for discoverability of trade secrets is to balance the need for disclosure against the harm that would ensue from disclosure. The potential harm that would come from public disclosure of the formulae for old Coke, new Coke, diet Coke, and caffeine free Coke is great, [c], but virtually all of that harm can be eliminated with stringent protective orders and other safeguards. Because plaintiffs are Coca-Cola bottlers, they will have an incentive to keep the formulae secret. The likelihood of harm is less than if defendant's trade secrets were disclosed in litigation to competitors. [Cc] The potential for harm from protected disclosure of the formulae for old Coke, new Coke, diet Coke, and caffeine free Coke is outweighed by the plaintiffs' need for the information. While plaintiffs' need for the experimental cola formulae is less strong, this lesser need is counterbalanced by the fact that the harm resulting from disclosure of these formulae would be less severe, because those colas have never been marketed and are less valuable trade secrets.

In sum, the product identity issue is important in these two cases, and analyses of the complete formulae will be a significant part of the proof on that issue. Plaintiffs' need for this information outweighs the harm that disclosure under protective order would cause. Disclosure will be ordered. ...

It has been held that defendant must disclose its complete formulae, including secret ingredients, for diet Coke, old Coke, new Coke, caffeine free Coke, and certain experimental low calorie colas, but not the formulae for TAB and caffeine free diet Coke. ... Given the proprietary nature of the formula information, however, a more stringent protective order than the one currently in effect is warranted to prevent public disclosure of the formulae. For example, it may be advisable to limit the disclosure of the formulae to plaintiffs' trial counsel and independent experts. [Cc] Because the parties have not addressed what additional protective measures would be satisfactory, the Court will not enter a new protective order at this time. Instead, the parties shall negotiate a protective order that both allows access to information and prevents disclosure of trade secrets. The parties shall submit that order within twenty days.

INQUIRY

Sanctions. Coca-Cola Co. refused to comply with the above opinion requiring disclosure of its secret formulas. What sanction would be most appropriate for that refusal? Rule 37(b)(2)(A) is a non-exhaustive list of the sanctions that a federal district court may impose for refusal to obey a discovery order. The list includes everything from monetary sanctions to dismissal or default. In a subsequent order in the same case, the district court decided not to default Coca-Cola Co. but to grant its opposing bottlers every possible inference from the refusal to disclose the formulas including that the formulas for old Coke and diet Coke were identical. The court also imposed monetary sanctions in the amount of the costs and attorney's fees that the bottlers had incurred in the motion to compel. Coca-Cola Bottling Co. v. Coca-Cola Co., 110 F.R.D. 363 (D. Del. 1986). Next consider a case imposing an attorney's fee award as a sanction for failing to produce documents and for evasive answers to admission requests. Notice how the trial court determined the basis for the fee award and its amount.

Poole v. Textron,

United States District Court for the District of Maryland
192 F.R.D. 494 (2000)

GAUVEY, United States Magistrate Judge. ...

This is a product liability case in which the plaintiff, Ryan W. Poole ("Poole"), has sued Textron, Inc. ("Textron") for alleged defects in a golf car, which resulted in serious injuries to him. The trial judge referred the undersigned all discovery disputes. ...

Before the Court is plaintiff's request for attorneys' fees and other expenses related to the three substantive discovery motions and other sanctions... . This Court has already ruled on the merits of these three motions. The current issue facing the Court is whether an award of expenses including attorneys' fees or other sanction is justified under the governing rules and case law and if so, the amount of expenses or sanction. ...

For the reasons stated below, the Court awards $37,258.39 in expenses, including attorneys' fees, but declines to award any other sanction under the rules or its inherent power. ...

... [T]his Court finds the sanctioning scheme of Rules 37 and 26 of the Federal Rules of Civil Procedure sufficient to redress the violations here without exercise of the inherent powers.

... Fed. R. Civ. P. 37 governs both the entitlement to expenses and the amount of such expenses. If such a motion is granted, the Rule provides, in pertinent part: "[T]he Court *shall* ... require the party ... whose conduct necessitated the motion or the ... attorney advising such conduct or both of them to pay to the moving party the *reasonable expenses* incurred in making the motion, *including attorneys' fees, unless* the Court finds that ... the opposing party's non-disclosure, response or objection was substantially justified, or that other circumstances make an award of expenses unjust." Fed. R. Civ. P. 37(a)(4)(A) (emphasis added). Where, as here, the motion is granted in part and denied in part, the court shall "apportion the reasonable expenses incurred in relation to the motion among the parties and persons in a just manner." Fed. R. Civ. P. 37(a)(4). The Court has determined that there was no substantial justification for Textron's non-disclosure, responses and objections and that there were no circumstances that made an award of expenses unjust.

Similarly, Rule 26(g)(3) provides, in pertinent part, that "if without substantial justification a certification is made in violation of the rule, the Court, upon motion or upon its own initiative *shall* impose upon the person who made the certification, the party on whose behalf the disclosure request, response, or objection is made, or both, an *appropriate sanction* which *may* include an order to pay the amount of *reasonable expenses* incurred because of the violation, *including a reasonable attorney's fee*" (emphasis added). By its language, Rule 26(g)(3) does not limit a court to the award of expenses only, but gives the Court latitude to fashion an "appropriate sanction," in addition to an award of expenses. Nevertheless, an award of attorneys' fees appear to be the sanction most commonly imposed in reported decisions. [C][fn] The Court has determined that while counsel for Textron signed the various discovery responses,[fn] counsel had not conducted the requisite "reasonable inquiry" and that the quality of the responses suggested an improper purpose, specifically "to cause unnecessary delay or needless cost of litigation." Fed. R. Civ. P. 26(g). Accordingly, there was no substantial justification for the certifications in violation of the rule. ...

Regarding plaintiff's motion for determination of the sufficiency of Textron's answers and objections to plaintiff's request for admissions, the Court finds under Rule 37, in conjunction with Rule 36, that Textron's responses or objections were not substantially justified. To the contrary, with one exception, the responses and objections appeared crafted to sabotage the legitimate use of request for admissions. Under the plain language of the rule, a party must *either* lodge an objection *or* an answer to a request, but cannot do both. ...

Rule 36 expressly permits a party to qualify an answer, but only "when good faith requires." ...

In almost every response, Textron impermissibly lodged both an objection and an answer. Moreover, when Textron filed an answer, its complexity "undermine[d] the efficacy of the rule by crediting disingenuous, hair-splitting distinctions whose unarticulated goal is unfairly to burden an opposing party." Thalheim[v. Eberheim], 124 F.R.D. [34,] 35 [(D. Conn. 1988)] (citations omitted).

Accordingly, this Court believes the defendant's responses and objections lacked substantial justification. As the Court granted relief as to 12 out of the 13 contested requests (or 92% of the requests), the Court grants that percentage of the attorney time and expenses reasonably related to this motion. *See* Fed. R. Civ. P. 37(a)(4). ...

In his motion for sanctions filed pursuant to Rule 37 and the inherent powers of the Court, plaintiff charged that defendant Textron engaged in "improper discovery tactics [which] were willful, inexcusable and not in good faith" [c] and asked for a finding of liability, or alternatively certain relief tailored to each of the alleged instances of discovery abuse. [C] The Court found that many of plaintiff's complaints of discovery abuse were meritorious, and ordered considerable relief in terms of further investigation and production of discovery responses.[fn] ...

The conduct this Court has found sanctionable violates Fed. R. Civ. P. 37, and, in some instances, Fed. R. Civ. P. 26(g) as well. Particularly egregious was Textron's lack of diligence in providing key, requested information, such as prior litigation involving the golf car model or testing... .

This Court has concluded, as plaintiff states, that "Textron did not perform an even minimally-adequate search for documents prior to Plaintiff's Motion for Sanctions." [C] ... Textron's initial inquiry in response to written discovery requests (as well as Rule 30(b)(6) corporate designation) started and largely, if not entirely, stopped with an inquiry to ... a Textron reliability engineer and E-Z-Go's designee in golf car litigation since 1981 and with a review of the official corporate records of Textron.[fn] It appears that Textron did not even contact its own employees in other corporate departments, such as the manager of Textron's Commercial and Media Relations, [c], to respond to the document requests or requests attached to the corporate designee notice. ...

However, another and perhaps greater proof of the inadequacy of the initial inquiry was ... the sheer volume of documents produced *after* plaintiff's motions and court order compared to that produced in response to discovery demands under the rules demonstrates the inadequacy of Textron's initial efforts. Textron initially produced a single page in response to plaintiff's document request. [C] ... After plaintiff filed his Motion for Sanctions, Textron produced 20 videotapes and more than 2,900 additional pages of documents that are responsive to the discovery requests. [C] Given the results of court-mandated efforts, it is clear that these documents were in the control of Textron and that a reasonable search would have located them.

Second, a review of Textron's responses to certain of plaintiff's specific discovery requests likewise demonstrates the lack of an adequate inquiry. For example, plaintiff had propounded a request for "[a]ll advertisements and promotional materials that concern or refer to the GX-440, X-440, GX-444, and X-444 for model years 1978 through 1990." [C] ... In response, Textron produced a single brochure. [C] ...

After the Court-ordered investigation, Textron produced 229 pages of advertising and promotional materials, [c], including photos of the golf cars on grassy slopes much like that on which the accident occurred here. ...

Similarly, plaintiff had propounded a request for "[a]ll documents that reflect, refer or relate to any tests performed on or concerning the GX-440, X-440, GX-444, and X-444 that pertain to stability, safety, rollovers, and warning labels." [C] Textron's first response was to object for a host of reasons, including that tests on golf cars other than the GX-440 are not relevant evidence. [C]

... But, in response to this Court's Order, Textron has now produced a list of thousands of tests performed by its E-Z-Go Division ([c]), many appearing to be relevant such as "Golf Car Slope Limits" and "Spring Rate Reduction and Effects on Rolls." [C] These additional tests, of course, were produced after much, if not all, of the discovery was complete, indeed after the discovery deadline.

Rule 26(g) of the Federal Rules of Procedure defines the duty of counsel in responding to discovery requests. That is, counsel must make "a reasonable effort to assure that the client has provided all the information and documents responsive to the discovery demand." Advisory Committee Notes to 1983 Amendments to Rule 26(g). ... In this case, it is clear that defendant's counsel did not make a reasonable effort under the Rule to assure that its client had complied fully with plaintiff's discovery requests and obtained all documents within its possession, custody and control. ...

In an attempt to ward off any sanction, Textron represents to this Court that its counsel spent at least 154.6 hours on document collection and investigation efforts to comply with the Court's May 22, 1999 Order, at a cost to Textron of $23,260... . Such an interpretation of the rules would encourage sharp practices and dilatory responses to legitimate discovery demands. If the only sanction for failing to comply with the discovery rules is having to comply with the discovery rules if you are caught, the diligent are punished and the less than diligent, rewarded. Indeed, Rule 37 itself defeats such an interpretation, as it provides, *inter alia,* that the Court shall award the moving party fees if the discovery is provided by ruling or simply after the motion is filed. Fed. R. Civ. P. 37(a)(4)(A).

This is clearly not a situation where justice should be tempered by mercy, given the comparative resources of the plaintiff and defendant, and the inescapable conclusion that Textron's stonewalling on discovery played on that disparity. … Rule 37 sanctions must be applied diligently both "to penalize those whose conduct may be deemed to warrant such a sanction, [and] to deter those who might be tempted to such conduct in the absence of such a deterrent." Nat'l Hockey League v. Metropolitan Hockey Club, 427 U.S. 639, 643[] (1976). Likewise, "Rule 26(g) is designed to curb discovery abuse by explicitly encouraging imposition of sanctions." Advisory Committee Notes to 1983 Amendments to Fed. R. Civ. P. 26. …

Having rejected Textron's argument that its remedial efforts were a sufficient sanction, the Court will consider the appropriate amount of the sanctions award.

Rule 37 is straight-forward and directive: Courts "shall ... require ... the party or attorney or both of them to pay to the moving party the reasonable expenses incurred in making the motion, including attorney's fees ... unless ... other circumstances make an award of expenses unjust." Similarly, Rule 26(g) provides that "[i]f without substantial justification a certification is made in violation of the rule, the court ... shall impose on the [attorney], the party ... or both, an appropriate sanction which may include an order to pay the amount of reasonable expenses incurred because of the violation, including a reasonable attorney's fee." …

… The reasonableness of the attorneys' fees is to be subject to an "independent" analysis by the court, [c,] and necessarily requires a review of contemporaneous timesheets to insure that the time expended in the motion was not excessive to the task and … a consideration of the hourly rate charged in light of fees charged in the legal community for services of like kind and quality.

Based on its independent analysis, this Court has concluded that the attorneys' fees and other expenses requested are, in the main, justifiable. As to the time expended, while the Court invited comment, Textron did not identif[y] any work as excessive or duplicative. While the total number of hours—260.4—and the attorneys' fees for those hours—$48,527—are staggering, review of the contemporaneous timesheets does not reveal any evident inefficiency or litigation overkill. Plaintiff's motions dealt with numerous disputes over a long discovery period. The complexity (and cost) of plaintiff's motions' effort could be seen as a result of Textron's obduracy on several discovery fronts. …

As to the hourly rate, Textron vigorously challenges the rates sought by plaintiff: $240 an hour for Mr. Freeman admitted to the bar in 1986; $235 an hour for Ms. McKee admitted to the bar in 1985; $155 an hour for Ms. Willis admitted to the bar in 1995; $265 an hour for Mr. Goldstein admitted to the bar in 1973; and $75 an hour for paralegals.[fn] Their affidavits demonstrate their admirable educational achievements and extensive experience. Their abilities are evident in the work in this case. Plaintiff has provided five affidavits from lawyers in the Baltimore legal community attesting to the customary rates charged for the same or similarly legal services in complex litigation. The rates sought here for plaintiff's four lawyers are within, with one or two exceptions, the rates attested to in all plaintiff's affidavits.[fn] …

In reaching the amount of $37,258.39 in reasonable attorneys' fees and expenses, the Court has applied the "success" rate in each motion to the hours documented for each motion and multiplied by the hourly rate.[fn] *See* Fed. R. Civ. P. 37(a)(4).

For all these reasons, the Court imposes a monetary sanction of $37,258.39 jointly and severally against Andrew Gendron of Goodell, DeVries, Leech and Gray and Textron, Inc.[fn] Mr. Thomas M. Goss is jointly and severally liable with Mr. Gendron and Textron for $4,206.24 of that $37,258.39, which are the fees and costs associated with the motion to determine the sufficiency of answers and objections to requests for admission.

Where, as here, a party has in-house counsel, the approach to discovery is rarely left entirely to outside counsel. Often defense strategy is largely dictated by the client's inside legal team. At a minimum, defense strategy is the product of the consensus of inside and outside counsel. … The Court will not attempt to determine how much fault lies with Textron and its inside counsel and how much fault lies with outside counsel. Accordingly, the award is joint and several. …

The Court takes no pleasure in the imposition of this considerable expense award against well known members of the bar and members of a respected Baltimore law firm. However, … [m]any fine defense counsel have accommodated their duty to the Court without sacrifice of their client's interest in a vigorous defense.

A separate Order will issue.

INQUIRY

Magistrate Judges. You may have noticed that United States magistrate judges made the decisions in several of the above cases including *Poole v. Textron, Hopson v. Mayor of Baltimore,* and *Chiquita International Ltd. v. M/V Bolero Reefer*. The president appoints and Senate confirms United States district court judges under the Constitution's Article III for lifetime appointment. By contrast, magistrate judges serve under 28 U.S.C. §631 to assist district court judges. The judges of each federal district vote on the appointment of magistrate judges, granting them 8-year terms. As further discussed in Chapter XII, magistrate judges have authority with consent of the parties to conduct trials of cases in place of the assigned district judge. United States district court judges may designate a magistrate judge to hear pretrial matters, although the authorizing statute reserves to the designating district court judge the right to reconsider any clearly erroneous or contrary-to-law ruling. 28 U.S.C. §636(b)(1)(A). FED. R. CIV. P. 72, set forth below in full, provides additional detail regarding the magistrate judge's order, objections to orders, and district judge review. Also, read FED. R. CIV. P. 78 on scheduling motion hearings.

FED. R. CIV. P. 72. Magistrate Judges: Pretrial Order

(a) NONDISPOSITIVE MATTERS. When a pretrial matter not dispositive of a party's claim or defense is referred to a magistrate judge to hear and decide, the magistrate judge must promptly conduct the required proceedings and, when appropriate, issue a written order stating the decision. A party may serve and file objections to the order within 14 days after being served with a copy. A party may not assign as error a defect in the order not timely objected to. The district judge in the case must consider timely objections and modify or set aside any part of the order that is clearly erroneous or is contrary to law.

(b) DISPOSITIVE MOTIONS AND PRISONER PETITIONS.

(1) *Findings and Recommendations.* A magistrate judge must promptly conduct the required proceedings when assigned, without the parties' consent, to hear a pretrial matter dispositive of a claim or defense or a prisoner petition challenging the conditions of confinement. A record must be made of all evidentiary proceedings and may, at the magistrate judge's discretion, be made of any other proceedings. The magistrate judge must enter a recommended disposition, including, if appropriate, proposed findings of fact. The clerk must promptly mail a copy to each party.

(2) *Objections.* Within 14 days after being served with a copy of the recommended disposition, a party may serve and file specific written objections to the proposed findings and recommendations. A party may respond to another party's objections within 14 days after being served with a copy. Unless the district judge orders otherwise, the objecting party must promptly arrange for transcribing the record, or whatever portions of it the parties agree to or the magistrate judge considers sufficient.

(3) *Resolving Objections.* The district judge must determine de novo any part of the magistrate judge's disposition that has been properly objected to. The district judge may accept, reject, or modify the recommended disposition; receive further evidence; or return the matter to the magistrate judge with instructions.

…

FED. R. CIV. P. 78. Hearing Motions; Submission on Briefs

(a) PROVIDING A REGULAR SCHEDULE FOR ORAL HEARINGS. A court may establish regular times and places for oral hearings on motions.

(b) PROVIDING FOR SUBMISSION ON BRIEFS. By rule or order, the court may provide for submitting and determining motions on briefs, without oral hearings.

INQUIRY

Summary. Parties anticipating litigation owe duties to preserve evidence. When litigation commences, they must produce evidence through initial voluntary disclosures and in response to other parties' requests. Discovery is a significant feature and extended stage of civil litigation during which many cases resolve and affecting the subsequent disposition by motion or at trial of many other cases. FED. R. CIV. P. 26 limits the scope of discovery to relevant, non-privileged information that is either admissible evidence or likely to lead to the discovery of admissible evidence. Parties need not produce attorney work product prepared anticipating litigation and reflecting an attorney's mental impressions about the case. Parties also need not produce information that is within the attorney-client privilege and other common-law privileges but must indicate by privilege log when that information is withheld. Parties may further limit discovery by showing that complying with it would be unduly burdensome or, in the case of electronically stored information, that it is not reasonably accessible. FED R. CIV. P. 37 authorizes parties to move to compel discovery responses from parties resisting discovery. Rule 37 also authorizes sanctions for the failure to respond and for refusing to respond when response was due. Sanctions may begin with awards of costs and attorney's fees and continue through issue preclusion all the way to dismissal or default.

Career

In what state do you expect to practice? Because individual state bars license lawyers, civil-litigation practices tend to remain within a state. Any single case may require depositions all over the country, but a lawyer will tend to file and try cases in a single state (the state in which the lawyer has a license). Lawyers share values based on their common education and training. Yet each state bar and professional community has its own history and culture. As you study civil procedure and read the cases, see if you can discern what some of those differences might be, and what might be your preference.

CHAPTER XI

ADJUDICATION BEFORE TRIAL

OBJECTIVE: That you be able to determine when a case is appropriate for summary judgment under the Supreme Court's articulation of the current Rule 56 standard.

Case Study: You have 45 days remaining for discovery in defense of an employer in an employment-rights case. You have taken the plaintiff's deposition and obtained the plaintiff's interrogatory answers and responses to document requests, indicating all of the evidence on which the plaintiff relies for the claim. Your client wants to know whether the court will now dismiss the case or allow it to proceed to trial. Articulate for the client the Rule 56 summary-judgment standard, giving examples of ways in which you could challenge the sufficiency of the plaintiff's case by motion for summary judgment.

Federal Rules of Civil Procedure this chapter reproduces and addresses:
FED. R. CIV. P. 16. Pretrial Conferences; Scheduling; Management
FED. R. CIV. P. 53. Masters
FED. R. CIV. P. 56. Summary Judgment
FED. R. CIV. P. 73. Magistrate Judges: Trial by Consent; Appeal

This chapter addresses pretrial conferences and orders, and summary judgment, relating to adjudications before trial. Here is how those subjects relate. Recently, total filings of new civil cases in the state and federal courts have dropped somewhat. Overall, clearance rates (the number of cases resolved versus the number filed) have improved slightly, reducing some backlogs. Yet the number and types of civil and criminal cases will certainly continue to fluctuate over time, responding to legislative, political, technological, social, and demographic trends. A single defective product like asbestos can significantly increase the number of new cases, as can social trends like rises in divorce and out-of-wedlock birth rates, and political issues like sentencing for drug-related crimes. Increased case filings interfere with the ability of the courts to manage their existing caseloads. Criminal trials have priority over civil trials due to constitutional and statutory speedy-trial rights. Overloaded and backlogged courts can have a severe effect on the timely resolution of civil cases.

The state courts tend to treat this phenomenon differently from the federal courts. Given the state courts' general jurisdiction, there is less of a sense of urgency or concern over public access to the state courts. If significantly more individuals and entities need civil justice in one area or another as trends rise and fall, then they should have it. State courts direct their concerns less toward limiting access and more toward whether the courts are adequately staffed and managed to respond. State courts suffer real crises due to increases in case filings and changes in litigation patterns. National Center for State Courts statistics from its report *Examining the Work of State Courts* (2005) indicate that a state-court trial judge carries an average docket of about 1,600 cases at any one time. Yet because there is no other justice system to which to turn, state courts tend to respond to increased litigation with specialty courts, temporary assignment of extra judicial resources, and other solutions that do not limit access.

By contrast, the federal courts have always been courts of limited jurisdiction. Congress can readily change that jurisdiction and routinely does so, for instance by increasing the monetary minimum for diversity jurisdiction. Thus, it is natural for the federal courts to view litigation management from the standpoint of controlling and limiting access to the federal justice system. Federal judges have an average caseload about one quarter to one third that of a state-court judge. Yet those figures do not mean that federal judges have it any easier than state-court judges. It is not solely the number of *cases* that determines whether a trial court can complete its work while functioning efficiently. Rather, it is the number and length of *trials*. A trial occupies several hours of every court day. Complex, high-stakes trials in federal court can easily last weeks. Just a handful of additional lengthy trials over the course of a year can make the difference between an efficiently functioning or severely backlogged court. Case-resolution rates thus become critical to a trial judge's ability to manage the court's docket. United States Department of Justice Bureau of Justice Statistics confirm what every practitioner knows, that as few as two percent of cases reach trial. Yet relatively small differences in trial rates and the pretrial stage when other cases resolve, with or without judicial intervention, can have a large impact on the ability of a court to manage its docket.

This dynamic creates critical points at the pretrial conference and summary judgment stages—the two points at which the federal district courts can most influence whether a case goes to trial and the two subjects of this chapter. There are statutory bases for federal pretrial adjudications. In 1990 Congress enacted the Civil Justice Reform Act, 28 U.S.C. §§471-482, requiring each federal judicial district to adopt a "civil justice expense and delay reduction plan." Then,

A. Pretrial Conference and Order

An introductory civil procedure course is not the place for detailed study of the skills necessary to pretrial procedures. Law schools offer specific courses on pretrial and trial skills, and clinical instruction covering both areas. You should understand the rules under which trial judges manage civil cases and the purposes and workings of those rules. FED. R. CIV. P. 16 and similar state-court rules govern pretrial practice. There can be significant differences in the way in which state and federal courts manage pretrial matters under that rule authority. Consider those differences before studying Rule 16.

It is relatively common in state courts for the trial judge to issue an automatic pretrial scheduling order as soon as there are appearances for all parties or a short while later. State-court practitioners will receive the pretrial order in the mail or perhaps at an informal pretrial conference held in the trial judge's chambers, enter the scheduled dates on their litigation calendars, and continue with their discovery and other pretrial preparation often without other significant involvement by the state court. Not so in federal court. The state-court practitioner who shows up in federal court expecting to walk into the judge's chambers for an informal pretrial should expect a very different welcome. Many federal judges conduct pretrial conferences from the bench on the record in open court. They or their staff will have studied the file closely enough to determine what to require of counsel to move the case forward—and not necessarily forward toward trial. The federal court may direct initial pretrial planning toward determining whether there are grounds to dismiss or for summary judgment, or opportunities to refer the case to another forum.

Practice

They met for the pretrial conference in the federal court's long marbled hallway. The plaintiff's lawyer immediately noticed a difference in the previously self-assured demeanor of the large-firm managing partner who was defending the case. "I've heard he's a real tiger," she said nervously to the plaintiff's lawyer, referring to the trial judge. The plaintiff's lawyer, who had been in the judge's courtroom many times before, nodded assent while trying to stifle a smile. They entered the empty courtroom and each sat at their respective counsel table. Precisely on the hour, the court staff marched solemnly in and remained standing, while the judicial secretary called all to rise. The trial judge entered brusquely through the door from chambers, causing the judicial secretary to tell the lawyers that they may sit.

Over the next half hour, the trial judge grilled counsel for both sides on their theories of the case, evidence in support, and expectations for discovery and trial. The plaintiff's lawyer smiled again when he saw defense counsel begin to relax—a mistake in this courtroom. Indeed, each time defense counsel rose to answer the trial judge's questions, she was rising a little lower, beginning first not to stand fully up and then gradually coming to the point where her seat was barely out of the chair when she answered—a common posture in relatively informal state court.

Then it happened. Right at the conclusion of the pretrial conference, defense counsel had spoken to the judge without rising from her chair. The judge exploded, excoriating defense counsel as if she were an elementary school truant rather than a distinguished managing partner from one of the state's most respected law firms. "You will stand in this courtroom and show the court its due respect," the trial judge was nearly yelling, piling on invective about large-firm lawyers, lawyers from the big city, lawyer incivility, and on and on. The court staff looked both embarrassed for defense counsel and amused.

It ended as quickly as it had begun, with the judge disappearing once again into chambers. The lawyers returned to the safe confines of the long marbled hallway. "Want to arbitrate this case?" defense counsel asked the plaintiff's lawyer. The plaintiff's lawyer again nodded assent while trying to stifle a sympathetic smile.

Rule 16(a) recognizes these purposes to expedite, control, and manage "so that the case will not be protracted because of lack of management." There are two primary means by which Rule 16 does so. The first means, authorized under Rule 16(b), is to issue a scheduling order within a specific time early in the case.

Rule 16(b)(3)(A) requires the order to limit the time within which parties join other parties, complete discovery, amend pleadings, and file motions. The point is not for an overzealous trial judge to require the parties to turn a pretrial order into something like a common law pleading. Yet there may be ways in which a trial judge can help the parties recognize and accept which are the central and supportable claims and defenses. The pretrial order may include other appropriate matters like limiting discovery, memorializing agreements concerning privileged information, setting a trial date, and memorializing agreements on producing electronically stored information.

Prudent practitioners recognize that pretrial orders do not merely establish voluntary schedules. They compel the parties to comply. The trial court may enforce its pretrial order as it would other court orders. *See* Fahim v. Marriott Hotel Services, Inc., 551 F.3d 344, 348 (5th Cir. 2008) (affirming denial of motion to modify pretrial scheduling order to amend pleadings); *see also* Kassner v. 2nd Avenue Delicatessen Inc., 496 F.3d 229 (2d Cir. 2007) (trial court may consider effect of Rule 16 scheduling order when deciding whether to permit late pleading amendment). Practitioners treat pretrial orders as they do other court orders, calendaring its dates, planning compliance, and requesting relief in advance when unable to comply. They fail to do so at their peril. Compliance with a pretrial order can be a prerequisite to relief that a party would otherwise be due and that may even be case dispositive. *See, e.g.,* Torres v. Commonwealth of Puerto Rico, 485 F.3d 5 (1st Cir 2007) (affirming denial of pretrial motion to dismiss based on sovereign immunity for failure to timely file it within terms of pretrial order). Tracinda Corp. v. DaimlerChrysler AG, 502 F.3d 212 (3d Cir. 2007), is a haunting example in which the appellate court upheld the trial court's sanction under Rule 16 of more than a half-million dollars for a party inadvertently not timely producing documents pursuant to the pretrial order.

The other means by which Rule 16 expedites cases is to authorize a pretrial conference. Rule 16(a) authorizes the court to direct counsel to appear with authority to stipulate to pretrial terms. Rule 16(c)(2) lists a wide range of 15 different specific pretrial matters conferences may address in addition to "facilitating in other ways the just, speedy, and inexpensive disposition of the action." Primary among those matters is to simplify the issues, eliminating unnecessary or insupportable claims and defenses. Amending pleadings, stipulating to facts, limiting testimony, planning summary judgment procedures, referring decision to magistrate judges or special masters, and timing discovery are other matters. Rule 16(c)(1) also authorizes the court to require parties to attend or be available to discuss settlement. See Chapter IX for issues that arise around Rule 16 settlement efforts. The breadth and detail of pretrial subjects, and the fact that Rule 16(f) authorizes sanctions where counsel fails to appear or appears unprepared, is a reminder to counsel of the opportunity and challenge that Rule 16 conferences can present. Read Rule 16 before considering two cases involving pretrial conferences and orders.

FED. R. CIV. P. 16. Pretrial Conferences; Scheduling; Management

(a) PURPOSES OF A PRETRIAL CONFERENCE. In any action, the court may order the attorneys and any unrepresented parties to appear for one or more pretrial conferences for such purposes as:

(1) expediting disposition of the action;

(2) establishing early and continuing control so that the case will not be protracted because of lack of management;

(3) discouraging wasteful pretrial activities;
(4) improving the quality of the trial through more thorough preparation; and
(5) facilitating settlement.
(b) SCHEDULING.
(1) *Scheduling Order.* Except in categories of actions exempted by local rule, the district judge—or a magistrate judge when authorized by local rule—must issue a scheduling order:
(A) after receiving the parties' report under Rule 26(f); or
(B) after consulting with the parties' attorneys and any unrepresented parties at a scheduling conference or by telephone, mail, or other means.
(2) *Time to Issue.* The judge must issue the scheduling order as soon as practicable, but in any event within the earlier of 120 days after any defendant has been served with the complaint or 90 days after any defendant has appeared.
(3) *Contents of the Order.*
(A) *Required Contents.* The scheduling order must limit the time to join other parties, amend the pleadings, complete discovery, and file motions.
(B) *Permitted Contents.* The scheduling order may:
(i) modify the timing of disclosures under Rules 26(a) and 26(e)(1);
(ii) modify the extent of discovery;
(iii) provide for disclosure or discovery of electronically stored information;
(iv) include any agreements the parties reach for asserting claims of privilege or of protection as trial preparation material after information is produced;
(v) set dates for pretrial conferences and for trial; and
(vi) include other appropriate matters.
(4) *Modifying a Schedule.* A schedule may be modified only for good cause and with the judge's consent.
(c) ATTENDANCE AND MATTERS FOR CONSIDERATION AT A PRETRIAL CONFERENCE.
(1) *Attendance.* A represented party must authorize at least one of its attorneys to make stipulations and admissions about all matters that can reasonably be anticipated for discussion at a pretrial conference. If appropriate, the court may require that a party or its representative be present or reasonably available by other means to consider possible settlement.
(2) *Matters for Consideration.* At any pretrial conference, the court may consider and take appropriate action on the following matters:
(A) formulating and simplifying the issues, and eliminating frivolous claims or defenses;
(B) amending the pleadings if necessary or desirable;
(C) obtaining admissions and stipulations about facts and documents to avoid unnecessary proof, and ruling in advance on the admissibility of evidence;
(D) avoiding unnecessary proof and cumulative evidence, and limiting the use of testimony under Federal Rule of Evidence 702;
(E) determining the appropriateness and timing of summary adjudication under Rule 56;
(F) controlling and scheduling discovery, including orders affecting disclosures and discovery under Rule 26 and Rules 29 through 37;
(G) identifying witnesses and documents, scheduling the filing and exchange of any pretrial briefs, and setting dates for further conferences and for trial;
(H) referring matters to a magistrate judge or a master;
(I) settling the case and using special procedures to assist in resolving the dispute when authorized by statute or local rule;
(J) determining the form and content of the pretrial order;
(K) disposing of pending motions;
(L) adopting special procedures for managing potentially difficult or protracted actions that may involve complex issues, multiple parties, difficult legal questions, or unusual proof problems;
(M) ordering a separate trial under Rule 42(b) of a claim, counterclaim, crossclaim, third-party claim, or particular issue;
(N) ordering the presentation of evidence early in the trial on a manageable issue that might, on the evidence, be the basis for a judgment as a matter of law under Rule 50(a) or a judgment on partial findings under Rule 52(c);
(O) establishing a reasonable limit on the time allowed to present evidence; and
(P) facilitating in other ways the just, speedy, and inexpensive disposition of the action.
(d) PRETRIAL ORDERS. After any conference under this rule, the court should issue an order reciting the action taken. This order controls the course of the action unless the court modifies it.
(e) FINAL PRETRIAL CONFERENCE AND ORDERS. The court may hold a final pretrial conference to formulate a trial plan, including a plan to facilitate the admission of evidence. The conference must be held as close to the start of trial as is reasonable, and must be attended by at least one attorney who will conduct the trial for each party and by any unrepresented party. The court may modify the order issued after a final pretrial conference only to prevent manifest injustice.
(f) SANCTIONS.
(1) *In General.* On motion or on its own, the court may issue any just orders, including those

authorized by Rule 37(b)(2)(A)(ii)–(vii), if a party or its attorney:
(A) fails to appear at a scheduling or other pretrial conference;
(B) is substantially unprepared to participate—or does not participate in good faith—in the conference; or
(C) fails to obey a scheduling or other pretrial order.

(2) *Imposing Fees and Costs.* Instead of or in addition to any other sanction, the court must order the party, its attorney, or both to pay the reasonable expenses—including attorney's fees—incurred because of any noncompliance with this rule, unless the noncompliance was substantially justified or other circumstances make an award of expenses unjust.

Sanders v. Union Pacific R.R. Co.,

United States Court of Appeals for the Ninth Circuit
193 F.3d 1080 (1999)

RYMER, Circuit Judge:

Phillip Sanders appeals the district court's sua sponte dismissal of his action with prejudice for failure to comply with the court's pretrial preparation order.

In June 1995, Sanders filed an action against Union Pacific Railroad Company under the Federal Employers' Liability Act (FELA), 45 U.S.C. §§51-60. The case was assigned to Judge James M. Ideman. The court set a trial date of November 19, 1996, and a pretrial conference date of November 8. Its standard form pretrial conference order also required the parties to submit certain documents twenty-one days before trial and others fourteen days before. The form order warned that failure to comply could result in sanctions, including dismissal.

As of the pretrial conference, Sanders's counsel had not filed a trial brief, memorandum of contentions of fact and law, responses to Union Pacific's motions in limine, or proposed voir dire questions as he should have. His motion in limine was filed six days late, and his witness, exhibit and expert witness lists were filed the day before the conference, two days late under the order. Counsel failed to meet and confer with Union Pacific despite requests that he do so, as a result of which no joint exhibit notebook, joint proposed jury instructions, or joint trial notebook was submitted.

The final pretrial conference was held as scheduled, except that Judge Ideman's law clerk presided. Sanders's counsel said that he had been involved in a complex FELA action in Nebraska and asked for an opportunity to explain to the judge why he had been unable to comply with the order. The law clerk told counsel for both parties that the trial date would be vacated and that the court would probably set the matter for hearing on an order to show cause.

Nevertheless, on November 15, Judge Ideman's courtroom deputy notified counsel that the case had been dismissed with prejudice. That same day the court issued a written order vacating the trial date and dismissing the case pursuant to Federal Rule of Civil Procedure 41(b).[fn] Sanders's counsel then filed a motion to set aside the judgment pursuant to Rule 60(b), which the court denied without a hearing.

Sanders urges us to hold that the court was obliged to warn counsel and client of imminent sua sponte dismissal and to have dismissed without prejudice instead of with prejudice, while Union Pacific argues that the court did not abuse its discretion because Sanders was warned in the order and had clearly failed to comply by the time the pretrial conference occurred. At the same time, Union Pacific acknowledges that the "pretrial conference" wasn't a pretrial conference in the normal sense and that our analysis is hampered by the lack of a record about what happened there.

We decline to dissect what happened in this case and to prescribe a recipe for how and when an action may be dismissed, with or without prejudice, for failure to follow the pretrial rules. This is a unique case. Suffice it to say that where, as here, the district judge allows his law clerk to conduct the final pretrial conference, declines to give counsel an opportunity to be heard before the court, and then dismisses the action sua sponte with prejudice, we cannot let the dismissal stand.

Counsel was plainly derelict in meeting his Rule 16 obligations, but so was the district judge. In different circumstances, where the district court exercises its own discretion in a deliberate, informed and reasonable way, we would accord it considerable deference.[fn] [C] But we cannot see how any deference is warranted in these circumstances. Accordingly, we vacate all orders entered after the pretrial conference and remand for another district judge to consider afresh how to proceed. [FN3. Judge Ideman resigned from the federal bench after the decision was rendered in this case. For this reason we do not need to decide whether this action should be reassigned to the calendar of a different district judge; it will necessarily be assigned to a new judge in any event.] In so doing, we express no opinion about how the new judge's discretion should be exercised. Rather, we simply put the parties back to square one.

REVERSED AND REMANDED.

TARSHIMA, Circuit Judge, with whom WARDLAW, Circuit Judge, joins, concurring:

I concur fully in Judge Rymer's majority opinion. I write separately to address an additional point[that a law clerk cannot conduct a Rule 16 pretrial conference]. ...

Rogan v. Menino,

United States Court of Appeals for the First Circuit
175 F.3d 75 (1999)

SELYA, Circuit Judge.

This appeal stems from a traffic accident that occurred in Boston, Massachusetts. It illustrates once again the dangers that lurk when busy trial courts, struggling to manage crowded dockets, do not turn square corners. The tale follows. ...

On March 15, 1996, a motor vehicle operated by plaintiff-appellant Shannon Rogan collided with a trolley car operated under the auspices of the Massachusetts Bay Transportation Authority (the MBTA). The MBTA has its own police force, [c], ... [sharing] jurisdiction over certain matters with the Boston Police Department (the BPD). In this instance, officers from both entities converged on the accident scene. Pursuant to departmental policy, the BPD officers, John McDonough and Robert Colburn, relinquished control of the investigation to their MBTA counterparts.

Displeased with the results of the investigation, Rogan sued Thomas Menino (Mayor of Boston), Paul Evans (Boston's police commissioner), Dennis DiMarzio (Boston's chief of operations), and the two responding officers in federal district court.[fn] Her complaint limned a plethora of claims—but Rogan voluntarily discontinued most of them, and only one remnant is relevant here. Invoking 42 U.S.C. §1983, Rogan asserted that the five City of Boston/BPD defendants, jointly and severally, hindered her access to the courts vis-à-vis her accident-related claim for personal injuries and property damage. The defendants were liable, Rogan theorized, because by abdicating responsibility for investigation of the accident they had aided and abetted the MBTA's attempts to cover up the trolley driver's negligence. ...

The district court disposed of these claims in two stages. First, acting on the defendants' motion, *see* Fed. R.Civ. P. 12(b)(6), it dismissed all claims against Menino, Evans, and DiMarzio in their individual capacities.[fn] Nearly a year later, at the final pretrial conference, the court, acting on its own initiative, brought closure to the suit by entering summary judgment [on the remaining claims]. Rogan now appeals ... entry of a sua sponte summary judgment. ...

When it jettisoned the claims brought against Evans and DiMarzio in their individual capacities, the district court kept alive Rogan's official-capacity claims against these same defendants, treating those as claims against the City of Boston. [C] The court also refused to dismiss the claims against McDonough and Colburn, reasoning that the complaint could be read to allege that they knew MBTA officers would not investigate the accident impartially.

At the final pretrial conference, *see* Fed.R.Civ.P. 16, the court demanded that Rogan marshal all the evidence at her disposal to defeat summary judgment. She attempted to comply with this directive, but the court found her proffer inadequate. Declaring that no reasonable jury could find for Rogan on the adduced evidence, the court, acting sua sponte, entered summary judgment in the defendants' favor on all remaining claims. Rogan assigns error.

It is apodictic that trial courts have the power to grant summary judgment sua sponte. [C] Withal, that power is not unbridled. To protect against erosion of the fairness principles embedded in Fed. R. Civ. P. 56, a court tempted to grant an unbesought summary judgment must hew to Rule 56's procedural strictures. [C] Thus, before the court can seriously consider sua sponte summary judgment, two conditions precedent must be satisfied: (1) the case must be sufficiently advanced in terms of pretrial discovery for the summary judgment target to know what evidence likely can be mustered, and (2) the target must have received appropriate notice. [Cc] Notice, in this context, has two aspects: the summary judgment target is entitled to know both the grounds that the district court will consider and the point at which her obligation to bring forth evidence supporting the elements of her claim accrues. [C]

Inasmuch as the lower court made its sua sponte ruling at the final pretrial conference, with discovery complete (or nearly so), the first condition precedent clearly was satisfied here. It is more problematic whether the court fulfilled the second condition. On one hand, the docket sheet reflects that no outstanding motion to dismiss or motion for summary judgment was extant when the court acted; the transcript of the penultimate pretrial conference intimates no warning of the court's intention to consider terminating the case at the final pretrial conference; nothing in the procedural order entered by the court preliminary to the final pretrial conference directed the parties to prepare for a hearing on dispositive motions; and there is no other record of a written notice that dispositive motions would be entertained at that conference. On the other hand, ... the court had in fact notified the parties during an unreported chambers conference (presumably held in connection with the penultimate pretrial conference) that "pursuant to Fed. R. Civ. P. 16, [it might] dismiss any or all of the defendants" at the final pretrial conference. Moreover, the defendants submitted several affidavits on the day before the final pretrial conference, presumably in anticipation that the court would consider terminating the case then and there. ...

Even so, the mere announcement that the court might dismiss the defendants at the final pretrial conference falls well short of the *specific* notice to which parties are entitled under Fed. R. Civ. P. 56. In the first place, Rule 56 obliges the moving party to inform the nonmovant of the grounds for the motion by "identifying those portions of the 'pleadings, depositions, answers to interrogatories, and admissions on file, together with the affidavits, if any,' which it believes demonstrate the absence of a genuine issue of material fact." Celotex Corp. v. Catrett, 477 U.S. 317, 323[] (1986) (quoting Fed. R. Civ. P. 56(c)). As far as the record in this case reveals, Rogan never received specific advance warning of this kind from either the defendants or the court.

In the second place, once the movant articulates his rationale for *brevis* disposition and submits the documentation (if any) on which he relies, Rule 56(c) in terms entitles the summary judgment target to no less than ten days within which to prepare a defense to the motion. This requirement persists even when the trial court aspires to grant summary judgment on its own initiative. [Cc] Here, however, the defendants filed several affidavits on the day before the final pretrial conference, and the court considered them without affording Rogan the benefit of the ten-day window that Rule 56 envisions. In doing so, the court erred. [C]

That the district court acted under the auspices of Fed. R. Civ. P. 16 provides no cover. To be sure, Rule 16 permits a court to dispose of marginal claims or issues that do not warrant a full-dress trial. *See* Fed. R. Civ. P. 16(c)(1) (authorizing district courts to "take appropriate action, with respect to ... the elimination of frivolous claims or defenses" at pretrial conferences). Nevertheless, when the district court employs summary judgment as the vehicle for the elimination of such detritus, Rule 16 does not trump the procedural prophylaxis of Rule 56. [C] Without advance notice of the basis of a looming dismissal, a targeted party lacks a "meaningful opportunity to cull the best evidence supporting his position, and to present that evidence, together with developed legal argumentation, in opposition to the entry of summary judgment." Berkovitz v. HBO, Inc., 89 F.3d [24,] 31[(1st Cir. 1996)]. And where, as here, the summary judgment loser was never afforded such an opportunity, sua sponte summary judgment cannot stand.[fn] *See id.* at 29 (holding that the trial court must provide a targeted party with an "adequate opportunity to dodge the bullet" before entering sua sponte summary judgment). ...

We need go no further. ... [D]espite our repeated calls for caution in the use of sua sponte summary judgments, [cc], the court below acted too hastily in dispatching the other claims in this case. Thus, we vacate the remainder of the judgment and remand for further proceedings in the district court.[fn] We take no view of the merit (or lack of merit) of Rogan's case.

Affirmed in part, vacated in part, and remanded. All parties to bear their own costs.

INQUIRY

Dismissals. FED. R. CIV. P. 16(c) authorizes the trial court to eliminate frivolous claims and defenses. Yet as the above *Rogan v. Menino* case illustrates, that authority is limited. When are Rule 16(c) dismissals appropriate? *Rogan v. Menino* would constrain Rule 16 dismissals based on insufficient evidence to instances where the party suffering dismissal had adequate notice and an opportunity to prepare and respond. Summary-judgment proceedings, designed to test factual support for claims and defenses, are certainly the preferred method for insufficient-evidence dismissals. May the court instead base dismissal on an insufficient legal theory or defects in the pleadings? There is case law supporting that Rule 16(c) authorizes the trial court to dismiss allegations that are in themselves senseless. *See* MacArthur v. San Juan County, 416 F.Supp.2d 1098, 1199 (D. Utah 2005) (Rule 16(c) dismissal appropriate when claims are "indisputably meritless legal theory or are footed upon conclusory assertions rather than specific facts").

Referral. Rule 16(c)(2)(H) mentions the possibility of the trial court "referring matters to a magistrate judge or a master." Referral does not dispose of the case. It does remove the case from the court's trial docket. Remember that it is not the number of cases but the number of trials or other evidentiary hearings that has the greater impact on the trial court's ability to manage its docket. When a trial judge refers a case to a magistrate judge or especially to a special master, it removes the case from the trial judge's direct management and limits involvement to review of the integrity of the referred proceeding. FED. R. CIV. P. 53 governs referral to masters, while FED. R. CIV. P. 73 governs referral to magistrates. Masters are often retired judges or lawyers of special expertise and high standing, compensated by the parties within the limits of Rule 53(a)(3) that the court must not impose unreasonable expense. As previously mentioned, the federal district court employs and compensates magistrate judges. Rule 53(c) authorizes masters to exercise the trial court's powers except as limited by the court's referring order. Rule 73 refers to a magistrate judge's authority under statute, 28 U.S.C. §636(c). Referral to a magistrate judge or master to resolve triable issues ordinarily requires the parties' consent. Rule 53(e) authorizes the trial court to reduce the master's report to an order or judgment, again if the parties have so consented on referral. Magistrate's judgments enter under statutory authority, 28 U.S.C. §636(c)(3). Review Rule 53 on masters, Rule 73 on magistrates, and 28 U.S.C. §636 governing a magistrate's statutory authority.

FED. R. CIV. P. 53. Masters
(a) APPOINTMENT.
(1) *Scope.* Unless a statute provides otherwise, a court may appoint a master only to:
(A) perform duties consented to by the parties;
(B) hold trial proceedings and make or recommend findings of fact on issues to be decided without a jury if appointment is warranted by:
(i) some exceptional condition; or

(ii) the need to perform an accounting or resolve a difficult computation of damages; or
(C) address pretrial and posttrial matters that cannot be effectively and timely addressed by an available district judge or magistrate judge of the district.
(2) *Disqualification.* A master must not have a relationship to the parties, attorneys, action, or court that would require disqualification of a judge under 28 U.S.C. §455, unless the parties, with the court's approval, consent to the appointment after the master discloses any potential grounds for disqualification.
(3) *Possible Expense or Delay.* In appointing a master, the court must consider the fairness of imposing the likely expenses on the parties and must protect against unreasonable expense or delay.
(b) ORDER APPOINTING A MASTER.
(1) *Notice.* Before appointing a master, the court must give the parties notice and an opportunity to be heard. Any party may suggest candidates for appointment.
(2) *Contents.* The appointing order must direct the master to proceed with all reasonable diligence and must state:
(A) the master's duties, including any investigation or enforcement duties, and any limits on the master's authority under Rule 53(c);
(B) the circumstances, if any, in which the master may communicate ex parte with the court or a party;
(C) the nature of the materials to be preserved and filed as the record of the master's activities;
(D) the time limits, method of filing the record, other procedures, and standards for reviewing the master's orders, findings, and recommendations; and
(E) the basis, terms, and procedure for fixing the master's compensation under Rule 53(g).
(3) *Issuing.* The court may issue the order only after:
(A) the master files an affidavit disclosing whether there is any ground for disqualification under 28 U.S.C. § 455; and
(B) if a ground is disclosed, the parties, with the court's approval, waive the disqualification.
(4) *Amending.* The order may be amended at any time after notice to the parties and an opportunity to be heard.
(c) MASTER'S AUTHORITY.
(1) *In General.* Unless the appointing order directs otherwise, a master may:
(A) regulate all proceedings;
(B) take all appropriate measures to perform the assigned duties fairly and efficiently; and
(C) if conducting an evidentiary hearing, exercise the appointing court's power to compel, take, and record evidence.
(2) *Sanctions.* The master may by order impose on a party any noncontempt sanction provided by Rule 37 or 45, and may recommend a contempt sanction against a party and sanctions against a nonparty.
(d) MASTER'S ORDERS. A master who issues an order must file it and promptly serve a copy on each party. The clerk must enter the order on the docket.
(e) MASTER'S REPORTS. A master must report to the court as required by the appointing order. The master must file the report and promptly serve a copy on each party, unless the court orders
otherwise.
(f) ACTION ON THE MASTER'S ORDER, REPORT, OR RECOMMENDATIONS.
(1) *Opportunity for a Hearing; Action in General.* In acting on a master's order, report, or recommendations, the court must give the parties notice and an opportunity to be heard; may receive evidence; and may adopt or affirm, modify, wholly or partly reject or reverse, or resubmit to the master with instructions.
(2) *Time to Object or Move to Adopt or Modify.* A party may file objections to—or a motion to adopt or modify—the master's order, report, or recommendations no later than 21 days after a copy is served, unless the court sets a different time.
(3) *Reviewing Factual Findings.* The court must decide de novo all objections to findings of fact made or recommended by a master, unless the parties, with the court's approval, stipulate that:
(A) the findings will be reviewed for clear error; or
(B) the findings of a master appointed under Rule 53(a)(1)(A) or (C) will be final.
(4) *Reviewing Legal Conclusions.* The court must decide de novo all objections to conclusions of law made or recommended by a master.
(5) *Reviewing Procedural Matters.* Unless the appointing order establishes a different standard of review, the court may set aside a master's ruling on a procedural matter only for an abuse of discretion.
(g) COMPENSATION.
(1) *Fixing Compensation.* Before or after judgment, the court must fix the master's compensation on the basis and terms stated in the appointing order, but the court may set a new basis and terms after giving notice and an opportunity to be heard.
(2) *Payment.* The compensation must be paid either:
(A) by a party or parties; or
(B) from a fund or subject matter of the action within the court's control.

(3) *Allocating Payment.* The court must allocate payment among the parties after considering the nature and amount of the controversy, the parties' means, and the extent to which any party is more responsible than other parties for the reference to a master. An interim allocation may be amended to reflect a decision on the merits.

(h) APPOINTING A MAGISTRATE JUDGE. A magistrate judge is subject to this rule only when the order referring a matter to the magistrate judge states that the reference is made under this rule.

...

Fed. R. Civ. P. 73. Magistrate Judges: Trial by Consent; Appeal

(a) TRIAL BY CONSENT. When authorized under 28 U.S.C. §636(c), a magistrate judge may, if all parties consent, conduct a civil action or proceeding, including a jury or nonjury trial. A record must be made in accordance with 28 U.S.C. §636(c)(5).

(b) CONSENT PROCEDURE.

(1) *In General.* When a magistrate judge has been designated to conduct civil actions or proceedings, the clerk must give the parties written notice of their opportunity to consent under 28 U.S.C. § 636(c). To signify their consent, the parties must jointly or separately file a statement consenting to the referral. A district judge or magistrate judge may be informed of a party's response to the clerk's notice only if all parties have consented to the referral.

(2) *Reminding the Parties About Consenting.* A district judge, magistrate judge, or other court official may remind the parties of the magistrate judge's availability, but must also advise them that they are free to withhold consent without adverse substantive consequences.

(3) *Vacating a Referral.* On its own for good cause—or when a party shows extraordinary circumstances—the district judge may vacate a referral to a magistrate judge under this rule.

(c) APPEALING A JUDGMENT. In accordance with 28 U.S.C. §636(c)(3), an appeal from a judgment entered at a magistrate judge's direction may be taken to the court of appeals as would any other appeal from a district-court judgment.

---

28 U.S.C. §636. Jurisdiction, powers, and temporary assignment.

(a) Each United States magistrate judge serving under this chapter shall have within the district in which sessions are held by the court that appointed the magistrate judge, at other places where that court may function, and elsewhere as authorized by law—

(1) all powers and duties conferred or imposed upon United States commissioners by law or by the Rules of Criminal Procedure for the United States District Courts;

(2) the power to administer oaths and affirmations, issue orders pursuant to section 3142 of title 18 concerning release or detention of persons pending trial, and take acknowledgements, affidavits, and depositions;

(3) the power to conduct trials under section 3401, title 18, United States Code, in conformity with and subject to the limitations of that section;

(4) the power to enter a sentence for a petty offense; and

(5) the power to enter a sentence for a class A misdemeanor in a case in which the parties have consented.

(b)(1) Notwithstanding any provision of law to the contrary—

(A) a judge may designate a magistrate judge to hear and determine any pretrial matter pending before the court, except a motion for injunctive relief, for judgment on the pleadings, for summary judgment, to dismiss or quash an indictment or information made by the defendant, to suppress evidence in a criminal case, to dismiss or to permit maintenance of a class action, to dismiss for failure to state a claim upon which relief can be granted, and to involuntarily dismiss an action. A judge of the court may reconsider any pretrial matter under this subparagraph (A) where it has been shown that the magistrate judge's order is clearly erroneous or contrary to law.

(B) a judge may also designate a magistrate judge to conduct hearings, including evidentiary hearings, and to submit to a judge of the court proposed findings of fact and recommendations for the disposition, by a judge of the court, of any motion excepted in subparagraph (A), of applications for posttrial relief made by individuals convicted of criminal offenses and of prisoner petitions challenging conditions of confinement.

(C) the magistrate judge shall file his proposed findings and recommendations under subparagraph (B) with the court and a copy shall forthwith be mailed to all parties. Within fourteen days after being served with a copy, any party may serve and file written objections to such proposed findings and recommendations as provided by rules of court. A judge of the court shall make a de novo determination of those portions of the report or specified proposed findings or recommendations to which objection is made. A judge of the court may accept, reject, or modify, in whole or in part, the findings or recommendations made by the magistrate judge. The judge may also receive further evidence or recommit the matter to the magistrate judge with instructions.

(2) A judge may designate a magistrate judge to serve as a special master pursuant to the applicable provisions of this title and the Federal Rules of Civil Procedure for the United States district courts. A judge may designate a magistrate judge to serve as a special master in any civil case, upon consent of the parties, without regard to the provisions of rule 53(b) of the Federal Rules of Civil Procedure for the United States district courts.

(3) A magistrate judge may be assigned such additional duties as are not inconsistent with the Constitution and laws of the United States.

(4) Each district court shall establish rules pursuant to which the magistrate judges shall discharge their duties.

(c) Notwithstanding any provision of law to the contrary—

(1) Upon the consent of the parties, a full-time United States magistrate judge or a part-time United States magistrate judge who serves as a full-time judicial officer may conduct any or all proceedings in a jury or nonjury civil matter and order the entry of judgment in the case, when specially designated to exercise such jurisdiction by the district court or courts he serves. Upon the consent of the parties, pursuant to their specific written request, any other part-time magistrate judge may exercise such jurisdiction, if such magistrate judge meets the bar membership requirements set forth in section 631(b)(1) and the chief judge of the district court certifies that a full-time magistrate judge is not reasonably available in accordance with guidelines established by the judicial council of the circuit. When there is more than one judge of a district court, designation under this paragraph shall be by the concurrence of a majority of all the judges of such district court, and when there is no such concurrence, then by the chief judge.

(2) If a magistrate judge is designated to exercise civil jurisdiction under paragraph (1) of this subsection, the clerk of court shall, at the time the action is filed, notify the parties of the availability of a magistrate judge to exercise such jurisdiction. The decision of the parties shall be communicated to the clerk of court. Thereafter, either the district court judge or the magistrate judge may again advise the parties of the availability of the magistrate judge, but in so doing, shall also advise the parties that they are free to withhold consent without adverse substantive consequences. Rules of court for the reference of civil matters to magistrate judges shall include procedures to protect the voluntariness of the parties' consent.

(3) Upon entry of judgment in any case referred under paragraph (1) of this subsection, an aggrieved party may appeal directly to the appropriate United States court of appeals from the judgment of the magistrate judge in the same manner as an appeal from any other judgment of a district court. The consent of the parties allows a magistrate judge designated to exercise civil jurisdiction under paragraph (1) of this subsection to direct the entry of a judgment of the district court in accordance with the Federal Rules of Civil Procedure. Nothing in this paragraph shall be construed as a limitation of any party's right to seek review by the Supreme Court of the United States.

(4) The court may, for good cause shown on its own motion, or under extraordinary circumstances shown by any party, vacate a reference of a civil matter to a magistrate judge under this subsection.

(5) The magistrate judge shall, subject to guidelines of the Judicial Conference, determine whether the record taken pursuant to this section shall be taken by electronic sound recording, by a court reporter, or by other means.

(d) The practice and procedure for the trial of cases before officers serving under this chapter shall conform to rules promulgated by the Supreme Court pursuant to section 2072 of this title.

(e) Contempt authority.—

(1) In general.—A United States magistrate judge serving under this chapter shall have within the territorial jurisdiction prescribed by the appointment of such magistrate judge the power to exercise contempt authority as set forth in this subsection. ...

...

(h) A United States magistrate judge who has retired may, upon the consent of the chief judge of the district involved, be recalled to serve as a magistrate judge in any judicial district by the judicial council of the circuit within which such district is located. ...

FED. R. CIV. P. Form 80. Notice of a Magistrate Judge's Availability

1. A magistrate judge is available under title 28 U.S.C. § 636(c) to conduct the proceedings in this case, including a jury or nonjury trial and the entry of final judgment. But a magistrate judge can be assigned only if all parties voluntarily consent.

2. You may withhold your consent without adverse substantive consequences. The identity of any party consenting or withholding consent will not be disclosed to the judge to whom the case is assigned or to any magistrate judge.

3. If a magistrate judge does hear your case, you may appeal directly to a United States court of appeals as you would if a district judge heard it.

A form called *Consent to an Assignment to a United States Magistrate Judge* is available from the court clerk's office.

FED. R. CIV. P. FORM 81. Consent to an Assignment to a Magistrate Judge

(Caption—See Form 1.)

I voluntarily consent to have a United States magistrate judge conduct all further proceedings in this case, including a trial, and order the entry of final judgment. (Return this form to the court clerk—not to a judge or magistrate judge.)

Date____________

____

Signature of the Party

FED. R. CIV. P. Form 82. Order of Assignment to a Magistrate Judge

(Caption—See Form 1.)

With the parties' consent it is ordered that this case be assigned to United States Magistrate Judge _______ of this district to conduct all proceedings and enter final judgment in accordance with 28 U.S.C. §636(c).

Date ___________

____

United States District Judge

B. Summary Judgment

In that vast majority of cases that do not reach trial, summary judgment is the most significant phase of civil litigation in which the trial court is directly involved. Trial courts dispose of a certain percentage of cases by Rule 12 motions to dismiss on the pleadings. As you have seen above and in the previous chapter, there is also some prospect that a party or its counsel will engage in some misconduct or make some lapse during discovery or in pretrial procedures that will vest the court with authority to dismiss the case as a sanction. Of course, the parties may also settle the case or decide to continue it in an alternative dispute-resolution forum. Each of these actions—pleading, discovery, and settlement—involves a party's voluntary action or counsel's technical performance more so than an actual judgment as to the merits of the case. The one hurdle that every case must pass to reach trial is a test of the sufficiency of the evidence. Summary judgment is the earliest and clearest point where the trial court applies law to fact, determining the sufficiency of both to support the claims and defenses. Summary proceedings in America predate the Constitution, although modern forms of summary judgment arose in the mid- to late-19th century and gained popularity in the early 20th century with the demise of writ pleading. *See* Jack H. Friedenthal & Joshua E. Gardner, *Judicial Discretion to Deny Summary Judgment in the Era of Managerial Judging,* 31 HOFSTRA L.REV. 91, 96 (2002).

Knowledge

Transfer of learning is critical to your legal education. Cognitive studies show that learning occurs in context. When you meet a new person, you may not recognize that person in a different setting until you have met them in several settings, by which time you have generalized their identity. The same phenomenon occurs with learning legal skills and knowledge. For example, the IRAC framework works well for case briefing, recitation, essay examination, legal memoranda, motions and briefs, oral argument, and bar examination. For another example, writing skills (grammar, punctuation, organization) work consistently across all the same school and practice settings, and in a variety of subjects and fields like torts, contracts, property, and constitutional law. You go through a necessary and natural process of relearning those skills in each setting until you have generalized the learning so that it is readily transferable. Seek out different settings in which to practice your learning, so that your learning will occur more quickly and surely.

Not every case involves a summary-judgment motion. In a substantial percentage of cases, it is so apparent that the plaintiff has evidence to support each element of the plaintiff's claims that there is no arguable basis for a summary-judgment motion. Even in those cases, though, the defense will have considered the possibility. Summary-judgment proceedings turn allegations into either triable claims or waste paper. In that sense, summary judgment relates closely to the nature of trials and their purpose. Clients and other non-lawyers perceive trials as places where parties recount events in order to see principles vindicated and justice done. In fact, though, trials resolve disputed fact issues. If there are no disputed fact issues, then there is no need for trial. The trial court can vindicate principles and do justice by motion for summary judgment. The theater and drama of trial are absent, but the judgment that results is equally enforceable.

FED. R. CIV. P. 56 and equivalent state-court rules state summary judgment's procedures and standard. *See, e.g.,* MICH. CT. RULE 2.116(C)(10) (summary disposition). Either side may move for summary judgment, as Rules 56(a) and (b) make clear. Rule 56(a) provides for motions by parties claiming relief (typically plaintiffs) and subrule (b) for motions by defending parties. Although either side may move, the side without the burden of proof, typically meaning the defendant, usually does so. A party without the burden of proof need not come forward with evidence meeting a burden of production. Rules 56(a) and (b) permit a motion "with or without supporting affidavits." Rather, the motion standard provides the key to how the trial court must decide the motion. Under Rule 56(c), the trial court should grant judgment "if the pleadings, the discovery and disclosure materials on file, and any affidavits show that there is no genuine issue as to any material fact and that the movant is entitled to judgment as a matter of law." The "no genuine issue as to any material fact" phrasing is so familiar to civil litigators that they could repeat its litany in their sleep. There must be evidence from which a reasonable jury could find in favor of the party opposing summary judgment.

Summary-judgment proceedings, though, are not quite that easy. Supreme Court case law excerpted below holds that the movant must point out (articulate) the absence of evidence creating a genuine issue of material fact on one or more elements of the claim. The party opposing summary judgment must then come forward with evidence showing a genuine issue of material fact. Rule 56(e) makes clear that when a movant has "properly made and supported" a motion for summary judgment, "an opposing party may not rely merely on allegations or denials in its own pleading... ." Rather, Rule 56(e) requires that the response must "set out specific facts showing a genuine issue for trial" and do so (in the usual case) supported by affidavits. The party opposing summary judgment bears the laboring oar in summary-judgment proceedings, not the moving party. Given that it is usually defendants who move and plaintiffs who respond, plaintiffs typically have the burden of showing evidence creating the genuine issue.

Given that summary judgment disposes of cases, litigators must know summary-judgment standards and procedures. Overall, the litigator's skill is in:

(1) predicting how the trial courts will apply the summary-judgment standard, (2) making or responding to the motion to require the trial court to do so, and (3) marshalling the proofs in support of or opposition to the motion. The motion itself, the marshalling of proofs to oppose it, and the predicting of outcomes are three interrelated, high-level, comprehensive skills, pulling together law, fact, strategy, and discernment. To appreciate how the trial courts apply these concepts, and how practitioners invoke and resist summary judgment, you should know summary judgment's trends and history. First, read Rule 56 for the above structure and its additional detail. Then, consider the series of Supreme Court cases that articulated its standard and procedures.

FED. R. CIV. P. 56. Summary Judgment

(a) BY A CLAIMING PARTY. A party claiming relief may move, with or without supporting affidavits, for summary judgment on all or part of the claim.

(b) BY A DEFENDING PARTY. A party against whom relief is sought may move, with or without supporting affidavits, for summary judgment on all or part of the claim.

(c) TIME FOR A MOTION, RESPONSE, AND REPLY; PROCEEDINGS.

(1) These times apply unless a different time is set by local rule or the court orders otherwise:

(A) a party may move for summary judgment at any time until 30 days after the close of all discovery;

(B) a party opposing the motion must file a response within 21 days after the motion is served or a responsive pleading is due, whichever is later; and

(C) the movant may file a reply within 14 days after the response is served.

(2) The judgment sought should be rendered if the pleadings, the discovery and disclosure materials on file, and any affidavits show that there is no genuine issue as to any material fact and that the movant is entitled to judgment as a matter of law.

(d) CASE NOT FULLY ADJUDICATED ON THE MOTION.

(1) *Establishing Facts.* If summary judgment is not rendered on the whole action, the court should, to the extent practicable, determine what material facts are not genuinely at issue. The court should so determine by examining the pleadings and evidence before it and by interrogating the attorneys. It should then issue an order specifying what facts—including items of damages or other relief—are not genuinely at issue. The facts so specified must be treated as established in the action.

(2) *Establishing Liability.* An interlocutory summary judgment may be rendered on liability alone, even if there is a genuine issue on the amount of damages.

(e) AFFIDAVITS; FURTHER TESTIMONY.

(1) *In General.* A supporting or opposing affidavit must be made on personal knowledge, set out facts that would be admissible in evidence, and show that the affiant is competent to testify on the matters stated. If a paper or part of a paper is referred to in an affidavit, a sworn or certified copy must be attached to or served with the affidavit. The court may permit an affidavit to be supplemented or opposed by depositions, answers to interrogatories, or additional affidavits.

(2) *Opposing Party's Obligation to Respond.* When a motion for summary judgment is properly made and supported, an opposing party may not rely merely on allegations or denials in its own pleading; rather, its response must—by affidavits or as otherwise provided in this rule—set out specific facts showing a genuine issue for trial. If the opposing party does not so respond, summary judgment should, if appropriate, be entered against that party.

(f) WHEN AFFIDAVITS ARE UNAVAILABLE. If a party opposing the motion shows by affidavit that, for specified reasons, it cannot present facts essential to justify its opposition, the court may:

(1) deny the motion;

(2) order a continuance to enable affidavits to be obtained, depositions to be taken, or other discovery to be undertaken; or

(3) issue any other just order.

(g) AFFIDAVIT SUBMITTED IN BAD FAITH. If satisfied that an affidavit under this rule is submitted in bad faith or solely for delay, the court must order the submitting party to pay the other party the reasonable expenses, including attorney's fees, it incurred as a result. An offending party or attorney may also be held in contempt.

Adickes v. S.H. Kress & Co.,

United States Supreme Court
398 U.S. 144 (1970)

Mr. Justice HARLAN delivered the opinion of the Court.

Petitioner, Sandra Adickes, a white school teacher from New York, brought this suit in the United States District Court for the Southern District of New York against respondent S. H. Kress & Co. ("Kress") to recover damages under 42 U.S.C. §1983[fn] for an alleged violation of her constitutional rights under the Equal Protection Clause of the Fourteenth Amendment. The suit arises out of Kress' refusal to serve lunch to Miss Adickes at its restaurant facilities in its Hattiesburg, Mississippi, store on August 14, 1964, and Miss Adickes' subsequent arrest upon her departure from the store by the Hattiesburg police on a charge of vagrancy. At the time of both the refusal to serve and the arrest, Miss Adickes was with six young people, all Negroes, who were her students in a Mississippi "Freedom School" where she was teaching that summer. Unlike Miss Adickes, the students were offered service, and were not arrested. …

… Petitioner sought, inter alia, to prove that the refusal to serve her was pursuant to a "custom of the community to segregate the races in public eating places." … [Miss Adickes tried the first count of her complaint to a jury, but the trial court directed a verdict against her for failure to adduce necessary evidence of a city custom of arrest following refusal of service.]

The second count of her complaint, alleging that both the refusal of service and her subsequent arrest were the product of a conspiracy between Kress and the Hattiesburg police, was dismissed before trial on a motion for summary judgment. The District Court ruled that petitioner had "failed to allege any facts from which a conspiracy might be inferred." [C] This determination was unanimously affirmed by the Court of Appeals, [c]. …

As explained in Part I, because the respondent failed to show the absence of any disputed material fact, we think the District Court erred in granting summary judgment. … [The trial court also erred by directing a verdict.] …

… In granting respondent's motion[for summary judgment], the District Court simply stated that there was "no evidence in the complaint or in the affidavits and other papers from which a 'reasonably-minded person' might draw an inference of conspiracy," [c]. Our own scrutiny of the factual allegations of petitioner's complaint, as well as the material found in the affidavits and depositions presented by Kress to the District Court, however, convinces us that summary judgment was improper here, for we think respondent failed to carry its burden of showing the absence of any genuine issue of fact. Before explaining why this is so, it is useful to state the factual arguments, made by the parties concerning summary judgment, and the reasoning of the courts below.

In moving for summary judgment, Kress argued that "uncontested facts" established that no conspiracy existed between any Kress employee and the police. To support this assertion, Kress pointed first to the statements in the deposition of the store manager (Mr. Powell) that (a) he had not communicated with the police,[fn] and that (b) he had, by a prearranged tacit signal,[fn] ordered the food counter supervisor to see that Miss Adickes was refused service only because he was fearful of a riot in the store by customers angered at seeing a "mixed group" of whites and blacks eating together.[fn] Kress also relied on affidavits from the Hattiesburg chief of police,[fn] and the two arresting officers,[fn] to the effect that store manager Powell had not requested that petitioner be arrested. Finally, Kress pointed to the statements in petitioner's own deposition that she had no knowledge of any communication between any Kress employee and any member of the Hattiesburg police, and was relying on circumstantial evidence to support her contention that there was an arrangement between Kress and the police.

Petitioner, in opposing summary judgment, pointed out that respondent had failed in its moving papers to dispute the allegation in petitioner's complaint, a statement at her deposition,[fn] and an unsworn statement by a Kress employee,[fn] all to the effect that there was a policeman in the store at the time of the refusal to serve her, and that this was the policeman who subsequently arrested her. Petitioner argued that although she had no knowledge of an agreement between Kress and the police, the sequence of events created a substantial enough possibility of a conspiracy to allow her to proceed to trial, especially given the fact that the noncircumstantial evidence of the conspiracy could only come from adverse witnesses. Further, she submitted an affidavit specifically disputing the manager's assertion that the situation in the store at the time of the refusal was "explosive," thus creating an issue of fact as to what his motives might have been in ordering the refusal of service.

We think that on the basis of this record, it was error to grant summary judgment. As the moving party, respondent had the burden of showing the absence of a genuine issue as to any material fact, and for these purposes the material it lodged must be viewed in the light most favorable to the opposing party.[fn] Respondent here did not carry its burden because of its failure to foreclose the possibility that there was a policeman in the Kress store while petitioner was awaiting service, and that this policeman reached an understanding with some Kress employee that petitioner not be served.

It is true that Mr. Powell, the store manager, claimed in his deposition that he had not seen or communicated with a policeman prior to his tacit signal to Miss Baggett, the supervisor of the food counter. But respondent did not submit any affidavits from Miss Baggett,[fn] or from Miss Freeman,[fn] the waitress who actually refused petitioner service, either of whom might well have seen and communicated with a policeman in the store. Further, we find it particularly noteworthy that the two officers involved in the arrest each failed in his affidavit to foreclose the possibility (1) that he was in the store while petitioner was there; and (2) that, upon seeing petitioner with Negroes, he communicated his disapproval to a Kress employee, thereby influencing the decision not to serve petitioner.

Given these unexplained gaps in the materials submitted by respondent, we conclude that respondent failed to fulfill its initial burden of demonstrating what is a critical element in this aspect of the case—that there was no policeman in the store. If a policeman were present, we think it would be open to a jury, in light of the sequence that followed, to infer from the circumstances that the policeman and a Kress employee had a "meeting of the minds" and thus reached an understanding that petitioner should be refused service. Because "(o)n summary judgment the inferences to be drawn from the underlying facts contained in (the moving party's) materials must be viewed in the light most favorable to the party opposing the motion," United States v. Diebold, Inc., 369 U.S. 654, 655[] (1962), we think respondent's failure to show there was no policeman in the store requires reversal.

Pointing to Rule 56(e), as amended in 1963,[fn] respondent argues that it was incumbent on petitioner to come forward with an affidavit properly asserting the presence of the policeman in the store, if she were to rely on that fact to avoid summary judgment. Respondent notes in this regard that none of the materials upon which petitioner relied met the requirements of Rule 56(e).[fn]

This argument does not withstand scrutiny, however, for both the commentary on and background of the 1963 amendment conclusively show that it was not intended to modify the burden of the moving party under Rule 56(c) to show initially the absence of a genuine issue concerning any material fact.[fn] …

If respondent had met its initial burden by, for example, submitting affidavits from the policemen denying their presence in the store at the time in question, Rule 56(e) would then have required petitioner to have done more than simply rely on the contrary allegation in her complaint. To have avoided conceding this fact for purposes of summary judgment, petitioner would have had to come forward with either (1) the affidavit of someone who saw the policeman in the store or (2) an affidavit under Rule 56(f) explaining why at that time it was impractical to do so. Even though not essential here to defeat respondent's motion, the submission of such an affidavit would have been the preferable course for petitioner's counsel to have followed. …

For the foregoing reasons we think petitioner is entitled to a new trial on the substantive count of her complaint.

The judgment of the Court of Appeals is reversed, and the case is remanded to that court for further proceedings consistent with this opinion.

It is so ordered.

Mr. Justice MARSHALL took no part in the decision of this case.

Mr. Justice BLACK, concurring in the judgment[, omitted].

Mr. Justice DOUGLAS, dissenting in part[, omitted].

INQUIRY

Favorable Light. Notice how the Supreme Court in *Adickes v. S.H. Kress & Co.* stated the trial court must view the evidence: in the light most favorable to the party opposing summary judgment. Why is that the case? Parties have the right to have juries decide disputed fact issues. Only where no reasonable juror could decide in the non-movant's favor would it be appropriate for the trial court to remove an issue from the purview of the jury. Even where the parties have not demanded a jury, and where the trial judge will decide disputed facts, the trial judge should do so in a trial or evidentiary hearing where the trial judge can observe the demeanor and judge the credibility of witnesses. Motion practice based on affidavits, deposition testimony, and exhibits is not suited for resolving disputed facts. It offers a cold record, without the important human element that helps a factfinder sort truth from fiction. Practitioners know that summary judgment requires the trial court to view the non-movant's evidence generously. Add the most-favorable-light litany to the no-genuine-issue litany.

Affidavits. FED. R. CIV. P. 56 has abundant detail regarding affidavits. What does it require, and why? When a movant files a summary-judgment motion testing the sufficiency of the evidence on one or more elements, the non-movant must come forward with that evidence. Affidavits are a usual means of presenting evidence when the court is not holding any hearing or trial but is instead reviewing court papers, as in the case of summary judgment. Affidavits have the effect of testimony in that the affiant swears to the truth of what an affidavit states, as certified by a notary public's endorsement at the end of the affidavit. Rule 56(e)(2) states that the non-movant may not rely on the pleadings but must set forth specific facts "by affidavits or as otherwise provided in this rule." Practitioners thus routinely submit affidavits opposing summary judgment. Some lawyers adopt a prophylactic practice of submitting an "affidavit of counsel" signed by the lawyer asserting that the facts stated in the response are true to the best of the lawyer's knowledge. Rule 56(e)(1) effectively negates that practice by requiring that affidavits be on personal knowledge of admissible evidence to which the affiant can testify at trial. Lawyers do not testify. Rule 56(e)(1) indicates that "[t]he court may permit an affidavit to be supplemented or opposed by depositions, answers to interrogatories, or additional affidavits." Affidavits often refer to attached exhibits. Practitioners thus routinely supplement and oppose affidavits with other evidentiary materials of all kinds. Some state-court rules give the trial court broader latitude than Rule 56 to consider those other evidentiary materials. *See, e.g.,* MICH. CT. RULE 2.116(G)(5) ("The affidavits, together with the pleadings, depositions, admissions, and documentary evidence then filed in the action or submitted by the parties, must be considered by the court... ."). Review the following state-court motion for summary judgment (or, as the applicable state rule denominates it, "summary disposition"). Although it is a state-court motion under state rules, does it meet Rule 56's requirements for stating and a motion for summary judgment, articulated by *Adickes v. S.H. Kress & Co.*?

STATE OF MICHIGAN
IN THE LEEWORTH COUNTY CIRCUIT COURT

COMMERCIAL GENERAL INSURANCE COMPANY, Plaintiff,	No. 05-01234-CK Hon. Roberta Sherlock
v	**DEFENDANT ABC'S RESPONSE MEMORANDUM BRIEF**
ABC DEVELOPMENT, INC., and **JACOB FORD,** Defendants.	**OPPOSING PLAINTIFF'S MOTION FOR SUMMARY DISPOSITION**

[names and addresses for counsel of record]

____

Response

Defendant ABC Development, Inc. ("ABC"), opposes plaintiff Commercial General Insurance Company's ("Commercial's") motion for summary disposition saying:

1. This case involves ABC's "business protector" coverage claim for allegedly negligent work resulting in physical damage to defendant Jacob Ford's residence.

2. Commercial argues that there is no evidence supporting a claim for business protector coverage because all of the damage was to ABC's work such that there was no "occurrence."

3. To the contrary, Mr. Ford's discovery responses show a genuine issue of material fact in ABC's favor that there was damage to property other than the work of ABC such that there is business protector coverage.

ON THESE GROUNDS, defendant ABC Development, Inc., prays under MCR 2.116(C)(10) that the Court deny plaintiff Commercial General Insurance Company's motion.

Memorandum Brief

Counter-Statement of Facts

Physical Damage. Commercial admits at page three of its brief that the building contract underlying this insurance coverage dispute was one "to build an addition to Mr. Ford's home"–to build *an addition* to an already existing home. Commercial also admits at page six of its brief that Mr. Ford alleges ABC's negligence in "failing to ascertain the need for pierings prior to beginning work on the project." Commercial cites Mr. Ford's Complaint at paragraph 28. Commercial also attaches to its motion and brief Mr. Ford's interrogatory answers where Mr. Ford claims that he "had to pay the following expenses as a result of ABC Development's poor and negligent workmanship" listing roofing costs, plumbing costs, heating and cooling expenses, drywall costs, and siding costs.

Policy Provisions. Commercial also admits at page six of its brief that it was ABC's insurer under a Business Protector Liability Coverage for property damage at Mr. Ford's residence. It further admits at page nine of its brief that for purposes of its motion "'property damage' is being claimed." Commercial then cites at page nine of its brief the "occurrence" requirement that its policy further defines as an "accident." These are the relevant material facts to this motion that raise a genuine issue in ABC's favor as follows.

Standard for Review

Under MCR 2.116(C)(10), summary disposition is only available when "[e]xcept as to the amount of damages, there is no genuine issue as to any material fact, and the moving party is entitled to judgment or partial judgment as a matter of law." The Court must grant the party opposing summary disposition the benefit of any reasonable doubt regarding material facts. Bertrand v Alan Ford, Inc., 449 Mich 606, 617-618, 537 NW2d 185 (1995). The Court should be liberal in finding a fact dispute. Porter v City of Royal Oak, 214 Mich App 478, 488, 542 NW2d 905 (1995). The Court may not make factual findings or weigh credibility. Barnell v Taubman Co., 203 Mich App 110, 115, 512 NW2d 13 (1993).

Authority and Analysis

Commercial admits at pages nine and ten of its brief that, "It is only where and to the extent that the damage is to property *other than the insured's work* that the 'property damage' will be deemed to be unforeseen, unexpected and unintended, and, therefore, caused by an 'occurrence.'" (Emphasis in original) Commercial correctly cites in support Radenbaugh v. Farm Bureau Ins. Co., 240 Mich App 134, 610 NW2d 272 (2000), citing Bundy Tubing Co. v. Royal Indemnity Co., 298 F2d 151 (6th Cir. 1962). ABC relies on this general proposition in opposing Commercial's motion. Mr. Ford does not restrict his property damage claim to only ABC's additions. To the contrary, Mr. Ford maintains that ABC damages Mr. Ford's already-constructed home. Although Mr. Ford also alleges damage to ABC's workmanship, Mr. Ford alleges damage to the home that existed before ABC began work on the premises. These allegations take this case out of the general principle on which Commercial relies.

Commercial also argues at pages 11 and 12 of its brief that the claim is excluded under its exclusion for property damage to "that particular part of real property on which you or any contractor or subcontractor is working directly or indirectly on your behalf...." Here again, Mr. Ford's allegations contradict that the only damage was to ABC's work. Mr. Ford instead alleges that the absence of pierings–not direct or indirect work but the omission of some precaution–caused property damage to the existing structure. A failure to take precaution, leading to property damage to a part of the structure not constructed or reconstructed by the insured contractor, is what "business protector" coverage protects. If not, then what? One has to ask what the purpose would be of a policy of that type covering property damage if it were construed to eliminate all property-damage coverage. Ambiguities are resolved against the drafter and exclusions strictly construed. *See* Universal Underwriters Ins. Co. v. Kneeland, 464 Mich 491, 496, 628 NW2d 491, 494 (2001). Commercial should pay for that damage. Mr. Ford also alleges damage to roof, plumbing, and other elements not a part of ABC's work. There are genuine issues of material fact such that the Court should not resolve the coverage claim by summary disposition.

Relief Requested

On this authority and analysis, defendant ABC Development, Inc., prays under MCR 2.116(C)(10) that the Court deny plaintiff Commercial General Insurance Company's motion.

Respectfully submitted,
[signature block for defendant ABC's counsel]

INQUIRY

Unavailable Evidence. Rule 56(f) further provides for situations in which the non-movant can show the trial court that the evidence on which the non-movant would rely to oppose summary judgment is unavailable. Rule 56(f) provides that when the non-movant shows by affidavit that "for specified reasons" it cannot present "facts essential to justify its opposition" to the motion, then the court may deny the motion, hold its decision in abeyance pending completion of discovery, or take other action. What situation does Rule 56(f) address? Parties occasionally move for summary judgment prematurely, before discovery is complete. The expense of discovery can itself create an incentive for an early motion for summary judgment. If the trial court is going to dismiss the case eventually, then why not dismiss it sooner rather than later? Rule 56(f) addresses the procedural unfairness to the non-movant when the non-movant has not yet been able to obtain the evidence necessary to oppose summary judgment. Rule 56(f)(2) provides specifically that the trial court's continuing the motion (reserving decision for later) may be to permit the non-movant to obtain affidavits, take depositions, or complete other discovery. Although one might mistakenly assume so, Rule 56(f) is not for dilatory non-movants. Rule 56(f) is for situations in which a non-movant does not anticipate a summary-judgment motion on a certain issue. The non-movant may have known all along exactly where to obtain the evidence but merely preferred to wait for trial to incur that expense. Notice how summary judgment thus forces parties to engage in discovery when they may not otherwise have done so. Has summary judgment reduced costs or increased them?

Movant's Burden. Until the following Supreme Court case a decade and a half later, the trial courts tended to misread *Adickes v. S.H. Kress & Co.* as requiring that the moving party produce affirmative evidence in its favor on the issue where it claimed the non-movant opposing party had no evidence. You can see how the trial courts might have thought so. *Adickes v. S.H. Kress & Co.* held that the moving party should have attempted to meet its initial burden by providing affidavits contradicting the non-movant's only workable theory. To conclude so, though, is to read *Adickes* too generously to the non-movant. *Adickes* involved a plaintiff who was trying to rely on circumstantial evidence to draw an inference of conspiracy from police officers' presence on the scene. So long as the inference remained, there would be a disputed fact issue, and the moving party would not be entitled to summary judgment. For the moving party to prevail on summary judgment, the moving party would have had to point out that the police officers were not even present and therefore could not possibly have engaged in a conspiracy. The following Supreme Court case confirmed that ordinarily, the moving party has no burden to come forward with any evidence. It was either that the lower courts had misread *Adickes v. S.H. Kress & Co.* or perhaps that the Supreme Court was changing summary judgment's emphasis to respond to changes in litigation in the ensuing years. See what you think as you read the first of three Supreme Court cases that reinvigorated summary-judgment practice.

Celotex Corp. v. Catrett,

United States Supreme Court
477 U.S. 317 (1986)

Justice REHNQUIST delivered the opinion of the Court.

The United States District Court for the District of Columbia granted the motion of petitioner Celotex Corporation for summary judgment against respondent Catrett because the latter was unable to produce evidence in support of her allegation in her wrongful-death complaint that the decedent had been exposed to petitioner's asbestos products. A divided panel of the Court of Appeals for the District of Columbia Circuit reversed, however, holding that petitioner's failure to support its motion with evidence tending to *negate* such exposure precluded the entry of summary judgment in its favor. ... We ... reverse the decision of the District of Columbia Circuit.

Respondent commenced this lawsuit in September 1980, alleging that the death in 1979 of her husband ... resulted from his exposure to products containing asbestos manufactured or distributed by 15 named corporations. ... Petitioner's motion ... argued that summary judgment was proper because respondent had "failed to produce evidence that any [Celotex] product ... was the proximate cause of the injuries... ." ... In response to petitioner's summary judgment motion, respondent then produced ... a transcript of a deposition of the decedent, a letter from an official of one of the decedent's former employers whom petitioner planned to call as a trial witness, and a letter from an insurance company to respondent's attorney, all tending to establish that the decedent had been exposed to petitioner's asbestos products... . Petitioner, in turn, argued that the three documents were inadmissible hearsay and thus could not be considered in opposition to the summary judgment motion.

... [T]he District Court granted ... petitioner's summary judgment motion because "there [was] no showing that the plaintiff was exposed to the defendant Celotex's product... ." [C] ... [A] divided panel of the District of Columbia Circuit reversed. The majority of the Court of Appeals held that petitioner's summary judgment motion was rendered "fatally defective" by the fact that petitioner "made no effort to adduce *any* evidence, in the form of affidavits or otherwise, to support its motion." [C] According to the majority, Rule 56(e) of the Federal Rules of Civil Procedure,[fn] and this Court's decision in Adickes v. S.H. Kress & Co., 398 U.S. 144, 159[] (1970), establish that "the party opposing the motion for summary judgment bears the burden of responding *only after* the moving party has met its burden of coming forward with proof of the absence of any genuine issues of material fact." [C] The majority therefore declined to consider petitioner's argument that none of the evidence produced by respondent in opposition to the motion for summary judgment would have been admissible at trial. ...

We think that the position taken by the majority of the Court of Appeals is inconsistent with the standard for summary judgment set forth in Rule 56(c) of the Federal Rules of Civil Procedure.[fn] Under Rule 56(c), summary judgment is proper "if the pleadings, depositions, answers to interrogatories, and admissions on file, together with the affidavits, if any, show that there is no genuine issue as to any material fact and that the moving party is entitled to a judgment as a matter of law." In our view, the plain language of Rule 56(c) mandates the entry of summary judgment, after adequate time for discovery and upon motion, against a party who fails to make a showing sufficient to establish the existence of an element essential to that party's case, and on which that party will bear the burden of proof at trial. In such a situation, there can be "no genuine issue as to any material fact," since a complete failure of proof concerning an essential element of the nonmoving party's case necessarily renders all other facts immaterial. The moving party is "entitled to a judgment as a matter of law" because the nonmoving party has failed to make a sufficient showing on an essential element of her case with respect to which she has the burden of proof. "[T]h[e] standard [for granting summary judgment] mirrors the standard for a directed verdict under Federal Rule of Civil Procedure 50(a)...." Anderson v. Liberty Lobby, Inc., 477 U.S. 242, 250[] (1986).

Of course, a party seeking summary judgment always bears the initial responsibility of informing the district court of the basis for its motion, and identifying those portions of "the pleadings, depositions, answers to interrogatories, and admissions on file, together with the affidavits, if any," which it believes demonstrate the absence of a genuine issue of material fact. But unlike the Court of Appeals, we find no express or implied requirement in Rule 56 that the moving party support its motion with affidavits or other similar materials *negating* the opponent's claim. On the contrary, Rule 56(c), which refers to "the affidavits, *if any*" (emphasis added), suggests the absence of such a requirement. ... Rules 56(a) and (b)... [also] provide that claimants and defendants, respectively, may move for summary judgment "*with or without supporting affidavits*" (emphasis added). ... One of the principal purposes of the summary judgment rule is to isolate and dispose of factually unsupported claims or defenses, and we think it should be interpreted in a way that allows it to accomplish this purpose.[fn]

... In cases like the instant one, where the nonmoving party will bear the burden of proof at trial on a dispositive issue, a summary judgment motion may properly be made in reliance solely on the "pleadings, depositions, answers to interrogatories, and admissions on file." Such a motion, whether or not accompanied by affidavits, will be "made and supported as provided in this rule," and Rule 56(e) therefore requires the nonmoving party to go beyond the pleadings and by her own affidavits, or by the "depositions, answers to interrogatories, and admissions on file," designate "specific facts showing that there is a genuine issue for trial."

We do not mean that the nonmoving party must produce evidence in a form that would be admissible at trial in order to avoid summary judgment. Obviously, Rule 56 does not require the nonmoving party to depose her own witnesses. Rule 56(e) permits a proper summary judgment motion to be opposed by any of the kinds of evidentiary materials listed in Rule 56(c), except the mere pleadings themselves, and it is from this list that one would normally expect the nonmoving party to make the showing to which we have referred.

The Court of Appeals in this case felt itself constrained, however, by language in our decision in Adickes v. S.H. Kress & Co., 398 U.S. 144[] (1970). There we held that summary judgment had been improperly entered in favor of the defendant restaurant in an action brought under 42 U.S.C. §1983. ... [T]he *Adickes* Court said that "both the commentary on and the background of the 1963 amendment conclusively show that it was not intended to modify the burden of the moving party ... to show initially the absence of a genuine issue concerning any material fact." *Id.*, at 159, 90 S.Ct., at 1609. ... [W]e fully agree with the *Adickes* Court ... [but] do not think the *Adickes* language quoted above should be construed to mean that the burden is on the party moving for summary judgment to produce evidence showing the absence of a genuine issue of material fact, even with respect to an issue on which the nonmoving party bears the burden of proof. Instead, as we have explained, the burden on the moving party may be discharged by "showing"—that is, pointing out to the district court—that there is an absence of evidence to support the nonmoving party's case. ...

Our conclusion is bolstered by the fact that district courts are widely acknowledged to possess the power to enter summary judgments *sua sponte,* so long as the losing party was on notice that she had to come forward with all of her evidence. [Cc] It would surely defy common sense to hold that the District Court could have entered summary judgment *sua sponte* in favor of petitioner in the instant case, but that petitioner's filing of a motion requesting such a disposition precluded the District Court from ordering it.

Respondent commenced this action in September 1980, and petitioner's motion was filed in September 1981. The parties had conducted discovery, and no serious claim can be made that respondent was in any sense "railroaded" by a premature motion for summary judgment. Any potential problem with such premature motions can be adequately dealt with under Rule 56(f),[fn] which allows a summary judgment motion to be denied, or the hearing on the motion to be continued, if the nonmoving party has not had an opportunity to make full discovery. ...

The Federal Rules of Civil Procedure have for almost 50 years authorized motions for summary judgment upon proper showings of the lack of a genuine, triable issue of material fact. Summary judgment procedure is properly regarded not as a disfavored procedural shortcut, but rather as an integral part of the Federal Rules as a whole, which are designed "to secure the just, speedy and inexpensive determination of every action." Fed. Rule Civ. Proc. 1; [c]. Before the shift to "notice pleading" accomplished by the Federal Rules, motions to dismiss a complaint or to strike a defense were the principal tools by which factually insufficient claims or defenses could be isolated and prevented from going to trial with the attendant unwarranted consumption of public and private resources. But with the advent of "notice pleading," the motion to dismiss seldom fulfills this function any more, and its place has been taken by the motion for summary judgment. Rule 56 must be construed with due regard not only for the rights of persons asserting claims and defenses that are adequately based in fact to have those claims and defenses tried to a jury, but also for the rights of persons opposing such claims and defenses to demonstrate in the manner provided by the Rule, prior to trial, that the claims and defenses have no factual basis.

The judgment of the Court of Appeals is accordingly reversed, and the case is remanded for further proceedings consistent with this opinion.

It is so ordered.

Justice WHITE, concurring.

I agree that the Court of Appeals was wrong in holding that the moving defendant must always support his motion with evidence or affidavits showing the absence of a genuine dispute about a material fact. I also agree that the movant may rely on depositions, answers to interrogatories, and the like, to demonstrate that the plaintiff has no evidence to prove his case and hence that there can be no factual dispute. But the movant must discharge the burden the Rules place upon him: It is not enough to move for summary judgment without supporting the motion in any way or with a conclusory assertion that the plaintiff has no evidence to prove his case.

A plaintiff need not initiate any discovery or reveal his witnesses or evidence unless required to do so under the discovery Rules or by court order. Of course, he must respond if required to do so; but he need not also depose his witnesses or obtain their affidavits to defeat a summary judgment motion asserting only that he has failed to produce any support for his case. It is the defendant's task to negate, if he can, the claimed basis for the suit. …

Justice BRENNAN, with whom THE CHIEF JUSTICE and Justice BLACKMUN join, dissenting.

This case requires the Court to determine whether Celotex satisfied its initial burden of production in moving for summary judgment on the ground that the plaintiff lacked evidence to establish an essential element of her case at trial. … [T]he Court has not clearly explained what is required of a moving party seeking summary judgment on the ground that the nonmoving party cannot prove its case.[fn] This lack of clarity is unfortunate: district courts must routinely decide summary judgment motions, and the Court's opinion will very likely create confusion. …

Where the moving party … seeks summary judgment on the ground that the nonmoving party—who will bear the burden of persuasion at trial—has no evidence, … a conclusory assertion that the nonmoving party has no evidence is insufficient. … Rather, as the Court confirms, a party who moves for summary judgment on the ground that the nonmoving party has no evidence must affirmatively show the absence of evidence in the record. [C] This may require the moving party to depose the nonmoving party's witnesses or to establish the inadequacy of documentary evidence. If there is literally no evidence in the record, the moving party may demonstrate this by reviewing for the court the admissions, interrogatories, and other exchanges between the parties that are in the record. Either way, however, the moving party must affirmatively demonstrate that there is no evidence in the record to support a judgment for the nonmoving party.

If the moving party has not fully discharged this initial burden of production, its motion for summary judgment must be denied... . Accordingly, the nonmoving party may defeat a motion for summary judgment that asserts that the nonmoving party has no evidence by calling the Court's attention to supporting evidence already in the record that was overlooked or ignored by the moving party. In that event, the moving party must respond by making an attempt to demonstrate the inadequacy of this evidence, for it is only by attacking all the record evidence allegedly supporting the nonmoving party that a party seeking summary judgment satisfies Rule 56's burden of production.[fn] ...

I do not read the Court's opinion to say anything inconsistent with or different than the preceding discussion. My disagreement with the Court concerns the application of these principles to the facts of this case.

Defendant Celotex sought summary judgment on the ground that plaintiff had "failed to produce" any evidence that her decedent had ever been exposed to Celotex asbestos.[fn] ...

Approximately three months earlier, Celotex had filed an essentially identical motion. Plaintiff responded to this earlier motion by producing three pieces of evidence which she claimed "[a]t the very least ... demonstrate that there is a genuine factual dispute for trial"... .

... [W]hen Celotex filed its second summary judgment motion, the record *did* contain evidence—including at least one witness—supporting plaintiff's claim. Indeed, counsel for Celotex admitted to this Court at oral argument that Celotex was aware of this evidence and of plaintiff's intention to call Mr. Hoff as a witness at trial when the second summary judgment motion was filed. [C] ...

On these facts, there is simply no question that Celotex failed to discharge its initial burden of production. Having chosen to base its motion on the argument that there was no evidence in the record to support plaintiff's claim, Celotex was not free to ignore supporting evidence that the record clearly contained. Rather, Celotex was required, as an initial matter, to attack the adequacy of this evidence. Celotex' failure to fulfill this simple requirement constituted a failure to discharge its initial burden of production under Rule 56, and thereby rendered summary judgment improper.[fn]

... Under the circumstances, then, remanding is a waste of time.

Justice STEVENS, dissenting[, omitted].

Practice

The plaintiff's lawyer opened the mail quickly, recognizing that it was the long-awaited opinion on the defendant's motion for summary judgment. The lawyers had argued the motion two months ago. The plaintiff's lawyer had begun painstaking trial preparations two weeks ago. Now, the lawyer skimmed the opinion's first page and then flipped to the end of the opinion with a sinking feeling. The trial judge had dismissed the case. It was going to be a tough call to the client, who had not been very understanding when the defense had first filed and argued the motion. A serious injury not of one's own making, followed by substantial uncompensated wage loss and medical expense, would make anyone unhappy. The lawyer did not look forward to trying to help the client understand that the justice system was not trying to wreak another injury.

INQUIRY

Burden to Point Out. A dissent in *Celotex Corp. v. Catrett* asserted that it was indistinguishable from *Adickes v. S.H. Kress & Co.* even though it reached the opposite conclusion. Members of the Court could not agree on that point, which we can probably do no better to resolve. Either *Celotex Corp. v. Catrett* changed the Rule 56 standard, or it did not. What is clear after *Celotex Corp. v. Catrett* is that the movant's Rule 56 obligation to "show" the absence of a genuine material issue is not a duty to produce evidence. Rather, the movant satisfies its Rule 56 obligation to show the absence of evidence by "pointing out to the district court" that absence. It is a duty to articulate or explain why there is no evidence on an element, not a duty to produce, establish, rebut, or otherwise overcome evidence. Do you see the difference that this standard (whether new or old) makes? From a practical standpoint, it is significantly easier for a moving party to criticize and dissect evidence than to produce it. One need not necessarily take onerous depositions of adverse witnesses or convince reluctant independent witnesses to cooperate to the point of signing affidavits. One need not necessarily locate critical electronically stored information or find key paper documents. The movant can simply examine the evidence available to the non-movant while pointing out to the trial court where it fails to establish a genuine issue. In any case, the lower courts embraced the clearer standard. *See* Adler v. Wal-Mart Stores, Inc., 144 F.3d 664, 670-671 (10th Cir. 1998) ("point out to the court a lack of evidence for the nonmovant on an essential element"); National State Bank v. Federal Reserve bank, 979 F.2d 1579, 1581-1582 (3d Cir. 1992) ("point to the lack of evidence supporting the non-movant's claim"). *Celotex Corp. v. Catrett* placed the burden of producing evidence back on the non-movant, where the Supreme Court in that case stated that it had always been. Consider another Supreme Court case decided the same year as *Celotex Corp. v. Catrett*, holding that a higher proof burden of clear and convincing evidence also matters when a trial court decides a summary-judgment motion.

Anderson v. Liberty Lobby, Inc.,

United States Supreme Court
477 U.S. 242 (1986)

Justice WHITE delivered the opinion of the Court.

In New York Times Co. v. Sullivan, 376 U.S. 254, 279-280[] (1964), we held that, in a libel suit brought by a public official, the First Amendment requires the plaintiff to show that in publishing the defamatory statement the defendant acted with actual malice—"with knowledge that it was false or with reckless disregard of whether it was false or not." We held further that such actual malice must be shown with "convincing clarity." *Id.* at 285-286[]. [C] These *New York Times* requirements we have since extended to libel suits brought by public figures as well. [C]

This case presents the question whether the clear-and-convincing-evidence requirement must be considered by a court ruling on a motion for summary judgment under Rule 56 of the Federal Rules of Civil Procedure in a case to which *New York Times* applies. The United States Court of Appeals for the District of Columbia Circuit held that that requirement need not be considered at the summary judgment stage. [C] ... We now reverse.

I

Respondent Liberty Lobby, Inc., is a not-for-profit corporation and self-described "citizens' lobby." Respondent Willis Carto is its founder and treasurer. In October 1981, The Investigator magazine published two articles... . These articles portrayed respondents as neo-Nazi, anti-Semitic, racist, and Fascist.

Respondents filed this diversity libel action in the United States District Court for the District of Columbia, alleging that some 28 statements and 2 illustrations in the 3 articles were false and derogatory. Named as defendants in the action were petitioner Jack Anderson, the publisher of The Investigator, petitioner Bill Adkins, president and chief executive officer of the Investigator Publishing Co., and petitioner Investigator Publishing Co. itself.

Following discovery, petitioners moved for summary judgment pursuant to Rule 56. In their motion, petitioners asserted that because respondents are public figures they were required to prove their case under the standards set forth in *New York Times.* Petitioners also asserted that summary judgment was proper because actual malice was absent as a matter of law. In support of this latter assertion, petitioners submitted the affidavit of Charles Bermant, an employee of petitioners and the author of the two longer articles.[fn] In this affidavit, Bermant stated that he had spent a substantial amount of time researching and writing the articles and that his facts were obtained from a wide variety of sources. He also stated that he had at all times believed and still believed that the facts contained in the articles were truthful and accurate. Attached to this affidavit was an appendix in which Bermant detailed the sources for each of the statements alleged by respondents to be libelous.

Respondents opposed the motion for summary judgment, asserting that there were numerous inaccuracies in the articles and claiming that an issue of actual malice was presented by virtue of the fact that in preparing the articles Bermant had relied on several sources that respondents asserted were patently unreliable. Generally, respondents charged that petitioners had failed adequately to verify their information before publishing. Respondents also presented evidence that William McGaw, an editor of The Investigator, had told petitioner Adkins before publication that the articles were "terrible" and "ridiculous."

... The District Court then held that Bermant's thorough investigation and research and his reliance on numerous sources precluded a finding of actual malice. Thus, the District Court granted the motion and entered judgment in favor of petitioners. ...

On appeal, the Court of Appeals affirmed as to 21 and reversed as to 9 of the allegedly defamatory statements. ... [T]he Court of Appeals ... held that for the purposes of summary judgment the requirement that actual malice be proved by clear and convincing evidence, rather than by a preponderance of the evidence, was irrelevant... .

II

A

... Rule 56(c) of the Federal Rules of Civil Procedure provides that summary judgment "shall be rendered forthwith if the pleadings, depositions, answers to interrogatories, and admissions on file, together with the affidavits, if any, show that there is no genuine issue as to any material fact and that the moving party is entitled to a judgment as a matter of law." By its very terms, this standard provides that the mere existence of *some* alleged factual dispute between the parties will not defeat an otherwise properly supported motion for summary judgment; the requirement is that there be no *genuine* issue of *material* fact. ...

... [S]ummary judgment will not lie if the dispute about a material fact is "genuine," that is, if the evidence is such that a reasonable jury could return a verdict for the nonmoving party. In First National Bank of Arizona v. Cities Service Co., 391 U.S. 253[] (1968), we affirmed a grant of summary judgment for an antitrust defendant where the issue was whether there was a genuine factual dispute as to the existence of a conspiracy. ... We went on to hold that, in the face of the defendant's properly supported motion for summary judgment, the plaintiff could not rest on his allegations of a conspiracy to get to a jury without "any significant probative evidence tending to support the complaint." *Id.* at 290[].

Again, in Adickes v. S.H. Kress & Co., 398 U.S. 144[] (1970), the Court emphasized that the availability of summary judgment turned on whether a proper jury question was presented. There, one of the issues was whether there was a conspiracy between private persons and law enforcement officers. The District Court granted summary judgment for the defendants, stating that there was no evidence from which reasonably minded jurors might draw an inference of conspiracy. We reversed, pointing out that the moving parties' submissions had not foreclosed the possibility of the existence of certain facts from which "it would be open to a jury ... to infer from the circumstances" that there had been a meeting of the minds. *Id.* at 158-159[].

Our prior decisions may not have uniformly recited the same language in describing genuine factual issues under Rule 56, but it is clear enough from our recent cases that at the summary judgment stage the judge's function is not himself to weigh the evidence and determine the truth of the matter but to determine whether there is a genuine issue for trial. As *Adickes, supra,* and *Cities Service, supra,* indicate, there is no issue for trial unless there is sufficient evidence favoring the nonmoving party for a jury to return a verdict for that party. [C] If the evidence is merely colorable, Dombrowski v. Eastland, 387 U.S. 82[] (1967) (*per curiam*), or is not significantly probative, *Cities Service, supra,* at 290[], summary judgment may be granted. ...

B

Progressing to the specific issue in this case, we are convinced that the inquiry involved in a ruling on a motion for summary judgment or for a directed verdict necessarily implicates the substantive evidentiary standard of proof that would apply at the trial on the merits. If the defendant in a run-of-the-mill civil case moves for summary judgment or for a directed verdict based on the lack of proof of a material fact, the judge must ask himself not whether he thinks the evidence unmistakably favors one side or the other but whether a fair-minded jury could return a verdict for the plaintiff on the evidence presented. The mere existence of a scintilla of evidence in support of the plaintiff's position will be insufficient; there must be evidence on which the jury could reasonably find for the plaintiff. The judge's inquiry, therefore, unavoidably asks whether reasonable jurors could find by a preponderance of the evidence that the plaintiff is entitled to a verdict… .

The case for the proposition that a higher burden of proof should have a corresponding effect on the judge when deciding whether to send the case to the jury was well made by the Court of Appeals for the Second Circuit in United States v. Taylor, 464 F.2d 240 (2d Cir. 1972)… .

… [T]he *Taylor* court thought that it was implicit in this Court's adoption of the clear-and-convincing-evidence standard for certain kinds of cases that there was a "concomitant duty on the judge to consider the applicable burden when deciding whether to send a case to the jury." 464 F.2d, at 243. Although the court thought that this higher standard would not produce different results in many cases, it could not say that it would never do so.

Just as the "convincing clarity" requirement is relevant in ruling on a motion for directed verdict, it is relevant in ruling on a motion for summary judgment. When determining if a genuine factual issue as to actual malice exists in a libel suit brought by a public figure, a trial judge must bear in mind the actual quantum and quality of proof necessary to support liability under *New York Times*. For example, there is no genuine issue if the evidence presented in the opposing affidavits is of insufficient caliber or quantity to allow a rational finder of fact to find actual malice by clear and convincing evidence.

Thus, in ruling on a motion for summary judgment, the judge must view the evidence presented through the prism of the substantive evidentiary burden. …

In sum, we conclude that the determination of whether a given factual dispute requires submission to a jury must be guided by the substantive evidentiary standards that apply to the case. … Thus, where the factual dispute concerns actual malice, clearly a material issue in a *New York Times* case, the appropriate summary judgment question will be whether the evidence in the record could support a reasonable jury finding either that the plaintiff has shown actual malice by clear and convincing evidence or that the plaintiff has not.[fn] …

IV

In sum, a court ruling on a motion for summary judgment must be guided by the *New York Times* "clear and convincing" evidentiary standard in determining whether a genuine issue of actual malice exists—that is, whether the evidence presented is such that a reasonable jury might find that actual malice had been shown with convincing clarity. Because the Court of Appeals did not apply the correct standard in reviewing the District Court's grant of summary judgment, we vacate its decision and remand the case for further proceedings consistent with this opinion.

It is so ordered.

Justice BRENNAN, dissenting[, omitted].

Justice REHNQUIST, with whom THE CHIEF JUSTICE joins, dissenting[, omitted].

INQUIRY

Proof Burdens. Appreciate the conceptual challenge that the decision in *Anderson v. Liberty Lobby, Inc.,* presents. Under Rule 56's summary-judgment standard, trial judges are not to weigh the evidence. They are not to make credibility judgments of witnesses or judge the quality and quantity of documentary evidence, as that evidence would weigh in favor of or against particular issues. Trial judges are to determine whether there is prima facie evidence for material propositions, meaning whether reasonable jurors could conclude that the evidence satisfies the disputed element. The summary-judgment standard is a threshold, not a scale. Yet requiring the trial judge to consider the higher clear-and-convincing proof burden in cases where that higher burden applies seems to require the trial judge to weigh evidence at least to some degree. The conceptual challenge is to recognize that the summary-judgment standard remains a threshold. The threshold has simply moved in those cases. *Anderson v. Liberty Lobby, Inc.,* was one of three cases the Supreme Court decided in the same year, each making summary judgment easier to obtain and harder to resist either in all or some cases. Consider next the third of those Supreme Court cases, in which the Court held that if the inferences one draws in the non-movant's favor from circumstantial evidence are implausible, then the non-movant must come forward with more persuasive evidence.

Matsushita Elec. Industries Co. v. Zenith Radio Corp.,

United States Supreme Court
475 U.S. 574 (1986)

Justice POWELL delivered the opinion of the Court.

This case requires that we again consider the standard district courts must apply when deciding whether to grant summary judgment in an antitrust conspiracy case.

I...

A

Petitioners, defendants below, are 21 corporations that manufacture or sell "consumer electronic products" (CEPs)—for the most part, television sets. Petitioners include both Japanese manufacturers of CEPs and American firms, controlled by Japanese parents, that sell the Japanese-manufactured products. Respondents, plaintiffs below, are Zenith Radio Corporation (Zenith) and National Union Electric Corporation (NUE). Zenith is an American firm that manufactures and sells television sets. NUE is the corporate successor to Emerson Radio Company, an American firm that manufactured and sold television sets until 1970, when it withdrew from the market after sustaining substantial losses. Zenith and NUE began this lawsuit in 1974,[fn] claiming that petitioners had illegally conspired to drive American firms from the American CEP market. ...

After several years of detailed discovery, petitioners filed motions for summary judgment on all claims against them. The District Court directed the parties to file, with preclusive effect, "Final Pretrial Statements" listing all the documentary evidence that would be offered if the case proceeded to trial. Respondents filed such a statement, and petitioners responded with a series of motions challenging the admissibility of respondents' evidence. In three detailed opinions, the District Court found the bulk of the evidence on which Zenith and NUE relied inadmissible.[fn]

The District Court then turned to petitioners' motions for summary judgment. In an opinion spanning 217 pages, the court found that the admissible evidence did not raise a genuine issue of material fact as to the existence of the alleged conspiracy. ... Summary judgment therefore was granted on respondents' claims... .

B

The Court of Appeals for the Third Circuit reversed.[fn] The court began by examining the District Court's evidentiary rulings, and determined that much of the evidence excluded by the District Court was in fact admissible. [C] ...

On the merits, and based on the newly enlarged record, the court found that the District Court's summary judgment decision was improper. The court acknowledged that "there are legal limitations upon the inferences which may be drawn from circumstantial evidence," [c], but it found that "the legal problem ... is different" when "there is direct evidence of concert of action." [C] Here, the court concluded, "there is both direct evidence of certain kinds of concert of action and circumstantial evidence having some tendency to suggest that other kinds of concert of action may have occurred." [C] ...

We granted certiorari to determine (i) whether the Court of Appeals applied the proper standards in evaluating the District Court's decision to grant petitioners' motion for summary judgment... . We reverse on the first issue... .

II...

The Court of Appeals found that respondents' allegation of a horizontal conspiracy to engage in predatory pricing,[fn] if proved,[fn] would be a *per se* violation of §1 of the Sherman Act. [C] Petitioners did not appeal from that conclusion. The issue in this case thus becomes whether respondents adduced sufficient evidence in support of their theory to survive summary judgment. We therefore examine the principles that govern the summary judgment determination.

III

To survive petitioners' motion for summary judgment,[fn] respondents must establish that there is a genuine issue of material fact as to whether petitioners entered into an illegal conspiracy that caused respondents to suffer a cognizable injury. Fed. Rule Civ. Proc. 56(e);[n] First National Bank of Arizona v. Cities Service Co., 391 U.S. 253, 288-289[] (1968). This showing has two components. First, respondents must show more than a conspiracy in violation of the antitrust laws; they must show an injury to them resulting from the illegal conduct. ...

Second, the issue of fact must be "genuine." Fed.Rules Civ.Proc. 56(c), (e). When the moving party has carried its burden under Rule 56(c),[fn] its opponent must do more than simply show that there is some metaphysical doubt as to the material facts. [Cc] In the language of the Rule, the nonmoving party must come forward with "specific facts showing that there is a *genuine issue for trial.*" Fed. Rule Civ. Proc. 56(e) (emphasis added). [C] Where the record taken as a whole could not lead a rational trier of fact to find for the non-moving party, there is no "genuine issue for trial." *Cities Service, supra,*[] at 289[].

It follows from these settled principles that if the factual context renders respondents' claim implausible—if the claim is one that simply makes no economic sense—respondents must come forward with more persuasive evidence to support their claim than would otherwise be necessary. *Cities Service* is instructive. The issue in that case was whether proof of the defendant's refusal to deal with the plaintiff supported an inference that the defendant willingly had joined an illegal boycott. Economic factors strongly suggested that the defendant had no motive to join the alleged conspiracy. [C] ... Since the defendant lacked any rational motive to join the alleged boycott, and since its refusal to deal was consistent with the defendant's independent interest, the refusal to deal could not by itself support a finding of antitrust liability. [C]

Respondents correctly note that "[o]n summary judgment the inferences to be drawn from the underlying facts ... must be viewed in the light most favorable to the party opposing the motion." United States v. Diebold, Inc., 369 U.S. 654, 655[] (1962). But antitrust law limits the range of permissible inferences from ambiguous evidence in a §1 case. ... To survive a motion for summary judgment or for a directed verdict, a plaintiff seeking damages for a violation of §1 must present evidence "that tends to exclude the possibility" that the alleged conspirators acted independently. [C] Respondents in this case, in other words, must show that the inference of conspiracy is reasonable in light of the competing inferences of independent action or collusive action that could not have harmed respondents. See *Cities Service, supra,* [] at 280[]. ...

IV

A

A predatory pricing conspiracy is by nature speculative. Any agreement to price below the competitive level requires the conspirators to forgo profits that free competition would offer them. The forgone profits may be considered an investment in the future. For the investment to be rational, the conspirators must have a reasonable expectation of recovering, in the form of later monopoly profits, more than the losses suffered. ...

The alleged conspiracy's failure to achieve its ends in the two decades of its asserted operation is strong evidence that the conspiracy does not in fact exist. ...

Nor does the possibility that petitioners have obtained supracompetitive profits in the Japanese market change this calculation. ...

B

... [C]ourts should not permit factfinders to infer conspiracies when such inferences are implausible, because the effect of such practices is often to deter procompetitive conduct. ...

V

As our discussion in Part IV-A shows, petitioners had no motive to enter into the alleged conspiracy. To the contrary, as presumably rational businesses, petitioners had every incentive *not* to engage in the conduct with which they are charged, for its likely effect would be to generate losses for petitioners with no corresponding gains. Cf. *Cities Service, [supra,]* at 279[]. The Court of Appeals did not take account of the absence of a plausible motive to enter into the alleged predatory pricing conspiracy. It focused instead on whether there was "direct evidence of concert of action." [C] The Court of Appeals erred in two respects: (i) the "direct evidence" on which the court relied had little, if any, relevance to the alleged predatory pricing conspiracy; and (ii) the court failed to consider the absence of a plausible motive to engage in predatory pricing. ...

That being the case, the absence of any plausible motive to engage in the conduct charged is highly relevant to whether a "genuine issue for trial" exists within the meaning of Rule 56(e). Lack of motive bears on the range of permissible conclusions that might be drawn from ambiguous evidence: if petitioners had no rational economic motive to conspire, and if their conduct is consistent with other, equally plausible explanations, the conduct does not give rise to an inference of conspiracy. See *Cities Service, supra,* [] at 278-280[]. ...

On remand, the Court of Appeals is free to consider whether there is other evidence that is sufficiently unambiguous to permit a trier of fact to find that petitioners conspired to price predatorily for two decades despite the absence of any apparent motive to do so. The evidence must "ten[d] to exclude the possibility" that petitioners underpriced respondents to compete for business rather than to implement an economically senseless conspiracy. [C] In the absence of such evidence, there is no "genuine issue for trial" under Rule 56(e), and petitioners are entitled to have summary judgment reinstated. ...

The decision of the Court of Appeals is reversed, and the case is remanded for further proceedings consistent with this opinion.

It is so ordered.

Justice WHITE, with whom Justice BRENNAN, Justice BLACKMUN, and Justice STEVENS join, dissenting[, omitted].

INQUIRY

Impact. Consider the substantial cumulative effect of the *Celotex* trilogy. One of the cases, *Celotex* itself, applies to the procedure for summary judgment, holding that the moving party need not produce evidence but may merely point out the defects in the non-movant's evidence. *Celotex* thus applies to all summary-judgment proceedings. The second of the cases, *Anderson v. Liberty Lobby, Inc.*, holding that the trial court must consider the proof burden, applies only to the relatively fewer cases involving the higher clear-and-convincing-evidence proof burden. Yet it may also represent a more general invitation to trial judges to look more closely at the evidence in light of whatever happens to be the applicable proof burden. The third of the cases, *Matsushita Elec. Industries Co. v. Zenith Radio Corp.*, holding that the non-movant must buttress implausible inferences with persuasive evidence, applies potentially to all cases and invites the trial judge to measure the plausibility of inferences. Consider next a case that cites all three cases in the *Celotex* trilogy to affirm summary judgment. While reading the case, think of what the trial and appellate court might have done if the only Supreme Court case extant on summary judgment was *Adickes v. S.H. Kress & Co.*, and the Supreme Court had never decided its *Celotex* trilogy. Also, think of which summary-judgment regime you prefer—one that disposes of more or fewer cases like the following case. Keep in mind that the Supreme Court cases are only a lens through which to view state-court summary-judgment practice. Individual states have their own history and trends, although in many instances both will look a lot like that reflected in the Supreme Court case law.

Bias v. Advantage International, Inc.,

United States Court of Appeals for the District of Columbia Circuit
905 F.2d 1558 (1990)

SENTELLE, Circuit Judge:

This case arises out of the tragic death from cocaine intoxication of University of Maryland basketball star Leonard K. Bias ("Bias"). James Bias, as Personal Representative of the Estate of Leonard K. Bias, deceased ("the Estate"), appeals an order of the District Court for the District of Columbia which granted summary judgment to defendants Advantage International, Inc. ("Advantage") and A. Lee Fentress on the Estate's claims arising out of a representation agreement between Bias and Advantage. ... For the reasons which follow, we affirm... .

I. BACKGROUND

On April 7, 1986, after the close of his college basketball career, Bias entered into a representation agreement with Advantage whereby Advantage agreed to advise and represent Bias in his affairs. Fentress was the particular Advantage representative servicing the Bias account. On June 17 of that year Bias was picked by the Boston Celtics in the first round of the National Basketball Association draft. On the morning of June 19, 1986, Bias died of cocaine intoxication. The Estate sued Advantage and Fentress for two separate injuries allegedly arising out of the representation arrangement between Bias and the defendants.[fn]

First, the Estate alleges that, prior to Bias's death, Bias and his parents directed Fentress to obtain a one-million dollar life insurance policy on Bias's life, that Fentress represented to Bias and Bias's parents that he had secured such a policy, and that in reliance on Fentress's assurances, Bias's parents did not independently seek to buy an insurance policy on Bias's life. ... [Defendants] did not secure any life insurance coverage for Bias prior to his death. ...

The District Court awarded the defendants summary judgment... . [T]he District Court held, in effect, that the Estate did not suffer any damage from the defendants' alleged failure to obtain life insurance for Bias because, even if the defendants had tried to obtain a one-million dollar policy on Bias's life, they would not have been able to do so. The District Court based this conclusion on the facts, about which it found no genuine issue, that Bias was a cocaine user and that no insurer in 1986 would have issued a one-million dollar life insurance policy, or "jumbo" policy, to a cocaine user unless the applicant made a misrepresentation regarding the applicant's use of drugs, thereby rendering the insurance policy void. ...

The Estate appeals..., arguing that there is a genuine issue as to Bias's insurability... .

II. SUMMARY JUDGMENT STANDARD...

The Supreme Court has stated that the moving party always bears the initial responsibility of informing the district court of the basis for its motion and identifying those portions of the record which it believes demonstrate the absence of a genuine issue of material fact. Celotex Corp. v. Catrett, 477 U.S. 317, 323[] (1986). The Supreme Court also explained that summary judgment is appropriate, no matter which party is the moving party, where a party fails to make a showing sufficient to establish the existence of an element essential to that party's case, and on which that party will bear the burden of proof at trial. *Id.* at 322[]. Thus, the moving party must explain its reasons for concluding that the record does not reveal any genuine issues of material fact, and must make a showing supporting its claims insofar as those claims involve issues on which it will bear the burden at trial.

Once the moving party has carried its burden, the responsibility then shifts to the nonmoving party to show that there is, in fact, a genuine issue of material fact. The Supreme Court has directed that the nonmoving party "must do more than simply show that there is some metaphysical doubt as to the material facts. " Matsushita Elec. Industrial Co. v. Zenith Radio, 475 U.S. 574, 586[] (1986)... . The nonmoving party "must come forward with 'specific facts showing that there is a *genuine issue for trial.*'" *Id.* at 587[] (emphasis in original). In evaluating the nonmovant's proffer, a court must of course draw from the evidence all justifiable inferences in favor of the nonmovant. Anderson v. Liberty Lobby, Inc., 477 U.S. 242, 255[] (1986).

III. THE INSURANCE ISSUE

The District Court's determination that there was no genuine issue involving Bias's insurability rests on two subsidiary conclusions: First, the District Court concluded that there was no genuine issue as to the fact that Bias was a drug user. Second, the District Court held that there was no dispute about the fact that as a drug user, Bias could not have obtained a jumbo life insurance policy. We can only affirm the District Court's award of summary judgment to the defendants on the insurance issue if both of these conclusions were correct.

A. *Bias's Prior Drug Use*

The defendants in this case offered the eyewitness testimony of two former teammates of Bias, Terry Long and David Gregg, in order to show that Bias was a cocaine user during the period prior to his death. Long and Gregg both described numerous occasions when they saw Bias ingest cocaine, and Long testified that he was introduced to cocaine by Bias and that Bias sometimes supplied others with cocaine.

Although on appeal the Estate attempts to discredit the testimony of Long and Gregg, the Estate did not seek to impeach the testimony of these witnesses before the District Court, and the Estate made no effort to depose these witnesses. Instead, the Estate offered affidavits from each of Bias's parents stating that Bias was not a drug user; the deposition testimony of Bias's basketball coach, Charles "Lefty" Driesell, who testified that he knew Bias well for four years and never knew Bias to be a user of drugs at any time prior to his death; and the results of several drug tests administered to Bias during the four years prior to his death which may have shown that, on the occasions when the tests were administered, there were no traces in Bias's system of the drugs for which he was tested.

Because the Estate's generalized evidence that Bias was not a drug user did not contradict the more specific testimony of teammates who knew Bias well and had seen him use cocaine on particular occasions, the District Court determined that there was no genuine issue as to the fact that Bias was a drug user. We agree.

There is no question that the defendants satisfied their initial burden on the issue of Bias's drug use. The testimony of Long and Gregg clearly tends to show that Bias was a cocaine user. We also agree with the District Court that the Estate did not rebut the defendants' showing. The testimony of Bias's parents to the effect that they knew Bias well and did not know him to be a drug user does not rebut the Long and Gregg testimony about Bias's drug use on particular occasions. The District Court properly held that rebuttal testimony either must come from persons familiar with the particular events to which the defendants' witnesses testified or must otherwise cast more than metaphysical doubt on the credibility of that testimony. Bias's parents and coach did not have personal knowledge of Bias's activities at the sorts of parties and gatherings about which Long and Gregg testified. The drug test results offered by the Estate may show that Bias had no cocaine in his system on the dates when the tests were administered, but, as the District Court correctly noted, these tests speak only to Bias's abstention during the periods preceding the tests. The tests do not rebut the Long and Gregg testimony that on a number of occasions Bias ingested cocaine in their presence.

The Estate could have deposed Long and Gregg, or otherwise attempted to impeach their testimony. The Estate also could have offered the testimony of other friends or teammates of Bias who were present at some of the gatherings described by Long and Gregg, who went out with Bias frequently, or who were otherwise familiar with his social habits. The Estate did none of these things. The Estate is not entitled to reach the jury merely on the supposition that the jury might not believe the defendants' witnesses. We thus agree with the District Court that there was no genuine issue of fact concerning Bias's status as a cocaine user.

B. *The Availability of a Jumbo Policy in Light of Bias's Prior Drug Use*

The defendants submitted affidavits from several experts who testified that in their expert opinions no insurer in 1986 would have issued a jumbo policy without inquiring, at some point in the application process, about the applicant's prior drug use. Dr. Francis Achampong, an Associate Professor of Business Law and Insurance and an occasional consultant for the insurance industry, asserted that life insurance companies will always and as a routine matter ask an applicant whether the applicant has ever used cocaine before issuing a term life policy of this size to that applicant. ... Bernard R. Wolfe, a licensed insurance agent experienced in evaluating the insurance needs of professional athletes, offered essentially the same opinion... .

... The Estate did not offer any testimony showing that a company existed at that time which would not have inquired about an applicant's prior drug use at *some* stage in the process. Moreover, the Estate did not offer any testimony tending to show that even if an applicant did admit to being a cocaine user, a company existed in 1986 which would have issued a jumbo policy to that applicant. The District Court thus concluded that the Estate had failed to rebut the defendants' showing that as a cocaine user Bias would have been unable to obtain a jumbo policy. The District Court recognized that Bias might have been able to obtain a policy by lying about his prior drug use, but rightly concluded that such a knowing and material misrepresentation in response to a direct question would have rendered void any policy which Bias thereby obtained. *See* D.C.Code Ann. § 35-414 (1988).

... The Estate failed to name a single particular company or provide other evidence that a single company existed which would have issued a jumbo policy in 1986 without inquiring about the applicant's drug use. Because the Estate has failed to do more than show that there is "some metaphysical doubt as to the material facts," *Matsushita Elec., [supra,]* at 586[], the District Court properly concluded that there was no genuine issue of material fact as to the insurability of a drug user. ...

V. CONCLUSION

In order to withstand a summary judgment motion once the moving party has made a prima facie showing to support its claims, the nonmoving party must come forward with specific facts showing that there is a genuine issue for trial. Fed.R.Civ.P. 56(e). The Estate has failed to come forward with such facts in this case, relying instead on bare arguments and allegations or on evidence which does not actually create a genuine issue for trial. For this reason, we affirm the District Court's award of summary judgment to the defendants in this case.[fn]

Biography

Mauricio E. Barreiro, who represented the appellant Bias Estate in the above case, practices as a sole practitioner in the firm of Mauricio E. Barreiro, LLC. Mr. Barreiro is a bilingual lawyer who for more than two decades has specialized in complex civil litigation in Maryland and the District of Columbia, primarily representing individuals. He has chaired a governor's commission on Hispanic affairs and the Baltimore County Human Relations Commission. In addition to business litigation and personal-injury, products-liability, and mass-torts cases, Mr. Barreiro also represents individual clients in white-collar crime and family law matters.

INQUIRY

Current Standard. Given that it has been about two-and-a-half decades since the *Celotex* trilogy, one might interpret the cases as representing the swing of a pendulum to its farthest point in one direction. While Rule 56 retains its centering effect that judges must still grant summary judgment only when there are no genuine material issues when viewing the evidence in the light most favorable to the non-movant, the *Celotex* trilogy emboldens trial judges to liberalize summary judgment. Research on the cases' effect has been inconclusive, with scholars disagreeing over whether it has led to more dismissals than previously. *Contrast* Martin H. Redish, *Summary Judgment and the Vanishing Trial: Implications of the Litigation Matrix,* 57 STANFORD L.REV.1329, 1330 (2005) (dramatic reduction in federal trials due in large part to new summary-judgment standard), *with* David L. Shapiro, *The Story of Celotex:*

The Role of Summary Judgment in the Administration of Justice, in KEVIN M. CLERMONT, ED., CIVIL PROCEDURE STORIES (2004) (sparse evidence of effects). Whatever the new standard's effect, there has been a definite trend away from jury trials beginning in the early 1970s, well before the *Celotex* trilogy in the mid-1980s. Has that trend abated? In the following recent case, the Supreme Court may have given the pendulum another push in the same direction, further liberalizing summary judgment. Note the degree to which the Court engages in a review, evaluation, and contrast of the evidence and its credibility.

Scott v. Harris,

United States Supreme Court
550 U.S. 372 (2007)

Justice SCALIA delivered the opinion of the Court. ...

In March 2001, a Georgia county deputy clocked respondent's vehicle traveling at 73 miles per hour on a road with a 55-mile-per-hour speed limit. The deputy activated his blue flashing lights indicating that respondent should pull over. Instead, respondent sped away, initiating a chase down what is in most portions a two-lane road, at speeds exceeding 85 miles per hour. The deputy radioed his dispatch to report that he was pursuing a fleeing vehicle, and broadcast its license plate number. Petitioner, Deputy Timothy Scott, heard the radio communication and joined the pursuit along with other officers. In the midst of the chase, respondent pulled into the parking lot of a shopping center and was nearly boxed in by the various police vehicles. Respondent evaded the trap by making a sharp turn, colliding with Scott's police car, exiting the parking lot, and speeding off once again down a two-lane highway.

Following respondent's shopping center maneuvering, which resulted in slight damage to Scott's police car, Scott took over as the lead pursuit vehicle. Six minutes and nearly 10 miles after the chase had begun, Scott decided to attempt to terminate the episode by employing a "Precision Intervention Technique ('PIT') maneuver, which causes the fleeing vehicle to spin to a stop." [C] Having radioed his supervisor for permission, Scott was told to "'[g]o ahead and take him out.'" [C] Instead, Scott applied his push bumper to the rear of respondent's vehicle.[fn] As a result, respondent lost control of his vehicle, which left the roadway, ran down an embankment, overturned, and crashed. Respondent was badly injured and was rendered a quadriplegic.

Respondent filed suit against Deputy Scott and others under ... 42 U.S.C. §1983, alleging, *inter alia,* a violation of his federal constitutional rights, viz. use of excessive force resulting in an unreasonable seizure under the Fourth Amendment. In response, Scott filed a motion for summary judgment based on an assertion of qualified immunity. The District Court denied the motion, finding that "there are material issues of fact on which the issue of qualified immunity turns which present sufficient disagreement to require submission to a jury." [C] On interlocutory appeal,[fn] the United States Court of Appeals for the Eleventh Circuit affirmed... . We ... now reverse. ...

In resolving questions of qualified immunity, courts are required to resolve a "threshold question: Taken in the light most favorable to the party asserting the injury, do the facts alleged show the officer's conduct violated a constitutional right? This must be the initial inquiry." Saucier v. Katz, 533 U.S. 194, 201[] (2001). ... We therefore turn to the threshold inquiry: whether Deputy Scott's actions violated the Fourth Amendment. ...

The first step in assessing the constitutionality of Scott's actions is to determine the relevant facts. As this case was decided on summary judgment, there have not yet been factual findings by a judge or jury, and respondent's version of events (unsurprisingly) differs substantially from Scott's version. When things are in such a posture, courts are required to view the facts and draw reasonable inferences "in the light most favorable to the party opposing the [summary judgment] motion." United States v. Diebold, Inc., 369 U.S. 654, 655[] (1962) *(per curiam);* [c]. In qualified immunity cases, this usually means adopting (as the Court of Appeals did here) the plaintiff's version of the facts.

There is, however, an added wrinkle in this case: existence in the record of a videotape capturing the events in question. There are no allegations or indications that this videotape was doctored or altered in any way, nor any contention that what it depicts differs from what actually happened. The videotape quite clearly contradicts the version of the story told by respondent and adopted by the Court of Appeals.[fn] For example, the Court of Appeals adopted respondent's assertions that, during the chase, "there was little, if any, actual threat to pedestrians or other motorists, as the roads were mostly empty and [respondent] remained in control of his vehicle." [C] Indeed, reading the lower court's opinion, one gets the impression that respondent, rather than fleeing from police, was attempting to pass his driving test.... .

The videotape tells quite a different story. There we see respondent's vehicle racing down narrow, two-lane roads in the dead of night at speeds that are shockingly fast. We see it swerve around more than a dozen other cars, cross the double-yellow line, and force cars traveling in both directions to their respective shoulders to avoid being hit.[fn] We see it run multiple red lights and travel for considerable periods of time in the occasional center left-turn-only lane, chased by numerous police cars forced to engage in the same hazardous maneuvers just to keep up. Far from being the cautious and controlled driver the lower court depicts, what we see on the video more closely resembles a Hollywood-style car chase of the most frightening sort, placing police officers and innocent bystanders alike at great risk of serious injury.[fn]

At the summary judgment stage, facts must be viewed in the light most favorable to the nonmoving party only if there is a "genuine" dispute as to those facts. Fed. Rule Civ. Proc. 56(c). As we have emphasized, "[w]hen the moving party has carried its burden under Rule 56(c), its opponent must do more than simply show that there is some metaphysical doubt as to the material facts.... Where the record taken as a whole could not lead a rational trier of fact to find for the nonmoving party, there is no 'genuine issue for trial.'" Matsushita Elec. Industrial Co. v. Zenith Radio Corp., 475 U.S. 574, 586-587[] (1986) (footnote omitted). "[T]he mere existence of *some* alleged factual dispute between the parties will not defeat an otherwise properly supported motion for summary judgment; the requirement is that there be no *genuine* issue of *material* fact." Anderson v. Liberty Lobby, Inc., 477 U.S. 242, 247-248[] (1986). When opposing parties tell two different stories, one of which is blatantly contradicted by the record, so that no reasonable jury could believe it, a court should not adopt that version of the facts for purposes of ruling on a motion for summary judgment.

That was the case here with regard to the factual issue whether respondent was driving in such fashion as to endanger human life. Respondent's version of events is so utterly discredited by the record that no reasonable jury could have believed him. The Court of Appeals should not have relied on such visible fiction; it should have viewed the facts in the light depicted by the videotape. …

Judging the matter on that basis, we think it is quite clear that Deputy Scott did not violate the Fourth Amendment. … The question we need to answer is whether Scott's actions were objectively reasonable.[fn] …

… [I]n judging whether Scott's actions were reasonable, we must consider the risk of bodily harm that Scott's actions posed to respondent in light of the threat to the public that Scott was trying to eliminate. Although there is no obvious way to quantify the risks on either side, it is clear from the videotape that respondent posed an actual and imminent threat to the lives of any pedestrians who might have been present, to other civilian motorists, and to the officers involved in the chase. [C] It is equally clear that Scott's actions posed a high likelihood of serious injury or death to respondent… . So how does a court go about weighing the perhaps lesser probability of injuring or killing numerous bystanders against the perhaps larger probability of injuring or killing a single person? We think it appropriate in this process to take into account not only the number of lives at risk, but also their relative culpability. It was respondent, after all, who intentionally placed himself and the public in danger by unlawfully engaging in the reckless, high-speed flight that ultimately produced the choice between two evils that Scott confronted. Multiple police cars, with blue lights flashing and sirens blaring, had been chasing respondent for nearly 10 miles, but he ignored their warning to stop. By contrast, those who might have been harmed had Scott not taken the action he did were entirely innocent. We have little difficulty in concluding it was reasonable for Scott to take the action that he did.[fn]

But wait, says respondent: Couldn't the innocent public equally have been protected, and the tragic accident entirely avoided, if the police had simply ceased their pursuit? We think the police need not have taken that chance and hoped for the best. Whereas Scott's action—ramming respondent off the road—was *certain* to eliminate the risk that respondent posed to the public, ceasing pursuit was not. …

… [W]e are loath to lay down a rule requiring the police to allow fleeing suspects to get away whenever they drive *so recklessly* that they put other people's lives in danger. It is obvious the perverse incentives such a rule would create: Every fleeing motorist would know that escape is within his grasp, if only he accelerates to 90 miles per hour, crosses the double-yellow line a few times, and runs a few red lights. The Constitution assuredly does not impose this invitation to impunity-earned-by-recklessness. Instead, we lay down a more sensible rule: A police officer's attempt to terminate a dangerous high-speed car chase that threatens the lives of innocent bystanders does not violate the Fourth Amendment, even when it places the fleeing motorist at risk of serious injury or death.

The car chase that respondent initiated in this case posed a substantial and immediate risk of serious physical injury to others; no reasonable jury could conclude otherwise. Scott's attempt to terminate the chase by forcing respondent off the road was reasonable, and Scott is entitled to summary judgment. The Court of Appeals' judgment to the contrary is reversed.

It is so ordered.

Justice GINSBURG, concurring[, omitted].

Justice BREYER, concurring.

... Because watching the video footage of the car chase made a difference to my own view of the case, I suggest that the interested reader take advantage of the link in the Court's opinion,
[http://www.supremecourtus.gov/opinions/video/scott_ v_ harris. rmvb]. ...

Justice **STEVENS**, dissenting[, omitted].

INQUIRY

Partial Summary Judgment. When the trial court is unable to grant summary judgment disposing of all triable issues, FED. R. CIV. P. 56(d) authorizes the trial court to determine what specific issues remain and to enter an order accordingly. Rule 56(d)(1) adds the curious statement that the trial judge may "interrogate" counsel to determine the specific facts that are no longer in issue. Rule 56(d)(1) surely means that the trial judge may inquire of counsel, contemplating no interrogation techniques. Rule 56(d)(1) does admonish the trial court that it should makes its determination of the settled facts "to the extent practicable" following which the parties and court must treat those facts as established in the action. Although Rule 56(d) does not explicitly use the phrase "partial summary judgment," courts and practitioners commonly do, and the Supreme Court has approved partial summary judgment as a trial judge's option. *See* Crawford-El v. Britton, 523 U.S. 574, 599 (1998). Rule 56(d)(2) contemplates that the trial court may grant summary judgment on liability without determining disputed damages. Summary judgment can be a flexible tool, not always an all-or-nothing proposition.

Summary. The trial courts take an active role in managing civil litigation at its outset. That role has as one substantial purpose, expressed frankly in FED. R. CIV. P. 16, disposing of cases before trial. Rule 16 and equivalent state-court rules authorize pretrial conferences at which the trial judge can examine the pleadings and inquire of counsel to set the case schedule, explore settlement, winnow issues by stipulation, and dispose of frivolous claims and defenses. A Rule 16 pretrial order follows the pretrial conference. Nearer the conclusion of pretrial proceedings, FED. R. CIV. P. 56 authorizes a party to move for summary judgment. The movant must point out to the trial court the absence of a genuine issue of material fact in the non-movant's favor on one or more elements. The non-movant must then come forward with affidavits or other admissible evidence showing a genuine material issue. The trial court must grant the motion when the moving party is entitled to judgment as a matter of law, after viewing the evidence in the light most favorable to the non-movant. The trial court must consider the proof burden and require more persuasive evidence when the only evidence in the non-movant's favor are implausible inferences.

Career

Which law school subjects do you most enjoy? Civil litigation covers every law subject. A single civil litigator may file, prepare, and try cases involving securities regulations, employment law, family law, civil rights, contract and other business disputes, probate issues, malpractice, and personal injury. If you appreciate a variety of law subjects, then know that you can engage them all in civil litigation. Yet many civil litigators concentrate their practices into one or a small number of law fields. Some lawyers do nothing other than collections work. Others do nothing but worker's compensation or Social Security disability. Others handle nothing but construction cases and others nothing but business or insurance disputes. As you read the cases, see if you have an affinity for one or a small number of law fields, or whether you might most appreciate engaging them all.

CHAPTER XII

TRIAL

OBJECTIVE: That you be able to sort jury-triable from bench-trial claims, articulate the procedures for drawing juries, and state the order and procedures for trial.

Case Study: The trial judge has set for jury trial a case in which you are representing an insurance company in defense of a builder's claim for coverage for damage done to a residence on which the builder worked. The insurance-company representative has asked you to prepare a report reflecting your strategy at each stage of the trial. Outline the procedural opportunities and issues you expect to face at each stage of trial.

Federal Rules of Civil Procedure this chapter reproduces and addresses
FED. R. CIV. P. 38. Right to a Jury Trial; Demand
FED. R. CIV. P. 39. Trial by Jury or by the Court
FED. R. CIV. P. 40. Scheduling Cases for Trial
FED. R. CIV. P. 43. Taking Testimony
FED. R. CIV. P. 44. Proving an Official Record
FED. R. CIV. P. 46. Objecting to a Ruling or Order
FED. R. CIV. P. 47. Selecting Jurors
FED. R. CIV. P. 48. Number of Jurors; Verdict; Polling
FED. R. CIV. P. 49. Special Verdict; General Verdict and Questions
FED. R. CIV. P. 50. Judgment as a Matter of Law in a Jury Trial; ... Motion for a New Trial; ... Ruling
FED. R. CIV. P. 51. Instructions to the Jury; Objections; Preserving a Claim of Error
FED. R. CIV. P. 52. Findings and Conclusions by the Court; Judgment on Partial Findings
FED. R. CIV. P. 57. Declaratory Judgment
FED. R. CIV. P. 63. Judge's Inability to Proceed
FED. R. CIV. P. 80. Stenographic Transcript as Evidence

This chapter addresses the right to jury trial and procedural issues having to do with the drawing and control of juries, and the order of trial. You have seen the many routes cases take leading to disposition before or resolution away from jury trial. The impression that nearly every case results in trial, or even that any substantial percentage of cases reaches trial, is highly inaccurate. For most civil litigators, including ones with thriving practices and substantial caseloads, jury trials are few and far between, perhaps on average a couple of times per year. Chapter I offers a very brief history of jury trials. Originally, in feudal England, they were active bodies investigating, testifying in, and deciding matters. Blackstone and others revered them as the glory of English law. Today, juries play an almost completely passive role until deliberation. Moreover, the number and percentage of jury trials has declined sharply in the past 30 years to the point of vanishing as a substantial aspect of litigation practice. The trial lawyers of yesterday are the litigators of today, conducting elaborate discovery and motion practice, hiring mediators and structured-settlement experts, and settling cases through alternative dispute resolution.

The impression that surprise, theatrics, and drama fill trials is also inaccurate given the scope of discovery and compelled disclosures, the effect of pretrial conferences and summary-judgment proceedings, and judicial regulation of the order and conduct of trial. Procedure wrings out any surprise or drama long before trial, particularly in the federal courts where judicial resources are comparatively greater, the lawyers participate in elaborate joint pretrial conferences producing detailed joint pretrial orders, and trial judges exercise strict control over jury voir dire, witness examination, and opening statement and closing arguments. The conduct of trials is largely predictable from the practitioners' standpoint, even if jury outcomes are somewhat less so. Litigators tend to know what to expect for everything but the outcome, and even there, experienced litigators develop a reasonable sense of the claims and defenses that juries are likely to accept. When they lack the relevant experience, they conduct mock jury trials, hire jury consultants, and research verdict and settlement databases.

Why, then, are trials so significant, if the federal courts conduct trials in only two percent or so of their civil cases, state courts conduct trials in only slightly higher percentages of civil cases, and their conduct is so highly regulated and reasonably predictable? The reason is in large part that the parties, counsel, and court view every other stage of civil litigation, from the initial pleadings right through to post-trial judgment, motions, and appeals, through the lens of trial. Every aspect of civil litigation is an effort to account for how the decisionmaker, whether judge or jury, will consider the claims and defenses when concentrated into a single, on-the-record, open-court trial. To borrow analogies, no recipe makes sense without the oven, no season without a championship, no ball without a dance, no assembly without a speaker, no course without an assessment. The preparation and even the outcome depend on the anticipated performance. Judges, masters, magistrates, mediators, lawyers, clients, insurers, and everyone else having any influence on the resolution or disposition of a case evaluate every case as if it were going to trial. Diligent lawyers tend to prepare every case as if it was going to trial. To a degree, even if civil litigators knew which 2% to 5% of their cases would go to trial, they would still prepare the other 95% to 98% of their cases as if those cases, too, were going to trial. Every litigator, even those who conduct primarily a motion practice, needs to know their way around both a jury trial and bench trial (a trial to a judge).

FED. R. CIV. P. 40. Scheduling Cases for Trial
Each court must provide by rule for scheduling trials. The court must give priority to actions entitled to priority by a federal statute.

…

FED. R. CIV. P. 63. Judge's Inability to Proceed
If a judge conducting a hearing or trial is unable to proceed, any other judge may proceed upon certifying familiarity with the record and determining that the case may be completed without prejudice to the parties. In a hearing or a nonjury trial, the successor judge must, at a party's request, recall any witness whose testimony is material and disputed and who is available to testify again without undue burden. The successor judge may also recall any other witness.

A. Jury Trial

In the current civil justice system in the United States, juries decide some cases, while judges decide others. Some cases involve multiple claims, some of which juries decide, and some of which judges decide. In all cases, judges control the proceedings. In those cases in which there is no jury, judges also decide the outcome. In those cases in which there is a jury, juries decide the outcome, provided that it be within the law that they do so. This section on the right to a jury trial begins by defining the scope of that right, answering the question as to which cases it applies. This section then addresses how the court, parties, and their counsel draw juries, meaning how they ensure that the jurors are qualified to sit as impartial decisionmakers representative of the community. This section ends with a study of how judges control juries through a division of authority in which the judge determines and states the law, and juries decide issues of fact. First consider the scope of the jury-trial right.

1. Right to Jury Trial

In federal court, the Seventh Amendment is the source of the right to a jury trial. The Constitution's drafters had contentious debate when omitting jury-trial rights from the body of the Constitution. Juries were then bulwarks against legislative, administrative, and judicial oppression, and thus another expression of the value of separating powers. As in the case of other foundational rights, the Constitution's drafters and supporters anticipated the omission's remedy in the subsequently adopted Bill of Rights. Unlike other rights guaranteed in the first ten Amendments in the Bill of Rights, the Supreme Court has not incorporated the Seventh Amendment through the 14th Amendment's due-process clause to apply to the states. Jury-trial rights in state courts depend on state constitutions. State constitutions and practice tend to recognize similar jury-trial rights but without interpreting them quite so expansively, either because of cost or the absence of influencing political history. *See, e.g.*, Strauss v. Summerhays, 204 Cal.Rptr. 227 (Cal. Ct. App. 1984) (affirming trial of equitable claims to the bench first resulting in loss of jury-trial right); Pelfrey v. Bank of Greer, 244 S.E.2d. 315 (S.C. 1978) (rejecting Supreme Court classification of shareholder derivative actions as jury triable).

Indeed, to assert that the Seventh Amendment determines jury-trial rights in the federal courts is the very broadest of possible brushes of a fascinating and complex historical subject. The Seventh Amendment was itself a compromise that did not guarantee a jury trial as broadly as it might. One cannot articulate the basis for federal jury-trial rights and predict its applicability in close cases without appreciating the Supreme Court case law that has interpreted the Seventh Amendment in light of its goals, language, and history. The Supreme Court gives the federal trial courts some discretion in determining which issues the court must try to a jury, constraining that discretion within the Seventh Amendment's historical references. *See* American Life Ins. Co. v. Stewart, 300 U.S. 203 (1937) (holding that the trial court had discretion either to try equitable claims or offer jury trial of legal claims). This section addresses that Supreme Court case law in the context of various issues that practitioners face when considering whether to advise their clients to demand a jury.

First, though, accept this brief explanation of the scope of the jury-trial right. Whether there is a right to a jury trial or not is an exceedingly simple question for most practitioners most of the time, with the answer readily determined by decades if not centuries of practice. In nearly all cases, all that a practitioner needs to know is that the asserted claims fit into one or another of the traditional categories under which the courts determine the right to a jury. For example, there is no right to a jury trial in family-law cases, meaning cases involving divorce, paternity, child custody, child support, and related equitable proceedings determining personal obligations and rights. By contrast, there is a right to a jury trial in torts and contract cases for money damages. *See, e.g.,* N.Y CODE P. §208 (1848) ("an action for the recovery of money ... must be tried by a jury"). Every practitioner knows so. The claims as to which the question begins to grow more complex are those in which a party claims equitable relief like specific performance of a contract or the partition of jointly owned land. Judges make orders, not juries. Hence, judges decide equitable claims involving injunctive relief, not juries. When a party combines a claim for money damages with a claim for equitable relief, in the ordinary case a jury will decide the former and the judge the latter. In an approach rejected by the federal courts, some states use a predominance test, not requiring a jury if the equitable claims predominate and the legal claims are merely incidental. *See, e.g.,* Hiatt v. Yergin, 284 N.E.2d 834 (Ind. Ct. App. 1972). There are other instances where the rights are not clear. Read the Seventh Amendment, FED. R. CIV. P. 38 recognizing the Seventh Amendment jury-trial right, and FED. R. CIV. P. 39 distinguishing trial by jury from trial by the court, before exploring the boundary issues.

U.S. CONST. AMEND. VII. Trial by Jury in Civil Cases
In Suits at common law, where the value in controversy shall exceed twenty dollars, the right of trial by jury shall be preserved, and no fact tried by a jury, shall be otherwise re-examined in any Court of the United States, than according to the rules of the common law.

FED. R. CIV. P. 38. Right to a Jury Trial; Demand
(a) RIGHT PRESERVED. The right of trial by jury as declared by the Seventh Amendment to the Constitution—or as provided by a federal statute—is preserved to the parties inviolate.
(b) DEMAND. On any issue triable of right by a jury, a party may demand a jury trial by:
(1) serving the other parties with a written demand—which may be included in a pleading—no later than 14 days after the last pleading directed to the issue is served; and
(2) filing the demand in accordance with Rule 5(d).
(c) SPECIFYING ISSUES. In its demand, a party may specify the issues that it wishes to have tried by a jury; otherwise, it is considered to have demanded a jury trial on all the issues so triable. If the party has demanded a jury trial on only some issues, any other party may—within 14 days after being served with the demand or within a shorter time ordered by the court—serve a demand for a jury trial on any other or all factual issues triable by jury.
(d) WAIVER; WITHDRAWAL. A party waives a jury trial unless its demand is properly served and filed. A proper demand may be withdrawn only if the parties consent.
(e) ADMIRALTY AND MARITIME CLAIMS. These rules do not create a right to a jury trial on issues in a claim that is an admiralty or maritime claim under Rule 9(h).
...

FED. R. CIV. P. 39. Trial by Jury or by the Court

(a) WHEN A DEMAND IS MADE. When a jury trial has been demanded under Rule 38, the action must be designated on the docket as a jury action. The trial on all issues so demanded must be by jury unless:
(1) the parties or their attorneys file a stipulation to a nonjury trial or so stipulate on the record; or
(2) the court, on motion or on its own, finds that on some or all of those issues there is no federal right to a jury trial.
(b) WHEN NO DEMAND IS MADE. Issues on which a jury trial is not properly demanded are to be tried by the court. But the court may, on motion, order a jury trial on any issue for which a jury might have been demanded.
(c) ADVISORY JURY; JURY TRIAL BY CONSENT. In an action not triable of right by a jury, the court, on motion or on its own:
(1) may try any issue with an advisory jury; or
(2) may, with the parties' consent, try any issue by a jury whose verdict has the same effect as if a jury trial had been a matter of right, unless the action is against the United States and a federal statute provides for a nonjury trial.

Practice

There was the usual scurrying when the jury passed a note to the bailiff that they had reached a verdict. The judge returned to the bench, the court reporter to the well, and the lawyers and their clients to counsel table. The bailiff called out, "All rise," and the jurors marched solemnly in.

The plaintiff's lawyer noticed immediately that the lone woman juror was crying. It was not a good sign. Maybe it was just relief, the plaintiff's lawyer thought, knowing otherwise but still hoping for a favorable verdict. Then it was over. The young bicyclist hit by a car and his wife, the personal-injury plaintiffs in the case, had lost. The defense had a no-cause verdict, with the tearful woman juror the lone holdout.

The cabal of male jurors gathered by the curb out in the courthouse parking lot, laughing and joking with defense counsel. The plaintiff's lawyer stopped for a moment to listen but then just shrugged and turned away from the callous banter. The tearful woman juror, too, walked right past, now looking angry. She paused briefly to apologize to the plaintiff's lawyer and ask if the young couple would be all right.

INQUIRY

Jury Demand. The Seventh Amendment and its interpreting case law speak of a *right* to a jury trial. When the law speaks of a right, it refers to a choice that resides with an individual. Courts do not have to use juries unless the parties want them to. In the first instance, the parties determine whether a jury or judge decides a case. FED. R. CIV. P. 38 and equivalent state-court rules require parties to demand a jury within specified periods by specified means. Under Rule 38(b), a party has 14 days after the last pleading within which to file and serve the demand. The practice is for the plaintiff who wants a jury to include a jury demand under that title when filing the complaint. The plaintiff has the option of waiting to see whether a defendant demands a jury (allowing the defendant to pay the jury fee if there is a fee) and then filing a demand within 14 days of the defendant's answer if not. When any party demands a jury, and there is a jury-trial right, the judge must try the case with a jury. It only takes one party to demand a jury for there to be a jury trial. If one party wants a bench trial but the other demands a jury trial, there will be a jury trial if there is a jury-trial right. There is no right to a bench trial. When neither party demands a jury, the judge must try the case without a jury. Rule 39(c) permits a judge to empanel an advisory jury, but instances of a judge doing so are understandably rare, given the additional time, trouble, and cost. Rule 39(c) also permits a judge to try a case to a jury without a party's demand, if the parties' consent. When a party fails to demand a jury but later wishes to have a jury, the party may move for a jury, and the court may grant the motion.

Suits at Common Law. The Seventh Amendment begins with an important qualification that the right to a jury trial applies only to "suits at common law." The reference is historical. The Seventh Amendment's reference is to the difference in the English common law between suits at common law tried to juries and suits in equity or admiralty tried to a judge. *See* Parsons v. Bedford, 28 U.S. (3 Pet.) 433, 436 (1830). Lest anyone miss the historical nature of the reference, the Seventh Amendment continues that the right to a jury trial "shall be preserved," meaning that it is the same as that which existed when the states adopted the Seventh Amendment. *See* Dimick v. Schiedt, 293 U.S. 474, 476 (1935). Parties have the right to a jury only in cases "at law," meaning those seeking legal rather than equitable remedies. As already indicated in the introduction above, jury-triable cases at law involving legal relief are those cases that demand damages for the violation of legal rights. Non-jury cases in equity are those cases involving injunctive relief where the legal remedy of damages would be inadequate. Parties must try to a judge cases that demand an injunction as the only relief. Parties may try to a jury cases that demand damages as the only relief. When the parties in a case demand both legal relief (damages) and equitable relief (injunction), the court tries the legal issue to a jury while the judge decides the equitable relief. See if you can sort the legal relief from the equitable relief in the following Supreme Court case.

Beacon Theatres, Inc. v. Westover,

United States Supreme Court
359 U.S. 500 (1959)

Mr. Justice BLACK delivered the opinion of the Court.

Petitioner, Beacon Theatres, Inc., sought by mandamus to require a district judge in the Southern District of California to vacate certain orders alleged to deprive it of a jury trial of issues arising in a suit brought against it by Fox West Coast Theatres, Inc. The Court of Appeals for the Ninth Circuit refused the writ, holding that the trial judge had acted within his proper discretion in denying petitioner's request for a jury. [C] We granted certiorari, [c], because "Maintenance of the jury as a fact-finding body is of such importance and occupies so firm a place in our history and jurisprudence that any seeming curtailment of the right to a jury trial should be scrutinized with the utmost care." Dimick v. Schiedt, 293 U.S. 474[, 486 (1935)].

Fox had asked for declaratory relief against Beacon alleging a controversy arising under the Sherman Antitrust Act, [] 15 U.S.C. §§1, 2[], and under the Clayton Act, [] 15 U.S.C. §15, which authorizes suits for treble damages against Sherman Act violators. According to the complaint Fox operates a movie theatre in San Bernardino, California, and has long been exhibiting films under contracts with movie distributors. These contracts grant it the exclusive right to show "first run" pictures in the "San Bernardino competitive area" and provide for "clearance"-a period of time during which no other theatre can exhibit the same pictures. After building a drive-in theatre about 11 miles from San Bernardino,

Beacon notified Fox that it considered contracts barring simultaneous exhibitions of first-run films in the two theatres to be overt acts in violation of the antitrust laws.[fn] Fox's complaint alleged that this notification, together with threats of treble damage suits against Fox and its distributors, gave rise to "duress and coercion" which deprived Fox of a valuable property right, the right to negotiate for exclusive first-run contracts. Unless Beacon was restrained, the complaint continued, irreparable harm would result. Accordingly, while its pleading was styled a "Complaint for Declaratory Relief," Fox prayed both for a declaration that a grant of clearance between the Fox and Beacon theatres is reasonable and not in violation of the antitrust laws, and for an injunction, pending final resolution of the litigation, to prevent Beacon from instituting any action under the antitrust laws against Fox and its distributors arising out of the controversy alleged in the complaint.[fn] Beacon filed an answer, a counterclaim against Fox, and a cross-claim against an exhibitor who had intervened. These denied the threats and asserted that there was no substantial competition between the two theatres, that the clearances granted were therefore unreasonable, and that a conspiracy existed between Fox and its distributors to manipulate contracts and clearances so as to restrain trade and monopolize first-run pictures in violation of the antitrust laws. Treble damages were asked.

Beacon demanded a jury trial of the factual issues in the case as provided by Federal Rule of Civil Procedure 38(b)[]. The District Court, however, viewed the issues raised by the "Complaint for Declaratory Relief," including the question of competition between the two theatres, as essentially equitable. Acting under the purported authority of Rules 42(b) and 57, it directed that these issues be tried to the court before jury determination of the validity of the charges of antitrust violations made in the counterclaim and cross-claim.[fn] A common issue of the "Complaint for Declaratory Relief," the counterclaim, and the cross-claim was the reasonableness of the clearances granted to Fox, which depended, in part, on the existence of competition between the two theatres. Thus the effect of the action of the District Court could be, as the Court of Appeals believed, "to limit the petitioner's opportunity fully to try to a jury every issue which has a bearing upon its treble damage suit," for determination of the issue of clearances by the judge might "operate either by way of res judicata or collateral estoppel so as to conclude both parties with respect thereto at the subsequent trial of the treble damage claim." [C]

The District Court's finding that the Complaint for Declaratory Relief presented basically equitable issues draws no support from the Declaratory Judgment Act, 28 U.S.C. §§2201, 2202[]; Fed. Rules Civ.Proc. 57. [C] That statute, while allowing prospective defendants to sue to establish their nonliability, specifically preserves the right to jury trial for both parties.[fn] It follows that if Beacon would have been entitled to a jury trial in a treble damage suit against Fox it cannot be deprived of that right merely because Fox took advantage of the availability of declaratory relief to sue Beacon first. Since the right to trial by jury applies to treble damage suits under the antitrust laws, and is, in fact, an essential part of the congressional plan for making competition rather than monopoly the rule of trade, [c], the Sherman and Clayton Act issues on which Fox sought a declaration were essentially jury questions.

Nevertheless the Court of Appeals ... held that the question of whether a right to jury trial existed was to be judged by Fox's complaint read as a whole. In addition to seeking a declaratory judgment, the court said, Fox's complaint can be read as making out a valid plea for injunctive relief, thus stating a claim traditionally cognizable in equity. A party who is entitled to maintain a suit in equity for an injunction, said the court, may have all the issues in his suit determined by the judge without a jury regardless of whether legal rights are involved. ... [I]t invoked the principle that a court sitting in equity could retain jurisdiction even though later a legal remedy became available. In such instances the equity court had discretion to enjoin the later lawsuit in order to allow the whole dispute to be determined in one case in one court.[fn] Reasoning by analogy, the Court of Appeals held it was not an abuse of discretion for the district judge, acting under Federal Rule of Civil Procedure 42(b), to try the equitable cause first even though this might, through collateral estoppel, prevent a full jury trial of the counterclaim and cross-claim which were as effectively stopped as by an equity injunction.[fn]

Beacon takes issue with the holding of the Court of Appeals that the complaint stated a claim upon which equitable relief could be granted. As initially filed the complaint alleged that threats of lawsuits by petitioner against Fox and its distributors were causing irreparable harm to Fox's business relationships. The prayer for relief, however, made no mention of the threats but asked only that pending litigation of the claim for declaratory judgment, Beacon be enjoined from beginning any lawsuits under the antitrust laws against Fox and its distributors arising out of the controversy alleged in the complaint. Evidently of the opinion that this prayer did not state a good claim for equitable relief, the Court of Appeals construed it to include a request for an injunction against threats of lawsuits. ... But this fact does not solve our problem. Assuming that the pleadings can be construed to support such a request and assuming additionally that the complaint can be read as alleging the kind of harassment by a multiplicity of lawsuits which would traditionally have justified equity to take jurisdiction and settle the case in one suit,[fn] we are nevertheless of the opinion that, under the Declaratory Judgment Act and the Federal Rules of Civil Procedure, neither claim can justify denying Beacon a trial by jury of all the issues in the antitrust controversy.

The basis of injunctive relief in the federal courts has always been irreparable harm and inadequacy of legal remedies.[fn] At least as much is required to justify a trial court in using its discretion under the Federal Rules to allow claims of equitable origins to be tried ahead of legal ones, since this has the same effect as an equitable injunction of the legal claims. And it is immaterial, in judging if that discretion is properly employed, that before the Federal Rules and the Declaratory Judgment Act were passed, courts of equity, exercising a jurisdiction separate from courts of law, were, in some cases, allowed to enjoin subsequent legal actions between the same parties involving the same controversy. This was because the subsequent legal action, though providing an opportunity to try the case to a jury, might not protect the right of the equity plaintiff to a fair and orderly adjudication of the controversy. [C] Under such circumstances the legal remedy could quite naturally be deemed inadequate. Inadequacy of remedy and irreparable harm are practical terms, however. As such their existence today must be determined, not by precedents decided under discarded procedures, but in the light of the remedies now made available by the Declaratory Judgment Act and the Federal Rules.[fn]

Viewed in this manner, the use of discretion by the trial court under Rule 42(b) to deprive Beacon of a full jury trial on its counterclaim and cross-claim, as well as on Fox's plea for declaratory relief, cannot be justified. Under the Federal Rules the same court may try both legal and equitable causes in the same action. Fed. Rules Civ. Proc., 1, 2, 18. Thus any defenses, equitable or legal, Fox may have to charges of antitrust violations can be raised either in its suit for declaratory relief or in answer to Beacon's counterclaim. On proper showing, harassment by threats of other suits, or other suits actually brought, involving the issues being tried in this case, could be temporarily enjoined pending the outcome of this litigation. Whatever permanent injunctive relief Fox might be entitled to on the basis of the decision in this case could, of course, be given by the court after the jury renders its verdict. In this way the issues between these parties could be settled in one suit giving Beacon a full jury trial of every antitrust issue. [C] By contrast, the holding of the court below while granting Fox no additional protection unless the avoidance of jury trial be considered as such, would compel Beacon to split his antitrust case, trying part to a judge and part to a jury.[fn] Such a result, which involves the postponement and subordination of Fox's own legal claim for declaratory relief as well as of the counterclaim which Beacon was compelled by the Federal Rules to bring,[fn] is not permissible.

Our decision is consistent with the plan of the Federal Rules and the Declaratory Judgment Act to effect substantial procedural reform while retaining a distinction between jury and nonjury issues and leaving substantive rights unchanged.[fn] Since in the federal courts equity has always acted only when legal remedies were inadequate,[fn] the expansion of adequate legal remedies provided by the Declaratory Judgment Act and the Federal Rules necessarily affects the scope of equity. Thus, the justification for equity's deciding legal issues once it obtains jurisdiction, and refusing to dismiss a case, merely because subsequently a legal remedy becomes available, must be re-evaluated in the light of the liberal joinder provisions of the Federal Rules which allow legal and equitable causes to be brought and resolved in one civil action.[fn] Similarly the need for, and therefore, the availability of such equitable remedies as Bills of Peace, Quia Timet and Injunction must be reconsidered in view of the existence of the Declaratory Judgment Act as well as the liberal joinder provision of the Rules.[fn] This is not only in accord with the spirit of the Rules and the Act but is required by the provision in the Rules that "(t)he right of trial by jury as declared by the Seventh Amendment to the Constitution or as given by a statute of the United States shall be preserved * * * inviolate."[fn]

If there should be cases where the availability of declaratory judgment or joinder in one suit of legal and equitable causes would not in all respects protect the plaintiff seeking equitable relief from irreparable harm while affording a jury trial in the legal cause, the trial court will necessarily have to use its discretion in deciding whether the legal or equitable cause should be tried first. Since the right to jury trial is a constitutional one, however, while no similar requirement protects trials by the court,[fn] that discretion is very narrowly limited and must, wherever possible, be exercised to preserve jury trial. ... [O]nly under the most imperative circumstances, circumstances which in view of the flexible procedures of the Federal Rules we cannot now anticipate,[fn] can the right to a jury trial of legal issues be lost through prior determination of equitable claims. [C] As we have shown, this is far from being such a case. ...

The judgment of the Court of Appeals is reversed.

Reversed.

Mr. Justice FRANKFURTER took no part in the consideration or decision of this case.

Mr. Justice STEWART, with whom Mr. Justice HARLAN and Mr. Justice WHITTAKER concur, dissenting. ...

The complaint filed by Fox stated a claim traditionally cognizable in equity. That claim, in brief, was that Beacon had wrongfully interfered with the right of Fox to compete freely with Beacon and other distributors for the licensing of films for first-run exhibition in the San Bernardino area. The complaint alleged that the plaintiff was without an adequate remedy at law and would be irreparably harmed unless the defendant were restrained from continuing to interfere-by coercion and threats of litigation-with the plaintiff's lawful business relationships.

... Instead of just putting in issue the allegations of the complaint, however, Beacon filed pleadings which affirmatively alleged the existence of a broad conspiracy among the plaintiff and other theatre owners to monopolize the first-run exhibition of films in the San Bernardino area to refrain from competing among themselves, and to discriminate against Beacon in granting film licenses. Based upon these allegations, Beacon asked damages in the amount of $300,000. Clearly these conspiracy allegations stated a cause of action triable as of right by a jury. What was demanded by Beacon, however, was a jury trial not only of this cause of action, but also of the issues presented by the original complaint.

Upon motion of Fox the trial judge ordered the original action for declaratory and equitable relief to be tried separately to the court and in advance of the trial of the defendant's counter-claim and cross-claim for damages. The court's order, which carefully preserved the right to trial by jury upon the conspiracy and damage issues raised by the counterclaim and cross-claim, was in conformity with the specific provisions of the Federal Rules of Civil Procedure.[fn] Yet it is decided today that the Court of Appeals must compel the district judge to rescind it.

... I cannot agree that the District Court must be compelled to try the counterclaim first.[fn] ...

... [T]he complaint in the present case, as the Court recognizes, presented issues of exclusively equitable cognizance, going well beyond a mere defense to any subsequent action at law. Fox sought from the court protection against Beacon's allegedly unlawful interference with its business relationships-protection which this Court seems to recognize might not have been afforded by a declaratory judgment, unsupplemented by equitable relief. The availability of a declaratory judgment did not, therefore, operate to confer upon Beacon the right to trial by jury with respect to the issues raised by the complaint. ...

It has been an established rule "that equitable jurisdiction existing at the filing of a bill is not destroyed because an adequate legal remedy may have become available thereafter."[fn] American Life Ins. Co. v. Stewart, 300 U.S. 203, 215[(1937)]. [C] It has also been long settled that the District Court in its discretion may order the trial of a suit in equity in advance of an action at law between the same parties, even if there is a factual issue common to both. ...

The Court today sweeps away these basic principles... . It suggests that the Federal Rules of Civil Procedure have somehow worked an "expansion of adequate legal remedies" so as to oust the District Courts of equitable jurisdiction, as well as to deprive them of their traditional power to control their own dockets. But obviously the Federal Rules could not and did not 'expand' the substantive law one whit.[fn]

Like the Declaratory Judgment Act, the Federal Rules preserve inviolate the right to trial by jury in actions historically cognizable at common law, as under the Constitution they must.[fn] They do not create a right of trial by jury where that right "does not exist under the Constitution or statutes of the United States." Rule 39(a). ... [T]he counterclaim [cannot] be held to have transformed Fox's original complaint into an action at law.[fn] [C]

The Rules make possible the trial of legal and equitable claims in the same proceeding, but they expressly affirm the power of a trial judge to determine the order in which claims shall be heard. Rule 42(b). Certainly the Federal Rules were not intended to undermine the basic structure of equity jurisprudence, developed over the centuries and explicitly recognized in the United States Constitution.[fn]

For these reasons I think the petition for a writ of mandamus should have been dismissed.

INQUIRY

Declaratory Relief. Declaratory-judgment actions are those cases in which a party requests that the court declare the relative rights of the parties. Examples include (1) which of two or more parties owns land in a title or boundary dispute, (2) what a contract requires of one of its parties in performing for the other party, and (3) whether an insurer owes an indemnity to an insured for a certain liability or loss. In a declaratory-judgment action, the court issues a judgment binding the parties to the court's interpretation of the parties' relative rights. It is a way of settling disputes before monetary losses arise—again for instance, before a claimant builds on disputed lands, a party to a contract refuses due performance to the other party's loss, or an insured incurs a liability or loss without due insurance. One might therefore think that declaratory-judgment actions are non-jury cases because there is no request for money damages and only a request for an interpreting order. To the contrary, the law generally construes a declaratory-judgment action to be a procedural form, not a substantive right, meaning that the courts will look to the issues on which the claim's disposition depends and the requested relief to determine whether there is a jury-trial right. Declaratory-judgment actions that raise contract or property disputes, anticipating future damages, are legal actions for which parties have jury-trial rights. *Beacon Theatres, Inc. v. Westover* implies that the federal Declaratory Judgment Act, 28 U.S.C. §§2201, 2202, "specifically preserves" jury-trial rights in federal cases seeking declaratory relief. Do you see any specific reference in the Act, reproduced below? The Declaratory Judgment Act is actually neutral as to jury-trial rights. On the other hand, FED. R. CIV. P. 57 governing declaratory-judgment actions specifically preserves whatever jury-trial rights may exist. One must look to the issues in the action.

28 U.S.C. §2201. Creation of remedy
(a) In a case of actual controversy within its jurisdiction, except with respect to Federal taxes other than actions brought under section 7428 of the Internal Revenue Code of 1986, a proceeding under section 505 or 1146 of title 11, or in any civil action involving an antidumping or countervailing duty proceeding regarding a class or kind of merchandise of a free trade area country (as defined in section 516A(f)(10) of the Tariff Act of 1930), as determined by the administering authority, any court of the United States, upon the filing of an appropriate pleading, may declare the rights and other legal relations of any interested party seeking such declaration, whether or not further relief is or could be sought. Any such declaration shall have the force and effect of a final judgment or decree and shall be reviewable as such.
(b) For limitations on actions brought with respect to drug patents see section 505 or 512 of the Federal Food, Drug, and Cosmetic Act.

28 U.S.C. §2202. Further relief
Further necessary or proper relief based on a declaratory judgment or decree may be granted, after reasonable notice and hearing, against any adverse party whose rights have been determined by such judgment.

FED. R. CIV. P. 57. Declaratory Judgment
These rules govern the procedure for obtaining a declaratory judgment under 28 U.S.C. §2201. Rules 38 and 39 govern a demand for a jury trial. The existence of another adequate remedy does not preclude a declaratory judgment that is otherwise appropriate. The court may order a speedy hearing of a declaratory judgment action.

INQUIRY

Priority. After the *Federal Rules of Civil Procedure* merged law and equity, *see* FED. R. CIV. P. 2, parties could readily combine legal and equitable claims in a single lawsuit. As *Beacon Theatres, Inc. v. Westover* shows, that combination can make it difficult to determine whether and when to offer a jury. There is no question of supremacy. Jury trial is a constitutional right. If the right exists in a particular case, then the party should have it. The problem has to do with timing. In *Beacon Theatres, Inc. v. Westover,* the first party to file suit requested only equitable relief while the request for legal relief came later. The Supreme Court still held that a jury should decide the legal issue first before the judge resolves the equitable issue, while indicating that the trial judge had only narrow discretion to do otherwise in imperative cases. *Beacon Theatres, Inc. v. Westover* presented a relatively easy case in that respect. The only harm was commercial, meaning that waiting for injunctive relief until after jury trial would work only commercial damage. Can you imagine cases, though, in which it would deprive a party of all effective equitable relief if the party had to wait for a jury trial before getting an injunction? Think of cases involving personal safety or the physical destruction of property having unique qualities. Trial judges have some discretion to enjoin parties even in cases where a jury may later offer legal relief. Moreover, when a trial judge grants equitable relief in one case, that determination can preclude the same parties from seeking related legal relief in a subsequent action even if those parties would have had a right to a jury trial in that subsequent legal action. *See* Parklane Hosiery v. Shore, 439 U.S. 322 (1979). Other imperative circumstances can warrant a judge providing a preemptive equitable remedy before jury trial on legal relief. In Katchen v. Landy, 382 U.S. 323 (1966), the Supreme Court held that a creditor against whom a debtor's trustee asserted a money-damages claim in bankruptcy court had no jury-trial right because Congress intended bankruptcy to facilitate prompt judicial resolution of disputed rights.

Framework. Aside from the issue of timing when a single case has both legal and equitable issues, there are cases in which it is just plain difficult to tell the difference between legal and equitable relief. Dairy Queen, Inc. v. Wood, 369 U.S. 469 (1962), was one such case in which the Supreme Court had to decide which aspect, legal or equitable, predominated. *Dairy Queen, Inc. v. Wood* involved a dispute over use of an ice-cream retailer's trademark, in which the parties claimed an accounting and injunction (both equitable forms of relief) and damages for breach of contract and trademark infringement. In doing so, the Supreme Court avoided traditional classifications and instead considered whether the case was so complex that only a judge, and not a jury, could make a reliable decision. The Court ultimately held that it was not, thus calling it a legal rather than equitable decision for the jury. Then, in Ross v. Bernhard, 396 U.S. 531 (1970), the Supreme Court articulated a framework for deciding close cases. The law first looks to the traditional classification of the claim before the law-equity merger, then to the form of remedy whether legal (damages) or equitable (injunctive), and then to the practical ability of a jury to parse the evidence to decide the issue. *Ross v. Bernhard* held that there is a jury right in shareholder-derivative cases, even though the equity courts would have tried those cases in 1791. The Supreme Court looked to the legal claims of the corporation that the shareholder asserts derivatively, as predominating over the equitable claim of the shareholder. Recognize that *Beacon Theatres, Dairy Queen,* and *Ross v. Bernhard* diminished the historical analysis while offering new interpretive tools. Consider a federal appellate case citing these cases while attempting to employ their framework. Only a few state courts have looked favorably on the Supreme Court's interpretive efforts in these cases. *See, e.g.,* Onvoy, Inc. v. Allete, Inc., 736 N.W.2d 611 (Minn. 2007).

Amoco Oil Co. v. Torcomian,

United States Court of Appeals for the Third Circuit
722 F.2d 1099 (1983)

BECKER, Circuit Judge.

The question presented by this appeal is whether the district court erred in refusing to afford defendants John Torcomian and Albert Torcomian a jury trial with respect to both the complaint of plaintiff Amoco and the Torcomians' compulsory counterclaim. The basis of the denial was that the claims, which arose out of the parties' dealings concerning an Amoco service station, were equitable in nature. The district court, following a bench trial, found for Amoco on all issues, and the Torcomians appeal. Because we hold that many components of Amoco's main claim and the Torcomians' counterclaim, as pleaded, presented legal issues and sought legal relief, the district court erred in refusing to grant the defendants a jury trial. ... The defendants' seventh amendment rights were therefore violated. Accordingly, the district court's judgment must be vacated and the entire case remanded for further proceedings.

I. THE RECORD RELEVANT TO THE JURY TRIAL ISSUE

The district court's initial determination of whether a jury trial is warranted must be based on the pleadings, including the pre-trial order. ... Amoco's complaint alleg[ed] violations of Pennsylvania state law and the Lanham Act, 15 U.S.C. §1053 et seq. (1976);[fn] the defendants' answer and compulsory counterclaim (which contained a timely jury demand) [was] based upon Amoco's alleged fraud and breach of contract... .

Amoco originally sought extensive relief including... ejectment of the defendants from [a] service station; ... permanent injunction restraining defendants from continued use, enjoyment and possession of [the service station]; ... a permanent injunction restraining defendants from use of the Amoco logo, tradename, service mark or trademark; ...[and] judgment in the amount of $46,675 for profits lost as a result of defendants' wrongful possession and fraudulent misrepresentations[, among other damages claims]. ...

Defendants' pleadings and their submissions in the pre-trial order state a claim that the defendants had a franchise relationship with Amoco... . ... [T]he defendants sought ... injunction enjoining plaintiff to comply with its franchise agreement [and] ... judgment against plaintiff in an amount in excess of $100,000.00 for profits lost [and other money damages]... .

II. WERE THE COMPONENTS OF AMOCO'S CLAIM LEGAL OR EQUITABLE?

It has long been settled law that neither joinder of an equitable claim with a legal claim nor joinder of a prayer for equitable relief with a claim for legal relief as to a legal claim can defeat an otherwise valid seventh amendment right to a jury trial. *See* Beacon Theatres, Inc. v. Westover, 359 U.S. 500[] (1959); Dairy Queen, Inc. v. Wood, 369 U.S. 469[] (1962). Thus, in order to assess the district court's denial of the defendants' demand for a jury trial as to the main claim, we must consider whether it comprised any legal claims seeking legal relief. If we find such claims, we must vacate the judgment, at least as to those claims, unless we are persuaded that Amoco was entitled to a directed verdict on those claims. [C]

At the outset, we note that on its surface Amoco's complaint appears to present a number of essentially legal claims.[fn] The complaint sought ejectment, a form of action long regarded as legal. *See* Redfield v. Parks, 132 U.S. 239, 244[] (1889) ("In the courts of the United States where the distinction between actions at law and suits in equity has always been maintained, the action of ejectment is an action at law ...."); United States v. King, 44 U.S. (3 How.) 773, 787-88[] (1845) (ejectment is legal). It also sought damages, a form of relief usually treated as legal. ...

> ... Pennsylvania's characterization of ejectment is irrelevant. (per curiam). As the Supreme Court there held, "[i]n diversity cases, of course, the substantive dimension of the claim asserted finds its source in state law ... but the characterization of that state-created claim as legal or equitable for purposes of whether a right to jury trial is indicated must be made by recourse to federal law." And federal law, as we have indicated, unequivocally holds actions seeking ejectment to be legal, not equitable.[fn]

III. WERE THE COMPONENTS OF THE DEFENDANTS' COUNTERCLAIM EQUITABLE OR LEGAL?

It is settled law in this Circuit and elsewhere, [cc], that even an equitable main claim cannot preclude a jury trial on a legal counterclaim, at least when the counterclaim is compulsory.[fn] A rule to the contrary would enable the preemptive filing of a complaint by the holder of an equitable claim, coupled with the doctrine of res judicata, to deprive the holder of a legal claim of his seventh amendment right to a jury trial. [C] Accordingly, we must consider whether there was an element present in the counterclaim which would have given rise to a right to jury trial.[fn]

Although the defendants did ask for equitable relief in their counterclaim (i.e., fulfillment of Amoco's obligation under the alleged franchise agreement), defendants also sought damages for the past breach of that agreement. A routine claim such as that presented here for damages stemming from breach of contract is legal. [C] ... [T]he fact that equitable relief is sought in addition to substantial legal relief does not eliminate a right to a jury trial.[fn] ...

V. CONCLUSION

We have concluded that both Amoco's main claim and the defendants' counterclaim contained a number of legal components to which the defendants were entitled to a jury trial under the seventh amendment. Accordingly, the judgment of the district court will be vacated and the case remanded for a new trial.

INQUIRY

New Claims. New interpretive tools regarding jury-trial rights were not the works of an activist Supreme Court. In certain cases, the historical analysis that the Seventh Amendment requires or urges simply does not provide an answer. The declaratory-judgment actions discussed above in *Beacon Theatres, Inc. v. Westover* did not exist in 1791 when the states adopted the Seventh Amendment. Congress has created many new actions that have no historical precedent and are statutory rights of action rather than actions at common law. Civil-rights claims are one example. The Supreme Court has avoided a categorical approach in those cases and instead asked whether the statutory claims are analogous to claims that were available at common law. For example, in Curtis v. Loether, 415 U.S. 189 (1974), the Supreme Court held that a jury-trial right exists for the priviate right of action Congress created for housing discrimination violating the fair-housing provision of the Civil Rights Act of 1968, 42 U.S.C. §3612. Housing-discrimination claims have no historical antedent and are statutory, not common law. Historical analysis, as the first step of the three-step framework of *Ross v. Bernhard,* gives no guidance other than that such actions were not a part of the common law. Yet damages claims for housing discrimination are like tort actions in that they involve demands for monetary relief for the invasion of personal rights. Because tort actions were at common law, analogous statutory actions requesting similar legal relief should have equivalent jury-trial rights under the second step in the *Ross v. Bernhard* framework. Juries should have no greater difficulty assessing those statutory claims than they would tort actions, confirming with the framework's third step that jury-trial rights are appropriate. The three-step framework of *Ross v. Bernhard* is especially helpful in cases where the step-one historical inquiry provides no clear answer. Consider another case involving a new right, where the Supreme Court had to decide without historical guidance whether there was a jury right.

Chauffeurs, Teamsters & Helpers, Local No. 391 v. Terry,

United States Supreme Court
494 U.S. 558 (1990)

Justice MARSHALL delivered the opinion of the Court except as to Part III-A.

This case presents the question whether an employee who seeks relief in the form of backpay for a union's alleged breach of its duty of fair representation has a right to trial by jury. We hold that the Seventh Amendment entitles such a plaintiff to a jury trial. ...

McLean Trucking Company and the Chauffeurs, Teamsters, and Helpers Local No. 391 (Union) were parties to a collective-bargaining agreement that governed the terms and conditions of employment at McLean's terminals. The 27 respondents were employed by McLean as truckdrivers in bargaining units covered by the agreement, and all were members of the Union. In 1982 McLean ... transferred respondents to the terminal located in Winston-Salem and agreed to give them special seniority rights... .

After working in Winston-Salem for approximately six weeks, respondents were alternately laid off and recalled several times. Respondents filed a grievance with the Union... . [T]he grievance committee ordered McLean to recall any respondent who was then laid off and ... to recognize respondents' special seniority rights... .

On the basis of this decision, McLean recalled respondents... . Soon after this, though, McLean [allowed recalled employees] to regain seniority rights over respondents. ... Accordingly, respondents filed another grievance... . [T]he committee held that McLean had not violated the committee's first decision.

McLean continued to engage in periodic layoffs and recalls of the workers at the Winston-Salem terminal. Respondents filed a third grievance with the Union, but the Union declined to refer the charges to a grievance committee on the ground that the relevant issues had been determined in the prior proceedings.

In July 1983, respondents filed an action in District Court, alleging that McLean had breached the collective-bargaining agreement ... and that the Union had violated its duty of fair representation. Respondents requested a permanent injunction requiring the defendants to cease their illegal acts and to reinstate them to their proper seniority status; in addition, they sought, *inter alia,* compensatory damages for lost wages and health benefits. In 1986 McLean filed for bankruptcy; subsequently, the action against it was voluntarily dismissed, along with all claims for injunctive relief.

Respondents had requested a jury trial in their pleadings. The Union moved to strike the jury demand on the ground that no right to a jury trial exists in a duty of fair representation suit. The District Court denied the motion to strike. After an interlocutory appeal, the Fourth Circuit affirmed the trial court, holding that the Seventh Amendment entitled respondents to a jury trial of their claim for monetary relief. [C] We granted the petition for certiorari to resolve a Circuit conflict on this issue,[fn] [c], and now affirm the judgment of the Fourth Circuit. ...

... The Seventh Amendment provides that "[i]n Suits at common law, where the value in controversy shall exceed twenty dollars, the right of trial by jury shall be preserved." The right to a jury trial includes more than the common-law forms of action recognized in 1791; the phrase "Suits at common law" refers to "suits in which *legal* rights [are] to be ascertained and determined, in contradistinction to those where equitable rights alone [are] recognized, and equitable remedies [are] administered." Parsons v. Bedford, [28 U.S. (]3 Pet.[)] 433, 447[] (1830); [c]. The right extends to causes of action created by Congress. Tull v. United States, 481 U.S. 412, 417[] (1987). Since the merger of the systems of law and equity, see Fed. Rule Civ. Proc. 2, this Court has carefully preserved the right to trial by jury where legal rights are at stake. [The Court cited and quoted Beacon Theatres, Inc. v. Westover, 359 U.S. 500, 501 (1959).]

To determine whether a particular action will resolve legal rights, we examine both the nature of the issues involved and the remedy sought. "First, we compare the statutory action to 18th-century actions brought in the courts of England prior to the merger of the courts of law and equity. Second, we examine the remedy sought and determine whether it is legal or equitable in nature." *Tull, supra,* [] at 417-418[] (citations omitted). The second inquiry is the more important in our analysis. Granfinanciera, S.A. v. Nordberg, 492 U.S. 33, 42[] (1989).[fn] ...

An action for breach of a union's duty of fair representation was unknown in 18th-century England; in fact, collective bargaining was unlawful. [C] We must therefore look for an analogous cause of action that existed in the 18th century to determine whether the nature of this duty of fair representation suit is legal or equitable.

The Union contends that this duty of fair representation action resembles a suit brought to vacate an arbitration award because respondents seek to set aside the result of the grievance process. In the 18th century, an action to set aside an arbitration award was considered equitable. [Cc]. ...

The arbitration analogy is inapposite, however, to the Seventh Amendment question posed in this case. ... [R]espondents' claim against the Union cannot be characterized as an action to vacate an arbitration award... .

The Union next argues that respondents' duty of fair representation action is comparable to an action by a trust beneficiary against a trustee for breach of fiduciary duty. Such actions were within the exclusive jurisdiction of courts of equity. [Cc] This analogy is far more persuasive than the arbitration analogy. Just as a trustee must act in the best interests of the beneficiaries, [c], a union, as the exclusive representative of the workers, must exercise its power to act on behalf of the employees in good faith, [c]. Moreover, just as a beneficiary does not directly control the actions of a trustee, [c], an individual employee lacks direct control over a union's actions taken on his behalf, [c].

The trust analogy extends to a union's handling of grievances. In most cases, a trustee has the exclusive authority to sue third parties who injure the beneficiaries' interest in the trust, [c], including any legal claim the trustee holds in trust for the beneficiaries, [c]. The trustee then has the sole responsibility for determining whether to settle, arbitrate, or otherwise dispose of the claim. [C] Similarly, the union typically has broad discretion in its decision whether and how to pursue an employee's grievance against an employer. [C] ...

Respondents contend that their duty of fair representation suit is less like a trust action than an attorney malpractice action, which was historically an action at law, [c]. ... [W]e find that, in the context of the Seventh Amendment inquiry, the attorney malpractice analogy does not capture the relationship between the union and the represented employees as fully as the trust analogy does.

The attorney malpractice analogy is inadequate in several respects. Although an attorney malpractice suit is in some ways similar to a suit alleging a union's breach of its fiduciary duty, the two actions are fundamentally different. The nature of an action is in large part controlled by the nature of the underlying relationship between the parties. Unlike employees represented by a union, a client controls the significant decisions concerning his representation. Moreover, a client can fire his attorney if he is dissatisfied with his attorney's performance. This option is not available to an individual employee who is unhappy with a union's representation, unless a majority of the members of the bargaining unit share his dissatisfaction. [C] Thus, we find the malpractice analogy less convincing than the trust analogy.

Nevertheless, the trust analogy does not persuade us to characterize respondents' claim as wholly equitable. ... As we observed in Ross v. Bernhard, 396 U.S. 531[, 538] (1970), "The Seventh Amendment question depends on the nature of the *issue* to be tried rather than the character of the overall action." [C] (emphasis added) (finding a right to jury trial in a shareholder's derivative suit, a type of suit traditionally brought in courts of equity, because plaintiffs' case presented legal issues of breach of contract and negligence). ... [T]o recover from the Union here, respondents must prove both that McLean violated §301 by breaching the collective-bargaining agreement and that the Union breached its duty of fair representation.[fn] When viewed in isolation, the duty of fair representation issue is analogous to a claim against a trustee for breach of fiduciary duty. The §301 issue, however, is comparable to a breach of contract claim-a legal issue.[fn]

Respondents' action against the Union thus encompasses both equitable and legal issues. The first part of our Seventh Amendment inquiry, then, leaves us in equipoise as to whether respondents are entitled to a jury trial. ...

Our determination under the first part of the Seventh Amendment analysis is only preliminary. [C] In this case, the only remedy sought is a request for compensatory damages representing backpay and benefits. Generally, an action for money damages was "the traditional form of relief offered in the courts of law." Curtis v. Loether, 415 U.S. 189, 196[] (1974). This Court has not, however, held that "any award of monetary relief must *necessarily* be 'legal' relief." *Ibid.* (emphasis added). [C] Nonetheless, because we conclude that the remedy respondents seek has none of the attributes that must be present before we will find an exception to the general rule and characterize damages as equitable, we find that the remedy sought by respondents is legal.

First, we have characterized damages as equitable where they are restitutionary, such as in "action[s] for disgorgement of improper profits," *Tull, [supra,]* at 424[]. [Cc] The backpay sought by respondents is not money wrongfully held by the Union, but wages and benefits they would have received from McLean had the Union processed the employees' grievances properly. Such relief is not restitutionary.

Second, a monetary award "incidental to or intertwined with injunctive relief" may be equitable. *Tull, supra,* [] at 424[]. [C] Because respondents seek only money damages, this characteristic is clearly absent from the case.[fn] ...

The Union argues that the backpay relief sought here must nonetheless be considered equitable because this Court has labeled backpay awarded under Title VII, of the Civil Rights Act of 1964, 42 U.S.C. § 2000e *et seq.* [], as equitable. See Albemarle Paper Co. v. Moody, 422 U.S. 405, 415-418[] (1975) (characterizing backpay awarded against employer under Title VII as equitable in context of assessing whether judge erred in refusing to award such relief). ...

The Court has never held that a plaintiff seeking backpay under Title VII has a right to a jury trial. See Lorillard v. Pons, 434 U.S. 575, 581-582[] (1978). ... Congress specifically characterized backpay under Title VII as a form of "equitable relief." 42 U.S.C. §2000e-5(g) [] ... . [C] Congress made no similar pronouncement regarding the duty of fair representation. ...

We hold, then, that the remedy of backpay sought in this duty of fair representation action is legal in nature. Considering both parts of the Seventh Amendment inquiry, we find that respondents are entitled to a jury trial on all issues presented in their suit. ...

On balance, our analysis of the nature of respondents' duty of fair representation action and the remedy they seek convinces us that this action is a legal one. Although the search for an adequate 18th-century analog revealed that the claim includes both legal and equitable issues, the money damages respondents seek are the type of relief traditionally awarded by courts of law. Thus, the Seventh Amendment entitles respondents to a jury trial, and we therefore affirm the judgment of the Court of Appeals.

It is so ordered.

Justice BRENNAN, concurring in part and concurring in the judgment.

I agree with the Court that respondents seek a remedy that is legal in nature and that the Seventh Amendment entitles respondents to a jury trial on their duty of fair representation claims. ... I believe the historical test can and should be simplified. ...

I believe that our insistence that the jury trial right hinges in part on a comparison of the substantive right at issue to forms of action used in English courts 200 years ago needlessly convolutes our Seventh Amendment jurisprudence. ... The time has come to borrow William of Occam's razor and sever this portion of our analysis. ...

... [M]odern statutory rights did not exist in the 18th century, and even the most exacting historical research may not elicit a clear historical analog.[fn] ... I have grappled with this kind of inquiry for three decades on this Court and have come to the realization that engaging in such inquiries is impracticable and unilluminating.

To rest the historical test required by the Seventh Amendment solely on the nature of the relief sought would not, of course, offer the federal courts a rule that is in all cases self-executing. Courts will still be required to ask which remedies were traditionally available at law and which only in equity. But this inquiry involves fewer variables and simpler choices, on the whole, and is far more manageable... .

We can guard this right and save our courts from needless and intractable excursions into increasingly unfamiliar territory simply by retiring that prong of our Seventh Amendment test which we have already cast into a certain doubt. If we are not prepared to accord the nature of the historical analog sufficient weight for this factor to affect the outcome of our inquiry, except in the rarest of hypothetical cases, what reason do we have for insisting that federal judges proceed with this arduous inquiry? It is time we read the writing on the wall, especially as we ourselves put it there.

Justice STEVENS, concurring in part and concurring in the judgment.

Because I believe the Court has made this case unnecessarily difficult by exaggerating the importance of finding a precise common-law analogue to the duty of fair representation, I do not join Part III-A of its opinion. ...

In my view, the evolution of this doctrine through suits tried to juries, the useful analogy to common-law malpractice cases, and the well-recognized duty to scrutinize any proposed curtailment of the right to a jury trial "with the utmost care," [c], provide a plainly sufficient basis for the Court's holding today. I therefore join its judgment and all of its opinion except for Part III-A.

Justice KENNEDY, with whom Justice O'CONNOR and Justice SCALIA join, dissenting.

This case asks whether the Seventh Amendment guarantees the respondent union members a jury trial in a duty of fair representation action against their labor union. The Court is quite correct, in my view, in its formulation of the initial premises that must govern the case. ...

I disagree with the analytic innovation of the Court that identification of the trust action as a model for modern duty of fair representation actions is insufficient to decide the case. ... Having made this decision in favor of an equitable action, our inquiry should end. Because the Court disagrees with this proposition, I dissent. ...

The Court must adhere to the historical test in determining the right to a jury because the language of the Constitution requires it. The Seventh Amendment "preserves" the right to jury trial in civil cases. We cannot preserve a right existing in 1791 unless we look to history to identify it. Our precedents are in full agreement with this reasoning and insist on adherence to the historical test.

No alternatives short of rewriting the Constitution exist. [Cc] If we abandon the plain language of the Constitution to expand the jury right, we may expect Courts with opposing views to curtail it in the future. ...

If Congress has not provided for a jury trial, we are confined to the Seventh Amendment to determine whether one is required. Our own views respecting the wisdom of using a jury should be put aside. Like Justice BRENNAN, I admire the jury process. Other judges have taken the opposite view. [C] But the judgment of our own times is not always preferable to the lessons of history. Our whole constitutional experience teaches that history must inform the judicial inquiry. Our obligation to the Constitution and its Bill of Rights, no less than the compact we have with the generation that wrote them for us, do not permit us to disregard provisions that some may think to be mere matters of historical form. ...

... I would deny a jury trial to the respondents here, but would leave these other questions for a later time. Because the Court has reached a different result, I dissent.

INQUIRY

Weight. The Supreme Court in *Chauffeurs, Teamsters & Helpers v. Terry* applied only the first two parts (historical analysis and form of relief) of the three-part framework of *Ross v. Bernhard.* The nature of the relief and claim in *Terry*, backpay for violating a duty of fair representation, raised no question implicating the third part of the *Ross v. Bernhard* framework—the jury's practical ability to reach a reliable decision. When considering the first two parts of the test, the *Terry* Supreme Court held that the second part having to do with the form of relief was more important than the historical analysis. Does the plain language of the Seventh Amendment, that the jury-trial right "at common law" "shall be preserved," permit the Supreme Court to lend greater credence to anything other than a historical analysis? You can appreciate the difficulty when there is no history. The Court continues to give greater weight to the form-of-relief test employed in *Terry. See, e.g.,* City of Monterey v. Del Monte Dunes, 526 U.S. 687, 709-711 (1999) (§1983 action requesting money damages is akin to common-law tort action due jury trial). Some federal appellate courts are particularly reluctant to consider the third part of the *Ross v. Bernhard* framework having to do with the jury's practical ability to decide a complex case, believing a complexity exception to be inconsistent with the Seventh Amendment's historical emphasis and the respect to afford a constitutional right. *See* In re United States Financial Secs. Litigation, 609 F.2d 411 (9th Cir. 1979), cert. denied, 446 U.S. 929 (1980).

Statutes. *Curtis v. Loether* and *Chauffeurs, Teamsters & Helpers v. Terry* involved statutory actions in which Congress had remained silent regarding jury-trial rights. May Congress expressly grant or limit jury-trial rights when it creates new statutory actions? Justice Kennedy's dissent in *Terry* excerpted above recognizes that Congress may, consistent with its control over federal-court jurisdiction, require jury trial where the Seventh Amendment does not. On the other hand, given the Seventh Amendment's supremacy over federal statutes, the

Supreme Court has understandably held that Congress may not limit the Seventh Amendment's jury-trial right. Granfinanciera, S.A. v. Nordberg, 492 U.S. 33, 36 (1989), is an example. Congress defines a bankruptcy trustee's action to recover a debtor's fraudulent conveyance as a core bankruptcy proceeding, meaning that parties must try those claims in the bankruptcy court where there are ordinarily no juries. Nonetheless, in *Granfinanciera, S.A. v. Nordberg*, the Supreme Court held that if the one from whom the trustee sought recovery had made no claim against the bankruptcy estate, then that person had a right to a jury trial. *Granfinanciera* may seem to conflict with *Katchen v Landy, supra,* in that *Katchen* held that creditors do not get juries when making claims in bankruptcy. *Granfinanciera*, though, dealt with a claim *against* a creditor who was not otherwise involved in the bankruptcy proceeding, not a claim *by* a creditor. In other words, voluntary resort to the administrative-like forum may be the difference. What is clear is that Congress cannot take away what the Seventh Amendment grants. *See* Carlson v. Green, 446 U.S. 14, 20-22 (1980) (Seventh Amendment right to jury in common-law *Bivens* action even though not under alternative Federal Tort Claims Act). Yet Congress can deny what the Seventh Amendment does not guarantee. *See* Lehman v. Makshian, 453 U.S. 156, 160 (1981) (no right to jury trial in claim against federal government, where Congress granted none and the Seventh Amendment required none). In addition, Congress may assign new statutory rights for which there would be Seventh Amendment jury-trial rights if maintained in the federal courts, for adjudication by an administrative agency where there is no jury-trial right. *See* Altlas Roofing Co. v. Occupational Health & Safety Review Commn., 430 U.S. 442, 450 (1977).

Number of Jurors. The number of jurors seated in a civil jury trial depends on the law of the jurisdiction. Twelve jurors is minimum number required by the common law, but after the Supreme Court held the practice constitutional in Colgrove v. Battin, 413 U.S. 149 (1973), the federal courts and many states now require as few as six jurors for civil jury trials. In general, more jurors mean less likelihood that a jury reaches an aberrant decision. More jurors also mean greater likelihood of diverse perspectives. No matter the minimum number of jurors, the court is likely to seat at least one and often two alternate jurors, especially in trials likely to last more than a few days. Occasionally, jurors fall ill or fail to return (risking contempt sanctions in the latter case). Alternate jurors ensure that the trial continues. Thus, in a jurisdiction requiring 12 jurors, 14 jurors will observe the entire trial until the court removes 2 alternate jurors just before deliberations begin. In a jurisdiction requiring just 6 jurors, 8 jurors will observe the entire trial until the court removes the 2 alternate jurors. The means of removing alternate jurors depends on the law or practice of the jurisdiction. In some jurisdictions, the court does not designate alternates until drawing them off. In other jurisdictions, the court designates alternates at the outset and excuses them if all regular jurors remain to begin deliberations. Some courts permit the parties to stipulate to having all jurors including alternates deliberate. One strong-willed juror can make a difference in outcomes. Whether to stipulate to deliberating alternates is one of the more intriguing strategic decisions lawyers make, especially when the court has not identified the alternates.

> ***Skills***
>
> Trial skills are obviously different from the skills associated with pleading, discovery, motion, and appellate practice. The reason has to do with the audience: jurors, not judges or lawyers. The skill involves switching from the language and conventions of lawyers to the language and conventions of non-lawyers—while still retaining the strategic sense and professional decorum of a lawyer. Jurors expect lawyers to act like lawyers. They expect lawyers to be firm advocates and believe in their cases but while treating others with civility. A trial lawyer must never speak down to jurors but must use words, phrases, images, and emotions with which the jurors can connect. You will know when you have made that connection. You will see it their attentive eyes, and their laughter and smiles. You will also know when you have not made that connection—when they look away, roll their eyes, and cross their arms across their chest. Appreciate the distinct skills of a trial lawyer.

Unanimity. Depending on the law, rule, and practice of the jurisdiction, civil juries either must deliberate until unanimous or may reach non-unanimous decisions of one, two, or even three dissenting jurors. Unanimity rules probably produce sharper juror debate and more vigorous scrutiny of the evidence. Unanimity rules also probably increase participation by jurors whose diversity might otherwise marginalize them. Some courts permit the parties to stipulate to different rules. Thus for example, in some jurisdictions, six regular and two alternate jurors may observe the trial, and counsel may then stipulate to all eight deliberating to a verdict of six out of eight. When the jury returns a verdict, the losing party typically requests that the court poll the jurors. Polling requires each juror to confirm assent to the verdict on the record in open court, ensuring the requisite unanimity or near-unanimity. Read FED. R. CIV. P. 48 governing the number and unanimity of jurors in civil trials in the federal courts.

FED. R. CIV. P. 48. Number of Jurors; Verdict; Polling

(a) NUMBER OF JURORS. A jury must begin with at least 6 and no more than 12 members, and each juror must participate in the verdict unless excused under Rule 47(c).

(b) VERDICT. Unless the parties stipulate otherwise, the verdict must be unanimous and must be returned by a jury of at least 6 members.

(c) POLLING. After a verdict is returned but before the jury is discharged, the court must on a party's request, or may on its own, poll the jurors individually. If the poll reveals a lack of unanimity or lack of assent by the number of jurors that the parties stipulated to, the court may direct the jury to deliberate further or may order a new trial.

---

2. Drawing Juries

The right to a jury trial is only a preliminary to the drawing of jurors. Courts have access to jury pools assembled from voter registration lists (the most common method), driver's licenses, tax rolls, public utility records, or similar means provided for by statute and rule. Federal statute requires use of voter registration lists supplemented by other information necessary to make a representative pool. 28 U.S.C. §1863(b). The choice of sources can influence representation in important ways. The means chosen should ensure the broadest representation of qualified jurors. The goal is to assemble jurors at random who will represent a fair cross section of the community. *See* 28 U.S.C. §1861. The Supreme Court has rejected practices that exclude certain classes of jurors. *See* Thiel v. Southern Pacific Co., 328 U.S. 217 (1946) (rejecting practice of striking daily-wage workers based on economic hardship); *see also* Galloway v. Superior Court, 816 F.Supp. 12 (D. D.C. 1993) (no automatic exclusion of the blind).

A court's jury clerk will estimate the number of jury trials likely to proceed in a given jury term and the number of prospective jurors needed for each trial. The jury clerk will send notices to an appropriate number of jurors that they may be called to appear at the courthouse at a specific time and on a specific date, on penalty of contempt sanction, to serve as jurors. The notice will include a juror questionnaire for the jurors to complete and return, disclosing basic demographic information such as age, education, marital and family status, employment, criminal history, and experience with the legal system as party, witness, or juror. The jury clerk will use that information to determine jurors' basic qualifications to serve by citizenship, age, literacy, and other statutory qualifications. *See* 28 U.S.C. §1865. The jury clerk will make the questionnaire information available to trial counsel, typically a few days before trial but no later than the time of trial. The jurors will assemble at the specified place, time, and date unless a call system has given them notice of adjournment. The court may show them a preliminary video or give them general written information about trials. At the scheduled time of trial, on the judge's call, the jury clerk will seat about 20 to 30 prospective jurors, known as the venire panel, in the courtroom's gallery. The judge and courtroom staff will then call enough of the prospective jurors forward to fill the requisite number of seats in the jury box. Consider the federal statutes on jury pools and juror qualifications.

28 U.S.C. §1861. Declaration of policy

It is the policy of the United States that all litigants in Federal courts entitled to trial by jury shall have the right to grand and petit juries selected at random from a fair cross section of the community in the district or division wherein the court convenes. It is further the policy of the United States that all citizens shall have the opportunity to be considered for service on grand and petit juries in the district courts of the United States, and shall have an obligation to serve as jurors when summoned for that purpose.

28 U.S.C. §1862. Discrimination prohibited

No citizen shall be excluded from service as a grand or petit juror in the district courts of the United States or in the Court of International Trade on account of race, color, religion, sex, national origin, or economic status.

28 U.S.C. §1863. Plan for random jury selection

(a) Each United States district court shall devise and place into operation a written plan for random selection of grand and petit jurors that shall be designed to achieve the objectives of sections 1861 and 1862 of this title... .

(b) Among other things, such plan shall—

(1) either establish a jury commission, or authorize the clerk of the court, to manage the jury selection process. ...

(2) specify whether the names of prospective jurors shall be selected from the voter registration lists or the lists of actual voters of the political subdivisions within the district or division. ...
(3) specify detailed procedures to be followed by the jury commission or clerk in selecting names from the sources specified in paragraph (2) of this subsection. These procedures shall be designed to ensure the random selection of a fair cross section of the persons residing in the community in the district or division wherein the court convenes. ...
(4) provide for a master jury wheel (or a device similar in purpose and function) into which the names of those randomly selected shall be placed. ...
(5)(A) except as provided in subparagraph (B), specify those groups of persons or occupational classes whose members shall, on individual request therefor, be excused from jury service. ...
(B) specify that volunteer safety personnel, upon individual request, shall be excused from jury service. ...
(6) specify that the following persons are barred from jury service on the ground that they are exempt: (A) members in active service in the Armed Forces of the United States; (B) members of the fire or police departments...; (C) public officers ... who are actively engaged in the performance of official duties. ...

28 U.S.C. §1864. Drawing of names from the master jury wheel; completion of juror qualification form
(a) From time to time as directed by the district court, the clerk or a district judge shall draw at random from the master jury wheel the names of as many persons as may be required for jury service. ... The clerk or jury commission shall mail to every person whose name is drawn from the master wheel a juror qualification form accompanied by instructions to fill out and return the form, duly signed and sworn, to the clerk or jury commission by mail within ten days. ...
(b) Any person summoned pursuant to subsection (a) of this section who fails to appear as directed shall be ordered by the district court forthwith to appear and show cause for his failure to comply with the summons. Any person who fails to appear pursuant to such order or who fails to show good cause for noncompliance with the summons may be fined not more than $1,000, imprisoned not more than three days, ordered to perform community service, or any combination thereof. Any person who willfully misrepresents a material fact on a juror qualification form for the purpose of avoiding or securing service as a juror may be fined not more than $1,000, imprisoned not more than three days, ordered to perform community service, or any combination thereof.

28 U.S.C. §1865. Qualifications for jury service
(a) The chief judge of the district court, or such other district court judge as the plan may provide, ... or the clerk under supervision of the court if the court's jury selection plan so authorizes, shall determine ... whether a person is unqualified for, or exempt, or to be excused from jury service. ...
(b) In making such determination the chief judge of the district court, or such other district court judge as the plan may provide, or the clerk if the court's jury selection plan so provides, shall deem any person qualified to serve on grand and petit juries in the district court unless he—
(1) is not a citizen of the United States eighteen years old who has resided for a period of one year within the judicial district;
(2) is unable to read, write, and understand the English language with a degree of proficiency sufficient to fill out satisfactorily the juror qualification form;
(3) is unable to speak the English language;

(4) is incapable, by reason of mental or physical infirmity, to render satisfactory jury service; or
(5) has a charge pending against him for the commission of, or has been convicted in a State or Federal court of record of, a crime punishable by imprisonment for more than one year and his civil rights have not been restored.

28 U.S.C. §1866. Selection and summoning of jury panels
(a) The jury commission, or in the absence thereof the clerk, shall maintain a qualified jury wheel and shall place in such wheel names of all persons drawn from the master jury wheel who are determined to be qualified as jurors and not exempt or excused pursuant to the district court plan. ...
(b) When the court orders a grand or petit jury to be drawn, the clerk or jury commission or their duly designated deputies shall issue summonses for the required number of jurors. Each person drawn for jury service may be served personally, or by registered, certified, or first-class mail addressed to such person at his usual residence or business address. ...

28 U.S.C. §1867. Challenging compliance with selection procedures
...
(c) In civil cases, before the voir dire examination begins, or within seven days after the party discovered or could have discovered, by the exercise of diligence, the grounds therefor, whichever is earlier, any party may move to stay the proceedings on the ground of substantial failure to comply with the provisions of this title in selecting the petit jury. ...

INQUIRY

Voir Dire. Then begins that stage of the trial known as jury voir dire, meaning examination of the jurors to ensure fairness and eliminate bias. Competent practitioners will have already scrutinized the juror questionnaires in order to be familiar with the general backgrounds of seated jurors. The trial judge controls jury voir dire. Some trial judges leave voir dire entirely to the lawyers except to ensure that the plaintiff's lawyer examines each juror first and the defense lawyer has equal opportunity. Lawyers prefer that deference because it gives them an opportunity not only to learn about the jurors but also to develop more of a relationship. Other trial judges conduct some, most, or all of the voir dire on their own, although in every case the trial judge will at least allow the lawyers to propose additional questions. Jurors are to answer the judge's and lawyers' questions truthfully. When they do not, and a party discovers the dissembling later, the party may demand a new trial if the party can show that a true answer would have subjected the juror to disqualification on challenge for cause. *See* McDonough Power Equipment v. Greenwood, 464 U.S 548 (1984). Some trial judges require the lawyers to submit proposed questions in advance of trial. Lawyers must not ask jurors their opinions about the case, but they may ask questions about juror bias surrounding issues in the case. Thus through the course of the voir-dire questions, the jurors gradually develop a sense of the case. Studies suggest that jurors tend to decide or at least form impressions early (the opposite of that which the trial judge instructs), and so practitioners may construct jury voir dire to influence jurors, a practice that the trial judge will recognize and discourage. Welcome to trial. Read FED. R. CIV. P. 47 governing jury selection in federal court. Then review the following proposed jury voir dire. Does it ask the right questions?

FED. R. CIV. P. 47. Selecting Jurors
(a) EXAMINING JURORS. The court may permit the parties or their attorneys to examine prospective jurors or may itself do so. If the court examines the jurors, it must permit the parties or their attorneys to make any further inquiry it considers proper, or must itself ask any of their additional questions it considers proper.
(b) PEREMPTORY CHALLENGES. The court must allow the number of peremptory challenges provided by 28 U.S.C. §1870.
(c) EXCUSING A JUROR. During trial or deliberation, the court may excuse a juror for good cause.

UNITED STATES DISTRICT COURT
FOR THE WESTERN DISTRICT OF MICHIGAN

MAYNARD RAY, JOHN W. BAINES, and **PAUL RUTTER,**
Plaintiffs,
v

No. CIV-01-01234

Hon. **************

WINDSOR COUNTY and **RON HOOPER** individually and in his official capacity as Sheriff of Windsor County,
Defendants.

PLAINTIFFS' JURY VOIR DIRE

[*Names, addresses, and telephone numbers of counsel omitted*]

Plaintiffs Maynard Ray, John Baines, and Paul Rutter respectfully request the following jury voir dire:

Proposed Statement of Case:
This case involves a claim by three deputies that their sheriff demoted and reassigned them because of their support of a losing candidate in a sheriff's election, violating their First Amendment rights. The sheriff denies the connection, saying that the demotions and reassignments were for management purposes.

By Trial Judge:
1. Do you know any of the parties or their attorneys in this case? (Attorneys are Ms. Leary and Mr. Edwards. Parties are Mr. Ray, Mr. Baines, Mr. Rutter, and Mr. Hooper.)
2. Do you know any of the witnesses in this case? (Witnesses are Don Rosen, Dave Zinski, Rink Miller, Roy Dammer, Denise Bailes, Rupert Locker, and Gail Mauer.)
3. Have you been a juror on any other case? What kind of case? What was the result? Was there anything about that experience that would influence you about this case?

4. Have you been a party to a civil lawsuit? Plaintiff or defendant? What kind of case? Was there anything about that experience that would influence you about this case?

5. Have you ever had a disagreement with a police officer? What was the nature of the dispute? Was there anything about that experience that would influence you about this case?

6. Have you ever held an elective or political office? What office? Was there anything about that experience that would influence you about this case?

7. Have any of you served in law enforcement or the military? Please describe your service.

8. Can you be a fair and impartial juror? Is there anything in your experience that would influence you for or against these parties, without knowing more facts?

By Plaintiffs' Counsel:

1. If you were in the place of my clients, would you want to have a fair jury? So will you be sure to tell me especially those views you hold that you think I would not want to hear?

2. My clients filed this lawsuit against their employer the Windsor County Sheriff Department. What do you think of people who file lawsuits? Can you think of an example when a lawsuit put right a wrong?

3. This lawsuit is against a public or government employer. Can you think of an example when government did something wrong? If government did something against your constitutional rights that affected you every day, would you file a lawsuit to set it right?

4. This lawsuit is also against the individual sheriff. Can you think of an example when a government official violated someone's constitutional rights? If a government official did something seriously wrong to you, would you trust a jury of your peers to put it right?

5. How important do you think your constitutional rights are? Have you ever seen or heard about something that made you realize how important your constitutional rights can be?

6. How important is your right to vote for the candidate of your choice? Should we allow government officials withhold important rights, depending on how you vote?

7. How important do you think law enforcement is to keeping us safe and free?

8. How important is this civil justice system, where people can bring their claims against others whom they believe are breaking the law by violating constitutional rights?

9. If you had a day in court to prove something very important to you, what kind of juror would you want? Can you be that kind of juror?

10. Do you have anything against lawyers who help those whose rights are violated? Do you think you would need a lawyer if you had to come to court to enforce your rights?

Respectfully submitted,
[Signature block for plaintiffs' counsel]

Dated: September 1, 2003

INQUIRY

Peremptory Challenges. What does one do with the information that jurors share during voir dire? Jury voir dire enables the parties to exercise intelligently their peremptory challenges. A peremptory challenge is one in which a party requests that the trial judge remove a juror for any lawful reason or no reason at all. In civil cases in the federal courts, statute limits each side to three peremptory challenges. *See* 28 U.S.C. §1870 (reproduced below). States allow between two and six peremptory challenges. Peremptory challenges are not a constitutional right. *See* Georgia v. McCollum, 505 U.S. 42, 57 (1992). The lawyer exercising a party's peremptory challenge announces to the trial judge that the party requests the court to remove a certain juror. If the party has a peremptory challenge remaining and makes the request, then the judge must remove the juror except in extraordinary circumstances discussed below. Exercising peremptory challenges is a fascinating skill that depends on a broad range of criteria and the lawyer's ability to evaluate those criteria. Criteria include: the verdict-inclination of jurors based on scant voir-dire and questionnaire information, and the juror's reaction to bare information disclosed about the case; the juror's reactions to the lawyer; the juror's likely ability to attend to trial detail (e.g., eyesight, hearing, attention, etc.); the juror's probable standing and influence among other jurors; the makeup of the jury as it would stand after the peremptory challenge (e.g., all male, all female, etc.); the likelihood that a peremptory challenge by one side will lead to challenges of other jurors by the other side; and the potential jurors that the court might yet draw from the remaining jury pool. The trial judge alternates peremptory challenges between sides. If one side declines to exercise a peremptory challenge, then the judge will give the other side an opportunity to do so. Although the plaintiff exercises a peremptory challenge first, meaning that the defendant gets to draw off the last juror, some plaintiff's lawyers like to pass early in order to get the last draw.

28 U.S.C. §1870. Challenges
In civil cases, each party shall be entitled to three peremptory challenges. Several defendants or several plaintiffs may be considered as a single party for the purposes of making challenges, or the court may allow additional peremptory challenges and permit them to be exercised separately or jointly. All challenges for cause or favor, whether to the array or panel or to individual jurors, shall be determined by the court.

INQUIRY

Discriminatory Challenges. Because information on jurors is limited, parties and their lawyers tend to rely for peremptory challenges on presumptions drawn from a variety of demographic characteristics including age, sex, education, and employment. Lawyers may develop profiles for the ideal juror based on presumed affinity for or against parties and witnesses, and other facts and circumstances of the case. Parties employ jury consultants and rely on experienced counsel to exercise the expertise to have the court draw off jurors whose profile does not appear to favor the case. At times, jury voir dire can involve professional judgment presuming juror attitudes drawn from their demographic characteristics—very nearly like unlawful discrimination, at least when the presumptions rest on protected characteristics like age, race, and sex. Although peremptory challenges are at the discretion of the parties, the Supreme Court held in Batson v. Kentucky, 476 U.S. 79 (1986), that the Fifth Amendment's due-process clause limits party discretion to peremptory challenges that do not discriminate based on race. Objections to peremptory challenges that appear to be race-based are known as *Batson* challenges. Five years later, the Supreme Court extended *Batson's* holding to civil cases in the following case. The same year, in J.E.B. v. Alabama ex rel. T.B., 511 U.S. 127, 130-131 (1991), the Supreme Court extended that prohibition to peremptory challenges based on gender. While fully appreciating the rationale stated in the following case, recognize also the sensitivity that a trial court must show to achieve its objective.

Edmonson v. Leesville Concrete Co.,

United States Supreme Court
500 U.S. 614 (1991)

Justice KENNEDY delivered the opinion of the Court.

We must decide in the case before us whether a private litigant in a civil case may use peremptory challenges to exclude jurors on account of their race. Recognizing the impropriety of racial bias in the courtroom, we hold the race-based exclusion violates the equal protection rights of the challenged jurors. This civil case originated in a United States District Court, and we apply the equal protection component of the Fifth Amendment's Due Process Clause. See Bolling v. Sharpe, 347 U.S. 497[] (1954).

I

... Edmonson sued Leesville Concrete Company for negligence in the United States District Court for the Western District of Louisiana, claiming that a Leesville employee permitted one of the company's trucks to roll backward and pin him against some construction equipment. Edmonson invoked his Seventh Amendment right to a trial by jury.

During *voir dire,* Leesville used two of its three peremptory challenges authorized by statute to remove black persons from the prospective jury. Citing our decision in Batson v. Kentucky, 476 U.S. 79[] (1986), Edmonson, who is himself black, requested that the District Court require Leesville to articulate a race-neutral explanation for striking the two jurors. The District Court denied the request on the ground that *Batson* does not apply in civil proceedings. As empaneled, the jury included 11 white persons and 1 black person. The jury rendered a verdict for Edmonson, assessing his total damages at $90,000. It also attributed 80% of the fault to Edmonson's contributory negligence, however, and awarded him the sum of $18,000.

Edmonson appealed... .

... A divided en banc panel affirmed the judgment of the District Court, holding that a private litigant in a civil case can exercise peremptory challenges without accountability for alleged racial classifications. [C] The court concluded that the use of peremptories by private litigants does not constitute state action and, as a result, does not implicate constitutional guarantees. ... We ... now reverse the Court of Appeals.

II...

In Powers v. Ohio, 499 U.S. 400[] (1991), we held that a criminal defendant, regardless of his or her race, may object to a prosecutor's race-based exclusion of persons from the petit jury. Our conclusion rested on a two-part analysis. First, following our opinions in *Batson* and in Carter v. Jury Commission of Greene County, 396 U.S. 320[] (1970), we made clear that a prosecutor's race-based peremptory challenge violates the equal protection rights of those excluded from jury service. [C] Second, we relied on well-established rules of third-party standing to hold that a defendant may raise the excluded jurors' equal protection rights. [C] ...

That an act violates the Constitution when committed by a government official, however, does not answer the question whether the same act offends constitutional guarantees if committed by a private litigant or his attorney. The Constitution's protections of individual liberty and equal protection apply in general only to action by the government. National Collegiate Athletic Assn. v. Tarkanian, 488 U.S. 179, 191[] (1988). Racial discrimination, though invidious in all contexts, violates the Constitution only when it may be attributed to state action. Moose Lodge No. 107 v. Irvis, 407 U.S. 163, 172[] (1972). Thus, the legality of the exclusion at issue here turns on the extent to which a litigant in a civil case may be subject to the Constitution's restrictions. ...

Although private use of state-sanctioned private remedies or procedures does not rise, by itself, to the level of state action, Tulsa Professional[Collection Services, Inc. v. Pope,] 485 U.S.[478,] 485[(1988)], our cases have found state action when private parties make extensive use of state procedures with "the overt, significant assistance of state officials." *Id.* at 486[]; [cc]. It cannot be disputed that, without the overt, significant participation of the government, the peremptory challenge system, as well as the jury trial system of which it is a part, simply could not exist. ...

The trial judge exercises substantial control over *voir dire* in the federal system. See Fed. Rule Civ. Proc. 47. The judge determines the range of information that may be discovered about a prospective juror, and so affects the exercise of both challenges for cause and peremptory challenges. In some cases, judges may even conduct the entire *voir dire* by themselves... . The judge oversees the exclusion of jurors for cause, in this way determining which jurors remain eligible for the exercise of peremptory strikes. In cases involving multiple parties, the trial judge decides how peremptory challenges shall be allocated among them. 28 U.S.C. §1870. When a lawyer exercises a peremptory challenge, the judge advises the juror he or she has been excused. ...

The principle that the selection of state officials, other than through election by all qualified voters, may constitute state action applies with even greater force in the context of jury selection through the use of peremptory challenges. Though the motive of a peremptory challenge may be to protect a private interest, the objective of jury selection proceedings is to determine representation on a governmental body. Were it not for peremptory challenges, there would be no question that the entire process of determining who will serve on the jury constitutes state action. The fact that the government delegates some portion of this power to private litigants does not change the governmental character of the power exercised. …

… Here, as in most civil cases, the initial decision whether to sue at all, the selection of counsel, and any number of ensuing tactical choices in the course of discovery and trial may be without the requisite governmental character to be deemed state action. That cannot be said of the exercise of peremptory challenges, however; when private litigants participate in the selection of jurors, they serve an important function within the government and act with its substantial assistance. If peremptory challenges based on race were permitted, persons could be required by summons to be put at risk of open and public discrimination as a condition of their participation in the justice system. The injury to excluded jurors would be the direct result of governmental delegation and participation.

Finally, we note that the injury caused by the discrimination is made more severe because the government permits it to occur within the courthouse itself. Few places are a more real expression of the constitutional authority of the government than a courtroom, where the law itself unfolds. Within the courtroom, the government invokes its laws to determine the rights of those who stand before it. In full view of the public, litigants press their cases, witnesses give testimony, juries render verdicts, and judges act with the utmost care to ensure that justice is done.

Race discrimination within the courtroom raises serious questions as to the fairness of the proceedings conducted there. Racial bias mars the integrity of the judicial system and prevents the idea of democratic government from becoming a reality. Rose v. Mitchell, 443 U.S. 545, 556[] (1979); Smith v. Texas, 311 U.S. 128, 130[] (1940). In the many times we have addressed the problem of racial bias in our system of justice, we have not "questioned the premise that racial discrimination in the qualification or selection of jurors offends the dignity of persons and the integrity of the courts." Powers[v. Ohio,] 499 U.S.[400,] 402[(1991)]. To permit racial exclusion in this official forum compounds the racial insult inherent in judging a citizen by the color of his or her skin. …

III

It remains to consider whether a prima facie case of racial discrimination has been established in the case before us, requiring Leesville to offer race-neutral explanations for its peremptory challenges. In *Batson,* we held that determining whether a prima facie case has been established requires consideration of all relevant circumstances, including whether there has been a pattern of strikes against members of a particular race. 476 U.S. at 96-97[]. The same approach applies in the civil context, and we leave it to the trial courts in the first instance to develop evidentiary rules for implementing our decision.

The judgment is reversed, and the case is remanded for further proceedings consistent with our opinion.

It is so ordered.

Justice O'CONNOR, with whom THE CHIEF JUSTICE and Justice SCALIA join, dissenting.

... Not everything that happens in a courtroom is state action. A trial, particularly a civil trial is by design largely a stage on which private parties may act; it is a forum through which they can resolve their disputes in a peaceful and ordered manner. The government erects the platform; it does not thereby become responsible for all that occurs upon it. As much as we would like to eliminate completely from the courtroom the specter of racial discrimination, the Constitution does not sweep that broadly. ...

Justice SCALIA, dissenting.

I join Justice O'CONNOR's dissent, which demonstrates that today's opinion is wrong in principle. I write to observe that it is also unfortunate in its consequences.

The concrete benefits of the Court's newly discovered constitutional rule are problematic. It will not necessarily be a net help rather than hindrance to minority litigants in obtaining racially diverse juries. ... *Both* sides have peremptory challenges, and they are sometimes used to *assure* rather than to *prevent* a racially diverse jury. ...

Although today's decision neither follows the law nor produces desirable concrete results, it certainly has great symbolic value. To overhaul the doctrine of state action in this fashion—what a magnificent demonstration of this institution's uncompromising hostility to race-based judgments, even by private actors! The price of the demonstration is, alas, high, and much of it will be paid by the minority litigants who use our courts. I dissent.

INQUIRY

Pretext. The prohibition of race-based peremptory challenges in *Edmonson v. Leesville Concrete Co.* and of gender-based peremptory challenges in *J.E.B. v. Alabama* means that when a party objects to an opposing party's peremptory challenge asserting one of those two impermissible bases, the party exercising the challenge must give race- and gender-neutral reasons. *See* Johnson v. California, 545 U.S. 162, 168 (2005). Given the breadth of permissible reasons to remove a juror peremptorily—literally, anything other than race or gender—one can imagine the ease with which a party could offer grounds that were pretext for impermissible race and gender reasons. The Supreme Court began to work out how the trial courts were to recognize pretext, in the years after *Batson, Edmonson,* and *J.E.B.* Initially, it appeared that the Supreme Court would be willing to accept as legitimate nearly any reason to exclude a juror even when circumstances suggested race. *See* Purkett v Elem, 514 U.S 765 (1995) (long hair, mustache, and beard). Eventually, though, in Miller-El v. Dretke, 545 U.S. 231, 239-240 (2005), the Supreme Court articulated how the trial court may distinguish genuine reasons from pretext. *Miller-El v. Dretke* involved a criminal case in which the prosecution used peremptory challenges to eliminate 10 of 11 African-American members of the venire, resulting a jury that had only 1 African American out of 12 members. The Supreme Court found that statistical disparity to be remarkable but also examined closely the prosecution's proffered rationale for the strikes, which the Court characterized ultimately as "afterthought." The

Court also permitted the defense to compare the qualifications of the stricken jurors with those of the jurors who remained. Assuming that the Court would apply the same standard in civil cases, it appears that a party must have extenuating and supportable explanations for strikes for which there could be a race or gender basis.

Challenges for Cause. Peremptory challenges are only one of two kinds of challenges. Parties may also challenge jurors for cause. To challenge for cause means to request that a court remove a juror for evident bias. The law does not limit the number of challenges for cause. Challenges for cause do not count against the party's three peremptory challenges. Parties routinely make peremptory challenges in most jury cases. By contrast, parties have less opportunity to challenge for cause and no guarantee whatsoever that the court will grant the challenge. Some jurors want to be removed—perhaps most of them. Yet most jurors will also deny any personal bias, even when (and perhaps especially when) something that the juror has already said indicates the potential for bias. In the usual instance of a challenge for cause, the juror will have given some indication of potential bias. When the that round of voir dire concludes, the trial judge will ask whether any party has a challenge for cause. The party against whom the bias would work will then make that challenge. The judge will then usually turn to opposing counsel asking for any objection to dismissing the juror for cause. In many instances, opposing counsel will object. The judge then rules or, as is oftent he case, inquires further of the juror to confirm or refute bias. Consider the following case in which the judge failed to "push" the juror to an adequate commitment, one way or the other.

Thompson v. Altheimer & Gray,

United States Court of Appeals for the Seventh Circuit
248 F.3d 621 (2003)

POSNER, Circuit Judge.

The plaintiff brought suit against her employer under Title VII of the Civil Rights Act of 1964, charging racial discrimination. The case was tried, the jury returned a verdict for the defendant, and the plaintiff appeals, arguing that a juror named Leiter should have been struck for cause. If the plaintiff is right, she is entitled to a new trial without having to show that Leiter's presence on the jury caused the jury to side with the defendant. Denial of the right to an unbiased tribunal is one of those trial errors that is not excused by being shown to have been harmless. Gray v. Mississippi, 481 U.S. 648, 668[] (1987); [cc]. …

… The important question is whether the plaintiff's constitutional right to an impartial tribunal was infringed. Let us see.

During the voir dire of the jury, the judge asked the members of the venire whether "there is something about this kind of lawsuit for money damages that would start any of you leaning for or against a particular party?" Leiter raised her hand and explained that she has "been an owner of a couple of businesses and am currently an owner of a business, and I feel that as an employer and owner of a business that will definitely sway my judgment in this case." The judge asked her whether "if I instructed you as to what the law is that you would be able to apply the law recognizing that you are a business owner?" To which she replied, "I think my experience will cloud my judgment, but I can do my best." The judge permitted the lawyers also to ask questions of the prospective jurors and Thompson's lawyer asked Leiter, "And you said earlier that you were concerned that your position as a business owner may cloud your judgment. Can you tell me how?" And she replied, "I am constantly faced with people that want various benefits or different positions in the company [what Thompson was seeking from her employer, the defendant, Altheimer & Gray] or better contacts or, you know, a myriad of issues that employers face on a regular basis, and I have to decide whether or not that person should get them." The lawyer then asked Leiter whether she was concerned "that if somebody doesn't get them [benefits sought from their employer] they're going to sue you," and she answered, "Of course." Asked then whether "you believe that people file lawsuits just because they don't get something they want?", she answered, "I believe there are some people that do." In answer to the next and last question, "Are you concerned that that might cloud your judgment in this case?" she said, "I think I bring a lot of background to this case, and I can't say that it's not going to cloud my judgment. I can try to be as fair as I can, as I do every day."

That was the end of the voir dire of Leiter. After refusing to strike her for cause (though urged to do so by the plaintiff's lawyer), and releasing the jurors who had not been selected for the jury (the defendant had also exercised its three peremptory challenges, none overlapping with the plaintiff's), the judge asked the eight remaining jurors, that is, the jurors selected to hear the case, whether they would follow his instructions on the law even if they didn't agree with them and whether they would be able to suspend judgment until they had heard all the evidence. The question was asked to the jurors at large and all either nodded their heads or said yes. The defendant, again perhaps dropping the ball, makes nothing of Leiter's failure at this stage to reiterate her doubts about her ability to exercise an unclouded judgment. The defendant is content to argue that the answers that Leiter gave to the earlier questions by the judge, and the questions by Thompson's lawyer, did not require that Leiter be struck for cause.

Our review of the trial judge's ruling with respect to a challenge for cause is deferential, [cc], but not completely supine, and it is pertinent to note that no issue of credibility is presented. There is no argument that Leiter was not telling the truth. The issue is interpretive: did what she say manifest a degree of bias such that the judge abused his discretion in failing to strike her for cause? …

When Leiter said that she believed that some people sue their employer just because they haven't gotten a promotion or a raise or some other benefit, she was not manifesting bias. She was expressing a prior belief (prior, that is, to hearing any evidence in this case) that was not only not irrational, but was undoubtedly true—there are indeed some people who will sue their employer just because of disappointment over the failure of the employer to give them something they want. In other words, there are spurious suits, in the employment domain as elsewhere. Leiter could not be thought biased for holding a true belief, or even for holding it unshakably if it is indubitably true. The belief that some employees make bogus claims against employers is so obviously true that it could not be shaken; but inability to set aside a clearly sound belief does not make for a biased juror. It makes for a realistic one.

Suppose a member of the venire in a case involving alleged sex discrimination by a fire department stated his belief that men on average have greater upper-body strength than women. Suppose he added that this belief was unshakable in the sense that if some social scientist testified otherwise, he would conclude that he was being fed junk science. Should this juror be disqualified? Not automatically, surely. The relevant questions would be whether he could distinguish averages from individuals, and thus recognize the possibility that a given woman might have greater upper-body strength than a given man, and whether he was so fixated on the average sex difference in upper-body strength that he was not open to the possibility that a woman whose upper-body strength was indeed less than that of the least strong firefighter in the fire department could nevertheless be as good a firefighter, or even a better one.

The question in this case was not whether Leiter's belief that some claims against employers are spurious was true or false (it was, as we have noted, true), but whether this belief would somehow impede her in giving due weight to the evidence and following the judge's instructions. That question was not adequately explored. The last thing Leiter said before the judge refused to strike her for cause was that she couldn't say the "background" she brought to this case wasn't going to "cloud" her judgment. She said she would *try* to be fair, but she expressed no confidence in being able to succeed in the attempt. She may have realized that because of bad experiences in the past, she might have difficulty separating the logically distinct propositions that some claims against employers are bogus and that this claim must be bogus because it is a claim against an employer.

Had she said she could *not* be fair, the judge would of course have had to strike her for cause. She did not say that, and so the judge ... should have followed up by asking her, as he later asked the jury *en masse*, whether she would follow his instructions on the law and suspend judgment until she had heard all the evidence.

Instead the matter was left dangling... . The judge didn't push hard enough to determine whether Leiter could relinquish her prior beliefs for purposes of deciding the case.

Had the judge pushed Leiter and had she finally given unequivocal assurances that he deemed credible, his ruling could not be disturbed. See Lockett v. Ohio, 438 U.S. 586, 595-96[] (1978); [cc]. But he failed to do that. ... A candid and thoughtful person, if one may judge from the transcript, Leiter would probably have made an excellent juror—in another case.

When a prospective juror manifests a prior belief that is both material and *contestable* (for, to repeat an earlier point, it is not bias to cling to a belief that no rational person would question), it is the judge's duty to determine whether the juror is capable of suspending that belief for the duration of the trial. When as in this case the record contains no assurances that the belief is "shakable," that the prospective juror can exercise a judgment unclouded by that belief, the verdict cannot stand. [Cc] "When a juror is unable to state that she will serve fairly and impartially despite being asked repeatedly for such assurances, we can have no confidence that the juror will 'lay aside' her biases or her prejudicial personal experiences and render a fair and impartial verdict." United States v. Gonzalez, 214 F.3d [1109,] 1114[(9th Cir. 2000)]. That's this case. Missing are those "unwavering affirmations of impartiality" that permitted the district judge in United States v. Garcia, 936 F.2d 648, 653 (2d Cir.1991), to find the challenged juror unbiased.

REVERSED AND REMANDED.

DIANE P. WOOD, Circuit Judge, concurring[, omitted].

---

3. Law-Fact Distinction

Once the parties have completed jury voir dire and the court has impaneled the jury, the court then swears the jury to uphold the law. At that point, though, the judicial role does not recede but has just begun. Trial judges retain control of trials even when juries are deciding disputed issues. They do so through a carefully drawn law-fact distinction. Judges determine and instruct as to the law, while juries decide disputed fact issues. A disputed fact issue is one the resolution of which depends on evaluating witness credibility, determining the weight and meaning of documentary evidence, or otherwise choosing among contrary inferences. Yet it is not simply that juries decide disputed fact issues. They also apply law to fact. For example, there was no dispute in Railroad Co. v. Stout, 84 U.S. (17 Wall) 657 (1873), that a child suffered serious injury playing on defendant's railroad turntable, but the Supreme Court approved that the jury decide whether defendant was negligent for having left the turntable unfenced and unlocked. For another example, the appellate court in Dobson v. Masonite Corp., 359 F.2d 921 (5th Cir. 1966), held that even though there was no dispute that the parties had entered into a certain written contract, a jury would nonetheless decide the contract's interpretation as a matter of fact. To say that juries decide disputed fact issues is really to say that they simultaneously determine facts while applying law to facts. The law binds up the concept of a legal fact within its law context.

A traditional way of justifying the law-fact distinction is that judges are experts in the law, while juries bring broader experience to decide matters of fact that are common to us all. The law bases the distinction in part on competence. Judges are better at law than jurors are, while jurors (collectively) are better at facts. Yet the law-fact distinction also plays an important structural role in dividing power. The power of a judge to determine and instruct as to the law checks lawless runaway juries. The power of a jury to decide contrary to the judge's view of the facts disburses power that trials would otherwise concentrate in the hands of the judge. Indeed, the law-fact distinction has its roots in the Seventh Amendment, under some of the same principles and case law as the preliminary question of a jury-trial right. *See* Edmonson v. Leesville Concrete Co., 500 U.S. 614, 624-625 (1991) ("the Constitution itself commits the trial of facts ... to the jury"). Consider the following Supreme Court case drawing out the law-fact distinction, articulating the authority on which it rests, and also suggesting its functional basis in the judge's greater expertise.

Markman v. Westview Instruments, Inc.,

United States Supreme Court
517 U.S. 370 (1996)

Justice SOUTER delivered the opinion of the Court.

The question here is whether the interpretation of a so-called patent claim, the portion of the patent document that defines the scope of the patentee's rights, is a matter of law reserved entirely for the court, or subject to a Seventh Amendment guarantee that a jury will determine the meaning of any disputed term of art about which expert testimony is offered. We hold that the construction of a patent, including terms of art within its claim, is exclusively within the province of the court.

I

... Petitioner in this infringement suit, Markman, owns United States Reissue Patent No. 33,054 for his "Inventory Control and Reporting System for Drycleaning Stores." The patent describes a system that can monitor and report the status, location, and movement of clothing in a dry-cleaning establishment. ...

Markman brought an infringement suit against Westview and Althon Enterprises, an operator of dry-cleaning establishments using Westview's products (collectively, Westview). ... The case was tried before a jury, which heard, among others, a witness produced by Markman who testified about the meaning of the claim language.

... [T]he jury ... found an infringement... . The District Court nevertheless granted Westview's deferred motion for judgment as a matter of law... . Under the trial court's construction of the patent, the production, sale, or use of a tracking system for dry cleaners would not infringe Markman's patent unless the product was capable of tracking articles of clothing throughout the cleaning process and generating reports about their status and location. Since Westview's system cannot do these things, the District Court directed a verdict... .

Markman appealed, arguing it was error for the District Court to substitute its construction of the disputed claim term "inventory" for the construction the jury had presumably given it. The United States Court of Appeals for the Federal Circuit affirmed, holding the interpretation of claim terms to be the exclusive province of the court and the Seventh Amendment to be consistent with that conclusion. [C] ... We now affirm.

II

... [W]e ask, first, whether we are dealing with a cause of action that either was tried at law at the time of the founding or is at least analogous to one that was, see, *e.g.,* Tull v. United States, 481 U.S. 412, 417[] (1987). If the action in question belongs in the law category, we then ask whether the particular trial decision must fall to the jury in order to preserve the substance of the common-law right as it existed in 1791. [C][fn]

A

As to the first issue, going to the character of the cause of action, ... there is no dispute that infringement cases today must be tried to a jury, as their predecessors were more than two centuries ago. [C]

B

This conclusion raises the second question, whether a particular issue occurring within a jury trial (here the construction of a patent claim) is itself necessarily a jury issue, the guarantee being essential to preserve the right to a jury's resolution of the ultimate dispute. In some instances the answer to this second question may be easy because of clear historical evidence that the very subsidiary question was so regarded under the English practice of leaving the issue for a jury. But when, as here, the old practice provides no clear answer, [c], we are forced to make a judgment about the scope of the Seventh Amendment guarantee without the benefit of any foolproof test.

The Court has repeatedly said that the answer to the second question "must depend on whether the jury must shoulder this responsibility *as necessary to preserve the 'substance of the common-law right of trial by jury.'*" Tull v. United States, *supra,* at 426[] (emphasis added) (quoting Colgrove v. Battin, 413 U.S. 149, 156[] (1973)); [c]. ...

The "substance of the common-law right" is, however, a pretty blunt instrument for drawing distinctions. We have tried to sharpen it, to be sure, by reference to the distinction between substance and procedure. [Cc] We have also spoken of the line as one between issues of fact and law. [Cc]

But the sounder course, when available, is to ... [use] the historical method, much as we do in characterizing the suits and actions within which they arise. Where there is no exact antecedent, the best hope lies in comparing the modern practice to earlier ones whose allocation to court or jury we do know, [cc], seeking the best analogy we can draw between an old and the new, [c].

C

"Prior to 1790 nothing in the nature of a claim had appeared either in British patent practice or in that of the American states," [c], and we have accordingly found no direct antecedent of modern claim construction in the historical sources. ...

D

Losing, then, on the contention that juries generally had interpretive responsibilities during the 18th century, Markman seeks a different anchor for analogy in the more modest contention that even if judges were charged with construing most terms in the patent, the art of defining terms of art employed in a specification fell within the province of the jury. Again, however, Markman has no authority from the period in question... .

III

Since evidence of common-law practice at the time of the framing does not entail application of the Seventh Amendment's jury guarantee to the construction of the claim document, we must look elsewhere to characterize this determination of meaning in order to allocate it as between court or jury. We accordingly consult existing precedent[fn] and consider both the relative interpretive skills of judges and juries and the statutory policies that ought to be furthered by the allocation.

A

The two elements of a simple patent case, construing the patent and determining whether infringement occurred, were characterized by the former patent practitioner, Justice Curtis.[fn] "The first is a question of law, to be determined by the court, construing the letters-patent, and the description of the invention and specification of claim annexed to them. The second is a question of fact, to be submitted to a jury." Winans v. Denmead, [50 U.S. 330,] 338 [(1853)]; [cc]. ...

... [No other case law] undercuts Justice Curtis's authority.

B

Where history and precedent provide no clear answers, functional considerations also play their part in the choice between judge and jury to define terms of art. We said in Miller v. Fenton, 474 U.S. 104, 114[] (1985), that when an issue "falls somewhere between a pristine legal standard and a simple historical fact, the fact/law distinction at times has turned on a determination that, as a matter of the sound administration of justice, one judicial actor is better positioned than another to decide the issue in question." So it turns out here, for judges, not juries, are the better suited to find the acquired meaning of patent terms.

The construction of written instruments is one of those things that judges often do and are likely to do better than jurors unburdened by training in exegesis. Patent construction in particular "is a special occupation, requiring, like all others, special training and practice. The judge, from his training and discipline, is more likely to give a proper interpretation to such instruments than a jury; and he is, therefore, more likely to be right, in performing such a duty, than a jury can be expected to be." Parker v. Hulme, 18 F. Cas.[1138,] 1140[(E.D. Pa. 1849)]. Such was the understanding nearly a century and a half ago, and there is no reason to weigh the respective strengths of judge and jury differently in relation to the modern claim... .

Markman would trump these considerations with his argument that a jury should decide a question of meaning peculiar to a trade or profession simply because the question is a subject of testimony requiring credibility determinations, which are the jury's forte. It is, of course, true that credibility judgments have to be made about the experts who testify in patent cases, and in theory there could be a case in which a simple credibility judgment would suffice to choose between experts whose testimony was equally consistent with a patent's internal logic. But our own experience with document construction leaves us doubtful that trial courts will run into many cases like that. In the main, we expect, any credibility determinations will be subsumed within the necessarily sophisticated analysis of the whole document, required by the standard construction rule that a term can be defined only in a way that comports with the instrument as a whole. [Cc] ... The decisionmaker vested with the task of construing the patent is in the better position to ascertain whether an expert's proposed definition fully comports with the specification and claims and so will preserve the patent's internal coherence. We accordingly think there is sufficient reason to treat construction of terms of art like many other responsibilities that we cede to a judge in the normal course of trial, notwithstanding its evidentiary underpinnings.

C

Finally, we see the importance of uniformity in the treatment of a given patent as an independent reason to allocate all issues of construction to the court. As we noted in General Elec. Co. v. Wabash Appliance Corp., 304 U.S. 364, 369[] (1938), "[t]he limits of a patent must be known for the protection of the patentee, the encouragement of the inventive genius of others and the assurance that the subject of the patent will be dedicated ultimately to the public." Otherwise, a "zone of uncertainty which enterprise and experimentation may enter only at the risk of infringement claims would discourage invention only a little less than unequivocal foreclosure of the field," United Carbon Co. v. Binney & Smith Co., 317 U.S. 228, 236[] (1942), and "[t]he public [would] be deprived of rights supposed to belong to it, without being clearly told what it is that limits these rights." Merrill v. Yeomans, 94 U.S. 568, 573[] (1877). It was just for the sake of such desirable uniformity that Congress created the Court of Appeals for the Federal Circuit as an exclusive appellate court for patent cases... .

Uniformity would, however, be ill served by submitting issues of document construction to juries. ...

Accordingly, we hold that the interpretation of the word "inventory" in this case is an issue for the judge, not the jury, and affirm the decision of the Court of Appeals for the Federal Circuit.

It is so ordered.

Skill

Successful professionals depend on probabilistic, methodological, and quantitative reasoning skills. In few places is that more true for lawyers than in predicting jury-trial outcomes. Each jury is different. The parties could try the same case twice and have a different outcome, as occasionally happens on remands for new trial. The uncertainty of jury trials makes advising clients regarding outcomes a matter not of logical analysis but of probabilities. The problem is that there are so few trials on which to base that reasoning. Many litigators today will not have tried enough cases to be able to make sound predictions based on personal experience. To remedy that shortcoming, lawyers research jury-verdict databases, try cases to mock juries, and consult with experienced trial counsel. Scholars criticize legal education for over-emphasizing logical reasoning to the detriment of probabilistic and quantitative reasoning necessary for effective counseling. *See* RANDALL KISER, BEYOND RIGHT AND WRONG—THE POWER OF EFFECTIVE DECISION MAKING FOR ATTORNEYS AND CLIENTS 144-158 (Springer 2010). Learn and appreciate the value of quantifying uncertainty.

4. Instructing Juries

In addition to determining the law, judges also instruct juries in the law to aid the juries in finding fact. Judges instruct juries at the outset of the case, occasionally during the case as the need arises, and at the conclusion of the case. The preliminary instructions that a trial judge reads to the jury at the beginning of a case, immediately after the parties draw and the court impanels and swears the jury, tend to be standard instructions applicable to all cases. Indeed, state supreme courts may adopt standard jury instructions and require that trial courts read them whenever they apply. Many of the standard instructions will be preliminary instructions having to do with the stages of trial. Others will be cautionary instructions such as not to visit the scene, do legal research, or begin deliberations. *See* In re Beverly Hills Fire Litigation, 695 F.2d 207 (6th Cir. 1982) (new trial ordered for juror having examined his home's wiring to tell jurors about it to help resolve trial issue over safety of aluminum wiring). Trial judges may give limiting or correcting instructions during trial, such as after an unprepared witness inadvertently discloses an irrelevant or unduly prejudicial matter, and the trial judge instructs the jury to disregard it. State law tends to strongly discourage judges from commenting on the evidence while instructing the jury in a way that will influence the outcome. Federal law does less so, although even in federal court there are some things that a trial judge cannot get away saying. *See* Quercia v. United States, 289 U.S. 466, 468 (1933) (reversing for trial judge telling jurors that witnesses like the defendant who wipe their hands while testifying are liars) (quoting trial judge as saying, "'and now I am going to tell you what I think of the defendant's testimony'"). Instruction should be neutral.

For trial lawyers, the main points of concentration and contention, though, arise with the trial judge's final instructions to the jury after the close of proofs and (usually) after closing arguments. FED. R. CIV. P. 51 and similar state-court rules govern jury instructions. It may surprise the novitiate to know that lawyers, not judges, draft jury instructions. Rule 51(a)(1) anticipates that the trial court will order that the parties submit proposed jury instructions during or shortly before trial, although competent counsel often compile jury instructions early in the case to guide pleading, discovery, and trial preparation. Rule 51(a)(2) anticipates that new issues may arise during trial that require counsel to submit additional instructions after the evidence closes. Some courts order joint submission of proposed jury instructions, making the lawyers for all sides attempt to negotiate and resolve points of contention. Other courts accept disparate submissions. Drafting jury instructions stating the law in non-argumentative fashion is an art more than a science. Lawyers draw on standard jury instructions formally adopted in specific jurisdictions pursuant to court rule. They also draw on pattern instructions that, while not formally adopted for specific courts, carry some weight by author and usage. They also modify standard and pattern instructions for particular cases and issues, and draft special instructions of their own for issues not addressed by standard or pattern instructions. Importantly, they also prepare the proposed verdict form.

Rule 51(b) then requires the trial judge to tell the lawyers before closing arguments and final instructions, what instructions the trial judge intends to give. Trial judges conduct in-chambers conferences, sorting through disparate sets of instructions and discussing which to adopt and which to reject or modify. As required by Rule 51(c), trial judges also conduct on-the-record hearings, noting instructions to which a party objects or which the court refused to give over objection, and the grounds for objections. Rule 51(b) requires these steps before closing argument, in order that the lawyers have the opportunity to shape their closing arguments to specific instructions. While lawyers rightly hesitate to tell jurors the law, lawyers commonly make closing-argument assertions that begin with statements like, "The judge will tell you that the plaintiff has the burden of proving the case by a preponderance of the evidence," and then proceed to advocate the facts and theories favorable to their clients. One must know the instructions in advance to do so. Some courts prepare copies of the instructions for each juror to read along as the judge reads them aloud or to take into deliberations, or both. Read Rule 51 and then review the following example of proposed jury instructions for an employment-rights case.

FED. R. CIV. P. 51. Instructions to the Jury; Objections; Preserving a Claim of Error
(a) REQUESTS.
(1) *Before or at the Close of the Evidence.* At the close of the evidence or at any earlier reasonable time that the court orders, a party may file and furnish to every other party written requests for the jury instructions it wants the court to give.
(2) *After the Close of the Evidence.* After the close of the evidence, a party may:
(A) file requests for instructions on issues that could not reasonably have been anticipated by an earlier time that the court set for requests; and
(B) with the court's permission, file untimely requests for instructions on any issue.
(b) INSTRUCTIONS. The court:
(1) must inform the parties of its proposed instructions and proposed action on the requests before instructing the jury and before final jury arguments;
(2) must give the parties an opportunity to object on the record and out of the jury's hearing before the instructions and arguments are delivered; and
(3) may instruct the jury at any time before the jury is discharged.
(c) OBJECTIONS.
(1) *How to Make.* A party who objects to an instruction or the failure to give an instruction must do so on the record, stating distinctly the matter objected to and the grounds for the objection.
(2) *When to Make.* An objection is timely if:
(A) a party objects at the opportunity provided under Rule 51(b)(2); or
(B) a party was not informed of an instruction or action on a request before that opportunity to object, and the party objects promptly after learning that the instruction or request will be, or has been, given or refused.
(d) ASSIGNING ERROR; PLAIN ERROR.
(1) *Assigning Error.* A party may assign as error:
(A) an error in an instruction actually given, if that party properly objected; or
(B) a failure to give an instruction, if that party properly requested it and—unless the court rejected the request in a definitive ruling on the record—also properly objected.
(2) *Plain Error.* A court may consider a plain error in the instructions that has not been preserved as required by Rule 51(d)(1) if the error affects substantial rights.

UNITED STATES DISTRICT COURT
FOR THE WESTERN DISTRICT OF MICHIGAN

MAYNARD RAY, JOHN W. BAINES, and **PAUL RUTTER,**
Plaintiffs,
v

WINDSOR COUNTY and **RON HOOPER** individually and in his official capacity as Sheriff of Windsor County,
Defendants.

No. CIV-01-01234

Hon. ***** *******

PLAINTIFFS' PROPOSED JURY INSTRUCTIONS

[*Names, addresses, and telephone numbers of counsel omitted*]

Plaintiffs submit the following Standardized Civil Jury Instructions for the Western District of Michigan (SCJI), special jury instructions from O'MALLEY, GRENIG, & LEE, FEDERAL JURY PRACTICE AND INSTRUCTIONS (CIVIL) (5th ed. 2001) (FJPI), having been reviewed and corrected by defense counsel.

[signature block of plaintiffs' counsel]

SCJI 2.01 Introduction
SCJI 2.01A More Than One Plaintiff

SCJI 2.01B	More Than One Defendant
SCJI 2.02	Jurors' Duties
SCJI 2.03	All Persons Equal Before Law – Organizations
SCJI 2.04	Evidence Defined
SCJI 2.05	Consideration of Evidence
SCJI 2.05A	Consideration of Evidence – Corporate
SCJI 2.06	Direct and Circumstantial Evidence
SCJI 2.07	Credibility of Witnesses
SCJI 2.08	Number of Witnesses and Evidence Presented
SCJI 2.08A	All Available Evidence Need Not Be Produced
SCJI 2.08B	Single Witness
SCJI 2.08C	Not Required to Accept Uncontradicted Testimony
SCJI 2.14	Lawyers' Objections
SCJI 3.01	Introduction
SCJI 3.02	Preponderance of the Evidence
SCJI 3.02A	Burden of Proof [also refer to special instructions below]
SCJI 3.03	Specific Elements of Claims [refer to special instructions]
SCJI 3.03A	Proximate Cause
SCJI 3.03B	Proximate Cause and Proximately Contributed
SCJI 3.04	Consider Damages Only If Necessary
SCJI 3.04A	Damages – Reasonable – Not Speculative
SCJI 3.04B	Recovery of Take-Home Pay Only
SCJI 3.04C	Future Damages – Reduction to Present Cash Value
SCJI 3.04E	Duty to Mitigate Damages
SCJI 3.05	Describe Damages For Specific Claims [see special instrs.]
SCJI 3.05A	Prejudgment Interest
SCJI 4.01	Introduction
SCJI 4.02A	Stipulations of Fact [refer to joint final pretrial order]
SCJI 4.06	Summaries Not Admitted in Evidence
SCJI 4.08	Impeachment by Prior Inconsistent Stmt. Not Under Oath
SCJI 9.01	Introduction
SCJI 9.02	Experiments, Research and Investigation
SCJI 9.04	Duty to Deliberate
SCJI 9.04A	Notes
SCJI 9.05	Verdict Form
SCJI 9.09	Court Has No Opinion
SCJI 10.02	Deposition as Substantive Evidence

FJPI §168.01 Nature of the Action

Plaintiffs claim that defendants, while acting "under color" of state law, intentionally deprived plaintiffs of plaintiffs' rights under the First Amendment of the U.S. Constitution. Plaintiffs claim that, while defendants were acting under color of state law, defendants transferred plaintiffs, demoted one of the plaintiffs, and otherwise affected the terms, conditions, and privileges of their employment, because of plaintiffs' exercise of the right of free speech.

Defendants deny violating plaintiffs' First Amendment rights in any way and assert that plaintiffs' transfer and the other affects on the terms, conditions, and privileges of their employment had nothing to do with plaintiffs' exercise of the right of free speech.

FJPI §168.10 Generally

Under the First Amendment to the Constitution, every public employee has the right to freedom of speech addressing issues of public concern. 42 U.S.C.

§1983 provides that a person may sue for an award of money damages against anyone who, "under color" of any state law or custom, intentionally violated the plaintiff's rights under the U.S. Constitution.

FJPI §168.21 Political Activity

Under the First Amendment to the U.S. Constitution, every citizen has the right to engage in political activity, such as holding meetings and hearing the views of political candidates, or running for office or supporting political candidates, without governmental interference or penalty. This means that, in the case of governmental or public employees [], public employees may not have the terms, conditions, or privileges of their employment affected by governmental authority because of political activity that is protected by the First Amendment.

The law further provides that a person may sue for an award of money damages against anyone who, "under color" of any state law or custom, intentionally violates plaintiff's rights under the U.S. Constitution.

In order to prevail on this claim, plaintiffs must prove each of the following facts by a preponderance of the evidence:

First: That the actions of defendants were "under color" of the authority of the State;

Second: That plaintiffs engaged in constitutionally protected political activity, a form of free speech, as previously defined, by supporting the former sheriff in elections;

Third: Such protected activity was a substantial or motivating factor in defendant's decision to affect one or more of plaintiffs' terms, conditions, or privileges of employment; and

Fourth: That defendants' acts were the proximate or legal cause of damages sustained by plaintiffs.

In this case the parties have stipulated or agreed that defendants acted "under color" of state law and you should, therefore, accept that fact as proven.

FJPI §168.50 Generally

If you find that plaintiffs have met the plaintiffs' burden of proof, then you must determine whether defendants have shown by a preponderance of the evidence that plaintiffs would have been transferred, demoted, and otherwise had their jobs affected even if the plaintiffs political association had not been considered, because of other reasons. If defendants show, by a preponderance of the evidence, that plaintiffs would have been transferred, demoted, or otherwise had their jobs affected in any event, then you should find for defendants.

FJPI §168.60 Actual Damages

If you find in favor of plaintiffs, then you must award plaintiffs such sums as you find from the preponderance of the evidence will fairly and justly compensate plaintiffs for any damages you find plaintiffs sustained and are reasonably certain to sustain in the future as a direct result of the defendants' conduct. You should consider the following elements of damages:

1. The mental and emotional suffering the plaintiffs have experienced and are reasonably certain to experience in the future;

2. The wages, salary, and benefits plaintiffs have lost and the reasonable value of the earning capacity the plaintiffs are reasonably certain to lose in the future.

Throughout your deliberations you must not engage in any speculation, guess, or conjecture and you must not award any damages under this instruction by way of punishment or through sympathy.

FJPI §168.61 Nominal Damages

If you find in favor of plaintiffs under these instructions, but you find that plaintiffs' damages have no monetary value, then you must return a verdict for plaintiffs in the nominal amount of one dollar.

FJPI §168.62 Punitive Damages

In addition to the damages mentioned in the other instructions, the law permits you to award an injured person punitive damages under certain circumstances in order to punish the defendants for some extraordinary misconduct and to serve as an example or waning to others not to engage in such conduct.

If you find in favor of plaintiffs and against defendants and if you find the conduct of defendants was recklessly and callously indifferent to plaintiffs rights of political association, then, in addition to any other damages to which you find the plaintiffs are entitled, you may, but are not required to, award plaintiffs an additional amount as punitive damages if you find it is appropriate to punish the defendants or deter defendants and others from like conduct in the future. Whether to award plaintiffs punitive damages and the amount of those damages are within your sound discretion.

INQUIRY

Choice of Instructions. Notice that the lawyer who drafted the above-proposed jury instructions drew some from standard instructions approved by the local federal district court and some from a well-known and locally accepted book of pattern instructions. When lawyers request that a trial judge instruct the jury using standard jury instructions, what discretion does the trial judge have in granting or denying the request? Some state cases and court rules require the trial judge to use formally adopted standard jury instructions when a party requests them and they apply to the case. Those provisions do not prohibit the trial judge from adopting non-standard instructions to address other issues for which there are no standard instructions. In any given case, would you rather have a committee drafting standard instructions that the trial judge must give when requested, or would you prefer to draft the proposed instructions yourself? Consider two such state-court rules in states whose jury-instruction committees have adopted hundreds of standard jury instructions.

MISSOURI RULE OF CIVIL PROCEDURE 70.02. Instructions to Juries

(a) Requests for Instructions. Any party may, and a party with the burden of proof on an issue shall, submit written requests for instructions on the law applicable to the issues. ... Each instruction shall be submitted with an original and one copy for the court and one copy for each party. Each copy shall indicate whether it was prepared at the court's direction or by which party it was tendered and shall contain a notation as follows: "MAI No. ___" or "MAI No. ___ modified" or "Not in MAI" as the case may be.

(b) Form of Instructions. Whenever Missouri Approved Instructions contains an instruction applicable in a particular case that the appropriate party requests or the court decides to submit, such instruction shall be given to the exclusion of any other instructions on the same subject. Where an MAI must be modified to fairly submit the issues in a particular case, or where there is no applicable MAI so that an instruction not in MAI must be given, then such modifications or such instructions shall be simple, brief, impartial, free from argument, and shall not submit to the jury or require findings of detailed evidentiary facts.

(c) Violation of Rule—Effect. The giving of an instruction in violation of the provisions of this Rule 70.02 shall constitute error, its prejudicial effect to be judicially determined, provided that objection has been timely made pursuant to Rule 70.03.

(d) Converse Instruction—Effect of Requesting. The request of a converse instruction shall not be deemed to waive any objection to the instruction conversed.

(e) Instructions Conference and Record. The court shall hold an instructions conference with counsel to determine the instructions to be given. ...

(f) Instructions—How and When Given. After a jury has been sworn to try a case but before opening statements, the court shall read to the jury Missouri Approved Instructions 2.01, which shall be marked and given to the jury along with the other instructions at the close of the case... . The final instructions on the law governing the case shall be read to the jury by the court and provided to the jury in writing.

MICH. COURT RULE 2.516. Instructions to Jury

(A) Request for Instructions.

(1) At a time the court reasonably directs, the parties must file written requests that the court instruct the jury on the law as stated in the requests. ...

(2) ... [A]fter the close of the evidence each party shall submit in writing to the court a statement of the issues and may submit the party's theory of the case as to each issue. ...

(B) Instructing the Jury.

(1) After the jury is sworn and before evidence is taken, the court shall give such preliminary instructions ... as are reasonably necessary to enable the jury to understand the proceedings. ...

(2) At any time during the trial, the court may, with or without request, instruct the jury on a point of law... .

(3) Before or after arguments or at both times, as the court elects, the court shall instruct the jury on the applicable law... .

(C) Objections. A party may assign as error the giving of or the failure to give an instruction only if the party objects on the record before the jury retires to consider the verdict... .

(D) Model Civil Jury Instructions.

(1) The Committee on Model Civil Jury Instructions appointed by the Supreme Court has the authority to adopt model civil jury instructions... .

(2) Pertinent portions of the instructions approved by the Committee on Model Civil Jury Instructions or its predecessor committee must be given in each action in which jury instructions are given if

(a) they are applicable,

(b) they accurately state the applicable law, and

(c) they are requested by a party.

(3) Whenever the committee recommends that no instruction be given on a particular matter, the court shall not give an instruction unless it specifically finds for reasons stated on the record that

(a) the instruction is necessary to state the applicable law accurately, and

(b) the matter is not adequately covered by other pertinent model civil jury instructions.
(4) This subrule does not limit the power of the court to give additional instructions on applicable law not covered by the model instructions. Additional instructions when given must be patterned as nearly as practicable after the style of the model instructions, and must be concise, understandable, conversational, unslanted, and nonargumentative.

INQUIRY

Objections. FED. R. CIV. P. 51(c) requires in most cases that parties object to instructions on the record before the trial judge reads them to the jury. The provision's purpose is to give the trial judge an opportunity to correct an erroneous instruction before given. Errors in instructions are great sources for appeal. Appellate courts can have great difficulty evaluating the basis for a jury verdict, the prejudicial effect of an improper comment by counsel, or the prejudicial effect of admitting inadmissible evidence. Appellate courts have no difficulty in recognizing law errors in jury instructions. Trial counsel work diligently to identify and preserve error to protect against potential adverse verdicts. In the usual case, trial lawyers argue vigorously over jury instructions that they believe are erroneous and prejudicial. Just to be sure, Rule 51(c) prevents trial counsel from sandbagging the trial judge as to erroneous jury instructions. Rule 51(d)(1) reiterates that a party may assign as error only those jury instructions to which the party objected. On the other hand, where a lawyer fails to timely object to an erroneous instruction, Rule 51(d)(2) provides an escape valve for some instructional errors. Rule 51(d)(2) provides that a party may request post-judgment relief based on an instructional error so plain that it affects the party's substantial rights.

5. Judicial Control of Juries

A trial judge's control of a jury trial does not end with determining the law and instructing the jury as to it. Trial judges monitor the proofs to ensure that there is sufficient evidentiary support on each issue to submit it to the jury. This authority, memorialized in FED. R. CIV. P. 50 and equivalent state-court rules, effectively prevents juries from reaching decisions for which there is inadequate evidentiary support. Judgment as a matter of law (formerly "directed verdict") does not usurp the jury's authority but confines it to its proper scope in deciding disputed issues. Issues for which there is inadequate evidentiary support are not genuinely disputed issues. A disputed issue is one for which there is adequate evidentiary support for reasonable jurors to decide on either side of the issue. Rule 50(a)(1)(A) authorizes the trial court to resolve issues on which a party has not supplied the requisite evidence to submit to the jury. The trial court must wait until that point in the trial, typically after the party rests its case, to find that the trial court has fully heard the party on the issue but that the evidence does not support a reasonable dispute. Rule 50(a)(1)(B) permits the trial court to enter judgment against a party who has not supplied the requisite evidence on an issue that is an essential element of the party's claim.

Rule 50 also dictates the timing and procedure for judgment as a matter of law. Under Rule 50(a)(2), parties may move for judgment as a matter of law at any time before the court submits the case to a jury for deliberations. Trial counsel should do so in any case in which there has been a failure of proof on a dispositive issue. If a party moves for judgment as a matter of law before the trial court submits the case to the jury, and the trial court denies the motion, then Rule 50(b) permits a party to renew the motion after trial and appeal its denial. Again, trial counsel should renew Rule 50 motions for judgment as a matter of law after trial. What Rule 50 may not state expressly but does implicitly provide is that failing to move for judgment as a matter of law before submission to the jury and renewing that motion after verdict but before appeal effectively bars appeals for judgment as a matter of law. Parties who fail to move for judgment as a matter of law and renew those motions may still move for new trial but may not appeal based on the trial court's failing to grant judgment as a matter of law. Read Rule 50 for these procedures, followed by a Supreme Court case illustrating a failure of proof in a negligence case.

FED. R. CIV. P. 50. Judgment as a Matter of Law in a Jury Trial; Related Motion for a New Trial; Conditional Ruling

(a) JUDGMENT AS A MATTER OF LAW.

(1) *In General.* If a party has been fully heard on an issue during a jury trial and the court finds that a reasonable jury would not have a legally sufficient evidentiary basis to find for the party on that issue, the court may:

(A) resolve the issue against the party; and

(B) grant a motion for judgment as a matter of law against the party on a claim or defense that, under the controlling law, can be maintained or defeated only with a favorable finding on that issue.

(2) *Motion.* A motion for judgment as a matter of law may be made at any time before the case is submitted to the jury. The motion must specify the judgment sought and the law and facts that entitle the movant to the judgment.

(b) RENEWING THE MOTION AFTER TRIAL; ALTERNATIVE MOTION FOR A NEW TRIAL. If the court does not grant a motion for judgment as a matter of law made under Rule 50(a), the court is considered to have submitted the action to the jury subject to the court's later deciding the legal questions raised by the motion. No later than 28 days after the entry of judgment—or if the motion addresses a jury issue not decided by a verdict, no later than 28 days after the jury was discharged—the movant may file a renewed motion for judgment as a matter of law and may include an alternative or joint request for a new trial under Rule 59. In ruling on the renewed motion, the court may:

(1) allow judgment on the verdict, if the jury returned a verdict;

(2) order a new trial; or

(3) direct the entry of judgment as a matter of law.

(c) GRANTING THE RENEWED MOTION; CONDITIONAL RULING ON A MOTION FOR A NEW TRIAL.

(1) *In General.* If the court grants a renewed motion for judgment as a matter of law, it must also conditionally rule on any motion for a new trial by determining whether a new trial should be granted if the judgment is later vacated or reversed. The court must state the grounds for conditionally granting or denying the motion for a new trial.

(2) *Effect of a Conditional Ruling.* Conditionally granting the motion for a new trial does not affect the judgment's finality; if the judgment is reversed, the new trial must proceed unless the appellate court orders otherwise. If the motion for a new trial is conditionally denied, the appellee may assert error in that denial; if the judgment is reversed, the case must proceed as the appellate court orders.

(d) TIME FOR A LOSING PARTY'S NEW-TRIAL MOTION. Any motion for a new trial under Rule 59 by a party against whom judgment as a matter of law is rendered must be filed no later than 28 days after the entry of the judgment.

(e) DENYING THE MOTION FOR JUDGMENT AS A MATTER OF LAW; REVERSAL ON APPEAL. If the court denies the motion for judgment as a matter of law, the prevailing party may, as appellee, assert grounds entitling it to a new trial should the appellate court conclude that the trial court erred in denying the motion. If the appellate court reverses the judgment, it may order a new trial, direct the trial court to determine whether a new trial should be granted, or direct the entry of judgment.

Pennsylvania Railroad v. Chamberlain,

United States Supreme Court
288 U.S. 333 (1933)

Mr. Justice SUTHERLAND delivered the opinion of the Court.

This is an action brought by respondent against petitioner to recover for the death of a brakeman, alleged to have been caused by petitioner's negligence. The complaint alleges that the deceased, at the time of the accident resulting in his death, was assisting in the yard work of breaking up and making up trains and in the classifying and assorting of cars operating in interstate commerce; that in pursuance of such work, while riding a cut of cars, other cars ridden by fellow employees were negligently caused to be brought into violent contact with those upon which deceased was riding, with the result that he was thrown therefrom to the railroad track and run over by a car or cars, inflicting injuries from which he died.

At the conclusion of the evidence, the trial court directed the jury to find a verdict in favor of petitioner. Judgment upon a verdict so found was reversed by the Court of Appeals, Judge Swan dissenting. [C] ...

The case for respondent rests wholly upon the claim that the fall of deceased was caused by a violent collision of the string of nine cars with the string ridden by deceased. Three employees, riding the nine-car string, testified positively that no such collision occurred. They were corroborated by every other employee in a position to see, all testifying that there was no contact between the nine-car string and that of the deceased. The testimony of these witnesses, if believed, establishes beyond doubt that there was no collision between these two strings of cars, and that the nine-car string contributed in no way to the accident. The only witness who testified for the respondent was one Bainbridge; and it is upon his testimony alone that respondent's right to recover is sought to be upheld. His testimony is concisely stated, in its most favorable light for respondent, in the prevailing opinion below by Judge Learned Hand, as follows:

> The plaintiff's only witness to the event, one Bainbridge, then employed by the road, stood close to the yardmaster's office... . He professed to have paid little attention to what went on, but he did see the deceased riding at the rear of his cars, whose speed when they passed him he took to be about eight or ten miles. Shortly thereafter a second string passed ... and this was followed by the nine, which, according to the plaintiff's theory, collided with the deceased's. After the nine cars had passed at a somewhat greater speed than the deceased's, Bainbridge paid no more attention to either string for a while, but looked again when the deceased, who was still standing in his place, had passed the switch and onto the assorting track where he was bound. At that time his speed had been checked to about three miles, but the speed of the following nine cars

> had increased. They were just passing the switch, about four or five cars behind the deceased. Bainbridge looked away again and soon heard what he described as a "loud crash," not however an unusual event in a switching yard. Apparently this did not cause him at once to turn, but he did so shortly thereafter, and saw the two strings together, still moving, and the deceased no longer in sight. Later still his attention was attracted by shouts and he went to the spot and saw the deceased between the rails. Until he left to go to the accident, he had stood fifty feet to the north of the track where the accident happened, and about nine hundred feet from where the body was found.

The court, although regarding Bainbridge's testimony as not only "somewhat suspicious in itself, but its contradiction ... so manifold as to leave little doubt," held, nevertheless, that the question was one of fact depending upon the credibility of the witnesses, and that it was for the jury to determine, as between the one witness and the many, where the truth lay.

... It, of course, is true, generally, that where there is a direct conflict of testimony upon a matter of fact, the question must be left to the jury to determine, without regard to the number of witnesses upon either side. But here there really is no conflict in the testimony as to the facts. The witnesses for petitioner flatly testified that there was no collision between the nine-car and the two-car strings. Bainbridge did not say there was such a collision. What he said was that he heard a "loud crash," which did not cause him at once to turn, but that shortly thereafter he did turn and saw the two strings of cars moving together with the deceased no longer in sight; that there was nothing unusual about the crash of cars—it happened every day; that there was nothing about this crash to attract his attention except that it was extra loud; that he paid no attention to it; that it was not sufficient to attract his attention. The record shows that there was a continuous movement of cars over and down the "hump," which were distributed among a large number of branch tracks within the yard, and that any two strings of these cars moving upon the same track might have come together and caused the crash which Bainbridge heard. There is no direct evidence that in fact the crash was occasioned by a collision of the two strings in question; and it is perfectly clear that no such fact was brought to Bainbridge's attention as a perception of the physical sense of sight or of hearing. At most there was an inference to that effect drawn from observed facts which gave equal support to the opposite inference that the crash was occasioned by the coming together of other strings of cars entirely away from the scene of the accident, or of the two-car string ridden by deceased and the seven-car string immediately ahead of it.

We, therefore, have a case belonging to that class of cases where proven facts give equal support to each of two inconsistent inferences; in which event, neither of them being established, judgment, as a matter of law, must go against the party upon whom rests the necessity of sustaining one of these inferences as against the other, before he is entitled to recover. [Cc]

The rule is succinctly stated in Smith v. First National Bank in Westfield, 99 Mass. 605, 611-612 [(1868)], quoted in [United States F. & G. Co. v. Des Moines National Bank, 145 F.273, 280 (8th Cir. 1906)]: "...When the evidence tends equally to sustain either of two inconsistent propositions, neither of them can be said to have been established by legitimate proof. A verdict in favor of the party bound to maintain one of those propositions against the other is necessarily wrong."

That Bainbridge concluded from what he himself observed that the crash was due to a collision between the two strings of cars in question is sufficiently indicated by his statements. But this, of course, proves nothing, since it is not allowable for a witness to resolve the doubt as to which of two equally justifiable inferences shall be adopted by drawing a conclusion, which, if accepted, will result in a purely gratuitous award in favor of the party who has failed to sustain the burden of proof cast upon him by the law. ...

Not only is Bainbridge's testimony considered as a whole suspicious, insubstantial, and insufficient, but his statement that when he turned shortly after hearing the crash the two strings were moving together is simply incredible, if he meant thereby to be understood as saying that he saw the two in contact; and if he meant by the words "moving together" simply that they were moving at the same time in the same direction but not in contact, the statement becomes immaterial. As we have already seen he was paying slight and only occasional attention to what was going on. The cars were eight or nine hundred feet from where he stood and moving almost directly away from him... . At that sharp angle and from that distance, near dusk of a misty evening (as the proof shows), the practical impossibility of the witness being able to see whether the front of the nine-car string was in contact with the back of the two-car string is apparent. And, certainly, in the light of these conditions, no verdict based upon a statement so unbelievable reasonably could be sustained as against the positive testimony to the contrary of unimpeached witnesses, all in a position to see, as this witness was not, the precise relation of the cars to one another. The fact that these witnesses were employees of the petitioner, under the circumstances here disclosed, does not impair this conclusion. [C]

We think, therefore, that the trial court was right in withdrawing the case from the jury. ...

The judgment of the Circuit Court of Appeals is reversed and that of the District Court is affirmed.

Mr. Justice STONE and Mr. Justice CARDOZO concur in the result.

INQUIRY

Shifting Burdens. *Pennsylvania Railroad v. Chamberlain* followed the equipoise rule for judgment as a matter of law where the evidence is equal and indistinguishable as to two contrasting inferences, one of which supports the claim and the other of which refutes it. That case involved inferences drawn from observations of physical events. In many cases, particularly civil-rights cases, the factual disputes involve not physical events but the state of mind of various actors and decisionmakers. When the disputed issue is what the critical decisionmakers were thinking at the time and there are several possible inferences, how should the courts treat those contrasting inferences as to state of mind in motions for judgment as a matter of law? The Supreme Court does not follow an equipoise rule. Instead, in McDonnell Douglas Corp. v. Green, 411 U.S. 792 (1973), the

Supreme Court developed a burden-shifting paradigm for civil-rights cases. Once the plaintiff establishes a prima-facie case of unlawful discrimination from the circumstantial evidence, the burden of production shifts to the defendant to offer lawful reasons for the decision challenged as discriminatory. If the defendant can offer no legitimate explanation, then the plaintiff prevails. Yet once the defendant offers a legitimate reason, the presumption of discrimination disappears, and the plaintiff retains the burden of proof to show that the proffered reason was pretext. Thus, the trial court may enter judgment as a matter of law, preventing the case from reaching the jury, at any one of three stages, if (1) the plaintiff fails to establish through circumstantial evidence a prima-facie case of unlawful discrimination, (2) the defendant fails to offer legitimate reasons after the plaintiff establishes a prima-facie circumstantial case, or (3) the plaintiff fails to offer evidence that the defendant's legitimate reasons were pretext. Consider the following Supreme Court case applying the *McDonnell Douglas* burden-shifting framework.

Reeves v. Sanderson Plumbing Products, Inc.,

United States Supreme Court
530 U.S. 133 (2000)

Justice O'CONNOR delivered the opinion of the Court.

This case concerns the kind and amount of evidence necessary to sustain a jury's verdict that an employer unlawfully discriminated on the basis of age. Specifically, we must resolve whether a defendant is entitled to judgment as a matter of law when the plaintiff's case consists exclusively of a prima facie case of discrimination and sufficient evidence for the trier of fact to disbelieve the defendant's legitimate, nondiscriminatory explanation for its action. We must also decide whether the employer was entitled to judgment as a matter of law under the particular circumstances presented here.

I

In October 1995, petitioner Roger Reeves was 57 years old and had spent 40 years in the employ of respondent, Sanderson Plumbing Products, Inc., a manufacturer of toilet seats and covers. [C] Petitioner worked in a department known as the "Hinge Room," where he supervised the "regular line." [C] Joe Oswalt, in his mid-thirties, supervised the Hinge Room's "special line," and Russell Caldwell, the manager of the Hinge Room and age 45, supervised both petitioner and Oswalt. [C] Petitioner's responsibilities included recording the attendance and hours of those under his supervision, and reviewing a weekly report that listed the hours worked by each employee. [C]

In the summer of 1995, Caldwell informed Powe Chesnut, the director of manufacturing and the husband of company president Sandra Sanderson, that "production was down" in the Hinge Room because employees were often absent and were "coming in late and leaving early." [C] Because the monthly attendance reports did not indicate a problem, Chesnut ordered an audit of the Hinge Room's timesheets for July, August, and September of that year. [C] According to Chesnut's testimony, that investigation revealed "numerous timekeeping errors and misrepresentations on the part of Caldwell, Reeves, and Oswalt." [C] Following the audit, Chesnut, along with Dana Jester, vice president of human resources, and Tom Whitaker, vice president of operations, recommended to company president Sanderson that petitioner and Caldwell be fired. [C] In October 1995, Sanderson followed the recommendation and discharged both petitioner and Caldwell. [C]

In June 1996, petitioner filed suit in the United States District Court for the Northern District of Mississippi, contending that he had been fired because of his age in violation of the Age Discrimination in Employment Act of 1967 (ADEA), [] 29 U.S.C. §621 *et seq.* At trial, respondent contended that it had fired petitioner due to his failure to maintain accurate attendance records, while petitioner attempted to demonstrate that respondent's explanation was pretext for age discrimination. [C] Petitioner introduced evidence that he had accurately recorded the attendance and hours of the employees under his supervision, and that Chesnut, whom Oswalt described as wielding "absolute power" within the company, [c], had demonstrated age-based animus in his dealings with petitioner. [C]

During the trial, the District Court twice denied oral motions by respondent for judgment as a matter of law under Rule 50 of the Federal Rules of Civil Procedure, and the case went to the jury. [C] The court instructed the jury that "[i]f the plaintiff fails to prove age was a determinative or motivating factor in the decision to terminate him, then your verdict shall be for the defendant." [C] So charged, the jury returned a verdict in favor of petitioner, awarding him $35,000 in compensatory damages, and found that respondent's age discrimination had been "willfu[l]." [C] The District Court accordingly entered judgment for petitioner in the amount of $70,000, which included $35,000 in liquidated damages based on the jury's finding of willfulness. [C] Respondent then renewed its motion for judgment as a matter of law and alternatively moved for a new trial, while petitioner moved for front pay. [C] The District Court denied respondent's motions and granted petitioner's, awarding him $28,490.80 in front pay for two years' lost income. [C]

The Court of Appeals for the Fifth Circuit reversed, holding that petitioner had not introduced sufficient evidence to sustain the jury's finding of unlawful discrimination. [C] ...

We granted certiorari, [c], to resolve a conflict among the Courts of Appeals as to whether a plaintiff's prima facie case of discrimination (as defined in McDonnell Douglas Corp. v. Green, 411 U.S. 792, 802[] (1973)), combined with sufficient evidence for a reasonable factfinder to reject the employer's nondiscriminatory explanation for its decision, is adequate to sustain a finding of liability for intentional discrimination. ...

II

Under the ADEA, it is "unlawful for an employer ... to fail or refuse to hire or to discharge any individual or otherwise discriminate against any individual with respect to his compensation, terms, conditions, or privileges of employment, because of such individual's age." 29 U.S.C. §623(a)(1). Recognizing that "the question facing triers of fact in discrimination cases is both sensitive and difficult," and that "[t]here will seldom be 'eyewitness' testimony as to the employer's mental processes," U.S. Postal Service Bd. of Governors v. Aikens, 460 U.S. 711, 716[] (1983), the Courts of Appeals, including the Fifth Circuit in this case, have employed some variant of the framework articulated in

McDonnell Douglas to analyze ADEA claims that are based principally on circumstantial evidence. [Cc] ...

McDonnell Douglas and subsequent decisions have "established an allocation of the burden of production and an order for the presentation of proof in ... discriminatory-treatment cases." St. Mary's Honor Center v. Hicks, 509 U.S. 502, 506[] (1993). First, the plaintiff must establish a prima facie case of discrimination. *Ibid.;* Texas Dept. of Community Affairs v. Burdine, 450 U.S. 248, 252-253[] (1981). It is undisputed that petitioner satisfied this burden here: (i) at the time he was fired, he was a member of the class protected by the ADEA..., (ii) he was otherwise qualified for the position of Hinge Room supervisor, (iii) he was discharged by respondent, and (iv) respondent successively hired three persons in their thirties to fill petitioner's position. [C] The burden therefore shifted to respondent to "produc[e] evidence that the plaintiff was rejected, or someone else was preferred, for a legitimate, nondiscriminatory reason." *Burdine, supra,* at 254[]. This burden is one of production, not persuasion; it "can involve no credibility assessment." *St. Mary's Honor Center, supra,* at 509[]. Respondent met this burden by offering admissible evidence sufficient for the trier of fact to conclude that petitioner was fired because of his failure to maintain accurate attendance records. [C] Accordingly, "the *McDonnell Douglas* framework—with its presumptions and burdens"—disappeared, [c], and the sole remaining issue was "discrimination *vel non,*" *Aikens, supra,* at 714[].

Although intermediate evidentiary burdens shift back and forth under this framework, "[t]he ultimate burden of persuading the trier of fact that the defendant intentionally discriminated against the plaintiff remains at all times with the plaintiff." *Burdine,* 450 U.S. at 253[]. And in attempting to satisfy this burden, the plaintiff—once the employer produces sufficient evidence to support a nondiscriminatory explanation for its decision—must be afforded the "opportunity to prove by a preponderance of the evidence that the legitimate reasons offered by the defendant were not its true reasons, but were a pretext for discrimination." *Ibid.;* [c]. That is, the plaintiff may attempt to establish that he was the victim of intentional discrimination "by showing that the employer's proffered explanation is unworthy of credence." *Burdine, supra,* at 256[]. Moreover, although the presumption of discrimination "drops out of the picture" once the defendant meets its burden of production, [c], the trier of fact may still consider the evidence establishing the plaintiff's prima facie case "and inferences properly drawn therefrom ... on the issue of whether the defendant's explanation is pretextual," *Burdine, supra,* at 255n.10[].

In this case, the evidence supporting respondent's explanation for petitioner's discharge consisted primarily of testimony by Chesnut and Sanderson and documentation of petitioner's alleged "shoddy record keeping." [C] Chesnut testified that a 1993 audit of Hinge Room operations revealed "a very lax assembly line" where employees were not adhering to general work rules. [C] As a result of that audit, petitioner was placed on 90 days' probation for unsatisfactory performance. [C] In 1995, Chesnut ordered another investigation of the Hinge Room, which, according to his testimony, revealed that petitioner was not correctly recording the absences and hours of employees. [C] Respondent introduced summaries of that investigation documenting several attendance violations by 12 employees under petitioner's supervision, and noting that each should have been disciplined in some manner. [Cc] ... Sanderson testified that she accepted the recommendation to discharge petitioner because he had "intentionally falsif[ied] company pay records." [C]

Petitioner, however, made a substantial showing that respondent's explanation was false. First, petitioner offered evidence that he had properly maintained the attendance records. ... [B]oth petitioner and Oswalt testified that the company's automated timeclock often failed to scan employees' timecards, so that the timesheets would not record any time of arrival. [Cc] ... On cross-examination, Chesnut acknowledged that the timeclock sometimes malfunctioned, and that if "people were there at their work station[s]" at the start of the shift, the supervisor "would write in seven o'clock." [C] Petitioner also testified that when employees arrived before or stayed after their shifts, he would assign them additional work so they would not be overpaid. [C] ...

Based on this evidence, the Court of Appeals concluded that petitioner "very well may be correct" that "a reasonable jury could have found that [respondent's] explanation for its employment decision was pretextual." [C] Nonetheless, the court held that this showing, standing alone, was insufficient to sustain the jury's finding of liability... . [I]n making this determination, the Court of Appeals ignored the evidence supporting petitioner's prima facie case and challenging respondent's explanation for its decision. [C] The court confined its review of evidence favoring petitioner to that evidence showing that Chesnut had directed derogatory, age-based comments at petitioner, and that Chesnut had singled out petitioner for harsher treatment than younger employees. [C] It is therefore apparent that the court believed that only this additional evidence of discrimination was relevant to whether the jury's verdict should stand. That is, the Court of Appeals proceeded from the assumption that a prima facie case of discrimination, combined with sufficient evidence for the trier of fact to disbelieve the defendant's legitimate, nondiscriminatory reason for its decision, is insufficient as a matter of law to sustain a jury's finding of intentional discrimination.

In so reasoning, the Court of Appeals misconceived the evidentiary burden borne by plaintiffs who attempt to prove intentional discrimination through indirect evidence. This much is evident from our decision in *St. Mary's Honor Center*. There we held that the factfinder's rejection of the employer's legitimate, nondiscriminatory reason for its action does not *compel* judgment for the plaintiff. 509 U.S. at 511[]. The ultimate question is whether the employer intentionally discriminated, and proof that "the employer's proffered reason is unpersuasive, or even obviously contrived, does not necessarily establish that the plaintiff's proffered reason ... is correct." *Id.* at 524[]. In other words, "[i]t is not enough ... to *dis* believe the employer; the factfinder must *believe* the plaintiff's explanation of intentional discrimination." *Id.* at 519.

In reaching this conclusion, however, we reasoned that it is *permissible* for the trier of fact to infer the ultimate fact of discrimination from the falsity of the employer's explanation. Specifically, we stated: "The factfinder's disbelief of the reasons put forward by the defendant ... may, together with the elements of the prima facie case, suffice to show intentional discrimination. Thus, rejection of the defendant's proffered reasons will *permit* the trier of fact to infer the ultimate fact of intentional discrimination." *Id.*, at 511[].

Proof that the defendant's explanation is unworthy of credence is simply one form of circumstantial evidence that is probative of intentional discrimination, and it may be quite persuasive. ... In appropriate circumstances, the trier of fact can reasonably infer from the falsity of the explanation that the employer is dissembling to cover up a discriminatory purpose. Such an inference is consistent with the general principle of evidence law that the factfinder is entitled to consider a party's dishonesty about a material fact as "affirmative evidence of guilt." Wright v. West, 505 U.S. 277, 296[] (1992); [cc]. ... Thus, a plaintiff's prima facie case, combined with sufficient evidence to find that the employer's asserted justification is false, may permit the trier of fact to conclude that the employer unlawfully discriminated.

This is not to say that such a showing by the plaintiff will *always* be adequate to sustain a jury's finding of liability. Certainly there will be instances where, although the plaintiff has established a prima facie case and set forth sufficient evidence to reject the defendant's explanation, no rational factfinder could conclude that the action was discriminatory. For instance, an employer would be entitled to judgment as a matter of law if the record conclusively revealed some other, nondiscriminatory reason for the employer's decision, or if the plaintiff created only a weak issue of fact as to whether the employer's reason was untrue and there was abundant and uncontroverted independent evidence that no discrimination had occurred. [Cc] To hold otherwise would be effectively to insulate an entire category of employment discrimination cases from review under Rule 50, and we have reiterated that trial courts should not "'treat discrimination differently from other ultimate questions of fact.'" *St. Mary's Honor Center, supra,* at 524[] (quoting *Aikens,* 460 U.S. at 716).

Whether judgment as a matter of law is appropriate in any particular case will depend on a number of factors. Those include the strength of the plaintiff's prima facie case, the probative value of the proof that the employer's explanation is false, and any other evidence that supports the employer's case and that properly may be considered on a motion for judgment as a matter of law. [C] ... [B]ecause a prima facie case and sufficient evidence to reject the employer's explanation may permit a finding of liability, the Court of Appeals erred in proceeding from the premise that a plaintiff must always introduce additional, independent evidence of discrimination.

III

A

The remaining question is whether, despite the Court of Appeals' misconception of petitioner's evidentiary burden, respondent was nonetheless entitled to judgment as a matter of law. Under Rule 50, a court should render judgment as a matter of law when "a party has been fully heard on an issue and there is no legally sufficient evidentiary basis for a reasonable jury to find for that party on that issue." Fed. Rule Civ. Proc. 50(a); [c]. ...

... [I]n entertaining a motion for judgment as a matter of law, the court should review all of the evidence in the record.

In doing so, however, the court must draw all reasonable inferences in favor of the nonmoving party, and it may not make credibility determinations or weigh the evidence. [Cc] Thus, although the court should review the record as a whole, it must disregard all evidence favorable to the moving party that the jury is not required to believe. [C] That is, the court should give credence to the evidence favoring the nonmovant... .

B

Applying this standard here, it is apparent that respondent was not entitled to judgment as a matter of law. In this case, in addition to establishing a prima facie case of discrimination and creating a jury issue as to the falsity of the employer's explanation, petitioner introduced additional evidence that Chesnut was motivated by age-based animus and was principally responsible for petitioner's firing. Petitioner testified that Chesnut had told him that he "was so old [he] must have come over on the Mayflower" and, on one occasion when petitioner was having difficulty starting a machine, that he "was too damn old to do [his] job." [C] ... Oswalt, roughly 24 years younger than petitioner, corroborated that there was an "obvious difference" in how Chesnut treated them. [C] ...

In holding that the record contained insufficient evidence to sustain the jury's verdict, the Court of Appeals misapplied the standard of review dictated by Rule 50. Again, the court disregarded critical evidence favorable to petitioner—namely, the evidence supporting petitioner's prima facie case and undermining respondent's nondiscriminatory explanation. [C] The court also failed to draw all reasonable inferences in favor of petitioner. ... [T]he Court of Appeals impermissibly substituted its judgment concerning the weight of the evidence for the jury's.

The ultimate question in every employment discrimination case involving a claim of disparate treatment is whether the plaintiff was the victim of intentional discrimination. Given the evidence in the record supporting petitioner, we see no reason to subject the parties to an additional round of litigation before the Court of Appeals rather than to resolve the matter here. ... Given that petitioner established a prima facie case of discrimination, introduced enough evidence for the jury to reject respondent's explanation, and produced additional evidence of age-based animus, there was sufficient evidence for the jury to find that respondent had intentionally discriminated. The District Court was therefore correct to submit the case to the jury, and the Court of Appeals erred in overturning its verdict.

For these reasons, the judgment of the Court of Appeals is reversed.

It is so ordered.

Justice GINSBURG, concurring[, omitted].

INQUIRY

Procedure. *Reeves v. Sanderson Plumbing Products, Inc.,* involved pre- and post-judgment review of the sufficiency of the evidence. The next chapter further explores challenges to verdicts and judgments. The point here is that parties first challenge the sufficiency of evidence at trial before submission to the jury and then again by renewing the motion after trial within the 28-day period Rule 50(b) specifies. Judgment as a matter of law is a procedural device that begins during trial as a challenge to the evidence and, if denied, one that a party must renew in the trial court after trial. The defendants in *Reeves v. Sanderson Plumbing Products, Inc.*, moved under Rule 50(a) for judgment as a matter of law not once but *twice* during the course of the trial before the trial judge submitted the case to the jury, and again in the trial court after trial. Other motions, particularly motions judgment notwithstanding the verdict and new trial, attack the jury's verdict, the conduct of opposing parties and counsel, and the overall conduct of the trial (even the trial judge's conduct). By contrast, Rule 50 motions for judgment as a matter of law are efforts to constrain or limit the jury's authority to its proper bounds in deciding disputed factual issues. A party must therefore first make a Rule 50 motion before the jury begins deliberations. Consider the following Supreme Court case highlighting the timing and significance of motions for judgment as a matter of law during and after trial, and before appeal.

Unitherm Food System, Inc. v. Swift-Ekrich, Inc.,

United States Supreme Court
546 U.S. 394 (2006)

Justice THOMAS delivered the opinion of the Court.

Ordinarily, a party in a civil jury trial that believes the evidence is legally insufficient to support an adverse jury verdict will seek a judgment as a matter of law by filing a motion pursuant to Federal Rule of Civil Procedure 50(a) before submission of the case to the jury, and then (if the Rule 50(a) motion is not granted and the jury subsequently decides against that party) a motion pursuant to Rule 50(b). In this case, however, the respondent filed a Rule 50(a) motion before the verdict, but did not file a Rule 50(b) motion after the verdict. Nor did respondent request a new trial under Rule 59. The Court of Appeals nevertheless proceeded to review the sufficiency of the evidence and, upon a finding that the evidence was insufficient, remanded the case for a new trial. Because our cases addressing the requirements of Rule 50 compel a contrary result, we reverse.

I

The genesis of the underlying litigation in this case was ConAgra's attempt to enforce its ['027] patent... . In early 2000, ConAgra issued a general warning to companies who sold equipment and processes for browning precooked meats explaining that it intended to "'aggressively protect all of [its] rights under [the '027] patent.'" [C] Petitioner Unitherm sold such processes, but did not receive ConAgra's warning. ... Jennie-O, a direct competitor, received ConAgra's correspondence and undertook an investigation to determine its rights and responsibilities with regard to the '027 patent. Jennie-O determined that the browning process it had purchased from Unitherm was the same as the process described in the '027 patent. Jennie-O further determined that the '027 patent was invalid because Unitherm's president had invented the process described in that patent six years before ConAgra filed its patent application.

Consistent with these determinations, Jennie-O and Unitherm jointly sued ConAgra in the Western District of Oklahoma[seeking] ... a declaration that the '027 patent was invalid and unenforceable, and alleg[ing] that ConAgra had violated §2 of the Sherman Act, [] 15 U.S.C. §2, by attempting to enforce a patent that was obtained by committing fraud on the Patent and Trademark Office

(PTO). See Walker Process Equipment, Inc. v. Food Machinery & Chemical Corp., 382 U.S. 172, 174[] (1965)... . The District Court construed the '027 patent and determined that it was invalid based on Unitherm's prior public use and sale of the process described therein. 35 U.S.C. § 102(b). After dismissing Jennie-O for lack of antitrust standing, the District Court allowed Unitherm's *Walker Process* claim to proceed to trial. Prior to the court's submission of the case to the jury, ConAgra moved for a directed verdict under Rule 50(a) based on legal insufficiency of the evidence. The District Court denied that motion.[fn] The jury returned a verdict for Unitherm, and ConAgra neither renewed its motion for judgment as a matter of law pursuant to Rule 50(b), nor moved for a new trial on antitrust liability pursuant to Rule 59.[fn]

On appeal to the Federal Circuit, ConAgra maintained that there was insufficient evidence to sustain the jury's *Walker Process* verdict. ...

... [T]he Federal Circuit concluded that, although Unitherm had presented sufficient evidence to support a determination that ConAgra had attempted to enforce a patent that it had obtained through fraud on the PTO, [c], Unitherm had failed to present evidence sufficient to support the remaining elements of its antitrust claim. [c] Accordingly, it vacated the jury's judgment in favor of Unitherm and remanded for a new trial. We ... now reverse.

II

Federal Rule of Civil Procedure 50 sets forth the procedural requirements for challenging the sufficiency of the evidence in a civil jury trial and establishes two stages for such challenges-prior to submission of the case to the jury, and after the verdict and entry of judgment. Rule 50(a) allows a party to challenge the sufficiency of the evidence prior to submission of the case to the jury, and authorizes the district court to grant such motions at the court's discretion... . Rule 50(b), by contrast, sets forth the procedural requirements for renewing a sufficiency of the evidence challenge after the jury verdict and entry of judgment. ...

This Court has addressed the implications of a party's failure to file a postverdict motion under Rule 50(b) on several occasions and in a variety of procedural contexts. This Court has concluded that, "[i]n the absence of such a motion" an "appellate court [is] without power to direct the District Court to enter judgment contrary to the one it had permitted to stand." Cone v. West Virginia Pulp & Paper Co., 330 U.S. 212, 218[] (1947). This Court has similarly concluded that a party's failure to file a Rule 50(b) motion deprives the appellate court of the power to order the entry of judgment in favor of that party where the district court directed the jury's verdict, Globe Liquor Co. v. San Roman, 332 U.S. 571[] (1948), and where the district court expressly reserved a party's preverdict motion for a directed verdict and then denied that motion after the verdict was returned, Johnson v. New York, N.H. & H.R. Co., 344 U.S. 48[] (1952). A postverdict motion is necessary because "[d]etermination of whether a new trial should be granted or a judgment entered under Rule 50(b) calls for the judgment in the first instance of the judge who saw and heard the witnesses and has the feel of the case which no appellate printed transcript can impart."[fn] *Cone, supra,* at 216[]. Moreover, the "requirement of a timely application for judgment after verdict is not an idle motion" because it "is ... an essential part of the rule, firmly grounded in principles of fairness." *Johnson, supra,* at 53[].

The foregoing authorities lead us to reverse the judgment below. ... This Court's observations about the necessity of a postverdict motion under Rule 50(b), and the benefits of the district court's input at that stage, apply with equal force whether a party is seeking judgment as a matter of law or simply a new trial. ... [T]his Court has determined that a party may only pursue on appeal a particular avenue of relief available under Rule 50(b), namely, the entry of judgment *or a new trial,* when that party has complied with the Rule's filing requirements by requesting that particular relief below. See *Johnson, supra,* at 54[]... .

Our determination that respondent's failure to comply with Rule 50(b) forecloses its challenge to the sufficiency of the evidence is further validated by the purported basis of respondent's appeal, namely, the District Court's denial of respondent's preverdict Rule 50(a) motion. As an initial matter, *Cone, Globe Liquor,* and *Johnson* unequivocally establish that the precise subject matter of a party's Rule 50(a) motion—namely, its entitlement to judgment as a matter of law—cannot be appealed unless that motion is renewed pursuant to Rule 50(b). ... [I]f, as in *Cone, Globe Liquor,* and *Johnson,* a litigant that has failed to file a Rule 50(b) motion is foreclosed from seeking the relief it sought in its Rule 50(a) motion—*i.e.,* the entry of judgment—then surely respondent is foreclosed from seeking a new trial, relief it did not and could not seek in its preverdict motion. In short, respondent never sought a new trial before the District Court, and thus forfeited its right to do so on appeal. Yakus v. United States, 321 U.S. 414, 444[] (1944) ("No procedural principle is more familiar to this Court than that a ... right may be forfeited ... by the failure to make timely assertion of the right before a tribunal having jurisdiction to determine it").

The text of Rule 50(b) confirms that respondent's preverdict Rule 50(a) motion did not present the District Court with the option of ordering a new trial. That text provides that a district court may only order a new trial on the basis of issues raised in a preverdict Rule 50(a) motion when "ruling on a renewed motion" under Rule 50(b). Accordingly, even if the District Court was inclined to grant a new trial on the basis of arguments raised in respondent's preverdict motion, it was without the power to do so under Rule 50(b) absent a postverdict motion pursuant to that Rule. Consequently, the Court of Appeals was similarly powerless. ...

... [T]he District Court's denial of respondent's preverdict motion cannot form the basis of respondent's appeal, because the denial of that motion was not error. It was merely an exercise of the District Court's discretion, in accordance with the text of the Rule and the accepted practice of permitting the jury to make an initial judgment about the sufficiency of the evidence. The only error here was counsel's failure to file a postverdict motion pursuant to Rule 50(b).[fn]

For the foregoing reasons, we hold that since respondent failed to renew its preverdict motion as specified in Rule 50(b), there was no basis for review of respondent's sufficiency of the evidence challenge in the Court of Appeals. The judgment of the Court of Appeals is reversed.[fn]

It is so ordered.

Justice STEVENS, with whom Justice KENNEDY joins, dissenting.

Murphy's law applies to trial lawyers as well as pilots. Even an expert will occasionally blunder. For that reason Congress has preserved the federal appeals courts' power to correct plain error, even though trial counsel's omission will ordinarily give rise to a binding waiver. This is not a case, in my view, in which the authority of the appellate court is limited by an explicit statute or controlling rule. The spirit of the Federal Rules of Civil Procedure favors preservation of a court's power to avoid manifestly unjust results in exceptional cases. ...

Nothing in Rule 50(b) limits this statutory grant of power to appellate courts; while a party's failure to make a Rule 50(b) motion precludes the *district court* from directing a verdict in that party's favor, the Rule does not purport to strip the courts of appeals of the authority to review district court judgments or to order such relief as "may be just under the circumstances." ...

I respectfully dissent.

INQUIRY

Re-Examination. If it is not clear from the above *Unitherm Food System* opinion, there is another reason beyond Rule 50 why trial judges may not substitute their judgment for the judgment of the jury unless a party first makes a Rule 50 motion before the jury begins its deliberations. Recall that the Seventh Amendment's second clause counsels that the court must not re-examine the facts supporting a jury verdict ("no fact tried by a jury, shall be otherwise re-examined"). The Amendment's plain language against *re*-examining facts implies what was historically the case that judges could initially *examine* them before the jury's verdict. *See* Baltimore & Carolina Line v. Redman, 295 U.S. 654 (1935) (post-verdict judgment as a matter of law is unconstitutional re-examination without motion before deliberations). Hence, we have today Rule 50's structure requiring in Rule 50(a) that a party make a motion for judgment as a matter of law before the jury begins deliberations and only later *renew* the motion after verdict and judgment. It may sound a little strained or technical, but to renew a motion means that the trial judge will look again at the facts as they existed at the time of the initial motion rather than to examine the facts in light of the jury's verdict. The practice that Rule 50 authorizes makes sense even if one could construe it as dodging the intent of the Seventh Amendment. Rule 50 permits a trial judge to reserve decision on a motion for judgment as a matter of law until after the trial judge sees if the jury agrees that the movant should prevail. If so, then the trial judge avoids an appealable decision. If not, then the trial judge still gets to rule consistent with the trial judge's evaluation of the sufficiency of the evidence.

Practice

The jury filed out of the courtroom to deliberate, for the first time looking not just solemn but weighted by the burden of responsibility. Not defense counsel. The moment that the door had closed behind the jurors, the hometown defense counsel was on his way up to the bench to chat amiably with his friends the trial judge, court reporter, and judicial secretary—so swiftly (the out-of-town plaintiff's lawyer noticed) that the trial judge hardly had time to call the court in recess. The trial judge melted away into chambers, while defense counsel and the court staff made loud wagers on how quickly the jury would return with a no-cause verdict. Twenty minutes was the prevailing guess.

The plaintiff's lawyer was not so sure. The plaintiff's lawyer thought that defense counsel had made a huge blunder when he left a pony-tailed biker on the jury, waiving peremptories. The defendant homemaker had hit the plaintiff motorcyclist at an intersection, crippling the motorcyclist who might have been speeding over a hill and hard for the homemaker to see. Yet it was not a case for the defense to be overly confident.

Suddenly, barely more than 20 minutes after the jury left, the bailiff poked his head in the courtroom saying that the jury had reached its verdict. Defense counsel and the court staff smiled broadly, laughing at their accurate wagers. The judge took the bench, and the jury filed back in. The judge asked the jurors if they had selected a foreperson. The biker rose. The plaintiff's lawyer glanced at defense counsel who looked like he had blanched. "And what is your verdict?" the trial judge intoned. "We find for the plaintiff," the biker answered.

Judicial Qualifications. Judicial control over jury proceedings raises an implicit issue having to do with judicial qualifications. Trial judges tend to be acutely aware of the prospect for appellate review. Trial judges know when an appellate court reverses them because they get the case back, often to repeat proceedings or conduct additional proceedings requiring the participation of one or more unhappy parties. Like anyone, trial judges do not like to have to do the same thing twice simply because of an error the first time. They also value their reputation before the local bench and bar, and regional and national professional associations. Like anyone, they do not like to be wrong and do not like to be embarrassed. Trial judges will on occasion brag of their high rate of appellate affirmance. Judicial codes of conduct also bind judges whose conduct is subject to judicial tenure commission review for code violations. Federal statute also authorizes a procedure for individuals to complain to the chief judge of a district about judicial misconduct. *See* 28 U.S.C. §§351 et seq. Trial judges' system of professional accountability is thus quite different from the accountability system—family members, friends, neighbors—of jurors.

Recusal. Trial judges are also subject to recusal in specific cases. Recusal is a process by which a party can challenge a trial judge's qualifications to serve, either based on circumstances or for specific demonstrated bias, causing the trial judge to voluntarily step aside or for the court to remove the judge. The federal recusal statutes, 28 U.S.C. §§144, 455, provide both specific and general grounds for recusal. Section 144 permits a party to have a trial judge removed based on an affidavit asserting personal bias or prejudice, reciting the grounds for the belief. The party must accompany the affidavit with counsel's certification that the party makes it in good faith. Section 455 requires trial judges to self-disqualify where "impartiality might reasonably be questioned" and in specific instances such as having previously served as a lawyer in the case or having a financial interest in the case. A party's decision whether to seek recusal is strategic in nature, particularly if a request fails, but even if the request succeeds. *See* Blank v. Sullivan & Cromwell, 418 F.Supp. 1 (S.D. N.Y. 1975) (African-American, female, former civil-rights lawyer judge denies motion to recuse from case involving African-American female civil rights plaintiff because "no judge on this court could hear this case" based on such race and sex profiling). There is a strong presumption that federal trial judges are qualified and would step voluntarily aside if warranted. Review the following federal recusal statutes before reading a recent Supreme Court case on recusal standards required by due process.

28 U.S.C. §144. Bias or prejudice of judge
Whenever a party to any proceeding in a district court makes and files a timely and sufficient affidavit that the judge before whom the matter is pending has a personal bias or prejudice either against him or in favor of any adverse party, such judge shall proceed no further therein, but another judge shall be assigned to hear such proceeding. The affidavit shall state the facts and the reasons for the belief that bias or prejudice exists, and shall be filed not less than ten days before the beginning of the term at which the proceeding is to be heard, or good cause shall be shown for failure to file it within such time. A party may file only one such affidavit in any case. It shall be accompanied by a certificate of counsel of record stating that it is made in good faith.

28 U.S.C. §455. Disqualification of justice, judge, or magistrate judge
(a) Any justice, judge, or magistrate judge of the United States shall disqualify himself in any proceeding in which his impartiality might reasonably be questioned.
(b) He shall also disqualify himself in the following circumstances:
(1) Where he has a personal bias or prejudice concerning a party, or personal knowledge of disputed evidentiary facts concerning the proceeding;
(2) Where in private practice he served as lawyer in the matter in controversy, or a lawyer with whom he previously practiced law served during such association as a lawyer concerning the matter, or the judge or such lawyer has been a material witness concerning it;
(3) Where he has served in governmental employment and in such capacity participated as counsel, adviser or material witness concerning the proceeding or expressed an opinion concerning the merits of the particular case in controversy;
(4) He knows that he, individually or as a fiduciary, or his spouse or minor child residing in his household, has a financial interest in the subject matter in controversy or in a party to the proceeding, or any other interest that could be substantially affected by the outcome of the proceeding;
(5) He or his spouse, or a person within the third degree of relationship to either of them, or the spouse of such a person:
(i) Is a party to the proceeding, or an officer, director, or trustee of a party;
(ii) Is acting as a lawyer in the proceeding;
(iii) Is known by the judge to have an interest that could be substantially affected by the outcome of the proceeding;
(iv) Is to the judge's knowledge likely to be a material witness in the proceeding.
(c) A judge should inform himself about his personal and fiduciary financial interests, and make a reasonable effort to inform himself about the personal financial interests of his spouse and minor children residing in his household. ...

Caperton v. A.T. Massey Coal Co.,

United States Supreme Court
__ U.S. __, 129 S.Ct. 2252 (2009)

Justice KENNEDY delivered the opinion of the Court.

In this case the Supreme Court of Appeals of West Virginia reversed a trial court judgment, which had entered a jury verdict of $50 million. Five justices heard the case, and the vote to reverse was 3 to 2. The question presented is whether the Due Process Clause of the Fourteenth Amendment was violated when one of the justices in the majority denied a recusal motion. The basis for the motion was that the justice had received campaign contributions in an extraordinary amount from, and through the efforts of, the board chairman and principal officer of the corporation found liable for the damages.

Under our precedents there are objective standards that require recusal when "the probability of actual bias on the part of the judge or decisionmaker is too high to be constitutionally tolerable." Withrow v. Larkin, 421 U.S. 35, 47[] (1975). Applying those precedents, we find that, in all the circumstances of this case, due process requires recusal.

I

In August 2002 a West Virginia jury returned a verdict that found respondents A.T. Massey Coal Co. and its affiliates (hereinafter Massey) liable for fraudulent misrepresentation, concealment, and tortious interference with existing contractual relations. The jury awarded petitioners ... Caperton ... the sum of $50 million in compensatory and punitive damages. ...

Don Blankenship is Massey's chairman, chief executive officer, and president. After the verdict but before the appeal, West Virginia held its 2004 judicial elections. Knowing the Supreme Court of Appeals of West Virginia would consider the appeal in the case, Blankenship decided to support an attorney who sought to replace Justice McGraw. Justice McGraw was a candidate for reelection to that court. The attorney who sought to replace him was Brent Benjamin.

In addition to contributing the $1,000 statutory maximum to Benjamin's campaign committee, Blankenship donated almost $2.5 million to "And For The Sake Of The Kids," a political organization formed under 26 U.S.C. §527. The §527 organization opposed McGraw and supported Benjamin. [C] Blankenship's donations accounted for more than two-thirds of the total funds it raised. [C] This was not all. Blankenship spent, in addition, just over $500,000 on independent expenditures—for direct mailings and letters soliciting donations as well as television and newspaper advertisements—"'to support ... Brent Benjamin.'" [C]

To provide some perspective, Blankenship's $3 million in contributions were more than the total amount spent by all other Benjamin supporters and three times the amount spent by Benjamin's own committee. [C] Caperton contends that Blankenship spent $1 million more than the total amount spent by the campaign committees of both candidates combined. [C]

Benjamin won. ...

In October 2005, before Massey filed its petition for appeal in West Virginia's highest court, Caperton moved to disqualify now-Justice Benjamin under the Due Process Clause and the West Virginia Code of Judicial Conduct, based on the conflict caused by Blankenship's campaign involvement. Justice Benjamin denied the motion in April 2006. He indicated that he "carefully considered the bases and accompanying exhibits proffered by the movants." But he found "no objective information ... to show that this Justice has a bias for or against any litigant, that this Justice has prejudged the matters which comprise this litigation, or that this Justice will be anything but fair and impartial." [C] In

December 2006 Massey filed its petition for appeal to challenge the adverse jury verdict. The West Virginia Supreme Court of Appeals granted review.

In November 2007 that court reversed the $50 million verdict against Massey. …

Caperton sought rehearing, and the parties moved for disqualification of three of the five justices who decided the appeal. Photos had surfaced of Justice Maynard vacationing with Blankenship in the French Riviera while the case was pending. [C] Justice Maynard granted Caperton's recusal motion. On the other side Justice Starcher granted Massey's recusal motion, apparently based on his public criticism of Blankenship's role in the 2004 elections. In his recusal memorandum Justice Starcher urged Justice Benjamin to recuse himself as well. He noted that "Blankenship's bestowal of his personal wealth, political tactics, and 'friendship' have created a cancer in the affairs of this Court." [C] Justice Benjamin declined Justice Starcher's suggestion and denied Caperton's recusal motion.

The court granted rehearing. Justice Benjamin, now in the capacity of acting chief justice, selected Judges Cookman and Fox to replace the recused justices. Caperton moved a third time for disqualification… . Caperton … included the results of a public opinion poll, which indicated that over 67% of West Virginians doubted Justice Benjamin would be fair and impartial. Justice Benjamin again refused to withdraw… .

In April 2008 a divided court again reversed the jury verdict, and again it was a 3-to-2 decision. …

We granted certiorari. [C]

II

… [T]he Court has recognized … [that] "most matters relating to judicial disqualification [do] not rise to a constitutional level." FTC v. Cement Institute, 333 U.S. 683, 702[] (1948). The early and leading case on the subject is Tumey v. Ohio, 273 U.S. 510, [523] (1927). There, the Court stated that "matters of kinship, personal bias, state policy, remoteness of interest, would seem generally to be matters merely of legislative discretion." [C]

The *Tumey* Court concluded that the Due Process Clause incorporated the common-law rule that a judge must recuse himself when he has "a direct, personal, substantial, pecuniary interest" in a case. *Ibid.* This rule reflects the maxim that "[n]o man is allowed to be a judge in his own cause; because his interest would certainly bias his judgment, and, not improbably, corrupt his integrity." The Federalist No. 10, p. 59 (J. Cooke ed.1961) (J. Madison); [c]. …

… [T]he Court has identified additional instances which, as an objective matter, require recusal. These are circumstances "in which experience teaches that the probability of actual bias on the part of the judge or decisionmaker is too high to be constitutionally tolerable." Withrow[v. Larkin], 421 U.S.[35,] 47[(1975)]. …

The first involved the emergence of local tribunals where a judge had a financial interest in the outcome of a case, although the interest was less than what would have been considered personal or direct at common law. …

This was the problem addressed in *Tumey*. There, the mayor of a village had the authority to sit as a judge (with no jury) to try those accused of violating a state law prohibiting the possession of alcoholic beverages. Inherent in this structure were two potential conflicts. First, the mayor received a salary supplement for performing judicial duties, and the funds for that compensation derived from the fines assessed in a case. No fines were assessed upon acquittal. The mayor-judge thus received a salary supplement only if he convicted the defendant. 273 U.S., at 520[]. Second, sums from the criminal fines were deposited to the village's general treasury fund for village improvements and repairs. *Id.* at 522[].

The Court held that the Due Process Clause required disqualification "both because of [the mayor-judge's] direct pecuniary interest in the outcome, and because of his official motive to convict and to graduate the fine to help the financial needs of the village." *Id.* at 535[]. ... The Court articulated the controlling principle: "Every procedure which would offer a possible temptation to the average man as a judge to forget the burden of proof required to convict the defendant, or which might lead him not to hold the balance nice, clear and true between the State and the accused, denies the latter due process of law." *Ibid.* The Court was thus concerned with more than the traditional common-law prohibition on direct pecuniary interest. It was also concerned with a more general concept of interests that tempt adjudicators to disregard neutrality.

This concern with conflicts resulting from financial incentives was elaborated in Ward v. Monroeville, 409 U.S. 57[] (1972), which invalidated a conviction in another mayor's court. In *Monroeville,* unlike in *Tumey,* the mayor received no money; instead, the fines the mayor assessed went to the town's general fisc. ... The principle, instead, turned on the "'possible temptation'" the mayor might face; the mayor's "executive responsibilities for village finances may make him partisan to maintain the high level of contribution [to those finances] from the mayor's court." *Ibid.* As the Court reiterated in another case that Term, "the [judge's] financial stake need not be as direct or positive as it appeared to be in *Tumey.*" Gibson v. Berryhill, 411 U.S. 564, 579[] (1973)... .

The second instance requiring recusal that was not discussed at common law emerged in the criminal contempt context, where a judge had no pecuniary interest in the case but was challenged because of a conflict arising from his participation in an earlier proceeding. ...

III

Based on the principles described in these cases we turn to the issue before us. This problem arises in the context of judicial elections, a framework not presented in the precedents we have reviewed and discussed.

Caperton contends that Blankenship's pivotal role in getting Justice Benjamin elected created a constitutionally intolerable probability of actual bias. Though not a bribe or criminal influence, Justice Benjamin would nevertheless feel a debt of gratitude to Blankenship for his extraordinary efforts to get him elected. That temptation, Caperton claims, is as strong and inherent in human nature as was the conflict the Court confronted in *Tumey* and *Monroeville* when a mayor-judge (or the city) benefited financially from a defendant's conviction, as well as the conflict ... when a judge was the object of a defendant's contempt.

Justice Benjamin was careful to address the recusal motions and explain his reasons why, on his view of the controlling standard, disqualification was not in order. ... We do not question his subjective findings of impartiality and propriety. Nor do we determine whether there was actual bias.

Following accepted principles of our legal tradition respecting the proper performance of judicial functions, judges often inquire into their subjective motives and purposes in the ordinary course of deciding a case. This does not mean the inquiry is a simple one. …

The difficulties of inquiring into actual bias, and the fact that the inquiry is often a private one, simply underscore the need for objective rules. Otherwise there may be no adequate protection against a judge who simply misreads or misapprehends the real motives at work in deciding the case. The judge's own inquiry into actual bias, then, is not one that the law can easily superintend or review, though actual bias, if disclosed, no doubt would be grounds for appropriate relief. In lieu of exclusive reliance on that personal inquiry, or on appellate review of the judge's determination respecting actual bias, the Due Process Clause has been implemented by objective standards that do not require proof of actual bias. See *Tumey,* 273 U.S. at 532[]; [cc]. In defining these standards the Court has asked whether, "under a realistic appraisal of psychological tendencies and human weakness," the interest "poses such a risk of actual bias or prejudgment that the practice must be forbidden if the guarantee of due process is to be adequately implemented." *Withrow,* 421 U.S. at 47[].

We turn to the influence at issue in this case. Not every campaign contribution by a litigant or attorney creates a probability of bias that requires a judge's recusal, but this is an exceptional case. [C] We conclude that there is a serious risk of actual bias—based on objective and reasonable perceptions—when a person with a personal stake in a particular case had a significant and disproportionate influence in placing the judge on the case by raising funds or directing the judge's election campaign when the case was pending or imminent. The inquiry centers on the contribution's relative size in comparison to the total amount of money contributed to the campaign, the total amount spent in the election, and the apparent effect such contribution had on the outcome of the election.

Applying this principle, we conclude that Blankenship's campaign efforts had a significant and disproportionate influence in placing Justice Benjamin on the case. …

Massey responds that Blankenship's support, while significant, did not cause Benjamin's victory. In the end the people of West Virginia elected him, and they did so based on many reasons other than Blankenship's efforts. Massey points out that every major state newspaper, but one, endorsed Benjamin. [C] It also contends that then-Justice McGraw cost himself the election by giving a speech during the campaign, a speech the opposition seized upon for its own advantage. [C] …

Whether Blankenship's campaign contributions were a necessary and sufficient cause of Benjamin's victory is not the proper inquiry. Much like determining whether a judge is actually biased, proving what ultimately drives the electorate to choose a particular candidate is a difficult endeavor, not likely to lend itself to a certain conclusion. … Due process requires an objective inquiry into whether the contributor's influence on the election under all the circumstances "would offer a possible temptation to the average ... judge to ... lead him not to hold the balance nice, clear and true." *Tumey, supra,* at 532[]. In an election decided by fewer than 50,000 votes… , Blankenship's campaign contributions—in comparison to the total amount contributed to the campaign, as well as the total amount spent in the election—had a significant and disproportionate influence on the electoral outcome. And the risk that Blankenship's influence engendered actual bias is sufficiently substantial that it "must be forbidden if the guarantee of due process is to be adequately implemented." *Withrow, supra,* at 47[].

The temporal relationship between the campaign contributions, the justice's election, and the pendency of the case is also critical. It was reasonably foreseeable, when the campaign contributions were made, that the pending case would be before the newly elected justice. …

IV

Our decision today addresses an extraordinary situation where the Constitution requires recusal. Massey and its *amici* predict that various adverse consequences will follow from recognizing a constitutional violation here—ranging from a flood of recusal motions to unnecessary interference with judicial elections. We disagree. The facts now before us are extreme by any measure. …

The judgment of the Supreme Court of Appeals of West Virginia is reversed, and the case is remanded for further proceedings not inconsistent with this opinion.

It is so ordered.

Chief Justice ROBERTS, with whom Justice SCALIA, Justice THOMAS, and Justice ALITO join, dissenting.

INQUIRY

Standard. Judicial campaigns have grown increasingly divisive, notorious, and expensive as the electorate perceives that the ideology or political party of the candidates will affect their judicial decisions on important issues of the day. With it, funding of judicial campaigns and the potential influence that funding might possibly buy is increasingly an administrative issue. Statutes, court rules, judicial-conduct rules, and professional norms on recusal have their own influence. *Caperton v. W.A. Massey Coal Co.* holds that recusal becomes a constitutional due-process issue only when there is a "serious risk of actual bias" based on "objective and reasonable perceptions." It further holds that due process requires recusal based on campaign contributions only when a party or party representative in a case before the judge "had a significant and disproportionate influence in placing the judge on the case by raising funds or directing the judge's election campaign when the case was pending or imminent." Further, "significant" and "disproportionate" influence depends on the contribution amount relative to the total campaign spending and its likely effect on the election's outcome. How workable is that standard? Is the *Caperton* ruling likely to reduce disproportionate campaign contributions? Do you think Blankenship would have made the same efforts and contributions on Justice Benjamin's behalf if the Supreme Court had already established (in a prior case) *Caperton's* constitutional standard for recusal?

B. Order of Trial

Trial skills courses address in detail the conduct of trial. Consider here trial's basic structure and the applicable *Federal Rules of Civil Procedure.* As you have seen above, jury trials begin with the court empaneling the jury. The trial judge has the jury sworn and reads preliminary instructions. Beyond that point, the trial judge actually has considerable discretion as to the conduct of trial and order of proofs. One might think that elaborate rules dictate trial procedures. They do not. There are few if any written rules of procedure governing the conduct of trial and order of proofs. The very few *Federal Rules of Civil Procedure* that directly address trial proofs have primarily to do with recording testimony, objections, and rulings in open court, not with the conduct of trial and order of proofs. Given the absence of rule guidance and the trial judge's virtually unfettered authority to conduct the trial and order the proofs as the trial judge best determines, one might think that trials are highly unpredictable. They are not. Trial judges seldom exercise their discretion. Instead, trial judges follow highly predictable and traditional customs in the conduct of trial and order of proofs. Read FED. R. CIV. P. 43, 44, 46, and 80, on the conduct of trial, where you will find no real guidance, before considering trial customs.

FED. R. CIV. P. 43. Taking Testimony
(a) IN OPEN COURT. At trial, the witnesses' testimony must be taken in open court unless a federal statute, the Federal Rules of Evidence, these rules, or other rules adopted by the Supreme Court provide otherwise. For good cause in compelling circumstances and with appropriate safeguards, the court may permit testimony in open court by contemporaneous transmission from a different location.
(b) AFFIRMATION INSTEAD OF AN OATH. When these rules require an oath, a solemn affirmation suffices.
(c) EVIDENCE ON A MOTION. When a motion relies on facts outside the record, the court may hear the matter on affidavits or may hear it wholly or partly on oral testimony or on depositions.
(d) INTERPRETER. The court may appoint an interpreter of its choosing; fix reasonable compensation to be paid from funds provided by law or by one or more parties; and tax the compensation as costs.
...

FED. R. CIV. P. 44. Proving an Official Record
(a) MEANS OF PROVING.
(1) *Domestic Record.* Each of the following evidences an official record—or an entry in it—that is otherwise admissible and is kept within the United States, any state, district, or commonwealth, or any territory subject to the administrative or judicial jurisdiction of the United States:
(A) an official publication of the record; or
(B) a copy attested by the officer with legal custody of the record—or by the officer's deputy—and accompanied by a certificate that the officer has custody. The certificate must be made under seal:
(i) by a judge of a court of record in the district or political subdivision where the record is kept; or
(ii) by any public officer with a seal of office and with official duties in the district or political subdivision where the record is kept.
(2) *Foreign Record.*
(A) *In General.* Each of the following evidences a foreign official record—or an entry in it—that is otherwise admissible:
(i) an official publication of the record; or
(ii) the record—or a copy—that is attested by an authorized person and is accompanied either by a final certification of genuineness or by a certification under a treaty or convention to which the United States and the country where the record is located are parties.
(B) *Final Certification of Genuineness.* A final certification must certify the genuineness of the signature and official position of the attester or of any foreign official whose certificate of genuineness relates to the attestation or is in a chain of certificates of genuineness relating to the attestation. A final certification may be made by a secretary of a United States embassy or

legation; by a consul general, vice consul, or consular agent of the United States; or by a diplomatic or consular official of the foreign country assigned or accredited to the United States.

(C) *Other Means of Proof.* If all parties have had a reasonable opportunity to investigate a foreign record's authenticity and accuracy, the court may, for good cause, either:

(i) admit an attested copy without final certification; or

(ii) permit the record to be evidenced by an attested summary with or without a final certification.

(b) LACK OF A RECORD. A written statement that a diligent search of designated records revealed no record or entry of a specified tenor is admissible as evidence that the records contain no such record or entry. For domestic records, the statement must be authenticated under Rule 44(a)(1). For foreign records, the statement must comply with (a)(2)(C)(ii).

(c) OTHER PROOF. A party may prove an official record—or an entry or lack of an entry in it—by any other method authorized by law.

...

FED. R. CIV. P. 46. Objecting to a Ruling or Order

A formal exception to a ruling or order is unnecessary. When the ruling or order is requested or made, a party need only state the action that it wants the court to take or objects to, along with the grounds for the request or objection. Failing to object does not prejudice a party who had no opportunity to do so when the ruling or order was made.

...

FED. R. CIV. P. 80. Stenographic Transcript as Evidence

If stenographically reported testimony at a hearing or trial is admissible in evidence at a later trial, the testimony may be proved by a transcript certified by the person who reported it.

INQUIRY

Customary Order. The customary order of trial begins with opening statements first by the plaintiff's lawyer and then by defense counsel. The plaintiff then presents a case in chief, calling witnesses for direct examination and offering exhibits through them. The defense may cross-examine each of the plaintiff's witnesses after each witness' direct examination. When the plaintiff completes its case in chief and rests, the defense may move for judgment as a matter of law (formerly "directed verdict"). If the court denies the motion, then the defense proceeds with a case in chief, calling witnesses for direct examination (and cross-examination by plaintiff's counsel) and offering exhibits through them. When the defense completes its case in chief, the plaintiff may move for judgment as a matter of law on affirmative defenses. The plaintiff may then present a rebuttal case of additional witnesses and exhibits on new and unanticipated issues that the defense's case in chief raised. Each party may alternate with rebuttal until there are no new issues and the proofs are complete. In the typical case of moderate complexity, rebuttal entails one or two additional witnesses called by the plaintiff. Simple cases may not entail rebuttal, whereas complex cases may entail two or more rounds. The plaintiff's lawyer then gives a closing argument. Defense counsel gives a closing argument, and the plaintiff's lawyer may rebut. The trial judge then instructs the jury, swears it to a verdict, and excuses it into the bailiff's care to deliberate. The jury returns to the courtroom to read its verdict in open court.

Multiple Parties. One area in which trial judges sometimes do exercise discretion to change the customary order of proofs is in aligning multiple parties to make the best sense of the opening statements, proofs, and closing arguments. Just because a case has, say, two plaintiffs, three defendants each with counterclaims and cross-claims, and four third-party defendants does not mean that there will be a dozen successive cases in chief. Trial judges may require all plaintiffs to share a single case in chief, all defendants to share a single case in chief, and all third-party defendants to share a single case in chief. Trial judges may require parties to include counterclaims, cross-claims, and third-party claims all within their single case in chief. If the interests of third-party defendants align well with the interests of the plaintiffs, which is relatively often the case, then the trial judge may require those parties to share a single case in chief. The trial judge may require similarly aligned parties to sit together at counsel table and to split time for opening statements and closing arguments. On rare occasions, a trial judge may switch the order of proofs so that a defendant goes first, when the defendant does not substantially contest the plaintiff's claim but does have a more substantial and contested counterclaim. Trial judges tend properly to look past theory to the quantity and alignment of proofs when deciding the order of presentation.

Conduct. The trial judge controls the conduct of parties, counsel, witnesses, court staff, and jurors throughout each of these stages of a jury trial. Misconduct by a party, counsel, witness, or juror can result in new trial. Given the number of interested persons and their conflicting roles, there are many different ways in which things can and do go wrong at trial. Parties may fail or refuse to appear, cooperate with counsel, and comply with court orders regarding impermissible testimony and activities. Witnesses may fail or refuse to appear, or may fail or refuse to bring subpoenaed exhibits, and may violate counsel instructions and court orders prohibiting disclosure of irrelevant, unduly prejudicial, or privileged information. Jurors may have unauthorized contact with parties, witnesses, or one another outside of the courtroom, visit the scene without authorization, or do unauthorized independent research to share with other jurors. The next chapter on judgments addresses motions for new trial and their grounds. Unfortunately, lawyers also engage in misconduct affecting the intergrity of the proceedings. Consider one such case.

Gilbert v. DaimlerChrysler Corp.,

Michigan Supreme Court
685 N.W.2d 391 (2004)

YOUNG, J.

In this appeal, defendant seeks reversal or remittitur of the largest recorded compensatory award for a single-plaintiff sexual harassment suit in the history of the United States. The $21 million verdict awarded, according to plaintiff, barely compensates her for the lasting effects of the sexual harassment she endured as an employee of defendant, DaimlerChrysler, by whom she is still employed and earning almost $100,000 a year. She contended during her trial that defendant's failure to deal adequately with sexual harassment in her plant led to a permanent change in her "brain chemistry" and a relapse into substance abuse and depression, and that these conditions will soon lead to her untimely and excruciating death.

The foundation for this theory of recovery was laid by the expert opinion testimony of a social worker who had a longstanding relationship with plaintiff's counsel. This witness not only lacked any training, education, or experience in medicine, but also testified falsely about his credentials. Nevertheless, plaintiff asked the jury to treat this witness's testimony as a "prognosis," and to compensate plaintiff for the loss of her health and, eventually, her life. Plaintiff's counsel evoked images of physical abuse and torture, compared his client to survivors of the Holocaust, and argued that defendant DaimlerChrysler thought of itself as "God Almighty," exempt from the legal norms that govern others. Thus, in defendant's view, the verdict was the product of inflammatory rhetoric, unscientific "expert" testimony, fraud on the court, and attorney misconduct.

We granted leave to appeal in order to determine whether the verdict was a legitimate estimate of plaintiff's losses, as plaintiff contends, or whether it was, as defendant argues, an unjust, excessive award procured through systematic misconduct by plaintiff's trial counsel and supported by dubious evidence. …

The people have declared in our Constitution that "equal protection of the laws" shall not be denied on the basis of national origin. [Cc] The observance of this fundamental principle cannot stop at the door of the courthouse. Indeed, it is within the courthouse that we ought be most concerned that the merits of a party's cause, not its alienage or status, should remain the exclusive focus of a jury's deliberations. … [D]efendant was entitled to a trial free of naked appeals to entice the jury to consider its passions and prejudice rather than the evidence.

A careful review of the record reveals that plaintiff's trial counsel engaged in a sustained and deliberate effort to divert the jury's attention from the facts and the law. In their stead, counsel interposed misleading argument, prejudice-baiting rhetoric, and pleas for punitive damages. This rhetoric had its intended result: the jury's verdict unmistakably reflects passion rather than reason and prejudice rather than impartiality.

We conclude that the trial court lacked any justification for denying defendant's postverdict motion for a new trial under MCR 2.611. Thus, the trial court abused its discretion in denying defendant's motion for a new trial. We reverse, and we remand to the trial court for further proceedings consistent with this opinion. …

Defendant moved for postjudgment relief on a number of grounds. One of the grounds was that the verdict was the product of prejudice and passion. According to defendant, plaintiff's counsel had repeatedly equated plaintiff's experiences to those of the victims of the Holocaust, and thereby associated defendant's new German co-owners with the Nazis who perpetrated that horror. This argument, according to defendant, was bolstered by the expert testimony of a social worker who suggested to the jury that sexual harassment had altered plaintiff's "brain chemistry" and would lead to her untimely and agonizing death. Defendant argued that the excessiveness of the verdict—a $21 million award—palpably reflected the passion and prejudice that plaintiff sought to instill in the jury. …

Having determined that the verdict is excessive, we also conclude excessiveness may be attributed to the effect of plaintiff's efforts to cause the jury to act on passion and prejudice. An objective review of the record leads to an unavoidable conclusion: plaintiff's counsel engaged in a systematic effort to divert the jury from its true task—that of appropriately compensating the plaintiff for any losses suffered as a result of defendant's violation of the [Civil Rights

Act]—and instead sought to inflame passion and to incite the jury to punish the defendant even while disclaiming that he was seeking punitive damages.

Plaintiff's counsel deliberately tried to provoke the jury by supplanting law, fact, and reason with prejudice, misleading arguments, and repeated *ad hominem* attacks against defendant based on its corporate status. Given the undeniable role of this inflammatory rhetoric, the trial court erred in denying defendant's motion for a new trial.[fn]

One of counsel's tactics in this vein was his repeated attempts to equate plaintiff with the victims of the Holocaust. This association began during the testimony of plaintiff's expert, Steven Hnat, when Mr. Hnat testified that plaintiff's psychological state was akin to that of concentration camp survivors. Plaintiff's counsel further developed this theme during his closing argument: "Never again. Never again. That is a line now used by the [sabras] in Israel, the land of Israel, to mean that the unspeakable horrors that were perpetrated on the people of Israel, on the Jews, must never be forgotten and must never happen again. Never again. Never again." Counsel also exhorted the jury to "provide full and complete justice and thereby, as I indicated at the start of this trial, raise the roof of this courthouse so that justice will ring loud and clear. No more." "As those young [sabras] said in the land of Israel, no more. We will not let this stand. We will not allow this to pass. We will not allow you, you, an equal with all of us in this, the great equalizer, to crush the health and the dreams of a woman who simply had the American dream." Even the final sentence of plaintiff's closing argument referenced the Holocaust theme: "Let's bury this prejudice once and for all so that we may appropriately say, never again."

This recurring rhetorical theme was especially virulent given the context of plaintiff's trial. In 1998, Chrysler had merged with Daimler Benz AG, a German automobile manufacturer. The merger was highly publicized-particularly in metropolitan Detroit, where plaintiff's trial was held. And if any of the jurors had failed to hear about the merger through media outlets, they were privy to the news once plaintiff's counsel pointed out during his closing argument that Chrysler was under German ownership: "Daimler-Chrysler may be powerful, but, my God, they are going to have to recognize, hopefully today by your verdict, that not only must they face justice in this case, they must obey the law." "We are a nation of laws, not powerful individuals. We are a nation of laws... ." "And, I can assure that verdict will be heard from the floor of that plant on Jefferson to the board room in Auburn Hills or Stuttgart... ." "Once they hear in Auburn Hills and in Germany about Linda ... it will stop." Continuing on this theme, counsel argued that the jury now had a chance to acquaint Chrysler's German owners with a distinctly *American* brand of justice: "[You must] ring that bell of justice even if you have to have it rung across the oceans of this land to their board rooms, wherever they may be." "Chrysler must take notice that it is responsible, under the Constitution and laws of this state, and that we are ringing the bell of justice so that she can walk a little taller and stand a little prouder."

Thus, counsel's closing argument had a clear rhetorical aim of making defendant's German ownership a critical issue in the minds of the jurors. By associating plaintiff with those who had endured inhuman treatment in concentration camps, counsel likened defendant DaimlerChrysler—which, as the jury was informed, was partially under German ownership—with the Nazis. This argument was an attempt to incite the jury to heap upon the *defendant* the moral outrage that is now reserved for the Nazis and those who assisted them in carrying out the Holocaust. It was, in other words, a naked appeal to passion and prejudice and an attempt to divert the jury from the facts and the law relevant to this case.

Besides associating defendant with one of the most destructive and inhumane forces in modern history, counsel attempted artfully to convince the jury that defendant itself had *physically* harmed plaintiff, when there was no record of physical injury in the record. In describing plaintiff's refusal to quit her position as a millwright, counsel argued: "She stayed. She was not going to give up. *You could kick her. You could torture her.* You could harass her. You could put her in hospitals, but she was going to claw. She was going to hold on. She was going to do whatever was necessary to not lose that last shred of humanity that made her pull—that constitutes the soul, the thread, that will live on forever after she is gone [Emphasis added]." Plaintiff's counsel also equated plaintiff with a dog that had been kicked, beaten, and physically abused on a daily basis. Although counsel was quick to point out that he was not saying that plaintiff was *actually* a dog, he failed to mention that there was absolutely no evidence that plaintiff had been physically abused in any way by any employee of defendant.

Plaintiff's counsel also played on prejudice against corporations, arguing that DaimlerChrysler thought that it did not have to obey the law simply because of its corporate status: "You [defendant] are not God Almighty sitting on the mountain. You are not Zeus... ." "We will hold you to the same standard we will hold to anyone else, because their attitude speaks volume [sic] of their belief that they are above being held to the same standard as a lowly woman millwright would be held to." ...

There was no evidence presented at trial suggesting that anyone employed by defendant thought incorporation relieved it of the obligation to follow the law. Nor was there evidence that anyone in the management of DaimlerChrysler approved of sexual harassment or would have responded differently had a corporate officer been the subject of sexual harassment. ...

Finally, plaintiff's counsel attempted to inject passion and prejudice into the adjudication of this matter by deliberately and repeatedly using language that calls for punitive rather than compensatory damages. A number of these pleas for punitive damages have already been cited. One request for punitive damages was particularly overt: "You must consider the days, the minutes, the hours, and the weeks that she went through for seven years, and for as long as God gives her on this plant [sic], God help her, and allows her to maintain on this plant [sic], despite the disease that she is suffering from, the diseases that she will suffer from, and that will kill her, you must consider that, and so that your verdict reflect the enormity of the wrong, the intolerable nature of the injury, the extent of the humiliation, the torture, the extent of the outrage perpetrated... ." "But I suggest to you that you award as full and complete justice for the seven years of past and for the future, whatever it holds, $140,000,000.00. You can break that any way you want... ." "[T]he hopes and dreams of all free Americans exist in Linda the way they do in all of us." "And to destroy those, and to subject anyone to the type of indignity and injustice and intolerable acts that this woman has been subjected to for the past seven years, that figure reflects a symbol, if you will, since you can't adequately compensate her for every... ." This soliloquy stopped briefly only when defense counsel objected to this use of punitive damages rhetoric and the court gave a curative instruction.

The verdict rendered by the jury, however, showed that the damage had been done—that counsel's inflammatory rhetoric had its intended effect. Instead of awarding plaintiff an amount that fully and fairly compensated her, the jury returned a verdict that responded to plaintiff's request that they "send a message" to Chrysler. …

… Plaintiff's counsel has been admonished in two published Court of Appeals opinions since this trial for precisely the same sort of hyperbolic and vitriolic argument he made on behalf of Linda Gilbert.[fn] Overreaching, prejudice-baiting rhetoric appears to be a calculated, routine feature of counsel's trial strategy. This deliberate use of improper argument, coupled with the astonishingly excessive verdict rendered against defendant, precludes us from concluding that counsel's misconduct was "innocuous" and "unintended." …

When faced with defendant's motion for postjudgment relief… , the trial court had no reason to deny relief and every reason to grant it. In making its ruling on defendant's posttrial motions, the trial court clearly ignored the prominence of prejudicial rhetoric in plaintiff's closing argument and the effect that this rhetoric had on the jury.

The trial court's failure to grant a new trial was, therefore, an abuse of discretion. We reverse the judgment of the Court of Appeals and remand this action to the circuit court for proceedings in accordance with this opinion. …

INQUIRY

Verdicts. Another area in which trial judges do exercise substantial control is in the taking of jury verdicts. FED. R. CIV. P. 49 and equivalent state-court rules provide for both special and general verdicts. A special verdict answers specific questions that control the outcome of the case. A general verdict decides which party wins and which party loses a case. Lawyers for the parties draft verdict forms for the trial judge's consideration, modification, and approval, and for the jury's use. Juries write answers on the verdict forms during deliberations and return to the courtroom for the foreperson to read aloud on the record the answers written on the form. The foreperson signs the form, and the trial court retains it in the court file. A trial court can combine general and special verdicts into a single form in which the jury both answers specific subsidiary questions and finds in general for and against the parties. Read Rule 49 followed by examples of special and general verdict forms.

FED. R. CIV. P. 49. Special Verdict; General Verdict and Questions

(a) SPECIAL VERDICT.

(1) *In General.* The court may require a jury to return only a special verdict in the form of a special written finding on each issue of fact. The court may do so by:

(A) submitting written questions susceptible of a categorical or other brief answer;

(B) submitting written forms of the special findings that might properly be made under the pleadings and evidence; or

(C) using any other method that the court considers appropriate.

(2) *Instructions.* The court must give the instructions and explanations necessary to enable the jury to make its findings on each submitted issue.

(3) *Issues Not Submitted.* A party waives the right to a jury trial on any issue of fact raised by the pleadings or evidence but not submitted to the jury unless, before the jury retires, the party demands its submission to the jury. If the party does not demand submission, the court may make a finding on the issue. If the court makes no finding, it is considered to have made a finding consistent with its judgment on the special verdict.

(b) GENERAL VERDICT WITH ANSWERS TO WRITTEN QUESTIONS.

(1) *In General.* The court may submit to the jury forms for a general verdict, together with written questions on one or more issues of fact that the jury must decide. The court must give the instructions and explanations necessary to enable the jury to render a general verdict and answer the questions in writing, and must direct the jury to do both.

(2) *Verdict and Answers Consistent.* When the general verdict and the answers are consistent, the court must approve, for entry under Rule 58, an appropriate judgment on the verdict and answers.

(3) *Answers Inconsistent with the Verdict.* When the answers are consistent with each other but one or more is inconsistent with the general verdict, the court may:

(A) approve, for entry under Rule 58, an appropriate judgment according to the answers, notwithstanding the general verdict;

(B) direct the jury to further consider its answers and verdict; or

(C) order a new trial.

(4) *Answers Inconsistent with Each Other and the Verdict.* When the answers are inconsistent with each other and one or more is also inconsistent with the general verdict, judgment must not be entered; instead, the court must direct the jury to further consider its answers and verdict, or must order a new trial.

UNITED STATES DISTRICT COURT
FOR THE WESTERN DISTRICT OF MICHIGAN

MAYNARD RAY, JOHN W. BAINES, and **PAUL RUTTER,**
Plaintiffs,
v

WINDSOR COUNTY and **RON HOOPER** individually and in his official capacity as Sheriff of Windsor County,
Defendants.

No. CIV-01-01234

Hon. ****** *******

GENERAL VERDICT FORM

FJPI §168.70 Verdict Form [Modified for Multiple Plaintiffs]

On the First Amendment claim of plaintiff Maynard Ray, we find in favor of (check one)

☐ Plaintiff Maynard Ray or
☐ Defendants.

On the First Amendment claim of plaintiff John Baines, we find in favor of (check one)

☐ Plaintiff John Baines or
☐ Defendants.

On the First Amendment claim of plaintiff Paul Rutter, we find in favor of (check one)

☐ Plaintiff Paul Rutter or
☐ Defendants.

Note: Complete the following paragraphs only if one or more of the above findings are in favor of plaintiffs. State the amount, or if you find that plaintiffs' damages have no monetary value, set forth a nominal amount such as $1. If all of the above findings are in favor of defendants, have your foreperson sign and date this form because you have completed your deliberations.

We find plaintiffs' damages as defined to be:
Maynard Ray: $__________________
John Baines: $__________________
Paul Rutter: $__________________

We assess punitive damages against defendants as follows:
As to Maynard Ray: $__________________
As to John Baines: $__________________
As to Paul Rutter: $__________________

____
Foreperson

Dated: _______________

SJI2d 241.01 SPECIAL VERDICT FORM

We, the jury, make the following answers to the questions submitted by the Court:

QUESTION NO. 1: Was there a contract for the sale of goods between the buyer and the seller?
Answer: ___ (yes or no)
If your answer is "no," do not answer any further questions.

QUESTION NO. 2: Were the goods that the buyer accepted nonconforming?
Answer: ___ (yes or no)
If your answer is "no," do not answer any further questions.

QUESTION NO. 3: Did the buyer notify the seller of the nonconformity within a reasonable time after the buyer discovered or should have discovered the nonconformity?
Answer: ___ (yes or no)
If your answer is "no," do not answer any further questions.
If your answer is "yes," make the following determinations:

The value the goods would have had if they had conformed to the contract:

$_______________.__

Subtract the value of the goods at the time and place of acceptance, their actual value:

$_______________.__

Subtotal for Question No. 3:

$_______________.__

QUESTION NO. 4: Did the buyer incur any reasonable expenses incident to the seller's delay or other breach?

Answer: ___ (yes or no)
If your answer is "yes," state the amount: $______________.__

QUESTION NO. 5: Did the buyer incur any other losses resulting from the general or particular requirements or needs which the seller had reason to know about at the time of contracting, and which the buyer could not reasonably have prevented?

Answer: ___ (yes or no)
If your answer is "yes," state the amount: $______________._

QUESTION NO. 6: Did the buyer sustain an injury to person or property as a proximate result of any breach of warranty?

Answer: ___(yes or no)
If your answer is "yes," state the amount: $_____________.___
ADD the amounts in the answers to Questions No. 4 through No. 6 to the subtotal in Question No. 3 for the buyer's TOTAL DAMAGES: $_____________.___

INQUIRY

Summary. The conduct and character of a trial depends in large part on whether it is a judge or jury trial. Parties have a right to jury trial in federal courts to the same extent that the right existed when in 1791 states adopted the Seventh Amendment. Parties have similar, though often somewhat more circumscribed, rights to jury trial in state court under state constitutional provisions. The Seventh Amendment guarantees jury trial in suits at common law, meaning suits for legal relief, not in suits in equity, meaning suits for injunctive relief. When a case combines legal and equitable claims and issues, the trial court must preserve jury-trial rights but may thereafter decide equitable issues. To classify a claim as legal or equitable, the Supreme Court looks first to the historical classification of the claim and then to the form of the requested relief and the jury's ability to decide the issue. In jury trials, judges decide questions of law while juries decide questions of fact. Judges preserve the law-fact distinction by instructing juries in the law throughout the proceeding but especially at its conclusion. Judges also limit juries to acting within the scope of their role by entering judgment as a matter of law under FED. R. CIV. P. 50 when a party fails to support a claim or defense with sufficient evidence for reasonable jurors to find in that party's favor. Trial judges also have broad discretion to control the order of proofs at trial but typically follow a highly predictable and customary order. Trial judges also enforce rules and norms having to do with the conduct of parties, their lawyers, witnesses, and jurors.

Career

Do you know graduates of your law school? Your law school has many graduates in civil-litigation practice, some of them highly experienced and others recent graduates. You can use your law school's alumni database to locate civil litigators in the subject field, firm size, and geographic area in which you wish to practice. Those alumni will discuss your career interests with you. You may have the opportunity to tour their law offices and hear about the kind, value, rewards, and challenges of the work that they do. When you read a civil-procedure case that sounds particularly interesting to you, consider using your school's alumni database to locate a civil litigator qualified to handle that kind of case, and then arrange to meet that alumni. Also, consider locating a recent graduate who is practicing civil litigation, to discuss the transition from school to practice in that field.

CHAPTER XIII

JUDGMENT

OBJECTIVE: That you be able to articulate the procedures for obtaining judgments, the grounds and procedure for challenging judgments, and the procedures for enforcing judgment.

Case Study: You and your plaintiff client, a commercial property owner and manager, have just retired to the local diner for a cup of coffee and sandwich after a nice jury-trial win. The client has asked what the next steps are to recover the disputed property and money damages that the jury awarded. Explain the procedures for obtaining and enforcing judgment, and the nature of any challenges to the judgment that your client might see along the way.

Federal Rules of Civil Procedure this chapter reproduces and addresses
FED. R. CIV. P. 52. Findings and Conclusions by the Court; Judgment on Partial Findings
FED. R. CIV. P. 54. Judgment; Costs
FED. R. CIV. P. 58. Entering Judgment
FED. R. CIV. P. 59. New Trial; Altering or Amending a Judgment
FED. R. CIV. P. 60. Relief from a Judgment or Order
FED. R. CIV. P. 61. Harmless Error
FED. R. CIV. P. 62. Stay of Proceedings to Enforce a Judgment
FED. R. CIV. P. 62.1. Indicative Ruling on a Motion for Relief That is Barred by a Pending Appeal
FED. R. CIV. P. 65. Injunctions and Restraining Orders
FED. R. CIV. P. 69. Execution
FED. R. CIV. P. 70. Enforcing a Judgment for a Specific Act
FED. R. CIV. P. 71. Enforcing Relief For or Against a Nonparty
FED. R. CIV. P. 77. Conducting Business; Clerk's Authority; Notice of an Order or Judgment
FED. R. CIV. P. 79. Records Kept by the Clerk

The word *judgment* has a finality to it that, when describing a stage of civil litigation, is both accurate and misleading. When parties engage in litigation, either voluntarily as plaintiffs or compelled as defendants, they seek resolution. Litigation is not an end in itself, at least so long as a party remains sound of mind. Indeed, although litigation is a career and practice of many lawyers, those lawyers must appreciate their clients' need not to treat litigation as an end but instead as a means to other, more productive and beneficial ends. It is a common enough criticism of lawyers that they do not price and conduct their legal services in ways that promote their efficient deployment. Process has a value. It is all well and good that the civil justice system is replete with elaborate procedures. Even so, it is ultimately not about the procedures but instead the purposes for which clients invoke them. When parties are unable to agree to the end of litigation, judgments are the first step in making them do so. Judgments do not magically appear. Lawyers craft them. Practitioners must know how and when to obtain judgments.

Yet judgments are only a first step toward full and final resolution. In many cases, a judgment becomes only the next event around which parties conduct the litigation and data point around which they continue to negotiate toward voluntary resolution. Judgments are not self-executing. Judgments provide information that helps the parties to evaluate the strengths and weaknesses of their positions, and the likelihood of protecting or promoting their interests. Judgments also provide a basis for further proceedings. Judgments become a weapon and a shield. Parties deploy judgments to threaten and usurp opposing parties' property interests, influence the behavior of opposing parties, and influence the behavior of non-parties. Parties also attack judgments in the trial courts and on appeal to higher courts, using judgments to demonstrate the injustice of their opponents, opponents' legal representatives, trial judges, society, and life. One might think that when the jury has spoken, it is over. It is not over. There are cases in which the post-verdict proceedings are longer, more substantial, and more uncertain than pretrial and trial. Consider the important subject of judgments.

A. Obtaining Judgment

There is both the act of obtaining judgment and the knowledge of knowing when it has been obtained. A judgment is a court paper usually bearing that title and providing for the final disposition of all claims in the case, "leav[ing] nothing for the court to do but execute the judgment." Catlin v. United States, 324 U.S. 229, 233 (1945). Judgments enter in both bench trials and jury trials. Judges make oral rulings from the bench. Judges also write opinions. Juries return verdicts. Oral rulings and jury verdicts are not judgments, although they can certainly be events on which the court may enter judgment. A judicial opinion can constitute a judgment depending on its scope and language. Lawyers must know when a judgment is available for the taking and when the court has already issued one. One must know when a judgment is available so as to timely take the necessary actions to obtain it, oppose it, and advise a client as to its effects. One must know when a court has already issued a judgment so as to timely take the necessary actions to challenge, appeal, or enforce it. Consider several *Federal Rules of Civil Procedure* having to do with the entry of judgment.

Skill

The joke is that intellectually capable and ambitious college graduates who nonetheless cannot handle numbers go to law school. The truth is that lawyers who have a facility for numbers can lend substantial service to clients. Basic mathematics and algebra can help in such areas as (a) working with financial statements and appraisals valuing client interests, (b) conceptualizing, proving, and challenging damages claims, (c) advising as to structured settlements, and (d) calculating judgments including compound interest. Lawyers who have no facility for numbers can at least engage other professionals who do and then supervise and review their work to ensure that it satisfies client needs. Respect the value of numerical skills, and work to develop and employ them.

FED. R. CIV. P. 54(a) defines a judgment as "any order from which an appeal lies." Rule 54(a)'s definition is technical and procedural, not substantive. The text immediately above defines a judgment differently in the way that lawyers usually think of it—as a court paper finally disposing of all remaining claims. Why does Rule 54(a) define a judgment by reference to appeal rights? The answer has to do with an important procedural doctrine known as the *final-judgment rule*. Federal statute defines the appellate jurisdiction of the United States Courts of Appeals as "appeals from all final decisions of the district courts of the United States... ." 28 U.S.C. 1291. Section 1291 is the federal codification of the final-judgment rule, that final judgments trigger appeal rights. By defining a judgment as an order from which appeal lies, Rule 54(a) points to §1291's final-judgment rule, while §1291 points to "final decisions" of the district courts. A judgment is a final decision of the trial court from which an appeal lies. Judgments often bear that title. Nearly as often, they do not. Final decisions may arise when a court grants a Rule 12(b) motion to dismiss or a Rule 56 motion for summary judgment. Any court paper that constitutes an order, whether or not titled "judgment," can constitute a judgment. The critical condition is that the order dispose of all remaining claims. Read Rule 54, §1291, and the following Supreme Court case on the final-judgment rule. We will return to the final-judgment rule in the next chapter on appeals.

FED. R. CIV. P. 54. Judgment; Costs

(a) DEFINITION; FORM. "Judgment" as used in these rules includes a decree and any order from which an appeal lies. A judgment should not include recitals of pleadings, a master's report, or a record of prior proceedings.

(b) JUDGMENT ON MULTIPLE CLAIMS OR INVOLVING MULTIPLE PARTIES. When an action presents more than one claim for relief—whether as a claim, counterclaim, crossclaim, or third-party claim—or when multiple parties are involved, the court may direct entry of a final judgment as to one or more, but fewer than all, claims or parties only if the court expressly determines that there is no just reason for delay. Otherwise, any order or other decision, however designated, that adjudicates fewer than all the claims or the rights and liabilities of fewer than all the parties does not end the action as to any of the claims or parties and may be revised at any time before the entry of a judgment adjudicating all the claims and all the parties' rights and liabilities.

(c) DEMAND FOR JUDGMENT; RELIEF TO BE GRANTED. A default judgment must not differ in kind from, or exceed in amount, what is demanded in the pleadings. Every other final judgment should grant the relief to which each party is entitled, even if the party has not demanded that relief in its pleadings.

(d) COSTS; ATTORNEY'S FEES.

(1) *Costs Other Than Attorney's Fees.* Unless a federal statute, these rules, or a court order provides otherwise, costs—other than attorney's fees—should be allowed to the prevailing party. But costs against the United States, its officers, and its agencies may be imposed only to the extent allowed by law. The clerk may tax costs on 14 days' notice. On motion served within the next 7 days, the court may review the clerk's action.

(2) *Attorney's Fees.*

(A) *Claim to Be by Motion.* A claim for attorney's fees and related nontaxable expenses must be made by motion unless the substantive law requires those fees to be proved at trial as an element of damages.

(B) *Timing and Contents of the Motion.* Unless a statute or a court order provides otherwise, the motion must:

(i) be filed no later than 14 days after the entry of judgment;

(ii) specify the judgment and the statute, rule, or other grounds entitling the movant to the award;

(iii) state the amount sought or provide a fair estimate of it; and

(iv) disclose, if the court so orders, the terms of any agreement about fees for the services for which the claim is made.

(C) *Proceedings.* Subject to Rule 23(h), the court must, on a party's request, give an opportunity for adversary submissions on the motion in accordance with Rule 43(c) or 78. The court may decide issues of liability for fees before receiving submissions on the value of services. The court must find the facts and state its conclusions of law as provided in Rule 52(a).

(D) *Special Procedures by Local Rule; Reference to a Master or a Magistrate Judge.* By local rule, the court may establish special procedures to resolve fee-related issues without extensive evidentiary hearings. Also, the court may refer issues concerning the value of services to a special master under Rule 53 without regard to the limitations of Rule 53(a)(1), and may refer a motion for attorney's fees to a magistrate judge under Rule 72(b) as if it were a dispositive pretrial matter.

(E) *Exceptions.* Subparagraphs (A)–(D) do not apply to claims for fees and expenses as sanctions for violating these rules or as sanctions under 28 U.S.C. §1927.

---

28 U.S.C. §1291. Final decisions of district courts
The courts of appeals (other than the United States Court of Appeals for the Federal Circuit) shall have jurisdiction of appeals from all final decisions of the district courts of the United States, the United States District Court for the District of the Canal Zone, the District Court of Guam, and the District Court of the Virgin Islands, except where a direct review may be had in the Supreme Court. The jurisdiction of the United States Court of Appeals for the Federal Circuit shall be limited to the jurisdiction described in sections 1292(c) and (d) and 1295 of this title.

Liberty Mutual Insurance Co. v. Wetzel,

United States Supreme Court
424 U.S. 737 (1976)

Mr. Justice REHNQUIST delivered the opinion of the Court.

Respondents filed a complaint in the United States District Court for the Western District of Pennsylvania in which they asserted that petitioner's employee insurance benefits and maternity leave regulations discriminated against women in violation of Title VII of the Civil Rights Act of 1964, [] 42 U.S.C. §2000e et seq.[]. The District Court ruled in favor of respondents on the issue of petitioner's liability under that Act, and petitioner appealed to the Court of Appeals for the Third Circuit. That court held that it had jurisdiction of petitioner's appeal under 28 U.S.C. §1291, and proceeded to affirm on the merits the judgment of the District Court. ... Though neither party has questioned the jurisdiction of the Court of Appeals to entertain the appeal, we are obligated to do so on our own motion if a question thereto exists. Mansfield, Coldwater & Lake Michigan R. Co. v. Swan, 111 U.S. 379[] (1884). Because we conclude that the District Court's order was not appealable to the Court of Appeals, we vacate the judgment of the Court of appeals with instructions to dismiss petitioner's appeal from the order of the District Court.

Respondents' complaint, after alleging jurisdiction and facts deemed pertinent to their claim, prayed for a judgment against petitioner embodying the following relief:

(a) requiring that defendant establish non-discriminatory hiring, payment, opportunity, and promotional plans and programs;

(b) enjoining the continuance by defendant of the illegal acts and practices alleged herein;

> (c) requiring that defendant pay over to plaintiffs and to the members of the class the damages sustained by plaintiffs and the members of the class by reason of defendant's illegal acts and practices, including adjusted backpay, with interest, and an additional equal amount as liquidated damages, and exemplary damages;
>
> (d) requiring that defendant pay to plaintiffs and to the members of the class the costs of this suit and a reasonable attorneys' fee, with interest; and
>
> (e) such other and further relief as the Court deems appropriate. [C]

After extensive discovery, respondents moved for partial summary judgment only as to the issue of liability. Fed. Rule Civ. Proc. 56(c). The District Court... , finding no issues of material fact in dispute, entered an order to the effect that petitioner's pregnancy-related policies violated Title VII of the Civil Rights Act of 1964. It also ruled that Liberty Mutual's hiring and promotion policies violated Title VII.[fn] Petitioner thereafter filed a motion for reconsideration which was denied by the District Court. Its order ... denying the motion for reconsideration, contains the following concluding language:

> In its Order the court stated it would enjoin the continuance of practices which the court found to be in violation of Title VII. The Plaintiffs were invited to submit the form of the injunction order and the Defendant has filed Notice of Appeal and asked for stay of any injunctive order. Under these circumstances the court will withhold the issuance of the injunctive order and amend the Order previously issued under the provisions of Fed.R.Civ.P. 54(b), as follows:
>
> And now this 20th day of February, 1974, it is directed that final judgment be entered in favor of Plaintiffs that Defendant's policy of requiring female employees to return to work within three months of delivery of a child or be terminated is in violation of the provisions of Title VII of the Civil Rights Act of 1964; that Defendant's policy of denying disability income protection plan benefits to female employees for disabilities related to pregnancies or childbirth are (sic) in violation of Title VII of the Civil Rights Act of 1964 and that it is expressly directed that Judgment be entered for the Plaintiffs upon these claims of Plaintiffs' Complaint; there being no just reason for delay. [C]

It is obvious from the District Court's order that respondents, although having received a favorable ruling on the issue of petitioner's liability to them, received none of the relief which they expressly prayed for in the portion of their complaint set forth above. They requested an injunction, but did not get one; they requested damages, but were not awarded any; they requested attorneys' fees, but received none.

Counsel for respondents when questioned during oral argument in this Court suggested that at least the District Court's order ... amounted to a declaratory judgment on the issue of liability pursuant to the provisions of 28 U.S.C. §2201. Had respondents sought only a declaratory judgment, and no other form of relief, we would of course have a different case. But even if we accept respondents' contention that the District Court's order was a declaratory judgment on the issue of liability, it nonetheless left unresolved respondents' requests for an injunction, for compensatory and exemplary damages, and for attorneys' fees. It finally disposed of none of respondents' prayers for relief.

The District Court and the Court of Appeals apparently took the view that because the District Court made the recital required by Fed. Rule Civ. Proc. 54(b) that final judgment be entered on the issue of liability, and that there was no just reason for delay, the orders thereby became appealable as a final decision pursuant to 28 U.S.C. §1291. We cannot agree with this application of the Rule and statute in question.

Rule 54(b)[fn] "does not apply to a single claim action... . It is limited expressly to multiple claims actions in which 'one or more but less than all' of the multiple claims have been finally decided and are found otherwise to be ready for appeal." Sears, Roebuck & Co. v. Mackey, 351 U.S. 427, 435[] (1956).[fn] Here, however, respondents set forth but a single claim: that petitioner's employee insurance benefits and maternity leave regulations discriminated against its women employees in violation of Title VII of the Civil Rights Act of 1964. They prayed for several different types of relief in the event that they sustained the allegations of their complaint, see Fed. Rule Civ. Proc. 8(a)(3), but their complaint advanced a single legal theory which was applied to only one set of facts.[fn] Thus, despite the fact that the District Court undoubtedly made the findings required under the Rule had it been applicable, those findings do not in a case such as this make the order appealable pursuant to 28 U.S.C. §1291. [C]

We turn to consider whether the District Court's order might have been appealed by petitioner to the Court of Appeals under any other theory. The order, viewed apart from its discussion of Rule 54(b), constitutes a grant of partial summary judgment limited to the issue of petitioner's liability. Such judgments are by their terms interlocutory, see Fed. Rule Civ. Proc. 56(c), and where assessment of damages or awarding of other relief remains to be resolved have never been considered to be "final" within the meaning of 28 U.S.C. §1291. [Cc] ...

Were we to sustain the procedure followed here, we would condone a practice whereby a district court in virtually any case before it might render an interlocutory decision on the question of liability of the defendant, and the defendant would thereupon be permitted to appeal to the court of appeals without satisfying any of the requirements that Congress carefully set forth. We believe that Congress... has been well aware of the dangers of an overly rigid insistence upon a "final decision" for appeal in every case, and has in [other] sections made ample provision for appeal of orders which are not "final" so as to alleviate any possible hardship. ...

The judgment of the Court of Appeals is therefore vacated, and the case is remanded with instructions to dismiss the petitioner's appeal.

It is so ordered.

Mr. Justice BLACKMUN took no part in the consideration or decision of this case.

INQUIRY

Recitals. In cases involving multiple claims or parties, FED. R. CIV. P. 54(b) permits a trial court to certify as final a decision on fewer than all claims and parties. Although it did not find them dispositive of the issue, *Liberty Mutual Insurance Co. v. Wetzel* referred to recitals required by Rule 54(b) for a party to take an appeal from a judgment in a case involving multiple claims or parties. What role do Rule 54(b) recitals play? As the above case illustrates, Rule 54(b) applies only to cases involving multiple claims or parties. In some cases in which a trial court disposes of one out of multiple claims, or disposes of all claims as to one of multiple parties, there is no reason to delay appeal as to that decided claim or party. The claim is sufficiently substantial and discrete, or the party sufficiently independent, that the appellate review is appropriate. Rule 54(b) enables a trial court to label as appealable those certain decisions in cases involving multiple claims or parties. Keep in mind that those decisions that the trial court certifies must still be final. *See* Sears, Roebuck & Co. v. Mackey, 351 U.S. 427, 435 (1956). Perhaps surprisingly, the Supreme Court has approved the practice of treating as final a trial court's decision on a main claim as to which there was an undecided counterclaim. *See* Curtiss-Wright Corp. v. General Electric Co., 446 U.S. 1, 8-9 (1980). The next chapter on appeals excerpts *Sears, Roebuck & Co. v. Mackey* and further discusses this issue.

Findings. FED. R. CIV. P. 52 provides for findings and conclusions by the trial judge when there is no jury or only an advisory jury. Rule 52(a)(1) requires that the trial judge find facts and state separate conclusions of law. Judges in federal cases cannot simply rule for one party or the other. They must state the factual and legal grounds. Constitutional due process requires not only an impartial decisionmaker—a qualified trial judge. It also requires independent and impartial review of a decision. Appellate judges must have a basis for affirming or reversing a trial judge's decision. Rule 52(a)(1)'s strictures ensure that trial judges give appellate courts that review basis, as Rule 52(a)(5) implies when it provides that a party "may later question the sufficiency of the evidence supporting the findings" of the trial judge. Rule 52(a)(6) cautions the appellate court that it must not set findings aside "unless clearly erroneous" and that it must "give due regard to the trial court's opportunity to judge the witnesses' credibility." Trial judges usually recite findings of fact and conclusions of law in written opinions, as any law student well knows from having read such opinions. If the trial court hears only a part of the case, the trial judge makes findings, and those findings dispose of a claim or defense, Rule 52(c) permits the trial judge to enter judgment. Read Rule 52 for these and other details.

FED. R. CIV. P. 52. Findings and Conclusions by the Court; Judgment on Partial Findings

(a) FINDINGS AND CONCLUSIONS.

(1) *In General.* In an action tried on the facts without a jury or with an advisory jury, the court must find the facts specially and state its conclusions of law separately. The findings and conclusions may be stated on the record after the close of the evidence or may appear in an opinion or a memorandum of decision filed by the court. Judgment must be entered under Rule 58.

(2) *For an Interlocutory Injunction.* In granting or refusing an interlocutory injunction, the court must similarly state the findings and conclusions that support its action.

(3) *For a Motion.* The court is not required to state findings or conclusions when ruling on a motion under Rule 12 or 56 or, unless these rules provide otherwise, on any other motion.

(4) *Effect of a Master's Findings.* A master's findings, to the extent adopted by the court, must be considered the court's findings.

(5) *Questioning the Evidentiary Support.* A party may later question the sufficiency of the evidence supporting the findings, whether or not the party requested findings, objected to them, moved to amend them, or moved for partial findings.

(6) *Setting Aside the Findings.* Findings of fact, whether based on oral or other evidence, must not be set aside unless clearly erroneous, and the

reviewing court must give due regard to the trial court's opportunity to judge the witnesses' credibility.
(b) AMENDED OR ADDITIONAL FINDINGS. On a party's motion filed no later than 28 days after the entry of judgment, the court may amend its findings—or make additional findings—and may amend the judgment accordingly. The motion may accompany a motion for a new trial under Rule 59.
(c) JUDGMENT ON PARTIAL FINDINGS. If a party has been fully heard on an issue during a nonjury trial and the court finds against the party on that issue, the court may enter judgment against the party on a claim or defense that, under the controlling law, can be maintained or defeated only with a favorable finding on that issue. The court may, however, decline to render any judgment until the close of the evidence. A judgment on partial findings must be supported by findings of fact and conclusions of law as required by Rule 52(a).

INQUIRY

Proposed Findings. Judges may request help making findings, and counsel for the parties are ordinarily quite willing to provide it. It is a relatively common practice that a trial judge will invite the parties to submit proposed findings of fact and conclusions of law in a bench trial. The lawyers for the parties know the case. They know what facts support what legal conclusions. When a trial judge requests proposed findings of fact and conclusions of law in advance of, during, or immediately after a bench trial, it gives the trial judge a clearer sense of the disputed issues and supportable claims and defenses. Trial judges may adopt wholesale one or another party's proposed findings of fact and conclusions of law, or adopt some findings and conclusions from each party, or use the proposed findings and conclusions as templates for modified findings and conclusions. Drafting proposed findings of fact and conclusions of law that are sufficiently clear, supportable, and non-argumentative is an art as much as a science. Consider the following example in a probate case in which one beneficiary claimed undue influence, violation of fiduciary duties, and surcharge of attorney's fees against another beneficiary. (The actual proposed findings and conclusions from which this example was drawn were significantly more detailed and numerous to respond fully to all included claims. The probate judge adopted them verbatim.)

**DEFENDANT'S PROPOSED FINDINGS OF FACT
AND CONCLUSIONS OF LAW**

Defendant Margaret Green proposes the following findings of fact and conclusions of law:

1. When the decedent Muriel Beeker died in 1990, she left a trust under which her daughter Mrs. Green would receive part of the family farm with her son plaintiff Mr. Beeker the remainder.

2. Mr. Beeker alleges that Mrs. Green violated fiduciary duties and influenced her mother Muriel to amend the trust to include Mrs. Green.

Findings of Fact

3. Muriel had sound reason to amend her estate plan independent of any influence or breach of duties by Mrs. Green.

4. Muriel independently determined to do what she believed she lawfully could, to equalize what Mr. Beeker and Mrs. Green received from Muriel's estate.

5. Muriel independently believed that Mr. Beeker's receiving everything was not right and fair, and that she wanted to treat her children equally.

6. Muriel independently reached her determination to amend the trust following an argument with Mr. Beeker.

7. When amending the trust Muriel was not under the influence of Mrs. Green.

8. Muriel's brother, not her daughter Mrs. Green, encouraged Muriel to change her estate plan.

9. Muriel instructed the estate attorney and Mrs. Green that she did not want her amendment disclosed to Mr. Beeker, for her own sound reasons having to do with her fear of Mr. Beeker.

10. Muriel had full power to change the disposition of the assets in the trust.

Conclusions of Law

11. Because Mrs. Green was not a trustee of her mother Muriel's trust when Muriel made the amendment, Mrs. Green did not have the fiduciary duties of a trustee.

12. Mrs. Green did not keep material information from Mr. Beeker or violate other fiduciary duties.

13. Mrs. Green did not unduly influence Muriel.

14. Assuming for argument's sake that Mrs. Green did violate duties, such violation did not affect the outcome.

15. There was no bad faith on Mrs. Green's part.

16. To surcharge Mrs. Green when she acted reasonably and in good faith would by inequitable and cause substantial material injustice.

Relief Requested

Defendant Margaret Green respectfully requests that this Court determine that no surcharge against her is warranted.

Respectfully submitted,
[signature block of defendant's counsel]

INQUIRY

Form. A judgment is quite different in form than judicial findings of fact or opinions. A judgment often takes the following form. It bears the case caption because the court will file it in the case file. It often bears the title "Judgment" while occasionally also reflecting parties ("... as to Third-Party Defendants"), claims ("... on Counterclaim," "... as to Declaratory and Injunctive Relief"), or outcomes ("... of Money Damages," "... of No Cause for Action," "... for Dismissal"). The judgment may begin with a recital or series of recitals including the nature of the claims, the identity of the parties, nature and date of hearings or trials held, and the results of those proceedings. The judgment then states the critical language of decision, such as "It is ordered... " or "It is adjudged... ." It then includes the specific relief supported by the trial judge's findings of fact and conclusions of law. Trial judges typically request that the lawyer for the prevailing party prepare the judgment, as was the case in the above Supreme Court case *Liberty Mutual Insurance Co. v. Wetzel.* That lawyer will draft the proposed judgment, circulating it among the lawyers for all other parties to attempt to obtain approval as to the judgment's form. When lawyers approve an opposing side's judgment as to form, they may sign below that statement ("Approved as to form only") at the end of the judgment. A lawyer who inadvertently indicates approval as to the substance of an adverse judgment may have waived the client's appeal rights. When lawyers cannot agree on a judgment's form, the lawyer for the prevailing party will move for entry of judgment. Consider two form judgments offered by the *Federal Rules of Civil Procedure* followed by a practice example. Also, read FED. R. CIV. P. 58 stating procedures for the entry of a properly drafted judgment, together with FED. R. CIV. P. 77 and 79 on other duties of the court clerk relating to filing and notice of judgment.

FED. R. CIV. P. FORM 70. Judgment on a Jury Verdict

(Caption—See Form 1.)

This action was tried by a jury with Judge _______ presiding, and the jury has rendered a verdict.

It is ordered that: [the plaintiff *name* recover from the defendant *name* the amount of $_______ with interest at the rate of ___%, along with costs.] [the plaintiff recover nothing, the action be dismissed on the merits, and the defendant *name* recover costs from the plaintiff *name*.]

Date _______

____

Clerk of Court

FED. R. CIV. P. Form 71. Judgment by the Court Without a Jury

(Caption—See Form 1.)

This action was tried by Judge _______ without a jury and the following decision was reached:

It is ordered that [the plaintiff *name* recover from the defendant *name* the amount of $_______, with prejudgment interest at the rate of ___%, postjudgment interest at the rate of ___%, along with costs.] [the plaintiff recover nothing, the action be dismissed on the merits, and the defendant *name* recover costs from the plaintiff *name*.]

Date_______________

____

Clerk of Court

Skills

Notice the difference between the form above and the example judgment below. The forms included with the *Federal Rules of Civil Procedure* are certainly appropriate representatives in the direct and plain language that they use. Their simplicity, though, belies the complexity of practice. In civil litigation, drafting is a critical skill, just as it is for transactional work. The *Federal Rules* forms do not represent this complexity. The following judgment, even though significantly more detailed than the above form, is itself relatively simple. Does it state more or less than it needs to state? Judgments tend to be much simpler than settlement agreements. Why? What should a judgment include, and what should it omit?

IN THE UNITED STATES DISTRICT COURT
FOR THE WESTERN DISTRICT OF MICHIGAN

*****************,
Plaintiffs,

No. 99-cv-01234

v.

Hon. ****** ** ********

*****************,
Defendants.

JUDGMENT CONFIRMING ARBITRATION AWARD

At a session of the Court held in the Courthouse in Lansing, Michigan, on ____________

This case was referred to arbitration by order dated March 21, 2000. The arbitrator issued an Opinion and Award dated May 2, 2001, together with costs and fees to the prevailing parties. The arbitrator subsequently issued a Determination dated June 29, 2001, as to the amounts of the awarded costs and fees, and then issued a Corrected Determination dated July 3, 2001. Plaintiffs applied to confirm the award, costs, and fees. The Court is otherwise adequately advised.

IT IS ORDERED AND ADJUDGED that the arbitration award is confirmed as a judgment of this Court, in favor of the plaintiffs and against defendants as provided for in the arbitrator's attached Opinion and Award, and further as to costs and fees in the amounts provided for in the arbitrator's attached Corrected Determination. Interest at the average of the federal statutory judgment interest rates during the period for which interest applies, shall run on the damage awards from the October 6, 1998 date of the filing of the Complaint, and shall run on the awarded costs and fees from the May 2, 2001 date of the arbitrator's Opinion and Award, until satisfied by defendants.

Hon. ****** ** ***********

Prepared and presented by:
[signature block of plaintiffs' counsel]

Fed. R. Civ. P. 58. Entering Judgment
(a) SEPARATE DOCUMENT. Every judgment and amended judgment must be set out in a separate document, but a separate document is not required for an order disposing of a motion:
(1) for judgment under Rule 50(b);
(2) to amend or make additional findings under Rule 52(b);
(3) for attorney's fees under Rule 54;
(4) for a new trial, or to alter or amend the judgment, under Rule 59; or
(5) for relief under Rule 60.
(b) ENTERING JUDGMENT.
(1) *Without the Court's Direction.* Subject to Rule 54(b) and unless the court orders otherwise, the clerk must, without awaiting the court's direction, promptly prepare, sign, and enter the judgment when:
(A) the jury returns a general verdict;
(B) the court awards only costs or a sum certain; or
(C) the court denies all relief.
(2) *Court's Approval Required.* Subject to Rule 54(b), the court must promptly approve the form of the judgment, which the clerk must promptly enter, when:
(A) the jury returns a special verdict or a general verdict with answers to written questions; or
(B) the court grants other relief not described in this subdivision (b).
(c) TIME OF ENTRY. For purposes of these rules, judgment is entered at the following times:
(1) if a separate document is not required, when the judgment is entered in the civil docket under Rule 79(a); or
(2) if a separate document is required, when the judgment is entered in the civil docket under Rule 79(a) and the earlier of these events occurs:
(A) it is set out in a separate document; or
(B) 150 days have run from the entry in the civil docket.
(d) REQUEST FOR ENTRY. A party may request that judgment be set out in a separate document as required by Rule 58(a).
(e) COST OR FEE AWARDS. Ordinarily, the entry of judgment may not be delayed, nor the time for appeal extended, in order to tax costs or award fees. But if a timely motion for attorney's fees is made under Rule 54(d)(2), the court may act before a notice of appeal has been filed and become effective to order that the motion have the same effect under Federal Rule of Appellate Procedure 4(a)(4) as a timely motion under Rule 59.
…

Fed. R. Civ. P. 77. Conducting Business; Clerk's Authority; Notice of an Order or Judgment
(a) WHEN COURT IS OPEN. Every district court is considered always open for filing any paper, issuing and returning process, making a motion, or entering an order.
(b) PLACE FOR TRIAL AND OTHER PROCEEDINGS. Every trial on the merits must be conducted in open court and, so far as convenient, in a regular courtroom. Any other act or proceeding may be done
or conducted by a judge in chambers, without the attendance of the clerk or other court official, and anywhere inside or outside the district. But no hearing—other than one ex parte—may be conducted outside the district unless all the affected parties consent.
(c) CLERK'S OFFICE HOURS; CLERK'S ORDERS.
(1) *Hours.* The clerk's office—with a clerk or deputy on duty—must be open during business hours every day except Saturdays, Sundays, and legal holidays. But a court may, by local rule or order, require that the office be open for specified hours on Saturday or a particular legal holiday other than one listed in Rule 6(a)(4)(A).
(2) *Orders.* Subject to the court's power to suspend, alter, or rescind the clerk's action for good cause, the clerk may:
(A) issue process;
(B) enter a default;
(C) enter a default judgment under Rule 55(b)(1); and
(D) act on any other matter that does not require the court's action.
(d) SERVING NOTICE OF AN ORDER OR JUDGMENT.
(1) *Service.* Immediately after entering an order or judgment, the clerk must serve notice of the entry, as provided in Rule 5(b), on each party who is not in default for failing to appear. The clerk must record the service on the docket. A party also may serve notice of the entry as provided in Rule 5(b).
(2) *Time to Appeal Not Affected by Lack of Notice.* Lack of notice of the entry does not affect the time for appeal or relieve—or authorize the court to relieve—a party for failing to appeal within the time allowed, except as allowed by Federal Rule of Appellate Procedure (4)(a).
…

FED. R. CIV. P. 79. Records Kept by the Clerk

(a) CIVIL DOCKET.

(1) *In General.* The clerk must keep a record known as the "civil docket" in the form and manner prescribed by the Director of the Administrative Office of the United States Courts with the approval of the Judicial Conference of the United States. The clerk must enter each civil action in the docket. Actions must be assigned consecutive file numbers, which must be noted in the docket where the first entry of the action is made.

(2) *Items to be Entered.* The following items must be marked with the file number and entered chronologically in the docket:

(A) papers filed with the clerk;

(B) process issued, and proofs of service or other returns showing execution; and

(C) appearances, orders, verdicts, and judgments.

(3) *Contents of Entries; Jury Trial Demanded.* Each entry must briefly show the nature of the paper filed or writ issued, the substance of each proof of service or other return, and the substance and date of entry of each order and judgment. When a jury trial has been properly demanded or ordered, the clerk must enter the word "jury" in the docket.

(b) CIVIL JUDGMENTS AND ORDERS. The clerk must keep a copy of every final judgment and appealable order; of every order affecting title to or a lien on real or personal property; and of any other order that the court directs to be kept. The clerk must keep these in the form and manner prescribed by the Director of the Administrative Office of the United States Courts with the approval of the Judicial Conference of the United States.

(c) INDEXES; CALENDARS. Under the court's direction, the clerk must:

(1) keep indexes of the docket and of the judgments and orders described in Rule 79(b); and

(2) prepare calendars of all actions ready for trial, distinguishing jury trials from nonjury trials.

(d) OTHER RECORDS. The clerk must keep any other records required by the Director of the Administrative Office of the United States Courts with the approval of the Judicial Conference of the United States.

INQUIRY

Injunctive Relief. Special procedures apply when a party requests judgment in the form of injunctive relief. Judgments typically dispose of property rights and interests, often in the form of money judgments that one party pay another but also in the form of declarations that one party holds an interest claimed by another. By contrast, injunctive relief restrains and enjoins a party from engaging in certain conduct that stands to irreparably harm the party seeking the injunction. In that sense, injunctive relief often has an urgency to it, that the restraint take hold before the harm, and an invasiveness, that a party's liberty to act (not merely its ability to control property or benefit from finances) is at stake. To protect rights while accommodating these interests, FED. R. CIV. P. 65 and equivalent state-court rules offer a three-step proceeding for injunctions. Rule 65(b)'s first step allows a party seeking an injunction to obtain the trial court's temporary restraining order ("TRO"), without notice to the other side ("ex parte") if the party is unable to give notice within the time necessary to prevent the harm or if the notice itself will engender the harm. Rule 65(a)'s second step allows the trial court to issue a preliminary injunction after notice to the party enjoined. The trial court must require the party obtaining a temporary restraining order or preliminary injunction to post a bond to secure the enjoined party against any loss due to an improvidently entered restraint. Rule 65 in general and its subrule (d) in particular anticipate the third and final step involving an injunction (sometimes called a permanent injunction to distinguish it from a preliminary injunction) after trial. Rule 65(a)(2) specifically anticipates that the trial court may condense the second and third steps, accelerating trial. Trial judges conduct hearings on preliminary injunction but must preserve jury-trial rights for final (permanent) injunctions. Read Rule 65 for these and other injunction particulars.

FED. R. CIV. P. 65. Injunctions and Restraining Orders

(a) PRELIMINARY INJUNCTION.

(1) *Notice.* The court may issue a preliminary injunction only on notice to the adverse party.

(2) *Consolidating the Hearing with the Trial on the Merits.* Before or after beginning the hearing on a motion for a preliminary injunction, the court may advance the trial on the merits and consolidate it with the hearing. Even when consolidation is not ordered, evidence that is received on the motion and that would be admissible at trial becomes part of the trial record and need not be repeated at trial. But the court must preserve any party's right to a jury trial.

(b) TEMPORARY RESTRAINING ORDER.

(1) *Issuing Without Notice.* The court may issue a temporary restraining order without written or oral notice to the adverse party or its attorney only if:

(A) specific facts in an affidavit or a verified complaint clearly show that immediate and irreparable injury, loss, or damage will result to the movant before the adverse party can be heard in opposition; and

(B) the movant's attorney certifies in writing any efforts made to give notice and the reasons why it should not be required.

(2) *Contents; Expiration.* Every temporary restraining order issued without notice must state the date and hour it was issued; describe the injury and state why it is irreparable; state why the order was issued without notice; and be promptly filed in the clerk's office and entered in the record. The order expires at the time after entry—not to exceed 14 days—that the court sets, unless before that time the court, for good cause, extends it for a like period or the adverse party consents to a longer extension. The reasons for an extension must be entered in the record.

(3) *Expediting the Preliminary-Injunction Hearing.* If the order is issued without notice, the motion for a preliminary injunction must be set for hearing at the earliest possible time, taking precedence over all other matters except hearings on older matters of the same character. At the hearing, the party who obtained the order must proceed with the motion; if the party does not, the court must dissolve the order.

(4) *Motion to Dissolve.* On 2 days' notice to the party who obtained the order without notice—or on shorter notice set by the court—the adverse party may appear and move to dissolve or modify the order. The court must then hear and decide the motion as promptly as justice requires.

© SECURITY. The court may issue a preliminary injunction or a temporary restraining order only if the movant gives security in an amount that the court considers proper to pay the costs and damages sustained by any party found to have been wrongfully enjoined or restrained. The United States, its officers, and its agencies are not required to give security.

(d) CONTENTS AND SCOPE OF EVERY INJUNCTION AND RESTRAINING ORDER.

(1) *Contents.* Every order granting an injunction and every restraining order must:

(A) state the reasons why it issued;

(B) state its terms specifically; and

(C) describe in reasonable detail—and not by referring to the complaint or other document—the act or acts restrained or required.

(2) *Persons Bound.* The order binds only the following who receive actual notice of it by personal service or otherwise:

(A) the parties;

(B) the parties' officers, agents, servants, employees, and attorneys; and

(C) other persons who are in active concert or participation with anyone described in Rule 65(d)(2)(A) or (B).

(e) OTHER LAWS NOT MODIFIED. These rules do not modify the following:

(1) any federal statute relating to temporary restraining orders or preliminary injunctions in actions affecting employer and employee;

(2) 28 U.S.C. §2361, which relates to preliminary injunctions in actions of interpleader or in the nature of interpleader; or

(3) 28 U.S.C. §2284, which relates to actions that must be heard and decided by a three-judge district court.

(f) COPYRIGHT IMPOUNDMENT. This rule applies to copyright-impoundment proceedings.

INQUIRY

Preliminary Injunction. FED. R. CIV. P. 65 does not state the well-known and oft-repeated standard for preliminary injunction. Under Rule 65(a)(1), preliminary injunctions are available only after notice giving the opposing party an opportunity for hearing. At that hearing, the party seeking preliminary injunction must show (1) a likelihood of success on the merits, (2) likelihood of irreparable harm if injunction does not issue, (3) that money damages are an inadequate remedy, and (4) that the moving party would face a greater hardship without the injunction than the party enjoined. *See* Chaplaincy of Full Gospel Churches v. England, 454 F.3d 290 (D.C. Cir. 2006); Save Our Sonoran, Inc. v. Flowers, 408 F.3d 1113 (9th Cir. 2005). The party opposing preliminary injunction can readily dispute any one or all four of the conditions. Irreparable harm and inadequacy of money damages are particularly difficult to establish, given that the kinds of harm often claimed are economic in nature. Thus, the Supreme Court has held that the federal courts are not to enjoin the transfer of assets to ensure that a plaintiff is able to collect on a contract claim for money damages. *See* Grupo Mexicano de Desarrollo, S.A. v. Alliance Bond Fund, Inc., 527 U.S. 308, 333 (1999). The just-cited case is a reminder that efforts at prejudgment attachment are similar to efforts to obtain a preliminary injunction. Although the standards for granting each form of prejudgment relief (attachment and preliminary injunction) are stated quite differently, they have the same roots in procedural fairness and substantial justice.

Practice

"Come on in, come on in," the elderly trial judge motioned to the new lawyer who stood at the door to the judge's chambers. "So how are we today?" the jovial judge added, sensing the new lawyer's trepidation. The lawyer began explaining to the trial judge the request for a TRO that necessitated the late-day emergency visit. "Well, let's see what we have here," the judge said as he looked over the motion, brief, affidavit, and proposed order. "How about if we just add this language and change this a little bit?" the judge said as he worked over the order with a pen, scratching out words and phrases and writing new ones in here and there. "All set to go, counselor," the judge said with a big smile, bidding the new lawyer a good day. The new lawyer walked out humbled with the power and responsibility that attends ex parte proceedings.

B. Challenging Judgment

When a judgment enters, the prevailing side thinks enforcement, and the losing side thinks appeal. Actually, though, there is first a post-judgment period during which either or both sides can challenge the judgment before its enforcement or appeal. Recall from the prior chapter on the conduct of trial that parties may move before jury deliberations for a Rule 50(a) motion for judgment as a matter of law (formerly directed verdict). If the trial court denies the motion and the party suffers an adverse verdict, then after the court enters judgment on the verdict the losing party may under Rule 50(b) renew that motion for judgment as a matter of law. A Rule 50(b) motion seeks what the law formerly called judgment notwithstanding the verdict or JNOV. The prior chapter addressed the conditions under which the trial court may grant Rule 50(a) judgment as a matter of law before jury deliberations—when the party opposing the motion has failed to adduce evidence in support of its claim or defense. The same conditions apply to a post-judgment Rule 50(b) motion for judgment as a matter of law. In essence, the trial judge gets a second chance or, prosaically, the moving party gets a second bite at the apple.

Judgment as a matter of law is not the only permissible challenge to a judgment. FED. R. CIV. P. 59 and equivalent state-court rules permit parties to move for new trial. For the moving party, a successful Rule 59 motion for new trial is not as welcome as would be a successful Rule 50(b) motion for judgment as a matter of law because it means going back and doing the trial over again, albeit under better conditions (without the error that justified the grant of new trial). Rule 59(b) requires parties to file new-trial motions within 28 days after entry of judgment. FED. R. CIV. P. 62(a) automatically stays enforcement of a judgment for 14 days, while Rule 62(b) permits the trial court to stay enforcement for longer periods including while the court resolves a motion for new trial. Thus, judgment does not end proceedings. Rather, a judgment begins new proceedings within new time periods unless the party subject to the judgment elects instead to satisfy or comply with it. See the next section for further discussion of stays, satisfaction, and enforcement.

Rule 59 does not state the grounds on which a party may move for new trial other than to refer to the traditional grounds "in an action at law." This phrase refers subtly to the Seventh Amendment's clause prohibiting re-examination of jury verdicts other "than according to the rules of the common law." Those grounds fall into two general categories. The first category involves defects in the proceedings such as misconduct by a party, lawyer, or witness, or errors by the trial judge in admitting or excluding evidence or instructing the jury. (Yes, trial judges do, after trial, reconsider erroneous rulings that they made in the heat of trial.) Chapter XII on trials showed an example of a case involving misconduct of counsel in making a closing argument that went beyond the evidence and invited the jury's bias and prejudice. Other procedural defects may involve mistaken interpretations and application of evidence rules, or instructional errors based on mistaken interpretations or applications of substantive law. Before considering the other category of defects warranting new trial, read Rule 59 followed by a case involving a procedural defect, the erroneous admission of expert testimony, in which the Supreme Court had to decide whether the parties should have a new trial under Rule 59 or the trial court should enter judgment as a matter of law under Rule 50.

FED. R. CIV. P. 59. New Trial; Altering or Amending a Judgment

(a) IN GENERAL.

(1) *Grounds for New Trial.* The court may, on motion, grant a new trial on all or some of the issues—and to any party—as follows:

(A) after a jury trial, for any reason for which a new trial has heretofore been granted in an action at law in federal court; or

(B) after a nonjury trial, for any reason for which a rehearing has heretofore been granted in a suit in equity in federal court.

(2) *Further Action After a Nonjury Trial.* After a nonjury trial, the court may, on motion for a new trial, open the judgment if one has been entered, take additional testimony, amend findings of fact and conclusions of law or make new ones, and direct the entry of a new judgment.

(b) TIME TO FILE A MOTION FOR A NEW TRIAL. A motion for a new trial must be filed no later than 28 days after the entry of judgment.
(c) TIME TO SERVE AFFIDAVITS. When a motion for a new trial is based on affidavits, they must be filed with the motion. The opposing party has 14 days after being served to file opposing affidavits. The court may permit reply affidavits.
(d) NEW TRIAL ON THE COURT'S INITIATIVE OR FOR REASONS NOT IN THE MOTION. No later than 28 days after the entry of judgment, the court, on its own, may order a new trial for any reason that would justify granting one on a party's motion. After giving the parties notice and an opportunity to be heard, the court may grant a timely motion for a new trial for a reason not stated in the motion. In either event, the court must specify the reasons in its order.
(e) MOTION TO ALTER OR AMEND A JUDGMENT. A motion to alter or amend a judgment must be filed no later than 28 days after the entry of the judgment.

Weisgram v. Marley Co.,

United States Supreme Court
528 U.S. 440 (2000)

Justice GINSBURG delivered the opinion of the Court.

This case concerns the respective authority of federal trial and appellate courts to decide whether, as a matter of law, judgment should be entered in favor of a verdict loser. The pattern we confront is this. Plaintiff in a product liability action gains a jury verdict. Defendant urges, unsuccessfully before the federal district court but successfully on appeal, that expert testimony plaintiff introduced was unreliable, and therefore inadmissible, under the analysis required by *Daubert v. Merrell Dow Pharmaceuticals, Inc.*, 509 U.S. 579[] (1993). Shorn of the erroneously admitted expert testimony, the record evidence is insufficient to justify a plaintiff's verdict. May the court of appeals then instruct the entry of judgment as a matter of law for defendant, or must that tribunal remand the case, leaving to the district court's discretion the choice between final judgment for defendant or a new trial of plaintiff's case?

Our decision is guided by Federal Rule of Civil Procedure 50, which governs the entry of judgment as a matter of law, and by the Court's pathmarking opinion in *Neely v. Martin K. Eby Constr. Co.*, 386 U.S. 317[] (1967). As *Neely* teaches, courts of appeals should "be constantly alert" to "the trial judge's first-hand knowledge of witnesses, testimony, and issues"; in other words, appellate courts should give due consideration to the first-instance decisionmaker's "'feel' for the overall case." *Id.* at 325[]. ... But if, as in the instant case, the court of appeals concludes that further proceedings are unwarranted because the loser on appeal has had a full and fair opportunity to present the case, including arguments for a new trial, the appellate court may appropriately instruct the district court to enter judgment against the jury-verdict winner. Appellate authority to make this determination is no less when the evidence is rendered insufficient by the removal of erroneously admitted testimony than it is when the evidence, without any deletion, is insufficient.

I

Firefighters arrived at the home of Bonnie Weisgram ... to discover flames around the front entrance. Upon entering the home, they found Weisgram in an upstairs bathroom, dead of carbon monoxide poisoning. Her son, petitioner

Chad Weisgram, individually and on behalf of Bonnie Weisgram's heirs, brought a diversity action in the United States District Court for the District of North Dakota seeking wrongful death damages. He alleged that a defect in an electric baseboard heater, manufactured by defendant (now respondent) Marley Company and located inside the door to Bonnie Weisgram's home, caused both the fire and his mother's death.[fn]

At trial, Weisgram introduced the testimony of three witnesses, proffered as experts, in an endeavor to prove the alleged defect in the heater and its causal connection to the fire. The District Court overruled defendant Marley's objections, lodged both before and during the trial, that this testimony was unreliable and therefore inadmissible under Federal Rule of Evidence 702 as elucidated by *Daubert.* At the close of Weisgram's evidence, and again at the close of all the evidence, Marley unsuccessfully moved under Federal Rule of Civil Procedure 50(a) for judgment as a matter of law on the ground that plaintiffs had failed to meet their burden of proof on the issues of defect and causation. The jury returned a verdict for Weisgram. Marley again requested judgment as a matter of law, and additionally requested, in the alternative, a new trial, pursuant to Rules 50 and 59; among arguments in support of its post-trial motions, Marley reasserted that the expert testimony essential to prove Weisgram's case was unreliable and therefore inadmissible. [C] The District Court denied the motions and entered judgment for Weisgram. [C]

The Court of Appeals for the Eighth Circuit held that Marley's motion for judgment as a matter of law should have been granted. [C] Writing for the panel majority, Chief Judge Bowman first examined the testimony of Weisgram's expert witnesses, the sole evidence supporting plaintiffs' product defect charge. [C] Concluding that the testimony was speculative and not shown to be scientifically sound, the majority held the expert evidence incompetent to prove Weisgram's case. [C] The court then considered the remaining evidence in the light most favorable to Weisgram, found it insufficient to support the jury verdict, and directed judgment as a matter of law for Marley. [C] In a footnote, the majority "reject[ed] any contention that [it was] required to remand for a new trial." [C] It recognized its discretion to do so under Rule 50(d), but stated: "[W]e can discern no reason to give the plaintiffs a second chance to make out a case of strict liability.... This is not a close case. The plaintiffs had a fair opportunity to prove their claim and they failed to do so." [C] ...

II

Federal Rule of Civil Procedure 50, ... governs motions for judgment as a matter of law in jury trials.[fn] ... Under this Rule, Weisgram urges, when a court of appeals determines that a jury verdict cannot be sustained due to an error in the admission of evidence, the appellate court may not order the entry of judgment for the verdict loser, but must instead remand the case to the trial court for a new trial determination. [C] Nothing in Rule 50 expressly addresses this question.[fn]

In a series of pre-1967 decisions, this Court refrained from deciding the question, while emphasizing the importance of giving the party deprived of a verdict the opportunity to invoke the discretion of the trial judge to grant a new trial. [Cc] Then, in *Neely,* the Court reviewed its prior jurisprudence and ruled definitively that if a motion for judgment as a matter of law is erroneously denied by the district court, the appellate court does have the power to order the entry of judgment for the moving party. 386 U.S. at 326[]; [c].

Neely first addressed the compatibility of appellate direction of judgment as a matter of law (then styled "judgment *n.o.v.*") with the Seventh Amendment's jury trial guarantee. It was settled, the Court pointed out, that a trial court, pursuant to Rule 50(b), could enter judgment for the verdict loser without offense to the Seventh Amendment. 386 U.S. at 321[] (citing Montgomery Ward & Co. v. Duncan, 311 U.S. 243[] (1940)). "As far as the Seventh Amendment's right to jury trial is concerned," the Court reasoned, "there is no greater restriction on the province of the jury when an appellate court enters judgment *n.o.v.* than when a trial court does"; accordingly, the Court concluded, "there is no constitutional bar to an appellate court granting judgment *n.o.v.*" 386 U.S. at 322[] (citing Baltimore & Carolina Line v. Redman, 295 U.S. 654[] (1935)). The Court next turned to "the statutory grant of appellate jurisdiction to the courts of appeals [in 28 U.S.C. §2106],"[fn] which it found "certainly broad enough to include the power to direct entry of judgment *n.o.v.* on appeal." 386 U.S. at 322[]. ...

... *Neely* ultimately clarified that if a court of appeals determines that the district court erroneously denied a motion for judgment as a matter of law, the appellate court may (1) order a new trial at the verdict winner's request or on its own motion, (2) remand the case for the trial court to decide whether a new trial or entry of judgment for the defendant is warranted, or (3) direct the entry of judgment as a matter of law for the defendant. *Id.* at 327-330[].

III

... Weisgram relies on cases holding that, in fairness to a verdict winner who may have relied on erroneously admitted evidence, courts confronting questions of judgment as a matter of law should rule on the record as it went to the jury, without excising evidence inadmissible under Federal Rule of Evidence 702. [Cc] These decisions are of questionable consistency with Rule 50(a)(1), which states that in ruling on a motion for judgment as a matter of law, the court is to inquire whether there is any "legally sufficient evidentiary basis for a reasonable jury to find for [the opponent of the motion]." Inadmissible evidence contributes nothing to a "legally sufficient evidentiary basis." See Brooke Group Ltd. v. Brown & Williamson Tobacco Corp., 509 U.S. 209, 242[] (1993) ("When an expert opinion is not supported by sufficient facts to validate it in the eyes of the law, or when indisputable record facts contradict or otherwise render the opinion unreasonable, it cannot support a jury's verdict.").[fn]

As *Neely* recognized, appellate rulings on post-trial pleas for judgment as a matter of law call for the exercise of "informed discretion," 386 U.S. at 329[], and fairness to the parties is surely key to the exercise of that discretion. But fairness concerns should loom as large when the verdict winner, in the appellate court's judgment, failed to present sufficient evidence as when the appellate court declares inadmissible record evidence essential to the verdict winner's case. In both situations, the party whose verdict is set aside on appeal will have had notice, before the close of evidence, of the alleged evidentiary deficiency. See Fed. Rule Civ. Proc. 50(a)(2) (motion for judgment as a matter of law "shall specify ... the law and facts on which the moving party is entitled to the judgment"). On appeal, both will have the opportunity to argue in support of the jury's verdict or, alternatively, for a new trial. And if judgment is instructed for the verdict loser, both will have a further chance to urge a new trial in a rehearing petition.[fn]

Since *Daubert,* moreover, parties relying on expert evidence have had notice of the exacting standards of reliability such evidence must meet. 509 U.S. 579[]; see also Kumho Tire Co. v. Carmichael, 526 U.S. 137[] (1999) (rendered shortly after the Eighth Circuit's decision in Weisgram's case);[fn] General Electric Co. v. Joiner, 522 U.S. 136[] (1997). It is implausible to suggest, post-*Daubert,* that parties will initially present less than their best expert evidence in the expectation of a second chance should their first try fail. We therefore find unconvincing Weisgram's fears that allowing courts of appeals to direct the entry of judgment for defendants will punish plaintiffs who could have shored up their cases by other means had they known their expert testimony would be found inadmissible. [C] In this case, for example, although Weisgram was on notice every step of the way that Marley was challenging his experts, he made no attempt to add or substitute other evidence. See Lujan v. National Wildlife Federation, 497 U.S. 871, 897[] (1990) ("[A] litigant's failure to buttress its position because of confidence in the strength of that position is always indulged in at the litigant's own risk.").

After holding Weisgram's expert testimony inadmissible, the Court of Appeals evaluated the evidence presented at trial, viewing it in the light most favorable to Weisgram, and found the properly admitted evidence insufficient to support the verdict. [C] ... The Eighth Circuit concluded that this was "not a close case." [c] In these circumstances, the Eighth Circuit did not abuse its discretion by directing entry of judgment for Marley, instead of returning the case to the District Court for further proceedings. ...

Neely recognized that there are myriad situations in which the determination whether a new trial is in order is best made by the trial judge. 386 U.S. at 325-326[]. *Neely* held, however, that there are also cases in which a court of appeals may appropriately instruct the district court to enter judgment as a matter of law against the jury-verdict winner. *Id.* at 326[]. We adhere to *Neely's* holding and rationale, and today hold that the authority of courts of appeals to direct the entry of judgment as a matter of law extends to cases in which, on excision of testimony erroneously admitted, there remains insufficient evidence to support the jury's verdict.

For the reasons stated, the judgment of the Court of Appeals for the Eighth Circuit is

Affirmed.

INQUIRY

Verdict Defects. The second category of new trial motions involves defects in the verdict. One form of verdict defect is when it is internally inconsistent, such as when answers to special questions on the verdict form do not support the general verdict, when fault percentages do not add to 100% as applicable tort law requires, or when there are errors in arithmetic on damages calculations. New trial is clearly warranted in those cases. The jury, long since dismissed and free to discuss the case with outsiders, has erred. A new jury must hear the case. Perhaps surprisingly, though, a party may also move under FED. R. CIV. P. 59 for new trial based on a verdict that is *against the great weight of the evidence*. If Rule 50(b) authorizes a party to renew a motion for judgment as a matter of law, what is the need for a Rule 59 motion for new trial based on a verdict against the great weight of the evidence? When, in other words, could a verdict be against the great weight warranting new trial but still sustained by enough evidence that the court may not enter judgment as a matter of law? It may be slicing the distinction thin, but there are cases in which although there is some evidence in support of the claim, a verdict in that party's favor is simply against the evidence's great weight. As you read the following case, see if you agree that the verdict was just enough to avoid judgment as a matter of law but yet against the great weight of the evidence.

Dadurian v. Underwriters at Lloyd's of London,

United States Court of Appeals for the First Circuit
787 F.2d 756 (1986)

LEVIN H. CAMPBELL, Chief Judge.

This diversity case arose out of the refusal of defendant-appellant Lloyd's, London ("Lloyd's")[fn] to indemnify plaintiff-appellee Paul Dadurian after he claimed the loss of certain jewelry that he allegedly owned and that had been insured under a Lloyd's insurance policy. As affirmative defenses to the suit for nonpayment, Lloyd's asserted that Dadurian's claim was fraudulent... . The jury entered special verdicts favorable to Dadurian, resulting in his recovering $267,000 plus interest. Lloyd's moved for judgment notwithstanding the verdict, or alternatively, for a new trial. The United States District Court for the District of Rhode Island denied the motion, and Lloyd's now appeals. As we find the jury's verdict was against the great weight of the evidence, we vacate and remand for a new trial. ...

Dadurian claimed that he purchased 12 pieces of "specialty" jewelry for investment purposes over a period of 30 months, from August 1977 to January 1980. ... Dadurian testified that he purchased all the jewelry from James Howe, a jeweler... , and paid for each item in cash. Dadurian did not present any sales slips, receipts or other documents of transfer reflecting any of his alleged purchases; and Howe not only presented no records of his sale of the jewelry to Dadurian, but he could not remember from whom he had originally obtained the jewelry and had no records showing that the jewelry had ever actually been in his possession. ...

Dadurian claimed that on or about April 12, 1980, armed robbers entered his home and forced him to open his safe, where the jewelry was kept. He was shot in the right shoulder, allegedly by one of the robbers, and was taken to the hospital. It is Dadurian's contention that the insured pieces of jewelry were stolen during the robbery. ...

Lloyd's argues on appeal that Dadurian swore falsely, and necessarily knowingly, with respect to at least two key issues, and that either instance of false swearing was sufficient to void the insurance policy. First, Dadurian is said to have clearly lied in asserting that he purchased and owned the 12 pieces of jewelry for which he later obtained the insurance; and second, he is said to have knowingly lied in telling Lloyd's, at the formal examination under oath conducted before this action was begun, that the cash he used to purchase the jewelry came from certain bank loans. Lloyd's contends that evidence presented at trial was so overwhelmingly against Dadurian on both these issues that no reasonable jury could have rendered a verdict in his favor. …

… Dadurian procured the Lloyd's insurance on the basis of written appraisals executed by Howe, the man from whom he allegedly purchased all 12 pieces. But he obtained no receipts nor did Howe have any records of the alleged sales to Dadurian. Moreover, although Dadurian testified to specific dates and prices paid for each of his jewelry purchases, in support of his story of ownership, his testimony that he had obtained that information from Howe's records was contradicted by testimony that Howe kept no such records.

But whatever may be thought of Dadurian's story, we cannot say, as a matter of law, that no jury could have properly found that Dadurian had purchased the jewelry as he claimed. … [T]he jury was entitled to overlook the lack of any documentation for the purchases. …

Lloyd's also argues that Dadurian knowingly lied under oath at the formal examination when he swore that certain specific bank loans were the source of the cash he used to buy the jewelry. If Dadurian swore falsely and knowingly on this issue, he is not entitled to recover under the insurance contract. … [I]t is undisputed that under the policy, [FN3] as well as under established case law,[fn] knowingly false testimony by Dadurian as to any fact considered "material" to his claim voids the policy.

… [W]here Dadurian got the cash was material to his insurance claim, since Dadurian insisted that he paid Howe a total of $233,000 in cash over a 30-month period for the jewelry, and the credibility of this story, and hence of Dadurian's ownership of the insured items, turned in part on his ability to explain plausibly where he obtained such large sums of cash.[Fn5. Lloyd's was understandably interested in hearing Dadurian's explanation of the source of his cash [because] the year Dadurian allegedly bought four of the twelve jewelry items for a total of $90,000 in cash, his income as reported in his federal tax return was only about $3,000.] …

… Confronted with … evidence[at trial], Dadurian essentially conceded that some, if not most, of the promissory notes he had [claimed were the source of his jewelry-buying funds] had been the wrong ones, and that his testimony as to the sources of the funds was therefore in part false. He insisted, however, that he had … been honestly mistaken.

Since it is thus uncontroverted that a substantial number of Dadurian's representations under oath about the sources of his cash were untrue, the only remaining question is whether Dadurian made these false statements *knowingly* or whether he was simply mistaken in good faith as he claims. …

After carefully considering the entire record, we find that the great weight of the evidence indicates overwhelmingly that Dadurian knew he was giving false testimony. At the formal examination under oath Dadurian specifically identified 13 promissory notes, apparently from those he had given Lloyd's sometime before the examination, and explicitly linked each note to a particular jewelry purchase. He did not qualify his identifications, but rather couched his testimony in terms of misleading certainty. Only when confronted at trial with the patent falsity of his earlier testimony did Dadurian testify, by way of explanation, that he had made his selections only to the "best of his recollection" in order to satisfy the insurance company's inquiries. It was only then that he explained that because he had "files and files" of such notes in his possession,[fn] he must have simply selected the wrong ones under pressure of time and circumstances.

This explanation strains credulity. This was not a case where Dadurian was confronted for the first time at the examination with "files and files" of his promissory notes and asked to come up with correct ones "on the spot." Rather it was Dadurian himself who originated and put forward the story that most of his cash had come from bank loans, and it was Dadurian who apparently first tendered the supposedly relevant promissory notes to Lloyd's at some time before the formal examination. ... The uncontested facts simply belie Dadurian's excuse that he was pressured into making identifications prematurely.

Dadurian had much to gain by providing a plausible explanation for the sources of his cash. By piecing together notes executed on dates close to the times of the alleged purchases, he could hope to create an impression of credibility. That he linked the notes to the jewelry purchases so positively—without bothering to ascertain readily available information showing that they were not so related—indicates, at the least, a wilful misrepresentation as to the state of his own knowledge concerning the matters to which he was testifying. We think the only fair inference from this kind of total indifference to the truth or falsity of his assertions was that Dadurian knew that he was not telling the truth. [C]

It follows, we believe, that the jury's verdict was against the clear weight of the evidence insofar as it found that Dadurian did not knowingly give false answers or information on any material subject when he was examined under oath before commencement of this suit.[fn] We emphasize that Dadurian himself conceded that some of his answers were incorrect, and it is clear the district court properly found them "material." ... We conclude that the jury's finding that Dadurian did not give knowingly false answers was contrary to the great weight of the evidence. For that aspect of the verdict to stand would, in our view, amount to a manifest miscarriage of justice. [C] We hold, therefore, that the district court abused its discretion in denying defendant's motion for a new trial, and remand the case for retrial by a new jury.

We are mindful of the alternative plea by Lloyd's that we should reverse the court's refusal to grant a judgment n.o.v. and, in effect, direct a finding for Lloyd's rather than order a new trial. Whether to do so is a very close question. A factor weighing against this alternative is that Lloyd's had the burden of proving that Dadurian was lying, and this circuit, like most courts, is reluctant to direct a verdict for the party having the burden of proof. [Cc] The issue, moreover, involves a determination of credibility. Hence, even though we find it hard to see how a reasonable jury could reach any result other than that Dadurian was knowingly lying, we believe that the more appropriate relief is a new trial. ...

Vacated and remanded for a new trial.

INQUIRY

Limits and Conditions. There is authority that the trial courts may limit new trial to issues or elements affected by the error. If, for instance, a jury found for the plaintiff on liability and damages while making an error in damages, or where there was a defect in the trial affecting only the damages issue, then the trial court could grant new trial solely as to damages. *See, e.g.,* Pingatore v. Montgomery Ward & Co., 419 F.2d 1138 (6th Cir. 1969), cert. denied, 398 U.S. 928 (1970). Doing so may be more consistent with reliable justice, that the trial court would not duplicate portions of the trial as to which there was no error, running the risk of inconsistent conclusions. It can also save judicial resources. In the procedure known as remittitur, trial courts can also grant a defendant new trial conditioned on the plaintiff rejecting the highest amount in damages that the proofs warranted. *See* Hetzel v. Prince William County, 523 U.S. 208 (1998) (plaintiff must have the choice); *see also* Donovan v. Penn Shipping Co., 429 U.S. 648, 649 (1977) (plaintiff may not both accept the remittitur and pursue an appeal but do one or the other). The Supreme Court has held unconstitutional the procedure known as additur, as violating the Seventh Amendment. *See* Dimick v. Schiedt, 293 U.S. 474 (1935). Additur is the obverse of remittitur in that it increases damages to the lowest amount the proofs permit while giving the defendant the opportunity to accept or reject the increased award. Can you discern why the Supreme Court would permit remittitur but prohibit additur? Once a jury awards too much, one might say that it has simultaneously awarded everything up to that amount. When a jury awards too little, one cannot say that it has awarded more. Some states continue to approve additur. *See, e.g.,* Jehl v. Southern Pacific Co., 427 P.2d 988 (Cal. 1967).

Jury Impeachment. Notice that none of the grounds for new trial so far discussed has relied on what jurors say later about their verdict. The law permits jurors to speak after they reach their verdict and the trial concludes. Some lawyers make a practice of interviewing willing jurors after trial, both for the lawyer's professional development and to learn more about the case in the event of an appeal, remand, and retrial. Juror interviews and observation of mock juries tend to suggest that jurors can misunderstand and misapply the law with alarming frequency. On occasion, a losing party will learn of juror errors in deliberation and attempt to make those errors a ground for new trial. The effort to use a juror's affidavit to undermine a verdict is known as jury impeachment. The courts frown on the practice. FED. R. EVID. 606(b) holds inadmissible a juror's testimony as to the mental impressions of jurors during deliberations. Can you articulate why? Consider the following case rejecting jury impeachment as a ground for new trial.

Peterson v. Wilson,

United States Court of Appeals for the Fifth Circuit
141 F.3d 573 (1998)

WIENER, Circuit Judge:

The case we review today was twice tried to verdict by civil juries. The first trial ended in a verdict favorable to Plaintiff-Appellant Sylvester L. Peterson and unfavorable to Defendant-Appellee Bobby Wilson, but the district court granted a new trial. The second trial ended in a verdict rejecting all of Peterson's claims and exonerating Wilson. This appeal turns on whether the district court abused its discretion when, at the conclusion of the first trial, it granted Wilson a new one: If that was error and was not harmless, we must reverse and remand for entry of judgment for Peterson... . Our review of the record of the first trial and the applicable law leads to the unavoidable conclusion that the district court abused its discretion in granting a new trial after the jury found for Peterson in the first trial, and that doing so was not harmless, i.e., it constituted reversible error. We therefore vacate the verdict and judgment from the second trial, reverse the district court's order granting the new trial, and remand this case to the district court with instructions to enter judgment for Peterson in accordance with the first jury verdict and to award appropriate costs, including attorneys' fees, and interest. ...

I

FACTS AND PROCEEDINGS...

Peterson filed this suit [against Wilson] in district court under 42 U.S.C. §... 1988 ... after he was fired as grant director at Texas Southern University (TSU). He claims that his property interest in his employment at TSU was damaged or destroyed when it was arbitrarily and capriciously terminated[by Wilson]. ... After five days of trial, conducted by the magistrate judge with the consent of the parties, the jury found for Peterson and awarded him $152,235 for lost pay and benefits and $35,000 for past and future mental anguish. Following the verdict, Wilson renewed his motion for j.m.l. and supplemented it with his bare-bones alternative motion for a new trial.

... [T]he district court granted the new trial ... for the following reason: "The court concludes, based on the jury's verdict and *comments the jurors made to the court after returning the verdict* [and outside the presence of the parties and their respective counsel], that the jury completely disregarded the Court's instructions. ... Accordingly, the Court deems it in the interest of justice to grant a new trial (emphasis added)." ... This ruling ... demonstrates beyond cavil that the court met with and interrogated the jurors after the verdict (concededly, outside the presence of the parties and counsel), and then acted on the comments of some of the jurors as though their remarks were newly discovered evidence. The inference is inescapable that, to impeach the jury's verdict, the district court relied on information gleaned from the jurors themselves during the court's post-verdict, *ex parte* meeting with the jury. The court voided the verdict because, in the court's own words, the jury "completely disregarded the Court's instructions." ...

Peterson timely filed a motion for reconsideration, which the district court did not grant. The case was re-tried in June 1996, and ended in a jury verdict in favor of Wilson, rejecting Peterson's claims. Peterson timely filed the notice of appeal that places the case before us today... .

Without reiterating every detail of the relevant testimony and documents, it suffices that the evidence heard and obviously credited by the jury [in the first trial] painted a picture of Peterson as a highly principled, apolitical, objective grant administrator who repeatedly refused to "play ball" with high ranking TSU administrators when they attempted to obtain expensive equipment for unauthorized personal use or sought to have unauthorized job positions created and funded with grant money for their special "friends."[fn] The jury also heard and obviously credited testimony of both direct and implied threats by Wilson of adverse job actions, including firing, that Peterson was in jeopardy of incurring if, on reflection, he should fail or refuse to accede to requests that would require the unauthorized expenditure of grant funds. ...

That the jury [in the first trial] unquestionably credited the testimony and documentation supporting Peterson's version of the facts and rejected Wilson's is confirmed by the "Yes" answer to Interrogatory No. I-A, "Do you find from a preponderance of the evidence that Dr. Bobby Wilson acted arbitrarily and capriciously in terminating Dr. Peterson?" In the interrogatory that followed, the jury awarded Peterson $152,235 in lost pay and benefits, and $35,000 for past and future mental anguish.

II

ANALYSIS...

"It is a well-settled rule in this circuit that 'a verdict can be against the "great weight of the evidence," and thus justify a new trial, even if there is substantial evidence to support it.'" [Rousseau v. Teledyne Movible Offshore, Inc., 812 F.2d 971, 972 (5th Cir.), cert. denied, 484 U.S. 827 (1987), citing Shows v. Jamison Bedding, Inc., 671 F.2d 927, 930 (5th Cir. 1982).] What courts cannot do ... is to grant a new trial "simply because [the court] would have come to a different conclusion then the jury did." [25 FEDERAL PROCEDURE, LAWYER'S EDITION § 58.13 (1984).] ...

The district court's succinct but cryptic, three-sentence explanation for granting a new trial demonstrates beyond question that, following the verdict, the court impermissibly met with and interrogated the jurors *outside the presence of the parties and their respective counsel,* and then proceeded to act in direct reliance on the jurors' comments as though they constituted newly discovered evidence of a kind that the court could properly consider. It was not. The conclusion is inescapable that, in impeaching the jury's verdict in this case, the district court relied on information obtained from the jurors in the court's post-verdict, *ex parte* meeting with them *and* that, by definition, any information thus obtained had to come directly from their internal deliberations qua jurors.[fn] ...

Rule 606(b) of the Federal Rules of Evidence (F.R.E.) tightly controls impeachment of jury verdicts. This rule states, in pertinent part:

> Upon an inquiry into the validity of a verdict ... , a juror may not testify as to any matter or statement occurring during the course of the jury's deliberations or to the effect of anything upon that or any other juror's mind or emotions as influencing the juror to assent to or dissent from the verdict ... or concerning the juror's mental processes in connection therewith, except that a juror may testify on the question whether extraneous prejudicial information was improperly brought to the jury's attention or whether any outside influence was improperly brought to the jury's attention or whether any outside influence was improperly brought to bear upon any juror. Nor may a juror's affidavit or evidence of any statement by the juror concerning a matter about which the juror would be precluded from testifying be received for these purposes.[fn]

... The landmark Supreme Court case on this issue is Tanner v. United States[, 483 U.S. 107 (1987).] After acknowledging that "[b]y the beginning of this century, if not earlier, the near-universal and firmly established common-law rule in the United States flatly prohibited the admission of juror testimony to impeach a jury verdict,"[fn] the Court observed that " Federal Rule of Evidence 606(b) is grounded in the common-law rule against admission of jury testimony to impeach a verdict and the exception for juror testimony relating to extraneous influences."[fn] Following *Tanner,* and more closely on point, we held in Robles v. Exxon Corp.[, 862 F.2d 1201 (5th Cir.), cert. denied, 490 U.S. 1051 (1989)], that receiving testimony from the jurors after they have returned their verdict, for the purpose of ascertaining that the jury misunderstood its instructions, is absolutely prohibited by F.R.E. 606(b).[fn] We underscored that holding by noting that "the legislative history of the rule unmistakably points to the conclusion that Congress made a conscious decision to disallow juror testimony as to the jurors' mental processes or *fidelity to the court's instructions.*"[fn] What is pellucid here, from the court's own unequivocal and unambiguous words, is that the jurors' statements to the court related directly to matters that transpired in the jury room, that these matters comprehended the mental processes of the jurors in their deliberations on the case, and that the jurors' statements formed the foundation of the court's impeachment of the verdict grounded in the jury's lack of "fidelity to the court's instructions."[fn] We cannot conceive of an example more explicitly violative of *Robles.* ...

... [F]or the trial court's abuse of discretion to be harmless and its order of a new trial to be sustained, we would have to conclude that, viewing all the evidence in the light most favorable to Peterson, the verdict is against the great weight of the evidence or the evidence is insufficient to support the verdict. The instant record cannot support any such conclusion. ...

As noted above, the jury in this case was presented with extensive evidence, principally testimonial evidence, much of which was in direct conflict, i.e., a "swearing match." Classically, the jury had the opportunity to view the witnesses' demeanor, look them in the eye, observe their body language, hear the timbre of their voices, and, finally, exercise the ultimate responsibility of the finder of fact by making credibility calls and deciding whom to believe and whom to disbelieve. We have now conducted the obligatory "cumbersome review" of the multi-volume trial record and find that both sides of the case—Peterson's and Wilson's—are supported by substantial evidence. One thing that is palpably absent from the record of the first trial, however, is a "great weight of evidence" either way. ...

Because our review of the entire record of the first trial eschews any possibility that the jury verdict was against the great weight of the evidence, or that the evidence is insufficient to support Peterson's claims, this ground cannot serve as a substitute basis for affirming the district court's grant of a new trial. It follows inescapably, then, that the court's abuse of discretion in violating F.R.E. 606(b) and of our rule in *Robles,* grounded in the Supreme Court's pronouncements in *Tanner,* was not harmless error. Rather, it was reversible error.

III
CONCLUSION

Our meticulous review of the record of the first trial of this case and our parsing of the ruling of the district court in granting a new trial satisfy us that such ruling must be reversed and a judgment must be rendered on the basis of the original jury verdict in favor of Peterson. ...

We are thus left with no choice but to reverse the district court's grant of a new trial, vacate the court's judgment rendered on the basis of the jury verdict in the second trial, and reinstate the results of the first trial. We therefore remand this case to the district court for entry of judgment in favor of Peterson and against Wilson in the principal sum of $187,235 ($152,235 for lost pay and benefits and $35,000 for past and future mental anguish), and for the assessment of appropriate interest and costs, including reasonable attorneys' fees incurred by Peterson in both trials and on appeal.

REVERSED and REMANDED with instructions.

INQUIRY

Harmless Error. Implicit in the discussion of new-trial motions so far, and explicit in the above opinion, is the condition that the party moving for new trial must show that the error about which the party complains affected a substantial right. Errors that are harmless, meaning those that have no probable effect on the outcome, are not grounds for relief from judgment. FED. R. CIV. P. 61 and equivalent state-court rules memorialize the harmless-error rule. The harmless-rule applies with equal force to the trial judge considering whether to grant a new trial and the appellate court reconsidering that decision. The next chapter on appeals further addresses harmless error. Read Rule 61 before considering another rule on which to challenge a judgment.

FED. R. CIV. P. 61. Harmless Error
Unless justice requires otherwise, no error in admitting or excluding evidence—or any other error by the court or a party—is ground for granting a new trial, for setting aside a verdict, or for vacating, modifying, or otherwise disturbing a judgment or order. At every stage of the proceeding, the court must disregard substantial rights.

INQUIRY

Relief from Judgment. There is another kind of challenge that a party can raise to a judgment that has less to do with what happened at trial than what happens after it. FED. R. CIV. P. 60 and equivalent state-court rules permit a party to move for relief from judgment. Motions for relief from judgment need not be made within a short time (such as Rule 59's 28 days) after trial. Rather, Rule 60(c) permits a motion for relief from judgment as late as one year after the judgment and, for certain grounds, at any later reasonable time. *Cf.* Arrieta v. Bataglia, 461 F.3d 861, 865 (7th Cir. 2006) (one-year limit on certain Rule 60 motions is jurisdictional and bars late-filed motions). The grounds that Rule 60(b) lists indicate why. They include clerical mistakes, newly discovered evidence, fraud by an opposing party, the judgment's satisfaction or release, and any other ground justifying relief. Either implicit or explicit in each of these grounds is the condition that the party moving for relief had no reasonable opportunity to obtain the relief at an earlier point before or during trial, or within the 28-day period within which the party might have moved under Rule 59 for new trial. Rule 60(b)(2) motions are extraordinary, and their success is rare. *See* Latshaw v. Trainer Wortham & Co., 452 F.3d 1097, 1103 (9th Cir. 2006) ("used sparingly ... only [in] extraordinary circumstances"). You can easily imagine why, given elaborate pretrial procedures for disclosure, discovery, and the scheduling and control of proceedings to ensure notice and opportunity for hearing that other civil procedures provide in general. *See* Scutieri v. Paige, 808 F.2d 785, 793 (11th Cir. 1987). Read Rule 60 before considering additional detail on relief from judgment. Also, note and read FED. R. CIV. P. 62.1. Rule 62.1 recognizes that Rule 60 motions for relief from judgment may occur while an appeal is pending that divests the trial court of jurisdiction to decide the motion. Rule 62.1 permits the trial court to indicate that it would grant relief if the appellate court remanded, giving the moving party an opportunity to so notify the appellate court.

FED. R. CIV. P. 60. Relief from a Judgment or Order

(a) CORRECTIONS BASED ON CLERICAL MISTAKES; OVERSIGHTS AND OMISSIONS. The court may correct a clerical mistake or a mistake arising from oversight or omission whenever one is found in a judgment, order, or other part of the record. The court may do so on motion or on its own, with or without notice. But after an appeal has been docketed in the appellate court and while it is pending, such a mistake may be corrected only with the appellate court's leave.

(b) GROUNDS FOR RELIEF FROM A FINAL JUDGMENT, ORDER, OR PROCEEDING. On motion and just terms, the court may relieve a party or its legal representative from a final judgment, order, or proceeding for the following reasons:

(1) mistake, inadvertence, surprise, or excusable neglect;

(2) newly discovered evidence that, with reasonable diligence, could not have been discovered in time to move for a new trial under Rule 59(b);

(3) fraud (whether previously called intrinsic or extrinsic), misrepresentation, or misconduct by an opposing party;

(4) the judgment is void;

(5) the judgment has been satisfied, released, or discharged; it is based on an earlier judgment that has been reversed or vacated; or applying it prospectively is no longer equitable; or

(6) any other reason that justifies relief.

© TIMING AND EFFECT OF THE MOTION.

(1) *Timing.* A motion under Rule 60(b) must be made within a reasonable time—and for reasons (1), (2), and (3) no more than a year after the entry of the judgment or order or the date of the proceeding.

(2) *Effect on Finality.* The motion does not affect the judgment's finality or suspend its operation.

(d) OTHER POWERS TO GRANT RELIEF. This rule does not limit a court's power to:

(1) entertain an independent action to relieve a party from a judgment, order, or proceeding;

(2) grant relief under 28 U.S.C. §1655 to a defendant who was not personally notified of the action; or

(3) set aside a judgment for fraud on the court.

(e) BILLS AND WRITS ABOLISHED. The following are abolished: bills of review, bills in the nature of bills of review, and writs of coram nobis, coram vobis, and audita querela.

...

FED. R. CIV. P. 62.1. Indicative Ruling on a Motion for Relief That is Barred by a Pending Appeal

(a) RELIEF PENDING APPEAL. If a timely motion is made for relief that the court lacks authority to grant because of an appeal that has been docketed and is pending, the court may:

(1) defer considering the motion;

(2) deny the motion; or

(3) state either that it would grant the motion if the court of appeals remands for that purpose or that the motion raises a substantial issue.

(b) NOTICE TO THE COURT OF APPEALS. The movant must promptly notify the circuit clerk under Federal Rule of Appellate Procedure 12.1 if the district court states that it would grant the motion or that the motion raises a substantial issue.

(c) REMAND. The district court may decide the motion if the court of appeals remands for that purpose.

INQUIRY

Excusable Neglect. FED. R. CIV. P. 60(b)(1) recognizes "excusable neglect" as a grounds for relief from judgment. Although they must be extraordinary and are thus rare, there are occasions on which a party may have notice of the proceeding and yet have an excuse not to respond. When is neglect excusable? Life goes on notwithstanding civil litigation. The inability of a party to attend to litigation because of family emergencies and the absence of a party from the country because of such emergencies can constitute excuse warranting relief from judgment. *See* Bateman v. U.S. Postal Service, 231 F.3d 1220 (9th Cir. 2000). The fact that party representatives live a great distance away from the forum in a region where communication is slow and difficult can be a basis for excusable neglect. FG Hemisphere Assocs., LLC v. Democratic Republic of Congo, 447 F.3d 835 (D.C. Cir. 2006). Addressing a similar bankruptcy-court rule, the Supreme Court in Pioneer Investment Services Co. v. Brunswick Assocs. Ltd. Partnership, 507 U.S. 380 (1993), held that the trial court should consider such factors as the length of delay, reason for delay, whether the party moving for relief controlled the delay, whether the moving party acted in good faith, and the extent to which the party obtaining the judgment would be prejudiced by the delay if the trial court set aside the judgment. If a party's lawyer neglects the proceeding, then one would ordinarily expect the only relief to be the party's malpractice action against the lawyer rather than Rule 60(b) relief from judgment. *But see* Community Dental Services v. Tani, 282 F.3d 1164 (9th Cir. 2002) (granting party Rule 60(b)(6) relief on grounds of lawyer's gross negligence).

Newly Discovered Evidence. Another ground for relief from judgment, newly discovered evidence, illustrates the significant limitation on relief, that the party moving for relief must not have had an earlier reasonable opportunity, before, during, or shortly after trial, to avoid, contest, or challenge the judgment. Rule 60(b)(2) limits relief for newly discovered evidence to evidence "that, with reasonable diligence, could not have been discovered in time to move for a new trial under Rule 59(b)... ." Parties do on rare occasions discover new evidence long after trial. The question then becomes why they did not discover it earlier, given elaborate discovery procedures. Trial courts faced with motions for relief for judgment based on newly discovered evidence require the moving party to show not only that the party exercised due diligence in discovery but also that the evidence is material, not cumulative, and would likely lead to a different result if a new trial were granted. *See* U.S. Steel v. M. DeMatteo Const. Co., 315 F.3d 43, 52 (1st Cir. 2002); Toole v. Baxter Healthcare Corp., 235 F.3d 1307, 1316 (11th Cir 2000). Instances where some additional evidence comes to light after trial are probably not that rare. Instances where the newly discovered evidence was not discoverable earlier, is not cumulative, and would likely make for a different outcome are exceedingly unusual.

Fraud. Rule 60(b)(3) identifies fraud, misrepresentation, or other party misconduct as additional grounds for relief from judgment. Obviously, the fraud must be as to the legal proceeding rather than be part of the underlying claim. One form of fraud, also covered by Rule 60(b)(2) regarding newly discovered evidence, would be for a party to conceal material evidence requested by an opposing party. *See, e.g.*, Green v. Foley, 856 F.2d 660 (4th Cir 1988). Given the reprehensibility of such fraud, that it is directed at destroying the integrity of the proceeding, and its direct implication of a party, trial courts may look more generously on Rule 60(b)(3)'s fraud grounds than on Rule 60(b)(2)'s grounds based on newly discovered evidence, even while requiring the moving party to prove by clear and convincing evidence another party's deliberate scheme to conceal the evidence. *See* Waddell v. Hendry County Sheriff's Office, 329 F.3d 1300, 1309 (11th Cir 2003); Yapp v. Excel Corp., 186 F.3d 1222 (10th Cir. 1999).

C. Enforcing Judgment

In some cases, the fact that the trial court has entered a judgment is all that the prevailing party needs to have accomplished its litigation goals, without any further enforcement action. For instance, a party who obtains a declaratory judgment clearing title to real property may need to do nothing more than record the judgment. The judgment requires no action by the losing party—no payment of money or relinquishing of personal property, for example. In most cases, though, the losing party must act in some manner, usually with the payment of money, for the judgment to accomplish its purpose. In some of those cases, entry of the judgment is alone enough to induce the losing party's action to comply with the judgment. In cases where an insurance company has indemnified the losing party for the judgment liability, insurers are generally responsible as to those obligations. They either promptly pay the judgment or authorize an appeal, retaining appellate counsel, posting bond, ensuring stay, and acting in other ways necessary to protect the losing party's assets.

When a party pays a money judgment, or the prevailing party obtains its payment, the lawyer for the prevailing party will prepare, sign, and file a court paper titled "Satisfaction of Judgment," indicating to the public that the judgment is no longer outstanding. Satisfied judgments are actually relatively rare. Given the vast number of unpaid financial obligations—rent, mortgage debt, credit-card debt, medical bills—unsatisfied judgments are common. There are vast numbers of cases in which the prevailing party must either attempt to force the losing party to act, invoke action by others to enforce the judgment, or decide whether that enforcement action is not worthwhile. Parties and their lawyers are usually sensitive to financial reality and ready to avoid fruitless procedures. The sayings are that one cannot get "blood from a turnip" or "water from a stone." It is not for lack of available procedures. Even though there is no debtor's prison in America (understanding that incarceration to induce payment can occur in connection with child support and tax obligations), state laws provide for ample alternative enforcement measures of civil judgments.

Parties enforce judgments using post-judgment procedures offered by the court that issued the judgment. When property or persons against whom a judgment creditor seeks to execute are located in a different state than the one in which the judgment-issuing court is located, the judgment creditor may file an enforcement action in the state's court under uniform reciprocal enforcement of judgment acts. The Constitution's Article IV full-faith-and-credit clause and 28 U.S.C. 1738 require the state and federal courts to recognize one another's judgments. FED. R. CIV. P. 69 refers the federal district courts to the forum state's law for enforcing federal-court judgments. Read Rule 69 before considering some of those state-law measures.

FED. R. CIV. P. 69. Execution
(a) IN GENERAL.
(1) *Money Judgment; Applicable Procedure.* A money judgment is enforced by a writ of execution, unless the court directs otherwise. The procedure on execution—and in proceedings supplementary to and in aid of judgment or execution—must accord with the procedure of the state where the court is located, but a federal statute governs to the extent it applies.
(2) *Obtaining Discovery.* In aid of the judgment or execution, the judgment creditor or a successor in interest whose interest appears of record may obtain discovery from any person—including the judgment debtor—as provided in these rules or by the procedure of the state where the court is located.
(b) AGAINST CERTAIN PUBLIC OFFICERS. When a judgment has been entered against a revenue officer in the circumstances stated in 28 U.S.C. §2006, or against an officer of Congress in the circumstances stated in 2 U.S.C. §118, the judgment must be satisfied as those statutes provide.

INQUIRY

Garnishment. Garnishment is a primary means of enforcement authorized by state law. Garnishment is a process by which a judgment creditor can control and acquire a judgment debtor's money held by a non-party. The judgment creditor requests that the court issue a writ of garnishment to a non-party, called the garnishee or garnishee defendant, who holds money belonging to the judgment debtor. The judgment creditor will have the garnishment writ served on the garnishee. The writ instructs the garnishee to turn the money or a portion of it over to the judgment creditor unless the judgment debtor objects within a defined period, in which instance the court will hear and resolve the objection. Bank accounts are a prime example. Banks hold checking, savings, and other accounts for their customers. When a judgment creditor learns that a judgment debtor has a bank account in a certain institution, the judgment creditor obtains a garnishment writ, serves it on the bank, and waits for the time for objection to expire before the bank turns it over to the judgment creditor. Paychecks are another example. Judgment creditors can garnish wages that an employer owes an employee. The employer must then pay a statutory portion of the wage (preserving a portion for the employee debtor's survival) to the judgment creditor. *See* 28 U.S.C. §1673(a) (defining garnishable proportion). Statutes exempt from garnishment certain obligations such as retirement accounts (IRAs, 401k's, etc.) and public benefits (Social Security and other welfare).

28 U.S.C. §1673. Restriction on garnishment
(a) *Maximum allowable garnishment*
Except as provided in subsection (b) of this section and in section 1675 of this title, the maximum part of the aggregate disposable earnings of an individual for any workweek which is subjected to garnishment may not exceed (1) 25 per

centum of his disposable earnings for that week, or (2) the amount by which his disposable earnings for that week exceed thirty times the Federal minimum hourly wage prescribed by section 206(a)(1) of Title 29 in effect at the time the earnings are payable, whichever is less. ...
(b) *Exceptions*
(1) The restrictions of subsection (a) of this section do not apply in the case of (A) any order for the support of any person issued by a court of competent jurisdiction or in accordance with an administrative procedure, which is established by State law, which affords substantial due process, and which is subject to judicial review; (B) any order of any court of the United States having jurisdiction over cases under chapter 13 of Title 11; (C) any debt due for any State or Federal tax.
(2) The maximum part of the aggregate disposable earnings of an individual for any workweek which is subject to garnishment to enforce any order for the support of any person shall not exceed—(A) where such individual is supporting his spouse or dependent child (other than a spouse or child with respect to whose support such order is used), 50 per centum of such individual's disposable earnings for that week; and (B) where such individual is not supporting such a spouse or dependent child described in clause (A), 60 per centum of such individual's disposable earnings for that week; ... .
(c) *Execution or enforcement of garnishment order or process prohibited*
No court of the United States or any State, and no State (or officer or agency thereof), may make, execute, or enforce any order or process in violation of this section.

INQUIRY

Execution. FED. R. CIV. P. 69 states that "[a] money judgment is enforced by a writ of execution, unless the court directs otherwise," before referring the federal district courts to the forum-state's law for the "procedure on execution." Execution thus refers to enforcement procedures generally, including the just-discussed garnishment procedures. Execution also has a narrower meaning as a specific form of enforcement. State procedures provide for a judgment creditor to request and a court to issue a writ of execution. A writ of execution commands the U.S. marshal, sheriff, or equivalent government official to take control of property, often real property, to auction or otherwise sell it in satisfaction of the judgment. A judgment debtor who receives notice that the judgment creditor has executed the judgment upon the debtor's home, vehicle, or other substantial property, and that the sheriff will soon be selling the property, may (if able) satisfy the judgment by other means to remove the threat and save the property. The judgment debtor may not attack the judgment except for non-service and lack of jurisdiction. *See* United States v. Bigford, 365 F.3d 859, 866 (10th Cir. 2004); United States v. Straits Steel & Wire Co., 810 F.Supp. 208, 211 (W.D. Mich. 1992). State law also exempts some property from execution, such as tools of a trade, and exempts other property up to certain values, such as a homestead and vehicle, so as not to make the debtor destitute of the means of self support. *See, e.g.,* N.Y. C.P.LR. §5205 (including exemptions for sewing machine, school books, Bible, stove, and wedding rings). Sophisticated debtors may be attracted to states having no limit to certain exemptions such as a homestead. Consider the following state scheme for exemptions from execution.

FLORIDA CONST. ART. 10, §4. Homestead; exemptions

(a) There shall be exempt from forced sale under process of any court, and no judgment, decree or execution shall be a lien thereon, except for the payment of taxes and assessments thereon, obligations contracted for the purchase, improvement or repair thereof, or obligations contracted for house, field or other labor performed on the realty, the following property owned by a natural person:

(1) a homestead, if located outside a municipality, to the extent of one hundred sixty acres of contiguous land and improvements thereon, which shall not be reduced without the owner's consent by reason of subsequent inclusion in a municipality; or if located within a municipality, to the extent of one-half acre of contiguous land, upon which the exemption shall be limited to the residence of the owner or the owner's family;

(2) personal property to the value of one thousand dollars.

(b) These exemptions shall inure to the surviving spouse or heirs of the owner.

(c) The homestead shall not be subject to devise if the owner is survived by spouse or minor child, except the homestead may be devised to the owner's spouse if there be no minor child. The owner of homestead real estate, joined by the spouse if married, may alienate the homestead by mortgage, sale or gift and, if married, may by deed transfer the title to an estate by the entirety with the spouse. If the owner or spouse is incompetent, the method of alienation or encumbrance shall be as provided by law.

In re Davis,

United States Court of Appeals for the Fifth Circuit (en banc)
170 F.3d 475 (1999)

EDITH H. JONES, Circuit Judge:

In 1987, Cullen and Karen Davis filed for bankruptcy relief and claimed as their exempt Texas homestead a residence valued at $500,000 which they owned free and clear. Cullen's former wife Sandra obtained a judgment from the bankruptcy court declaring that her $250,000-plus claim for alimony, child support, and maintenance was nondischargeable under 11 U.S.C. §523(a)(5). To enforce the nondischargeability judgment, Sandra sought turnover relief in the form of an order permitting her to foreclose on Cullen's and Karen's homestead. The bankruptcy court and the district court held that she could not levy on the debtors' homestead because it is protected from execution under Texas law, and 11 U.S.C. §522(c)(1), a provision of the Bankruptcy Code, did not preempt the debtors' state-law rights. A split panel of this court reversed the lower courts. [C] This case was selected for en banc rehearing because of its importance to federal bankruptcy law and to state exemption rules. We conclude that the lower courts were essentially correct and affirm their judgments denying Sandra the relief she seeks.

FACTUAL AND PROCEDURAL HISTORY

When Sandra and Cullen divorced in 1968, they executed a property settlement, support and child custody agreement, and divorce judgment (collectively "divorce judgment"), and Cullen agreed to make monthly payments to Sandra through January 1, 1991, with certain contingent payments thereafter. In 1979, Cullen married Karen Davis. In 1984, Cullen and Karen purchased a house and lot for $750,000.

In 1987, Cullen and Karen stopped making payments to Sandra as required by the divorce judgment and filed for Chapter 7 bankruptcy relief, followed later by conversion to Chapter 11. As has been noted, Cullen's and Karen's costly, lien-free home was claimed as exempt property pursuant to §522(b)(2)(A) and valued at $500,000 on their schedules.

Armed with the bankruptcy court's judgment that Cullen owed her $300,000 in nondischargeable alimony, maintenance and child support obligations and associated attorneys' fees, Sandra requested that the bankruptcy court seize and sell the debtors' homestead under ... Fed. R. Civ. P. 69. Because a debtor's homestead is exempt from attachment, execution, or seizure under Tex. Const. art. XVI §50 and Texas Property Code §41.002(a), the bankruptcy court determined that the debtors' homestead was not subject to the Texas turnover statute. In so doing, the court rejected Sandra's argument that §522(c)(1) of the Bankruptcy Code preempted the Texas homestead exemption for nondischargeable debts related to family support as defined in §523(a)(5). ...

THE BANKRUPTCY EXEMPTION STATUTE

At issue in this case are the meaning and preemptive force, if any, of 11 U.S.C. §522(c), a provision that is part of the Bankruptcy Code's framework for the treatment of exempt property. ...

Federal bankruptcy law affords debtors a fresh start by enjoining collection of discharged debts, §524, and by permitting the debtors to retain certain limited amounts and types of exempt property, §522. Exemptions have been perennially controversial, because they reduce assets potentially available to pay creditors and arouse charges of abuse of bankruptcy. Exemptions are also fought over by states'-rights advocates, who value the traditional state legislative prerogative to adjust exemptions to local economic conditions, and by advocates of federal uniformity, who want to raise—or lower—exemptions based on conceptions of national equity. Congress allayed the controversy between state and federal advocates by providing in the 1978 Bankruptcy Code that states could opt out of prescribed federal exemptions altogether or could allow their citizens to select either schedule. *See* 11 U.S.C. §522(b).

Exemptions are easy to claim. The debtor files a list of exempt property protected by applicable federal or state law with the court. [C] If the exemptions are not objected to, the property becomes exempt and unavailable to be levied on by pre-petition creditors or managed by the trustee.

The right to claim exemptions is closely guarded. Waivers are unenforceable. [C] A debtor may claim exemptions even on property recovered by the trustee from third parties. [C] The debtor may "avoid the fixing of a lien" to the extent it impairs an exemption. [C] Both husband and wife may claim exemptions individually. [C]

The consequences of claiming exemptions are delineated in §522(c). Generally, unless a case is dismissed, exempt property may not be held liable to repay any pre-petition debt of the debtor. ...

In order to prevail in this case, Sandra must demonstrate that §522(c) creates a basis for execution on Cullen's homestead to enforce her nondischargeable divorce judgment and that, in enacting this provision, Congress expressly or impliedly preempted the Texas homestead law.[fn]

Sandra's argument as to § 522(c) is simple. She reads the section to say that property exempt from payment of discharged debts is "liable" for the types of debts listed as exceptions. But the statute does not say this. Rather, it states that exempt property "is not liable ... for any debt ... except ... [a nondischargeable divorce judgment]." Her argument did not persuade the bankruptcy court, who wrote:

> [Section 522(c)] does not create or establish liability. It enjoins most liability imposed by non-bankruptcy law upon exempt property but does not enjoin all liability for all debts. While it does not impose an injunction against liability on exempt property for §523(a)(1) or (a)(5) debts, it also does not prevent non-bankruptcy law from imposing such an injunction. Indeed, Texas has done so. [C]

At best, the statutory language is ambiguous from the standpoint of imposing the liability Sandra seeks. Viewed in light of the exemption framework outlined above, however, Judge Felsenthal's explanation is more plausible than Sandra's. In other words, §522(c) sought to leave exempt property exposed to postbankruptcy liability only to the extent it would have been exposed if the bankruptcy had not occurred. This interpretation is the most plausible reading of §522(c) for several reasons.

Unless Congress expressly legislates otherwise, ... , the policies of bankruptcy law have little bearing on property after it is exempt from the debtor's estate. Such property is no longer available for distribution to creditors, and it is not subject to charge for bankruptcy administrative fees. The debtor may use the exempt property without claims of pre-petition creditors hanging over his head. Of course, Congress deemed necessary some narrow exceptions to this policy of a fresh start for the debtor's exempt property. Thus, purchase money liens on exempt property had to be protected to insure a free flow of credit for purchases of property in markets like residential real estate. Further, tax liens were preserved against exempt property because the contrary result—voiding, e.g., school tax liens on a homestead—is unthinkable. Section 522(c)(2) deals with these claims by simply leaving them unaltered on exempt property. The section does not "create" or "impose" liability, nor does it override or add to state law or federal tax law. The holders of those sorts of unaltered claims would have to proceed via applicable non-bankruptcy collection schemes to realize on their security against exempt property.[fn]

... When Sandra contends that the language "creates" a "liability" over and above the protection her lien is accorded in state law, she means that the bankruptcy court can order execution on the homestead to satisfy the divorce judgment. This contention flatly contradicts standard canons of statutory interpretation, for the same language in a single statutory provision cannot have two different meanings. *See* Sullivan v. Stroop, 496 U.S. 478, 484[] (1990) (espousing "normal rule of statutory construction" that "identical words used in different parts of the same act are intended to have the same meaning"). ...

Notwithstanding our view that Sandra's construction of §522(c) creates internal inconsistencies in that provision, bits of legislative history and the import of §522(f) may be cited to bolster her position. These arguments are not without force, but they are ultimately unconvincing. ...

Sandra also contends that §522(c)(1) is not intended to serve simply as a lien preservation provision, because that purpose is fulfilled by §522(f), which provides in part that while a debtor may avoid the fixing of a lien on exempt property, the debtor may not avoid a judicial lien for alimony or family support. If §522(c)(1) does not have the broader purpose of permitting execution against exempt property, then it is allegedly redundant of the lien preservation function of §522(f)(1)(A)(i). But §522(c) is not duplicative of §522(f)(1)(A). The former provision states the effect of an exemption on liability for each kind of debt specified, while the latter provision states when a party may avoid the fixing of a pre-petition lien on exempt property. The two sections overlap in part, but their scope and purpose differ. ...

A holistic reading of §522(c)(1) undermines Sandra's theory that the provision is literally self-executing. She has confused her right with her remedy. This error is exposed by applying her reasoning to other debts that §522(c) preserves notwithstanding property exemptions, i.e. certain tax debts, federal depository regulators' debts, and debts already secured by a valid lien. If Sandra's reading of §522(c) is correct, then a homestead could be sold to repay non-liened tax debt, made nondischargeable according to §523(a)(1), or indeed to pay off an obligation owed to the FDIC without recourse to federal or state lien or homestead protection laws. The impact of such a construction would put the preferred creditors in a better position after the debtor has filed bankruptcy than before and may create an incentive for filing involuntary bankruptcies. In effect, Sandra's proffered construction of §522(c) does not merely withhold any special protection offered by bankruptcy law, but overrides nonbankruptcy law and has the effect of denying the debtor even exemptions that would have been available outside of bankruptcy. Further, this interpretation seriously disadvantages a debtor subject to the listed obligations, and it actively discourages a large number of potential debtors who are faced with the types of obligations excepted from §522(c) from seeking bankruptcy relief. Congress surely would not have reached this consequential result without legislating more explicitly.[fn]

For all these reasons, we conclude that §522(c)(1) does not "create" "liability" of exempt property for specified debts following bankruptcy. Instead, the section permits creditors holding such claims to proceed against the property after bankruptcy based on the rights and remedies they would have had under state law if bankruptcy had not been filed.

PREEMPTION

To prevail in her approach to §522(c), Sandra must show that it preempts Texas law, thus subjecting Cullen's homestead to seizure and sale to satisfy her nondischargeable divorce judgment, despite the express prohibition on such foreclosure contained in the Texas constitution and statutes. [C]

The Supremacy Clause enables Congress to override state laws if it so intends. Deference to our federalism counsels a presumption that areas of law traditionally reserved to the states, like police powers or property law, are not to be disturbed absent the "clear and manifest purpose of Congress."[fn] But preemption may be implied if state and federal laws conflict or a state law thwarts the "accomplishment and execution" of congressional intent. [C] Moreover, if

Congress has passed a pervasive federal legislative scheme leaving states no room to supplement, then state law will also be preempted. [C]

The Bankruptcy Code's "policy" of strengthening enforcement of family support obligations is a weak reed on which to support implied preemption. Although §522(c) entitles these obligations to special status against property otherwise exempt in bankruptcy, neither that provision nor §523(a)(5), the provision for nondischargeability of family support obligations, which §522(c) incorporates, expresses the full intent of the Code. A debtor who owes family support obligations is afforded a great deal of latitude and protection. First, the filing of the bankruptcy case automatically stays payments of support obligations, as it does all other payments to pre-petition creditors. [C] An ex-spouse deprived of certain family support payments must file an adversary proceeding in bankruptcy court to enforce nondischargeability, and even then, the court may order reduction of certain payments if it finds that the defaulting spouse would suffer "hardship." [C] A debtor may obtain a Chapter 7 discharge or confirm a Chapter 13 plan without being current in family support obligations. Bankruptcy law presently contains neither a pervasive or consistent approach toward family support obligations. ...

Reliance on the exemption provision of the Code as a source of implied preemption is also misplaced. Congress specifically preserved state exemptions under §522(b), rejecting a proposal for uniform federal exemptions.[fn] Congress allowed states to define the existence and limits of exemptions.[fn] By expressly preserving a role for the state law in the Bankruptcy Code, it is clear that Congress has not devised a policy on federal exemptions so pervasive as to leave no room for a state to supplement bankruptcy law with respect to exemptions.

Even more important, there is no direct conflict between compliance with the Bankruptcy Code and the Texas homestead law. We concluded earlier that in specifying certain debts for which the exempt property is still liable, §522(c) leaves the parties to their state law collection rights. To execute a judgment against Texas property, a judgment creditor must rely on the state mechanism for enforcement. Although Texas law does not permit the seizure of a homestead for a family support obligation, Sandra can still perfect a judgment lien against the property in question, even if it is a homestead. The property is thus liable, although it is immune from seizure while it is a homestead.[fn] This is all §522(c)(1) requires. [C] Section 522(c)(1) assures that the debtor remains ultimately liable, and the property or proceeds from the sale of property may be subject to seizure if the property ever ceases to be the debtor's homestead.[fn] Because the Texas homestead law does not bar the attachment of a perfected lien to homestead property, it does not conflict with §522(c)(1). ...

Section 522(c) also fails to conflict with Texas law because it is not self-executing, it provides no means for enforcing the creditor's right. Fed. R. Civ. P. 69(a) explains why:

> Process to enforce a judgment for the payment of money shall be a writ of execution.... The procedure on execution, in proceedings on and in aid of a judgment, and in proceedings on and in aid of execution *shall be in accordance with the practice and procedure of the state in which the district court is held,* existing at the time the remedy is sought, *except*

that any statute of the United States governs to the extent that it is applicable.

(emphasis added). Pursuant to Rule 69(a), incorporated by Bankr. R. 7069, Texas's enforcement mechanisms govern in bankruptcy court in the absence of a federal execution statute. The Texas turnover statute does not permit seizure and sale of a homestead to satisfy a family support obligation. [C]

CONCLUSION

Cullen and Karen Davis were entitled to exempt their homestead from claims of creditors under Texas and federal bankruptcy law, and they did so. Sandra is entitled, under §522(c)(1), to enforce her nondischargeable judgment for family support obligations notwithstanding the exemption claim, but her remedy must be in accord with Texas law, since §522(c) is not an execution statute and does not preempt relevant Texas law. Either Texas or, perhaps, the U.S. Congress could alter this situation, but it is our duty to enforce the present statute.

The judgment of the district court, affirming the judgment of the bankruptcy court, is AFFIRMED.

INQUIRY

Discovery. Notice that Rule 69(a)(2) provides for discovery of judgment debtors. Parties do not have the right to discover the assets of opposing parties before the trial court enters a judgment making relevant the extent and location of those assets. Once a judgment enters, the party who is the judgment creditor may invoke discovery procedures to ascertain the nature and extent of those assets and their location. Rule 69(a)(2) permits a party to use federal or forum-state discovery procedures. Subpoenas to non-parties to obtain financial records are common. So are record requests to the judgment debtor. Depositions of judgment debtors are somewhat less common because of the cost. States authorize procedures for debtor's examinations, requiring the judgment debtor to appear at the courthouse for the judgment creditor's lawyer to ask questions of the debtor under oath. The trial judge may swear the debtor, but the examinations occur outside of the courtroom so as not to take court time. When a debtor fails to appear for examination, the trial court may issue an order to show cause and then a bench (arrest) warrant. Special procedures of this type can challenge a recalcitrant debtor sufficiently to increase the likelihood of judgment compliance when debtors are able. State laws provide other procedures to protect against fraudulent conveyance of assets to avoid enforcement of judgment.

Practice

It took about eight years of intensive post-judgment litigation, but when the case finally resolved with the payment of most of the judgment, the plaintiff's lawyer felt that the effort had been worth every single minute. The defendant businessman had raped a young woman jogger in the roadside weeds before capture, plea, and criminal conviction. Although the subsequent civil trial ended quickly with a six-figure judgment, by then the businessman had conveyed away his ongoing business interest. Post-judgment pleadings, discovery, hearings, and appeals challenged and eventually overturned the conveyance, forcing the businessman to finally settle. Some fights, the lawyer thought, are worth finishing to the very end.

Collections. Lawyers call the work of invoking judgment-enforcement procedures "collection practice." Although trial lawyers know and occasionally invoke collection procedures, lawyers tend to specialize in collection practice in part because of the uniqueness of the procedures but also for economic reasons. Collection practice tends to be a volume service. Clients who have large numbers of routine collection matters usually pursued on default judgments, or in which the simplicity of the claim and assuredness of the debt truncate pretrial and trial procedures, hire lawyers who have organized their practices for collection work both from an administrative and economic standpoint. Given the small or non-existent returns in many cases, systems and efficiency are essential to collection work. Lawyers practicing collections will manage many more cases at once, will rely more heavily on standardized forms and practices, and will also rely more on legal assistants and other support personnel to process standard paperwork.

Stay. As mentioned in the previous section, FED. R. CIV. P. 62 provides an automatic 14-day stay against enforcement, permits the trial court to extend the stay pending disposition of new trial and other post-judgment motions, and links those motions stays to the movant providing security for the judgment. Rule 62(c) also authorizes the trial court to stay enforcement of a judgment pending disposition of an appeal, provided that the appellant posts a bond to secure the judgment and the trial court approves the bond. A bond is a written assurance that the entity giving the bond will pay the judgment in the event of certain conditions such as an unfavorable resolution of the appeal and the failure of the judgment debtor to pay. Trial courts approve bonds only from entities recognized as capable of making payment. Appellees do not typically oppose the posting of a stay bond, given that it removes the significant question of an appellant's ultimate ability to pay. Read Rule 62 on stays and bonds for security before considering a related issue having to do with how a party might secure a judgment even before obtaining it.

FED. R. CIV. P. 62. Stay of Proceedings to Enforce a Judgment

(a) AUTOMATIC STAY; EXCEPTIONS FOR INJUNCTIONS, RECEIVERSHIPS, AND PATENT ACCOUNTINGS. Except as stated in this rule, no execution may issue on a judgment, nor may proceedings be taken to enforce it, until 14 days have passed after its entry. But unless the court orders otherwise, the following are not stayed after being entered, even if an appeal is taken:

(1) an interlocutory or final judgment in an action for an injunction or a receivership; or

(2) a judgment or order that directs an accounting in an action for patent infringement.

(b) STAY PENDING THE DISPOSITION OF A MOTION. On appropriate terms for the opposing party's security, the court may stay the execution of a judgment—or any proceedings to enforce it—pending disposition of any of the following motions:

(1) under Rule 50, for judgment as a matter of law;

(2) under Rule 52(b), to amend the findings or for additional findings;

(3) under Rule 59, for a new trial or to alter or amend a judgment; or

(4) under Rule 60, for relief from a judgment or order.

(c) INJUNCTION PENDING AN APPEAL. While an appeal is pending from an interlocutory order or final judgment that grants, dissolves, or denies an injunction, the court may suspend, modify, restore, or grant an injunction on terms for bond or other terms that secure the opposing party's rights. If the judgment appealed from is rendered by a statutory three-judge district court, the order must be made either:

(1) by that court sitting in open session; or
(2) by the assent of all its judges, as evidenced by their signatures.
(d) STAY WITH BOND ON APPEAL. If an appeal is taken, the appellant may obtain a stay by supersedeas bond, except in an action described in Rule 62(a)(1) or (2). The bond may be given upon or after filing the notice of appeal or after obtaining the order allowing the appeal. The stay takes effect when the court approves the bond.
(e) STAY WITHOUT BOND ON AN APPEAL BY THE UNITED STATES, ITS OFFICERS, OR ITS AGENCIES. The court must not require a bond, obligation, or other security from the appellant when granting a stay on an appeal by the United States, its officers, or its agencies or on an appeal directed by a department of the federal government.
(f) STAY IN FAVOR OF A JUDGMENT DEBTOR UNDER STATE LAW. If a judgment is a lien on the judgment debtor's property under the law of the state where the court is located, the judgment debtor is entitled to the same stay of execution the state court would give.
(g) APPELLATE COURT'S POWER NOT LIMITED. This rule does not limit the power of the appellate court or one of its judges or justices:
(1) to stay proceedings—or suspend, modify, restore, or grant an injunction—while an appeal is pending; or
(2) to issue an order to preserve the status quo or the effectiveness of the judgment to be entered.
(h) STAY WITH MULTIPLE CLAIMS OR PARTIES. A court may stay the enforcement of a final judgment entered under Rule 54(b) until it enters a later judgment or judgments, and may prescribe terms necessary to secure the benefit of the stayed judgment for the party in whose favor it was entered.

INQUIRY

Security. Effective enforcement of a judgment may depend on the prevailing party first having secured property or financial interests on which to execute. A lawsuit in which the defendant has a substantial risk of incurring a substantial uninsured financial obligation creates an incentive to protect financial interests. On notice of a lawsuit, defendants might give, sell, loan, encumber, or otherwise burden, conceal, or dispose of the property on which the plaintiff expects to execute after judgment. Although the common law did not recognize prejudgment garnishment, state laws have offered claimants some protection against such actions through various means of securing respondents' property before judgment. State laws have offered prejudgment garnishment of accounts and even wages, attachment of real property and intangible interests at the time of filing of the complaint, sequestration of disputed property in the hands of an independent non-party, and replevin procedures permitting claimants to seize goods before service of process. As mentioned in Chapter III on notice and opportunity for hearing, FED. R. CIV. P. 64 authorizes federal-court litigants to employ the prejudgment procedures for security in anticipation of judgment that the forum state recognizes. Rule 64(b) mentions specifically that those procedures may include garnishment, attachment, replevin, and sequestration. Rule 64(b) also mentions civil arrest, but that remedy is not generally available in the kinds of civil actions filed in the federal courts.

Due Process. Involuntary prejudgment securing of a party's property raises Fifth Amendment (and in the state courts, Fourteenth Amendment) due-process concerns, especially when there is no notice of the action, no opportunity for the respondent to argue against the securing, and the action harms the respondent's interest. Prejudgment garnishment, attachment, and replevin can prevent a person from drawing on lines of credit, selling goods in the ordinary course of business, and otherwise conducting routine financial affairs. It can also trigger default in mortgages and other obligations. Civil procedures, including especially hearing or trial before judgment and execution, ensure fair resolution of claims. Procedures that jump-start enforcement by securing claims before hearing or trial run the risk of interfering with a party's property when the court may not ultimately find the party liable. The Supreme Court worked out permissible contours of prejudgment garnishment procedures in Connecticut v. Doehr, 501 U.S. 1 (1991), addressed in Chapter III on notice and opportunity for hearing. *Connecticut v. Doehr* avoided hard-and-fast rules and instead considered factors including: (a) whether the attached property is a subject of the dispute; (b) whether attachment will leave the property in its owner's hands; (c) whether attachment depends on review by a judge; (d) whether there is notice of attachment; (e) whether there is hearing before or soon after attachment; (f) the probability of the plaintiff prevailing; (g) the nature of the claim (tort or contract debt); (h) the harm on attachment; and (i) the harm if the court refuses attachment. *See also* Mathews v. Eldridge, 424 U.S. 319, 334 (1976). While some practices are clearly unconstitutional, in many cases the availability of prejudgment procedures to secure an anticipated judgment will depend on evaluating several of these factors as to the particular case.

Specific Acts. Not all judgments are solely for money. Some judgments anticipate that the losing party will engage in a specific act. Judgments that are not self-executing or upon which a party cannot execute through independent cooperative non-parties like banks and employers, and that instead require losing parties to act cooperatively, are naturally problematic. Losers are usually not happy about losing. The loss may implicate a range of interests that to the loser can look more substantial than the consequences of failing or refusing to comply with the judgment. FED. R. CIV. P. 70 and equivalent state-court rules increase the consequences of non-compliance with a range of alternative remedies. Rule 70(e) authorizes contempt sanctions against a disobedient party. *See* Spallone v. United States, 493 U.S. 265 (1990) (daily fine until judgment compliance). Contempt sanctions can include incarceration pending performance—the strongest of inducements. Rule 70(a) provides an attractive alternative, that if the losing party fails to act timely, the court may order a willing non-party to do the act for the losing party at the party's expense. For the right price (at the losing party's cost), the prevailing party may be able to find someone to do that which the losing party ought to have done. Rule 70(b) offers another attractive alternative, that the court may enter a judgment that has the effect of conveying away real or personal property that the losing party should have conveyed to comply with the judgment, or otherwise extinguishing the losing party's lost interest. Read Rule 70 and its companion Rule 71 regarding non-party relief.

FED. R. CIV. P. 70. Enforcing a Judgment for a Specific Act

(a) PARTY'S FAILURE TO ACT; ORDERING ANOTHER TO ACT. If a judgment requires a party to convey land, to deliver a deed or other document, or to perform any other specific act and the party fails to comply within the time specified, the court may order the act to be done—at the disobedient party's expense—by another person appointed by the court. When done, the act has the same effect as if done by the party.

(b) VESTING TITLE. If the real or personal property is within the district, the court—instead of ordering a conveyance—may enter a judgment divesting any party's title and vesting it in others. That judgment has the effect of a legally executed conveyance.

(c) OBTAINING A WRIT OF ATTACHMENT OR SEQUESTRATION. On application by a

party entitled to performance of an act, the clerk must issue a writ of attachment or sequestration against the disobedient party's property to compel obedience.
(d) OBTAINING A WRIT OF EXECUTION OR ASSISTANCE. On application by a party who obtains a judgment or order for possession, the clerk must issue a writ of execution or assistance.
(e) HOLDING IN CONTEMPT. The court may also hold the disobedient party in contempt.

FED. R. CIV. P. 71. Enforcing Relief For or Against a Nonparty

When an order grants relief for a nonparty or may be enforced against a nonparty, the procedure for enforcing the order is the same as for a party.

INQUIRY

Summary. When a court finds facts and reaches conclusions of law, or a jury reaches its verdict, the court must still enter a judgment that properly disposes of the parties' claims and defenses. The court may enter judgment on its own or request a party to prepare a judgment for the court's entry, or a party may move for entry of judgment following findings or verdict. A judgment is a court paper that disposes of claims or defenses. The final-judgment rule, embodied in FED. R. CIV. P. 54 and 28 U.S.C. §1291, provides that final decisions of a trial court that dispose of all claims trigger the right to and periods for post-judgment motions and appeals. Parties may attack a judgment with renewed Rule 50 motions for judgment as a matter of law (JNOV), Rule 59 motions for new trial, or Rule 60 motions for relief from judgment. A Rule 50 motion for judgment as a matter of law must show that there was no evidence to support one or more elements of the claim supporting the judgment. A Rule 59 motion for new trial may rely on defects in the proceeding or in the verdict affecting a substantial right of the losing party. A verdict against the great weight of the evidence is one such defect. A Rule 60 motion for relief from judgment must show mistake, excusable neglect, newly discovered evidence, or similar extraordinary grounds for relief. Rule 61's harmless-error rule requires that a party moving for new trial show likelihood that the error affected the outcome. Under Rule 64, parties enforce federal-court judgments under the laws of the forum state. Those state laws typically provide for garnishment of interests, execution on property, and discovery of assets, while also providing for stay of enforcement on appeal with bond for security. State law may also provide for prejudgment securing of anticipated judgment, as limited by due-process concerns around notice and opportunity for hearing.

Career

Have you researched any specific attorneys and their employers? One does not have to meet and get to know a lawyer in order to draw on that lawyer as a model and inspiration. Many lawyers have drawn their inspiration from Abraham Lincoln and other famous and not-so-famous civil litigators. Information is widely available today on the Internet and through your law school's library about individual civil litigators and their law firms. When you read a recent civil procedure case that interests you, look up in an electronic research database the names of the lawyers who prepared and argued that case. (The databases often give the names of the lawyers after the caption and headnotes and before the opinion.) Then research those lawyers to see what kind of civil-litigation firm and practice they maintain, and what qualifications they claim. Find your inspiration among the many fine civil litigators who file, prepare, and try these cases, and argue the appeals, producing the opinions you read. They are real lawyers with fascinating practices.

CHAPTER XIV

APPEAL

OBJECTIVE: That you be able to identify when a party has an appeal of right or opportunity for appeal, state how to perfect the appeal, and identify the appeal standard of review.

Case Study: You represent the defendant subcontractor in a construction-defect case brought against it by the plaintiff general contractor and plaintiff developer. You filed a motion for summary judgment on your client subcontractor's behalf arguing the economic-loss doctrine as to the general contractor's claim but lost. Your client and its insurer then settled the general contractor's claim. At trial, you moved for judgment as a matter of law at the close of the plaintiff developer's proofs but lost. The jury then returned a verdict against your client subconstractor. You have renewed the motion for judgment as a matter of law and alternatively moved for new trial for errors in the admission of evidence. Your client and its insurer want to know what appeal rights the subcontractor will have as to all parties and claims if you lose the post-trial motions, when you must file the appeal, and what the appeal review standards will be. What is your advice?

Federal Rules of Appellate Procedure this chapter reproduces:
FED. R. APP. P. 1. Scope of Rules; Title
FED. R. APP. P. 2. Suspension of Rules
FED. R. APP. P. 3. Appeal as of Right—How Taken
FED. R. CIV. P. 4. Appeal as of Right—When Taken
FED. R. APP. P. 5. Appeal by Permission
FED. R. APP. P. 21. Writs of Mandamus and Prohibition, and Other Extraordinary Writs
FED. R. APP. P. 38. Frivolous Appeal—Damages and Costs

As the number and percentage of federal civil trials has dwindled to the figurative point of disappearing, it should not be surprising that the number of federal civil appeals has increased substantially. State appellate dockets show similar increases. On the other hand, the increase in appeals is curious in that only small percentages of civil appeals (about 10 to 20 percent in federal court) result in reversal. It may also surprise you to know that the Supreme Court has not explicitly recognized appeals as a federal constitutional right. So long as a state provides a full and fair trial on the merits, the Fourteenth Amendment does not require the state to offer an appeal. *See* Griffin v. Illinois, 351 U.S. 12 (1956).

Independent review of final decisions is so prevalent because we accept it as a hallmark of due process. The authority exercised by the federal courts is delegated authority, meaning that it requires constitutional and (in most instances) legislative sanction. State judges operate under similar constitutional and statutory sanction. The delegation of judicial authority implies a higher authority than that which trial judges exercise. The existence of a higher authority implies a right of appeal to that authority. Appeal is something that even unschooled children (at least those with offender siblings) recognize as an inherent right. Nothing about the structure of government and the courts suggests anything less. To the extent that government offers a higher authority than the official who makes a decision, citizens ought to have the right to appeal to that higher authority when the lower official makes an error affecting important interests. Not to offer an appeal would undermine public trust in the civil justice system.

The aims of appeal thus include to foster public trust and respect, properly represent the nature of delegated authority, and (of course) correct erroneous and unjust decisions. Implicated in the last aim of correcting error is that appeals also establish and constantly modify and renew a body of common law that carries enormous value for the liberty, productivity, order, and general welfare of the world's most prosperous nation. As concerned as it is with ends, though, civil procedure deals primarily with process. When it comes to appeals, process is particularly important. The *Federal Rules of Appellate Procedure* reflects a more technical appellate culture in several provisions including (among other examples) FED. R. CIV. P. 10 (content of the record), 11 (forwarding the record), 12 (docketing the appeal), 25 (filing and service), 27 (motions), 28 (briefs), 30 (appendices), and 32 (form of briefs). Appellate practice is not for those who prefer informality and generality to detail.

The substantial process issues surrounding appeals, though, begin with the questions of when appeal is available and to whom. The law uses the concept of finality (more specifically, the final-judgment rule) as a framework for answering the *when* and *who* appeal issues. As you should already have discovered in Chapter XIII on judgments, the final-judgment rule is an interpretive rather than certain framework. The final-judgment rule offers alternative formulations to accommodate parties having varying interests in challenging a trial court's decision and has several exceptions to accommodate other interests. This chapter explores those formulations and exceptions. The law also uses standards for review, including particularly the harmless-error rule, to control who may appeal. The appellate courts use review standards not only to decide who may appeal but also the degree to which the appellate court will defer to the trial court's decision. In other words, appeals not only raise the issues of *when* and *who* but also *how* to decide the appeal. Review standards answer that question of how the appellate courts evaluate an appeal. The second part of this chapter addresses review standards.

Begin this chapter, though, with a practical question: what procedural steps must a lawyer take in order to perfect a client's appeal? The answer to that practical question is important because everything else having to do with an appeal depends on success in taking that initial step of proper filing. There is no appeal unless a party properly files it. One might think that one initiates an appeal by filing a notice in the appellate court. FED. R. CIV. P. 3(a)(1) provides otherwise for the federal courts, that a party must file a notice with the district-court clerk within the time allowed by FED. R. CIV. P. 4 in order to take an appeal of right. Indeed, Rule 3(a)(1) states expressly that a party takes an appeal *only* by filing that notice with the district-court clerk. Rule 3(a)(2) reinforces the significance of that filing by stating that "any step other than the timely filing of a notice of appeal does not affect the validity of the appeal," leaving the clear implication that timely filing of a notice of appeal with the district-court clerk is jurisdictional. Rule 3(d)(1) then requires the district-court clerk to serve the notice on the court of appeals clerk and on counsel of record or unrepresented parties. Rule 3(c) dictates the contents of the notice and refers to an official form. It may be surprising to you that the notice does not include grounds for the appeal. Read Rule 3, noting the simplicity of the official form that follows. Note also the introductory Rules 1 and 2.

FED. R. APP. P. 1. Scope of Rules; Title.
(a) SCOPE OF RULES.
(1) These rules govern procedure in the United States courts of appeals.
(2) When these rules provide for filing a motion or other document in the district court, the procedure must comply with the practice of the district court.
(b) [Abrogated.]
(c) *Title*. These rules are to be known as the Federal Rules of Appellate Procedure.

FED. R. APP. P. 2. Suspension of Rules.
On its own or a party's motion, a court of appeals may—to expedite its decision or for other good cause—suspend any provision of these rules in a particular case and order proceedings as it directs, except as otherwise provided in Rule 26(b).

FED. R. APP. P. 3. Appeal as of Right—How Taken.
(a) FILING THE NOTICE OF APPEAL.
(1) An appeal permitted by law as of right from a district court to a court of appeals may be taken only by filing a notice of appeal with the district clerk within the time allowed by Rule 4. At the time of filing, the appellant must furnish the clerk with enough copies of the notice to enable the clerk to comply with Rule 3(d).
(2) An appellant's failure to take any step other than the timely filing of a notice of appeal does not affect the validity of the appeal, but is ground only for the court of appeals to act as it considers appropriate, including dismissing the appeal.
(3) An appeal from a judgment by a magistrate judge in a civil case is taken in the same way as an appeal from any other district court judgment.
(4) An appeal by permission under 28 U.S.C. §1292(b) or an appeal in a bankruptcy case may be taken only in the manner prescribed by Rules 5 and 6, respectively.
(b) JOINT OR CONSOLIDATED APPEALS.
(1) When two or more parties are entitled to appeal from a district-court judgment or order, and their interests make joinder practicable, they may file a joint notice of appeal. They may then proceed on appeal as a single appellant.
(2) When the parties have filed separate timely notices of appeal, the appeals may be joined or consolidated by the court of appeals.
(c) CONTENTS OF THE NOTICE OF APPEAL.
(1) The notice of appeal must:
(A) specify the party or parties taking the appeal by naming each one in the caption or body of the notice, but an attorney representing more than one party may describe those parties with such terms as ''all plaintiffs,'' ''the defendants,'' ''the plaintiffs A, B, et al.,'' or ''all defendants except X'';
(B) designate the judgment, order, or part thereof being appealed; and
(C) name the court to which the appeal is taken.
(2) A pro se notice of appeal is considered filed on behalf of the signer and the signer's spouse and minor children (if they are parties), unless the notice clearly indicates otherwise.
(3) In a class action, whether or not the class has been certified, the notice of appeal is sufficient if it names one personqualified to bring the appeal as representative of the class.
(4) An appeal must not be dismissed for informality of form or title of the notice of appeal, or for failure to name a party whose intent to appeal is otherwise clear from the notice.
(5) Form 1 in the Appendix of Forms is a suggested form of a notice of appeal.
(d) SERVING THE NOTICE OF APPEAL.
(1) The district clerk must serve notice of the filing of a notice of appeal by mailing a copy to each party's counsel of record—excluding the appellant's—or, if a party is proceeding pro se, to the party's last known address. When a defendant in a criminal case appeals, the clerk must also serve a copy of the notice of appeal on the defendant, either by personal service or

by mail addressed to the defendant. The clerk must promptly send a copy of the notice of appeal and of the docket entries—and any later docket entries—to the clerk of the court of appeals named in the notice. The district clerk must note, on each copy, the date when the notice of appeal was filed.
(2) If an inmate confined in an institution files a notice of appeal in the manner provided by Rule 4(c), the district clerk must also note the date when the clerk docketed the notice.
(3) The district clerk's failure to serve notice does not affect the validity of the appeal. The clerk must note on the docket the names of the parties to whom the clerk mails copies, with the date of mailing. Service is sufficient despite the death of a party or the party's counsel.
(e) PAYMENT OF FEES. Upon filing a notice of appeal, the appellant must pay the district clerk all required fees. The district clerk receives the appellate docket fee on behalf of the court of appeals.

FED. R. APP. P. Form 1. Notice of Appeal to a Court of Appeals From a Judgment or Order of a District Court

United States District Court for the _____
District of _______
File No. ____________

A.B., Plaintiff)
)
v.) *Notice of Appeal*
)
C.D., Defendant)

Notice is hereby given that [(here name all parties taking the appeal), (plaintiffs) (defendants) in the above named case, hereby appeal to the United States Court of Appeals for the _______ Circuit (from the final judgment) (from an order (describing it)) entered in this action on the _______ day of _______, 20___.

(s)

____
Attorney for [_________________]
[Address: ____________________]

A. Finality

Chapter XIII on judgments has already introduced you to the final-judgment rule. Recall that FED. R. CIV. P. 54(a) defines a judgment as "any order from which an appeal lies," while federal statute defines the appellate jurisdiction of the United States Courts of Appeals as "appeals from all final decisions of the district courts of the United States… ," 28 U.S.C. 1291. Section 1291 triggers appeal rights, as the federal codification of the final-judgment rule. For purposes of §1291, a final decision is "'ends the litigation on the merits and leaves nothing for the court to do but execute the judgment.'" Van Cauwenberghe v. Biard, 486 U.S. 517, 521 (1988), *quoting* Catlin v. United States, 324 U.S. 229, 233 (1945). When the district court reaches a final decision, meaning that it has disposed of all claims and defenses in the case, and there is nothing more to decide (setting aside the question of enforcing the judgment), then appeal of that decision lies under §1291. Although the law calls it the final-*judgment* rule, in fact, final decisions may arise after not only the filing of a court paper titled "judgment" after trial but also when a court grants a Rule 12(b) motion to dismiss or a Rule 56 motion for summary judgment disposing of all claims and defenses. Any court paper that constitutes an order, whether or not titled "judgment," can constitute a final decision and thus trigger appeal rights under §1291, as long as there remain no additional claims or defenses to decide.

Although one would think that whether orders and judgments are final decisions involves an easy determination made along a bright line, final decisions are not always so easy to recognize. Indeed, there can even be instances where a literal reading of the final-judgment rule's usual requirement that there remain no claims or defenses to decide would defeat the rule's own purposes to discourage appellate interference with trial-court management, maintain order in the separate proceedings, preserve judicial resources, and provide for finality (at least in stages). Interpretations of finality are not necessarily technical but may be pragmatic. For example, in Brown Shoe Co. v. United States, 370 U.S. 294, 304-310 (1962), the Supreme Court permitted appeal of an antitrust divestiture order even though the federal district court had not yet approved a specific plan for divestiture. Divestiture plans can require time-consuming negotiation and drafting, when it is the initial divestiture decision and order that have by far the greater significance for appeal purposes. In allowing appeal, the Supreme Court articulated these guiding principles:

> The requirement that a final judgment shall have been entered in a case by a lower court before a right of appeal attaches has an ancient history in federal practice, first appearing in the Judiciary Act of 1789.[fn] With occasional modifications, the requirement has remained a cornerstone of the structure of appeals in the federal courts.[fn] The Court has adopted essentially practical tests for identifying those judgments which are, and those which are not, to be considered "final." [Cc] A pragmatic approach to the question of finality has been considered essential to the achievement of the "just, speedy, and inexpensive determination of every action":[Fn. FED. R. CIV. P. 1.] the touchstones of federal procedure. [370 U.S. at 306.]

The finality question is not theoretical but practical in two respects. First, the time within which one must take an appeal or lose the right to do so depends on determining when the judgment became final. Appeal periods run with final judgments, not preliminary orders or partial judgments. Knowing when a judgment is final is critical to determining when to appeal. Yet finality also determines whether there is a right to appeal. Appeals of right are from final judgments, not preliminary orders or partial judgments. One might attempt an appeal well within any applicable time limit (indeed, before the time even began to run) but not succeed in perfecting the appeal because there was simply no right to it. On the other hand, there are several exceptions to the final-judgment rule. There are also state variations on it and, indeed, some states that grant generous rights to interlocutory appeals. Consider, then, the following sections on the time for appeal, exceptions to the final-judgment rule, and state variations on it.

Practice

It was one of the trial lawyer's toughest days ever. The afternoon before trial, the judge had granted the defense's motion in limine prohibiting the plaintiff former officer from using graphic documentary evidence showing that the officer who had replaced him was unfit for office, which the entire department knew. The erroneous ruling looked to gut the plaintiff's case, which was now entirely circumstantial. And as if just to make it harder, the judge had excoriated the trial lawyer for even thinking of offering the evidence. The trial lawyer called a partner back at the law office, but they agreed that there was no chance of making an interlocutory appeal. But the next day, the jury draw went pretty well. So did opening statement, and then the plaintiff's case in chief and cross-examination of the defense witnesses. By closing argument, the trial lawyer was thinking that the adverse ruling the day before trial, as wrong as it was, may have actually made the plaintiff's case better. It had let the plaintiff take the high road at trial. The ruling had also eliminated a potential appeal issue for the defense to raise in case the plaintiff won. And win the plaintiff did, a nice verdict that both made the plaintiff whole and also punished the defendant. The trial judge even invited counsel for both sides into chambers to say how well they had tried the case. On the long drive home, the trial lawyer thought again how curious life is, that sometimes you get what you ask for, while other times you don't, and the not-getting is often better.

1. Time to Appeal

The time for an appeal is jurisdictional, meaning that failing to appeal within the proscribed time bars the appeal. FED. R. APP. P. 4(a)(1)(A) provides a 30-day period within which to file the appeal (60 days for appeals involving the United States). *See also* 28 U.S.C. §2107(a). Reading together Rule 4(a)(1)(A)'s time provision, Rule 3(a)(1) on how to perfect an appeal, and §1291's final-judgment rule, an appellant satisfies the appeal period by filing a notice of appeal with the district-court clerk within 30 days of the court's final decision. As you can see, appellate practice can depend on a close reading of multiple interrelated rules. It is not for the cavalier. As you can see from Rule 4, appellate practice generally and federal appellate practice under the *Federal Rules of Appellate Procedure* in particular are not for the cavalier and uninitiated. There are protocols, interpretations, details, and complexities that are not always so pronounced in trial-court practice, where the trial courts exercise greater latitude to accommodate the practices and preferences of the parties and their counsel. Read Rule 4 for its basic time provision and its abundant additional detail on time-related issues.

FED. R. CIV. P. 4. Appeal as of Right—When Taken.

(a) APPEAL IN A CIVIL CASE.

(1) *Time for Filing a Notice of Appeal.*

(A) In a civil case, except as provided in Rules 4(a)(1)(B), 4(a)(4), and 4(c), the notice of appeal required by Rule 3 must be filed with the district clerk within 30 days after the judgment or order appealed from is entered.

(B) When the United States or its officer or agency is a party, the notice of appeal may be filed by any party within 60 days after the judgment or order appealed from is entered.

(C) An appeal from an order granting or denying an application for a writ of error *coram nobis* is an appeal in a civil case for purposes of Rule 4(a).

(2) *Filing Before Entry of Judgment.* A notice of appeal filed after the court announces a

decision or order—but before the entry of the judgment or order—is treated as filed on the date of and after the entry.

(3) *Multiple Appeals.* If one party timely files a notice of appeal, any other party may file a notice of appeal within 14 days after the date when the first notice was filed, or within the time otherwise prescribed by this Rule 4(a), whichever period ends later.

(4) *Effect of a Motion on a Notice of Appeal.*

(A) If a party timely files in the district court any of the following motions under the Federal Rules of Civil Procedure, the time to file an appeal runs for all parties from the entry of the order disposing of the last such remaining motion:

(i) for judgment under Rule 50(b);

(ii) to amend or make additional factual findings under Rule 52(b), whether or not granting the motion would alter the judgment;

(iii) for attorney's fees under Rule 54 if the district court extends the time to appeal under Rule 58;

(iv) to alter or amend the judgment under Rule 59;

(v) for a new trial under Rule 59; or

(vi) for relief under Rule 60 if the motion is filed no later than 28 days after the judgment is entered.

(B)

(i) If a party files a notice of appeal after the court announces or enters a judgment—but before it disposes of any motion listed in Rule 4(a)(4)(A)—the notice becomes effective to appeal a judgment or order, in whole or in part, when the order disposing of the last such remaining motion is entered.

(ii) A party intending to challenge an order disposing of any motion listed in Rule 4(a)(4)(A), or a judgment's alteration or amendment upon such a motion, must file a notice of appeal, or an amended notice of appeal—in compliance with Rule 3(c) within the time prescribed by this Rule measured from the entry of the order disposing of the last such remaining motion.

(iii) No additional fee is required to file an amended notice.

(5) *Motion for Extension of Time.*

(A) The district court may extend the time to file a notice of appeal if:

(i) a party so moves no later than 30 days after the time prescribed by this Rule 4(a) expires; and

(ii) regardless of whether its motion is filed before or during the 30 days after the time prescribed by this Rule 4(a) expires, that party shows excusable neglect or good cause.

(B) A motion filed before the expiration of the time prescribed in Rule 4(a)(1) or (3) may be ex parte unless the court requires otherwise. If the motion is filed after the expiration of the prescribed time, notice must be given to the other parties in accordance with local rules.

(C) No extension under this Rule 4(a)(5) may exceed 30 days after the prescribed time or 14 days after the date when the order granting the motion is entered, whichever is later.

(6) *Reopening the Time to File an Appeal.* The district court may reopen the time to file an appeal for a period of 14 days after the date when its order to reopen is entered, but only if all the following conditions are satisfied:

(A) the court finds that the moving party did not receive notice under Federal Rule of Civil Procedure 77(d) of the entry of the judgment or order sought to be appealed within 21 days after entry;

(B) the motion is filed within 180 days after the judgment or order is entered or within 14 days after the moving party receives notice under Federal Rule of Civil Procedure 77(d) of the entry, whichever is earlier; and

(C) the court finds that no party would be prejudiced.

(7) *Entry Defined.*

(A) A judgment or order is entered for purposes of this
Rule 4(a):

(i) if Federal Rule of Civil Procedure 58(a)(1) does not require a separate document, when the judgment or order is entered in the civil docket under Federal Rule of Civil Procedure 79(a); or

(ii) if Federal Rule of Civil Procedure 58(a)(1) requires a separate document, when the judgment or order is entered in the civil docket under Federal Rule of Civil Procedure 79(a) and when the earlier of these events occurs:

• the judgment or order is set forth on a separate document, or

• 150 days have run from entry of the judgment or order in the civil docket under Federal Rule of Civil Procedure 79(a).

(B) A failure to set forth a judgment or order on a separate document when required by Federal Rule of Civil Procedure 58(a)(1) does not affect the validity of an appeal from that judgment or order.

(b) APPEAL IN A CRIMINAL CASE.

(1) *Time for Filing a Notice of Appeal.*

(A) In a criminal case, a defendant's notice of appeal must be filed in the district court within 14 days after the later of:

(i) the entry of either the judgment or the order being appealed; or

(ii) the filing of the government's notice of appeal.

(B) When the government is entitled to appeal, its notice of appeal must be filed in the district court within 30 days after the later of:

(i) the entry of the judgment or order being appealed; or

(ii) the filing of a notice of appeal by any defendant.

(2) *Filing Before Entry of Judgment.* A notice of appeal filed after the court announces a decision, sentence, or order—but before the entry of the judgment or order—is treated as filed on the date of and after the entry.

(3) *Effect of a Motion on a Notice of Appeal.*

(A) If a defendant timely makes any of the following motions under the Federal Rules of Criminal Procedure, the notice of appeal from a judgment of conviction must be filed within 14 days after the entry of the order disposing of the last such remaining motion, or within 14 days after the entry of the judgment of conviction, whichever period ends later. This provision applies to a timely motion:

(i) for judgment of acquittal under Rule 29;

(ii) for a new trial under Rule 33, but if based on newly discovered evidence, only if the motion is made no later than 14 days after the entry of the judgment; or

(iii) for arrest of judgment under Rule 34.

(B) A notice of appeal filed after the court announces a decision, sentence, or order—but before it disposes of any of the motions referred to in Rule 4(b)(3)(A)—becomes effective upon the later of the following:

(i) the entry of the order disposing of the last such remaining motion; or

(ii) the entry of the judgment of conviction.

(C) A valid notice of appeal is effective—without amendment—to appeal from an order disposing of any of the motions referred to in Rule 4(b)(3)(A).

(4) *Motion for Extension of Time.* Upon a finding of excusable neglect or good cause, the district court may—before or after the time has expired, with or without motion and notice—extend the time to file a notice of appeal for a period not to exceed 30 days from the expiration of the time otherwise prescribed by this Rule 4(b).

(5) *Jurisdiction.* The filing of a notice of appeal under this Rule 4(b) does not divest a district court of jurisdiction to correct a sentence under Federal Rule of Criminal Procedure 35(a), nor does the filing of a motion under 35(a) affect the validity of a notice of appeal filed before entry of the order disposing of the motion. The filing of a motion under Federal Rule of Criminal Procedure 35(a) does not suspend the time for filing a notice of appeal from a judgment of conviction.

(6) *Entry Defined.* A judgment or order is entered for purposes of this Rule 4(b) when it is entered on the criminal docket.

(c) APPEAL BY AN INMATE CONFINED IN AN INSTITUTION.

(1) If an inmate confined in an institution files a notice of appeal in either a civil or a criminal case, the notice is timely if it is deposited in the institution's internal mail system on or before the last day for filing. If an institution has a system designed for legal mail, the inmate must use that system to receive the benefit of this rule. Timely filing may be shown by a declaration in compliance with 28 U.S.C. §1746 or by a notarized statement, either of which must set forth the date of deposit and state that first-class postage has been prepaid.

(2) If an inmate files the first notice of appeal in a civil case under this Rule 4(c), the 14-day period provided in Rule 4(a)(3) for another party to file a notice of appeal runs from the date when the district court dockets the first notice.

(3) When a defendant in a criminal case files a notice of appeal under this Rule 4(c), the 30-day period for the government to file its notice of appeal runs from the entry of the judgment or order appealed from or from the district court's docketing of the defendant's notice of appeal, whichever is later.

(d) MISTAKEN FILING IN THE COURT OF APPEALS. If a notice of appeal in either a civil or a criminal case is mistakenly filed in the court of appeals, the clerk of that court must note on the notice the date when it was received and send it to the district clerk. The notice is then considered filed in the district court on the date so noted.

INQUIRY

Early Appeals. FED. R. APP. P. 58 attempts to make even clearer the moment of judgment, requiring that the trial court "set out in a separate document" each judgment and amended judgment. There is nonetheless occasional confusion as to when and whether the trial court has actually satisfied Rule 58's separate-document requirement. The trial judge may rule from the bench or in a written opinion indicating that the final judgment is to follow, and the clerk then makes a docket notation indicating the disposition. Did the clerk trigger the appeal period? The Supreme Court accentuated the concern over literal rather than fair interpretations of Rule 58 when in United States v.

Indrelunas, 411 U.S. 216 (1973), it "mechanically applied" the rule to hold an appeal ineffective when the party filed the notice before (rather than within the appeal period after) the separate document reflecting the final judgment. Yet the Supreme Court subsequently disavowed that aspect of *Indrelunas* in Bankers Trust Co. v. Mallis, 435 U.S. 381 (1978), permitting an appeal that, though it may not have exactly met Rule 58's separate-document requirement, did meet the district court's intent and parties' understanding. The Court subsequently amended Rule 4(a) to reflect its disavowal of *Indrelunas.* Currently, if the appellant files the appeal too early, then Rule 4(a)(4) permits the trial court to hold the filing in abeyance until the judgment becomes final and appealable by the filing of a separate document indicating the disposition. Too early is now once again better than too late. *See* FirsTier Mortgage Co. v. Investors Mortgage Ins. Co., 498 U.S. 269 (1991) (permitting appeal filed after oral ruling indicating intent to grant summary judgment but before written order).

Late Appeals. Although it is often the lawyers who draft the judgment and submit it for signature and entry, judges sometimes prepare judgments of their own for the clerk to enter. What happens to appeal rights if the district-court clerk enters a separate document indicating a case's final disposition but does so without notice to the losing party? FED. R. CIV. P. 77(d)(1) provides that the clerk must immediately serve notice of a judgment's entry. Rule 77(d)(1) is obviously to require the clerk to alert unsuspecting parties for appeal, enforcement, stay, and other post-judgment responsibilities. Perhaps surprisingly, Rule 77(d)(2) specifically provides that the clerk's failure to give the required notice does not affect the appeal period. Instead, a party aggrieved by the clerk's failure or having other good cause for delayed appeal must turn for relief to FED. R. APP. P. 4(a)(5) and 28 U.S.C. §2107, each permitting the district court to extend the time for appeal on motion showing excusable neglect or good cause, or more specifically to FED. R. APP. P. 4(a)(6) permitting the district court to "reopen the appeal period" for the clerk's failure. Read §2107 reiterating the 30-day appeal period and extension provisions of FED. R. APP. P. 4.

28 U.S.C. §2107. Time for appeal to court of appeals

(a) Except as otherwise provided in this section, no appeal shall bring any judgment, order or decree in an action, suit or proceeding of a civil nature before a court of appeals for review unless notice of appeal is filed, within thirty days after the entry of such judgment, order or decree.

(b) In any such action, suit or proceeding in which the United States or an officer or agency thereof is a party, the time as to all parties shall be sixty days from such entry.

(c) The district court may, upon motion filed not later than 30 days after the expiration of the time otherwise set for bringing appeal, extend the time for appeal upon a showing of excusable neglect or good cause. In addition, if the district court finds—

(1) that a party entitled to notice of the entry of a judgment or order did not receive such notice from the clerk or any party within 21 days of its entry, and

(2) that no party would be prejudiced, the district court may, upon motion filed within 180 days after entry of the judgment or order or within 14 days after receipt of such notice, whichever is earlier, reopen the time for appeal for a period of 14 days from the date of entry of the order reopening the time for appeal.

(d) This section shall not apply to bankruptcy matters or other proceedings under Title 11.

INQUIRY

Jurisdiction. To say that the established time for an appeal is jurisdictional means that the district court cannot alter the time without specific authority. You may have noticed that FED. R. APP. P. 4(a)(5) and §2107 each authorize the district court to extend the period for filing a notice only by *14 days* on a party's showing good cause or excusable neglect. Similarly, FED. R. APP. P. 4(a)(6) authorizes the district court to extend the appeal period only by 14 days on a party's showing that the clerk did not give the required notice of entry of final judgment. What if the district court purports to grant the losing party more than 14 days? In the following case, the Supreme Court held that the district court cannot create appeal jurisdiction where the rules and statutes do not provide it. It bears stating again that appellate practice can have a technicality and inflexibility that would be unusual in trial-court practice.

Bowles v. Russell,

United States Supreme Court
551 U.S. 205 (2007)

Justice THOMAS delivered the opinion of the Court.

In this case, a District Court purported to extend a party's time for filing an appeal beyond the period allowed by statute. We must decide whether the Court of Appeals had jurisdiction to entertain an appeal filed after the statutory period but within the period allowed by the District Court's order. We have long and repeatedly held that the time limits for filing a notice of appeal are jurisdictional in nature. Accordingly, we hold that petitioner's untimely notice—even though filed in reliance upon a District Court's order—deprived the Court of Appeals of jurisdiction.

I

In 1999, an Ohio jury convicted petitioner Keith Bowles of murder for his involvement in the beating death of Ollie Gipson. The jury sentenced Bowles to 15-years-to-life imprisonment. Bowles unsuccessfully challenged his conviction and sentence on direct appeal.

Bowles then filed a federal habeas corpus application on September 5, 2002. On September 9, 2003, the District Court denied Bowles habeas relief. After the entry of final judgment, Bowles had 30 days to file a notice of appeal. Fed. Rule App. Proc. 4(a)(1)(A); 28 U.S.C. §2107(a). He failed to do so. On December 12, 2003, Bowles moved to reopen the period during which he could file his notice of appeal pursuant to Rule 4(a)(6), which allows district courts to extend the filing period for 14 days from the day the district court grants the order to reopen, provided certain conditions are met. See §2107(c).

On February 10, 2004, the District Court granted Bowles' motion. But rather than extending the time period by 14 days, as Rule 4(a)(6) and § 2107(c) allow, the District Court inexplicably gave Bowles 17 days—until February 27—to file his notice of appeal. Bowles filed his notice on February 26—within the 17 days allowed by the District Court's order, but after the 14-day period allowed by Rule 4(a)(6) and §2107(c).

On appeal, respondent Russell argued that Bowles' notice was untimely and that the Court of Appeals therefore lacked jurisdiction to hear the case. The Court of Appeals agreed. It first recognized that this Court has consistently held the requirement of filing a timely notice of appeal is "mandatory and jurisdictional." 432 F.3d 668, 673 (C.A. 6 2005) (citing Browder v. Director, Dept. of Corrections of Ill., 434 U.S. 257, 264[] (1978)). The court also noted that courts of appeals have uniformly held that Rule 4(a)(6)'s 180-day period for filing a motion to reopen is also mandatory and not susceptible to equitable modification. [C] Concluding that "the fourteen-day period in Rule 4(a)(6) should be treated as strictly as the 180-day period in that same Rule," [c], the Court of Appeals held that it was without jurisdiction. We ... now affirm.

II

According to 28 U.S.C. §2107(a), parties must file notices of appeal within 30 days of the entry of the judgment being appealed. District courts have limited authority to grant an extension of the 30-day time period. Relevant to this case, if certain conditions are met, district courts have the statutory authority to grant motions to reopen the time for filing an appeal for 14 additional days. §2107(c). Rule 4 of the Federal Rules of Appellate Procedure carries §2107 into practice. In accord with §2107(c), Rule 4(a)(6) describes the district court's authority to reopen and extend the time for filing a notice of appeal after the lapse of the usual 30 days... .

It is undisputed that the District Court's order in this case purported to reopen the filing period for more than 14 days. Thus, the question before us is whether the Court of Appeals lacked jurisdiction to entertain an appeal filed outside the 14-day window allowed by §2107(c) but within the longer period granted by the District Court.

A

This Court has long held that the taking of an appeal within the prescribed time is "mandatory and jurisdictional." Griggs v. Provident Consumer Discount Co., 459 U.S. 56, 61[] (1982) *(per curiam)* ...;[fn] [cc]. Indeed, even prior to the creation of the circuit courts of appeals, this Court regarded statutory limitations on the timing of appeals as limitations on its own jurisdiction. See Scarborough v. Pargoud, 108 U.S. 567, 568[] (1883) ...; United States v. Curry, 6 How. 106, 113[] (1848) ... .

... [I]t is indisputable that time limits for filing a notice of appeal have been treated as jurisdictional in American law for well over a century. ...

Although several of our recent decisions have undertaken to clarify the distinction between claims-processing rules and jurisdictional rules, none of them calls into question our longstanding treatment of statutory time limits for taking an appeal as jurisdictional. Indeed, those decisions have also recognized the jurisdictional significance of the fact that a time limitation is set forth in a statute. ...

This Court's treatment of its certiorari jurisdiction also demonstrates the jurisdictional distinction between court-promulgated rules and limits enacted by Congress. According to our Rules, a petition for a writ of certiorari must be filed within 90 days of the entry of the judgment sought to be reviewed. See this Court's Rule 13.1. That 90-day period applies to both civil and criminal cases. But the 90-day period for civil cases derives from both this Court's Rule 13.1 and 28 U.S.C. §2101(c). We have repeatedly held that this statute-based filing period for civil cases is jurisdictional. *See, e.g.,* Federal Election Comm'n v. NRA Political Victory Fund, 513 U.S. 88, 90[] (1994). …

Jurisdictional treatment of statutory time limits makes good sense. Within constitutional bounds, Congress decides what cases the federal courts have jurisdiction to consider. Because Congress decides whether federal courts can hear cases at all, it can also determine when, and under what conditions, federal courts can hear them. [C]

The resolution of this case follows naturally from this reasoning. Like the initial 30-day period for filing a notice of appeal, the limit on how long a district court may reopen that period is set forth in a statute, 28 U.S.C. §2107(c). Because Congress specifically limited the amount of time by which district courts can extend the notice-of-appeal period in §2107(c), that limitation is more than a simple "claim-processing rule."

B

…

Today we make clear that the timely filing of a notice of appeal in a civil case is a jurisdictional requirement. Because this Court has no authority to create equitable exceptions to jurisdictional requirements, use of the "unique circumstances" doctrine is illegitimate. … We see no compelling reason to resurrect the doctrine from its 40-year slumber. Accordingly, we reject Bowles' reliance on the doctrine… .

C

If rigorous rules like the one applied today are thought to be inequitable, Congress may authorize courts to promulgate rules that excuse compliance with the statutory time limits. …

III

The Court of Appeals correctly held that it lacked jurisdiction to consider Bowles' appeal. The judgment of the Court of Appeals is affirmed.

It is so ordered.

Justice SOUTER, with whom Justice STEVENS, Justice GINSBURG, and Justice BREYER join, dissenting.

The District Court told petitioner Keith Bowles that his notice of appeal was due on February 27, 2004. He filed a notice of appeal on February 26, only to be told that he was too late because his deadline had actually been February 24. It is intolerable for the judicial system to treat people this way, and there is not even a technical justification for condoning this bait and switch. I respectfully dissent. …

I have to admit that Bowles's counsel … probably just trusted that the date given was correct, and there was nothing unreasonable in so trusting. The other side let the order pass without objection, either not caring enough to make a fuss or not even noticing the discrepancy; the mistake of a few days was probably not enough to ring the alarm bell to send either lawyer to his copy of the federal rules and then off to the courthouse to check the docket.[fn] This would be a different case if the year were wrong on the District Court's order, or if opposing counsel had flagged the error. But on the actual facts, it was reasonable to rely on a facially plausible date provided by a federal judge. …

I would vacate the decision of the Court of Appeals and remand for consideration of the merits.

> ***Skills***
>
> As rule-dependent and convention-bound as appellate practice is, there is yet within it real opportunity for the exercise of complex skills and for professional development. The lawyer who is willing to patiently study appellate rules, while becoming a student of appellate norms and conventions, can significantly expand professional networks and practice. Trial lawyers tend to operate within a professional community of other trial lawyers. There is a separate circle of lawyers who specialize in appellate practice. Some lawyers, though, master both trial and appellate practice. By doing so, they may better serve some clients while also improving their skill in both fields. Just as masterful appellate judges often begin as masterful trial judges, so, too, can a masterful trial lawyer sometimes make for a very special appellate advocate.

2. Exceptions

You have just seen how strict the appellate courts can be in following the literal requirements of procedural rules to avoid deciding appeals for which there is no jurisdiction. Yet the great increase in the importance of discovery and pretrial proceedings over trials and final judgments has increased the need for appeals before final judgment. Given the above *Bowles v. Russell* case, it may surprise you that the Supreme Court and appellate courts have responded to the need for more pre-trial appeals with new interpretations of the final-judgment rule, creating routes around it, and with exceptions to it. Where the final-judgment rule appears to apply to bar an appeal because of undecided claims and defenses, the parties may yet be able to appeal. Statute establishes some alternative routes to the appellate courts, while other routes are the product of case law, and still others the *Federal Rules of Appellate Procedure* confirm. Some routes provide in essence for appeals of right, while others require both the district court and appellate court to exercise discretion. A route to appellate review may be available as to trial-court decisions involving injunctions, receiverships, admiralty decisions, or collateral orders, or through mandamus, or when the trial court certifies a decision for appeal to materially advance the litigation's termination. Consider each route in turn.

The following statute, 28 U.S.C. §1292 contains important exceptions to the final-judgment rule, providing a route to appellate review. Section 1292(a) permits appellate review of injunction decisions, decisions on receivership, and admiralty decisions. There is good reason that parties may appeal trial-court decisions whether to grant, modify, or dissolve an injunction. Cases involving injunctive relief often include requests for money damages. Those cases are often primarily about the injunction and only subsidiarily about the money damages. When a trial court denies an injunction, the money-damages claim may yet require discovery and trial, effectively delaying appeal of the injunction denial until a time when injunction may no longer be meaningful and irreparable harm may have resulted. Section 1292's other exception is for when the district-court judge states that appeal of a non-appealable order decided on a substantial ground for difference of opinion "may materially advance the ultimate termination of the litigation." 28 U.S.C. §1292(b). Section 1292(b) gives the trial judge the opportunity to request that the appellate court review the decision, when the trial judge believes that appeal is a swifter or at least more efficient route to the litigation's termination.

Do not over-estimate the appellate courts' willingness to entertain interlocutory appeals certified under §1292(b) in this manner. *See* Michael Solomine, *Revitalizing Interlocutory Appeals in the Federal Courts,* 58 GEO. WASH. L.REV. 1165 (100 interlocutory appeals granted out of 300 certified, compared to 40,000 federal appeals of right in the study period). As inviting as §1292(b) sounds, it takes both the federal district court and court of appeals to agree to grant a §1292(b) appeal, when it is easy to contest that an appeal will "materially advance the ultimate termination of the litigation." Read §1292 and the curt opinion declining an interlocutory appeal that follows it. Also, read FED. R. APP. P. 5 stating the procedure for appeals by permission. Note that in the case of interlocutory appeals requiring the appellate court's exercise of discretion, Rule 5 requires the party to file with the circuit-court clerk, not the district-court clerk.

28 U.S.C. §1292. Interlocutory decisions

(a) Except as provided in subsections (c) and (d) of this section, the courts of appeals shall have jurisdiction of appeals from:

(1) Interlocutory orders of the district courts of the United States ... granting, continuing, modifying, refusing or dissolving injunctions, or refusing to dissolve or modify injunctions, except where a direct review may be had in the Supreme Court;

(2) Interlocutory orders appointing receivers, or refusing orders to wind up receiverships or to take steps to accomplish the purposes thereof, such as directing sales or other disposals of property;

(3) Interlocutory decrees of such district courts or the judges thereof determining the rights and liabilities of the parties to admiralty cases in which appeals from final decrees are allowed.

(b) When a district judge, in making in a civil action an order not otherwise appealable under this section, shall be of the opinion that such order involves a controlling question of law as to which there is substantial ground for difference of opinion and that an immediate appeal from the order may materially advance the ultimate termination of the litigation, he shall so state in writing in such order. The Court of Appeals which would have jurisdiction of an appeal of such action may thereupon, in its discretion, permit an appeal to be taken from such order, if application is made to it within ten days after the entry of the order: *Provided, however,* That application for an appeal hereunder shall not stay proceedings in the district court unless the district judge or the Court of Appeals or a judge thereof shall so order. ...

FED. R. APP. P. 5. Appeal by Permission.

(a) PETITION FOR PERMISSION TO APPEAL.

(1) To request permission to appeal when an appeal is within the court of appeals' discretion, a party must file a petition permission to appeal. The petition must be filed with the circuit clerk with proof of service on all other parties to the district-court action.

(2) The petition must be filed within the time specified by the statute or rule authorizing the appeal or, if no such time is specified, within the time provided by Rule 4(a) for filing a notice of appeal.

(3) If a party cannot petition for appeal unless the district court first enters an order granting permission to do so or stating that the necessary conditions are met, the district court may amend its order, either on its own or in response to a party's motion, to include the required permission or statement. In that event, the time to petition runs from entry of the amended order.

(b) CONTENTS OF THE PETITION; ANSWER OR CROSS-PETITION; ORAL ARGUMENT.
(1) The petition must include the following:
(A) the facts necessary to understand the question presented;
(B) the question itself;
(C) the relief sought;
(D) the reasons why the appeal should be allowed and is authorized by a statute or rule; and
(E) an attached copy of:
(i) the order, decree, or judgment complained of and any related opinion or memorandum, and
(ii) any order stating the district court's permission to appeal or finding that the necessary conditions are met.
(2) A party may file an answer in opposition or a cross-petition within 10 days after the petition is served.
(3) The petition and answer will be submitted without oral argument unless the court of appeals orders otherwise.
(c) FORM OF PAPERS; NUMBER OF COPIES. All papers must conform to Rule 32(c)(2). Except by the court's permission, a paper must not exceed 20 pages, exclusive of the disclosure statement, the proof of service, and the accompanying documents required by Rule 5(b)(1)(E). An original and 3 copies must be filed unless the court requires a different number by local rule or by order in a particular case.
(d) GRANT OF PERMISSION; FEES; COST BOND; FILING THE RECORD.
(1) Within 14 days after the entry of the order granting permission to appeal, the appellant must:
(A) pay the district clerk all required fees; and
(B) file a cost bond if required under Rule 7.
(2) A notice of appeal need not be filed. The date when the order granting permission to appeal is entered serves as the date of the notice of appeal for calculating time under these rules.
(3) The district clerk must notify the circuit clerk once the petitioner has paid the fees. Upon receiving this notice, the circuit clerk must enter the appeal on the docket. The record must be forwarded and filed in accordance with Rules 11 and 12(c).

Atlantic City Elec. Co. v. General Elec. Co.,

United States Court of Appeals for the Second Circuit
337 F.2d 844 (1964)

PER CURIAM.

The district court has certified pursuant to section 1292(b), 28 U.S.C.A., that its order, sustaining objections to interrogatories designed to discover whether damages were actually sustained by plaintiffs who may have shifted such damages, if any, to their customers of electricity, involves a controlling question of law in these litigations and that there is substantial ground for differences of opinion. The court noted in its opinion that the Court of Appeals for the Seventh Circuit has permitted an appeal to be taken from a similar order.[fn]

In sustaining the objections to the interrogatories posed, the district court has, in effect, foreclosed defendants from pre-trial discovery of facts relating to a defense that plaintiffs have "passed-on" to their customers any damages incurred by plaintiffs and hence are not entitled to recover to the extent that defendants can prove such passing-on.

Upon this application for leave to appeal it would not be appropriate to isolate and endeavor to decide before an appeal from any final judgment this particular question of law. Pre-trial leave to appeal applications must be decided against the background of the entire case. Many important questions of law will undoubtedly arise in these cases but the problem now confronting us is the feasibility and advisability of trying to decide this particular question in advance of trial.

If pre-trial discovery were allowed as defendants request it could easily develop into a multitude of full scale rate cases which would dwarf in time and testimony the already extensive pre-trial proceedings. If the district court is in error, as to which no opinion is expressed, defendants will have full opportunity in the event of an adverse judgment, if based in whole or in part upon this error, to have it corrected upon appeal together with any other errors which may be urged. It is doubtful that any discoveries or hearings required to establish the extent of any damages, if the passing-on doctrine applies, would be more burdensome then than now. Since defendants' rights to this defense are not being taken away or prejudiced on any ultimate appeal by denial of the pre-trial appeal now sought, we believe that the ultimate disposition of these cases would be delayed rather than advanced by granting this application.

Application denied.

INQUIRY

Multiple Claims and Parties. You have already seen in Chapter XIII on challenging judgments that FED. R. CIV. P. 54(b) includes another exception to the final-judgment rule, this one for cases involving multiple claims or parties. Under Rule 54(b), if the district court disposes of a claim in a case in which there are multiple claims or of a party in a case in which there are multiple parties, then the district court may recite in the order that there is no just reason to delay an appeal of that order. The claim may have been sufficiently substantial and discrete, or the party sufficiently independent, that appellate review is appropriate. Essentially, Rule 54(b) enables a trial court to label certain decisions as appealable if the appellate court is willing to hear them, so long as those decisions are in themselves final. A plaintiff who loses on the central claims may still voluntarily dismiss the remaining claims in order to ensure an appeal of right. *See* James v. Price Stern Sloan, Inc., 283 F.3d 1064 (9th Cir. 2002). Yet in other cases, the remaining claims may be substantial enough that the case will continue in the district court, even while it is just and expedient that a party have an opportunity to appeal dismissed claims or the dismissal of certain parties. As noted in the previous chapter, the Supreme Court has even approved treating as final a trial court's decision on a main claim as to which there was an undecided counterclaim. *See* Curtiss-Wright Corp. v. General Electric Co., 446 U.S. 1, 8-9 (1980). Consider an early Supreme Court case illustrating the multiple parties-multiple claims exception.

Sears, Roebuck & Co. v. Mackey,

United States Supreme Court
351 U.S. 427 (1956)

Mr. Justice BURTON delivered the opinion of the Court.

This action, presenting multiple claims for relief, was brought by Mackey and another in the United States District Court for the Northern District of Illinois, Eastern Division, in 1953. The court expressly directed that judgment be entered for the defendant, Sears, Roebuck & Co., on two, but less than all, of the claims presented. It also expressly determined that there was no just reason for delay in making the entry. After Mackey's notice of appeal from that judgment to the Court of Appeals for the Seventh Circuit, Sears, Roebuck & Co. moved to dismiss the appeal for lack of appellate jurisdiction. The Court of Appeals upheld its jurisdiction and denied the motion, relying upon 28 U.S.C. §1291[] and Rule 54(b) of the Federal Rules of Civil Procedure, [c]. Because of the importance of the issue in determining appellate jurisdiction and because of a conflict of judicial views on the subject,[fn] we granted certiorari. [C] For the reasons hereafter stated, we sustain the Court of Appeals and its appellate jurisdiction.

Although we are here concerned with the present appealability of the judgment of the District Court and not with its merits, we must examine the claims stated in the complaint so as to consider adequately the issue of appealability. ...

In Count I, ... Mackey charges Sears with conduct violating the Sherman Antitrust Act in a manner prejudicial to three of Mackey's commercial ventures [as to Metalcraft, Vascoloy, and Time Saver] causing him $190,000 damages, for which he seeks $570,000 as treble damages. ...

In Count II, Mackey ... incorporates the allegations of Count I as to the Metalcraft transactions and asks for $250,000 damages for Sears' wilful destruction of the business of Metalcraft, plus $50,000 for Mackey's loss on obligations guaranteed by him.

In Count III, Mackey seeks $75,000 in a common-law proceeding against Sears for unlawfully inducing a breach of his Vascoloy commission contract.

In Count IV, Time Saver seeks $200,000 in a common-law proceeding against Sears for unlawfully destroying Time Saver's business by unfair competition and patent infringement.

The jurisdiction of the Court of Appeals to entertain Mackey's appeal from the District Court's judgment depends upon 28 U.S.C. §1291[], which provides that "The courts of appeals shall have jurisdiction of appeals from all final decisions of the district courts of the United States... ." (Emphasis supplied.)

If Mackey's complaint had contained only Count I, there is no doubt that a judgment striking out that count and thus dismissing, in its entirety, the claim there stated would be both a final and an appealable decision within the meaning of §1291. Similarly, if his complaint had contained Counts I, II, III and IV, there is no doubt that a judgment striking out all four would be a final and appealable decision under §1291. The controversy before us arises solely because, in this multiple claims action, the District Court has dismissed the claims stated in Counts I and II, but has left unadjudicated those stated in Counts III and IV.[fn]

Before the adoption of the Federal Rules of Civil Procedure in 1939, such a situation was generally regarded as leaving the appellate court without jurisdiction of an attempted appeal. It was thought that, although the judgment was a final decision on the respective claims in Counts I and II, it obviously was not a final decision of the whole case, and there was no authority for treating anything less than the whole case as a judicial unit for purposes of appeal.[fn] This construction of the judicial unit was developed from the common law which had dealt with litigation generally less complicated than much of that of today.[fn]

With the Federal Rules of Civil Procedure, there came an increased opportunity for the liberal joinder of claims in multiple claims actions. This, in turn, demonstrated a need for relaxing the restrictions upon what should be treated as a judicial unit for purposes of appellate jurisdiction. Sound judicial administration did not require relaxation of the standard of finality in the disposition of the individual adjudicated claims for the purpose of their appealability. It did, however, demonstrate that, at least in multiple claims actions, some final decisions, on less than all of the claims, should be appealable without waiting for a final decision on all of the claims. Largely to meet this need, in 1939, Rule 54(b) was promulgated in its original form through joint action of Congress and this Court.[fn] …

… [Rule 54(b)] does not relax the finality required of each decision, as an individual claim, to render it appealable, but it does provide a practical means of permitting an appeal to be taken from one or more final decisions on individual claims, in multiple claims actions, without waiting for final decisions to be rendered on all the claims in the case. …

To meet the demonstrated need for flexibility, the District Court is used as a "dispatcher." It is permitted to determine, in the first instance, the appropriate time when each "final decision" upon "one or more but less than all" of the claims in a multiple claims action is ready for appeal. This arrangement already has lent welcome certainty to the appellate procedure. Its "negative effect" has met with uniform approval. The effect so referred to is the rule's specific requirement that for "one or more but less than all" multiple claims to become appealable, the District Court must make both "an express determination that there is no just reason for delay" and "an express direction for the entry of judgment." A party adversely affected by a final decision thus knows that his time for appeal will not run against him until this certification has been made.[fn]

In the instant case, the District Court made this certification, but Sears, Roebuck & Co. nevertheless moved to dismiss the appeal for lack of appellate jurisdiction under §1291. …

… [T]here is no doubt that each of the claims dismissed is a "claim for relief" within the meaning of Rule 54(b), or that their dismissal constitutes a "final decision" on individual claims. Also, it cannot well be argued that the claims stated in Counts I and II are so inherently inseparable from, or closely related to, those stated in Counts III and IV that the District Court has abused its discretion in certifying that there exists no just reason for delay. They certainly can be decided independently of each other. …

… [T]he instant case affords an excellent illustration of the value of the amended rule… . The District Court cannot, in the exercise of its discretion, treat as "final" that which is not "final" within the meaning of §1291. But the District Court may, by the exercise of its discretion in the interest of sound judicial administration, release for appeal final decisions upon one or more, but less than all, claims in multiple claims actions. The timing of such a release is, with good reason, vested by the rule primarily in the discretion of the District Court as the one most likely to be familiar with the case and with any justifiable reasons for delay. With equally good reason, any abuse of that discretion remains reviewable by the Court of Appeals.

Rule 54(b), in its original form, thus may be said to have modified the single judicial unit practice which had been developed by court decisions. …

Rule 54(b) … does not supersede any statute controlling appellate jurisdiction. It scrupulously recognizes the statutory requirement of a "final decision" under §1291 as a basic requirement for an appeal to the Court of Appeals. It merely administers that requirement in a practical manner in multiple claims actions and does so by rule instead of by judicial decision. By its negative effect, it operates to restrict in a valid manner the number of appeals in multiple claims actions. ...

Accordingly, the appellate jurisdiction of the Court of Appeals is sustained,[fn] and its judgment denying the motion to dismiss the appeal for lack of appellate jurisdiction is affirmed.

Affirmed.

Mr. Justice FRANKFURTER, whom Mr. Justice HARLAN joins, concurring in No. 34 and dissenting in No. 76. ...

... [T]he Court rightly states, even if it does not hold, that §1291 is unimpaired by Rule 54(b). Section 1291 is what a long course of decision has construed it to be. The unifying principle of decisions for over a century is observance of hostility in the federal judicial system to piecemeal appellate review (with a few strictly defined exceptions not here relevant, see 28 U.S.C. §1292[]) of one litigation, no matter how many phases or parts there may be to a single judicial proceeding, so long as no part has become separated from, and independent of, the others. This rooted principle against piecemeal appeals of an organic whole—the core of §1291—is not left unimpaired when its enforcement is committed without guidance to the individualized notions about finality of some two hundred and fifty district judges, themselves accountable to the discordant views of eleven essentially independent courts of appeals. Allowing such leeway to the district courts and courts of appeals is not flexibility but anarchy.

INQUIRY

Collateral Orders. In the next case excerpted below, Cohen v. Beneficial Industries Loan Corp., 337 U.S. 541 (1949), the Supreme Court articulated another route around §1291's final-judgment rule, known as the collateral-order doctrine. Some trial-court orders decide important rights that are collateral to the central claim raised by the case and yet have a way of undermining or unduly burdening pursuit of the case. The collateral-order doctrine permits the appellate court to treat those decisions as final. *Cohen*, for instance, involved a decision to require the plaintiff to post a substantial security bond before proceeding. The Supreme Court permitted appeal under the collateral-order doctrine in *Cohen*, just as it did in the following other cases in which it found a basis for determining that the appealed orders were sufficiently collateral to the claims remaining in the trial court: Quackenbush v. Allstate Ins. Co., 517 U.S. 706 (1996) (remand order based on abstention); Puerto Rico Aqueduct & Sewer Auth. v. Metcalf & Eddy, 506 U.S. 139 (1993) (order denying Eleventh Amendment immunity); Mitchell v. Forsyth, 472 U.S. 511 (1985) (involving a trial court's decision to deny a claim of qualified immunity); Nixon v. Fitzgerald, 457 U.S. 731 (1982) (involving a trial court's refusal to dismiss on absolute immunity grounds a suit against the President). To give the Supreme Court even broader latitude than re-interpreting §1291's final-judgment rule to allow interlocutory appeals, Congress amended the Rules Enabling Act, 28 U.S.C. §2072(c), to allow the Supreme Court to specifically "define when a ruling of a district court is final for the purposes of appeal under section 1291 of this title."

The Supreme Court's only effort to do so, so far, has been FED. R. CIV. P. 23(f) permitting interlocutory appeals from class-certification decisions.

Limits. Do not interpret the collateral-order doctrine too broadly. In Lauro Lines, S.R.L. v. Chaser, 490 U.S. 495 (1989), a case addressing liability for the terrorist hijacking of the cruise ship Achille Lauro, the Supreme Court rejected the collateral-order doctrine's application. *Lauro Lines* held that the appellant must show that the trial court's decision: (1) conclusively determined the question; (2) resolved an important issue completely separate from the case's merits; and (3) would be effectively unreviewable if left for appeal until after resolution of the case's merits. Other recent Supreme Court cases rejecting interlocutory appeal of arguably collateral orders include Will v. Hallock, 546 U.S. 345 (2006) (ruling denying public-official immunity); Cunningham v. Hamilton County, 527 u.S. 198 (1999) (order sanctioning attorney for discovery violations); Digital Equip. Corp. v. Desktop Direct, Inc., 511 U.S. 863 (1994) (order holding settlement agreement did not release party from alleged liability); Van Cauwenberghe v. Biard, 486 U.S. 517 (1988) (no interlocutory appeal of ruling denying motion to dismiss for inconvenient forum); Richardson-Merrell, Inc. v. Koller, 472 U.S. 424 (1985) (no interlocutory appeal from order to disqualify party's lawyer). For the cases seeking interlocutory appeal of immunity decisions, the Supreme Court holds that collateral-order appeals are available if the immunity decision rested on an interpretation of law, *see* Behrens v. Pelletier, 516 U.S. 299 (1996), but not disputed fact, *see* Johnson v. Jones, 515 U.S. 304 (1995). Read the following excerpts of *Cohen* confirming the collateral-order doctrine and excerpts of *Lauro Lines* limiting it, for the policy and rationale of these holdings.

Cohen v. Beneficial Industries Loan Corp.,

United States Supreme Court
337 U.S. 541 (1949)

Mr. Justice JACKSON delivered the opinion of the Court.

The ultimate question here is whether a federal court, having jurisdiction of a stockholder's derivative action only because the parties are of diverse citizenship, must apply a statute of the forum state which makes the plaintiff, if unsuccessful, liable for all expenses, including attorney's fees, of the defense and requires security for their payment as a condition of prosecuting the action.

Petitioners' decedent as plaintiff, brought in the United States District Court for New Jersey an action in the right of the Beneficial Industrial Loan Corporation, a Delaware corporation doing business in New Jersey. The defendants were the corporation and certain of its managers and directors. The complaint alleged generally that since 1929 the individual defendants engaged in a continuing and successful conspiracy to enrich themselves at the expense of the corporation. Specific charges of mismanagement and fraud extended over a period of eighteen years and the assets allegedly wasted or diverted thereby were said to exceed $100,000,000. The stockholder had demanded that the corporation institute proceedings for its recovery but, by their control of the corporation, the individual defendants prevented it from doing so. This stockholder, therefore, sought to assert the right of the corporation. One of 16,000 stockholders, he owned 100 of its more than two million shares, so that his holdings, together with

150 shares held by the intervenor, approximated 0.0125% of the outstanding stock and had a market value that had never exceeded $9,000.

The action was brought in 1943, and various proceedings had been taken therein when, in 1945, New Jersey enacted the statute which is here involved.[fn] Its general effect is to make a plaintiff having so small an interest liable for all expenses and attorney's fees of the defense if he fails to make good his complaint and to entitle the corporation to indemnity before the case can be prosecuted. These conditions are made applicable to pending actions. The corporate defendant therefore moved to require security, pointed to its by-laws by which it might be required to indemnify the individual defendants, and averred that a bond of $125,000 would be appropriate.

The District Court was of the opinion that the state enactment is not applicable to such an action when pending in a federal court, [c]. The Court of Appeals were of a contrary opinion and reversed, [c], and we granted certiorari. [C] ...

At the threshold we are met with the question whether the District Court's order refusing to apply the statute was an appealable one. Title 28 U.S.C. §1291, provides, as did its predecessors, for appeal only "from all final decisions of the district courts," except when direct appeal to this Court is provided. Section 1292 allows appeals also from certain interlocutory orders, decrees and judgments, not material to this case except as they indicate the purpose to allow appeals from orders other than final judgments when they have a final and irreparable effect on the rights of the parties. It is obvious that, if Congress had allowed appeals only from those final judgments which terminate an action, this order would not be appealable.

The effect of the statute is to disallow appeal from any decision which is tentative, informal or incomplete. Appeal gives the upper court a power of review, not one of intervention. So long as the matter remains open, unfinished or inconclusive, there may be no intrusion by appeal. But the District Court's action upon this application was concluded and closed and its decision final in that sense before the appeal was taken.

Nor does the statute permit appeals, even from fully consummated decisions, where they are but steps towards final judgment in which they will merge. The purpose is to combine in one review all stages of the proceeding that effectively may be reviewed and corrected if and when final judgment results. But this order of the District Court did not make any step toward final disposition of the merits of the case and will not be merged in final judgment. When that time comes, it will be too late effectively to review the present order and the rights conferred by the statute, if it is applicable, will have been lost, probably irreparably. We conclude that the matters embraced in the decision appealed from are not of such an interlocutory nature as to affect, or to be affected by, decision of the merits of this case.

This decision appears to fall in that small class which finally determine claims of right separable from, and collateral to, rights asserted in the action, too important to be denied review and too independent of the cause itself to require that appellate consideration be deferred until the whole case is adjudicated. The Court has long given this provision of the statute this practical rather than a technical construction. [Cc]

We hold this order appealable because it is a final disposition of a claimed right which is not an ingredient of the cause of action and does not require consideration with it. But we do not mean that every order fixing security is subject to appeal. Here it is the right to security that presents a serious and unsettled question. If the right were admitted or clear and the order involved only an exercise of discretion as to the amount of security, a matter the statute makes subject to reconsideration from time to time, appealability would present a different question.

Since this order may be reviewed on appeal, the petition in No. 512, whereby the corporation asserts the right to compel security by mandamus, is dismissed. ...

The judgment of the Court of Appeals is affirmed.

Affirmed.

Mr. Justice DOUGLAS, with whom Mr. Justice FRANKFURTER concurs, dissenting in part[, omitted].

Mr. Justice RUTLEDGE, dissenting[, omitted].

Lauro Lines s.r.l. v. Chasser,

United States Supreme Court
490 U.S. 495 (1989)

Justice BRENNAN delivered the opinion of the Court.

We granted certiorari to consider whether an interlocutory order of a United States District Court denying a defendant's motion to dismiss a damages action on the basis of a contractual forum-selection clause is immediately appealable under 28 U.S.C. §1291 as a collateral final order. We hold that it is not.

I

The individual respondents were, or represent the estates of persons who were, passengers aboard the cruise ship Achille Lauro when it was hijacked by terrorists in the Mediterranean in October 1985. Petitioner Lauro Lines s.r.l., an Italian company, owns the Achille Lauro. Respondents filed suits against Lauro Lines in the District Court for the Southern District of New York to recover damages for injuries sustained as a result of the hijacking and for the wrongful death of passenger Leon Klinghoffer. Lauro Lines moved before trial to dismiss the actions, citing the forum-selection clause printed on each passenger ticket. This clause purported to obligate the passenger to institute any suit arising in connection with the contract in Naples, Italy, and to renounce the right to sue elsewhere.

The District Court denied petitioner's motions to dismiss, holding that the ticket as a whole did not give reasonable notice to passengers that they were waiving the opportunity to sue in a domestic forum. Without moving for certification for immediate appeal pursuant to 28 U.S.C. §1292(b), Lauro Lines sought to appeal the District Court's orders. The Court of Appeals for the Second Circuit dismissed petitioner's appeal on the ground that the District Court's orders denying petitioner's motions to dismiss were interlocutory and not appealable under §1291. The court held that the orders did not fall within the exception to the rule of nonappealability carved out for collateral final orders in Cohen v. Beneficial Industrial Loan Corp., 337 U.S. 541[] (1949). [C] We granted certiorari to resolve a disagreement among the Courts of Appeals. [C] ... We now affirm.

II

Title 28 U.S.C. §1291 provides for appeal to the courts of appeals only from "final decisions of the district courts of the United States." For purposes of §1291, a final judgment is generally regarded as "a decision by the district court that 'ends the litigation on the merits and leaves nothing for the court to do but execute the judgment.'" Van Cauwenberghe v. Biard, 486 U.S. 517, 521[] (1988), quoting Catlin v. United States, 324 U.S. 229, 233[] (1945). An order denying a motion to dismiss a civil action on the ground that a contractual forum-selection clause requires that such suit be brought in another jurisdiction is not a decision on the merits that ends the litigation. On the contrary, such an order "ensures that litigation will continue in the District Court." Gulfstream Aerospace Corp. v. Mayacamas Corp., 485 U.S. 271, 275[] (1988). Section 1291 thus permits an appeal only if an order denying a motion to dismiss based upon a forum-selection clause falls within the "narrow exception to the normal application of the final judgment rule [that] has come to be known as the collateral order doctrine." Midland Asphalt Corp. v. United States, 489 U.S. 794, 798[] (1989). That exception is for a "small class" of pre-judgment orders that "finally determine claims of right separable from, and collateral to, rights asserted in the action [and that are[too important to be denied review and too independent of the cause itself to require that appellate consideration be deferred until the whole case is adjudicated." *Cohen, supra,* [] at 546. We have held that to fall within the *Cohen* exception, an order must satisfy at least three conditions: "It must 'conclusively determine the disputed question,' 'resolve an important issue completely separate from the merits of the action,' and 'be effectively unreviewable on appeal from a final judgment.'" Richardson-Merrell Inc. v. Koller, 472 U.S. 424, 431[] (1985), quoting Coopers & Lybrand v. Livesay, 437 U.S. 463, 468[] (1978). For present purposes, we need not decide whether an order denying a dismissal motion based upon a contractual forum-selection clause conclusively determines a disputed issue, or whether it resolves an important issue that is independent of the merits of the action, for the District Court's orders fail to satisfy the third requirement of the collateral order test.

We recently reiterated the "general rule" that an order is "effectively unreviewable" only "where the order at issue involves 'an asserted right the legal and practical value of which would be destroyed if it were not vindicated before trial.'" *Midland Asphalt Corp., supra,* [] at 799[], quoting United States v. MacDonald, 435 U.S. 850, 860[] (1978). If it is eventually decided that the District Court erred in allowing trial in this case to take place in New York, petitioner will have been put to unnecessary trouble and expense, and the value of its contractual right to an Italian forum will have been diminished. It is always true, however, that "there is value ... in triumphing before trial, rather than after it," *MacDonald, supra,* at 860n. 7[], and this Court has declined to find the costs associated with unnecessary litigation to be enough to warrant allowing the immediate appeal of a pretrial order, see *Richardson-Merrell Inc., supra,* [] at 436[] ("[T]he possibility that a ruling may be erroneous and may impose additional litigation expense is not sufficient to set aside the finality requirement imposed by Congress" in §1291). Instead, we have insisted that the right asserted be one that is essentially destroyed if its vindication must be postponed until trial is completed.

We have thus held in cases involving criminal prosecutions that the deprivation of a right *not to be tried* is effectively unreviewable after final judgment and is immediately appealable. Helstoski v. Meanor, 442 U.S. 500[] (1979) ... ; Abney v. United States, 431 U.S. 651[] (1977) ... . See *Midland Asphalt Corp., supra,* [] at 801[] ("A right not to be tried in the sense relevant to the *Cohen* exception rests upon an explicit statutory or constitutional guarantee *that trial will not occur*") (emphasis added). Similarly, in civil cases, we have held that the denial of a motion to dismiss based upon a claim of absolute immunity from suit is immediately appealable prior to final judgment, Nixon v. Fitzgerald, 457 U.S. 731, 742-743[] (1982), "for the essence of absolute immunity is its possessor's entitlement not to have to answer for his conduct in a civil damages action," Mitchell v. Forsyth, 472 U.S. 511, 525[] (1985). And claims of qualified immunity may be pursued by immediate appeal, because qualified immunity too "is an *immunity from suit.*" *Id.* at 526[] (emphasis in original).

On the other hand, we have declined to hold the collateral order doctrine applicable where a district court has denied a claim, not that the defendant has a right not to be sued at all, but that the suit against the defendant is not properly before the particular court because it lacks jurisdiction. In Van Cauwenberghe v. Biard, 486 U.S. 517[] (1988), a civil defendant moved for dismissal on the ground that he had been immune from service of process because his presence in the United States had been compelled by extradition to face criminal charges. We noted that, after *Mitchell,* "[t]he critical question ... is whether 'the essence' of the claimed right is a right not to stand trial," 486 U.S. at 524[], and held that the immunity from service of process defendant asserted did not amount to an immunity from suit—even though service was essential to the trial court's jurisdiction over the defendant. See also *Catlin v. United States,* 324 U.S. at 236[] (order denying motion to dismiss petition for condemnation of land not immediately appealable, "even when the motion is based upon jurisdictional grounds").

... [P]etitioner is obviously not entitled under the forum-selection clause of its contract to avoid suit altogether, and an entitlement to avoid suit is different in kind from an entitlement to be sued only in a particular forum. Petitioner's claim that it may be sued only in Naples, while not perfectly secured by appeal after final judgment, is adequately vindicable at that stage—surely as effectively vindicable as a claim that the trial court lacked personal jurisdiction over the defendant—and hence does not fall within the third prong of the collateral order doctrine.

Petitioner argues that there is a strong federal policy favoring the enforcement of foreign forum-selection clauses, citing The Bremen v. Zapata Off-Shore Co., 407 U.S. 1[] (1972), and that "the essential concomitant of this strong federal policy ... is the right of immediate appellate review of district court orders denying their enforcement." [C] A policy favoring enforcement of forum-selection clauses, however, would go to the merits of petitioner's claim that its ticket agreement requires that any suit be filed in Italy and that the agreement should be enforced by the federal courts. Immediate appealability of a prejudgment order denying enforcement, insofar as it depends upon satisfaction of the third prong of the collateral order test, turns on the precise contours of the right asserted, and not upon the likelihood of eventual success on the merits. The Court of Appeals properly dismissed petitioner's appeal, and its judgment is

Affirmed.

Justice SCALIA, concurring. ...

While it is true, therefore, that the "right not to be sued elsewhere than in Naples" is not fully vindicated—indeed, to be utterly frank, is positively destroyed—by permitting the trial to occur and reversing its outcome, that is vindication enough because the right is not sufficiently important to overcome the policies militating against interlocutory appeals. We have made that judgment when the right not to be tried in a particular court has been created through jurisdictional limitations established by Congress or by international treaty, see *Van Cauwenberghe, supra.* The same judgment applies—if anything, *a fortiori*—when the right has been created by private agreement.

INQUIRY

Mandamus. Where a party is unable to establish jurisdiction for an appeal under the collateral-order doctrine or a statutory or court-rulel exception, mandamus may provide an alternative route. Mandamus is a court proceeding through which a party may obtain a writ requiring that a lower-court judge or other official to act consistent with the legal obligations of the office. In LaBuy v. Howes Leather Co., 352 U.S. 249 (1957), the Supreme Court held that mandamus is available in the federal Courts of Appeals through the All Writs Act, 28 U.S.C. §1651(a), in extreme cases involving exceptional circumstances. The Supreme Court case of *Beacon Theatres, Inc. v. Westover*, excerpted and discussed in Chapter XII on jury-trial rights, is another example of mandamus, used in that case to review a trial-court decision to deny jury trial. In Schlagenhauf v. Holder, 379 U.S. 104 (1964), the Supreme Court further defined what constitutes extreme circumstances warranting mandamus, holding mandamus available when a federal district court judge usurps judicial power in a way that raises a substantial issue of first impression. *Schlagenhauf v. Holder* involved a district-court order for medical examination of a defendant whose medical condition was not in controversy. In reversing the order, the Supreme Court articulated guidelines for the exercise of mandamus. The following excerpt from *Schlagenhauf* states those guidelines, followed by the All Writs Act:

> It is, of course, well settled, that the writ [of mandamus] is not to be used as a substitute for appeal, [c], even though hardship may result from delay and perhaps unnecessary trial, [c]. The writ is appropriately issued, however, when there is "usurpation of judicial power" or a clear abuse of discretion, Bankers Life & Casualty Co. v. Holland, 346 U.S.[379,] 383[(1953)].
>
> Here petitioner's basic allegation was lack of power in a district court to order a mental and physical examination of a defendant. That this issue was substantial is underscored by the fact that the challenged order requiring examination of a defendant appears to be the first of its kind in any reported decision in the federal courts under Rule 35,[fn] and we have found only one

such modern case in the state courts.[fn] The Court of Appeals recognized that it had the power to review on a petition for mandamus the basic, undecided question of whether a district court could order the mental or physical examination of a defendant. We agree that, under these unusual circumstances and in light of the authorities, the Court of Appeals had such power. ...

We recognize that in the ordinary situation where the sole issue presented is the district court's determination that "good cause" has been shown for an examination, mandamus is not an appropriate remedy, absent, of course, a clear abuse of discretion. See Bankers Life & Casualty Co. v. Holland, supra[]. Here, however, the petition was properly before the court on a substantial allegation of usurpation of power in ordering any examination of a defendant, an issue of first impression that called for the construction and application of Rule 35 in a new context. The meaning of Rule 35's requirements of "in controversy" and "good cause" also raised issues of first impression. In our view, the Court of Appeals should have..., under these special circumstances, determined the "good cause" issue, so as to avoid piecemeal litigation and to settle new and important problems.

Thus we believe that the Court of Appeals had power to determine all of the issues presented by the petition for mandamus.[fn]

---

28 U.S.C. §1651. Writs

(a) The Supreme Court and all courts established by Act of Congress may issue all writs necessary or appropriate in aid of their respective jurisdictions and agreeable to the usages and principles of law.

(b) An alternative writ or rule nisi may be issued by a justice or judge of a court which has jurisdiction.

INQUIRY

Mandamus Procedures. The All Writs Act, 28 U.S.C. §1651, gives no real guidance as to how to institute mandamus actions. FED. R. APP. P. 21 provides that guidance. The party seeking mandamus begins the action by filing a petition with the circuit-court clerk, serving copies on all parties including the allegedly offending trial-court judge. Rule 21 then establishes a flexible proceeding that allows the appellate court either to quickly dispose of the allegation without requiring the opposing parties and trial-court judge to respond or, if the allegations appear to have merit, then to require opposing parties and trial-court judge to answer, followed by briefing and oral argument as the appellate court deems necessary. Rule 21 gives the appellate court the flexibility necessary to protect trial-court judges from the burden of responding to unwarranted mandamus challenges. Read Rule 21, followed by another Supreme Court case *Kerr v. United States District Court* discussing mandamus as an alternative remedy:

FED. R. APP. P. 21. Writs of Mandamus and Prohibition, and Other Extraordinary Writs

(a) MANDAMUS OR PROHIBITION TO A COURT: PETITION, FILING, SERVICE, AND DOCKETING.

(1) A party petitioning for a writ of mandamus or prohibition directed to a court must file a petition with the circuit clerk with proof of service on all parties to the proceeding in the trial court. The party must also provide a copy

to the trial-court judge. All parties to the proceeding in the trial court other than the petitioner are respondents for all purposes.
(2)(A) The petition must be titled ''In re [name of petitioner].''
(B) The petition must state:
(i) the relief sought;
(ii) the issues presented;
(iii) the facts necessary to understand the issue presented by the petition; and
(iv) the reasons why the writ should issue.
(C) The petition must include a copy of any order or opinion or parts of the record that may be essential to understand the matters set forth in the petition.
(3) Upon receiving the prescribed docket fee, the clerk must docket the petition and submit it to the court.
(b) DENIAL; ORDER DIRECTING ANSWER; BRIEFS; PRECEDENCE.
(1) The court may deny the petition without an answer. Otherwise, it must order the respondent, if any, to answer within a fixed time.
(2) The clerk must serve the order to respond on all persons directed to respond.
(3) Two or more respondents may answer jointly.
(4) The court of appeals may invite or order the trial-court judge to address the petition or may invite an amicus curiae to do so. The trial-court judge may request permission to address the petition but may not do so unless invited or ordered to do so by the court of appeals.
(5) If briefing or oral argument is required, the clerk must advise the parties, and when appropriate, the trial-court judge or amicus curiae.
(6) The proceeding must be given preference over ordinary civil cases.
(7) The circuit clerk must send a copy of the final disposition to the trial-court judge.
(c) OTHER EXTRAORDINARY WRITS. An application for an extraordinary writ other than one provided for in Rule 21(a) must be made by filing a petition with the circuit clerk with proof of service on the respondents. Proceedings on the application must conform, so far as is practicable, to the procedures prescribed in Rule 21(a) and (b).
(d) FORM OF PAPERS; NUMBER OF COPIES. All papers must conform to Rule 32(c)(2). Except by the court's permission, a paper must not exceed 30 pages, exclusive of the disclosure statement, the proof of service, and the accompanying documents required by Rule 21(a)(2)(C). An original and 3 copies must be filed unless the court requires the filing of a different number by local rule or by order in a particular case.

Kerr v. United States District Court,

United States Supreme Court
426 U.S. 394 (1976)

Mr. Justice MARSHALL delivered the opinion of the Court.

Petitioners, defendants in a class action, sought issuance of writs of mandamus from the United States Court of Appeals for the Ninth Circuit to compel the District Court to vacate two discovery orders. The Court of Appeals refused to issue the writs. We hold that in the circumstances of this case and particularly in light of the availability of an alternative, less extreme, path to modification of the challenged discovery orders issuance of the writ is inappropriate. We therefore affirm.

I

Seven prisoners in the custody of the Department of Corrections of the State of California filed a class action in the United States District Court for the Northern District of California on behalf of themselves and "on behalf of all adult male felons who now are, as well as all adult male felons who in the future will be, in the custody of the California Department of Corrections, whether confined in an institution operated by the Department or on parole." [C][fn] Among the defendants in the action are petitioners in this case: the individual members of the California Adult Authority, the Administrative Officer of the California Adult Authority, and the Director of Corrections of the State of California. Plaintiffs' complaint alleges substantial constitutional violations in the manner in which the

California Adult Authority carries out its function of determining the length and conditions of punishment for convicted criminal offenders.

In the course of discovery, plaintiffs submitted requests for the production of a number of documents pursuant to Fed. Rule Civ. Proc. 34. Petitioners' subsequent two petitions for writs of mandamus were concerned with two classes of documents that were part of these requests. The first class, part of a series of requests first made in June 1973, and which will be referred to here as the "Adult Authority files," is generally composed of the personnel files of all members and employees of the Adult Authority, all Adult Authoritydocuments relating to its past, present, or future operation, and all memoranda written by the Chairman of the Adult Authority within the preceding five years.[fn] The second class of documents with which we are concerned was first requested by plaintiffs in November 1973, and will be referred to here as the "prisoners' files." Plaintiffs requested the opportunity to examine the files of every twentieth inmate at each California Department of Corrections institution, [c]; the class of documents, therefore, is composed of the correctional files of a sample of the prisoners in the custody of the California Department of Corrections.

When presented with the request for the Adult Authority files, petitioners objected, claiming that the files were irrelevant, confidential, and privileged, and suggesting that they should not be required to turn over the files to plaintiffs without prior in camera review by the District Court to evaluate the claims of privilege. Plaintiffs moved, pursuant to Fed. Rule Civ. Proc. 37, for an order compelling discovery. [C] ... The District Court accepted the Magistrate's recommendations and ordered the production of the documents. Seeking to limit distribution of the personnel files of the Adult Authority members and their employees, however, the District Court issued a protective order limiting the number of people associated with the plaintiffs who could examine those documents... .

Dissatisfied with the District Court's ruling, petitioners filed a petition for a writ of mandamus under 28 U.S.C. §1651(a),[fn] requesting the Court of Appeals for the Ninth Circuit to vacate the District Court's order granting plaintiffs' motion to compel discovery. The Court of Appeals denied the petition... . According to the Court of Appeals, discovery of the documents was part of "a proper line of attack" in the underlying lawsuit. [C] The court went on to observe that petitioners had no absolute privilege that would allow them to avoid production of the documents at issue. ... [T]he Court of Appeals indicated that because the assertions of privilege were not personally made by high-level officials of the California Adult Authority and because the assertions of privilege were lacking in what it saw to be the requisite specificity, issuance of the writ on grounds of privilege was inappropriate... .

A similar course was followed with regard to the requests for the prisoners' files. ...

II

The remedy of mandamus is a drastic one, to be invoked only in extraordinary situations. Will v. United States, 389 U.S. 90, 95[] (1967); Bankers Life & Cas. Co. v. Holland, 346 U.S. 379, 382-385[] (1953); Ex parte Fahey, 332 U.S. 258, 259[] (1947). As we have observed, the writ "has traditionally been used in the federal courts only 'to confine an inferior court to a lawful exercise of its prescribed jurisdiction or to compel it to exercise its authority when it is its duty to do so.'" *Will v. United States, supra,* [] at 95[], quoting Roche v. Evaporated Milk Assn., 319 U.S. 21, 26[] (1943). And, while we have not limited the use of mandamus by an unduly narrow and technical understanding of what constitutes a matter of "jurisdiction," *Will v. United States, supra,* at 95[], the fact still remains that "only exceptional circumstances amounting to a judicial 'usurpation of power' will justify the invocation of this extraordinary remedy." Ibid.

Our treatment of mandamus within the federal court system as an extraordinary remedy is not without good reason. As we have recognized before, mandamus actions such as the one involved in the instant case "have the unfortunate consequence of making the (district court) judge a litigant, obliged to obtain personal counsel or to leave his defense to one of the litigants (appearing) before him" in the underlying case. *Bankers Life & Cas. Co. v. Holland, supra,* [] at 384-385[], quoting *Ex parte Fahey, supra*, [] at 260[]. More importantly, particularly in an era of excessively crowded lower court dockets, it is in the interest of the fair and prompt administration of justice to discourage piecemeal litigation. It has been Congress' determination since the Judiciary Act of 1789 that as a general rule "appellate review should be postponed . . . until after final judgment has been rendered by the trial court." *Will v. United States, supra,* [] at 96[]; Parr v. United States, 351 U.S. 513, 520-521[] (1956).[fn] A judicial readiness to issue the writ of mandamus in anything less than an extraordinary situation would run the real risk of defeating the very policies sought to be furthered by that judgment of Congress.

As a means of implementing the rule that the writ will issue only in extraordinary circumstances, we have set forth various conditions for its issuance. Among these are that the party seeking issuance of the writ have no other adequate means to attain the relief he desires, *Roche v. Evaporated Milk Assn., supra,* [] at 26[], and that he satisfy "the burden of showing that (his) right to issuance of the writ is 'clear and indisputable.'" *Banker's Life & Cas. Co. v. Holland, [supra,]* at 384[], quoting United States ex rel. Bernardin v. Duell, 172 U.S. 576, 582[] (1899); [c]. Moreover, it is important to remember that issuance of the writ is in large part a matter of discretion with the court to which the petition is addressed. Schlagenhauf v. Holder, 379 U.S. 104, 112n. 8[] (1964); [c]. [Cc].

When looked at in the framework of these factors, it would appear that the actions of the Court of Appeals in this case should be affirmed. What petitioners are seeking here is not a declaration that the documents in question are absolutely privileged and that plaintiffs can never have access to any of them. On the contrary, petitioners request only that "production of the confidential documents not be compelled without a prior informed determination by the district court that plaintiffs' need for them in the action below outweighs their confidentiality." [C] Petitioners ask in essence only that the District Court review the challenged documents in camera before passing on whether each one individually should or should not be disclosed. But the Court of Appeals' opinion dealing with the Adult Authority files did not foreclose the possible necessity of such in camera review. Its denial of the writ was based largely on the grounds that the governmental privilege had not been asserted personally by anyone eligible to assert it, and that it had not been asserted with the requisite specificity. The court apparently left open the opportunity for petitioners to return to the District Court, assert the privilege more specifically and through responsible officials, and then have their request for an in camera review of the materials by the District Court reconsidered in a different light… .

We are thus confident that the Court of Appeals did in fact intend to afford the petitioners the opportunity to apply for and, upon proper application, receive in camera review. Accordingly the orders of the Court of Appeals are affirmed.

So ordered.

Mr. Justice STEVENS took no part in the consideration or decision of this case.

INQUIRY

Extraordinary Cases. The above *Kerr* case cautions to be sure to reserve mandamus for the extraordinary case, citing (among other cases) Will v. United States, 389 U.S. 90 (1967). *Will* involved the prosecution's request for a writ of mandamus to overturn an order that the defendant have discovery of the prosecution's case. The Supreme Court in *Will* denied the writ even though without it there could not be appellate guidance on discovery by defendants in criminal cases, given that prosecutors cannot appeal acquittals, and only on an acquittal could the prosecution show prejudice from defense discovery. The truly extraordinary case would be one like United States v. Nixon, 418 U.S. 683 (1974), in which the Supreme Court found All Writs Act jurisdiction to hear and deny the petition of the President of the United States for immunity from a grand jury subpoena to produce Oval Office recordings connected with Watergate. Consider Cheney v. United States District Court, 542 U.S. 367 (2004), for another example of an extraordinary case worthy of mandamus. Immediately upon winning office, President George W. Bush appointed an advisory committee headed by Vice President Cheney and comprised solely of federal officials to develop a national energy policy. Government watchdog groups sued under federal laws requiring open meetings and citizen participation on advisory panels. When the district court ordered discovery of committee materials, the Vice President sought mandamus to re-determine the issue of executive privilege. Although the federal appellate court initially denied mandamus, the Supreme Court reversed and held mandamus appropriate, stating:

> We now come to the central issue in the case—whether the Court of Appeals was correct to conclude it "ha[d] no authority to exercise the extraordinary remedy of mandamus," [c], on the ground that the Government could protect its rights by asserting executive privilege in the District Court.

The common-law writ of mandamus against a lower court is codified at 28 U.S.C. §1651(a)... . This is a "drastic and extraordinary" remedy "reserved for really extraordinary causes." Ex parte Fahey, 332 U.S. 258, 259-260[] (1947). "The traditional use of the writ in aid of appellate jurisdiction both at common law and in the federal courts has been to confine [the court against which mandamus is sought] to a lawful exercise of its prescribed jurisdiction." Roche v. Evaporated Milk Assn., 319 U.S. 21, 26[] (1943). Although courts have not "confined themselves to an arbitrary and technical definition of 'jurisdiction,'" Will v. United States, 389 U.S. 90, 95[] (1967), "only exceptional circumstances amounting to a judicial 'usurpation of power,'" *ibid.*, or a "clear abuse of discretion," Bankers Life & Casualty Co. v. Holland, 346 U.S. 379, 383[] (1953), "will justify the invocation of this extraordinary remedy," *Will,* 389 U.S. at 95[].

As the writ is one of "the most potent weapons in the judicial arsenal," *id.*, at 107[], three conditions must be satisfied before it may issue. Kerr v. United States Dist. Court for Northern Dist. of Cal., 426 U.S. 394, 403[] (1976). First, "the party seeking issuance of the writ [must] have no other adequate means to attain the relief he desires," *ibid.*—a condition designed to ensure that the writ will not be used as a substitute for the regular appeals process, *Fahey, supra,* at 260[]. Second, the petitioner must satisfy "'the burden of showing that [his] right to issuance of the writ is "clear and indisputable."'" *Kerr, supra,* at 403[] (quoting *Bankers Life & Casualty Co., supra,* at 384[]). Third, even if the first two prerequisites have been met, the issuing court, in the exercise of its discretion, must be satisfied that the writ is appropriate under the circumstances. *Kerr, supra,* at 403[] (citing Schlagenhauf v. Holder, 379 U.S. 104, 112n.8[] (1964)). These hurdles, however demanding, are not insuperable. This Court has issued the writ to restrain a lower court when its actions would threaten the separation of powers by "embarrass[ing] the executive arm of the Government," Ex parte Peru, 318 U.S. 578, 588[] (1943), or result in the "intrusion by the federal judiciary on a delicate area of federal-state relations," *Will, supra,* at 95[], (citing Maryland v. Soper (No. 1), 270 U.S. 9[] (1926)).

Were the Vice President not a party in the case, the argument that the Court of Appeals should have entertained an action in mandamus, notwithstanding the District Court's denial of the motion for certification, might present different considerations. Here, however, the Vice President and his comembers on the NEPDG are the subjects of the discovery orders. The mandamus petition alleges that the orders threaten "substantial intrusions on the process by which those in closest operational proximity to the President advise the President." [C] These facts and allegations remove this case from the category of ordinary discovery orders where interlocutory appellate review is unavailable, through mandamus or otherwise. [542 U.S. at 380-381.]

Contempt. Contempt orders can make the extraordinary case for mandamus. Nixon v. Sirica, 487 F.2d 700 (D.C. Cir. 1973), was another Watergate case in which the appellate court granted mandamus but denied the President's request to quash a grand jury subpoena for Oval Office tapes. In finding jurisdiction to hear the President's petition, the appellate court in *Nixon v. Sirica* considered that the only other option the President had to mandamus was to disobey the subpoena, suffer contempt, and then appeal the contempt order—not a very attractive option for most litigants, including an embattled President. In the ordinary case, though, that is exactly what the courts expect: that a party, compelled by order to do some act such as comply with a subpoena, will either do the act or suffer contempt and then appeal the contempt order. *See* United States v. Ryan, 402 U.S. 530 (1971). Non-parties have that option for interlocutory appeal of a contempt order, as do both parties and non-parties held in criminal contempt. Parties held in civil contempt must await final judgment to appeal. *See* Fox v. Capital Co., 299 U.S. 105, 107 (1936). In any case, Congress has provided that the Supreme Court and federal courts of appeals have the authority to do as they see fit with lower court orders brought before them for review. Read 28 U.S.C. §2106 confirming that authority.

28 U.S.C. §2106. Determination
The Supreme Court or any other court of appellate jurisdiction may affirm, modify, vacate, set aside or reverse any judgment, decree, or order of a court lawfully brought before it for review, and may remand the cause and direct the entry of such appropriate judgment, decree, or order, or require such further proceedings to be had as may be just under the circumstances.

---

3. State Variations

While the final-judgment rule is certainly a part of federal appellate jurisdiction, not all states follow the final-judgment rule. New York is an example. There is much broader opportunity for interlocutory appeals under New York's statute for appeals to the appellate division from its supreme and county courts (keeping in mind that New York's supreme court is a trial court, not an appellate court). With certain exceptions, parties may appeal orders deciding a motion that "involves some part of the merits" or "affects a substantial right." Which do you prefer, the federal regime just described above, with provisions that are simultaneously jurisdictional, rigidly applied, and yet interpreted with exceptions, or a state regime in which the parties can choose whether to appeal early and piecemeal, if necessary? State regimes for liberal appeal rights reject or minimize the federal regime's goals of certainty, finality, and efficiency, in favor of access to appellate justice. That access can have its own efficiencies in reassuring parties that they may obtain prompt correction of erroneous rulings. Read New York's statute, as you consider the benefits of each regime.

N.Y. C.P. L.R. §5701. Appeals to appellate division from supreme and county courts
(a) Appeals as of right. An appeal may be taken to the appellate division as of right in an action, originating in the supreme court or a county court:
1. from any final or interlocutory judgment except one entered subsequent to an order of the appellate division which disposes of all the issues in the action; or
2. from an order not specified in subdivision (b), where the motion it decided was made upon notice and it:
(i) grants, refuses, continues or modifies a provisional remedy; or
(ii) settles, grants or refuses an application to resettle a transcript or statement on appeal; or
(iii) grants or refuses a new trial; except where specific questions of fact arising upon the issues in an action triable by the court have been tried by a jury, pursuant

to an order for that purpose, and the order grants or refuses a new trial upon the merits; or
(iv) involves some part of the merits; or
(v) affects a substantial right; or
(vi) in effect determines the action and prevents a judgment from which an appeal might be taken; or
(vii) determines a statutory provision of the state to be unconstitutional, and the determination appears from the reasons given for the decision or is necessarily implied in the decision; or
(viii) grants a motion for leave to reargue made pursuant to subdivision (d) of rule 2221 or determines a motion for leave to renew made pursuant to subdivision (e) of rule 2221; or
3. from an order, where the motion it decided was made upon notice, refusing to vacate or modify a prior order, if the prior order would have been appealable as of right under paragraph two had it decided a motion made upon notice.
(b) Orders not appealable as of right. An order is not appealable to the appellate division as of right where it:
1. is made in a proceeding against a body or officer pursuant to article 78; or
2. requires or refuses to require a more definite statement in a pleading; or
3. orders or refuses to order that scandalous or prejudicial matter be stricken from a pleading.
(c) Appeals by permission. An appeal may be taken to the appellate division from any order which is not appealable as of right in an action originating in the supreme court or a county court by permission of a judge who made the order granted before application to a justice of the appellate division; or by permission of a justice of the appellate division in the department to which the appeal could be taken, upon refusal by the judge who made the order or upon direct application.

B. Standard for Review

Properly filing an appeal so as to invoke the appellate court's jurisdiction is a big first step. There can be several important smaller steps to follow before a party has perfected an appeal for the appellate court's decision. Court rules may require the appealing party to order transcripts of hearings and trial, certify those transcript orders, order the trial court's docket sheet, and complete and file appeal checklists and case-information sheets. Counsel for both sides may have to prepare and submit a joint appendix. Of course, each side must prepare and file an appeal brief, often after exhaustive research including studies of the decisions of the appellate judges assigned to the appeal panel. The appealing party may also file a rebuttal brief. Both sides may solicit and coordinate briefs with amici curiae ("friends of the court," meaning non-parties whose interests the appeal outcome may affect) who will then file their own briefs advocating a decision that will advance or protect their own interests. These efforts all point toward preparing the case for appellate review. The appeals judges do their own work to evaluate appeals, reading all or part of the trial court's record, researching and writing, communicating with one another, and using law clerks or staff attorneys to prepare bench memoranda and draft opinions. The appellate court will likely offer oral argument (the practice except in relatively rare cases such as a sanction for a late-filed brief), and the lawyers for both sides will likely accept the offer (although some litigants waive oral arguments).

When a party timely files and otherwise perfects an appeal of right, the appellate court must have a standard under which to decide the appeal. The question of the standard for review actually implicates two closely related but conceptually distinct questions: (1) what deference the appellate court should give the trial court's decision; and (2) what decisions or parts of decisions the appellate court may review, in other words, what is the scope of review. The appellate courts use a law-fact distinction to determine the first question of the degree of deference the appellate court should afford the trial-court decision. The appellate courts show greater deference to fact decisions and lesser deference to law decisions, as the next section explains. Another way to put it is that the degree of deference depends on the scope of review, whether law or fact. The appellate courts use the harmless-error rule to answer the second question as to the scope of review. The appellate courts do not review harmless errors but review only material errors, meaning those having a likelihood of having affected the trial court's decision. Another way to put it is that the scope of review depends on the deference the appellate court will show for the trial court's management of the case through preliminary orders. Thus, the two questions of deference and scope relate closely to one another. The greater the deference, the more narrow the scope of review, while, equally, the more narrow the scope of review, the greater the deference. Consider first the law-fact distinction followed by the harmless-error rule.

1. Law and Fact

The federal appellate courts apply one of three review standards, depending on the type of issue—either law or fact—that the trial court is deciding. The lowest review standard giving the least deference to the trial court's decision (indeed giving no deference at all) is *de novo* review. De novo review means to make the decision anew as if not previously made. The appellate courts reserve de novo review for a trial court's decisions of law. Examples of trial-court decisions of law would include the decision of which law (state or federal) to apply, how to instruct the jury as to the parties' substantive rights, claims, and defenses, and whether to grant judgment as a matter of law. *See also* Cooper Indus., Inc., v. Leatherman Tool Group, Inc., 532 U.S. 424 (2001) (de novo review of constitutionality of punitive-damages award); Salve Regina College v. Russell, 499 U.S. 225 (1991) (de novo review of determination of state law in diversity action). In theory, statements of the law are either wrong or right. Trial judges and appellate judges should be operating under the same understanding of the law, with the same or similar legal education and training. On those understandings, an appellate judge owes a trial judge no deference as to rulings on the law.

On the other hand, when trial judges make determinations of fact, they are necessarily making judgments of credibility based on observation of the testifying witnesses. They may also be inspecting tangible and documentary evidence in the context of that testimony, and even visiting the scene (although rarely). Appellate judges have none of those advantages when deciding on the cold appellate record. Thus, the appellate courts offer a higher review standard for a trial judge's determination of fact, one that defers to the trial judge's superior vantage point. That higher review standard requires the appealing party to show a clear error, FED. R. CIV. P. 52(a), meaning a clearly erroneous decision that leaves the appellate court with the definite and firm conviction that the trial made a mistake. *See* Anderson v. City of Bessemer City, 470 U.S. 564, 565 (1985); United States v. U.S. Gysum Co., 333 U.S. 364, 395 (1948). A party appealing a trial judge's determination of fact must show that it was clearly erroneous. Determinations of fact arise primarily when the trial judge is acting without a jury such as in bench trials or evidentiary hearings.

A still-higher standard of review permits reversal of a trial judge's decision only for an abuse of discretion, wherever the trial judge had discretion to manage pretrial and trial proceedings. That discretion exists for such matters as scheduling trial and pretrial conferences, determining the contents of pretrial orders, determining the order of proofs, limiting the number of witnesses, limiting the presentation of documentary evidence so that it is not cumulative, and keeping parties to reasonable time limits in opening statements, examination of witnesses, and closing arguments. The abuse-of-discretion standard is the most deferential of the three standards, meant to protect trial judges' rulings wherever those rulings have a rational and lawful basis, even where the appellate court would have decided differently. *See* General Electric v. Joiner, 522 U.S. 136 (1997) (reversing too stringent of a review under abuse-of-discretion standard).

The above law-fact distinction has historical and constitutional bases. Historically, equity courts reviewed written records. They did not conduct trials involving oral testimony. Because an appellate judge could read a written record as well as a trial judge, appellate courts adopted a de novo review standard for equity cases. Law cases, in which the trials involved oral testimony, were different. The factfinder (judge or jury) could make, and indeed in most cases had to make, credibility determinations based on that observation. The review standard needed to accommodate that evaluative function. When the *Federal Rules of Civil Procedure* merged law and equity, the appellate review standards remained, justified by their functional basis. FED. R. CIV. P. 52(a)(6) confirms that appellate courts must not set aside "[f]indings of fact, whether based on oral or documentary evidence," "unless clearly erroneous." In appropriate cases, an appellate court may apply more than one review standard to different issues arising on appeal. In Cooter & Gell v. Hartmax Corp., 469 U.S. 384 (1990), involving Rule 11 sanctions, the Supreme Court applied the clearly erroneous standard to the trial judge's finding that the lawyer had failed to adequately investigate, while applying the abuse-of-discretion standard to the question of the complaint's legal sufficiency and the sanction to impose.

The constitutional basis for the law-fact distinction lies in the Seventh Amendment. The Seventh Amendment's re-examination clause prohibits direct appellate review of jury verdicts determining fact issues, except as at common law. In a strict sense, there is no review standard for a jury's fact determination because there is no review. Yet the appellate courts do review trial-court decisions to deny new trial, which can like reviewing the jury's decision. Appellate review of new-trial denials was not available at the time of the Seventh Amendment's adoption. Indeed, it may burden Seventh Amendment jury-trial rights for an appellate court to throw out a jury verdict that the trial judge approved when denying a motion for new trial. *See* Lightfoot v. Union Carbide

Corp., 110 F.3d 898, 910 (2d Cir. 1997). Federal appellate courts may not review trial-court decisions to grant new trial until after the trial court conducts the new trial, when it may review those decisions only under the abuse-of-discretion standard. *See* Adams v. Travelers Indem. Co., 465 F.3d 156, 163 (5th Cir. 2006); Christoper v. Florida, 449 F.3d 1360, 1365 (11th Cir. 2006). The Seventh Amendment has to do with jury-trial rights. It does not protect findings of fact made by a judge in a bench trial. As indicated above, the appellate courts review a judge's findings of fact based on a standard of clear error and must determine those findings to be clearly erroneous before reversing. Consider the following seminal Supreme Court case illustrating the clearly erroneous review standard. As you read, notice the length and detail of the opinion (even though edited), which is itself a reflection of the deference due a trial judge's fact determinations.

Anderson v. City of Bessemer City,

United States Supreme Court
470 U.S. 564 (1985)

Justice WHITE delivered the opinion of the Court.

In Pullman-Standard v. Swint, 456 U.S. 273[] (1982), we held that a District Court's finding of discriminatory intent in an action brought under Title VII of the Civil Rights Act of 1964, [] 42 U.S.C. §2000e *et seq.*, is a factual finding that may be overturned on appeal only if it is clearly erroneous. In this case, the Court of Appeals for the Fourth Circuit concluded that there was clear error in a District Court's finding of discrimination and reversed. Because our reading of the record convinces us that the Court of Appeals misapprehended and misapplied the clearly-erroneous standard, we reverse.

I

Early in 1975, officials of respondent Bessemer City, North Carolina, set about to hire a new Recreation Director for the city. Although the duties that went with the position were not precisely delineated, the new Recreation Director was to be responsible for managing all of the city's recreational facilities and for developing recreational programs-athletic and otherwise-to serve the needs of the city's residents. A five-member committee selected by the Mayor was responsible for choosing the Recreation Director. Of the five members, four were men; the one woman on the committee, Mrs. Auddie Boone, served as the chairperson.

Eight persons applied for the position of Recreation Director. Petitioner, at the time a 39-year-old schoolteacher with college degrees in social studies and education, was the only woman among the eight. The selection committee reviewed the resumés submitted by the applicants and briefly interviewed each of the jobseekers. Following the interviews, the committee offered the position to Mr. Donald Kincaid, a 24-year-old who had recently graduated from college with a degree in physical education. All four men on the committee voted to offer the job to Mr. Kincaid; Mrs. Boone voted for petitioner.

Believing that the committee had passed over her in favor of a less qualified candidate solely because she was a woman, petitioner filed discrimination charges with the Charlotte District Office of the Equal Employment Opportunity Commission. In July 1980 (five years after petitioner filed the charges), the EEOC's District Director found that there was reasonable cause to believe that petitioner's charges were true and invited the parties to attempt a resolution of petitioner's grievance through conciliation proceedings. The EEOC's efforts proved unsuccessful, and in due course, petitioner received a right-to-sue letter.

Petitioner then filed this Title VII action in the United States District Court for the Western District of North Carolina. After a 2-day trial during which the court heard testimony from petitioner, Mr. Kincaid, and the five members of the selection committee, the court issued a brief memorandum of decision setting forth its finding that petitioner was entitled to judgment because she had been denied the position of Recreation Director on account of her sex. In addition to laying out the rationale for this finding, the memorandum requested that petitioner's counsel submit proposed findings of fact and conclusions of law expanding upon those set forth in the memorandum. Petitioner's counsel complied with this request by submitting a lengthy set of proposed findings ([c]); the court then requested and received a response setting forth in detail respondent's objections to the proposed findings ([c])—objections that were, in turn, answered by petitioner's counsel in a somewhat less lengthy reply ([c]). After receiving these submissions, the court issued its own findings of fact and conclusions of law. [C]

As set forth in the formal findings of fact and conclusions of law, the court's finding that petitioner had been denied employment by respondent because of her sex rested on a number of subsidiary findings. First, the court found that at the time the selection committee made its choice, petitioner had been better qualified than Mr. Kincaid to perform the range of duties demanded by the position. The court based this finding on petitioner's experience as a classroom teacher responsible for supervising schoolchildren in recreational and athletic activities, her employment as a hospital recreation director in the late 1950's, her extensive involvement in a variety of civic organizations, her knowledge of sports acquired both as a high school athlete and as a mother of children involved in organized athletics, her skills as a public speaker, her experience in handling money (gained in the course of her community activities and in her work as a bookkeeper for a group of physicians), and her knowledge of music, dance, and crafts. The court found that Mr. Kincaid's principal qualifications were his experience as a student teacher and as a coach in a local youth basketball league, his extensive knowledge of team and individual sports, acquired as a result of his lifelong involvement in athletics, and his formal training as a physical education major in college. Noting that the position of Recreation Director involved more than the management of athletic programs, the court concluded that petitioner's greater breadth of experience made her better qualified for the position.

Second, the court found that the male committee members had in fact been biased against petitioner because she was a woman. The court based this finding in part on the testimony of one of the committee members that he believed it would have been "real hard" for a woman to handle the job and that he would not want his wife to have to perform the duties of the Recreation Director. The finding of bias found additional support in evidence that another male committee member had told Mr. Kincaid, the successful applicant, of the vacancy and had also solicited applications from three other men, but had not attempted to recruit any women for the job.

Also critical to the court's inference of bias was its finding that petitioner, alone among the applicants for the job, had been asked whether she realized the job would involve night work and travel and whether her husband approved of her applying for the job. The court's finding that the committee had pursued this line of inquiry only with petitioner was based on the testimony of petitioner that these questions had been asked of her and the testimony of Mrs. Boone that similar questions had not been asked of the other applicants. Although Mrs. Boone also testified that during Mr. Kincaid's interview, she had made a "comment" to him regarding the reaction of his new bride to his taking the position of Recreation Director, the court concluded that this comment was not a serious inquiry, but merely a "facetious" remark prompted by Mrs. Boone's annoyance that only petitioner had been questioned about her spouse's reaction. The court also declined to credit the testimony of one of the male committee members that Mr. Kincaid had been asked about his wife's feelings "in a way" and the testimony of another committeeman that all applicants had been questioned regarding their willingness to work at night and their families' reaction to night work. The court concluded that the finding that only petitioner had been seriously questioned about her family's reaction suggested that the male committee members believed women had special family responsibilities that made certain forms of employment inappropriate.

Finally, the court found that the reasons offered by the male committee members for their choice of Mr. Kincaid were pretextual. The court rejected the proposition that Mr. Kincaid's degree in physical education justified his choice, as the evidence suggested that where male candidates were concerned, the committee valued experience more highly than formal training in physical education.[fn] The court also rejected the claim of one of the committeemen that Mr. Kincaid had been hired because of the superiority of the recreational programs he planned to implement if selected for the job. The court credited the testimony of one of the other committeemen who had voted for Mr. Kincaid that the programs outlined by petitioner and Mr. Kincaid were substantially identical.

On the basis of its findings that petitioner was the most qualified candidate, that the committee had been biased against hiring a woman, and that the committee's explanations for its choice of Mr. Kincaid were pretextual, the court concluded that petitioner had met her burden of establishing that she had been denied the position of Recreation Director because of her sex. Petitioner having conceded that ordering the city to hire her would be an inappropriate remedy under the circumstances, the court awarded petitioner backpay in the amount of $30,397 and attorney's fees of $16,971.59.

The Fourth Circuit reversed the District Court's finding of discrimination. [C] In the view of the Court of Appeals, three of the District Court's crucial findings were clearly erroneous: the finding that petitioner was the most qualified candidate, the finding that petitioner had been asked questions that other applicants were spared, and the finding that the male committee members were biased against hiring a woman. Having rejected these findings, the Court of Appeals concluded that the District Court had erred in finding that petitioner had been discriminated against on account of her sex.

II

We must deal at the outset with the Fourth Circuit's suggestion that "close scrutiny of the record in this case [was] justified by the manner in which the opinion was prepared," *id.*, at 156—that is, by the District Court's adoption of petitioner's proposed findings of fact and conclusions of law. The court recalled that the Fourth Circuit had on many occasions condemned the practice of announcing a decision and leaving it to the prevailing party to write the findings of fact and conclusions of law. [Cc] The court rejected petitioner's contention that the procedure followed by the trial judge in this case was proper because the judge had given respondent an opportunity to object to the proposed findings and had not adopted petitioner's findings verbatim. According to the court, the vice of the procedure lay in the trial court's solicitation of findings after it had already announced its decision and in the court's adoption of the "substance" of petitioner's proposed findings.

We, too, have criticized courts for their verbatim adoption of findings of fact prepared by prevailing parties, particularly when those findings have taken the form of conclusory statements unsupported by citation to the record. See, *e.g.*, United States v. El Paso Natural Gas Co., 376 U.S. 651, 656-657[] (1964); United States v. Marine Bancorporation, 418 U.S. 602, 615n. 13[] (1974). We are also aware of the potential for overreaching and exaggeration on the part of attorneys preparing findings of fact when they have already been informed that the judge has decided in their favor. [C] Nonetheless, our previous discussions of the subject suggest that even when the trial judge adopts proposed findings verbatim, the findings are those of the court and may be reversed only if clearly erroneous. *United States v. Marine Bancorporation, supra,* at 615 n. 13[]; *United States v. El Paso Natural Gas Co., supra,* [] at 656-657.

In any event, the District Court in this case does not appear to have uncritically accepted findings prepared without judicial guidance by the prevailing party. The court itself provided the framework for the proposed findings when it issued its preliminary memorandum, which set forth its essential findings and directed petitioner's counsel to submit a more detailed set of findings consistent with them. Further, respondent was provided and availed itself of the opportunity to respond at length to the proposed findings. Nor did the District Court simply adopt petitioner's proposed findings: the findings it ultimately issued—and particularly the crucial findings regarding petitioner's qualifications, the questioning to which petitioner was subjected, and bias on the part of the committeemen—vary considerably in organization and content from those submitted by petitioner's counsel. Under these circumstances, we see no reason to doubt that the findings issued by the District Court represent the judge's own considered conclusions. There is no reason to subject those findings to a more stringent appellate review than is called for by the applicable rules.

III

Because a finding of intentional discrimination is a finding of fact, the standard governing appellate review of a district court's finding of discrimination is that set forth in Federal Rule of Civil Procedure 52(a): "Findings of fact shall not be set aside unless clearly erroneous, and due regard shall be given to the opportunity of the trial court to judge of the credibility of the witnesses." The question before us, then, is whether the Court of Appeals erred in holding the District Court's finding of discrimination to be clearly erroneous.

Although the meaning of the phrase "clearly erroneous" is not immediately apparent, certain general principles governing the exercise of the appellate court's power to overturn findings of a district court may be derived from our cases. The foremost of these principles, as the Fourth Circuit itself recognized, is that "[a] finding is 'clearly erroneous' when although there is evidence to support it, the reviewing court on the entire evidence is left with the definite and firm conviction that a mistake has been committed." United States v. United States Gypsum Co., 333 U.S. 364, 395[] (1948). This standard plainly does not entitle a reviewing court to reverse the finding of the trier of fact simply because it is convinced that it would have decided the case differently. The reviewing court oversteps the bounds of its duty under Rule 52(a) if it undertakes to duplicate the role of the lower court. "In applying the clearly erroneous standard to the findings of a district court sitting without a jury, appellate courts must constantly have in mind that their function is not to decide factual issues *de novo*." Zenith Radio Corp. v. Hazeltine Research, Inc., 395 U.S. 100, 123[] (1969). If the district court's account of the evidence is plausible in light of the record viewed in its entirety, the court of appeals may not reverse it even though convinced that had it been sitting as the trier of fact, it would have weighed the evidence differently. Where there are two permissible views of the evidence, the factfinder's choice between them cannot be clearly erroneous. United States v. Yellow Cab Co., 338 U.S. 338, 342[] (1949); see also Inwood Laboratories, Inc. v. Ives Laboratories, Inc., 456 U.S. 844[] (1982).

This is so even when the district court's findings do not rest on credibility determinations, but are based instead on physical or documentary evidence or inferences from other facts. To be sure, various Courts of Appeals have on occasion asserted the theory that an appellate court may exercise *de novo* review over findings not based on credibility determinations. [Cc] This theory has an impressive genealogy, having first been articulated in an opinion written by Judge Frank and subscribed to by Judge Augustus Hand, [c], but it is impossible to trace the theory's lineage back to the text of Rule 52(a), which states straightforwardly that "findings of fact shall not be set aside unless clearly erroneous." That the Rule goes on to emphasize the special deference to be paid credibility determinations does not alter its clear command… .

The rationale for deference to the original finder of fact is not limited to the superiority of the trial judge's position to make determinations of credibility. The trial judge's major role is the determination of fact, and with experience in fulfilling that role comes expertise. Duplication of the trial judge's efforts in the court of appeals would very likely contribute only negligibly to the accuracy of fact determination at a huge cost in diversion of judicial resources. In addition, the parties to a case on appeal have already been forced to concentrate their energies and resources on persuading the trial judge that their account of the facts is the correct one; requiring them to persuade three more judges at the appellate level is requiring too much. As the Court has stated in a different context, the trial on the merits should be "the 'main event'... rather than a 'tryout on the road.'" Wainwright v. Sykes, 433 U.S. 72, 90[] (1977). For these reasons, review of factual findings under the clearly-erroneous standard—with its deference to the trier of fact—is the rule, not the exception.

When findings are based on determinations regarding the credibility of witnesses, Rule 52(a) demands even greater deference to the trial court's findings; for only the trial judge can be aware of the variations in demeanor and tone of voice that bear so heavily on the listener's understanding of and belief in what is said. See Wainwright v. Witt, 469 U.S. 412[] (1985). This is not to suggest that the trial judge may insulate his findings from review by denominating them credibility determinations, for factors other than demeanor and inflection go into the decision whether or not to believe a witness. Documents or objective evidence may contradict the witness' story; or the story itself may be so internally inconsistent or implausible on its face that a reasonable factfinder would not credit it. Where such factors are present, the court of appeals may well find clear error even in a finding purportedly based on a credibility determination. [C] But when a trial judge's finding is based on his decision to credit the testimony of one of two or more witnesses, each of whom has told a coherent and facially plausible story that is not contradicted by extrinsic evidence, that finding, if not internally inconsistent, can virtually never be clear error. [C]

IV

Application of the foregoing principles to the facts of the case lays bare the errors committed by the Fourth Circuit in its employment of the clearly-erroneous standard. In detecting clear error in the District Court's finding that petitioner was better qualified than Mr. Kincaid, the Fourth Circuit improperly conducted what amounted to a *de novo* weighing of the evidence in the record. The District Court's finding was based on essentially undisputed evidence regarding the respective backgrounds of petitioner and Mr. Kincaid and the duties that went with the position of Recreation Director. The District Court, after considering the evidence, concluded that the position of Recreation Director in Bessemer City carried with it broad responsibilities for creating and managing a recreation program involving not only athletics, but also other activities for citizens of all ages and interests. The court determined that petitioner's more varied educational and employment background and her extensive involvement in a variety of civic activities left her better qualified to implement such a rounded program than Mr. Kincaid, whose background was more narrowly focused on athletics.

The Fourth Circuit, reading the same record, concluded that the basic duty of the Recreation Director was to implement an athletic program, and that the essential qualification for a successful applicant would be either education or experience specifically related to athletics.[fn] Accordingly, it seemed evident to the Court of Appeals that Mr. Kincaid was in fact better qualified than petitioner.

Based on our own reading of the record, we cannot say that either interpretation of the facts is illogical or implausible. Each has support in inferences that may be drawn from the facts in the record; and if either interpretation had been drawn by a district court on the record before us, we would not be inclined to find it clearly erroneous. The question we must answer, however, is not whether the Fourth Circuit's interpretation of the facts was clearly erroneous, but whether the District Court's finding was clearly erroneous. [C] The District Court determined that petitioner was better qualified, and, as we have stated above, such a finding is entitled to deference notwithstanding that it is not based on credibility determinations. When the record is examined in light of the appropriately deferential standard, it is apparent that it contains nothing that mandates a finding that the District Court's conclusion was clearly erroneous.

Somewhat different concerns are raised by the Fourth Circuit's treatment of the District Court's finding that petitioner, alone among the applicants for the position of Recreation Director, was asked questions regarding her spouse's feelings about her application for the position. Here the error of the Court of

Appeals was its failure to give due regard to the ability of the District Court to interpret and discern the credibility of oral testimony. The Court of Appeals rested its rejection of the District Court's finding of differential treatment on its own interpretation of testimony by Mrs. Boone-the very witness whose testimony, in the view of the District Court, supported the finding. In the eyes of the Fourth Circuit, Mrs. Boone's testimony that she had made a "comment" to Mr. Kincaid about the feelings of his wife (a comment judged "facetious" by the District Court) conclusively established that Mr. Kincaid, and perhaps other male applicants as well, had been questioned about the feelings of his spouse.

... But Mrs. Boone several times stated that other candidates had not been questioned about the reaction of their wives—at least, "not in the same context" as had petitioner. And even after recalling and calling to the attention of the court that she had made a comment on the subject to Mr. Kincaid, Mrs. Boone denied that she had "asked" Mr. Kincaid about his wife's reaction. Mrs. Boone's testimony on these matters is not inconsistent with the theory that her remark was not a serious inquiry into whether Mr. Kincaid's wife approved of his applying for the position. Whether the judge's interpretation is actually correct is impossible to tell from the paper record, but it is easy to imagine that the tone of voice in which the witness related her comment, coupled with her immediate denial that she had questioned Mr. Kincaid on the subject, might have conclusively established that the remark was a facetious one. We therefore cannot agree that the judge's conclusion that the remark was facetious was clearly erroneous.

Once the trial court's characterization of Mrs. Boone's remark is accepted, it is apparent that the finding that the male candidates were not seriously questioned about the feelings of their wives cannot be deemed clearly erroneous. ... Under these circumstances, the trial court's decision to credit Mrs. Boone was not clearly erroneous.

... Given that that finding was not clearly erroneous, the finding of bias cannot be termed erroneous: it finds support not only in the treatment of petitioner in her interview, but also in the testimony of one committee member that he believed it would have been difficult for a woman to perform the job and in the evidence that another member solicited applications for the position only from men.[fn]

Our determination that the findings of the District Court regarding petitioner's qualifications, the conduct of her interview, and the bias of the male committee members were not clearly erroneous leads us to conclude that the court's finding that petitioner was discriminated against on account of her sex was also not clearly erroneous. The District Court's findings regarding petitioner's superior qualifications and the bias of the selection committee are sufficient to support the inference that petitioner was denied the position of Recreation Director on account of her sex. Accordingly, we hold that the Fourth Circuit erred in denying petitioner relief under Title VII.

In so holding, we do not assert that our knowledge of what happened 10 years ago in Bessemer City is superior to that of the Court of Appeals; nor do we claim to have greater insight than the Court of Appeals into the state of mind of the men on the selection committee who rejected petitioner for the position of Recreation Director. Even the trial judge, who has heard the witnesses directly and who is more closely in touch than the appeals court with the milieu out of which the controversy before him arises, cannot always be confident that he "knows" what happened. Often, he can only determine whether the plaintiff has succeeded in presenting an account of the facts that is more likely to be true than not. Our task—and the task of appellate tribunals generally—is more limited still: we must determine whether the trial judge's conclusions are clearly erroneous. On the record before us, we cannot say that they are. Accordingly, the judgment of the Court of Appeals is

Reversed.

Justice POWELL, concurring[, omitted].

Justice BLACKMUN, concurring in the judgment[, omitted].

INQUIRY

Clearly Erroneous. Were you able to find in the above lengthy opinion the Supreme Court's articulations of the clearly erroneous review standard for the appellate review of trial judges' fact determinations? The Court acknowledged in *Anderson v. City of Bessemer City* that the definition is not obvious. Rather, certain principles govern its application. One is that the appellate court must review all the evidence. Another is that the appellate court's review of all the evidence must leave it with a definite and firm conviction as to the trial court's mistake. Another is that the appellate court must not reverse simply because it would have decided differently. The appellate court must avoid de novo review and not duplicate the trial court's role. The appellate court must preserve the trial court's role, recognizing not only the trial court's greater opportunity to observe and evaluate the evidence but also its greater expertise at those skills. The appellate court must not reverse a trial-court determination that is plausible on the whole record. Finally, if the trial-court determination was one of two or more permissible inferences, the appellate court must affirm the determination even if other inferences seem to the appellate court more attractive. From a strategic standpoint, the clearly erroneous review standard makes significant the law-fact distinction. Law decisions are reversed far more often under a de novo review standard than fact determinations under a clearly erroneous review standard. As a practitioner reviewing a trial record for error to support an appeal, one would ordinarily far prefer to find a questionable interpretation of law than a questionable fact determination.

2. Harmless Error

As indicated above, the appellate courts also evaluate appeals under a harmless-error review standard. As also indicated above, the harmless-error standard has to do with who gets to appeal or, depending on how you look at it, with the scope of review. The appellate courts review only errors having a likelihood of having affected the trial-court outcome. In some cases, trial courts make many pretrial decisions or even many decisions at trial, only a few of which are genuinely likely to affect the outcome. The decisions may even have been material to the outcome at the time but made moot by later decisions of the court or parties. For efficiency's sake, the appellate court does not want to decide matters that have no need of being decided. It will certainly not remand a case for a trial court to have to repeat proceedings under conditions that, though correct, will not change the outcome. Just as significantly, an appellate court properly shows deference to the trial court's management of the case through preliminary orders. Trial courts have the responsibility and expertise for that management, and the greater opportunity to evaluate and decide on management techniques. There is thus more than one rationale for the harmless-error rule. Note the following statute, 28 U.S.C. 2111, requiring the federal appellate courts to recognize and abide by the harmless-error rule, and a similar state-court rule. Then consider one such case in which the appellate court held a trial court's error to be harmless.

28 U.S.C. §2111. Harmless error
On the hearing of any appeal or writ of certiorari in any case, the court shall give judgment after an examination of the record without regard to errors or defects which do not affect the substantial rights of the parties.

MICHIGAN COURT RULE 2.613. Limitations on Corrections of Error
(A) Harmless Error. An error in the admission or the exclusion of evidence, an error in a ruling or order, or an error or defect in anything done or omitted by the court or by the parties is not ground for granting a new trial, for setting aside a verdict, or for vacating, modifying, or otherwise disturbing a judgment or order, unless refusal to take this action appears to the court inconsistent with substantial justice.
(B) Correction of Error by Other Judges. A judgment or order may be set aside or vacated, and a proceeding under a judgment or order may be stayed, only by the judge who entered the judgment or order, unless that judge is absent or unable to act. If the judge who entered the judgment or order is absent or unable to act, an order vacating or setting aside the judgment or order or staying proceedings under the judgment or order may be entered by a judge otherwise empowered to rule in the matter.
(C) Review of Findings by Trial Court. Findings of fact by the trial court may not be set aside unless clearly erroneous. In the application of this principle, regard shall be given to the special opportunity of the trial court to judge the credibility of the witnesses who appeared before it.

Harnden v. Jayco, Inc.,

United States Court of Appeals for the Sixth Circuit
496 F.3d 579 (2007)

BOYCE F. MARTIN, JR., Circuit Judge.

Plaintiff Glenn Harnden appeals the district court's order granting summary judgment to defendant Jayco as to Harnden's claims based on alleged defects in a Jayco-manufactured Recreational Vehicle. For the reasons below, we **AFFIRM** the judgment of the district court. ...

On June 15, 2002, Harnden purchased a new 2001 Jayco Eagle Recreational Vehicle ("RV"). The total purchase price of the RV was $51,451.22. The chassis of the RV was manufactured by Ford Motor Company and the "home" portion of the RV was manufactured by Jayco. When Ford completed its part of the RV, it sent it to Jayco, which completed the assembly. Jayco sold the RV to Lloyd Bridges, an independent dealer, which in turn sold it to Harnden. Following his purchase of the RV, Harnden returned it several times to Ford and Jayco for repair of various defects.

... Harnden filed a complaint in Michigan state court against ... Jayco ... alleging ... violation of the Michigan Consumer Protection Act ("MCPA"), [c]; ... breach of written warranty under the Magnuson-Moss Warranty Act ("MMWA"), [c]; ... breach of implied warranty under the MMWA; ... breach of express warranty; ... [and] breach of implied warranty of merchantability... . [T]he defendants removed the case to federal court based on Harnden's federal claim under the MMWA. ...

... Jayco moved for summary judgment on all claims against it, relying in part on an expert report prepared by Randy Zonker, a Jayco employee. ... [T]he district court granted Jayco's motion for summary judgment on all remaining claims. [C] ... Harnden now appeals the district court's order granting Jayco summary judgment on Harnden's breach-of-express-warranty claim and his claims under the MMWA and MCPA. ...

A report detailing a series of tests performed by Jayco employee Randy Zonker was submitted along with Jayco's Motion for Summary Judgment ... . [C] Based on these tests, Zonker ultimately concluded that in his expert opinion the RV was in good condition. He noted just two minor leaks, neither of which was a substantial defect. Zonker reported that neither defect substantially impaired the value of the RV and that both were common in the RV industry. Further, one leak did not affect a Jayco-manufactured part and thus was not covered by the warranty. Zonker concluded that repairing a leaky compartment manufactured by Jayco would be easy, in that "[m]ost likely, the compartment just needs some more sealant at the lip, where the door closes." [C] Zonker recommended that in order to be sure the problem was fixed, he would remove some of the molding in the exterior of the compartment and then clean and seal the entire compartment. [C] He claimed that this repair, plus re-testing, would cost no more than $250. Harnden has offered no evidence rebutting Zonker's conclusions that these were the only defects, that these defects were insubstantial, and that these defects were easily repairable for little cost.

Jayco and Harnden dispute the admissibility of this report. At the summary judgment hearing ... , Harnden's attorney objected to the admission of the expert report because it was not in the form of an affidavit or sworn statement, as required under Fed. R. Civ. P. 56(e). Thus, according to Harnden, Zonker's report was inadmissible hearsay. Jayco's attorney responded that he was willing to submit the report in an admissible form, but the district court did not take him up on his offer. The district court considered Zonker's report in conducting its analysis. [C]

Even if Zonker's unsworn testimony was in the form of inadmissible evidence for purposes of Rule 56, thus rendering its consideration to be in error, such error may be considered harmless if it "does not affect the substantial rights of the parties." *See* Fed. R. Civ. P. 61; United States v. Markwood, 48 F.3d 969, 981 (6th Cir. 1995) (holding that reversal is required only where the district court's error affected a party's substantial rights and the party was prejudiced by the district court's error).

We hold that admission of this report was harmless error. Notably, sending this case back to the district court will simply result in the affidavit being re-submitted in admissible form, and the district court granting summary judgment again. We reject Harnden's contention that if Jayco were given the opportunity to re-file its motion with the report in admissible form, Harnden would have the opportunity to "present additional evidence showing that summary judgment is improper that is not currently part of the record." [C] First, this argument implies that Zonker's report was a surprise for which Harnden did not have adequate time to prepare; but, in fact, Jayco submitted this report along with its motion for summary judgment… . Harnden knew of the content of Zonker's report well in advance, and had ample time to procure his own expert report and/or evidence.[fn] Thus, Harnden appears to be arguing that had Jayco submitted this same report at the same time, but in admissible form, Harnden would have obtained an expert of his own. Given that Harnden had advance warning of Zonker's testimony, we cannot find that the district court's error affected Harnden's substantial rights, and most certainly, Harnden was not prejudiced by this error. …

… [T]he district court … properly considered Randy Zonker's report. Having had the benefit of oral argument, and having considered the record on appeal and the parties' briefs, we have conducted a *de novo* review and conclude that the district court's order granting summary judgment to Jayco was correct. The district court thoroughly and accurately set forth the undisputed facts and the governing law. Issuing an opinion conducting a complete analysis of these claims would serve no jurisprudential purpose and would be duplicative. Therefore, we affirm the grant of summary judgment on the basis of the district court's well-reasoned opinion… .

For the foregoing reasons, we **AFFIRM** the judgment of the district court.

INQUIRY

Mootness. The harmless-error rule is not merely a rule of convenience to save judicial resources. It has constitutional underpinnings in Article III's actual-case-or-controversy requirement. An appeal that is merely pro forma rather than deciding a disputed controversy would run afoul of the Constitution. What, then, about appeals that presented an actual controversy when filed but that time made moot? Ordinarily, the appellate courts do not decide moot appeals. If something happens after a party appeals to render the appeal moot, then the appellate court will ordinarily dismiss rather than decide the appeal. There are exceptions. For an example, in Sosna v. Iowa, 419 U.S. 393 (1975), the appellant challenged the state's one-year residency requirement for divorce. The appellant satisfied the one-year residency requirement while the appeal was pending, which is hardly surprising given the time it takes (routinely more than a year) to lose in the trial court and have an appellate court decide that loss. The Supreme Court held that it could still review the matter because others would in the future find themselves in a similar situation. Where there is no prospect for an appeal because of mootness, but litigants are likely to face and raise the issue again, then an appellate court may decide the moot appeal for its precedential value. Should an appellate court get to decide an appeal that the parties moot by settling? The Supreme Court held in U.S. Bancorp Mortgage Co. v. Bonner Mall, 513 U.S. 18, (1994), that the parties retain no right to appeal after settling the controversy. On the other hand, there is some authority for an appellate court setting aside a trial court's decision as part of a settlement. *See* Neary v. University of California, 834 P.2d 119 (Ca. 1992).

Partial Relief. That the appellant received some relief in the trial court will not bar an appeal of the trial court's denial of additional relief. A party's obtaining some relief, and perhaps even substantial relief, does not make harmless its inability to obtain full relief due to trial-court error. In some cases, justice limited is justice denied. For example, in Forney v. Apfel, 524 U.S. 266 (1998), the federal district court remanded for redetermination a Social Security claimant's unsuccessful administrative claim. In other words, the claimant won in the district court at least to the extent of a second chance with the Social Security Administration. The Supreme Court nonetheless held that the claimant could appeal the district court's decision to remand because the district court had denied her request for an order for benefits. Half a loaf is less than full. One may appeal for the full loaf when given half. In a somewhat different situation, the Supreme Court held that a class member may appeal the federal district court's approval of a class-action settlement that the class representatives accepted. Devlin v. Scardelletti, 536 U.S. 1 (2002). Partial relief for some class members does not bar another class member from objecting and appealing.

Practice

The lawyer opened the telltale envelope from the appellate court immediately. The lawyer had long ago learned not to procrastinate over receiving and communicating results, good or bad, to clients. Anyway, things tended to move pretty quickly when an appeal result came in. There were nearly always some economic consequences with which to deal, and the sooner the better. Sometimes it was ordering a check from the insurance company. Other times it was preparing a bill of costs. Other times it was calculating judgment interest, drafting a satisfaction of judgment, and preparing a settlement statement. There might instead be a petition for a higher court to review the appellate decision. But even so, with the envelope in the lawyer's hands, the period for that action was also now running. So the lawyer slid the telltale light-pink paper of an appellate opinion out of the envelope, quickly read the first paragraph and, when it did not reveal the result, flipped to the last page, briefly noting the several-page length of the opinion. There would be time to read the opinion later. First, though, the lawyer's damp palms, uneasy stomach, and ringing ears meant that the lawyer needed to know the result. Lawyers suffer little stress when in control. The hardest part is when they know that they are not.

Interlocutory Rulings. The harmless-error rule also applies to interlocutory rulings, particularly rulings that occur before summary judgment and trial proceedings, independent of the final disposition of the case. Unless the losing party can demonstrate that the interlocutory ruling influenced the outcome, the appellate court need not review it for error. Any error would have been harmless. As to interlocutory rulings, one can think of the harmless-error rule not so much as setting the standard for review as limiting the scope of review. The harmless-error rule has a corollary effect on parties who prevail in the final judgment after having suffered an adverse interlocutory ruling. Prevailing parties may not appeal adverse interlocutory rulings. *See* Kotteakos v. United States, 328 U.S. 750, 764-765 (1946).

Preserving Error. The harmless-error rule relates to a rule that you have already studied in Chapter XII on trial, that parties must notify the trial court on the record of error that is likely to affect a ruling, in order to preserve an appeal over that error. A party must ordinarily object to an erroneous jury instruction before the trial judge gives it, or the party will have waived appeal rights. FED. R. CIV. P. 51(d)(2). A failure to object the giving of an erroneous instruction ordinarily makes the error unreviewable. A trial lawyer must also challenge most erroneous evidentiary rulings by contemporaneous objection, to preserve appeal rights. *See* FED. R. EVID. 103(a); *see also* FED. R. CIV. P. 46 (although formal exception is unnecessary, party must object to erroneous rulings, stating the grounds for the objection). An evidentiary objection or request for jury instruction at trial is ordinarily necessary even if the party moved for equivalent relief before trial and the trial court denied it. *See* Mims v. Central Mfrs. Mut. Ins. Co., 178 F.2d 56, 59 (5th Cir. 1949).

Plain Error. Notice the qualification in the preceding paragraph that objections are *ordinarily* necessary. Objections are not necessary when the trial court's decision involved *plain error*. The plain-error rule permits an appellate court to review a trial court's ruling to which the aggrieved party (the appellant) did not object. The plain-error rule is not merely a lawyer's free pass, although to the lawyer who failed to object to an appealable ruling, it could certainly feel that way. The plain-error rule finds its theoretical justification in the presumption that the trial judge should know well-established points of law without a lawyer having to call those points to the judge's attention by objection. *See* Douglas v. U.S.A.A., 79 F.3d 1415 (5th Cir. 1996); Troupe v. Chicago, Duluth & Georgian Bay Transit Co., 234 F.2d 253, 261 (2d Cir. 1956) (Frank, J., concurring). What is a plain error? Appellate courts have used several conditions to qualify plain error, including that the error (1) must affect the appellant's substantial rights (often meaning affect the case outcome), (2) involve a well-established and substantial (perhaps constitutional) point of law, and (3) affect the public's view of the integrity of the proceeding. *See* United States v. Marcus, __ U.S. __ (2010 WL 2025203). The latter condition highlights that it is not so much the unfairness to the appellant that justifies the plain-error rule—after all, the appellant failed to object at trial—but the larger concern about the integrity of the law and court.

Cross-Appeals. Cross-appeals involve a somewhat different application of the harmless-error rule. Not every trial results in a complete win by one side and complete loss by the other. Indeed, many decisions leave both sides with something about which to complain. When both sides suffer adverses decision in the trial court, both sides may appeal, or to put it more accurately, when one party appeals the opposing party may cross-appeal. When only one side appeals, may the other side (the appellee) argue that the trial court erred in some way adverse to the appellee? The answer is only to support affirmance. The Supreme Court stated in United States v. American Railway Express Co., 265 U.S. 425, 435 (1923), that "the appellee may not attack the decree with a view either to enlarging his own rights thereunder or of lessening the rights of his adversary... ." On the other hand, an appellee "may, without taking a cross-appeal, urge in support of a decree any matter appearing in the record, although his argument may involve an attack upon the reasoning of the lower court or an insistence upon a matter overlooked or ignored by it." If a party does not cross-appeal, then the presumption is that the outcome is favorable to it. That party must not argue errors that are harmless to the presumed-favorable outcome.

Frivolous Appeals. The thought of a party arguing harmless error on appeal should have made you think not only of the fruitlessness of that action but of the offense to the opposing party and appellate court. FED. R. APP. P. 38 authorizes sanction of frivolous appeals. The sanction can include "just damages and single or double costs to the appellee." A much more common treatment of meritless appeals is for the appellate court to simply grant summary affirmance. The federal appellate courts tend not to use Rule 38 to police filings to the same extent as the federal trial courts are willing to use FED. R. CIV. P. 11. That fact should not give any aid or comfort to the practitioner considering making frivolous arguments. Lawyers have ethical duties and reputational interests that extend well beyond what they might get away with in appellate litigation. Read Rule 38 before considering one last appeal issue.

FED. R. APP. P. 38. Frivolous Appeal—Damages and Costs.
If a court of appeals determines that an appeal is frivolous, it may, after a separately filed motion or notice from the court and reasonable opportunity to respond, award just damages and single or double costs to the appellee.

INQUIRY

Burdening Appeal. Given the increase in appellate filings, appeals courts have similar interests to trial courts in limiting appeals or resolving them before they run their full course. Legislatures whose budgets must fund the courts share that interest. To what extent may a court or legislature discourage meritorious appeal? Given that the Supreme Court has not recognized a federal constitutional right to appeal, *see* Griffin v. Illinois, 351 U.S. 12 (1956), the answer may be that there is no limit. For example, in Bankers Life & Casualty Co. v. Crenshaw, 486 U.S. 71 (1988), the Supreme Court upheld as constitutional a state statute that imposed a penalty on unsuccessful appeals, without regard to their merit, in the amount of 15 percent of the appealed money judgment. The seven-figure judgment in that case, upheld on appeal, resulted in a $243,000 penalty, despite that the appeal was not frivolous. In another case, Lindsey v. Normet, 405 U.S. 56, 77-79 (1972), the Supreme Court struck a state statute under which tenants had to post an appeal bond of double their rent accruing during the appeal period, but the Court did so on equal-protection grounds, not as a matter of due process. On the other hand, the Supreme Court in M.L.B. v. S.L.J., 519 U.S. 102 (1996), held as a matter of due process that a state may not use filing and transcript costs to withhold an appeal from an indigent litigant who has suffered loss of an important right. *Cf.* Pennzoil Co. v. Texaco, Inc., 481 U.S. 1 (1987) (refusing for jurisdictional reasons to hear challenge to multi-billion-dollar bond requirement).

Summary. Appellate practice is an important aspect of civil procedure, given the diminishing number of trials and the increased number of cases dismissed by summary proceedings. A party aggrieved by a trial-court order or judgment must timely appeal or lose the right of review. Timely filing of notice of appeal with the district-court clerk is jurisdictional. Final judgments trigger appeal periods such as the 30-day period FED. R. CIV. P. 4(a) provides in most cases in the federal courts. A final judgment is one that disposes of all claims and defenses in the trial court, so that there is nothing remaining for the trial court to do beyond enforcing the judgment. Parties may have some opportunity to appeal some interlocutory (non-final) orders in certain cases, such as those involving injunctions or receivers, or where the trial court certifies and the appellate court accepts that interlocutory appeal will advance the litigation's termination. Once a party perfects an appeal, the appellate court must apply a review standard appropriate to the nature of the decision the appellate court reviews. Under the Seventh Amendment, the federal appellate courts do not review fact determinations by juries, although they do review denials of new trial motions by the trial courts. For trial judge decisions, the appellate courts use a bifurcated review standard, reviewing decisions of law de novo but reviewing fact determinations under a clearly erroneous standard. Appellate courts review other decisions having to do with the trial courts' management of trials under for an abuse of discretion.

Career

Have you met with your law school's career advisor? There are many kinds of civil litigation and many routes into civil-litigation practice. Career advisors are trained in professional development. They have many career-exploration resources and broad experience directing students through a process and into opportunities that help students discern career goals. Starting early with your career advisor can better prepare you to make the inevitable big decisions that will come later. See your career advisor about opportunities to explore civil litigation while you are still in law school.

CHAPTER XV

EFFECT OF JUDGMENT

OBJECTIVE: That you be able to determine when prior adjudication precludes relitigation of claims and issues.

Case Study: You are meeting with in-house counsel for a corporate client. In-house counsel just accepted service of a summons and complaint in a federal district court action naming the corporate client as defendant. In-house counsel explains to you that this action is the third legal proceeding brought against the corporate client or its subsidiary by the same plaintiff. The first action was an administrative proceeding and the second a state-court case. In-house counsel wants to know if the law precludes this third action, and if so, then what procedure you can invoke to dispose most efficiently of the action. Determine the questions you need to ask, state the general advice you can give without yet knowing the answers to those questions, and outline the procedure assuming that the law precludes the third action.

Judgments have important effects beyond their direct enforcement. Judgments end matters. Authority must have an attribute of finality about it, or it is not authority. There must be an end to litigation if it is to be law-based and just—if it is to be more than a war of attrition. Law offers finality in several ways. Statutes of repose bar claims (even before some arise) within a reasonable period after risk-producing actions. Statutes of limitation bar claims within reasonable periods after claims arise. Substantive law itself, whether based on codes or case decisions, can reduce the number and scope of disputes over rights and obligations. The structure of courts including their number and appellate levels also limits litigation, as do the availability of lawyers and legal resources. Yet when substantive law, courts and their dockets, and lawyers and their means do not limit the availability of litigation, civil procedure at some point must. It does so through the doctrines of claim preclusion and issue preclusion. *See* Allen v. McCurry, 449 U.S. 90, 94 (1980) (preclusion rules "relieve parties of the cost and vexation of multiple lawsuits, conserve judicial resources, and … encourage reliance on adjudication"). Each doctrine addresses the finality of judgments, not as to whether a party may appeal but to answer the question whether and when a party may bring a subsequent related action. How many times may a party sue over the same matter? Claim and issue preclusion answer that question. In claim preclusion, former adjudication bars relitigation between the same parties of matters that they could have raised in the prior litigation. The common law precludes the same parties from litigating claims that they could have litigated in a prior proceeding that reached final judgment on the merits. In issue preclusion, former adjudication bars relitigation of an issue that the prior litigation actually decided. The common law precludes a party from relitigating an issue that the party already actually litigated to final judgment.

You should suspect by now that claim and issue preclusion raise several conceptual and boundary issues. First, though, get some nomenclature straight before reading claim- and issue-preclusion cases addressing those issues. Until fairly recently, lawyers and judges referred to claim preclusion as res judicata (literally, the thing adjudicated) and to issue preclusion as collateral estoppel, with variations in defining and applying those terms. *See, e.g.*, Allen v. McCurry, 449 U.S. 90, 94 (1980); Brown v. Felsen, 442 U.S. 127 (1979). One variation was for res judicata to refer to both claim and issue preclusion, and collateral estoppel only to issue preclusion. *See, e.g.*, Baker v. General Motors Corp., 522 U.S. 222, 233n.5 (1998); Migra v. Warren City School Dist. Bd. of Educ., 452 U.S. 394 (1981); 18 C. WRIGHT, A. MILLER, & E. COOPER, FEDERAL PRACTICE AND PROCEDURE §4402 (1981). Reaching further back, lawyers and judges knew claim preclusion by the doctrines of merger and bar. If the plaintiff pled and prevailed on a claim, the law merged all other related claims into the judgment to preclude subsequent litigation. If the plaintiff pled but lost on a claim, the law barred all related claims in subsequent litigation. The law also refers to claim preclusion, res judicata, and merger and bar as the rule against splitting claims. *See, e.g.*, Consolidated Edison Co. v. Bodman, 445 F.3d 438, 450-451 (D.C. Cir. 2006); Mathews v. New York Racing Assn., Inc., 193 F.Supp. 293 (S.D. N.Y. 1961).

The variation in terms and their change over time are due to different ways of conceiving of and administering the law, requiring continual clarification and adaptation of old terms, not to carelessness of former generations. Because the common-law writ system recognized only specific forms of action, pursuing claims based on different theories or rights in some instances required different cases before different courts. The law associated the claim with a violated obligation and vindicated right, not with the underlying facts and transaction. As code and notice pleading gradually replaced writ pleading, and the law permitted parties to plead multiple claims in a single proceeding, the law had to redefine traditional claim-preclusion doctrines. As the fundamental unit around which parties organized litigation changed from the discrete right or legal theory to the transaction or occurrence, the law under which courts precluded relitigation had to change in the same way. Redefinition will surely continue because what today is acceptably clear will tomorrow seem arcane. Be patient with your legal forebears that following generations be patient with you. Now, look more closely at claim preclusion before moving on to issue preclusion.

Practice

It ended with a whimper, not a bang. After eleven years of litigation involving two trials, three significant evidentiary hearings, and four appeals through mid-level and state supreme courts, with one state-supreme-court reversal, the partner held the state supreme court's one-line final order denying the opposing party's final motion for reconsideration. The opposing party had raised every plausible objection, filed every possible motion, and sought every available rehearing or reconsideration, at every stage of the litigation. An ordinary one- to two-year civil litigation among family members after the death of the family's matriarch instead devolved into an endless proceeding. During its course, family members married, had children, moved, change jobs, and divorced while the litigation dragged on and on, due entirely to the efforts of the one family member who was capable of financing the litigation. What that one family member did not anticipate was that the other family members would find a lawyer willing to carry their legal fees over the decade-plus of litigation, into a six-figure receivable. Now, it had ended. With deeds recorded and interests confirmed, the proceeding had finally divided the great homestead. It was over. The partner considered framing the one-line order.

A. Claim Preclusion

As stated above, the law precludes the same parties from litigating claims that they could have litigated in a prior proceeding that reached final judgment on the merits. Rush v. City of Maple Heights, 147 N.E.2d 599 (Ohio Sup. Ct.), cert. denied, 358 U.S. 814 (1958), is an example in which the plaintiff won a $100 judgment in municipal court for damage to personal property following a motorcycle accident. The plaintiff then sued again in county court for personal injuries from the same accident. Although the plaintiff won a $12,000 judgment after jury verdict in that second case, the state supreme court reversed and ordered the second case's dismissal, holding (consistent with the majority rule against splitting claims) that the plaintiff should have brought the claims together. In broad outline, the party who advocates claim preclusion must satisfy four conditions: (1) that the claim in the new action was or could have been raised in the prior adjudication; (2) that the parties in the new action are the same parties as those in the prior adjudication; and (3) that the prior matter reached final judgment on the merits. Each of these conditions raises boundary issues. For instance, on the first condition requiring the same claims, must the claims that the parties could have raised be identical, or is it enough that the claims would arise out of the same transaction or occurrence? On the second condition, must the parties be precisely the same, or does a representative party (for example, a guardian or ward) bind the represented? Then, what is a final judgment "on the merits? The subsections below address these questions. First, though, to illustrate the conditions for and boundary issues as to claim preclusion, consider another straightfoward case in which the plaintiff tried but failed to split claims arising out of a transaction or occurrence.

Mathews v. New York Racing Assn., Inc.,

United States District Court for the Southern District of New York
193 F.Supp. 293 (1961)

McMahon, District Judge.

Defendants move for summary judgment, pursuant to Rule 56(b), Federal Rules on Civil Procedure, [c], on the ground that a judgment in a prior action in this court is res judicata as to the claim alleged in the complaint.

New York Racing Association Inc. is a New York corporation which operates Jamaica Race Track. It employs defendant Thoroughbred Racing Protective Association Inc., a private detective agency, for security purposes.

Plaintiff brings this action against the Association and Thoroughbred alleging that on April 4, 1958, at Jamaica Race Track, he was "assaulted," "kidnaped," "falsely arrested," and "falsely imprisoned" by employees of Thoroughbred. He further alleges that the defendants charged him with disorderly conduct and maliciously caused him to be prosecuted and convicted in the Magistrate's Court of the City of New York on April 10, 1958. He prays for relief in the form of money damages and an injunction restraining the defendants from interfering with his attendance at race tracks, from publication of libelous statements, and from acting as peace officers.

The prior judgment on which defendants rely was entered in this court on June 30, 1960 following a trial before Judge Palmieri sitting without a jury. The complaint in that action alleged, among other matters, that plaintiff was assaulted by the defendant's private investigators at Jamaica Race Track on April 4, 1958. It also alleged that the employees of the defendants had made libelous statements concerning the plaintiff on several occasions, including plaintiff's trial for disorderly conduct on April 10, 1958. The relief prayed for in that action was also money damages and an injunction from further interference with plaintiff's attendance at race tracks within the United States. ...

The doctrine of res judicata operates as a bar to subsequent suits involving the same parties, or those in privity with them, based on a claim which has once reached a judgment on the merits. Lawlor v. National Screen Service, [] 349 U.S. 322, 326[(1955)]. There can be no doubt that the parties in this action are in privity with those in the earlier suit. A corporation acts only through its agents, and if the agents are not at fault, there is no basis for corporate liability. [C] ...

The Association owns the race track, Thoroughbred is its agent, and the individual defendants, who removed plaintiff from Jamaica Race Track on April 4, 1958 and who testified at his trial on April 10, 1958, were employees of Thoroughbred. The present corporate defendants are, therefore, so identified in interest with their agents, the individual defendants in the earlier action, that they stand or fall with them. [C]

The classic situation in which the doctrine of res judicata comes into play is where a second claim between the same parties is based on the same operative facts as the earlier one. The issues tried in the first claim and any other issues which could have been dealt with there are forever barred by the first judgment. Angel v. Bullington, [] 330 U.S. 183, 192-193[(1947)].

Thus, the question is whether the claim alleged in this complaint is the same as that in the suit concluded earlier. The term "claim" refers to a group of facts limited to a single occurrence or transaction without particular reference to the resulting legal rights. It is the facts surrounding the occurrence which operate to make up the claim, not the legal theory upon which a plaintiff relies. [C]

The facts upon which plaintiff predicates this action occurred on two days, separated by almost a week, but they are so interrelated as to constitute a single claim. The ejection from the race track on April 4, 1958 was the subject of the subsequent trial for disorderly conduct on April 10, 1958.

The facts relevant to the incident at Jamaica Race Track on April 4, 1958, along with three other separate claims based on different facts, were tried to a conclusion in the earlier suit. There, the plaintiff relied on the acts of the agents occurring on April 4, 1958 as the basis of a claim against them on the theory of assault. Now, he asserts these same acts as the basis of a claim against the agents' principals on the theory of false arrest. In the earlier action, plaintiff relied on the statements of the agents made on April 10, 1958 as the basis of a claim against them on the theory of libel. Now, he asserts those same statements as the basis of a claim against their principals on the theory of malicious prosecution. Clearly, any liability of the defendants for the acts or statements of their agents must be predicated upon the familiar principle of respondeat superior. Thus, if the agents committed no actionable wrong against the plaintiff, neither did their principals. [C]

Essentially, therefore, the same facts are the basis for liability in each suit. The testimony of the witnesses who took part in or saw the ejection of the plaintiff on April 4, 1958 is the same under any theory of liability. The evidence that agents of the defendants characterized plaintiff as undesirable is the same in each suit, whether plaintiff claims the words the agents used are actionable under a theory of libel or under a theory of malicious prosecution.

The plaintiff cannot be permitted to splinter his claim into a multiplicity of suits and try them piecemeal at his convenience. Baltimore S.S. Co. v. Phillips, [] 274 U.S. 316, 322-323[(1927)]. "The plaintiff having alleged operative facts which state a cause of action because he tells of defendant's misconduct and his own harm has had his day in court. He does not get another day after the first lawsuit is concluded by giving a different reason than he gave in the first for recovery of damages for the same invasion of his rights. The problem of his rights against the defendant based upon the alleged wrongful acts is fully before the court whether all the reasons for recovery were stated to the court or not." Williamson v. Columbia Gas & Electric Corp., [] 186 F.2d 464, 470[(3d Cir. 1950)], cert[.] denied[], 341 U.S. 921[(1951)]; [cc].

The issues relating to plaintiff's ejection from Jamaica Race Track on April 4, 1958 and his trial on April 10, 1958 were tried and determined by Judge Palmieri, who found that upon the facts and law plaintiff had shown no right to relief. He specifically found that plaintiff had physically resisted removal from the track, and that the defendants' employees had used no more force than was reasonably necessary to effect his removal. Therefore, plaintiff is estopped, both directly and collaterally, from maintaining this action. [C]

The court is cognizant of the fact that plaintiff appears pro se, but as the law provides a beginning for litigation, it must also provide an end. The doctrine of res judicata is a barrier against needless multiplication of litigation. "Litigation is the means for vindicating rights, but it may also involve unwarranted friction and waste. The doctrine ... reflects the refusal of law to tolerate needless litigation. Litigation is needless if, by fair process, a controversy has once gone through the courts to conclusion." Angel v. Bullington, supra, [] at [] 192-193[]. [C].

Plaintiff had the opportunity to consolidate this action with the earlier one, which he was told arose out of the same claim. The earlier decision in this action sustaining the sufficiency of the complaint showed him the propriety of consolidation. He failed to accept either that suggestion in this action or judicial advice that he retain an attorney in a third action growing out of the same facts. [C]

Plaintiff has had his day in court. The doctrine of res judicata must now take effect, putting an end to this litigation. Accordingly, defendants' motion is granted.

So ordered.

Practice

The associate smiled appreciatively as the partner handed over the new file. Inside, it was a sad and pained smile. The file included a summons and complaint in the tenth case that the unrepresented former philosophy student had filed in the local state trial court against his former university raising similar claims arising out of the same transaction. Each case had minor differences in its recited law that the former philosophy student seemed to have picked up from scattered reading of law texts and codes. The claims leaned heavily toward conspiracy theories—he was highly paranoid and likely schizophrenic—but also included antitrust, interference with contract, intentional infliction, and the flavor of the day. The new associate had managed to get the trial court to dismiss every one of the cases, lacking coherence (no less a factual basis) as they did. Partners in law firms assign new associates work that helps develop their skills while carrying less risk. Unrepresented litigants are the bane of new associates. The probability of losing to an unrepresented litigant may be low, but for the new associate, that fact only raises the stakes (like losing to one's baby sister in an argument or fight). Unrepresented litigants do not know or follow procedural rules, making the new associate's conduct of the litigation circuitous adventure rather than a routine. Along the way, the new associate had learned a little about the former student including that he wrote his voluminous pleadings and court papers on his job at an overnight answering service. The student would pepper his appellate briefs (yes, he appealed every dismissal) with cartoons and quotes mocking case participants, which does not endear one to appellate judges. The new associate had met the student—even more eccentric, gray of pallor, and disheveled than the usual philosophy student—a couple of times at motion hearings, though the trial court had soon taken to ruling without hearing. The student's onslaught finally petered out with case eleven, not a case too soon for the new associate.

INQUIRY

Governing Law. You may have noticed that this chapter has yet to cite and discuss any rule from the *Federal Rules of Civil Procedure.* FED. R. CIV. P. 41(b) provides specifically for when adjudication is on the merits, thus implying that it addresses claim preclusion. The Supreme Court rejected that implication in *Semtek Intl., Inc. v. Lockheed Martin Corp.* (excerpted in a following section), relying in part on the Rules Enabling Act's prohibition that the *Federal Rules* "shall not abridge, enlarge or modify any substantive right." 28 U.S.C. §2072(b). So then, what law (code, rule, common law, and state or federal) was the federal court applying in the above case? The substantive law was of course state tort law. Yet which law (state or federal) was the federal court applying when it decided that its prior judgment barred the current case? Claim-preclusion law can be either federal law or state law, depending on the forum court, the forum court in the prior case, the subject-matter jurisdiction of the prior case, and the grounds for the prior case's dismissal. The following *Migra v. Warren City School Dist. Bd. of Educ.* case illustrates how federalism and choice of law affect claim-preclusion decisions. Federal courts must generally apply the claim-preclusion rules of their forum state when determining the preclusive effect of prior state-court judgments. Shelar v. Shelar, 910 F.Supp. 1307 (N.D. Ohio 1995), is an example in which the plaintiff obtained a state-court divorce judgment and then sued her former husband a second time for intentional infliction of emotional distress within the marriage. The husband removed the case to federal court based on diversity jurisdiction, where the federal court applied the state's claim-preclusion law to hold the second case precluded. Ignoring potential inequities in any one case, that governing-law rule makes sense. If the federal courts applied different claim-preclusion law from their forum states, then forum-shopping parties might angle for a more advantageous federal forum in order to avoid the state's claim-preclusion law. Before studying the specifics of claim preclusion in the following sections, read the *Migra v. Warren City School Dist. Bd. of Educ.* case and the statute that it cites, while appreciating the case's federalism principles and choice-of-law rules.

28 U.S.C. §1738. State and Territorial statutes and judicial proceedings; full faith and credit
The Acts of the legislature of any State, Territory, or Possession of the United States, or copies thereof, shall be authenticated by affixing the seal of such State, Territory or Possession thereto. The records and judicial proceedings of any court of any such State, Territory or Possession, or copies thereof, shall be proved or admitted in other courts within the United States and its Territories and Possessions by the attestation of the clerk and seal of the court annexed, if a seal exists, together with a certificate of a judge of the court that the said attestation is in proper form. Such Acts, records and judicial proceedings or copies thereof, so authenticated, shall have the same full faith and credit in every court within the United States and its Territories and Possessions as they have by law or usage in the courts of such State, Territory or Possession from which they are taken.

Migra v. Warren City School Dist. Bd. of Educ.,

United States Supreme Court
452 U.S. 394 (1981)

Justice BLACKMUN delivered the opinion of the Court.

This case raises issues concerning the claim preclusive effect[fn] of a state-court judgment in the context of a subsequent suit, under 42 U.S.C. §§ 1983 and 1985[], in federal court. ...

Petitioner, Dr. Ethel D. Migra, was employed by the Warren [Ohio] City School District Board of Education from August 1976 to June 1979. She served as supervisor of elementary education. Her employment was on an annual basis under written contracts for successive school years.

On April 17, 1979, at a regularly scheduled meeting, the Board, with all five of its members present, unanimously adopted a resolution renewing Dr. Migra's employment as supervisor for the 1979-1980 school year. Being advised of this, she accepted the renewed appointment by letter dated April 18 delivered to a member of the Board on April 23. Early the following morning her letter was passed on to the Superintendent of Schools and to the Board's President[who convened a special meeting at which three of the four attending board members voted not to renew Dr. Migra's contract.] ...

Petitioner brought suit in the Court of Common Pleas of Trumbull County, Ohio, against the Board and its three members who had voted not to renew her employment. The complaint ... presented ... two causes of action, namely, breach of contract by the Board, and wrongful interference by the individual members with petitioner's contract of employment. The state court … ruled that under Ohio law petitioner had accepted the employment proffered for 1979-1980, that this created a binding contract between her and the Board, and that the Board's subsequent action purporting not to renew the employment relationship had no legal effect. [C] The court awarded Dr. Migra reinstatement to her position and compensatory damages. [C] Thereafter, petitioner moved the state trial court to dismiss without prejudice "the issue of the conspiracy and individual board member liability." [C] That motion was granted. [C] The Ohio Court of Appeals, Eleventh District, in an unreported opinion, affirmed the judgment of the Court of Common Pleas. Review was denied by the Supreme Court of Ohio.[fn]

In July 1980, Dr. Migra filed the present action in the United States District Court for the Northern District of Ohio against the Board, its then individual members, and the Superintendent of Schools. [C] Her complaint alleged that Dr. Migra had become the director of a commission appointed by the Board to fashion a voluntary plan for the desegregation of the District's elementary schools; that she had prepared a social studies curriculum; that the individual defendants objected to and opposed the curriculum and resisted the desegregation plan; that hostility and ill will toward petitioner developed; and that, as a consequence, the individual defendants determined not to renew petitioner's contract of employment. [C] Many of the alleged facts had been proved in the earlier state-court litigation. Dr. Migra claimed that the Board's actions were intended to punish her for the exercise of her First Amendment rights. She also claimed that the actions deprived her of property without due process and denied her equal protection. Her federal claim thus arose under the First, Fifth and Fourteenth Amendments and 42 U.S.C. §§1983 and 1985. She requested injunctive relief and compensatory and punitive damages. [C] Answers were filed in due course and shortly thereafter the defendants moved for summary judgment on the basis of res judicata and the bar of the statute of limitations. [C]

The District Court granted summary judgment for the defendants and dismissed the complaint. [C] The United States Court of Appeals for the Sixth Circuit, by a short unreported order, affirmed. [Cc][fn] …

The Constitution's Full Faith and Credit Clause[fn] is implemented by the Federal Full Faith and Credit Statute, 28 U.S.C. §1738. That statute reads in pertinent part: "Such Acts, records and judicial proceedings or copies thereof, so authenticated, shall have the same full faith and credit in every court within the United States and its Territories and Possessions as they have by law or usage in the courts of such State, Territory or Possession from which they are taken."

It is now settled that a federal court must give to a state-court judgment the same preclusive effect as would be given that judgment under the law of the State in which the judgment was rendered. In Allen v. McCurry, 449 U.S. 90[, 96] (1980), this Court said: "Indeed, though the federal courts may look to the common law or to the policies supporting res judicata and collateral estoppel in assessing the preclusive effect of decisions of other federal courts, Congress has specifically required all federal courts to give preclusive effect to state-court judgments whenever the courts of the State from which the judgments emerged would do so...." [C] This principle was restated in Kremer v. Chemical Construction Corp., 456 U.S. 461[, 466] (1982): "Section 1738 requires federal courts to give the same preclusive effect to state court judgments that those judgments would be given in the courts of the State from which the judgments emerged." [Cc] Accordingly, in the absence of federal law modifying the operation of §1738, the preclusive effect in federal court of petitioner's state-court judgment is determined by Ohio law. …

… This Court[explained in *Allen v. McCurry, supra*, that]: "[N]othing in the language of §1983 remotely expresses any congressional intent to contravene the common-law rules of preclusion or to repeal the express statutory requirements of the predecessor of 28 U.S.C. §1738. ..." 449 U.S. at 97-99. *Allen* therefore made clear that issues actually litigated in a state-court proceeding are entitled to the same preclusive effect in a subsequent federal §1983 suit as they enjoy in the courts of the State where the judgment was rendered. …

The Court in *Allen* left open the possibility, however, that the preclusive effect of a state-court judgment might be different as to a federal issue that a §1983 litigant could have raised but did not raise in the earlier state-court proceeding.[fn] [C] That is the central issue to be resolved in the present case. Petitioner did not litigate her §1983 claim in state court…

It is difficult to see how the policy concerns underlying § 1983 would justify a distinction between the issue preclusive and claim preclusive effects of state-court judgments. … Any distrust of state courts that would justify a limitation on the preclusive effect of state judgments in §1983 suits would presumably apply equally to issues that actually were decided in a state-court as well as to those that could have been. If §1983 created an exception to the general preclusive effect accorded to state-court judgments, such an exception would seem to require similar treatment of both issue preclusion and claim preclusion. Having rejected in *Allen* the view that state-court judgments have no issue preclusive effect in §1983 suits, we must reject the view that §1983 prevents the judgment in petitioner's state-court proceeding from creating a claim preclusion bar in this case.

Petitioner suggests that to give state-court judgments full issue preclusive effect but not claim preclusive effect would enable litigants to bring their state claims in state court and their federal claims in federal court, thereby taking advantage of the relative expertise of both forums. Although such a division may seem attractive from a plaintiff's perspective, it is not the system established by §1738. That statute embodies the view that it is more important to give full faith and credit to state-court judgments than to ensure separate forums for federal and state claims. This reflects a variety of concerns, including notions of comity, the need to prevent vexatious litigation, and a desire to conserve judicial resources. …

… We hold, therefore, that petitioner's state-court judgment in this litigation has the same claim preclusive effect in federal court that the judgment would have in the Ohio state courts. …

It appears to us that preclusion law in Ohio has experienced a gradual evolution, and that Ohio courts recently have applied preclusion concepts more broadly than in the past. …

In reading the opinion of the District Court in the present litigation, we are unable to determine whether that court was applying what it thought was the Ohio law of preclusion. … Our holding today makes clear that Ohio state preclusion law is to be applied to this case. Prudence also dictates that it is the District Court, in the first instance, not this Court, that should interpret Ohio preclusion law and apply it.

The judgment of the Court of Appeals, accordingly, is vacated and the case is remanded to that court so that it may instruct the District Court to conduct such further proceedings as are required by, and are consistent with, this opinion.

It is so ordered.

Justice WHITE, with whom THE CHIEF JUSTICE and Justice POWELL join, concurring[omitted].

INQUIRY

Full Faith and Credit. The above *Migra v. Warren City School Dist. Bd. of Educ.* case states that, "The Constitution's Full Faith and Credit Clause is implemented by the Federal Full Faith and Credit Statute, 28 U.S.C. §1738." To elaborate, the Constitution's full-faith-and-credit clause, found in Article IV, §4, requires the courts of each state to recognize the judgments of the courts of other states to the same extent as the home-state courts would recognize their own judgments. State courts must do so even for other states' judgments that are against the policy of the courts' home state. *See* Fauntleroy v. Lum, 210 U.S. 230 (1908). The Constitution's full-faith-and-credit clause does not expressly apply to the federal courts, meaning that under the Constitution alone, federal courts need not give full faith and credit to state-court judgments. Yet Congress provided in §1738 that federal courts must recognize state-court judgments to the same extent as state courts must under the Constitution's full-faith-and-credit clause. Congress can alter §1738's general rule, as can the Constitution. For example (outside of civil litigation), claim-preclusion law does not prevent federal courts from reviewing state-court convictions under the Constitution's writ of habeas corpus, also authorized by federal statute, 28 U.S.C. §§2241-2255.

1. Same Claim

Now consider within this constitutional context the basic claim-preclusion rules requiring (1) the same claim, (2) same parties, and (3) final judgment on the merits. Claim preclusion requires that the parties raised or could have raised the same claims in the prior adjudication. Satisfying this requirement is simple when a party pleads an identical subsequent claim. Issues arise when the prior and present claims are different in one or more respects. Those differences can include the relief that the party requests (compensatory or punitive damages, declaratory or injunctive relief, attorney's fees), the particular theories that a party alleges (fraudulent or negligent misrepresentation, breach of contract or quantum meruit), or the law under which the party sues (common law or statutory, state or federal). Given the variety of possible differences, the lack of principled bases on which to distinguish them, the multiplicity of categorial rules the law would need to distinguish them, and a party's ability to manipulate those rules, most courts have adopted and applied a transactional test associated with the Restatement (Second) of Judgments §24. The transactional test requires that the court determine whether the prior claim arose out of the same transaction or series of transactions.

Claims arise out of the same transaction if they share the same nucleus of operative facts. *See, e.g.*, Berrety v. Asarco Inc., 439 F.3d 636, 646n.8 (10th Cir. 2006); Petro-Hunt, L.L.C. v. United States, 365 F.3d 385 (5th Cir. 2004). Difficulties arise when there is a continuing course of conduct in which events are related but spread over time, causing an accumulating injury. The case of *Mathews v. New York Racing Assn., Inc.*, excerpted above, is an example in which the alleged assault, false imprisonment, and defamation spread over days. Preclusion was nonetheless an easy decision because the incidents all related to the patron's removal from the racetrack. If the conduct continues after the first suit, then surely the judgment would not preclude a second suit. Yet there is no perfect formula. Restatement (Second) of Judgments §24(b) indicates that claims share operative facts when those facts are "related in time, space, origin, or motivation," and "form a convenient trial unit," and "their treatment as a unit conforms to the parties' expectations or business understanding or usage." *See* Interoceania Corp. v. Sound Pilots, Inc., 107 F.3d 86, 90 (2d Cir. 1997) (quoting Restatement); Porn v. National Grange Mut. Ins. Co., 93 F.3d 31, 34 (1st Cir. 1996) (applying Restatement). That the transactions are between the same parties and similar or even identical is not enough if they are separate transactions giving rise to separate causes of action accruing at different times. A judgment on one or more obligations arising out of a series of maturing notes or interest coupons does not preclude a subsequent action on the remaining obligations. *See* Nesbit v. Independent District of Riverside, 144 U.S. 610, 619 (1892).

The same-claim rule applies whether a party files the subsequent case in the same or a different court. Adjudication in a court of one state can bar adjudication of the same claim in another state. Also, as the above federal cases illustrate, adjudication in a state court can bar subsequent adjudication in a federal court, and vice versa. What matters under the transactional test is whether they arose out of the same transaction. Yet although the transactional test is an excellent starting point, it is not the endpoint of the same-claim analysis. There are exceptions where adjudication of one claim will not bar subsequent adjudication of another claim arising out of the same transaction. One of those exceptions is where the party was unable to raise aspects of the same claim in the prior case, for lack of subject-matter jurisdiction or other reason. Consider one such case.

Nestor v. Pratt & Whitney,

United States Court of Appeals for the Second Circuit
466 F.3d 65 (2006)

DENNIS JACOBS, Chief Judge.

Plaintiff-Appellant ... Nestor... filed a complaint with the Connecticut Commission on Human Rights and Opportunities ("CCHRO") against her former employer ... Pratt & Whitney ... alleging that her employment had been terminated by reason of her sex. She prevailed in the CCHRO ... and collected damages of back pay and interest. She later filed this action in the United States District Court for the District of Connecticut... pursuant to Title VII of the Civil Rights Act of 1964, 42 U.S.C. § 2000e et seq... , seeking damages that were unavailable in the CCHRO proceedings: attorney's fees, compensatory damages for emotional distress, and punitive damages... .[fn]

Pratt successfully moved for summary judgment on the ground that Nestor's action is barred by Connecticut's doctrine of res *judicata* (or "claim preclusion"). We vacate the judgment and remand for further proceedings consistent with this opinion. ...

The issue presented on appeal is whether a Title VII plaintiff who prevailed on her discrimination claims before a state administrative agency and in appeals of the agency decision to state court can subsequently file suit in federal court seeking relief that was unavailable in the state proceedings. This issue has split our sister circuit courts. [Cc]

It is undisputed that the relief Nestor seeks under Title VII was unavailable in the state administrative proceedings. [C] ...

... The doctrine of res *judicata* bears on "the effect of a judgment in foreclosing litigation of a matter that never has been litigated, because of a determination that it should have been advanced in an earlier suit." Migra v. Warren City School Dist. Bd. of Education, 465 U.S. 75, 77[] (1984).[fn] It is a rule against the splitting of actions that could be brought and resolved together. See Restatement (Second) of Judgments §24 (providing "General Rule Concerning 'Splitting'").

The doctrine varies in its effect from jurisdiction to jurisdiction, depending chiefly on how courts define the claims that have or could have been litigated, and on how much weight is put on the goals of preclusion (e.g., finality and efficiency). The parties to this appeal vigorously dispute whether the issue of preclusion is governed by federal law or Connecticut law; however, since Nestor's action survives either way, we do not decide the question, which implicates difficult issues of federalism. Marrese v. American Acad. of Orthopaedic Surgeons, 470 U.S. 373, 383[] (1985); *see* Lyng v. N.W. Indian Cemetery Protective Assn., 485 U.S. 439, 445[] (1988) ("A fundamental and long-standing principle of judicial restraint requires that courts avoid reaching constitutional questions in advance of the necessity of deciding them."); [cc].

1. Federal Preclusion Law [fn]

In considering the preclusive effect of a state court judgment on a subsequent federal action, under the Full Faith and Credit Act, 28 U.S.C. §1738, we usually consult the preclusion laws of the state in which the judgment was issued. *See Migra,[supra,]* at 81[]; *see also Marrese,[supra,]* at 380[] ("Section 1738 embodies concerns of comity and federalism that allow the States to determine, subject to the requirements of the statute and the Due Process Clause, the preclusive effect of judgments in their own courts."). We consider whether the statute creating the federal cause of action (i.e., Title VII) preempted the application of state preclusion law only if the action would be barred under state law. *See Marrese, [supra,]* at 381[].

Our usual approach to preemption is, however, seemingly inapplicable here. The Supreme Court held in New York Gaslight Club, Inc. v. Carey, 447 U.S. 54[, 66-68] (1980), that a complainant who succeeds on a discrimination claim that is filed in a state administrative agency and that is upheld on appeal can sue in federal court under Title VII to recover attorney's fees that were incurred in the state proceedings but that are not awardable under state law. [C] In holding that Congress intended to authorize a suit under Title VII "solely to obtain an award of attorney's fees for legal work done in state and local proceedings" irrespective of whether such a claim for fees would be permissible under state law, the Court did not consider Title VII to have preempted the application of state law, but rather considered the federal action for damages to be a "supplement" to state remedies "when the State does not provide prompt or complete relief." *Id.* at 65-68[]. As the Court explained, allowing recovery in federal court of fees incurred in the state proceedings furthers the goals of Congress… .

Pratt argues that *Carey* has been eroded by Kremer v. Chem. Const. Corp., 456 U.S. 461[] (1982), in which the Supreme Court held that a state court judgment affirming the denial of a Title VII claim precluded the claimant from bringing a federal action to relitigate the liability determination. *Kremer* explained that, in enacting Title VII, Congress did not intend "to override the historic respect that federal courts accord state court judgments." 456 U.S. at 471-72[].[fn] However, nothing in *Kremer* (or in any subsequent Supreme Court holdings) overturns *Carey,* and we can read the two cases together as holding that a state court's decision on the merits of a discrimination claim is entitled to full faith and credit, but that Title VII permits a claimant to seek-in federal court-"supplemental" relief that was unavailable in the state court.[fn] …

Pratt contends that it is unfair to allow the plaintiff to (in effect) relitigate damages while binding the defendant to liability findings, particularly when (as here) liability was decided in an administrative forum that did not afford such basic procedures as discovery. … In Title VII cases, federal courts do not give preclusive effect to state agency decisions unless they have been reviewed in court. *See* Univ. of Tennessee v. Elliott, 478 U.S. 788[] (1986); *Kremer,* 456 U.S. at 470n. 7[]. The CCHRO's liability determination binds Pratt only because Pratt appealed and lost in state court.

2. Connecticut Preclusion Law [fn]

Even if state preclusion law controls, Nestor's action survives. In Connecticut, "under the doctrine of *res judicata,* or claim preclusion, a former judgment on a claim, if rendered on the merits, is an absolute bar to a subsequent action [between the same parties or those in privity with them] on the same claim ... [or any claim based on the same operative facts that] *might have been made."* Connecticut National Bank v. Rytman, []694 A.2d 1246, 1256-57 (Conn. 1997) (emphasis in original; … internal quotation marks omitted); [c]. …

In determining what claims were or could have been litigated in a prior action, Connecticut law applies the "transactional" test described in Section 24 of the Restatement (Second) of Judgments: "The claim [that is] extinguished includes all rights of the plaintiff to remedies against the defendant with respect to all or any part of the transaction, or series of connected transactions, out of which the action arose." [Cc] Therefore, Pratt contends, *res judicata* in Connecticut operates to extinguish all rights regarding the transaction, even if claims for additional remedies could not have been made in the prior proceeding. This argument overlooks an exception.

Section 26(1)(c) of the Restatement (Second) of Judgments provides an exception to the rule against splitting an action where "[t]he plaintiff was unable to rely on a certain theory of the case or to seek a certain remedy or form of relief in the first action because of the limitations on the subject matter jurisdiction of the courts or restrictions on their authority to entertain multiple theories or demands for multiple remedies or forms of relief in a single action, and the plaintiff desires in the second action to rely on that theory or to seek that remedy or form of relief...." This Restatement provision has been adopted as Connecticut law, [c] ... .

We see no reason why this exception is not equally applicable in the Title VII context. ... Connecticut and the federal government share an interest in having employment discrimination claims adjudicated in state agencies. Thus Connecticut set up the CCHRO as a faster and less expensive alternative to litigation in the trial courts; we doubt that Connecticut would apply res *judicata* in a way that would limit the relief available to claimants who use the CCHRO, and thereby furnish an incentive to litigate in court. ...

The judgment is vacated, and the case is remanded for further proceedings.

INQUIRY

Procedure. How did the defendant obtain the trial court's claim-preclusion ruling in the above case? Courts do have the inherent authority to raise preclusion on their own, *see* Burrell v. Armijo, 456 F.3d 1159, 1176 (10th Cir. 2006), even though the Supreme Court has stated that only special circumstances (such as a court taking notice of its own prior judgments) warrant doing so, *see* Arizona v. California, 530 U.S. 392, 412 (2000). Courts do have jurisdiction over precluded claims. *See* Scherer v. Equitable Life Assurance Socy., 347 F.3d 394, 398n.4 (2d Cir. 2003). Ordinarily, the defendant must plead preclusion, *see* FED. R. CIV. P. 8(c), unless the defendant's failure to do so results in no unfair surprise or undue prejudice to the opposing party, *see* Lafreniere Park Foundation v. Broussard, 221 F.3d 804, 908 (5th Cir. 2000). The defendant then moves to dismiss under FED. R. CIV. P. 12(b)(6) failure to state a claim or, if the motion requires looking beyond the pleadings, then under FED. R. CIV. P. 56.

2. Same Parties

Claim preclusion's next requirement, that the prior adjudication have involved the same parties as the subsequent action, is equally simple when the parties in the actions are identical. Identical parties in the prior and subsequent actions satisfies claim preclusion's same-parties requirement. Issues arise when the parties are not identical but so closely related that it seems just to bind them. Courts will judge the parties to be in effect the same when privity or similar relationship in fairness should bind them—as some courts state, when they are *substantially* the same parties. The next case, *Richards v. Jefferson County*, is an example of a state supreme court holding that the parties were substantially the same and further litigation therefore precluded under state claim-preclusion rules. What makes *Richards v. Jefferson County* especially helpful, though, are the federalism and due-process principles necessary to its resolution. Because *Richards v. Jefferson County* involved a state-court dismissal of a subsequent case based on a prior adjudication in state court, under *Migra v. Warren City School Dist. Bd. of Educ.* and federalism principles, the state courts should have been free to make their own claim-preclusion rules. However, in the *Richards v. Jefferson County* opinion below, the Supreme Court held that state courts must not preclude a claim without ensuring due process to the deprived litigant. Under *Richards v. Jefferson County*, a state court must not define its same-parties requirement so expansively as to preclude a claim based on a prior adjudication about which the precluded party had no constitutional notice. *Richards v. Jefferson* illustrates a same-parties analysis while showing how the Constitution's due-process clause affects claim-preclusion doctrine.

Richards v. Jefferson County,

United States Supreme Court
517 U.S. 793 (1996)

Justice STEVENS delivered the opinion of the Court.

In Hansberry v. Lee, 311 U.S. 32, 37[] (1940), we held that it would violate the Due Process Clause of the Fourteenth Amendment to bind litigants to a judgment rendered in an earlier litigation to which they were not parties and in which they were not adequately represented. The decision of the Supreme Court of Alabama that we review today presents us with the same basic question in a somewhat different context. ...

Jason Richards and Fannie Hill (petitioners) are privately employed in Jefferson County, Alabama. ... They ... commenced this action in the Circuit Court of Jefferson County.

Petitioners represent a class of all nonfederal employees subject to [Jefferson C]ounty's occupation tax.[fn] Petitioners alleged that the tax ... violates the Due Process and Equal Protection Clauses of the Fourteenth Amendment and similar provisions of the Alabama Constitution. ...

The county moved for summary judgment on the ground that petitioners' claims were barred by a prior adjudication of the tax in an earlier action brought by the acting director of finance for the city of Birmingham and the city itself. That earlier action had been consolidated for trial with a separate suit brought by three county taxpayers, and the Supreme Court of Alabama upheld the tax in the resulting appeal. See Bedingfield v. Jefferson County, 527 So.2d 1270 (1988). After examining the course of this prior litigation, the trial court granted the county's motion for summary judgment as to the state constitutional claims, but refused to do so as to the federal claims because they had not been decided by either the trial court or the Alabama Supreme Court in *Bedingfield.*

On appeal, the county argued that the federal claims as well as the state claims were barred by the adjudication in *Bedingfield.* The Alabama Supreme Court agreed. The majority opinion noted that in Alabama, as in most States, a prior judgment on the merits rendered by a court of competent jurisdiction precludes the relitigation of a claim if there is a "substantial identity of the parties" and if the "same cause of action" is presented in both suits. [C] Moreover, the court explained, the prior judgment is generally "'res judicata not only as to all matters litigated and decided by it, but as to all relevant issues which could have been but were not raised and litigated in the suit.'" [Cc] ...

We now conclude that the State Supreme Court's holding that petitioners are bound by the adjudication in *Bedingfield* deprived them of the due process of law guaranteed by the Fourteenth Amendment.[fn] ...

State courts are generally free to develop their own rules for protecting against the relitigation of common issues or the piecemeal resolution of disputes.

Postal Telegraph Cable Co. v. Newport, 247 U.S. 464, 475[] (1918). We have long held, however, that extreme applications of the doctrine of res judicata may be inconsistent with a federal right that is "fundamental in character." *Id.* at 476.[fn]

The limits on a state court's power to develop estoppel rules reflect the general consensus "'in Anglo-American jurisprudence that one is not bound by a judgment *in personam* in a litigation in which he is not designated as a party or to which he has not been made a party by service of process.' Hansberry v. Lee, 311 U.S. 32, 40[] (1940)... ." Martin v. Wilks, 490 U.S. 755, 761-762[] (1989). As a consequence, "[a] judgment or decree among parties to a lawsuit resolves issues as among them, but it does not conclude the rights of strangers to those proceedings." *Id.* at 762[]; [c].

Of course, these principles do not always require one to have been a party to a judgment in order to be bound by it. Most notably, there is an exception when it can be said that there is "privity" between a party to the second case and a party who is bound by an earlier judgment. ...

In addition, as we explained in *Wilks:* "We have recognized an exception to the general rule when, in certain limited circumstances, a person, although not a party, has his interests adequately represented by someone with the same interests who is a party. See *Hansberry v. Lee,* 311 U.S. 32, 41-42[] (1940) ('class' or 'representative' suits); Fed. Rule Civ. Proc. 23 (same); Montana v. United States, 440 U.S. 147, 154-155[] (1979) (control of litigation on behalf of one of the parties in the litigation). Additionally, where a special remedial scheme exists expressly foreclosing successive litigation by nonlitigants, as for example in bankruptcy or probate, legal proceedings may terminate pre-existing rights if the scheme is otherwise consistent with due process. [Cc]"

Here, the Alabama Supreme Court concluded that res judicata applied because petitioners were adequately represented in the *Bedingfield* action. [C] We now consider the propriety of that determination. ...

We begin by noting that the parties to the *Bedingfield* case failed to provide petitioners with any notice that a suit was pending which would conclusively resolve their legal rights. That failure is troubling because, as we explained in Mullane v. Central Hanover Bank & Trust Co., 339 U.S. 306[, 314] (1950), the right to be heard ensured by the guarantee of due process "has little reality or worth unless one is informed that the matter is pending and can choose for himself whether to appear or default, acquiesce or contest." [Cc] Nevertheless, respondents ask us to excuse the lack of notice on the ground that petitioners, as the Alabama Supreme Court concluded, were adequately represented in *Bedingfield.*[fn]

Our answer is informed by our decision in *Hansberry v. Lee, [supra,* at 42-43, ... in which w]e recognized the "familiar doctrine ... that members of a class not present as parties to the litigation may be bound by the judgment where they are in fact adequately represented by parties who are present, or ... the relationship between the parties present and those who are absent is such as legally to entitle the former to stand in judgment for the latter." [C] We concluded, however, that because the interests of those class members who had been a party to the prior litigation were in conflict with the absent members who were the defendants in the subsequent action, the doctrine of representation of absent parties in a class suit could not support the decree.

Even assuming that our opinion in *Hansberry* may be read to leave open the possibility that in some class suits adequate representation might cure a lack of notice, [cc], it may not be read to permit the application of res judicata here. Our opinion explained that a prior proceeding, to have binding effect on absent parties, would at least have to be "so devised and applied as to insure that those present are of the same class as those absent and that the litigation is so conducted as to insure the full and fair consideration of the common issue." 311 U.S. at 43[]; [c]. It is plain that the *Bedingfield* action, like the prior proceeding in *Hansberry* itself, does not fit such a description.

The Alabama Supreme Court concluded that the "taxpayers in the *Bedingfield* action adequately represented the interests of the taxpayers here," [c], but the three county taxpayers who were parties in *Bedingfield* did not sue on behalf of a class; their pleadings did not purport to assert any claim against or on behalf of any nonparties; and the judgment they received did not purport to bind any county taxpayers who were nonparties. That the acting director of finance for the city of Birmingham also sued in his capacity as both an individual taxpayer and a public official does not change the analysis. Even if we were to assume, as the Alabama Supreme Court did not, that by suing in his official capacity, the finance director intended to represent the pecuniary interests of all city taxpayers, and not simply the corporate interests of the city itself, he did not purport to represent the pecuniary interests of *county* taxpayers like petitioners.[fn]

As a result, there is no reason to suppose that the *Bedingfield* court took care to protect the interests of petitioners in the manner suggested in *Hansberry.* Nor is there any reason to suppose that the individual taxpayers in *Bedingfield* understood their suit to be on behalf of absent county taxpayers. Thus, to contend that the plaintiffs in *Bedingfield* somehow represented petitioners, let alone represented them in a constitutionally adequate manner, would be "to attribute to them a power that it cannot be said that they had assumed to exercise." *Hansberry, [supra,]* at 46[].

... Accordingly, due process prevents the former from being bound by the latter's judgment. ...

Because petitioners received neither notice of, nor sufficient representation in, the *Bedingfield* litigation, that adjudication, as a matter of federal due process, may not bind them and thus cannot bar them from challenging an allegedly unconstitutional deprivation of their property. Accordingly, the judgment of the Alabama Supreme Court is reversed, and the case is remanded to that court for further proceedings not inconsistent with this opinion.

It is so ordered.

INQUIRY

Due Process. Even before *Richards v. Jefferson County, supra*, the courts tended to interpret claim preclusion's same-parties requirement consistent with the contours of due process. *See, e.g.,* Benson and Ford, Inc. v. Wanda Petroleum Co., 833 F.2d 1172 (5th Cir, 1987). Although the cases tend to state that parties in privity are bound to the same extent as identical parties, *privity* in claim-preclusion parlance means something different from privity's contract-law connotation. Privity can include non-parties (1) who succeeded to the same interest held by a party in the prior adjudication, (2) who controlled the prior adjudication, or (3) whose interests a party adequately represented in the prior adjudication. *See* Freeman v. Lester Coggins Trucking, Inc., 771 F.2d 860, 864 (5th Cir. 1985). Where does one find succession of interests? Purchasers of real property or going business concerns succeed to their sellers' interests. Who controls litigation? Insurers control the litigation of insureds, presidents the litigation of corporations, and corporate parents the litigation of subsidiaries. *Id.*; *see also* Montana v. United States, 440 U.S. 147, 155 (1979) (government bound by prior adjudication where it required, reviewed, paid for, and directed appeal of it). What is adequate representation? Claim preclusion construes representation narrowly. The Restatement (Second) of Judgments §41(1) gives as examples (a) nonparty beneficiaries represented by party trustees, executors, administrators, guardians, conservators, or other fiduciaries, (b) persons represented by agencies or officials charged by law, and (c) certified class members represented by approved class representatives. Some courts recognize what they designate as *virtual* representation. *See* Southwest Airlines Co. v. Texas Intl. Airlines, 546 F.2d 84, 98-101 (5th Cir. 1977) (private entities precluded by the same public agency effort in prior adjudication); Rynsburger v. Dairymen's Fertilizer Coop., 72 Cal. Rptr. 102 (Cal. Ct. App. 1968). Consider a more recent Supreme Court case rejecting virtual representation as a grounds on which to preclude a claim but recognizing traditional equivalents.

Taylor v. Sturgell,

United States Supreme Court
553 U.S. 880 (2008)

Justice GINSBURG delivered the opinion of the Court.

"It is a principle of general application in Anglo-American jurisprudence that one is not bound by a judgment *in personam* in a litigation in which he is not designated as a party or to which he has not been made a party by service of process." Hansberry v. Lee, 311 U.S. 32, 40[] (1940). Several exceptions, recognized in this Court's decisions, temper this basic rule. In a class action, for example, a person not named as a party may be bound by a judgment on the merits of the action, if she was adequately represented by a party who actively participated in the litigation. See *id.*, at 41[]. In this case, we consider for the first time whether there is a "virtual representation" exception to the general rule against precluding nonparties. Adopted by a number of courts, including the courts below in the case now before us, the exception so styled is broader than any we have so far approved.

The virtual representation question we examine in this opinion arises in the following context. Petitioner Brent Taylor filed a lawsuit under the Freedom of Information Act seeking certain documents from the Federal Aviation Administration. Greg Herrick, Taylor's friend, had previously brought an unsuccessful suit seeking the same records. The two men have no legal relationship, and there is no evidence that Taylor controlled, financed, participated in, or even had notice of Herrick's earlier suit. Nevertheless, the D.C. Circuit held Taylor's suit precluded by the judgment against Herrick because, in that court's assessment, Herrick qualified as Taylor's "virtual representative."

We disapprove the doctrine of preclusion by "virtual representation," and hold, based on the record as it now stands, that the judgment against Herrick does not bar Taylor from maintaining this suit.

I

... The courts below held the instant FOIA suit barred by the judgment in earlier litigation seeking the same records. ...

... [T]he District Court in D.C. concluded that Taylor's suit was barred by claim preclusion; accordingly, it granted summary judgment to Fairchild and the FAA. The court acknowledged that Taylor was not a party to Herrick's suit[but ...] held that a nonparty may be bound by a judgment if she was "virtually represented" by a party. [C] ...

The D.C. Circuit affirmed. It observed, first, that other Circuits "vary widely" in their approaches to virtual representation. [C] In this regard, the D.C. Circuit contrasted the multifactor balancing test applied by the Eighth Circuit and the D.C. District Court with the Fourth Circuit's narrower approach, which "treats a party as a virtual representative only if the party is 'accountable to the nonparties who file a subsequent suit' and has 'the tacit approval of the court' to act on the nonpart[ies'] behalf." [Q]uoting Klugh v. United States, 818 F.2d 294, 300 (C.A.4 1987)[].

Rejecting both of these approaches, the D.C. Circuit announced its own five-factor test. The first two factors—"identity of interests" and "adequate representation"—are necessary but not sufficient for virtual representation. [C] In addition, at least one of three other factors must be established: "a close relationship between the present party and his putative representative," "substantial participation by the present party in the first case," or "tactical maneuvering on the part of the present party to avoid preclusion by the prior judgment." [C]

Applying this test to the record in Taylor's case, the D.C. Circuit found both of the necessary conditions for virtual representation well met. ...

We granted certiorari, [c], to resolve the disagreement among the Circuits over the permissibility and scope of preclusion based on "virtual representation."[fn]

II

The preclusive effect of a federal-court judgment is determined by federal common law. See Semtek Intl. Inc. v. Lockheed Martin Corp., 531 U.S. 497, 507-508[] (2001). ... The federal common law of preclusion is, of course, subject to due process limitations. See Richards v. Jefferson County, 517 U.S. 793, 797[] (1996). ...

Though hardly in doubt, the rule against nonparty preclusion is subject to exceptions. For present purposes, the recognized exceptions can be grouped into six categories.[fn]

First, "[a] person who agrees to be bound by the determination of issues in an action between others is bound in accordance with the terms of his agreement." 1 Restatement (Second) of Judgments §40, p. 390 (1980) (hereinafter Restatement). ...

Second, nonparty preclusion may be justified based on a variety of pre-existing "substantive legal relationship[s]" between the person to be bound and a party to the judgment. [C] See also *Richards,* 517 U.S., at 798[]. Qualifying relationships include, but are not limited to, preceding and succeeding owners of property, bailee and bailor, and assignee and assignor. [C]

Third, we have confirmed that, "in certain limited circumstances," a nonparty may be bound by a judgment because she was "adequately represented by someone with the same interests who [wa]s a party" to the suit. *Richards,* 517 U.S. at 798[]. Representative suits with preclusive effect on nonparties include properly conducted class actions, [cc], and suits brought by trustees, guardians, and other fiduciaries, [cc].

Fourth, a nonparty is bound by a judgment if she "assume[d] control" over the litigation in which that judgment was rendered. [Cc] ...

Fifth, a party bound by a judgment may not avoid its preclusive force by relitigating through a proxy. Preclusion is thus in order when a person who did not participate in a litigation later brings suit as the designated representative of a person who was a party to the prior adjudication. [Cc] And although our decisions have not addressed the issue directly, it also seems clear that preclusion is appropriate when a nonparty later brings suit as an agent for a party who is bound by a judgment. [C]

Sixth, in certain circumstances a special statutory scheme may "expressly foreclos[e] successive litigation by nonlitigants ... if the scheme is otherwise consistent with due process." *Martin,* 490 U.S. at 762n.2[]. Examples of such schemes include bankruptcy and probate proceedings, [c], and *quo warranto* actions or other suits that, "under [the governing] law, [may] be brought only on behalf of the public at large," *Richards,* 517 U.S. at 804[].

III

Reaching beyond these six established categories, some lower courts have recognized a "virtual representation" exception to the rule against nonparty preclusion. ...

Fairchild and the FAA ... ask us to abandon the attempt to delineate discrete grounds and clear rules altogether. Preclusion is in order, they contend, whenever "the relationship between a party and a non-party is 'close enough' to bring the second litigant within the judgment." [Cc] ...

We reject this argument for three reasons. First, our decisions emphasize the fundamental nature of the general rule that a litigant is not bound by a judgment to which she was not a party. [C] Accordingly, we have endeavored to delineate discrete exceptions that apply in "limited circumstances." [C] Respondents' amorphous balancing test is at odds with the constrained approach to nonparty preclusion our decisions advance. ...

Our second reason for rejecting a broad doctrine of virtual representation rests on the limitations attending nonparty preclusion based on adequate representation. A party's representation of a nonparty is "adequate" for preclusion purposes only if, at a minimum: (1) the interests of the nonparty and her representative are aligned, [c]; and (2) either the party understood herself to be acting in a representative capacity or the original court took care to protect the interests of the nonparty, [cc]. In addition, adequate representation sometimes requires (3) notice of the original suit to the persons alleged to have been represented, [c].[fn] ...

Third, a diffuse balancing approach to nonparty preclusion would likely create more headaches than it relieves. Most obviously, it could significantly complicate the task of district courts faced in the first instance with preclusion questions. An all-things-considered balancing approach might spark wide-ranging, time-consuming, and expensive discovery tracking factors potentially relevant under seven- or five-prong tests. And after the relevant facts are established, district judges would be called upon to evaluate them under a standard that provides no firm guidance. [C] Preclusion doctrine, it should be recalled, is intended to reduce the burden of litigation on courts and parties. [C] ...

IV

For the foregoing reasons, we disapprove the theory of virtual representation on which the decision below rested. The preclusive effects of a judgment in a federal-question case decided by a federal court should instead be determined according to the established grounds for nonparty preclusion described in this opinion. [C]

Although references to "virtual representation" have proliferated in the lower courts, our decision is unlikely to occasion any great shift in actual practice. Many opinions use the term "virtual representation" in reaching results at least arguably defensible on established grounds. [C] In these cases, dropping the "virtual representation" label would lead to clearer analysis with little, if any, change in outcomes. [C]

In some cases, however, lower courts have relied on virtual representation to extend nonparty preclusion beyond the latter doctrine's proper bounds. We now turn back to Taylor's action to determine whether his suit is such a case, or whether the result reached by the courts below can be justified on one of the recognized grounds for nonparty preclusion. ...

It is uncontested that four of the six grounds for nonparty preclusion have no application here: There is no indication that Taylor agreed to be bound by Herrick's litigation, that Taylor and Herrick have any legal relationship, that Taylor exercised any control over Herrick's suit, or that this suit implicates any special statutory scheme limiting relitigation. Neither the FAA nor Fairchild contends otherwise.

It is equally clear that preclusion cannot be justified on the theory that Taylor was adequately represented in Herrick's suit. Nothing in the record indicates that Herrick understood himself to be suing on Taylor's behalf, that Taylor even knew of Herrick's suit, or that the Wyoming District Court took special care to protect Taylor's interests. ...

That leaves only the fifth category: preclusion because a nonparty to an earlier litigation has brought suit as a representative or agent of a party who is bound by the prior adjudication. Taylor is not Herrick's legal representative and he has not purported to sue in a representative capacity. He concedes, however, that preclusion would be appropriate if respondents could demonstrate that he is acting as Herrick's "undisclosed agen[t]." [C]

Respondents argue here, as they did below, that Taylor's suit is a collusive attempt to relitigate Herrick's action. [Cc] The D.C. Circuit considered a similar question in addressing the "tactical maneuvering" prong of its virtual representation test. [C] The Court of Appeals did not, however, treat the issue as one of agency, and it expressly declined to reach any definitive conclusions due to "the ambiguity of the facts." [C] We therefore remand to give the courts below an opportunity to determine whether Taylor, in pursuing the instant FOIA suit, is acting as Herrick's agent. Taylor concedes that such a remand is appropriate. [C]

We have never defined the showing required to establish that a nonparty to a prior adjudication has become a litigating agent for a party to the earlier case. Because the issue has not been briefed in any detail, we do not discuss the matter elaboratively here. We note, however, that courts should be cautious about finding preclusion on this basis. A mere whiff of "tactical maneuvering" will not suffice; instead, principles of agency law are suggestive. They indicate that preclusion is appropriate only if the putative agent's conduct of the suit is subject to the control of the party who is bound by the prior adjudication. [C][fn] ...

For the reasons stated, the judgment of the United States Court of Appeals for the District of Columbia Circuit is vacated, and the case is remanded for further proceedings consistent with this opinion.

It is so ordered.

Biography

Adina Rosenbaum represented the prevailing petitioner Brent Taylor in the above Supreme Court case. Ms. Rosenbaum is a staff attorney for the Public Citizen Litigation Group in Washington, D.C., where she litigates public-interest cases involving open government, consumer safety, and First Amendment issues. Before joining Public Citizen in 2004, Ms. Rosenbaum served a judicial clerkship for the Honorable Martha Craig Daugherty of the United States Court of Appeals for the Sixth Circuit. She graduated from law school in 2003, meaning that she had a Supreme Court win in her first five years as a lawyer.

3. Final Judgment on the Merits

The last condition for claim preclusion, that the prior adjudication has been final and on the merits, actually has three aspects. The prior adjudication must have been valid, meaning for instance that there must have been personal jurisdiction, notice and opportunity for hearing, and subject-matter jurisdiction. A claim-preclusion challenge can be a good time for the opposing party to contest the prior adjudication based on those or other substantial defects. The following Supreme Court case, *Federated Department Stores, Inc. v. Moitie*, illustrates a validity inquiry. A foreign judgment can preclude relitigation so long as the process that resulted in the judgment was impartial, without fraud, with jurisdiction, and otherwise bore acceptable hallmarks of justice. *See* Black Clawson Co. v. Kroenert Corp., 245 F.3d 759, 763 (8th Cir. 2001). The prior adjudication must also have been final, meaning that there are no further proceedings available in the prior adjudication other than post-judgment enforcement (garnishment, execution, etc.). *See* Firestone Tire & Rubber Co. v. Risjord, 449 U.S. 368, 373 (1981). The law treats a judgment that is on appeal as final, understanding that whatever happens on appeal is part of the final judgment. *See* Crawford v. Chabot, 202 F.R.D. 223 (W.D. Mich. 1998), affirmed, 229 F.3d 1151 (6th Cir. 2000); Restatement (Second) of Judgments §13, comment f ("The better view is that a judgment otherwise final remains so despite the taking of an appeal unless what is called an appeal actually consists of a trial de novo."). These first two requirements of validity and finality are straightforward.

The last requirement, that the prior adjudication must have been on the merits, is less so. Consistent with state-court practices, the Supreme Court stated in Morris v. Jones, 329 U.S. 545, 550-551 (1947), that a default judgment is a final judgment on the merits for claim preclusion, even though defaults are procedural devices barring contests over liability. To hold otherwise would destroy the utility of default procedures. A judgment entered after trial is certainly on the merits. So, too, is summary judgment after briefing and review of evidentiary materials. In each of those instances, the trial court would have reached the substance of the claim and decided whether it was tenable. On the other hand, dismissals under FED. R. CIV. P. 12(b) on its various enumerated grounds, some more technical than substantive, are problematic. The following Supreme Court case, *Federated Department Stores, Inc. v. Moitie*, held that a Rule 12(b)(6) dismissal for failure to state a claim is a dismissal on the merits.

Federated Department Stores, Inc. v. Moitie,

United States Supreme Court
452 U.S. 394 (1981)

Justice REHNQUIST delivered the opinion of the Court.

The only question presented in this case is whether the Court of Appeals for the Ninth Circuit validly created an exception to the doctrine of res judicata. The court held that res judicata does not bar relitigation of an unappealed adverse judgment where, as here, other plaintiffs in similar actions against common defendants successfully appealed the judgments against them. We disagree with the view taken by the Court of Appeals for the Ninth Circuit and reverse. ...

In 1976 the United States brought an antitrust action against petitioners, owners of various department stores, alleging that they had violated §1 of the Sherman Act, 15 U.S.C. §1, by agreeing to fix the retail price of women's clothing sold in northern California. Seven parallel civil actions were subsequently filed by private plaintiffs ... including that of respondent Moitie in state court (*Moitie I*) and respondent Brown (*Brown I*) in the United States District Court... . All of the actions originally filed in the District Court were assigned to a single federal judge, and the *Moitie I* case was removed there... . The District Court dismissed all of the actions "in their entirety" on the ground that plaintiffs had not alleged an "injury" to their "business or property" within the meaning of §4 of the Clayton Act, 15 U.S.C. §15. [C]

Plaintiffs in five of the suits appealed that judgment... . The single counsel representing Moitie and Brown, however, chose not to appeal and instead refiled the two actions in state court, *Moitie II* and *Brown II*.[fn] Although the complaints purported to raise only state-law claims, they made allegations similar to those made in the prior complaints... . Petitioners removed these new actions to the District Court for the Northern District of California and moved to have them dismissed on the ground of res judicata. In a decision rendered July 8, 1977, the District Court ... concluded that because *Moitie II* and *Brown II* involved the "same parties, the same alleged offenses, and the same time periods" as *Moitie I* and *Brown I*, the doctrine of res judicata required that they be dismissed. This time, Moitie and Brown appealed.

Pending that appeal, this Court ... decided Reiter v. Sonotone Corp., 442 U.S. 330[(1979)], holding that retail purchasers can suffer an "injury" to their "business or property" as those terms are used in §4 of the Clayton Act. On June 25, 1979, the Court of Appeals for the Ninth Circuit reversed and remanded the five cases which had been decided with *Moitie I* and *Brown I*, the cases that had been appealed, for further proceedings in light of *Reiter*.

When *Moitie II* and *Brown II* finally came before the Court of Appeals for the Ninth Circuit, the court reversed the decision of the District Court dismissing the cases. [C][fn] Though the court recognized that a "strict application of the doctrine of *res judicata* would preclude our review of the instant decision," [c] it refused to apply the doctrine to the facts of this case. It observed that the other five litigants in the *Weinberg* cases had successfully appealed the decision against them. It then asserted that "non-appealing parties may benefit from a reversal when their position is closely interwoven with that of appealing parties," [c], and concluded that "[b]ecause the instant dismissal rested on a case that has been effectively overruled," the doctrine of res judicata must give way to "public policy" and "simple justice." [C] We granted certiorari, [c], to consider the validity of the Court of Appeals' novel exception to the doctrine of res judicata. ...

... A final judgment on the merits of an action precludes the parties or their privies from relitigating issues that were or could have been raised in that action. Commissioner v. Sunnen, 333 U.S. 591, 597[] (1948); Cromwell v. County of Sac, 94 U.S. 351, 352-353[] (1877). Nor are the res judicata consequences of a final, unappealed judgment on the merits altered by the fact that the judgment may have been wrong or rested on a legal principle subsequently overruled in another case. Angel v. Bullington, 330 U.S. 183, 187[] (1947); Chicot County Drainage District v. Baxter State Bank, 308 U.S. 371[] (1940); Wilson's Executor v. Deen, 121 U.S. 525, 534[] (1887). As this Court explained in Baltimore S.S. Co. v. Phillips, 274 U.S. 316, 325[] (1927), an "erroneous conclusion" reached by the court in the first suit does not deprive the defendants in the second action "of their right to rely upon the plea of *res judicata*.... A judgment merely voidable because based upon an erroneous view of the law is not open to collateral attack, but can be corrected only by a direct review and not by bringing another action upon the same cause [of action]." We have observed that "[t]he indulgence of a contrary view would result in creating elements of uncertainty and confusion and in undermining the conclusive character of judg ments, consequences which it was the very purpose of the doctrine of *res judicata* to avert." Reed v. Allen, 286 U.S. 191, 201[] (1932).

In this case, the Court of Appeals conceded that the "strict application of the doctrine of *res judicata*" required that *Brown II* be dismissed. By that, the court presumably meant that the "technical elements" of res judicata had been satisfied, namely, that the decision in *Brown I* was a final judgment on the merits and involved the same claims and the same parties as *Brown II*.[FN3. The dismissal for failure to state a claim under Federal Rule of Civil Procedure 12(b)(6) is a "judgment on the merits." See Angel v. Bullington, 330 U.S. 183, 190[] (1947); Bell v. Hood, 327 U.S. 678[] (1946).] The court, however, declined to dismiss *Brown II* because, in its view, it would be unfair to bar respondents from relitigating a claim so "closely interwoven" with that of the successfully appealing parties. We believe that such an unprecedented departure from accepted principles of res judicata is unwarranted. Indeed, the decision below is all but foreclosed by our prior case law.[fn] ...

... [T]his Court recognizes no general equitable doctrine, such as that suggested by the Court of Appeals, which countenances an exception to the finality of a party's failure to appeal merely because his rights are "closely interwoven" with those of another party. ... Respondents here seek to be the windfall beneficiaries of an appellate reversal procured by other independent parties, who have no interest in respondents' case, not a reversal in interrelated cases procured, as in *Reed*, by the same affected party. ... [I]t is apparent that respondents here made a calculated choice to forgo their appeals. [C]

The Court of Appeals also rested its opinion in part on what it viewed as "simple justice." But we do not see the grave injustice which would be done by the application of accepted principles of res judicata. "Simple justice" is achieved when a complex body of law developed over a period of years is evenhandedly applied. The doctrine of res judicata serves vital public interests beyond any individual judge's ad hoc determination of the equities in a particular case. There is simply "no principle of law or equity which sanctions the rejection by a federal court of the salutary principle of *res judicata*." Heiser v. Woodruff, 327 U.S. 726, 733[] (1946). The Court of Appeals' reliance on "public policy" is similarly misplaced. This Court has long recognized that "[p]ublic policy dictates that there be an end of litigation; that those who have contested an issue shall be bound by the result of the contest, and that matters once tried shall be considered forever settled as between the parties." Baldwin v. Traveling Men's Assn., 283 U.S. 522, 525[] (1931). We have stressed that "[the] doctrine of *res judicata* is not a mere matter of practice or procedure inherited from a more technical time than ours. It is a rule of fundamental and substantial justice, 'of public policy and of private peace,' which should be cordially regarded and enforced by the courts...." Hart Steel Co. v. Railroad Supply Co., 244 U.S. 294, 299[] (1917). ...

... *Brown I* is res judicata as to respondents' federal-law claims. Accordingly, the judgment of the Court of Appeals is reversed, and the cause is remanded for proceedings consistent with this opinion.

It is so ordered.

Justice BLACKMUN, with whom Justice MARSHALL joins, concurring in the judgment[, omitted].

Justice BRENNAN, dissenting[, omitted].

INQUIRY

Stating Claims. Given that it was a Supreme Court decision, federal courts follow the holding of *Federated Department Stores, Inc. v. Moitie* that dismissals under FED. R. CIV. P. 12(b)(6) for failure to state a claim are on the merits and preclude relitigation of those claims between the same parties. *See, e.g.,* Wagh v. Metris Direct, Inc., 363 F.3d 821, 832 (9th Cir. 2003). State courts, on the other hand, may develop their own claim-preclusion rules when the dismissal is for failure to state a claim under state rules of procedure. Some state courts do not deem dismissal for failure to state a claim to be a claim-preclusive decision on the merits. *See* In re Estate of Cochrane, 391 N.E.2d 35 (Ill. Ct. App. 1979); Keidatz v. Albany, 249 P.2d 264 (1952). The anomaly of holding preclusive a Rule 12(b)(6)-type dismissal is that sometimes the failure is in the pleading, not the underlying claim. Pleaders do not always get it right the first time. Under some states' claim-preclusion rules, dismissal of a claim because the complaint that alleged it failed to recite sufficient facts will not bar a subsequent claim based on a complaint that sets forth the missing facts. *See In re Estate of Cochrane, supra.* The claim-preclusion rule of *Federated Department Stores, Inc. v. Moitie* raises the pleader's stakes. In the next case, appreciate that states might treat differently a dismissal based not on the failure to state a claim but on a statute of limitation.

Semtek Intl. Inc. v. Lockheed Martin Corp.,

United States Supreme Court
531 U.S. 497 (2001)

Justice SCALIA delivered the opinion of the Court.

This case presents the question whether the claim-preclusive effect of a federal judgment dismissing a diversity action on statute-of-limitations grounds is determined by the law of the State in which the federal court sits.

I

Petitioner filed a complaint against respondent in California state court, alleging inducement of breach of contract and various business torts. Respondent removed the case to the United States District Court for the Central District of California on the basis of diversity of citizenship, see 28 U.S.C. §§1332, 1441[], and successfully moved to dismiss petitioner's claims as barred by California's 2-year statute of limitations. In its order of dismissal, the District Court, adopting language suggested by respondent, dismissed petitioner's claims "in [their] entirety on the merits and with prejudice." [C] Without contesting the District Court's designation of its dismissal as "on the merits," petitioner appealed to the Court of Appeals for the Ninth Circuit, which affirmed the District Court's order. [C] Petitioner also brought suit against respondent in the State Circuit Court for Baltimore City, Maryland, alleging the same causes of action, which were not time barred under Maryland's 3-year statute of limitations. Respondent sought injunctive relief against this action from the California federal court under the All Writs Act, 28 U.S.C. §1651... . Following a hearing, the Maryland state court granted respondent's motion to dismiss on the ground of res judicata. ... Petitioner ... appealed the Maryland trial court's order of dismissal to the Maryland Court of Special Appeals. The Court of Special Appeals affirmed, holding that, regardless of whether California would have accorded claim-preclusive effect to a statute-of-limitations dismissal by one of its own courts, the dismissal by the California federal court barred the complaint filed in Maryland, since the res judicata effect of federal diversity judgments is prescribed by federal law, under which the earlier dismissal was on the merits and claim preclusive. [C] ...

II

Petitioner contends that the outcome of this case is controlled by Dupasseur v. Rochereau, [88 U.S. (]21 Wall.[)] 130, 135[] (1874), which held that the res judicata effect of a federal diversity judgment "is such as would belong to judgments of the State courts rendered under similar circumstances," and may not be accorded any "higher sanctity or effect." Since, petitioner argues, the dismissal of an action on statute-of-limitations grounds by a California state court would not be claim preclusive, it follows that the similar dismissal of this diversity action by the California federal court cannot be claim preclusive. While we agree that this would be the result demanded by *Dupasseur,* the case is not dispositive because it was decided under the Conformity Act of 1872, 17 Stat. 196, which required federal courts to apply the procedural law of the forum State in nonequity cases. . . .

Respondent, for its part, contends that the outcome of this case is controlled by Federal Rule of Civil Procedure 41(b), which provides as follows: "Involuntary Dismissal: Effect Thereof. ... Unless the court in its order for dismissal otherwise specifies, a dismissal under this subdivision and any dismissal not provided for in this rule, other than a dismissal for lack of jurisdiction, for improper venue, or for failure to join a party under Rule 19, operates as an adjudication upon the merits." Since the dismissal here did not "otherwise specif[y]" (indeed, it specifically stated that it *was* "on the merits"), and did not pertain to the excepted subjects of jurisdiction, venue, or joinder, it follows, respondent contends, that the dismissal "is entitled to claim preclusive effect." [C]

Implicit in this reasoning is the unstated minor premise that all judgments denominated "on the merits" are entitled to claim-preclusive effect. That premise is not necessarily valid. The original connotation of an "on the merits" adjudication is one that actually "pass[es] directly on the substance of [a particular] claim" before the court. Restatement §19, Comment *a,* at 161. That connotation remains common to every jurisdiction of which we are aware. See *ibid.* ("The prototyp[ical] [judgment on the merits is] one in which the merits of [a party's] claim are in fact adjudicated [for or] against the [party] after trial of the substantive issues"). And it is, we think, the meaning intended in those many statements to the effect that a judgment "on the merits" triggers the doctrine of res judicata or claim preclusion. See, e.g., Parklane Hosiery Co. v. Shore, 439 U.S. 322, 326n.5[] (1979) ("Under the doctrine of res judicata, a judgment on the merits in a prior suit bars a second suit involving the same parties or their privies based on the same cause of action"); [c].

But over the years the meaning of the term "judgment on the merits" "has gradually undergone change," R. Marcus, M. Redish, & E. Sherman, Civil Procedure: A Modern Approach 1140-1141 (3d ed.2000), and it has come to be applied to some judgments (such as the one involved here) that do *not* pass upon the substantive merits of a claim and hence do *not* (in many jurisdictions) entail claim-preclusive effect. [Cc] That is why the Restatement of Judgments has abandoned the use of the term—"because of its possibly misleading connotations," Restatement § 19, Comment *a,* at 161.

In short, it is no longer true that a judgment "on the merits" is necessarily a judgment entitled to claim-preclusive effect; and there are a number of reasons for believing that the phrase "adjudication upon the merits" does not bear that meaning in Rule 41(b). To begin with, Rule 41(b) sets forth nothing more than a default rule for determining the import of a dismissal (a dismissal is "upon the merits," with the three stated exceptions, unless the court "otherwise specifies"). This would be a highly peculiar context in which to announce a federally prescribed rule on the complex question of claim preclusion, saying in effect, "All federal dismissals (with three specified exceptions) preclude suit elsewhere, unless the court otherwise specifies."

And even apart from the purely default character of Rule 41(b), it would be peculiar to find a rule governing the effect that must be accorded federal judgments by other courts ensconced in rules governing the internal procedures of the rendering court itself. Indeed, such a rule would arguably violate the jurisdictional limitation of the Rules Enabling Act: that the Rules "shall not abridge, enlarge or modify any substantive right," 28 U.S.C. §2072(b). Cf. Ortiz v. Fibreboard Corp., 527 U.S. 815, 842[] (1999) (adopting a "limiting construction" of Federal Rule of Civil Procedure 23(b)(1)(B) in order to "minimiz[e] potential conflict with the Rules Enabling Act, and [to] avoi[d] serious constitutional concerns"). In the present case, for example, if California law left petitioner free to sue on this claim in Maryland even after the California statute of limitations had expired, the federal court's extinguishment of that right (through Rule 41(b)'s mandated claim-preclusive effect of its judgment) would seem to violate this limitation.

Moreover, as so interpreted, the Rule would in many cases violate the federalism principle of Erie R. Co. v. Tompkins, 304 U.S. 64, 78-80[] (1938), by engendering "'substantial' variations [in outcomes] between state and federal litigation" which would "[l]ikely ... influence the choice of a forum," Hanna v. Plumer, 380 U.S. 460, 467-468[] (1965). [Cc] With regard to the claim-preclusion issue involved in the present case, for example, the traditional rule is that expiration of the applicable statute of limitations merely bars the remedy and does not extinguish the substantive right, so that dismissal on that ground does not have claim-preclusive effect in other jurisdictions with longer, unexpired limitations periods. See Restatement (Second) of Conflict of Laws §§142(2), 143 (1969); Restatement of Judgments §49, Comment *a* (1942). Out-of-state defendants sued on stale claims in California and in other States adhering to this traditional rule would systematically remove state-law suits brought against them to federal court—where, unless otherwise specified, a statute-of-limitations dismissal would bar suit everywhere.[fn]

Finally, if Rule 41(b) did mean what respondent suggests, we would surely have relied upon it in our cases recognizing the claim-preclusive effect of federal judgments in federal-question cases. Yet for over half a century since the promulgation of Rule 41(b), we have not once done so. [Cc]

We think the key to a more reasonable interpretation of the meaning of "operates as an adjudication upon the merits" in Rule 41(b) is to be found in Rule 41(a), which, in discussing the effect of voluntary dismissal by the plaintiff, makes clear that an "adjudication upon the merits" is the opposite of a "dismissal without prejudice": "Unless otherwise stated in the notice of dismissal or stipulation, the dismissal is without prejudice, except that a notice of dismissal operates as an adjudication upon the merits when filed by a plaintiff who has once dismissed in any court of the United States or of any state an action based on or including the same claim." [Cc] The primary meaning of "dismissal without prejudice," we think, is dismissal without barring the plaintiff from returning later, to the same court, with the same underlying claim. That will also ordinarily (though not always) have the consequence of not barring the claim from *other* courts, but its primary meaning relates to the dismissing court itself. Thus, Black's Law Dictionary (7th ed.1999) defines "dismissed without prejudice" as "removed from the court's docket in such a way that the plaintiff may refile the same suit on the same claim," *id.*, at 482, [c], and defines "dismissal without prejudice" as "[a] dismissal that does not bar the plaintiff from refiling the lawsuit within the applicable limitations period," *ibid.*

We think, then, that the effect of the "adjudication upon the merits" default provision of Rule 41(b)—and, presumably, of the explicit order in the present case that used the language of that default provision—is simply that, unlike a dismissal "without prejudice," the dismissal in the present case barred refiling of the same claim in the United States District Court for the Central District of California. That is undoubtedly a necessary condition, but it is not a sufficient one, for claim-preclusive effect in other courts.[fn]

III

... [W]e turn to consideration of what determines the issue. ...

... [W]e have long held that States cannot give [federal-court] judgments [in federal-question cases] merely whatever effect they would give their own judgments, but must accord them the effect that this Court prescribes. See Stoll v. Gottlieb, 305 U.S. 165, 171-172[] (1938); Gunter v. Atlantic Coast Line R. Co., 200 U.S. 273, 290-291[] (1906); Deposit Bank v. Frankfort, 191 U.S. 499, 514-515[] (1903). The reasoning of that line of cases suggests, moreover, that even when States are allowed to give federal judgments (notably, judgments in diversity cases) no more than the effect accorded to state judgments, that disposition is by direction of *this* Court, which has the last word on the claim-preclusive effect of *all* federal judgments... . In short, federal common law governs the claim-preclusive effect of a dismissal by a federal court sitting in diversity. [C]

It is left to us, then, to determine the appropriate federal rule. ... [W]e think the result decreed by *Dupasseur* continues to be correct for diversity cases. Since state, rather than federal, substantive law is at issue there is no need for a uniform federal rule. And indeed, nationwide uniformity in the substance of the matter is better served by having the same claim-preclusive rule (the state rule) apply whether the dismissal has been ordered by a state or a federal court. This is, it seems to us, a classic case for adopting, as the federally prescribed rule of decision, the law that would be applied by state courts in the State in which the federal diversity court sits. [Cc] As we have alluded to above, any other rule would produce the sort of "forum-shopping ... and ... inequitable administration of the laws" that *Erie* seeks to avoid, *Hanna,* 380 U.S. at 468[], since filing in, or removing to, federal court would be encouraged by the divergent effects that the litigants would anticipate from likely grounds of dismissal. [C] ...

Because the claim-preclusive effect of the California federal court's dismissal "upon the merits" of petitioner's action on statute-of-limitations grounds is governed by a federal rule that in turn incorporates California's law of claim preclusion (the content of which we do not pass upon today), the Maryland Court of Special Appeals erred in holding that the dismissal necessarily precluded the bringing of this action in the Maryland courts. The judgment is reversed, and the case remanded for further proceedings not inconsistent with this opinion.

It is so ordered.

INQUIRY

On the Merits. The above Supreme Court case, *Semtek Intl. Inc. v. Lockheed Martin Corp.*, held that the prior judgment that stated it was "on the merits" under FED. R. CIV. P. 41(b) providing for "on the merits" dismissal in federal was *not* on the merits for claim-preclusion purposes in state court. Can you articulate why the decision makes theoretical and practical sense? As to the theory, Rule 41(b) governs actions in federal court, not state court. A party should not refile in the same or another federal court a federal-court action dismissed under uniform federal law and rules. That federal dismissal may mean that the party could still maintain the same action in state court. The *Semtek Intl. Inc. v. Lockheed Martin Corp.* decision is theoretically sound. Yet it is also practical. A trial court can, at the urging of the prevailing party, put whatever it wishes in the final judgment including that it was "on the merits." Lawyers draft judgments and orders for judges to sign and the court to enter. The particular words that they choose should not necessarily govern procedural and substantive rights that depend on other circumstances. Judgments, other than those taken by consent, are not contracts. When it comes to interpreting the effect of a judgment, the law of judgments binds parties, not necessarily the mistaken, inarticulate, or incomplete words of the judgment itself. The point of *Semtek Intl. Inc. v. Lockheed Martin Corp.* is that when it comes to claim preclusion, it is the substance that counts, not the nomenclature. If the prior adjudication reached the substance of the claim, then it should preclude relitigation. If on the other hand it was a procedural dismissal, it should not. *See* Styskal v. Weld County Bd. of Commrs., 365 F.3d 855, 858 (10th Cir. 2004) (preclusion rules look at substantive basis, not descriptive nomenclature).

Consent Judgments. What, though, about the finality and claim-preclusive effect of a consent judgment? Do consent judgments, which the lawyers negotiate and draft, and to which the parties stipulate, preclude litigation of claims not expressly resolved by the judgment but which the parties could have raised? The general rule is that consent judgments do preclude subsequent litigation of claims not expressly resolved by the judgment unless the judgment provides expressly otherwise. *See* Arizona v. California, 530 U.S. 392, 414 (2000). Consent judgments have the character of a contract, meaning that the intent of the parties to it should control. Presumably, the lawyers who advise their clients regarding the claim-preclusive effect of final judgments know the preclusive effect of consent judgments and so advise their clients to state expressly any claims they wish to reserve. On some occasions, such as to facilitate post-judgment settlement, both sides may wish to avoid a judgment's preclusive effect. A trial court may accept the parties' stipulation to do so, with (once again) the intent of the parties' controlling. An appellate court may even accept the parties' stipulation to reverse or vacate a lower-court judgment to avoid its preclusive effect, *see* Neary v. Regents of the University of California, 834 P.2d 119 (1992), although the Supreme Court has held that only extraordinary circumstances warrant doing so, *see* U.S. Bancorp Mortgage Co. v. Bonner Mall Partnership, 513 U.S. 18 (1994).

Governing Law. Notice how the Supreme Court in *Semtek Intl. Inc. v. Lockheed Martin Corp.* treated the governing-law issue the case presented. Recall from the discussion of *Migra v. Warren City School Dist. Bd. of Educ.* above, that when a federal court evaluates the preclusive effect of a state-court judgment, it must apply the claim-preclusion law of the judgment's state. *See also* Parsons Steel, Inc. v. First Alabama Bank, 474 U.S. 518 (1986) (state decision rejecting that federal decision under state law was preclusive precludes subsequent federal action). The Supreme Court faced a different situation in *Semtek Intl. Inc. v. Lockheed Martin Corp.*, involving the preclusive effect of a federal-court judgment, not (as in *Migra*) a state-court judgment. In *Semtek Intl. Inc. v. Lockheed Martin Corp.*, the Supreme Court held that for federal-court judgments in diversity cases decided under state substantive law, federal common law requires that the federal court apply the claim-preclusion rules of the forum state. That governing-law rule makes the same sense as *Migra's* rule for state-court judgments, in that it prevents parties from forum shopping between the federal and state courts. They should have the same claim-preclusion rules for cases decided under state law. Yet *Semtek Intl. Inc. v. Lockheed Martin Corp.* also stated that federal claim-preclusion law, not the forum state's claim-preclusion law, governs the preclusive effect of a federal-court judgment in federal-question cases. Again, that governing-law rule makes sense that parties trying to avoid the preclusive effect of a federal-court federal-question judgment should not get to shop for a forum state with more favorable claim-preclusion rules. *See, e.g.*, Maher v. GSI Lumonics, Inc., 433 F.3d 123, 126 (1st Cir 2005). That said, federal claim-preclusion law might be identical to state law in many instances. *Id.* (federal preclusion requires identity of claims and parties, and final judgment on the merits). When federal and state claim-preclusion law is not identical, the federal defense that federal claim-preclusion law would bar a claim does not give the defendant the right to remove from state to federal court. *See* Rivet v. Regions Bank, 522 U.S. 470 (1998). Removal under 28 U.S.C. §1441(b) depends on the law of the claim, not of the defense.

Dismissal as Sanction. Although the case did not involve it and the discussion is therefore only dicta, the opinion in *Semtek Intl. Inc. v. Lockheed Martin Corp.* stated that a federal court might still appropriately ignore state-law claim-preclusion rules if those rules were incompatible with federal-court interests. The opinion gave as an example a federal-court dismissal as a sanction for the refusal to comply with discovery orders. If that sanctions-based dismissal were of a state-law claim filed under the federal court's diversity-of-citizenship jurisdiction, then state-law claim-preclusion law should apply in the subsequent federal proceeding in which the defendant raised the sanctions dismissal as a preclusion defense. To preserve the integrity of its sanction, the federal court could treat the dismissal as preclusive, even if the forum state's claim-preclusion law would have held otherwise. State courts have similar interests in the integrity of their proceedings and judgments. In Gargallo v. Merrill, Lynch, Pierce, Fenner & Smith, 918 F.2d 658 (6th Cir. 1990), the federal court held that it would give preclusive effect to a state-court dismissal for refusal to comply with discovery orders because the state court would also have given that ruling preclusive effect. Marrese v. American Academy of Orthopaedic Surgeons, 470 U.S. 373 (1985) and 28 U.S.C. §1738 required that *Gargallo* respect the state-court judgment. The twist in *Gargallo*, though, was that the state court did not have subject-matter jurisdiction over the claim in the first place. Because the forum state's law would not have given preclusive effect to a prior adjudication by a court without subject-matter jurisdiction, *Gargallo* held the subsequent claim not precluded.

Exceptions. There can be instances where claim preclusion is inappropriate even though it meets each of the above conditions that the prior adjudication involved the same claim (or that the parties could have raised it), the same parties or their privies, and a final judgment on the merits. The Restatement (Second) of Judgments §26(1) lists five such circumstances including: (a) when the parties agree that claim preclusion should not apply; (b) where the court made it a condition of the prior adjudication that it not preclude a subsequent adjudication; (c) where the prior court was unable for lack of subject-matter jurisdiction to offer relief sought in the subsequent action; (d) a statutory or constitutional scheme warrants allowing a subsequent adjudication; or (e) there is a continuing wrong that warrants splitting claims. The same Restatement subsection would allow a trial court to forgo claim preclusion for any other "extraordinary reason, such as the apparent invalidity of a continuing restraint or condition having a vital relation to personal liberty... ." Considering some of the historically bad decisions even from so well-informed a body as the Supreme Court, the law of claim preclusion has to acknowledge that sometimes, a court just gets it wrong the first time.

B. Issue Preclusion

The doctrine of issue preclusion, formerly known as collateral estoppel, addresses a gap left by claim preclusion. Both claim preclusion and issue preclusion are affirmative doctrines on which a party may rely to bar relitigation. They each depend on a prior judgment that is both valid and final. They each apply the same rules for validity and finality. They each apply not only to parties but also to their privies, again applying the same rules for who constitutes a privy. Yet despite the comprehensive scope of claim-preclusion doctrine, something yet remains for issue preclusion to address. Issue preclusion differs from claim preclusion in several subtle respects. Claim preclusion involves a prior adjudication barring a subsequent proceeding between the same parties or their privies involving the same claim or a claim that a party could have raised. Issue preclusion involves the prior adjudication of an issue barring a party whom that prior adjudication bound from contesting that issue in a subsequent proceeding, even when the issue arises in a different claim. *See* New Hampshire v. Maine, 532 U.S. 742, 748-749 (2001). Notice the differences. An issue is narrower than a claim. A court may adjudicate the same issue in a prior case (notice, agency, duty, fraud, causation, damages, immunity, etc.) without having resolved the same claim. Foremost, issue preclusion allows a party to rely in a new case involving a new claim on a prior adjudication of an old issue. Finality and judicial efficiency justify issue preclusion. *See* Nasem v. Brown, 595 F.2d 801 (D.C. Cir. 1979).

There is a degree of uncertainty in allowing old, resolved issues to affect new claims. To eliminate that uncertainty and ensure that the courts apply the doctrine equitably, issue preclusion is a more precise doctrine than claim preclusion. With issue preclusion, the issues in the prior and subsequent cases must be the same, not (as with claim preclusion) that they simply arose out of the same transaction. Any material dissimilarity in the issues will mean that issue preclusion is not available. For a party to be able to claim issue preclusion, the issues in the prior and subsequent cases must be identical. In addition, with issue preclusion, the prior case must have actually litigated the issue, not (as with claim preclusion) simply that the parties could have litigated it. If the prior case could have but did not litigate the issue, then issue preclusion is not available as a defense in the subsequent proceeding. In addition, with issue preclusion, the issue's adjudication must have been necessary to the resolution of the prior case, not (as with claim preclusion) simply that the court might or could have decided it. If the party in the subsequent proceeding cannot demonstrate definitively that the prior case decided the issue, then that party cannot rely in the subsequent case on issue preclusion. The following sections address each of these differences in detail.

One final difference between claim preclusion and issue preclusion arose in preclusion doctrine's recent history. The same-parties requirement of claim preclusion means that there must be the same parties (or their privies) on both sides of the dispute. If the prior adjudication involved an individual suing a corporation, then for claim preclusion to apply in a subsequent proceeding, the same individual (or privies) would need to be suing the same corporation (or privies). Claim preclusion applies only when its preclusive effect is mutual. Both sides in the subsequent case must have been bound by the adjudication in the prior case. In recent years, federal law and the law of a majority of states have abandoned the mutuality requirement for issue preclusion. Issue preclusion still requires that the party whom the doctrine will bind in the second case must have been a party to the prior adjudication. As a matter of due process, judgments bind parties, not non-parties. Yet a person who or entity that was not a party to the prior adjudication may be able to use issue preclusion offensively to prevent a party who was bound in the prior adjudication from contesting the same issue in the subsequent proceeding. Alternatively, the party bound in the prior adjudication might hope to use issue preclusion defensively to prevent a non-party's claim in a subsequent proceeding. These non-mutuality issues are the subject of the final section.

1. Same Issues

The first condition for issue preclusion to apply is that the issue that the court decided in the prior adjudication must be the same issue that the party in the subsequent adjudication wishes to preclude. Courts decide issues when they grant or deny motions, determine matters of law or make findings of fact in opinions and orders, and receive jury verdicts and enter them as judgments. The inquiry involves examining what issues the parties' claims and defenses placed in dispute and what the court decided when it disposed of those claims. The subsequent case in which a party raises issue preclusion will involve new claims. If it involved the same claims, then claim preclusion would apply. Yet new claims can raise old issues. For instance, the parties may have had a disputed course of dealing involving several discrete and separable transactions. While the violation of rights in each individual transaction could give rise to new claims, prior adjudications may already have resolved material or even dispositive issues having to do with notice, agency, control, duty, title, priority, a party's competency, or any of the other myriad of issues that litigation can raise. Resolving identical issues differently from proceeding to proceeding may be unjust, revealing an uncertainty of outcomes that should not be too great a part of civil litigation. It may also be expensive, requiring parties and court to redo that which they have already done in some cases at considerable expense. One party may be more able to bear that expense and thus able to manipulate the process to achieve a result based on available litigation resources rather than the merits.

Consider an illustrative case. The following case involved the United States government's effort to quiet its title to vast tracts of California lands it had received under the Treaty of Guadalupe Hidalgo. After receiving the lands, Congress had authorized railroads to file maps under which they could claim ownership to thousands of acres of that land. In the prior adjudication, the United States and the Southern Pacific Railroad Co. established that the Atlantic & Pacific Railroad Company had failed to file a sufficiently definite map to establish its claim. When in the second case the United States maintained that the lands had thus reverted to the United States, the Southern Pacific Railroad Co. took the contrary position that the Atlantic & Pacific Railroad Company had filed a sufficiently definite map but that for other reasons the Southern Pacific Railroad Co. had acceded to the Atlantic & Pacific Railroad Company's claim. Should Southern Pacific get to have it both ways? In the opinion below, the Supreme Court found that the first case had already decided the same issue of the insufficiency of the Atlantic & Pacific Railroad Company's map, thus barring relitigation of that issue in the subsequent case. In litigation vernacular, you get only one bite at the apple.

Southern Pacific Railroad Co. v. United States,

United States Supreme Court
168 U.S. 1 (1897)

Mr. Justice HARLAN... delivered the opinion of the court.

The pleadings in the former suits show that the government based its claim to relief upon certain grounds that were distinctly controverted by the Southern Pacific Railroad Company. Those grounds were: ...

That, the Atlantic & Pacific Railroad Company having failed to meet the conditions of the grant by constructing its road in California, the lands ... were not left, upon such statutory forfeiture, to be earned by the Southern Pacific Railroad Company under the junior grant.

The Southern Pacific Railroad Company controverted the material allegations of the government's bill and amended bill, and made defense upon these among other grounds: ...

That ... the right of the Southern Pacific Railroad Company to those lands attached and became complete upon the forfeiture of the lands and rights granted to the Atlantic & Pacific Railroad Company... .

In those cases the circuit court denied the relief asked, and dismissed the bills filed by the United States. [C] But this court reversed the judgment so rendered, holding: ...

That, upon the forfeiture by congress of the rights granted to the Atlantic & Pacific Railroad Company, the lands to which its grant had attached upon the filing and acceptance of its map of definite location in 1872 did not inure to the benefit of the Southern Pacific Railroad Company; ... .

The present suit was brought by the United States against the Southern Pacific Railroad Company ... [on] a mortgage executed by that company on the

1st day of April, 1875 (the same trustees and mortgage referred to in the former cases), ... to quiet the title of the United States to the lands involved in this suit. It was pending at the time the former cases were decided in this court. ...

... [A]ll the lands now in dispute are within the limits of the grant to the Atlantic & Pacific Railroad Company... .

... [I]t was distinctly adjudged in the former cases, as between the government and the Southern Pacific Railroad Company (146 U. S. 570, 596[]), that the maps filed in 1872 sufficiently identified the lands granted to the Atlantic & Pacific Railroad Company on the contemplated line between the Colorado river and San Buenaventura on the Pacific coast...; that is, those maps were directly adjudged to be maps adequately fixing or locating the line of the road under the act of 1866. The records of those cases having been introduced in the present suit, there is no room for doubt (if those records are competent evidence) as to what was in issue and what was adjudged in the former cases. The maps which in this case are relied upon by the United States as maps of definite location, and which the Southern Pacific Railroad Company denies to be of that character, are the identical maps which the government relied on in the former cases, and the same which that company referred to and made part of its answer in the former litigation, and which were adjudged by this court, in conformity with the contention of the government, to be valid maps of definite location, the acceptance of which made it impossible for the Southern Pacific Railroad Company to acquire any interest in any lands granted to the Atlantic & Pacific Railroad Company that were forfeited to the United States by the act of 1886.

It is said, however, that, under the pleadings and evidence in this collateral proceeding, it is open to the Southern Pacific Railroad Company to renew the contest as to the sufficiency of the maps of 1872 filed by the Atlantic & Pacific Railroad Company, and to show that they were not maps of definite location.

Is this position consistent with the settled rule of law as to the conclusiveness, between parties and their privies, of the final determination by a court of competent jurisdiction of matters put in issue by the pleadings? ...

The general principle announced in numerous cases is that a right, question, or fact distinctly put in issue, and directly determined by a court of competent jurisdiction, as a ground of recovery, cannot be disputed in a subsequent suit between the same parties or their privies; and, even if the second suit is for a different cause of action, the right, question, or fact once so determined must, as between the same parties or their privies, be taken as conclusively established, so long as the judgment in the first suit remains unmodified. This general rule is demanded by the very object for which civil courts have been established, which is to secure the peace and repose of society by the settlement of matters capable of judicial determination. Its enforcement is essential to the maintenance of social order; for the aid of judicial tribunals would not be invoked for the vindication of rights of person and property if, as between parties and their privies, conclusiveness did not attend the judgments of such tribunals in respect of all matters properly put in issue, and actually determined by them. ...

In view of these adjudications, it would seem that the controlling inquiry is whether, under the pleadings in the former cases, the sufficiency of the Atlantic & Pacific maps of 1872 as maps of definite location was a matter in issue, and determined, as between the United States and the Southern Pacific Railroad Company. That that matter was in issue, and was actually decided, in the former cases, is too clear to admit of doubt. That it was material is equally clear, for, upon its determination depended the question whether the grant of public lands to the Atlantic & Pacific Railroad Company attached to any specific lands along its line to which the forfeiture act of 1886 could apply. ... [T]he Southern Pacific Railroad Company, holding the junior grant, took none of the lands appertaining to that line by reason of the definite location and construction of its line. ...

The only way in which, in the former cases, the court could have avoided a decision as to the character of those maps, was to have held that, whether they were maps of definite location or not, the rights of the Southern Pacific Railroad Company attached, upon the declaration of forfeiture, to the lands then in dispute, and that congress was without power to restore them to the public domain. So far from sustaining that view, the court expressly adjudged that, upon the acceptance of the Atlantic & Pacific maps of 1872, the rights of that company in the lands granted attached as of the date of the grant of 1866; and that it was not possible for the Southern Pacific Railroad Company, by the location of its road, whether located before or after the acceptance of the maps of 1872, to acquire any interest whatever in the lands there in dispute... .

That the record and judgment in the former cases were admissible in evidence without being specially pleaded, we entertain no doubt. And, when before the court as admissible evidence, the only inquiry was whether the sufficiency of the maps of 1872 was a matter in issue and determined between the parties to those cases. ... [T]he former judgment, if admissible in evidence at all, is conclusive of the matters put in issue and actually determined by it. ...

For the reasons stated, we are of opinion that it must be taken in this case to have been conclusively adjudicated in the former cases as between the United States and the Southern Pacific Railroad Company—

(1) That the maps filed by the Atlantic & Pacific Railroad Company in 1872 were sufficient, as maps of definite location, to identify the lands granted to that company by the act of 1866.

(2) That upon the acceptance of those maps by the land department, the rights of that company in the lands so granted attached, by relation, as of the date of the act of 1866; and

(3) That, in view of the conditions attached to the grant, and of the reservations of power in congress contained in the act of 1866, such lands became, upon the passage of the forfeiture act of 1886, the property of the United States, and by force of that act were restored to the public domain, without the Southern Pacific Railroad Company having acquired any interest therein that affected the power of the United States to forfeit and restore them to the public domain.

The result is that the decree must be affirmed in all respects as to the Southern Pacific Railroad Company, as well as to the trustees in the mortgage executed by that company, and affirmed also as to the other defendants, subject, however, to the right of the government to proceed in the circuit court to a final decree as to those defendants.

It is so ordered.

2. Actually Litigated

The second condition for issue preclusion is that the prior adjudication have actually litigated and decided the issue. *See, e.g.,* Gargallo v. Merrill, Lynch, Pierce, Fenner & Smith, 918 F.2d 658 (6th Cir 1990) (issue preclusion does not apply where court dismissed prior adjudication as discovery sanction without actually litigating issues). It is not enough (as it would be for claim preclusion) that the parties could have raised the issue in the prior litigation. For instance, consent judgments do not satisfy the actually litigated condition so as to have issue-preclusive effect. *See* Arizona v. California, 530 U.S. 392, 414 (2000). It is also not enough that the parties did raise the issue but that the court did not decide it. Some cases are easier than other for determining what the court adjudicated. For instance, when a jury verdict form has special interrogatories that required the jury to decide specific issues, the inquiry is as simple as examining the jury's answers. If after a bench trial the trial judge has made specific findings of fact or has written an opinion detailed enough to define and decide underlying issues, then again the inquiry is as simple as reading the findings or interpreting the opinion. Decisions on dispositive motions uniformly contain sufficiently detailed reasoning to discern the basis for the ruling. There are instances, such as a general verdict without explication, where the court will not have made the issues sufficiently clear. In those cases, the parties' pleadings and court papers, and trial and hearing transcripts, may make sufficiently clear the decided issues. If not, issue preclusion will fail. It is a precise doctrine. Consider the following Supreme Court case illustrating the relative ease and difficulty that courts can have discerning what issue the prior adjudication decided.

Cromwell v. County of Sac,

United States Supreme Court
94 U.S. (4 Otto) 351 (1876)

Mr. Justice FIELD delivered the opinion of the court.

This was an action on four bonds of the county of Sac, in the State of Iowa, each for $1,000, and four coupons for interest, attached to them, each for $100. The bonds were issued in 1860, and were made payable to bearer, in the city of New York, in the years 1868, 1869, 1870, and 1871, respectively, with annual interest at the rate of ten per cent a year.

To defeat this action, the defendant relied upon the estoppel of a judgment rendered in favor of the county in a prior action brought by one Samuel C. Smith upon certain earlier maturing coupons on the same bonds, accompanied with proof that the plaintiff Cromwell was at the time the owner of the coupons in that action, and that the action was prosecuted for his sole use and benefit.

In considering the operation of this judgment, it should be borne in mind… that there is a difference between the effect of a judgment as a bar or estoppel against the prosecution of a second action upon the same claim or demand, and its effect as an estoppel in another action between the same parties upon a different claim or cause of action. In the former case, the judgment, if rendered upon the merits, constitutes an absolute bar to a subsequent action. It is a finality as to the claim or demand in controversy, concluding parties and those in privity with them, not only as to every matter which was offered and received to sustain or defeat the claim or demand, but as to any other admissible matter which might have been offered for that purpose. Thus, for example, a judgment rendered upon a promissory note is conclusive as to the validity of the instrument and the amount due upon it, although it be subsequently alleged that perfect defences actually existed, of which no proof was offered, such as forgery, want of consideration, or payment. If such defences were not presented in the action, and established by competent evidence, the subsequent allegation of their existence is of no legal consequence. The judgment is as conclusive, so far as future proceedings at law are concerned, as though the defences never existed. The language, therefore, which is so often used, that a judgment estops not only as to every ground of recovery or defence actually presented in the action, but also as to every ground which might have been presented, is strictly accurate, when applied to the demand or claim in controversy. ...

But where the second action between the same parties is upon a different claim or demand, the judgment in the prior action operates as an estoppel only as to those matters in issue or points controverted, upon the determination of which the finding or verdict was rendered. In all cases, therefore, where it is sought to apply the estoppel of a judgment rendered upon one cause of action to matters arising in a suit upon a different cause of action, the inquiry must always be as to the point or question actually litigated and determined in the original action, not what might have been thus litigated and determined. Only upon such matters is the judgment conclusive in another action.

The difference in the operation of a judgment in the two classes of cases mentioned is seen through all the leading adjudications upon the doctrine of estoppel. Thus, in the case of *Outram* v. *Morewood*, 3 East, 346, the defendants were held estopped from averring title to a mine, in an action of trespass for digging out coal from it, because, in a previous action for a similar trespass, they had set up the same title, and it had been determined against them. In commenting upon a decision cited in that case, Lord Ellenborough, in his elaborate opinion, said: "It is not the recovery, but the matter alleged by the party, and upon which the recovery proceeds, which creates the estoppel. The recovery of itself in an action of trespass is only a bar to the future recovery of damages for the same injury; but the estoppel precludes parties and privies from contending to the contrary of that point or matter of fact, which, having been once distinctly put in issue by them, or by those to whom they are privy in estate or law, has been, on such issue joined, solemnly found against them." ...

These cases, usually cited in support of the doctrine that the determination of a question directly involved in one action is conclusive as to that question in a second suit between the same parties upon a different cause of action, negative the proposition that the estoppel can extend beyond the point actually litigated and determined. The argument in these cases, that a particular point was necessarily involved in the finding in the original action, proceeded upon the theory that, if not thus involved, the judgment would be inoperative as an estoppel. ...

It is not believed that there are any cases going to the extent that because in the prior action a different question from that actually determined might have arisen and been litigated, therefore such possible question is to be considered as excluded from consideration in a second action between the same parties on a different demand... . On principle, a point not in litigation in one action cannot be received as conclusively settled in any subsequent action upon a different cause, because it might have been determined in the first action

Various considerations, other than the actual merits, may govern a party in bringing forward grounds of recovery or defence in one action, which may not exist in another action upon a different demand, such as the smallness of the amount or the value of the property in controversy, the difficulty of obtaining the necessary evidence, the expense of the litigation, and his own situation at the time. A party acting upon considerations like these ought not to be precluded from contesting in a subsequent action other demands arising out of the same transaction. A judgment by default only admits for the purpose of the action the legality of the demand or claim in suit: it does not make the allegations of the declaration or complaint evidence in an action upon a different claim. …

If, now, we consider the main question presented for our determination by the light of the views thus expressed and the authorities cited, its solution will not be difficult. It appears from the findings in the original action of Smith, that the county of Sac, by a vote of its people, authorized the issue of bonds to the amount of $10,000, for the erection of a court-house; that bonds to that amount were issued by the county judge, and delivered to one Meserey, with whom he had made a contract for the erection of the court-house; that immediately upon receipt of the bonds the contractor gave one of them as a gratuity to the county judge; and that the court-house was never constructed by the contractor, or by any other person pursuant to the contract. It also appears that the plaintiff had become, before their maturity, the holder of twenty-five coupons, which had been attached to the bonds; but there was no finding that he had ever given any value for them. The court below held, upon these findings, that the bonds were void as against the county, and gave judgment accordingly. The case coming here on writ of error, this court held that the facts disclosed by the findings were sufficient evidence of fraud and illegality in the inception of the bonds to call upon the holder to show that he had given value for the coupons; and, not having done so, the judgment was affirmed. Reading the record of the lower court by the opinion and judgment of this court, it must be considered that the matters adjudged in that case were these: that the bonds were void as against the county in the hands of parties who did not acquire them before maturity and give value for them, and that the plaintiff, not having proved that he gave such value, was not entitled to recover upon the coupons. Whatever illegality or fraud there was in the issue and delivery to the contractor of the bonds affected equally the coupons for interest attached to them. The finding and judgment upon the invalidity of the bonds, as against the county, must be held to estop the plaintiff here from averring to the contrary. But as the bonds were negotiable instruments, … they would be held as valid obligations against the county in the hands of *a bona fide* holder taking them for value before maturity, according to repeated decisions of this court upon the character of such obligations. If, therefore, the plaintiff received the bond and coupons in suit before maturity for value, as he offered to prove, he should have been permitted to show that fact. There was nothing adjudged in the former action in the finding that the plaintiff had not made such proof in that case which can preclude the present plaintiff from making such proof here. The fact that a party may not have shown that he gave value for one bond or coupon is not even presumptive, much less conclusive, evidence that he may not have given value for another and different bond or coupon. The exclusion of the evidence offered by the plaintiff was erroneous, and for the ruling of the court in that respect the judgment must be reversed and a new trial had. …

Upon the second question presented, we think the court below ruled correctly. Evidence showing that the action of Smith was brought for the sole use and benefit of the present plaintiff was, in our judgment, admissible. The finding that Smith was the holder and owner of the coupons in suit went only to this extent, that he held the legal title to them, which was sufficient for the purpose of the action, and was not inconsistent with an equitable and beneficial interest in another.

Judgment reversed, and cause remanded for a new trial.

INQUIRY

Default Judgments. Should issue preclusion ever arise from a default judgment? The actually litigated requirement would suggest not. Defaults do not reach and decide issues. Defaults enter because of failure to appear or as sanctions, presuming that there may be genuine issues but prohibiting the defaulted party from addressing them and obtaining a decision. Yet any judgment, whether default or contested, presumes the resolution of certain issues. There might in the rare case be reason to recognize issue preclusion arising out of a default judgment simply to preserve the integrity of the prior adjudication. *See, e.g.*, Braxton v. Litchalk, 223 N.W.2d 316 (Mich. Ct. App. 1974). Precluding an issue based on a prior default judgment may be especially warranted when the default was due to party misconduct. *See* In re Sammy Daily, 47 F.3d 365 (9th Cir. 1995) (party deliberately preventing issue resolution by misconduct may be bound as if court resolved issue). *In re Sammy Daily* allowed issue preclusion where there was "substantial participation in an adversary contest in which the party is afforded a reasonable opportunity to defend himself on the merits but chooses not to do so" by obstructing the litigation rather than simply failing to appear. *Id.* at 368. It is an anomalous case.

Law of the Case. The actually litigated requirement suggests an even simpler form of issue preclusion. So far, you have been considering issue preclusion from a prior adjudication to a subsequent adjudication, across cases. Yet there are plenty of occasions within a single litigation in which the court may decide an issue and then have it arise again later in the same litigation. A party who lost an issue at an early stage of the litigation, perhaps by motion or after evidentiary hearing, may at a later stage of the litigation wish to raise the issue again. Even a party who *won* an issue at an early stage of the litigation may later, for strategic reasons because of changes in interests, wish to contest the issue, seeking a different result. What bars the party from doing so? Once a court decides an issue, that issue becomes the law of the case. A decided issue is the law, at least within that same case. The doctrine of the law of the case bars a party from contesting an issue in the same proceeding in which the court has already decided it. In Christianson v. Colt Indus. Operating Corp., 486 U.S. 800, 815-816 (1988), the Supreme Court described the law-of-the-case doctrine as holding that "when a court decides upon a rule of law, that decision should continue to govern the same issues in subsequent stages in the same case." We should take the Court's statement to mean that the fact issue remains decided, not just the formulation of the law that the court will apply to it. The law of the case continues on appeal and after remand unless an appellate court reverses it.

3. Necessary to Decision

A third condition to issue preclusion (to which the above *Cromwell v. County of Sac* opinion alludes briefly) is that the issue's prior adjudication must have been necessary to the outcome. *See, e.g.,* Illinois Central Gulf Railroad v. Parks, 390 N.E.2d 1078 (Ind. Ct. App. 1979) (no issue preclusion where court might have rendered prior judgment without reaching contributory-negligence issue). The necessary-to-the-decision requirement is in part to ensure that the prior adjudication did actually decide the issue. As the Supreme Court stated in Russell v. Place, 94 U.S. (4 Otto) 606, 608 (1876), "if it appear that several distinct matters may have been litigated upon one or more of which the judgment may have passed, without indicating which of them was thus litigated, and upon which the judgment was rendered," then "the whole subject-matter of the action will be at large, and open to a new contention... ." Rather, "it must appear, either upon the face of the record or be shown by extrinsic evidence, that the precise question was raised and [necessarily] determined in the former suit." *Id.*

Another common instance in which parties are unable to satisfy issue preclusion's necessary-to-the-decision requirement is when the prior adjudication decided the issue in the alternative. The thought may at first seem odd, but courts do decide issues in the alternative when they have no need to. Deciding in the alternative can save judicial resources while precluding or discouraging appeals whenever there is doubt about the soundness of one or more issues. Why not, then, take as precluded all decided issues, even when the court decided them in the alternative? Parties and courts may devote greater or lesser attention to alternative issues. A court may be sure in its decision on one issue, only incidentally reaching and deciding an alternative issue, and therefore using less of its resources and requiring less of the parties in its proof. Parties may for a variety of reasons contest vigorously some but not other alternative issues, when in subsequent litigation they would have other need to. The condition that the prior adjudication must have necessarily decided the issue ensures the integrity of the process by which the court reached and resolved the prior issue. Discern these strategies and circumstances as you read the following illustrative case.

Rios v. Davis,

Texas Court of Civil Appeals
373 S.W.2d 386 (1963)

COLLINGS, Justice.

Juan C. Rios brought this suit against Jessie Hubert Davis in the District Court to recover damages in the sum of $17,500.00, alleged to have been sustained as a result of personal injuries received on December 24, 1960, in an automobile collision. Plaintiff alleged that his injuries were proximately caused by negligence on the part of the defendant. The defendant answered alleging that Rios was guilty of contributory negligence. Also, among other defenses, the defendant urged a plea of res judicata and collateral estoppel based upon the findings and the judgment entered on December 17, 1962, in a suit between the same parties in the County Court at Law of El Paso County. The plea of res judicata was sustained and judgment was entered in favor of the defendant Jessie Hubert Davis. Juan C. Rios has appealed.

It is shown by the record that on April 11, 1961, Popular Dry Goods Company brought suit against appellee Davis in the El Paso County Court at Law, seeking to recover for damages to its truck in the sum of $443.97, alleged to have been sustained in the same collision here involved. Davis answered alleging contributory negligence on the part of Popular and joined appellant Juan C. Rios as a third party defendant and sought to recover from Rios $248.50, the alleged amount of damages to his automobile. The jury in the County Court at Law found that Popular Dry Goods Company and Rios were guilty of negligence proximately causing the collision. However, the jury also found that Davis was guilty of negligence proximately causing the collision, and judgment was entered in the County Court at Law denying Popular Dry Goods any recovery against Davis and denying Davis any recovery against Rios.

Appellant Rios in his third point contends that the District Court erred in sustaining appellee's plea of res judicata based upon the judgment of the County Court at Law because the findings on the issues regarding appellant's negligence and liability in the County Court at Law case were immaterial because the judgment entered in that case was in favor of appellant. We sustain this point. We are unable to agree with appellee's contention that the findings in the County Court at Law case that Rios was guilty of negligence in failing to keep a proper lookout and in driving on the left side of the roadway, and that such negligent acts were proximate causes of the accident were essential to the judgment entered therein. The sole basis for the judgment in the County Court at Law as between Rios and Davis was the findings concerning the negligence of Davis. The finding that Rios was negligent was not essential or material to the judgment and the judgment was not based thereon. On the contrary, the finding in the County Court at Law case that Rios was negligent proximately causing the accident would, if it had been controlling, led to a different result. Since the judgment was in favor of Rios he had no right or opportunity to complain of or to appeal from the finding that he was guilty of such negligence even if such finding had been without any support whatever in the evidence. The right of appeal is from a judgment and not from a finding. The principles controlling the fact situation here involved are, in our opinion, stated in the following quoted authorities and cases. The annotation in 133 A.L.R. 840, page 850 states: "According to the weight of authority, a finding of a particular fact is not res judicata in a subsequent action, where the finding not only was not essential to support the judgment, but was found in favor of the party against whom the judgment was rendered, and, if allowed to control, would have led to a result different from that actually reached." In the case of Word v. Colley, Tex.Civ.App., 173 S.W. 629, at page 634 of its opinion (Error Ref.), the court stated as follows: "It is the judgment, and not the verdict or the conclusions of fact, filed by a trial court which constitutes the estoppel, and a finding of fact by a jury or a court which does not become the basis or one of the grounds of the judgment rendered is not conclusive against either party to the suit." ...

For the reasons stated the court erred in entering judgment for Jessie Hubert Davis based upon his plea of res judicata and collateral estoppel. The judgment is, therefore, reversed and the cause is remanded.

INQUIRY

Exceptions. Even where a party asserting issue preclusion satisfies the doctrine's same-issue, actually litigated, and necessary-to-decision requirements, there may be cases in which the trial court should not preclude an issue's relitigation. Based on your reading of the above cases, can you articulate any? The Restatement (Second) of Judgments §28 lists several such circumstances including: (1) the party in the prior action had no opportunity to appeal; (2) the law on which the court decided the issue has changed; (3) the second action offers better procedures for deciding the issue; (4) the burden of proof in the subsequent action requires less of the party against whom issue preclusion would work; (5) the public would not be served by issue preclusion; (6) the party against whom preclusion would work could not have foreseen its likelihood; or (7) the party against whom preclusion would work had inadequate opportunity or incentive to litigate the issue in the prior action. On the other hand, should there be instances where issue preclusion applies even though one or more of the same-issue, actually litigated, and necessary-to-decision requirements are *not* met? *See, e.g.,* Kovach v. District of Columbia, 805 A.2d 957 (D.C. Ct. App. 2002) (barring relitigation of traffic violation in civil-rights action despite that the prior administrative action did not actually and necessarily litigate the issue, and there were subsequent material events).

Administrative Adjudications. The case of *Kovach v. District of Columbia* just cited involved a prior adjudication (by simple payment) of a traffic fine in an administrative proceeding. Should administrative decisions preclude parties from raising the same issues in subsequent judicial proceedings? Issue preclusion applies only when the agency conducted the prior administrative proceeding in a judicial rather than rule-making or legislative manner. *See* United States v. Utah Construction & Mining Co., 384 US. 394, 421-422 (1966); *see also* Holmberg v. State, Division of Risk Management, 796 P.2d 823 (1990) (prior worker's compensation board decision could carry issue-preclusive effect). To act in a judicial capacity is to resolve disputed fact issues affecting the rights of a private party to the proceeding. Agencies often do act in a judicial capacity, having administrative law judges who hold contested hearings on an administrative record for such purposes as granting, denying, or revoking licenses. The procedures those hearings afford are sufficiently fair, comprehensive, and consistent with due process that issue adjudications in those proceedings could readily preclude issues raised later in the civil courts. By contrast, agencies also decide issues in legislative-like, rule-making hearings that do not necessarily afford individuals due process over private interests that might later be disputed in civil court actions. Issue preclusion does not arise out of those decisions.

4. Parties and Non-Mutuality

You should have a sense by now of how flexible issue preclusion can be depending on the case circumstances. Now consider the same-parties parameter as to which, once again, there is variety in issue-preclusion rules and doctrine. Due-process constraints ensure that issue preclusion works against only those who were parties to the prior adjudication in which the court decided the issue. *See* Martin v. Wilks, 490 U.S. 755, 762 (1989) ("A judgment or decree among parties to a lawsuit resolves issues as among them, but it does not conclude the rights of strangers to those proceedings."). Issue preclusion does not bind non-parties to the prior adjudication of the issue. For issue preclusion, the same-parties requirement means that the party to be bound in the subsequent action must have been a party to the prior adjudication in which the court decided the issue. Due process requires that the one who opposes issue adjudication—the party in the subsequent action whom issue preclusion will bind if allowed—must have been a party to the prior adjudication or must have been adequately represented in the action by privies under the same rules that apply to claim preclusion.

The question remains whether non-parties to the prior adjudication may in the subsequent adjudication bind a party to the prior adjudication of the issue. In other words, must issue preclusion be mutual for it to apply at all? We know that the one who opposes issue preclusion must have been a party to the prior adjudication. Due process requires it. Yet must the one who asserts issue preclusion also have been a party to the prior adjudication? Claim preclusion requires this mutuality. For claim preclusion, both the asserting and opposing parties must have been parties to the prior adjudication. It is in the very nature of a claim that it exists between parties. Change the identity of one of those parties, and it is a new claim, not previously decided. Yet change the identity of one of those parties, and the issue may remain the same such that it would be fair to bind a party to its adjudication (even if not the non-party). Issue preclusion can more justly tolerate non-mutuality. A majority of jurisdictions including the federal courts do recognize non-mutual issue preclusion. A case meets issue preclusion's same-parties requirement when both the asserting and opposing parties are the same in the prior and subsequent adjudication. In many jurisdictions, a case also meets issue preclusion's same-parties requirement when *only* the party opposing issue preclusion, and not the party asserting it, was a party to the prior adjudication.

There are two ways in which a non-party to the prior adjudication might use issue preclusion in the subsequent proceeding. The law labels them offensive and defensive issue preclusion. Defensive issue preclusion is when in a subsequent proceeding a party to the prior adjudication claims against a non-party to the prior adjudication, and the non-party then defends with the assertion that issue preclusion binds the party to a decision on an issue in the prior action. The non-party in essence asserts, "You lost that issue to someone else before, so do not think that you can win it against me." The non-party defends using issue preclusion. Offensive issue preclusion is when in a subsequent proceeding a non-party to the prior adjudication claims against a party to the prior adjucation by asserting that issue preclusion binds the party to a decision on an issue in the prior action. The non-party in essence asserts, "You lost that issue to someone else before, so you are going to lose it again to me." The non-party goes on the offense using issue preclusion.

Notice that the difference between offensive and defensive issue preclusion is how the *non-party*, not the party, uses the doctrine. Parties to the prior adjudication cannot use issue preclusion against non-parties to the prior adjudication. Due process prevents it. The question in non-mutual applications is always whether the issue preclusion will work against the party to the prior adjudication, not whether it will work against the non-party. More courts recognize defensive issue preclusion than offensive issue preclusion, holding it fairer to bar a party from proceeding against a non-party on an issue the party previously lost than to bar a party from defending against a non-party on an issue the party previously lost. As you read the following landmark state-court case recognizing non-mutual issue preclusion followed by the Supreme Court case citing and relying on it, consider further the fairness of and policy grounds for recognizing non-mutual issue preclusion.

Bernhard v. Bank of America Nat. Trust & Sav. Assn.,

California Supreme Court
122 P.2d 892 (1942)

TRAYNOR, Justice.

In June, 1933, Mrs. Clara Sather, an elderly woman, made her home with Mr. and Mrs. Charles O. Cook in San Dimas, California. Because of her failing health, she authorized Mr. Cook and Dr. Joseph Zeiler to make drafts jointly against her commercial account in the Security First National Bank of Los Angeles. On August 24, 1933 Mrs. Cook opened a commercial account at the First National Bank of San Dimas in the name of "Clara Sather by Charles O. Cook." No authorization for this account was ever given to the bank by Mrs. Sather. Thereafter, a number of checks drawn by Cook and Zeiler on Mrs. Sather's commercial account in Los Angeles were deposited in the San Dimas account and checks were drawn upon that account signed "Clara Sather by Charles O. Cook" to meet various expenses of Mrs. Sather.

On October 26, 1933, a teller from the Los Angeles Bank called on Mrs. Sather at her request to assist in transferring her money from the Los Angeles bank to the San Dimas Bank. In the presence of this teller, the cashier of the San Dimas Bank, Mr. Cook, and her physician, Mrs. Sather signed by mark an authorization directing the Security First National Bank of Los Angeles to transfer the balance of her savings account in the amount of $4,155.68 to the First National Bank of San Dimas ... "for credit to the account of Mrs. Clara Sather." The order was credited by the San Dimas Bank to the account of "Clara Sather by Charles O. Cook." Cook withdrew the entire balance from that account and opened a new account in the same bank in the name of himself and his wife. He subsequently withdrew the funds from this last mentioned account and deposited them in a Los Angeles Bank in the names of himself and his wife.

Mrs. Sather died in November, 1933. Cook qualified as executor of the estate and proceeded with its administration. After a lapse of several years he filed an account at the instance of the probate court accompanied by his resignation. The account made no mention of the money transferred by Mrs. Sather to the San Dimas Bank; and Helen Bernhard, Beaulah Bernhard, Hester

Burton, and Iva LeDoux, beneficiaries under Mrs. Sather's will, filed objections to the account for this reason. After a hearing on the objections the court settled the account, and as part of its order declared that the decedent during her lifetime had made a gift to Charles O. Cook of the amount of the deposit in question.

After Cook's discharge, Helen Bernhard was appointed administratrix with the will annexed. She instituted this action against defendant, the Bank of America, successor to the San Dimas Bank, seeking to recover the deposit on the ground that the bank was indebted to the estate for this amount because Mrs. Sather never authorized its withdrawal. In addition to a general denial, defendant pleaded two affirmative defenses: (1) That the money on deposit was paid out to Charles O. Cook with the consent of Mrs. Sather and (2) that this fact is res judicata by virtue of the finding of the probate court... . The trial court ... gave judgment for defendant on the ground that Cook's ownership of the money was conclusively established by the finding of the probate court. Plaintiff has appealed, denying that the doctrine of res judicata is applicable to the instant case... .

Plaintiff contends that the doctrine of res judicata does not apply because the defendant who is asserting the plea was not a party to the previous action nor in privity with a party to that action and because there is no mutuality of estoppel.

The doctrine of res judicata precludes parties or their privies from relitigating a cause of action that has been finally determined by a court of competent jurisdiction. Any issue necessarily decided in such litigation is conclusively determined as to the parties or their privies if it is involved in a subsequent lawsuit on a different cause of action. [Cc] The rule is based upon the sound public policy of limiting litigation by preventing a party who has had one fair trial on an issue from again drawing it into controversy. [Cc] The doctrine also serves to protect persons from being twice vexed for the same cause. [Cc] It must, however, conform to the mandate of due process of law that no person be deprived of personal or property rights by a judgment without notice and an opportunity to be heard. [Cc]

Many courts have stated the facile formula that the plea of res judicata is available only when there is privity and mutuality of estoppel. [Cc] Under the requirement of privity, only parties to the former judgment or their privies may take advantage of or be bound by it. [Cc] ... The estoppel is mutual if the one taking advantage of the earlier adjudication would have been bound by it, had it gone against him. [Cc]

The criteria for determining who may assert a plea of res judicata differ fundamentally from the criteria for determining against whom a plea of res judicata may be asserted. The requirements of due process of law forbid the assertion of a plea of res judicata against a party unless he was bound by the earlier litigation in which the matter was decided. [Cc] He is bound by that litigation only if he has been a party thereto or in privity with a party thereto. [Cc] There is no compelling reason, however, for requiring that the party asserting the plea of res judicata must have been a party, or in privity with a party, to the earlier litigation.

No satisfactory rationalization has been advanced for the requirement of mutuality. Just why a party who was not bound by a previous action should be precluded from asserting it as res judicata against a party who was bound by it is difficult to comprehend. [C] Many courts have abandoned the requirement of mutuality and confined the requirement of privity to the party against whom the plea of res judicata is asserted. [Cc] The commentators are almost unanimously in accord. [Cc] The courts of most jurisdictions have in effect accomplished the same result by recognizing a broad exception to the requirements of mutuality and privity, namely, that they are not necessary where the liability of the defendant asserting the plea of res judicata is dependent upon or derived from the liability of one who was exonerated in an earlier suit brought by the same plaintiff upon the same facts. [Cc] Typical examples of such derivative liability are master and servant, principal and agent, and indemnitor and indemnitee. Thus, if a plaintiff sues a servant for injuries caused by the servant's alleged negligence within the scope of his employment, a judgment against the plaintiff of the grounds that the servant was not negligent can be pleaded by the master as res judicata if he is subsequently sued by the same plaintiff for the same injuries. Conversely, if the plaintiff first sues the master, a judgment against the plaintiff on the grounds that the servant was not negligent can be pleaded by the servant as res judicata if he is subsequently sued by the plaintiff. In each of these situations the party asserting the plea of res judicata was not a party to the previous action nor in privity with such a party under the accepted definition of a privy set forth above. Likewise, the estoppel is not mutual since the party asserting the plea, not having been a party or in privity with a party to the former action, would not have been bound by it had it been decided the other way. The cases justify this exception on the ground that it would be unjust to permit one who has had his day in court to reopen identical issues by merely switching adversaries.

In determining the validity of a plea of res judicata three questions are pertinent: Was the issue decided in the prior adjudication identical with the one presented in the action in question? Was there a final judgment on the merits? Was the party against whom the plea is asserted a party or in privity with a party to the prior adjudication? …

In the present case, therefore, the defendant is not precluded by lack of privity or of mutuality of estoppel from asserting the plea of res judicata against the plaintiff. Since the issue as to the ownership of the money is identical with the issue raised in the probate proceeding, and since the order of the probate court settling the executor's account was a final adjudication of this issue on the merits ([c]), it remains only to determine whether the plaintiff in the present action was a party or in privity with a party to the earlier proceeding. The plaintiff has brought the present action in the capacity of administratrix of the estate. In this capacity she represents the very same persons and interests that were represented in the earlier hearing on the executor's account. … The plea of res judicata is therefore available against plaintiff as a party to the former proceeding despite her formal change of capacity. …

The judgment is affirmed.

GIBSON, C.J., and SHENK, CURTIS, EDMONDS, HOUSER, and CARTER, J.J., concurred.

INQUIRY

Multiple Inconsistent Verdicts. As sensible as *Bernhard v. Bank of America Nat. Trust & Sav. Assn.* makes non-mutual issue preclusion seem, the doctrine can in any one case have its problems. Think, for instance, of the unfairness of the doctrine if a defendant were to win the same dispositive issue in nine actions in a row by brought by nine different plaintiffs but then lose the same issue in the tenth action by yet another plaintiff. All subsequent plaintiffs bringing the same claims could assert issue preclusion. *See* Harrison v. Celotex Corp., 583 F.Supp. 1497 (E.D. Tenn. 1984) (single anomalous decision can have preclusive effect). There must be very few instances in which this hypothetical would actually arise, but something like it has happened. *See* State Farm Fire & Cas. Co. v. Century Home Components, 550 P.2d 1185 (Or. Sup. Ct. 1976). The *State Farm Fire & Cas. Co.* case involved 48 consolidated cases in which the defendant won one of the first cases to go to trial but then lost two subsequent cases, after which the trial court held the defendant precluded from contesting subsequent cases. How should the courts resolve this anomaly? In *State Farm Fire & Cas. Co.,* the appellate court reversed, holding that trial courts must exercise discretion in such instances and at least consider declining issue preclusion to avoid unfairness. The Supreme Court opinion below mentions this possibility and, in dicta, reaches the same conclusion. As you read the following opinion, appreciate the policy favoring and disfavoring non-mutual issue preclusion.

Parklane Hosiery Co. v. Shore,

United States Supreme Court
439 U.S. U.S. 322 (1979)

Mr. Justice STEWART delivered the opinion of the Court.

This case presents the question whether a party who has had issues of fact adjudicated adversely to it in an equitable action may be collaterally estopped from relitigating the same issues before a jury in a subsequent legal action brought against it by a new party.

The respondent brought this stockholder's class action against the petitioners in a Federal District Court. The complaint alleged that the petitioners, Parklane Hosiery Co., Inc. (Parklane), and 13 of its officers, directors, and stockholders, had issued a materially false and misleading proxy statement in connection with a merger.[fn] The proxy statement, according to the complaint, had violated §§14(a), 10(b), and 20(a) of the Securities Exchange Act of 1934, [] 15 U.S.C. §§78n(a), 78j(b), and 78t(a), as well as various rules and regulations promulgated by the Securities and Exchange Commission (SEC). The complaint sought damages, rescission of the merger, and recovery of costs.

Before this action came to trial, the SEC filed suit against the same defendants in the Federal District Court, alleging that the proxy statement that had been issued by Parklane was materially false and misleading in essentially the same respects as those that had been alleged in the respondent's complaint. Injunctive relief was requested. After a 4-day trial, the District Court found that the proxy statement was materially false and misleading in the respects alleged, and entered a declaratory judgment to that effect. [C] The Court of Appeals for the Second Circuit affirmed this judgment. [C]

The respondent in the present case then moved for partial summary judgment against the petitioners, asserting that the petitioners were collaterally estopped from relitigating the issues that had been resolved against them in the action brought by the SEC.[fn] [Although the prior action found the proxy solicitation false and misleading, the respondent private plaintiff still had to prove causation and damages. *See* Mills v. Electric Auto-Lite Co., 396 U.S. 375, 386-390 (1970).] The District Court denied the motion on the ground that such an application of collateral estoppel would deny the petitioners their Seventh Amendment right to a jury trial. The Court of Appeals for the Second Circuit reversed, holding that a party who has had issues of fact determined against him after a full and fair opportunity to litigate in a nonjury trial is collaterally estopped from obtaining a subsequent jury trial of these same issues of fact. [C] The appellate court concluded that "the Seventh Amendment preserves the right to jury trial only with respect to issues of fact, [and] once those issues have been fully and fairly adjudicated in a prior proceeding, nothing remains for trial, either with or without a jury." [C] Because of an inter-circuit conflict,[fn] we granted certiorari. [C]

I

The threshold question to be considered is whether, quite apart from the right to a jury trial under the Seventh Amendment, the petitioners can be precluded from relitigating facts resolved adversely to them in a prior equitable proceeding with another party under the general law of collateral estoppel. Specifically, we must determine whether a litigant who was not a party to a prior judgment may nevertheless use that judgment "offensively" to prevent a defendant from relitigating issues resolved in the earlier proceeding.[Fn4. In this context, offensive use of collateral estoppel occurs when the plaintiff seeks to foreclose the defendant from litigating an issue the defendant has previously litigated unsuccessfully in an action with another party. Defensive use occurs when a defendant seeks to prevent a plaintiff from asserting a claim the plaintiff has previously litigated and lost against another defendant.]

A

Collateral estoppel, like the related doctrine of res judicata,[fn] has the dual purpose of protecting litigants from the burden of relitigating an identical issue with the same party or his privy and of promoting judicial economy by preventing needless litigation. Blonder-Tongue Laboratories, Inc. v. University of Illinois Foundation, 402 U.S. 313, 328-329[(1971)]. Until relatively recently, however, the scope of collateral estoppel was limited by the doctrine of mutuality of parties. Under this mutuality doctrine, neither party could use a prior judgment as an estoppel against the other unless both parties were bound by the judgment.[fn] Based on the premise that it is somehow unfair to allow a party to use a prior judgment when he himself would not be so bound,[Fn7. It is a violation of due process for a judgment to be binding on a litigant who was not a party or a privy and therefore has never had an opportunity to be heard. Blonder-Tongue Laboratories, Inc. v. University of Illinois Foundation, 402 U.S. 313, 329 (1971); Hansberry v. Lee, 311 U.S. 32, 40 (1940).] the mutuality requirement provided a party who had litigated and lost in a previous action an opportunity to relitigate identical issues with new parties.

By failing to recognize the obvious difference in position between a party who has never litigated an issue and one who has fully litigated and lost, the mutuality requirement was criticized almost from its inception.[Fn.8. This criticism was summarized in the Court's opinion in *Blonder-Tongue Laboratories, Inc. v. University of Illinois Foundation, supra*, 402 U.S. at 322-327[]. The opinion of Justice Traynor for a unanimous California Supreme Court in Bernhard v. Bank of America Nat. Trust & Savings Assn., [] 122 P.2d 892, 895 [(Cal. Sup. Ct. 1942)], made the point succinctly:"No satisfactory rationalization has been advanced for the requirement of mutuality. Just why a party who was not bound by a previous action should be precluded from asserting it as res judicata against a party who was bound by it is difficult to comprehend."] Recognizing the validity of this criticism, the Court in *Blonder-Tongue Laboratories, Inc. v. University of Illinois Foundation, supra,* abandoned the mutuality requirement, at least in cases where a patentee seeks to relitigate the validity of a patent after a federal court in a previous lawsuit has already declared it invalid.[fn] The "broader question" before the Court, however, was "whether it is any longer tenable to afford a litigant more than one full and fair opportunity for judicial resolution of the same issue." 402 U.S. at 328[]. The Court strongly suggested a negative answer to that question.... .

B

The *Blonder-Tongue* case involved defensive use of collateral estoppel—a plaintiff was estopped from asserting a claim that the plaintiff had previously litigated and lost against another defendant. The present case, by contrast, involves offensive use of collateral estoppel—a plaintiff is seeking to estop a defendant from relitigating the issues which the defendant previously litigated and lost against another plaintiff. In both the offensive and defensive use situations, the party against whom estoppel is asserted has litigated and lost in an earlier action. Nevertheless, several reasons have been advanced why the two situations should be treated differently.[fn]

First, offensive use of collateral estoppel does not promote judicial economy in the same manner as defensive use does. Defensive use of collateral estoppel precludes a plaintiff from relitigating identical issues by merely "switching adversaries." *Bernhard v. Bank of America Nat. Trust & Savings Assn., [supra,]* at 895.[fn] Thus defensive collateral estoppel gives a plaintiff a strong incentive to join all potential defendants in the first action if possible. Offensive use of collateral estoppel, on the other hand, creates precisely the opposite incentive. Since a plaintiff will be able to rely on a previous judgment against a defendant but will not be bound by that judgment if the defendant wins, the plaintiff has every incentive to adopt a "wait and see" attitude, in the hope that the first action by another plaintiff will result in a favorable judgment. [Cc] Thus offensive use of collateral estoppel will likely increase rather than decrease the total amount of litigation, since potential plaintiffs will have everything to gain and nothing to lose by not intervening in the first action.[Fn.13. The Restatement (Second) of Judgments §§88(3) (Tent. Draft No. 2, Apr. 15, 1975) provides that application of collateral estoppel may be denied if the party asserting it "could have effected joinder in the first action between himself and his present adversary."]

A second argument against offensive use of collateral estoppel is that it may be unfair to a defendant. If a defendant in the first action is sued for small or nominal damages, he may have little incentive to defend vigorously, particularly if future suits are not foreseeable. The Evergreens v. Nunan, 141 F.2d 927, 929 ([2d. Cir. 1944]); cf. Berner v. British Commonwealth Pac. Airlines, 346 F.2d 532 ([2d. Cir. 1965]) (application of offensive collateral estoppel denied where defendant did not appeal an adverse judgment awarding damages of $35,000 and defendant was later sued for over $7 million). Allowing offensive collateral estoppel may also be unfair to a defendant if the judgment relied upon as a basis for the estoppel is itself inconsistent with one or more previous judgments in favor of the defendant.[Fn14. In Professor Currie's familiar example, a railroad collision injures 50 passengers all of whom bring separate actions against the railroad. After the railroad wins the first 25 suits, a plaintiff wins in suit 26. Professor Currie argues that offensive use of collateral estoppel should not be applied so as to allow plaintiffs 27 through 50 automatically to recover. [Cc]] Still another situation where it might be unfair to apply offensive estoppel is where the second action affords the defendant procedural opportunities unavailable in the first action that could readily cause a different result.[Fn.15. If, for example, the defendant in the first action was forced to defend in an inconvenient forum and therefore was unable to engage in full scale discovery or call witnesses, application of offensive collateral estoppel may be unwarranted. Indeed, differences in available procedures may sometimes justify not allowing a prior judgment to have estoppel effect in a subsequent action even between the same parties, or where defensive estoppel is asserted against a plaintiff who has litigated and lost. The problem of unfairness is particularly acute in cases of offensive estoppel, however, because the defendant against whom estoppel is asserted typically will not have chosen the forum in the first action. [C]]

C

We have concluded that the preferable approach for dealing with these problems in the federal courts is not to preclude the use of offensive collateral estoppel, but to grant trial courts broad discretion to determine when it should be applied.[fn] The general rule should be that in cases where a plaintiff could easily have joined in the earlier action or where, either for the reasons discussed above or for other reasons, the application of offensive estoppel would be unfair to a defendant, a trial judge should not allow the use of offensive collateral estoppel.

In the present case, however, none of the circumstances that might justify reluctance to allow the offensive use of collateral estoppel is present. The application of offensive collateral estoppel will not here reward a private plaintiff who could have joined in the previous action, since the respondent probably could not have joined in the injunctive action brought by the SEC even had he so desired.[fn] Similarly, there is no unfairness to the petitioners in applying offensive collateral estoppel in this case. First, in light of the serious allegations made in the SEC's complaint against the petitioners, as well as the foreseeability of subsequent private suits that typically follow a successful Government judgment, the petitioners had every incentive to litigate the SEC lawsuit fully and vigorously.[fn] Second, the judgment in the SEC action was not inconsistent with any previous decision. Finally, there will in the respondent's action be no procedural opportunities available to the petitioners that were unavailable in the first action of a kind that might be likely to cause a different result.[fn]

We conclude, therefore, that none of the considerations that would justify a refusal to allow the use of offensive collateral estoppel is present in this case. Since the petitioners received a "full and fair" opportunity to litigate their claims in the SEC action, the contemporary law of collateral estoppel leads inescapably to the conclusion that the petitioners are collaterally estopped from relitigating the question of whether the proxy statement was materially false and misleading.

II

The question that remains is whether, notwithstanding the law of collateral estoppel, the use of offensive collateral estoppel in this case would violate the petitioners' Seventh Amendment right to a jury trial.[fn] ...

The petitioners have advanced no persuasive reason, however, why the meaning of the Seventh Amendment should depend on whether or not mutuality of parties is present. ...

The Seventh Amendment has never been interpreted in the rigid manner advocated by the petitioners. On the contrary, many procedural devices developed since 1791 that have diminished the civil jury's historic domain have been found not to be inconsistent with the Seventh Amendment. See Galloway v. United States, 319 U.S. 372, 388-393[(1943)] (directed verdict does not violate the Seventh Amendment); [cc].[fn]

The *Galloway* case is particularly instructive. There the party against whom a directed verdict had been entered argued that the procedure was unconstitutional under the Seventh Amendment. In rejecting this claim, the Court said: "The Amendment did not bind the federal courts to the exact procedural incidents or details of jury trial according to the common law in 1791, any more than it tied them to the common-law system of pleading or the specific rules of evidence then prevailing. ... The more logical conclusion, we think, and the one which both history and the previous decisions here support, is that the Amendment was designed to preserve the basic institution of jury trial in only its most fundamental elements, not the great mass of procedural forms and details, varying even then so widely among common-law jurisdictions." 319 U.S. at 390, 392[] (footnote omitted).

The law of collateral estoppel, like the law in other procedural areas defining the scope of the jury's function, has evolved since 1791. Under the rationale of the *Galloway* case, these developments are not repugnant to the Seventh Amendment simply for the reason that they did not exist in 1791. Thus if, as we have held, the law of collateral estoppel forecloses the petitioners from relitigating the factual issues determined against them in the SEC action, nothing in the Seventh Amendment dictates a different result, even though because of lack of mutuality there would have been no collateral estoppel in 1791.[fn]

The judgment of the Court of Appeals is

Affirmed.

Mr. Justice REHNQUIST, dissenting[, omitted. Justice Rehnquist's dissent argued that the Seventh Amendment jury-trial right prohibits preclusion under these circumstances.]

INQUIRY

Factors. Given that non-mutual issue preclusion is available in the federal and many state courts, but there seems the clear need for trial courts to exercise discretion in some cases. when should the trial court offer it? The Restatement (Second) of Judgments §29 lists seven factors including whether: (1) preclusion would interfere with a remedy scheme in the actions; (2) the second forum has additional procedures to arrive at a more reliable decision; (3) the party seeking to avoid preclusion could have joined in the earlier action the party seeking to rely on it in the later action; (4) the precluding decision is consistent with other decisions on the same issue; (5) the relationship of the parties in the first action was any different; (6) preclusion would complicate the later action; and (7) the court in the later action should give the legal rule on which preclusion would rely further consideration. The Restatement also encourages the trial court to consider other "compelling circumstances [that] make it appropriate that the party be permitted to relitigate the issue." Applying these and other considerations, the courts have generally avoided applying issue preclusion to mass torts like asbestos litigation, instead relying on patterns in varying verdicts and judgments to establish settlement parameters. Would you rather be counsel for the plaintiff party who had to try an asbestos case to provide the information on which other plaintiffs would settle their cases, or would you rather represent the settling plaintiff?

Government. The Supreme Court embraced non-mutual issue preclusion in *Parklane Hosiery Co. v. Shore, supra.* Odd as it may seem, just five years later the Supreme Court held in United States v. Mendoza, 464 U.S. 154 (1984), that the *Parklane Hosiery Co. v. Shore* holding does not apply against the federal government. A party cannot assert non-mutual issue preclusion against the United States. The Supreme Court's rejection of non-mutual issue preclusion as to the United States in the *Mendoza* case highlights the potential unfairness of the doctrine's non-mutual form. The United States has relatively unlimited resources out of which to satisfy judgments. It also has the special role toward its citizens of any national government. It may justifiably base its decisions on which cases to pursue, defend, and appeal with what resources, on considerations broader than the prospects of issue preclusion in future cases. The federal government does not and should not act strategically to the same extent as other litigants. Non-mutual issue preclusion should therefore not bind the federal government as it would bind othe parties. Convinced?

Summary. Claim preclusion bars a party from relitigating a claim that the party asserted or court have asserted in a prior litigation between the same parties. There must be a mutuality of parties or their privies in the prior and subsequent litigation. Issue preclusion bars a person from relitigating an issue that the court actually and necessarily litigated in a prior adjudication to which the person was a party. Many jurisdictions including the federal courts do not require mutuality of parties for issue preclusion, although because of due-process constraints, claim and issue preclusion apply against only those who were parties to the decision on the claim or issue in the prior adjudication.

Conclusion

Chapter I's introduction suggested that civil procedure is about more than process. The subject's deeper roots lie in how one recognizes and approaches authority. Everything both real and artificial depends on the authority of law. The universe represents authority. Nothing is greater than authority. Matter and energy are utterly subject to physical laws representative of authority. Lawyers have no greater liberty to discount, ignore, offend, or act contrary to authority. Lawyers possess no authority. Rather, a lawyer's skill is to invoke authority.

Every power that lawyers exercise, we derive from an authority outside of ourselves—a source that we must respect and whose requirements we must follow. Lawyers who hope to invoke authority with power and purpose must know its requirements. Authority will forgive a lawyer's mistake in the exercise of power. Authority cannot forgive a lawyer's abuse of itself. Lawyers must draw properly from authority if they expect to have any power to serve clients. Authority is not a personal attribute, not even of judges. Authority anoints a judge only so long as the judge remains subject to it and within its boundaries. Civil procedure instructs lawyers in authority, as physical laws instruct auto mechanics in the possibilities of locomotive power. Without civil procedure, lawyers can no more gain authoritative results for their clients than a mechanic could fix a car by arguing with it. The civil justice system manifests authority. While lawyers direct its authority attempting to resolve their clients' matters, the civil justice system demands that lawyers and clients acknowledge authority. Lawyers and clients meet and come to know and embrace authority through the civil justice system's redemptive power.

Civil procedure would be as simple as Esther approaching the king, if the persons and institutions vested with authority were infallible. Civil procedure is instead complex because delegated authorities are fallible. Rules on the authority of a court to adjudicate are necessary because we cannot trust courts to know those limits without their contested definition. It is a profound proposition that lawyers have civil procedure's authority to stand before courts arguing that the courts have no authority. Procedures for adjudication are necessary because we cannot trust courts to know a case without demonstrating it to them. Rules on the enforcement and effect of judgments exist because we cannot trust the justice system with enforcement without procedures to prove and contest it. Do not think of civil procedure's detail and complexity as wasteful. It is instead powerful and necessary. A lawyer need only stand once before an unjust judge to fully appreciate the many stages and doctrines of civil procedure that divide, shape, and constrain delegated authority. Yet fallibility extends as much to lawyers as to the courts. Rules for authority, procedures, and enforcement exist not just to govern the courts but to guide the lawyers who invoke the civil justice system's delegated authority.

Even when judges are wrong, indeed especially when they are wrong, lawyers submit to their delegated authority, while lawyers invoke higher authority to correct them. The lawyer who rebels against an erroneous trial judge's delegated authority rebels against law itself. The law does not hold lawyers responsible for judicial errors. It does hold lawyers responsible for following judgments and orders. Lawyers direct their obedience not to the person of the judge but to the authority of the law as it lies on the judge. It must be a perfect obedience, or at least lawyers must aspire toward its perfection. The lawyer who does not seek subjection to law's authority corrupts the lawyer's own delegated authority. The power of a lawyer is therefore made perfect not in the lawyer's professional strength but in the lawyer's personal weakness. Lawyers who attempt out of personal hubris to exercise authority that they do not possess lose the delegated authority that they once possessed. Lawyers submit to authority. They obey only that which is authoritative. The skill of a lawyer is to maintain a submissive attitude toward authority but one that obeys only the authoritative—to know the difference between what is and is not authoritative, and who carries delegated authority under what circumstances and with what conditions. Civil procedure draws that line. The study of civil procedure answers those questions.

The lawyer who knows authority seeks it. Lawyers seek and find authority that clients cannot recognize. Lawyers must be sensitive to recognize authority. Wins do not teach lawyers the sensitivity to locate, recognize, and draw on authority. Losses teach authority. Fear of mistaking authority teaches sensitivity to it. Lawyers who know authority readily sense the rebellion of others to it. Lawyers counsel clients effectively by leading them to authority. Lawyers do not exercise their delegated authority carelessly. They guard it jealously because in exercising it beyond its scope they lose it. Authority flows through the lawyer from its source only insofar as the lawyer is fit for it. Knowledge of civil procedure makes the lawyer fit to exercise and appeal to delegated authority. At its core, civil procedure is not about techniques, strategies, forms, and methods. It is about authority. The lawyer who knows authority appreciates civil procedure.

Practice

The lawyer slipped quietly into the back of the courtroom, motioned to opposing counsel to confirm that they were checked in, and settled into a bench near the back. Some lawyers liked to sit in front of the rail to wait their turn to argue motions. The lawyer liked to sit in the gallery as far back as possible to get a better view of everything going on in the courtroom. The long late-fall sun glinted in through the tall windows behind the judge, causing the lawyer to reminisce.

Courtrooms present such turning points for most litigants. Marriages and businesses dissolved, titles contested and quieted, estates opened and closed, guardianships established and terminated. No one can know a community without spending some time in its courtroom, where they might learn that the local hospital sues more people by far than anyone else or that one out of every eight children in the county is under a family-court order. The justice system reveals the community's pain as much as it holds the community's redemption. Parties enter the courtroom expecting vindication. Some get it. Others get a mirror into their own souls. Vindication is good, self-revelation better.

Just then, the lawyer noticed opposing counsel stirring. The lawyer glanced through notes in the slim court file. When the judge nodded to them, they rose together from their different locations in the courtroom, met at the lectern to shake hands, and began their arguments. The whole scene seemed so familiar to both of them that they could have been arguing any one of dozens of different motions down through the years. Maybe they were. Maybe the judge was right then weighing the sum total of their many civil skirmishes to determine who should win and who lose this time, knowing all the while that the masterful skill of both lawyers would likely bring about the right resolution long before the judge had to exercise the full and final weight of that authority. So is the fundamental nature of civil procedure, that it affords every lawyer the opportunity to be tested by an authority having no superior.

APPENDIX I

FEDERAL RULES OF CIVIL PROCEDURE

TITLE I. SCOPE OF RULES; FORM OF ACTION

FED. R. CIV. P. 1. Scope and Purpose.
These rules govern the procedure in all civil actions and proceedings in the United States district courts, except as stated in Rule 81. They should be construed and administered to secure the just, speedy, and inexpensive determination of every action and proceeding.

FED. R. CIV. P. 2. One Form of Action
There is one form of action—the civil action.

TITLE II. COMMENCING AN ACTION; SERVICE OF PROCESS, PLEADINGS, MOTIONS, AND ORDERS

FED. R. CIV. P. 3. Commencing an Action.
A civil action is commenced by filing a complaint with the court.

FED. R. CIV. P. 4. Summons.
(a) CONTENTS; AMENDMENTS.
(1) *Contents.* A summons must:
(A) name the court and the parties;
(B) be directed to the defendant;
(C) state the name and address of the plaintiff's attorney or—if unrepresented—of the plaintiff;
(D) state the time within which the defendant must appear and defend;
(E) notify the defendant that a failure to appear and defend will result in a default judgment against the defendant
for the relief demanded in the complaint;
(F) be signed by the clerk; and
(G) bear the court's seal.
(2) *Amendments.* The court may permit a summons to be amended.
(b) ISSUANCE. On or after filing the complaint, the plaintiff may present a summons to the clerk for signature and seal. If the summons is properly completed, the clerk must sign, seal, and issue it to the plaintiff for service on the defendant. A summons—or a copy of a summons that is addressed to multiple defendants—must be issued for each defendant to be served.
(c) SERVICE.
(1) *In General.* A summons must be served with a copy of the complaint. The plaintiff is responsible for having the summons and complaint served within the time allowed by Rule 4(m) and must furnish the necessary copies to the person who makes service.
(2) *By Whom.* Any person who is at least 18 years old and not a party may serve a summons and complaint.
(3) *By a Marshal or Someone Specially Appointed.* At the plaintiff's request, the court may order that service be made by a
United States marshal or deputy marshal or by a person specially appointed by the court. The court must so order if the
plaintiff is authorized to proceed in forma pauperis under 28 U.S.C. §1915 or as a seaman under 28 U.S.C. §1916.
(d) WAIVING SERVICE.
(1) *Requesting a Waiver.* An individual, corporation, or association that is subject to service under Rule 4(e), (f), or (h) has a duty to avoid unnecessary expenses of serving the summons. The plaintiff may notify such a defendant that an action has been commenced and request that the defendant waive service of a summons. The notice and request must:
(A) be in writing and be addressed:
(i) to the individual defendant; or
(ii) for a defendant subject to service under Rule 4(h), to an officer, a managing or general agent, or any
other agent authorized by appointment or by law to receive service of process;
(B) name the court where the complaint was filed;
(C) be accompanied by a copy of the complaint, 2 copies of a waiver form, and a prepaid means for returning the form;

(D) inform the defendant, using text prescribed in Form 5, of the consequences of waiving and not waiving service;
(E) state the date when the request is sent;
(F) give the defendant a reasonable time of at least 30 days after the request was sent—or at least 60 days if sent to the defendant outside any judicial district of the United States—to return the waiver; and
(G) be sent by first-class mail or other reliable means.
(2) *Failure to Waive.* If a defendant located within the United States fails, without good cause, to sign and return a waiver requested by a plaintiff located within the United States, the court must impose on the defendant:
(A) the expenses later incurred in making service; and
(B) the reasonable expenses, including attorney's fees, of any motion required to collect those service expenses.
(3) *Time to Answer After a Waiver.* A defendant who, before being served with process, timely returns a waiver need not serve an answer to the complaint until 60 days after the request was sent—or until 90 days after it was sent to the defendant outside any judicial district of the United States.
(4) *Results of Filing a Waiver.* When the plaintiff files a waiver, proof of service is not required and these rules apply as if a summons and complaint had been served at the time of filing the waiver.
(5) *Jurisdiction and Venue Not Waived.* Waiving service of a summons does not waive any objection to personal jurisdiction or to venue.
(e) SERVING AN INDIVIDUAL WITHIN A JUDICIAL DISTRICT OF THE UNITED STATES. Unless federal law provides otherwise, an individual—other than a minor, an incompetent person, or a person whose waiver has been filed—may be served in a judicial district of the United States by:
(1) following state law for serving a summons in an action brought in courts of general jurisdiction in the state where the district court is located or where service is made; or
(2) doing any of the following:
(A) delivering a copy of the summons and of the complaint to the individual personally;
(B) leaving a copy of each at the individual's dwelling or usual place of abode with someone of suitable age and discretion who resides there; or
(C) delivering a copy of each to an agent authorized by appointment or by law to receive service of process.
(f) SERVING AN INDIVIDUAL IN A FOREIGN COUNTRY. Unless federal law provides otherwise, an individual—other than a minor, an incompetent person, or a person whose waiver has been filed—may be served at a place not within any judicial district of the United States:
(1) by any internationally agreed means of service that is reasonably calculated to give notice, such as those authorized by the Hague Convention on the Service Abroad of Judicial and Extrajudicial Documents;
(2) if there is no internationally agreed means, or if an international agreement allows but does not specify other means, by a method that is reasonably calculated to give notice:
(A) as prescribed by the foreign country's law for service in that country in an action in its courts of general jurisdiction;
(B) as the foreign authority directs in response to a letter rogatory or letter of request; or
(C) unless prohibited by the foreign country's law, by:
(i) delivering a copy of the summons and of the complaint to the individual personally; or
(ii) using any form of mail that the clerk addresses and sends to the individual and that requires a signed
receipt; or
(3) by other means not prohibited by international agreement, as the court orders.
(g) SERVING A MINOR OR AN INCOMPETENT PERSON. A minor or an incompetent person in a judicial district of the United States must be served by following state law for serving a summons or like process on such a defendant in an action brought in the courts of general jurisdiction of the state where service is made. A minor or an incompetent person who is not within any judicial district of the United States must be served in the manner prescribed by Rule 4(f)(2)(A), (f)(2)(B), or (f)(3).
(h) SERVING A CORPORATION, PARTNERSHIP, OR ASSOCIATION. Unless federal law provides otherwise or the defendant's waiver has been filed, a domestic or foreign corporation, or a partnership or other unincorporated association that is subject to suit under a common name, must be served:
(1) in a judicial district of the United States:
(A) in the manner prescribed by Rule 4(e)(1) for serving an individual; or
(B) by delivering a copy of the summons and of the complaint to an officer, a managing or general agent, or any other agent authorized by appointment or by law to receive service of process and—if the agent is one authorized by statute and the statute so requires—by also mailing a copy of each to the defendant; or
(2) at a place not within any judicial district of the United States, in any manner prescribed by

Rule 4(f) for serving an individual, except personal delivery under (f)(2)(C)(i).

(i) SERVING THE UNITED STATES AND ITS AGENCIES, CORPORATIONS, OFFICERS, OR EMPLOYEES.

(1) *United States.* To serve the United States, a party must:

(A)(i) deliver a copy of the summons and of the complaint to the United States attorney for the district where the action is brought—or to an assistant United States attorney or clerical employee whom the United States attorney designates in a writing filed with the court clerk—or

(ii) send a copy of each by registered or certified mail to the civil-process clerk at the United States attorney's office;

(B) send a copy of each by registered or certified mail to the Attorney General of the United States at Washington, D.C.; and

(C) if the action challenges an order of a nonparty agency or officer of the United States, send a copy of each by registered or certified mail to the agency or officer.

(2) *Agency; Corporation; Officer or Employee Sued in an Official Capacity.* To serve a United States agency or corporation, or a United States officer or employee sued only in an official capacity, a party must serve the United States and also send a copy of the summons and of the complaint by registered or certified mail to the agency, corporation, officer, or employee.

(3) *Officer or Employee Sued Individually.* To serve a United States officer or employee sued in an individual capacity for an act or omission occurring in connection with duties performed on the United States' behalf (whether or not the officer or employee is also sued in an official capacity), a party must serve the United States and also serve the officer or employee under Rule 4(e), (f), or (g).

(4) *Extending Time.* The court must allow a party a reasonable time to cure its failure to:

(A) serve a person required to be served under Rule 4(i)(2), if the party has served either the United States attorney or the Attorney General of the United States; or

(B) serve the United States under Rule 4(i)(3), if the party has served the United States officer or employee.

(j) SERVING A FOREIGN, STATE, OR LOCAL GOVERNMENT.

(1) *Foreign State.* A foreign state or its political subdivision, agency, or instrumentality must be served in accordance with 28 U.S.C. §1608.

(2) *State or Local Government.* A state, a municipal corporation, or any other state-created governmental organization that is subject to suit must be served by:

(A) delivering a copy of the summons and of the complaint to its chief executive officer; or

(B) serving a copy of each in the manner prescribed by that state's law for serving a summons or like process on such a defendant.

(k) TERRITORIAL LIMITS OF EFFECTIVE SERVICE.

(1) *In General.* Serving a summons or filing a waiver of service establishes personal jurisdiction over a defendant:

(A) who is subject to the jurisdiction of a court of general jurisdiction in the state where the district court is located;

(B) who is a party joined under Rule 14 or 19 and is served within a judicial district of the United States and not more than 100 miles from where the summons was issued; or

(C) when authorized by a federal statute.

(2) *Federal Claim Outside State-Court Jurisdiction.* For a claim that arises under federal law, serving a summons or filing a waiver of service establishes personal jurisdiction over a defendant if:

(A) the defendant is not subject to jurisdiction in any state's courts of general jurisdiction; and

(B) exercising jurisdiction is consistent with the United States Constitution and laws.

(*l*) PROVING SERVICE.

(1) *Affidavit Required.* Unless service is waived, proof of service must be made to the court. Except for service by a United States marshal or deputy marshal, proof must be by the server's affidavit.

(2) *Service Outside the United States.* Service not within any judicial district of the United States must be proved as follows:

(A) if made under Rule 4(f)(1), as provided in the applicable treaty or convention; or

(B) if made under Rule 4(f)(2) or (f)(3), by a receipt signed by the addressee, or by other evidence satisfying the court that the summons and complaint were delivered to the addressee.

(3) *Validity of Service; Amending Proof.* Failure to prove service does not affect the validity of service. The court may permit proof of service to be amended.

(m) TIME LIMIT FOR SERVICE. If a defendant is not served within 120 days after the complaint is filed, the court—on motion or on its own after notice to the plaintiff—must dismiss the action without prejudice against that defendant or order that service be made within a specified time. But if the plaintiff shows good cause for the failure, the court must extend the time for service for an appropriate period. This subdivision (m) does not apply to service in a foreign country under Rule 4(f) or 4(j)(1).

(n) ASSERTING JURISDICTION OVER PROPERTY OR ASSETS.

(1) *Federal Law.* The court may assert jurisdiction over property if authorized by a federal statute. Notice to claimants of the property must be given as provided in the statute or by serving a summons under this rule.
(2) *State Law.* On a showing that personal jurisdiction over a defendant cannot be obtained in the district where the action is brought by reasonable efforts to serve a summons under this rule, the court may assert jurisdiction over the defendant's assets found in the district. Jurisdiction is acquired by seizing the assets under the circumstances and in the manner provided by state law in that district.

FED. R. CIV. P. 4.1. Serving Other Process
(a) IN GENERAL. Process—other than a summons under Rule 4 or a subpoena under Rule 45—must be served by a United States marshal or deputy marshal or by a person specially appointed for that purpose. It may be served anywhere within the territorial limits of the state where the district court is located and, if authorized by a federal statute, beyond those limits. Proof of service must be made under Rule 4(*l*).
(b) ENFORCING ORDERS: COMMITTING FOR CIVIL CONTEMPT. An order committing a person for civil contempt of a decree or injunction issued to enforce federal law may be served and enforced in any district. Any other order in a civil-contempt proceeding may be served only in the state where the issuing court is located or elsewhere in the United States within 100 miles from where the
order was issued.

FED. R. CIV. P. 5. Serving and Filing Pleadings and Other Papers
(a) SERVICE: WHEN REQUIRED.
(1) *In General.* Unless these rules provide otherwise, each of the following papers must be served on every party:
(A) an order stating that service is required;
(B) a pleading filed after the original complaint, unless the court orders otherwise under Rule 5(c) because there are numerous defendants;
(C) a discovery paper required to be served on a party, unless the court orders otherwise;
(D) a written motion, except one that may be heard ex parte; and
(E) a written notice, appearance, demand, or offer of judgment, or any similar paper.
(2) *If a Party Fails to Appear.* No service is required on a party who is in default for failing to appear. But a pleading that asserts a new claim for relief against such a party must be served on that party under Rule 4.
(3) *Seizing Property.* If an action is begun by seizing property and no person is or need be named as a defendant, any service required before the filing of an appearance, answer, or claim must be made on the person who had custody or possession of the property when it was seized.
(b) SERVICE: HOW MADE.
(1) *Serving an Attorney.* If a party is represented by an attorney, service under this rule must be made on the attorney unless the court orders service on the party.
(2) *Service in General.* A paper is served under this rule by:
(A) handing it to the person;
(B) leaving it:
(i) at the person's office with a clerk or other person in charge or, if no one is in charge, in a conspicuous
place in the office; or
(ii) if the person has no office or the office is closed, at the person's dwelling or usual place of abode with
someone of suitable age and discretion who resides there;
(C) mailing it to the person's last known address—in which event service is complete upon mailing;
(D) leaving it with the court clerk if the person has no known address;
(E) sending it by electronic means if the person consented in writing—in which event service is complete upon transmission, but is not effective if the serving party learns that it did not reach the person to be served; or
(F) delivering it by any other means that the person consented to in writing—in which event service is complete when the person making service delivers it to the agency designated to make delivery.
(3) *Using Court Facilities.* If a local rule so authorizes, a party may use the court's transmission facilities to make service under Rule 5(b)(2)(E).
(c) SERVING NUMEROUS DEFENDANTS.
(1) *In General.* If an action involves an unusually large number of defendants, the court may, on motion or on its own, order that:
(A) defendants' pleadings and replies to them need not be served on other defendants;
(B) any crossclaim, counterclaim, avoidance, or affirmative defense in those pleadings and replies to them will be treated as denied or avoided by all other parties; and
(C) filing any such pleading and serving it on the plaintiff constitutes notice of the pleading to all parties.
(2) *Notifying Parties.* A copy of every such order must be served on the parties as the court directs.
(d) FILING.
(1) *Required Filings; Certificate of Service.* Any paper after the complaint that is required to be

served—together with a certificate of service—must be filed within a reasonable time after service. But disclosures under Rule 26(a)(1) or (2) and the following discovery requests and responses must not be filed until they are used in the proceeding or the court orders filing: depositions, interrogatories, requests for documents or tangible things or to permit entry onto land, and requests for admission.

(2) *How Filing Is Made—In General.* A paper is filed by delivering it:

(A) to the clerk; or

(B) to a judge who agrees to accept it for filing, and who must then note the filing date on the paper and promptly send it to the clerk.

(3) *Electronic Filing, Signing, or Verification.* A court may, by local rule, allow papers to be filed, signed, or verified by electronic means that are consistent with any technical standards established by the Judicial Conference of the United States. A local rule may require electronic filing only if reasonable exceptions are allowed. A paper filed electronically in compliance with a local rule is a written paper for purposes of these rules.

(4) *Acceptance by the Clerk.* The clerk must not refuse to file a paper solely because it is not in the form prescribed by these rules or by a local rule or practice.

FED. R. CIV. P. 5.1. Constitutional Challenge to a Statute—Notice, Certification, and Intervention

(a) NOTICE BY A PARTY. A party that files a pleading, written motion, or other paper drawing into question the constitutionality of a federal or state statute must promptly:

(1) file a notice of constitutional question stating the question and identifying the paper that raises it, if:

(A) a federal statute is questioned and the parties do not include the United States, one of its agencies, or one of its officers or employees in an official capacity; or

(B) a state statute is questioned and the parties do not include the state, one of its agencies, or one of its officers or employees in an official capacity; and

(2) serve the notice and paper on the Attorney General of the United States if a federal statute is questioned—or on the state attorney general if a state statute is questioned—either by certified or registered mail or by sending it to an electronic address designated by the attorney general for this purpose.

(b) CERTIFICATION BY THE COURT. The court must, under 28 U.S.C. §2403, certify to the appropriate attorney general that a statute has been questioned.

(c) INTERVENTION; FINAL DECISION ON THE MERITS. Unless the court sets a later time, the attorney general may intervene within 60 days after the notice is filed or after the court certifies the challenge, whichever is earlier. Before the time to intervene expires, the court may reject the constitutional challenge, but may not enter a final judgment holding the statute unconstitutional.

(d) NO FORFEITURE. A party's failure to file and serve the notice, or the court's failure to certify, does not forfeit a constitutional claim or defense that is otherwise timely asserted.

FED. R. CIV. P. 5.2. Privacy Protection For Filings Made with the Court

(a) REDACTED FILINGS. Unless the court orders otherwise, in an electronic or paper filing with the court that contains an individual's social-security number, taxpayer-identification number, or birth date, the name of an individual known to be a minor, or a financial-account number, a party or nonparty making the filing may include only:

(1) the last four digits of the social-security number and taxpayer- identification number;

(2) the year of the individual's birth;

(3) the minor's initials; and

(4) the last four digits of the financial-account number.

(b) EXEMPTIONS FROM THE REDACTION REQUIREMENT. The redaction requirement does not apply to the following:

(1) a financial-account number that identifies the property allegedly subject to forfeiture in a forfeiture proceeding;

(2) the record of an administrative or agency proceeding;

(3) the official record of a state-court proceeding;

(4) the record of a court or tribunal, if that record was not subject to the redaction requirement when originally filed;

(5) a filing covered by Rule 5.2(c) or (d); and

(6) a pro se filing in an action brought under 28 U.S.C. §§2241, 2254, or 2255.

(c) LIMITATIONS ON REMOTE ACCESS TO ELECTRONIC FILES; SOCIAL SECURITY APPEALS AND IMMIGRATION CASES. Unless the court orders otherwise, in an action for benefits under the Social Security Act, and in an action or proceeding relating to an order of removal, to relief from removal, or to immigration benefits or detention, access to an electronic file is authorized as follows:

(1) the parties and their attorneys may have remote electronic access to any part of the case file, including the administrative record;

(2) any other person may have electronic access to the full record at the courthouse, but may have remote electronic access only to:
(A) the docket maintained by the court; and
(B) an opinion, order, judgment, or other disposition of the court, but not any other part of the case file or the administrative record.
(d) FILINGS MADE UNDER SEAL. The court may order that a filing be made under seal without redaction. The court may later unseal the filing or order the person who made the filing to file a redacted version for the public record.
(e) PROTECTIVE ORDERS. For good cause, the court may by order in a case:
(1) require redaction of additional information; or
(2) limit or prohibit a nonparty's remote electronic access to a document filed with the court.
(f) OPTION FOR ADDITIONAL UNREDACTED FILING UNDER SEAL. A person making a redacted filing may also file an unredacted copy under seal. The court must retain the unredacted copy as part of the record.
(g) OPTION FOR FILING A REFERENCE LIST. A filing that contains redacted information may be filed together with a reference list that identifies each item of redacted information and specifies an appropriate identifier that uniquely corresponds to each item listed. The list must be filed under seal and may be amended as of right. Any reference in the case to a listed identifier will be construed to refer to the corresponding item of information.
(h) WAIVER OF PROTECTION OF IDENTIFIERS. A person waives the protection of Rule 5.2(a) as to the person's own information by filing it without redaction and not under seal.

FED. R. CIV. P. 6. Computing and Extending Time; Time for Motion Papers

(a) COMPUTING TIME. The following rules apply in computing any time period specified in these rules, in any local rule or court order, or in any statute that does not specify a method of computing time.
(1) *Period Stated in Days or a Longer Unit.* When the period is stated in days or a longer unit of time:
(A) exclude the day of the event that triggers the period;
(B) count every day, including intermediate Saturdays, Sundays, and legal holidays; and
(C) include the last day of the period, but if the last day is a Saturday, Sunday, or legal holiday, the period continues to run until the end of the next day that is not a Saturday, Sunday, or legal holiday.
(2) *Period Stated in Hours.* When the period is stated in hours:
(A) begin counting immediately on the occurrence of the event that triggers the period;
(B) count every hour, including hours during intermediate Saturdays, Sundays, and legal holidays; and
(C) if the period would end on a Saturday, Sunday, or legal holiday, the period continues to run until the same time on the next day that is not a Saturday, Sunday, or legal holiday.
(3) *Inaccessibility of the Clerk's Office.* Unless the court orders otherwise, if the clerk's office is inaccessible:
(A) on the last day for filing under Rule 6(a)(1), then the time for filing is extended to the first accessible day that is not a Saturday, Sunday, or legal holiday; or
(B) during the last hour for filing under Rule 6(a)(2), then the time for filing is extended to the same time on the first accessible day that is not a Saturday, Sunday, or legal holiday.
(4) *''Last Day'' Defined.* Unless a different time is set by a statute, local rule, or court order, the last day ends:
(A) for electronic filing, at midnight in the court's time zone; and
(B) for filing by other means, when the clerk's office is scheduled to close.
(5) *''Next Day'' Defined.* The ''next day'' is determined by continuing to count forward when the period is measured after an event and backward when measured before an event.
(6) *''Legal Holiday'' Defined.* ''Legal holiday'' means:
(A) the day set aside by statute for observing New Year's Day, Martin Luther King Jr.'s Birthday, Washington's Birthday, Memorial Day, Independence Day, Labor Day, Columbus Day, Veterans' Day, Thanksgiving Day, or Christmas Day;
(B) any day declared a holiday by the President or Congress; and
(C) for periods that are measured after an event, any other day declared a holiday by the state where the district court is located.
(b) EXTENDING TIME.
(1) *In General.* When an act may or must be done within a specified time, the court may, for good cause, extend the time:
(A) with or without motion or notice if the court acts, or if a request is made, before the original time or its extension expires; or
(B) on motion made after the time has expired if the party failed to act because of excusable neglect.
(2) *Exceptions.* A court must not extend the time to act under Rules 50(b) and (d), 52(b), 59(b), (d), and (e), and 60(b).

(c) MOTIONS, NOTICES OF HEARING, AND AFFIDAVITS.
(1) *In General.* A written motion and notice of the hearing must be served at least 14 days before the time specified for the hearing, with the following exceptions:
(A) when the motion may be heard ex parte;
(B) when these rules set a different time; or
(C) when a court order—which a party may, for good cause, apply for ex parte—sets a different time.
(2) *Supporting Affidavit.* Any affidavit supporting a motion must be served with the motion. Except as Rule 59(c) provides otherwise, any opposing affidavit must be served at least 7 days before the hearing, unless the court permits service at another time.
(d) ADDITIONAL TIME AFTER CERTAIN KINDS OF SERVICE. When a party may or must act within a specified time after service and service is made under Rule 5(b)(2)(C), (D), (E), or (F), 3 days are added after the period would otherwise expire under Rule 6(a).

TITLE III. PLEADINGS AND MOTIONS

FED. R. CIV. P. 7. Pleadings Allowed; Form of Motions and Other Papers
(a) PLEADINGS. Only these pleadings are allowed:
(1) a complaint;
(2) an answer to a complaint;
(3) an answer to a counterclaim designated as a counterclaim;
(4) an answer to a crossclaim;
(5) a third-party complaint;
(6) an answer to a third-party complaint; and
(7) if the court orders one, a reply to an answer.
(b) MOTIONS AND OTHER PAPERS.
(1) *In General.* A request for a court order must be made by motion. The motion must:
(A) be in writing unless made during a hearing or trial;
(B) state with particularity the grounds for seeking the order; and
(C) state the relief sought.
(2) *Form.* The rules governing captions and other matters of form in pleadings apply to motions and other papers.

FED. R. CIV. P. 7.1. Disclosure Statement
(a) WHO MUST FILE; CONTENTS. A nongovernmental corporate party must file 2 copies of a disclosure statement that:
(1) identifies any parent corporation and any publicly held corporation owning 10% or more of its stock; or
(2) states that there is no such corporation.
(b) TIME TO FILE; SUPPLEMENTAL FILING. A party must:
(1) file the disclosure statement with its first appearance, pleading, petition, motion, response, or other request addressed to the court; and
(2) promptly file a supplemental statement if any required information changes.

FED. R. CIV. P. 8. General Rules of Pleading
(a) CLAIM FOR RELIEF. A pleading that states a claim for relief must contain:
(1) a short and plain statement of the grounds for the court's jurisdiction, unless the court already has jurisdiction and the claim needs no new jurisdictional support;
(2) a short and plain statement of the claim showing that the pleader is entitled to relief; and
(3) a demand for the relief sought, which may include relief in the alternative or different types of relief.
(b) DEFENSES; ADMISSIONS AND DENIALS.
(1) *In General.* In responding to a pleading, a party must:
(A) state in short and plain terms its defenses to each claim asserted against it; and
(B) admit or deny the allegations asserted against it by an opposing party.
(2) *Denials—Responding to the Substance.* A denial must fairly respond to the substance of the allegation.
(3) *General and Specific Denials.* A party that intends in good faith to deny all the allegations of a pleading—including the jurisdictional grounds—may do so by a general denial. A party that does not intend to deny all the allegations must either specifically deny designated allegations or generally deny all except those specifically admitted.
(4) *Denying Part of an Allegation.* A party that intends in good faith to deny only part of an allegation must admit the part that is true and deny the rest.
(5) *Lacking Knowledge or Information.* A party that lacks knowledge or information sufficient to form a belief about the truth of an allegation must so state, and the statement has the effect of a denial.
(6) *Effect of Failing to Deny.* An allegation—other than one relating to the amount of damages—is admitted if a responsive pleading is required and the allegation is not denied. If a responsive pleading is not required, an allegation is considered denied or avoided.
(c) AFFIRMATIVE DEFENSES.
(1) *In General.* In responding to a pleading, a party must affirmatively state any avoidance or affirmative defense, including:
• accord and satisfaction;
• arbitration and award;
• assumption of risk;
• contributory negligence;

- discharge in bankruptcy;
- duress;
- estoppel;
- failure of consideration;
- fraud;
- illegality;
- injury by fellow servant;
- laches;
- license;
- payment;
- release;
- res judicata;
- statute of frauds;
- statute of limitations; and
- waiver.

(2) *Mistaken Designation.* If a party mistakenly designates a defense as a counterclaim, or a counterclaim as a defense, the court must, if justice requires, treat the pleading as though it were correctly designated, and may impose terms for doing so.

(d) PLEADING TO BE CONCISE AND DIRECT; ALTERNATIVE STATEMENTS; INCONSISTENCY.

(1) *In General.* Each allegation must be simple, concise, and direct. No technical form is required.

(2) *Alternative Statements of a Claim or Defense.* A party may set out 2 or more statements of a claim or defense alternatively or hypothetically, either in a single count or defense or in separate ones. If a party makes alternative statements, the pleading is sufficient if any one of them is sufficient.

(3) *Inconsistent Claims or Defenses.* A party may state as many separate claims or defenses as it has, regardless of consistency.

(e) CONSTRUING PLEADINGS. Pleadings must be construed so as to do justice.

FED. R. CIV. P. 9. Pleading Special Matters

(a) CAPACITY OR AUTHORITY TO SUE; LEGAL EXISTENCE.

(1) *In General.* Except when required to show that the court has jurisdiction, a pleading need not allege:

(A) a party's capacity to sue or be sued;

(B) a party's authority to sue or be sued in a representative capacity; or

(C) the legal existence of an organized association of persons that is made a party.

(2) *Raising Those Issues.* To raise any of those issues, a party must do so by a specific denial, which must state any supporting facts that are peculiarly within the party's knowledge.

(b) FRAUD OR MISTAKE; CONDITIONS OF MIND. In alleging fraud or mistake, a party must state with particularity the circumstances constituting fraud or mistake. Malice, intent, knowledge, and other conditions of a person's mind may be alleged generally.

(c) CONDITIONS PRECEDENT. In pleading conditions precedent, it suffices to allege generally that all conditions precedent have occurred or been performed. But when denying that a condition precedent has occurred or been performed, a party must do so with particularity.

(d) OFFICIAL DOCUMENT OR ACT. In pleading an official document or official act, it suffices to allege that the document was legally issued or the act legally done.

(e) JUDGMENT. In pleading a judgment or decision of a domestic or foreign court, a judicial or quasi-judicial tribunal, or a board or officer, it suffices to plead the judgment or decision without showing jurisdiction to render it.

(f) TIME AND PLACE. An allegation of time or place is material when testing the sufficiency of a pleading.

(g) SPECIAL DAMAGES. If an item of special damage is claimed, it must be specifically stated.

(h) ADMIRALTY OR MARITIME CLAIM.

(1) *How Designated.* If a claim for relief is within the admiralty or maritime jurisdiction and also within the court's subject- matter jurisdiction on some other ground, the pleading may designate the claim as an admiralty or maritime claim for purposes of Rules 14(c), 38(e), and 82 and the Supplemental Rules for Admiralty or Maritime Claims and Asset Forfeiture Actions. A claim cognizable only in the admiralty or maritime jurisdiction is an admiralty or maritime claim for those purposes, whether or not so designated.

(2) *Designation for Appeal.* A case that includes an admiralty or maritime claim within this subdivision (h) is an admiralty case within 28 U.S.C. §1292(a)(3).

FED. R. CIV. P. 10. Form of Pleadings

(a) CAPTION; NAMES OF PARTIES. Every pleading must have a caption with the court's name, a title, a file number, and a Rule 7(a) designation. The title of the complaint must name all the parties; the title of other pleadings, after naming the first party on each side, may refer generally to other parties.

(b) PARAGRAPHS; SEPARATE STATEMENTS. A party must state its claims or defenses in numbered paragraphs, each limited as far as practicable to a single set of circumstances. A later pleading may refer by number to a paragraph in an earlier pleading. If doing so would promote clarity, each claim founded on a separate transaction or occurrence—and each defense other than a denial—must be stated in a separate count or defense.

(c) ADOPTION BY REFERENCE; EXHIBITS. A statement in a pleading may be adopted by reference elsewhere in the same pleading or in any other pleading or motion. A copy of a written instrument that is an exhibit to a pleading is a part of the pleading for all purposes.

FED. R. CIV. P. 11. Signing Pleadings, Motions, and Other Papers; Representations to the Court; Sanctions

(a) SIGNATURE. Every pleading, written motion, and other paper must be signed by at least one attorney of record in the attorney's name—or by a party personally if the party is unrepresented. The

paper must state the signer's address, e-mail address, and telephone number. Unless a rule or statute specifically states otherwise, a pleading need not be verified or accompanied by an affidavit. The court must strike an unsigned paper unless the omission is promptly corrected after being called to the attorney's or party's attention.

(b) REPRESENTATIONS TO THE COURT. By presenting to the court a pleading, written motion, or other paper—whether by signing, filing, submitting, or later advocating it—an attorney or unrepresented party certifies that to the best of the person's knowledge, information, and belief, formed after an inquiry reasonable under the circumstances:

(1) it is not being presented for any improper purpose, such as to harass, cause unnecessary delay, or needlessly increase the cost of litigation;

(2) the claims, defenses, and other legal contentions are warranted by existing law or by a nonfrivolous argument for extending, modifying, or reversing existing law or for establishing new law;

(3) the factual contentions have evidentiary support or, if specifically so identified, will likely have evidentiary support after a reasonable opportunity for further investigation or discovery; and

(4) the denials of factual contentions are warranted on the evidence or, if specifically so identified, are reasonably based on belief or a lack of information.

(c) SANCTIONS.

(1) *In General.* If, after notice and a reasonable opportunity to respond, the court determines that Rule 11(b) has been violated, the court may impose an appropriate sanction on any attorney, law firm, or party that violated the rule or is responsible for the violation. Absent exceptional circumstances, a law firm must be held jointly responsible for a violation committed by its partner, associate, or employee.

(2) *Motion for Sanctions.* A motion for sanctions must be made separately from any other motion and must describe the specific conduct that allegedly violates Rule 11(b). The motion must be served under Rule 5, but it must not be filed or be presented to the court if the challenged paper, claim, defense, contention, or denial is withdrawn or appropriately corrected within 21 days after service or within another time the court sets. If warranted, the court may award to the prevailing party the reasonable expenses, including attorney's fees, incurred for the motion.

(3) *On the Court's Initiative.* On its own, the court may order an attorney, law firm, or party to show cause why conduct specifically described in the order has not violated Rule 11(b).

(4) *Nature of a Sanction.* A sanction imposed under this rule must be limited to what suffices to deter repetition of the conduct or comparable conduct by others similarly situated. The sanction may include nonmonetary directives; an order to pay a penalty into court; or, if imposed on motion and warranted for effective deterrence, an order directing payment to the movant of part or all of the reasonable attorney's fees and other expenses directly resulting from the violation.

(5) *Limitations on Monetary Sanctions.* The court must not impose a monetary sanction:

(A) against a represented party for violating Rule 11(b)(2); or

(B) on its own, unless it issued the show-cause order under Rule 11(c)(3) before voluntary dismissal or settlement of the claims made by or against the party that is, or whose attorneys are, to be sanctioned.

(6) *Requirements for an Order.* An order imposing a sanction must describe the sanctioned conduct and explain the basis for the sanction.

(d) INAPPLICABILITY TO DISCOVERY. This rule does not apply to disclosures and discovery requests, responses, objections, and motions under Rules 26 through 37.

FED. R. CIV. P. 12. Defenses and Objections: When and How Presented; Motion for Judgment on the Pleadings; Consolidating Motions; Waiving Defenses; Pretrial Hearing

(a) TIME TO SERVE A RESPONSIVE PLEADING.

(1) *In General.* Unless another time is specified by this rule or a federal statute, the time for serving a responsive pleading is as follows:

(A) A defendant must serve an answer:

(i) within 21 days after being served with the summons and complaint; or

(ii) if it has timely waived service under Rule 4(d), within 60 days after the request for a waiver was sent, or within 90 days after it was sent to the defendant outside any judicial district of the United States.

(B) A party must serve an answer to a counterclaim or crossclaim within 21 days after being served with the pleading that states the counterclaim or crossclaim.

(C) A party must serve a reply to an answer within 21 days after being served with an order to reply, unless the order specifies a different time.

(2) *United States and Its Agencies, Officers, or Employees Sued in an Official Capacity.* The United States, a United States agency, or a United States officer or employee sued only in an
official capacity must serve an answer to a complaint, counterclaim, or crossclaim within 60 days after service on the United States attorney.

(3) *United States Officers or Employees Sued in an Individual Capacity.* A United States officer or employee sued in an individual capacity for an act or omission occurring in connection with duties performed on the United States' behalf must serve an answer to a complaint, counterclaim, or crossclaim within 60 days after service on the officer or employee or service on the United States attorney, whichever is later.

(4) *Effect of a Motion.* Unless the court sets a different time, serving a motion under this rule alters these periods as follows:

(A) if the court denies the motion or postpones its disposition until trial, the responsive pleading must be served within 14 days after notice of the court's action; or

(B) if the court grants a motion for a more definite statement, the responsive pleading must be served within 14 days after the more definite statement is served.

(b) HOW TO PRESENT DEFENSES. Every defense to a claim for relief in any pleading must be asserted in the responsive pleading if one is required. But a party may assert the following defenses by motion:

(1) lack of subject-matter jurisdiction;

(2) lack of personal jurisdiction;

(3) improper venue;

(4) insufficient process;

(5) insufficient service of process;

(6) failure to state a claim upon which relief can be granted; and

(7) failure to join a party under Rule 19.

A motion asserting any of these defenses must be made before pleading if a responsive pleading is allowed. If a pleading sets out a claim for relief that does not require a responsive pleading, an opposing party may assert at trial any defense to that claim. No defense or objection is waived by joining it with one or more other defenses or objections in a responsive pleading or in a motion.

(c) MOTION FOR JUDGMENT ON THE PLEADINGS. After the pleadings are closed—but early enough not to delay trial—a party may move for judgment on the pleadings.

(d) RESULT OF PRESENTING MATTERS OUTSIDE THE PLEADINGS. If, on a motion under Rule 12(b)(6) or 12(c), matters outside the pleadings are presented to and not excluded by the court, the motion must be treated as one for summary judgment under Rule 56. All parties must be given a reasonable opportunity to present all the material that is pertinent to the motion.

(e) MOTION FOR A MORE DEFINITE STATEMENT. A party may move for a more definite statement of a pleading to which a responsive pleading is allowed but which is so vague or ambiguous that the party cannot reasonably prepare a response. The motion must be made before filing a responsive pleading and must point out the defects complained of and the details desired. If the court orders a more definite statement and the order is not obeyed within 14 days after notice of the order or within the time the court sets, the court may strike the pleading or issue any other appropriate order.

(f) MOTION TO STRIKE. The court may strike from a pleading an insufficient defense or any redundant, immaterial, impertinent, or scandalous matter. The court may act:

(1) on its own; or

(2) on motion made by a party either before responding to the pleading or, if a response is not allowed, within 21 days after being served with the pleading.

(g) JOINING MOTIONS.

(1) *Right to Join.* A motion under this rule may be joined with any other motion allowed by this rule.

(2) *Limitation on Further Motions.* Except as provided in Rule 12(h)(2) or (3), a party that makes a motion under this rule must not make another motion under this rule raising a defense or objection that was available to the party but omitted from its earlier motion.

(h) WAIVING AND PRESERVING CERTAIN DEFENSES.

(1) *When Some Are Waived.* A party waives any defense listed in Rule 12(b)(2)–(5) by:

(A) omitting it from a motion in the circumstances described in Rule 12(g)(2); or

(B) failing to either:

(i) make it by motion under this rule; or

(ii) include it in a responsive pleading or in an amendment allowed by Rule 15(a)(1) as a matter of course.

(2) *When to Raise Others.* Failure to state a claim upon which relief can be granted, to join a person required by Rule 19(b), or to state a legal defense to a claim may be raised:

(A) in any pleading allowed or ordered under Rule 7(a);

(B) by a motion under Rule 12(c); or

(C) at trial.

(3) *Lack of Subject-Matter Jurisdiction.* If the court determines at any time that it lacks subject-matter jurisdiction, the court must dismiss the action.

(i) HEARING BEFORE TRIAL. If a party so moves, any defense listed in Rule 12(b)(1)–(7)—whether made in a pleading or by motion— and a motion under Rule 12(c) must be heard and decided before trial unless the court orders a deferral until trial.

FED. R. CIV. P. 13. Counterclaim and Crossclaim

(a) COMPULSORY COUNTERCLAIM.

(1) *In General.* A pleading must state as a counterclaim any claim that—at the time of its service—the pleader has against an opposing party if the claim:

(A) arises out of the transaction or occurrence that is the subject matter of the opposing party's claim; and

(B) does not require adding another party over whom the court cannot acquire jurisdiction.

(2) *Exceptions.* The pleader need not state the claim if:

(A) when the action was commenced, the claim was the subject of another pending action; or

(B) the opposing party sued on its claim by attachment or other process that did not establish personal jurisdiction over the pleader on that claim, and the pleader does not assert any counterclaim under this rule.

(b) PERMISSIVE COUNTERCLAIM. A pleading may state as a counterclaim against an opposing party any claim that is not compulsory.

(c) RELIEF SOUGHT IN A COUNTERCLAIM. A counterclaim need not diminish or defeat the recovery sought by the opposing party. It may request relief that exceeds in amount or differs in kind from the relief sought by the opposing party.

(d) COUNTERCLAIM AGAINST THE UNITED STATES. These rules do not expand the right to assert a counterclaim—or to claim a credit— against the United States or a United States officer or agency.

(e) COUNTERCLAIM MATURING OR ACQUIRED AFTER PLEADING. The court may permit a party to file a supplemental pleading asserting a counterclaim that matured or was acquired by the party after serving an earlier pleading.

(f) [ABROGATED.]

(g) CROSSCLAIM AGAINST A COPARTY. A pleading may state as a crossclaim any claim by one party against a coparty if the claim arises out of the transaction or occurrence that is the subject matter of the original action or of a counterclaim, or if the claim relates to any property that is the subject matter of the original action. The crossclaim may include a claim that the coparty is or may be liable to the crossclaimant for all or part of a claim asserted in the action against the crossclaimant.

(h) JOINING ADDITIONAL PARTIES. Rules 19 and 20 govern the addition of a person as a party to a counterclaim or crossclaim.

(i) SEPARATE TRIALS; SEPARATE JUDGMENTS. If the court orders separate trials under Rule 42(b), it may enter judgment on a counterclaim or crossclaim under Rule 54(b) when it has jurisdiction to do so, even if the opposing party's claims have been dismissed or otherwise resolved.

FED. R. CIV. P. 14. Third-Party Practice

(a) WHEN A DEFENDING PARTY MAY BRING IN A THIRD PARTY.

(1) *Timing of the Summons and Complaint.* A defending party may, as third-party plaintiff, serve a summons and complaint on a nonparty who is or may be liable to it for all or part of the claim against it. But the third-party plaintiff must, by motion, obtain the court's leave if it files the third-party complaint more than 14 days after serving its original answer.

(2) *Third-Party Defendant's Claims and Defenses.* The person served with the summons and third-party complaint—the "third-party defendant":

(A) must assert any defense against the third-party plaintiff's claim under Rule 12;

(B) must assert any counterclaim against the third-party plaintiff under Rule 13(a), and may assert any counterclaim against the third-party plaintiff under Rule 13(b) or any crossclaim against another third-party defendant under Rule 13(g);

(C) may assert against the plaintiff any defense that the third-party plaintiff has to the plaintiff's claim; and

(D) may also assert against the plaintiff any claim arising out of the transaction or occurrence that is the subject matter of the plaintiff's claim against the third-party plaintiff.

(3) *Plaintiff's Claims Against a Third-Party Defendant.* The plaintiff may assert against the third-party defendant any claim arising out of the transaction or occurrence that is the subject matter of the plaintiff's claim against the third-party plaintiff. The third-party defendant must

then assert any defense under Rule 12 and any counterclaim under Rule 13(a), and may assert any counterclaim under Rule 13(b) or any crossclaim under Rule 13(g).

(4) *Motion to Strike, Sever, or Try Separately.* Any party may move to strike the third-party claim, to sever it, or to try it separately.

(5) *Third-Party Defendant's Claim Against a Nonparty.* A thirdparty defendant may proceed under this rule against a nonparty who is or may be liable to the third-party defendant for all or part of any claim against it.

(6) *Third-Party Complaint In Rem.* If it is within the admiralty or maritime jurisdiction, a third-party complaint may be in rem. In that event, a reference in this rule to the ''summons'' includes the warrant of arrest, and a reference to the defendant or third-party plaintiff includes, when appropriate, a person who asserts a right under Supplemental Rule C(6)(a)(i) in the property arrested.

(b) WHEN A PLAINTIFF MAY BRING IN A THIRD PARTY. When a claim is asserted against a plaintiff, the plaintiff may bring in a third party if this rule would allow a defendant to do so.

(c) ADMIRALTY OR MARITIME CLAIM.

(1) *Scope of Impleader.* If a plaintiff asserts an admiralty or maritime claim under Rule 9(h), the defendant or a person who asserts a right under Supplemental Rule C(6)(a)(i) may, as a third-party plaintiff, bring in a third-party defendant who may be wholly or partly liable—either to the plaintiff or to the third-party plaintiff—for remedy over, contribution, or otherwise on account of the same transaction, occurrence, or series of transactions or occurrences.

(2) *Defending Against a Demand for Judgment for the Plaintiff.* The third-party plaintiff may demand judgment in the plaintiff's favor against the third-party defendant. In that event, the third-party defendant must defend under Rule 12 against the plaintiff's claim as well as the third-party plaintiff's claim; and the action proceeds as if the plaintiff had sued both the third-party defendant and the third-party plaintiff.

FED. R. CIV. P. 15. Amended and Supplemental Pleadings

(a) AMENDMENTS BEFORE TRIAL.

(1) *Amending as a Matter of Course.* A party may amend its pleading once as a matter of course within:

(A) 21 days after serving it, or

(B) if the pleading is one to which a responsive pleading is required, 21 days after service of a responsive pleading or 21 days after service of a motion under Rule 12(b), (e), or (f), whichever is earlier.

(2) *Other Amendments.* In all other cases, a party may amend its pleading only with the opposing party's written consent or the court's leave. The court should freely give leave when justice so requires.

(3) *Time to Respond.* Unless the court orders otherwise, any required response to an amended pleading must be made within the time remaining to respond to the original pleading or within 14 days after service of the amended pleading, whichever is later.

(b) AMENDMENTS DURING AND AFTER TRIAL.

(1) *Based on an Objection at Trial.* If, at trial, a party objects that evidence is not within the issues raised in the pleadings, the court may permit the pleadings to be amended. The court should freely permit an amendment when doing so will aid in presenting the merits and the objecting party fails to satisfy the court that the evidence would prejudice that party's action or defense on the merits. The court may grant a continuance to enable the objecting party to meet the evidence.

(2) *For Issues Tried by Consent.* When an issue not raised by the pleadings is tried by the parties' express or implied consent, it must be treated in all respects as if raised in the pleadings. A party may move—at any time, even after judgment—to amend the pleadings to conform them to the evidence and to raise an unpleaded issue. But failure to amend does not affect the result of the trial of that issue.

(c) RELATION BACK OF AMENDMENTS.

(1) *When an Amendment Relates Back.* An amendment to a pleading relates back to the date of the original pleading when:

(A) the law that provides the applicable statute of limitations allows relation back;

(B) the amendment asserts a claim or defense that arose out of the conduct, transaction, or occurrence set out—or attempted to be set out—in the original pleading; or

(C) the amendment changes the party or the naming of the party against whom a claim is asserted, if Rule 15(c)(1)(B) is satisfied and if, within the period provided by Rule 4(m) for serving the summons and complaint, the party to be brought in by amendment:

(i) received such notice of the action that it will not be prejudiced in defending on the merits; and

(ii) knew or should have known that the action would have been brought against it, but for a mistake

concerning the proper party's identity.

(2) *Notice to the United States.* When the United States or a United States officer or agency is added as a defendant by amendment, the notice requirements of Rule 15(c)(1)(C)(i) and

(ii) are satisfied if, during the stated period, process was delivered or mailed to the United States attorney or the United States attorney's designee, to the Attorney General of the United States, or to the officer or agency.

(d) SUPPLEMENTAL PLEADINGS. On motion and reasonable notice, the court may, on just terms, permit a party to serve a supplemental pleading setting out any transaction, occurrence, or event that happened after the date of the pleading to be supplemented. The court may permit supplementation even though the original pleading is defective in stating a claim or defense. The court may order that the opposing party plead to the supplemental pleading within a specified time.

FED. R. CIV. P. 16. Pretrial Conferences; Scheduling; Management

(a) PURPOSES OF A PRETRIAL CONFERENCE. In any action, the court may order the attorneys and any unrepresented parties to appear for one or more pretrial conferences for such purposes as:

(1) expediting disposition of the action;

(2) establishing early and continuing control so that the case will not be protracted because of lack of management;

(3) discouraging wasteful pretrial activities;

(4) improving the quality of the trial through more thorough preparation; and

(5) facilitating settlement.

(b) SCHEDULING.

(1) *Scheduling Order.* Except in categories of actions exempted by local rule, the district judge—or a magistrate judge when authorized by local rule—must issue a scheduling order:

(A) after receiving the parties' report under Rule 26(f); or

(B) after consulting with the parties' attorneys and any unrepresented parties at a scheduling conference or by telephone, mail, or other means.

(2) *Time to Issue.* The judge must issue the scheduling order as soon as practicable, but in any event within the earlier of 120 days after any defendant has been served with the complaint or 90 days after any defendant has appeared.

(3) *Contents of the Order.*

(A) *Required Contents.* The scheduling order must limit the time to join other parties, amend the pleadings, complete discovery, and file motions.

(B) *Permitted Contents.* The scheduling order may:

(i) modify the timing of disclosures under Rules 26(a) and 26(e)(1);

(ii) modify the extent of discovery;

(iii) provide for disclosure or discovery of electronically stored information;

(iv) include any agreements the parties reach for asserting claims of privilege or of protection as trialpreparation material after information is produced;

(v) set dates for pretrial conferences and for trial; and

(vi) include other appropriate matters.

(4) *Modifying a Schedule.* A schedule may be modified only for good cause and with the judge's consent.

(c) ATTENDANCE AND MATTERS FOR CONSIDERATION AT A PRETRIAL CONFERENCE.

(1) *Attendance.* A represented party must authorize at least one of its attorneys to make stipulations and admissions about all matters that can reasonably be anticipated for discussion at a pretrial conference. If appropriate, the court may require that a party or its representative be present or reasonably available by other means to consider possible settlement.

(2) *Matters for Consideration.* At any pretrial conference, the court may consider and take appropriate action on the following matters:

(A) formulating and simplifying the issues, and eliminating frivolous claims or defenses;

(B) amending the pleadings if necessary or desirable;

(C) obtaining admissions and stipulations about facts and documents to avoid unnecessary proof, and ruling in advance on the admissibility of evidence;

(D) avoiding unnecessary proof and cumulative evidence, and limiting the use of testimony under Federal Rule of Evidence 702;

(E) determining the appropriateness and timing of summary adjudication under Rule 56;

(F) controlling and scheduling discovery, including orders affecting disclosures and discovery under Rule 26 and Rules 29 through 37;

(G) identifying witnesses and documents, scheduling the filing and exchange of any pretrial briefs, and setting dates for further conferences and for trial;

(H) referring matters to a magistrate judge or a master;

(I) settling the case and using special procedures to assist in resolving the dispute when authorized by statute or local rule;

(J) determining the form and content of the pretrial order;

(K) disposing of pending motions;

(L) adopting special procedures for managing potentially difficult or protracted actions that may involve complex issues, multiple parties, difficult legal questions, or unusual proof problems;

(M) ordering a separate trial under Rule 42(b) of a claim, counterclaim, crossclaim, third-party claim, or particular issue;
(N) ordering the presentation of evidence early in the trial on a manageable issue that might, on the evidence, be the basis for a judgment as a matter of law under Rule 50(a) or a judgment on partial findings under Rule 52(c);
(O) establishing a reasonable limit on the time allowed to present evidence; and
(P) facilitating in other ways the just, speedy, and inexpensive disposition of the action.
(d) PRETRIAL ORDERS. After any conference under this rule, the court should issue an order reciting the action taken. This order controls the course of the action unless the court modifies it.
(e) FINAL PRETRIAL CONFERENCE AND ORDERS. The court may hold a final pretrial conference to formulate a trial plan, including a plan to facilitate the admission of evidence. The conference must be held as close to the start of trial as is reasonable, and must be attended by at least one attorney who will conduct the trial for each party and by any unrepresented party. The court may modify the order issued after a final pretrial conference only to prevent manifest injustice.
(f) SANCTIONS.
(1) *In General.* On motion or on its own, the court may issue any just orders, including those authorized by Rule 37(b)(2)(A)(ii)–(vii), if a party or its attorney:
(A) fails to appear at a scheduling or other pretrial conference;
(B) is substantially unprepared to participate—or does not participate in good faith—in the conference; or
(C) fails to obey a scheduling or other pretrial order.
(2) *Imposing Fees and Costs.* Instead of or in addition to any other sanction, the court must order the party, its attorney, or both to pay the reasonable expenses—including attorney's fees—incurred because of any noncompliance with this rule, unless the noncompliance was substantially justified or other circumstances make an award of expenses unjust.

Fed. R. Civ. P. 17. Plaintiff and Defendant; Capacity; Public Officers
(a) REAL PARTY IN INTEREST.
(1) *Designation in General.* An action must be prosecuted in the name of the real party in interest. The following may sue in their own names without joining the person for whose benefit the action is brought:
(A) an executor;
(B) an administrator;
(C) a guardian;
(D) a bailee;
(E) a trustee of an express trust;
(F) a party with whom or in whose name a contract has been made for another's benefit; and
(G) a party authorized by statute.
(2) *Action in the Name of the United States for Another's Use or Benefit.* When a federal statute so provides, an action for another's use or benefit must be brought in the name of the United States.
(3) *Joinder of the Real Party in Interest.* The court may not dismiss an action for failure to prosecute in the name of the real party in interest until, after an objection, a reasonable time has been allowed for the real party in interest to ratify, join, or be substituted into the action. After ratification, joinder, or substitution, the action proceeds as if it had been originally commenced by the real party in interest.
(b) CAPACITY TO SUE OR BE SUED. Capacity to sue or be sued is determined as follows:
(1) for an individual who is not acting in a representative capacity, by the law of the individual's domicile;
(2) for a corporation, by the law under which it was organized; and
(3) for all other parties, by the law of the state where the court is located, except that:
(A) a partnership or other unincorporated association with no such capacity under that state's law may sue or be sued in its common name to enforce a substantive right existing under the United States Constitution or laws; and
(B) 28 U.S.C. §§754 and 959(a) govern the capacity of a receiver appointed by a United States court to sue or be sued in a United States court.
(c) MINOR OR INCOMPETENT PERSON.
(1) *With a Representative.* The following representatives may sue or defend on behalf of a minor or an incompetent person:
(A) a general guardian;
(B) a committee;
(C) a conservator; or
(D) a like fiduciary.
(2) *Without a Representative.* A minor or an incompetent person who does not have a duly appointed representative may sue by a next friend or by a guardian ad litem. The court must appoint a guardian ad litem—or issue another appropriate order—to protect a minor or incompetent person who is unrepresented in an action.
(d) PUBLIC OFFICER'S TITLE AND NAME. A public officer who sues or is sued in an official capacity may be designated by official title rather than by name, but the court may order that the officer's name be added.

Fed. R. Civ. P. 18. Joinder of Claims

(a) IN GENERAL. A party asserting a claim, counterclaim, crossclaim, or third-party claim may join, as independent or alternative claims, as many claims as it has against an opposing party.

(b) JOINDER OF CONTINGENT CLAIMS. A party may join two claims even though one of them is contingent on the disposition of the other; but the court may grant relief only in accordance with the parties' relative substantive rights. In particular, a plaintiff may state a claim for money and a claim to set aside a conveyance that is fraudulent as to that plaintiff, without first obtaining a judgment for the money.

Fed. R. Civ. P. 19. Required Joinder of Parties

(a) PERSONS REQUIRED TO BE JOINED IF FEASIBLE.

(1) *Required Party.* A person who is subject to service of process and whose joinder will not deprive the court of subjectmatter jurisdiction must be joined as a party if:

(A) in that person's absence, the court cannot accord complete relief among existing parties; or

(B) that person claims an interest relating to the subject of the action and is so situated that disposing of the action in the person's absence may:

(i) as a practical matter impair or impede the person's ability to protect the interest; or

(ii) leave an existing party subject to a substantial risk of incurring double, multiple, or otherwise inconsistent obligations because of the interest.

(2) *Joinder by Court Order.* If a person has not been joined as required, the court must order that the person be made a party. A person who refuses to join as a plaintiff may be made either a defendant or, in a proper case, an involuntary plaintiff.

(3) *Venue.* If a joined party objects to venue and the joinder would make venue improper, the court must dismiss that party.

(b) WHEN JOINDER IS NOT FEASIBLE. If a person who is required to be joined if feasible cannot be joined, the court must determine whether, in equity and good conscience, the action should proceed among the existing parties or should be dismissed. The factors for the court to consider include:

(1) the extent to which a judgment rendered in the person's absence might prejudice that person or the existing parties;

(2) the extent to which any prejudice could be lessened or avoided by:

(A) protective provisions in the judgment;

(B) shaping the relief; or

(C) other measures;

(3) whether a judgment rendered in the person's absence would be adequate; and

(4) whether the plaintiff would have an adequate remedy if the action were dismissed for nonjoinder.

(c) PLEADING THE REASONS FOR NONJOINDER. When asserting a claim for relief, a party must state:

(1) the name, if known, of any person who is required to be joined if feasible but is not joined; and

(2) the reasons for not joining that person.

(d) EXCEPTION FOR CLASS ACTIONS. This rule is subject to Rule
23.

Fed. R. Civ. P. 20. Permissive Joinder of Parties

(a) PERSONS WHO MAY JOIN OR BE JOINED.

(1) *Plaintiffs.* Persons may join in one action as plaintiffs if:

(A) they assert any right to relief jointly, severally, or in the alternative with respect to or arising out of the same transaction, occurrence, or series of transactions or occurrences; and

(B) any question of law or fact common to all plaintiffs will arise in the action.

(2) *Defendants.* Persons—as well as a vessel, cargo, or other property subject to admiralty process in rem—may be joined in one action as defendants if:

(A) any right to relief is asserted against them jointly, severally, or in the alternative with respect to or arising out of the same transaction, occurrence, or series of transactions or occurrences; and

(B) any question of law or fact common to all defendants will arise in the action.

(3) *Extent of Relief.* Neither a plaintiff nor a defendant need be interested in obtaining or defending against all the relief demanded. The court may grant judgment to one or more plaintiffs according to their rights, and against one or more defendants according to their liabilities.

(b) PROTECTIVE MEASURES. The court may issue orders—including an order for separate trials—to protect a party against embarrassment, delay, expense, or other prejudice that arises from including a person against whom the party asserts no claim and who asserts no claim against the party.

Fed. R. Civ. P. 21. Misjoinder and Nonjoinder of Parties

Misjoinder of parties is not a ground for dismissing an action. On motion or on its own, the court may at any time, on just terms, add or drop a party. The court may also sever any claim against a party.

FED. R. CIV. P. 22. Interpleader

(a) GROUNDS.

(1) *By a Plaintiff.* Persons with claims that may expose a plaintiff to double or multiple liability may be joined as defendants and required to interplead. Joinder for interpleader is proper even though:

(A) the claims of the several claimants, or the titles on which their claims depend, lack a common origin or are adverse and independent rather than identical; or

(B) the plaintiff denies liability in whole or in part to any or all of the claimants.

(2) *By a Defendant.* A defendant exposed to similar liability may seek interpleader through a crossclaim or counterclaim.

(b) RELATION TO OTHER RULES AND STATUTES. This rule supplements— and does not limit—the joinder of parties allowed by Rule 20. The remedy this rule provides is in addition to—and does not supersede or limit—the remedy provided by 28 U.S.C. §§1335, 1397, and 2361. An action under those statutes must be conducted under these rules.

FED. R. CIV. P. 23. Class Actions

(a) PREREQUISITES. One or more members of a class may sue or be sued as representative parties on behalf of all members only if:

(1) the class is so numerous that joinder of all members is impracticable;

(2) there are questions of law or fact common to the class;

(3) the claims or defenses of the representative parties are typical of the claims or defenses of the class; and

(4) the representative parties will fairly and adequately protect the interests of the class.

(b) TYPES OF CLASS ACTIONS. A class action may be maintained if Rule 23(a) is satisfied and if:

(1) prosecuting separate actions by or against individual class members would create a risk of:

(A) inconsistent or varying adjudications with respect to individual class members that would establish incompatible standards of conduct for the party opposing the class; or

(B) adjudications with respect to individual class members that, as a practical matter, would be dispositive of the interests of the other members not parties to the individual adjudications or would substantially impair or impede their ability to protect their interests;

(2) the party opposing the class has acted or refused to act on grounds that apply generally to the class, so that final injunctive relief or corresponding declaratory relief is appropriate respecting the class as a whole; or

(3) the court finds that the questions of law or fact common to class members predominate over any questions affecting only individual members, and that a class action is superior to other available methods for fairly and efficiently adjudicating the controversy. The matters pertinent to these findings include:

(A) the class members' interests in individually controlling the prosecution or defense of separate actions;

(B) the extent and nature of any litigation concerning the controversy already begun by or against class members;

(C) the desirability or undesirability of concentrating the litigation of the claims in the particular forum; and

(D) the likely difficulties in managing a class action.

(c) CERTIFICATION ORDER; NOTICE TO CLASS MEMBERS; JUDGMENT; ISSUES CLASSES; SUBCLASSES.

(1) *Certification Order.*

(A) *Time to Issue.* At an early practicable time after a person sues or is sued as a class representative, the court must determine by order whether to certify the action as a class action.

(B) *Defining the Class; Appointing Class Counsel.* An order that certifies a class action must define the class and the class claims, issues, or defenses, and must appoint class counsel under Rule 23(g).

(C) *Altering or Amending the Order.* An order that grants or denies class certification may be altered or amended before final judgment.

(2) *Notice.*

(A) *For (b)(1) or (b)(2) Classes.* For any class certified under Rule 23(b)(1) or (b)(2), the court may direct appropriate notice to the class.

(B) *For (b)(3) Classes.* For any class certified under Rule 23(b)(3), the court must direct to class members the best notice that is practicable under the circumstances, including individual notice to all members who can be identified through reasonable effort. The notice must clearly and concisely state in plain, easily understood language:

(i) the nature of the action;

(ii) the definition of the class certified;

(iii) the class claims, issues, or defenses;

(iv) that a class member may enter an appearance through an attorney if the member so desires;

(v) that the court will exclude from the class any member who requests exclusion;

(vi) the time and manner for requesting exclusion; and

(vii) the binding effect of a class judgment on members under Rule 23(c)(3).

(3) *Judgment.* Whether or not favorable to the class, the judgment in a class action must:
(A) for any class certified under Rule 23(b)(1) or (b)(2), include and describe those whom the court finds to be class members; and
(B) for any class certified under Rule 23(b)(3), include and specify or describe those to whom the Rule 23(c)(2) notice was directed, who have not requested exclusion, and whom the court finds to be class members.
(4) *Particular Issues.* When appropriate, an action may be brought or maintained as a class action with respect to particular issues.
(5) *Subclasses.* When appropriate, a class may be divided into subclasses that are each treated as a class under this rule.
(d) CONDUCTING THE ACTION.
(1) *In General.* In conducting an action under this rule, the court may issue orders that:
(A) determine the course of proceedings or prescribe measures to prevent undue repetition or complication in presenting evidence or argument;
(B) require—to protect class members and fairly conduct the action—giving appropriate notice to some or all class members of:
(i) any step in the action;
(ii) the proposed extent of the judgment; or
(iii) the members' opportunity to signify whether they consider the representation fair and adequate, to intervene and present claims or defenses, or to otherwise come into the action;
(C) impose conditions on the representative parties or on intervenors;
(D) require that the pleadings be amended to eliminate allegations about representation of absent persons and that the action proceed accordingly; or
(E) deal with similar procedural matters.
(2) *Combining and Amending Orders.* An order under Rule 23(d)(1) may be altered or amended from time to time and may be combined with an order under Rule 16.
(e) SETTLEMENT, VOLUNTARY DISMISSAL, OR COMPROMISE. The claims, issues, or defenses of a certified class may be settled, voluntarily dismissed, or compromised only with the court's approval. The following procedures apply to a proposed settlement, voluntary dismissal, or compromise:
(1) The court must direct notice in a reasonable manner to all class members who would be bound by the proposal.
(2) If the proposal would bind class members, the court may approve it only after a hearing and on finding that it is fair, reasonable, and adequate.
(3) The parties seeking approval must file a statement identifying any agreement made in connection with the proposal.
(4) If the class action was previously certified under Rule 23(b)(3), the court may refuse to approve a settlement unless it affords a new opportunity to request exclusion to individual class members who had an earlier opportunity to request exclusion but did not do so.
(5) Any class member may object to the proposal if it requires court approval under this subdivision (e); the objection may be withdrawn only with the court's approval.
(f) APPEALS. A court of appeals may permit an appeal from an order granting or denying class-action certification under this rule if a petition for permission to appeal is filed with the circuit clerk within 14 days after the order is entered. An appeal does not stay proceedings in the district court unless the district judge or the court of appeals so orders.
(g) CLASS COUNSEL.
(1) *Appointing Class Counsel.* Unless a statute provides otherwise, a court that certifies a class must appoint class counsel. In appointing class counsel, the court:
(A) must consider:
(i) the work counsel has done in identifying or investigating potential claims in the action;
(ii) counsel's experience in handling class actions, other complex litigation, and the types of claims asserted in the action;
(iii) counsel's knowledge of the applicable law; and
(iv) the resources that counsel will commit to representing the class;
(B) may consider any other matter pertinent to counsel's ability to fairly and adequately represent the interests of the class;
(C) may order potential class counsel to provide information on any subject pertinent to the appointment and to propose terms for attorney's fees and nontaxable costs;
(D) may include in the appointing order provisions about the award of attorney's fees or nontaxable costs under Rule 23(h); and
(E) may make further orders in connection with the appointment.
(2) *Standard for Appointing Class Counsel.* When one applicant seeks appointment as class counsel, the court may appoint that applicant only if the applicant is adequate under Rule 23(g)(1) and (4). If more than one adequate applicant seeks appointment, the court must appoint the applicant best able to represent the interests of the class.
(3) *Interim Counsel.* The court may designate interim counsel to act on behalf of a putative class before determining whether to certify the action as a class action.
(4) *Duty of Class Counsel.* Class counsel must fairly and adequately represent the interests of the class.

(h) ATTORNEY'S FEES AND NONTAXABLE COSTS. In a certified class action, the court may award reasonable attorney's fees and nontaxable costs that are authorized by law or by the parties' agreement. The following procedures apply:
(1) A claim for an award must be made by motion under Rule 54(d)(2), subject to the provisions of this subdivision (h), at a time the court sets. Notice of the motion must be served on all parties and, for motions by class counsel, directed to class members in a reasonable manner.
(2) A class member, or a party from whom payment is sought, may object to the motion.
(3) The court may hold a hearing and must find the facts and state its legal conclusions under Rule 52(a).
(4) The court may refer issues related to the amount of the award to a special master or a magistrate judge, as provided in Rule 54(d)(2)(D).

FED. R. CIV. P. 23.1. Derivative Actions
(a) PREREQUISITES. This rule applies when one or more shareholders or members of a corporation or an unincorporated association bring a derivative action to enforce a right that the corporation or association may properly assert but has failed to enforce. The derivative action may not be maintained if it appears that the plaintiff does not fairly and adequately represent the interests of shareholders or members who are similarly situated in enforcing the right of the corporation or association.
(b) PLEADING REQUIREMENTS. The complaint must be verified and must:
(1) allege that the plaintiff was a shareholder or member at the time of the transaction complained of, or that the plaintiff's share or membership later devolved on it by operation of law;
(2) allege that the action is not a collusive one to confer jurisdiction that the court would otherwise lack; and
(3) state with particularity:
(A) any effort by the plaintiff to obtain the desired action from the directors or comparable authority and, if necessary, from the shareholders or members; and
(B) the reasons for not obtaining the action or not making the effort.
(c) SETTLEMENT, DISMISSAL, AND COMPROMISE. A derivative action may be settled, voluntarily dismissed, or compromised only with the court's approval. Notice of a proposed settlement, voluntary dismissal, or compromise must be given to shareholders or members in the manner that the court orders.

FED. R. CIV. P. 23.2. Actions Relating to Unincorporated Associations
This rule applies to an action brought by or against the members of an unincorporated association as a class by naming certain members as representative parties. The action may be maintained only if it appears that those parties will fairly and adequately protect the interests of the association and its members. In conducting the action, the court may issue any appropriate orders corresponding with those in Rule 23(d), and the procedure for settlement, voluntary dismissal, or compromise must correspond with the procedure in Rule 23(e).

FED. R. CIV. P. 24. Intervention
(a) INTERVENTION OF RIGHT. On timely motion, the court must permit anyone to intervene who:
(1) is given an unconditional right to intervene by a federal statute; or
(2) claims an interest relating to the property or transaction that is the subject of the action, and is so situated that disposing of the action may as a practical matter impair or impede the movant's ability to protect its interest, unless existing parties adequately represent that interest.
(b) PERMISSIVE INTERVENTION.
(1) *In General.* On timely motion, the court may permit anyone to intervene who:
(A) is given a conditional right to intervene by a federal statute; or
(B) has a claim or defense that shares with the main action a common question of law or fact.
(2) *By a Government Officer or Agency.* On timely motion, the court may permit a federal or state governmental officer or agency to intervene if a party's claim or defense is based on:
(A) a statute or executive order administered by the officer or agency; or
(B) any regulation, order, requirement, or agreement issued or made under the statute or executive order.
(3) *Delay or Prejudice.* In exercising its discretion, the court must consider whether the intervention will unduly delay or prejudice the adjudication of the original parties' rights.
(c) NOTICE AND PLEADING REQUIRED. A motion to intervene must be served on the parties as provided in Rule 5. The motion must state the grounds for intervention and be accompanied by a pleading that sets out the claim or defense for which intervention is sought.

FED. R. CIV. P. 25. Substitution of Parties
(a) DEATH.
(1) *Substitution if the Claim Is Not Extinguished.* If a party dies and the claim is not extinguished, the court may order substitution of the proper party. A motion for substitution may be made by

any party or by the decedent's successor or representative. If the motion is not made within 90 days after service of a statement noting the death, the action by or against the decedent must be dismissed.

(2) *Continuation Among the Remaining Parties.* After a party's death, if the right sought to be enforced survives only to or against the remaining parties, the action does not abate, but proceeds in favor of or against the remaining parties. The death should be noted on the record.

(3) *Service.* A motion to substitute, together with a notice of hearing, must be served on the parties as provided in Rule 5 and on nonparties as provided in Rule 4. A statement noting death must be served in the same manner. Service may be made in any judicial district.

(b) INCOMPETENCY. If a party becomes incompetent, the court may, on motion, permit the action to be continued by or against the party's representative. The motion must be served as provided in Rule 25(a)(3).

(c) TRANSFER OF INTEREST. If an interest is transferred, the action may be continued by or against the original party unless the court, on motion, orders the transferee to be substituted in the action or joined with the original party. The motion must be served as provided in Rule 25(a)(3).

(d) PUBLIC OFFICERS; DEATH OR SEPARATION FROM OFFICE. An action does not abate when a public officer who is a party in an official capacity dies, resigns, or otherwise ceases to hold office while the action is pending. The officer's successor is automatically substituted as a party. Later proceedings should be in the substituted party's name, but any misnomer not affecting the parties' substantial rights must be disregarded. The court may order substitution at any time, but the absence of such an order does not affect the substitution.

FED. R. CIV. P. 26. Duty to Disclose; General Provisions Governing Discovery

(a) REQUIRED DISCLOSURES.

(1) *Initial Disclosure.*

(A) *In General.* Except as exempted by Rule 26(a)(1)(B) or as otherwise stipulated or ordered by the court, a party must, without awaiting a discovery request, provide to the other parties:

(i) the name and, if known, the address and telephone number of each individual likely to have discoverable information—along with the subjects of that information— that the disclosing party may use to support its claims or defenses, unless the use would be solely for impeachment;

(ii) a copy—or a description by category and location— of all documents, electronically stored information, and tangible things that the disclosing party has in its possession, custody, or control and may use to support its claims or defenses, unless the use would be solely for impeachment;

(iii) a computation of each category of damages claimed by the disclosing party—who must also make available for inspection and copying as under Rule 34 the documents or other evidentiary material, unless privileged or protected from disclosure, on which each computation is based, including materials bearing on the nature and extent of injuries suffered; and

(iv) for inspection and copying as under Rule 34, any insurance agreement under which an insurance business may be liable to satisfy all or part of a possible judgment in the action or to indemnify or reimburse for payments made to satisfy the judgment.

(B) *Proceedings Exempt from Initial Disclosure.* The following proceedings are exempt from initial disclosure:

(i) an action for review on an administrative record;

(ii) a forfeiture action in rem arising from a federal statute;

(iii) a petition for habeas corpus or any other proceeding to challenge a criminal conviction or sentence;

(iv) an action brought without an attorney by a person in the custody of the United States, a state, or a state subdivision;

(v) an action to enforce or quash an administrative summons or subpoena;

(vi) an action by the United States to recover benefit payments;

(vii) an action by the United States to collect on a student loan guaranteed by the United States;

(viii) a proceeding ancillary to a proceeding in another court; and

(ix) an action to enforce an arbitration award.

(C) *Time for Initial Disclosures—In General.* A party must make the initial disclosures at or within 14 days after the parties' Rule 26(f) conference unless a different time is set by stipulation or court order, or unless a party objects during the conference that initial disclosures are not appropriate in this action and states the objection in the proposed discovery plan. In ruling on the objection, the court must determine what disclosures, if any, are to be made and must set the time for disclosure.

(D) *Time for Initial Disclosures—For Parties Served or Joined Later.* A party that is first served or otherwise joined after the Rule 26(f) conference must make the initial disclosures within 30 days after being served or joined, unless a different time is set by stipulation or court order.

(E) *Basis for Initial Disclosure; Unacceptable Excuses.* A party must make its initial disclosures based on the information then reasonably available to it. A party is not excused from making its disclosures because it has not fully investigated the case or because it challenges the sufficiency of another party's disclosures or because another party has not made its disclosures.

(2) *Disclosure of Expert Testimony.*

(A) *In General.* In addition to the disclosures required by Rule 26(a)(1), a party must disclose to the other parties the identity of any witness it may use at trial to present evidence under Federal Rule of Evidence 702, 703, or 705.

(B) *Written Report.* Unless otherwise stipulated or ordered by the court, this disclosure must be accompanied by a written report—prepared and signed by the witness—if the witness is one retained or specially employed to provide expert testimony in the case or one whose duties as the party's employee regularly involve giving expert testimony. The report must contain:

(i) a complete statement of all opinions the witness will express and the basis and reasons for them;

(ii) the data or other information considered by the witness in forming them;

(iii) any exhibits that will be used to summarize or support them;

(iv) the witness's qualifications, including a list of all publications authored in the previous 10 years;

(v) a list of all other cases in which, during the previous 4 years, the witness testified as an expert at trial or by deposition; and

(vi) a statement of the compensation to be paid for the study and testimony in the case.

(C) *Time to Disclose Expert Testimony.* A party must make these disclosures at the times and in the sequence that the court orders. Absent a stipulation or a court order, the disclosures must be made:

(i) at least 90 days before the date set for trial or for the case to be ready for trial; or

(ii) if the evidence is intended solely to contradict or rebut evidence on the same subject matter identified by another party under Rule 26(a)(2)(B), within 30 days after the other party's disclosure.

(D) *Supplementing the Disclosure.* The parties must supplement these disclosures when required under Rule 26(e).

(3) *Pretrial Disclosures.*

(A) *In General.* In addition to the disclosures required by Rule 26(a)(1) and (2), a party must provide to the other parties and promptly file the following information about the evidence that it may present at trial other than solely for impeachment:

(i) the name and, if not previously provided, the address and telephone number of each witness—separately identifying those the party expects to present and those it may call if the need arises;

(ii) the designation of those witnesses whose testimony the party expects to present by deposition and, if not taken stenographically, a transcript of the pertinent parts of the deposition; and

(iii) an identification of each document or other exhibit, including summaries of other evidence—separately identifying those items the party expects to offer and those it may offer if the need arises.

(B) *Time for Pretrial Disclosures; Objections.* Unless the court orders otherwise, these disclosures must be made at least 30 days before trial. Within 14 days after they are made, unless the court sets a different time, a party may serve and promptly file a list of the following objections: any objections to the use under Rule 32(a) of a deposition designated by another party under Rule 26(a)(3)(A)(ii); and any objection, together with the grounds for it, that may be made to the admissibility of materials identified under Rule 26(a)(3)(A)(iii). An objection not so made—except for one under Federal Rule of Evidence 402 or 403—is waived unless excused by the court for good cause.

(4) *Form of Disclosures.* Unless the court orders otherwise, all disclosures under Rule 26(a) must be in writing, signed, and served.

(b) DISCOVERY SCOPE AND LIMITS.

(1) *Scope in General.* Unless otherwise limited by court order, the scope of discovery is as follows: Parties may obtain discovery regarding any nonprivileged matter that is relevant to any party's claim or defense—including the existence, description, nature, custody, condition, and location of any documents or other tangible things and the identity and location of persons who know of any discoverable matter. For good cause, the court may order discovery of any matter relevant to the subject matter involved in the action. Relevant information need not be admissible at the trial if the discovery appears reasonably calculated to lead to the discovery of admissible evidence. All discovery is subject to the limitations imposed by Rule 26(b)(2)(C).

(2) *Limitations on Frequency and Extent.*

(A) *When Permitted.* By order, the court may alter the limits in these rules on the number of depositions and interrogatories or on the length of depositions under Rule 30. By order or local rule, the court may also limit the number of requests under Rule 36.

(B) *Specific Limitations on Electronically Stored Information.* A party need not provide discovery of electronically stored information from sources that the party identifies as not reasonably accessible because of undue burden or cost. On motion to compel discovery or for a protective order, the party from whom discovery is sought must show that the information is not reasonably accessible because of undue burden or cost. If that showing is made, the court may nonetheless order discovery from such sources if the requesting party shows good cause, considering the limitations of Rule 26(b)(2)(C). The court may specify conditions for the discovery.

(C) *When Required.* On motion or on its own, the court must limit the frequency or extent of discovery otherwise allowed by these rules or by local rule if it determines that:

(i) the discovery sought is unreasonably cumulative or duplicative, or can be obtained from some other source that is more convenient, less burdensome, or less expensive;

(ii) the party seeking discovery has had ample opportunity to obtain the information by discovery in the action; or

(iii) the burden or expense of the proposed discovery outweighs its likely benefit, considering the needs of the case, the amount in controversy, the parties' resources, the importance of the issues at stake in the action, and the importance of the discovery in resolving the issues.

(3) *Trial Preparation: Materials.*

(A) *Documents and Tangible Things.* Ordinarily, a party may not discover documents and tangible things that are prepared in anticipation of litigation or for trial by or for another party or its representative (including the other party's attorney, consultant, surety, indemnitor, insurer, or agent). But, subject to Rule 26(b)(4), those materials may be discovered if:

(i) they are otherwise discoverable under Rule 26(b)(1); and

(ii) the party shows that it has substantial need for the materials to prepare its case and cannot, without undue hardship, obtain their substantial equivalent by other means.

(B) *Protection Against Disclosure.* If the court orders discovery of those materials, it must protect against disclosure of the mental impressions, conclusions, opinions, or legal theories of a party's attorney or other representative concerning the litigation.

(C) *Previous Statement.* Any party or other person may, on request and without the required showing, obtain the person's own previous statement about the action or its subject matter. If the request is refused, the person may move for a court order, and Rule 37(a)(5) applies to the award of expenses. A previous statement is either:

(i) a written statement that the person has signed or otherwise adopted or approved; or

(ii) a contemporaneous stenographic, mechanical, electrical, or other recording—or a transcription of it—that recites substantially verbatim the person's oral statement.

(4) *Trial Preparation: Experts.*

(A) *Expert Who May Testify.* A party may depose any person who has been identified as an expert whose opinions may be presented at trial. If Rule 26(a)(2)(B) requires a report from the expert, the deposition may be conducted only after the report is provided.

(B) *Expert Employed Only for Trial Preparation.* Ordinarily, a party may not, by interrogatories or deposition, discover facts known or opinions held by an expert who has been retained or specially employed by another party in anticipation of litigation or to prepare for trial and who is not expected to be called as a witness at trial. But a party may do so only:

(i) as provided in Rule 35(b); or

(ii) on showing exceptional circumstances under which it is impracticable for the party to obtain facts or opinions on the same subject by other means.

(C) *Payment.* Unless manifest injustice would result, the court must require that the party seeking discovery:

(i) pay the expert a reasonable fee for time spent in responding to discovery under Rule 26(b)(4)(A) or (B); and

(ii) for discovery under (B), also pay the other party a fair portion of the fees and expenses it reasonably incurred in obtaining the expert's facts and opinions.

(5) *Claiming Privilege or Protecting Trial-Preparation Materials.*

(A) *Information Withheld.* When a party withholds information otherwise discoverable by claiming that the information is privileged or subject to protection as trial-preparation material, the party must:

(i) expressly make the claim; and

(ii) describe the nature of the documents, communications, or tangible things not produced or disclosed— and do so in a manner that, without revealing information itself privileged or protected, will enable other parties to assess the claim.

(B) *Information Produced.* If information produced in discovery is subject to a claim of privilege or of protection as trial-preparation material, the party making the claim may notify any party that received the information of the claim and the basis for it. After being notified, a party must promptly return, sequester, or destroy the specified information and any copies it has; must not use or disclose the information until the claim is resolved; must take reasonable steps to retrieve the information if the party disclosed it before being notified; and may promptly present the information to the court under seal for a determination of the claim. The producing party must preserve the information until the claim is resolved.

(c) PROTECTIVE ORDERS.

(1) *In General.* A party or any person from whom discovery is sought may move for a protective order in the court where the action is pending—or as an alternative on matters relating to a deposition, in the court for the district where the deposition will be taken. The motion must include a certification that the movant has in good faith conferred or attempted to confer with other affected parties in an effort to resolve the dispute without court action. The court may, for good cause, issue an order to protect a party or person from annoyance, embarrassment, oppression, or undue burden or expense, including one or more of the following:

(A) forbidding the disclosure or discovery;

(B) specifying terms, including time and place, for the disclosure or discovery;

(C) prescribing a discovery method other than the one selected by the party seeking discovery;

(D) forbidding inquiry into certain matters, or limiting the scope of disclosure or discovery to certain matters;

(E) designating the persons who may be present while the discovery is conducted;

(F) requiring that a deposition be sealed and opened only on court order;

(G) requiring that a trade secret or other confidential research, development, or commercial information not be revealed or be revealed only in a specified way; and

(H) requiring that the parties simultaneously file specified documents or information in sealed envelopes, to be opened as the court directs.

(2) *Ordering Discovery.* If a motion for a protective order is wholly or partly denied, the court may, on just terms, order that any party or person provide or permit discovery.

(3) *Awarding Expenses.* Rule 37(a)(5) applies to the award of expenses.

(d) TIMING AND SEQUENCE OF DISCOVERY.

(1) *Timing.* A party may not seek discovery from any source before the parties have conferred as required by Rule 26(f), except in a proceeding exempted from initial disclosure under Rule 26(a)(1)(B), or when authorized by these rules, by stipulation, or by court order.

(2) *Sequence.* Unless, on motion, the court orders otherwise for the parties' and witnesses' convenience and in the interests of justice:

(A) methods of discovery may be used in any sequence; and

(B) discovery by one party does not require any other party to delay its discovery.

(e) SUPPLEMENTING DISCLOSURES AND RESPONSES.

(1) *In General.* A party who has made a disclosure under Rule 26(a)—or who has responded to an interrogatory, request for production, or request for admission—must supplement or correct its disclosure or response:

(A) in a timely manner if the party learns that in some material respect the disclosure or response is incomplete or incorrect, and if the additional or corrective information has not otherwise been made known to the other parties during the discovery process or in writing; or

(B) as ordered by the court.

(2) *Expert Witness.* For an expert whose report must be disclosed under Rule 26(a)(2)(B), the party's duty to supplement extends both to information included in the report and to information given during the expert's deposition. Any additions or changes to this information must be disclosed by the time the party's pretrial disclosures under Rule 26(a)(3) are due.

(f) CONFERENCE OF THE PARTIES; PLANNING FOR DISCOVERY.

(1) *Conference Timing.* Except in a proceeding exempted from initial disclosure under Rule 26(a)(1)(B) or when the court orders otherwise, the parties must confer as soon as practicable—and in any event at least 21 days before a scheduling conference is to be held or a scheduling order is due under Rule 16(b).

(2) *Conference Content; Parties' Responsibilities.* In conferring, the parties must consider the nature and basis of their claims and defenses and the possibilities for promptly settling or resolving the case; make or arrange for the disclosures required by Rule 26(a)(1); discuss any issues about preserving discoverable information; and develop a proposed discovery plan. The attorneys of record and all unrepresented parties that have appeared in the case are jointly responsible for arranging the conference, for attempting in good faith to agree on the proposed discovery plan, and for submitting to the court within 14 days after the conference a written report outlining the plan. The court may order the parties or attorneys to attend the conference in person.

(3) *Discovery Plan.* A discovery plan must state the parties' views and proposals on:

(A) what changes should be made in the timing, form, or requirement for disclosures under Rule 26(a), including a statement of when initial disclosures were made or will be made;

(B) the subjects on which discovery may be needed, when discovery should be completed, and whether discovery should be conducted in phases or be limited to or focused on particular issues;

(C) any issues about disclosure or discovery of electronically stored information, including the form or forms in which it should be produced;
(D) any issues about claims of privilege or of protection as trial-preparation materials, including—if the parties agree on a procedure to assert these claims after production— whether to ask the court to include their agreement in an order;
(E) what changes should be made in the limitations on discovery imposed under these rules or by local rule, and what other limitations should be imposed; and
(F) any other orders that the court should issue under Rule 26(c) or under Rule 16(b) and (c).
(4) *Expedited Schedule.* If necessary to comply with its expedited schedule for Rule 16(b) conferences, a court may by local rule:
(A) require the parties' conference to occur less than 21 days before the scheduling conference is held or a scheduling order is due under Rule 16(b); and
(B) require the written report outlining the discovery plan to be filed less than 14 days after the parties' conference, or excuse the parties from submitting a written report and permit them to report orally on their discovery plan at the Rule 16(b) conference.
(g) SIGNING DISCLOSURES AND DISCOVERY REQUESTS, RESPONSES, AND OBJECTIONS.
(1) *Signature Required; Effect of Signature.* Every disclosure under Rule 26(a)(1) or (a)(3) and every discovery request, response, or objection must be signed by at least one attorney of record in the attorney's own name—or by the party personally, if unrepresented—and must state the signer's address, email address, and telephone number. By signing, an attorney or party certifies that to the best of the person's knowledge, information, and belief formed after a reasonable inquiry:
(A) with respect to a disclosure, it is complete and correct as of the time it is made; and
(B) with respect to a discovery request, response, or objection, it is:
(i) consistent with these rules and warranted by existing law or by a nonfrivolous argument for extending, modifying, or reversing existing law, or for establishing new law;
(ii) not interposed for any improper purpose, such as to harass, cause unnecessary delay, or needlessly increase the cost of litigation; and
(iii) neither unreasonable nor unduly burdensome or expensive, considering the needs of the case, prior discovery in the case, the amount in controversy, and the importance of the issues at stake in the action.
(2) *Failure to Sign.* Other parties have no duty to act on an unsigned disclosure, request, response, or objection until it is signed, and the court must strike it unless a signature is promptly supplied after the omission is called to the attorney's or party's attention.
(3) *Sanction for Improper Certification.* If a certification violates this rule without substantial justification, the court, on motion or on its own, must impose an appropriate sanction on the signer, the party on whose behalf the signer was acting, or both. The sanction may include an order to pay the reasonable expenses, including attorney's fees, caused by the violation.

FED. R. CIV. P. 27. Depositions to Perpetuate Testimony

(a) BEFORE AN ACTION IS FILED.
(1) *Petition.* A person who wants to perpetuate testimony about any matter cognizable in a United States court may file a verified petition in the district court for the district where any expected adverse party resides. The petition must ask for an order authorizing the petitioner to depose the named persons in order to perpetuate their testimony. The petition must be titled in the petitioner's name and must show:
(A) that the petitioner expects to be a party to an action cognizable in a United States court but cannot presently bring it or cause it to be brought;
(B) the subject matter of the expected action and the petitioner's interest;
(C) the facts that the petitioner wants to establish by the proposed testimony and the reasons to perpetuate it;
(D) the names or a description of the persons whom the petitioner expects to be adverse parties and their addresses, so far as known; and
(E) the name, address, and expected substance of the testimony of each deponent.
(2) *Notice and Service.* At least 21 days before the hearing date, the petitioner must serve each expected adverse party with a copy of the petition and a notice stating the time and place of the hearing. The notice may be served either inside or outside the district or state in the manner provided in Rule 4. If that service cannot be made with reasonable diligence on an expected adverse party, the court may order service by publication or otherwise. The court must appoint an attorney to represent persons not served in the manner provided in Rule 4 and to cross-examine the deponent if an unserved person is not otherwise represented. If any expected adverse party is a minor or is incompetent, Rule 17(c) applies.
(3) *Order and Examination.* If satisfied that perpetuating the testimony may prevent a failure or delay of justice, the court must issue an order that designates or describes the persons whose depositions may be taken, specifies the subject

matter of the examinations, and states whether the depositions will be taken orally or by written interrogatories. The depositions may then be taken under these rules, and the court may issue orders like those authorized by Rules 34 and 35. A reference in these rules to the court where an action is pending means, for purposes of this rule, the court where the petition for the deposition was filed.

(4) *Using the Deposition.* A deposition to perpetuate testimony may be used under Rule 32(a) in any later-filed districtcourt action involving the same subject matter if the deposition either was taken under these rules or, although not so taken, would be admissible in evidence in the courts of the state where it was taken.

(b) PENDING APPEAL.

(1) *In General.* The court where a judgment has been rendered may, if an appeal has been taken or may still be taken, permit a party to depose witnesses to perpetuate their testimony for use in the event of further proceedings in that court.

(2) *Motion.* The party who wants to perpetuate testimony may move for leave to take the depositions, on the same notice and service as if the action were pending in the district court. The motion must show:

(A) the name, address, and expected substance of the testimony of each deponent; and

(B) the reasons for perpetuating the testimony.

(3) *Court Order.* If the court finds that perpetuating the testimony may prevent a failure or delay of justice, the court may permit the depositions to be taken and may issue orders like those authorized by Rules 34 and 35. The depositions may be taken and used as any other deposition taken in a pending district- court action.

(c) PERPETUATION BY AN ACTION. This rule does not limit a court's power to entertain an action to perpetuate testimony.

FED. R. CIV. P. 28. Persons Before Whom Depositions May Be Taken

(a) WITHIN THE UNITED STATES.

(1) *In General.* Within the United States or a territory or insular possession subject to United States jurisdiction, a deposition must be taken before:

(A) an officer authorized to administer oaths either by federal law or by the law in the place of examination; or

(B) a person appointed by the court where the action is pending to administer oaths and take testimony.

(2) *Definition of "Officer."* The term "officer" in Rules 30, 31, and 32 includes a person appointed by the court under this rule or designated by the parties under Rule 29(a).

(b) IN A FOREIGN COUNTRY.

(1) *In General.* A deposition may be taken in a foreign country:

(A) under an applicable treaty or convention;

(B) under a letter of request, whether or not captioned a "letter rogatory";

(C) on notice, before a person authorized to administer oaths either by federal law or by the law in the place of examination; or

(D) before a person commissioned by the court to administer any necessary oath and take testimony.

(2) *Issuing a Letter of Request or a Commission.* A letter of request, a commission, or both may be issued:

(A) on appropriate terms after an application and notice of it; and

(B) without a showing that taking the deposition in another manner is impracticable or inconvenient.

(3) *Form of a Request, Notice, or Commission.* When a letter of request or any other device is used according to a treaty or convention, it must be captioned in the form prescribed by that treaty or convention. A letter of request may be addressed "To the Appropriate Authority in [name of country]."

A deposition notice or a commission must designate by name or descriptive title the person before whom the deposition is to be taken.

(4) *Letter of Request—Admitting Evidence.* Evidence obtained in response to a letter of request need not be excluded merely because it is not a verbatim transcript, because the testimony was not taken under oath, or because of any similar departure from the requirements for depositions taken within the United States.

(c) DISQUALIFICATION. A deposition must not be taken before a person who is any party's relative, employee, or attorney; who is related to or employed by any party's attorney; or who is financially interested in the action.

FED. R. CIV. P. 29. Stipulations About Discovery Procedure

Unless the court orders otherwise, the parties may stipulate that:

(a) a deposition may be taken before any person, at any time or place, on any notice, and in the manner specified—in which event it may be used in the same way as any other deposition; and

(b) other procedures governing or limiting discovery be modified— but a stipulation extending the time for any form of discovery must have court approval if it would interfere with the time set for completing discovery, for hearing a motion, or for trial.

FED. R. CIV. P. 30. Depositions by Oral Examination

(a) WHEN A DEPOSITION MAY BE TAKEN.

(1) *Without Leave.* A party may, by oral questions, depose any person, including a party, without leave of court except as provided in Rule 30(a)(2). The deponent's attendance may be compelled by subpoena under Rule 45.

(2) *With Leave.* A party must obtain leave of court, and the court must grant leave to the extent consistent with Rule 26(b)(2):

(A) if the parties have not stipulated to the deposition and:

(i) the deposition would result in more than 10 depositions being taken under this rule or Rule 31 by the plaintiffs, or by the defendants, or by the third-party defendants;

(ii) the deponent has already been deposed in the case; or

(iii) the party seeks to take the deposition before the time specified in Rule 26(d), unless the party certifies in the notice, with supporting facts, that the deponent is expected to leave the United States and be unavailable for examination in this country after that time; or

(B) if the deponent is confined in prison.

(b) NOTICE OF THE DEPOSITION; OTHER FORMAL REQUIREMENTS.

(1) *Notice in General.* A party who wants to depose a person by oral questions must give reasonable written notice to every other party. The notice must state the time and place of the deposition and, if known, the deponent's name and address. If the name is unknown, the notice must provide a general description sufficient to identify the person or the particular class or group to which the person belongs.

(2) *Producing Documents.* If a subpoena duces tecum is to be served on the deponent, the materials designated for production, as set out in the subpoena, must be listed in the notice or in an attachment. The notice to a party deponent may be accompanied by a request under Rule 34 to produce documents
and tangible things at the deposition.

(3) *Method of Recording.*

(A) *Method Stated in the Notice.* The party who notices the deposition must state in the notice the method for recording the testimony. Unless the court orders otherwise, testimony may be recorded by audio, audiovisual, or stenographic means. The noticing party bears the recording costs. Any party may arrange to transcribe a deposition.

(B) *Additional Method.* With prior notice to the deponent and other parties, any party may designate another method for recording the testimony in addition to that specified in the original notice. That party bears the expense of the additional record or transcript unless the court orders otherwise.

(4) *By Remote Means.* The parties may stipulate—or the court may on motion order—that a deposition be taken by telephone or other remote means. For the purpose of this rule and Rules
28(a), 37(a)(2), and 37(b)(1), the deposition takes place where the deponent answers the questions.

(5) *Officer's Duties.*

(A) *Before the Deposition.* Unless the parties stipulate otherwise, a deposition must be conducted before an officer appointed or designated under Rule 28. The officer must begin the deposition with an on-the-record statement that includes:

(i) the officer's name and business address;

(ii) the date, time, and place of the deposition;

(iii) the deponent's name;

(iv) the officer's administration of the oath or affirmation to the deponent; and

(v) the identity of all persons present.

(B) *Conducting the Deposition; Avoiding Distortion.* If the deposition is recorded nonstenographically, the officer must repeat the items in Rule 30(b)(5)(A)(i)–(iii) at the beginning of each unit of the recording medium. The deponent's and attorneys' appearance or demeanor must not be distorted through recording techniques.

(C) *After the Deposition.* At the end of a deposition, the officer must state on the record that the deposition is complete and must set out any stipulations made by the attorneys about custody of the transcript or recording and of the exhibits, or about any other pertinent matters.

(6) *Notice or Subpoena Directed to an Organization.* In its notice or subpoena, a party may name as the deponent a public or private corporation, a partnership, an association, a governmental agency, or other entity and must describe with reasonable particularity the matters for examination. The named organization must then designate one or more officers, directors, or managing agents, or designate other persons who consent to testify on its behalf; and it may set out the matters on which each person designated will testify. A subpoena must advise a nonparty organization of its duty to make this designation. The persons designated must testify about information known or reasonably available to the organization. This paragraph (6) does not preclude a deposition by any other procedure allowed by these rules.

(c) EXAMINATION AND CROSS-EXAMINATION; RECORD OF THE EXAMINATION; OBJECTIONS; WRITTEN QUESTIONS.

(1) *Examination and Cross-Examination.* The examination and cross-examination of a deponent proceed as they would at trial under the Federal Rules of Evidence, except Rules 103 and 615. After putting the deponent under oath or affirmation, the officer must record the testimony by the method designated under Rule 30(b)(3)(A). The testimony must be recorded by theofficer personally or by a person acting in the presence and under the direction of the officer.

(2) *Objections.* An objection at the time of the examination— whether to evidence, to a party's conduct, to the officer's qualifications, to the manner of taking the deposition, or to any other aspect of the deposition—must be noted on the record, but the examination still proceeds; the testimony is taken subject to any objection. An objection must be stated concisely in a nonargumentative and nonsuggestive manner. A person may instruct a deponent not to answer only when necessary to preserve a privilege, to enforce a limitation ordered by the court, or to present a motion under Rule 30(d)(3).

(3) *Participating Through Written Questions.* Instead of participating in the oral examination, a party may serve written questions in a sealed envelope on the party noticing the deposition, who must deliver them to the officer. The officer must ask the deponent those questions and record the answers verbatim.

(d) DURATION; SANCTION; MOTION TO TERMINATE OR LIMIT.

(1) *Duration.* Unless otherwise stipulated or ordered by the court, a deposition is limited to 1 day of 7 hours. The court must allow additional time consistent with Rule 26(b)(2) if needed to fairly examine the deponent or if the deponent, another person, or any other circumstance impedes or delays the examination.

(2) *Sanction.* The court may impose an appropriate sanction— including the reasonable expenses and attorney's fees incurred by any party—on a person who impedes, delays, or frustrates the fair examination of the deponent.

(3) *Motion to Terminate or Limit.*

(A) *Grounds.* At any time during a deposition, the deponent or a party may move to terminate or limit it on the ground that it is being conducted in bad faith or in a manner that unreasonably annoys, embarrasses, or oppresses the deponent or party. The motion may be filed in the court where the action is pending or the deposition is being taken. If the objecting deponent or party so demands, the deposition must be suspended for the time necessary to obtain an order.

(B) *Order.* The court may order that the deposition be terminated or may limit its scope and manner as provided in Rule 26(c). If terminated, the deposition may be resumed only by order of the court where the action is pending.

(C) *Award of Expenses.* Rule 37(a)(5) applies to the award of expenses.

(e) REVIEW BY THE WITNESS; CHANGES.

(1) *Review; Statement of Changes.* On request by the deponent or a party before the deposition is completed, the deponent must be allowed 30 days after being notified by the officer that the transcript or recording is available in which:

(A) to review the transcript or recording; and

(B) if there are changes in form or substance, to sign a statement listing the changes and the reasons for making them.

(2) *Changes Indicated in the Officer's Certificate.* The officer must note in the certificate prescribed by Rule 30(f)(1) whether a review was requested and, if so, must attach any changes the deponent makes during the 30-day period.

(f) CERTIFICATION AND DELIVERY; EXHIBITS; COPIES OF THE TRANSCRIPT OR RECORDING; FILING.

(1) *Certification and Delivery.* The officer must certify in writing that the witness was duly sworn and that the deposition accurately records the witness's testimony. The certificate must accompany the record of the deposition. Unless the court orders otherwise, the officer must seal the deposition in an envelope or package bearing the title of the action and marked "Deposition of [witness's name]" and must promptly send it to the attorney who arranged for the transcript or recording. The attorney must store it under conditions that will protect it against loss, destruction, tampering, or deterioration.

(2) *Documents and Tangible Things.*

(A) *Originals and Copies.* Documents and tangible things produced for inspection during a deposition must, on a party's request, be marked for identification and attached to the deposition. Any party may inspect and copy them. But if the person who produced them wants to keep the originals, the person may:

(i) offer copies to be marked, attached to the deposition, and then used as originals—after giving all parties a fair opportunity to verify the copies by comparing them with the originals; or

(ii) give all parties a fair opportunity to inspect and copy the originals after they are marked—in which event the originals may be used as if attached to the deposition.

(B) *Order Regarding the Originals.* Any party may move for an order that the originals be attached to the deposition pending final disposition of the case.

(3) *Copies of the Transcript or Recording.* Unless otherwise stipulated or ordered by the court, the officer must retain the stenographic notes of a deposition taken stenographically or a copy of the recording of a deposition taken by another method. When paid reasonable charges,

the officer must furnish a copy of the transcript or recording to any party or the deponent.
(4) *Notice of Filing.* A party who files the deposition must promptly notify all other parties of the filing.
(g) FAILURE TO ATTEND A DEPOSITION OR SERVE A SUBPOENA; EXPENSES. A party who, expecting a deposition to be taken, attends in person or by an attorney may recover reasonable expenses for attending, including attorney's fees, if the noticing party failed to:
(1) attend and proceed with the deposition; or
(2) serve a subpoena on a nonparty deponent, who consequently did not attend.

FED. R. CIV. P. 31. Depositions by Written Questions
(a) WHEN A DEPOSITION MAY BE TAKEN.
(1) *Without Leave.* A party may, by written questions, depose any person, including a party, without leave of court except as provided in Rule 31(a)(2). The deponent's attendance may be compelled by subpoena under Rule 45.
(2) *With Leave.* A party must obtain leave of court, and the court must grant leave to the extent consistent with Rule 26(b)(2):
(A) if the parties have not stipulated to the deposition and:
(i) the deposition would result in more than 10 depositions being taken under this rule or Rule 30 by the plaintiffs, or by the defendants, or by the third-party defendants;
(ii) the deponent has already been deposed in the case; or
(iii) the party seeks to take a deposition before the time specified in Rule 26(d); or
(B) if the deponent is confined in prison.
(3) *Service; Required Notice.* A party who wants to depose a person by written questions must serve them on every other party, with a notice stating, if known, the deponent's name and address. If the name is unknown, the notice must provide a general description sufficient to identify the person or the particular class or group to which the person belongs. The notice must also state the name or descriptive title and the address of the officer before whom the deposition will be taken.
(4) *Questions Directed to an Organization.* A public or private corporation, a partnership, an association, or a governmental agency may be deposed by written questions in accordance with Rule 30(b)(6).
(5) *Questions from Other Parties.* Any questions to the deponent from other parties must be served on all parties as follows: cross-questions, within 14 days after being served with the notice and direct questions; redirect questions, within 7 days after being served with cross-questions; and recross-questions, within 7 days after being served with redirect questions. The court may, for good cause, extend or shorten these times.
(b) DELIVERY TO THE OFFICER; OFFICER'S DUTIES. The party who noticed the deposition must deliver to the officer a copy of all the questions served and of the notice. The officer must promptly proceed in the manner provided in Rule 30(c), (e), and (f) to:
(1) take the deponent's testimony in response to the questions;
(2) prepare and certify the deposition; and
(3) send it to the party, attaching a copy of the questions and of the notice.
(c) NOTICE OF COMPLETION OR FILING.
(1) *Completion.* The party who noticed the deposition must notify all other parties when it is completed.
(2) *Filing.* A party who files the deposition must promptly notify all other parties of the filing.

FED. R. CIV. P. 32. Using Depositions in Court Proceedings
(a) USING DEPOSITIONS.
(1) *In General.* At a hearing or trial, all or part of a deposition may be used against a party on these conditions:
(A) the party was present or represented at the taking of the deposition or had reasonable notice of it;
(B) it is used to the extent it would be admissible under the Federal Rules of Evidence if the deponent were present and testifying; and
(C) the use is allowed by Rule 32(a)(2) through (8).
(2) *Impeachment and Other Uses.* Any party may use a deposition to contradict or impeach the testimony given by the deponent as a witness, or for any other purpose allowed by the Federal Rules of Evidence. (3) *Deposition of Party, Agent, or Designee.* An adverse party may use for any purpose the deposition of a party or anyone who, when deposed, was the party's officer, director, managing agent, or designee under Rule 30(b)(6) or 31(a)(4).
(4) *Unavailable Witness.* A party may use for any purpose the deposition of a witness, whether or not a party, if the court finds:
(A) that the witness is dead;
(B) that the witness is more than 100 miles from the place of hearing or trial or is outside the United States, unless it appears that the witness's absence was procured by the party offering the deposition;
(C) that the witness cannot attend or testify because of age, illness, infirmity, or imprisonment;
(D) that the party offering the deposition could not procure the witness's attendance by subpoena; or

(E) on motion and notice, that exceptional circumstance make it desirable—in the interest of justice and
with due regard to the importance of live testimony in open court—to permit the deposition to be used.
(5) *Limitations on Use.*
(A) *Deposition Taken on Short Notice.* A deposition must not be used against a party who, having received less than 14 days' notice of the deposition, promptly moved for a protective order under Rule 26(c)(1)(B) requesting that it not be taken or be taken at a different time or place—and this motion was still pending when the deposition was taken.
(B) *Unavailable Deponent; Party Could Not Obtain an Attorney.* A deposition taken without leave of court under the unavailability provision of Rule 30(a)(2)(A)(iii) must not be used against a party who shows that, when served with the notice, it could not, despite diligent efforts, obtain an attorney to represent it at the deposition.
(6) *Using Part of a Deposition.* If a party offers in evidence only part of a deposition, an adverse party may require the offeror to introduce other parts that in fairness should be considered with the part introduced, and any party may itself introduce any other parts.
(7) *Substituting a Party.* Substituting a party under Rule 25 does not affect the right to use a deposition previously taken.
(8) *Deposition Taken in an Earlier Action.* A deposition lawfully taken and, if required, filed in any federal- or state-court action may be used in a later action involving the same subject matter between the same parties, or their representatives or successors in interest, to the same extent as if taken in the later action. A deposition previously taken may also be used as allowed by the Federal Rules of Evidence.
(b) OBJECTIONS TO ADMISSIBILITY. Subject to Rules 28(b) and 32(d)(3), an objection may be made at a hearing or trial to the admission of any deposition testimony that would be inadmissible if the witness were present and testifying.
(c) FORM OF PRESENTATION. Unless the court orders otherwise, a party must provide a transcript of any deposition testimony the party offers, but may provide the court with the testimony in nontranscript form as well. On any party's request, deposition testimony offered in a jury trial for any purpose other than impeachment must be presented in nontranscript form, if available, unless the court for good cause orders otherwise.
(d) WAIVER OF OBJECTIONS.
(1) *To the Notice.* An objection to an error or irregularity in a deposition notice is waived unless promptly served in writing on the party giving the notice.
(2) *To the Officer's Qualification.* An objection based on disqualification of the officer before whom a deposition is to be taken is waived if not made:
(A) before the deposition begins; or
(B) promptly after the basis for disqualification becomes known or, with reasonable diligence, could have been known.
(3) *To the Taking of the Deposition.*
(A) *Objection to Competence, Relevance, or Materiality.* An objection to a deponent's competence—or to the competence, relevance, or materiality of testimony—is not waived by a failure to make the objection before or during the deposition, unless the ground for it might have been corrected at that time.
(B) *Objection to an Error or Irregularity.* An objection to an error or irregularity at an oral examination is waived if:
(i) it relates to the manner of taking the deposition, the form of a question or answer, the oath or affirmation, a party's conduct, or other matters that might have been corrected at that time; and
(ii) it is not timely made during the deposition.
(C) *Objection to a Written Question.* An objection to the form of a written question under Rule 31 is waived if not served in writing on the party submitting the question within the time for serving responsive questions or, if the question is a recross-question, within 7 days after being served with it.
(4) *To Completing and Returning the Deposition.* An objection to how the officer transcribed the testimony—or prepared, signed, certified, sealed, endorsed, sent, or otherwise dealt with the deposition—is waived unless a motion to suppress is made promptly after the error or irregularity becomes known or, with reasonable diligence, could have been known.

Fed. R. Civ. P. 33. Interrogatories to Parties

(a) IN GENERAL.
(1) *Number.* Unless otherwise stipulated or ordered by the court, a party may serve on any other party no more than 25 written interrogatories, including all discrete subparts. Leave to serve additional interrogatories may be granted to the extent consistent with Rule 26(b)(2).
(2) *Scope.* An interrogatory may relate to any matter that may be inquired into under Rule 26(b). An interrogatory is not objectionable merely because it asks for an opinion or contention that relates to fact or the application of law to fact, but the court may order that the interrogatory need not be answered until

designated discovery is complete, or until a pretrial conference or some other time.

(b) ANSWERS AND OBJECTIONS.

(1) *Responding Party.* The interrogatories must be answered:

(A) by the party to whom they are directed; or

(B) if that party is a public or private corporation, a partnership, an association, or a governmental agency, by any officer or agent, who must furnish the information available to the party.

(2) *Time to Respond.* The responding party must serve its answers and any objections within 30 days after being served with the interrogatories. A shorter or longer time may be stipulated to under Rule 29 or be ordered by the court. (3) *Answering Each Interrogatory.* Each interrogatory must, to the extent it is not objected to, be answered separately and fully in writing under oath.

(4) *Objections.* The grounds for objecting to an interrogatory must be stated with specificity. Any ground not stated in a timely objection is waived unless the court, for good cause, excuses the failure.

(5) *Signature.* The person who makes the answers must sign them, and the attorney who objects must sign any objections.

(c) USE. An answer to an interrogatory may be used to the extent allowed by the Federal Rules of Evidence.

(d) OPTION TO PRODUCE BUSINESS RECORDS. If the answer to an interrogatory may be determined by examining, auditing, compiling, abstracting, or summarizing a party's business records (including electronically stored information), and if the burden of deriving or ascertaining the answer will be substantially the same for either party, the responding party may answer by:

(1) specifying the records that must be reviewed, in sufficient detail to enable the interrogating party to locate and identify them as readily as the responding party could; and

(2) giving the interrogating party a reasonable opportunity to examine and audit the records and to make copies, compilations, abstracts, or summaries.

FED. R. CIV. P. 34. Producing Documents, Electronically Stored Information, and Tangible Things, or Entering onto Land, for Inspection and Other Purposes

(a) IN GENERAL. A party may serve on any other party a request within the scope of Rule 26(b):

(1) to produce and permit the requesting party or its representative to inspect, copy, test, or sample the following items in the responding party's possession, custody, or control:

(A) any designated documents or electronically stored information—including writings, drawings, graphs, charts, photographs, sound recordings, images, and other data or data compilations—stored in any medium from which information can be obtained either directly or, if necessary, after translation by the responding party into a reasonably usable form; or

(B) any designated tangible things; or

(2) to permit entry onto designated land or other property possessed or controlled by the responding party, so that the requesting party may inspect, measure, survey, photograph, test, or sample the property or any designated object or operation on it.

(b) PROCEDURE.

(1) *Contents of the Request.* The request:

(A) must describe with reasonable particularity each item or category of items to be inspected;

(B) must specify a reasonable time, place, and manner for the inspection and for performing the related acts; and

(C) may specify the form or forms in which electronically stored information is to be produced.

(2) *Responses and Objections.*

(A) *Time to Respond.* The party to whom the request is directed must respond in writing within 30 days after being served. A shorter or longer time may be stipulated to under Rule 29 or be ordered by the court.

(B) *Responding to Each Item.* For each item or category, the response must either state that inspection and related activities will be permitted as requested or state an objection to the request, including the reasons.

(C) *Objections.* An objection to part of a request must specify the part and permit inspection of the rest.

(D) *Responding to a Request for Production of Electronically Stored Information.* The response may state an objection to a requested form for producing electronically stored information. If the responding party objects to a requested form—or if no form was specified in the request—the party must state the form or forms it intends to use.

(E) *Producing the Documents or Electronically Stored Information.* Unless otherwise stipulated or ordered by the court, these procedures apply to producing documents or electronically stored information:

(i) A party must produce documents as they are kept in the usual course of business or must organize and label them to correspond to the categories in the request;

(ii) If a request does not specify a form for producing electronically stored information, a party must
produce it in a form or forms in which it is ordinarily maintained or in a reasonably usable form or forms; and
(iii) A party need not produce the same electronically stored information in more than one form.
(c) NONPARTIES. As provided in Rule 45, a nonparty may be compelled to produce documents and tangible things or to permit an inspection.

Fed. R. Civ. P. 35. Physical and Mental Examinations

(a) ORDER FOR AN EXAMINATION.
(1) *In General.* The court where the action is pending may order a party whose mental or physical condition—including blood group—is in controversy to submit to a physical or mental examination by a suitably licensed or certified examiner. The court has the same authority to order a party to produce for examination a person who is in its custody or under its legal control.
(2) *Motion and Notice; Contents of the Order.* The order:
(A) may be made only on motion for good cause and on notice to all parties and the person to be examined; and
(B) must specify the time, place, manner, conditions, and scope of the examination, as well as the person or persons who will perform it.
(b) EXAMINER'S REPORT.
(1) *Request by the Party or Person Examined.* The party who moved for the examination must, on request, deliver to the requester a copy of the examiner's report, together with like reports of all earlier examinations of the same condition. The request may be made by the party against whom the examination order was issued or by the person examined.
(2) *Contents.* The examiner's report must be in writing and must set out in detail the examiner's findings, including diagnoses, conclusions, and the results of any tests.
(3) *Request by the Moving Party.* After delivering the reports, the party who moved for the examination may request—and is entitled to receive—from the party against whom the examination order was issued like reports of all earlier or later examinations of the same condition. But those reports need not be delivered by the party with custody or control of the person examined if the party shows that it could not obtain them.
(4) *Waiver of Privilege.* By requesting and obtaining the examiner's report, or by deposing the examiner, the party examined waives any privilege it may have—in that action or any other action involving the same controversy—concerning testimony about all examinations of the same condition.
(5) *Failure to Deliver a Report.* The court on motion may order—on just terms—that a party deliver the report of an examination. If the report is not provided, the court may exclude the examiner's testimony at trial.
(6) *Scope.* This subdivision (b) applies also to an examination made by the parties' agreement, unless the agreement states otherwise. This subdivision does not preclude obtaining an examiner's report or deposing an examiner under other rules.

Fed. R. Civ. P. 36. Requests for Admission

(a) SCOPE AND PROCEDURE.
(1) *Scope.* A party may serve on any other party a written request to admit, for purposes of the pending action only, the truth of any matters within the scope of Rule 26(b)(1) relating to:
(A) facts, the application of law to fact, or opinions about either; and
(B) the genuineness of any described documents.
(2) *Form; Copy of a Document.* Each matter must be separately stated. A request to admit the genuineness of a document must be accompanied by a copy of the document unless it is, or has been, otherwise furnished or made available for inspection and copying.
(3) *Time to Respond; Effect of Not Responding.* A matter is admitted unless, within 30 days after being served, the party to whom the request is directed serves on the requesting party a written answer or objection addressed to the matter and signed by the party or its attorney. A shorter or longer time for responding may be stipulated to under Rule 29 or be ordered by the court.
(4) *Answer.* If a matter is not admitted, the answer must specifically deny it or state in detail why the answering party cannot truthfully admit or deny it. A denial must fairly respond to the substance of the matter; and when good faith requires that a party qualify an answer or deny only a part of a matter, the answer must specify the part admitted and qualify or deny the rest. The answering party may assert lack of knowledge or information as a reason for failing to admit or deny only if the party states that it has made reasonable inquiry and that the information it knows or can readily obtain is insufficient to enable it to admit or deny.
(5) *Objections.* The grounds for objecting to a request must be stated. A party must not object solely on the ground that the request presents a genuine issue for trial.
(6) *Motion Regarding the Sufficiency of an Answer or Objection.* The requesting party may move to determine the sufficiency of an answer

or objection. Unless the court finds an objection justified, it must order that an answer be served. On finding that an answer does not comply with this rule, the court may order either that the matter is admitted or that an amended answer be served. The court may defer its final decision until a pretrial conference or a specified time before trial. Rule 37(a)(5) applies to an award of expenses.

(b) EFFECT OF AN ADMISSION; WITHDRAWING OR AMENDING IT. A matter admitted under this rule is conclusively established unless the court, on motion, permits the admission to be withdrawn or amended. Subject to Rule 16(e), the court may permit withdrawal or amendment if it would promote the presentation of the merits of the action and if the court is not persuaded that it would prejudice the requesting party in maintaining or defending the action on the merits. An admission under this rule is not an admission for any other purpose and cannot be used against the party in any other proceeding.

FED. R. CIV. P. 37. Failure to Make Disclosures or to Cooperate in Discovery; Sanctions

(a) MOTION FOR AN ORDER COMPELLING DISCLOSURE OR DISCOVERY.

(1) *In General.* On notice to other parties and all affected persons, a party may move for an order compelling disclosure or discovery. The motion must include a certification that the movant has in good faith conferred or attempted to confer with the person or party failing to make disclosure or discovery in an effort to obtain it without court action.

(2) *Appropriate Court.* A motion for an order to a party must be made in the court where the action is pending. A motion for an order to a nonparty must be made in the court where the discovery is or will be taken.

(3) *Specific Motions.*

(A) *To Compel Disclosure.* If a party fails to make a disclosure required by Rule 26(a), any other party may move to compel disclosure and for appropriate sanctions.

(B) *To Compel a Discovery Response.* A party seeking discovery may move for an order compelling an answer, designation, production, or inspection. This motion may be made if:

(i) a deponent fails to answer a question asked under Rule 30 or 31;

(ii) a corporation or other entity fails to make a designation under Rule 30(b)(6) or 31(a)(4);

(iii) a party fails to answer an interrogatory submitted under Rule 33; or

(iv) a party fails to respond that inspection will be permitted—or fails to permit inspection—as requested under Rule 34.

(C) *Related to a Deposition.* When taking an oral deposition, the party asking a question may complete or adjourn the examination before moving for an order.

(4) *Evasive or Incomplete Disclosure, Answer, or Response.* For purposes of this subdivision (a), an evasive or incomplete disclosure, answer, or response must be treated as a failure to disclose, answer, or respond.

(5) *Payment of Expenses; Protective Orders.*

(A) *If the Motion Is Granted (or Disclosure or Discovery Is Provided After Filing).* If the motion is granted—or if the disclosure or requested discovery is provided after the motion was filed—the court must, after giving an opportunity to be heard, require the party or deponent whose conduct necessitated the motion, the party or attorney advising that conduct, or both to pay the movant's reasonable expenses incurred in making the motion, including attorney's fees. But the court must not order this payment if:

(i) the movant filed the motion before attempting in good faith to obtain the disclosure or discovery without court action;

(ii) the opposing party's nondisclosure, response, or objection was substantially justified; or

(iii) other circumstances make an award of expenses unjust.

(B) *If the Motion Is Denied.* If the motion is denied, the court may issue any protective order authorized under Rule 26(c) and must, after giving an opportunity to be heard, require the movant, the attorney filing the motion, or both to pay the party or deponent who opposed the motion its reasonable expenses incurred in opposing the motion, including attorney's fees. But the court must not order this payment if the motion was substantially justified or other circumstances make an award of expenses unjust.

(C) *If the Motion Is Granted in Part and Denied in Part.* If the motion is granted in part and denied in part, the court may issue any protective order authorized under Rule 26(c) and may, after giving an opportunity to be heard, apportion the reasonable expenses for the motion.

(b) FAILURE TO COMPLY WITH A COURT ORDER.

(1) *Sanctions in the District Where the Deposition Is Taken.* If the court where the discovery is taken orders a deponent to be sworn or to answer a question and the deponent fails to obey, the failure may be treated as contempt of court.

(2) *Sanctions in the District Where the Action Is Pending.*

(A) *For Not Obeying a Discovery Order.* If a party or a party's officer, director, or managing agent—or a witness designated under Rule

30(b)(6) or 31(a)(4)—fails to obey an order to provide or permit discovery, including an order under Rule 26(f), 35, or 37(a), the court where the action is pending may issue further just orders. They may include the following:
(i) directing that the matters embraced in the order or other designated facts be taken as established for purposes of the action, as the prevailing party claims;
(ii) prohibiting the disobedient party from supporting or opposing designated claims or defenses, or from
introducing designated matters in evidence;
(iii) striking pleadings in whole or in part;
(iv) staying further proceedings until the order is obeyed;
(v) dismissing the action or proceeding in whole or in part;
(vi) rendering a default judgment against the disobedient party; or
(vii) treating as contempt of court the failure to obey any order except an order to submit to a physical or mental examination.
(B) *For Not Producing a Person for Examination.* If a party fails to comply with an order under Rule 35(a) requiring it to produce another person for examination, the court may issue any of the orders listed in Rule 37(b)(2)(A)(i)–(vi), unless the disobedient party shows that it cannot produce the other person.
(C) *Payment of Expenses.* Instead of or in addition to the orders above, the court must order the disobedient party, the attorney advising that party, or both to pay the reasonable expenses, including attorney's fees, caused by the failure, unless the failure was substantially justified or other circumstances make an award of expenses unjust.
(c) FAILURE TO DISCLOSE, TO SUPPLEMENT AN EARLIER RESPONSE, OR TO ADMIT.
(1) *Failure to Disclose or Supplement.* If a party fails to provide information or identify a witness as required by Rule 26(a) or
(e), the party is not allowed to use that information or witness to supply evidence on a motion, at a hearing, or at a trial, unless the failure was substantially justified or is harmless. In addition to or instead of this sanction, the court, on motion and after giving an opportunity to be heard:
(A) may order payment of the reasonable expenses, including attorney's fees, caused by the failure;
(B) may inform the jury of the party's failure; and
(C) may impose other appropriate sanctions, including any of the orders listed in Rule 37(b)(2)(A)(i)–(vi).
(2) *Failure to Admit.* If a party fails to admit what is requested under Rule 36 and if the requesting party later proves a document to be genuine or the matter true, the requesting party may move that the party who failed to admit pay the reasonable expenses, including attorney's fees, incurred in making that proof. The court must so order unless:
(A) the request was held objectionable under Rule 36(a);
(B) the admission sought was of no substantial importance;
(C) the party failing to admit had a reasonable ground to believe that it might prevail on the matter; or
(D) there was other good reason for the failure to admit.
(d) PARTY'S FAILURE TO ATTEND ITS OWN DEPOSITION, SERVE ANSWERS TO INTERROGATORIES, OR RESPOND TO A REQUEST FOR INSPECTION.
(1) *In General.*
(A) *Motion; Grounds for Sanctions.* The court where the action is pending may, on motion, order sanctions if:
(i) a party or a party's officer, director, or managing agent—or a person designated under Rule 30(b)(6) or 31(a)(4)—fails, after being served with proper notice, to appear for that person's deposition; or
(ii) a party, after being properly served with interrogatories under Rule 33 or a request for inspection under Rule 34, fails to serve its answers, objections, or written response.
(B) *Certification.* A motion for sanctions for failing to answer or respond must include a certification that the movant has in good faith conferred or attempted to confer with the party failing to act in an effort to obtain the answer or response without court action.
(2) *Unacceptable Excuse for Failing to Act.* A failure described in Rule 37(d)(1)(A) is not excused on the ground that the discovery sought was objectionable, unless the party failing to act has a pending motion for a protective order under Rule 26(c).
(3) *Types of Sanctions.* Sanctions may include any of the orders listed in Rule 37(b)(2)(A)(i)–(vi). Instead of or in addition to these sanctions, the court must require the party failing to act, the attorney advising that party, or both to pay the reasonable expenses, including attorney's fees, caused by the failure, unless the failure was substantially justified or other circumstances make an award of expenses unjust.
(e) FAILURE TO PROVIDE ELECTRONICALLY STORED INFORMATION.
Absent exceptional circumstances, a court may not impose sanctions under these rules on a party

for failing to provide electronically stored information lost as a result of the routine, good-faith operation of an electronic information system.
(f) FAILURE TO PARTICIPATE IN FRAMING A DISCOVERY PLAN. If a party or its attorney fails to participate in good faith in developing and submitting a proposed discovery plan as required by Rule
59 FEDERAL RULES OF CIVIL PROCEDURE **Rule 39** 26(f), the court may, after giving an opportunity to be heard, require that party or attorney to pay to any other party the reasonable expenses, including attorney's fees, caused by the failure.

FED. R. CIV. P. 38. Right to a Jury Trial; Demand

(a) RIGHT PRESERVED. The right of trial by jury as declared by the Seventh Amendment to the Constitution—or as provided by a federal statute—is preserved to the parties inviolate.
(b) DEMAND. On any issue triable of right by a jury, a party may demand a jury trial by:
(1) serving the other parties with a written demand—which may be included in a pleading—no later than 14 days after the last pleading directed to the issue is served; and
(2) filing the demand in accordance with Rule 5(d).
(c) SPECIFYING ISSUES. In its demand, a party may specify the issues that it wishes to have tried by a jury; otherwise, it is considered to have demanded a jury trial on all the issues so triable. If the party has demanded a jury trial on only some issues, any other party may—within 14 days after being served with the demand or within a shorter time ordered by the court—serve a demand for a jury trial on any other or all factual issues triable by jury.
(d) WAIVER; WITHDRAWAL. A party waives a jury trial unless its demand is properly served and filed. A proper demand may be withdrawn only if the parties consent.
(e) ADMIRALTY AND MARITIME CLAIMS. These rules do not create a right to a jury trial on issues in a claim that is an admiralty or maritime claim under Rule 9(h).

FED. R. CIV. P. 39. Trial by Jury or by the Court

(a) WHEN A DEMAND IS MADE. When a jury trial has been demanded under Rule 38, the action must be designated on the docket as a jury action. The trial on all issues so demanded must be by jury unless:
(1) the parties or their attorneys file a stipulation to a nonjury trial or so stipulate on the record; or
(2) the court, on motion or on its own, finds that on some or all of those issues there is no federal right to a jury trial.
(b) WHEN NO DEMAND IS MADE. Issues on which a jury trial is not properly demanded are to be tried by the court. But the court may, on motion, order a jury trial on any issue for which a jury might have been demanded.
(c) ADVISORY JURY; JURY TRIAL BY CONSENT. In an action not triable of right by a jury, the court, on motion or on its own:
(1) may try any issue with an advisory jury; or
(2) may, with the parties' consent, try any issue by a jury whose verdict has the same effect as if a jury trial had been a matter of right, unless the action is against the United States and a federal statute provides for a nonjury trial.

FED. R. CIV. P. 40. Scheduling Cases for Trial

Each court must provide by rule for scheduling trials. The court must give priority to actions entitled to priority by a federal statute.

FED. R. CIV. P. 41. Dismissal of Actions

(a) VOLUNTARY DISMISSAL.
(1) *By the Plaintiff.*
(A) *Without a Court Order.* Subject to Rules 23(e), 23.1(c), 23.2, and 66 and any applicable federal statute, the plaintiff may dismiss an action without a court order by filing:
(i) a notice of dismissal before the opposing party serves either an answer or a motion for summary judgment; or
(ii) a stipulation of dismissal signed by all parties who have appeared.
(B) *Effect.* Unless the notice or stipulation states otherwise, the dismissal is without prejudice. But if the plaintiff previously dismissed any federal- or state-court action based on or including the same claim, a notice of dismissal operates as an adjudication on the merits.
(2) *By Court Order; Effect.* Except as provided in Rule 41(a)(1), an action may be dismissed at the plaintiff's request only by court order, on terms that the court considers proper. If a defendant has pleaded a counterclaim before being served with the plaintiff's motion to dismiss, the action may be dismissed over the defendant's objection only if the counterclaim can remain pending for independent adjudication. Unless the order states otherwise, a dismissal under this paragraph (2) is without prejudice.
(b) INVOLUNTARY DISMISSAL; EFFECT. If the plaintiff fails to prosecute or to comply with these rules or a court order, a defendant may move to dismiss the action or any claim against it. Unless the dismissal order states otherwise, a dismissal under this subdivision

(b) and any dismissal not under this rule—except one for lack of jurisdiction, improper venue, or failure to join a party under Rule 19—operates as an adjudication on the merits.
(c) DISMISSING A COUNTERCLAIM, CROSSCLAIM, OR THIRD-PARTY CLAIM. This rule applies to a dismissal of any counterclaim, crossclaim, or third-party claim. A claimant's voluntary dismissal under Rule 41(a)(1)(A)(i) must be made:
(1) before a responsive pleading is served; or
(2) if there is no responsive pleading, before evidence is introduced at a hearing or trial.
(d) COSTS OF A PREVIOUSLY DISMISSED ACTION. If a plaintiff who previously dismissed an action in any court files an action based on or including the same claim against the same defendant, the
court:
(1) may order the plaintiff to pay all or part of the costs of
that previous action; and (2) may stay the proceedings until the plaintiff has complied.

Fed. R. Civ. P. 42. Consolidation; Separate Trials
(a) CONSOLIDATION. If actions before the court involve a common question of law or fact, the court may:
(1) join for hearing or trial any or all matters at issue in the actions;
(2) consolidate the actions; or
(3) issue any other orders to avoid unnecessary cost or delay.
(b) SEPARATE TRIALS. For convenience, to avoid prejudice, or to expedite and economize, the court may order a separate trial of one or more separate issues, claims, crossclaims, counterclaims, or third-party claims. When ordering a separate trial, the court must preserve any federal right to a jury trial.

Fed. R. Civ. P. 43. Taking Testimony
(a) IN OPEN COURT. At trial, the witnesses' testimony must be taken in open court unless a federal statute, the Federal Rules of Evidence, these rules, or other rules adopted by the Supreme Court provide otherwise. For good cause in compelling circumstances and with appropriate safeguards, the court may permit testimony in open court by contemporaneous transmission from a different location.
(b) AFFIRMATION INSTEAD OF AN OATH. When these rules require an oath, a solemn affirmation suffices.
(c) EVIDENCE ON A MOTION. When a motion relies on facts outside the record, the court may hear the matter on affidavits or may hear it wholly or partly on oral testimony or on depositions.
(d) INTERPRETER. The court may appoint an interpreter of its choosing; fix reasonable compensation to be paid from funds provided by law or by one or more parties; and tax the compensation as costs.

Fed. R. Civ. P. 44. Proving an Official Record
(a) MEANS OF PROVING.
(1) *Domestic Record.* Each of the following evidences an official record—or an entry in it—that is otherwise admissible and is kept within the United States, any state, district, or commonwealth, or any territory subject to the administrative or judicial jurisdiction of the United States:
(A) an official publication of the record; or
(B) a copy attested by the officer with legal custody of the record—or by the officer's deputy—and accompanied by a certificate that the officer has custody. The certificate must be made under seal:
(i) by a judge of a court of record in the district or political subdivision where the record is kept; or
(ii) by any public officer with a seal of office and with official duties in the district or political subdivision where the record is kept.
(2) *Foreign Record.*
(A) *In General.* Each of the following evidences a foreign official record—or an entry in it—that is otherwise admissible:
(i) an official publication of the record; or
(ii) the record—or a copy—that is attested by an authorized person and is accompanied either by a final certification of genuineness or by a certification under a treaty or convention to which the United States and the country where the record is located are parties.
(B) *Final Certification of Genuineness.* A final certification must certify the genuineness of the signature and official position of the attester or of any foreign official whose certificate of genuineness relates to the attestation or is in a chain of certificates of genuineness relating to the attestation. A final certification may be made by a secretary of a United States embassy or legation; by a consul general, vice consul, or consular agent of the United States; or by a diplomatic or consular official of the foreign country assigned or accredited to the United States.
(C) *Other Means of Proof.* If all parties have had a reasonable opportunity to investigate a foreign record's authenticity and accuracy, the court may, for good cause, either:
(i) admit an attested copy without final certification; or
(ii) permit the record to be evidenced by an attested summary with or without a final certification.

(b) LACK OF A RECORD. A written statement that a diligent search of designated records revealed no record or entry of a specified tenor is admissible as evidence that the records contain no such record or entry. For domestic records, the statement must be authenticated under Rule 44(a)(1). For foreign records, the statement must comply with (a)(2)(C)(ii).

(c) OTHER PROOF. A party may prove an official record—or an entry or lack of an entry in it—by any other method authorized by law.

Fed. R. Civ. P. 44.1. Determining Foreign Law

A party who intends to raise an issue about a foreign country's law must give notice by a pleading or other writing. In determining foreign law, the court may consider any relevant material or source, including testimony, whether or not submitted by a party or admissible under the Federal Rules of Evidence. The court's determination must be treated as a ruling on a question of law.

Fed. R. Civ. P. 45. Subpoena

(a) IN GENERAL.

(1) *Form and Contents.*

(A) *Requirements—In General.* Every subpoena must:

(i) state the court from which it issued;

(ii) state the title of the action, the court in which it is pending, and its civil-action number;

(iii) command each person to whom it is directed to do the following at a specified time and place: attend

and testify; produce designated documents, electronically stored information, or tangible things in that person's possession, custody, or control; or permit the inspection of premises; and

(iv) set out the text of Rule 45(c) and (d).

(B) *Command to Attend a Deposition—Notice of the Recording Method.* A subpoena commanding attendance at a deposition must state the method for recording the testimony.

(C) *Combining or Separating a Command to Produce or to Permit Inspection; Specifying the Form for Electronically Stored Information.* A command to produce documents, electronically stored information, or tangible things or to permit the inspection of premises may be included in a subpoena commanding attendance at a deposition, hearing, or trial, or may be set out in a separate subpoena. A subpoena may specify the form or forms in which electronically stored information is to be produced.

(D) *Command to Produce; Included Obligations.* A command in a subpoena to produce documents, electronically stored information, or tangible things requires the responding party to permit inspection, copying, testing, or sampling of the materials.

(2) *Issued from Which Court.* A subpoena must issue as follows:

(A) for attendance at a hearing or trial, from the court for the district where the hearing or trial is to be held;

(B) for attendance at a deposition, from the court for the district where the deposition is to be taken; and

(C) for production or inspection, if separate from a subpoena commanding a person's attendance, from the court for the district where the production or inspection is to be made.

(3) *Issued by Whom.* The clerk must issue a subpoena, signed but otherwise in blank, to a party who requests it. That party must complete it before service. An attorney also may issue and sign a subpoena as an officer of:

(A) a court in which the attorney is authorized to practice; or

(B) a court for a district where a deposition is to be taken or production is to be made, if the attorney is authorized to practice in the court where the action is pending.

(b) SERVICE.

(1) *By Whom; Tendering Fees; Serving a Copy of Certain Subpoenas.* Any person who is at least 18 years old and not a party may serve a subpoena. Serving a subpoena requires delivering a copy to the named person and, if the subpoena requires that person's attendance, tendering the fees for 1 day's attendance and the mileage allowed by law. Fees and mileage need not be tendered when the subpoena issues on behalf of the United States or any of its officers or agencies. If the subpoena commands the production of documents, electronically stored information, or tangible things or the inspection of premises before trial, then before it is served, a notice must be served on each party.

(2) *Service in the United States.* Subject to Rule 45(c)(3)(A)(ii), a subpoena may be served at any place:

(A) within the district of the issuing court;

(B) outside that district but within 100 miles of the place specified for the deposition, hearing, trial, production, or inspection;

(C) within the state of the issuing court if a state statute or court rule allows service at that place of a subpoena issued by a state court of general jurisdiction sitting in the place specified for the deposition, hearing, trial, production, or inspection; or

(D) that the court authorizes on motion and for good cause, if a federal statute so provides.

(3) *Service in a Foreign Country.* 28 U.S.C. § 1783 governs issuing and serving a subpoena directed to a United States national or resident who is in a foreign country.

(4) *Proof of Service.* Proving service, when necessary, requires filing with the issuing court a statement showing the date and manner of service and the names of the persons served. The statement must be certified by the server.

(c) PROTECTING A PERSON SUBJECT TO A SUBPOENA.

(1) *Avoiding Undue Burden or Expense; Sanctions.* A party or attorney responsible for issuing and serving a subpoena must take reasonable steps to avoid imposing undue burden or expense on a person subject to the subpoena. The issuing court must enforce this duty and impose an appropriate sanction— which may include lost earnings and reasonable attorney'sfees—on a party or attorney who fails to comply.

(2) *Command to Produce Materials or Permit Inspection.*

(A) *Appearance Not Required.* A person commanded to produce documents, electronically stored information, or tangible things, or to permit the inspection of premises, need not appear in person at the place of production or inspection unless also commanded to appear for a deposition, hearing, or trial.

(B) *Objections.* A person commanded to produce documents or tangible things or to permit inspection may serve on the party or attorney designated in the subpoena a written objection to inspecting, copying, testing or sampling any or all of the materials or to inspecting the premises— or to producing electronically stored information in the form or forms requested. The objection must be served before the earlier of the time specified for compliance or 14 days after the subpoena is served. If an objection is made, the following rules apply:

(i) At any time, on notice to the commanded person, the serving party may move the issuing court for an order compelling production or inspection.

(ii) These acts may be required only as directed in the order, and the order must protect a person who is neither a party nor a party's officer from significant expense resulting from compliance.

(3) *Quashing or Modifying a Subpoena.*

(A) *When Required.* On timely motion, the issuing court must quash or modify a subpoena that:

(i) fails to allow a reasonable time to comply;

(ii) requires a person who is neither a party nor a party's officer to travel more than 100 miles from where that person resides, is employed, or regularlytransacts business in person—except that, subject to

Rule 45(c)(3)(B)(iii), the person may be commanded to attend a trial by traveling from any such place within the state where the trial is held;

(iii) requires disclosure of privileged or other protected matter, if no exception or waiver applies; or

(iv) subjects a person to undue burden.

(B) *When Permitted.* To protect a person subject to or affected by a subpoena, the issuing court may, on motion, quash or modify the subpoena if it requires:

(i) disclosing a trade secret or other confidential research, development, or commercial information;

(ii) disclosing an unretained expert's opinion or information that does not describe specific occurrences in dispute and results from the expert's study that was not requested by a party; or

(iii) a person who is neither a party nor a party's officer to incur substantial expense to travel more than 100 miles to attend trial.

(C) *Specifying Conditions as an Alternative.* In the circumstances described in Rule 45(c)(3)(B), the court may, instead of quashing or modifying a subpoena, order appearance or production under specified conditions if the serving party:

(i) shows a substantial need for the testimony or material that cannot be otherwise met without undue hardship; and

(ii) ensures that the subpoenaed person will be reasonably compensated.

(d) DUTIES IN RESPONDING TO A SUBPOENA.

(1) *Producing Documents or Electronically Stored Information.* These procedures apply to producing documents or electronically stored information:

(A) *Documents.* A person responding to a subpoena to produce documents must produce them as they are kept in the ordinary course of business or must organize and label them to correspond to the categories in the demand.

(B) *Form for Producing Electronically Stored Information Not Specified.* If a subpoena does not specify a form for producing electronically stored information, the person responding must produce it in a form or forms in which it is ordinarily maintained or in a reasonably usable form or forms.

(C) *Electronically Stored Information Produced in Only One Form.* The person responding need not produce the same electronically stored information in more than one form.

(D) *Inaccessible Electronically Stored Information.* The person responding need not provide discovery of electronically stored information from sources that the person identifies as not reasonably accessible because of undue burden or cost. On motion to compel discovery or for a protective order, the person responding must show that the information is not reasonably accessible because of undue burden or cost. If that showing is made, the court may nonetheless order discovery from such sources if the requesting party shows good cause, considering the limitations of Rule 26(b)(2)(C). The court may specify conditions for the discovery.

(2) *Claiming Privilege or Protection.*

(A) *Information Withheld.* A person withholding subpoenaed information under a claim that it is privileged or subject to protection as trial-preparation material must:

(i) expressly make the claim; and

(ii) describe the nature of the withheld documents, communications, or tangible things in a manner that, without revealing information itself privileged or protected, will enable the parties to assess the claim.

(B) *Information Produced.* If information produced in response to a subpoena is subject to a claim of privilege or of protection as trial-preparation material, the person making the claim may notify any party that received the information of the claim and the basis for it. After being notified, a party must promptly return, sequester, or destroy the specified information and any copies it has; must not use or disclose the information until the claim is resolved; must take reasonable steps to retrieve the information if the party disclosed it before being notified; and may promptly present the information to the court under seal for a determination of the claim. The person who produced the information must preserve the information until the claim is resolved.

(e) CONTEMPT. The issuing court may hold in contempt a person who, having been served, fails without adequate excuse to obey the subpoena. A nonparty's failure to obey must be excused if the subpoena purports to require the nonparty to attend or produce at a place outside the limits of Rule 45(c)(3)(A)(ii).

FED. R. CIV. P. 46. Objecting to a Ruling or Order

A formal exception to a ruling or order is unnecessary. When the ruling or order is requested or made, a party need only state the action that it wants the court to take or objects to, along with the grounds for the request or objection. Failing to object does not prejudice a party who had no opportunity to do so when the ruling or order was made.

FED. R. CIV. P. 47. Selecting Jurors

(a) EXAMINING JURORS. The court may permit the parties or their attorneys to examine prospective jurors or may itself do so. If the court examines the jurors, it must permit the parties or their attorneys to make any further inquiry it considers proper, or must itself ask any of their additional questions it considers proper.

(b) PEREMPTORY CHALLENGES. The court must allow the number of peremptory challenges provided by 28 U.S.C. § 1870.

(c) EXCUSING A JUROR. During trial or deliberation, the court may excuse a juror for good cause.

FED. R. CIV. P. 48. Number of Jurors; Verdict; Polling

(a) NUMBER OF JURORS. A jury must begin with at least 6 and no more than 12 members, and each juror must participate in the verdict unless excused under Rule 47(c).

(b) VERDICT. Unless the parties stipulate otherwise, the verdict must be unanimous and must be returned by a jury of at least 6 members.

(c) POLLING. After a verdict is returned but before the jury is discharged, the court must on a party's request, or may on its own, poll the jurors individually. If the poll reveals a lack of unanimity or lack of assent by the number of jurors that the parties stipulated to, the court may direct the jury to deliberate further or may order a new trial.

FED. R. CIV. P. 49. Special Verdict; General Verdict and Questions

(a) SPECIAL VERDICT.

(1) *In General.* The court may require a jury to return only a special verdict in the form of a special written finding on each issue of fact. The court may do so by:

(A) submitting written questions susceptible of a categorical or other brief answer;

(B) submitting written forms of the special findings that might properly be made under the pleadings and evidence; or

(C) using any other method that the court considers appropriate.

(2) *Instructions.* The court must give the instructions and explanations necessary to enable the jury to make its findings on each submitted issue.

(3) *Issues Not Submitted.* A party waives the right to a jury trial on any issue of fact raised by the pleadings or evidence but not submitted to the jury unless, before the jury retires, the party demands its submission to the jury. If the party does not demand submission, the court may make a finding on the issue. If the court makes no finding, it is considered to have made a finding consistent with its judgment on the special verdict.

(b) GENERAL VERDICT WITH ANSWERS TO WRITTEN QUESTIONS.

(1) *In General.* The court may submit to the jury forms for a general verdict, together with written questions on one or more issues of fact that the

jury must decide. The court must give the instructions and explanations necessary to enable the jury to render a general verdict and answer the questions in writing, and must direct the jury to do both.
(2) *Verdict and Answers Consistent.* When the general verdict and the answers are consistent, the court must approve, for entry under Rule 58, an appropriate judgment on the verdict and answers.
(3) *Answers Inconsistent with the Verdict.* When the answers are consistent with each other but one or more is inconsistent with the general verdict, the court may:
(A) approve, for entry under Rule 58, an appropriate judgment according to the answers, notwithstanding the general verdict;
(B) direct the jury to further consider its answers and verdict; or
(C) order a new trial.
(4) *Answers Inconsistent with Each Other and the Verdict.* When the answers are inconsistent with each other and one or more is also inconsistent with the general verdict, judgment must not be entered; instead, the court must direct the jury to further consider its answers and verdict, or must order a new trial.

Fed. R. Civ. P. 50. Judgment as a Matter of Law in a Jury Trial; Related Motion for a New Trial; Conditional Ruling
(a) JUDGMENT AS A MATTER OF LAW.
(1) *In General.* If a party has been fully heard on an issue during a jury trial and the court finds that a reasonable jury would not have a legally sufficient evidentiary basis to find for the party on that issue, the court may:
(A) resolve the issue against the party; and
(B) grant a motion for judgment as a matter of law against the party on a claim or defense that, under the controlling law, can be maintained or defeated only with a favorable finding on that issue.
(2) *Motion.* A motion for judgment as a matter of law may be made at any time before the case is submitted to the jury. The motion must specify the judgment sought and the law and facts that entitle the movant to the judgment.
(b) RENEWING THE MOTION AFTER TRIAL; ALTERNATIVE MOTION FOR A NEW TRIAL. If the court does not grant a motion for judgment as a matter of law made under Rule 50(a), the court is considered to have submitted the action to the jury subject to the court's later deciding the legal questions raised by the motion. No later than 28 days after the entry of judgment—or if the motion addresses a jury issue not decided by a verdict, no later than 28 days after the jury was discharged—the movant may file a renewed motion for judgment as a matter of law and may include an alternative or joint request for a new trial under Rule 59. In ruling on the renewed motion, the court may:
(1) allow judgment on the verdict, if the jury returned a verdict;
(2) order a new trial; or
(3) direct the entry of judgment as a matter of law.
(c) GRANTING THE RENEWED MOTION; CONDITIONAL RULING ON A MOTION FOR A NEW TRIAL.
(1) *In General.* If the court grants a renewed motion for judgment as a matter of law, it must also conditionally rule on any motion for a new trial by determining whether a new trial should be granted if the judgment is later vacated or reversed. The court must state the grounds for conditionally granting or denying the motion for a new trial.
(2) *Effect of a Conditional Ruling.* Conditionally granting the motion for a new trial does not affect the judgment's finality; if the judgment is reversed, the new trial must proceed unless the appellate court orders otherwise. If the motion for a new trial is conditionally denied, the appellee may assert error in that denial; if the judgment is reversed, the case must proceed as the appellate court orders.
(d) TIME FOR A LOSING PARTY'S NEW-TRIAL MOTION. Any motion for a new trial under Rule 59 by a party against whom judgment as a matter of law is rendered must be filed no later than 28 days after the entry of the judgment.
(e) DENYING THE MOTION FOR JUDGMENT AS A MATTER OF LAW; REVERSAL ON APPEAL. If the court denies the motion for judgment as a matter of law, the prevailing party may, as appellee, assert grounds entitling it to a new trial should the appellate court conclude that the trial court erred in denying the motion. If the appellate court reverses the judgment, it may order a new trial, direct the trial court to determine whether a new trial should be granted, or direct the entry of judgment.

Fed. R. Civ. P. 51. Instructions to the Jury; Objections; Preserving a Claim of Error
(a) REQUESTS.
(1) *Before or at the Close of the Evidence.* At the close of the evidence or at any earlier reasonable time that the court orders, a party may file and furnish to every other party written requests for the jury instructions it wants the court to give.
(2) *After the Close of the Evidence.* After the close of the evidence, a party may:
(A) file requests for instructions on issues that could not reasonably have been anticipated by an earlier time that the court set for requests; and

(B) with the court's permission, file untimely requests for instructions on any issue.
(b) INSTRUCTIONS. The court:
(1) must inform the parties of its proposed instructions and proposed action on the requests before instructing the jury and before final jury arguments;
(2) must give the parties an opportunity to object on the record and out of the jury's hearing before the instructions and arguments are delivered; and
(3) may instruct the jury at any time before the jury is discharged.
(c) OBJECTIONS.
(1) *How to Make.* A party who objects to an instruction or the failure to give an instruction must do so on the record, stating distinctly the matter objected to and the grounds for the objection.
(2) *When to Make.* An objection is timely if:
(A) a party objects at the opportunity provided under Rule 51(b)(2); or
(B) a party was not informed of an instruction or action on a request before that opportunity to object, and the party objects promptly after learning that the instruction or request will be, or has been, given or refused.
(d) ASSIGNING ERROR; PLAIN ERROR.
(1) *Assigning Error.* A party may assign as error:
(A) an error in an instruction actually given, if that party properly objected; or
(B) a failure to give an instruction, if that party properly requested it and—unless the court rejected the request in a definitive ruling on the record—also properly objected.
(2) *Plain Error.* A court may consider a plain error in the instructions that has not been preserved as required by Rule 51(d)(1) if the error affects substantial rights.

FED. R. CIV. P. 52. Findings and Conclusions by the Court; Judgment on Partial Findings
(a) FINDINGS AND CONCLUSIONS.
(1) *In General.* In an action tried on the facts without a jury or with an advisory jury, the court must find the facts specially and state its conclusions of law separately. The findings and conclusions may be stated on the record after the close of the evidence or may appear in an opinion or a memorandum of decision filed by the court. Judgment must be entered under Rule 58.
(2) *For an Interlocutory Injunction.* In granting or refusing an interlocutory injunction, the court must similarly state the findings and conclusions that support its action.
(3) *For a Motion.* The court is not required to state findings or conclusions when ruling on a motion under Rule 12 or 56 or, unless these rules provide otherwise, on any other motion.
(4) *Effect of a Master's Findings.* A master's findings, to the extent adopted by the court, must be considered the court's findings.
(5) *Questioning the Evidentiary Support.* A party may later question the sufficiency of the evidence supporting the findings, whether or not the party requested findings, objected to them, moved to amend them, or moved for partial findings.
(6) *Setting Aside the Findings.* Findings of fact, whether based on oral or other evidence, must not be set aside unless clearly erroneous, and the reviewing court must give due regard to the trial court's opportunity to judge the witnesses' credibility.
(b) AMENDED OR ADDITIONAL FINDINGS. On a party's motion filed no later than 28 days after the entry of judgment, the court may amend its findings—or make additional findings—and may amend the judgment accordingly. The motion may accompany a motion for a new trial under Rule 59.
(c) JUDGMENT ON PARTIAL FINDINGS. If a party has been fully heard on an issue during a nonjury trial and the court finds against the party on that issue, the court may enter judgment against the party on a claim or defense that, under the controlling law, can be maintained or defeated only with a favorable finding on that issue. The court may, however, decline to render any judgment until the close of the evidence. A judgment on partial findings must be supported by findings of fact and conclusions of law as required by Rule 52(a).

FED. R. CIV. P. 53. Masters
(a) APPOINTMENT.
(1) *Scope.* Unless a statute provides otherwise, a court may appoint a master only to:
(A) perform duties consented to by the parties;
(B) hold trial proceedings and make or recommend findings of fact on issues to be decided without a jury if appointmen is warranted by:
(i) some exceptional condition; or
(ii) the need to perform an accounting or resolve a difficult computation of damages; or
(C) address pretrial and posttrial matters that cannot be effectively and timely addressed by an available district judge or magistrate judge of the district.
(2) *Disqualification.* A master must not have a relationship to the parties, attorneys, action, or court that would require disqualification of a judge under 28 U.S.C. § 455, unless the parties, with the court's approval, consent to the appointment after the master discloses any potential grounds for disqualification.
(3) *Possible Expense or Delay.* In appointing a master, the court must consider the fairness of

imposing the likely expenses on the parties and must protect against unreasonable expense or delay.

(b) ORDER APPOINTING A MASTER.

(1) *Notice.* Before appointing a master, the court must give the parties notice and an opportunity to be heard. Any party may suggest candidates for appointment.

(2) *Contents.* The appointing order must direct the master to proceed with all reasonable diligence and must state:

(A) the master's duties, including any investigation or enforcement duties, and any limits on the master's authority under Rule 53(c);

(B) the circumstances, if any, in which the master may communicate ex parte with the court or a party;

(C) the nature of the materials to be preserved and filed as the record of the master's activities;

(D) the time limits, method of filing the record, other procedures, and standards for reviewing the master's orders, findings, and recommendations; and

(E) the basis, terms, and procedure for fixing the master's compensation under Rule 53(g).

(3) *Issuing.* The court may issue the order only after:

(A) the master files an affidavit disclosing whether there is any ground for disqualification under 28 U.S.C. § 455; and

(B) if a ground is disclosed, the parties, with the court's approval, waive the disqualification.

(4) *Amending.* The order may be amended at any time after notice to the parties and an opportunity to be heard.

(c) MASTER'S AUTHORITY.

(1) *In General.* Unless the appointing order directs otherwise, a master may:

(A) regulate all proceedings;

(B) take all appropriate measures to perform the assigned duties fairly and efficiently; and

(C) if conducting an evidentiary hearing, exercise the appointing court's power to compel, take, and record evidence.

(2) *Sanctions.* The master may by order impose on a party any noncontempt sanction provided by Rule 37 or 45, and may recommend a contempt sanction against a party and sanctions against a nonparty.

(d) MASTER'S ORDERS. A master who issues an order must file it and promptly serve a copy on each party. The clerk must enter the order on the docket.

(e) MASTER'S REPORTS. A master must report to the court as required by the appointing order. The master must file the report and promptly serve a copy on each party, unless the court orders
otherwise.

(f) ACTION ON THE MASTER'S ORDER, REPORT, OR RECOMMENDATIONS.

(1) *Opportunity for a Hearing; Action in General.* In acting on a master's order, report, or recommendations, the court must give the parties notice and an opportunity to be heard; may receive evidence; and may adopt or affirm, modify, wholly or partly reject or reverse, or resubmit to the master with instructions.

(2) *Time to Object or Move to Adopt or Modify.* A party may file objections to—or a motion to adopt or modify—the master's order, report, or recommendations no later than 21 days after a copy is served, unless the court sets a different time.

(3) *Reviewing Factual Findings.* The court must decide de novo all objections to findings of fact made or recommended by a master, unless the parties, with the court's approval, stipulate that:

(A) the findings will be reviewed for clear error; or

(B) the findings of a master appointed under Rule 53(a)(1)(A) or (C) will be final.

(4) *Reviewing Legal Conclusions.* The court must decide de novo all objections to conclusions of law made or recommended by a master.

(5) *Reviewing Procedural Matters.* Unless the appointing order establishes a different standard of review, the court may set aside a master's ruling on a procedural matter only for an abuse of discretion.

(g) COMPENSATION.

(1) *Fixing Compensation.* Before or after judgment, the court must fix the master's compensation on the basis and terms stated in the appointing order, but the court may set a new basis and terms after giving notice and an opportunity to be heard.

(2) *Payment.* The compensation must be paid either:

(A) by a party or parties; or

(B) from a fund or subject matter of the action within the court's control.

(3) *Allocating Payment.* The court must allocate payment among the parties after considering the nature and amount of the controversy, the parties' means, and the extent to which any party is more responsible than other parties for the reference to a master. An interim allocation may be amended to reflect a decision on the merits.

(h) APPOINTING A MAGISTRATE JUDGE. A magistrate judge is subject to this rule only when the order referring a matter to the magistrate judge states that the reference is made under this rule.

FED. R. CIV. P. 54. Judgment; Costs

(a) DEFINITION; FORM. "Judgment" as used in these rules includes a decree and any order from which an appeal lies. A judgment should not include recitals of pleadings, a master's report, or a record of prior proceedings.

(b) JUDGMENT ON MULTIPLE CLAIMS OR INVOLVING MULTIPLE PARTIES. When an action presents more than one claim for relief—whether as a claim, counterclaim, crossclaim, or third-party claim—or when multiple parties are involved, the court may direct entry of a final judgment as to one or more, but fewer than all, claims or parties only if the court expressly determines that there is no just reason for delay. Otherwise, any order or other decision, however designated, that adjudicates fewer than all the claims or the rights and liabilities of fewer than all the parties does not end the action as to any of the claims or parties and may be revised at any time before the entry of a judgment adjudicating all the claims and all the parties' rights and liabilities.

(c) DEMAND FOR JUDGMENT; RELIEF TO BE GRANTED. A default judgment must not differ in kind from, or exceed in amount, what is demanded in the pleadings. Every other final judgment should grant the relief to which each party is entitled, even if the party has not demanded that relief in its pleadings.

(d) COSTS; ATTORNEY'S FEES.

(1) *Costs Other Than Attorney's Fees.* Unless a federal statute, these rules, or a court order provides otherwise, costs—other than attorney's fees—should be allowed to the prevailing party. But costs against the United States, its officers, and its agencies may be imposed only to the extent allowed by law. The clerk may tax costs on 14 days' notice. On motion served within the next 7 days, the court may review the clerk's action.

(2) *Attorney's Fees.*

(A) *Claim to Be by Motion.* A claim for attorney's fees and related nontaxable expenses must be made by motion unless the substantive law requires those fees to be proved at trial as an element of damages.

(B) *Timing and Contents of the Motion.* Unless a statute or a court order provides otherwise, the motion must:

(i) be filed no later than 14 days after the entry of judgment;

(ii) specify the judgment and the statute, rule, or other grounds entitling the movant to the award;

(iii) state the amount sought or provide a fair estimate of it; and

(iv) disclose, if the court so orders, the terms of any agreement about fees for the services for which the claim is made.

(C) *Proceedings.* Subject to Rule 23(h), the court must, on a party's request, give an opportunity for adversary submissions on the motion in accordance with Rule 43(c) or 78. The court may decide issues of liability for fees before receiving submissions on the value of services. The court must find the facts and state its conclusions of law as provided in Rule 52(a).

(D) *Special Procedures by Local Rule; Reference to a Master or a Magistrate Judge.* By local rule, the court may establish special procedures to resolve fee-related issues without extensive evidentiary hearings. Also, the court may refer issues concerning the value of services to a special master under Rule 53 without regard to the limitations of Rule 53(a)(1), and may refer a motion for attorney's fees to a magistrate judge under Rule 72(b) as if it were a dispositive pretrial matter.

(E) *Exceptions.* Subparagraphs (A)–(D) do not apply to claims for fees and expenses as sanctions for violating these rules or as sanctions under 28 U.S.C. §1927.

FED. R. CIV. P. 55. Default; Default Judgment

(a) ENTERING A DEFAULT. When a party against whom a judgment for affirmative relief is sought has failed to plead or otherwise defend, and that failure is shown by affidavit or otherwise, the clerk must enter the party's default.

(b) ENTERING A DEFAULT JUDGMENT.

(1) *By the Clerk.* If the plaintiff's claim is for a sum certain or a sum that can be made certain by computation, the clerk— on the plaintiff's request, with an affidavit showing the amount due—must enter judgment for that amount and costs against a defendant who has been defaulted for not appearing

and who is neither a minor nor an incompetent person.

(2) *By the Court.* In all other cases, the party must apply to the court for a default judgment. A default judgment may be entered against a minor or incompetent person only if represented by a general guardian, conservator, or other like fiduciary who has appeared. If the party against whom a default judgment is sought has appeared personally or by a representative, that party or its representative must be served with written notice of the application at least 7 days before the hearing. The court may conduct hearings or make referrals— preserving any federal statutory right to a jury trial—when, to enter or effectuate judgment, it needs to:

(A) conduct an accounting;

(B) determine the amount of damages;

(C) establish the truth of any allegation by evidence; or

(D) investigate any other matter.

(c) SETTING ASIDE A DEFAULT OR A DEFAULT JUDGMENT. The court may set aside an entry of default for good cause, and it may set aside a default judgment under Rule 60(b).

(d) JUDGMENT AGAINST THE UNITED STATES. A default judgment may be entered against the United States, its officers, or its agencies only if the claimant establishes a claim or right to relief by evidence that satisfies the court.

FED. R. CIV. P. 56. Summary Judgment

(a) BY A CLAIMING PARTY. A party claiming relief may move, with or without supporting affidavits, for summary judgment on all or part of the claim.

(b) BY A DEFENDING PARTY. A party against whom relief is sought may move, with or without supporting affidavits, for summary judgment on all or part of the claim.

(c) TIME FOR A MOTION, RESPONSE, AND REPLY; PROCEEDINGS.

(1) These times apply unless a different time is set by local rule or the court orders otherwise:

(A) a party may move for summary judgment at any time until 30 days after the close of all discovery;

(B) a party opposing the motion must file a response within 21 days after the motion is served or a responsive pleading is due, whichever is later; and

(C) the movant may file a reply within 14 days after the response is served.

(2) The judgment sought should be rendered if the pleadings, the discovery and disclosure materials on file, and any affidavits show that there is no genuine issue as to any material fact and that the movant is entitled to judgment as a matter of law.

(d) CASE NOT FULLY ADJUDICATED ON THE MOTION.

(1) *Establishing Facts.* If summary judgment is not rendered on the whole action, the court should, to the extent practicable, determine what material facts are not genuinely at issue. The court should so determine by examining the pleadings and evidence before it and by interrogating the attorneys. It should then issue an order specifying what facts—including items of damages or other relief—are not genuinely at issue. The facts so specified must be treated as established in the action.

(2) *Establishing Liability.* An interlocutory summary judgment may be rendered on liability alone, even if there is a genuine issue on the amount of damages.

(e) AFFIDAVITS; FURTHER TESTIMONY.

(1) *In General.* A supporting or opposing affidavit must be made on personal knowledge, set out facts that would be admissible in evidence, and show that the affiant is competent to testify on the matters stated. If a paper or part of a paper is referred to in an affidavit, a sworn or certified copy must be attached to or served with the affidavit. The court may permit an affidavit to be supplemented or opposed by depositions, answers to interrogatories, or additional affidavits.

(2) *Opposing Party's Obligation to Respond.* When a motion for summary judgment is properly made and supported, an opposing party may not rely merely on allegations or denials in its own pleading; rather, its response must—by affidavits or as otherwise provided in this rule—set out specific facts showing a genuine issue for trial. If the opposing party does not so respond, summary judgment should, if appropriate, be entered against that party.

(f) WHEN AFFIDAVITS ARE UNAVAILABLE. If a party opposing the motion shows by affidavit that, for specified reasons, it cannot present facts essential to justify its opposition, the court may:

(1) deny the motion;

(2) order a continuance to enable affidavits to be obtained, depositions to be taken, or other discovery to be undertaken; or

(3) issue any other just order.

(g) AFFIDAVIT SUBMITTED IN BAD FAITH. If satisfied that an affidavit under this rule is submitted in bad faith or solely for delay, the court must order the submitting party to pay the other party the reasonable expenses, including attorney's fees, it incurred as a result. An offending party or attorney may also be held in contempt.

FED. R. CIV. P. 57. Declaratory Judgment

These rules govern the procedure for obtaining a declaratory judgment under 28 U.S.C. §2201. Rules 38 and 39 govern a demand for a jury trial. The existence of another adequate remedy does not preclude a declaratory judgment that is otherwise appropriate. The court may order a speedy hearing of a declaratoryjudgment action.

FED. R. CIV. P. 58. Entering Judgment

(a) SEPARATE DOCUMENT. Every judgment and amended judgment must be set out in a separate document, but a separate document is not required for an order disposing of a motion:

(1) for judgment under Rule 50(b);

(2) to amend or make additional findings under Rule 52(b);

(3) for attorney's fees under Rule 54;

(4) for a new trial, or to alter or amend the judgment, under Rule 59; or

(5) for relief under Rule 60.

(b) ENTERING JUDGMENT.

(1) *Without the Court's Direction.* Subject to Rule 54(b) and unless the court orders otherwise, the clerk must, without awaiting the court's

direction, promptly prepare, sign, and enter the judgment when:
(A) the jury returns a general verdict;
(B) the court awards only costs or a sum certain; or
(C) the court denies all relief.
(2) *Court's Approval Required.* Subject to Rule 54(b), the court must promptly approve the form of the judgment, which the clerk must promptly enter, when:
(A) the jury returns a special verdict or a general verdict with answers to written questions; or
(B) the court grants other relief not described in this subdivision (b).
(c) TIME OF ENTRY. For purposes of these rules, judgment is entered at the following times:
(1) if a separate document is not required, when the judgment is entered in the civil docket under Rule 79(a); or
(2) if a separate document is required, when the judgment is entered in the civil docket under Rule 79(a) and the earlier of these events occurs:
(A) it is set out in a separate document; or
(B) 150 days have run from the entry in the civil docket.
(d) REQUEST FOR ENTRY. A party may request that judgment be set out in a separate document as required by Rule 58(a).
(e) COST OR FEE AWARDS. Ordinarily, the entry of judgment may not be delayed, nor the time for appeal extended, in order to tax costs or award fees. But if a timely motion for attorney's fees is
made under Rule 54(d)(2), the court may act before a notice of appeal has been filed and become effective to order that the motion have the same effect under Federal Rule of Appellate Procedure 4(a)(4) as a timely motion under Rule 59.

FED. R. CIV. P. 59. New Trial; Altering or Amending a Judgment

(a) IN GENERAL.
(1) *Grounds for New Trial.* The court may, on motion, grant a new trial on all or some of the issues—and to any party—as follows:
(A) after a jury trial, for any reason for which a new trial has heretofore been granted in an action at law in federal court; or
(B) after a nonjury trial, for any reason for which a rehearing has heretofore been granted in a suit in equity in federal court.
(2) *Further Action After a Nonjury Trial.* After a nonjury trial, the court may, on motion for a new trial, open the judgment if one has been entered, take additional testimony, amend findings of fact and conclusions of law or make new ones, and direct the entry of a new judgment.
(b) TIME TO FILE A MOTION FOR A NEW TRIAL. A motion for a new trial must be filed no later than 28 days after the entry of judgment.
(c) TIME TO SERVE AFFIDAVITS. When a motion for a new trial is based on affidavits, they must be filed with the motion. The opposing party has 14 days after being served to file opposing affidavits. The court may permit reply affidavits.
(d) NEW TRIAL ON THE COURT'S INITIATIVE OR FOR REASONS NOT IN THE MOTION. No later than 28 days after the entry of judgment, the court, on its own, may order a new trial for any reason that would justify granting one on a party's motion. After giving the parties notice and an opportunity to be heard, the court may grant a timely motion for a new trial for a reason not stated in the motion. In either event, the court must specify the reasons in its order.
(e) MOTION TO ALTER OR AMEND A JUDGMENT. A motion to alter or amend a judgment must be filed no later than 28 days after the entry of the judgment.

FED. R. CIV. P. 60. Relief from a Judgment or Order

(a) CORRECTIONS BASED ON CLERICAL MISTAKES; OVERSIGHTS AND OMISSIONS. The court may correct a clerical mistake or a mistake arising from oversight or omission whenever one is found in a judgment, order, or other part of the record. The court may do so on motion or on its own, with or without notice. But after an appeal has been docketed in the appellate court and while it is pending, such a mistake may be corrected only with the appellate court's leave.
(b) GROUNDS FOR RELIEF FROM A FINAL JUDGMENT, ORDER, OR PROCEEDING. On motion and just terms, the court may relieve a party or its legal representative from a final judgment, order, or proceeding for the following reasons:
(1) mistake, inadvertence, surprise, or excusable neglect;
(2) newly discovered evidence that, with reasonable diligence, could not have been discovered in time to move for a new trial under Rule 59(b);
(3) fraud (whether previously called intrinsic or extrinsic), misrepresentation, or misconduct by an opposing party;
(4) the judgment is void;
(5) the judgment has been satisfied, released, or discharged; it is based on an earlier judgment that has been reversed or vacated; or applying it prospectively is no longer equitable; or
(6) any other reason that justifies relief.
(c) TIMING AND EFFECT OF THE MOTION.

(1) *Timing.* A motion under Rule 60(b) must be made within a reasonable time—and for reasons (1), (2), and (3) no more than a year after the entry of the judgment or order or the date of the proceeding.
(2) *Effect on Finality.* The motion does not affect the judgment's
finality or suspend its operation.
(d) OTHER POWERS TO GRANT RELIEF. This rule does not limit a court's power to:
(1) entertain an independent action to relieve a party from a judgment, order, or proceeding;
(2) grant relief under 28 U.S.C. §1655 to a defendant who was not personally notified of the action; or
(3) set aside a judgment for fraud on the court.
(e) BILLS AND WRITS ABOLISHED. The following are abolished: bills of review, bills in the nature of bills of review, and writs of coram nobis, coram vobis, and audita querela.

FED. R. CIV. P. 61. Harmless Error
Unless justice requires otherwise, no error in admitting or excluding evidence—or any other error by the court or a party—is ground for granting a new trial, for setting aside a verdict, or for vacating, modifying, or otherwise disturbing a judgment or order. At every stage of the proceeding, the court must disregard
substantial rights.

FED. R. CIV. P. 62. Stay of Proceedings to Enforce a Judgment
(a) AUTOMATIC STAY; EXCEPTIONS FOR INJUNCTIONS, RECEIVERSHIPS, AND PATENT ACCOUNTINGS. Except as stated in this rule, no execution may issue on a judgment, nor may proceedings be taken to enforce it, until 14 days have passed after its entry. But unless the court orders otherwise, the following are not stayed after being entered, even if an appeal is taken:
(1) an interlocutory or final judgment in an action for an injunction or a receivership; or
(2) a judgment or order that directs an accounting in an action for patent infringement.
(b) STAY PENDING THE DISPOSITION OF A MOTION. On appropriate terms for the opposing party's security, the court may stay the execution of a judgment—or any proceedings to enforce it—pending disposition of any of the following motions:
(1) under Rule 50, for judgment as a matter of law;
(2) under Rule 52(b), to amend the findings or for additional findings;
(3) under Rule 59, for a new trial or to alter or amend a judgment; or
(4) under Rule 60, for relief from a judgment or order.
(c) INJUNCTION PENDING AN APPEAL. While an appeal is pending from an interlocutory order or final judgment that grants, dissolves, or denies an injunction, the court may suspend, modify, restore, or grant an injunction on terms for bond or other terms that secure the opposing party's rights. If the judgment appealed from is rendered by a statutory three-judge district court, the order must be made either:
(1) by that court sitting in open session; or
(2) by the assent of all its judges, as evidenced by their signatures.
(d) STAY WITH BOND ON APPEAL. If an appeal is taken, the appellant may obtain a stay by supersedeas bond, except in an action described in Rule 62(a)(1) or (2). The bond may be given upon or after filing the notice of appeal or after obtaining the order allowing the appeal. The stay takes effect when the court approves the bond.
(e) STAY WITHOUT BOND ON AN APPEAL BY THE UNITED STATES, ITS OFFICERS, OR ITS AGENCIES. The court must not require a bond, obligation, or other security from the appellant when granting a stay on an appeal by the United States, its officers, or its agencies or on an appeal directed by a department of the federal government.
(f) STAY IN FAVOR OF A JUDGMENT DEBTOR UNDER STATE LAW. If a judgment is a lien on the judgment debtor's property under the law of the state where the court is located, the judgment debtor is entitled to the same stay of execution the state court would give.
(g) APPELLATE COURT'S POWER NOT LIMITED. This rule does not limit the power of the appellate court or one of its judges or justices:
(1) to stay proceedings—or suspend, modify, restore, or grant an injunction—while an appeal is pending; or
(2) to issue an order to preserve the status quo or the effectiveness of the judgment to be entered.
(h) STAY WITH MULTIPLE CLAIMS OR PARTIES. A court may stay the enforcement of a final judgment entered under Rule 54(b) until it enters a later judgment or judgments, and may prescribe terms necessary to secure the benefit of the stayed judgment for the party in whose favor it was entered.

FED. R. CIV. P. 62.1. Indicative Ruling on a Motion for Relief That is Barred by a Pending Appeal
(a) RELIEF PENDING APPEAL. If a timely motion is made for relief that the court lacks authority to grant because of an appeal that has been docketed and is pending, the court may:
(1) defer considering the motion;
(2) deny the motion; or

(3) state either that it would grant the motion if the court of appeals remands for that purpose or that the motion raises a substantial issue.
(b) NOTICE TO THE COURT OF APPEALS. The movant must promptly notify the circuit clerk under Federal Rule of Appellate Procedure 12.1 if the district court states that it would grant the motion or that the motion raises a substantial issue.
(c) REMAND. The district court may decide the motion if the court of appeals remands for that purpose.

FED. R. CIV. P. 63. Judge's Inability to Proceed
If a judge conducting a hearing or trial is unable to proceed, any other judge may proceed upon certifying familiarity with the record and determining that the case may be completed without prejudice to the parties. In a hearing or a nonjury trial, the successor judge must, at a party's request, recall any witness whose testimony is material and disputed and who is available to testify again without undue burden. The successor judge may also recall any other witness.

FED. R. CIV. P. 64. Seizing a Person or Property
(a) REMEDIES UNDER STATE LAW—IN GENERAL. At the commencement of and throughout an action, every remedy is available that, under the law of the state where the court is located, provides for seizing a person or property to secure satisfaction of the potential judgment. But a federal statute governs to the extent it applies.
(b) SPECIFIC KINDS OF REMEDIES. The remedies available under this rule include the following—however designated and regardless of whether state procedure requires an independent action:
• arrest;
• attachment;
• garnishment;
• replevin;
• sequestration; and
• other corresponding or equivalent remedies.

FED. R. CIV. P. 65. Injunctions and Restraining Orders
(a) PRELIMINARY INJUNCTION.
(1) *Notice.* The court may issue a preliminary injunction only on notice to the adverse party.
(2) *Consolidating the Hearing with the Trial on the Merits.* Before or after beginning the hearing on a motion for a preliminary injunction, the court may advance the trial on the merits and consolidate it with the hearing. Even when consolidation is not ordered, evidence that is received on the motion and that would be admissible at trial becomes part of the trial record and need not be repeated at trial. But the court must preserve any party's right to a jury trial.
(b) TEMPORARY RESTRAINING ORDER.
(1) *Issuing Without Notice.* The court may issue a temporary restraining order without written or oral notice to the adverse party or its attorney only if:
(A) specific facts in an affidavit or a verified complaint clearly show that immediate and irreparable injury, loss, or damage will result to the movant before the adverse party can be heard in opposition; and
(B) the movant's attorney certifies in writing any efforts made to give notice and the reasons why it should not be required.
(2) *Contents; Expiration.* Every temporary restraining order issued without notice must state the date and hour it was issued; describe the injury and state why it is irreparable; state why the order was issued without notice; and be promptly filed in the clerk's office and entered in the record. The order expires at the time after entry—not to exceed 14 days—that the court sets, unless before that time the court, for good cause, extends it for a like period or the adverse party consents to a longer extension. The reasons for an extension must be entered in the record.
(3) *Expediting the Preliminary-Injunction Hearing.* If the order is issued without notice, the motion for a preliminary injunction must be set for hearing at the earliest possible time, taking precedence over all other matters except hearings on older matters of the same character. At the hearing, the party who obtained the order must proceed with the motion; if the party does not, the court must dissolve the order.
(4) *Motion to Dissolve.* On 2 days' notice to the party who obtained the order without notice—or on shorter notice set by the court—the adverse party may appear and move to dissolve or modify the order. The court must then hear and decide the motion as promptly as justice requires.
(c) SECURITY. The court may issue a preliminary injunction or a temporary restraining order only if the movant gives security in an amount that the court considers proper to pay the costs and damages sustained by any party found to have been wrongfully enjoined or restrained. The United States, its officers, and its agencies are not required to give security.
(d) CONTENTS AND SCOPE OF EVERY INJUNCTION AND RESTRAINING ORDER.
(1) *Contents.* Every order granting an injunction and every restraining order must:
(A) state the reasons why it issued;
(B) state its terms specifically; and

(C) describe in reasonable detail—and not by referring to the complaint or other document—the act or acts restrained or required.
(2) *Persons Bound.* The order binds only the following who receive actual notice of it by personal service or otherwise:
(A) the parties;
(B) the parties' officers, agents, servants, employees, and attorneys; and
(C) other persons who are in active concert or participation with anyone described in Rule 65(d)(2)(A) or (B).
(e) OTHER LAWS NOT MODIFIED. These rules do not modify the following:
(1) any federal statute relating to temporary restraining orders or preliminary injunctions in actions affecting employer and employee;
(2) 28 U.S.C. §2361, which relates to preliminary injunctions in actions of interpleader or in the nature of interpleader; or
(3) 28 U.S.C. §2284, which relates to actions that must be heard and decided by a three-judge district court.
(f) COPYRIGHT IMPOUNDMENT. This rule applies to copyright-impoundment proceedings.

FED. R. CIV. P. 65.1. Proceedings Against a Surety

Whenever these rules (including the Supplemental Rules for Admiralty or Maritime Claims and Asset Forfeiture Actions) require or allow a party to give security, and security is given through a bond or other undertaking with one or more sureties, each surety submits to the court's jurisdiction and irrevocably appoints the court clerk as its agent for receiving service of any papers that affect its liability on the bond or undertaking. The surety's liability may be enforced on motion without an independent action. The motion and any notice that the court orders may be served on the court clerk, who must promptly mail copy of each to every surety whose address is known.

FED. R. CIV. P. 66. Receivers

These rules govern an action in which the appointment of a receiver is sought or a receiver sues or is sued. But the practice in administering an estate by a receiver or a similar court-appointed officer must accord with the historical practice in federal courts or with a local rule. An action in which a receiver has been appointed may be dismissed only by court order.

FED. R. CIV. P. 67. Deposit into Court

(a) DEPOSITING PROPERTY. If any part of the relief sought is a money judgment or the disposition of a sum of money or some other deliverable thing, a party—on notice to every other party and by leave of court—may deposit with the court all or part of the money or thing, whether or not that party claims any of it. The depositing party must deliver to the clerk a copy of the order permitting deposit.
(b) INVESTING AND WITHDRAWING FUNDS. Money paid into court under this rule must be deposited and withdrawn in accordance with 28 U.S.C. §§2041 and 2042 and any like statute. The money must be deposited in an interest-bearing account or invested in a court-approved, interest-bearing instrument.

FED. R. CIV. P. 68. Offer of Judgment

(a) MAKING AN OFFER; JUDGMENT ON AN ACCEPTED OFFER. At least 14 days before the date set for trial, a party defending against a claim may serve on an opposing party an offer to allow judgment on specified terms, with the costs then accrued. If, within 14 days after being served, the opposing party serves written notice accepting the offer, either party may then file the offer and notice of acceptance, plus proof of service. The clerk must then enter judgment.
(b) UNACCEPTED OFFER. An unaccepted offer is considered withdrawn, but it does not preclude later offer. Evidence of an unaccepted offer is not admissible except in a proceeding to determine costs.
(c) OFFER AFTER LIABILITY IS DETERMINED. When one party's liability to another has been determined but the extent of liability remains to be determined by further proceedings, the party held liable may make an offer of judgment. It must be served within a reasonable time—but at least 14 days—before the date set for a hearing to determine the extent of liability.
(d) PAYING COSTS AFTER AN UNACCEPTED OFFER. If the judgment that the offeree finally obtains is not more favorable than the unaccepted offer, the offeree must pay the costs incurred after the offer was made.

FED. R. CIV. P. 69. Execution

(a) IN GENERAL.
(1) *Money Judgment; Applicable Procedure.* A money judgment is enforced by a writ of execution, unless the court directs otherwise. The procedure on execution—and in proceedings supplementary to and in aid of judgment or execution—must accord with the procedure of the state where the court is located, but a federal statute governs to the extent it applies.
(2) *Obtaining Discovery.* In aid of the judgment or execution, the judgment creditor or a successor in interest whose interest appears of record may obtain discovery from any person—including the judgment debtor—as provided in

these rules or by the procedure of the state where the court is located.

(b) AGAINST CERTAIN PUBLIC OFFICERS. When a judgment has been entered against a revenue officer in the circumstances stated in 28 U.S.C. § 2006, or against an officer of Congress in the circumstances stated in 2 U.S.C. § 118, the judgment must be satisfied as those statutes provide.

FED. R. CIV. P. 70. Enforcing a Judgment for a Specific Act

(a) PARTY'S FAILURE TO ACT; ORDERING ANOTHER TO ACT. If a judgment requires a party to convey land, to deliver a deed or other document, or to perform any other specific act and the party fails to comply within the time specified, the court may order the act to be done—at the disobedient party's expense—by another person appointed by the court. When done, the act has the same effect as if done by the party.

(b) VESTING TITLE. If the real or personal property is within the district, the court—instead of ordering a conveyance—may enter a judgment divesting any party's title and vesting it in others. That judgment has the effect of a legally executed conveyance.

(c) OBTAINING A WRIT OF ATTACHMENT OR SEQUESTRATION. On application by a party entitled to performance of an act, the clerk must issue a writ of attachment or sequestration against the disobedient party's property to compel obedience.

(d) OBTAINING A WRIT OF EXECUTION OR ASSISTANCE. On application by a party who obtains a judgment or order for possession, the clerk must issue a writ of execution or assistance.

(e) HOLDING IN CONTEMPT. The court may also hold the disobedient party in contempt.

FED. R. CIV. P. 71. Enforcing Relief For or Against a Nonparty

When an order grants relief for a nonparty or may be enforced against a nonparty, the procedure for enforcing the order is the same as for a party.

FED. R. CIV. P. 71.1. Condemning Real or Personal Property

(a) APPLICABILITY OF OTHER RULES. These rules govern proceedings to condemn real and personal property by eminent domain, except as this rule provides otherwise.

(b) JOINDER OF PROPERTIES. The plaintiff may join separate pieces of property in a single action, no matter whether they are owned by the same persons or sought for the same use.

(c) COMPLAINT.

(1) *Caption.* The complaint must contain a caption as provided in Rule 10(a). The plaintiff must, however, name as defendants both the property—designated generally by kind, quantity, and location—and at least one owner of some part of or interest in the property.

(2) *Contents.* The complaint must contain a short and plain statement of the following:

(A) the authority for the taking;

(B) the uses for which the property is to be taken;

(C) a description sufficient to identify the property;

(D) the interests to be acquired; and

(E) for each piece of property, a designation of each defendant who has been joined as an owner or owner of an interest in it.

(3) *Parties.* When the action commences, the plaintiff need join as defendants only those persons who have or claim an interest in the property and whose names are then known. But before any hearing on compensation, the plaintiff must add as defendants all those persons who have or claim an interest and whose names have become known or can be found by a reasonably diligent search of the records, considering both the property's character and value and the interests to be acquired. All others may be made defendants under the designation "Unknown Owners."

(4) *Procedure.* Notice must be served on all defendants as provided in Rule 71.1(d), whether they were named as defendants when the action commenced or were added later. A defendant may answer as provided in Rule 71.1(e). The court, meanwhile, may order any distribution of a deposit that the facts warrant.

(5) *Filing; Additional Copies.* In addition to filing the complaint, the plaintiff must give the clerk at least one copy for the defendants' use and additional copies at the request of the clerk or a defendant.

(d) PROCESS.

(1) *Delivering Notice to the Clerk.* On filing a complaint, the plaintiff must promptly deliver to the clerk joint or several notices directed to the named defendants. When adding defendants, the plaintiff must deliver to the clerk additional notices directed to the new defendants.

(2) *Contents of the Notice.*

(A) *Main Contents.* Each notice must name the court, the title of the action, and the defendant to whom it is directed. It must describe the property sufficiently to identify it, but need not describe any property other than that to be taken from the named defendant. The notice must also state:

(i) that the action is to condemn property;

(ii) the interest to be taken;

(iii) the authority for the taking;

(iv) the uses for which the property is to be taken;
(v) that the defendant may serve an answer on the plaintiff's attorney within 21 days after being served with the notice;
(vi) that the failure to so serve an answer constitutes consent to the taking and to the court's authority to proceed with the action and fix the compensation; and
(vii) that a defendant who does not serve an answer may file a notice of appearance.
(B) *Conclusion.* The notice must conclude with the name, telephone number, and e-mail address of the plaintiff's attorney and an address within the district in which the action is brought where the attorney may be served.
(3) *Serving the Notice.*
(A) *Personal Service.* When a defendant whose address is known resides within the United States or a territory subject to the administrative or judicial jurisdiction of the United States, personal service of the notice (without a copy of the complaint) must be made in accordance with Rule 4.
(B) *Service by Publication.*
(i) A defendant may be served by publication only when the plaintiff's attorney files a certificate stating that the attorney believes the defendant cannot be personally served, because after diligent inquiry within the state where the complaint is filed, the defendant's place of residence is still unknown or, if known, that it is beyond the territorial limits of personal service. Service is then made by publishing the notice—once a week for at least 3 successive weeks—in a newspaper published in the county where the property is located or, if there is no such newspaper, in a newspaper with general circulation where the property is located. Before the last publication, a copy of the notice must also be mailed to every defendant who cannot be personally served but whose place of residence is then known. Unknown owners may be served by publication in the same manner by a notice addressed to "Unknown Owners."
(ii) Service by publication is complete on the date of the last publication. The plaintiff's attorney must prove publication and mailing by a certificate, attach a printed copy of the published notice, and mark on the copy the newspaper's name and the dates of publication.
(4) *Effect of Delivery and Service.* Delivering the notice to the clerk and serving it have the same effect as serving a summons under Rule 4.
(5) *Amending the Notice; Proof of Service and Amending the Proof.* Rule 4(a)(2) governs amending the notice. Rule 4(*l*) governs proof of service and amending it.
(e) APPEARANCE OR ANSWER.
(1) *Notice of Appearance.* A defendant that has no objection or defense to the taking of its property may serve a notice of appearance designating the property in which it claims an interest. The defendant must then be given notice of all later proceedings affecting the defendant.
(2) *Answer.* A defendant that has an objection or defense to the taking must serve an answer within 21 days after being served with the notice. The answer must:
(A) identify the property in which the defendant claims an interest;
(B) state the nature and extent of the interest; and
(C) state all the defendant's objections and defenses to the taking.
(3) *Waiver of Other Objections and Defenses; Evidence on Compensation.* A defendant waives all objections and defenses not stated in its answer. No other pleading or motion asserting an additional objection or defense is allowed. But at the trial on compensation, a defendant—whether or not it has previously appeared or answered—may present evidence on the amount of compensation to be paid and may share in the award.
(f) AMENDING PLEADINGS. Without leave of court, the plaintiff may—as often as it wants—amend the complaint at any time before the trial on compensation. But no amendment may be made if it would result in a dismissal inconsistent with Rule 71.1(i)(1) or
(2). The plaintiff need not serve a copy of an amendment, but must serve notice of the filing, as provided in Rule 5(b), on every affected party who has appeared and, as provided in Rule 71.1(d), on every affected party who has not appeared. In addition, the plaintiff must give the clerk at least one copy of each amendment for the defendants' use, and additional copies at the request of the clerk or a defendant. A defendant may appear or answer in the time and manner and with the same effect as provided in Rule
71.1(e).
(g) SUBSTITUTING PARTIES. If a defendant dies, becomes incompetent, or transfers an interest after being joined, the court may, on motion and notice of hearing, order that the proper party be substituted. Service of the motion and notice on a nonparty must be made as provided in Rule 71.1(d)(3).
(h) TRIAL OF THE ISSUES.
(1) *Issues Other Than Compensation; Compensation.* In an action
involving eminent domain under federal law, the court tries all issues, including compensation, except when compensation must be determined:
(A) by any tribunal specially constituted by a federal statute to determine compensation; or
(B) if there is no such tribunal, by a jury when a party demands one within the time to answer or

within any additional time the court sets, unless the court appoints a commission.

(2) *Appointing a Commission; Commission's Powers and Report.*

(A) *Reasons for Appointing.* If a party has demanded a jury, the court may instead appoint a three-person commission to determine compensation because of the character, location, or quantity of the property to be condemned or for other just reasons.

(B) *Alternate Commissioners.* The court may appoint up to two additional persons to serve as alternate commissioners to hear the case and replace commissioners who, before a decision is filed, the court finds unable or disqualified to perform their duties. Once the commission renders its final decision, the court must discharge any alternate who has not replaced a commissioner.

(C) *Examining the Prospective Commissioners.* Before making its appointments, the court must advise the parties of the identity and qualifications of each prospective commissioner and alternate, and may permit the parties to examine them. The parties may not suggest appointees, but for good cause may object to a prospective commissioner or alternate.

(D) *Commission's Powers and Report.* A commission has the powers of a master under Rule 53(c). Its action and report are determined by a majority. Rule 53(d), (e), and (f) apply to its action and report.

(i) DISMISSAL OF THE ACTION OR A DEFENDANT.

(1) *Dismissing the Action.*

(A) *By the Plaintiff.* If no compensation hearing on a piece of property has begun, and if the plaintiff has not acquired title or a lesser interest or taken possession, the plaintiff may, without a court order, dismiss the action as to that property by filing a notice of dismissal briefly describing the property.

(B) *By Stipulation.* Before a judgment is entered vesting the plaintiff with title or a lesser interest in or possession of property, the plaintiff and affected defendants may, without a court order, dismiss the action in whole or in part by filing a stipulation of dismissal. And if the parties so stipulate, the court may vacate a judgment already entered.

(C) *By Court Order.* At any time before compensation has been determined and paid, the court may, after a motion and hearing, dismiss the action as to a piece of property. But if the plaintiff has already taken title, a lesser interest, or possession as to any part of it, the court must award compensation for the title, lesser interest, or possession taken.

(2) *Dismissing a Defendant.* The court may at any time dismiss a defendant who was unnecessarily or improperly joined.

(3) *Effect.* A dismissal is without prejudice unless otherwise stated in the notice, stipulation, or court order.

(j) DEPOSIT AND ITS DISTRIBUTION.

(1) *Deposit.* The plaintiff must deposit with the court any money required by law as a condition to the exercise of eminent domain and may make a deposit when allowed by statute.

(2) *Distribution; Adjusting Distribution.* After a deposit, the court and attorneys must expedite the proceedings so as to distribute the deposit and to determine and pay compensation. If the compensation finally awarded to a defendant exceeds the amount distributed to that defendant, the court must enter judgment against the plaintiff for the deficiency. If the compensation awarded to a defendant is less than the amount distributed to that defendant, the court must enter judgment against that defendant for the overpayment.

(k) CONDEMNATION UNDER A STATE'S POWER OF EMINENT DOMAIN.This rule governs an action involving eminent domain under state law. But if state law provides for trying an issue by jury—or for trying the issue of compensation by jury or commission or both—that law governs.

(*l*) COSTS. Costs are not subject to Rule 54(d).

FED. R. CIV. P. 72. Magistrate Judges: Pretrial Order

(a) NONDISPOSITIVE MATTERS. When a pretrial matter not dispositive of a party's claim or defense is referred to a magistrate judge to hear and decide, the magistrate judge must promptly conduct the required proceedings and, when appropriate, issue a written order stating the decision. A party may serve and file objections to the order within 14 days after being served with a copy. A party may not assign as error a defect in the order not timely objected to. The district judge in the case must consider timely objections and modify or set aside any part of the order that is clearly erroneous or is contrary to law.

(b) DISPOSITIVE MOTIONS AND PRISONER PETITIONS.

(1) *Findings and Recommendations.* A magistrate judge must promptly conduct the required proceedings when assigned, without the parties' consent, to hear a pretrial matter dispositive of a claim or defense or a prisoner petition challenging the conditions of confinement. A record must be made of all evidentiary proceedings and may, at the magistrate judge's discretion, be made of any other proceedings. The magistrate judge must

enter a recommended disposition, including, if appropriate, proposed findings of fact. The clerk must promptly mail a copy to each party.
(2) *Objections.* Within 14 days after being served with a copy of the recommended disposition, a party may serve and file specific written objections to the proposed findings and recommendations. A party may respond to another party's objections within 14 days after being served with a copy. Unless the district judge orders otherwise, the objecting party must promptly arrange for transcribing the record, or whatever portions of it the parties agree to or the magistrate judge considers sufficient.
(3) *Resolving Objections.* The district judge must determine de novo any part of the magistrate judge's disposition that has been properly objected to. The district judge may accept, reject, or modify the recommended disposition; receive further evidence; or return the matter to the magistrate judge with instructions.

FED. R. CIV. P. 73. Magistrate Judges: Trial by Consent; Appeal
(a) TRIAL BY CONSENT. When authorized under 28 U.S.C. § 636(c), a magistrate judge may, if all parties consent, conduct a civil action or proceeding, including a jury or nonjury trial. A record must be made in accordance with 28 U.S.C. § 636(c)(5).
(b) CONSENT PROCEDURE.
(1) *In General.* When a magistrate judge has been designated to conduct civil actions or proceedings, the clerk must give the parties written notice of their opportunity to consent under 28 U.S.C. §636(c). To signify their consent, the parties must jointly or separately file a statement consenting to the referral. A district judge or magistrate judge may be informed of a party's response to the clerk's notice only if all parties have consented to the referral.
(2) *Reminding the Parties About Consenting.* A district judge, magistrate judge, or other court official may remind the parties of the magistrate judge's availability, but must also advise them that they are free to withhold consent without adverse substantive consequences.
(3) *Vacating a Referral.* On its own for good cause—or when a party shows extraordinary circumstances—the district judge may vacate a referral to a magistrate judge under this rule.
(c) APPEALING A JUDGMENT. In accordance with 28 U.S.C. § 636(c)(3), an appeal from a judgment entered at a magistrate judge's direction may be taken to the court of appeals as would any other appeal from a district-court judgment.

FED. R. CIV. P. 74. [Abrogated (Apr. 11, 1997, eff. Dec. 1, 1997).]
FED. R. CIV. P. 75. [Abrogated (Apr. 11, 1997, eff. Dec. 1, 1997).]
FED. R. CIV. P. 76. [Abrogated (Apr. 11, 1997, eff. Dec. 1, 1997).]

FED. R. CIV. P. 77. Conducting Business; Clerk's Authority; Notice of an Order or Judgment
(a) WHEN COURT IS OPEN. Every district court is considered always open for filing any paper, issuing and returning process, making a motion, or entering an order.
(b) PLACE FOR TRIAL AND OTHER PROCEEDINGS. Every trial on the merits must be conducted in open court and, so far as convenient, in a regular courtroom. Any other act or proceeding may be done
or conducted by a judge in chambers, without the attendance of the clerk or other court official, and anywhere inside or outside the district. But no hearing—other than one ex parte—may be conducted outside the district unless all the affected parties consent.
(c) CLERK'S OFFICE HOURS; CLERK'S ORDERS.
(1) *Hours.* The clerk's office—with a clerk or deputy on duty—must be open during business hours every day except Saturdays, Sundays, and legal holidays. But a court may, by local rule or order, require that the office be open for specified hours on Saturday or a particular legal holiday other than one listed in Rule 6(a)(4)(A).
(2) *Orders.* Subject to the court's power to suspend, alter, or rescind the clerk's action for good cause, the clerk may:
(A) issue process;
(B) enter a default;
(C) enter a default judgment under Rule 55(b)(1); and
(D) act on any other matter that does not require the court's action.
(d) SERVING NOTICE OF AN ORDER OR JUDGMENT.
(1) *Service.* Immediately after entering an order or judgment, the clerk must serve notice of the entry, as provided in Rule 5(b), on each party who is not in default for failing to appear. The clerk must record the service on the docket. A party also may serve notice of the entry as provided in Rule 5(b).
(2) *Time to Appeal Not Affected by Lack of Notice.* Lack of notice of the entry does not affect the time for appeal or relieve—or authorize the court to relieve—a party for failing to appeal within the time allowed, except as allowed by Federal Rule of Appellate Procedure (4)(a).

FED. R. CIV. P. 78. Hearing Motions; Submission on Briefs

(a) PROVIDING A REGULAR SCHEDULE FOR ORAL HEARINGS. A court may establish regular times and places for oral hearings on motions.

(b) PROVIDING FOR SUBMISSION ON BRIEFS. By rule or order, the court may provide for submitting and determining motions on briefs, without oral hearings.

FED. R. CIV. P. 79. Records Kept by the Clerk

(a) CIVIL DOCKET.

(1) *In General.* The clerk must keep a record known as the "civil docket" in the form and manner prescribed by the Director of the Administrative Office of the United States Courts with the approval of the Judicial Conference of the United States. The clerk must enter each civil action in the docket. Actions must be assigned consecutive file numbers, which must be noted in the docket where the first entry of the action is made.

(2) *Items to be Entered.* The following items must be marked with the file number and entered chronologically in the docket:

(A) papers filed with the clerk;

(B) process issued, and proofs of service or other returns showing execution; and

(C) appearances, orders, verdicts, and judgments.

(3) *Contents of Entries; Jury Trial Demanded.* Each entry must briefly show the nature of the paper filed or writ issued, the substance of each proof of service or other return, and the substance and date of entry of each order and judgment. When a jury trial has been properly demanded or ordered, the clerk must enter the word "jury" in the docket.

(b) CIVIL JUDGMENTS AND ORDERS. The clerk must keep a copy of every final judgment and appealable order; of every order affecting title to or a lien on real or personal property; and of any other order that the court directs to be kept. The clerk must keep these in the form and manner prescribed by the Director of the Administrative Office of the United States Courts with the approval of the Judicial Conference of the United States.

(c) INDEXES; CALENDARS. Under the court's direction, the clerk must:

(1) keep indexes of the docket and of the judgments and orders described in Rule 79(b); and

(2) prepare calendars of all actions ready for trial, distinguishing jury trials from nonjury trials.

(d) OTHER RECORDS. The clerk must keep any other records required by the Director of the Administrative Office of the United States Courts with the approval of the Judicial Conference of the United States.

FED. R. CIV. P. 80. Stenographic Transcript as Evidence

If stenographically reported testimony at a hearing or trial is admissible in evidence at a later trial, the testimony may be proved by a transcript certified by the person who reported it.

FED. R. CIV. P. 81. Applicability of the Rules in General; Removed Actions

(a) APPLICABILITY TO PARTICULAR PROCEEDINGS.

(1) *Prize Proceedings.* These rules do not apply to prize proceedings in admiralty governed by 10 U.S.C. §§7651–7681.

(2) *Bankruptcy.* These rules apply to bankruptcy proceedings to the extent provided by the Federal Rules of Bankruptcy Procedure.

(3) *Citizenship.* These rules apply to proceedings for admission to citizenship to the extent that the practice in those proceedings is not specified in federal statutes and has previously conformed to the practice in civil actions. The provisions of 8 U.S.C. § 1451 for service by publication and for answer apply in proceedings to cancel citizenship certificates.

(4) *Special Writs.* These rules apply to proceedings for habeas corpus and for quo warranto to the extent that the practice in those proceedings:

(A) is not specified in a federal statute, the Rules Governing Section 2254 Cases, or the Rules Governing Section 2255 Cases; and

(B) has previously conformed to the practice in civil actions.

(5) *Proceedings Involving a Subpoena.* These rules apply to proceedings to compel testimony or the production of documents through a subpoena issued by a United States officer or agency under a federal statute, except as otherwise provided by statute, by local rule, or by court order in the proceedings.

(6) *Other Proceedings.* These rules, to the extent applicable, govern proceedings under the following laws, except as these laws provide other procedures:

(A) 7 U.S.C. §§292, 499g(c), for reviewing an order of the Secretary of Agriculture;

(B) 9 U.S.C., relating to arbitration;

(C) 15 U.S.C. §522, for reviewing an order of the Secretary of the Interior;

(D) 15 U.S.C. §715d(c), for reviewing an order denying a certificate of clearance;

(E) 29 U.S.C. §§159, 160, for enforcing an order of the National Labor Relations Board;

(F) 33 U.S.C. §§918, 921, for enforcing or reviewing a compensation order under the

Longshore and Harbor Workers' Compensation Act; and

(G) 45 U.S.C. §159, for reviewing an arbitration award in a railway-labor dispute.

(b) SCIRE FACIAS AND MANDAMUS. The writs of scire facias and mandamus are abolished. Relief previously available through them may be obtained by appropriate action or motion under these rules.

(c) REMOVED ACTIONS.

(1) *Applicability.* These rules apply to a civil action after it is removed from a state court.

(2) *Further Pleading.* After removal, repleading is unnecessary unless the court orders it. A defendant who did not answer before removal must answer or present other defenses or objections under these rules within the longest of these periods:

(A) 21 days after receiving—through service or otherwise— a copy of the initial pleading stating the claim for relief;

(B) 21 days after being served with the summons for an initial pleading on file at the time of service; or

(C) 7 days after the notice of removal is filed.

(3) *Demand for a Jury Trial.*

(A) *As Affected by State Law.* A party who, before removal, expressly demanded a jury trial in accordance with state law need not renew the demand after removal. If the state law did not require an express demand for a jury trial, a party need not make one after removal unless the court orders the parties to do so within a specified time. The court must so order at a party's request and may so order on its own. A party who fails to make a demand when so ordered waives a jury trial.

(B) *Under Rule 38.* If all necessary pleadings have been served at the time of removal, a party entitled to a jury trial under Rule 38 must be given one if the party serves a demand within 14 days after:

(i) it files a notice of removal; or

(ii) it is served with a notice of removal filed by another party.

(d) LAW APPLICABLE.

(1) *''State Law'' Defined.* When these rules refer to state law, the term ''law'' includes the state's statutes and the state's judicial decisions.

(2) *''State'' Defined.* The term ''state'' includes, where appropriate, the District of Columbia and any United States commonwealth or territory.

(3) *''Federal Statute'' Defined in the District of Columbia.* In the United States District Court for the District of Columbia, the term ''federal statute'' includes any Act of Congress that applies locally to the District.

FED. R. CIV. P. 82. Jurisdiction and Venue Unaffected

These rules do not extend or limit the jurisdiction of the district courts or the venue of actions in those courts. An admiralty or maritime claim under Rule 9(h) is not a civil action for purposes of 28 U.S.C. §§1391–1392.

FED. R. CIV. P. 83. Rules by District Courts; Judge's Directives

(a) LOCAL RULES.

(1) *In General.* After giving public notice and an opportunity for comment, a district court, acting by a majority of its district judges, may adopt and amend rules governing its practice. A local rule must be consistent with—but not duplicate— federal statutes and rules adopted under 28 U.S.C. §§2072 and 2075, and must conform to any uniform numbering system prescribed by the Judicial Conference of the United States. A local rule takes effect on the date specified by the district court and remains in effect unless amended by the court or abrogated by the judicial council of the circuit. Copies of rules and amendments must, on their adoption, be furnished to the judicial council and the Administrative Office of the United States Courts and be made available to the public.

(2) *Requirement of Form.* A local rule imposing a requirement of form must not be enforced in a way that causes a party to lose any right because of a nonwillful failure to comply.

(b) PROCEDURE WHEN THERE IS NO CONTROLLING LAW. A judge may regulate practice in any manner consistent with federal law, rules adopted under 28 U.S.C. §§2072 and 2075, and the district's local rules. No sanction or other disadvantage may be imposed for noncompliance with any requirement not in federal law, federal rules, or the local rules unless the alleged violator has been furnished in the particular case with actual notice of the requirement.

FED. R. CIV. P. 84. Forms

The forms in the Appendix suffice under these rules and illustrate the simplicity and brevity that these rules contemplate.

FED. R. CIV. P. 85. Title

These rules may be cited as the Federal Rules of Civil Procedure.

FED. R. CIV. P. 86. Effective Dates

(a) IN GENERAL. These rules and any amendments take effect at the time specified by the Supreme Court, subject to 28 U.S.C. §2074. They govern:

(1) proceedings in an action commenced after their effective date; and

(2) proceedings after that date in an action then pending unless:

(A) the Supreme Court specifies otherwise; or
(B) the court determines that applying them in a particular action would be infeasible or work an injustice.
(b) DECEMBER 1, 2007 AMENDMENTS. If any provision in Rules 1–5.1, 6–73, or 77–86 conflicts with another law, priority in time for the purpose of 28 U.S.C. §2072(b) is not affected by the amendments taking effect on December 1, 2007.

APPENDIX II

FEDERAL RULES OF APPELLATE PROCEDURE

TITLE I. APPLICABILITY OF RULES

FED. R. APP. P. 1. Scope of Rules; Title.
(a) SCOPE OF RULES.
(1) These rules govern procedure in the United States courts of appeals.
(2) When these rules provide for filing a motion or other document in the district court, the procedure must comply with the practice of the district court.
(b) [Abrogated.]
(c) *Title.* These rules are to be known as the Federal Rules of Appellate Procedure.

FED. R. APP. P. 2. Suspension of Rules.
On its own or a party's motion, a court of appeals may—to expedite its decision or for other good cause—suspend any provision of these rules in a particular case and order proceedings as it directs, except as otherwise provided in Rule 26(b).

TITLE II. APPEAL FROM A JUDGMENT OR ORDER OF A DISTRICT COURT

FED. R. APP. P. 3. Appeal as of Right—How Taken.
(a) FILING THE NOTICE OF APPEAL.
(1) An appeal permitted by law as of right from a district court to a court of appeals may be taken only by filing a notice of appeal with the district clerk within the time allowed by Rule 4. At the time of filing, the appellant must furnish the clerk with enough copies of the notice to enable the clerk to comply with Rule 3(d).
(2) An appellant's failure to take any step other than the timely filing of a notice of appeal does not affect the validity of the appeal, but is ground only for the court of appeals to act as it considers appropriate, including dismissing the appeal.
(3) An appeal from a judgment by a magistrate judge in a civil case is taken in the same way as an appeal from any other district court judgment.
(4) An appeal by permission under 28 U.S.C. §1292(b) or an appeal in a bankruptcy case may be taken only in the manner prescribed by Rules 5 and 6, respectively.
(b) JOINT OR CONSOLIDATED APPEALS.
(1) When two or more parties are entitled to appeal from a district-court judgment or order, and their interests make joinder practicable, they may file a joint notice of appeal. They may then proceed on appeal as a single appellant.
(2) When the parties have filed separate timely notices of appeal, the appeals may be joined or consolidated by the court of appeals.
(c) CONTENTS OF THE NOTICE OF APPEAL.
(1) The notice of appeal must:
(A) specify the party or parties taking the appeal by naming each one in the caption or body of the notice, but an attorney representing more than one party may describe those parties with such terms as ''all plaintiffs,'' ''the defendants,'' ''the plaintiffs A, B, et al.,'' or ''all defendants except X'';
(B) designate the judgment, order, or part thereof being appealed; and
(C) name the court to which the appeal is taken.
(2) A pro se notice of appeal is considered filed on behalf of the signer and the signer's spouse and minor children (if they are parties), unless the notice clearly indicates otherwise.
(3) In a class action, whether or not the class has been certified, the notice of appeal is sufficient if it names one personqualified to bring the appeal as representative of the class.
(4) An appeal must not be dismissed for informality of form or title of the notice of appeal, or for failure to name a party whose intent to appeal is otherwise clear from the notice.
(5) Form 1 in the Appendix of Forms is a suggested form of a notice of appeal.

(d) SERVING THE NOTICE OF APPEAL.

(1) The district clerk must serve notice of the filing of a noticeof appeal by mailing a copy to each party's counsel of record—excluding the appellant's—or, if a party is proceeding pro se, to the party's last known address. When a defendant in a criminal case appeals, the clerk must also serve a copy of the notice of appeal on the defendant, either by personal service or by mail addressed to the defendant. The clerk must promptly send a copy of the notice of appeal and of the docket entries—and any later docket entries—to the clerk of the court of appeals named in the notice. The district clerk must note, on each copy, the date when the notice of appeal was filed.

(2) If an inmate confined in an institution files a notice of appeal in the manner provided by Rule 4(c), the district clerk must also note the date when the clerk docketed the notice.

(3) The district clerk's failure to serve notice does not affect the validity of the appeal. The clerk must note on the docket the names of the parties to whom the clerk mails copies, with the date of mailing. Service is sufficient despite the death of a party or the party's counsel.

(e) PAYMENT OF FEES. Upon filing a notice of appeal, the appellant must pay the district clerk all required fees. The district clerk receives the appellate docket fee on behalf of the court of appeals.

FED. R. CIV. P. 4. Appeal as of Right—When Taken.

(a) APPEAL IN A CIVIL CASE.

(1) *Time for Filing a Notice of Appeal.*

(A) In a civil case, except as provided in Rules 4(a)(1)(B), 4(a)(4), and 4(c), the notice of appeal required by Rule 3 must be filed with the district clerk within 30 days after the judgment or order appealed from is entered.

(B) When the United States or its officer or agency is a party, the notice of appeal may be filed by any party within 60 days after the judgment or order appealed from is entered.

(C) An appeal from an order granting or denying an application for a writ of error *coram nobis* is an appeal in a civil case for purposes of Rule 4(a).

(2) *Filing Before Entry of Judgment.* A notice of appeal filed after the court announces a decision or order—but before the entry of the judgment or order—is treated as filed on the date of and after the entry.

(3) *Multiple Appeals.* If one party timely files a notice of appeal, any other party may file a notice of appeal within 14 days after the date when the first notice was filed, or within the time otherwise prescribed by this Rule 4(a), whichever period ends later.

(4) *Effect of a Motion on a Notice of Appeal.*

(A) If a party timely files in the district court any of the following motions under the Federal Rules of Civil Procedure, the time to file an appeal runs for all parties from the entry of the order disposing of the last such remaining motion:

(i) for judgment under Rule 50(b);

(ii) to amend or make additional factual findings under Rule 52(b), whether or not granting the motion would alter the judgment;

(iii) for attorney's fees under Rule 54 if the district court extends the time to appeal under Rule 58;

(iv) to alter or amend the judgment under Rule 59;

(v) for a new trial under Rule 59; or

(vi) for relief under Rule 60 if the motion is filed no later than 28 days after the judgment is entered.

(B)

(i) If a party files a notice of appeal after the court announces or enters a judgment—but before it disposes of any motion listed in Rule 4(a)(4)(A)—the notice becomes effective to appeal a judgment or order, in whole or in part, when the order disposing of the last such remaining motion is entered.

(ii) A party intending to challenge an order disposing of any motion listed in Rule 4(a)(4)(A), or a judgment's alteration or amendment upon such a motion, must file a notice of appeal, or an amended notice of appeal—in compliance with Rule 3(c) within the time prescribed by this Rule measured from the entry of the order disposing of the last such remaining motion.

(iii) No additional fee is required to file an amended notice.

(5) *Motion for Extension of Time.*

(A) The district court may extend the time to file a notice of appeal if:

(i) a party so moves no later than 30 days after the time prescribed by this Rule 4(a) expires; and

(ii) regardless of whether its motion is filed before or during the 30 days after the time prescribed by this Rule 4(a) expires, that party shows excusable neglect or good cause.

(B) A motion filed before the expiration of the time prescribed in Rule 4(a)(1) or (3) may be ex parte unless the court requires otherwise. If the motion is filed after the expiration of the prescribed time, notice must be given to the other parties in accordance with local rules.

(C) No extension under this Rule 4(a)(5) may exceed 30 days after the prescribed time or 14 days after the date when the order granting the motion is entered, whichever is later.

(6) *Reopening the Time to File an Appeal.* The district court may reopen the time to file an appeal for a period of 14 days after the date

when its order to reopen is entered, but only if all the following conditions are satisfied:
(A) the court finds that the moving party did not receive notice under Federal Rule of Civil Procedure 77(d) of the entry of the judgment or order sought to be appealed within 21 days after entry;
(B) the motion is filed within 180 days after the judgment or order is entered or within 14 days after the moving party receives notice under Federal Rule of Civil Procedure 77(d) of the entry, whichever is earlier; and
(C) the court finds that no party would be prejudiced.
(7) *Entry Defined.*
(A) A judgment or order is entered for purposes of this
Rule 4(a):
(i) if Federal Rule of Civil Procedure 58(a)(1) does not require a separate document, when the judgment or order is entered in the civil docket under Federal Rule of Civil Procedure 79(a); or
(ii) if Federal Rule of Civil Procedure 58(a)(1) requires a separate document, when the judgment or order is entered in the civil docket under Federal Rule of Civil Procedure 79(a) and when the earlier of these events occurs:
• the judgment or order is set forth on a separate document, or
• 150 days have run from entry of the judgment or order in the civil docket under Federal Rule of Civil Procedure 79(a).
(B) A failure to set forth a judgment or order on a separate document when required by Federal Rule of Civil Procedure 58(a)(1) does not affect the validity of an appeal from that judgment or order.
(b) APPEAL IN A CRIMINAL CASE.
(1) *Time for Filing a Notice of Appeal.*
(A) In a criminal case, a defendant's notice of appeal must be filed in the district court within 14 days after the later of:
(i) the entry of either the judgment or the order being appealed; or
(ii) the filing of the government's notice of appeal.
(B) When the government is entitled to appeal, its notice of appeal must be filed in the district court within 30 days after the later of:
(i) the entry of the judgment or order being appealed; or
(ii) the filing of a notice of appeal by any defendant.
(2) *Filing Before Entry of Judgment.* A notice of appeal filed after the court announces a decision, sentence, or order—but before the entry of the judgment or order—is treated as filed on the date of and after the entry.
(3) *Effect of a Motion on a Notice of Appeal.*
(A) If a defendant timely makes any of the following motions under the Federal Rules of Criminal Procedure, the notice of appeal from a judgment of conviction must be filed within 14 days after the entry of the order disposing of the last such remaining motion, or within 14 days after the entry of the judgment of conviction, whichever period ends later. This provision applies to a timely motion:
(i) for judgment of acquittal under Rule 29;
(ii) for a new trial under Rule 33, but if based on newly discovered evidence, only if the motion is made no later than 14 days after the entry of the judgment; or
(iii) for arrest of judgment under Rule 34.
(B) A notice of appeal filed after the court announces a decision, sentence, or order—but before it disposes of any of the motions referred to in Rule 4(b)(3)(A)—becomes effective upon the later of the following:
(i) the entry of the order disposing of the last such remaining motion; or
(ii) the entry of the judgment of conviction.
(C) A valid notice of appeal is effective—without amendment—to appeal from an order disposing of any of the motions referred to in Rule 4(b)(3)(A).
(4) *Motion for Extension of Time.* Upon a finding of excusable neglect or good cause, the district court may—before or after the time has expired, with or without motion and notice—extend the time to file a notice of appeal for a period not to exceed 30 days from the expiration of the time otherwise prescribed by this Rule 4(b).
(5) *Jurisdiction.* The filing of a notice of appeal under this Rule 4(b) does not divest a district court of jurisdiction to correct a sentence under Federal Rule of Criminal Procedure 35(a), nor does the filing of a motion under 35(a) affect the validity of a notice of appeal filed before entry of the order disposing of the motion. The filing of a motion under Federal Rule of Criminal Procedure 35(a) does not suspend the time for filing a notice of appeal from a judgment of conviction.
(6) *Entry Defined.* A judgment or order is entered for purposes of this Rule 4(b) when it is entered on the criminal docket.
(c) APPEAL BY AN INMATE CONFINED IN AN INSTITUTION.
(1) If an inmate confined in an institution files a notice of appeal in either a civil or a criminal case, the notice is timely if it is deposited in the institution's internal mail system on or before the last day for filing. If an institution has a system designed for legal mail, the inmate must use that system to receive the benefit of this rule. Timely filing may be shown by a declaration in compliance with 28 U.S.C. § 1746 or by a notarized statement, either of

which must set forth the date of deposit and state that first-class postage has been prepaid.
(2) If an inmate files the first notice of appeal in a civil case under this Rule 4(c), the 14-day period provided in Rule 4(a)(3) for another party to file a notice of appeal runs from the date when the district court dockets the first notice.
(3) When a defendant in a criminal case files a notice of appeal under this Rule 4(c), the 30-day period for the government to file its notice of appeal runs from the entry of the judgment or order appealed from or from the district court's docketing of the defendant's notice of appeal, whichever is later.
(d) MISTAKEN FILING IN THE COURT OF APPEALS. If a notice of appeal in either a civil or a criminal case is mistakenly filed in the court of appeals, the clerk of that court must note on the notice the date when it was received and send it to the district clerk. The notice is then considered filed in the district court on the date so noted.

FED. R. APP. P. 5. Appeal by Permission.
(a) PETITION FOR PERMISSION TO APPEAL.
(1) To request permission to appeal when an appeal is within the court of appeals' discretion, a party must file a petition permission to appeal. The petition must be filed with the circuit clerk with proof of service on all other parties to the district-court action.
(2) The petition must be filed within the time specified by the statute or rule authorizing the appeal or, if no such time is specified, within the time provided by Rule 4(a) for filing a notice of appeal.
(3) If a party cannot petition for appeal unless the district court first enters an order granting permission to do so or stating that the necessary conditions are met, the district court may amend its order, either on its own or in response to a party's motion, to include the required permission or statement. In that event, the time to petition runs from entry of the amended order.
(b) CONTENTS OF THE PETITION; ANSWER OR CROSS-PETITION; ORAL ARGUMENT.
(1) The petition must include the following:
(A) the facts necessary to understand the question presented;
(B) the question itself;
(C) the relief sought;
(D) the reasons why the appeal should be allowed and is authorized by a statute or rule; and
(E) an attached copy of:
(i) the order, decree, or judgment complained of and any related opinion or memorandum, and
(ii) any order stating the district court's permission to appeal or finding that the necessary conditions are met.
(2) A party may file an answer in opposition or a cross-petition within 10 days after the petition is served.
(3) The petition and answer will be submitted without oral argument unless the court of appeals orders otherwise.
(c) FORM OF PAPERS; NUMBER OF COPIES. All papers must conform to Rule 32(c)(2). Except by the court's permission, a paper must not exceed 20 pages, exclusive of the disclosure statement, the proof of service, and the accompanying documents required by Rule 5(b)(1)(E). An original and 3 copies must be filed unless the court requires a different number by local rule or by order in a particular case.
(d) GRANT OF PERMISSION; FEES; COST BOND; FILING THE RECORD.
(1) Within 14 days after the entry of the order granting permission to appeal, the appellant must:
(A) pay the district clerk all required fees; and
(B) file a cost bond if required under Rule 7.
(2) A notice of appeal need not be filed. The date when the order granting permission to appeal is entered serves as the date of the notice of appeal for calculating time under these rules.
(3) The district clerk must notify the circuit clerk once the petitioner has paid the fees. Upon receiving this notice, the circuit clerk must enter the appeal on the docket. The record must be forwarded and filed in accordance with Rules 11 and 12(c).

[FED. R. APP. P. 5.1. Appeal by Leave under 28 U.S.C. § 636(c)(5)] (Abrogated Apr. 24, 1998, eff. Dec. 1, 1998)

FED. R. APP. P. 6. Appeal in a Bankruptcy Case From a Final Judgment, Order, or Decree of a District Court or Bankruptcy Appellate Panel.
(a) APPEAL FROM A JUDGMENT, ORDER, OR DECREE OF A DISTRICT COURT EXERCISING ORIGINAL JURISDICTION IN A BANKRUPTCY CASE. An appeal to a court of appeals from a final judgment, order, or decree of a district court exercising jurisdiction under 28 U.S.C. § 1334 is taken as any other civil appeal under these rules.
(b) APPEAL FROM A JUDGMENT, ORDER, OR DECREE OF A DISTRICT COURT OR BANKRUPTCY APPELLATE PANEL EXERCISING APPELLATE JURISDICTION IN A BANKRUPTCY CASE.
(1) *Applicability of Other Rules.* These rules apply to an appeal to a court of appeals under 28 U.S.C. § 158(d) from a final judgment, order,

or decree of a district court or bankruptcy appellate panel exercising appellate jurisdiction under 28 U.S.C. §158(a) or (b). But there are 3 exceptions:

(A) Rules 4(a)(4), 4(b), 9, 10, 11, 12(b), 13–20, 22–23, and 24(b) do not apply;

(B) the reference in Rule 3(c) to ''Form 1 in the Appendix of Forms'' must be read as a reference to Form 5; and

(C) when the appeal is from a bankruptcy appellate panel, the term ''district court,'' as used in any applicable rule, means ''appellate panel.''

(2) *Additional Rules.* In addition to the rules made applicable by Rule 6(b)(1), the following rules apply:

(A) MOTION FOR REHEARING.

(i) If a timely motion for rehearing under Bankruptcy Rule 8015 is filed, the time to appeal for all parties runs from the entry of the order disposing of the motion. A notice of appeal filed after the district court or bankruptcy appellate panel announces or enters a judgment, order, or decree—but before disposition of the motion for rehearing—becomes effective when the order disposing of the motion for rehearing is entered.

(ii) Appellate review of the order disposing of the motion requires the party, in compliance with Rules 3(c) and 6(b)(1)(B), to amend a previously filed notice of appeal. A party intending to challenge an altered or amended judgment, order, or decree must file a notice of appeal or amended notice of appeal within the time prescribed by Rule 4—excluding Rules 4(a)(4) and 4(b)— measured from the entry of the order disposing of the motion.

(iii) No additional fee is required to file an amended notice.

(B) *The record on appeal.*

(i) Within 14 days after filing the notice of appeal, the appellant must file with the clerk possessing the record assembled in accordance with Bankruptcy Rule 8006—and serve on the appellee—a statement of the issues to be presented on appeal and a designation of the record to be certified and sent to the circuit clerk.

(ii) An appellee who believes that other parts of the record are necessary must, within 14 days after being served with the appellant's designation, file with the clerk and serve on the appellant a designation of additional parts to be included.

(iii) The record on appeal consists of:

• the redesignated record as provided above;

• the proceedings in the district court or bankruptcy

• appellate panel; and

• a certified copy of the docket entries prepared by the clerk under Rule 3(d).

(C) *Forwarding the record.*

(i) When the record is complete, the district clerk or bankruptcy appellate panel clerk must number the documents constituting the record and send them promptly to the circuit clerk together with a list of the documents correspondingly numbered and reasonably identified. Unless directed to do so by a party or the circuit clerk, the clerk will not send to the court of appeals documents of unusual bulk or weight, physical exhibits other than documents, or other parts of the record designated for omission by local rule of the court of appeals. If the exhibits are unusually bulky or heavy, a party must arrange with the clerks in advance for their transportation and receipt.

(ii) All parties must do whatever else is necessary to enable the clerk to assemble and forward the record. The court of appeals may provide by rule or order that a certified copy of the docket entries be sent in place of the redesignated record, but any party may request at any time during the pendency of the appeal that the redesignated record be sent.

(D) *Filing the record.* Upon receiving the record—or a certified copy of the docket entries sent in place of the redesignated record—the circuit clerk must file it and immediately notify all parties of the filing date.

FED. R. APP. P. 7. Bond for Costs on Appeal in a Civil Case.

In a civil case, the district court may require an appellant to file a bond or provide other security in any form and amount necessary to ensure payment of costs on appeal. Rule 8(b) applies to a surety on a bond given under this rule.

FED. R. APP. P. 8. Stay or Injunction Pending Appeal.

(a) MOTION FOR STAY.

(1) *Initial Motion in the District Court.* A party must ordinarily move first in the district court for the following relief:

(A) a stay of the judgment or order of a district court

pending appeal;

(B) approval of a supersedeas bond; or

(C) an order suspending, modifying, restoring, or granting an injunction while an appeal is pending.

(2) *Motion in the Court of Appeals; Conditions on Relief.* A motion for the relief mentioned in Rule 8(a)(1) may be made to the court of appeals or to one of its judges.

(A) The motion must:

(i) show that moving first in the district court would be impracticable; or

(ii) state that, a motion having been made, the district court denied the motion or failed to

afford the relief requested and state any reasons given by the district court for its action.
(B) The motion must also include:
(i) the reasons for granting the relief requested and the facts relied on;
(ii) originals or copies of affidavits or other sworn statements supporting facts subject to dispute; and
(iii) relevant parts of the record.
(C) The moving party must give reasonable notice of the motion to all parties.
(D) A motion under this Rule 8(a)(2) must be filed with the circuit clerk and normally will be considered by a panel of the court. But in an exceptional case in which time requirements make that procedure impracticable, the motion may be made to and considered by a single judge.
(E) The court may condition relief on a party's filing a bond or other appropriate security in the district court.
(b) PROCEEDING AGAINST A SURETY. If a party gives security in the form of a bond or stipulation or other undertaking with one or more sureties, each surety submits to the jurisdiction of the district court and irrevocably appoints the district clerk as the surety's agent on whom any papers affecting the surety's liability on the bond or undertaking may be served. On motion, a surety's liability may be enforced in the district court without the necessity of an independent action. The motion and any notice that the district court prescribes may be served on the district clerk, who must promptly mail a copy to each surety whose address is known.
(c) STAY IN A CRIMINAL CASE. Rule 38 of the Federal Rules of Criminal Procedure governs a stay in a criminal case.

FED. R. APP. P. 9. Release in a Criminal Case.
(a) RELEASE BEFORE JUDGMENT OF CONVICTION.
(1) The district court must state in writing, or orally on the record, the reasons for an order regarding the release or detention of a defendant in a criminal case. A party appealing from the order must file with the court of appeals a copy of the district court's order and the court's statement of reasons as soon as practicable after filing the notice of appeal. An appellant who questions the factual basis for the district court's order must file a transcript of the release proceedings or an explanation of why a transcript was not obtained.
(2) After reasonable notice to the appellee, the court of appeals must promptly determine the appeal on the basis of the papers, affidavits, and parts of the record that the parties present or the court requires. Unless the court so orders, briefs need not be filed.
(3) The court of appeals or one of its judges may order the defendant's release pending the disposition of the appeal.
(b) RELEASE AFTER JUDGMENT OF CONVICTION. A party entitled to do so may obtain review of a district-court order regarding release after a judgment of conviction by filing a notice of appeal from that order in the district court, or by filing a motion in the court of appeals if the party has already filed a notice of appeal from the judgment of conviction. Both the order and the review are subject to Rule 9(a). The papers filed by the party seeking review must include a copy of the judgment of conviction.
(c) CRITERIA FOR RELEASE. The court must make its decision regarding release in accordance with the applicable provisions of 18 U.S.C. §§3142, 3143, and 3145(c).

FED. R. APP. P. 10. The Record on Appeal.
(a) COMPOSITION OF THE RECORD ON APPEAL. The following items constitute the record on appeal:
(1) the original papers and exhibits filed in the district court;
(2) the transcript of proceedings, if any; and
(3) a certified copy of the docket entries prepared by the district clerk.
(b) THE TRANSCRIPT OF PROCEEDINGS.
(1) *Appellant's Duty to Order.* Within 14 days after filing the notice of appeal or entry of an order disposing of the last timely remaining motion of a type specified in Rule 4(a)(4)(A), whichever is later, the appellant must do either of the following:
(A) order from the reporter a transcript of such parts of the proceedings not already on file as the appellant considers necessary, subject to a local rule of the court of appeals and with the following qualifications:
(i) the order must be in writing;
(ii) if the cost of the transcript is to be paid by the United States under the Criminal Justice Act, the order must so state; and
(iii) the appellant must, within the same period, file a copy of the order with the district clerk; or
(B) file a certificate stating that no transcript will be ordered.
(2) *Unsupported Finding or Conclusion.* If the appellant intends to urge on appeal that a finding or conclusion is unsupported by the evidence or is contrary to the evidence, the appellant must include in the record a transcript of all evidence relevant to that finding or conclusion.
(3) *Partial Transcript.* Unless the entire transcript is ordered:

(A) the appellant must—within the 14 days provided in Rule 10(b)(1)—file a statement of the issues that the appellant intends to present on the appeal and must serve on the appellee a copy of both the order or certificate and the statement;
(B) if the appellee considers it necessary to have a transcript of other parts of the proceedings, the appellee must, within 14 days after the service of the order or certificate and the statement of the issues, file and serve on the appellant a designation of additional parts to be ordered; and
(C) unless within 14 days after service of that designation the appellant has ordered all such parts, and has so notified the appellee, the appellee may within the following 14 days either order the parts or move in the district court for an order requiring the appellant to do so.
(4) *Payment.* At the time of ordering, a party must make satisfactory arrangements with the reporter for paying the cost of the transcript.
(c) STATEMENT OF THE EVIDENCE WHEN THE PROCEEDINGS WERE NOT RECORDED OR WHEN A TRANSCRIPT IS UNAVAILABLE. If the transcript of a hearing or trial is unavailable, the appellant may prepare a statement of the evidence or proceedings from the best available means, including the appellant's recollection. The statement must be served on the appellee, who may serve objections or proposed amendments within 14 days after being served. The statement and any objections or proposed amendments must then be submitted to the district court for settlement and approval. As settled and approved, the statement must be included by the district clerk in the record on appeal.
(d) AGREED STATEMENT AS THE RECORD ON APPEAL. In place of the record on appeal as defined in Rule 10(a), the parties may prepare, sign, and submit to the district court a statement of the case showing how the issues presented by the appeal arose and were decided in the district court. The statement must set forth only those facts averred and proved or sought to be proved that are essential to the courts resolution of the issues. If the statement is truthful, it—together with any additions that the district court may consider necessary to a full presentation of the issues on appeal— must be approved by the district court and must then be certified to the court of appeals as the record on appeal. The district clerk must then send it to the circuit clerk within the time provided by Rule 11. A copy of the agreed statement may be filed in place of the appendix required by Rule 30.
(e) CORRECTION OR MODIFICATION OF THE RECORD.
(1) If any difference arises about whether the record truly discloses what occurred in the district court, the difference must be submitted to and settled by that court and the record conformed accordingly.
(2) If anything material to either party is omitted from or misstated in the record by error or accident, the omission or misstatement may be corrected and a supplemental record may be certified and forwarded:
(A) on stipulation of the parties;
(B) by the district court before or after the record has been forwarded; or
(C) by the court of appeals.
(3) All other questions as to the form and content of the record must be presented to the court of appeals.

FED. R. APP. P. 11. Forwarding the Record.
(a) APPELLANT'S DUTY. An appellant filing a notice of appeal must comply with Rule 10(b) and must do whatever else is necessary to enable the clerk to assemble and forward the record. If there are multiple appeals from a judgment or order, the clerk must forward a single record.
(b) DUTIES OF REPORTER AND DISTRICT CLERK.
(1) *Reporter's Duty to Prepare and File a Transcript.* The reporter must prepare and file a transcript as follows:
(A) Upon receiving an order for a transcript, the reporter must enter at the foot of the order the date of its receipt and the expected completion date and send a copy, so endorsed, to the circuit clerk.
(B) If the transcript cannot be completed within 30 days of the reporters receipt of the order, the reporter may request the circuit clerk to grant additional time to complete it. The clerk must note on the docket the action taken and notify the parties.
(C) When a transcript is complete, the reporter must file it with the district clerk and notify the circuit clerk of the filing.
(D) If the reporter fails to file the transcript on time, the circuit clerk must notify the district judge and do whatever else the court of appeals directs.
(2) *District Clerk's Duty to Forward.* When the record is complete, the district clerk must number the documents constituting the record and send them promptly to the circuit clerk together with a list of the documents correspondingly numbered and reasonably identified. Unless directed to do so by a party or the circuit clerk, the district clerk will not send to the court of appeals documents of unusual bulk or weight, physical exhibits other than documents, or other parts of the record designated for omission by local rule of the court of appeals. If the exhibits are

unusually bulky or heavy, a party must arrange with the clerks in advance for their transportation and receipt.

(c) RETAINING THE RECORD TEMPORARILY IN THE DISTRICT COURT FOR USE IN PREPARING THE APPEAL. The parties may stipulate, or the district court on motion may order, that the district clerk retain the record temporarily for the parties to use in preparing the papers on appeal. In that event the district clerk must certify to the circuit clerk that the record on appeal is complete. Upon receipt of the appellee's brief, or earlier if the court orders or the parties agree, the appellant must request the district clerk to forward the record.

(d) [Abrogated.]

(e) RETAINING THE RECORD BY COURT ORDER.

(1) The court of appeals may, by order or local rule, provide that a certified copy of the docket entries be forwarded instead of the entire record. But a party may at any time during the appeal request that designated parts of the record be forwarded.

(2) The district court may order the record or some part of it retained if the court needs it while the appeal is pending, subject, however, to call by the court of appeals.

(3) If part or all of the record is ordered retained, the district clerk must send to the court of appeals a copy of the order and the docket entries together with the parts of the original record allowed by the district court and copies of any parts of the record designated by the parties.

(f) RETAINING PARTS OF THE RECORD IN THE DISTRICT COURT BY STIPULATION OF THE PARTIES. The parties may agree by written stipulation filed in the district court that designated parts of the record be retained in the district court subject to call by the court of appeals or request by a party. The parts of the record so designated remain a part of the record on appeal.

(g) RECORD FOR A PRELIMINARY MOTION IN THE COURT OF APPEALS. If, before the record is forwarded, a party makes any of the following motions in the court of appeals:

- for dismissal;
- for release;
- for a stay pending appeal;
- for additional security on the bond on appeal or on a supersedeas
- bond; or
- for any other intermediate order—
- the district clerk must send the court of appeals any parts of the record designated by any party.

FED. R. APP. P. 12. Docketing the Appeal; Filing a Representation Statement; Filing the Record.

(a) DOCKETING THE APPEAL. Upon receiving the copy of the notice of appeal and the docket entries from the district clerk under Rule 3(d), the circuit clerk must docket the appeal under the title of the district-court action and must identify the appellant, adding the appellant's name if necessary.

(b) FILING A REPRESENTATION STATEMENT. Unless the court of appeals designates another time, the attorney who filed the notice of appeal must, within 14 days after filing the notice, file a statement with the circuit clerk naming the parties that the attorney represents on appeal.

(c) FILING THE RECORD, PARTIAL RECORD, OR CERTIFICATE. Upon receiving the record, partial record, or district clerk's certificate as provided in Rule 11, the circuit clerk must file it and immediately notify all parties of the filing date.

(As amended Apr. 1, 1979, eff. Aug. 1, 1979; Mar. 10, 1986, eff. July 1, 1986; Apr. 22, 1993, eff. Dec. 1, 1993; Apr. 24, 1998, eff. Dec. 1, 1998; Mar. 26, 2009, eff. Dec. 1, 2009.)

FED. R. APP. P. 12.1. Remand After an Indicative Ruling by the District Court on a Motion for Relief That Is Barred by a Pending Appeal.

(a) NOTICE TO THE COURT OF APPEALS. If a timely motion is made in the district court for relief that it lacks authority to grant because of an appeal that has been docketed and is pending, the movant must promptly notify the circuit clerk if the district court states either that it would grant the motion or that the motion raises a substantial issue.

(b) REMAND AFTER AN INDICATIVE RULING. If the district court states that it would grant the motion or that the motion raises a substantial issue, the court of appeals may remand for further proceedings but retains jurisdiction unless it expressly dismisses the appeal. If the court of appeals remands but retains jurisdiction, the parties must promptly notify the circuit clerk when the district court has decided the motion on remand.

TITLE III. REVIEW OF A DECISION OF THE UNITED STATES TAX COURT

FED. R. APP. P. 13. Review of a Decision of the Tax Court.

(a) HOW OBTAINED; TIME FOR FILING NOTICE OF APPEAL.

(1) Review of a decision of the United States Tax Court is commenced by filing a notice of appeal with the Tax Court clerk within 90 days after the entry of the Tax Court's

decision. At the time of filing, the appellant must furnish the clerk with enough copies of the notice to enable the clerk to comply with Rule 3(d). If one party files a timely notice of appeal, any other party may file a notice of appeal within 120 days after the Tax Court's decision is entered.

(2) If, under Tax Court rules, a party makes a timely motion to vacate or revise the Tax Court's decision, the time to file a notice of appeal runs from the entry of the order disposing of the motion or from the entry of a new decision, whichever is later.

(b) NOTICE OF APPEAL; HOW FILED. The notice of appeal may be filed either at the Tax Court clerk's office in the District of Columbia or by mail addressed to the clerk. If sent by mail the notice is considered filed on the postmark date, subject to §7502 of the Internal Revenue Code, as amended, and the applicable regulations.

(c) CONTENTS OF THE NOTICE OF APPEAL; SERVICE; EFFECT OF FILING AND SERVICE. Rule 3 prescribes the contents of a notice of appeal, themanner of service, and the effect of its filing and service. Form 2 in the Appendix of Forms is a suggested form of a notice of appeal.

(d) THE RECORD ON APPEAL; FORWARDING; FILING.

(1) An appeal from the Tax Court is governed by the parts of Rules 10, 11, and 12 regarding the record on appeal from a district court, the time and manner of forwarding and filing, and the docketing in the court of appeals. References in those rules and in Rule 3 to the district court and district clerk are to be read as referring to the Tax Court and its clerk.

(2) If an appeal from a Tax Court decision is taken to more than one court of appeals, the original record must be sent to the court named in the first notice of appeal filed. In an appeal to any other court of appeals, the appellant must apply to that other court to make provision for the record.

FED. R. APP. P. 14. Applicability of Other Rules to the Review of a Tax Court Decision. All provisions of these rules, except Rules 4–9, 15–20, and 22–23, apply to the review of a Tax Court decision.

TITLE IV. REVIEW OR ENFORCEMENT OF AN ORDER OF AN ADMINISTRATIVE AGENCY, BOARD, COMMISSION, OR OFFICER

FED. R. APP. P. 15. Review or Enforcement of an Agency Order—How Obtained; Intervention.

(a) PETITION FOR REVIEW; JOINT PETITION.

(1) Review of an agency order is commenced by filing, within the time prescribed by law, a petition for review with the clerk of a court of appeals authorized to review the agency order. If their interests make joinder practicable, two or more persons may join in a petition to the same court to review the same order.

(2) The petition must:

(A) name each party seeking review either in the caption or the body of the petition—using such terms as "et al.," "petitioners," or "respondents" does not effectively name the parties;

(B) name the agency as a respondent (even though not named in the petition, the United States is a respondent if required by statute); and

(C) specify the order or part thereof to be reviewed.

(3) Form 3 in the Appendix of Forms is a suggested form of a petition for review.

(4) In this rule "agency" includes an agency, board, commission, or officer; "petition for review" includes a petition to enjoin, suspend, modify, or otherwise review, or a notice of appeal, whichever form is indicated by the applicable statute.

(b) APPLICATION OR CROSS-APPLICATION TO ENFORCE AN ORDER; ANSWER; DEFAULT.

(1) An application to enforce an agency order must be filed with the clerk of a court of appeals authorized to enforce the order. If a petition is filed to review an agency order that the court may enforce, a party opposing the petition may file a cross-application for enforcement.

(2) Within 21 days after the application for enforcement is filed, the respondent must serve on the applicant an answer to the application and file it with the clerk. If the respondent fails to answer in time, the court will enter judgment for the relief requested.

(3) The application must contain a concise statement of the proceedings in which the order was entered, the facts upon which venue is based, and the relief requested.

(c) SERVICE OF THE PETITION OR APPLICATION. The circuit clerk must serve a copy of the petition for review, or an application or crossapplication to enforce an agency order, on each respondent as prescribed by Rule 3(d), unless a different manner of service is prescribed by statute. At the time of filing, the petitioner must:

(1) serve, or have served, a copy on each party admitted to participate in the agency proceedings, except for the respondents;

(2) file with the clerk a list of those so served; and

(3) give the clerk enough copies of the petition or application to serve each respondent.
(d) Intervention. Unless a statute provides another method, a person who wants to intervene in a proceeding under this rule must file a motion for leave to intervene with the circuit clerk and serve a copy on all parties. The motion—or other notice of intervention authorized by statute—must be filed within 30 days after the petition for review is filed and must contain a concise statement of the interest of the moving party and the grounds for intervention.
(e) PAYMENT OF FEES. When filing any separate or joint petition for review in a court of appeals, the petitioner must pay the circuit clerk all required fees.

FED. R. APP. P. 15.1. Briefs and Oral Argument in a National Labor Relations Board Proceeding.
In either an enforcement or a review proceeding, a party adverse to the National Labor Relations Board proceeds first on briefing and at oral argument, unless the court orders otherwise.

FED. R. APP. P. 16. The Record on Review or Enforcement.
(a) COMPOSITION OF THE RECORD. The record on review or enforcement of an agency order consists of:
(1) the order involved;
(2) any findings or report on which it is based; and
(3) the pleadings, evidence, and other parts of the proceedings
before the agency.
(b) OMISSIONS FROM OR MISSTATEMENTS IN THE RECORD. The parties may at any time, by stipulation, supply any omission from the record or correct a misstatement, or the court may so direct. If necessary, the court may direct that a supplemental record be prepared and filed.

FED. R. APP. P. 17. Filing the Record.
(a) AGENCY TO FILE; TIME FOR FILING; NOTICE OF FILING. The agency must file the record with the circuit clerk within 40 days after being served with a petition for review, unless the statute authorizing review provides otherwise, or within 40 days after it files an application for enforcement unless the respondent fails to answer or the court orders otherwise. The court may shorten or extend the time to file the record. The clerk must notify all parties of the date when the record is filed.
(b) FILING – WHAT CONSTITUTES.
(1) The agency must file:
(A) the original or a certified copy of the entire record or parts designated by the parties; or
(B) a certified list adequately describing all documents, transcripts of testimony, exhibits, and other material constituting the record, or describing those parts designated by the parties.
(2) The parties may stipulate in writing that no record or certified list be filed. The date when the stipulation is filed with the circuit clerk is treated as the date when the record is filed.
(3) The agency must retain any portion of the record not filed with the clerk. All parts of the record retained by the agency are a part of the record on review for all purposes and, if the court or a party so requests, must be sent to the court regardless of any prior stipulation.

FED. R. APP. P. 18. Stay Pending Review.
(a) MOTION FOR A STAY.
(1) *Initial Motion Before the Agency.* A petitioner must ordinarily move first before the agency for a stay pending review of its decision or order.
(2) *Motion in the Court of Appeals.* A motion for a stay may be made to the court of appeals or one of its judges.
(A) The motion must:
(i) show that moving first before the agency would be impracticable; or
(ii) state that, a motion having been made, the agency denied the motion or failed to afford the relief requested and state any reasons given by the agency for its action.
(B) The motion must also include:
(i) the reasons for granting the relief requested and the facts relied on;
(ii) originals or copies of affidavits or other sworn statements supporting facts subject to dispute; and
(iii) relevant parts of the record.
(C) The moving party must give reasonable notice of the motion to all parties.
(D) The motion must be filed with the circuit clerk and normally will be considered by a panel of the court. But in an exceptional case in which time requirements make that procedure impracticable, the motion may be made to and considered by a single judge.
(b) BOND. The court may condition relief on the filing of a bond or other appropriate security.

FED. R. APP. P. 19. Settlement of a Judgment Enforcing an Agency Order in Part.
When the court files an opinion directing entry of judgment enforcing the agency's order in part, the agency must within 14 days file with the clerk and serve on each other party a proposed judgment conforming to the opinion. A party who disagrees with the agency's proposed judgment must within 10 days file

with the clerk and serve the agency with a proposed judgment that the party believes conforms to the opinion. The court will settle the judgment and direct entry without further hearing or argument.

FED. R. APP. P. 20. Applicability of Rules to the Review or Enforcement of an Agency Order.

All provisions of these rules, except Rules 3–14 and 22–23, apply to the review or enforcement of an agency order. In these rules, ''appellant'' includes a petitioner or applicant, and ''appellee'' includes a respondent.

TITLE V. EXTRAORDINARY WRITS

FED. R. APP. P. 21. Writs of Mandamus and Prohibition, and Other Extraordinary Writs

(a) MANDAMUS OR PROHIBITION TO A COURT: PETITION, FILING, SERVICE, AND DOCKETING.

(1) A party petitioning for a writ of mandamus or prohibition directed to a court must file a petition with the circuit clerk with proof of service on all parties to the proceeding in the trial court. The party must also provide a copy to the trial-court judge. All parties to the proceeding in the trial court other than the petitioner are respondents for all purposes.

(2)(A) The petition must be titled ''In re [name of petitioner].''

(B) The petition must state:

(i) the relief sought;

(ii) the issues presented;

(iii) the facts necessary to understand the issue presented by the petition; and

(iv) the reasons why the writ should issue.

(C) The petition must include a copy of any order or opinion or parts of the record that may be essential to understand the matters set forth in the petition.

(3) Upon receiving the prescribed docket fee, the clerk must docket the petition and submit it to the court.

(b) DENIAL; ORDER DIRECTING ANSWER; BRIEFS; PRECEDENCE.

(1) The court may deny the petition without an answer. Otherwise, it must order the respondent, if any, to answer within a fixed time.

(2) The clerk must serve the order to respond on all persons directed to respond.

(3) Two or more respondents may answer jointly.

(4) The court of appeals may invite or order the trial-court judge to address the petition or may invite an amicus curiae to do so. The trial-court judge may request permission to address the petition but may not do so unless invited or ordered to do so by the court of appeals.

(5) If briefing or oral argument is required, the clerk must advise the parties, and when appropriate, the trial-court judge or amicus curiae.

(6) The proceeding must be given preference over ordinary civil cases.

(7) The circuit clerk must send a copy of the final disposition to the trial-court judge.

(c) OTHER EXTRAORDINARY WRITS. An application for an extraordinary writ other than one provided for in Rule 21(a) must be made by filing a petition with the circuit clerk with proof of service on the respondents. Proceedings on the application must conform, so far as is practicable, to the procedures prescribed in Rule 21(a) and (b).

(d) FORM OF PAPERS; NUMBER OF COPIES. All papers must conform to Rule 32(c)(2). Except by the court's permission, a paper must not exceed 30 pages, exclusive of the disclosure statement, the proof of service, and the accompanying documents required by Rule 21(a)(2)(C). An original and 3 copies must be filed unless the court requires the filing of a different number by local rule or by order in a particular case.

TITLE VI. HABEAS CORPUS; PROCEEDINGS IN FORMA PAUPERIS

FED. R. APP. P. 22. Habeas Corpus and Section 2255 Proceedings.

(a) APPLICATION FOR THE ORIGINAL WRIT. An application for a writ of habeas corpus must be made to the appropriate district court. If made to a circuit judge, the application must be transferred to the appropriate district court. If a district court denies an application made or transferred to it, renewal of the application before a circuit judge is not permitted. The applicant may, under 28 U.S.C. §2253, appeal to the court of appeals from the district court's order denying the application.

(b) CERTIFICATE OF APPEALABILITY.

(1) In a habeas corpus proceeding in which the detention complained of arises from process issued by a state court, or in a 28 U.S.C. §2255 proceeding, the applicant cannot take an appeal unless a circuit justice or a circuit or district judge issues a certificate of appealability under 28 U.S.C. §2253(c). If an applicant files a notice of appeal, the district clerk must send to the court of appeals the certificate (if any) and the statement described in Rule 11(a) of the Rules Governing Proceedings Under 28 U.S.C. §2254 or §2255 (if any), along with the notice of appeal and the file of the district-court proceedings. If the district judge has denied the certificate, the applicant may request a circuit judge to issue it.

(2) A request addressed to the court of appeals may be considered by a circuit judge or judges, as the court prescribes. If no express request for a certificate is filed, the notice of appeal constitutes a request addressed to the judges of the court of appeals.
(3) A certificate of appealability is not required when a state or its representative or the United States or its representative appeals.

FED. R. APP. P. 23. Custody or Release of a Prisoner in a Habeas Corpus Proceeding.
(a) TRANSFER OF CUSTODY PENDING REVIEW. Pending review of a decision in a habeas corpus proceeding commenced before a court, justice, or judge of the United States for the release of a prisoner, the person having custody of the prisoner must not transfer custody to another unless a transfer is directed in accordance with this rule. When, upon application, a custodian shows the need for a transfer, the court, justice, or judge rendering the decision under review may authorize the transfer and substitute the successor custodian as a party.
(b) DETENTION OR RELEASE PENDING REVIEW OF DECISION NOT TO RELEASE. While a decision not to release a prisoner is under review, the court or judge rendering the decision, or the court of appeals, or the Supreme Court, or a judge or justice of either court, may order that the prisoner be:
(1) detained in the custody from which release is sought;
(2) detained in other appropriate custody; or
(3) released on personal recognizance, with or without surety.
(c) RELEASE PENDING REVIEW OF DECISION ORDERING RELEASE. While a decision ordering the release of a prisoner is under review, the prisoner must—unless the court or judge rendering the decision, or the court of appeals, or the Supreme Court, or a judge or justice of either court orders otherwise—be released on personal recognizance, with or without surety.
(d) MODIFICATION OF THE INITIAL ORDER ON CUSTODY. An initial order governing the prisoner's custody or release, including any recognizance or surety, continues in effect pending review unless for special reasons shown to the court of appeals or the Supreme Court, or to a judge or justice of either court, the order is modified or an independent order regarding custody, release, or surety is issued.

FED. R. APP. P. 24. Proceeding in Forma Pauperis.
(a) LEAVE TO PROCEED IN FORMA PAUPERIS.
(1) *Motion in the District Court.* Except as stated in Rule 24(a)(3), a party to a district-court action who desires to appeal in forma pauperis must file a motion in the district court. The party must attach an affidavit that:
(A) shows in the detail prescribed by Form 4 of the Appendix of Forms the party's inability to pay or to give security for fees and costs;
(B) claims an entitlement to redress; and
(C) states the issues that the party intends to present on appeal.
(2) *Action on the Motion.* If the district court grants the motion, the party may proceed on appeal without prepaying or giving security for fees and costs, unless a statute provides otherwise. If the district court denies the motion, it must state its reasons in writing.
(3) *Prior Approval.* A party who was permitted to proceed in forma pauperis in the district-court action, or who was determined to be financially unable to obtain an adequate defense in a criminal case, may proceed on appeal in forma pauperis without further authorization, unless:
(A) the district court—before or after the notice of appeal is filed—certifies that the appeal is not taken in good faith or finds that the party is not otherwise entitled to proceed in forma pauperis and states in writing its reasons for the certification or finding; or
(B) a statute provides otherwise.
(4) *Notice of District Court's Denial.* The district clerk must immediately notify the parties and the court of appeals when the district court does any of the following:
(A) denies a motion to proceed on appeal in forma pauperis;
(B) certifies that the appeal is not taken in good faith; or
(C) finds that the party is not otherwise entitled to proceed in forma pauperis.
(5) *Motion in the Court of Appeals.* A party may file a motion to proceed on appeal in forma pauperis in the court of appeals within 30 days after service of the notice prescribed in Rule 24(a)(4). The motion must include a copy of the affidavit filed in the district court and the district court's statement of reasons for its action. If no affidavit was filed in the district court, the party must include the affidavit prescribed by Rule 24(a)(1).
(b) LEAVE TO PROCEED IN FORMA PAUPERIS ON APPEAL OR REVIEW OF AN ADMINISTRATIVE-AGENCY. When an appeal or review of a proceeding before an administrative agency, board, commission, or officer (including for the purpose of this rule the United States Tax Court) proceeds directly in a court of appeals, a party may file in the court of appeals a motion for leave to proceed on appeal in forma pauperis with an affidavit prescribed by Rule 24(a)(1).

(c) LEAVE TO USE ORIGINAL RECORD. A party allowed to proceed on appeal in forma pauperis may request that the appeal be heard on the original record without reproducing any part.

TITLE VII. GENERAL PROVISIONS

Fed. R. App. P. 25. Filing and Service.
(a) FILING.
(1) *Filing with the Clerk.* A paper required or permitted to be filed in a court of appeals must be filed with the clerk.
(2) FILING: METHOD AND TIMELINESS.
(A) *In general.* Filing may be accomplished by mail addressed to the clerk, but filing is not timely unless the clerk receives the papers within the time fixed for filing.
(B) *A brief or appendix.* A brief or appendix is timely filed, however, if on or before the last day for filing, it is:
(i) mailed to the clerk by First-Class Mail, or other class of mail that is at least as expeditious, postage prepaid; or
(ii) dispatched to a third-party commercial carrier for delivery to the clerk within 3 days.
(C) *Inmate filing.* A paper filed by an inmate confined in an institution is timely if deposited in the institution's internal mailing system on or before the last day for filing. If an institution has a system designed for legal mail, the inmate must use that system to receive the benefit of this rule. Timely filing may be shown by a declaration in compliance with 28 U.S.C. §1746 or by a notarized statement, either of which must set forth the date of deposit and state that first-class postage has been prepaid.
(D) *Electronic filing.* A court of appeals may by local rule permit or require papers to be filed, signed, or verified by electronic means that are consistent with technical standards, if any, that the Judicial Conference of the United States establishes. A local rule may require filing by electronic means only if reasonable exceptions are allowed. A paper filed by electronic means in compliance with a local rule constitutes a written paper for the purpose of applying these rules.
(3) *Filing a Motion with a Judge.* If a motion requests relief that may be granted by a single judge, the judge may permit the motion to be filed with the judge; the judge must note the filing date on the motion and give it to the clerk.
(4) *Clerk's Refusal of Documents.* The clerk must not refuse to accept for filing any paper presented for that purpose solely because it is not presented in proper form as required by these rules or by any local rule or practice.
(5) *Privacy Protection.* An appeal in a case whose privacy protection was governed by Federal Rule of Bankruptcy Procedure 9037, Federal Rule of Civil Procedure 5.2, or Federal Rule of Criminal Procedure 49.1 is governed by the same rule on appeal. In all other proceedings, privacy protection is governed by Federal Rule of Civil Procedure 5.2, except that Federal Rule of Criminal Procedure 49.1 governs when an extraordinary writ is sought in a criminal case.
(b) SERVICE OF ALL PAPERS REQUIRED. Unless a rule requires service by the clerk, a party must, at or before the time of filing a paper, serve a copy on the other parties to the appeal or review. Service on a party represented by counsel must be made on the party's counsel.
(c) MANNER OF SERVICE.
(1) Service may be any of the following:
(A) personal, including delivery to a responsible person at the office of counsel;
(B) by mail;
(C) by third-party commercial carrier for delivery within 3 days; or
(D) by electronic means, if the party being served consents in writing.
(2) If authorized by local rule, a party may use the court's transmission equipment to make electronic service under Rule 25(c)(1)(D).
(3) When reasonable considering such factors as the immediacy of the relief sought, distance, and cost, service on a party must be by a manner at least as expeditious as the manner used to file the paper with the court.
(4) Service by mail or by commercial carrier is complete on mailing or delivery to the carrier. Service by electronic means is complete on transmission, unless the party making service is notified that the paper was not received by the party served.
(d) PROOF OF SERVICE.
(1) A paper presented for filing must contain either of the following:
(A) an acknowledgment of service by the person served; or
(B) proof of service consisting of a statement by the person who made service certifying:
(i) the date and manner of service;
(ii) the names of the persons served; and
(iii) their mail or electronic addresses, facsimile numbers, or the addresses of the places of delivery, as appropriate for the manner of service.
(2) When a brief or appendix is filed by mailing or dispatch in accordance with Rule 25(a)(2)(B), the proof of service must also state the date and manner by which the document was mailed or dispatched to the clerk.
(3) Proof of service may appear on or be affixed to the papers filed.
(e) NUMBER OF COPIES. When these rules require the filing or furnishing of a number of

copies, a court may require a different number by local rule or by order in a particular case.

FED. R. APP. P. 26. Computing and Extending Time.

(a) COMPUTING TIME. The following rules apply in computing any time period specified in these rules, in any local rule or court order, or in any statute that does not specify a method of computing time.

(1) *Period Stated in Days or a Longer Unit.* When the period is stated in days or a longer unit of time:

(A) exclude the day of the event that triggers the period;

(B) count every day, including intermediate Saturdays, Sundays, and legal holidays; and

(C) include the last day of the period, but if the last day is a Saturday, Sunday, or legal holiday, the period continues to run until the end of the next day that is not a Saturday, Sunday, or legal holiday.

(2) *Period Stated in Hours.* When the period is stated in hours:

(A) begin counting immediately on the occurrence of the event that triggers the period;

(B) count every hour, including hours during intermediate Saturdays, Sundays, and legal holidays; and

(C) if the period would end on a Saturday, Sunday, or legal holiday, the period continues to run until the same time on the next day that is not a Saturday, Sunday, or legal holiday.

(3) *Inaccessibility of the Clerk's Office.* Unless the court orders otherwise, if the clerk's office is inaccessible:

(A) on the last day for filing under Rule 26(a)(1), then the time for filing is extended to the first accessible day that is not a Saturday, Sunday, or legal holiday; or

(B) during the last hour for filing under Rule 26(a)(2), then the time for filing is extended to the same time on the first accessible day that is not a Saturday, Sunday, or legal holiday.

(4) *''Last Day'' Defined.* Unless a different time is set by a statute, local rule, or court order, the last day ends:

(A) for electronic filing in the district court, at midnight in the court's time zone;

(B) for electronic filing in the court of appeals, at midnight in the time zone of the circuit clerk's principal office;

(C) for filing under Rules 4(c)(1), 25(a)(2)(B), and 25(a)(2)(C)—and filing by mail under Rule 13(b)—at the latest time for the method chosen for delivery to the post office, third-party commercial carrier, or prison mailing system; and

(D) for filing by other means, when the clerk's office is scheduled to close.

(5) *''Next Day'' Defined.* The ''next day'' is determined by continuing to count forward when the period is measured after an event and backward when measured before an event.

(6) *''Legal Holiday'' Defined.* ''Legal holiday'' means:

(A) the day set aside by statute for observing New Year's Day, Martin Luther King Jr.'s Birthday, Washington's Birthday, Memorial Day, Independence Day, Labor Day, Columbus Day, Veterans' Day, Thanksgiving Day, or Christmas Day;

(B) any day declared a holiday by the President or Congress; and

(C) for periods that are measured after an event, any other day declared a holiday by the state where either of the following is located: the district court that rendered the challenged judgment or order, or the circuit clerk's principal office.

(b) EXTENDING TIME. For good cause, the court may extend the time prescribed by these rules or by its order to perform any act, or may permit an act to be done after that time expires. But the court may not extend the time to file:

(1) a notice of appeal (except as authorized in Rule 4) or a petition for permission to appeal; or

(2) a notice of appeal from or a petition to enjoin, set aside, suspend, modify, enforce, or otherwise review an order of an administrative agency, board, commission, or officer of the United States, unless specifically authorized by law.

(c) ADDITIONAL TIME AFTER SERVICE. When a party may or must act within a specified time after service, 3 days are added after the period would otherwise expire under Rule 26(a), unless the paper is delivered on the date of service stated in the proof of service. For purposes of this Rule 26(c), a paper that is served electronically is not treated as delivered on the date of service stated in the proof of service.

FED. R. APP. P. 26.1. Corporate Disclosure Statement.

(a) WHO MUST FILE. Any nongovernmental corporate party to a proceeding in a court of appeals must file a statement that identifies any parent corporation and any publicly held corporation that owns 10% or more of its stock or states that there is no such corporation.

(b) TIME FOR FILING; SUPPLEMENTAL FILING. A party must file the Rule 26.1(a) statement with the principal brief or upon filing a motion, response, petition, or answer in the court of appeals, whichever occurs first, unless a local rule requires earlier filing. Even if the statement has already been filed, the party's principal brief must include the

statement before the table of contents. A party must supplement its statement whenever the information that must be disclosed under Rule 26.1(a) changes.
(c) NUMBER OF COPIES. If the Rule 26.1(a) statement is filed before the principal brief, or if a supplemental statement is filed, the party must file an original and 3 copies unless the court requires a different number by local rule or by order in a particular case.

Fed. R. App. P. 27. Motions.
(a) IN GENERAL.
(1) *Application for Relief.* An application for an order or other relief is made by motion unless these rules prescribe another form. A motion must be in writing unless the court permits otherwise.
(2) *Contents of a Motion.*
(A) *Grounds and relief sought.* A motion must state with particularity the grounds for the motion, the relief sought, and the legal argument necessary to support it.
(B) *Accompanying documents.*
(i) Any affidavit or other paper necessary to support a motion must be served and filed with the motion.
(ii) An affidavit must contain only factual information, not legal argument.
(iii) A motion seeking substantive relief must include a copy of the trial court's opinion or agency's decision as a separate exhibit.
(C) *Documents barred or not required.*
(i) A separate brief supporting or responding to a motion must not be filed.
(ii) A notice of motion is not required.
(iii) A proposed order is not required.
(3) *Response.*
(A) *Time to file.* Any party may file a response to a motion; Rule 27(a)(2) governs its contents. The response must be filed within 10 days after service of the motion unless the court shortens or extends the time. A motion authorized by Rules 8, 9, 18, or 41 may be granted before the 10-day period runs only if the court gives reasonable notice to the parties that it intends to act sooner.
(B) *Request for affirmative relief.* A response may include a motion for affirmative relief. The time to respond to the new motion, and to reply to that response, are governed by Rule 27(a)(3)(A) and (a)(4). The title of the response must alert the court to the request for relief.
(4) *Reply to Response.* Any reply to a response must be filed within 7 days after service of the response. A reply must not present matters that do not relate to the response.
(b) DISPOSITION OF A MOTION FOR A PROCEDURAL ORDER. The court may act on a motion for a procedural order including a motion under Rule 26(b)—at any time without awaiting a response, and may, by rule or by order in a particular case, authorize its clerk to act on specified types of procedural motions. A party adversely affected by the court's, or the clerk's, action may file a motion to reconsider, vacate, or modify that action. Timely opposition filed after the motion is granted in whole or in part does not constitute a request to reconsider, vacate, or modify the disposition; a motion requesting that relief must be filed.
(c) POWER OF A SINGLE JUDGE TO ENTERTAIN A MOTION. A circuit judge may act alone on any motion, but may not dismiss or otherwise determine an appeal or other proceeding. A court of appeals may provide by rule or by order in a particular case that only the court may act on any motion or class of motions. The court may review the action of a single judge.
(d) FORM OF PAPERS; PAGE LIMITS; AND NUMBER OF COPIES.
(1) *Format.*
(A) *Reproduction.* A motion, response, or reply may be reproduced by any process that yields a clear black image on light paper. The paper must be opaque and unglazed. Only one side of the paper may be used.
(B) *Cover.* A cover is not required, but there must be a caption that includes the case number, the name of the court, the title of the case, and a brief descriptive title indicating the purpose of the motion and identifying the party or parties for whom it is filed. If a cover is used, it must be white.
(C) *Binding.* The document must be bound in any manner that is secure, does not obscure the text, and permits the document to lie reasonably flat when open.
(D) *Paper size, line spacing, and margins.* The document must be on 8½ by 11 inch paper. The text must be doublespaced, but quotations more than two lines long may be indented and single-spaced. Headings and footnotes may be single-spaced. Margins must be at least one inch on all four sides. Page numbers may be placed in the margins, but no text may appear there.
(E) *Typeface and type styles.* The document must comply with the typeface requirements of Rule 32(a)(5) and the type-style requirements of Rule 32(a)(6).
(2) *Page Limits.* A motion or a response to a motion must not exceed 20 pages, exclusive of the corporate disclosure statement and accompanying documents authorized by Rule 27(a)(2)(B), unless the court permits or directs otherwise. A reply to a response must not exceed 10 pages.
(3) *Number of Copies.* An original and 3 copies must be filed unless the court requires a

different number by local rule or by order in a particular case.

(e) *Oral Argument.* A motion will be decided without oral argument unless the court orders otherwise.

Fed. R. App. P. 28. Briefs.

(a) APPELANT'S BRIEF. The appellant's brief must contain, under appropriate headings and in the order indicated:

(1) a corporate disclosure statement if required by Rule 26.1;

(2) a table of contents, with page references;

(3) a table of authorities—cases (alphabetically arranged), statutes, and other authorities—with references to the pages of the brief where they are cited;

(4) a jurisdictional statement, including:

(A) the basis for the district court's or agency's subjectmatter jurisdiction, with citations to applicable statutory provisions and stating relevant facts establishing jurisdiction;

(B) the basis for the court of appeals' jurisdiction, with citations to applicable statutory provisions and stating relevant facts establishing jurisdiction;

(C) the filing dates establishing the timeliness of the appeal or petition for review; and

(D) an assertion that the appeal is from a final order or judgment that disposes of all parties' claims, or information establishing the court of appeals' jurisdiction on some other basis;

(5) a statement of the issues presented for review;

(6) a statement of the case briefly indicating the nature of the case, the course of proceedings, and the disposition below;

(7) a statement of facts relevant to the issues submitted for review with appropriate references to the record (see Rule 28(e));

(8) a summary of the argument, which must contain a succinct, clear, and accurate statement of the arguments made in the body of the brief, and which must not merely repeat the argument headings;

(9) the argument, which must contain:

(A) appellant's contentions and the reasons for them, with citations to the authorities and parts of the record on which the appellant relies; and

(B) for each issue, a concise statement of the applicable standard of review (which may appear in the discussion of the issue or under a separate heading placed before the discussion of the issues);

(10) a short conclusion stating the precise relief sought; and

(11) the certificate of compliance, if required by Rule 32(a)(7).

(b) APPELLEE'S BRIEF. The appellee's brief must conform to the requirements of Rule 28(a)(1)–(9) and (11), except that none of the following need appear unless the appellee is dissatisfied with the appellant's statement:

(1) the jurisdictional statement;

(2) the statement of the issues;

(3) the statement of the case;

(4) the statement of the facts; and

(5) the statement of the standard of review.

(c) REPLY BRIEF. The appellant may file a brief in reply to the appellee's brief. Unless the court permits, no further briefs may be filed. A reply brief must contain a table of contents, with page references, and a table of authorities—cases (alphabetically arranged), statutes, and other authorities—with references to the pages of the reply brief where they are cited.

(d) REFERENCES TO PARTIES. In briefs and at oral argument, counsel should minimize use of the terms ''appellant'' and ''appellee.'' To make briefs clear, counsel should use the parties' actual names or the designations used in the lower court or agency proceeding, or such descriptive terms as ''the employee,'' ''the injured person,'' ''the taxpayer,'' ''the ship,'' ''the stevedore.''

(e) REFERENCES TO THE RECORD. References to the parts of the record contained in the appendix filed with the appellant's brief must be to the pages of the appendix. If the appendix is prepared after the briefs are filed, a party referring to the record must follow one of the methods detailed in Rule 30(c). If the original record is used under Rule 30(f) and is not consecutively paginated, or if the brief refers to an unreproduced part of the record, any reference must be to the page of the original document. For example:

- Answer p. 7;
- Motion for Judgment p. 2;
- Transcript p. 231.

Only clear abbreviations may be used. A party referring to evidence whose admissibility is in controversy must cite the pages of the appendix or of the transcript at which the evidence was identified, offered, and received or rejected.

(f) REPRODUCTION OF STATUTES, RULES, REGULATIONS, ETC. If the court's determination of the issues presented requires the study of statutes, rules, regulations, etc., the relevant parts must be set out in the brief or in an addendum at the end, or may be supplied to the court in pamphlet form.

(g) [RESERVED]

(h) [RESERVED]

(i) BRIEFS IN A CASE INVOLVING MULTIPLE APPELLANTS OR APPELLEES. In a case involving more than one appellant or appellee, including consolidated cases, any number of appellants or appellees may join in a brief, and any party may adopt by reference a part of another's brief. Parties may also join in reply briefs.

(j) CITATION OF SUPPLEMENTAL AUTHORITIES. If pertinent and significant authorities come to a party's attention after the party's brief has been filed—or after oral argument but before decision—a party may promptly advise the circuit clerk by letter, with a copy to all other parties, setting forth the citations. The letter must state the reasons for the supplemental citations, referring either to the page of the brief or to a point argued orally. The body of the letter must not exceed 350 words. Any response must be made promptly and must be similarly limited.

FED. R. APP. P. 28.1. Cross-Appeals.

(a) APPLICABILITY. This rule applies to a case in which a cross-appeal is filed. Rules 28(a)–(c), 31(a)(1), 32(a)(2), and 32(a)(7(A)–(B) do not apply to such a case, except as otherwise provided in this rule.

(b) DESIGNATION OF APPELLANT. The party who files a notice of appeal first is the appellant for the purposes of this rule and Rules 30 and 34. If notices are filed on the same day, the plaintiff in the proceeding below is the appellant. These designations may be modified by the parties' agreement or by court order.

(c) BRIEFS. In a case involving a cross-appeal:

(1) *Appellant's Principal Brief.* The appellant must file a principal brief in the appeal. That brief must comply with Rule 28(a).

(2) *Appellee's Principal and Response Brief.* The appellee must file a principal brief in the cross-appeal and must, in the same brief, respond to the principal brief in the appeal. That appellee's brief must comply with Rule 28(a), except that the brief need not include a statement of the case or a statement of the facts unless the appellee is dissatisfied with the appellant's statement.

(3) *Appellant's Response and Reply Brief.* The appellant must file a brief that responds to the principal brief in the cross-appeal and may, in the same brief, reply to the response in the appeal. That brief must comply with Rule 28(a)(2)–(9) and (11), except that none of the following need appear unless the appellant is dissatisfied with the appellee's statement in the cross-appeal:

(A) the jurisdictional statement;

(B) the statement of the issues;

(C) the statement of the case;

(D) the statement of the facts; and

(E) the statement of the standard of review.

(4) *Appellee's Reply Brief.* The appellee may file a brief in reply to the response in the cross-appeal. That brief must comply with Rule 28(a)(2)–(3) and (11) and must be limited to the issues presented by the cross-appeal.

(5) *No Further Briefs.* Unless the court permits, no further briefs may be filed in a case involving a cross-appeal.

(d) COVER. Except for filings by unrepresented parties, the cover of the appellant's principal brief must be blue; the appellee's principal and response brief, red; the appellant's response and reply brief, yellow; the appellee's reply brief, gray; and intervenor's or amicus curiae's brief, green; and any supplemental brief, tan. The front cover of a brief must contain the information required by Rule 32(a)(2).

(e) LENGTH.

(1) *Page Limitation.* Unless it complies with Rule 28.1(e)(2) and (3), the appellant's principal brief must not exceed 30 pages; the appellee's principal and response brief, 35 pages; the appellant's response and reply brief, 30 pages; and the appellee's reply brief, 15 pages.

(2) *Type-Volume Limitation.*

(A) The appellant's principal brief or the appellant's response and reply brief is acceptable if:

(i) it contains no more than 14,000 words; or

(ii) it uses a monospaced face and contains no more than 1,300 lines of text.

(B) The appellee's principal and response brief is acceptable if:

(i) it contains no more than 16,500 words; or

(ii) it uses a monospaced face and contains no more than 1,500 lines of text.

(C) The appellee's reply brief is acceptable if it contains no more than half of the type volume specified in Rule 28.1(e)(2)(A).

(3) *Certificate of Compliance.* A brief submitted under Rule 28.1(e)(2) must comply with Rule 32(a)(7)(C).

(f) TIME TO SERVE AND FILE A BRIEF. Briefs must be served and filed as follows:

(1) the appellant's principal brief, within 40 days after the record is filed;

(2) the appellee's principal and response brief, within 30 days after the appellant's principal brief is served;

(3) the appellant's response and reply brief, within 30 days after the appellee's principal and response brief is served; and

(4) the appellee's reply brief, within 14 days after the appellant's response and reply brief is served, but at least 7 days before argument unless the court, for good cause, allows a later filing.

Rule 29. Brief of an Amicus Curiae.

(a) WHEN PERMITTED. The United States or its officer or agency, or a State, Territory, Commonwealth, or the District of Columbia may file an amicus-curiae brief without the

consent of the parties or leave of court. Any other amicus curiae may file a brief only by leave of court or if the brief states that all parties have consented to its filing.
(b) MOTION FOR LEAVE TO FILE. The motion must be accompanied by the proposed brief and state:
(1) the movant's interest; and
(2) the reason why an amicus brief is desirable and why the matters asserted are relevant to the disposition of the case.
(c) CONTENTS AND FORM. An amicus brief must comply with Rule 32. In addition to the requirements of Rule 32, the cover must identify the party or parties supported and indicate whether the brief supports affirmance or reversal. If an amicus curiae is a corporation, the brief must include a disclosure statement like that required of parties by Rule 26.1. An amicus brief need not comply with Rule 28, but must include the following:
(1) a table of contents, with page references;
(2) a table of authorities—cases (alphabetically arranged), statutes and other authorities—with references to the pages of the brief where they are cited;
(3) a concise statement of the identity of the amicus curiae, its interest in the case, and the source of its authority to file;
(4) an argument, which may be preceded by a summary and which need not include a statement of the applicable standard of review; and
(5) a certificate of compliance, if required by Rule 32(a)(7).
(d) LENGTH. Except by the court's permission, an amicus brief may be no more than one-half the maximum length authorized by these rules for a party's principal brief. If the court grants a party permission to file a longer brief, that extension does not affect the length of an amicus brief.
(e) TIME FOR FILING. An amicus curiae must file its brief, accompanied by a motion for filing when necessary, no later than 7 days after the principal brief of the party being supported is filed. An amicus curiae that does not support either party must file its
brief no later than 7 days after the appellant's or petitioner's principal brief is filed. A court may grant leave for later filing, specifying the time within which an opposing party may answer.
(f) REPLY BRIEF. Except by the court's permission, an amicus curiae may not file a reply brief.
(g) ORAL ARGUMENT. An amicus curiae may participate in oral argument only with the court's permission.

Fed. R. App. P. 30. Appendix to the Briefs.
(a) APPELLANT'S RESPONSIBILITY..
(1) *Contents of the Appendix.* The appellant must prepare and file an appendix to the briefs containing:
(A) the relevant docket entries in the proceeding below;
(B) the relevant portions of the pleadings, charge, findings, or opinion;
(C) the judgment, order, or decision in question; and
(D) other parts of the record to which the parties wish to direct the court's attention.
(2) *Excluded Material.* Memoranda of law in the district court should not be included in the appendix unless they have independent relevance. Parts of the record may be relied on by the court or the parties even though not included in the appendix.
(3) *Time to File; Number of Copies.* Unless filing is deferred under Rule 30(c), the appellant must file 10 copies of the appendix with the brief and must serve one copy on counsel for each party separately represented. An unrepresented party proceeding in forma pauperis must file 4 legible copies with the clerk, and one copy must be served on counsel for each separately represented party. The court may by local rule or by order in a particular case require the filing or service of a different number.
(b) ALL PARTIES' RESPONSIBILITIES.
(1) *Determining the Contents of the Appendix.* The partiesare encouraged to agree on the contents of the appendix. In the absence of an agreement, the appellant must, within 14 days after the record is filed, serve on the appellee a designation of the parts of the record the appellant intends to include in the appendix and a statement of the issues the appellant intends to present for review. The appellee may, within 14 days after receiving the designation, serve on the appellant a designation of additional parts to which it wishes to direct the court's attention. The appellant must include the designated parts in the appendix. The parties must not engage in unnecessary designation of parts of the record, because the entire record is available to the court. This paragraph applies also to a cross-appellant and a cross-appellee.
(2) *Costs of Appendix.* Unless the parties agree otherwise, the appellant must pay the cost of the appendix. If the appellant considers parts of the record designated by the appellee to be unnecessary, the appellant may advise the appellee, who must then advance the cost of including those parts. The cost of the appendix is a taxable cost. But if any party causes unnecessary parts of the record to be included in the appendix, the court may impose the cost of those parts on that party. Each circuit must, by local rule, provide for sanctions against attorneys who unreasonably

and vexatiously increase litigation costs by including unnecessary material in the appendix.

(c) DEFERRED APPENDIX.

(1) *Deferral Until After Briefs Are Filed.* The court may provide by rule for classes of cases or by order in a particular case that preparation of the appendix may be deferred until after the briefs have been filed and that the appendix may be filed 21 days after the appellee's brief is served. Even though the filing of the appendix may be deferred, Rule 30(b) applies; except that a party must designate the parts of the record it wants included in the appendix when it serves its brief, and need not include a statement of the issues presented.

(2) *References to the Record.*

(A) If the deferred appendix is used, the parties may cite in their briefs the pertinent pages of the record. When the appendix is prepared, the record pages cited in the briefs must be indicated by inserting record page numbers, in brackets, at places in the appendix where those pages of the record appear.

(B) A party who wants to refer directly to pages of the appendix may serve and file copies of the brief within the time required by Rule 31(a), containing appropriate references to pertinent pages of the record. In that event, within 14 days after the appendix is filed, the party must serve and file copies of the brief, containing references to the pages of the appendix in place of or in addition to the references to the pertinent pages of the record. Except for the correction of typographical errors, no other changes may be made to the brief.

(d) FORMAT OF THE APPENDIX. The appendix must begin with a table of contents identifying the page at which each part begins. The relevant docket entries must follow the table of contents. Other parts of the record must follow chronologically. When pages from the transcript of proceedings are placed in the appendix, the transcript page numbers must be shown in brackets immediately before the included pages. Omissions in the text of papers or of the transcript must be indicated by asterisks. Immaterial formal matters (captions, subscriptions, acknowledgments, etc.) should be omitted.

(e) REPRODUCTION OF EXHIBITS. Exhibits designated for inclusion in the appendix may be reproduced in a separate volume, or volumes, suitably indexed. Four copies must be filed with the appendix, and one copy must be served on counsel for each separately represented party. If a transcript of a proceeding before an administrative agency, board, commission, or officer was used in a district- court action and has been designated for inclusion in the appendix, the transcript must be placed in the appendix as an exhibit.

(f) APPEAL ON THE ORIGINAL RECORD WITHOUT AN APPENDIX. The court may, either by rule for all cases or classes of cases or by order in a particular case, dispense with the appendix and permit an appeal to proceed on the original record with any copies of the record, or relevant parts, that the court may order the parties to file.

Fed. R. App. P. 31. Serving and Filing Briefs

(a) TIME TO SERVE AND FILE A BRIEF.

(1) The appellant must serve and file a brief within 40 days after the record is filed. The appellee must serve and file a brief within 30 days after the appellant's brief is served. The appellant may serve and file a reply brief within 14 days after service of the appellee's brief but a reply brief must be filed at least 7 days before argument, unless the court, for good cause, allows a later filing.

(2) A court of appeals that routinely considers cases on the merits promptly after the briefs are filed may shorten the time to serve and file briefs, either by local rule or by order in a particular case.

(b) NUMBER OF COPIES. Twenty-five copies of each brief must be filed with the clerk and 2 copies must be served on each unrepresented party and on counsel for each separately represented party. An unrepresented party proceeding in forma pauperis must file 4 legible copies with the clerk, and one copy must be served on each unrepresented party and on counsel for each separately represented party. The court may by local rule or by order in a particular case require the filing or service of a different number.

(c) CONSEQUENCE OF FAILURE TO FILE. If an appellant fails to file a brief within the time provided by this rule, or within an extended time, an appellee may move to dismiss the appeal. An appellee who fails to file a brief will not be heard at oral argument unless the court grants permission.

Fed. R. App. P. 32. Form of Briefs, Appendices, and Other Papers

(a) FORM OF A BRIEF.

(1) *Reproduction.*

(A) A brief may be reproduced by any process that yields a clear black image on light paper. The paper must be opaque and unglazed. Only one side of the paper may be used.

(B) Text must be reproduced with a clarity that equals or exceeds the output of a laser printer.

(C) Photographs, illustrations, and tables may be reproduced by any method that results in a good copy of the original; a glossy finish is acceptable if the original is glossy.

(2) *Cover.* Except for filings by unrepresented parties, the cover of the appellant's brief must be blue; the appellee's, red; an intervenor's or amicus curiae's, green; any reply brief, gray and any supplemental brief, tan. The front cover of a brief must contain:
(A) the number of the case centered at the top;
(B) the name of the court;
(C) the title of the case (see Rule 12(a));
(D) the nature of the proceeding (e.g., Appeal, Petition for Review) and the name of the court, agency, or board below;
(E) the title of the brief, identifying the party or parties for whom the brief is filed; and
(F) the name, office address, and telephone number of counsel representing the party for whom the brief is filed.
(3) *Binding.* The brief must be bound in any manner that is secure, does not obscure the text, and permits the brief to lie reasonably flat when open.
(4) *Paper Size, Line Spacing, and Margins.* The brief must be on 8½ by 11 inch paper. The text must be double-spaced, but quotations more than two lines long may be indented and single- spaced. Headings and footnotes may be single-spaced. Margins must be at least one inch on all four sides. Page numbers may be placed in the margins, but no text may appear there.
(5) *Typeface.* Either a proportionally spaced or a monospaced face may be used.
(A) A proportionally spaced face must include serifs, but sans-serif type may be used in headings and captions. A proportionally spaced face must be 14-point or larger.
(B) A monospaced face may not contain more than 10½ characters per inch.
(6) *Type Styles.* A brief must be set in a plain, roman style, although italics or boldface may be used for emphasis. Case names must be italicized or underlined.
(7) *Length.*
(A) *Page limitation.* A principal brief may not exceed 30 pages, or a reply brief 15 pages, unless it complies with Rule 32(a)(7)(B) and (C).
(B) *Type-volume limitation.*
(i) A principal brief is acceptable if:
• it contains no more than 14,000 words; or
• it uses a monospaced face and contains no more
• than 1,300 lines of text.
(ii) A reply brief is acceptable if it contains no more than half of the type volume specified in Rule 32(a)(7)(B)(i).
(iii) Headings, footnotes, and quotations count toward the word and line limitations. The corporate disclosure statement, table of contents, table of citations, statement with respect to oral argument, any addendum containing statutes, rules or regulations, and any certificates of counsel do not count toward the limitation.
(C) *Certificate of compliance.*
(i) A brief submitted under Rules 28.1(e)(2) or 32(a)(7)(B) must include a certificate by the attorney, or an unrepresented party, that the brief complies with the type-volume limitation. The person preparing the certificate may rely on the word or line count of the word-processing system used to prepare the brief. The certificate must state either:
• the number of words in the brief; or
• the number of lines of monospaced type in the brief.
(ii) Form 6 in the Appendix of Forms is a suggested form of a certificate of compliance. Use of Form 6 must be regarded as sufficient to meet the requirements of Rules 28.1(e)(3) and 32(a)(7)(C)(i).
(b) FORM OF AN APPENDIX. An appendix must comply with Rule 32(a)(1), (2), (3), and (4), with the following exceptions:
(1) The cover of a separately bound appendix must be white.
(2) An appendix may include a legible photocopy of any document found in the record or of a printed judicial or agency decision.
(3) When necessary to facilitate inclusion of odd-sized documents such as technical drawings, an appendix may be a size other than 8½ by 11 inches, and need not lie reasonably flat when opened.
(c) FORM OF OTHER PAPERS.
(1) *Motion.* The form of a motion is governed by Rule 27(d).
(2) *Other Papers.* Any other paper, including a petition for panel rehearing and a petition for hearing or rehearing en banc, and any response to such a petition, must be reproduced in the manner prescribed by Rule 32(a), with the following exceptions:
(A) A cover is not necessary if the caption and signature page of the paper together contain the information required by Rule 32(a)(2). If a cover is used, it must be white.
(B) Rule 32(a)(7) does not apply.
(d) SIGNATURE. Every brief, motion, or other paper filed with the court must be signed by the party filing the paper or, if the party is represented, by one of the party's attorneys.
(e) LOCAL VARIATION. Every court of appeals must accept documents that comply with the form requirements of this rule. By local rule or order in a particular case a court of appeals may accept documents that do not meet all of the form requirements of this rule.

FED. R. APP. P. 32.1. Citing Judicial Dispositions.

(a) CITATION PERMITTED. A court may not prohibit or restrict the citation of federal

judicial opinions, orders, judgments, or other written dispositions that have been:
(i) designated as ''unpublished,'' ''not for publication,'' ''nonprecedential,'' ''not precedent,'' or the like; and
(ii) issued on or after January 1, 2007.
(b) COPIES REQUIRED. If a party cites a federal judicial opinion, order, judgment, or other written disposition that is not available in a publicly accessible electronic database, the party must file and serve a copy of that opinion, order, judgment, or disposition with the brief or other paper in which it is cited.

Fed. R. App. P. 33. Appeal Conferences.
The court may direct the attorneys—and, when appropriate, the parties—to participate in one or more conferences to address any matter that may aid in disposing of the proceedings, including simplifying the issues and discussing settlement. A judge or other person designated by the court may preside over the conference, which may be conducted in person or by telephone. Before a settlement conference, the attorneys must consult with their clients and obtain as much authority as feasible to settle the case. The court may, as a result of the conference, enter an order controlling the course of the proceedings or implementing any settlement agreement.

Fed. R. App. P. 34. Oral Argument.
(a) IN GENERAL.
(1) *Party's Statement.* Any party may file, or a court may require by local rule, a statement explaining why oral argument should, or need not, be permitted.
(2) *Standards.* Oral argument must be allowed in every case unless a panel of three judges who have examined the briefs and record unanimously agrees that oral argument is unnecessary for any of the following reasons:
(A) the appeal is frivolous;
(B) the dispositive issue or issues have been authoritatively decided; or
(C) the facts and legal arguments are adequately presented in the briefs and record, and the decisional process would not be significantly aided by oral argument.
(b) NOTICE OF ARGUMENT; POSTPONEMENT. The clerk must advise all parties whether oral argument will be scheduled, and, if so, the date, time, and place for it, and the time allowed for each side. A motion to postpone the argument or to allow longer argument must be filed reasonably in advance of the hearing date.
(c) ORDER AND CONTENTS OF ARGUMENT. The appellant opens and concludes the argument. Counsel must not read at length from briefs, records, or authorities.
(d) CROSS-APPEALS AND SEPARATE APPEALS. If there is a cross-appeal, Rule 28.1(b) determines which party is the appellant and which is the appellee for purposes of oral argument. Unless the court directs otherwise, a cross-appeal or separate appeal must be argued when the initial appeal is argued. Separate parties should avoid duplicative argument.
(e) NONAPPEARANCE OF A PARTY. If the appellee fails to appear for argument, the court must hear appellant's argument. If the appellant fails to appear for argument, the court may hear the appellee's argument. If neither party appears, the case will be decided on the briefs, unless the court orders otherwise.
(f) SUBMISSION ON BRIEFS. The parties may agree to submit a case for decision on the briefs, but the court may direct that the case be argued.
(g) USE OF PHYSICAL EXHIBITS AT ARGUMENT; REMOVAL. Counsel intending to use physical exhibits other than documents at the argument must arrange to place them in the courtroom on the day of the argument before the court convenes. After the argument, counsel must remove the exhibits from the courtroom, unless the court directs otherwise. The clerk may destroy or dispose of the exhibits if counsel does not reclaim them within a reasonable time after the clerk gives notice to remove them.

Fed. R. App. P. 35. En Banc Determination.
(a) WHEN HEARING OR REHEARING EN BANC MAY BE ORDERED. A majority of the circuit judges who are in regular active service and who are not disqualified may order that an appeal or other proceeding be heard or reheard by the court of appeals en banc. An en banc hearing or rehearing is not favored and ordinarily will not be ordered unless:
(1) en banc consideration is necessary to secure or maintain uniformity of the court's decisions; or
(2) the proceeding involves a question of exceptional importance.
(b) PETITION FOR HEARING OR REHEARING EN BANC. A party may petitionfor a hearing or rehearing en banc.
(1) The petition must begin with a statement that either:
(A) the panel decision conflicts with a decision of the United States Supreme Court or of the court to which the petition is addressed (with citation to the conflicting case or cases) and consideration by the full court is therefore necessary to secure and maintain uniformity of the court's decisions; or
(B) the proceeding involves one or more questions of exceptional importance, each of which must be concisely stated; for example, a

petition may assert that a proceeding presents a question of exceptional importance if it involves an issue on which the panel decision conflicts with the authoritative decisions of other United States Courts of Appeals that have addressed the issue.
(2) Except by the court's permission, a petition for an en banc hearing or rehearing must not exceed 15 pages, excluding material not counted under Rule 32.
(3) For purposes of the page limit in Rule 35(b)(2), if a party files both a petition for panel rehearing and a petition for rehearing en banc, they are considered a single document even if they are filed separately, unless separate filing is required by local rule.
(c) TIME FOR PETITION FOR HEARING OR REHEARING EN BANC. A petition that an appeal be heard initially en banc must be filed by the date when the appellee's brief is due. A petition for a rehearing enbanc must be filed within the time prescribed by Rule 40 for filing a petition for rehearing.
(d) NUMBER OF COPIES. The number of copies to be filed must be prescribed by local rule and may be altered by order in a particular case.
(e) RESPONSE. No response may be filed to a petition for an en banc consideration unless the court orders a response.
(f) CALL FOR A VOTE. A vote need not be taken to determine whether the case will be heard or reheard en banc unless a judge calls for a vote.

FED. R. APP. P. 36. Entry of Judgment; Notice.
(a) ENTRY. A judgment is entered when it is noted on the docket. The clerk must prepare, sign, and enter the judgment:
(1) after receiving the court's opinion—but if settlement of the judgment's form is required, after final settlement; or
(2) if a judgment is rendered without an opinion, as the court instructs.
(b) NOTICE. On the date when judgment is entered, the clerk must serve on all parties a copy of the opinion—or the judgment, if no opinion was written—and a notice of the date when the judgment was entered.

FED. R. APP. P. 37. Interest on Judgment.
(a) WHEN THE COURT AFFIRMS. Unless the law provides otherwise, if a money judgment in a civil case is affirmed, whatever interest is allowed by law is payable from the date when the district court's judgment was entered.
(b) WHEN THE COURT REVERSES. If the court modifies or reverses a judgment with a direction that a money judgment be entered in the district court, the mandate must contain instructions about the allowance of interest.

FED. R. APP. P. 38. Frivolous Appeal—Damages and Costs.
If a court of appeals determines that an appeal is frivolous, it may, after a separately filed motion or notice from the court and reasonable opportunity to respond, award just damages and single or double costs to the appellee.

FED. R. APP. P. 39. Costs.
(a) AGAINST WHOM ASSESSED. The following rules apply unless the law provides or the court orders otherwise:
(1) if an appeal is dismissed, costs are taxed against the appellant, unless the parties agree otherwise;
(2) if a judgment is affirmed, costs are taxed against the appellant;
(3) if a judgment is reversed, costs are taxed against the appellee;
(4) if a judgment is affirmed in part, reversed in part, modified, or vacated, costs are taxed only as the court orders.
(b) COSTS FOR AND AGAINST THE UNITED STATES. Costs for or against the United States, its agency, or officer will be assessed under Rule 39(a) only if authorized by law.
(c) COSTS OF COPIES. Each court of appeals must, by local rule, fix the maximum rate for taxing the cost of producing necessary copies of a brief or appendix, or copies of records authorized by Rule 30(f). The rate must not exceed that generally charged for such work in the area where the clerk's office is located and should encourage economical methods of copying.
(d) BILL OF COSTS: OBJECTIONS; INSERTION IN MANDATE.
(1) A party who wants costs taxed must—within 14 days after entry of judgment—file with the circuit clerk, with proof of service, an itemized and verified bill of costs.
(2) Objections must be filed within 14 days after service of the bill of costs, unless the court extends the time.
(3) The clerk must prepare and certify an itemized statement of costs for insertion in the mandate, but issuance of the mandate must not be delayed for taxing costs. If the mandate issues before costs are finally determined, the district clerk must—upon the circuit clerk's request—add the statement of costs, or any amendment of it, to the mandate.
(e) COSTS ON APPEAL TAXABLE IN THE DISTRICT COURT. The following costs on appeal are taxable in the district court for the benefit of the party entitled to costs under this rule:

(1) the preparation and transmission of the record;
(2) the reporter's transcript, if needed to determine the appeal;
(3) premiums paid for a supersedeas bond or other bond to preserve rights pending appeal; and
(4) the fee for filing the notice of appeal.

FED. R. APP. P. 40. Petition for Panel Rehearing

(a) TIME TO FILE; CONTENTS; ANSWER; ACTION BY THE COURT IF GRANTED.
(1) *Time.* Unless the time is shortened or extended by order or local rule, a petition for panel rehearing may be filed within 14 days after entry of judgment. But in a civil case, if the United States or its officer or agency is a party, the time within which any party may seek rehearing is 45 days after entry of judgment, unless an order shortens or extends the time.
(2) *Contents.* The petition must state with particularity each point of law or fact that the petitioner believes the court has overlooked or misapprehended and must argue in support of the petition. Oral argument is not permitted.
(3) *Answer.* Unless the court requests, no answer to a petition for panel rehearing is permitted. But ordinarily rehearing will not be granted in the absence of such a request.
(4) *Action by the Court.* If a petition for panel rehearing is granted, the court may do any of the following:
(A) make a final disposition of the case without reargument;
(B) restore the case to the calendar for reargument or resubmission; or
(C) issue any other appropriate order.
(b) FORM OF PETITION; LENGTH. The petition must comply in form with Rule 32. Copies must be served and filed as Rule 31 prescribes. Unless the court permits or a local rule provides otherwise, a petition for panel rehearing must not exceed 15 pages.

FED. R. APP. P. 41. Mandate: Contents; Issuance and Effective Date; Stay.

(a) CONTENTS. Unless the court directs that a formal mandate issue, the mandate consists of a certified copy of the judgment, a copy of the court's opinion, if any, and any direction about costs.
(b) WHEN ISSUED. The court's mandate must issue 7 days after the time to file a petition for rehearing expires, or 7 days after entry of an order denying a timely petition for panel rehearing, petition for rehearing en banc, or motion for stay of mandate, whichever is later. The court may shorten or extend the time.
(c) EFFECTIVE DATE. The mandate is effective when issued.
(d) STAYING THE MANDATE.
(1) *On Petition for Rehearing or Motion.* The timely filing of a petition for panel rehearing, petition for rehearing en banc, or motion for stay of mandate, stays the mandate until disposition of the petition or motion, unless the court orders otherwise.
(2) *Pending Petition for Certiorari.*
(A) A party may move to stay the mandate pending the filing of a petition for a writ of certiorari in the Supreme Court. The motion must be served on all parties and must show that the certiorari petition would present a substantial question and that there is good cause for a stay.
(B) The stay must not exceed 90 days, unless the period is extended for good cause or unless the party who obtained the stay files a petition for the writ and so notifies the circuit clerk in writing within the period of the stay. In that case, the stay continues until the Supreme Court's final disposition.
(C) The court may require a bond or other security as a condition to granting or continuing a stay of the mandate.
(D) The court of appeals must issue the mandate immediately when a copy of a Supreme Court order denying the petition for writ of certiorari is filed.

FED. R. APP. P. 42. Voluntary Dismissal.

(a) DISMISSAL IN THE DISTRICT COURT. Before an appeal has been docketed by the circuit clerk, the district court may dismiss the appeal on the filing of a stipulation signed by all parties or on the appellant's motion with notice to all parties.
(b) DISMISSAL IN THE COURT OF APPEALS. The circuit clerk may dismiss a docketed appeal if the parties file a signed dismissal agreement specifying how costs are to be paid and pay any fees that are due. But no mandate or other process may issue without a court order. An appeal may be dismissed on the appellant's motion on terms agreed to by the parties or fixed by the court.

FED. R. APP. P. 43. Substitution of Parties.

(a) DEATH OF A PARTY.
(1) *After Notice of Appeal Is Filed.* If a party dies after a notice of appeal has been filed or while a proceeding is pending in the court of appeals, the decedent's personal representative may be substituted as a party on motion filed with the circuit clerk by the representative or by any party. A party's motion must be served on the representative in accordance with Rule 25. If the decedent has no representative, any party may suggest the

death on the record, and the court of appeals may then direct appropriate proceedings.
(2) *Before Notice of Appeal Is Filed—Potential Appellant.* If a party entitled to appeal dies before filing a notice of appeal, the decedent's personal representative—or, if there is no personal representative, the decedent's attorney of record—may file a notice of appeal within the time prescribed by these rules. After the notice of appeal is filed, substitution must be in accordance with Rule 43(a)(1).
(3) *Before Notice of Appeal Is Filed—Potential Appellee.* If a party against whom an appeal may be taken dies after entry of a judgment or order in the district court, but before a notice of appeal is filed, an appellant may proceed as if the death had not occurred. After the notice of appeal is filed, substitution must be in accordance with Rule 43(a)(1).
(b) SUBSTITUTION FOR A REASON OTHER THAN DEATH. If a party needs to be substituted for any reason other than death, the procedure prescribed in Rule 43(a) applies.
(c) PUBLIC OFFICER: IDENTIFICATION; SUBSTITUTION.
(1) *Identification of Party.* A public officer who is a party to an appeal or other proceeding in an official capacity may be described as a party by the public officer's official title rather than by name. But the court may require the public officer's name to be added.
(2) *Automatic Substitution of Officeholder.* When a public officer who is a party to an appeal or other proceeding in an official capacity dies, resigns, or otherwise ceases to hold office, the action does not abate. The public officer's successor is automatically substituted as a party. Proceedings following the substitution are to be in the name of the substituted party, but any misnomer that does not affect the substantial rights of the parties may be disregarded. An order of substitution may be entered at any time, but failure to enter an order does not affect the substitution.

Fed. R. App. P. 44. Case Involving a Constitutional Question When the United States or the Relevant State is Not a Party.
(a) CONSTITUTIONAL CHALLENGE TO FEDERAL STATUTE. If a party questions the constitutionality of an Act of Congress in a proceeding in which the United States or its agency, officer, or employee is not a party in an official capacity, the questioning party must give written notice to the circuit clerk immediately upon the filing of the record or as soon as the question is raised in the court of appeals. The clerk must then certify that fact to the Attorney General.
(b) CONSTITUTIONAL CHALLENGE TO STATE STATUTE. If a party questions the constitutionality of a statute of a State in a proceeding in which that State or its agency, officer, or employee is not a party in an official capacity, the questioning party must give written notice to the circuit clerk immediately upon the filing of the record or as soon as the question is raised in the court of appeals. The clerk must then certify that fact to the attorney general of the State.

Fed. R. App. P. 45. Clerk's Duties.
(a) GENERAL PROVISIONS.
(1) *Qualifications.* The circuit clerk must take the oath and post any bond required by law. Neither the clerk nor any deputy clerk may practice as an attorney or counselor in any court while in office.
(2) *When Court Is Open.* The court of appeals is always open for filing any paper, issuing and returning process, making a motion, and entering an order. The clerk's office with the clerk or a deputy in attendance must be open during business hours on all days except Saturdays, Sundays, and legal holidays. A court may provide by local rule or by order that the clerk's office be open for specified hours on Saturdays or on legal holidays other than New Year's Day, Martin Luther King, Jr.'s Birthday, Washington's Birthday, Memorial Day, Independence Day, Labor Day, Columbus Day, Veterans' Day, Thanksgiving Day, and Christmas Day.
(b) RECORDS.
(1) *The Docket.* The circuit clerk must maintain a docket and an index of all docketed cases in the manner prescribed by the Director of the Administrative Office of the United States Courts. The clerk must record all papers filed with the clerk and all process, orders, and judgments.
(2) *Calendar.* Under the court's direction, the clerk must prepare a calendar of cases awaiting argument. In placing cases
on the calendar for argument, the clerk must give preference to appeals in criminal cases and to other proceedings and appeals entitled to preference by law.
(3) *Other Records.* The clerk must keep other books and records required by the Director of the Administrative Office of the United States Courts, with the approval of the Judicial Conference of the United States, or by the court.
(c) NOTICE OF AN ORDER OR JUDGMENT. Upon the entry of an order or judgment, the circuit clerk must immediately serve a notice of entry on each party, with a copy of any opinion, and must note the date of service on the docket. Service on a party

represented by counsel must be made on counsel.
(d) CUSTODY OF RECORDS AND PAPERS. The circuit clerk has custody of the court's records and papers. Unless the court orders or instructs otherwise, the clerk must not permit an original record or paper to be taken from the clerk's office. Upon disposition of the case, original papers constituting the record on appeal or review must be returned to the court or agency from which they were received. The clerk must preserve a copy of any brief, appendix, or other paper that has been filed.

Fed. R. App. P. 46. Attorneys.
(a) ADMISSION TO THE BAR.
(1) *Eligibility.* An attorney is eligible for admission to the bar of a court of appeals if that attorney is of good moral and professional character and is admitted to practice before the Supreme Court of the United States, the highest court of a state, another United States court of appeals, or a United States district court (including the district courts for Guam, the Northern Mariana Islands, and the Virgin Islands).
(2) *Application.* An applicant must file an application for admission, on a form approved by the court that contains the applicant's personal statement showing eligibility for membership. The applicant must subscribe to the following oath or affirmation: ''I, lllllllllll, do solemnly swear [or affirm] that I will conduct myself as an attorney and counselor of this court, uprightly and according to law; and that I will support the Constitution of the United States.''
(3) *Admission Procedures.* On written or oral motion of a member of the court's bar, the court will act on the application. An applicant may be admitted by oral motion in open court. But, unless the court orders otherwise, an applicant need not appear before the court to be admitted. Upon admission, an applicant must pay the clerk the fee prescribed by local rule or court order.
(b) SUSPENSION OR DISBARMENT.
(1) *Standard.* A member of the court's bar is subject to suspension or disbarment by the court if the member:
(A) has been suspended or disbarred from practice in any other court; or
(B) is guilty of conduct unbecoming a member of the court's bar.
(2) *Procedure.* The member must be given an opportunity to show good cause, within the time prescribed by the court, why the member should not be suspended or disbarred.
(3) *Order.* The court must enter an appropriate order after the member responds and a hearing is held, if requested, or after the time prescribed for a response expires, if no response is made.
(c) DISCIPLINE. A court of appeals may discipline an attorney who practices before it for conduct unbecoming a member of the bar or for failure to comply with any court rule. First, however, the court must afford the attorney reasonable notice, an opportunity to show cause to the contrary, and, if requested, a hearing.

Fed. R. App. P. 47. Local Rules by Courts of Appeals.
(a) LOCAL RULES.
(1) Each court of appeals acting by a majority of its judges in regular active service may, after giving appropriate public notice and opportunity for comment, make and amend rules governing its practice. A generally applicable direction to parties or lawyers regarding practice before a court must be in a local rule rather than an internal operating procedure or standing order. A local rule must be consistent with—but not duplicative of—Acts of Congress and rules adopted under 28 U.S.C. §2072 and must conform to any uniform numbering system prescribed by the Judicial Conference of the United States. Each circuit clerk must send the Administrative Office of the United States Courts a copy of each local rule and internal operating procedure when it is promulgated or amended.
(2) A local rule imposing a requirement of form must not be enforced in a manner that causes a party to lose rights because of a nonwillful failure to comply with the requirement.
(b) PROCEDURE WHEN THERE IS NO CONTROLLING LAW. A court of appeals may regulate practice in a particular case in any manner consistent with federal law, these rules, and local rules of the circuit. No sanction or other disadvantage may be imposed for noncompliance with any requirement not in federal law, federal rules, or the local circuit rules unless the alleged violator has been furnished in the particular case with actual notice of the requirement.

Fed. R. App. P. 48. Masters.
(a) APPOINTMENT; POWERS. A court of appeals may appoint a special master to hold hearings, if necessary, and to recommend factual findings and disposition in matters ancillary to proceedings in the court. Unless the order referring a matter to a master specifies or limits the master's powers, those powers include, but are not limited to, the following:
(1) regulating all aspects of a hearing;
(2) taking all appropriate action for the efficient performance of the master's duties under the order;

(3) requiring the production of evidence on all matters embraced in the reference; and

(4) administering oaths and examining witnesses and parties.

(b) COMPENSATION. If the master is not a judge or court employee, the court must determine the master's compensation and whether the cost is to be charged to any party.

INDEX

Access to justice, ethics, 15
Adjudication before trial, 619
  summary judgment, 633
    affidavits, 639
    burden to point out, 648
    current standard for, 659
    most favorable light std., 638
    movant's burden, 642
    partial, grant of, 663
    proof burdens, and, 652
    summary of subject, 665
    unavailable evidence, 642
Admissions, 592
Alienage jurisdiction, 179
Alternative dispute resolution, 465
  arbitration, 494
    jurisdiction to enforce, 497
    nonbinding, 498
    unconscionable agreement to, 497
  mediation, 484
    results of, 490
  negotiation, 469
  neutral evaluation, 490
    factfinding, 493
  offer of judgment, 482
    fee award as to, 484
  settlement, 474
    agreement form, 474
    breach of agreement, 476
    confidentiality, 475
    content, 475
    fees, and, 476
  voluntariness of, 468
Amending pld., 338 (*see also* Pleading)
Ancillary jurisdiction, 186
Answer, 325 (*see also* Pleading)
  admissions in, 328
  defenses, 325,333
  denials, 329
  indirection in, 333
  lack of information as to, 332
Appeal, generally, 789
  burdening, 837
  collateral orders, 807
    limit on doctrine, 808
  cross-appeals, 836
  early appeals, 796
  finality of judgment for, 792
    exceptions, 801
  frivolous appeal, 837
  interlocutory, 802
  jurisdiction, 798
  late appeals, 797
  mandamus as substitute for, 814
    contempt orders, 819
    extraordinary cases, 818
    procedures, 814
  multiple claims & parties, 804
  plain error, 836
  preserving error, 836
  review standard, 821
    clearly erroneous, 831
    harmless error, 831
      interlocutory rulings, 835
      plain error, 836
      preserving error, 836
    law and fact, 822
    mootness, 834
    partial relief, 835
  state variations on rules, 820
  summary of subject, 837
  time for, 794
Appearance, 318
  as consent to jurisdiction, 98
Arbitrary particularization, 45
Arbitration, 494
  jurisdiction to enforce, 497
  nonbinding, 498

unconscionable agreement to, 497
Assigned case, 20

Barreiro, Mauricio E., biography, 659
Bos, Carole, biography, 427
Brinkman, Beth, biography, 482
Broder, Sherry, biography, 392

Calendar systems, 314
Candor, ethical rule for, 206
Capacity, 373
Caption, 275
Case-selection skill, 18
Case management, 300
Choice of law, 99
Citizenship, for diversity jurisd., 176
Civil or criminal law, career, 127
Civil-law systems, 17
Claim preclusion, 841
final judgment on merits, 860
dismissal as sanction, 869
exceptions, 870
on the merits, 868
stating claims, 863
governing law, 844
full faith & credit, 848
same claim, 848
procedure, 852
same parties, 852
due process, 855
Claims, joinder of, 362 (*see* Joinder)
Class Action Fairness Act, 174,452
Class actions, generally, 418
adequacy, 430
approve settlement-only, 460
certification, 420
notice, 436
prerequisites, 423
choice of law, and, 451
Class Action Fairness Act, 452
common fund, 461
diversity of citizenship, and, 438
due process, and, 442
fees, attorney's, 460
personal jurisdiction, and, 445
reach, 437
removal of, 440
resolution of, 451
securities litigation, 441
settlement only classes, 454
approval, 460
summary of subject, 463
supplemental jurisd. as to, 196
types of, 431
common fund, 461
Coaching witness, ethics of, 591
Cognovit, 100
Collateral attack on jurisdiction, 126
Collections, 784
Comparative procedure, 16-17
Competence, ethics of, 418
Complaint, 271 (*see also* Pleading)
ad damnum, 274
calendar systems, 314
caption, 275
consistency & inconsistency, 275
form of, 272
forms for, 275
frivolous, 285
general rules, 271
heightened standards for, 283
plausibility standard for, 295
possibilities, 281
privacy as to, 273
responding, 313 (*see* Pleading)
Rule 12 motions on, 285
sufficiency, 286
Concept map for knowledge, 69
Conflicts of law, 229,264
determining foreign law, 266
Content structure, 7-8
Contribution, 397
Corporations
citizenship, diversity jurisd., 183
service on, 154
venue, and, 212
Counterclaims, 365 (*see* Joinder)
Cybersquatting, 109

Default, 313 (*see* Pleading)
affidavit of, 317
process for, 316
setting aside, 317
Depositions, 584
corporations, of, 592
cost, 592
objections, 591
priority of, 591

Devereaux, James O., biography, 96
Discovery, generally, 501
 devices, 567
  admission requests, 592
  depositions, 584
   corporations, of, 592
   cost, 592
   objections, 591
   priority of, 591
  document production, 567
  document requests, 568
   format of ESI, 571
   non-parties and, 570
   producing things, 571
   interrogatories, 576
  examination, phys. & ment., 596
   conditions for, 597
   in-controversy requ., 597
 disputes, 600
  ignoring requests, 606
  magistrate judges, 615
  sanctions, 610
 electronically stored info., 535
  accessibility, 543
  claw back, 543
  format when produced, 571
  metadata, 571
  sampling, 543
 interrogatories, 576
  business records, 584
  discovery of theories, 581
  number of, 580
 limitations on, 525
  balancing interests, 529
  burden & proportionality, 529
  electronically stored info., 535
 metadata, 571
 nonparties, of, 522
 perpetuating testimony, 507
 presuit investigation, 507
 privilege, 544
  attorney-client, 544
  attorney work product, 555,566
   anticipation of litigation, 560
   scope of privilege, 555
   substantial need, 561
  evidence rule for, 553
  non-waiver agreements, 548
  privilege logs, 561
  waiver, 548
 required disclosures, 561
 scope of, 518
  nonparties, of, 522
  "reasonably calculated," 523
 skill in discovery, 561
 spoliation of evidence, 509
  statutes regarding, 518
 stipulations as to, 567
 subpoenas, 523
 summary of subject, 616
Diversity jurisdiction, 174
 See Subject matter jurisdiction

Effect of judgment, generally, 839
 claim preclusion, 841
  final judgment on merits, 860
   dismissal as sanction, 869
   exceptions, 870
   on the merits, 868
   stating claims, 863
  governing law, 844
   full faith & credit, 848
  same claim, 848
   procedure, 852
  same parties, 852
   due process, 855
 issue preclusion, 870
  actually litigated, 875
  administrative adjudications, 881
  default judgments, 878
  exceptions, 881
  inconsistent verdicts, 885
  law of the case, 878
  necessary to decision, 879
  non-mutuality of parties, 882
   factors for, 890
   government, and, 891
  same issues, 871
  summary of subject, 891
Electronically stored info., 535
 accessibility, 543
 claw back, 543
 format when produced, 571
 metadata, 571
 sampling, 543
Erie doctrine, 230,234,255
 See Governing law
Examination, phys. & ment., 596

conditions for, 597
in-controversy requ., 597
Execution, 776

Family law, diversity jurisd., 183
Federal-question jurisdiction, 166
See Subject matter jurisdiction
Federal common law, 241
See Governing law
Fee agreements, 14
Fee shifting, 10
Financing litigation, 10
Foreign service of process, 154
Forum-selection clauses, 98
Forum non conveniens, 220
See Venue
Forum shopping, 57
Forums as career guide, 22
Frivolous pleadings, ethics of, 285

Garnishment, writ, 157,776
General jurisdiction, 83
Gidari, Jr., Albert, biography, 535
Gilmore, Grant, 4
Governing law, generally, 229
balancing interests, 248
certification to state court, 263
conflicts of law, 264
determining foreign law, 266
constitutional issues, 234,241,250
diversity jurisdiction, and, 233
Erie doctrine, 230,234
relevance of, 255
standard established by, 255
federal common law, 241
guesswork as to state law, 262
certification to state court, 263
outcome-determinative test, 246
realism, and, 245
reconciliation of cases on, 254
Rules Enabling Act, 249
Rules of Decision Act, 230
state law in federal court, 230
statutory construction, and, 242
substance versus procedure, 242
summary of subject, 266
Government, serv. of process on, 155

Hague Convention, 155
Harmless error, 772

In personam jurisdiction, 36,46
In rem jurisdiction, 28,101
Indemnity, 396
Indiano, David, biography, 196
Indigency, 13
Insurance, 14
Interpleader, 400
diversity of citizenship, 402
injunctions, 407
procedure for, 407
Interrogatories, 576
business records, 584
discovery of theories, 581
number of, 580
Intervention, 407
alignment, 413
joinder, and, 414
significantly protectable int., 413
timing, 417
Involuntary dismissal, 324
Issue preclusion, 870
actually litigated, 875
administrative adjudications, 881
default judgments, 878
exceptions, 881
inconsistent verdicts, 885
law of the case, 878
necessary to decision, 879
non-mutuality of parties, 882
factors for, 890
government, and, 891
same issues, 871
summary of subject, 891

Joinder, generally, 361
claims, 362
case or controversy, 370
claim preclusion, 364
counterclaims, 365
crossclaims, 371
jurisdiction for, 363
logical-relationship test, 369
multiple claims, 362
pleading, 370
policy for, 369
state courts, in, 363
compulsory joinder, 381

consolidation, 380
counterclaims, 365
crossclaims, 371
feasibility of, 384
indispensable parties, 385
interpleader, 400
diversity of citizenship, 402
injunctions, 407
procedure for, 407
intervention, 407
alignment, 413
joinder, and, 414
significantly protectable int., 413
timing, 417
necessary parties, 384
parties, 372
capacity, 373
compulsory joinder, 381
equity and conscience, 385
feasibility of, 384
indispensable parties, 385
misjoinder, 376
necessary parties, 384
nonjoinder, 376
permissive joinder, 375
substitution of, 375
tactics as to joinder of, 380
third parties, 393
contribution, 397
derivative liability, 396
further pleading by, 400
indemnity, 396
jurisdiction, 397
Judges, qualifications, 727
bias or prejudice, 728
recusal, 727
constitutional standard for, 733
Judging, 45
Judgment, 320,745
challenging, 759
harmless error, 772
limits to, 768
jury impeachment, 768
new trial, 760
verdict defects, 764
effect of judgment, 839
claim preclusion, 841
issue preclusion, 870
enforcing, 775
collections, 784
discovery, 783
due process, 786
execution, 776,777
garnishment, writ, 157,776
security for stay, 785
specific acts, 786
stay as to, 784
security for, 785
entering, 756
execution, 776,777
finality, for appeal, 792
findings, 751
form of, 753
injunctive relief, 757
obtaining, 746
preliminary injunction, 758
proposed findings, 752
recitals, 750
relief from, 772
excusable neglect, 774
fraud, 774
newly discovered evidence, 774
summary of subject, 787
Judgment as a matter of law, 713
shifting burdens, 716
Judgment, as practice skill, 165
Judicial system, 8
Jurisdiction, generally, 23
absence of, 35-36
agreement for, 98
alienage jurisdiction, 179
arbitrary particularization, 45
balancing interests as to, 51
challenging, 122
procedure for, 125
special appearance, by, 123
collateral attack on, 126
consent to, 36, 96
by appearance, 98
constitutional basis for, 35
current challenges as to, 69
defined, 23
development, 28
doing business as basis for, 39
effects test for, 69
estoppel as to, 99
factors influencing, 68
forum-selection clauses, 98

fairness of, 99
forum shopping and, 57
general jurisdiction, 83
implied consent to, 37
in personam, 36,46
in rem, 28,101
long-arm statutes, 110
statutory construction of, 117
minimum contacts, 47
modern bases for, 40
nationwide contacts, 121
predicting, skill of, 46
property, based on, 101
purposeful acts, 52
quasi in rem, 28,101
reach of the federal courts, 120
recent developments as to, 79
registration as basis for, 100
resident agents and, 96
sovereignty and, 51
special appearance to challenge, 123
specific jurisdiction, 46
state long-arm statutes, 110
statutory construction of, 117
statutory authority for, 110
traditional bases, 28
transient jurisdiction, 90
websites and, 79
worldwide contacts, 122

Lawsuits, number of, 8
Legal terms used differently, 24
Lieber, Francis, 183
Litigiousness, 3
Llewellyn, Karl, 3
Long-arm statutes, 110
statutory construction of, 117

Magna Carta, 15
Magistrate judges, 615
referrals to, 628
Mail, service by, 139
Maine, Sir Henry, 4
Mandamus, 814
contempt orders, 819
extraordinary cases, 818
procedures, 814
Masters, 628
Mediation, 484
results of, 490
Motion for more def. statement, 321
Motion to strike, 322
Multi-jurisdictional practice, 36
Multiparty, Multiforum Trial
Jurisdiction Act, 174

Nationwide contacts, jurisd. on, 121
Negotiation, 469
judge's role in, 473
settlement agreement, form, 474
breach, 476
confidentiality, 475
content, 475
fees, and, 476
Neutral evaluation, 490
factfinding, 493
Notice and opport. for hearing, 129
constitutional requirem. for, 131
service of process, and, 319

Offer of judgment, 482
fee award as to, 484
Opportunity for hearing, 156

Pendent jurisdiction, 189
Perpetuating testimony, 507
Personal jurisdiction, 23
Pleading, 267
abuses, 350
other sanctions, 358
Rule 11 violations, 350
safe harbors, 358
signing pleadings, 351
admissions in, 328
amending, 338
at trial, 344
culpability to deny, 343
general rules, 338
prejudice to deny, 343
relation back of amendt., 344
answer, 325
admissions in, 328
defenses, 325,333
denials, 329
indirection in, 333
lack of information as to, 332
appearance, and, 318
burdens of, 337

shifting, 337
calculating time to respond, 314
calendar systems, 314
case management as to, 300
complaint, 271
see Complaint
computing time for, 315
default, 313
affidavit of, 317
process for, 316
setting aside, 317
defenses, 325,333
denials, 329
evaluating rules for, 349
evolution of rules for, 295
filing of, 319
frivolous, ethics of, 285
functions of, 270
heightened standards for, 283
history of, 269
involuntary dismissal, 324
liberality of, 302
motion for more def. statement, 321
motion to strike, 322
particularity, 303
plausibility standard for, 295
possibilities, 281
real and personal prop. actions, 309
responding, 313
calculating time to, 314
computing time for, 315
default, 313
delay in, 322
Rule 11, abuses of, 359
Rule 11 violations, 350
other sanctions, 358
safe harbors, 358
signing pleadings, 351
Rule 12 motions, 286
safe harbors, 358
service of, 319
serving and filing, 319
shifting burdens, 337
signing, 351
special damages, 304
special rules as to, 301
state decisions, 301
state rules as to, 269
statutory standards for, 304
strategy, 285
sufficiency, 286
summary of subject, 360
supplemental, 339,349
voluntary dismissal of, 322
discretion as to, 324
Posting, service by, 138
Pre-answer motion, 321
more definite statement, 321
motion to strike, 322
Predicting, skill of, 46
Pretrial conference, 620
dismissals at, 628
referrals at, 628
Pretrial order, 620
Pro-bono assignment, 20
Process, defined, 130
See Service of process
Public-interest organizations, 15
Publication, service by, 138
Purpose of rules, multiple, 28

Reach of the federal courts, 120
Recusal of judges, 727
constitutional standard for, 733
Registration of corporation, 100
Relation back of amendments, 344
Remand after removal, 202
Removal, generally, 197
basis for, 198
procedure for, 199
remand after, 202
scope of jurisdiction after, 199
strategy for, 198
Replevin, writ of, 157
Representation by counsel, 21
Representative case, 17
Required discl., 561 (*see* Discovery)
Resident agents and jurisdiction, 96
Rule 16 conference, 622
Rules Enabling Act, 7,249
Rules of Decision Act, 230

Sanctions, discovery, 610
Seizure of property, 157
Service of process, 27,120,130,319
alternative forms of, 150
corporations, on, 154
favored means of, 150

foreign, 154
government, on, 155
impracticality of, 146
mail, by, 139
mechanics of, 148
posting, by, 138
proving, 156
publication, by, 138
substituted service, 156
waiver, form, 149
Settlement, 474
agreement form, 474
breach of agreement, 476
confidentiality, 475
content, 475
fees, and, 476
results, getting, 479
Sides, choosing, for career, 162
Significance of civil procedure, 2
Signing pleadings, 351
Solicitation, ethics of, 460
Sources for civil procedure, 15
Special appearance to challenge jurisdiction, 123
Spoliation of evidence, 509
statutes regarding, 518
Statement of jurisdiction, form, 185
Stay of judgment, 784
security for, 785
Structure of civil procedure, 4
Subject matter jurisd., generally, 163
challenging, 173
constitutional basis of, 165
constitutional framework for, 163
diversity jurisdiction, 174
alienage jurisdiction, 179
amount in controv., 175,184
citizenship, 176
collusive joinder as to, 179
complete, 178
corporations, citizenship, 183
family-law cases, 183
governing law, and, 233
minimal, 178
nominal joinder as to, 179
federal-question jurisdiction, 166
arising under test, 167
artful-drafting doctr., the, 167
federal int. as basis for, 173
federal stds. as basis for, 169
well-pled complaint rule, 167
statement of, form, 185
summary of, 203
Subpoenas, 523
Substance versus procedure, 209
Substituted service of process, 156
Summary judgment, 633
affidavits, 639
burden to point out, 648
current standard for, 659
most favorable light std., 638
movant's burden, 642
partial, grant of, 663
proof burdens, and, 652
summary of subject, 665
unavailable evidence, 642
Summons, 25,120
contents of, 147
form, 147
Supplemental jurisdiction, 185,190
class actions and, 196
counterclaims, and, 197
discretionary denial, 197
exceptions to, 189
pendent jurisdiction, 189
Supplemental pleadings, 339,349

Technology, use of pleading, 301,328
Third parties, 393 (*see* Joinder, part.)
Transfer of venue, 215
Transient jurisdiction, 90
Trial, generally, 665
conduct of, 736
instructions, jury, 705
choice of, 710
objections to, 712
judgment as a matter of law, 713
shifting burdens, 716
jurors, 686
discriminatory challenges, 693
pretext justifying, 697
drawing, 687
instructing, 705
judicial control of, 712
number of, 686
peremptory challenges, 693
unanimity of, 687
voir dire, 690

jury, 667
declaratory relief, and, 675
demand for, 669
framework for right, 677
impeachment of, 768
new claims, and right to, 679
right to, 667
Seventh Amendment, 668
statutory actions, and, 685
suits at common law, 670
law-fact distinction, 701
multiple parties, 735
order of, 734
customary order, 735
scheduling, 666
shifting burdens, 716
summary of subject, 743
verdicts, 741

United States Courts of Appeals, 9
United States District Courts, 9
United States justice, value of, 226
United States Supreme Court, 9

Venue, generally, 250
access, 226
arguing motion for change of, 214
challenging venue, 214
corporations, 212
discretion as to, 216
limits on discretion, 217
drafting mot. for change of, 219
fallback provisions, 212
federal court, 209
forum law, 217
forum non conveniens, 220
inconvenience, 225
jurisdiction, 225
inconvenience, 225
justice, United States, 226
local-action doctrine, 213
location of events, 211
multidistrict litig., and, 216,217
multiple claims, 213
original, 206
residence, 211
special statutes, 212
state court, 206
specific provisions, 209
transfers, 218
summary of, 226
transfer of venue, 215
United States justice, 226
waiver of defects as to, 215
Voluntary dismissal, 322
discretion, 324

Waiver of service, form, 149
Websites, effect of on jurisd., 79
Witness coaching, ethics of, 591
Worldwide contacts, jurisd. on, 122
Writ system, 16

CPSIA information can be obtained at www.ICGtesting.com
Printed in the USA
BVOW09*0738110515

398517BV00004B/4/P